Canadian Human Resource Management

ELEVENTH EDITION

Dr. Hermann F. Schwind

Saint Mary's University

Dr. Krista Uggerslev

Northern Alberta Institute of Technology

Dr. Terry H. Wagar

Saint Mary's University

Dr. Neil Fassina

Northern Alberta Institute of Technology

Julie Bulmash

George Brown College

McGraw Hill Education

Canadian Human Resource Management
Eleventh Edition

The Internet addresses listed in the text were accurate at the time of publication. The inclusion of a Web site does not indicate an endorsement by the authors or McGraw-Hill Ryerson, and McGraw-Hill Ryerson does not guarantee the accuracy of the information presented at these sites.

978-1-25-908762-2

1-25-908762-X

1 2 3 4 5 6 7 8 9 10   TCP   1 9 8 7 6

Printed and bound in Canada.

Care has been taken to trace ownership of copyright material contained in this text; however, the publisher will welcome any information that enables them to rectify any reference or credit for subsequent editions.

Director of Product Management: Rhondda McNabb
Group Product Manager: Kim Brewster
Marketing Manager: Cathie Lefebvre
Product Developer: Lindsay MacDonald
Senior Product Team Associate: Stephanie Giles
Supervising Editors: Cathy Biribauer, Jeanette McCurdy
Photo/Permissions Researcher: Monika Schurmann
Copy Editor: Cat Haggert
Plant Production Coordinator: Michelle Saddler
Manufacturing Production Coordinator: Emily Hickey
Cover and Interior Design: Dave Murphy
Cover Image: © Fountainview Academy Orchestra and Singers, Lillooet, BC Canada
Composition: Laserwords Private
Printer: Transcontinental Printing Group

About the Authors

DR. HERMANN F. SCHWIND

Dr. Schwind is Professor Emeritus (Human Resource Management) at Saint Mary's University in Halifax. He received his Ph.D. from the University of British Columbia, B.B.A. and M.B.A. degrees from the University of Washington, and mechanical and industrial engineering degrees from German institutions. He has 15 years of industrial experience and has taught as Visiting Professor at the University of Ottawa, in Japan at Sophia University in Tokyo, and at the Institute for International Studies and Training in Fujinomiya, a Japanese management training centre.

Dr. Schwind was a founding member and Vice-President of the British Columbia Society for Training and Development, President of the Halifax and District Personnel Association (1984/86; now the Human Resource Association of Nova Scotia), and President of the Administrative Science Association of Canada. His research and publications focused on Performance Appraisal, Training and Development, Motivation and Compensation, and Cross-Cultural Management. He also worked as a human resource consultant for 25 years.

DR. KRISTA UGGERSLEV

Dr. Krista Uggerslev is the Applied Research Chair in Leadership and Talent at the Northern Alberta Institute of Technology. Krista holds Ph.D. and M.Sc. degrees in Industrial and Organizational Psychology from the University of Calgary, and was a tenured Associate Professor in the Asper School of Business at the University of Manitoba.

In her research, Krista is a co-founder of metaBUS, creating Big Data tools for locating, curating, and synthesizing scientific research to propel the speed of science and disseminate information for evidence-based practice. Krista explores: (a) demographic and economic changes in Canada and ways of addressing Canada's impending war for talent, (b) talent management and leadership pipelines, and (c) the impact of recruitment practices on applicant attraction to organizations. Krista's research has appeared and continues to appear in the world's top academic journals in applied psychology and business, and has been presented to national and international audiences including NATO.

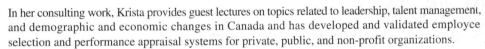

In her consulting work, Krista provides guest lectures on topics related to leadership, talent management, and demographic and economic changes in Canada and has developed and validated employee selection and performance appraisal systems for private, public, and non-profit organizations.

DR. TERRY H. WAGAR

Terry H. Wagar is a Professor of Human Resource Management/Industrial Relations at Saint Mary's University in Halifax. He has also taught at the University of South Australia, Wilfrid Laurier University, and the University of Western Australia. Dr. Wagar's degrees include an M.B.A. from the University of Toronto, a Master of Industrial Relations from Queen's University, an LL.B. from the University of Ottawa Law School, and a Ph.D. in labour relations, human resource management, and statistics/research methods from Virginia Tech.

Dr. Wagar has been a Visiting Scholar/Professor at several universities, including Flinders University of South Australia, University of Kentucky, University of Waikato, Queen's University, and the University of Western Australia. His research has been published in Canada, the United States, Europe, Asia, Australia, and New Zealand.

DR. NEIL FASSINA

Dr. Neil Fassina is the Provost and Vice President, Academic at the Northern Alberta Institute of Technology (NAIT). He received his Ph.D. in Management from the Rotman School of Business at the University of Toronto and his B.Sc. in Psychology from the University of Calgary. Neil has a Certified Human Resource Professional (CHRP) designation and an Institute of Corporate Directors (ICD.D) designation.

In his research, Dr. Fassina addresses questions related to the areas of applied decision making—such as negotiations and strategic decision making—as well as social exchange relationships and talent management. As an educator, Dr. Fassina delivers seminars and workshops on effective negotiation strategies, strategic planning, conflict management, and communications among other human resource–related topics to clients at all levels of private, public, and not-for-profit organizations.

JULIE BULMASH

Julie Bulmash is a professor at George Brown College in Toronto, where she coordinates the Human Resource program and teaches courses in organizational behaviour, human resource management, compensation, management of change, and organizational effectiveness. She also teaches at the University of Toronto in the Centre for Management of Technology and Entrepreneurship.

Julie has extensive business experience in the design, development, and delivery of human resource strategies intended to assist organizations in achieving their objectives. She has developed compensation and benefit systems, redesigned performance management programs, implemented human resource information systems, and has worked to ensure the effective management of change in both profit and not-for-profit sectors. Julie is a recipient of the award for Excellence in Teaching and Learning, which recognizes an instructor's ability to motivate and inspire through quality teaching methods. Currently Julie is the faculty representative on the Board of Governors for George Brown College. Julie obtained her undergraduate degree in psychology from Concordia University in Montreal. She did graduate work in assessment and counselling at the University of Toronto, and obtained her M.B.A. from Heriot-Watt University in Edinburgh, Scotland.

Letter to Students

Dear Student,

This book was written with you, our customer, in mind. We have tried to make it readable and, wherever possible, we have included practical "how-to-do" steps.

Each chapter includes many common elements, such as learning objectives, terms for review, and case studies. We hope the following guide will help you make maximum use of the textbook so that you will be successful with your studies in human resource management.

At the beginning of each chapter, we offer a quote from an expert on the subject matter to give you an insight into the concepts or issues discussed. Following the opening quote, you will find the chapter learning objectives. These will give you an overview of the chapter content. They will also appear in the page margins, as numbered LOs, wherever appropriate.

Within all chapters, you will find a *Spotlight on HRM* box. These timely articles from journals and magazines in the field illustrate a manager's or consultant's point of view on HRM or offer a sharing of practical HRM experiences relevant to the chapter. Each chapter also contains a *Spotlight on Ethics,* where an ethics issue relevant to the chapter content is raised. It is ideally suited for class discussion.

Photos of real job situations offer insights into work environments the book is discussing. Cartoons add some humour to the otherwise quite serious content. We highlight important terms and concepts with boldface and italic type in the text. All terms appearing in boldface are also defined separately in the text and referenced in the *Terms for Review* section at the end of each chapter and in the Subject Index, highlighted in a secondary colour. Students interested in earning the Certified Human Resource Professional (CHRP) designation will find topics relevant for exams marked with an *HRC (Human Resource Competencies)* icon in the text, and can reference the specific number of the seven Body of Knowledge domains in the Preface.

An end-of-chapter summary offers you an abbreviated version of the chapter content for review. The *Terms for Review*, where all important terms (and buzzwords) are listed, is an excellent tool for conducting another self-test. Similarly, the *Review and Discussion Questions* will help you test your understanding of the most critical topics in the chapter. For a higher level of self-testing, the *Critical Thinking Questions* help you to discover whether you are able to see the broader relationships and interactions of the concepts discussed.

The *Web Research Assignments* offer you the opportunity to make use of a computer and the Internet to search for additional information. As a self-test, it assesses your ability to conduct online research.

The *Incident* is a short case that usually does not require extensive analytical work, unlike the more comprehensive case studies later in the chapter, which test your thorough understanding of concepts and their impact on an organization.

Exercises are usually conducted under the supervision of your instructor; however, they can also be used as part of a group exercise, away from the classroom.

The *References* provide you with the sources for the information given in the chapter. They can also be used as a starting point for more detailed research.

If you have any feedback regarding the readability of the textbook or suggestions on how we could improve the next edition, please contact us via the e-mail addresses given below.

Good luck with your studies!

hermann.schwind@smu.ca
kristau@nait.ca
terry.wagar@smu.ca
nfassina@nait.ca
jbulmash@georgebrown.ca

Brief Table of Contents

Table of Contents

◉ PART 3   Attracting Human Resources   157

CHAPTER 4 Legal Requirements and Managing Diversity   158

CHAPTER 5 Recruitment   215

PART 5   Motivating and Rewarding Human Resources   417

CHAPTER 9 Compensation Management   418

CHAPTER 10 Employee Benefits and Services   465

PART 6   Maintaining High Performance   497

CHAPTER 11 Managing Employee Relations   498

Preface

We believe that human resource departments will play a critical role in determining the success of Canadian organizations in the twenty-first century.

—THE AUTHORS

Teachers and students ultimately determine the value of any university textbook. *Canadian Human Resource Management: A Strategic Approach* is no exception. Its tenth edition passed the test of the marketplace by earning adoptions and re-adoptions in more than sixty colleges and universities in Canada and becoming the best-selling human resource management text in this country. The book's thrust on presenting the key concepts, issues, and practices of this exciting field without being encyclopedic; its practical focus; and its emphasis on readability have endeared it to hundreds of instructors and thousands of students in Canada. Equally gratifying to the authors is that a large number of students retained this book for their professional libraries after course completion, suggesting that they found real value in the book.

Balanced Coverage

We attribute the book's popularity to its balanced coverage of both theory and practice, and both traditional materials and emerging concerns. Regardless of their orientation, readers will sense our belief that people are the ultimate resource for any employer. How well an organization obtains, maintains, and retains its human resources determines its success or failure. And the success or failure of our organizations shapes the well-being of every individual on this planet. If the events of the last decade are any indication, the human race is entering a totally new phase in its evolution. The breakup of protectionist trade barriers and ideological walls that separate countries of the world may mean that the manager of the twenty-first century has to operate in a more complex and dynamic global setting that is also much more interdependent. Training in human resource management (HRM) will become even more critical in this new setting.

The eleventh edition of *Canadian Human Resource Management: A Strategic Approach* builds on the strengths of the tenth edition. The book is divided into seven parts.

- **Part 1: The Strategic Human Resource Management Model** introduces the strategic model that will be used as a guide through all chapters.

- **Part 2: Planning Human Resources** describes the two pre-hiring processes, analyzing the jobs in question and planning for future staff needs. New job options have to be integrated into the organization as part of the planning process.

- **Part 3: Attracting Human Resources** covers the legal aspects of any hiring decision and discusses recruitment and selection processes and the management of a diverse workforce.

- **Part 4: Placing, Development, and Evaluation of Human Resources** discusses the importance of preparing employees for new challenges through training and development and providing timely performance feedback.

- **Part 5: Motivating and Rewarding Human Resources** reviews the many ways a human resource department can contribute to a more effective organization through a fair and equitable compensation system and proficient benefits administration. Creating a motivating environment is another responsibility of the HR manager.

- **Part 6: Maintaining High Performance** brings up the issues related to workplace safety, which is of concern to every manager. This concern has to be conveyed to all employees through an effective communication system. Good interpersonal relations require appropriate and fair discipline procedures.

This part also discusses in detail the union-management framework, union organizing, collective bargaining, and collective agreement administration.

- **Part 7: Human Resource Management in a Global Context,** the final part, examines the proper preparation of employees destined for a job abroad and the many challenges facing human resource managers when working with expatriate or foreign staff.

Updated in the Eleventh Edition

The chapters in the new edition have been streamlined and organized for easier reading and retention of material by students. The focus of the text continues to be the strategic contribution of HR function in organizations; but an explicit recognition of the relationship between HR strategies, tactics, and systems has been incorporated into the model and throughout the text material. Within this format, both present and emerging concerns of a significant nature are highlighted. Key terms are bolded and an extensive glossary of HR terms is included at the end of the text.

This edition has a very thorough coverage of Canadian human rights legislation and an in-depth discussion of the *Canadian Charter of Rights and Freedoms.* A number of recent trends and potentially promising HRM strategies have been incorporated into appropriate chapters of the new edition. HRM has recently played a more important role in the overall strategy of companies. This trend is strongly reflected in the new edition. All chapters now include a discussion of how the topic dealt with in the chapter should be mirrored in the HRM strategy and how this strategy fits into the overall strategy of the organization. This edition also discusses the national Certified Human Resource Professional (CHRP) designation requirements and the Human Resource Competencies (HRCs) identified by the task force on this matter.

All chapters have been updated. Information on legislative changes, especially in the area of employment equity (women, sexual orientation, the disabled, and First Nations People), statistics, and demographics, is the latest available. New work options provide organizations not only with opportunities to be more effective but also offer employees more flexible work opportunities, better suited to their needs. Growing international trade dictates that Canadians may be required to go abroad to manage subsidiaries or to work in joint ventures. Thorough pre-departure training is a must. Addressed also are issues related to managing international staff and the reintegration of expatriates into the home organization. The text provides over one hundred examples and anecdotes of Canadian and global firms—private and public, local and national, and large and small.

Some reviewers suggested that more emphasis be placed on the "how to do it" discussions. This suggestion has been followed in almost all chapters and, whenever possible, a step-by-step approach has been used.

Key Features

In addition to new features, important key features from previous editions have been retained.

Running Cases—This is the only Canadian HR text to have two cases anchored to material in every single chapter. Maple Leaf Shoes Limited symbolizes traditional HR practices—mostly responding to problems in a reactive fashion. In contrast, Canadian Pacific and International Bank Limited symbolizes the progressive, proactive, and strategic role of HR in today's organizations. By comparing the practices of the two firms, the student should be able to learn how HR can make a significant contribution to organizational success and growth.

CASE STUDY

Maple Leaf Shoes Ltd.

Legal Challenges

Maple Leaf Shoes Ltd. is a medium-sized manufacturer of leather and vinyl shoes located in Wilmington, Ontario. It was started in 1969 and currently employs about 400 persons in its Wilmington plant and some 380 more in offices and warehouses throughout Canada and internationally. More information on the firm and its operations is provided at the end of Chapter 1.

Eva White was the operator of a leather-cutting machine. When Eva heard the bell ring, indicating the end of the workday, she shut down her cutting machine and headed toward the women's locker room. It had been a long day and standing for eight hours on the machine didn't do her back any good. When she approached her locker, she saw that Rosetta Maurizio, who used the locker next to hers, was already there, changing into her street clothing. Eva and Rosetta had been hired together 10 months earlier. They had not known each other before, and, although they worked in different parts of the building, they kept each other company in the cafeteria during their lunch breaks. As her name indicated, Rosetta was of Italian descent. She had immigrated to Canada from Italy with her parents several years before, but her Italian accent was still quite noticeable.

Spotlights—Most chapters provide a "Spotlight on HRM" focusing on an emerging practice, issue, or HR opportunity. Some Spotlights from previous editions have been retained at the request of reviewers; the new ones reflect current trends and practices.

Spotlight *on* HRM

Using MOOCs in Corporate Training

Given the popularity of using massive open online courses (MOOCs) in higher education, it is no wonder that training executives and chief learning officers are excited about their potential in corporate settings. Although a 2013 study of a million MOOC students found low course engagement and high drop-out rates, with only 4 percent completing courses, corporate training experts believe business MOOCs may be valuable and cost-effective future training platforms.

MOOCs at AT&T

In 2013 AT&T partnered with MOOC-provider Udacity Inc. and Georgia Tech University to create one of the first accredited degree programs using the MOOC teaching model. With significantly lower tuition costs than an on-campus master's degree and tuition covered by the company, more than 200 AT&T employees have registered in the MOOC format Master's in Computer Science program.

The company needs more skilled software and network engineers to meet its evolving business in wireless, cloud-based products and services, and MOOCs can deliver leading-edge knowledge in those areas. AT&T senior vice president of human resources, Scott Smith, said "The MOOCs are a complement to the training we deliver internally, and they enable employees to access content 24/7 in ways that fit their work schedules and lifestyles. The format gives us a way to provide additional learning that in some cases may be too expensive to do internally, or when we may not have the instructors or content that a Georgia Tech or Udacity can offer."

Corporate MOOC Design

The key to MOOC success in the corporate domain may rest with motivated learners and MOOC design. Corporate learners may not seek to complete full courses, but rather seek information to address a specific issue or problem they are facing at work. So the drop-out rates that plague higher education MOOCs may not be of concern; learners will engage in the MOOC for only the portions providing the knowledge they seek. In organizations where MOOC completion is desired, some companies may provide "badges" for corporate profiles (e.g., AT&T) or certificates (Yahoo).

Ethics Box—A significant feature is the "Spotlight on Ethics," in which an ethics issue relevant to the chapter content is discussed.

Spotlight *on* ETHICS

The Hiring Dilemma

The manager of an accounting department has to hire the replacement for a retiring accountant. Over twenty applicants have applied and three were put onto the short list. One of the shortlisted candidates is a 60-year-old CPA, more experienced than the other two, who also have a CPA designation. The manager knows that the department will change accounting practices in the near future (no date has been set yet) and introduce new accounting software, which will require extensive retraining of current staff. If the more experienced candidate is hired, the manager will be faced with the question of whether it is justified to invest a considerable amount in retraining a person who may retire soon after. But if one of the younger candidates is hired, the company might face an age discrimination charge. What should the manager do?

Web Research—To assist students in making optimal use of the Internet for more information on HR topics, HR related websites are provided throughout the text and hotlinked in the ebook. To facilitate class discussion, a web research question has been added at the end of every chapter. We have also included a handy reference list of important homepages related to human resource management on Connect.

> Global Knowledge <http://www.globalknowledge.ca>, a leader in business and IT training, in conjunction with Deloitte <http://www.deloitte.ca>, a leading professional services firm, was awarded gold honours by the Canadian Society for Training and Development (CSTD) for their Managers 1 and 2 programs. These programs are designed to prepare the new managers to increase their confidence and capability. The program offered originality, instructional design, virtual class elearning, self-paced elearning, live labs, and a knowledge centre that included webinars, blogs, mobile apps, and special reports. The programs focused on the day-to-day realities that new managers face and provided them with the tools to manage these situations using technology.[41]

In-Text Glossary—Important terms and concepts are highlighted with boldface type in the text. Allowing students to find critical definitions at a glance, all terms appearing in boldface are also defined in the text between two separation lines and referenced in the Terms for Review section at the end of each chapter. They can also be found in the Subject Index, highlighted in a secondary colour. Finally, a full list of glossary terms is also provided in the end matter of the text.

HRC Icons—The specific content relating to the national CHRP designation requirements are identified by Human Resource Competencies (HRC) icons in the text, where relevant.

HRC #1 - Strategy

HRC #2 - Professional Practice

HRC #3 - Engagement

HRC #4 - Workforce Planning and Talent Management

HRC #5 - Employee and Labour Relations

HRC #6 - Total Rewards

HRC #7 - Learning and Development

HRC #8 - Health, Wellness, and Safe Workplaces

HRC #9 - Human Resource Metrics, Reporting, and Financial Management

Source: http://www.hrma.ca/wp-content/uploads/2014/09/CHRP-competency-framework.pdf

Learning and Pedagogical Devices

Also retained from previous editions are the following features:

Figures—Charts and diagrams are included to illustrate relevant ideas and concepts.

FIGURE 4-6

Steps in Managing Diversity

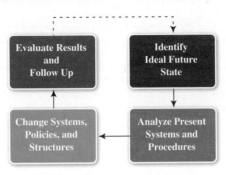

SOURCE: Adapted from Hari Das, *Strategic Organizational Design: For Canadian Firms in a Global Economy,* Scarborough, ON: Prentice Hall, 1998, p. 340. Reprinted with permission of Pearson Education Canada Inc.

Terms for Review—All important terms and buzzwords are included. It is an excellent tool for self-testing.

Learning Objectives—This useful tool enables students to gauge their progress and understanding while working through each chapter.

End-of-Chapter Summaries—the authors provide an abbreviated version of the main ideas, theories, and strategies of each chapter.

SUMMARY

Government is a significant variable that strongly shapes the role of human resource management. It influences human resources through laws governing the employment relationship. The application of the Charter of Rights and Freedoms was awaited with high expectations from both labour and management. However, its impact on the human resource management field has been mixed.

The two sources of equal employment laws are the federal and provincial human rights statutes. The *Canadian Human Rights Act* applies to federal government departments and agencies, Crown corporations, and businesses and industries under federal jurisdiction, such as banks, airlines, and railway companies. Areas not under federal jurisdiction are protected by provincial human rights laws. Each of Canada's provinces and territories has its own antidiscrimination laws that are broadly similar to the federal law.

Review and Discussion Questions—Review and Discussion Questions test students' understanding of the chapter material and suggest topics for class or group discussions.

REVIEW AND DISCUSSION QUESTIONS

1. Suppose that during your first job interview after graduation you are asked, "Why should a company have an employment equity program?" How would you respond?

2. List the major prohibitions of the *Canadian Human Rights Act*.

3. Since a human resource department is not a legal department, what role does it play in the area of equal employment law?

4. Suppose that you are told that your first duty as a human resource specialist is to construct an employment equity program. What would you do? What types of information would you seek?

5. What conditions would have to be met before you could bring suit against an employer who discriminated against you because of your sex?

6. A job candidate answers "yes" to the question of whether she is a smoker. She is well qualified, but you decide not to hire her. Does she have legal recourse?

7. Why is management of diversity important for an organization today?

8. What are the steps in implementing a diversity management program?

Critical Thinking Questions—These questions challenge students to expand on what they have just learned, discussing broader relationships and interactions of the concepts in the chapter.

CRITICAL THINKING QUESTIONS

1. If you are a supervisor in a bank and an employee demands to be allowed to miss work on Fridays for religious reasons, what would you do? Under what circumstances would you have to let the employee have time off? Under what circumstances could you prohibit it?

2. You have a job opening for a warehouse helper, a position that sometimes requires heavy lifting, up to 50 kilograms. A woman applies for the job and claims that she is able to do the work. She looks rather petite, and you are afraid that she may hurt herself. When you deny her the job, she threatens to complain to the Human Rights Commission. What do you do?

3. Choose an organization that you are familiar with. Are any of its rules, practices, or policies likely to be found undesirable by its female, minority, or older employees? Why?

4. If 40 percent of your employees are women, but if women account for only 2 percent of the executive group and 4 percent of the managerial group, what steps will you take to improve the status of women in your organization?

Incident—These short cases test students' understanding of concepts and their impact on the organization.

INCIDENT 4-1

Metropolitan Hospital's Employment Equity Needs

A large metropolitan hospital in Ontario recently developed an employment equity program. Under the program, the hospital agreed to promote two women into supervisory ranks for each man promoted. This practice was to continue until 40 to 45 percent of all supervisory jobs in the hospital were held by women.

The need for the first supervisory promotion occurred in the medical records department. The manager of medical records was one of the few female managers in the hospital. Nevertheless, she argued that Roy Biggs should become a medical records supervisor, as he was best qualified. Roy had two years of medical school and was a graduate of a medical records program at the local community college. The assistant director of hospital operations agreed that Roy should get the promotion. The equal employment compliance specialist in the human resource department argued that Kate VanDam should get the promotion, because of the employment equity program and because she had more seniority and experience in the department than Roy. The records manager, the assistant administrator, and the compliance specialist decided that the human resource manager should make the final decision.

Exercises—These offer students the opportunity to apply strategies to specific situations and arrive at their own conclusions or discuss with the instructor and fellow students.

EXERCISE 4-1

Carver Jewellery Company

Carver Jewellery Company Ltd. has the following workforce composition:

Job Classes	Male	Female	White	Black	Asian	Native Peoples
Executive	9	1	10	0	0	0
Management	71	9	79	0	1	0
Salaried/commission	43	31	74	0	0	0
Hourly paid	24	164	168	10	8	2

Subject Index—All chapter topics are indexed by subject. Glossary terms and page references are included in a secondary colour.

Reference Notes—Specific cases and other source references are gathered at the end of the text for more detailed research purposes.

References

CHAPTER 1

1. Leif Edvinsson, http://hrfirst.co.in; downloaded February 3, 2012.
2. How stuff works, http://www.howstuffworks.com/innovation/inventions/top-5-nasa-inventions.htm#page=1; downloaded March 12, 2015.
3. National Aeronautical and Space Administration, http://mars.jpl.nasa.gov/mars2020/; downloaded March 12, 2015
4. James Harder, "Engage your long-time employees to improve performance," *Harvard Business Review,* downloaded March 23, 2015, from: https://hbr.org/2015/03/engage-your-long-time-employees-to-improve-performance.
5. Dave Ulrich and Wayne Brockbank, *The HR Value Proposition.* Harvard Business Press: Boston, MA, 2005.
6. C. Brewster, G. Wood, M. Brookes, and J. Van Ommeren, J., "What determines the size of the HR function? A cross-national analysis," *Human Resource Management,*

18. Ibid.
19. Ibid.
20. World Economic Forum, *The Global Competitiveness Report 2014–2015,* http://www.weforum.org/reports/global-competitiveness-report-2014-2015; downloaded March 27, 2015.
21. Bruce Little, "We're Less Dependent but More Entangled," *The Globe and Mail,* May 15, 2000, p. A2.
22. Saba Colakoglu, Dave P. Lepak, and Ying Hong, "Measuring HRM Effectiveness: Considering a global context," *Human Resource Management Review,* Vol. 17, 2006, pp. 77–92.
23. World Economic Forum, *The Global Competitiveness Report 2014–2015,* http://www.weforum.org/reports/global-competitiveness-report-2014-2015; downloaded March 27, 2015.
24. Conference Board of Canada, "Innovation Overview," February 2010, http://sso.conferenceboard.ca/HCP/overview/Innovation-overview.aspx; downloaded

GID=0&GK=0&GRP=1&PID=105617&PRID=0&PTYPE=105277&S=0&SHOWALL=0&SUB=0&Temporal=2013&THEME=96&VID=0&VNAMEE=&VNAMEF=; downloaded March 27, 2015.
34. Working.com, http://www.working.com/story_print.html?id=bc7b53a1-4cf4-4624-9c23-b28c6ee8e559&sponsor; downloaded March 30, 2012.
35. "5 Telework Pitfalls to Avoid," *Canadian HR Reporter,* October 20, 2008, p. 2.
36. D. Mota, "Keeping data safe takes several solutions," 2015, http://insurancenewsnet.com/oarticle/2015/03/02/keeping-data-safe-takes-several-solutions-a-602265.html#.VRX1bPnF-OM; downloaded March 27, 2015.
37. "McCarthy's Reinvents the Practice," *The Globe and Mail,* December 6, 1999, p. M1.
38. R. Dobbs, S. Ramaswamy, e. Stephenson, E., and S. P. Viguerie, "Management intuition for the next 50 years," *McKinsey Quarterly.* 2014, http://www.mckinsey.com/insights/strategy/management_intuition_for_the

Glossary—The most comprehensive glossary in the HR field—over 600 items—completes the book, allowing students to find definitions of most HR terms and concepts.

Glossary

360-degree performance appraisal Combination of self, peer, supervisor, and subordinate performance evaluation.

ability tests Tests that assess an applicant's capacity or aptitude to function in a certain way.

ads Advertisements in a newspaper, magazine, and so on that solicit job applicants for a position.

alternate work arrangements Nontraditional work arrangements (e.g., flextime, telecommuting) that provide more flexibility to employees while meeting organizational goals.

alumni associations Associations of alumni of schools, colleges, or other training facilities.

applicant tracking systems (ATS) Databases of potential candidates that enable a good match between job requirements and applicant characteristics and also enlarge the recruitment pool.

apprenticeships A form of on-the-job training in which junior employees learn a trade from an experienced person.

financial management, internal operations, and customer management.

behavioural description interviews Interviews that attempt to find out how job applicants responded to specific work situations in the past.

behaviourally anchored rating scales (BARS) Evaluation tools that rate employees along a rating scale by means of specific behaviour examples on the scale.

benefit audit A system to control the efficiency of a benefit program.

biographical information blank (BIB) A type of application blank that uses a multiple-choice format to measure a job candidate's education, experiences, opinions, attitudes, and interests.

blind ads Job ads that do not identify the employer.

blog A web log—an online journal, diary, or serial published by a person or group of people.

bona fide occupational requirement

Canadian Human Rights Commission (CHRC) Supervises the implementation and adjudication of the *Canadian Human Rights Act.*

Canadian Labour Congress (CLC) An organization, with a membership of about 3.3 million, that represents many unions in Canada.

Canadian Occupational Projection System (COPS) Provides up to 10-year projection of Canadian economy and human resource needs.

career development A lifelong series of activities undertaken by individuals in their pursuit of a career.

career management A series of formal and less formal activities designed and managed by the organization to influence the career development of one or more employees.

career planning The process through which someone becomes more aware of their interests and needs, motivations, etc. in terms of their career.

MARKET LEADING TECHNOLOGY

Mc Graw Hill Education CONNECT

Learn without Limits

McGraw-Hill Connect® is an award-winning digital teaching and learning platform that gives students the means to better connect with their coursework, with their instructors, and with the important concepts that they will need to know for success now and in the future. With Connect, instructors can take advantage of McGraw-Hill Education's trusted content to seamlessly deliver assignments, quizzes, and tests online. McGraw-Hill Connect is the only learning platform that continually adapts to each student, delivering precisely what they need, when they need it, so class time is more engaging and effective. Connect makes teaching and learning personal, easy, and proven.

Connect Key Features:

SmartBook®

As the first and only adaptive reading experience, SmartBook is changing the way students read and learn. SmartBook creates a personalized reading experience by highlighting the most important concepts a student needs to learn at that moment in time. As a student engages with SmartBook, the reading experience continuously adapts by highlighting content based on what each student knows and doesn't know. This ensures that he or she is focused on the content needed to close specific knowledge gaps, while it simultaneously promotes long-term learning.

Connect Insight®

Connect Insight is Connect's new one-of-a-kind visual analytics dashboard—now available for both instructors and students—that provides at-a-glance information regarding student performance, which is immediately actionable. By presenting assignment, assessment, and topical performance results together with a time metric that is easily visible for aggregate or individual results, Connect Insight gives the user the ability to take a just-in-time approach to teaching and learning, which was never before available. Connect Insight presents data that empowers students and helps instructors improve class performance in a way that is efficient and effective.

Simple Assignment Management

With Connect, creating assignments is easier than ever, so instructors can spend more time teaching and less time managing.

- Assign SmartBook learning modules.

- Instructors can edit existing questions and create their own questions.

- Draw from a variety of text-specific questions, resources, and test bank material to assign online.

- Streamline lesson planning, student progress reporting, and assignment grading to make classroom management more efficient than ever.

Smart Grading

When it comes to studying, time is precious. Connect helps students learn more efficiently by providing feedback and practice material when they need it, where they need it.

- Automatically score assignments, giving students immediate feedback on their work and comparisons with correct answers.

- Access and review each response; manually change grades or leave comments for students to review.

- Track individual student performance—by question, assignment, or in relation to the class overall—with detailed grade reports.

- Reinforce classroom concepts with practice tests and instant quizzes.

- Integrate grade reports easily with Learning Management Systems including Blackboard, D2L, and Moodle.

Instructor Library

The Connect Instructor Library is a repository for additional resources to improve student engagement in and out of the class. It provides all the critical resources instructors need to build their course.

- Access Instructor resources.

- View assignments and resources created for past sections.

- Post your own resources for students to use.

INSTRUCTOR RESOURCES

Instructor Resources

- Instructor's Manual

- Computerized Test Bank

- Microsoft® PowerPoint® Presentation Slides

- Videos

- Manager's HotSeat Videos

- CCH Canada BusinessWorks©

SUPERIOR LEARNING SOLUTIONS AND SUPPORT

The McGraw-Hill Education team is ready to help instructors assess and integrate any of our products, technology, and services into your course for optimal teaching and learning performance. Whether it's helping your students improve their grades, or putting your entire course online, the McGraw-Hill Education team is here to help you do it. Contact your Learning Solutions Consultant today to learn how to maximize all of McGraw-Hill Education's resources.

For more information, please visit us online: http://www.mheducation.ca/he/solutions

Acknowledgements

The writing of a textbook requires the co-operation and support of many people. *Canadian Human Resource Management* is no exception. We are deeply indebted to the following persons for their time, expertise, and guidance in reviewing and commenting on the eleventh edition:

Stan Arnold	Humber College
Gordon Barnard	Durham College
Anna Bortolon	Conestoga College
Vilma Coutino-Hill	Carleton University
Gerry Culina	McMaster University
Raymond Lee	University of Manitoba
Sean MacDonald	University of Manitoba
Darragh McManamon	Memorial University
Cheryl Meheden	University of Lethbridge
Lisa Phillips	Douglas College
Carol Ann Samhaber	Algonquin College
Helen Stavaris	Dawson College
Kathryn Taft	Capilano University
Andrew Templer	University of Windsor
Spring Tompkins	St. Lawrence College
Roger Wheeler	Okanagan College

We are also thankful to the many students, instructors, researchers, and practitioners who have used and commented on our last edition. Ultimately, it is the users of a book who can tell us about what we did right in the past and what we should do in the future. We hope the readers will find this eleventh edition even more useful in teaching and learning about human resource management.

A very special thank you goes to the editorial staff of McGraw-Hill Ryerson: Kim Brewster, Publisher/Group Product Manager; Lindsay MacDonald, Product Developer; Cathie Lefebvre, Marketing Manager; Cathy Biribauer and Jeanette McCurdy, Supervising Editors; and Cat Haggert, Copy Editor, who, with their special expertise, guided us toward a better product.

Julie Bulmash would like to extend a special note of thanks to Courtney Fuller, a student in the post-graduate human resources program at George Brown College, for her research assistance, support, and insights.

And finally, we would like to express our deeply felt thanks to those who assisted us in many tangible and intangible ways: Ruth, Neil, Leslie, and Krista.

Hermann F. Schwind
Krista Uggerslev
Terry H. Wagar
Neil Fassina
Julie Bulmash

The Strategic Human Resource Management Model

Human resource management helps organizations and their employees attain their goals. This section explores some of the challenges facing organizations and outlines how strategic human resource management provides a framework for success upon which the rest of this book builds.

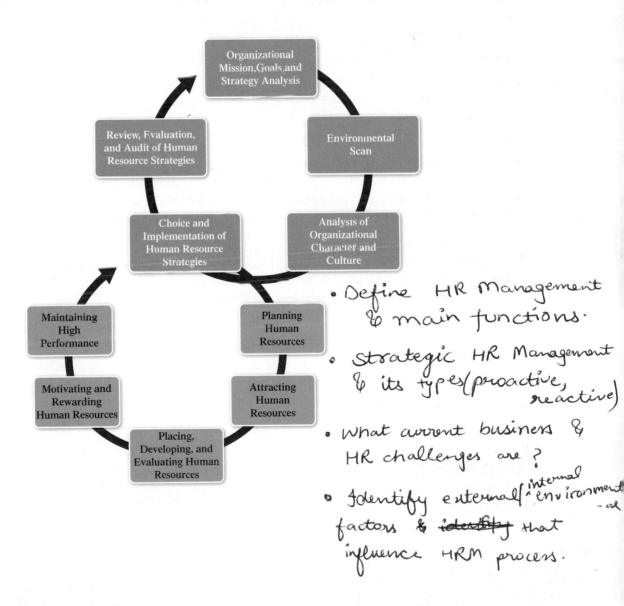

- Define HR Management & main functions.

- Strategic HR Management & its types (proactive, reactive)

- What current business & HR challenges are?

- Identify external/internal environmental factors & ~~identify~~ that influence HRM process.

CHAPTER 1

Strategic Human Resource Management

The only vital value an enterprise has is the experience, skills, innovativeness, and insights of its people.

LEIF EDVINSSON[1]

LEARNING OBJECTIVES

After studying this chapter, you should be able to:

LO1 Discuss the objectives of human resource management.

LO2 Identify steps in strategic management of human resources.

LO3 Explain how human resource departments are organized and function.

LO4 Discuss the role of human resource professionals in today's organization.

Consider for a moment the impact organizations have on your daily life. From the products you consume to the services you use, to the post-secondary institution you are attending, the vast majority of our time is spent interacting with organizations, their products, or services. One element ties all of these organizations together: people.

People are at the core of all social organizations—from the sole proprietor who owns and operates a small coffee shop to a multimillion dollar organization like George Weston Limited <http://www.weston.ca>. They create the goals, the innovations, and the accomplishments for which organizations are praised. They create the work environments that win awards like the "Canada's Best Managed Companies" <https://www.bestmanagedcompanies.ca>. When looked at from the perspective of the organization, people are resources. They are not inanimate resources, such as land and capital; instead, they are *human* resources. Without them, organizations would not exist.

At the beginning of the 1960s, the National Aeronautics and Space Administration (NASA) <http://www.nasa.gov> was trying to figure out how to build a spacecraft that would allow humans to return safely to earth.[2] At the time, an aeronautical engineer named Charles Yost developed what was called "slow spring back foam." This product was later adapted and is now referred to as "memory foam" and is found in football helmets, airline seats, and pillows.

Although NASA's balance sheet did not list its human "assets," these resources were at work. Before the foam discovery, a casual observer would have considered NASA's tangible infrastructure as the company's most important asset. With each discovery and innovation necessary to enable space travel, NASA's assets continued to grow. A keen observer would note that neither the tangible assets nor the innovation would be of great value without capable people to manage them. Amazingly, today NASA faces similar challenges; however, rather than returning from the moon safely, a major innovation challenge is how to return humans safely from Mars.[3]

Organizational success depends upon careful attention to human resources. An organization's strategies are dependent on the people brought together to create them. In turn, the success of an organization relative to these strategies are dependent upon the practices used to organize and lead human resources. Some of the best managed and most successful Canadian organizations are those that effectively make employees meet organizational challenges creatively:

In high-tech organizations, it is critical to motivate the engineers to come out with creative designs and systems; in research organizations, fostering creativity and free flow of ideas among researchers may be the key to success; in some manufacturing organizations, cost control or new innovations spells success; while in retail and service industries, the difference between growth and extinction is marked by the quality of service. In all instances, it is the employees who enable a firm's future and success.

LO1 HRC 1

What Is Human Resource Management?

To understand what human resource management is, we need to first consider why people come together to form organizations. In short, organizations bring people together in a coordinated manner to accomplish goals or objectives that could not be accomplished by a single individual. The goals that organizations set may be as varied as the organizations themselves. Many **organizational goals**, however, may be categorized into economic (e.g., profit, shareholder value), social (e.g., ethical practices), and environmental (e.g., reduction of carbon footprint) goals. For an organization to achieve its goals, employees must engage in actions and behaviours that move the organization toward accomplishing them. If employees do not contribute to an organization's goals—or worse, engage in behaviours or actions that move the organization away from its goals—the organization will stagnate and potentially fail.

organizational goals

An organization's short- and long-term goals that human resource management aims to support and enable.

At its core, **human resource management** is the leadership and management of people within an organization using systems, methods, processes, and procedures that recruit, select, motivate and enable employees to achieve outcomes individually and collectively that in turn enhance employees' positive contribution to the organization's goals. Thus, human resource management is not an end in itself; it is a means of structuring the organization to facilitate and enable the organization to achieve its organizational objectives. The role of human resource management is therefore critical to the success—indeed, even the very survival—of the organization.

human resource management

The leadership and management of people within an organization using systems, methods, processes, and procedures that enable employees to optimize their performance and in turn their contribution to the organization and its goals.

Human resource management as a specialist function evolved from very small beginnings (See Appendix A at the end of this chapter for the growth of human resource functions over time). Inseparable from key organizational goals, product-market plans, technology and innovation, and an organization's strategy, the field of human resource management comprises numerous activities—many of them discussed in depth throughout this textbook. Although each topic within human resources is addressed individually, it is important to recognize that the activities within human resource management are all interconnected. Figure 1-1 highlights some of this interconnectedness. When a change is made to one activity, it often has an impact on another activity. For example, if an organization acts to engage long-term employees in order to prevent them from leaving, it may spend fewer dollars recruiting and hiring new employees.[4] For human resource management systems, practices, and activities to be effective, leaders must consider how changes may affect the system overall.

FIGURE 1-1

The Interconnectivity of Human Resource Management Activities

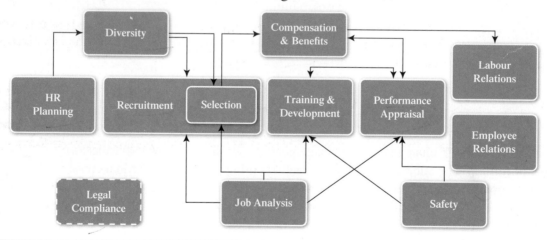

The Difference between Human Resource Management and a Human Resource Department

Before moving on, it is important to differentiate between the field of human resource management and a human resource department. Although human resource management is central to all organizations, not all organizations will have a dedicated human resource department. The field of human resource management thus focuses on what leaders and managers should do as it relates to organizing human resource systems, policies, and procedures. These systems, in turn, create value by facilitating and enabling employees to achieve individual goals that in turn contribute to corporate or organization goals.[5]

A human resource department, on the other hand, is a specialized group with the primary focus of ensuring the most effective use of human resource systems across an organization to enhance employee performance and accomplish organizational goals. The contribution of a human resource department should be kept at a level appropriate to the organization's needs and resources. In a new venture or micro-business, human resource management may be performed by the entrepreneur or one individual who has numerous other duties within the organization. As the organization grows, the organization may decide to hire a professional human resource manager. Within large-scale organizations, it is not uncommon to have numerous people dedicated to organizing human resource practices. However, resources are wasted when the human resource department is more or less sophisticated than the organization demands. A 2006 study on the size of human resource departments in European nations found that, on average, organizations had three human resource staff for every 200 employees.[6]

Regardless of the size of an organization and whether or not the organization has a human resource department, the responsibility for the day-to-day management of human resources most often rests with individual managers throughout the organization.

Strategic Human Resource Management

Human resource management must operate within the framework of an organization. Like other activities, human resource management activities must contribute to the organization's goals and performance.[7] In response to a growing call for accountability, recent decades have witnessed an increased attention to strategic human resource management. Strategic human resource management seeks to recognize that the choice of human resource tools will depend on what the organization is trying to achieve. That is, the human resource management activities must align and contribute to the organization's strategies.

A strategy is similar to a game plan: It involves large-scale, future-oriented, integrated plans to achieve organizational goals and respond to uncertain and competitive environments facing the organization. In part, a strategy identifies how the organization will create value.[8]

Strategies are often formulated at three levels: *corporate*, involving the entire organization; *business*, involving a major activity, business, or division in a large multi-business organization; and *functional*, involving managers of different activities, services (e.g., finance, marketing), or geographical areas.[9] Depending on organizational conditions, strategies may be developed at any or all of these three levels. Strategies can vary significantly, even within the same market.

> Walmart <http://www.walmart.ca/en> uses a slogan of "Save money. Live Better."[10] As a result, Walmart tends to follow a low-cost strategy. Target <http://www.target.com>, on the other hand, has a slogan of "Expect more. Pay less."[11] As a result, Target tends to follow a value-based strategy.

Strategic human resource management is the process of integrating the strategic needs of an organization into our choice of human resource management systems and practices to support the organization's overall mission, strategies, and performance. Strategic human resource management is a value driven, proactive focus on how best to deploy human resource practices and activities to enable an organization of any size to achieve its goals while at the same time recognizing that the people who make up an organizations human resources will have needs and goals of their own. We start with a discussion of strategic human resource management because it lays a foundation from which the topics discussed throughout this textbook can be integrated into a human resource system.

---

strategic human resource management

Integrating the strategic needs of an organization into our choice of human resource management systems and practices to support the organization's overall mission, strategies, and performance.

At the core, it is important that human resource strategies and tactics be mutually consistent and that they reflect the larger organizational mission and strategy. Even the best-laid strategies may fail if they are not accompanied by sound human resource programs or procedures.

> Costco Wholesalers <www.costco.ca> has a strategy based partly on high volume and value-based sales. To support this strategy, they have few people on the retail floor to help shoppers and instead employ a large number of cashiers to process orders more quickly. This could be compared to Holt Renfrew <www.holtrenfrew.com> that has a strategy based partly on high quality and high value products. As such, Holt Renfrew employs proportionately more sales associates to assist shoppers in product choice and fewer cashiers.

By integrating corporate strategies with the choice of human resource practices, human resource managers can remain proactive and anticipate challenges or problems both inside and outside the organization and make adjustments before they impact the organization or its people. This is often referred to as **proactive human resource management.** The alternative is **reactive human resource management**, which occurs when decision makers respond to problems or challenges as they arise.

proactive human resource management

A human resource management approach wherein decision makers anticipate problems or challenges both inside and outside the organization and take action before they impact the organization.

reactive human resource management

A human resource management approach wherein decision makers respond to problems or challenges as they arise rather than anticipate them.

> To contend with the demand for talent in retail locations, a number of large organizations such as McDonald's <http://www.mcdonalds.ca/ca/en.html>, Home Depot <http://www.homedepot.ca/>, and Walmart have turned to recruiting and hiring retired workers to complement traditional recruitment and selection practices focused on the youth.

The strategy of attracting talent from nontraditional labour pools is an example of how proactive strategies can better meet the needs of organizations than reactive ones. In the examples above, the human resource departments of these companies did not wait for a resurgence in the youth population—indeed, a population that continues to shrink. Rather, they sought out talent from a growing population—retiring workers. The importance of understanding the forces that may impact organizations and their strategies are critical in strategic human resource management and will be discussed later in this chapter.

Just as each member of an organization is expected to generate positive contributions to the accomplishment of an organization's goals, so too is every human resource system. That is, each and every human resource system, practice, process, or tactic should generate value for the organization. The challenge for managers of human resources is to understand that within a system of people, a decision to change one thing will often have an impact on other human resource practices or activities. Moreover, these decisions are often influenced by the organization and its environment. To this end, managers of human resources need to be able to integrate and synthesize information about an organization, its environment, its culture, and its strategies to make the most effective human resource decisions for the organization. For example:

> A number of organizations are installing workout facilities within the organization's physical space. At first glance, this may appear to be simply a cost centre for an organization with respect to the installation and ongoing maintenance and operation of the facility. A closer consideration, however, may reveal an increase

in employee morale, decreased expenses associated with sick days and health benefits, and a time savings for employees who no longer need to leave the office early to drive to a gym.

Although HR managers must be consistently strategic in their mindset, human resource issues are also dominating corporate strategic priorities. Part of this focus is based on the observation that employee salaries may account for more than 50 percent of the operating expenses in many organizations.[12] As a result, the expectations for human resource departments are regularly on the rise:

> A survey of 200 CEOs and other top executives in the United States, United Kingdom, France, Spain, Germany, and Australia indicates that four of the five top strategic priorities most commonly identified by business executives are HR related (ranks in parentheses): attracting and retaining skilled staff (1); improving workforce performance (3); changing leadership and management behaviours (4); and changing organizational culture and employee attitudes (5). The other priority, rated second overall, was increasing customer service—while a marketing priority, customer service is still closely linked to HR activities such as training, compensation, and performance management. Only 13 percent of the respondents, however, reported satisfaction with the way their HR departments achieved these priorities, thus underscoring the major strides HR has to make to fulfill organizational expectations.[13]

LO2
Understanding the Strategic Human Resource Management Process

To be effective, a human resource management strategy and system should be formulated after careful consideration of an organization's environment, mission and objectives, strategies, and internal strengths and weaknesses, including its culture. Often, the human resource strategy formulation and implementation process consists of the five steps as outlined in Figure 1-2.

Step 1: Organizational Mission, Goals, and Strategy Analysis

As the line between human resource management and strategic human resource management becomes less clear, a greater integration of human resource systems and priorities into an organization's overall mission, goals, and strategies becomes ever more important. An organizational analysis, involving a close look at the organization's overall mission, goals, and strategies, is the first integral aspect of identifying human resource strategies.

The way in which an organization defines its mission often significantly influences human resource strategies. A **mission statement** specifies what activities the organization intends to pursue and what course is charted for the future. It is a concise statement of "who we are, what we do, and where we are headed" and gives an organization its own special identity, character, and path of development.

mission statement
Statement outlining the purpose, long-term objectives, and activities the organization will pursue and the course for the future.

> For example, two similar pork producers may have varying missions. One may define the mission as "to be a sustainable pork producer," while the other may define it as "to be a leading pork producer." The associated strategies are likely to show significant differences. Apart from finding efficient ways to raise hogs, the former may also seek ways to improve the effectiveness and safety of manure recycling or seek strategies to raise antibiotic-free hogs while the focus of the second producer may be expansion and profitability.

FIGURE 1-2

A Model of Strategic Human Resource Management

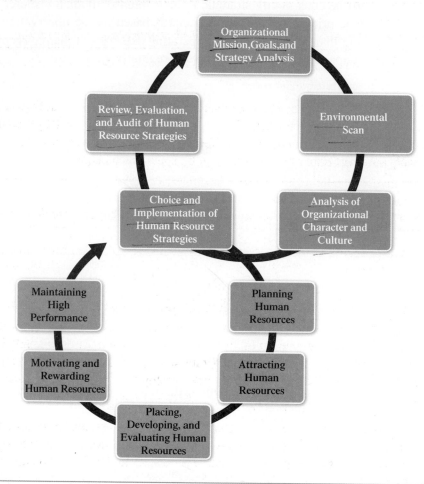

Even organizations with similar goals may show remarkable differences in their strategies to achieve those goals. There are at least three major generic strategies that a firm may pursue: cost leadership, differentiation, or focus.[14]

Firms that pursue a **cost leadership strategy** aim to gain a competitive advantage through lower costs. They aggressively seek efficiencies in production and use tight controls (especially in managing costs) to gain an advantage over their competitors.

cost leadership strategy

Strategy to gain competitive advantage through lower costs of operations and lower prices for products.

The Bic Pen Company <http://ca.bicworld.com/> is a good example of a firm that attempts to compete successfully by producing pens as cheaply as possible. Similar cost leadership strategy is seen in the cases of Timex watches <http://www.timex.ca/en/> and FedEx <http://www.fedex.com/ca_english/> overnight package delivery.

Product **differentiation strategy** focuses on creating a distinctive or even unique product that is unsurpassed in quality, innovative design, or other features. This may be accomplished through product design, unique technology, or even through carefully planned advertising and promotion. Firms that use this strategy may even be able to charge higher-than-average prices for their products.

differentiation strategy

Strategy to gain competitive advantage by creating a distinct product or offering a unique service.

Nikon cameras <http://en.nikon.ca> and Calvin Klein fashion apparel <http://www.calvinkleininc.com> are firms that employ a differentiation strategy.

Under the **focus strategy**, a firm concentrates on a segment of the market and attempts to satisfy it with a low-priced or a highly distinctive product. Within this specific market or target customer group, a focused firm may compete on the basis of either differentiation or cost leadership. The target market in this instance is usually set apart either by geography or by specialized needs.

focus strategy

Strategy to gain a competitive advantage by focusing on the needs of a specific segment of the total market.

An automobile manufacturer sells its sport utility vehicles primarily in North America because of the local demand. The same firm sells its smaller and fuel-efficient economy car in less-developed countries because consumers there have lower disposable income or require smaller vehicles.

Regardless of an organization's strategic focus, human resources are required to formulate and eventually accomplish those strategies. In all cases, the human resource strategies that are chosen should seek to enable successful completion of these strategies. In some cases, a single human resource strategy may be used to accomplish different corporate strategies. Many organizations are also now including specific strategies that directly consider their employees. For example, many organizations have set as a strategy to become one of Canada's "Top 50 Best Managed Companies."[15]

The challenge facing human resource leaders is that often the human resource strategy needs to be put in place before the corporate strategy can be successful. That is, the human resource strategy needs to be implemented so that the right people are in the right place at the right time to even initiate the corporate strategy. This creates new challenges for human resource professionals, such as needing to predict and respond to numerous forces, some of which are discussed in step 2.

Step 2: Environmental Scan

Through careful and continuous monitoring of economic, social, and labour market trends and by noting changes in governmental policies, legislation, and public policy statements, effective human resource management will be able to identify environmental threats and opportunities that in turn serve as a foundation for new action guidelines. Some of the strongest environmental forces facing Canadian organizations today are listed in Figure 1-3. For discussion purposes, the major forces facing a Canadian organization (especially those affecting human resource management) can be grouped under five headings: *economic* (e.g., recession), *technological* (e.g., automation), *demographic* (e.g., workforce composition), *cultural* (e.g., ethnic diversity), and *legal* (e.g., changing laws). The first four forces will be discussed in this chapter. The critical importance of legal compliance for the human resource function warrants a more elaborate review of the subject matter. Hence, this topic is discussed in detail in Chapter 4.

FIGURE 1-3

Major Forces Facing Canadian Business

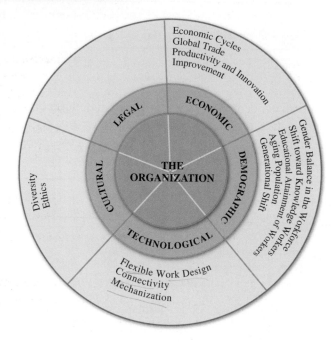

Economic Forces

Economic Force: Economic Cycles

The first of four critical **economic forces** is *economic cycles*.

---

economic forces

Economic factors facing Canadian business today, including global trade forces and the force to increase one's own competitiveness and productivity levels.

Economies go through boom and bust business cycles. The Canadian economy is no exception to this. In today's globally connected world, misfortunes originating in one economy are soon passed on to others. This further complicates the challenges that human resource professionals must consider in designing practices, policies, and the broader system. For instance, human resource managers face special challenges during a recessionary period, as they often have to carry out the unpleasant task of planning, communicating, and implementing employee layoffs. Often, wage concessions have to be sought from labour for the sheer survival of the firm. The workforce morale, by and large, is low during a recessionary period; supplementary employee counselling may become necessary. At times, the entire organization may assume a crisis management posture, which creates new challenges for the human resource manager with respect to policy formulation, communication, and implementation.

The challenges are equally daunting coming out of a recession, as human resource managers consider how best to grow the organization's talent base. During growth cycles, organizations may be faced with the opportunity of recruiting employees with a different skill set than those that may have been let go during the recessionary cycle.

By the end of 2011 Canada had endured a global recession better than most other industrialized countries and was the only Group of Eight (G8) country to recover all outputs and jobs lost during the recession.[16] By 2014, Canada had fared better than any other Group of Seven (G7) Country in employment improvement.[17] 1,054,000 jobs were recovered between July 2009 and December 2014, improving the unemployment rate to 7.0 percent, down from a peak of 8.7 percent during the recession.[18]

It is important to recognize that boom and bust cycles may not be experienced the same across the country. For instance, the manufacturing sector in Southern Ontario often cycles based on the value of the Canadian dollar against the American dollar. The oil and gas sector in Alberta, on the other hand, tends to vary based on the price of crude oil on the world market. This results in localized challenges for finding talent. Between 2009 and 2013, the job vacancy rate in Alberta rose from 2.9% to 6.1%. During the same period, the job vacancy rate in Ontario rose from 3.5% to 4.0%.[19]

Economic Force: Global Trade

International trade has always been critical to Canada's prosperity and growth. Canada ranks high among exporting nations: on a per capita basis, we export much more than either the United States or Japan. The combination of a relatively small population and a large natural resource base gives Canada an international trade advantage.

While our ability to compete in the international marketplace has been generally strong, recently there has been erosion in our overall competitiveness. In 2011, Canada was the twelfth most competitive nation in the world; however, in 2015, we had fallen to fifteenth (Figure 1-4).[20]

FIGURE 1-4

How Competitive Is Canada vis-à-vis Other Nations?

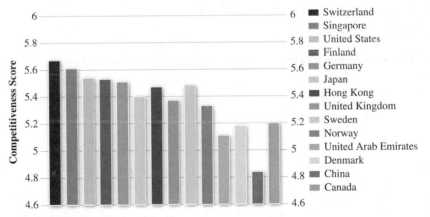

SOURCE: Table 3: "The Global Competitiveness Index 2013-2014 rankings and 2012-2013 comparisons", World Economic Forum, Switzerland (2014). Used with permission.

The ever-growing shift toward the global marketplace forces organizations to consider how they manage their employees. The emergence of open borders has presented newer opportunities to Canadian firms and professionals—resulting in Canadians working abroad as well as an increase in economic immigration to Canada. Progressive human resource practices and new government policies may be critical to meet these growing realities.[21]

Economic Force: Productivity and Innovation Improvement

Productivity refers to the ratio of an organization's outputs (e.g., goods and services) to its inputs (e.g., people, capital, materials, and energy). Productivity increases as an organization finds new ways to use fewer resources to produce its output. For example:

---

productivity

The ratio of a firm's outputs (goods and services) divided by its inputs (people, capital, materials, energy).

A restaurant may seek to improve productivity through using fewer ingredients in recipes (reduction in raw materials), asking a server to also clear, clean, and reset tables (increase in responsibility and associated reduction in the need for additional staff), or alternatively seek to increase the number of outputs by having more people come to the restaurant. The latter, however, may require increased marketing efforts, which would result in an increase in inputs.

In a business environment, productivity optimization is essential for long-run success. Individuals can even gain accreditation in optimization processes through organizations like International Association for Six Sigma Certification <http://www.iassc.org>. Through gains in productivity, managers can reduce costs, save scarce resources, and enhance profits. In turn, improved profits allow an organization to provide better pay, benefits, and working conditions. The result can be a higher quality of work life for employees, who are more likely to be motivated toward further improvements in productivity. Human resource professionals contribute to improved productivity directly by finding better, more efficient ways to meet their objectives and indirectly by improving the quality of work life for employees.

Unfortunately, optimizing productivity is not simply a matter of increasing outputs or decreasing inputs. In either case, it is a question of asking people to do more for less. As a result, a major challenge facing Canadian managers is productivity optimization while maintaining a high quality of work life for the employees. Moreover, strategic human resource management seeks to address more than just financial productivity.[22] Some of the strategies to address productivity will be discussed in Chapter 3.

What is worrisome today is the gap in the productivity levels of Canada and its biggest trade partner, the United States.[23] For over a decade, U.S. productivity has been consistently outpacing that of this country. Canada is steadily losing its ability to innovate and create wealth compared with other countries, according to a study by the Massachusetts Institute of Technology <http://web.mit.edu>. In this study, which ranked the 16 leading members of the Organisation for Economic Co-operation and Development <http://www.oecd.org>, Canada had slipped to ninth spot from sixth a decade before. Even more troublesome is the study's forecast that unless Canada changes its course soon, the country will lose more ground early in this millennium.[24] By 2013, Canada had slipped to 13 of 16 peer nations on innovation performance.[25]

A study by the Science, Technology, and Innovation Council <http://www.stic-csti.ca> released in 2009 that tracked Canada's performance by an array of measures including federal and business spending on research and development, the number of citizens with advanced degrees, venture capital investment, and basic literacy among workforce gave the country a mediocre grade compared to other nations.[26]

If Canada is to improve—even maintain—its competitiveness, innovation on two fronts, namely people management and technology, are a must.

Together the United States and Japan accounted for over 60 percent of all world patents, but Canada's share was approximately a mere 2 percent—a "D" grade in innovation according to the Conference Board of

Canada.[27] Canada ranks second to last for the number of trademarks filed per million population, with Switzerland ranking first.[28]

Without innovation, productivity differences tend to increase. As such, without innovation, Canadian employers and the human resource professionals will be faced with the challenge of creating additional productivity improvements. As a progressive human resource strategy, numerous organizations are starting to recruit or develop innovative staff to create a culture of innovation within the organization.

Technological Forces

Technological Force: Flexible Work Design

Technology influences organizations and the way people work. Often it can affect an entire industry, as the following example illustrates:

> With a history dating back to 1880, Kodak <http://www.kodak.ca> was among the major producers of photographic film. The advent of digital photography and technology is among the factors that contributed to Kodak filing for bankruptcy in 2012. Of note, Kodak had invented the digital photography technology, but chose not to commercialize it.[29]

Canada has witnessed the rapid growth of technology and access to high-speed information transmission systems affecting almost all walks of life. An unprecedented degree of technology has changed the way we work, play, study, and even entertain ourselves. Access to information has affected the way several organizations conduct their business. Nevertheless, Canada lags behind a number of developed nations in technology development and use.

> The government has actively encouraged initiatives, including the development of digital and broadband networks, to develop high-speed access throughout the country suitable for wireless and Internet applications.[30] Canada ranks eleventh in the OECD countries, down from second place in 2002. In addition, Canada's broadband market continues to rank poorly with regard to price and speed.[31]

Technology brings considerable flexibility into when and where work is carried out. In several instances, employees can work without ever leaving their homes. Such *telecommuting* has been found to cut employee stress and boost worker productivity in several instances, while also reducing the costs of operations.[32] More than 18 percent of Canada's working population works from a nontraditional workplace such as their home.[33]

> Telus Communications <http://telus.com> intends to arrange for half of its 30,000 employees to be able to work from home if they choose. In a 2006 pilot, Telus found that having 170 employees working from home saved 114 tonnes of greenhouse gases and 14,000 hours of traffic time. In the same pilot, Telus found that morale as well as productivity increased as a result of telecommuting.[34]

Telecommuting, however, is not without its human resource challenges. For instance, a challenge related to telecommuting is how an organization can best ensure that the employee's home workstation is safe.

Not all jobs lend themselves to less traditional workspaces; but with the advances in technology, virtually any job—or any part of a job—that involves work that is independent of other people and special equipment could be performed away from the workplace. Careful planning, training, and piloting may be required before telecommuting is rolled out in an organization, as managing from a distance is simply different from managing in person.[35]

More recently, a greater focus has been placed on cyber security.[36] With employees working distally, the probability of data breaches is also likely to climb. From a strategic human resource perspective, some organizations have taken to hiring cyber security experts to not only protect their sensitive data, but also make attempts to breach their security systems in an effort to better protect their data.

Technological Force: Connectivity

Connectivity and technology have disrupted the way organizations operate, often reducing costs or capitalizing on new opportunities.

McCarthy Tetrault <http://www.mccarthy.ca>, Canada's biggest law firm, saw technology as an area of opportunity and began recruiting lawyers with high-tech expertise. This in turn enabled the firm to take advantage of the opportunities in intellectual capital management.[37]

More effective *knowledge management*—the process of capturing organizational knowledge and making it available for sharing and building new knowledge—has been another outcome of digital information systems. It has given rise to potentially boundless information.[38] Intranets and integrated information systems help store and access information quickly and accurately. Information management systems capture an incredible amount of digital information about an employee, giving rise to human resource data analytics.[39] For instance, they can store what the employee learns during various training programs (or over a time period) and give evidence of performance improvement. When the annual performance interview is conducted, managers can identify the on-the-job competencies of an employee. The aggregation of the skill sets and competencies of all employees help the organization manage its human capital more effectively.[40]

Even the field of human resources is being shaped by big data trends. For instance, metaBUS <http://www.metabus.org> is a technology-based start-up that is seeking to bring together and synthesize every correlation within the field of human resources over a twenty-five year period to enable human resource practitioners make better data-informed decisions about their practices and systems.

The Internet is a platform for communication and interaction, which has had a profound impact on human resource management activities. Social networking sites, video-sharing sites, wikis, blogs, and other interactive opportunities allow users to own and control data as well as add value to the applications they use. This has resulted in rapid use of the technology for a variety of human resource purposes. It has also resulted in organizations needing to create human resource policies about the limitations of social networking within organizations.

Technological Force: Mechanization

Mechanization continues to be a technological force and opportunity that has affected Canadian organizations and their human resource management practices.

---

mechanization

The shift toward converting work that was traditionally done by hand to being completed by mechanical or electronic devices.

Organizations tend to mechanize for speed, reliability, or flexibility. Competition from other countries has made it imperative that we improve the speed of our manufacturing practices if we want to stay competitive. This trend has led to the development of mechatronics programs at some post-secondary institutions.

By moving to a mechanized process, better service may be provided to the customer through *increased predictability and reliability* in operations and *higher standards* of quality in production. Machines do not go on strike, nor do they ask for raises.

Mechanization allows for *flexibility* in operations. In several automated production facilities, even small production batches become economically viable since the time, cost, and effort involved in changing setups are minimal. The ability to produce small batches in turn enables a firm to focus on the needs of different customers and market segments and speed up delivery schedules.

Shapeways <http://www.shapeways.com> is an organization that specializes in rapid prototyping and small batch production through three-dimensional printing in materials such as plastic and metal. These products can be created in minutes.

Mechanization and automation is not without human resource challenges. Negative union attitudes toward mechanization are a barrier to the introduction of technology in the workplace. Automation may result in a smaller workforce together with fewer opportunities for socialization on the job. To use expensive technology effectively (during an automation), more and more manufacturing facilities may find it necessary to work two or three shifts a day. In addition, the technologies used in industries such as additive manufacturing may require highly skilled designers, operators, and technicians.

Improvements in technology and automation have helped the British Columbia lumber industry to increase its production by 25 percent with 6,000 fewer workers. In the pulp and paper industry, production has increased by a quarter; however, we have 9 percent fewer jobs now (having lost 12,000 jobs in the change process).[41] These are not jobs lost temporarily to adjust to a business cycle or to make short-term adjustments to competition—the new ways of working mean that these positions are lost forever.

In summary, the technology employed by different firms shows considerable variation. In organizations such as a large steel factory or lumber mill, the production processes are fairly routine. In several such organizations, improving predictability of operations assumes great importance. This often requires human resource managers to focus more on predictability of employee performance (e.g., by providing explicit job descriptions, job-specific training, and focusing on performance monitoring). In contrast, in firms with nonroutine production processes (such as advertising firms and software developers), flexible human resource practices that foster creativity, innovation, and entrepreneurship may add more value.

Robots are increasingly being used in places not yet seen before. The neuroArm developed at the University of Calgary is a surgical robotic system that is controlled by a surgeon working at a computer and guided by continuous magnetic resonance images.

Courtesy of Neuroarm, University of Calgary.

Demographic Forces

Demographic Force: Gender Balance in the Workforce

The demographics of the labour force describe the composition of the workforce: the education levels, the age levels, the percentage of the population participating in the workforce, and other population characteristics. While **demographic changes** occur slowly and can be predicted in most instances, they still exert considerable influence on organizational decisions. Each demographic change will have a different impact on the choice of human resource practices and activities, but may also have an additive effect. As a result, managers of human resources must consider demographic shifts both in isolation and as an integrated system.

---

demographic changes

Changes in the demographics of the labour force (e.g., education levels, age levels, participation rates) that occur slowly and are usually known in advance.

As of January 2015, Canada's labour force consisted of almost 19.1 million people aged 15 years or older, up from 14.2 million in 1990.[42] Nearly 48 percent of the workforce in 2015 are women.[43] Moreover, the participation rate of women in management, law, engineering, and medical fields also continues to grow (see Figure 1-5). The fact that women accounted for 70 percent of the total employment growth in Canada in the last two decades has underscored issues of child care, work–family balance, dual-career families, and employment equity.[44] Partly due to factors such as these, more women than men tend to work part-time (see Figure 1-6).

FIGURE 1-5

Distribution of Gender in the Workforce in Different Industries

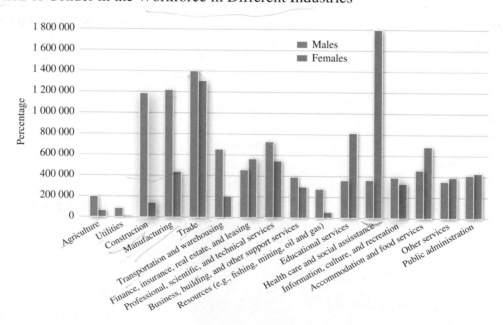

SOURCE: Adapted from Statistics Canada, "Labour force survey estimates by sex and detailed age group," CANSIM, table 282-0002.

FIGURE 1-6

Labour Force Employed Full-Time and Part-Time among Men and Women between 1990 and 2014

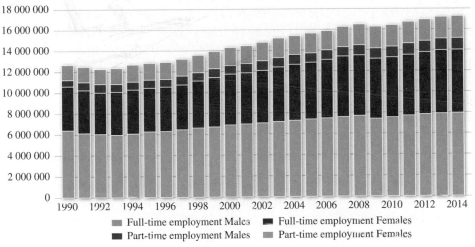

SOURCE: Adapted from Statistics Canada, "Labour force survey estimates by sex and detailed age group," CANSIM, table 282-0002.

Demographic Force: Shift toward Knowledge Workers

Currently there is a shift from employment in primary and extractive industries (such as mining and fishing) to service, technical, and professional jobs. The relative contribution to Canada's employment in various industries is shown in Figure 1-7. Service industries such as education, health care, tourism, trade, and public administration make significant contributions to our national wealth today—all services combined currently account for more than 75 percent of the gross domestic product (GDP).[45] Over 78 percent of the total labour force is employed in service-producing industries.[46]

FIGURE 1-7

Employment by Industry in Canada

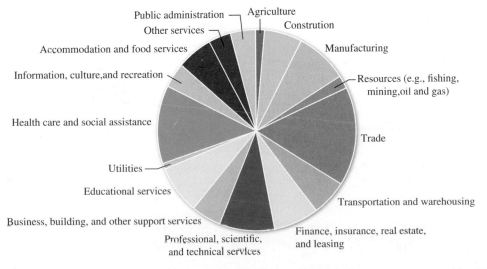

SOURCE: Adapted from Statistics Canada, "Employment by industry," CANSIM, table 282-0008 and Catalogue no. 71F0004XCB.

The move away from extractive industries increases the need for innovation. In part, it creates an environment that requires not only knowledge workers, but individuals who bring innovative thinking to their organization.

Knowledge workers have been the fastest-growing type of workers in the Canadian labour force over the last quarter century or so.[47] Although total employment grew at an average rate of 2.1 percent per year in the past two decades, the employment of knowledge workers grew at a rate of 5.2 percent per year. This is twice the pace of service workers, the second-fastest-growing group of workers over that period. It is estimated that by 2021, there will be a shortage of over 40,000 knowledge workers in the province of Alberta alone.[48]

---

knowledge workers

Members of occupations generating, processing, analyzing, or synthesizing ideas and information (like scientists and management consultants).

The ability of organizations to find, keep, and continually retrain these workers might spell success in the coming years. This is not only a trend in North America. China has taken great strides toward moving away from a factory-based to a knowledge-based economy.[49] With an increased reliance on knowledge workers, organizations also start to face challenges associated with employees hiding and withholding knowledge.[50] A further challenge facing human resource professionals in a growing knowledge-based economy is that educational attainment is not keeping pace.

Demographic Force: Educational Attainment of Workers

A look at the **educational attainment** of Canadian workers presents an intriguing picture. The educational attainment of Canadians has increased dramatically over the past several years and is expected to maintain its upward trend (see Figure 1-8).

---

educational attainment

The highest educational level attained by an individual worker, employee group, or population.

FIGURE 1-8

Educational Attainment of Canadian Workforce

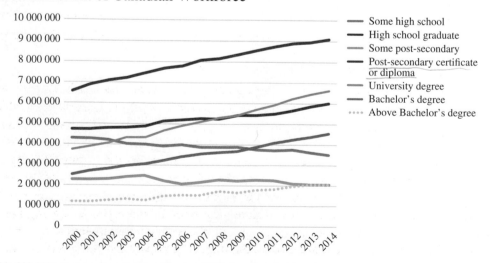

SOURCE: Table 282-0004 "Labour force survey estimates (LFS), by educational attainment, sex, and age group," from Statistics Canada, CANSIM.

In 2010, 68 percent of Canadians aged 25 to 44 years and 57 percent of Canadians aged 45 to 64 years were post-secondary graduates.[51] Over 19 percent of Canadian men and 17 percent of women aged 25 or above hold a university degree or better (the corresponding figure a decade ago was less than 10 percent).[52]

Primary and secondary education systems play a key role in generating the new supply of skills needed by our post-industrial society. By and large, Canadian schools appear to be ready for this task.

> In one study, approximately 30,000 students from more than 1,000 Canadian schools were compared on their mathematical and scientific literacy with students in 31 other countries. Canadian students performed well compared to others, ranking second in reading, seventh in science, and eighth in mathematics. In a majority of provinces, students' performance in reading, science, and mathematics placed these provinces among the top-ranked countries.[53]

The disturbing news, however, is that 15 percent of Canadians aged 16 or over fall in the lowest levels of literacy.[54] They have difficulty understanding printed materials and most likely experience problems reading any written words. Not only do such low literacy rates reduce the overall productivity levels in our industries, they may also be a major contributor to safety violations and accidents. Moreover, as the nature of work shifts to that of knowledge-based industries, the demand for individuals with post-secondary education will outpace the rate at which people attain a post-secondary education.

> About 9 percent of women and 15 percent of men drop out of school before they graduate.[55] It is estimated that currently more than 5.2 million Canadians lack a basic school certificate or diploma.[56] What is worse, our education system still frequently produces persons who do not have basic literary and numerical skills.

Some of the more progressive employers have recognized workplace literacy as a serious issue and have taken proactive action to minimize its adverse consequences.

> Durabelt Inc. <http://www.durabeltinc.com>, a company based in Prince Edward Island that manufactures conveyor belts for vegetable harvesters, was nominated for a national award for excellence in workplace literacy. The "Duraschool project," which has been in operation since 1997, converts the lunchroom and offices into classrooms for two evenings each week where several employees and family members routinely gather to update their math, reading, and writing skills.[57]

Faced with this disheartening prospect, the Corporate Council on Education identified a set of "employability skills" consisting of basic academic skills (e.g., communication, thinking, learning), personal management skills (e.g., positive attitudes and behaviours, ability to accept responsibility, adaptability to new challenges), and teamwork skills (e.g., ability to work with others, ability to lead a team). These skills were considered to be the foundation skills for employability in the future.[58]

Demographic Force: Aging Population

One of the impending issues for human resource managers is what *Maclean's* termed our old age crisis.[59] In 1996, about 28 percent of the population (or almost 7.6 million Canadians) were more than 50 years old. Beginning in 2012, the proportion of the population in the age group 65 and over will continue to expand rapidly, reinforced by a low birth rate and longer life expectancy. In 2016, the age group comprising those age 65 and over will form 16.5 percent of the population. By 2060, this proportion will increase to 25.4 percent. Conversely, the age category between 15 and 30 years old will decrease from 19.3 percent to 16.9 percent of the population over the same time frame.[60] In short, human resource professionals will face an ever-increasing trend of more people leaving the workforce than entering it. This is because the average age of the Canadian population has been steadily increasing (see Figure 1-9). Like economic cycles, the impact of population aging is different depending on your location.

FIGURE 1-9

Population Projections for Canada

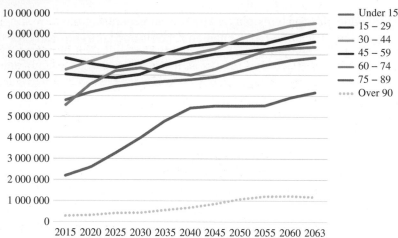

SOURCE: Adapted from Statistics Canada, "Projected population, by projection scenario, age and sex, as of July 1, Canada, provinces and territories," CANSIM, table 052-0005.

In 2016, the provinces with the highest proportion of the labour force aged 65 and over were Quebec, New Brunswick, Nova Scotia, and Prince Edward Island, all at 19 percent compared to 16.5 percent for Canada as a whole.[61] At the other end of the scale, Nunavut has only 7 percent of their population over the age of 65 in 2016. By 2038, Prince Edward Island will pull in front with 32 percent of their population over the age of 65, whereas Nunavut will continue to have the lowest percentage at 15 percent.

The exact consequences of this trend for the human resource management function are hard to predict. An increasingly hectic scramble for jobs (especially in the traditional sectors) may be one consequence. This is because the fear of post-retirement poverty (fuelled by uncertainty about government-sponsored pension plans and the recent volatility in the stock market which eroded the savings of many Canadians) may motivate employees to hold on to their current jobs. This may create unprecedented bottlenecks in professional and unionized industries.

According to Statistics Canada, the age of retirement has been on the rise since the 1990s. The average age for retirement in 2000 was 61.6, whereas the same number in 2014 was 63.[62]

Pressures for expanded retirement benefits, variable work schedules, coordination of government benefits (e.g., Canada/Quebec Pension Plan benefits) with company benefits, and retraining programs are just a few of the challenges that await human resource specialists in the future. This effect is compounded by recent changes to old age security. Specifically, workers now have to wait until they are 67 to claim old age security.

One major challenge facing Canadian organizations is retaining older, more experienced, and skilled employees whose expertise is in demand in the labour market. The past view of people as expendable cogs who are responsible for managing their own careers has encouraged employees to leave their employers as soon as a better opportunity emerges elsewhere. To retain older workers, employers have to show respect and appreciation, facilitate career growth within the organization, offer flexible work and opportunities to telecommute, and recognize their skills and experience.[63]

The abolition of mandatory retirement has also brought in new challenges as well as opportunities. An aging population affects many human resource functions, especially recruitment and selection, job design, training, appraisal, and compensation and benefits administration.

The availability of retirees provides an opportunity to employers who are looking for experienced, part-time employees. The reduction in the supply of young workers (a staple source of recruits by many fast-food restaurants and grocery chains) may be compensated by the availability of older workers willing to work part-time. Experienced and highly motivated retirees may be a welcome source of recruits for employers and nonprofit/voluntary agencies searching for persons who can accept supervisory responsibilities.

The age crisis is not limited to older generations. A declining youth population—those under age 25—entering the workforce has implications for Canada on a global scale. While Canada's youth population is falling in relation to the population overall, developing economies such as India are experiencing an increase in the youth population relative to the population overall.

Demographic Force: Generational Shift

Generation X (also sometimes called the Nexus generation) employees, who are born between 1966 and 1980, are considered to be different from the baby boomers (the previous generation). While Generation Xers are not averse to hard work, they place a premium on work–life balance and like to be active participants in decision making.[64] They are likely to show disdain for a "command and control" culture and are likely to have more loyalty to their profession and competency building than to their employers.

> Some writers claim that Gen Xers think of work as a job while boomers view it as a career. Xers are unfazed by power and authority; boomers are impressed and attracted by it. Xers mistrust most business practices; boomers instituted many of them. Xers are self-reliant; boomers are team-oriented.[65]

The newest generation in the labour market, Generation Y, is qualitatively different from either of the above groups:

> Generation Yers—those people who are entering the workforce today for the first time—may not respond well to traditional management practices. While it is risky to over-generalize about any group, significant numbers of Gen Yers seek continuous learning, ongoing feedback, teamwork, up-to-date technology, security, respect, and work–life balance. Their biggest fear is boredom. Some consider these new entrants to the workplace to hold unrealistically high expectations of themselves and others, often resulting in the setting of unrealistic targets and resultant frustration.[66]

In today's workplace, leaders may be faced with up to four generations—Generation Y, Generation X, baby boomers, and traditionalists. This generational diversity creates an interpersonal dynamic for all leaders regardless of age in that they must be aware of the different motivators for each of the generations and be able to tailor activities to different age demographics.

Generational shifts in North America are also having complex implications for human resource managers that are somewhat outside their control. For example, certain industries will be facing an impending skilled trades shortage in part because of the increasing average age of the skilled trade worker and in part because of challenges attracting young people to the skilled trades in post-secondary education.

Cultural Forces

Cultural Force: Diversity

As cultural values change, human resource departments discover new challenges. While several **cultural forces** face Canadian managers, we will only discuss diversity and ethics briefly here as an important consideration in the formulation of HR strategy. Cultural diversity will be discussed with greater detail in Chapter 14.

cultural forces

Challenges facing a firm's decision makers because of cultural differences among employees or changes in core cultural or social values occurring at the larger societal level.

In 1971, Canada became the first country to declare multiculturalism as a state policy.[67] By 2006, the Canadian population was made up of over 200 ethnic origins.[68] The coexistence of numerous national, racial, and ethnic groups, each with its unique cultural and social background, makes Canadian society a **cultural mosaic**.[69] Economic immigrants have often acted as engines of economic growth in this country, while shifts in the country of origin of immigrants have added to the cultural diversity and richness of this country.

cultural mosaic

Canadian ideal of encouraging each ethnic, racial, and social group to maintain its own cultural heritage, forming a national mosaic of different cultures.

Canada's workplaces become more and more diverse as each visible minority is encouraged to maintain his or her unique cultural heritage. What potential conflicts can develop because of this "encouragement"?

© Blue Images/Corbis

Unlike the American notion of the "melting pot," Canada has encouraged each ethnic minority to maintain its unique cultural heritage to form part of the Canadian cultural mosaic. Canada is no longer a two-language nation; millions of Canadians have neither English nor French as their mother tongue.

Today, over 3.6 million Canadians are referred to as *allophones*, which literally means "other speaking." For example, today, more Canadians speak Chinese than Italian and it is the most common nonofficial language.[70]

For the practising manager, this cultural diversity simultaneously brings additional opportunities and challenges. Often, it is the human resource department's responsibility to maximize the beneficial outcomes and minimize the challenges posed by a diverse workforce.

Cultural Force: Ethics

There is also a greater demand today for more ethical conduct of business. The unethical practices of several large companies including Bre-X, Enron, and WorldCom underscored the social costs of unethical and fraudulent business practices. Businesses, especially big corporations, have been accused of acting totally out of self-interest and furthering the interest of a few members of the top management. In recent years, a variety of unethical practices have been reported including creative accounting, insider trading, securities fraud, excessive payments made to top management not reflective of their contributions, and bribery and kickbacks. Indeed, greed and short-term orientation accompanied by creative accounting played no small role in the stock market meltdown and the acceleration of personal bankruptcies in 2008.

> A survey of Canadian firms indicated that 57 percent of respondents had been victims of fraudulent activities such as secret commissions, inflated expense reports, and personal use of company property. The most important ethical issues confronting Canadian firms today would seem to relate to avoiding conflicts of interest and maintaining honest governance, employee and client privacy, environmental protection, and security of information.[71]

This has resulted in many Canadian firms instituting a code of ethics or code of conduct for their employees. Over 70 percent of the responding firms in a survey[72] had also instituted a program to promote ethical values and practices. Needless to say, the human resource department will be a key player in this important activity.

Spotlight *on* ETHICS

What Is a "Right" Behaviour?

Ethics are moral principles that guide human behaviours and are often based on a society's cultural values, norms, customs, and beliefs, which means that different cultures and even individuals within the same society have widely varying standards of behaviour. How are we to differentiate "right" from "wrong" or "good" from "bad"? There are no simple answers. Many adopt one of the following postures in dealing with such ambiguous situations:

1. Universalist approach: Persons who embrace this view assert that some moral standards are universally applicable. In other words, regardless of society or place, a bad act (such as killing or stealing) is bad. There are no exceptions to moral "rights" and "wrongs."

2. Situational approach: What is good or bad depends essentially on the situation or culture surrounding the actor. While telling the truth is desirable, there may be situations in which lying is acceptable or even necessary, or other cultures may not value truth to the same extent. Similarly, while killing is bad, there may be situations in which this act is justified. It all depends on the situation. While high morals are to be followed, an individual may have to make exceptions when outcomes justify them.

3. Subjectivist approach: In this approach, the individual decision maker facing a situation determines what is right and wrong after considering all aspects of the situation. Moral decisions are based on personal values and preferences. Needless to say, the standards imposed by individuals are vastly different depending on their upbringing, current circumstances, values, and beliefs.

Another useful model to understand and guide ethical behaviour is offered by Lawrence Kohlberg. Kohlberg, an American psychologist, posits six stages that form an invariant and universal sequence in individual development; thus, everyone is supposed to go through the same stages in the same sequence. It is,

(Continued)

however, possible for a person to be "stuck" at one of the following stages and not proceed to the next level. The six stages of moral development identified by Kohlberg[73] are:

Stage 1: Obedience and Punishment Stage: The only reason for a person to perform the "right" act at this stage is obedience to others who have the power to punish.

Stage 2: Reciprocity Stage: Here, the individual enters into reciprocal agreements with others so that he or she receives the greatest good or reward. The focus is on achieving one's own objectives and on self-interest; for this, the individual concerned is willing to take actions that others want him or her to take.

Stage 3: Interpersonal Conformity Stage: What is "right" is determined by expectations of others who are close to the individual. Close relatives, friends, and other "reference groups" help the individual identify the "right" action in any setting.

Stage 4: Law and Order Stage: Doing one's duty and obeying society's rules is considered the "right" behaviour at this stage.

Stage 5: The Social Contract Stage: Here, the individual goes beyond the minimal standards established by laws and rules. "The greatest good of the greatest number" in the society is the maxim that guides the individual's behaviour at this stage.

Stage 6: Universal Ethical Principles Stage: At this stage, the individual is guided by high moral principles. People are to be treated as ends in themselves, not just as means to one's ends or even to the ends of a whole group or society. People are considered as inherently valuable and to be treated in the "right" way. Very few individuals reach this level.

The field of human resource management is full of situations that involve hard choices between good and bad, right and wrong, desirable and undesirable. Indeed, 52 percent of the 462 American HR professionals surveyed in the 2003 Business Ethics Survey[74] reported feeling at least some pressure to compromise their organization's ethical standards. The reasons most often cited for engaging in unethical behaviours were a need to follow the boss's orders (49 percent of the respondents), pressure to meet overly aggressive business objectives (48 percent), and helping the organization to survive (40 percent). Also mentioned frequently was pressure to be a "team player."

The Spotlight on Ethics feature in this book will introduce you to one or more ethical challenges associated with the topic discussed in each chapter. Once you have identified your responses, compare your answer to those of your friends or family members. Find out why each person chose differently. Try to categorize the responses under the three categories and six stages of moral development listed above. Which approach seems to be used by most of your friends and acquaintances? At what stage of moral development are you and your friends? Why? What are the implications for yourself and your employer? What prevents you and your friends from moving to the next stage?

Instructions: Consider the following situation. Make a note of your answer on a separate sheet and compare it with those of your friends and acquaintances.

Your organization currently offers a pension plan that provides employees with a defined benefit of 2 percent of employees' salary at retirement per year of service. Your pension fund manager has just informed you the pension fund cannot sustain the current defined benefit because of the combination of an extraordinary number of predicted retirements in the next ten years, the cumulative years of service provided by retiring employees, and a general increase in life expectancy. The pension fund manager has suggested that the fund be amended such that the defined benefit would be reduced to 1.8 percent of employees' salary per year of service. What would you do?

Step 3: Analysis of Organizational Character and Culture

In addition to external scans, human resource strategies should be formed only after a careful consideration of the internal environment and elements such as character and culture. Similarities between organizations can be found among their parts, but each whole organization has a unique character. **Organization character** is the product of all of an organization's features: its employees, its objectives, its technology, its size, its age, its unions, its policies, its successes, and its failures. Organization character reflects the past and shapes the future.[75] Human resource specialists should be familiar with and adjust to the character of the organization. For example, sometimes objectives can be achieved in several acceptable ways. This idea, often overlooked, is called *equifinality*, which means there are usually many paths to any given objective. The key to success is choosing the path that best fits the organization's character.

---

organization character

The product of all of an organization's features—people, objectives, technology, size, age, unions, policies, successes, and failures.

Human resource manager Aaron Chu feared that his request to hire a training assistant would be turned down. So instead of asking for funds to hire someone, Aaron expressed concern that poor supervisory skills were contributing to employee complaints and some resignations. He observed at the weekly management meeting that unskilled replacements might lead to rising labour costs. Knowing that top management was concerned that the company remain a low-cost producer, Aaron was not surprised when the plant manager suggested hiring "someone to do training around here." Aaron received a budget increase for training. By adjusting to the organization's character, he achieved his objective.

Often, several key managerial decisions and values are a "given" for the human resource manager. In some organizations, the top management may follow an autocratic decision-making style and foster a strong organizational hierarchy. In contrast, other organizations consciously make an effort to create an egalitarian, participative, and entrepreneurial work climate. HR practices such as seniority- and rank-based pay and top-down communication channels are likely to work best in the former situation while results-oriented (and competency-based) pay and up-and-down communication channels are likely to work best in the latter instance.

The managerial philosophy also influences the type of organization structure and the HR department's role within the firm. For instance, in a highly formal bureaucracy that is structured along functional lines (e.g., marketing, finance, production, etc.), HR's role is often to preserve the existing division of work through clear job descriptions, hiring of specialists for each division, and introducing training systems that foster functional expertise. In contrast, in organizations that have flexible structures, socialization of employees to create an organization-wide perspective, creation of broad job classes, etc. may assume greater importance. Finally, an **organizational culture**, the core beliefs and assumptions that are widely shared by all organizational members, shapes work-related and other attitudes and significantly influences overall job commitment and performance. Clearly, human resource management has a role in shaping this; however, even here, the culture has to be consistent with the overall mission and strategy of the organization concerned.

---

organizational culture

The core beliefs and assumptions that are widely shared by all organizational members.

Step 4: Choice and Implementation of Human Resource Strategies

Giving consideration to both the internal and external environments provides the opportunity for the human resource professional to begin evaluating potential human resource practices and activities and whether each is viable. Unsuitable strategic options must be dropped from consideration. The ones that appear viable should be scrutinized in detail for their advantages and weaknesses before being accepted for implementation.

Strategic choice and implementation involves identifying, securing, organizing, and directing the use of resources both within and outside the organization. Ultimately, there should be a clear line of sight between the human resource strategy and the corporate goals (see Figure 1-10). Consider the following example:

> Maple Leaf Grocers Ltd., which operated grocery stores in six residential districts in a large metropolitan city, had followed a strategy of high volume, low margin, limited selection, and limited service in the past. Recently, a new grocery chain, Trans Canada Superstores, made a major breakthrough in several other cities by operating large warehouse-style stores with rock-bottom prices. The typical "superstore" was about three times as large as a Maple Leaf store, and offered little service, but had considerably more variety of produce at prices that were 10 to 15 percent lower. The superstore was planning to start a new unit close to where one of the Maple Leaf stores was situated. Unable to match the competitor's low prices and wider selection, and not inclined to move to a new, more spacious location, the management at Maple Leaf decided to follow a new strategy based on superior customer service and "a family atmosphere." This required all cashiers and store personnel (including the store manager) to receive additional training in listening to and serving customers. Greater emphasis was placed on each employee knowing about all major products in at least three different store departments; special assistance was provided to the elderly and single parents who shopped there (the shop also allocated a portion of its floor space for a mini playpen). Store management and staff were actively encouraged to participate in community activities and to donate to neighbourhood parties and sports activities. When the superstore began operations in the area about a year later, Maple Leaf Grocers was able to retain over 80 percent of its customers.

FIGURE 1-10

Line of Sight in Human Resource Strategy

As the above example shows, the human resource strategy must reflect every change in the organizational strategy and support it. Simply stating that "we are strategic in our focus" does not, in fact, result in a contribution to organizational strategy.

> A 2008 survey of 700 HR professionals found that 66 percent of the respondents felt that many human resource professionals who think they are strategic are simply not so in their actions. Only 4 percent of the respondents felt that human resource professionals are, on the whole, strategic and recognized for their strategic thinking by relevant others. However, 73 percent of the respondents believe that the word "strategic" is overused in human resources.[76]

Identifying the HR strategy of an organization is often a complex task. It is not unusual to see the same organization adopting somewhat different employment practices for different employee groups or in different regions.[77] Although in any given organization, there tends to be a *dominant* HR strategy, multiple bundles of HR practices are likely to develop to cater to the unique needs of organizations in a subgroup or industry.[78] Mere use of the term "strategic" without clear actions that support it simply reduces the credibility of the HR profession and its members. In formulating strategies, the human resource department must continuously focus on the following five major groups of activities:

1. PLANNING HUMAN RESOURCES Human resource planning enables the determination of demand and supply of various types of human resources within the firm. It is also a systematic review of the current state of human resource practices in an organization and the identification of needed human resource processes, tools, and activities. The results of human resource planning shape the overall human resource strategies in the short run and identify any gaps in people or processes that need to be fulfilled.

A second element of the planning process is the eventual choice of appropriate human resource practices. While details of this choice will be discussed in the chapters that follow, some of the initial questions managers are able to ask themselves and others are:

- whether their assumptions are realistic?
- does the organization have the skills and resources to make the organization's strategy viable?
- does the organizational strategy hang together with the organization's character or will the strategy be at risk due to the character?
- what are the risks of the strategy and can we afford them?
- what do we need to do to make the strategy viable?

2. ATTRACTING HUMAN RESOURCES Following the planning of human resources, managers must begin to take action in filling apparent gaps in either people or practices. For instance, in recruiting and selecting workers, a human resource manager should meet all legal requirements (e.g., equal employment opportunity laws, affirmative action policies). Recruitment is the process of finding and attracting capable individuals to apply for employment and to accept a job offer if/when one is made to them. The selection process is a series of specific steps used to decide which recruits should be hired, and aims to match job requirements with an applicant's capabilities.

3. PLACING, DEVELOPING, AND EVALUATING HUMAN RESOURCES With the right talent in the right place, attention must turn to optimizing both the employee's time as well as the activities and processes that guide human resources in a company. Once hired, new employees need to be oriented to the organization's policies and procedures and placed in their new job positions. Since new workers seldom fit the organization's needs exactly, they must be trained to perform effectively. They must also be prepared for future responsibilities through systematic career planning.

Performance appraisals give employees feedback on their performance and can help the human resource department identify future training needs. This activity also indicates how well human resource activities have been carried out since poor performance might often mean that selection or training activities need to be redesigned.

4. MOTIVATING EMPLOYEES When employees perform acceptably, they must receive compensation. Some employee benefits are required (for example, Canada/Quebec Pension Plan), while several others are voluntary (for example, dental plans). Since employee motivation is also partially determined by internal work procedures, climate, and schedules, these must be continually modified to maximize performance.

> It has often been observed that people leave their bosses, not their organizations. Many a time, an employee may quit because the boss does not inspire, make good decisions, possess relevant knowledge, or treat employees fairly and with respect. Recognizing this fact, many progressive HR departments have initiated actions to identify problems before they cause an employee to leave the firm. An example is BMO Financial <http://www.bmo.com/home>, which fosters a culture to address problem managers. One tool used is the employee opinion survey with its specific questions on managers. The other is the employee call centre, which allows employees to convey their problems anonymously. A few times a year, a representative of the HR department conducts an "employee relations visit" to investigate a potential problem and find solutions.[79]

5. MAINTAINING HIGH PERFORMANCE The human resource strategy should ensure that the productive contribution from every member is at the maximum possible level. Most effective organizations have well-established employee relations practices, including good communication between managers and employees, standardized disciplinary procedures, and counselling systems. In today's work setting, internal work procedures and organizational policies must be continuously monitored to ensure that they meet the needs of a diverse workforce and ensure safety to every individual. In many organizations, employees may decide to join together and form unions. When this occurs, management is confronted with a new situation: union–management relations. To respond to the collective demands by employees, human resource specialists may have to negotiate a collective agreement and administer it.

> Canada's record in work stoppages is by no means flattering. In the recent past, Canada lost over 4 million person-days due to strikes and lockouts. Most of Canada's largest telecoms, Bell <http://www.bell.ca/>, Telus, MTS <http://www.mts.ca>, and Aliant <http://www.bellaliant.net/>, have been involved in work stoppages; so have Canada Post <http://www.canadapost.ca>, the CBC <http://www.cbc.ca/>, Videotron <http://www.videotron.com>, and Bell's subsidiary, Entourage <http://www.solutionstech.bell.ca>. Other significant stoppages occurred in the supermarket sector, in meat packing, and in paper and wood products industries.[80]

To be effective, a strategy should also have clearly defined action plans with target achievement dates (see Figure 1-11). Otherwise, it will simply end up being an exercise on paper.

What will the world of work look like in the next decade?

> PricewaterhouseCoopers <http://www.pwc.co.uk/> in the United Kingdom examined what the world of work will look like in year 2020. It came out with three (or possibly four) alternate scenarios. A "blue world" characterized by large corporations that often resemble mini states and exert considerable influence on the larger society; an "orange world" where focus is on specialization and the rise of collaborative networks of employees; or a "green world" where the environmental agenda drives the business strategy. It is also conceivable that a fourth scenario emerges where all the above three co-exist. Needless to point out, HR's role in each case will be significantly different. This means that the HR function, today, should prepare itself for vastly different future roles.[81]

FIGURE 1-11

Metro Hospital's Strategic Approach to Human Resource Management Background Information

Background Information

Metro Hospital, a large hospital in a major Canadian city, currently faces an 18 percent turnover among its nursing staff. In fact, the turnover among nurses has been on the increase in the last two years. Kim Cameron, the hospital's newly appointed human resource manager, would like to reverse this trend and bring down the turnover rate to under 5 percent in the near future. As a first step, she looked through all available company records to find out more about the background of nurses who left the organization. She interviewed 14 nurses who had left the hospital recently and another 10 nurses who are currently employed in the hospital. Here are some of Cameron's findings:

- Forty percent of the nurses who left the hospital commented that their supervisors did not "treat them well"; only about 25 percent of the nurses who are currently with the hospital made the same comment.

- Six of the nurses who left and five of the present staff complained that the heating and air conditioning systems in the hospital do not work well so that it is very hot inside the hospital in the summer months and too cold in the winter.

- Fifty-five percent of those she talked to said that the fringe benefits in the hospital were not as good as elsewhere, while the salary level was found to be similar to that available elsewhere.

- Research of hospital records indicated that only about 10 percent of the nursing supervisors had undergone any type of supervisory leadership skills training in the past.

Kim Cameron's Objective

After her initial research, Kim Cameron identified the following as one of her major objectives for the immediate future: "To reduce the turnover among nursing staff from the present 18 percent to 4 percent by July 1, 2014, by incurring costs not exceeding $—— (at current dollars)."

Kim Cameron's Overall Strategy

To achieve the above goal, Kim Cameron realized that it was critical that the overall job satisfaction of nurses (especially their satisfaction with supervisors, working conditions, and rewards) be monitored and improved (if necessary). She set out the following action plans for the immediate future for herself and others in her department.

Kim Cameron's Action Plans

Action Number	Action Description	Person Responsible for Action	Date by Which Action to Be Completed	Budget Allocated
1.	Conduct an attitude survey among all nurses; collect information on their attitudes toward their job, supervisor, pay, benefits, working conditions, and colleagues	Asst. HRM	31-3-2013	$5,000
2.	Identify steps for improving morale among nurses	Self (in consultation with others)	30-5-2013	_____
3.	Ask physical plant to check condition of A/C and heating systems	Self	25-1-2013	_____
4.	Complete training program for 50 percent of nursing supervisors	Training manager	15-2-2014	$9,000
5.	(Depending on the survey findings, other actions that have to be initiated will be listed here.)			

Without a future orientation, the human resource department becomes reactive, not proactive. And reactive approaches allow minor problems to become major ones.

Step 5: Review, Evaluation, and Audit of Human Resource Strategies

Human resource strategies, however effective they prove to be, must be examined regularly. An organization's contextual factors, such as technology, environments, government policies, and so on, change continuously; so do several of its internal factors, such as membership characteristics, role definitions, and internal procedures. All these changes necessitate regular strategy evaluation to ensure their continued appropriateness.

> For example, a study by Statistics Canada reported that attempts at innovative human resources have actually increased labour turnover in Canadian manufacturing operations. The study examined how six specific alternative work practices—problem-solving teams, self-managed teams, flexible job design, profit sharing, merit pay, and formal training on team work—affect turnover. Although the professionals have always argued that innovative practices cause lower turnover, this particular study did not support the claim.[82]

> Since 2005, Hewlett-Packard <http://www8.hp.com/ca> has carried out formal research to identify links between employee experience and the firm's operational performance. The company grouped employees based on their function, recognizing that certain functions have more direct impact on operational outcomes. Results from the study indicate that "effective collaboration" combined with "empowerment to make decisions" tend to be related to customer attitudes.[83]

Results of program evaluation such as the above produce valuable *feedback*, which is information to help evaluate success or failure. Such information, in turn, helps the firm to fine tune its practices or even abandon some actions that do not seem to have performance potential. Alternatively, in the case of successful projects, additional resources can be allocated to them to reap full benefits.

A holistic review of the human resource strategies in an organization with the intention of identifying and correcting deficiencies is referred to as a **human resource audit**. The audit may include one division or an entire company.

---

human resource audit

An examination of the human resource policies, practices, and systems of a firm (or division) to eliminate deficiencies and improve ways to achieve goals.

The benefits from a human resource audit are many and include the following:

- It helps align the human resource department's goals with larger organizational strategies.
- It almost invariably uncovers better ways for the department to contribute to societal, organizational, and employee objectives. This, in turn, clarifies the human resource department's duties and responsibilities.
- It ensures timely compliance with legal requirements.
- It discloses how well managers are meeting their human resource duties.
- It uncovers critical human resource problems and possible solutions.
- It reduces human resource costs through more effective procedures.
- It provides specific, verifiable data on the human resource department's contributions.
- It stimulates uniformity of human resource policies and practices.
- It helps review and improve the human resource department's information system.
- It enhances the professional image of the department among various stakeholders.

Human resource research grows more important with each passing year. Several reasons account for this. First, human resource work carries with it many legal implications for the employer. Failure to comply with equal employment or safety laws, for example, subjects the organization to lawsuits. Second, "people costs" are significant. Pay and benefits often are a major operating expense for most employers. Improper compensation plans can be costly, even fatal, to the company's survival. Third, the department's activities help shape an organization's productivity and its employees' quality of work life. Fourth, the critical resource in many organizations today is not capital, but rather, information, knowledge, and expertise.[84] This means that an audit of the calibre of a critical resource—namely, human resources—is necessary for the success of the organization. Human resource audits provide the information needed by human resource managers to validate the alignment (or misalignment) of human resource strategies with those of the organization as well as the organization's key performance indicators.

Finally, the growing complexity of human resource work makes research necessary. Today, more than ever before, human resource activities aimed at productivity improvement, succession planning, and organization's cultural change arc critical to competitive survival. More and more executives expect the department to make strategic contributions and place the function at a higher level in the organizational hierarchy.

Over 50 percent of 520 Canadian organizations surveyed in one study were found to have a vice-president in charge of human resources. Over 78 percent of these organizations employed at least one trained professional to deal with human resource matters.[85]

How effective are human resource departments in achieving various organizational and employee objectives? One study of 650 Canadian organizations[86] found that on criteria such as employee satisfaction and commitment, most Canadian organizations receive satisfactory, though not exemplary, ratings. Today, organizations are participating in human resource metric benchmarking. Through this process, organizations contribute information about human resource practices and associated metrics. In return, the participating organizations have access to aggregated data about other organizations so that they may benchmark their own practices and performance.[87]

The metrics established through an audit also result in the initiation of new programs such as literacy training and better responses to employees with disabilities, which can significantly improve employee productivity and morale. The major areas covered in a human resource audit are outlined in Figure 1-12 and major areas covered are described in Figure 1-13.

FIGURE 1-12

Steps in a Human Resource Audit

FIGURE 1-13

Major Areas Covered in a Human Resource Audit

Human Resource Management Information System	
Human rights legislation	**Human resource plans**
• Information on compliance	• Supply and demand estimates
	• Skills inventories
	• Replacement charts and summaries
Job analysis information	**Compensation administration**
• Job standards	• Wage and salary levels
• Job descriptions	• Benefit package
• Job specifications	• Employer-provided services
Staffing and Development	
Recruiting	**Selection**
• Source of recruits	• Selection ratios
• Availability of recruits	• Selection procedures
• Employment applications	• Human rights legislation compliance
Training and orientation	**Career development**
• Orientation program	• Internal placement success
• Training objectives and procedures	• Career planning program
• Learning rate	• Human resource development effort
Performance appraisals	**Labour–management relations**
• Standards and measures of performance	• Legal compliance
• Performance appraisal techniques	• Management rights
• Evaluation interviews	• Dispute resolution problems
Human resource controls	**Human resource audits**
• Employee communications	• Human resource function
• Discipline procedures	• Operating managers
• Change and development procedures	• Employee feedback on human resource department

Preparing for the Future

Evaluations and audits are necessary, but they are backward-looking. They uncover only the results of past decisions. Although past performance should be evaluated, human resource departments also should look to the future to be proactive. A proactive approach requires human resource managers and their staff to develop a future orientation. They must constantly scan their professional and social environment for clues about the future. New developments may mean new challenges.

For example, high divorce rates may lead to more employer-provided child care facilities and flexible work schedules so that working parents can fulfill their parental duties.

LO3 HRC 1 & 4

The Organization of Human Resource Management

The responsibility for human resource management activities rests with each manager. If a manager does not accept this responsibility, then human resource activities may be done only partially or not at all. When a manager finds that HRM work seriously disrupts other responsibilities, this work may be reassigned. The assignment might be to a worker or a specialized department that handles human resource matters. This process of getting others to share the work is called delegation. But delegation requires the manager to assign duties, grant authority, and create a sense of responsibility; if these three elements are not explained clearly to the delegate, delegation often fails. And even though others may have been asked to handle human resource activities, the manager still remains responsible. Delegation does not reduce a manager's responsibility; it only allows the sharing of that responsibility with others.

For example, many managers ask a senior worker to train new employees. However, if the senior worker errs and the new employee makes a costly mistake, the manager will appropriately be held responsible by superiors.

A separate department usually emerges only when human resource activities would otherwise become a burden to other departments in the organization—that is, when the expected benefits of a human resource department usually exceed its costs. Until then, managers handle human resource activities themselves or delegate them to subordinates. When a human resource department emerges, it is typically small and reports to some middle-level manager. Figure 1-14 illustrates a common placement of a human resource department at the time it is first formed. The activities of such a department are usually limited to maintaining employee records and helping managers find new recruits. Whether the department performs other activities depends upon the needs of other managers in the firm.

FIGURE 1-14

The Human Resource Department in a Small Organization

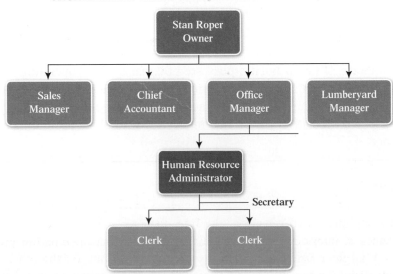

ORGANIZATION CHART FOR STAN'S LUMBER COMPANY

As demands on the department grow, it increases in importance and complexity. Figure 1-15 demonstrates the increased importance by showing the head of human resources reporting directly to the chief operating officer, who is the company president in this figure. The greater importance of the head of human resources may be signified by a change in title to vice-president. In practice, increased complexity also results as the organization grows and new demands are placed on the department, or jobs in the department become more specialized. As the department expands and specializes, it may become organized into highly specialized subdepartments.

FIGURE 1-15

A Large Human Resource Department

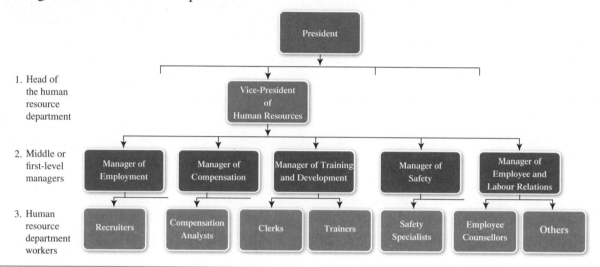

The Service Role of the Human Resource Department

While strategic partners, human resource departments continue to be service and support departments. They exist to assist employees, managers, and the organization. Their managers do not have the authority to order other managers in other departments to accept their ideas. Instead, the department has only **staff authority**, which is the authority to advise, not direct, managers in other departments.

---

staff authority

Authority to advise, but not to direct, others.

In contrast to staff authority, **line authority**, possessed by managers of operating departments, allows these managers to make decisions about production, performance, and people. It is the operating managers who normally are responsible for promotions, job assignments, and other people-related decisions. Human resource specialists advise line managers, who alone are ultimately responsible for employee performance.

---

line authority

Authority to make decisions about production, performance, and people.

For something like recruitment and retention, the line manager may provide details of performance standards and job success, interview job candidates, and utilize the information provided by human resources to make a final decision. The human resource professional, on the other hand, will ensure compliance with human rights laws and organizational policies regarding equity in addition to planning and organizing all of the activities related to recruiting, interviewing, hiring, and communicating about a new employee. In the case of employee and labour relations, the line manager is likely to communicate with the employee, implement motivational structures, coach employees, provide conflict resolution, and promote teamwork. The human resource professional is then left to focus on establishing grievance handling procedures, negotiating with the bargaining unit, and planning and initiating change initiatives. In short, human resource departments tend to provide the technical expertise while line managers use this expertise to effectively manage their subordinates.

In highly technical or extremely routine situations, the human resource department may be given functional authority. **Functional authority** gives the department the right to make decisions usually made by line managers or top management. For example, decisions about fringe benefits are technically complex, so the top manager may give the human resource department the functional authority to decide the type of benefits offered to employees. If each department manager made separate decisions about benefits, there might be excessive costs and inequities. To provide control, uniformity, and the use of expertise, functional authority allows human resource specialists to make crucial decisions effectively.

---

functional authority

Authority that allows staff experts to make decisions and take actions normally reserved for line managers.

LO4 HRC 1

Today's Human Resource Management Professional

In the last thirty years, there has been a surge in the number of human resource managers. In 1971, there were only 4,055 human resource managers in this country; in 1999, the corresponding number was estimated to be over 43,000.[88] However, the status of human resource professionals within organizations historically has not been high. In a national survey of chief human resources officers, it was found that only 60 percent of respondents report directly to the chief executive officers and only 62 percent were members of their organization's executive committee.[89]

Thus, despite its enormous growth, human resource management has been slow to evolve into a full-fledged profession. Since the actual capability of practising human resource experts varies widely, it became increasingly evident that professionalism of the human resource management field was needed. To meet these ever-increasing challenges, human resource managers were expected to possess a number of competencies, including the following:[90]

- **MASTERY OF HUMAN RESOURCE MANAGEMENT TOOLS** As professionals, they should be familiar with state-of-the-art tools in areas such as staffing, training, compensation planning, performance appraisal and planning, employee relations and communication, and organizational change interventions. Along with CHRP designation (see below), an MBA or Master's degree with specialization in HR is considered a very attractive background for HR professionals who are looking to climb the executive ranks.[91]

- **CHANGE MASTERY** Not only should HR professionals possess an abundance of problem-solving, critical thinking, negotiation, and interpersonal skills, they should also be well versed in using these to bring about changes in the organization and its various subsystems. Strong communication skills combined with strong networking skills facilitate HR managers' attempts to influence others;[92] reputation as a team player is a necessary prerequisite in most settings for successful change initiatives.

- **PERSONAL CREDIBILITY** The HR professional should project an image of a trustworthy, ethical, socially responsive, courageous leader who can build relationships and inspire others to work for larger causes.

In a recent study, a majority of CEOs reported that HR professionals need to further develop business acumen and a deeper connection to the business in order to enrich the value of HR.[93] Furthermore, human resource professionals need to be well versed in data-driven decision making and financial operations.[94]

To achieve these goals, accreditation and/or certification of the HR professional was considered as an imperative. The Canadian Council of Human Resource Associations (CCHRA) is a collaborative effort of Human Resource Associations across Canada that currently represents the interests of most HR practitioners in this country and coordinates the nationally recognized designation in HR called the **Certified Human Resources Professional** (CHRP) based on a series of national standards. Although the CHRP is granted by each provincial HR association, it is recognized and transferable across Canada.

Certified Human Resources Professional (CHRP)

Human resource practitioner, formally accredited to practice, who reflects a threshold professional level of practice.

Based on extensive national and regional consultations with employers, human resource professionals, and researchers, CCHRA has identified a set of competencies referred to as the "Certified Human Resource Professional Competency Framework" in key HR areas such as strategy, professional practice, engagement, workplace planning and talent management, labour and employee relations, total rewards, health, wellness, safe workplaces, metrics, reporting, and financial management. These standards are regularly being reviewed and updated. For a summary of the requirements for the CHRP designation, see the CCHRA website <http://www.cchra.ca>, as the architecture is different across provinces.

A second credentialing body for human resource professionals is the International Personnel Management Association <http://ipma-aigp.com>.

Certification or designation alone does not make human resource management a profession or improve its status in the eyes of organizations. One approach to improving the human resource manager's status within the organization may be to strengthen the position's contribution to the enhancement of organizational performance and effectiveness. This is already beginning to take place. The higher status given to human resource experts in job ads and organizational charts indicates that the importance of human resource management activity is being recognized.

The Framework Used in This Book

This textbook is divided into seven parts.

PART 1: THE STRATEGIC HUMAN RESOURCE MANAGEMENT MODEL offers a strategic model of managing human resources in Chapter 1. The key objectives of the human resource function are outlined here along with the steps for implementing a strategic HR approach in practice.

PART 2: PLANNING HUMAN RESOURCES is contained in two chapters. Chapter 2 deals with the important topic of job analysis—detailing the various methods of collecting data about jobs, the steps involved in writing job descriptions and job specifications and setting performance standards. Chapter 3 discusses the various factors that need to be considered when planning the supply and demand for human resources in organizations.

PART 3: ATTRACTING HUMAN RESOURCES deals with the various steps in acquiring human resources. Chapter 4 details key provisions of human rights legislation and the Canadian Constitution along with their implications for hiring employees. It also discusses the issue of diversity. Chapters 5 (Recruitment) and 6 (Selection) deal with the various tools, options, and strategies open to the human resource manager in attracting and selecting qualified applicants for the job.

PART 4: PLACING, DEVELOPING, AND EVALUATING HUMAN RESOURCES deals with all key activities involved in orienting, training, developing, and evaluating employees. Chapter 7 outlines the key steps involved in the orientation and training of employees; it also focuses on the development of employees to take on greater responsibilities in the future, including career counselling to staff. Chapter 8 deals with various appraisal techniques that help an organization to monitor and improve employee performance.

PART 5: MOTIVATING HUMAN RESOURCES discusses the critical tasks of motivating and rewarding employees. Chapter 9 deals with direct compensation, including methods of evaluating the worth of each job and the incentive schemes currently available. Chapter 10 discusses how careful planning enables an organization to make the most out of its benefits package. It also deals with various work options and other arrangements that have implications for employee motivation.

PART 6: MAINTAINING HIGH PERFORMANCE focuses on the various human resource actions to ensure high performance. Chapter 11 details the methods of improving communication and enforcing discipline when employees violate organizational policies. Chapter 12 discusses two types of security offered by modern human resource departments: financial and physical. Chapter 13 discusses strategies for dealing with unions and outlines the human resource manager's role during negotiations with unions.

PART 7: HUMAN RESOURCE MANAGEMENT IN A GLOBAL CONTEXT finally brings us an international level. Chapter 14 examines a variety of issues related to managing human resources from a global and cross-cultural perspective.

Spotlight *on* HRM

Human Capital: The Key to Productivity Improvement

A 1997 article in the *Canadian HR Reporter* described how organizations historically turned to improvements in technology as the basis for improving productivity. Today, however, this approach is not sufficient for Canada to keep pace with the productivity improvements in other developed or developing nations. These technology improvements are easily accessible and often easily duplicated. As a result, an increased focus is being placed on the role of human capital in creating long-term and sustainable productivity improvements.

The author noted that the key to human capital is the ability for people to apply their knowledge, skills, and abilities in ever-changing contexts to find improvements. Moreover, the ability for individuals to create and introduce new innovations to business products, services, and business processes is also important.

(Continued)

The role of human talent in creating long-term sustainable economic and social benefits to organizations and communities through productivity necessitates a collaborative and long-term approach between organizations, governments, communities, and numerous other support structures.

Because knowledge is a necessary precursor to realizing the full potential of human capital in creating productivity improvements, governments, communities, and education systems must come together in the development and enhancement of the overall knowledge base of citizens. To this end, a key focus must remain on continuously improving primary, secondary, and post-secondary education systems. Similarly, Canadian communities must also understand the importance of life-long learning. The time required for learners to progress through education systems underscores the importance of a long-term approach to planning in relation to the development of human talent.

Despite the importance of education systems, organizations must also take on an active role in creating productivity improvements specific to their line of business. Human resource professionals must consider how the knowledge that employees gain through education can be combined with job-specific training and development to create the most effective behaviours from employees. Moreover, human resource professionals must consider how the organization's culture will impact and be impacted by the ever-developing knowledge base of their employees.

More recently, we have seen growing examples of how productivity enhancements are often found through new innovations. Similar to developing a learning city, significant lead time and planning is needed to create a community in which innovation thrives. Examples abound of communities that have come together to create ecosystems in which innovation and entrepreneurism are strong (e.g., Silicon Valley).

Finally, individuals need to take an active part in continuously developing their own knowledge, skills, and abilities throughout life.

In short, productivity enhancement becomes everyone's responsibility if Canada is to stay competitive relative to other countries and continue to create social and economic benefits to Canadians.

SOURCE: Based on *Canadian HR Reporter*, December 29, 1997, pp. 18–19. www.hrreporter.com.

SUMMARY

The central challenge for organizations today is to survive and prosper in a very turbulent world. To do this, most organizations find it necessary to maintain high productivity and effectiveness levels and have a global focus. Strategic management of organizations is suggested as one method for coping with this environmental turbulence. **Human resource management** *aims to optimize the contribution of employees to the organization's goals.* The field of human resource management thus focuses on what managers—especially human resource specialists—do and what they should do.

It was pointed out that human resource management is the responsibility of every manager. The human resource department provides a service to other departments in the organization. In the final analysis, however, the performance and well-being of each worker is the dual responsibility of that worker's immediate supervisor and the human resource department.

Strategic human resource management is systematically linked to the strategic needs of an organization and aims to provide it with an effective workforce while meeting the needs of its members and other stakeholders. It is important that human resource strategies and tactics are mutually consistent and provide direct support to the organization's mission, goals, and strategies. Even the best-laid strategies may fail if they are not accompanied by sound programs or procedures and aligned with organizational strategies.

Strategic human resource management necessitates an exhaustive evaluation of an organization's internal and external environments. Factors that should be reviewed before formulating human resource strategies were discussed. These include economic, technological, demographic, and cultural challenges. Continuous evaluation of strategy and proactive management were pointed out as critical to ensure the successful management of human resources.

This section of the text has emphasized a strategic approach to human resource management. This is because, increasingly, human resource managers are expected to contribute to the organization's strategic thinking. Marketing, production, and financial strategies depend upon the abilities of the firm's human resources to execute these plans. The status of the human resource function within an organization is likely to be determined by its contribution to the organization's overall success. Strategic management of human resources may be one key to this success. To assist with the "people side" of implementation, human resource directors will be forced to uncover, through audits and research, the causes of and solutions to people-related problems. Their diagnostic abilities to assess present and potential human resource issues will be needed as they and their staff increasingly serve as internal consultants to others who are facing human resource–related challenges.[95] They then will be called on to facilitate changes in the organization that maximize the human contribution. In short, the traditional administrative skills associated with human resource management must grow to accommodate diagnostic, assessment, consulting, and facilitative skills.

TERMS FOR REVIEW

Certified Human Resources Professionals (CHRP)
cost leadership strategy
cultural forces
cultural mosaic
demographic changes
differentiation strategy
economic forces
educational attainment
focus strategy
functional authority
human resource audit
human resource management
knowledge workers
line authority
mechanization
mission statement
organization character
organizational culture
organizational goals
proactive human resource management
productivity
reactive human resource management
staff authority
strategic human resource management

SELF-ASSESSMENT EXERCISE

How Knowledgeable Are You about Human Resource Management?

A successful human resource manager should possess knowledge in a number of areas, including job design, human resource planning, recruitment, selection and training of employees, and employee relations. The following self-test helps you assess your present knowledge level in some of these areas. Read each statement and indicate whether the statement is true or false.

1. A human resource manager should take corrective actions only after a problem has been crystallized and well understood.	T	(F)
2. When assigning jobs to employees, I should ensure that there is no significant variation in job challenges from one employee to the next.	T	(F)
3. Two experienced workers and three trainees can complete a project in 10 days; three experienced workers and two trainees can do the same project in 8 days. If I hire two experienced workers and one trainee, they should be able to complete the project in 11½ days.	T	(F)
4. When designing a job application form, I should make sure to ask for the social insurance number of the applicant in order to complete the employee file.	T	(F)
5. When I visit campuses to recruit graduates, I should focus on the quality of education they received in the school rather than whether they meet specific job requirements.	T	(F)
6. When hiring an administrative assistant, the best way to assess the candidate's skills is by requiring the person to undergo a word processing or other performance test.	(T)	F
7. The best way to teach a person a new accounting program is to give a short lecture on the subject matter.	T	(F)
8. Measuring the students' learning before they begin this course and again at the end of the course may be a better indicator of this course's effectiveness than asking the students about their satisfaction level about what they learned in this course.	(T)	F
9. Today, in Canada, women and men get paid equally in all occupations.	T	(F)
10. If a person has to choose between two jobs that are alike in all respects, except that one job pays $45,000 in straight salary and the second one pays $35,000 in salary and $10,000 in benefits, the individual is better off accepting the second job.	(T)	F

SCORING

For statements 1, 2, 3, 4, 5, 7, and 9, if you answered false, you get one point each. For questions 6, 8, and 10, if you answered true, you get one point each. Add up your scores.

Scores of 8–10: Wow! You already know several important HR concepts. You can build on these by carefully studying the text chapters and actively participating in class discussions. You will also be a valuable source of information to others. So, participate actively in and outside the classroom!

Scores Less Than 8: As you read the various chapters in this text, you will find the rationale behind the above statements. (The question numbers correspond to the chapter in this book in which this material is discussed.) Human resource management is an exciting profession—it also means that several assumptions that are popularly considered to be true are not. Keep reading!

REVIEW AND DISCUSSION QUESTIONS

1. What are the goals of a human resource department? Choose an organization that you are familiar with and indicate which of these goals will be more important in this organization and discuss why.

2. Draw a diagram of a human resource department in a firm that employs over 5,000 persons and name the likely components of such a department. Which of these functions are likely to be eliminated in a small firm employing 50 persons?

3. Identify and briefly describe three major external challenges (choosing one each from economic, technological, and demographic categories) facing human resource managers in Canada, and their implications.

4. Outline the three major strategies pursued by Canadian businesses. What implications do they have for the human resource function within the firms? Illustrate your answer with suitable examples.

5. What are four trends (or attributes) in the Canadian labour market that have implications for a human resource manager? Explain your answer, citing which of the human resource functions will be affected and how.

CRITICAL THINKING QUESTIONS

1. Suppose your employer is planning a chain of high-quality restaurants to sell food products that it already produces. Outline which areas of human resource management will be affected.

2. If a bank is planning to open a new branch in a distant city, with what inputs will the human resource department be concerned? What activities will the department need to undertake in the transition to a fully staffed and operating branch? What type of feedback do you think the department should seek after the branch has been operating for six months?

3. Find two recent news items and explain how these developments might affect the demands made on the human resource department of an organization.

4. If the birthrate during the early 2010s was to double from the low rates of earlier decades, what are its implications in the years 2030 and 2040 for (a) grocery stores, (b) fast-food restaurants, (c) the Canadian Armed Forces, (d) large metropolitan universities?

5. Assume you were hired as the human resource manager in a firm that historically has given low importance to the function. Most of the human resource management systems and procedures in the firm are outdated. Historically, this function was given a low-status, "record-keeping" role within the firm. Armed with sophisticated HR training, you recently entered the firm and want to upgrade the HR systems and status of the department. In other words, you want to make the management recognize the true importance of sound HR practices for strategic success. What actions will you take in the short and long term to achieve your goal? Be specific in your action plans and illustrate your steps where relevant.

ETHICS QUESTION

After graduation, you were hired as a management trainee in the human resource department of a large organization with widely held stock. Your boss, the human resource manager, is away on holidays and asked you to make all decisions in her absence, including the hiring of an assistant in your department. A senior manager in the company recently indicated to you how much he would like the position to be given to Bob, his nephew who had applied for the position. When you looked through the records, you found that while Bob meets the basic requirements, there were at least two other better candidates—a male far superior than Bob and a female. (Your firm had recently indicated a commitment to employment equity initiatives.) You realize that the senior manager has considerable influence in the company and may even be able to influence your career progress within the firm.

WEB RESEARCH EXERCISE

Select three jobs: one knowledge-based, one manufacturing, and one in the service sector. Based on your search of websites of Employment and Social Development Canada, Statistics Canada, and other relevant online sources, what patterns in employment and job vacancies do you see? What are the implications for large human resource departments in these industries?

INCIDENT 1-1

Human Resource Decision Making at Calgary Importers Ltd.

Calgary Importers Ltd. (CIL) is a large importer of linens, china, and crystal from a number of Asian, European, and South American countries. While nearly 55 percent of linens are imported from China, nearly 70 percent of crystals and diamond items originate in India. Most of the china comes from European and South American countries. Several other handicrafts and household products are imported from other East European countries and Japan. Different geographical offices of CIL specialize in different products; for example, the Toronto and Vancouver offices primarily deal with suppliers in India (specializing in different industry groups), while the Calgary office conducts all negotiations with South America. CIL's offices in Montreal and Halifax primarily deal with their European counterparts. Over time, management practices, including HR activities, in various CIL offices have begun to show considerable differences, posing problems for the senior managers. Recently, the following conversation took place between the vice-president of human resources and the vice-president of distribution.

Rob Whittier: You may not agree with me, but if we are going to have consistency in our human resource policies, then key decisions about those policies must be centralized in the human resource department. Otherwise, branch managers will continue to make their own decisions, focusing on different aspects. Besides, the department has the experts. If you needed financial advice, you would not ask your doctor; you would go to a banker or other financial expert. When it comes to deciding compensation packages or hiring new employees, those decisions should be left to experts in salary administration or selection. To ask a branch manager or supervisor to make those decisions deprives our firm of all of the expertise we have in the department.

Henri DeLahn: I have never questioned your department's expertise. Sure, the people in human resources are more knowledgeable than the line managers. But if we want those managers to be responsible for the performance of their branches, then we must not deprive them of their authority to make human resource decisions. Those operating managers must be able to decide whom to hire and whom to reward with raises. If they cannot make those decisions, then their effectiveness as managers will suffer.

DISCUSSION QUESTIONS

1. If you were the president of Calgary Importers Ltd. and were asked to resolve this dispute, whose argument would you agree with? Why?

2. Can you suggest a compromise that would allow line managers to make these decisions consistently?

INCIDENT 1-2

Canadian Bio-Medical Instruments Ltd.

Canadian Bio-Medical Instruments Ltd., founded 10 years ago, manufactures a variety of bio-medical instruments used by physicians and surgeons both in their clinics and in hospitals. The high quality of its products led to quick market success, especially for products such as artificial heart valves, operating-room pumps, and respiratory modules. The company, which had sales of less than $900,000 in the first year, today enjoys an annual turnover of $150 million. However, the industry is competitive and the research development and promotional budgets of some of the key players in the industry are several times that of the firm.

Given the successful track record for its existing products and the competitiveness of the North American market, the management of the firm believed that gaining new market shares in Europe would be easier than expanding against well-entrenched domestic producers. Preliminary market studies supported management's thinking.

A decision was made to open a small sales office in Europe, probably in Frankfurt, Germany, given the nonstop flight facilities that currently exist from Toronto, where the firm's head office is located. Three employees were sent to Germany to identify possible office sites and to learn about European testing procedures and what documentation would be legally required to prove the safety and effectiveness of the company's medical instruments. All three employees were fluent in German. If the reports on Germany are favourable, the firm expects to have about 20 employees working in Europe within the next year.

DISCUSSION QUESTIONS

1. Assume you are the vice-president in charge of human resources. What additional information would you want these three employees to find out?

2. What human resource issues or policies are you likely to confront in the foreseeable future?

CASE STUDY

Maple Leaf Shoes Ltd.

A Strategic Management Exercise*

Maple Leaf Shoes Ltd. is a medium-sized manufacturer of leather and vinyl shoes located near Wilmington, Ontario. It began operations in 1969 and currently employs about 400 people in its Ontario plant and 380 others in offices and warehouses across Canada and internationally.

HISTORY

Maple Leaf was the brainchild of Mario Mansini, an Italian immigrant who left his native country to begin a new life in Canada in the late 1950s. After a couple of unsuccessful ventures (a stage show and a sailboat business), Mansini hit upon the idea of starting a shoe factory. "As long as people walk, they need shoes," he is said to have told the bank, which asked for a financial guarantee, given his past failures. Though not well educated (he dropped out of Grade 8), Mansini was an extravert and a flamboyant man who could impress and inspire others around him. In the end, his personality and optimism swayed the bank manager to extend a small loan for the new venture.

With the bank loan and financial assistance from some friends and relatives, Mansini built a small plant near Wilmington—two floors of shoes and about a dozen temporary sheds where employees lived and slept. In 1969, the firm formally opened for business.

What began as a small operation quickly grew into a regional and national operation. Despite his lack of education, Mansini was an astute businessman and he was also able to successfully recruit skilled workers. The folklore is that many of his erstwhile artist friends worked for practically no wages in his factory during the day and played music and rehearsed plays in the evenings. He had very close friendships with his employees, and many were willing to pitch in whenever he needed help. The firm quickly developed a reputation for quality footwear, especially shoes used for outdoor and sports purposes. Apart from a couple of major footwear firms in the United States, competition was virtually absent and the firm thrived.

Mansini worked long hours to make Maple Leaf a success. He was a loyal citizen (the firm's original name was Quality Footware; Mansini changed it to Maple Leaf Shoes). He also employed a paternalistic management style. He knew most workers by name and always took the time to inquire about their welfare. No one but Maple Leaf workers lived in the area where the factory was located. Over time, the location where Maple Leaf operated became unofficially known as "Leaf Town," although the closest town was Wilmington. For most workers, their houses were close enough to work to enable them to walk home for lunch. There was a Maple Leaf Grocery Store, Maple Leaf Recreation Hall, Maple Leaf teams, Maple Leaf Drug Store and Dispensary, and Maple Leaf Club for the higher echelon of the workforce. There was even a Leaf Cinema and Leaf Pub. Virtually everything was available in Leaf Town; residents only had to travel to nearby Wilmington for schools and medical assistance.

Consistent with his management style, Mansini had few organized procedures or systems in place. He noted: "If you lose touch with your men, you lose them. Systems come and go; people are more

---

* Case prepared by Professor Hari Das of the Department of Management, Saint Mary's University, Halifax, Canada. All rights retained by the author. Das © 2002.

important." There were few formal procedures—each event was looked at for its unique features and responded to accordingly. Mansini often worked 15 to 18 hours a day—he was involved in most decisions including hiring of personnel, product planning, financing strategy, shoe design, and handling employee grievances. During his time, efforts were made by local and international unions to organize the workers; however, they were unsuccessful (in the most recent attempt, the union was able to get less than 10 percent of the workers to sign up).

But Mansini's first love was music and arts. So, when a national conglomerate approached him with an offer to purchase a controlling share of Maple Leaf in the mid-1980s, he was only too willing to sell it. "I don't have any children to take over the firm," he said. (He died a bachelor soon after the sale of the company; a part of his estate was donated to Leaf Art Guild and Sports Team and the remainder was divided among his relatives and the Canadian Cancer Society.) "In any case, how long can a man spend his life looking at what is under the feet rather than what is above?" he mused.

SINCE THE TAKEOVER

The group that took over the firm modernized the manufacturing operations and attempted to extend its operations both nationally and internationally. During these efforts, it found that many of the company's past practices were archaic and inefficient. There was an attempt to improve efficiency and gross margin. New equipment was installed and several routine activities were automated or otherwise mechanized to reduce costs. While attempts were also made to update management practices, the firm was slow in this regard. Unfortunately, there was also above-average turnover in the top management team in the company in the initial years. Robert Clark, who was hired as the CEO of the firm, has now been with the firm for eight years and holds a significant share of the company stock apart from holding options.

While Maple Leaf Shoes makes shoes of all kinds, descriptions, and sizes today, it specializes in the manufacture of women's and youth athletic shoes. The company's designers were successful in producing a product that was both stylish and yet comfortable to wear and durable. The firm's shoes, marketed under the brand names of *Fluffy Puppy, Cariboo*, and *Madonna*, were very popular among ladies in the 19–40 age group. Its *Young Athlete* brand, aimed at boys and girls in the 9–14 age group, was a market leader in the children's sports shoes market in British Columbia. Historically, the shoes produced by the firm were cheaper than those of its competitors. This price advantage was a critical aspect of the company's marketing strategy in the past.

EMERGING CHALLENGES

Recently, the company has faced a number of issues that require immediate attention by its management. *First*, the cost of production at Maple Leaf Shoes has been rising slowly but steadily. Labour costs currently account for over 45 percent of manufacturing costs and have been increasing rapidly. The productivity levels of the employees have not shown any increase in the preceding three years. If the present trend continues, the firm is likely to lose its price advantage over its competitors. Already, for two out of six popular brands sold by Maple Leaf Shoes, the prices for the firm's products are equal to or higher than its competition. This has stalled the firm's growth and profitability. Some financial details of the firm are shown in Table 1. Figure 1 shows the firm's stock price during the preceding five years. The market reaction to the firm's potential has not been very positive, as indicated by the overall decline of its share price from a high of $25 about five years ago. The market meltdown in 2002 further worsened this picture, pulling the share price down to about $11, from which it has not yet recovered to any significant extent.

TABLE 1

Recent Financial Information on Maple Leaf Shoes Ltd.

	Current Year	Last Year	Year Before	3-Year Growth Rate
Total revenue ($000)	1,512,904	1,461,604	1,488,840	1.45%
Earnings before interest and tax ($000)	65,645	65,772	59,200	8.06%
Profit/loss ($000)	26,258	29,597	29,008	–10.53%
Earnings per share	1.33	1.47	1.35	–7.85%
Dividends per share	0.30	0.33	0.35	
Total assets ($000)	617,814	622,469	660,241	
Number of employees	783	843	897	

FIGURE 1

Maple Leaf Stock Price

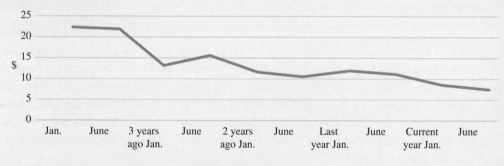

Second, over 60 percent of the company's staff are unionized. There are indications that remaining nonmanagerial staff are also about to be unionized. Management believes that this will reduce the already limited autonomy it possesses in hiring, terminating, and managing employees.

Third, in the recent past, competition in the shoe industry has been intense. Over the years, trade barriers across countries have disappeared, which has meant that cheaper, high-quality shoes made in countries such as Korea, Taiwan, Singapore, India, and Mexico pose serious competition to the firm within and outside Canadian markets. Despite this, Maple Leaf Shoes has been able to perform fairly well in the export markets. Currently, over 15 percent of its production is exported—mainly to western parts of the United States and Europe (the corresponding figure five years back was a tiny 2 percent). While the company increased its U.S. sales after the Canada–U.S. Free Trade Agreement, it is somewhat apprehensive about the future. Robert Clark, president of Maple Leaf Shoes, commented:

> The market has changed dramatically in the last five years. The Asians and the Chinese are fast conquering the world footwear market. How can we compete with the Malaysians, Thais, and the Indians, who pay a fraction of the wages we pay here? In China, from where most of the shoes sold in North

America originate, the labour is cheap and employment standards are low. And mind you, those Asian workers are good. It will be a totally new game now with a new set of rules… We simply would not be able to compete with them on labour costs … but what we have on our side is technology. We will constantly need to think of new products and newer strategies if we are to survive.

The firm's past strategy of responding to these challenges has been to automate its manufacturing functions and to downsize. It has also sold off some of its nonperforming assets and facilities and contracted out some of the services in a bid to cut costs. This strategy, while it has resulted in some improvements in the financial picture, has also brought with it negative union reaction and a decline in employee morale.

Maple Leaf recently signed an agreement with the producers of *Bumpy Bears*, a popular TV series aimed at young children. Under this agreement, the firm will have exclusive rights to reproduce the various animal characters seen in the show on its footwear. *Ticky* the black bear, *Rumpy* the arctic bear, and *Moosy* the white bear are beloved characters in the show. This is expected to increase the sales of children's shoes; however, the embossing technology is expensive and may require initial heavy capital investments and additional training for some members of the workforce.

Finally, the need for managerial training is felt now more than ever. The firm expects its activities to grow; however, given market conditions, it is not keen on expanding the size of its managerial cadre significantly. Instead, it would like to provide managerial and team-management skills to more of its employees and empower them to make decisions.

In a recent interview, Robert Clark identified a number of issues that require immediate attention:

1. Contracts with two of the four unions in the company will expire in another eight months. The remaining two unions will not start their contract negotiations for another 18 months; however, what happens in the negotiations with these two unions could have a significant impact on all future contract negotiations. One of the unions with which negotiations are to begin soon, the Leather Workers' Association, recently elected a leader who is rumoured to be militant and highly focused on results. A strike in the immediate future could paralyze the firm, and it is doubtful whether the firm would recover from its debilitating results for quite some time.

2. Recently, two complaints of sex discrimination were filed by women employees. One complaint was settled internally in consultation with the concerned union, while the other had to go before the provincial Human Rights Commission. The decision of the commission was in favour of the employee who had filed the grievance.

3. The management of Maple Leaf Shoes believes that growth through expanded activities is critical now, especially given the competitive challenge. Growth is possible only by expanding its operations within and outside Canada. The management would like to expand its operations to Atlantic Canada and Quebec in the next three years—a new plant in Quebec is being considered for entry into that market because the product styling must be somewhat modified to meet the demands of the French market. It is felt that the same plant can produce footwear that can be exported to France and other parts of Europe. Currently, Maple Leaf shoes are sold (although in small numbers) in Belgium and Luxembourg. These markets were developed almost accidentally: a few years back, a cousin of Robert Clark, the president, took samples of Young Athlete shoes for display in his sports equipment shops in Belgium and Luxembourg; the shoes became popular locally. Maple Leaf Shoes also sells its shoes through a home-building and hardware store in England. However, about 80 percent of its foreign sales are in Oregon and California, where the shoes are displayed and sold through fashion boutiques.

4. Production levels in Maple Leaf Shoes have been continuously increasing; however, management has fought hard not to increase its workforce. The company currently uses a large number of part-time and contract employees for various services. While this strategy has resulted in some reduction in costs, it has also been accompanied by negative reactions from workers, supervisors, and unions. This is expected to be a major issue during the next bargaining session.

5. As far as possible, the company attempts to fill managerial positions through internal promotions and transfers; however, this has meant that management training is more critical today than ever before.

6. In an effort to take advantage of cheap labour abroad, the firm, in the recent past, has attempted to enter into joint venture partnerships with firms in Indonesia, Mexico, and India. However, this has also resulted in exposing the firm to additional risks characteristic of international operations. While its negotiations with the Mexican and Indian partners have been proceeding according to schedule, its experience in Indonesia was less than satisfactory. The firm's Indonesian partner fell victim to the "Asian crisis" of 1997–1998, when the Indonesian currency, the rupiah, fell by more than 33 percent in a matter of days. Its partner was on the verge of declaring insolvency. Maple Leaf is currently looking for another Indonesian partner.

Added to the above is the void created by the resignation of John McAllister, the personnel manager who left the firm to take up a similar position in the west. Currently, the position of personnel manager in the firm is vacant. Pat Lim, general manager (marketing), is currently in charge of the human resource function, although all routine decisions and procedures are handled by Jane Reynolds, special assistant to the personnel manager. (Indeed, because of increased national and international marketing activities, Lim is often away from the office.) Robert Clark recently decided to rename the function as "human resource manager" to reflect the increasing importance of the activity. The management recognizes that a number of human resource procedures and systems within the firm are antiquated and must be replaced; however, cost pressures and day-to-day priorities have prevented the firm from systematizing various HR functions such as hiring, orientation, training, appraisal, and compensation. The firm hopes to hire a new human resource manager (HRM, as the position is now called) in the near future, who will bring about the needed changes.

McAllister was with the company for only about three years. While he was credited with having "run a tight ship," several of his colleagues complained about his dominating and centralized leadership style. One of the managers went as far as saying that *"Maple Leaf Shoes would not have been unionized this fast and to this extent but for John."* McAllister's predecessor, Tim Donovan, was not a popular personnel manager either. Donovan, who resigned his position after a mere ten-month stay at Maple Leaf Shoes, did not have positive things to say about the company and its management. On the eve of his departure, he is reported to have confided in an associate: *"The management system here is primitive. It's as if you are surrounded by forces of darkness. Of course, I could stay here and fight it out—maybe I would win in the end. But then I'm not masochistic!"*

DISCUSSION QUESTIONS

1. What are some changes within Maple Leaf Shoes and in its environment that have caused a shift in its strategy? List the challenges facing the company using the classification provided in your text.

2. Assume that you are hired as a consultant to help the firm hire a new human resource manager. What immediate and long-term job responsibilities will you identify for the new job incumbent?

3. Identify three sample objectives of the human resource department at Maple Leaf Shoes and list associated strategy and action plans to be implemented by the department.

CASE STUDY

Canadian Pacific and International Bank*

Canadian Pacific and International Bank (CPIB) is one of Canada's premier financial institutions, with assets of over $150 billion. CPIB, which began as a "western" bank in the early 1950s with its head office in Vancouver, British Columbia, spread its operations all over Canada and the United States by the mid-1960s. Originally called Pacific and Western Bank, the bank changed its name about 15 years ago to reflect its international character. Today, more than 25,000 employees provide personal, commercial, corporate, and investment banking services to individuals and businesses in 33 countries. Some recent financial and employee statistics for CPIB are shown in Figure 1.

FIGURE 1

Summary of Financial and Employee Statistics

	This Year	Last Year	Year Before	3-Year Growth
Total revenue ($000)	13,442,571	11,309,142	8,979,429	20.02%
Earnings before interest and tax ($000)	3,980,571	2,806,286	2,435,143	26.16%
Profit/loss ($000)	2,555,143	960,857	932,571	48.12%
Earnings per share	4.20	1.55	1.52	49.17%
Total assets ($000)	183,786,000	155,855,140	140,444,570	18.18%
Dividends per share	0.62	0.57	0.48	
Return on equity	27.39	12.77	14.05	
Employees	25,059	26,594	24,500	

CPIB, through its strategic initiatives, was successful in building long-term value for its shareholders while providing regular return on their investments. The market price of CPIB's share increased by over 40 percent in the preceding two years, bringing the bank's total market capitalization to nearly $18 billion, up from $10 billion just a few years back. In the current year, the share price has remained more or less static largely due to investor preferences for Internet stocks over "conservative" bank stocks.

Globally, CPIB serves more than 6 million customers in three key areas: personal and commercial banking, wealth management, and wholesale and corporate banking—marketed under the name CPIB Securities (see Figure 2).

---

* Case written by Professor Hari Das of the Department of Management, Saint Mary's University, Halifax, Canada. All rights retained by the author © 2002.

FIGURE 2

CPIB Operations

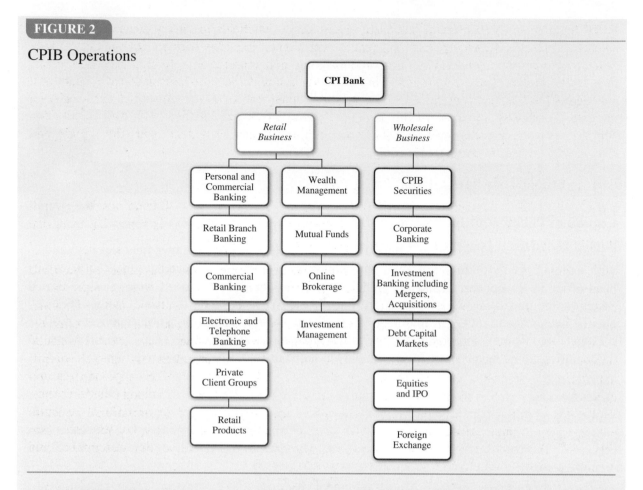

Personal and Commercial Banking: Through its 673 retail outlets, CPIB offers a wide variety of products and services. In addition, *CP Anytime*, CPIB's electronic banking service, offers customers access to retail products, services, and accounts via telephone banking. The 1,781 automated banking machines that form the Purple Touch network, CP Web Banking, and CP Day-Night Investor provide service around the clock. In a recent independent survey, the bank was cited as number two in four out of seven dimensions of customer service, including friendliness and customer responsiveness. The bank aims to further enhance customer service levels and flexibility (e.g., a single-number dial or a single Web site to meet all retailing and investment needs of small-volume customers). Through such efforts, it aims to build market share in small and medium-sized businesses.

Wealth Management: CPIB's wealth management business includes its discount brokerage and mutual fund operations. CPIB Investment is one of Canada's leading discount brokerages, currently with over 1 million customer accounts in the United States and Canada and a growing clientele in Australia, the United Kingdom, and Japan. Although smaller than TD Canada Trust's TD Waterhouse Group or Royal Bank's Action Direct, CPIB is attempting to make fast inroads into this highly competitive but lucrative sector of banking. Historically, CPIB had charged lower commissions ($25 for most transactions compared to $29 charged by TD Waterhouse and Action Direct). In the near future, the firm plans to increase its market penetration ratio. Currently, CPIB manages nearly $24 billion in mutual funds, pension funds, trusts, and endowments. In the near future, the bank wants to reorganize and integrate wealth management activities to improve customer service and sales support for all products.

CPIB Securities: CPIB offers a full range of services to its clients in all key areas of finance and specialized solutions for corporate and government clients. Included here are investment banking (which includes merchant banking, corporate banking, and syndications), foreign exchange, loans, debt capital markets (including initial public offerings and underwritings), mergers and acquisitions, and derivatives. In a recent ranking by a business magazine of North American firms offering integrated corporate services, CPIB was rated eighth in North America. The bank's priorities continue to be developing stronger client relationships, expanding industry specialty groups, and achieving maximum operating efficiency.

ORGANIZATION OF THE BANK

Since CPIB is an extremely large organization with operations in over 30 countries, the overall structure of the bank is very complex and not easily depicted. It also varies somewhat from one country to another to better respond to the local realities and challenges.

The chair and chief executive officer of the bank is Michael Bennett, who is also chair of the board of directors to which he is accountable. The 18-member board (17 men, 1 woman) represents a cross-section of top leaders in manufacturing and service industries and academic and professional institutions in Canada. The board has several committees entrusted with special tasks. Examples: audit and risk management committee, which, among other duties, reviews the audited financial statements and approves policies related to risk and liquidity management and internal control; management resources committee, which reviews and approves senior office appointments and executive compensation plans; and corporate governance committee, which, among other activities, deliberates on the board composition and functioning. CPIB's hybrid organizational structure attempts to maximize the advantages of functional, product-based, and geographic structures (see Figure 3). The bank has a 472-page manual that describes in detail the position descriptions and required competencies of various managerial positions.

The chair, assisted by a deputy chair and five vice-chairs, approves all critical decisions affecting the bank's future. Three of the vice-chairs are in charge of personal and commercial banking, wealth management, and CPIB Securities; the fourth is in charge of global operations and the last one in charge of overall administration. The seven senior vice-presidents are in charge of retail banking, commercial banking, mutual funds and brokerage, investment management, corporate and investment banking, human resources, and global operations. Below the senior vice-presidents are heads of various divisions including human resources, economic analysis, securities and foreign exchange, retail banking, real estate operations, and risk management. There are 36 heads of divisions or groups or regions currently. With the bank's expansion into electronic banking and foreign markets, more group heads and even vice-presidents may have to be hired in the near future. The three foreign division heads are located outside Canada: Asian Division in Singapore, European Division in London, and Middle East and African Division in Istanbul.

For ease of administration and to better respond to customer requirements, the domestic banking is divided into five regions (head offices in parentheses): Atlantic (Halifax), Quebec (Montreal), Ontario (Toronto), Prairie (Winnipeg), and Pacific (Vancouver). The corporate head office is also located in Vancouver. Several other functions are centralized at the head office to reap economies of scale and facilitate communication. Example: CP Economics Division that monitors Canadian and world economic trends and prepares routine and special reports for use by the bank in its various investment and client divisions. Some of the other functions (e.g., CP Ombudsperson) are located at the head office but with strong regional presence and frequent meetings with staff at various regions and branches to better respond to their queries and proactively deal with emerging issues or likely problems.

FIGURE 3

An Overview of CPIB Organization

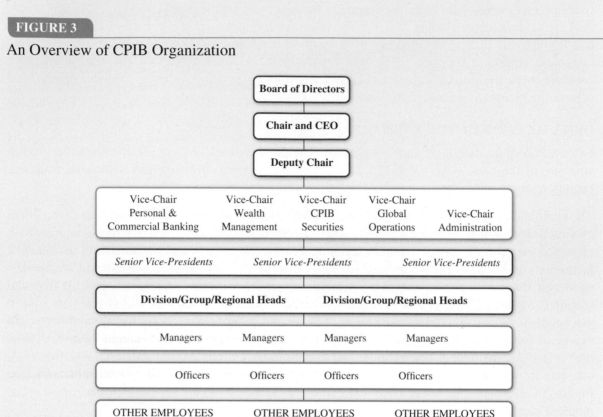

CORPORATE STRATEGIES

CPIB, which is known for its ability to capitalize on opportunities, was one of the first Canadian banks to enter Asian and Latin American markets, introduce automated tellers throughout Canada, begin a Web-based brokerage, and offer integrated wealth management and financial counselling services. Its extensive online delivery of wealth management and banking services has made CPIB a key player in the development of ecommerce and places it in the top dozen financial services firms in the world as measured by the number of online customer accounts. In a bid to dominate the market, CPIB recently acquired Maple Leaf Trust, a large trust firm with its head office in Toronto. CPIB is currently concluding negotiations for the acquisition of International Investors Inc., a large stock exchange brokerage firm located in New York. When completed (it is expected that the deal will be finalized in less than two months), the new investment arm of CPIB, namely Canadian and International Investors, will be among the top dozen financial services firms in the world. Reflecting its strategy of investing in the future of financial services, CPIB is progressing in the new millennium as a leader in online delivery.

CPIB has always prided itself on its record of enhancing shareholder value. Its consistently high net incomes (in some years, reflecting record growth for the entire banking industry in this country) and its focus on running a lean operation have resulted in considerable increase in shareholder value over the years. To finance its newer acquisitions, the firm plans to make initial public offerings

(IPOs) soon. Already, a number of large investors and brokerage firms have expressed considerable interest in the IPOs.

CPIB has a solid reputation as a good corporate citizen, having increased its charitable donations by 9.2 percent to $7.3 million last year. Two years ago, the bank created the slogan "Bank for Your Community" and began contributing 1 percent of pre-tax domestic income to improve the community. Its donations have focused primarily on children's health and education, university scholarships (its Canadian University Scholarship is a coveted award), and donations for art and sports events (over 100 children attend minor league sports or the Canadian Conservatory of Music each year). The bank is a major sponsor of Save the Children Network, a network of hospitals serving over a million children across Canada. In the future, the bank wants to expand its community service to include foreign countries as well.

IMMEDIATE CHALLENGES

CPIB recognizes that it has no time to rest on its laurels. To maintain and improve its competitive position, it must innovate and grow. Big competitors such as Royal Bank <http://www.rbcroyalbank.com>, TD Canada Trust <http://www.tdcanadatrust.com>, Canadian Imperial Bank of Commerce , Bank of Nova Scotia <http://www.scotiabank.com>, and Bank of Montreal <https://www.bmo.com> have been making fast inroads into electronic banking and foreign markets while smaller banks and credit unions, because of their small volumes, are able to provide more personal service compared to the large banks. Standardization and automation brought in considerable predictability and efficiency in operations, but it was also fraught with the risk of impersonal service and bureaucratic red tape. How to improve efficiency and predictability while offering personal and custom service? How to reap the advantages of smaller organizations such as flexibility without losing the economies of scale? There seem to be no simple answers.

More recently, a large number of "virtual banks" have appeared on the scene. These banks pay 4 to 5 percent interest even on small balances irrespective of the type of accounts (most Canadian banks do not pay any significant interest on chequing accounts). Because of the absence of any overhead costs, these virtual banks have been able to offer premium interest rates on other types of accounts as well as offer loans at cheaper rates. How can the bank compete with the virtual banks without losing the advantages of traditional banking and sacrificing the security and reputation?

Some have predicted that future societies may be "money-free"—in an Internet age, where most commodities can be virtually traded (including air miles, bonus points issued by gas stations, Canadian Tire coupons, and gift certificates), there is no reason why people should continue to use only currency notes or bank cheques as media of transaction.[96] If this scenario occurs, what will be the fate of traditional banks? No one quite knows.

While computerization and Internet trading have brought substantial benefits, they have also exposed banks and their systems to hackers and computer viruses that paralyze trading and, in some instances, wipe out a bank's entire computer memory. For instance, in early 2000, the "Love Bug" infected more than 2 million computer files around the world—over 90 percent of the sites being in North America—causing damage exceeding US$1 billion.[97] In the future, when banks increase their reliance on computerized trading, the risk element is only likely to grow.

In recent years, "shareholder democracy" has been gaining momentum. Organizations such as the Association for the Protection of Quebec Savers and Investors (APQSI) have been demanding a greater voice in bank decisions. In a recent Bank of Montreal shareholders' meeting,[98] APQSI proposed a course of action that was accepted by majority shareholders—even when the bank management recommended voting against it. The banks have been the focus of activist efforts because they are all widely held national institutions with a great deal of power. In the near future, there may be greater accountability of directors and senior bank executives to shareholders who are asking tough questions on all aspects of their operations. How can the bank respond to shareholder concerns without losing managerial authority and decision-making power? That is the question many bank managers ask themselves today.

Canada's banks operate in a highly regulated environment. Among the various restrictions they face is the complicated approval process needed for any merger. (In 1999, when Royal Bank and Bank of Montreal wanted to merge, the necessary approval was not granted.) In early 2001, the federal government was drafting legislation that could impose an even more complicated approval process on any merger among the big banks.[99] When the legislation is complete, any banking merger would require extensive public hearings on practically every aspect of the deal—a factor causing considerable frustration for Canadian banks, which find that their global status is coming down (the U.S. and Japanese banks have considerable resources and opportunity for cross-ownership of banks). In Royal Bank CEO John Cleghorn's words, "We are in a highly competitive game and we are hamstrung in our ability to deal with it."[100] Canadian bankers have also been complaining about intrusive consumer regulations that risk putting them at a disadvantage in relation to their U.S. competitors. The existing and proposed regulations will restrict the banks from using their customer databases to sell products to a targeted audience, including selling insurance through the branches. This is especially worrisome since large credit card companies have no similar restrictions imposed on them in this regard. "I worry a bit about the propensity to put consumer-type safeguards on banks only," Peter Godsoe, chairman of Bank of Nova Scotia, pointed out. "I think it has some dangers in it because database marketers can sit in the United States and sell the databases and all sorts of products."[101]

As an international organization, the bank is susceptible to all political and economic uncertainties in foreign countries. In the recent past, there was a significant slowdown in several Asian economies, resulting in, at times, massive losses to all major banks including CPIB. There were also instances where foreign governments suddenly changed their investment policies, prohibiting repatriation of capital and profits.[102] How can the bank expand without overexposing itself to risk? Clearly, there are no easy answers.

HUMAN RESOURCE FUNCTION

While its financial goals have been the driving force behind CPIB's externally focused strategies, management always recognized that it could not have achieved any of these results but for its highly competent and motivated employees—whether they are senior executives or clerks in remote branches. From its inception, the bank was committed to progressive human resource management practices in all its operations. It was one of the first banks to institute standardized selection and performance appraisal procedures, a well-designed human resource planning system, a detailed counselling system for employees, and financial assistance for university education for its employees. While occasional layoffs and staff reduction have been inevitable to cut costs, this has been done as humanely as possible. Mary Keddy, senior vice-president—human resources, an MBA from Saint Mary's specializing in human resources with an outstanding performance record in the steel industry, joined the firm six years ago. Since her arrival, she has tried to introduce state-of-the-art techniques and systems to the management of human resources. Compared to other banks, the staff turnover rate in CPIB is 2 percent lower. Past employee surveys have indicated that staff morale is high and rising. In Keddy's words,

I know it is a cliché to say that "human resources are our most important assets." Many organizations proclaim this as their policy, but then it is business as usual. Honestly, I do believe in the maxim and what is fortunate for me, CPIB also believes in it. My predecessor, John Galsworthy, was a progressive human resource manager. He was one of those visionaries—he realized the potential of humans and was determined to tap that to the fullest extent. What is more, he genuinely cared for the employees. I am told that he knew several tellers in distant branches by their first names. Even a year before his retirement from the bank, he was found to spend long hours—often 12 to 13 hours—in his office to refine our HR practices. Fitting into his shoes, naturally, was a daunting task initially. But he also left a good system to build on. And that is what I have been doing: building on our strengths.

Keddy's views on the importance of human resources are echoed by several senior executives, including the CEO. At a time when several Canadian banks had their HR function represented only at the divisional or group level, CPIB raised its status to a vice-president level. In the foreseeable future, especially if the present expansion and merger plans proceed according to plans, HR may be elevated to vice-chair level, adding organizational change to the function.

Most of the specialized HR functions are located at the Vancouver head office. The regional offices do have their own HR managers and staff, but all major policy decisions are made at the head office—of course, after extensive consultations with all concerned (see Figure 4).

FIGURE 4

Structure of HR Function at CPIB Head Office

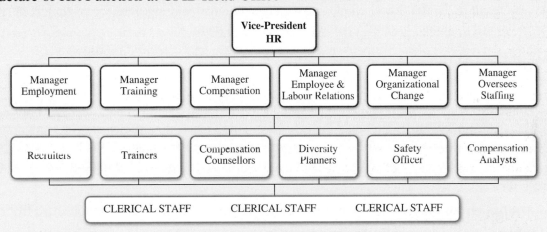

According to Keddy, some areas that HR is currently investigating are as follows:

While the bank has been a progressive employer, the number of female senior managers in its ranks continues to be low. At the junior levels of management, the ratio between male and female managers is currently 65:35; however, as one goes up the hierarchy, the ratio changes drastically in favour of the males. Of the eight vice-presidents, only one is a woman; of the remaining senior managers, less than 5 percent are women. While the bank has been aware of the situation and would like to correct it, it has not been easy. There is also a larger turnover among female managers, making the task even more difficult. An examination of the employee records does not show any significant differences between males and females either in terms of educational qualifications or prior work experience. Also, at lower levels, in many branches, female employees seem to score higher on tenure and overall productivity. The situation, thus, is somewhat perplexing.

In many large cities such as Toronto and Vancouver, the percentage of visible minorities in the general population and labour market has been significant—often totalling 40 percent of the workforce. CPIB has also a number of clerks and lower-level staff who belong to this group. However, even at the supervisory and junior managerial level, the percentage of minorities has been insignificant (often less than one-tenth of 1 percent). The bank would like to encourage more minorities and people with physical disabilities to reach middle-level and senior managerial levels.

After the merger with Investors, all duplication in services needs to be eliminated, which is likely to result in some job losses. How can the bank minimize job losses and employee anxiety? Keddy is currently heading a human resource steering committee that is looking into this matter and deliberating on staff reductions. She also wants to regularize communication flow to the employees on the matter to minimize rumours. The new employees from Investors also need to be socialized into CPIB's culture.

In recent months, Keddy and some of her senior colleagues have been seriously debating an ethical issue. Several manufacturers in developing economies employ young children (often aged seven or eight years) at very low wages (sometimes as low as less than a dollar per day) for long hours (12 hours and more in some cases) to produce cheap products such as soccer balls and volleyballs, jeans, and shoes. These manufacturers are important customers of the bank—often accounting for 25 percent or more of its loans in some regions. Keddy believes that the bank has a moral responsibility to do what is ethically right, but is not sure how it can influence the events in other countries.

Finally, how to reduce labour costs while minimizing the adverse impact on employee morale and customer satisfaction? Automation and computerization can reduce labour costs significantly, but could also result in layoffs, lower employee morale, and longer waiting lines for customers in some cases. What is the optimal tradeoff between efficiency and morale?

IMMEDIATE GOALS

For the next year, the bank has the following financial objectives:

Efficiency ratio: This ratio (also called "productivity" ratio) measures non-interest expenses as a percentage of revenue; the lower the percentage, the greater the efficiency. The bank aims to maintain an efficiency ratio of 58 percent (the six other major Canadian banks have productivity ratios ranging from 63 to 68 percent) compared to 61.6 percent last year and 63.8 percent two years ago.

Earnings on share: The bank aims to generate growth in earnings per common share from the present $4.20 to $4.62, or a 10 percent increase.

Return on equity: The bank wants to maintain its earning premium over risk-free Government of Canada Bonds, which currently translates into a return on equity (on cash basis) of about 17 percent. The bank wants to improve its overall return by 1 percentage point.

Provision for credit losses: Most Canadian banks average 0.37 percent (some banks with as high a rate as 0.5 percent) of net average loans as provision for credit losses. CPIB would like to keep it at 0.40 percent. CPIB had found that the bank's previous year's credit losses were far higher than normal because of the meltdown of the high-tech and telecom sectors and the general downturn of the U.S. and foreign economies in 2001–2002. The bank had also made significant loans to firms operating in Argentina, Japan, and Brazil—all of which had considerable loan defaults in the immediate past.

Market ratings for debt: The bank's credit ratings from Moody's and Standard Poor are strong at AA3 and AAMinus respectively. The bank would like to improve these.

DISCUSSION QUESTIONS

1. What are some major challenges facing CPIB?

2. What are the specific implications for the human resource function?

3. What suggestions do you have for the current challenges faced by the HR function?

PART-ENDING VIDEOS

"Creative Corporation"

Source: © MHHE Management Library.

"Southwest CEO"

Source: © MHHE Management Library.

"HR in Alignment"

Source: © MHHE Management Library.

"Leadership at Every Level"

Source: © 2012. Produced by Kantola Productions. Copyright protected by Kantola Productions and cannot be duplicated, transmitted, or placed on a network without prior written permission.

Go to Connect to access the videos.

ROLE-PLAY 1: IMPORTANCE OF HR MANAGEMENT ACTIVITIES

Time required: 40–50 minutes

OBJECTIVES OF THE ROLE-PLAY

1. To sensitize the student to differences in perceptions of the importance of HR activities in organizations.

2. To enhance their negotiating skills as future HR managers during budget negotiations.

3. To enhance their communication skills in conveying HR priorities.

PRIOR PREPARATION

1. Study Chapter 1 of the text.

2. Read the descriptions of Maple Leaf Shoes Ltd. at the ends of Chapters 1 and 2 in the text.

GUIDELINES FOR CONDUCTING THE ROLE-PLAY

The role-play enacts a meeting between Jane Reynolds, Special Assistant to the Human Resource Manager, with Tim MacDonald, General Manager of Finance. Ms. Reynolds is requesting an increase in the budget for training and HR system improvement. Ms. Reynolds and Mr. MacDonald hold differing views on the role of HR management in the company.

1. Two students, one for the role of Jane Reynolds and the other for Tim MacDonald, should be identified.

2. Students should read their own role description in the Instructor Resource Manual along with the company details given at the ends of Chapters 1 and 2.

3. The instructor should signal the beginning and the end of the meeting. The meeting will last a maximum length of 30 minutes. It may be ended earlier.

4. The remainder of the class time is used for discussion of the behaviours observed during the role-play and outcomes.

5. Observers should be asked to make notes against the questions listed below and discuss their findings at the end of the role-play.

6. The instructor should sum up by highlighting the differing HR strategies and their implications for organizational practices and outcomes.

INSTRUCTIONS FOR OBSERVERS

As you observe the meeting between Jane Reynolds and Tim MacDonald, make notes against each of the questions below. Pay particular attention to the behaviours and verbal and nonverbal expressions of each person.

1. Are there differences in the assumptions of the two parties about the role and importance of HR? How?

2. How did Jane begin the meeting?

3. Was there open communication between the two?

4. Did Jane get what she wanted?

5. Is there anything Jane could have done to change Tim's attitude? What?

6. Would you have done anything differently? If so, what?

APPENDIX A

Origins of Human Resource Management

The origins of human resource management are unknown. Probably the first cave dwellers struggled with problems of utilizing human resources. Even the Bible records selection and training problems faced by Moses. Moses was confronted with one of the earliest recorded personnel challenges when Jethro, his father-in-law, advised: "And thou shalt teach them ordinances and laws, and shalt shew them the way wherein they must walk, and the work they must do. Moreover, thou shalt provide out of all the people able men... to be rulers" (Exod. 18: 20–21).

During the thousands of years between Moses and the Industrial Revolution, there were few large organizations. Except for religious orders (the Roman Catholic Church, for example) or governments (particularly the military), small groups did most of the work. Whether on the farm, in small shops, or in the home, the primary work unit was the family. There was little need for formal study of human resource management.

The Industrial Revolution changed the nature of work. Mechanical power and economies of scale required large numbers of people to work together. Large textile mills, foundries, and mines sprung up in England and then in North America. Collectively, people were still an important resource, but the Industrial Revolution meant greater mechanization and unpleasant working conditions for many workers.

By the late 1800s, a few employers reacted to the human problems caused by industrialization and created the post of welfare secretary. Welfare secretaries existed to meet worker needs and to prevent workers from forming unions. Social secretaries, as they were sometimes called, helped employees with personal problems such as education, housing, and medical needs. These early forerunners of human resource specialists sought to improve working conditions for workers. The emergence of welfare secretaries prior to 1900 demonstrates that the personnel activities in large organizations had already become more extensive than some top operating managers alone could handle. Thus, social secretaries marked the birth of specialized human resource management, as distinct from the day-to-day supervision of personnel by operating managers.

Scientific Management and Human Needs

The next noteworthy development was scientific management. The scientific management proponents showed the world that the systematic, scientific study of work could lead to improved efficiency. Their arguments for specialization and improved training furthered the need for HR management. The first decades of the twentieth century saw primitive "personnel departments" replace welfare secretaries. These new departments contributed to organizational effectiveness by maintaining wages at proper levels, screening job applicants, and handling grievances. They also assumed the welfare secretary's role of improving working conditions, dealing with unions, and meeting other employee needs.

By the First World War, personnel departments were becoming common among very large industrial employers. But these early departments were not important parts of the organizations they served. They were record depositories with advisory authority only. At that time, production, finance, and marketing problems overshadowed the role of personnel management. The importance of personnel departments grew slowly as their contribution and responsibilities increased.

From the end of the First World War until the Great Depression of the 1930s, personnel departments assumed growing roles in handling compensation, testing, unions, and employee needs. More and more attention was paid to employee needs. The importance of individual needs became even more pronounced as a result of the research studies in the United States at Western Electric's Hawthorne plant during this period. These studies showed that the efficiency goals of scientific management had to be balanced by considerations of human needs. These observations eventually had a profound impact on personnel management. But the Depression and the Second World War diverted attention to more urgent matters of organizational and national survival.

Modern Influences

The Depression of the 1930s led citizens to lose faith in the ability of business to meet society's needs. They turned to government. Government intervened to give workers minimum wages and the right to join labour unions. In 1940, Canada started an unemployment insurance program to help alleviate financial problems during the transition from one job to another. In general, the government's emphasis was on improving employee security and working conditions.

This drafting of legislation during the 1930s helped to shape the present role of personnel departments by adding legal obligations. Organizations now had to consider societal objectives and the need for legal compliance, which elevated the importance of personnel departments. In practice, personnel departments were made responsible for discouraging unionization among employees. But with newfound legal protection, unions grew dramatically. These organizing successes startled many organizations into rethinking their use of paternalism, their "management knows best" approach to employee welfare. Personnel departments began replacing a paternalistic approach with more proactive approaches that considered employee desires. When workers did organize, responsibility for dealing with unions also fell to the personnel department, sometimes renamed the industrial relations department to reflect these new duties.

Personnel departments continued to increase in importance during the 1940s and 1950s. The recruiting and training demands of the Second World War added to the credibility of the personnel departments that successfully met these challenges. After the war, personnel departments grew in importance as they contended with unions and an expanding need for professionals such as engineers and accountants. The increasing attention given to behavioural findings led to concern for improved human relations. These findings helped underscore the importance of sound personnel management practices.

In the 1960s and 1970s, the central influence on personnel was again legislation. Several laws were passed that affected the working conditions, wage levels, safety, and health and other benefits of employees. These acts began to provide personnel department managers with a still larger voice—a voice that began to equal that of production, finance, and marketing executives in major corporations.

Human resource management—as the personnel function is known today—did not emerge until recently. It is only very recently that human resource specialists have started to exert great influence on organizational strategy or have been chosen as chief executives. But today, in many organizations, there is a genuine recognition that human resources spell the difference between strategic success and organizational decline. The emphasis placed on strategic human resource management and formal certification of HR specialists are evidence of this growing role of human resource management.

Planning Human Resources

This part introduces you to the important task of planning for human resources. Chapter 2 discusses the various approaches to conducting a job analysis. Steps to create valid job descriptions, specifications, and performance standards are outlined in this chapter. Chapter 3 discusses the various factors that need to be considered when forecasting the demand for and supply of human resources. It also outlines several popular techniques for making such forecasts. Together, these two chapters help you to identify the type, number, and degree of sophistication of human resources needed by your firm.

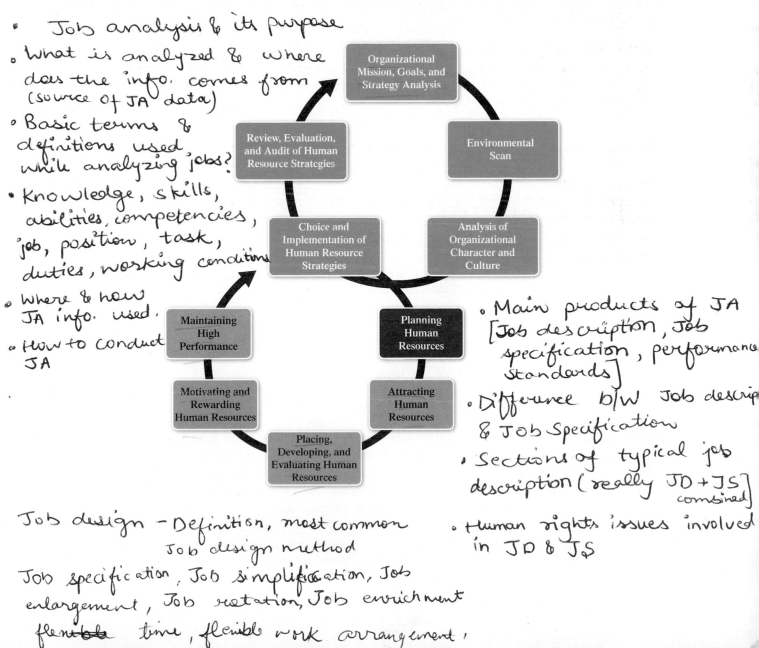

- Job analysis & its purpose
- What is analyzed & where does the info. comes from (source of JA data)
- Basic terms & definitions used while analyzing jobs?
- Knowledge, skills, abilities, competencies, job, position, task, duties, working conditions
- Where & how JA info. used.
- How to conduct JA

- Main products of JA [Job description, Job specification, performance standards]
- Difference b/w Job descrip & Job Specification
- Sections of typical job description (really JD + JS combined)
- Human rights issues involved in JD & JS

Job design - Definition, most common Job design method
Job specification, Job simplification, Job enlargement, Job rotation, Job enrichment flexible time, flexible work arrangement,

CHAPTER 2

Job Analysis
and
Design*

The data generated by job analyses have significant use in nearly every phase of human resource administration: designing jobs and reward systems; staffing and training; performance control and more. Few other processes executed by organizations have the potential for being such a powerful aid to management decision making.

PHILIP C. GRANT[1]

LEARNING OBJECTIVES

After studying this chapter, you should be able to:

LO1 Describe the uses of job analysis information for human resource managers.

LO2 Discuss the various steps in conducting job analysis and methods of job data collection.

LO3 Describe the contents of a job description and a job specification.

LO4 Discuss the various approaches to setting performance standards.

LO5 Outline the key considerations in job design.

In this part of the book, we will explain how knowledge about jobs and their requirements must be collected through **job analysis** (see: <www.job-analysis.net>) before any other HR functions can begin. From making the right selection decision, to developing training programs, to dismissing employees who are not performing to expectations and more, decision-makers need accurate information about a variety of aspects of the job in question.

*It has been suggested to reverse the sequence of Chapters 2 and 3—that is, to discuss human resource planning before job analysis. However, we feel that job analyses come first. Without them no human resource planning is possible.

job analysis

Systematic study of a job to discover its specifications, skill requirements, and so on, for wage-setting, recruitment, training, or job-design purposes.

Job analysis and design knowledge is vital to the effective functioning of an organization, as shown in the following example:

> At Purolator <http://www.purolator.ca>, which employs 11,600 Canadians including 3,000 couriers, 300 linehaul truck drivers, and 500 call centre operators, the Worker's Compensation Board bill came in at $13 million. Purolator traced 90 percent of the workers' compensation claims to employees in two occupations: couriers and sorters. These two jobs require constant lifting, hauling, pushing, and pulling, leading to soft tissue, orthopedic, and joint injuries—and the majority of the WCB claims. By conducting job analyses for the 25 jobs where most of the injuries were occurring, Purolator was able to identify suitable modified or transitional duties for injured workers. Through its early and safe back-to-work initiative, Purolator was able to reduce its lost day severity, total number of lost days, and number of modified or accommodated days, and keep workers engaged within their workgroups.[2]

Jobs are at the core of every organization's productivity. If they are not well designed and done right, productivity suffers, profits fall, and the organization is less able to meet the demands of society, customers, employees, and other stakeholders. The importance of well-designed jobs is perhaps best illustrated by an example:

> A small construction company, consisting of the owner, two administrators, and fourteen bricklayers and carpenters, experienced rapid growth, but the performance per staff member declined. A consultant found that the company had no job descriptions, causing uncertainty in employees about job responsibilities and performance expectations. Job analyses clarified everybody's role in the organization and established performance standards based on industry data. Job performance and quality improved significantly, as did job satisfaction, resulting in lower turnover.

For a human resource department to be effective, its members must have a clear understanding of the jobs found throughout the organization. A **job** consists of a group of related activities and duties. A job may be held by a single employee or several persons. The collection of tasks and responsibilities performed by an individual employee is called a **position**.

job

Group of related activities and duties.

position

Collection of tasks and responsibilities performed by an individual.

> In a department with one supervisor, three animators, and twelve programmers, there are sixteen positions, but only three jobs.

With hundreds—or even thousands—of positions, it is nearly impossible for the human resource professionals in large companies to know the details of every one. It is, however, unnecessary to collect information on identical positions separately. Consider this example:

> One transmedia company has 20 game developers. Each position is the same. Rather than study each position separately, the job analyst can collect data from a random sample of the positions to generate an accurate understanding of the game developer job.

LO1

Figure 2-1 lists major human resource actions that rely on job analysis information. For example, without job analysis information, human resource specialists will find it difficult to evaluate how environmental challenges or specific job requirements affect employees' quality of work life. To match job applicants to openings, human resource specialists must understand what each job requires and know what information to place in job advertisements. Similarly, compensation analysts cannot determine a fair salary without detailed knowledge of each job. Human resource departments formalize the collection, evaluation, and organization of this information.

FIGURE 2-1

Major Human Resource Management Activities That Rely on Job Analysis Information

1. Careful study of jobs to improve employee productivity levels.

2. Elimination of unnecessary job requirements that can cause discrimination in employment.

3. Creation of job advertisements used to generate a pool of qualified applicants.

4. Matching of job applicants to job requirements.

5. Planning of future human resource requirements.

6. Determination of employee orientation and training needs.

7. Fair and equitable compensation of employees.

8. Identification of realistic and challenging performance standards.

9. Redesign of jobs to improve performance, employee morale, and/or quality of work life.

10. Fair and accurate appraisal of employee performance.

This chapter describes the information sought by job analysts and the techniques to collect it. The chapter also describes how the data are converted into a useful *human resource information system (HRIS)*. A sophisticated HRIS permits easy retrieval of relevant job details; it also provides a variety of information about the job, jobholders, and past performance standards. Further details about designing an HRIS are in the next chapter.

LO2 HRC 4

Steps in the Job Analysis Process

Job analysis has three phases: preparation, collection of job information, and use of job information for improving organizational effectiveness (see Figure 2-2). Each phase consists of several actions discussed below.

Phase 1: Preparation for Job Analysis

Three key activities are performed in this phase:

Step 1: Familiarization with the Organization and Its Jobs

Before studying jobs, it is important to have an awareness of an organization's objectives, strategies, structure, inputs (people, materials, and procedures), and desired outcomes. Job analysis procedures are influenced by the organization character, discussed in Chapter 1. In unionized organizations, job analysis steps also have to meet the various provisions of the collective agreement between the management and the union (more details about this relationship are discussed in Chapter 13). Job analysts may also study industry and government reports about the jobs to be analyzed. In all instances, the intent is to collect relevant and accurate information about jobs and factors determining job success.

FIGURE 2-2

The Job Analysis Process

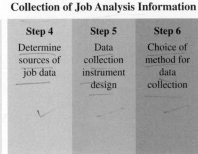

Phase 1			Phase 2			Phase 3
Preparation for Job Analysis			**Collection of Job Analysis Information**			**Use of Job Analysis Information**
Step 1	**Step 2**	**Step 3**	**Step 4**	**Step 5**	**Step 6**	• Job description
Familiarize with the organization and the jobs	Determine uses of job analysis	Identify jobs to be analyzed	Determine sources of job data	Data collection instrument design	Choice of method for data collection	• Job specification • Job performance standards • Job redesign • Designing HRIS • Changing HR systems (e.g., compensation) • Organization change (e.g., redesigning workflow in plant)

Step 2: Determine Uses of Job Analysis Information

As shown in Figure 2-1, job analysis plays a critical role for many HR functions. Although the most common uses are in the recruitment process, designing performance appraisal, compensation systems, and training,[3] job analysis may also be done to ensure fair treatment across all employee groups[4] or to assist in job redesign. In some cases, job analysis aids other objectives such as identifying non-traditional career paths for employees, as shown in the following example:

> One job analysis study[5] found that the skills, knowledge, and abilities essential for performance in secretarial and clerical positions are very similar to those needed in entry-level management positions. If female or minority employees are concentrated in secretarial or clerical positions, this information can be used to move them into managerial positions. Employees may also use this information to make the best use of their work experience and training to develop specific career paths.

The details collected during a job analysis are influenced by the objectives of the study; hence, it is critical to define the objectives early on.

Step 3: Identify Jobs to Be Analyzed

Although almost all jobs might benefit from an in-depth analysis, resource and time constraints often preclude organizations from conducting job analyses. Likely targets of job analysis are jobs that are critical to the success of an organization; jobs that are difficult to learn or perform (to determine the extent of training); jobs in which the firm continuously hires new employees (identification of clear job requirements assumes great importance); or jobs that exclude members of the protected classes described in Chapter 4. Jobs should also be analyzed if new technology or altered work environments affect how the job is performed (see: <www.hr-guide.com>).

If inappropriate job requirements are used, the organization may even be in violation of laws, as the following example illustrates:

> In the past, the Vancouver Fire Department <http://vancouver.ca/fire> required that all successful job applicants be at least 175 centimetres (five feet, nine inches) tall. After one of the applicants complained, the Human Rights Board looked into the department's selection practices and could not find any correlation between the height of a firefighter and injuries or productivity of the employees. The department was found to be in violation of the Human Rights Act.[6]

Discriminatory practices for firefighters are prohibited as long as a person is able to do the job. Women usually áre able to carry less weight than men. Should that be taken into account during hiring?

© Tyler Stableford/Stone/Getty Images

In general, senior management and all key supervisors of the firm should be consulted before selecting jobs for in-depth analysis, as the jobs selected for analysis can affect the strategic success and overall human resource policies (e.g., hiring, training) of the firm. The type, number, and geographical dispersion of the jobs selected for analysis also influence the choice of data collection method.

Phase 2: Collection of Job Analysis Information

This phase contains three interrelated activities: determining the source of job data, data collection instrument design, and choosing the method of collection.

Step 4: Determine Sources of Job Data

Although the most direct source of information about a job is the jobholder, various other sources—both human and nonhuman—may be used for this purpose. Figure 2-3 lists alternative sources of job information.

Occasionally, materials published in professional journals and magazines provide information about how jobs are performed in other organizations and settings. This information can be valuable when establishing performance standards and benchmarks for quality. The *National Occupational Classification (NOC)* in Canada (discussed in greater detail later in this chapter), and the U.S. Department of Labor Employment and Training Administration's electronic database, the *Occupational Information Network (O*NET)*, provide information on various jobs. Web sites of several professional associations and private consulting firms offer a wealth of material relevant to job analysis and job descriptions.

The jobholders, their supervisors, and colleagues provide the most valid information about the way jobs are performed. However, other parties can also provide important information about jobs:

> In the case of a salesperson, contacting past customers provides additional insights about job behaviours. In the case of college or university faculty, students may be able to provide important information on in-class behaviours related to effective job performance.

Sources of Job Data

Nonhuman Sources	Human Sources
Existing job descriptions and specifications	Job incumbents
Equipment design blueprints	Supervisors
Equipment maintenance manuals and records	Job experts
Training and safety manuals	Work colleagues
Organization charts and other company records	Subordinates
National Occupational Classification	Customers
Videos/films supplied by appliance/machine manufacturers	
Professional journals/magazines/publications	
Internet research	

Step 5: Data Collection Instrument Design

To study jobs, analysts most often develop **job analysis questionnaires**. These questionnaires are used to collect job information uniformly. They uncover the duties, responsibilities, human abilities, and performance standards of the jobs investigated.

---

job analysis questionnaires

Checklists used to collect information about jobs in a uniform manner.

Questionnaires are particularly important when collecting information from human sources. Even in the case of nonhuman sources, the quality and comparability of information collected can be enhanced by the use of common checklists. It is important to use the same questionnaire on similar jobs. Analysts want differences in job information to reflect differences in the jobs, not differences in the questions asked. Uniformity is especially hard to maintain in large organizations; where analysts study similar jobs in different departments; only a uniform questionnaire results in usable data.

Figure 2-4 shows an abbreviated sample form for conducting job analyses that can be modified to suit the needs of specific situations. Most standardized forms attempt to measure the following items:

- **IDENTIFICATION** The information in this section includes job title, division, and title of supervisor(s), and sometimes a job identification number such as a NOC code. Without these entries, users of job analysis data may rely on outdated information or apply the information retrieved to the wrong job. Because most jobs change over time, outdated information may misdirect other human resource activities:

  At IC&RC, the world leader in addiction-related credentialing, a new job analysis for Alcohol and Drug Counselors was released in February 2015. All new candidates seeking the Alcohol and Drug Counselor designation have to complete a test based on the four domains revealed in the job analysis to be essential for practice and knowledge in that field: Screening, Assessment, and Engagement; Treatment Planning, Collaboration, and Referral; Counseling; and Professional and Ethical Responsibilities. The job analysis for Alcohol and Drug Counselors is updated every five to seven years to stay relevant to current trends and practices for counselling people with alcohol and drug addictions.[7]

- **DUTIES AND RESPONSIBILITIES** A job analysis explains the purpose of the job, what the job accomplishes, and how the job is performed. Whereas the summary provides a quick overview, the specific duties and responsibilities are listed to give more detailed insight into the position. Questions on responsibility are expanded significantly when the checklist is applied to management jobs. Additional questions map areas of responsibility for decision making, controlling, organizing, planning, and other management functions.

- **HUMAN CHARACTERISTICS AND WORKING CONDITIONS** Besides information about the job, analysts need to uncover the particular skills, abilities, training, education, experience, and other characteristics that jobholders need. This information is invaluable when filling job openings or advising workers about new job assignments. Information about the job environment improves understanding of the job. Working conditions may explain the need for particular skills, training, knowledge, or even a particular job design. Likewise, jobs must be free from recognizable health and safety hazards. Knowledge of hazards allows the human resource department to redesign the job or protect workers through training and safety equipment.

- **PERFORMANCE STANDARDS** The job analysis questionnaire also seeks information about standards, which are used to evaluate performance. Performance standards describe to what level an employee needs to be doing the job to be a good performer versus an average or a poor performer. This information is collected on jobs with objective standards of performance. When standards are not readily apparent, job analysts may ask supervisors or industrial engineers to develop reasonable standards of performance.

FIGURE 2-4

Job Analysis Questionnaire

Maple Leaf Department Stores Job Analysis Questionnaire (Form 18-JAQ)
A. Job Analysis Status
1. Job analysis form revised on _____
2. Previous revisions on _____
3. Date of job analysis for specified job _____
4. Previous analysis on _____
5. Job analysis is conducted by _____
6. Verified by _____
B. Job Identification
1. Job title _____
2. Other titles _____
3. Division(s) _____
4. Department(s) _____
5. Title of supervisor(s) _____
C. Job Summary
Briefly describe purpose of job, what is done, and how.
_____

(Continued)

D. Duties

1. The primary duties of this job are best classified as:

   Managerial _____   Technical _____

   Professional _____   Clerical _____

2. List **major** duties and the proportion of time each involves:

   a. _____%

   b. _____%

   c. _____%

3. List other duties and the proportion of time each involves:

   a. _____%

   b. _____%

   c. _____%

4. What constitutes successful performance of these duties?   _____

5. How much training is needed for normal performance of these duties?   _____

E. Responsibility

1. What are the responsibilities involved in this job and how great are these responsibilities?

Extent of Responsibility	Minor	Major
Responsibility for:		
a. Equipment operation	_____	_____
b. Use of tools	_____	_____
c. Materials usage	_____	_____
d. Protection of equipment	_____	_____
e. Protection of tools	_____	_____
f. Protection of materials	_____	_____
g. Personal safety	_____	_____
h. Safety of others	_____	_____
i. Others' work performance	_____	_____
j. Other (Specify _____)	_____	_____

F. Human Characteristics

1. What physical attributes are necessary to perform the job?   _____

2. Of the following characteristics, which ones are needed and how important are they?

Characteristic	Unneeded	Helpful	Essential
1. Vision	_____	_____	_____
2. Hearing	_____	_____	_____
3. Talking	_____	_____	_____
4. Sense of smell	_____	_____	_____
5. Sense of touch	_____	_____	_____
6. Sense of taste	_____	_____	_____
7. Eye–hand coordination	_____	_____	_____
8. Overall coordination	_____	_____	_____
9. Strength	_____	_____	_____
10. Height	_____	_____	_____
11. Health	_____	_____	_____
12. Initiative	_____	_____	_____
13. Ingenuity	_____	_____	_____
14. Judgment	_____	_____	_____
15. Attention	_____	_____	_____

(Continued)

16. Reading _____ _____ _____
17. Arithmetic _____ _____ _____
18. Writing _____ _____ _____
19. Education (Level) _____ _____ _____
20. Other (Specify) _____ _____ _____

3. Experience for this job:
_____ a. Unimportant
_____ b. Includes _____ (months) as (job title)

4. Can training be substituted for experience?
_____ Yes   How: _____
_____ No   Why: _____

G. Working Conditions
1. Describe the physical conditions under which this job is performed.
2. Are there unusual psychological demands connected with this job?
3. Describe any unusual conditions under which the job is performed.

H. Health or Safety Features
1. Describe fully any health or safety hazards associated with this job.
2. Is any safety training or equipment required?

I. Performance Standards
1. How is the performance of this job measured?
2. What identifiable factors contribute most to the successful performance this job?

J. Miscellaneous Comments
Are there any aspects of this job that should be especially noted? _____
_____
_____
_____

Job Analyst's Signature   Date Completed

Various standardized forms are currently available for job analysis (two of the more popular ones are O*NET and Position Analysis Questionnaire):

- **OCCUPATIONAL INFORMATION NETWORK (O*NET)** On the O*NET website (<http://www.onetcenter.org>) there are generic questionnaires for specific domains of information (e.g., abilities, generalized work activities, work context) that can be easily customized to particular organizational needs and branded with the company logo.

- **FLEISHMAN JOB ANALYSIS SYSTEM (F-JAS)** The F-JAS is a well-researched job analysis method based on a list of 52 cognitive, psychomotor, physical, and sensory abilities.[8] The actual scales use a seven-point anchor indicating the different levels of abilities. The scale is used mainly in the U.S. market.

- **POSITION ANALYSIS QUESTIONNAIRE (PAQ)** Designed to apply to all types of jobs, the PAQ[9] offers an even more quantitative and finely tuned description of jobs than the F-JAS. It aims to determine the degree to which 194 different task elements in six divisions (information input, mental processes, work output including physical activities and tools, relationships with others, job context including the physical and social environment, and other job characteristics such as pace and structure) are involved in performing a particular job. The PAQ allows grouping of job elements in a logical and quantitative manner, and enables easy comparisons between jobs. Past research, however, has indicated the PAQ to be more useful for lower-level jobs.[10] Job analysts must purchase the PAQ for each job they analyze.

- **CRITICAL INCIDENT METHOD (CIM)** The CIM involves identifying and describing specific events (or incidents) when an employee performed really well and when they performed very poorly (such as inducing an accident). From these incidents, the job analyst identifies critical components of the job relating to the situation leading up to the event, the employee's actions, the results of the employee's actions, and the effectiveness of the employee's behaviour. The goal of the CIM is to create a behaviourally focused description of work and related performance standards, in particular, those that differentiate excellent from average or poor performance.

> When asked to provide critical incidents, train engineers from CP Rail <http://www.cpr.ca> may recall a train derailment near Golden, British Columbia, on December 27, 2011.[11] The job analyst will ask the train engineers about the behaviours and circumstances that led up to the event as well as the duties and tasks that are necessary to prevent this type of incident.

The job analyst will translate descriptions of critical incidents into specific job responsibilities, like these for the position of train engineer found on O*NET:

- Observe tracks to detect obstructions.
- Interpret train orders, signals, or railroad rules and regulations that govern the operation of locomotives.
- Confer with conductors or traffic control centre personnel via radiophones to issue or receive information concerning stops, delays, or oncoming trains.[12]

For job analysis purposes, about 10 statements will suffice.

Step 6: Choice of Method for Data Collection

There is no one best way to collect job analysis information. Analysts must evaluate the trade-offs between time, cost, and accuracy associated with each method.[13] Once they decide which trade-offs are most important, they use interviews, focus groups, questionnaires, employee logs, observations, or some combination of these techniques.

Interviews

Interviews are an effective way to collect job information. The analyst has the job analysis questionnaire as a guide, but can add other questions where needed. Although the process is slow and expensive, it allows the interviewer to explain unclear questions and probe into uncertain answers. Typically, both jobholders and supervisors are interviewed. The analyst usually talks with a limited number of workers first and then interviews supervisors to verify the information. This pattern ensures a high level of accuracy. The validity of the information received depends on the representativeness of the sample of the respondents and the types of questions used. Some guidelines for conducting interviews are as follows:

---

interview

Approach to collecting job- and performance-related information by a face-to-face meeting with jobholder, typically using a standardized checklist of questions.

---

1. Interviews should be conducted with the jobholders, as well as with all others who may be expected to be knowledgeable about the job's duties and responsibilities.

2. The interviewer should establish rapport with the interviewee before getting into the main theme. The interviewee should be briefed about the objectives of the interview and offered all relevant information to reduce defensiveness.

3. A structured checklist of questions similar to Figure 2-4 should be used. In any case, the checklist should collect information on a variety of matters, including:

    *   major purpose and outcomes of the job and the recipients of its outcomes;
    *   major duties and percentage of time spent on each;
    *   major responsibilities, including the type of equipment and processes used;
    *   education, skills, competencies, and experience levels needed;
    *   current performance standards and improvements needed; and
    *   physical demands, working conditions, and safety and health issues.

4. In those instances in which the respondent does not perform routine duties, the jobholder should be asked to list all duties, their relative importance to the overall success of the job, and the frequency of their occurrence.

5. The information collected should be reviewed and verified by both the interviewee and the immediate supervisor.

Focus Groups

In a **focus group**, typically five to seven jobholders or others who are knowledgeable about the job are brought together by a facilitator to interactively discuss the job's duties and responsibilities. Focus groups are useful to allow ideas from participants to build off of one another and to gain consensus on job duties and responsibilities. One caution is whether jobholders will be willing to share their opinions if a supervisor is included in the focus group as well.

---

focus group

A face-to-face meeting with five to seven knowledgeable experts on a job and a facilitator to collect job- and performance-related information.

Questionnaires

A fast and less costly option is to survey employees using a **questionnaire**. This can be done electronically, through internal (or interoffice) mail, or through Canada Post. This approach allows many jobs to be studied at once and at little cost. However, there is less accuracy because of the likelihood of misunderstood questions, incomplete responses, and low response rates. Supervisors can also be given questionnaires to verify employee responses.

---

questionnaires

Standardized surveys to collect information about jobs, working conditions, and other performance-related information.

Employee Log

In an **employee log**, workers periodically summarize their tasks and activities. If entries are made over the entire job cycle, the diary can prove quite accurate. Logs are not a popular technique. They are time-consuming for jobholders and human resource specialists, which makes them costly. Managers and workers often see them as a nuisance and resist their introduction. Moreover, after the novelty wears off, accuracy tends to decline as entries become less frequent.

employee log

Approach to collecting job- and performance-related information by asking the jobholder to summarize tasks, activities, and challenges in a diary format.

Observation

Another approach is direct **observation**. It is slow, costly, and potentially less accurate than other methods. Accuracy may be low because the analysts may miss irregularly occurring activities, and workers may perform differently when they know they are being watched. But observation is the preferred method in some situations. When analysts question data from other techniques, observation may confirm or remove doubts. The existence of language barriers with foreign-language-speaking workers may also necessitate the observation approach.

observation

An approach to collecting job- and performance related information by direct observation of jobholders by a specialist.

Combinations

Since each method has its shortcomings, analysts often use a **combination** of two or more techniques concurrently:

combination

Concurrent use of two or more job analysis techniques (e.g., interviews and observation).

A lumber company had six facilities scattered across Canada and the United States. To interview a few workers and supervisors at each facility was considered prohibitively expensive; to rely only on questionnaire data was thought to be too inaccurate. Therefore, the human resource department interviewed selected employees at the home office and sent questionnaires to other facilities.

A recent survey of 459 HR professionals revealed the most common job analysis methods used in their organizations as shown in Figure 2-5.[14] Key considerations in the choice of job analysis method should include method–purpose fit, practical feasibility, cost, and reliability of the data collected for making valid decisions.

FIGURE 2 5

Job Analysis Methods in Common Use

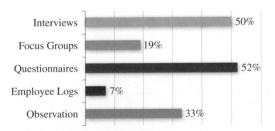

SOURCE: Based on SHRM Survey Findings: Job Analysis Activities. December 11, 2014.
http://www.shrm.org/research/surveyfindings/articles/pages/2014-Job-Analysis-Activities.aspx

Phase 3: Use of Job Analysis Information

The information collected about various jobs is put into such usable forms as job descriptions, job specifications, and job standards, and more recently, competency models (see <www.jobsetc.gc.ca/eng/pieces1.jsp?category_id=2803&root_id=2801>). Together, these applications of job analysis information provide the minimum human resource information system and data necessary to formulate various HR strategies. The remainder of this chapter discusses using job analysis to assist with job design.

Job Description

A **job description** is a written statement that explains the duties, working conditions, and other aspects of a specified job.

---

job description

A recognized list of functions, tasks, accountabilities, working conditions, and competencies for a particular occupation or job.

LO3
Contents of a Typical Job Description

Within a firm, all the job descriptions follow the same style, although between organizations, form and content may vary. One approach is to write a narrative description that covers the job in a few paragraphs. Another typical style breaks the description down into several subparts, as shown in Figure 2-6. This figure shows a job description that parallels the job analysis checklist that originally generated the data (see Figure 2-4).

The key parts of a job description are as follows: job identity, job summary, job duties, and working conditions. Most job descriptions also identify the author, the work supervisor, and the date on which it was prepared.

Job Identity

The section on **job identity** typically includes job title, job location, job code, job grade, and its status (whether or not exempted from overtime laws). **Job codes** use numbers, letters, or both to provide a quick summary of the job. These codes are useful for comparing jobs. Figure 2-7 explains the coding used in the **National Occupational Classification (NOC)**, and Figure 2-8 gives some sample NOC codes. The two major attributes of jobs that were used as classification criteria in developing the NOC were *skill level* (amount and type of education and training) and *skill type* (type of work performed). Other factors, such as industry and occupational mobility, were also taken into consideration.[15]

---

job identity

Key part of a job description, including job title, location, and status.

---

job code

A code that uses numbers, letters, or both to provide a quick summary of the job and its content.

National Occupational Classification (NOC)

An occupational classification created by the federal government, using skill level and skill types of jobs.

- **SKILL LEVEL** Four skill level categories are identified in the NOC, describing the educational and training requirements of occupations.
- **SKILL TYPE** Skill type is defined generally as the type of work performed. Ten broad occupational categories (0 to 9) are identified in the NOC.

FIGURE 2-6

A Job Description

Maple Leaf Department Stores
Job Description

Job Title: _____   Job Code: _____

Date: _____   Author: _____

Job Location: _____   Job Grade: _____

Report To: _____   Status: _____

Job Summary: Interacts with customers on a daily basis, promptly responding to all inquiries in a courteous and efficient manner. Encourages the sale of company products at every opportunity and applies exemplary customer relation skills that promote a superior company image. Provides information to customers about product features and substitutes when asked.

Responsibilities: Responds to customer inquiries on product features, prices, services, and delivery terms.

Takes customer orders for products and communicates these accurately to supply and servicing personnel in the company.

Accepts returns of merchandise by customers and gives them credit for the same.

Displays and stocks merchandise on shelves.

Appropriately prices items based on instructions received from the supervisor.

Prepares necessary documents and transmits/files copies to relevant offices within the company.

Responds to other miscellaneous inquiries especially those related to warranties, delivery terms, servicing frequencies (in the case of equiment).

Undertakes other tasks assigned by the supervisor.

Operates cash register and balances accounts at the end of the shift.

Working Conditions: Works in a well-ventilated office. Must be able to work shifts.

The above information is correct as approved by:

(Signed) _____   (Signed) _____
     Customer Service Representative   Customer Service Supervisor

FIGURE 2-7

NOC Skill Type and Skill Level Categories

When the First Digit Is …	the Skill Type Category Is …
1	Business, Finance, and Administrative Occupations
2	Natural and Applied Sciences and Related Occupations
3	Health Occupations
4	Occupations in Education, Law and Social, Community and Government Services
5	Occupations in Art, Culture, Recreation, and Sport
6	Sales and Service Occupations
7	Trades, Transport and Equipment Operators, and Related Occupations
8	Natural Resources, Agriculture, and Related Production Occupations
9	Occupations in Manufacturing, and Utilities

When the Second Digit Is …	the Skill Level Category Is …	and the Education Level Is …
1	Skill Level A	Professional Occupations
2 or 3	Skill Level B	Technical, Paraprofessional, and Skilled Occupations
4 or 5	Skill Level C	Intermediate Occupations
6	Skill Level D	Labouring and Elemental Occupations

SOURCE: Employment and Social Development Canada, National Occupation Classification. Reproduced with permission of the Minister of Public Works and Government Services Canada, 2011.

FIGURE 2-8

Examples of NOC Unit Groups and Codes

NOC Coding System. A two-digit code is assigned at the major group level. A third digit is added at the minor group level, and a fourth digit is added at the unit group level. For example:

- Major Group 31—Professional Occupations in Health
- Minor Group 314—Professional Occupations in Therapy and Assessment
- Unit Group 3142—Physiotherapists

Using the above coding system, some sample occupations with codes include:

0211	Engineering Managers
0212	Architecture and Science Managers
2231	Civil Engineering Technologists and Technicians
4163	Marketing Consultant – Market Research
6531	Tour and Travel Guides
4012	Tutor – Post-Secondary Teaching Assistant
5241	Graphic Designers and Illustrators
1226	Conference and Event Planners
1123	Professional Occupations in Advertising, Marketing and Public Relations

SOURCE: Employment and Social Development Canada, National Occupation Classification. Reproduced with permission of the Minister of Public Works and Government Services Canada, 2011.

Job Summary and Duties

Following the job identification section (in Figure 2-6), the next part of the description is the job summary. It summarizes the job in a few sentences, telling what the job is, how it is done, and why.

Then, in a simple, action-oriented style, the job description lists the job's responsibilities, or duties. In essence, this section explains what the job requires. The effectiveness of other human resource actions depends upon this understanding, because each major duty is described in terms of the actions expected.

Working Conditions

A job description also explains **working conditions**, which may go beyond descriptions of the physical environment. Hours of work, safety and health hazards, travel requirements, and other features of the job expand the meaning of this section.

working conditions

Facts about the situation in which the worker acts. Includes physical environment, hours, hazards, travel requirements, and so on, associated with a job.

Approvals

Because job descriptions affect most human resource decisions, their accuracy should be reviewed by selected jobholders and their supervisors. Then supervisors are asked to approve the description. This approval serves as a further test of the job description and a further check on the collection of job analysis information.

There are many form-fillable templates available online to assist in creating job descriptions. One useful template can be found at hrcouncil.ca (<www.hrcouncil.ca/docs/Template_JD.doc>). Employment and Social Development Canada (ESDC) has a downloadable handbook to guide generating job descriptions on the NOC website (<http://www5.hrsdc.gc.ca/NOC/English/NOC/2011/pdf/JobDescriptions.pdf>).

Job Specifications

Whereas the job description focuses on the job tasks and duties, the **job specification** indicates the human knowledge, skills, abilities, and other characteristics (KSAOs) necessary to do a job. These requirements include experience, training, education, and physical and mental demands. Whether part of a job description or a separate document, job specifications include the information illustrated in Figure 2-9. The data to compile specifications also come from the job analysis checklist.

job specification

A written statement that explains what a job demands of jobholders and the human skills and factors required.

A job specification should include specific tools, actions, experiences, education, and training (i.e., the individual requirements of the job).[16] For example, it should describe "physical effort" in terms of the special actions demanded by the job. "Lifts 40-kilogram bags" is better and more specific than "Lifts heavy weights." Clear behaviour statements give a better picture than vague generalities. Specifications of mental effort help human resource experts to determine the intellectual abilities needed to perform the job. Figure 2-9 contains several examples of the kind of information about physical and mental efforts needed by customer service representatives working for a department store.

Do the working conditions make any unusual demands on jobholders? The working conditions found in job descriptions may be translated by job specifications into demands faced by workers. Figure 2-10 provides examples for the job of hospital orderly and helps to show how tasks and duties from a job description can produce human requirements for a job specification. It shows that a simple statement of working conditions found in the job description can have significant implications for jobholders. For example, compare points 2 and 3 under the job description column with points 2 and 3 under job specifications.

FIGURE 2-9

A Job Specification Sheet

Maple Leaf Department Stores
Job Specification

Job Title: _____   Job Code: _____

Date: _____   Author: _____

Job Location: _____   Job Grade: _____

Report To: _____   Status: _____

Skill Factors

Education: Ten years of general education or equivalent.

Experience: Prior selling experience in a consumer-goods industry is desirable.

Communication: Strong interpersonal skills a must.

                     Ability to empathize with customer needs when communicating.

                     Knowledge of French highly desirable.

                     Should have strong oral communication skills.

Effort Factors

Physical Demands: Normally limited to those associated with clerical jobs although long periods of standing may be required in some instances.

                     Should be able to lift products weighing 10 kilograms or less.

                     Finger dexterity to operate a computer keyboard and cash register is essential.

Mental Demands: Ability to respond to customer inquiries regarding prices, service terms, etc. a must. This requires good short-term memory.

                     Ability to learn and remember product codes of popular items.

Working Conditions: Works in a well-ventilated office.

                     May have to work outdoors in the case of lawn/gardening-related equipment.

The above information is correct as approved by:

(Signed) _____   (Signed) _____

        Customer Service Representative   Customer Service Supervisor

FIGURE 2-10

Translation of Working Conditions for Job Description to Job Specification

Hospital Orderly	
Job Description Statement of Working Conditions	Job Specifications Interpretation of Working Conditions
1. Works in physically comfortable surroundings.	1. (Omitted. This item on the job description makes no demands on jobholders.)
2. Deals with physically ill and diseased patients.	2. Exposed to unpleasant situations and communicable diseases.
3. Deals with mentally ill patients.	3. May be exposed to verbal and physical abuse.

The job specifications for these hydro workers should clearly state that working outdoors under extreme conditions is a regular part of the job. What consequences could there be if that information was not provided?

CP/Fred Chartrand.

When preparing specifications, it is critical not to include needless job requirements, as the following example illustrates:

> In one instance, an employer required a high-school diploma for nearly all jobs within the company except those in the labour pool. When the need for a diploma was challenged, the employer could not show that it was absolutely necessary to perform many of the jobs for which it was officially required, and although this requirement was applied equally to all applicants, it had an unequal impact on applicants from minority groups. As a result, many persons belonging to such groups were offered labour-pool jobs only.

Further, needless job requirements exclude potentially qualified individuals from consideration, which may reduce the effectiveness not only of hiring, but also of other human resource activities.

LO4

Job Performance Standards

Job analysis has a third application, **job performance standards**. These standards serve two functions. First, they become objectives or targets for employee efforts. The challenge or pride of meeting objectives may serve to motivate employees. Once standards are met, workers may feel accomplishment and achievement. This outcome contributes to employee satisfaction.

---

job performance standards

The work performance expected from an employee on a particular job.

Second, standards are criteria against which job success is measured. They are indispensable to managers or human resource specialists who attempt to promote good work performance. Without standards, there is no yardstick for good versus average or poor job performance.

Job performance standards are developed from job analysis information, and then actual employee performance is measured. When measured performance strays from the job standard, corrective action is taken. The corrective action, in turn, may result in changes in either the standards (if they were inappropriate) or feedback to improve actual job performance.

In the Calgary Trust Company, current standards dictated that each loan supervisor review 350 mortgage-loan applications per month. Yet the actual output averaged 290. When more recent job information was collected, analysts discovered that since the standards had been first set, several new duties had been added for each supervisor. Corrective action resulted in new job designs, revised job descriptions, and more realistic standards.

Spotlight *on* HRM

The Many Uses of a Job Description

In an article about job descriptions, Mary Massa described how business owners are finding numerous uses for employee job descriptions.

If created properly, a job description can also be used in performance management to set goals relative to the description. Similarly, it can be used in compensation to create standardized compensation programs across jobs. An effective job description may also be used in return to work programs by identifying how work may be lightened or modified. Job descriptions are also proving to be important for essential job function analysis. That is, the job description provides a detailed breakdown of essential job functions. With this list in hand, employers are able to create appropriate accommodations in creating inclusive work environments.

As the nature of jobs evolves and becomes more dynamic, increased flexibility in job descriptions will become necessary. One solution is to generate more generic job descriptions that emphasize expectations and deliverables as compared to specific job tasks.

SOURCE: Based on: "Importance of a Job Description", by Mary Massad, *Entrepreneur Magazine*, June 22, 2005.

When the standards are wrong, as in the trust company example, they alert managers and human resource specialists to problems that need correction. The example also underscores the need for keeping job analysis information current.

Job standards are obtained either from job analysis information or from alternative sources. For example, industry standards may be used as benchmarks for performance in certain jobs (especially service functions such as human resource management function).[17] Job analysis information is usually sufficient for jobs that have the following features:

- Performance is quantified.
- Performance is easily measurable.
- Performance standards are understood by workers and supervisors.
- Performance requires little interpretation.

Jobs with short work cycles often exhibit these features. An example is an assembly-line job. For these jobs, questions on the job analysis checklist may generate specific, quantitative answers. When confirmed by supervisors, this information becomes the job performance standard. In the case of some service jobs, quantifiable "outputs" may not be readily available; but even here, performance can be appraised by looking at the behaviours of the jobholders. More details of behaviourally oriented performance appraisals will be discussed in Chapter 8.

Competency Models

More recently, competency-based job descriptions and specifications have become increasingly popular. A **competency** is a knowledge, skill, ability, or behaviour required to be successful on the job.[18] Competencies are broader in scope than the KSAOs discussed earlier in this chapter; examples are communication, innovation, team orientation, and leadership.[19] A **competency model** (or **competency framework**) describes a group of competencies required in a particular job, with typical jobs defined with between 10 and 15 competencies. Competency models can be developed for individuals, specific jobs, teams, work units, or the total organization.

competency

A knowledge, skill, ability, or behaviour associated with successful job performance.

competency model (competency framework)

A list of competencies required in a particular job.

There are three key differences between competency-based job analyses and other forms of job analyses. First, whereas duties or tasks might apply only to a single job within an organization, competencies may be job spanning, meaning that they contribute to success on multiple jobs (or even all jobs) within the organization. All jobs within the organization may require a particular competency, albeit how the competency should be enacted for strong performance will vary across jobs.

> At Maple Leaf Department Stores, a Product Knowledge competency may span multiple jobs including sales associates and product maintenance staff. However, Product Knowledge may be demonstrated differently in the varying roles. Whereas sales associates might demonstrate their Product Knowledge by answering customer inquiries on product features, prices, services, and delivery terms, Product Knowledge for maintenance staff might include troubleshooting when a product is not functioning properly.

A second difference is that job-spanning competencies may vary in importance across job roles. A **competency matrix** lists different levels of skill for a combination of competencies, and indicates to what level multiple jobs across the firm should have mastery of each competency. Figure 2-11 shows an example of a competency matrix in an engineering firm. Each of the six competencies is measured at seven levels (Level 1 being the lowest, Level 7 the highest). Employees may be expected to possess all competencies, though to varying degrees. An engineer may be required to possess high technical expertise and medium problem-solving abilities, while a manager may have to possess more sophisticated higher problem-solving skills and lower levels of technical expertise; both are expected to have adequate communication abilities. Use of a competency matrix shifts the focus from performing specific duties to developing broader skills needed. It also empowers employees to assume new responsibilities. Such a system must be supported by an effective training and development strategy and a competency-based compensation system. These will be discussed in later chapters.

competency matrix

A list of the level of each competency required for each of a number of jobs.

FIGURE 2-11

An Example of a Competency Matrix in an Engineering Firm

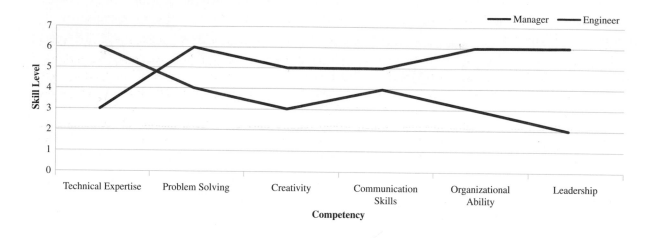

A third distinct feature of competency-based job analyses is that competencies contribute not only to job performance, but also to the success of the organization. Competencies explicitly support the vision, strategic direction, and values of the firm.

> At the YMCA of Greater Toronto <http://www.ymcagta.org>, seven association-wide competencies and seven leadership competencies support the organization's vision, values, and strategic plan, and they are the foundation for all jobs. The 14-competencies framework helps employees to understand what is expected of them, how to be successful, and how they will be rewarded. These competencies are used in job descriptions, training and development, recruitment and selection, performance evaluation, and succession planning. They are also a critical component used in the Y's employment branding.[20]

Some organizations have used competencies as the foundation for job design, new performance management systems, selection and career pathing, compensation, training and development, and, in a few cases, a highly integrated human resource management system called *competency-based management*. Competencies are identified after a careful analysis of the work of high performers and thorough examination of the organization's strategic direction. This may be done through observation, listings of critical incidents at work, interviews, focus groups, employee logs, or otherwise, and examining the organization's mission, vision, and values. In generating job-specific competencies, the process of data collection and sources discussed earlier in the chapter for job analysis will be useful.

However, it is important to offer one cautionary note: When competencies become increasingly job-spanning and are no longer supported by specific duties and tasks, the legal defensibility of decisions based on these competencies is unknown. As competency models are tested within the legal system in Canada over the coming years, HR professionals will have a better indication of how broad or narrow competencies can be to support their staffing practices and decisions and to avoid unintentional discrimination.

Spotlight *on* ETHICS

Job Design: Happy Workers or Higher Profits?

A small manufacturer of snowboards and skateboards faces a dilemma. His 15 employees work in loose production teams on cutting, layering, edging, pressing, drilling, painting, drying, mounting, and printing the boards. Job satisfaction is high and there is almost no turnover. But because of competition, the company had small profits for the last two years and he wants to change that. His choice is to ask his employees to accept a significant pay cut, switch to an assembly-line system, or, the most profitable solution, install an automated machine, which would require only 3 workers, making the remaining 12 redundant. All of his employees are married and have children and have been with him for 15 and more years. He feels a strong obligation toward them, but is convinced that a workflow change is necessary.

Of what nature are his obligations toward his employees? What is the optimal solution for (a) His employees? (b) His company? (c) Himself?

LO5

Job Design

Worldwide competition, complex technology, and increasing worker expectations have necessitated redesign of many jobs. Technological advances have brought about a revolution that has changed millions of jobs. While some jobs have grown more challenging, others are increasingly being automated or eliminated altogether. And yet, despite this vast increase in automation and computerization, human resources have become more, not less, important in today's organizations:

> For example, the cost of human error in a nuclear plant* or in flying a supersonic jet can be enormous. Whether it is the high speed computers or the traditional auto assembly plant now run by robotics, the contribution of human beings continues to be critical. Indeed, new technologies may be dangerous or unforgiving when operated by uncommitted or poorly skilled persons.

How well people perform is shaped, at least in part, by the characteristics designed into their jobs. Not only is productivity affected, but quality of work life is also tied to **job design**.[21] Jobs are the central link between employees and the organization. Poorly designed jobs not only lead to low productivity, but they can cause employee turnover, absenteeism, complaints, sabotage, unionization, resignations, and other problems. One high-end purse and bag maker's experience of redesigning jobs is noteworthy in this context:

---

job design

Identification of job duties, characteristics, competencies, and sequences taking into consideration technology, workforce, organization character, and environment.

> At Louis Vuitton, each worker had narrowly defined responsibilities such as cutting leather or canvas, attaching zippers or buckles, and stitching seams. Each worker performed a specific function and sent the product to the next person in the line of 20 or 30 workers. The result was that no one was responsible for completion of a single product. In 2006, Vuitton moved to a team-based design where workers were trained to complete multiple tasks and could shift production quickly according to consumer demands. Workers learned new skills, job satisfaction went up, and the time to produce the same bag dropped from eight days to one day.[22]

*A good example is the meltdown in the reactor of the Chernobyl nuclear power station in April 1986 in Ukraine, caused by a faulty test execution. The explosion released 100 times more radiation than the atomic bomb explosions in Hiroshima and Nagasaki. The long-term impact to the health of over seven million people is still unfolding. The contamination stretched to Norway and Germany.

In this case, the company had to consider the various environmental, organizational, and employee-related factors before redesigning the jobs. Typically, job redesign results in some trade-offs. Under the new structure at Vuitton, each worker needed to have knowledge of several activities. Therefore, more training for these workers was necessary. And, as the workers became more qualified, the company needed to pay them higher salaries.

Figure 2-12 illustrates five critical elements that deserve consideration when designing jobs: organizational, ergonomic, employee, job specialization, and environmental considerations. Each is discussed below.

FIGURE 2-12

Key Considerations in Job Design

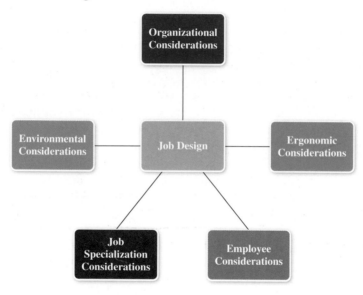

Organizational Considerations

Simply put, each job should contribute to the overall organizational objectives effectively and efficiently. The overall organizational mission is accomplished through a series of interrelated tasks or activities. If the organization is to remain successful and grow, these tasks and activities should be performed in a timely, effective, and efficient manner. This involves focus on two interrelated concepts: efficiency and work flow.

Efficiency

Concern for high task **efficiency**, or achieving maximum output with minimum expenditure of time, effort, or other resources, was first underscored by *scientific management* around the turn of the twentieth century. *Industrial engineering*, which evolved from this movement, focuses on analyzing work methods and establishing optimal time standards by finding the best ways to do jobs.[23] As discussed earlier, time standards are established by recording the time needed to complete each element in a work cycle. Industrial engineers study work cycles to determine which, if any, job elements can be combined, modified, or eliminated to reduce the overall time needed to perform the task. *Task specialization* was suggested as a key strategy to improve efficiency. According to these engineers, when workers are limited to a few repetitive tasks, output is usually higher, because specialized jobs lead to *short job cycles*. The automotive industry is a good example of such industrial engineering practices:[24]

efficiency

Achieving maximal output with minimal input.

> For example, an assembly-line worker may pick up a headlight, plug it in, twist the adjustment screws, and pick up the next headlight within 30 seconds. Completing these tasks in 30 seconds means this worker's job cycle takes half a minute. The job cycle begins when the next headlight is picked up.

Headlight installation is a specialized job, so specialized that training takes only a few minutes. The short job cycle means that the assembler gains much experience in a short time. Said another way, short job cycles require small investments in training and allow the worker to learn the job quickly. Training costs remain low because the worker needs to master only one job.

The above approach stresses efficiency in effort, time, labour costs, training, and employee learning time. Today, this technique is still widely used in assembly operations. But the efficient design of jobs also considers such organizational elements as work flow, ergonomics, and work practices.

Work Flow

The **work flow** in an organization is strongly influenced by the nature of the product or service. The product or service usually suggests the sequence of, and balance between, jobs if the work is to be done efficiently. For example, the frame of a car must be built before the fenders and doors can be added. Once the sequence of jobs is determined, the balance between jobs is established:

work flow

The sequence of and balance between jobs in an organization needed to produce the firm's goods or services.

> Suppose it takes one person 30 seconds to install each headlight. In two minutes, an assembler can put on four headlights. If, however, it takes four minutes to install the necessary headlight receptacles, the job designer must balance these two interrelated jobs by assigning two people to install the receptacles. Otherwise, a production bottleneck results. Therefore, the work flow demands two receptacle installers for each headlight installer.

Ergonomic Considerations

Optimal productivity requires that the physical relationship between the worker and the work be considered in designing jobs. Derived from the Greek words *ergo* meaning "work" and *nomos* meaning "laws," **ergonomics** in a general sense means the "laws of work" and focuses on how human beings physically interface with their work.[25] The study of ergonomics is multidisciplinary, using principles drawn from biology (especially anatomy and physiology), the behavioural sciences (psychology and sociology), and physics and engineering. Although the nature of job tasks may not vary when ergonomic factors are considered, the locations of tools, switches, and the work product itself are evaluated and placed in a position for ease of use. In other words, ergonomics focuses on fitting the task to the worker in many instances rather than simply forcing employees to adapt to the task.[26]

---

ergonomics

The study of relationships between physical attributes of workers and their work environment to reduce physical and mental strain and increase productivity and quality of work life.

On an automobile assembly line, for example, a car frame may actually be elevated at a work station so that the worker does not become fatigued from stooping. Similarly, the location of dashboard instruments in a car is ergonomically engineered to make driving easier.

Attention to details of work settings can lead to significant improvements in efficiency and productivity:

As seen in the video clip <http://www.youtube.com/watch?v=0lsZvPInD6w&feature=relmfu>, Ford <http://www.ford.ca> uses state-of-the art manufacturing and job design techniques—including industrial engineering, ergonomics, and behavioural considerations. Cars pass through the assembly line on hydraulic lifts that allow employees to raise or lower the cars to suit their own height. Employees are allowed to ride the platform to minimize their steps walking to and from cars, thereby conserving energy. Industrial engineers videotape employee actions and simplify operations to minimize motion.

Ergonomic considerations are also important to maintain safety at the workplace. Ignoring a proper fit between work station and worker can be catastrophic.[27]

In Canada in 2013, 640,000 workplace accidents were reported to the provincial Worker's Compensation Boards. These claims came at a cost to Canadian firms of $11.7 billion.[28] A significant percentage of these accidents stemmed from poor workplace or task design.[29]

If an employee has to remain in a seated position for many hours, an ergonomically correct seat and a suitably placed monitor are essential. What are other benefits of ergonomic considerations?

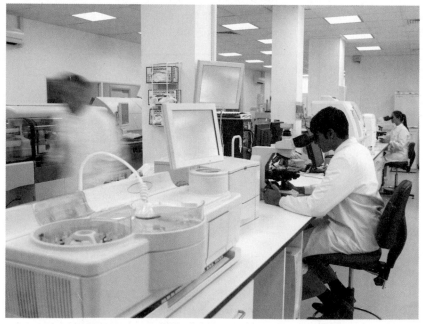

© Adam Gault/age fotostock

Ergonomics will become more important in the future as the Canadian workforce ages:

On July 1, 2014, 15.7 percent of Canada's population (nearly one in six Canadians) was aged 65 and older, up from only 10 percent thirty years prior. In 2016, projections suggest that the number of seniors in Canada will surpass the number of children 15 and under. The number of people aged 15 to 24 in Canada (the age when people typically enter the workforce), is now smaller than the number of people aged 55 to 64 (the age when people typically exit the workforce). Thirty years ago, there were two people aged 15 to 24 for every person aged 55 to 64.[30] Because aging results in a decrease in several hand functions (e.g., grip strength, precision), lowered muscular strength, and reduced vision and hearing, the need for ergonomics-based work improvements to reduce physical demands will be higher than ever before. Items such as mechanical assists for lifting (e.g., tilters, vacuum lifts) and for assembly (e.g., screw-guns, adjustable tables) will be essential. Such improvements will also be needed for lighting arrangements and size of character displays in terminals to respond to older workers' diminished visual capabilities.[31]

Employee Considerations

Jobs cannot be designed by using only those elements that aid efficiency. To do so overlooks the human needs of the people who are to perform the work. Instead, job designers draw heavily on behavioural research to provide a work environment that helps satisfy individual needs. In general, jobs have to be designed not only to maximize productivity, but also to help the employees achieve better work–life balance.

> Research studies indicate that employee productivity can be up to 20 percent higher in organizations that implement work–life balance programs.[32]

This section briefly describes the Job Characteristics Model, shown in Figure 2-13, which discusses the importance of high autonomy, variety, task identity, feedback, and task significance in a job design context.[33] According to this model, these five characteristics result in three psychological states: meaningfulness, responsibility, and knowledge of outcomes. Employees who find themselves in jobs that provide these experiences tend to have higher motivation, job satisfaction, and productivity.

FIGURE 2-13

The Job Characteristics Model

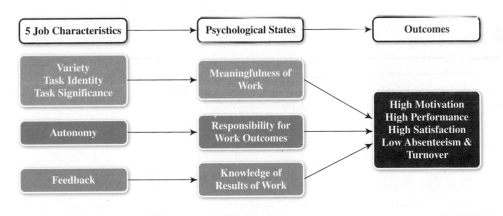

Autonomy

Autonomy refers to the concept of assuming responsibility for what one does. It is the freedom to control one's response to the environment. Jobs that give workers the authority to make decisions tend to increase employees' sense of recognition, self-esteem, job satisfaction, and performance. The absence of autonomy, on the other hand, can cause employee apathy or poor performance:

autonomy

In a job context, independence—having control over one's work and one's response to the work environment.

A common problem in many production operations is that employees develop an indifferent attitude because they believe they have no control over their jobs. On the bottling line of a small brewery, however, teams of workers were allowed to speed up or slow down the rate of the bottling line as long as they met daily production goals. Although total output per shift did not change, there were fewer cases of capping machines jamming or breaking down for other reasons. When asked about this unexpected development, the supervisor concluded, "Employees pride themselves on meeting the shift quota. So they are more careful to check for defective bottle caps before they load the machine."

Variety

A lack of **variety** may cause boredom. Boredom in turn leads to fatigue, and fatigue causes errors. By injecting variety into jobs, human resource specialists can reduce fatigue-caused errors.

---

variety

An attribute of jobs wherein the worker has the opportunity to use different skills and abilities, or perform different activities.

Being able to control the speed of the bottling line in the brewery example added variety to the pace of work and probably reduced both boredom and fatigue.

Past research studies have found that variety in work may be related to effective performance and can be a major contributor to employee satisfaction.

Task Identity

One problem with some jobs is that they lack any **task identity**. Workers contribute to one part of the piece of work, but do not get to point to some complete piece of work. They have little sense of responsibility, may lack pride in the results, and have little sense of accomplishment. When tasks are grouped so that employees feel they are making an identifiable contribution—to see the job through to completion—job satisfaction may be increased significantly.

---

task identity

The feeling of responsibility or pride that results from doing an entire piece of work, not just a small part of it.

In the earlier Louis Vuitton example, we saw that productivity and satisfaction increased when employees became responsible for an identifiable and sensible group of tasks.

Feedback

When jobs do not give the workers any **feedback** on how well they are doing, there is little guidance or motivation to perform better.

---

feedback

Information that helps evaluate the success or failure of an action or system.

For example, by letting employees know how they are doing relative to the daily production quota, the brewery gives workers feedback that allows them to adjust their efforts. Providing feedback leads to improved motivation.

Task Significance

Closely related to the above dimensions is **task significance**. Doing an identifiable piece of work makes the job more satisfying for employees. Task significance, knowing that the work is important to others within the organization or outside it, makes the job even more meaningful for incumbents. Their personal sense of self-importance is enhanced because they know that others depend on what they do. Pride, commitment, motivation, satisfaction, and better performance are likely to result.

---

task significance

Knowing that the work one does is important to others in the organization or to outsiders.

A good example was the Porsche <http://www.porsche.com/canada> car company. Mechanics, who assembled complete engines, punched their names into the engine block, a cause of extreme pride, but also useful for feedback purposes. Rationalization eliminated this procedure, resulting in lower satisfaction, lower quality, and higher turnover.

Job Specialization

As workers become more educated and affluent, routine jobs that are very specialized, such as assembly-line positions, hold less and less appeal for many people. These jobs seldom offer opportunities for accomplishment, recognition, psychological growth, or other sources of satisfaction. To increase the quality of work life for those who hold such jobs, human resource departments often use a combination of *job rotation, job enlargement, job enrichment,* and *employee involvement and work teams*.

Job Rotation

Job rotation moves employees from job to job. Jobs are not actually changed; only the workers are rotated. Rotation breaks the monotony of highly specialized work by calling on different skills and abilities. The organization benefits because workers become competent in several jobs rather than one. Knowing a variety of jobs improves self-image, provides personal growth, and makes the worker more valuable to the organization.

---

job rotation

Moving employees from one job to another to allow them more variety and to learn new skills.

Job rotation was introduced by the Volvo <http://www.volvo.com> car company in 1973 to reduce the monotony of the assembly line. Work teams exchanged jobs during the day. Job satisfaction increased and turnover decreased.

A caution about the use of job rotation: it does not improve the jobs, as the relationships between tasks, activities, and objectives remain unchanged. It may even delay the use of more effective techniques while adding to training costs. Implementation should occur only after other techniques have been considered.

Job Enlargement

Job enlargement expands the number of related tasks in the job. It adds similar duties to provide greater variety although the duties are not more complex. Enlargement reduces monotony by expanding the job cycle and drawing on a wider range of employee skills.

---

job enlargement

Adding more tasks to a job to increase the job cycle and draw on a wider range of employee skills.

IBM <http://www.ibm.com> reported that job enlargement led to higher wages and more inspection equipment, but improved quality and worker satisfaction offset these costs. Maytag Company <http://www.maytag.ca> claimed that production quality was improved, labour costs declined, worker satisfaction and overall efficiency were increased, and management production schedules became more flexible.[34]

Job Enrichment

Job enrichment adds new sources of needs satisfaction to jobs. It increases responsibility, autonomy, and control. Adding these elements to jobs is sometimes called *vertical loading*. Enrichment views jobs as consisting of three elements: *plan, do*, and *control*. Whereas job enlargement (or horizontal loading) adds more related tasks, enrichment (vertical loading) attempts to add more *planning* and *control* responsibilities. This, coupled with rethinking the job itself, often leads to increased motivation and other improvements:

---

job enrichment

Adding more responsibilities and autonomy to a job, giving the worker greater powers to plan, do, and evaluate job performance.

Since 1999, every year Statistics Canada has sampled information from over 6,000 Canadian workplaces about workforce characteristics and job organization, with specific questions regarding decision making, quality circles, teams, suggestion programs, feedback, and self-directed work. Two researchers used the data to determine whether enriched jobs result in higher motivation and job satisfaction. The study included feedback from 43,917 employees. The results strongly support the hypothesis that enriched jobs increase motivation and satisfaction.[35]

Job enrichment, however, is not a cure-all—if it were, this book could end here! Job enrichment techniques are merely tools, and they are not applicable universally. When the diagnosis indicates that jobs are unchallenging and limit employee motivation and satisfaction, human resource departments may find job enrichment to be the most appropriate strategy.

Employee Involvement and Work Teams

To increase employee involvement at the workplace, work teams are increasingly used. Work itself is increasingly being organized around teams and processes rather than activities or functions. Over 40 percent of the respondents in a national survey by the Conference Board of Canada reported use of teams in their workplaces.[36] Self-managed and autonomous work teams have become a normal part of many Canadian organizations including CIBC, Xerox Canada <http://www.xerox.ca>, and Vancouver City Savings <https://www.vancity.com>. These and other employee involvement approaches are discussed in detail in Chapter 11. The intent of all such approaches, however, is to provide more autonomy, feedback, and task significance to workers, and may also lead to increased innovation:

Multinational giant IBM uses innovation portals in the form of specially designated chat rooms, where employees with new ideas or projects can recruit team members, secure resources, or tap into location or domain expertise across the entire firm within hours. More than 90,000 IBM employees have worked on these global teams, decreasing project launch times from six months to 30 days.[37]

As in the case of job enrichment, employee involvement and teams may not be appropriate for all organizations or all situations. The complexity of the task involved, the prevalence of the shift system, and the skill levels of employees involved may moderate the applicability of such systems in a particular situation.[38] The introduction of team management, if not accompanied by changes in other systems (e.g., performance appraisal, compensation), may cause frustration. To be successful, top management has to be truly committed to the notion of employee empowerment—that is, granting employees the power to initiate change and take charge of what they do.

Use of Job Families in HR Decisions

Often, in the context of job design, the human resource manager looks at **job families** rather than single jobs. Job families are groups of jobs that are closely related by similar duties, responsibilities, skills, or job elements. The jobs of clerk, word processor, clerk-typist, and secretary constitute a job family, for example.

---

job families

Groups of different jobs that are closely related by similar duties, responsibilities, skills, or job elements.

Job families can be constructed in several ways. One way is by careful study of existing job analysis information. Matching the data in job descriptions can identify jobs with similar requirements. A second method is to use the codes in the National Occupational Classification discussed earlier in this chapter. Similarities in the job codes indicate similarities in the jobs. A third approach is to use the Position Analysis Questionnaire, also discussed earlier in this chapter, and statistically analyze information on tasks and worker traits to identify clusters of similar jobs.

Job families allow human resource managers to plan job rotation programs and make employee transfer decisions. The compensation levels of jobs that form a family should also be comparable; this means that equitable compensation strategies cannot be formed without considering the entire job family. In some instances, it may also be economical to use similar recruitment methods and sources to hire individuals who belong to the same job family.

Environmental Considerations

The environments within which the firm and job exist also need to be considered when redesigning jobs. As with most human resource activities, job designers cannot ignore **environmental considerations**—the influence of the external environment, which affects workforce availability, values, and practices.

---

environmental considerations

The influence of the external environment on job design. Includes employee ability, availability, and social expectations.

Workforce Availability

Efficiency considerations must be balanced against the abilities and availability of the people who will actually do the work. An extreme example underlines this point:

> Governments of less developed countries often think they can "buy" progress. To be "up to date," they seek the most advanced equipment they can find. Leaders of one country ordered a computerized oil refinery, necessitating a level of technology that exceeded the abilities of the country's available workforce. As a result, these government leaders have now hired Europeans to operate the refinery.

In less developed nations, the major risk is jobs that are too complex. But in industrialized nations with highly educated workers, jobs that are too simple can produce equally disturbing problems.

For example, even when unemployment rates are high, many simple and overly specialized jobs are sometimes hard to fill, as longstanding newspaper ads for janitors attest.

Social Expectations

The acceptability of a job's design is also influenced by **social expectations**. For example, working conditions that would have been acceptable to some early Canadian immigrants are no longer acceptable to our present generation.

---

social expectations

The larger society's expectations about job challenge, working conditions, and quality of work life.

When rail lines were being laid across Canada, many persons were willing to work long hours of hard labour. They had fled countries where jobs were unavailable, which made a job—any job—acceptable to them. Today, industrial workers are much better educated and have higher expectations about the quality of work life.

Even where work flow might suggest a particular job design, the job must meet the expectations of workers. Failure to consider these expectations can create dissatisfaction, poor motivation, and low quality of work life.

Work Practices

Work practices are set ways of performing work. These methods may arise from tradition or from the collective wishes of employees. Either way, the human resource department's flexibility to design jobs is limited, especially when such practices are part of a union–management relationship. Failure to consider work practices can have undesired outcomes:

---

work practices

The set ways of performing work in an organization.

General Motors <http://www.gm.com> decided to increase productivity at one of its American plants by eliminating some jobs and adding new tasks to others. These design changes caused workers to stage a strike for several weeks because traditional practices at the plant had required a slower rate of production and less work by the employees. The additional demands on their jobs by management were seen as an attempt by the company to disregard past work practices.

LO1 HRC 4

Job Analysis in Tomorrow's "Jobless" World

Global competition, fast technological obsolescence, changing worker profiles, and rapid increases in knowledge requirements for various jobs have made accurate and timely job descriptions difficult. Indeed, some writers have gone so far as to say that jobs as we see them today may not exist in the future.[39] Today's global village has resulted in "boundary-less" and "de-jobbed" organizations, in which traditional boundaries between a firm, its suppliers, customers, and even competitors have disappeared and "jobs" as we knew them in the past have begun to disappear.[40] Many employees are no longer responsible for producing specific outcomes; rather, they are members of teams entrusted with many responsibilities. In tomorrow's world, a firm may be valued by its ideas rather than its assets or products.[41]

How do organizations that operate in such fast-changing environments conduct valid job analyses? How can the task and person requirements identified today be relevant for an unknown tomorrow?

Of course, there are no simple solutions. A few attempts have been made to meet the newfound challenges. One strategy has been to adopt a future-oriented style when describing job activities and specifications. Rather than asking what the current jobholder does, the focus is on what the jobholder must do to effectively carry out and further organizational strategies and the new competencies required of the jobholder. Thus, present and future requirements, rather than past actions, guide job descriptions and the hiring and training of employees.

Further, job analysis will continue to be relevant for legal compliance and defensibility in the event of a court action.[42] Traditional sources of information (such as jobholders, supervisors) may, however, need to be supplemented by data emerging from customers, peers, and technical experts to incorporate the ever-changing job demands.

SUMMARY

Job analysis information provides the foundations of an organization's human resource information system. Analysts seek to gain a general understanding of the organization and the work it performs. Then they design job analysis questionnaires to collect specific data about jobs, jobholder characteristics, and job performance standards. Job analysis information can be collected through interviews, focus groups, questionnaires, employee logs, direct observation, or some combination of these techniques. Once collected, the data are converted into such useful applications as job descriptions, job specifications, job standards, and competency models.

Job analysis information is important because it tells human resource specialists what duties and responsibilities are associated with each job. This information is then used when these specialists undertake other human resource management activities such as job design, recruiting, and selection. Jobs are the link between organizations and their human resources. The combined accomplishment of every job allows the organization to meet its objectives. Similarly, jobs represent not only a source of income to workers but also a means of fulfilling their needs. For the organization and its employees to receive these mutual benefits, jobs must provide also a high quality of work life. This means that when designing jobs, organizational priorities (e.g., efficiency) alone should not play the decisive role. The needs of employees as well as environmental realities also play critical roles in job design efforts. This is especially true with the emergence of a "de-jobbed" and "boundary-less" work world where employees are expected to take initiative and solve problems creatively.

TERMS FOR REVIEW

autonomy
combination
competency
competency matrix
competency model (competency framework)
efficiency
employee log
environmental considerations
ergonomics
feedback
focus group
interview

job
job analysis
job analysis questionnaires
job code
job description
job design
job enlargement
job enrichment
job families
job identity
job performance standards
job rotation
job specification
questionnaires
National Occupational Classification (NOC)
observation
position
questionnaires
social expectations
task identity
task significance
variety
work flow
work practices
working conditions

SELF-ASSESSMENT EXERCISE

How Enjoyable Was That Work or Project?

Consider a job that you held in the past. If you have no work experience, consider a course project or other effort where you had to work for a reward. Please respond to the following questions frankly:

Statement about Your Work/Project	Strongly Disagree	Disagree	Agree	Strongly Agree
1. I felt that I had control over the quality and performance of my job.				
2. I was not allowed to plan the optimal pace at which I could work.				
3. The work/project involved various activities.				

(Continued)

4. It was the same routine every day; I did the same things day after day.				
5. At the end of a day, I could see a finished job or part of the project.				
6. There were many days when I had little sense of accomplishment.				
7. My boss/supervisor always told me whether I did the work well or poorly.				
8. I got little feedback from anyone about how well I performed during the course of the project.				
9. The work I did (or the project I completed) was an important one.				
10. Often I felt that it made little difference how I did on this job/project.				

SCORING

For the odd-numbered statements, assign a score of 1, 2, 3, or 4 for Strongly Disagree, Disagree, Agree, and Strongly Agree, respectively. For the even-numbered statements, reverse the scoring—that is, Strongly Disagree gets a score of 4 and Strongly Agree gets a score of 1. Add up your scores for all 10 statements.

Your score should lie somewhere between 10 and 40. If you received a score of 32 or higher, you had an enjoyable experience with your past work or assignment—at least most of the time. If you scored less than 20, it is unlikely that you had much fun doing the job or project.

While this is not a validated instrument, statements 1 and 2 above indicate the overall autonomy you had in doing the project; 3 and 4 measure the dimension of variety; 5 and 6 reflect task identity; 7 and 8 measure feedback; and 9 and 10 measure task significance. On each dimension, your scores can range anywhere from 2 to 8. It is possible for you to get a high score on one dimension and a low score on another, although an "enriched" project would have had high scores on all dimensions.

REVIEW AND DISCUSSION QUESTIONS

1. Suppose you work for an organization that does not conduct job analysis. What arguments will you make to introduce it? What method(s) of collecting job analysis information will you recommend and why?

2. Define job descriptions and job specifications, illustrating how the two are related yet different.

3. Why are clear job specifications important? What are the costs of imprecise specifications?

4. How can performance standards be set for production jobs when job analysis information is insufficient? How would you set performance standards for a research scientist if you were chief scientist?

5. What factors need to be considered when redesigning jobs? Of these, which is (are) most important?

CRITICAL THINKING QUESTIONS

1. Suppose you were assigned to write the job descriptions for a shirt factory in British Columbia employing mostly Chinese immigrants who spoke little English. What methods would you use to collect job analysis data?

2. You work in the human resource department of a large brewery in Atlantic Canada. You are in the process of writing job descriptions for all managerial and supervisory staff. One manager who is in the production division of the brewery refuses to complete a job analysis questionnaire.

   a. What reasons would you use to persuade that individual to complete it?

   b. If, after your best efforts at persuasion failed, you still wanted job analysis information on the manager's job, how would you get it?

3. Suppose that you have been assigned to design the job of ticket clerk for a regional airline in Ontario. How would you handle the following trade-offs?

   a. Would you recommend highly specialized job designs to minimize training or very broad job designs with all clerks cross-trained to handle multiple tasks? Why?

   b. Would you change your answer if you knew that employees tended to quit the job of ticket clerk within the first six months? Why or why not?

4. Assume that you are told to evaluate a group of jobs in a boat-building business. After studying each job for a considerable amount of time, you identify the following activities associated with each job. What job redesign techniques would you recommend for these jobs, if any?

   a. **Sailmaker:** Cuts and sews materials with very little variety in the type of work from day to day. Job is highly skilled and takes years to learn.

   b. **Sander:** Sands rough wood and fibreglass edges almost continuously. Little skill is required in this job.

   c. **Sales representative:** Talks to customers, answers phone inquiries, suggests customized additions to special-order boats.

   d. **Boat preparer:** Cleans up completed boats, waxes fittings, and generally makes the boat ready for customer delivery. Few skills are required for this job.

5. What are the key performance dimensions of the instructor who is teaching this course? How will you go about setting performance standards for the individual? Establish performance standards and associated time-bound, specific objectives in any two areas of your choice.

ETHICS QUESTION

Your firm, an importer of a large number of consumer goods including garments, sent you to a developing country to negotiate a deal with a local exporter. Under the proposed contract, your firm will invest 25 percent of the capital necessary to open a new garment tailoring plant, with the exporter investing the balance. During your week-long stay in the country, you realize that child labour is fairly common in this country, although a number of local employers categorically refuse to employ anyone under 18 years of age in their plants. During discussions with the local plant manager, you understand that he plans to use 12- to- 15-year-old children in the factory, and the children will have performance standards at levels equal to or higher than a typical adult Canadian worker in the same industry. You know that a couple of other foreign firms are currently interested in reaching a deal with this exporter because he has a reputation for reliability and quality. This is your first visit to this country.

What action, if any, will you take?

WEB RESEARCH EXERCISE

Select any job position (e.g., a financial accountant) of your choice. Consider various recruiters on the web. (Chapter 5, on recruitment, provides some websites for you to begin your search.) Are there any differences in the job specifications listed by different recruiters? Are any patterns visible across industry groups?

INCIDENT 2-1

Hillary Home Appliances Corporation

Hillary Home Appliances and Furnishings Corporation (HHAC) is a medium-sized manufacturer of home appliances. Historically, the firm has followed a low-cost strategy to successfully operate in a highly competitive industry. Recently, increasing global competition has made it necessary for the firm to revise its strategy in favour of improved customer service. The organization had paid virtually no attention to the human resource function; its human resource department (called "personnel and staffing department") focused primarily on compensation administration and staffing. Now, however, the top management of the firm is convinced of the need for strategic use of its human resources. An indication of this new thrust is the hiring of Leslie Wong, who has a reputation as a results-oriented HR manager (in two previous organizations), and the renaming of the department to "Human Resources." However, progressive HR practices have been slow to find acceptance at lower levels. In a recent meeting with two work supervisors, Jeff Gidoe and Mike Tarson, Leslie Wong, the newly hired human resource manager, faced these arguments:

Jeff Gidoe: I agree that good employee relations are important. But I simply cannot afford to let the HR staff interrupt our daily work with job analysis. Already, with the arrival of two new competitors, we have lost most of our cost advantage. Spending time on activities such as this further reduces our production and increases our costs.

Mike Tarson: Your plan to invite ideas from employees for product improvement is good; however, I should warn you that many of the workers in my section are school dropouts. They simply cannot accept responsibility. They care only for the wages they get and are constantly looking at the clock for quitting time.

Jeff Gidoe: At least a few of my employees will object to the time spent on job analysis. As you know, we have a production bonus plan in this plant. Every minute they spend on activities such as this costs them money. Already, several of them feel that the production standards are too high.

Mike Tarson: Your new idea of employee involvement teams is also likely to create problems. Already, they waste a fair bit of time each day jesting and horseplaying. If you put them into groups, things will only get worse, not better.

Leslie Wong: I value your comments. As supervisors, you know your employees best. I recognize that you are experts in your production areas. However, I can tell you this: the facts you have provided have simply reconfirmed the need for job analysis. Even more, it tells me that HR has a key role to play in this firm. I'll tell you why.

DISCUSSION QUESTIONS

1. What prompted the HR manager to make the above statement?

2. If you were the HR manager, what arguments would you provide to convince the two supervisors of the desirability of job analysis and employee involvement teams?

EXERCISE 2-1

A Good Work Environment

Think of some work-related situation that you have found enjoyable. Think of the job and identify the features that made it more enjoyable than other jobs that you have held. The job need not have been a formal, full-time job. It may simply have been some temporary job or even some chore you have had to perform. Make a list of those characteristics of the job that made it so enjoyable.

1. In reviewing your answers with others, do you find any similarities between your list and the lists of others who did different jobs?

2. Do these characteristics indicate what job features provide a good work situation?

EXERCISE 2-2

Strengths and Weaknesses of Job Descriptions*

Step 1. Students should bring several job descriptions to class.

Step 2. Create teams of three. Discuss the job descriptions. Do they adequately reflect the responsibilities and KSAOs that the employee will need to perform? Compare the job descriptions to the information in your text. What are the weaknesses and strengths of the job descriptions? What specific changes would make the job descriptions more measurable?

*Exercise suggestion: C. Fitzgerald, Okanagan College, Kelowna, B.C.

CASE STUDY

Maple Leaf Shoes Ltd

An Exercise in Job Analysis[*]

Maple Leaf Shoes Ltd. is a medium-sized manufacturer of leather and vinyl shoes located near Wilmington, Ontario. It began operations in 1969 and currently employs about 400 persons in its Ontario plant and some 380 more in offices and warehouses throughout Canada and internationally. In recent months, the company has experienced a number of challenges and problems (see the Case Study in Chapter 1 for further background). Added to these problems was the departure of John McAllister, the company's human resource manager. McAllister had been with the company for a little over three years and was reputed to have "run a tight ship."

Robert Clark, president and a major shareholder of Maple Leaf Shoes, decided to re-evaluate the role of the company's human resource manager before hiring a new person. Tim Lance, a graduate of the University of Manitoba and now the chief executive and owner of Productivity Systems, a management consulting operation located in Saskatoon, was hired to "look into the present and future role of Maple Leaf's human resource department and suggest appropriate action plans to improve its contribution to the organization and help the company meet its future challenges."

VIEWS OF THE SENIOR MANAGERS

Lance began his assignment by interviewing the senior managers of Maple Leaf Shoes. He made a short checklist of questions to prepare for his interview with the managers (see Figure 1). He was, however, determined not to restrict his interview to these questions. By keeping an informal and free flowing format, he felt that he could gain a better understanding of the structure, processes, and culture of the organization. His intent, therefore, was to use these questions as a springboard for letting the interviewee speak out and pursue any point that he or she may consider relevant. Lance was able to meet two of the five "key" managers in the company, plus the president. Figure 2 shows an approximate chain of command in the company. At the time Lance conducted his study, André Cardin, manager of Design & Research, was away on holidays. Lance was also unable to have an interview with the production manager, Bob Smith, because he was away on trips to Montreal and Winnipeg investigating the potential of expanding the company's operations to those cities. Lance felt that the half-hour interview with Robert Clark (interrupted by three or four phone calls "on urgent matters that unexpectedly arose") was totally inadequate for his purpose. However, Clark was due to leave town the next day, and Lance could not wait until Clark's return to proceed with his study.

After going through his notes, Lance realized that the human resource function was viewed very differently by the three people with whom he spoke. Clark had told him:

> I believe that we need a mover and shaker here. McAllister was all right, but he did not have the time or inclination to have a good system in place. He made most of the human resource decisions himself. I'm not saying that they weren't the correct decisions for those occasions; but he wasn't a popular man with either the employees or several managers. And as you know, this is one job where you need a lot of rapport with people at all levels.

[*]Case written by Professor Hari Das of the Department of Management, Saint Mary's University. All rights reserved by the author. © 2002.

Excerpts from Lance's interview with Clark follow:

I believe that the new person should be able to work with the people. In fact, not simply working with the people, but leading them. He or she should be able to look beyond today's needs … into the technological and other challenges that will face this company and our managers in the future. …

The future of Maple Leaf Shoes? I have mixed feelings on this. On the one hand, shoes are something that everyone needs—every day, every week, and throughout their lives. Also, most persons don't mind buying an extra pair if the price is right. But there's the catch. It's a pretty competitive market and what we do here and how well we do it depends quite a bit on how good our competitors are. To succeed, we need to have a clear market segment, control our costs, and meet our customers' needs. Two of our brands, which were leaders in the western Canada shoe market, are facing intense competition from products manufactured in China, Indonesia, and Korea. … The currency crisis in Asia (especially in Korea and Indonesia) can both hurt and help us. On the one hand, the prices of the imported shoes are getting lower by the day, thus cutting into our markets. The other side is that Western investments in these countries may slow down—at least in the short run. This means that we have breathing room to cope with this onslaught. … So, all in all … who knows?

FIGURE 1

Checklist Prepared by Lance for Interviewing the Senior Managers

- What do you expect from the human resource department in this company?
- What is your evaluation of the human resource department's contributions in the past?
- What activities should the human resource department of this company carry out?
- Which of these are done now? How well are you satisfied with the performance of the department in those fields?
- Overall, are you happy with the human resource staff? Why?
- What are the major challenges facing Maple Leaf Shoes in the next five years?
- What are the unique needs of your department?
- What new services or information should the human resource department provide you?

The most immediate problem? I should say we have two pressing issues: first, we must upgrade our production processes if we are to improve our efficiency and competitiveness. I personally believe that we have more employees than we need. If we could automate many of the production processes, we could improve the efficiency and reduce costs. But that is easier said than done. We have strong unions, and firing someone is going to be awfully hard in the future. At the same time, the reality is that no customer is going to pay 15 or 20 percent extra for our shoes if we cannot give a damn good reason for that. With the free trade worldwide, the market is flooded with Asian and South American products. We simply cannot compete with the Chinese and the Mexicans on the labour costs. … Our survival may very well depend on technological upgrading and improving worker productivity.

A second and related issue is dealing with unions. We have four major unions and I would term two of them as militant. Actually, our workers are pretty good—many of them have been with us for several years now—it's the union leadership that's causing much of the problem. The new human resource manager hired must be tough with the unions, yet caring and understanding. In the last three or four years, union–management relations have gone from bad to worse. We have to turn a new leaf now or else all of us will sink.

The responses to Lance's questions from the other two senior managers at Maple Leaf Shoes were varied. Excerpts from his interview with Tim McDonald, general manager, finance, are provided below:

I don't think human resource management is the most critical activity in the management of a shoe company. True, we have to pay the employees adequately and there must be a system for keeping employee records. But, beyond that, I don't think that the human resource department has anything major to offer that has a significant impact on an organization's working. What we really should focus on now is how to control our costs and come out with a sound marketing program. We especially need a good advertising campaign; we need to hire competent sales staff and upgrade the skills of the present sales force. …

FIGURE 2

An Approximate Chain of Command in Maple Leaf Shoes Ltd.

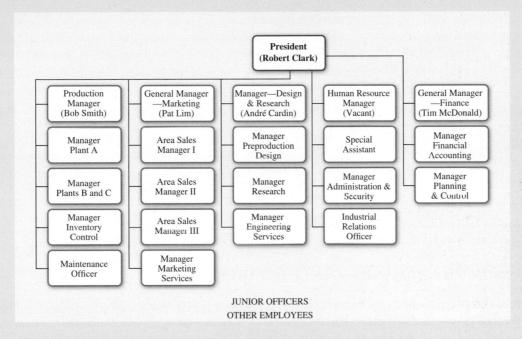

The human resource department here hasn't done much, if you ask me. They haven't had any input into job design or organizational planning. Part of the problem stems from the fact that there has been little continuity in that department. A typical manager in the human resource department stays for about three years before he moves out. Neither McAllister nor his predecessor stayed in the company for five years. Tony Rezkov, the manager in charge of administration and security, is new; so are several of the other junior officers and staff in the department. … I do believe there is a problem there. …

Oh, don't get me wrong. The human resource department staff are very friendly and cooperative. McAllister had a few rough edges, but overall he was someone whom I grew to like. He was one of those tough guys—straight out of an old John Wayne movie. He made fast decisions and was sort of a troubleshooter here. …

The big challenge? Global competition, of course. We'd better be prepared to meet the Koreans, the Chinese, and the Mexicans. Unless we maintain our competitiveness, we are just not going to survive. It's as simple as that. …

Of course, global free trade also brings with it a great opportunity. NAFTA gave us access to a market now that is several times the size of our local market. Freer trade in Asia and Eastern Europe will do the same. … But can we make use of this opportunity? That's the big question.

Pat Lim, general manager, marketing (and who was currently overseeing the human resource function until a new HR manager is appointed), had a somewhat different vision of the role of the human resource department:

It's probably one of the most important functions in this company. In my university days, I was taught that human resources are the single most important asset of any organization. After working for nearly 25 years in the management area, I've grown to realize how true that statement is. In my mind, people make all the difference. You can have all the resources you want, but in the absence of good employees, all those resources are worthless. The human resource department is the backbone of our employee relations…

What do I expect from the human resource department? Quite a lot, I should say. I believe that the department can play a leadership and developmental role. Until now, it has played a somewhat low-key, record-keeping, staff role. It's time the department became involved seriously in employee planning, job redesign, career planning, organizational design, and other development activities. Gone are the days when it could simply play a support role. Look at all the successful companies in this country and the United States, especially those that are listed in books such as *In Search of Excellence*. It's the people and people management that differentiate them from the common crop. …

The new human resource manager should be an expert—an expert on systems and people. We need new ideas here, and with a growing workforce we need more formal procedures and systems, whether it's orientation or performance appraisal. Right now, many of the human resource activities are done on an ad hoc basis.

Above all, I believe that the new human resource manager needs to bring a new philosophy to deal with the unions. In the past several months, there has been an increasing degree of hostility between the unions and management. I'm not blaming anyone for this. But I do believe that we, as part of the management team, have the responsibility to solve some of these problems. It's up to us to take the initiative to improve the situation. Isn't that the essence of good management?

VIEW FROM THE HUMAN RESOURCE DEPARTMENT

As part of the study, Lance met with the three key staff members in the human resource department: Jane Reynolds, special assistant to the human resource manager; Tony Rezkov, manager of administration and security; and Joseph McDonald, the industrial relations officer (no relation to Tim McDonald). Rezkov, being new on the job, was unable to tell Lance much about his position or the human resource function. In Lance's opinion, his two meetings (lasting approximately an hour each) with Jane Reynolds were more productive.

Lance studied the various comments made by Reynolds:

The possibilities here are simply enormous. With a little determination and the right type of resources, we can make this one of the best human resource departments in this country. To be really effective, I believe that human resource management must be well integrated with the strategic and operational planning in a firm. That has not occurred here yet…

When I joined this company two years ago, it didn't have any system—at least, not anything that is worth mentioning. My job since I arrived has been to introduce new procedures and decision support systems. For example, recently, we started a formal orientation program for all plant workers. We are also in the process of developing two performance appraisal instruments—one for the plant employees and the other for administrative staff. We are beginning to provide absenteeism and turnover data to various department and section managers. But I want to emphasize that these are just the beginning. With the right support, we can do wonders here…

Why do I sound pessimistic? Well, look at our department's staff strength compared to human resource departments in similar-sized organizations in this part of the country. We probably employ less than 50 percent of the number you would see elsewhere. As a cost-cutting strategy, when we downsized the organization, we lost two positions in our department. We also do not have the software programs and support to do an adequate job. …

Sure, despite everything, we could have still done better if we had the will to do it. I will be totally frank with you. You will keep my observations confidential, won't you? Not that I mind too much if someone comes to know about it. It's as if we are a poor cousin here. Being in human resources is just not considered to be important or very useful. We're looked upon by many others as an unnecessary appendage.

Lance found that Joseph McDonald ("Call me Joe, everyone does"), the industrial relations officer, was the toughest to handle. McDonald was very friendly and supportive, but did not give a direct or coherent answer to any of Lance's questions. Lance felt that McDonald was one of those people who talked to you for hours at a time nonstop without giving any useful information. Lance realized that he got only two points of information out of his 45-minute meeting with McDonald. First, one of the unions in the company was very militant and might go on strike when its contract expired in the next few months; and second, McDonald's son was planning to go to medical school—Lance knew the former fact already and didn't care to know about the latter.

In less than 10 days, Lance was scheduled to meet Robert Clark to give a summary of his findings and recommendations. Already, Lance had received a call from his office in Saskatoon informing him that one of his consultants had been injured in an automobile accident and would not be returning to work for the next several weeks. This meant that Lance had to return to his office soon to complete that project himself. Given the time constraints, Lance was wondering how he should proceed from here.

DISCUSSION QUESTIONS

1. What is your evaluation of Lance's approach to the project?
2. What would you do if you were in Lance's position right now?

CASE STUDY

Canadian Pacific and International Bank

*Redefining Jobs for the Future**

After computerizing Canadian Pacific and International Bank (CPIB) is a premier Canadian financial institution with assets of over $150 billion and operations across Canada and internationally. Today, its 25,000-plus employees provide personal, commercial, corporate, and investment banking services to individuals and businesses in 33 countries. More details of the bank are given at the end of Chapter 1.

CPIB, through its strategic initiatives, was successful in building long-term value for its shareholders while providing regular returns on their investments. A vital component of its recent strategy is growth through acquisition of smaller banks and other financial institutions in this country and internationally. The passage of the bill relating to bank mergers in June 2000 in Parliament accelerated this process for CPIB.

Last month, the bank acquired Central Canadian Trust Company (CCTC), a trust company located in Ontario employing over 3,000 employees. While the trust company was a very successful player in the financial industry in Ontario and Quebec, CPIB management felt that the human resource practices in the firm were inferior to those of the bank.

Initially, the identity of CCTC will be maintained; however, over the next year or so, all branches will be converted into CPIB branches. This means that, with immediate effect, CCTC staff must be trained to offer the highest quality of customer service that CPIB clients have come to expect. Compared to CPIB, CCTC is also far behind in allowing internet funds transfers and web banking. CPIB expects all its managers to be able to offer extensive client counselling (including areas such as portfolio management, margin trading, and using the budgeting tools and calculators provided to clients on their webpages); in contrast, CCTC being a trust company, historically had underplayed this role and concentrated on pension fund management and loan/mortgage services. CPIB also has a culture of transferring its employees to help them gain international experience whereas CCTC is primarily a regional institution where staff transfers are less common.

During the pre-acquisition survey, Mary Keddy, senior vice-president of human resources at CPIB, observed that CCTC did not have any regular job analysis procedure built into its HR systems. Since CPIB was contemplating the installation of a bank-wide electronic job data system (called the "Job Bank") in the next six months, Keddy decided to use the present opportunity to test the new system. Given the relatively small number of employees involved in CCTC (compared to CPIB), it was easier to fix all the "bugs" there before implementing it in its entirety in CPIB.

Under the proposed system, through their personal computers and other consoles, all managers will be able to store and retrieve human resource data from the company's mainframe computer. This means that when managers or human resource specialists needed a job description, they could simply obtain one from the computer.

After computerizing all human resource information in CCTC, HR staff began to notice that job descriptions, job specifications, and job standards were constantly being changed by jobholders. It seemed that whenever a manager or worker reviewed a job description or job specification that seemed outdated, he or she would make updates and save the later version. Thus, although in the beginning human resource specialists were pleased that workers were showing an interest by updating the electronic job analysis information, they eventually became worried because workers with the same job titles had different views of their jobs. Changes would come from almost anyone, and there was no consistency in style or content.

The HR staff at CPIB were bewildered. On the one hand, they did not want to introduce too many restrictions on employees updating their job descriptions; this was also contrary to the "open" culture that existed in CPIB. On the other hand, if not controlled, the problem could get out of hand, especially when implemented within such a large and diverse multilingual workforce.

DISCUSSION QUESTIONS

1. Assume you are invited as a consultant by CPIB. What procedures would you introduce that would ensure that the restudied job information was correct?

2. Given the ability of most managers to "communicate" directly with the HR files, can CPIB use this to its advantage in collecting job analysis information? Explain.

3. What additional skills and competencies would you focus on while planning a training program for CCTC staff? How should CPIB establish performance and skill standards for CCTC staff?

Sukhman
Komal

CHAPTER 3

Human Resource Planning

Human resource planning is ... designed to translate strategic objectives into targeted quantitative and qualitative skill requirements, identify the human resource strategies and objectives necessary to fulfill those requirements ... and ... to assess progress.

ABDUL RAHMAN BIN IDRIS AND DEREK ELDRIDGE[1]

LEARNING OBJECTIVES

After studying this chapter, you should be able to:

LO1 Explain the importance of human resource plans for strategic success.

LO2 Describe the human resource planning process.

LO3 Discuss methods for estimating an organization's demand for human resources.

LO4 Explain the various methods of estimating a firm's supply of human resources.

LO5 Identify solutions to shortages or surpluses of human resources.

LO6 Discuss the major contents of a human resource information system (HRIS).

LO7 Explain how HRIS has contributed to enhancing HR service delivery.

In Chapter 1, we addressed how different organizational strategies and tactical plans require different human resource practices, strategies, and tactics to be successful. In this chapter, we elaborate on this concept by addressing human resource planning—a fundamental step in strategic human resource management. Recall that strategic human resource management enabled leaders and human resource professionals alike to align the human resource systems, policies, and practices to the organizational strategy. Human resource planning, in turn, enables organizations to ensure that the right people are in the right place at the right time to support the completion of organizational strategies. Perhaps, more than any other human resource activity, planning allows the human resource department to be proactive. Planning is a critical HR process—particularly over the long term, since without planning an organization may find itself with a plant or an office without the employees to run it productively. The plans themselves may range from simple projections based on past trends to sophisticated predictive models. However, it is important that some form of planning exists.

In 1924, International Business Machines was created. Better known today as IBM, the company has made major shifts in business strategy over the last 95 years. With origins in creating and manufacturing hardware (including clocks), IBM has undertaken a strategy of "making markets by transforming industries and professions with data."[2] To undertake a strategy focused on big data and data analytics, an appropriate shift in human resources would have needed to take place to ensure that the right individuals with the right skill sets were in place well in advance of executing on this strategy. Without an appropriate human resource plan, the leaders at IBM would likely be addressing the age old phenomena. That is, they would be rushing to hire people in a reactive way rather than in a proactive way.

LO1 HRC 1 & 4

Relationship of Human Resource Planning to Strategic Planning

Human resource planning (HRP) is a process used to determine future human resource requirements by anticipating future business demands, analyzing the impacts of these demands on the organization, determining the current availability of human resources, and making decisions on how to effectively acquire and utilize firms' human resources. It helps identify what human resources are needed to ensure that the organization can respond to change and provides plans to help the organization respond effectively.[3] The term "human resource planning" has been used interchangeably with other terms such as *employment planning, human capital planning, human capital management*, and *strategic human resource planning*. Whatever term is used, planning denotes a proactive human resource process to manage future resource requirements.

human resource planning

A process used to determine future human resource requirements by anticipating future business demands, analyzing the impacts of these demands on the organization, determining the current availability of human resources, and making decisions on how to effectively acquire and utilize firms' human resources.

The major objective of human resource planning is to ensure that the organization has the *right people with the right skills at the right time* in order for the organization to fulfill organizational objectives.[4] Complementing the "people resource" element, planning also involves planning for the appropriate human resource practices and activities. The desired outcomes of planning focus on business competitiveness through effectively allocating "people" resources and prioritizing human resource initiatives.[5] By anticipating the number and types of employees and the activities that will be needed, the human resource department helps improve the utilization of its human resources, attempts to achieve economies of scale by securing the right type of resources, and aligns its activities with the overall strategic direction of the organization.

Before proceeding, it is important to note that getting the right people in the right place at the right time does not ensure organizational success. Having the appropriate human resource practices in place to create the *right environment* and enable and motivate people to do *the right things* is equally important. For example, consider an organization planning a major expansion into a new market when employees are resistant to change, lack trust in leadership, and have generally low morale. In a case like this, human resources will need to figure out how to attract, hire, and retain more employees while simultaneously developing and implementing strategies to improve the organization's culture. For discussion purposes, this chapter focuses on creating human resource plans and introduces concepts and tools that will be more fully developed throughout Part 2 of the text. Enabling and motivating "people" resources to do the right things is the focus of Part 3 of this text.

Different Strategies Require Different Human Resource Plans

In Chapter 1, we discussed organizational strategies related to differentiation, cost, and focus. Different corporate strategies will lead to different human resource strategies. For example, an organization's growth or expansion strategy is usually accompanied by aggressive hiring, training, and promotion of employees.

> One such company with a diversification strategy is Intel Corporation <http://www.intel.com>. When Paul Otellini took the helm at Intel as CEO, he embarked on a business strategy that was set to change the way Intel did business. The company decided to revise its business strategy and to extend its product offerings due to the fact that the personal computer (PC) market was shrinking and revenue growth was impacted. The old model was primarily focused on providing memory chips for PCs. The new strategy is focused on creating all types of chips and software, bringing together what Intel called "platforms" for consumer electronics, communications, and health care industries. Otellini decided to reorganize the company by putting its 98,000 employees in new jobs. In addition, he added 20,000 new employees targeting specific skill sets. The resource planning for these jobs involved identifying the types of skills needed to ensure optimum deployment of the business strategy. He brought in more employees with marketing skills—sociologists, ethnographers, and doctors—and shifted the focus onto marketing. In doing so, he deliberately created a new culture that focused more on teamwork, thinking about the customer, communicating to the customer about what Intel can do for them, and creating a more global mindset.[6]

In contrast, a retrenchment or cost reduction strategy often necessitates layoffs and early retirement of surplus employees.

> After reporting a loss of $12.7 billion, Ford Motor Company announced plans to close 16 plants and eliminate 30,000 hourly workers represented by the United Auto Workers (UAW) union as part of its "Way Forward" plan to return to profitability. With no confidence that the UAW would resist the destruction of jobs, 38,000 workers, nearly half of Ford's workforce, took the buyout.[7]

Linking Strategy to Planning

In Chapter 1, we outlined a number of forces—both internal and external—that would impact an organization's ability to successfully achieve their goals. Adopting a strategic focus on human resources enables managers to proactively anticipate the long term "people" needs of an organization and create a human resources strategy. It is important to recognize, however, that a firm's long-range strategic plan is accomplished by the thoughtful execution of a series of short-range, tactical (or operational) plans that focus on current needs and operations. Purchasing a new information management system to improve efficiency, recalling a defective product, and managing inventory more effectively are some examples of tactical planning. Whatever the plan, it is made and carried out by people, which necessitates the proper staffing of an organization. As such, each tactic also requires managers and leaders to consider the short-range human resource plan.

> Toyota Motor Manufacturing Company <http://www.tmmc.ca> identified a significant increase in market share for its RAV4 sport utility vehicle. As a result, Toyota determined through its year-end planning process that for this increased production demand to be met, it would require 800 more workers for a second shift in its assembly

operations in Woodstock, Ontario, by the following March.[8] As a result, the human resource department needed to embark on an aggressive hiring initiative to fill those jobs.

Nordstrom <http://shop.nordstrom.com>, an upscale U.S. retailer, announced that it would open a flagship store in Toronto. It began construction in 2014 and expects the outlet to be open in 2016. To be ready to execute this major initiative, Nordstrom must have the proper staff available with specific skills. For example, to staff its stores, Nordstrom will need retail clerks, managers, merchandizers, and cashiers. In addition, it will require regional managers, a country manager, and an executive to oversee this expansion.[9]

Figure 3-1 shows the relationship between strategic plans of an organization and its human resource plans. As can be seen, the overall organizational strategy defines the human resource objectives that are accomplished through the implementation of appropriate human resource plans. Successful organizations— both large and small, and public as well as private—recognize the importance of *intellectual* or *human capital*. An effective human resource plan is a critical tool to take advantage of this valuable asset.

FIGURE 3-1

Relationship between Strategic and Human Resource Plans

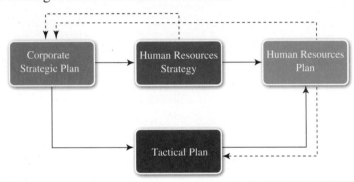

HR Planning Can Vary from Capturing Basic Information to a More Sophisticated Approach

Organizations are unique; they use different approaches for planning the allocation of human resources.

In one large electronics firm, strategic business planning begins with "top down" revenue and profit targets established by the company's policy committee. Then executives of the different business areas develop the strategies and sales volumes needed to achieve these goals. From here, various divisions create functional strategies for development, manufacturing, marketing, and service. Line managers are responsible for folding the functional plans into divisional ones. The human resource department's role is to review all divisional plans before they are sent to the top management. Although line managers have wide latitude in addressing human resource issues, human resource concerns are injected into the business plans by proactive human resource specialists who work closely with divisional managers. These managers are encouraged to involve human resource staff in decision making because the business plans will be reviewed for human resource considerations before they are finalized. Through their involvement in the strategic business planning process, the human resource planners in this firm are better able to develop their corporate and functional human resource plans.

This example illustrates an organization which engages in *robust* planning activities that are structured, tied to the business plan, integrated with HR functions, and dynamic in nature. It is typical to expect that, as organizations grow, they develop more robust planning practices largely due to the significant impact on labour costs. Large Canadian employers such as Onex (240,000 employees; <http://www.onex.ca>), George Weston (155,000 employees), Magna International (97,000 employees; <http://www.magna.com>), and Royal Bank (80,000 employees) pay considerable attention to employment planning since even a 1 percent increase or decrease in the total workforce can result in significantly different labour costs. In some cases, organizations have hired "Chief People Officers," asserting that organizations need to bring together strategy, research, data, planning, and employee engagement and well-being to create high performance organizations.[10] However, this type of planning is exceptional. Some organizations think very short term, their planning is informal, and the resource plan is static. One author has described these differences in terms of levels of planning sophistication.[11] From this perspective, organizations may be categorized into one of five levels of planning (see Figure 3-2).

FIGURE 3-2

The Five Levels of Planning Activities

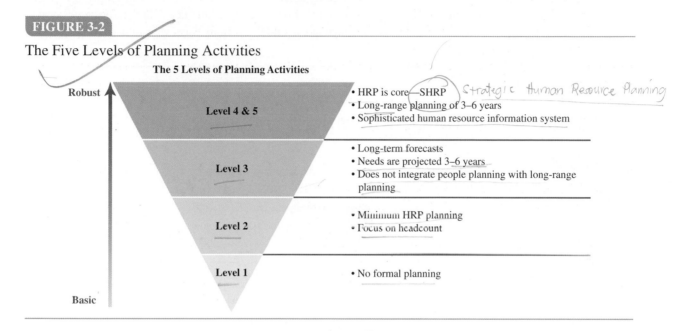

The 5 Levels of Planning Activities

LEVEL ONE companies can be described as not engaging in any form of planning, whether it is business or human resource related. Recruitment and training are considered an afterthought. An example would be family-owned small organizations where the leadership style is paternalistic in nature.

LEVEL TWO companies do engage in some long-term business planning, but minimal human resource planning. Resource planning is solely focused on how many people will be needed in the future. However, the planning is static in nature and receives minimal weight in terms of importance within the organization.

LEVEL THREE companies engage in moderate planning activities, creating longer-term forecasts, projecting their needs three to five years ahead. However, these organizations still do not integrate their people planning efforts into the long-term business plan.

LEVELS FOUR AND FIVE companies are considered advanced in terms of their planning sophistication, engaging in long-range human resource planning, spanning three to six years. Human resource planning now becomes a core process and is considered a key priority. Managers are enthusiastic about planning and there is a growing recognition that anticipating resource requirements for the future is imperative to ensure organizational sustainability. The plan is formal, flexible, and dynamic. It adjusts to change as circumstances dictate. The human resource components are fully integrated with the business plan. Recruitment and training are anticipated and succession planning is considered a critical activity to ensure sustainability. The key difference between level 4 and 5 is that level 5 organizations utilize *robust* evaluation tools and highly sophisticated technology to create long-range plans to improve returns on investment.

This is not to suggest that all organizations eventually progress through the levels. In some cases, an organization may not make it past level 1. This may be due to a lack of knowledge or simply a lack of time.

The behaviours described in level five require a great deal of resources and time. For some organizations, this investment is not only important, it is essential, to the point that they are turning to companies like SAP <http//www.sap.com> to create software solutions to predict certain events such as employee turnover.[12]

This has created a new challenge for human resource professionals. Namely, how to use data analytics without creating concern from employees.[13]

Next, we will discuss the steps to follow in the HR Planning Process (see Figure 3-3). The discussion begins with a look at factors causing human resource demand, followed by strategies to estimate demand and supply, and match current and future supply with demand. The chapter ends with a brief look at the human resource information system (HRIS), the importance of using these systems to manage talent, and the various ways we can use the information to effectively utilize our human resource capabilities.

LO2 HRC 4

The Human Resource Planning Process

FIGURE 3-3

The Human Resource Planning Process

As seen in Figure 3-3, human resource planning is a process with a specific order of activities helping managers to focus on the issues that are most important so they can plan effectively to ensure organizational objectives are met.

The steps are as follows:

Step 1: Forecast Demand for Resources

This activity answers the questions: *how many* human resources will we need, *when* will we need them, and *where* will we need them? It forecasts demand by looking at the many factors that cause a labour need to exist and uses various forms of forecasting techniques.

Step 2: Assess Internal and External Supply of Resources

This phase assesses the internal and external supply of labour. It answers the question: *what resources* do we have available both inside the organization and in the external environment and *what skills and competencies* do these resources possess?

Step 3: Develop HR Objectives

This step identifies what the planners expect to accomplish as a result of their actions. Planners carry out an analysis to determine the differences between demand and supply, and write HR objectives that will determine the choice of programs.

Step 4: Design and Implement HRM Programs

Here the planners decide what type of human resource programs will be developed to achieve their objectives. These programs attempt to balance demand and supply. For example, if the organization is projecting a shortage, it may choose to outsource or use overtime or, if a surplus is expected, it may decide to allow employees to job share as opposed to downsize.

Step 5: Establish Program Evaluation

With any process it is important to evaluate its effectiveness, using some form of quantitative or qualitative measurement. Evaluation of the process answers the question: Is there a tangible link between investments in human resource programs and organizational sustainability and to what degree?[14]

Forecasting Labour Demand

A challenge facing organizations is that "people" resources are rarely in a state of being perfectly balanced. Because organizations and their environments are continually changing, organizations quite likely will find themselves either in a position of having too many employees or not enough. This underscores the importance of effective human resource planning. While it may not completely eliminate it, a good human resource plan reduces the risk of being out of balance. To have an effective human resource plan, organizations need to have a clear understanding of what they need in terms of employees, what they have, and what the difference is between the two. Moreover, a good human resource plan will identify and anticipate shifts in either an organization's demand or supply of human resources.

The best place to begin is to forecast the need for resources. To this end, we need to consider the factors that cause a demand to exist.

Forecasting: Identifying the Causes that Will Drive Demand

To understand how to forecast demand, we need to consider what would cause an organization's need for employees or specific skill sets to change in one direction or another. It is important to note that the examples provided are not exhaustive, but rather provide some illustration of what may impact human resources demand. It is also important to note that some forces may create either an undersupply or oversupply depending on other factors. For example, sales projections may create an oversupply if sales projections are falling or an undersupply if sales projections are increasing. Some of these causes are within the organization's control and others are not. Human resource **forecasts** are attempts to predict an organization's future demand for employees.

---

forecasts

Estimates of future resource needs and changes.

Demographic Impacts

In Chapter 1, a series of demographic impacts were identified including age and gender. Like national, regional, or even local demographics, each organization will have a demographic profile of its own. This profile helps inform human resource leaders regarding impending changes in their workforce. For instance, human resource leaders may capture the average age of employees against the average retirement ages to gain insight into future retirements.

Turnover

Turnover is the departure of employees from an organization. In some cases, the decision to leave the organization is made by the employee, such as resignations. In some cases, the employer makes the decision, such as in terminations. In yet other cases, the turnover may be temporary (e.g., leaves of absence). As will be discussed later in the text, turnover may be functional (i.e., good) or dysfunctional (i.e., bad). Regardless of the cause, effective human resource planning needs to be prepared to understand and predict employee departures as best as possible.

Legal Changes

Changes occurring in social, political, and legal spheres are easier to predict, but their implications are seldom clear. As demographics change, so do employee attitudes toward work and their employers. The impact on human resource planning of the *Canadian Human Rights Act*, passed more than 20 years ago, is still somewhat unclear. Major judicial verdicts, changes in employment laws (such as minimum wages), and federal and provincial government regulations all have great implications for the human resource planner. Although many large firms have established employment equity programs, the results of a change from the notion of equal pay for equal work to that of equal pay for work of equal value (see Chapter 4) will have profound implications.

Technological Changes

Technological changes, which are normally difficult to predict, can affect both demand for, and supply of, human resources.[15] As an example, many thought the computer would mean mass unemployment. While it is true that computerization has eliminated certain types of jobs, the computer industry today employs hundreds of thousands of people and is a high-growth business. Very often, technological changes tend to reduce employment in one department while increasing it in another, making planning tricky.

The rapid computerization and automation[16] of many work activities may necessitate new skills on the part of employees, which may be hard to predict accurately.

Competitors

Competitors affect an organization's demand for human resources, though not in any uniform manner. Employment in some of the traditional sectors (such as the steel industry) barely grows because of foreign competition and a push for productivity improvement. But in the high-tech and electronics industries, competition causes lower prices, larger markets, and additional employment. In yet other cases, the arrival of a competitor may create demand because employees leave to work for the competitor.

Strategic Plan

As discussed earlier in the text, the organization's strategic plan commits the firm to long-range objectives, such as growth rates, new products, markets, or services. These objectives determine the numbers and types of employees needed in the future. Obviously, a fast-growing firm has more beginning-level vacancies. The number of higher-level openings also depends on how well the human resource department assists employees to develop their capabilities. If workers are not encouraged to expand their capabilities, they may not be ready to fill future vacancies.

Budgets and Revenue Forecasts

Budget increases or cuts are the most significant short-run influence on human resource needs. Related to budgets are revenue forecasts. While less exact than budgets, revenue forecasts may provide even quicker notice of short-run changes in human resource demand:

The human resource manager for a nationwide chain of furniture outlets observed a sharp decline in sales, brought on by a recession. The manager quickly discarded the short-run human resource plan and imposed an employment freeze on all outlets' hiring plans.

Historical sales and production forecasts can be used as the operational index to which HR planning forecasts its future human resource demands.

New Ventures

New ventures mean new human resource demands. When initiated internally to the organization, the lead time may allow planners to develop short-run and long-run employment plans. But new ventures begun by acquisitions and mergers cause an immediate revision of human resource demands. A reorganization, especially after a merger or an acquisition, can radically alter human resource needs. Several positions or jobs may have to be eliminated to avoid duplication, while new integrating roles may have to be created for smooth operating of merged units.

Organizational and Job Design

Changes in the organization structure have major implications for human resource needs. In some cases, new roles may be created. In others, roles may be eliminated.

Prior to its 2012 buyout by U.S. giant Semtech <http://www.semtech.com>, Gennum Corporation, a Canadian high-tech company that designed and manufactured silicon integrated circuits, changed from its existing function-based structure (employing specialist functional departments like marketing and production) to a product-based structure. Under the new structure, there were separate divisions for video and for hearing instrument products. This decision created new positions as well as the need to generate new employee competencies—especially at supervisory and managerial levels—resulting in changes in HR functions such as hiring and training.[17]

LO3

Forecasting Techniques for Estimating Human Resource Demand

As Figure 3-4 shows, forecasting techniques range from the informal to the sophisticated. Even the most sophisticated methods are not perfectly accurate; instead, they are best viewed as approximations. Most firms make only casual estimates about the immediate future. As they gain experience with forecasting human resource needs, they may use more sophisticated techniques (especially if they can afford specialized staff). Each of the forecasting methods in Figure 3-4 is explained below.

FIGURE 3-4

Techniques for Estimating Future Human Resource Needs

Expert	Trend	Other
• Informal and instant decisions	• Extrapolation	• Budget and planning analysis
• Formal expert survey	• Indexation	• New-venture analysis
• Delphi technique	• Statistical analysis	• Computer models

Expert Forecasts

Expert forecasts rely on those who are knowledgeable to estimate future human resource needs. At the first level of complexity, the manager may simply be convinced that the workload justifies another employee:

Manager: How come the credit card balance statements haven't gone out yet?

Billing clerk: I know they should have, but we're short-handed. The new computer system has some bugs that haven't been fixed yet. Right now, the two computer systems are not mutually compatible. We've been working overtime on this, but nothing helps.

Manager: Yes, I talked to Janet about it. It seems it will take at least another four months for the new system to be fully operational. Meanwhile, I'll ask the HR department to get us a temporary employee. The salary will be more than recovered by the cost of overtime and lost interest in unpaid accounts.

The example above illustrates an informal and instant forecast. But it is not part of a systematic planning effort. A better method is for planners to survey managers, who are the experts, about their department's future employment needs. The centralization of this information permits formal plans that identify the organization's future demand.

The survey may be an informal poll, a written questionnaire, or a focused discussion using the **nominal group technique** (NGT). The NGT presents a group of managers with a problem statement, such as, "What will cause our staffing needs to change over the next year?" Then each of the 5 to 15 participants writes down as many answers as he or she can imagine. These ideas are then shared in round-table fashion until all written ideas and any new ones they stimulated have been recorded. The group's ideas are then discussed and ranked by having each member of the group vote for the three to five most important ones.[18]

---

nominal group technique

A focused group discussion where members meet face-to-face, write down their ideas, and share them. All new thoughts on a topic are recorded and ranked for importance.

If the experts cannot be brought together, sophistication can be added to the survey approach with the **Delphi technique**. This technique solicits estimates from a group of experts, usually managers. Then human resource department planners act as intermediaries, summarizing the various responses and reporting the findings to the experts. The experts are surveyed again after they get this feedback. Summaries and surveys are repeated until the experts' opinions begin to agree on future developments. For example, the human resource department may survey all production supervisors and managers until an agreement is reached on the number of replacements needed during the next year. The main difference between the two techniques is that in the NGT they meet face-to-face, whereas in the Delphi technique they utilize a lead coordinator to collect, summarize, and disseminate the information to and from the experts.

Delphi technique

The soliciting of predictions about specified future events from a panel of experts, using repeated surveys until convergence in opinions occurs.

Trend Projection Forecasts

Perhaps the quickest forecasting technique is to project past trends. The two simplest methods are extrapolation and indexation. **Extrapolation** involves extending past rates of change into the future. For example, if an average of 20 production workers were hired each month for the past two years, extrapolation indicates that 240 production workers will probably be added during the upcoming year.

---

extrapolation

Extending past rates of change into the future.

Indexation is a method of estimating future employment needs by matching employment growth with a selected index. A common example is the ratio of production employees to sales. For example, planners may discover that for each million-dollar increase in sales, the production department requires 10 new assemblers.

Figure 3-5 shows an example of the indexation method in the case of a direct marketing firm. The relevant business factor here is sales figures in dollars. An overall productivity index for all relevant sales personnel is computed. This ratio, with appropriate modifications, enables the firm to estimate its demand for personnel for the next period. However, it should be noted that the growth or decline rate in the labour force may be different during growth and downsizing periods (typically, the growth of the management tier happens at a somewhat faster pace than its compression). When using indexation, this factor must be recognized.

indexation

A method of estimating future employment needs by matching employment growth with a selected index, such as the ratio of production employees to sales.

FIGURE 3-5

An Illustration of the Indexation Method

Plastics, Mugs, and Housewares (PMH), a direct marketer of household plastics products with its head office in Calgary, began operations in 1998. PMH, which began as a very small firm, soon grew rapidly and employed 530 persons in 2015. The firm hopes to have even higher growth rates in the next two years. The dollar sales value and the staff strength for the last seven years (for which company information is readily available) are shown below. The firm forecasts it will have a 20 percent increase in sales in 2016 and another 15 percent (over 2016 figures) in year 2017. Because of technological improvements and improved training, the sales productivity is expected to show a 15 percent improvement in 2016. (No substantial improvement is expected for the year after.) PMH is currently attempting to forecast its human resource needs for 2016 and 2017.

One possible approach here is as follows:

Year	Number of Employees	Dollar Sales (000s)	Sales Productivity Index (dollar sales divided by number of employees)
2009	300	150	0.5000
2010	310	160	0.5161
2011	400	210	0.5250
2012	430	222	0.5163
2013	430	228	0.5302
2014	520	273	0.5250
2015	530	280	0.5283

Sales targets for the next two years are:

Year	Number of Employees	Dollar Sales (000s)	Sales Productivity Index
2016	?	336	0.6075
2017	?	386.4	0.6075

Since the target sales are expected to rise by 20 percent in 2016 and 15 percent in 2017, the figures for the two years will be: 336 in 2016 (280 × 1.2) and 386.4 (336 × 1.15) in 2017. The labour productivity is expected to increase by 15 percent in 2016 (or reach 0.6075).

The human resource needs for the next two years will, hence, be:

2016 = 336   divided by 0.6075 = 553.09, and

2017 = 386.4   divided by 0.6075 = 636.05

This means that the firm will need to hire approximately 23 (or 553 − 530) persons for 2016 and 83 persons (636 − 553) a year later. Of course, the exact numbers can be arrived at only after a detailed look at the various types of job positions within the organization, their interdependencies, and differences in productivity levels across job positions. These figures also do not include hiring needed to replace employees who retire or otherwise leave the organization.

By analyzing the staffing needs of existing oil rigs, planners of a new rig can forecast their human resource needs until changes in technology occur. How can planners react to shortages of skilled staff?

PhotoLink/Getty Images.

Extrapolation and indexation are crude, short-run approximations because they assume that the causes of demand—external, organizational, and workforce factors—remain constant, which is seldom the case. They are very inaccurate for long-range human resource projections. More sophisticated statistical analyses make allowances for changes in the underlying causes of demand.

Other Forecasting Methods

There are several other ways planners can estimate the future demand for human resources.

Budget and Planning Analysis

Organizations that need human resource planning generally have detailed budgets and long-range plans.

A study of department budgets reveals the financial authorizations for more employees. These data plus extrapolations of workforce changes (resignations, terminations, and the like) can provide short-run estimates of human resource needs. Long-term estimates can be made from each department or division's long-range plans.

New-Venture Analysis

When new ventures complicate employment planning, planners can use *new-venture analysis*. New-venture analysis requires planners to estimate human resource needs by comparison with firms that already perform similar operations.

For example, an integrated steel company that owns steel plants and iron ore mines decides to explore iron ore at a new site. The management can estimate its employment needs in the new mine by looking at employment levels of other iron ore mines and making necessary adjustments for productivity improvements.

Computer-Based Simulation and Predictive Models

As we discussed earlier, the most sophisticated organizations used robust technology to forecasting effectively. *Computer models* are a series of mathematical formulas that simultaneously use extrapolation, indexation, survey results, and estimates of workforce changes to compute future human resource needs. They simulate and forecast changes in demand for human resources caused by various internal and external factors.

Converting a Forecast into Human Resource Requirements

Forecasts translate the causes of demand into short-range and long-range statements of need. The resulting long-range plans are, of necessity, general statements of probable needs. Specific numbers are either omitted or estimated. To summarize forecasts, organizations often turn to creating staffing tables.

A **staffing table** lists the future employment needs for each type of job, as in Figure 3-6. The listing may be a specific number or an approximate range of needs, depending on the accuracy of the underlying forecast. Staffing tables are neither complete nor wholly accurate. They are only approximations. But these estimates allow human resource specialists to match short-run demand and supply. They assist HR departments in writing HR objectives, they help operating departments run more smoothly, and can enhance the image of the human resource department with specific estimates of future human resource needs, allowing human resource specialists to become more proactive and systematic.

FIGURE 3-6

A Partial Staffing Table for a City Government

Metropolis City Government Staffing Table

Date Compiled:

Budget Code Number	Job Title (as found on job description)	Using Department(s)	Anticipated Openings by Month of the Year												
			Total	1	2	3	4	5	6	7	8	9	10	11	12
100-32	Police Recruit	Police	128	32			32			32			32		
100-33	Police Dispatcher	Police	3	2					1						
100-84	Meter Reader	Police	24	2	2	2	2	2	2	2	2	2	2	2	2
100-85	Traffic Supervisor	Police	5	2			1			1			1		
100-86	Team Supervisor — Police (Sergeant)	Police	5	2			1			1			1		
100-97	Duty Supervisor — Police (Staff Sergeant)	Police	2	1					1						
100-99	Shift Officer— Police (Inspector)	Police	1	1											
200-01	Car Washer	Motor Pool	4	1			1			1			1		
200-12	Mechanic's Assistant	Motor Pool	3				1			1			1		
200-13	Mechanic III	Motor Pool	2	1									1		
200-14	Mechanic II	Motor Pool	1						1						
200-15	Mechanic I (Working Supervisor)	Motor Pool	1	1											
300-01	Clerk IV	Administration	27	10			5			6			6		

---

staffing table

A list of anticipated employment openings for each type of job.

For example, a review of Figure 3-6 shows that the city's human resource department must hire 32 police academy recruits every three months. This knowledge allows recruiters in the human resource department to plan their recruiting campaign so that it peaks about six weeks before the beginning of the next police academy class. The advanced planning allows the department to screen applicants and notify them at least three weeks before the class begins. For those still in school or otherwise unable to be ready that quickly, recruiters can inform them when the following class begins. If the human resource department waited for the police department to notify them, notification might come too late to allow a systematic recruiting and screening process. Staffing tables enable recruiters to be proactive and to better plan their activities.

LO4

The Supply of Human Resources

Once the human resource department makes projections about future human resource demands, the next major concern is filling projected openings. There are two sources of supply: internal and external. The internal supply consists of present employees who can be promoted, transferred, or demoted to meet anticipated needs.

> For example, Jean-Marie Gasse (to continue the example of Figure 3-6) works in the police department of Metropolis, but is applying for a transfer into the human resource department. She is part of the internal supply of human resources to the city government. The external supply consists of people in the labour market who do not work for the city. These include employees of other organizations and those who are unemployed.

Internal Supply Estimates

Estimating the internal supply involves more than merely counting the number of employees in an organization. Planners audit the present workforce to learn about the capabilities of present workers. This information allows planners to estimate tentatively which openings can be filled by present employees. These tentative assignments usually are recorded on a replacement chart. Considering present employees for future job openings is important if workers are to have careers with their employer and feel engaged. The patterns of employee transitions among jobs must be carefully assessed and taken into consideration. Audits, replacement charts, and employee transition matrices (more popularly called Markov analysis and discussed in detail below) also are important additions to the human resource department's information base. With greater knowledge of employees, the department can more effectively plan recruiting, training, and career-planning activities. A human resource department can also help meet its employment equity goals by identifying internal minority candidates for job openings.

Human Resource Audits

Human resource audits summarize the employee's knowledge skills, and abilities and generate skills and management and leadership inventories that, in turn, facilitate the preparation of a replacement chart and replacement summaries. Below is a brief discussion of skills inventories in the context of human resource planning.

Skills Inventories

An inventory catalogues the capabilities found in the organization's workforce. **Skills inventories** may be applied to both managerial and nonmanagerial roles.

skills inventories

Summaries of each worker's skills and abilities.

An example of a skills inventory is found in Figure 3-7. This example is divided into four parts. Part I can be completed by the human resource department from employee records. It identifies the employee's job title, experience, age, and previous jobs. Part II seeks information about skills, duties, responsibilities, and education of the worker. From these questions, planners learn about the mix of employee abilities. The human resource department may collect these data by phone or in face-to-face interviews. Or the questions may be sent to the employee through the company mail.

The employee's potential is briefly summarized by the immediate supervisor in Part III. Performance, readiness for promotion, and any deficiencies are noted here. Part IV is added as a final check for completeness and for the addition of recent employee evaluations, which give more insight into past performance.

To be useful, inventories of human resources must be updated periodically. Updating every two years is sufficient for most organizations if employees are encouraged to report major changes to the human resource department when they occur. Major changes include new skills, degree completions, changed job duties, and the like. Failure to update skills inventories can lead to present employees being overlooked for job openings within the organization and may create an inaccurate profile of the organization's available skills. As the average length of term employees have with a company decreases, managers may need to reconsider the length of time between refreshing information. To make the process easier and more efficient, inventories are being conducted more often electronically. For example, Cognology <http//www.cognology.com.au> has developed a digital skills audit platform.[19]

Some organizations are complementing skills audits with competency audits. As the nature of work continues to change, having a robust understanding of employees' competencies allows human resource managers to mitigate the risks associated with and under- or oversupply of human resources.

Management and Leadership Inventories

An audit of management talent is called **management or leadership inventory**. As in the case of skills inventories, these are comprehensive reports of available management and leadership capabilities in the organization. Like skills inventories, management inventories should be updated periodically, since they also are used for key human resource–related decisions. In fact, some employers use the same form for managers and nonmanagers. When the forms differ, the management inventory requests information about management activities. Common topics include:

management or leadership inventory

Comprehensive reports of available management capabilities in the organization.

- Number of employees supervised
- Types of employees supervised
- Total budget managed
- Management training received
- Duties of subordinates
- Previous management duties

FIGURE 3-7

Skills Inventory Form for Metropolis City Government

Part I (To be completed by human resource department)

1. Name _____   2. Employee Number _____

3. Job Title _____   4. Experience _____ years

5. Age _____   6. Years with City _____

7. Other Jobs Held:

With City: Title _____ From _____ to _____

Title _____ From _____ to _____

Elsewhere: Title _____ From _____ to _____

Title _____ From _____ to _____

Part II (To be completed by employee)

8. **Special Skills.** List below any skills you possess, even if they are not used in your present job. Include types and names of machines or tools with which you are experienced.

Skills _____

Machines _____

Tools _____

9. **Duties.** Briefly describe your present duties. _____
_____

10. **Responsibilities.** Briefly describe your responsibilities for:

City Equipment: _____

City Funds: _____

Employee Safety: _____

Employee Supervision: _____

11. **Education.** Briefly describe your education and training background:

	Years Completed	**Year of Graduation**	**Degree and Major**
High School:	_____	_____	_____
University:	_____	_____	_____
Job Training:	_____	_____	_____
Special Courses:	_____	_____	_____

Part III (To be completed by human resource department with supervisory inputs)

12. Overall Evaluation of Performance _____

13. Overall Readiness for Promotion _____

To What Job(s): _____

Comments: _____

14. Current Deficiencies:
_____

15. Supervisor's Signature _____ Date: _____

Part IV (To be completed by human resource department representative)

16. Are the two most recent performance evaluations attached? _____ Yes _____ No

17. Prepared by _____ Date: _____

Recently, a great deal of attention has been paid to the domain of talent management. Understanding who in an organization may be transferred into a management or leadership role is a fundamental component of talent management. In some organizations, leaders at all levels are issued leadership profiles such as the Leadership Practice Inventory (LPI).[20] By accumulating information on employees' leadership behaviours, organizations are able to more accurately identify who from within the organization may be suitable to be put in a leadership role.

Replacement Charts

Replacement charts are a visual representation of who will replace whom in the event of a job opening. The information for constructing the chart comes from the human resource audit. Figure 3-8 illustrates a typical replacement chart. It shows the replacement status of only a few jobs in the administration of a large city.

replacement charts

Visual representations of who will replace whom when a job opening occurs.

FIGURE 3-8

A Partial Replacement Chart for a Municipal Government

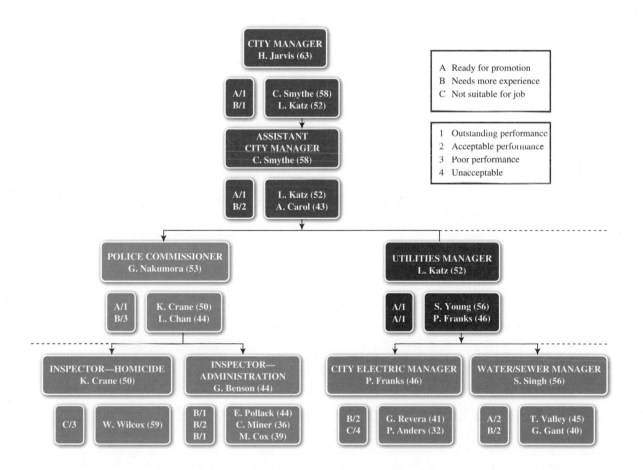

As mandatory retirement gets abolished, it becomes increasingly unnecessary to include age in replacement charts. It may, however, be desirable to gather retirement intentions to facilitate long-term planning.

Although different firms may seek to summarize different information in their replacement charts, the figure indicates the minimum information usually included or needed. The chart, which is much like an organization chart, depicts the various jobs in the organization and shows the status of likely candidates. Replacement status consists of two variables: present performance and promotability. Present performance is determined largely from supervisory evaluations. Opinions of other managers, peers, and subordinates may contribute to the appraisal of present performance. Future promotability is based primarily on present performance and the estimates by immediate superiors of future success in a new job. The human resource department may contribute to these estimates through the use of psychological tests, interviews, and other methods of assessment.

Human resource and management decision makers find these charts provide a quick reference. Their shortcoming is that they are built on the assumption that the organizational structure is quite static. They also contain little information.[21] To address the lack of information, replacement summaries may be prepared as discussed next.

Replacement Summaries

To supplement the chart—and, increasingly, to supplant it—human resource specialists develop **replacement summaries**. Replacement summaries list likely replacements and their relative strengths and weaknesses for each job. As Figure 3-9 shows, the summaries provide considerably more data than the replacement chart. This additional information allows decision makers to make more informed decisions.

---

replacement summaries

Lists of likely replacements for each job and their relative strengths and weaknesses.

Transition Matrices and Markov Analysis

Markov analysis is a fairly simple method of predicting the internal supply of human resources in the future. This is particularly useful in organizations where employees move from one job (or rank) to another on a regular basis. It is also useful in organizations where jobs do not fluctuate rapidly due to external (e.g., technological) or internal (e.g., strategic) change.

Markov analysis

Forecast of a firm's future human resource supplies, using transitional probability matrices reflecting historical or expected movements of employees across jobs.

Markov analysis reflects the patterns in these human resource movements using **transition matrices**. A transition matrix describes the probabilities of an incumbent staying in his or her present job for the forecast time period (usually one year), moving to another job position in the organization, or leaving the organization. When this matrix is multiplied by the number of employees in each job at the beginning of a year, the forecaster is easily able to identify the number of persons who will remain in the job at the end of the year.

---

transition matrices

Describe the probabilities of how quickly a job position turns over and what an incumbent employee may do over a forecast period of time, such as stay in the current position, move to another position within the firm, or accept a job in another organization.

FIGURE 3-9

A Replacement Summary for the Position of City Manager

Replacement Summary for the Position of City Manager			
Present Office Holder Harold Jarvis		**Age**	63
Probable Opening In two years		**Reason**	Retirement
Salary Grade 99 ($86,000)		**Experience**	8 years
Candidate 1	Clyde Smythe		
Current Position	Assistant City Manager		
Current Performance	Outstanding	**Explanation** Clyde's performance evaluations by the City Manager are always the highest possible.	
Promotability	Ready now for promotion	**Explanation** During an extended illness of the City Manager, Clyde assumed all duties successfully, including major policy decisions and negotiations with city unions.	
Training Needs	None		
Age	58		
Experience	4 years		
Candidate 2	Larry Katz		
Current Position	Utilities Manager		
Current Performance	Outstanding	**Explanation** Larry's performance has kept costs of utilities to citizens 10 to 15 percent below that of comparable city utilities through careful planning.	
Promotability	Needs more experience	**Explanation** Larry's experience is limited to utilities management. Although successful, he needs more broad administrative experience in other areas. (He is ready for promotion to Assistant City Manager at this time.)	
Training Needs	Training in budget preparation and public relations would be desirable before promotion to City Manager.		
Age	52		
Experience	5 years		

Figure 3-10 shows a sample transition matrix. It indicates that 80 percent (or 0.8) of the incumbents in Job A remain in their present position at the end of the year, 10 percent (or 0.1) move to Job B, 5 percent (or 0.05) more to Job C, none to Job D, and 5 percent (or 0.05) leave the organization (through resignations or otherwise). When these probabilities are multiplied by the number of persons in Job A at the beginning of the year (namely, 200), we see that 160 of them remain in their present position, 20 of them move to Job B, 10 of them move to Job C, and the remaining 10 leave the organization. When similar calculations are performed for all the jobs (in the case of this firm, for Jobs A, B, C, and D), we are able to predict the approximate number of employees who will remain in each job position.

Many firms use the previous year's transition rates for predicting next year's movements. However, if the previous year was atypical, the predictions may be erroneous. [22] Markov analysis is popular because of the ease of its use. However, it is only as good as the transition probabilities used. The probabilities are not very reliable if there are only a few incumbents in each job. Generally, Markov analysis works best if there are at least 50 employees in each job position. [23] This makes it more appropriate only for medium-sized and large organizations.

FIGURE 3-10

An Example of Markov Analysis

(a) Transition Probability Matrix

Year Beginning			Year End		
	Job A	Job B	Job C	Job D	Exit
Job A	0.80	0.10	0.05	0.00	0.05
Job B	0.10	0.70	0.00	0.10	0.10
Job C	0.00	0.00	0.90	0.05	0.05
Job D	0.00	0.00	0.00	0.90	0.10

(b) Expected Movements of Employees

	Initial Staffing Level	Job A	Job B	Job C	Job D	Exit
Job A	200	160	20	10	0	10
Job B	70	7	49	0	7	7
Job C	60	0	0	54	3	3
Job D	100	0	0	0	90	10
Predicted End-of-the-Year Staffing Level		167	69	64	100	30

Markov analysis can also be used speculatively to assess the impact of possible changes in transition analysis. Thus, "what if" analyses can be undertaken to understand the impact of possible future scenarios. For example, "What if the quit rate for Job A doubles from its present 6 percent per year?" This makes it a useful tool for human resource forecasting, especially in the context of strategic planning.

External Supply Estimates

Not every future opening can be met with present employees. Some jobs lack replacements to fill an opening when it occurs. Other jobs are entry-level positions; that is, they are beginning jobs that are filled by people who do not presently work for the organization. When there are no replacements or when the opening is for an entry-level job, there is a need for external supplies of human resources.

When estimating external supplies, three major factors must be examined: trends in the labour market, community attitudes, and demographic trends. These are briefly outlined below.

Labour Market Analysis

The human resource department's success in finding new employees depends on an accurate **labour market analysis**. Even when unemployment rates are high, many needed skills are difficult to find. This is a key distinction for human resource managers. A labour market analysis defines the people potentially available for work. A skills market, however, narrows the available people to those that have the appropriate skill set.

labour market analysis

The study of a firm's labour market to evaluate the present or future availability of different types of workers.

In the short run, the national unemployment rate serves as an approximate measure of how difficult it is to acquire new employees. Human resource specialists realize that this rate varies for different groups, as well as from province to province and city to city. A couple of regional differences were highlighted in Chapter 1.

A significant challenge with using employment rates as a measure of potential employee recruitment opportunities is that it represents only a moment in time. That is, it provides a measure of how many people are unemployed during a certain historical period. It does not identify what the future looks like. To address this shortcoming, some jurisdictions have undertaken an analysis to determine what the future supply and demand is for specific occupations.

> The province of Alberta conducts analyses on both a short-term basis and long-term basis. The Alberta's short-term employment forecast analysis predicts surplus or undersupply of potential employees in Alberta over a three year period for a series of jobs types.[24] The same province conducts a longer-term analysis that predicts labour markets in Alberta through to 2023.[25]

Regardless of the unemployment rate or regional demand outlook, external needs may be met by attracting employees who work for others or in other regions. In some professions—such as teachers and engineers—labour mobility between provinces is quite high.[26] In other industries, such as the infrastructure trades professional, there is less mobility relative to university graduates.[27]

In the long run, local developments and demographic trends have the most significant impact on labour markets. Local developments include community growth rates and attitudes.

> For example, many farm towns find their population declining. When they attempt to attract new business, employers fear that a declining population may mean future shortages in the local labour market. So the new businesses often locate elsewhere.[28]

The lack of jobs results in still more people leaving the local labour market. This is particularly so in the case of minorities and other disadvantaged groups of society.

During a recessionary period, the job prospects of minorities and new immigrants are more adversely affected. One estimate shows that immigrants lose their jobs at more than three times the rate of Canadian-born workers. In the Toronto region, almost 50 percent of residents are born outside Canada, which means that what happens to their jobs can have a profound impact on the overall economy.[29]

While people move across labour markets, language and cultural barriers may often act as deterrents. Sometimes, migrants from other areas may receive a hostile welcome in the local labour market as happened in Saint John, New Brunswick:

> When contract workers from Alberta were brought in to Saint John to build a new storage tank for a New Brunswick energy project, the local residents were furious at what they viewed as carpetbaggers taking scarce jobs. Protesters massed repeatedly outside the hotel where the migrant workers stayed despite a police injunction that they keep their distance from the new arrivals.[30]

A strong source of external workers for Canadian employers is the Canadian Temporary Foreign Worker Program.[31] This program came under scrutiny in 2014 and was overhauled to ensure that employers were putting Canadian workers first in their hiring decisions.[32]

Community Attitudes

Community attitudes also affect the nature of the labour market. Anti-business or nongrowth attitudes may cause present employers to move elsewhere. An example of this is activist investing.

In 2013, an activist investor group tried to break apart Agrium—a Calgary-based fertilizer company—into its wholesale and retail businesses. This action would have divided Agrium into two companies and would likely have had a dramatic effect on the employee pool.[33]

The loss of jobs forces middle-class workers to relocate, and the shrinking workforce discourages new businesses from becoming established.

Demographic Trends

Chapter 1 provided a detailed account of a number of demographic influences on an organization. Demographic trends are another long-term development that affects the availability of external supply. Fortunately for planners, these trends are known years in advance of their impact. Two examples serve to illustrate:

Consider a recent research study released by the Information and Communication Technology Council. They found that a major technology labour crunch is looming in Canada. The study predicted that there will be 106,000 openings in the next five years in the Information and Technology sector and the study highlights the specific skills sets needed.[34] Driven by baby boom retirements, the lack of hiring during the recent recession, and the significant changes in technology requirements, there exists a major shortage for these types of skills.

Another example relates to the shipping industry. A worldwide shortage of ship officers is forecast to reach 27,000 as fewer people enter this industry. A career at sea is not one that most people aspire to and, as a result, this industry is experiencing a staffing shortage. Finding ways to attract people to merchant marine careers is very difficult. There are programs that offer courses such as the Marine Institute in St. John's, Newfoundland, as well as distance learning programs focusing on nautical science. The industry itself has developed robust career paths for individuals who want to pursue a career in this field.[35]

There are several sources of information available to planners. For example, major sources of data are Statistics Canada <http//www.statcan.gc.ca> and Employment and Social Development Canada (EDSC) <http://www.esdc.gc.ca>. The latter also offers a job futures program. Another source of information is the Conference Board of Canada <http://www.conferenceboard.ca/>, which generates excellent research reports on many other HR related topics.

Statistics Canada publishes reports on labour force conditions on a monthly, quarterly, annual, and occasional basis. Information available on total labour force projections includes geographic, demographic, and occupational variables, and labour income, census data, and population projections by sex and province over various years.

The **Canadian Occupational Projection System (COPS)** was designed by Employment and Social Development Canada. The COPS provides a highly detailed projection of the Canadian economy up to 10 years in the future.[36]

Canadian Occupational Projection System (COPS)
Provides up to 10-year projection of Canadian economy and human resource needs.

Job Bank <http://www.jobbank.gc.ca/> is a group of products available from ESDC that identifies trends in the world of work. It outlines job outlooks by occupation as well as by field of study, and estimates the prospect of finding jobs in a specific occupation or field in a specific location. Job Bank provides Canadians with the latest information available about work—information that is important for anyone in the process of making decisions or advising others in the area of career planning.

For example, Job Bank forecasts that the chance of finding work as a registered nurse in Edmonton, Alberta, and Kenora, Ontario, is very strong. Of note, however, it also identifies the average wage in Edmonton is $41.00/hour whereas the rate in Kenora is $34.00/hour.

Figure 3-11 provides a summary of the HR tools used to estimate internal and external supply of labour.

FIGURE 3-11

Summary of HR Tools Used to Estimate Internal and External Supply of Labour

Internal Supply Indicators	External Supply Indicators
• Human Resource Audits	• Labour market analysis
• Skill inventories	• Community attitudes
• Management inventories	• Demographic trends
• Replacement charts/summaries	
• Transition matrices & Markov analysis	

HR Objectives

The identification of supply and demand forecasts and summaries only provides the human resource professional with context and information. It does not address the process by which any gaps can be addressed. As such, the next step in the process identifies what the organization expects to accomplish as a result of its actions. It directs the planning process of the organization, identifies what the planner will do to achieve its goals, and sets a baseline to determine whether the organization has achieved its goals. For example, if the organization's strategy were to grow its market share by 20 percent, the HR objective would be to add a certain number of "headcount" with a certain set of skills by a predetermined date. However, if the organization's objective is to reduce labour costs by 20 percent, then the objective might be to reduce the workforce in each department by 5 percent by a certain date, carefully taking into account the preservation of individuals with critical skills sets and significant ongoing potential. Once these objectives are identified, then the planner can decide what specific HR programs and strategies will be appropriate.

LO5

HRM Strategies to Achieve Objectives in Supply and Demand

Typically, human resource planners face two decision situations: they find that the available supply of human resources is either less or greater than their future needs. It is only the rare fortunate planner who finds that the supply and demand are equal. Each of the above two situations requires somewhat different corrective actions, which are discussed below.

Strategies to Manage an Oversupply of Human Resources

When the internal supply of workers exceeds the firm's demand, a human resource surplus exists. There are various strategies that HR can consider. We can group each of these strategies under three main headings: headcount reduction, attrition, and work arrangements.

Headcount Reduction

Here are four main ways to ensure a headcount reduction: layoffs, leaves without pay, incentives for voluntary separation, and termination.

Layoffs

Layoffs, the temporary withdrawal of employment to workers, are used in cases of a short-run surplus. Layoffs are the separation of employees from the organization for economic or business reasons. The separation may last only a few weeks if its purpose is to adjust inventory levels or to allow the factory to retool for a new product. When caused by a business cycle, the layoffs may last many months or even years. However, if the layoff is the result of restructuring or rescaling of an industry, the "temporary" layoffs may be permanent.

As unpleasant as layoffs are for both workers and management, they may be required when attrition (see below) is insufficient to reduce employment to acceptable levels. In some organizations, each employee who is laid off may receive a supplemental employment benefit over and above government EI benefits. However, during severe economic downturns, the employer's ability to provide these benefits may be seriously jeopardized.

While the terms of a collective agreement dictate layoff procedures in unionized settings, nonunion employers may have to consider other factors or be exposed to constructive dismissal claims.

> For example, in Ontario, the province's Employment Standards Act permits a temporary layoff of an employee without pay for up to 13 weeks in a consecutive 20-week period. If the unpaid layoff exceeds that period, it will no longer be deemed "temporary" and the employer will become liable for reasonable notice and severance pay, if applicable.[37]

When the layoffs are expected to be of a short duration—as when an automobile plant temporarily closes to change its tooling for a new model—layoffs may not follow the normal pattern of forcing the most recently hired employees to accept unemployment. Rather than following seniority, some contracts have "juniority" clauses. Juniority provisions require that layoffs be offered first to senior workers. If the senior worker wants to accept the layoff, that person collects employment insurance and the other organizational benefits and the juniors keep their jobs. Senior workers are likely to accept layoffs of short duration because they receive almost the same take-home pay without working. When the layoff is of an unknown duration, the seniors usually decline to exercise their juniority rights and fewer senior employees are put on layoff.

Leave without Pay

One way to temporarily reduce the number of employees on the payroll is to give them an opportunity to take a leave of absence without pay either to attend college or university or to pursue other personal interests. Employees who are offered this leave are usually those who are financially able to leave the organization for a little while and whose jobs may be eliminated in the future. Thus, this strategy might help some employees to prepare for oncoming changes.

Incentives for Voluntary Separation

Sometimes organizations decide to offer employees some form of an "enticement" to leave the organization early. This practice is referred to as a "buyout." At one large telecom during the recession, employees were offered a buyout. It was called "Voluntary Severance Package" (VSP) and contained a cash bonus, bridging for one's pension, and outplacement services.

Termination

Termination is a broad term that encompasses the permanent separation from the organization for any reason. Usually this term implies that the employee was fired as a form of discipline. When employees are discharged for business or economic reasons, it is commonly, although not always, called a layoff. Sometimes, however, the employer needs to separate some employees for business reasons and has no plans to rehire them. Rather than being laid off, those workers are simply terminated.

The blow of discharge may be softened through formal **outplacement** procedures, which help present employees find new jobs with other firms These efforts may include the provision of office space, secretarial services, photocopying machines, long-distance phone calls, counselling, instructions of how to look for work, and even invitations to competitors to meet with employees. Not only do such efforts help the former employee, but they also give evidence to the remaining employees of management's commitment to their welfare.

outplacement

Assisting employees to find jobs with other employers.

Attrition Strategies

Attrition is the normal separation of employees from an organization as a result of *resignation, retirement,* or *death.* It is initiated by the individual worker and not by the company. In most organizations, the key component of attrition is resignation, which is a voluntary separation. Although attrition is a slow way to reduce the employment base in an organization, it presents the fewest problems. Voluntary departures simply create a vacancy that is not filled and the staffing level declines without anyone being forced out of a job. Two common attrition strategies are hiring freeze and early and phased retirement offers.

attrition

Loss of employees due to their voluntary departures from the firm through resignation, retirement, or death.

Hiring Freeze

Most employers initially respond to a surplus with a hiring freeze. This freeze stops the human resource department from filling openings with external applicants. Instead, present employees are reassigned.

> Faced with a drop in heavy oil commodity prices in early 2015, Suncor cut 1,000 jobs and announced a hiring freeze.[38]

Early and Phased Retirement Offers

A special form of attrition is *early retirement*. It is one form of separation that the human resource department can actively control. It is used to reduce staffing levels and to create internal job openings. Early retirement plans are designed to encourage long-service workers to retire before the normal retirement age in the organization (say, 65 years). Since employees who retire before age 65 will draw benefits longer, their monthly retirement benefits may be reduced proportionately.

Some companies are allowing older employees to reduce their work activity and gradually *phase into* retirement without loss or reduction of pension benefits. The most typical pattern in **phased retirement** is to allow gradually shortened workweeks, a preferred schedule among older workers according to some surveys.[39] Most companies in the survey required that an employee first work a minimum of five years in the firm and be at least 55 years old in order to participate in a phased retirement program, and over half allowed employees to later change their minds. An example of phased retirement is provided by McGill University:

phased retirement

Gradual phase into retirement with loss or reduction of pension benefits.

> McGill University <http://www.mcgill.ca> in Montreal offers its faculty members a pre-retirement package that allows a faculty member to choose to teach only half of his or her normal teaching load for 65 percent of the salary. This assumes that faculty members will still carry on with their normal administrative work, e.g., attending department and other committee meetings and being available for student counselling.[40]

Alternative Work Arrangements

If the headcount of employees is not to change, other options are to adjust the work term either by reducing the number of work hours by using part time workers, job sharing, transferring employees where resources are needed, or loaning employees to other organizations.

Job Sharing

Reducing the number of total work hours through **job sharing** is the first of the above options to adjust the work term. Job sharing, also called *job splitting*, involves dividing duties of a single position between two or more employees. From the employer's perspective, this eliminates the need to lay off one employee completely. But the employees also benefit by having more free time at their disposal and maintain employment.

---

job sharing

A plan whereby available work is spread among all workers in a group to reduce the extent of layoffs when production requirements cause a substantial decline in available work.

"It makes good business sense for us to offer work sharing," says Norma Tombari, Director of Global Diversity, about the Royal Bank of Canada's work and family program. "We get to recruit and keep good employees, and our customers benefit because employees who feel the company is supporting them provide better service." The program is particularly popular with the female employees of the bank. Women constitute a large percentage of RBC's workforce.[41]

Work sharing programs are also used to avoid layoffs. A major initiative is the federal work sharing program administered by ESDC. It allows employees to voluntarily reduce their hours to spread available work around.[42]

The major advantage claimed for job sharing is increased productivity from workers who are not fatigued. Problems arise from the increased paperwork and administrative burden associated with two employees doing the job of one. Another problem is that of benefits. Human resource specialists are forced to decide whether job sharers should be given benefits equal with other employees or benefits that are scaled down in proportion to the employee's hours.[43]

Using Part-Time Employees

Eliminating full-time positions and replacing them with part-time positions, thus reducing the total work hours and labour costs, is another strategy used in several settings.

Since part-timers earn only a fraction of the salary earned by full-time employees, employers find it economical to use part-time employees.[44]

Very often, **part-time employees** are paid no benefits. The significant decrease in total benefit costs, especially health care and pensions, provides a great incentive for employers to make more use of regular *part-time work*, defined as "less than full-time work by employees on a company's regular payroll."[45] Employers that do pay benefits tend to be in the public sector, such as health care facilities and municipal governments. Another advantage of part-time work is that it increases flexibility so that employers can match the workforce with peak demands. Part-time employment is also popular for a few other reasons, such as the following:

- The growing number of women in the labour force, with a preference for part-time positions
- The higher demand in the service industries, which employ more than 40 percent of all part-timers[46]
- The need for cost-cutting

---

part-time employees

Persons working fewer than the required hours for categorization as full-time workers and who are ineligible for many supplementary benefits offered by employers.

Part-time work has public costs. Part-time employees have limited entitlement to government-run employment insurance and disability benefits, resulting in potentially serious financial problems should they be unable to work. Without disability benefits they have no income and may end up on the welfare rolls. In some settings, converting full-time to part-time work may be fraught with legal challenges as well.

Some employers have recognized the hidden costs of using a part-time workforce and begun to move in the opposite direction. Consider Loblaws's example:

> Canada's largest grocery chain, Loblaws <http://www.loblaws.ca>, was planning to convert about 10 percent of its part-time workforce to create 10,000 full-time jobs. The organization felt that this move would benefit not only the organization by improving employee morale and loyalty, but also the local economy overall. Management felt that the additional costs incurred by the company in creating the full-time jobs would be more than offset by the improvement in customer service, reduction in labour turnover, and improvement in overall productivity.[47]

Strategies to Manage Shortages of Employees

A **labour shortage** occurs when there is not enough qualified talent to fill the demand for labour and organizations cannot fill their open positions. A skill shortage refers to specific skills that the organization requires. It occurs when the demand for workers with specific skills exceeds the available supply of workers with these specialized skills.

---

labour shortage

Insufficient supply of qualified talent to fill the demand for labour.

Organizations that are effective at HR planning utilize a variety of staffing strategies to ensure that they have the right people with the right skills at the right place and at the right time to do the right things. There are several staffing options available to choose from depending on the sense of urgency, economic conditions, and productivity gains. The staffing options to consider are: to hire employees, contract out the work to another firm, develop existing employees, and leverage existing work arrangements. A summary of these options is shown below in Figure 3-12.

FIGURE 3-12

Alternative Staffing Strategies

Hire Employees	Source Service Providers	Develop Employees Internally	Existing Work Arrangements
• Full-time • Part-time	• Independent contractor • Third party • Outsource • Crowdsource	• Replacement charts • Succession planning • Career development • Float & transfer	• Overtime • Flexible schedules • Flexible time and location • Flex policies

Hire Employees

One way to address a labour shortage is simply to hire an employee to fill the open position. However, whether to hire a full-time or part-time employee, or to hire an internal or an external candidate, is an important decision that managers make. A more fulsome discussion of the hiring process is found later in the text.

Full-Time Employees

For several positions hiring **full-time employees** is the only alternative. This may be the case for key roles such as the CEO. Many organizations are averse to this strategy since it incurs additional fixed costs. Hiring full-time staff also requires a more detailed look at their competencies in terms of the organization's long-term strategies.

Some organizations have sought to mitigate some of the risk of hiring full-time employees by bringing them on first as probationary employees. These employees are hired on a full-time basis, but can be released from the organization at any time during their probationary period for any reason. This enables organizations to more effectively assess the skill set of a full-time employee before committing indefinitely to them.[48]

---

full-time employees

Work 37.5 to 40 hours in a workweek.

Part-Time Employees

An increasingly popular strategy for meeting human resource needs is to use part-time employees. Part-time employees are an attractive option to the employer since it adds flexibility in scheduling. Traditionally, part-timers have been employed by service businesses such as restaurants and retail stores that experience considerable fluctuation in demand during peak and off-peak times. However, more recently, many firms, after a downsizing or restructuring, employ part-timers to provide services that had previously been offered by full timers.

> For example, in the past, United Parcel Service <http://www.ups.com/> created 25-hour-per-week part-time jobs for shipping clerks and supervisors who sort packages at its distribution centres. Until the change, full-time staff carried out the same jobs.

Employment of part-timers reduces overall payroll costs since part-timers are, typically, not eligible for several of the expensive benefits offered to the full-time workforce. However, there are variations across provinces and the human resource manager should carefully check the legal requirements before introducing new policies. For example, Saskatchewan has extended a number of benefits to part-time workers under specific conditions:

> In Saskatchewan, a full-time employee is anyone who works 30 hours or more per week. All businesses with 10 or more full-time equivalent employees must provide benefits to eligible part-time employees. To qualify, part-time employees must have been employed for 26 consecutive weeks and have worked 390 hours in those 26 weeks. To maintain eligibility, the employee should work for at least 780 hours in a calendar year. Eligible benefits include dental plans, group life, accidental death or dismemberment plans, and prescription drug plans.[49]

Contract Out the Work

The next alternative that organizations may consider to manage a labour shortage is to enter into a service agreement with a **contract (or contingent) worker**. A contract worker is a freelancer who is not part of the regular workforce and who provides goods or services to another entity under the terms of a specific contract. Contractors are not employees of an organization. They are governed under contract law, not employment legislation. The contractor typically invoices the organization and the organization pays for these services via the accounting function. The contractor's "contract" ends when his services, that he had agreed to provide, are complete and the services have been delivered. On occasion, organizations will choose to engage a "consultant." **Consultants**, by definition, are professionals who provide expert advice and counsel in a particular area.

---

contract (or contingent) worker

A freelancer (self-employed, temporary, or leased employee) who is not part of the regular workforce who provides goods or services to another entity under the terms of a specific contract.

---

consultants

Professionals who provide expert advice and counsel in a particular area.

Contractors determine their own work hours, typically have their own offices, and can work on multiple contracts at the same time. They can hire other persons to perform the work, they are not eligible for benefits, and they provide their own equipment and supplies. Revenue Canada has provided a number of tests that can be used to determine whether someone is a contractor. They are strict and assess companies' practices to ensure that the relationship is arm's length. The tests are related to control, ownership of tools, chance of profit, and risk of loss and payment (see Figure 3-13).

FIGURE 3-13

Five Key Tests to Determine Contractor/Employee Status

Control	• Is the person under the direction and control of another with respect to the time the person works, where the person works. and the way in which the work is done?
	• The greater the control, the more likely the person is an employee. The contractor determines the result. As an employee, the employer has the right to determine the way the task is carried out.
Ownership of Tools	• Does the person use the tools, space, supplies, and/or equipment owned by someone else? If so, this may be an indicator.
	• Contractors supply their own tools.
Profit	• Does the person make a profit?
	• If the person profits, then he could be a contractor. If the person's income is the difference between the cost of providing the service and the price charged, then the person is deemed an independent contractor.
Risk of Loss	• An employee has no risk of loss.
	• If the person risks losing money if the cost of doing the job is more than the price charged, then she can be considered to have contractor status.
Payment	• If the person receives payments at regular intervals regardless of customer satisfaction, then she may be an employee.

Outsourcing

The term outsourcing has been used extensively in the past decade. **Outsourcing** work refers to a formal agreement an organization makes with a third party to perform a service rather than using internal resources. Outsourcing or "contracting out" work is typically associated with work that is *non-core* to that organization and one where the outsourcing firm has special skills, technology, and expertise to manage this work. Outsourcing is a business decision made by executives, not human resource planners. It allows the organization to save money, improve quality, or free company resources for other activities so that the organization can focus on those activities that it does best. A subset of the term (*off shoring*) also implies transferring jobs to another country, either by hiring local subcontractors or building a facility in an area where labour is cheap.

outsourcing

Contracting tasks to outside agencies or persons.

A recent trend has been for firms to outsource some of their HR related functions.

In an effort to manage costs and focus on its core competencies, Bank of Montreal (BMO) decided to outsource its human resource processing functions to alleviate its administrative burden and utilize the technologies of the outsourcing firm. The agreement between BMO and Exult Inc. (purchased in 2004 by Hewitt Associates) was valued at $750 million over ten years and made about 250 HR positions redundant.[50]

Human resource management plays a significant role when HR is outsourced. It must focus on service delivery and ensure that the transition is seamless. Ultimately, human resource management has direct responsibility for service quality and results and it must manage the vendor to ensure that the service is value added and business objectives are met.

Crowdsourcing—A Novel Way to "Source Talent"

Crowdsourcing is a new term which describes a novel way for companies to meet their resource requirements. It is an action taken by a company that takes a function once performed by employees and outsources it to an undefined (and generally large) network of people in the form of an open call.

---

crowdsourcing

The act of a company or institution taking a function once performed by employees and outsourcing it to an undefined (and generally large) network of people in the form of an open call.

In this model, the organization has a need for human resources. It then communicates this need to the public via the Internet. It is an *open call* to interested parties on the web who decide, based on their own interests and their own time, whether they want to help the organization with its problem, provide a service, or fill the need in some way. There exists a large network of potential labour. These individuals use their time to help the company solve their problems. The work is done outside the traditional company walls. If the organization feels that the contribution is valuable, the organization will pay the contributors for their efforts in some way.

In outsourcing, the organization typically sends out a formal *Request for Proposal (RFP)* and it reviews potential vendors before deciding on the best one. Typically, lower paid professionals do the work itself. In crowdsourcing, the problem is communicated through the net for those individuals who are interested to respond.

The main advantage of crowdsourcing is that innovative ideas can be explored at relatively low cost. Furthermore, it also helps reduce costs and makes use of the *crowd* to communicate its requirements.

> Rather than hiring a specific creative artist, Skyreader Media Inc. is a Toronto-based interactive production studio that plans to use crowdsourcing to generate ideas for characters in a new online interactive emagazine in partnership with Disney.[51]

Developing Employees Internally

Another option to be considered, which can address a shortage in human capital, looks at leveraging the current supply of existing employees within an organization. This option considers the strength of an organization's internal workforce with respect to the skills and knowledge employees possess and the future skills and knowledge employees will need for the organization to meet its human capital requirements. Organizations use various mechanisms such as promotions and replacement charts and succession and career plans to ascertain employees' interests, the types of training and development required, and when employees will be ready to fill a future labour requirement. Organizations utilize their internal HR related processes to facilitate these activities, optimizing their human resources' talent pool. Chapter 7 will discuss this option in more detail.

Creating Flexible Work Arrangements

The last staffing option focuses on the various types of work arrangements. A **work arrangement** refers to a firm's use of work hours, schedules, and location to ensure that the goals of the organization and the needs of employees are optimally met. We will be discussing three types of arrangements: overtime, flexible retirement, and float and transfer.

---

work arrangement

A firm's use of work hours, schedules, and location to ensure that the goals of the organization and the needs of employees are optimally met.

These types of arrangements are all based on *choices*: the organization can make a choice to offer these options to the employees and the employees make a choice whether to accept. In this reciprocal relationship, both the employer and employees typically receive a benefit as a result. For example, if employees agree to overtime, then they will receive money or time off in lieu, and the organization will be able to meets its staffing shortage.

Overtime

A popular strategy is to ask existing employees to work beyond the normal hours. Indeed, even during a non-shortage situation, regular overtime has become a fact of life in many firms that do not want to incur additional fixed expenses of hiring permanent employees.

In many organizations, employees—especially, supervisory and managerial staff—are expected to work overtime, most of it unpaid. The culture of the organization requires the employee to put in the extra effort without expecting any reward. This is particularly so in non-unionized settings.

Higher employee fatigue, stress levels, accident and wastage rates, and so on, are some of the unwanted consequences of using overtime on a recurring basis. Recognizing this fact, some progressive employers have gone against the mainstream—namely reducing the number of work hours—and ended up improving their productivity levels and competitiveness in the labour market. One U.S. manufacturer's experience is noteworthy:

Metro Plastics Technologies Inc. <http://www.metroplastics.com> in Columbus, Indiana, could not fill eight vacancies in its plant as the unemployment rate in the area hovered between one and three percent. To get a recruiting advantage, it adopted an innovative "30-hour work week for 40-hour pay" strategy under which an employee had to put in only 30 hours a week instead of the traditional 40 hours. A single newspaper ad brought hundreds of qualified applicants to the firm and the firm was able to fill the vacancies immediately. The benefits did not stop there. Within two years, customer returns had fallen by 72 percent and many internal costs had dropped dramatically. The same results have been reported in a number of other plants, in a variety of industries.[52]

Flexible Retirements

Another opportunity for firms to manage shortages is to target those employees who are close to retirement with a view to extending their contributions. The challenge has been how to balance the needs of these employees with the needs of the organization. A relatively new approach to managing retirement is called **flexible retirement**. This term has been used to describe a novel approach to optimizing the talent of these recent retirees, thus extending their contributions and continuing their engagement in organizational activities. Called "retiree-return" programs, these programs provide retirees with the opportunity to work after they have retired and provide them with significant flexibility in terms of how they work, what they work on, when they work, and where. These programs are flexible in the sense that they take into account the retirees' needs and tailor the work accordingly. These programs typically begin prior to retirement and continue after the employee has *officially* retired. One can say that these retirees take on an *active* retiree status, whereby they continue their involvement in the organizations long after they have *officially* retired.

---

flexible retirement

Programs that provide retirees with the opportunity to work after they have retired and provide them with significant flexibility in terms of how they work, what they work on, when they work, and where.

The benefits are substantial as the organization will be able to retain its intellectual capital long after employees have *left* the organization. The firm will be able to retain its talent to fill unexpected gaps, institutional knowledge and transfer of this knowledge will not be lost, and the organization will be able to control its labour costs, as *retirees* do not receive any additional benefits. It is projected that phased retirement programs will double over over the next several years, from 26 to 55 percent. In a recent William Mercer study, 23 percent of the companies surveyed had some form of program to provide mature workers with flexibility.[53]

Float and Transfer

Another flexible arrangement that organizations use to manage shifts in work is to use a flexible policy that enables its full-time resources to be transferred when needed, or, if the need is for a very short time, they *float* the worker. These organizations rely on their training programs to ensure that their employees are cross-trained and that they can secure these resources when they need them and for the length of time. Another term that we can use to describe this arrangement is *job rotation*. For example, Capital One <http://www.capitalone.ca> used this arrangement when it had significant demand in its payment processing area. Employees who normally worked in other areas were deployed to work in the payment processing area when the demand increased.[54]

Arrangements such as the above not only enhance organizational flexibility and efficiency and help reduce costs, but also enable human resource departments to better respond to employee needs. To ensure that HR is actually achieving these goals, evaluation and measurement must be an integral part of the HRP process.

Spotlight *on* ETHICS

Cutting Costs

Like other human resource management activities, HR planners often face ethical challenges. Consider the following two situations and respond to them. Once you have written down your answers, compare them with those of your team or classmates. Are there differences in your approaches? What facts and arguments seem to justify one action over the other?

Facing fierce price-based competition, your firm, which employs over 470 persons, has been trying to reduce costs in a variety of ways.

1. One action currently being considered is to move Production Unit 1 from its present location in an interior Canadian town to a developing country. Your manufacturing unit is the sole employer in that town and currently employs 128 persons. Most of the employees are semi-skilled and would find it hard to find employment elsewhere immediately. You know that in the case of many employees, they are the sole breadwinner for their families. Your firm located in this town because of a variety of tax advantages and subsidies the province offered to you for the first two years of your operations. Under those terms, your firm was expected to operate for a minimum period of four years. This is your sixth year in the province.

2. Your firm is also considering converting a number of your full-time employees in the head office and Production Unit 2 to a part-time workforce (You may assume that this is legal in the province where you are employed). Approximately 200 persons will be affected by this plan. This can generate significant savings for your firm, since a number of benefits currently offered to full-time employees need not be offered any more to the part-timers. You realize that a number of your employees depend on the company benefits to take care of their children and the elderly in the family.

Program Measurement and Evaluation

A major goal of human resource measurement is to enhance decisions about human capital and to connect human resources to strategy. The final step in the process is to evaluate the HR activities to determine if in fact the goals have been met. W. Schiemann has used the term "**people equity**," which refers to how an organization measures and manages its human capital to maximize its value.[55] The concept of people equity comprises three main elements and looks at how a firm optimizes its return on investment. He referred to these three elements as Alignment, Capabilities, and Engagement (ACE). Alignment refers to the degree of fit between strategy and people's activities. Capabilities are the talent resources to execute the strategy, and engagement is the degree of commitment that people have to the organization. To measure human capital effectively, the planner is responsible for evaluating its processes and continuously improving over the technical and strategic aspects of this process. For example, a measure of effectiveness might be the percent of internal versus external candidates who are hired within a given year.

---

people equity

How organizations measure and manage their human capital to maximize its value.

This improvement must be evident from year to year. To ensure continuous improvement, all processes must be measured, a baseline developed, and initiatives put in place. It is imperative that the human resource professional use key business metrics and develop a thorough understanding of how human resource planning can contribute to the bottom line. Evaluation is dependent on the criteria the organization uses to discern whether the human resource planning function is effective. Typically, processes are measured in terms of time and cost associated with their deployment. They can be assessed with respect to their usefulness, consistency, variability, and how robust they are.[56] For example a measure might be the time it took to find an appropriate resource to fill a particular position and include the cost of recruiting and time to interview.

There are a variety of mechanisms or tools that can be used to ascertain this value, and the ability to do this in a comprehensive way largely depends on the level of technological sophistication of the organization and the robust nature of the tools chosen. One such tool is the HRIS. Another is the use of applicable and proactive accounting methods that consider how investments in human capital can be measured in order to determine the financial returns on an organization. This method is called human resource accounting (HRA). Next, we will briefly discuss both of these tools.

LO6

Human Resource Information Systems

A **human resource information system (HRIS)** is used to collect, record, store, analyze, and retrieve data concerning an organization's human resources. These systems are comprised of different software applications that work with an electronic database. All good human resource decisions require timely and accurate information. A good HRIS enables the HR department to be responsive to its customers' needs and is critical for the effective functioning of the HR department and the larger organization. The major stakeholders who use the information from an HRIS are HR professionals, managers, and employees. Each of these "customers" expects a responsive HR department that can provide accurate and timely information. The larger the organization and the more dynamic an organization's environments, the greater the need for a sophisticated HRIS.

---

human resource information system (HRIS)

Gathers, analyzes, summarizes, and reports important data for formulating and implementing strategies by HR specialists and line managers.

Consider Chevron:

Chevron Corporation <http://www.chevron.com>, a large, international oil company with several thousands of employees working in over 50 countries, in the past initiated a sophisticated information system called "CHRIS" (Chevron Human Resource Information System). CHRIS can provide all necessary information on the firm's human resources to the managers of this conglomerate (containing 13 distinct companies) widely separated geographically.[57]

HRIS Functions—Breadth and Size

Not all HRISs are the same. In fact, there are many different systems to choose from depending on the organizational requirements. Key considerations that organizations take into account when deciding on an appropriate HRIS to match their needs, include:

- The size of the organization
- What information needs to be captured
- The volume of information transmitted
- The firm's objectives
- Managerial decision needs
- The importance of reporting capability
- Technical capabilities
- Available resources

Typically, a small firm may begin with a simple HRIS as its information needs are very basic and used solely for the purposes of HR administration. The type of employee information captured may include the employee name, address, emergency contact, employment status, position held, how much the employee is paid, benefit coverage, birth date, and sex. The technology is also low tech as these firms typically use generic software applications like Excel, and their entire database is maintained on one computer or a few networked computers and in one database. The application itself is "nonrelational," meaning that information on employee name, home address, job title, pay rate, and so on, will have to be separately entered into the payroll file, the benefits file, performance appraisal records, and several other places. Any change in employee information will have to be updated separately in each file. The probability of an error in inputting information is very high in nonrelational systems. Probability of delays and inconsistencies in information updating is also higher.

As organizations grow and their information needs become more complex, organizations typically require a more sophisticated HRIS. These systems can vary considerably in price depending on their degree of functionality and system integration capabilities. Because of the increase in importance related to human resource data, more and more companies are beginning to adopt mainstream HRIS systems as part of their core IT needs.[58]

Firms may choose an HRIS that is self-contained and relational, meaning that each HR module relates to one another. In this type of system information about an employee only needs to be entered once. In addition, these systems have the capabilities to prevent errors and catch inconsistencies. This feature, called *referential integrity*, ensures that an organization's policies are operationalized or implemented consistently throughout the organization. Referential integrity is a very important function as it enables HR to build into the HRIS its policies and set up parameters. An example below illustrates this function.

Take sick leave. A company's policy might require a doctor's note after 4 days and in terms of pay, an employee may be entitled to 100 percent pay for 4 weeks and then 60 percent of pay for the balance of leave. The system will flag this parameter and a report will be generated indicating the action required. An example of a relational system with referential integrity is Sage HRMS Software.[59]

Firms may also choose what is called a "gold standard" system. These systems not only have significant relational abilities within the HR environment, but they are also part of an enterprise-wide IT infrastructure. These systems are typically found in very large corporations such as AT&T <http://www.att.com> and CIBC. They are called "**enterprise-wide systems**" and link an organization's entire software application environment into a single enterprise solution. This means a seamless integration of data from the various functions such as sales, operations, distribution, and HR. This integration offers a single and shared view.

Therefore, the information is not only entered once, but it is accessible within other system applications and can be viewed in real time.

---

enterprise-wide systems

Link an organization's entire software application environment into a single enterprise solution.

For instance, an organization has decided on an annual salary increase for all employees. The information will appear on the employee file and also in the general ledger within the financial module instantly. The transaction is seamless and updated in "real time" only once. This information will appear in all appropriate tables (viewed on all permissible computer screens and resonant in the appropriate files). The computer program behind the HRIS will know how to use this new information for all relevant decisions affecting this employee—for example, compensation, skills listing, performance competencies, benefits, and so on.

These systems often possess several technological features. They have the ability to offer web-based applications, linking to the employer's **intranet**, an organization's internal website. A common feature of a web-based system is to offer intranet applications such as **employee self-service (ESS)** and **manager self-service (MSS)** functions. ESS allows employees to access and view their own records and make changes where applicable. An example would be updating address or banking information. MSS refers to managers being able to access their employee's records and view and add relevant information such as a performance appraisal rating or review their employee's performance record. In addition to these web-based applications, these systems also possess exceptional reporting capabilities, and seamlessly link to payroll and benefit providers. Examples of these systems are Oracle <http://www.oracle.com> and their affiliated application People Soft, and SAP.

---

intranet

An organization-specific internal computer network.

---

employee self-service (ESS)

A feature of an HRIS that allows employees to access and view their own records and make changes where applicable.

---

manager self-service (MSS)

A feature of an HRIS that allows managers to view and access their employee's records and add relevant information.

Enterprise information management is a growing industry. In many respects, it has emerged out of the risks identified by companies in relation to the data they create, collect, and store. HRIS is a key element of enterprise information and may become a cornerstone in predictive data analytics and knowledge transfer.

Components of an HR System and Common Data Fields

The most common components of an HRIS are recruitment and applicant tracking, time and attendance, training and development, performance management, career planning, compensation, benefits and pension administration, employment equity information, performance evaluation, health and safety, and labour relations (see Figure 3-14). However, the number of data fields, where information can be stored, will largely depend on the functionality of the system. For example, within the training component some common data fields available would be the type of training an employee took, the cost of the training, the vendor who delivered the training, and the method of training delivery. Within the performance module, the data fields might be the performance appraisal rating of the employees, the actual appraisal details, and various productivity data for a particular role. Some systems allow the organization to identify which data fields are important to them while other systems have the data fields predetermined and hard coded. Having a robust data set enables HR to generate more meaningful reports. Next we will discuss the types of reporting capabilities and why this information is so important for organizational effectiveness. Examples of the types of information contained within an HRIS and common reporting capabilities of the system are shown in Figure 3-15.

FIGURE 3-14

Components of a Human Resource Information System with Relational Features

Type of Outputs—Reporting Capabilities

All HRISs produce some regular reports, such as employee records, salary and benefit details, retirement benefits, and so on. However, as a firm's HRIS increases in sophistication, it goes beyond these regular reports and is able to produce special reports, answer questions interactively, and play an important role in supporting organizational decision makers.

For example, suppose an organization is considering a new dental benefit program. In a sophisticated HRIS, it will be able to generate predictions of not only how many employees are likely to qualify for and probably accept the new program, but also how much it will cost the firm over a specific period of time, how it will affect recruitment success, employee turnover, and other relevant data.

Today, even moderately sophisticated HRISs have a number of modules that perform specific functions such as applicant tracking, recruitment source evaluation and costing, performance appraisal recording, compensation and payroll, training records maintenance, and human resource forecasts.

For example, the University of Manitoba's HRIS enables the institution to pay employees and scholarship recipients, enroll and de-enroll employees in benefit plans, and record all hires, terminations, leaves, and salary increases, applying all the appropriate rules that pertain. It will provide timely reports and will automatically calculate service, statutory holiday pay, sick time, vacation entitlements, and much more.[60]

Access to HRIS Information—Privacy and Security Considerations

Who should have access to the information contained in an HRIS? Obviously, HR staff and key managers should have access to all information that enables them to make informed decisions; however, this should be weighed against the need for confidentiality and the need to respect employees' privacy. Most HRISs collect and retain only the employee information needed for business or legal reasons and establish controls for internal use and external release of this information. Sensitive information—such as security and medical reports, investigative and grievance files, insurance and benefit records, information related to performance and disciplinary actions, and so on—should be tightly protected and offered to persons only on a *need-to-know* basis. The decision about who should have the right to change input data is also critical. On the one hand, restricting data entry to a few persons can improve consistency and prevent errors; on the other hand, it can also result in delays and a complete lack of flexibility.

FIGURE 3-15

HRIS Database Information and Reporting Outcomes

HR Function	Typical Information Contained within an HRIS	HRIS Reporting Outcomes
HR Administration	• Employee information/demographics (all relevant data for tax and pension plan purposes, staff profiles, etc.) • Organizational data (structure, levels, reporting pattern) • HR policies	• Time and attendance data; absenteeism data • Division, department, and job categories • Employee records and employment histories • Employee positions and progressions
Compensation/Payroll	• Pay structure • Wage/salary histories of employees • Raises received by employees • Types of benefits and choices available	• Salary budget information • Pension and retirement plan information • Benefits utilization categorized by benefit type or employee group • Cost summaries and projections of benefits programs • Job evaluation information
Recruitment & Selection	• Job postings • Job descriptions/specifications • Selection decision criteria	• Applicant tracking • Recruitment costs • Number of job postings filled • Number of external hires vs. internal promotions • Employment equity reports • Diversity statistics
Training & Development	• Types, dates offered, training records of employees, training needs of personnel, training costs)	• Training data on courses and vendors • Career paths • Training ROI
Health & Safety	• Accidents, costs, tolerance limits for various dangerous substances	• Health and safety records and trends • Short- and long-term disability records
Performance Management	• Performance records, appraisals, productivity data	• Performance records—performance appraisal data • Employee rating percentages
Strategic HR Planning	• Succession plans (skills, specialties, work experience, performance record, promotion capabilities of employees), career planning—job families (jobs, number, training needs, salary)	• Turnover indices • Employee movements/redeployments • Skills inventories • Succession plans • Human resource plans
Labour Relations	• Grievances (types, frequency, decisions by adjudicator)	• Union contract details • Grievance statistics • Costing models

A key feature of any HRIS is how effective it is at providing the tools with which to manage these security issues. The more robust systems enable the organization to set up "security profiles." These profiles are based on "role" and whether the holder of the role can *view* the information or *change* it and what *data fields* are accessible. For example, what information can an HR consultant, payroll staff, or manager view? Should these roles have the ability to view or change information? Consider Social Insurance Numbers. The only role that can view this number is the employee and the payroll department. What about banking information? The only role that can view and change this information would be the payroll department, once the employee provides the appropriate documentation. An employee will be able to view it, but only payroll can change it. Consider emergency contact information. Should a manager, HR, and payroll have access to this information? Security profiles take a lot of time to create and to set up, but they are critical to ensure that proper security measures are in place.

LO7

HRIS—An Important Tool for Strategic HRM

As previously noted, the major stakeholders who use the information from HRISs are HR professionals, managers in each functional area, and the employees. With the increasing need for HR professionals to meet the needs of all its stakeholders, HR professionals recognize the importance of leveraging the system capabilities to deliver greater value-added services. By leveraging the automation and system capabilities, HR professionals can spend more time working at the strategic level rather than at the transactional level. As a result, the HR role has evolved in several ways to enhance its service delivery to the organization. There are several ways that illustrate HR's transformation.

Increased Efficiency—Enhanced Service Delivery

Advances in technology have enabled HR to decrease its involvement in administrative transactions and compliance requirements. HR has successfully automated the day-to-day activities and, where possible, downloaded the data entry at the source. It has established applicable security profiles and assigned relevant roles, identified key reporting criteria, developed meaningful reporting practices, and purchased applications that implemented self-service options using web-based technology. Not only is the information more readily available, but it is more accurate, timely, and accessible. As a result, HR is better equipped to provide *just-in-time* service delivery to all its stakeholders on an as-needed basis. Consider this example:

> When employees need to change their address or their emergency contact information in a system that has a self-service option, these employees no longer have to contact anyone, fill in any paperwork, or get approvals. They simply log on to the system into their employee file, enter the new information, and save it. The payroll department will automatically have an updated address so that the pay stub can be sent to the correct address and the HR department will automatically have the correct emergency contact in case a need arises.

Increased Effectiveness—Helping Stakeholders Make Better Decisions

Fewer transactions means that the HR department can focus more on strategic issues. Now HR has the time to focus on understanding which HR metrics are important to help the organization achieve its business goals and objectives. Choosing the appropriate data and analyzing them has become an integral part of how HR helps managers make better decisions. Using predictive analysis, HR helps managers to detect trends. **Predictive analysis** is the process of selecting, exploring, analyzing, and modelling data to create better business outcomes.[61] From this system, HR can collect applicable information, analyze it, and use it to *predict* how best to address future events, develop future strategies, or manage human resource–related issues. Consider these two examples to illustrate how HR data can be used to help managers make better decisions.

predictive analysis

The process of selecting, exploring, analyzing, and modelling data to create better business outcomes.

HRIS data can help managers *predict* a future headcount requirement. Due to an increase in market share a manager may need to hire 10 new salespeople to fill 10 new sales roles in any given quarter. Assuming the organization has a policy of "promote from within," data that would be important to collect would be the number of internal employees who are ready for a promotion and have the requisite skill, the performance ratings of these individuals, and the number of turnovers expected within this job class. Generating these reports and analyzing the data to help managers understand the internal supply of talent available is one way HR can help managers make a better decision.

The data can help managers *predict future* productivity levels—for managers to effectively ensure resource availability they need to understand their employees' attendance records. These records are found in the time and attendance module. An absenteeism pattern is one aspect of attendance that is important. How many employees were off sick in a given month? Were some employees only off sick on Mondays and Fridays? Is there a particular time of year that someone is constantly off? Managers will need to reflect on whether there might be a discipline issue. Generating reports and analyzing the information to establish a trend is one way HR can help managers manage more effectively.

Increased Contribution to Organizational Sustainability—Talent Management

Throughout the text we refer to how important it is for organizations to value their human resources and to effectively manage its talent, optimizing the skills and competencies resonant within the firm. The term *talent management* was coined by McKinsey and Company in 1997 and appeared in their report on the "War on Talent." This report took into account a number of HR processes critical for organizational sustainability. **Talent management** refers to "a systemic attraction, identification, development, engagement/retention and deployment of those individuals with high potential who are of particular value to the organization."[62]

---

talent management

A systemic attraction, identification, development, engagement/retention, and deployment of those individuals with high potential who are of particular value to the organization.

The information that is generated from the HRIS helps managers and HR leverage these employees' capabilities and skills and to design opportunities for development. A robust HRIS such as SAP and People Soft will possess several development modules such as Career Planning, Succession Planning, and Training & Development. On the infrastructure side, HR can populate these modules with career paths and the corresponding skills and competencies needed. They can create replacement charts and succession models and then generate a list of employees who have the skills and are ready to move into the next role or what type of development would be appropriate for these individuals to pursue. The opportunity to use this information to ensure that the organization can deploy its high potential workforce when need is invaluable to organizational sustainability, especially as organizations manage unforeseen challenges. We will discuss talent management in more detail in Chapter 7.

Increased Visibility—Enhanced HR Competencies

Not only has technology enabled HR to provide greater value-added services, but it has also afforded the HR professional the opportunity to interact at a more sophisticated level with its client groups regarding their business informational needs. Clients expect HR to possess knowledge of their financial and strategic business challenges and to explore the various technological solutions that will meet their needs. This expectation has enabled HR to demonstrate a greater degree of professionalism and has raised the credibility of the human resource professionals' knowledge within the organization. In addition, HR has had to work with IT departments to integrate and maintain these systems. This has resulted in HR becoming more technologically savvy, gaining greater credibility with IT departments, and working with IT as a strategic business partner instead of using them as a service department.

Human Resource Accounting

More recently, some progressive organizations have considered examining the impact of human resource capital development in organizations using a financial model. This approach considers "human resources" as an asset and an investment and measures from a financial perspective the return of those investments.[63] This value is quantified using a process method called **human resource accounting (HRA)**. HRA is the process of identifying, measuring, accounting, and forecasting the value of human resources in order to facilitate effective management of an organization.[64] HRA attempts to put a dollar figure on the human assets of an organization using cost or value models.[65] The cost model is based on some kind of cost calculation—acquisition, replacement, or opportunity costs—while the value-based models strive to evaluate human resources on the basis of their economic value to the organization.

---

human resource accounting (HRA)

A process to measure the present cost and value of human resources as well as their future worth to the organization.

HRA is a managerial tool that can help managers make better decisions. It can be a blessing to salary administrators, trainers, human resource planners, and union–management negotiators if it provides them with the kind of objective and reliable information they have long needed to plan these functions.

Spotlight *on* HRM

Focus on Generational Similarities not Differences

By Trish Maguire

When it comes to talent management, leaders shouldn't be focusing solely on how to harness the boomers. If we accept the view that in good economies talent matters and in bad economies talent matters even more, surely the real opportunity for leaders is in attracting, retaining and engaging an intergenerational workforce.

HR talent strategies have historically focused on having the right people with the right skills in the right place at the right time. But now there is a far more interesting dimension, driven predominantly by generation Y and the baby boomers: A growing need for people to find meaningful and purposeful work.

No single program or policy can be the panacea. This emerging dynamic suggests a new opportunity may rest in creating intergenerational strategies that address people's most pressing career, life and occupational concerns.

Yes, the recession has delayed the expected flood of retirees. But, more importantly, it has contributed to encouraging people, not just baby boomers, to rethink how they want to live and work. Until recently, age was a chronological condition where people were expected to work until they hit "that time" in their life and retire. Thanks to modern medicine, the middle years are now described as the prime of life and life expectancy has increased significantly. If leaders believe people are mission-critical for the organization, then it's time to put the word "retirement" out to pasture and explore and pioneer fresh ideas for talent management strategies.

Imagine the benefits organizations could gain by integrating these myth-breaking facts with additional myth-breaking data such as:

- Different generations have essentially the same values.

- All generations see lack of respect as a key challenge.

- There is no significant difference in motivational factors among the generations.

- Young people are just as loyal to their firms as everybody else.

- How many surveys will convince leaders there is a growing need for:

  - balancing work with personal obligations

(Continued)

- reinventing roles where people feel fulfilled
- encouraging personal control and choice with people's occupational goals
- respecting people's knowledge and abilities
- encouraging people to expand their talent capacity?

Ultimately, leaders need to build motivating organizational cultures by leveraging intergenerational talent strategies around sameness, not differences.

Trish Maguire is a commentator for SCNetwork on leadership in action and founding principal of Synergyx Solutions. She has held senior leadership roles in HR and organizational development in education, manufacturing and entrepreneurial organizations and can be reached at <synergyx@sympatico.ca>.

SOURCE: With the permission of Trish Maguire, MALT, CHRP, CHRL. Founder & President of Synergyx Solutions, a Talent Management & Leadership Development Coaching Practice. Trish is a long standing Human Resources Professional Association, a Board member of Canadian Women In Food and an ICF Certified coach. You can read many of her articles on "Leadership in Action" in the *Canadian HR Reporter* or connect through trish@synergyxsolutions.com or www.linkedin.com/in/trishmaguiresynergyxsolutions.

SUMMARY

Human resource planning is a proactive approach to ensuring that the organization has the right people at the right place with the right skills at the right time. The human resource planning process signals the beginning of an organization's ability to "manage its talent." The planning process directs the organization to decide what talent it needs and suggests several ways in which to source that talent. It is an attempt by companies to estimate their future needs and supplies of human resources. Through an understanding of the factors that influence the demand for workers, planners can forecast specific short- and long-term needs. Given some anticipated level of demand, planners try to estimate the availability of present workers both internal and external to the organization to meet that demand. Such estimates begin with an audit of present employees. Possible replacements are then identified. Internal shortages are resolved by seeking new employees in the external labour markets. Surpluses are reduced by normal attrition, leaves of absence, layoffs, or terminations. Both external and internal staffing strategies can be used to meet human resource needs.

Planners use various tools to gather information and analyze the data, such as HRIS and HRA, so that they can provide meaningful information to its stakeholders. Effective use of technology has afforded HR the opportunity to demonstrate enhanced service delivery and offer greater strategic services to its stakeholder.

The HR plan can be considered as a *road map* for HR professionals, as it directs the recruitment, selection, and training and development processes. Once HR professionals understand an organization's human resource needs and available supply, then they will be able to decide how best to recruit that resource and establish the framework for the selection criteria. Once onboard, employees' capabilities will need to be understood and their talents and skills optimized so they can perform effectively. Future value-added contributions will depend on how the organization develops its employees and successfully aligns its needs with its employees' developmental paths. Talent management is an important HR activity to ensure organizational sustainability. Later, in Chapters 5, 6, and 7, we will discuss those HR functions which support effective talent management processes.

Before that, it is important to study the impact of governmental policies on a firm's human resource policies and practices. This will be attempted in the next chapter.

TERMS FOR REVIEW

attrition
Canadian Occupational Projection System (COPS)
consultants
contract (or contingent) worker
crowdsourcing
Delphi technique
employee self-service (ESS)
enterprise-wide systems
extrapolation
flexible retirement
forecasts
full-time employees
human resource accounting (HRA)
human resource information system (HRIS)
human resource planning
indexation
intranet
job sharing
labour market analysis
labour shortage
management or leadership inventory
manager self-service (MSS)
Markov analysis
nominal group technique
outplacement
outsourcing
part-time employees
people equity
phased retirement
predictive analysis
replacement charts
replacement summaries
skills inventories
staffing table
talent management
transition matrices
work arrangement

SELF-ASSESSMENT EXERCISE

How Do External Supplies Affect Your Chosen Career?

Consider the job you plan to search for after graduation. (If you are already working and do not plan to leave your present job, you can look at the job rank [or grade] you want to have in five years after graduation.) This self-test involves looking at the external labour market and forming conclusions about how it affects your career. If you are not familiar with the labour market conditions, you may have to conduct an Internet search to identify answers to the following questions. You can start with Statistics Canada and Employment and Social Development Canada websites, but need not restrict your search to these. Once you have done this, please respond to the following statements.

Statement	Strongly Agree	Agree	Undecided	Disagree	Strongly Disagree
1. The way the job is done is significantly affected by technological changes.					
2. The growth rate in the number of jobs in this profession/job category is more than rate of employment growth rate.					
3. The career/job position I aspire to is likely to be found attractive by persons in all age and social groups.					
4. Because of demographic changes, there are fewer persons like me likely to be applying for a job/career such as the one I am aspiring to.					
5. The job position I have in mind is a glamorous or high-paying one.					
6. Most persons in my age or socio-economic group are unlikely to apply for the job position that I have in mind.					
7. The job I have in mind is likely to be found attractive by even individuals who live thousands of kilometres away.					
8. The location or the nature of the job may make it unattractive to persons who live in other provinces.					
9. Currently the unemployment rate in this job category is over 6 percent.					
10. There is hardly any unemployment in this job category, especially if a person is prepared to relocate.					

SCORING

For statements 1, 3, 5, 7, and 9, assign a score of 5, 4, 3, 2, and 1 for Strongly Agree, Agree, Undecided, Disagree, and Strongly Disagree respectively. For statements 2, 4, 6, 8, and 10, assign a score of 1, 2, 3, 4, and 5 for Strongly Agree, Agree, Undecided, Disagree, and Strongly Disagree. Add up the scores for all 10 statements.

INTERPRETATION

The total score may lie anywhere between 10 and 50. If the score is 33 or higher, you are aspiring for a job position that is very much in demand and likely to be found attractive by a large number of persons. This means that you have to equip yourself with additional competencies or unique skills to be attractive to employers. Even if the total score is lower, changes in economy or technology may change the picture considerably any time in the future!

REVIEW AND DISCUSSION QUESTIONS

1. What are the key steps in human resource planning in organizations? Which of your actions, if any, would be different if you were planning human resources for a smaller firm (that employs fewer than 50 persons in all) instead of a larger firm (which has 500 employees)?

2. What are staffing tables and replacement charts? Of what use are they to a human resource manager?

3. Discuss any three techniques for estimating the demand for human resources. Provide examples where relevant.

4. What are some popular approaches to match the supply and demand of human resources? Briefly discuss two approaches (each) for situations when demand exceeds and is less than supply of human resources, highlighting their advantages and limitations.

5. "Alternate work arrangements are useful approaches for both the employer and the employee." Discuss.

6. What are some of the security considerations organizations must understand when implementing a human resource information system? Provide an example of one way that security profiles are set up.

CRITICAL THINKING QUESTIONS

1. Suppose human resource planners estimated that due to several technological innovations your firm will need 25 percent fewer employees in three years. What actions would you take today?

2. Suppose you managed a restaurant in a winter resort area. During the summer it was profitable to keep the business open, but you needed only one-half the cooks, table servers, and bartenders. What actions would you take in April when the peak tourist season ended?

3. If your company locates its research and development offices in downtown Windsor, Ontario, the city is willing to forgo city property taxes on the building for 10 years. The city is willing to make this concession to help reduce its high unemployment rate. Calgary, Alberta, your company's other choice, has a low unemployment rate and is not offering any tax breaks. Based on just these considerations, which city would you recommend and why?

4. Assume you are the human resource manager in a Canadian university employing approximately 300 faculty members. Since these faculty members constitute a "valuable" resource of your organization, you decide to install an accounting procedure for changes in the value of this asset. How will you go about it? What problems do you anticipate in the process?

5. For a high-tech organization where the job specifications and customer needs continually change, which of the forecasting techniques discussed in the text are likely to be relevant? Why?

6. Some fire departments and hospital staff are using the 3-day, 36-hour schedule. Do you see any negative aspects to this schedule?

7. Assume you work for a firm that employs 30 managerial and 70 clerical/sales employees. As a cost-cutting strategy, your firm is forced to terminate the services of 10 percent of your managers and 5 percent of your clerical staff. What specific actions will you take to help the departing employees?

ETHICS QUESTION

Two months ago, you joined Canada Construction and Design Incorporated, an engineering firm that designs and builds large residential and office complexes, as its human resource manager. Of the 320 employees in the firm, 84 are engineers with various specializations. You find that engineers work routinely for 60–70 hours a week, often taking their work home or coming to the office even on the weekends or in the late evenings. Under the firm's job classification, the engineers are considered to be managerial or supervisory and hence not eligible for any overtime benefits. You also recognize that the culture of the organization expects people, especially managerial and supervisory staff, to put in extra effort. While there is no formal rule requiring overtime, it is clear that "nonperforming" engineers do not receive promotions or even merit increases. You are concerned about the impact of the current setup on the long-term mental health and family welfare of the engineers, yet don't know whether you should "make waves" so soon after your arrival in the firm. However, you feel that it is morally wrong to make an individual work without giving any rewards.

What actions, if any, will you take? Why?

WEB RESEARCH EXERCISE

Visit the websites of agencies such as Statistics Canada and ESDC and identify trends in employment and occupational demand patterns for the following positions in one western and one Atlantic province: electricians, fishers, nurses, and blue-collar workers in the paper and pulp industry. What patterns do you see? What are the implications for students about to graduate from high schools this year? For employers? Compare your findings and present your summary findings to the class.

INCIDENT 3-1

Case Incident: Zebra Ltd.*

Zebra Ltd. is a mid-size IT organization with revenues of over one million. It currently employs 250 employees and is located in Canada and the U.S. Zebra is very well known in the industry for providing software that helps organizations address their internet/intranet security needs and is well respected for its strong focus on R & D activities.

Recently Zebra had a major breakthrough, inventing a new and innovative software program that will ensure better encryption of data across the web. The industry is truly impressed with this innovation. The blogs are all talking about the technical genius and several articles have been written about this company appearing in the national newspaper and in IT related publications. The CEO, Brent Talver, is very pleased with the attention and with this attention the organization has experienced a significant demand for its products and services over the past several months. In fact, the VP of Sales is projecting an increase of 50 percent with respect to new orders within the next 12–15 months.

Brent Talver is wondering how the organization is going to manage the volume of work. He is thinking about the kinds of labour resources he will need, when these resources will be needed, and where. Notably, he is concerned about cost and availability of some critical skills sets especially in light of the current economic recession. His senior employees have all spoken to him about the need for more resources. The VP of Sales says she needs more sales representatives, the engineering dept is asking for more software engineers, HR is overwhelmed by the sudden need to hire, and new employees are complaining that they are not being signed up on the company benefit plans in a timely fashion.

Brent has asked you for advice as to what should he do to manage this volume of work.

---

*Case Incident written by Professor Julie Bulmash of the School of Business, George Brown College. Case reproduced from J. Bulmash, N. Chhinzer, and E. Speers, *Strategic Planning for Human Resources*, Toronto, ON: McGraw-Hill Ryerson, 2010.

QUESTIONS

1. What staffing options does he have available? Determine what the advantages may be for each option.

2. What specific skills would he need? How would he go about finding out this information?

3. Where should he go to find these skills? Can some skills sets be sourced locally or will the organization need to go nationally?

4. Assuming the organization is going to hire contract employees, what advice would you give the managers with respect to managing this group?

INCIDENT 3-2

Case Incident: What Does the Weather Have to Do with HRP? El Nino Impacts?*

The fallout from global warming will be felt for more than 1,000 years. There is significant evidence that the world is heating up! The arctic ice cap is melting much faster than expected and is now about thirty years ahead of what was originally predicted.[66] Significant increases in heat waves, rainstorms, increases in severe hurricanes and typhoons and a warming of the earth's core are predicted. The climate has been projected to change significantly over the several decades, ocean currents will slow by as much as 25 percent, global temperatures will be 1.7 to 4 degrees higher, and sea levels are expected to rise. If this trend continues, global warming of 1.9 to 4.6 degrees can lead to a complete elimination of the Greenland ice sheet and a rise in sea levels of about seven meters.

The warming of the climate system is going to continue. In fact, 11 out of the 12 years rank among the warmest since the 1950s.[67] What does this mean for specific industries? Consider the sporting goods industry or those manufacturing firms which make boots and winter apparel or snow equipment, or perhaps the travel industry which specializes in ski vacations. What challenges do you think these firms will face?

DISCUSSION QUESTIONS

1. What industries do you think would be most affected by this?

2. Identify some specific jobs that would be in demand.

3. Identify some specific jobs that might be comprised and when there may be an oversupply if these trends continue.

*Case Incident written by Professor Julie Bulmash of the School of Business, George Brown College. Case reproduced from J. Bulmash, N. Chhinzer, and E. Speers, *Strategic Planning for Human Resources*, Toronto, ON: McGraw-Hill Ryerson, 2010.

CASE STUDY

Maple Leaf Shoes Ltd.

*A Human Resource Planning Exercise**

Maple Leaf Shoes Ltd. is a medium-sized manufacturer of leather and vinyl shoes located near Wilmington, Ontario. It began operations in 1969 and currently employs about 400 persons in its Ontario plant and some 380 more in offices and warehouses throughout Canada and internationally. More information on the firm and its operations is provided at the end of Chapter 1.

The cost of production at Maple Leaf Shoes has been rising slowly but steadily. Labour costs currently account for over 53 percent of manufacturing costs and have been increasing rapidly. The productivity

*Case written by Professor Hari Das of the Department of Management, Saint Mary's University, Halifax. All rights retained by the author. Das © 2003. Revised © 2009.

levels of the employees have not shown any significant increase in recent years. Concerned with the situation, Maple Leaf Shoes' management has been attempting to introduce more sophisticated technology in its various plants. More capital-intensive, automated production processes are being considered by the management as part of the solution to the productivity challenge facing the firm.

The company is now in the midst of a strategic reorientation. As part of the exercise, Robert Clark, the president, has asked Jane Reynolds, Special Assistant in the Human Resources Division in the firm, to prepare a human resource forecast for the company.

Reynolds examined the company records that were likely to help her in her task. To her dismay, she found that very few plans or systematic procedures existed that would assist her in human resource planning. She decided to begin her analysis with the division in charge of shoes for children and youths (commonly—and half humorously—referred to as the "juvenile division" in the company). It currently employed fewer than 150 persons in total and seemed to have the most complete records related to employee hiring, transfers, exits, and training. But even here, production and labour statistics for several years were incomplete or inaccurate.

Her survey of company records resulted in the information given below. Reynolds also met with key managers in the firm (including Clark) several times to find out more about their goals and action plans for the immediate future. Her findings are also summarized below.

1. All of the juvenile division's manufacturing operations were located in Ontario. Reynolds considered that there were four distinct manufacturing stages: cutting, shaping, assembling, and finishing. (Of course, each of these stages contained several tasks; for example, "shaping" involved several subtasks such as bending the leather, vinyl, or plastic; making lace holes; attaching reinforcers, padding, and so on.) Reynolds also found that the operations progressively became more complex, from "cutting" to "finishing." Workers were normally hired as cutters and then progressively moved up to do shaping, assembling, and then finishing as they gained experience.

2. Cutting and shaping were more repetitive and boring, while assembling and finishing required greater attention and expertise and therefore were more challenging. Despite this, a few workers who were doing assembling chose to do shaping since the latter almost always fetched them more overtime work (and significantly higher earnings). No one doing final finishing had so far asked for reassignment to shaping or cutting. Employee movements during 2011–2012 among the four operations are shown in Table 1.

TABLE 1

Movement of Workers across the Four Operations (2011–2012)

From:	To:					
	Cutting	Shaping	Assembling	Finishing	Exits	Total
Cutting	21	3	1	0	1	26
Shaping	0	32	4	2	2	40
Assembling	0	2	26	5	0	33
Finishing	0	0	0	37	0	37
Total at the end (after accounting for exits)						133

3. The firm's labour productivity has not shown any significant improvement in the recent past. This has also been true of the juvenile division. Table 2 shows the production and staffing records of the entire division.

TABLE 2

Production and Workforce Statistics in the Juvenile Division

Year	Production (000s of pairs)	Number of Employees
1978	50	65
—	—	—
1989	75	91
—	—	—
2002	90	110
2003	92	120
2004	93	122
2005	98	125
2006	102	127
2007	110	140
2008	109	140
2009	106	136
2010	105	133
2011	101	130
2012	98	128
2013*	93	125

4. Through the introduction of computer-integrated technology and automated work systems, the firm expects to increase the division's productivity level by 25 percent in 2013 over its 2012 record. Much of this will be achieved by automating much of the cutting operations. It is expected that automation will reduce the need for 33 percent of cutters. The productivity of other operations (namely, shaping, assembling, and finishing) is also expected to increase, but at lower levels than in the case of cutting. The productivity improvement in these operations is expected to be equal. Workers who lose their jobs as a result of automation and computerization will receive severance pay.

5. Compared to other divisions, the juvenile division has an aging workforce. (On average, 3 to 8 percent of the division's workforce retires each year.) For calculation purposes, Reynolds is planning to use a flat 5 percent retirement figure. Table 1 figures do not include exits through retirement.

6. There are 10 persons in sales and order processing associated with the juvenile division products. Another 15 clerical staff are involved in a variety of related activities (such as billing, product movement, and so on) in the division. There are four managerial persons in the division.

---

*(Projected figures based on first eight months' production)

7.   As a cost-cutting measure, two of the above managerial positions will be eliminated in the next year. Because of the computerized billing initiated recently, the productivity of the clerical staff is expected to increase by 50 percent, making some of the clerical positions redundant. Where possible, the displaced workers will be transferred to other divisions or trained to do other activities in the firm.

8.   The firm plans to open two new sales outlets in the next year. It is estimated that each outlet will require one supervisor and two sales assistants initially.

9.   The percentage of women workers in the four operations were as follows: cutting, 72 percent; shaping, 70 percent; assembling, 63 percent; and finishing, 61 percent. Women account for 68 percent of the sales assistants and 55 percent of the clerical staff. No woman occupies a managerial position in the juvenile division.

10. A number of women in the past have requested job sharing and flextime work arrangements. The firm currently has no provision for nontraditional work arrangements.

11. Estimated production (based on projected market demand for shoes) for 2013 is 93,000 pairs of shoes. As is the case with several shoe manufacturers in this country (and the U.S.), footwear production has declined each year due to international competition.

DISCUSSION QUESTIONS

1.   Prepare a human resource plan for the juvenile division for 2014.

2.   What other suggestions and comments would you make to the management if you were in Reynolds' position?

CASE STUDY

Canadian Pacific and International Bank

Planning Supply and Demand for a Call Centre at CPIB*

Canadian Pacific and International Bank (CPIB) is a premier Canadian financial institution with assets over $150 billion and operations across Canada and in 33 countries. Today, its more than 25,000 employees provide personal, commercial, corporate, and investment banking services to individuals and businesses around the world. More details on the bank were given at the end of Chapter 1.

The bank has several call centres that offer exceptional customer services providing advice on banking products, services, and benefits. Currently their inbound call centre in Halifax, Nova Scotia, is in the process of conducting an HR planning exercise. They have estimated employee movements throughout the organization and have mapped this information onto the following Markov matrix:

	A	B	C	D	Exits
A. Shift Manager (n = 6)	0.70	0.05	0.00	0.00	0.25
B. Department Supervisor (n = 18)	0.13	0.82	0.03	0.00	0.02
C. Team Leader (n = 105)	0.05	0.10	0.72	0.05	0.08
D. Customer Service Representative (n = 590)	0.00	0.00	0.22	0.54	0.24

*Case revised from J. Bulmash, N. Chhinzer, and E. Speers, *Strategic Planning for Human Resources*, Toronto, ON: McGraw-Hill Ryerson, 2010.

1. Outline employee movement projections and the supply estimates for each level for next year.

2. What trends in the predicted workforce movement should be highlighted as potentially problematic?

In addition, the HR department suggests that three percent of the workforce this year will be retiring next year. These departures are expected to be experienced proportionately at all levels in the organization. These are not included in the exit estimates. After you have completed your Markov analysis, factor in these exits in your supply estimates based on this year's HR supply to help get a more accurate prediction of next year's estimates.

This year, the call centre had 5,200,000 clients. Due to a new project, the call centre expects an additional 1,500,000 clients in the next year. No changes are anticipated in the distribution of the workforce. What HR demand estimates would you calculate for CPIB?

DISCUSSION QUESTION

1. Comparing the forecasted HR supply and demand, conduct a needs assessment. What levels have a labour surplus and what levels have a labour shortage? How many employees would the company need to meet demands for next year?

PART-ENDING VIDEOS

"High Anxiety"

SOURCE: *Venture*, show number 918, March 14, 2004, running time 7:41.

Go to Connect to access the videos.

Attracting Human Resources

A company hires employees to meet its objectives. First, it has to identify potential employees and find the ways and means to get the necessary information to them, taking into account the requirements of human rights legislation. Then it has to select those candidates who best meet its needs.

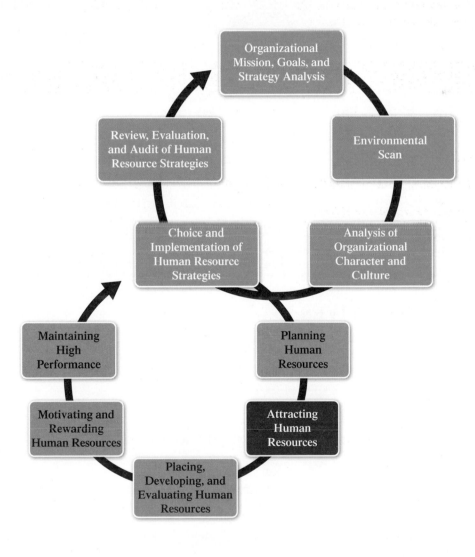

CHAPTER 4

Legal Requirements and Managing Diversity

All human beings are born free and equal in dignity and rights.

ARTICLE 1, UNIVERSAL DECLARATION OF HUMAN RIGHTS, DECEMBER 1948, UNITED NATIONS
<HTTP://WWW.OHCHR.ORG/EN/UDHR/PAGES/INTRODUCTION.ASPX>

All individuals should have an equal opportunity to make for themselves the lives that they are able and wish to have, consistent with their duties and obligations as members of society, without being hindered in or prevented from doing so by discriminatory practices based on race, national or ethnic origin, colour, religion, age, sex, sexual orientation, marital status, family status, disability or conviction for an offence for which a pardon has been granted.

SECTION 2, *CANADIAN HUMAN RIGHTS ACT*

LEARNING OBJECTIVES

After studying this chapter, you should be able to:

LO1 Explain the impact of government on human resource management.

LO2 List the major provisions of the *Canadian Human Rights Act*.

LO3 Define harassment and explain what is meant by the term sexual harassment.

LO4 Outline an employment equity program.

LO5 Explain the effect of human rights legislation on the role of human resource specialists.

LO6 Define diversity management and discuss the strategic importance of managing diversity.

LO7 Discuss the various steps in managing diversity.

LO1 HRC 1, 2, 4, 5 & 8

Government Impact

Few challenges encountered by human resource departments are as overwhelming as those presented by government. Government, through the enforcement of laws, has a direct and immediate impact on the human resource function. The federal and provincial laws that regulate the employee–employer relationship challenge the methods human resource departments use. The impact of these laws has helped elevate the importance of human resource decisions.

Many aspects of human resource management are affected by human rights legislation. This chapter will focus on compliance with government legislation and the challenges associated with managing diversity. At appropriate points throughout this book, employee-related laws are explained to illustrate the challenges modern human resource departments encounter and the actions they must take.

To avoid flooding the courts with complaints and the prosecution of relatively minor infractions, federal and provincial governments often create special regulatory bodies, such as commissions, tribunals, and boards, to enforce compliance with the law and to aid in its interpretation. Examples are the various human rights commissions and labour relations boards, which evaluate complaints and develop legally binding rules, called **regulations**. Human resource specialists become involved because legislation and regulations affect the employment relationship. The involvement creates three important responsibilities. First, human resource experts must stay abreast of the laws and the interpretation of the laws by regulatory bodies and court rulings. Second, they must develop and administer programs that ensure company compliance. Failure to do so may lead to the loss of government contracts, poor public relations, and suits by regulatory bodies or affected individuals. Third, they must pursue their traditional roles of obtaining, maintaining, and retaining an optimal workforce.

---

regulations

Legally enforceable rules developed by governmental agencies to ensure compliance with laws that the agency administers.

HRC 1, 2, 4, 5 & 8

The Charter of Rights and Freedoms

An example of government legislation that has profound implications for employers is the *Constitution Act* of 1982, which contains the **Canadian Charter of Rights and Freedoms**.[1] The Charter provides some fundamental rights to every Canadian. These are as follows:

Canadian Charter of Rights and Freedoms

Federal law enacted in 1982, guaranteeing individuals equal rights before the law.

- freedom of conscience and religion;
- freedom of thought, belief, opinion, and expression, including freedom of the press and other media of communication;
- freedom of peaceful assembly; and
- freedom of association.

The Charter provides protection to every Canadian in the following specific areas:[2]

- fundamental freedoms;
- democratic rights;
- the right to live and seek employment anywhere in Canada;
- legal rights: the right to life, liberty, and personal security;
- equality rights for all individuals;
- officially recognized languages of Canada;
- minority language education rights;
- Canada's multicultural heritage; and
- Aboriginal peoples' rights.

The Canadian Charter of Rights and Freedoms is probably the most far-reaching legal challenge for human resource managers. A review of the application of the Charter to human resource and industrial relations issues reveals that its impact has been important, but limited at times. One reason is that it takes considerable time for cases to reach the Supreme Court, the ultimate interpreter of the Charter.

Section 1 of the Charter guarantees rights and freedoms "subject only to such reasonable limits prescribed by law as can be demonstrably justified in a free and democratic society." Of course, such adjectives as "reasonable" and "demonstrably justified" will lead to different interpretations by different judges. This is one of the reasons why many cases are winding their way through the judicial system up to the Supreme Court, just to get a final opinion. Every time a court invokes one of the rights or freedoms, it must determine if the infringement is justified.

Section 2 of the Charter guarantees freedom of association, a very important aspect in industrial relations, especially for unions. A key question in this context is whether the freedom to associate carries with it the right to bargain collectively and the right to strike, the main reasons for the existence of unions. As will be shown, these rights cannot be taken for granted anymore.

Section 15—the equality rights part—came into effect on April 17, 1985, having been delayed to allow the federal government and the provinces to create or change laws to ensure compliance with the Charter. It states in its first paragraph:

> Every individual is equal before the law and under the law and has the right to the equal protection and benefit of the law without discrimination and, in particular, without discrimination based on race, national or ethnic origin, colour, religion, sex, age, or mental or physical disability.

This section of the Charter was expected to—and has—caused a flood of litigation that will take many years to resolve.

The Charter of Rights and Freedoms applies only to individuals dealing with federal and provincial governments and agencies under their jurisdiction, but its impact is far-reaching, since potentially every law can be challenged. Courts have the delicate task of balancing individual and collective rights. Consider this arbitration case:

> Quebec arbitrator Jean-Pierre Lussier ruled that a collective agreement provision providing for 24-hour shifts at the McGill University Health Centre violated both the Canadian Charter of Rights and Freedoms and the Quebec Charter of Human Rights and Freedoms. Grievor Alain Bestawros and other residents claimed that the long shifts affected their health and safety, reduced the ability to concentrate, resulted in fatigue when driving home, and led to difficulty in remembering common knowledge. According to Arbitrator Lussier, "a

condition of employment exposing a doctor to greater risk of physical or mental injury for himself, higher risk of errors, incorrect diagnoses and even causing injury to individuals when his mission is to take care of them is an unfair, unreasonable condition of employment."[3]

HRC 1, 2, 4 & 5

Human Rights Legislation

While the Charter of Rights and Freedoms guarantees equality before the law for every Canadian, the *Human Rights Act* seeks to provide equal employment opportunities without regard to people's race, national or ethnic origin, colour, religion, age, sex, sexual orientation, marital status, family status, disability, or conviction for an offence for which a pardon has been granted. Common sense dictates such a policy, but the human rights legislation requires every employer to ensure that equal opportunities are, in fact, reality and that there is no discrimination either intentional or unintentional. No other laws rival the impact human rights legislation has on human resource management.[4]

Scope

Usually, employment-related laws and regulations are limited in scope; their impact on the human resource management process is confined to a single human resource activity. For example, minimum-wage laws specify the lowest amount an employer can pay for each hour worked; in spite of their importance, these laws affect only the compensation management function. Other human resource activities—selection, training, and labour relations—are largely unaffected.

Human rights legislation, however, is an exception. Its role is not limited to a single human resource activity. Instead, human rights legislation affects nearly every human resource function: human resource planning, recruiting, selection, training, compensation, and labour relations.

HRC 5

Overview

Human rights legislation is a family of federal and provincial acts that have as a common objective the provision of equal employment opportunity for members of protected groups. Figure 4-1 summarizes these two layers of employment laws. Discrimination between workers on the basis of their effort, performance, or other work-related criteria remains both permissible and advisable:

> A waitress at a Winnipeg restaurant whose uncle was dying of cancer decided to shave off her hair to show support for her relative. The manager of the restaurant fired the woman, stating that her new look was inappropriate for the restaurant. The Manitoba Human Rights Commission denied the woman a hearing on the grounds that dress-code issues are generally within the employer's discretion. The Commission's Executive Director indicated that if a person undergoing chemotherapy shaves their head, there would be an obligation on the employer to accommodate the employee. In addition, there may be grounds for a complaint if male employees are permitted to shave their head but female employees are not.[5]

FIGURE 4-1

Types, Sources, Objectives, and Jurisdiction of Canadian Human Rights Legislation

Type	Source	Objectives and Jurisdiction
Federal Law	Passed by Parliament and enforced by federal Human Rights Commission/Tribunal	To ensure equal employment opportunities with employers under federal jurisdiction
Provincial Law	Enacted by provincial governments and enforced by provincial human rights commissions/tribunals	To ensure equal employment opportunities with employers under provincial jurisdiction

Human rights legislation permits employers to reward outstanding performers and penalize insufficient productivity. Its only requirement is that the basis for rewards and punishments be work-related, not based on a person's race, sex, age, or other prohibited criteria.

The following discussion focuses on federal human rights legislation, because **provincial human rights laws** tend to differ only slightly, mainly in terminology (e.g., some provinces use "national origin," others use "ethnic origin"). The examples used in the discussion of federal legislation are also quite typical of provincial situations. The major exceptions are pay equity and employment equity.

provincial human rights laws

All provinces have their own human rights laws with discrimination criteria, regulations, and procedures.

LO2   HRC 5

The *Canadian Human Rights Act*

The ***Canadian Human Rights Act*** was passed by Parliament on July 14, 1977, and took effect in March 1978. The Act proclaims:

Canadian Human Rights Act

A federal law prohibiting discrimination.

> The purpose of this Act is to extend the laws in Canada to give effect, within the purview of matters coming within the legislative authority of Parliament, to the principle that all individuals should have an opportunity equal with other individuals to make for themselves the lives that they are able and wish to have and to have their needs accommodated, consistent with their duties and obligations as members of society, without being hindered in or prevented from doing so by discriminatory practices based on race, national or ethnic origin, colour, religion, age, sex, sexual orientation, marital status, family status, disability or conviction for an offence for which a pardon has been granted.[6]

The Act applies to all federal government departments and agencies, Crown corporations, and business and industry under federal jurisdiction, such as banks, airlines, railways, and interprovincial communication (radio and TV) companies–in their dealings with the public and in their employment policies.

In areas not under federal jurisdiction, protection is given by provincial human rights laws. Each of Canada's provinces and territories—with the exception of Nunavut, which is still under federal jurisdiction, has its own antidiscrimination laws, which are broadly similar to the federal law. Figure 4-2 compares federal and individual provincial human rights legislation as to different grounds of discrimination prohibited in employment. While discrimination in the provision of services is also prohibited, the grounds are often very similar to employment and are not provided in the table.

Discrimination Defined

Webster's New World Dictionary of the American Language defines discrimination as: "a showing of partiality or prejudice in treatment; specific action or policies directed against the welfare of minority groups."

Former Iraq hostage James Loney says that a Catholic youth camp, where he was on staff, was ordered to close down because he is gay. Should sexual orientation play a role in staffing decisions in religious organizations?
CP/Bernard Weil.

Discrimination is not defined in the Charter of Rights and Freedoms, nor in any federal or provincial human rights legislation with the exception of Quebec. Section 10 of the Quebec Charter states:

Every person has a right to full and equal recognition and exercise of his human rights and freedoms without distinction, exclusion, or preference based on race, colour, sex, sexual orientation, civil status, religion, political convictions, language, ethnic or national origin, social condition, or the fact that he is a handicapped person, or that he uses any means to palliate his handicap. Discrimination exists where such a distinction, exclusion, or preference has the effect of nullifying or impairing such a right.

FIGURE 4-2

Prohibited Grounds of Discrimination in Canada (Employment)*

Prohibited Ground	Jurisdiction	Comments
Race or Colour	All jurisdictions	In addition, Saskatchewan prohibits discrimination on the basis of "perceived race."
Religion	All jurisdictions	Manitoba's Code and Yukon's Act read "religion or creed, or religious belief, religious association or religious activity." In addition, Saskatchewan prohibits discrimination on the basis of "religious creed." Ontario uses the term "creed." Nunavut's Act says "creed [and] religion."
Physical or Mental Disability	All jurisdictions	Quebec uses the phrase "handicap or use of any means to palliate a handicap." Ontario has prohibition on the basis of "both current and previous disabilities as well as the perception that one may have or have had a disability." Nunavut uses the word "disability."
Dependence on Alcohol or Drugs	All except Yukon and Northwest Territories	Policy to accept complaints in British Columbia, Alberta, Saskatchewan, Manitoba, Ontario, New Brunswick, Northwest Territories and Prince Edward Island. Included in "handicap" ground in Quebec. Previous dependence only in New Brunswick and Nova Scotia. Included in "disability" ground in the Yukon, Alberta, and Nunavut.
Age	All jurisdictions	British Columbia: 19+; Alberta: 18+; Saskatchewan: 18+; Ontario: 18+; Newfoundland: 19+; Quebec: except as provided for by law; Nunavut: applies with no age restrictions in the Act.
Sex (includes pregnancy and childbirth)	All jurisdictions	Alberta uses the term "gender"; Manitoba includes gender-determined characteristics; British Columbia and Ontario include breastfeeding; Ontario recognizes the protection of transgendered persons and accepts complaints related to "gender identity"; Ontario accepts complaints related to female genital mutilation; in Quebec, pregnancy as such is considered a ground of discrimination; in the Northwest Territories, gender identity as such is considered a ground of discrimination; Nunavut Act says "sex, sexual orientation, marital status, family status, pregnancy."
Marital Status	All jurisdictions	Quebec uses the term "civil status."
Family Status	All except New Brunswick and Newfoundland	Saskatchewan defines as being in a parent–child relationship; Quebec uses the term "civil status"; Northwest Territories have prohibition on the grounds of "family status" as well as "family affiliation."
Sexual Orientation	All jurisdictions	The Supreme Court of Canada read sexual orientation into the *Alberta Human Rights, Citizenship and Multiculturalism Act* in 1998.
National or Ethnic Origin (including linguistic background)	All except British Columbia	Saskatchewan and Northwest Territories use the term "nationality"; Manitoba Code uses "nationality" or "national origin"; Manitoba Code uses "ethnic background or origin"; Ontario's Code includes both "ethnic origin" and "citizenship"; Alberta uses the term "place of origin."

(Continued)

Ancestry or Place of Origin	Yukon, British Columbia, Alberta, Saskatchewan, Manitoba, Northwest Territories, Ontario, Nunavut, and New Brunswick	
Language	Ontario, Quebec, New Brunswick, Northwest Territories, and Yukon	Ontario accepts complaints on the grounds of ancestry, ethnic origin, place of origin, and race; New Brunswick and the Northwest Territories will accept language-related complaints filed on the basis of ancestry, although it is not an enumerated ground; included under "linguistic background" in Yukon; Nunavut: no specific mention in the Act.
Social Condition or Origin	Quebec, Northwest Territories, New Brunswick, and Newfoundland	
Source of Income	Alberta, Saskatchewan, Manitoba, Quebec, Yukon, Prince Edward Island, and Nova Scotia	Defined as "receipt of public assistance" in Saskatchewan; included under social condition in Quebec and New Brunswick; Nunavut says "lawful source of income."
Assignment, Attachment, or Seizure of Pay	Newfoundland and Quebec	Included under "social condition" in Quebec.
Based on Association	Yukon, Manitoba, Ontario, New Brunswick, Nova Scotia, Northwest Territories, Nunavut, and Prince Edward Island	Northwest Territories has prohibition on basis of "political association."
Political Belief	Yukon, Newfoundland, British Columbia, Manitoba, Quebec, Nova Scotia, Prince Edward Island, New Brunswick, and Northwest Territories	Newfoundland has prohibition on basis of "political opinion"; Manitoba Code includes political activity and political association.
Record of Criminal Conviction	Yukon, Manitoba, British Columbia, Quebec, Ontario, and Prince Edward Island	Manitoba and Yukon's Act read "criminal charges or criminal record"; Ontario has prohibition on basis of "record of offences."
Pardoned Conviction	Federal, Yukon, Ontario, Nunavut, and Northwest Territories	Ontario has prohibition on basis of "record of offences."

*This document provides comparative information on the grounds of discrimination covered by federal, provincial, and territorial human rights legislation in Canada. In some instances, prohibited grounds for employment differ from those for the provision of services.

SOURCE: Canadian Human Rights Commission, "Prohibited Grounds of Discrimination in Canada," September 2006, <www.chrc-ccdp.ca/publications/pdg_mdi-eng.aspx>. Reproduced with the permission of the Minister of Public Works and Government Services, 2012.

What grounds of discrimination occur most frequently? When examining the annual reports of the various human rights commissions/tribunals, the ground alleged most frequently is discrimination on the basis of disability (alleged in about 45 to 60 percent of claims). For example, in the federal jurisdiction for 2013, about 55 percent of the claims involved disability (with about 40 percent of these claims related to mental health), 17 percent were based on sex, 16 percent on national or ethnic origin, and 14 percent on race. In New Brunswick, 51 percent of the complaints involved disability (29 percent were physical and 22 percent were mental disability). Note that a complainant may allege more than one ground of discrimination.[7]

One area that is particularly challenging for employers involves "competing rights" cases. For example, what if a male employee refuses to work on a team with female workers? According to lawyer

Katherine Ford, the employer has a duty of accommodate but none of the rights is absolute and there is no hierarchy of rights. It is important to determine if the request is a right or preference and recognize that each case will be decided on its merits.[8]

Direct Versus Indirect (Systemic) Discrimination

Normally, intentional direct discrimination on grounds specified in the human rights legislation is illegal. However, under certain circumstances intentional direct discrimination is acceptable. A fashion store catering to women will be allowed to advertise for female models, and schools controlled by religious groups are permitted to limit their hiring to members of the specific faith. This legal discrimination is called a **bona fide occupational requirement (BFOR).**

bona fide occupational requirement (BFOR)

A justified business reason for discriminating against a member of a protected class. Also known as bona fide occupational qualification (BFOQ).

Indirect, unintentional, or **systemic discrimination** takes place if there is no intention to discriminate, but the system, arrangements, or policies allow it to happen. Such employment practices may appear to be neutral and may be implemented impartially, but they exclude specific groups of people for reasons that are not job-related or required for safe or efficient business operations. As a chief commissioner of the Ontario Human Rights Commission put it:

systemic discrimination

Any company policy, practice, or action that is not openly or intentionally discriminatory, but has an indirect discriminatory impact or effect.

> The traditional flight of stairs leading into a building was not put there specifically to keep people with mobility impairments out. There's nothing intentional about it; it simply was the way that buildings were designed. But it operates as a very real and substantial and inappropriate barrier to access and entry by people with mobility impairment. That's systemic discrimination.[9]

Examples include

- minimum height and weight requirements for employment with police forces, which make it more difficult for women and Canadians of Asian origin to be hired;
- minimum scores on employment tests, which discriminate against distinct groups (e.g., the use of culturally biased intelligence tests, which tend to screen out a disproportionate number of minorities);
- internal hiring policies, word-of-mouth hiring, or the requirement to submit a photograph with the application form;
- limited accessibility of buildings and facilities, which often makes it impossible for persons with disabilities to be employed with organizations using such places;
- psychological inability of people to deal with persons with disabilities;
- unavailability of alternative formats or forms of tools (e.g., publications in Braille for the blind or telephone devices for the deaf);

- job evaluation systems that tend to undervalue jobs traditionally held by women (e.g., give more points to compensable factors that favour men, such as physical strength, and fewer points to such factors as dexterity);
- promotion criteria that favour factors such as seniority and experience in traditionally male-dominated organizations in which women have not had the chance to acquire either;
- an organizational culture in which minority groups feel unwelcome and uneasy, resulting in a disproportionate turnover rate for such groups; and
- lack of explicit anti-harassment guidelines, which allows an atmosphere of abuse to develop in the workplace.

Indirect or systemic discrimination is more difficult to detect and to fight, because often it is hidden and requires a special effort to deal with effectively. The **Canadian Human Rights Commission (CHRC)** has taken specific steps to define and detect the causes and sources of indirect or systemic discrimination. It initiated a number of surveys to assess the accessibility of federal government offices and the availability of facilities, tools, and services for persons with disabilities. The Commission believes that the Charter of Rights and Freedoms gives it the legal basis to combat such discrimination.[10]

Canadian Human Rights Commission (CHRC)

Supervises the implementation and adjudication of the Canadian Human Rights Act.

Race and Colour

It is sometimes difficult to see which of these two characteristics is the actual basis of discrimination; often both are involved. The discrimination can be intentional or unintentional, subtle or very open:

> A number of years ago, a bank in a small town advertised a position specifying that the applicant should have a pleasing appearance and requested that a recent photograph be submitted. The bank personnel were all Caucasian. A black community leader filed a discrimination complaint, which was settled when the bank agreed to include human rights training in its courses on interviewing, human resource selection, and counselling.

Of course, not all cases end in favour of the complainant.

> Daljit Dhanjal, a Sikh, was employed in the engineering branch of Air Canada. He claimed that he was harassed and subjected to racial slurs by his supervisor, who at one point hit him. Shortly after this latter incident, he was offered an early retirement package. Mr. Dhanjal contended that he was forced to accept this offer because of the atmosphere of discrimination prevailing in this workplace. A human rights tribunal found the complaint to be unsubstantiated: Mr. Dhanjal was not a victim of racial harassment, race, or religion. The tribunal accepted the employer's evidence that Mr. Dhanjal was a poor employee who had trouble getting along with his fellow workers.

There is an interesting side issue in this case. In the tribunal's words, "the poor performance reviews received by the complainant [were] due to the fact that Mr. Dhanjal refused to accept the overbearing and authoritarian management style of his supervisor and that he interpreted this management style subjectively as colonialist and racist behaviour toward him while, in fact, the supervisor was behaving in the same manner toward all of his subordinates." In other words, the supervisor did not discriminate in his abusive behaviour.[11]

A *Canadian HR Reporter* survey found that almost 75 percent of the 235 participants agreed that First Nations people are underutilized in the workforce. Less than one-third of respondents indicated that their organization had a clear mission to recruit First Nations candidates. The most important factors limiting the recruitment of First Nations people included lack of candidates (67 percent), lack of academic qualifications (55 percent), lack of appropriate experience (47 percent), and location of candidates (35 percent).[12]

National or Ethnic Origins

It is also illegal for human resource decisions to be influenced by the national or ethnic origins of applicants or of their forebears. Although discrimination on the basis of national or ethnic origins may be indirect, on some occasions there is clear, documented evidence:

> Ottawa Valley Cleaning and Restoration was ordered to pay $8,000 to a foreign-born job applicant after a human rights tribunal found multiple violations of discrimination based on the applicant's race, colour, and place of origin. Among the text messages sent to the applicant, who during an initial phone call indicated that he was not from Canada, were "Try learning English you will have better luck I don't hire foreners [sic] I keep the white man working," and "Go file a complaint he will probably be a white man and he will probably laugh at you and tell you to go away."[13]

Does your name affect the likelihood of getting a callback after applying for a job? A study from Metropolis British Columbia probed the impact of name discrimination. The study authors sent out about 8,000 résumés to online job postings in three Canadian cities (Toronto, Montreal, and Vancouver). Some résumés had common Anglophone names while others contained common Chinese, Greek, or Indian names. The results revealed that applicants with Anglophone names were 47 percent more likely to get a callback compared with individuals with Chinese or Indian names in Toronto, 39 percent more likely in Montreal, and 20 percent more likely in Vancouver. The authors suggest that subconscious or implicit discrimination may help explain why applicants with non-Anglophone names were less likely to receive a callback.[14]

Religion

A person's religious beliefs and practices should not affect employment decisions. An employer has a **duty to accommodate** an employee's religious practices, unless those practices present undue hardship to the employer:

---

duty to accommodate

Requirement that an employer must accommodate the employee to the point of "undue hardship."

> A Muslim employee of a communications company lost his job over the question of having time off each week to attend prayers at his mosque. After conciliation, a settlement was reached, which did not impose undue hardships on the employer and by which the employee was allowed to take one-and-a-half hours per week of leave without pay. He was reinstated with retroactive pay and benefits.

If an employer does not make a reasonable attempt to accommodate workers' religious practices, he or she can be found guilty of violating the *Human Rights Act*.

The terms "undue hardship" and "duty to accommodate" were examined in an important decision by the Supreme Court of Canada in a ruling against Central Alberta Dairy Pool (1990). The complainant worked at a milk-processing plant. After becoming a member of the Worldwide Church of God, he requested unpaid leave for a particular Monday in order to observe a holy day of his church. The request was refused because Mondays were especially busy days at the plant. When the employee did not report for work, he was fired.

The court ruled that Dairy Pool had discriminated on the basis of religion. Although the company had not done so directly, it had an adverse effect on the complainant due to his religion. It is of importance to note that the court stated that the employer must meet the "duty to accommodate" up to the point of "undue hardship."

The court did not define "undue hardship." However, it stated that relevant considerations would include financial cost, health and safety, disruption of a collective agreement, interference with other workers' rights, the size of the operation, problems of morale of other employees, and interchangeability of workforce and facilities. It found that Dairy Pool could cope with employee absences on Mondays because of illnesses. Therefore, it could also accommodate a single instance for absence due to religious reasons, particularly if the employee had tried to accommodate the employer.[15]

Age

The use of age as an employment criterion has also received considerable attention in the past. Many employers consider that establishing a minimum or maximum age for certain jobs is justified, although evidence is rarely available that age is an accurate indication of one's ability to perform a given type of work: In recent years, we have seen the abolishment of mandatory retirement in jurisdictions across the country. Still, older workers may be the victims of indirect or subtle discrimination.

A Supreme Court judgment forced the RCMP to accommodate its Sikh officers' religious requirement to wear a turban at all times. Should Jewish men be accommodated to wear a yarmulke?

Paul Henry/Sun Media.

Home Depot is very active in recruiting older workers and has partnered with CARP (using career fairs, newsletters, and advertising campaigns) to make older workers aware of job opportunities. About 31 percent of Home Depot's employees are 50 and older, and 6 percent are 65 or older. However, a survey of small and medium-sized employers revealed that more than 70 percent of respondents said it is unlikely that job openings now or in the future will be filled by a person who is as least 65 years of age. The main reason given by employers is that they want to hire people who may stay with the organization for a long period of time.[16]

In December 2011, a section of the *Canadian Human Rights Act* was officially repealed. As a result, the approximately 12,000 federally regulated employers are no longer able to force employees to retire. According to David Langtry, acting chief commissioner of the Canadian Human Rights Commission, "We're not born with date stamps saying our fitness for work expires at 65. Age discrimination is age discrimination, pure and simple."[17]

Do Canadians want to retire? The 2015 *Sunlife Retirement Index* revealed that for 2014, 32 percent of Canadians expect to be working full-time at age 66 (compared with only 16 percent in 2009). About 59 percent reported that they would be working because they need to (compared to 41 percent who want to continue working) and a recent HSBC survey revealed that about 17 percent of Canadians report that they will never have sufficient funds to retire.[18] Some employers have developed programs to assist in the transition to retirement. For instance, Jane McVeigh, VP of HR at C4 Systems International <http://www.gdc4s.com>, found that the use of a phased-in retirement program (where employees reduce their time at work over a year or two) has been very successful in her company.[19]

As mentioned earlier, the law may make an exception for certain occupations when it comes to retirement age. It is not considered a discriminatory practice if a person's employment is terminated because that person has reached the normal age of retirement for employees working in similar positions. The last few years have seen a growth in age discrimination lawsuits. It is important that employers are aware of ageism discrimination and are able to provide clear evidence that employment-related decisions relating to older workers are based on legitimate business reasons.

In one recent case, a 60 year-old was not selected for an interview because the organization was looking for applicants who were "more junior in their experience and salary expectations." Putting pressure on an older worker to retire or trying to "push an older worker out the door" could lead to a human rights complaint. Rather, it is advisable to rely on the performance management system to distinguish between good and poor performers.[20]

Sex

The *Canadian Human Rights Act* also prevents discrimination on the basis of an individual's sex (often erroneously referred to as *gender*; the Act specifically uses the term *sex*). Consider the following case from Prince Edward Island:

> A PEI woman was fired after informing her former employer Inn on the Hill <http://www.innonthehill.com/> that she was pregnant. A human rights panel held that the hotel discriminated against the woman and ordered that it pay $11,700 for lost wages and lost employment insurance benefits and $3,500 for hurt feelings and humiliation.[21]

In another case, the employer tried to force an employee to quit:

> The new owner of a Vancouver sports bar reduced the number of shifts of a server who was six months pregnant from four to about one per week in an effort to get the employee to quit. The tribunal held that the server was in an inhospitable, discriminatory work environment and the bar was unable to show that not being pregnant was a bona fide occupational requirement. Consequently, the server was awarded $2,000 in lost wages and $7,500 for injury to dignity and self-respect.[22]

It should be noted that the Ontario Human Rights Commission recently updated its policy on discrimination on the basis of pregnancy to include protection for women trying to become pregnant[23] and the Supreme Court of Canada, in *Dionne v. Commission scolaire des Patriots*, made it clear that an employer may not discriminate against a pregnant employee who refuses to work because of a risk to the person's health and safety. In the case, Dionne refused work because her doctor advised her that she was susceptible to several harmful viruses and thus her work environment constituted a health risk because children are frequent carriers of a number of viruses.[24]

Not only is it illegal to recruit, hire, and promote employees because of their sex, it is unlawful to have separate policies for men and women. For example, it is discriminatory to reserve some jobs for men only or women only. It is even illegal to apply similar standards to men and women when such standards arbitrarily discriminate more against one sex than against the other. When standards discriminate against one sex (or race, national or ethnic origin, religion, age, or marital status), the burden is on the employer to prove that the standards are necessary:

> A woman complained that she had been refused an interview for a job as a bus driver because she was under the minimum height requirement of 173 centimetres (five feet, eight inches). She claimed that this requirement discriminated against women. After conciliation, the case was settled, with the company discontinuing the practice of requiring applicants to be 173 centimetres tall for drivers' jobs. Two women under that height have since been hired. As part of the settlement, the company agreed that the Commission would monitor the company's driver application records for one year. The complainant was paid $3,500 for lost wages and general damages.

Although the standard did not discriminate against women per se, the arbitrary height requirement tended to exclude most female applicants. To keep the height rule, since it discriminates against women, the employer must show that it is necessary given the nature of the job. If this cannot be shown, the employer can be compelled to drop the requirement.

Spotlight *on* ETHICS

The Hiring Dilemma

The manager of an accounting department has to hire the replacement for a retiring accountant. Over twenty applicants have applied and three were put onto the short list. One of the shortlisted candidates is a 60-year-old CPA, more experienced than the other two, who also have a CPA designation. The manager knows that the department will change accounting practices in the near future (no date has been set yet) and introduce new accounting software, which will require extensive retraining of current staff. If the more experienced candidate is hired, the manager will be faced with the question of whether it is justified to invest a considerable amount in retraining a person who may retire soon after. But if one of the younger candidates is hired, the company might face an age discrimination charge. What should the manager do?

A recent study showed that the words used in job ads had little effect on men but for women, words stereotypically associated with men (such as independent, aggressive, or analytical) made the ad less appealing and decreased the likelihood that a woman would apply for the position. The research suggests that subtle cues may impact on how an ad is perceived.[25] A Catalyst study revealed that women tend to get fewer "hot job" opportunities (such as those with mission-critical roles, C-suite visibility, and international experience) which are critical for advancement in global organizations. About 62 percent of respondents indicated that high profile assignments providing leadership experience had the greatest impact on their career while only 10 percent said that formal training had the largest impact.[26]

A far-reaching Supreme Court decision relating to sex discrimination concerns the earlier mentioned bona fide occupational requirement. The case involved a woman who had been employed by the Province of British Columbia in an elite firefighting unit for more than two years.

> In 1994, Ms. Meiorin failed one of several new fitness tests, a 2.5-kilometre run to be completed in 11 minutes, and lost her employment. A subsequent grievance launched by her union was appealed to the Supreme Court. The court decided in favour of Ms. Meiorin, agreeing with an earlier arbitrator's ruling that the government had failed to justify the test as a BFOR by providing credible evidence that her inability to meet the standard created a safety risk.[27]

The court established three new criteria to assess the appropriateness of a BFOR:

1. Is the standard rationally connected to the performance of the job?

2. Was the standard established in an honest belief that it was necessary to accomplish the purpose identified in stage one?

3. Is the standard reasonably necessary to accomplish its purpose?

The stricter rules may make it more difficult for human resource managers to establish and defend BFORs. However, one report suggests that the promise of Meiorin—that human rights legislation would take adverse effects discrimination seriously—is under attack, with intensified efforts to prevent complainants from going beyond the prima facie stage of discrimination. According to the authors, "for many people with disabilities, the duty to accommodate as it is being applied today, simply does not go far enough to ensure their equality and inclusion in the world they live in."[28]

Sexual Orientation

Consider this recent case:

> Robert Ranger, a gay correctional officer, alleged harassment and discrimination based on his sexual orientation. While the main antagonist was a fellow union member, the employer knew the environment was poisoned and did nothing to accommodate Ranger when he was able to return to work. Ranger suffered from "profoundly humiliating homophobic harassment" and eventually went on long-term disability. He still suffers from anxiety attacks and depression. Ranger was awarded $53,000 in compensatory damages for the employer's failure to accommodate, $244,000 for lost wages, and $45,000 in compensatory damages for discrimination, harassment, and a poisoned workplace. In the words of vice-chair Deborah Leighton, "there is no case before me where the complainant has suffered such extensive harm."[29]

As stated in the 1999 Canadian Human Rights Commission's annual report, that year may come to be regarded as a watershed year for gay and lesbian Canadians. The issue of discrimination against same-sex relationships was effectively addressed by the Supreme Court of Canada when it decided that same-sex couples must be treated the same way as heterosexual couples.

In 1996, a human rights tribunal ordered the federal government to extend medical and dental benefits to the same-sex partners of its employees. The same year, the government amended the *Human Rights Act* to add sexual orientation as a prohibited ground of discrimination. Since then, several Supreme Court decisions have forced provinces to amend their benefit and tax laws to include same-sex couples into their considerations. In 2000, Parliament passed legislation treating same-sex partners the same as legally married and common-law couples for all purposes of federal law, but left the traditional definition of marriage as between a man and a woman. Finally, in June 2005, Parliament also changed the definition of marriage to include same-sex couples.[30]

We are also seeing changing attitudes toward lesbian, gay, bisexual, and transgender employees:

> A survey by the Canadian Gay and Lesbian Chamber of Commerce of almost 1,000 lesbian, gay, bisexual, and transgender (LBGT) employees across the country indicated that attitudes toward LGBT people at work have improved over the past five years, with 72 percent of participants agreeing with that statement. However,

about 40 percent of respondents reported having been victims of discrimination at work, with social exclusion (43 percent) and ridicule (42 percent) being the most common forms of discrimination. More than 25 percent of participants indicated that they are worried about negative consequences if they come out at work (and more than 20 percent of that group believe that coming out may impair their opportunities for advancement).[31]

Gender Identity

As of March 2015, seven Canadian provinces and territories (Manitoba, Newfoundland and Labrador, Northwest Territories, Nova Scotia, Ontario, Prince Edward Island, and Saskatchewan) explicitly protect "gender identity" or "gender identity and expression" in their human rights legislation. Although not expressly protected in the *Alberta Human Rights Act*, the *Alberta Bill of Rights* has been amended (coming into force on June 1, 2015) to include gender identity and expression. Other jurisdictions, including the federal jurisdiction, indicate that while gender identity and expression are not expressly contained in the legislation, protections are interpreted under other prohibited grounds such as sex or gender.

A transgender bill (C-279) passed by the House of Commons in March 2013 is caught up in delays at Senate. The bill would add gender identity as a protected characteristic under the Canadian Human Rights Code and would also add it to the list of distinguishing characteristics of identifiable groups protected by Criminal Code hate speech provisions. Prime Minister Stephen Harper is opposed to the bill and NDP MP Randall Garrison believes that "their intention is to kill the bill by delay."[32]

A number of employers may not have policies relating to transgendered employees. Brian Kreissl, Managing Editor at Consult Carswell, makes the following suggestions: (1) meet with the employee beforehand to determine how and what should be communicated, (2) hold information sessions with other employees before the transgendered employee commences work, (3) have a respectful workplace policy, (4) inform employees to call the employee by his or her chosen name and pronoun, (5) allow the employee to dress in accordance with the dress code matching his or her gender identity, and (6) permit the employee to use washroom facilities consistent with the person's gender identity.[33]

Marital Status

The idea of what constitutes a family has undergone considerable change in Canadian society in recent years. Single-parent families, or nontraditional families, such as those resulting from common-law marriages, are now far more numerous than in the past. But there is still a strong feeling that the traditional family is a unique institution deserving special consideration.

The *Canadian Human Rights Act* spells out quite clearly that any discrimination based on marital status is illegal:

> A woman was denied a job with the CBC because her husband was already employed by the corporation at the same station. After a complaint and hearing, the CBC changed its employment practices, which formerly discriminated on the basis of marital status, and placed the woman in a position in the same station in which her husband was employed.

Family Status

In a widely cited case regarding family status, the CHRC initiated action against the Canada Employment Insurance Commission (CEIC) <http://www.esdc.gc.ca/en/ei/commission.page>.

> Ms. Ina Lang alleged that the CEIC denied her application for funding under the Challenge 86 program because she wished to hire her daughter to help in her family child care business. A tribunal held that the

CEIC had discriminated against Ms. Lang on the basis of her family status when it denied her the funding she sought, and awarded her $1,000 for hurt feelings. The CEIC appealed the decision to the Federal Court of Appeal, but the court upheld the decision.

A Canadian airline found out that *nepotism* is a form of discrimination based on family status. The airline had a policy of hiring the children of its employees for summer jobs. The CHRC ruled that this amounted to discrimination and a federal court rejected an appeal of this decision.

Some recent human rights decisions relating to family status suggest that employers may have a duty to accommodate employees with child care obligations unless such accommodation results in undue hardship. A number of the cases have dealt with work schedule issues and whether the employer would adjust the timing of shifts. However, it appears that voluntary family activities (such as vacations or extracurricular sporting events) would not fall under the duty to accommodate.[34]

Disability

No person should be denied employment solely for the reason of his or her being disabled. Of course, there are exceptions. A blind person cannot be a truck driver, or a deaf person a telephone operator. However, the principle of **reasonable accommodation** has been established. It means that an employer can be expected to take reasonable measures to make available a suitable job to a person with a physical handicap if it does not impose undue hardships on the organization:

reasonable accommodation

Voluntary adjustments to work or workplace that allow employees with special needs to perform their job effectively.

Coffee giant Starbucks <http://www.starbucks.com> was sued by a barista in El Paso, Texas. The woman, who is a dwarf, was hired on a trial basis and requested that she be able to use a stool or step ladder to help her perform her job. The company decided that using a stool was not reasonable accommodation considering the work environment and argued that the woman could represent a danger to customers and co-workers. The case was ultimately settled with Starbucks agreeing to pay the woman $75,000 and to provide training on disability issues to all managers and supervisory staff in its El Paso locations.[35]

The labour force participation rate is about 54 percent for people with disabilities and almost 800,000 Canadians are not working although their disability does not prevent them from doing so (with about half of the people having post-secondary education).[36]

Mackenzie Whitney has a math degree from the University of Alberta but was stuck working at marginal jobs because he is autistic. A year ago, he started working at Meticulon Consulting <http://meticulon.com> in Calgary as a junior tester monitoring quality assurance. Company co-founder Garth Johnson stated that he looks for people with autism because they offer unique skills such as precision, diligence, attention to detail, and an ability to sustain focus.[37]

Many organizations have established rigid physical standards for certain jobs without being able to show that these standards are truly relevant to the requirements of the job. Some complainants have been refused jobs when their disability might be a problem in a speculative situation; for example, the firm might argue that a deaf person would be unable to hear a fire alarm. Other complainants have been disqualified for jobs not because they are physically disabled now, but because they may become so in the future.

Being alcohol or drug-dependent can also be interpreted as a disability. Employees with dependency on drugs or alcohol must be reasonably accommodated to the point of undue hardship on the employer. Typical requirements include providing an employee assistance program or giving an employee time off to attend such a program. However, an employer is not obligated to accept long-term absences unrelated to rehabilitation.[38]

In its 2001 annual report, the Canadian Human Rights Commission <http://www.chrc-ccdp.ca/eng> suggested a new approach to dealing with barriers to the hiring of disabled persons. As an example, the chief commissioner pointed to new legislation in Ontario, the *Ontarians with Disabilities Act*, 2001. This Act allowed for the establishment of barrier-free standards on accessibility matters such as building access and public transportation. It required architects to consider the regulations of the Act during the planning process for a building. It was the first example in Canada of a standards-based barrier removal legislation.[39] Recent Ontario legislation is further addressing workplace issues relevant to employees with disabilities:

> In Ontario, the *Accessibility for Ontarians with Disabilities Act* (AODA) requires employers to make workplaces accessible to members of the public with disabilities. It is estimated that one in seven people in Ontario has a disability and that number is projected to increase. As of January 1, 2012, the Integrated Accessibility Standards Regulation requires that emergency procedures and plans be available in accessible formats if requested and employers must develop an individualized workplace emergency response plan for employees with a disability.[40]

However, several employers are in violation of the legislation. Ontario businesses with more than 20 employees were to have filed online reports by the end of 2012 indicating how they accommodate customers with disabilities, train employees, and obtain customer feedback. However, 65 percent of firms still have not filed their 2012 reports and the plan is to reduce the number of compliance inspections in 2015.[41]

Scotiabank changed its funding relating to accommodation to include services:

> According to Deanna Matzanke, Director, Global Employment Strategies (Diversity & Inclusion; HR Policy & Compliance) at the bank, "a lot of episodic disabilities (such as multiple sclerosis and chronic fatigue syndrome) don't actually need assistive technology or an electronic door. What they need more often are types of services like a job coach to help organize the workplace." About one-third of employers indicated that their knowledge of how to support people with episodic disabilities was low. Accommodations for people with episodic disabilities may include such things as flextime, working from home, adjusting work duties, and providing a private space at the workplace where employees can take medications or rest.[42]

Also consider the experience of a Tim Hortons franchisor:

> Mark Wafer is a Tim Hortons <http://www.timhortons.com> franchisor with six stores. Several years ago he hired an employee with an intellectual disability and by 2011 had 28 employees with intellectual disabilities. Wafer notes that he has "created an inclusive workplace where people with disabilities are treated as equals." Wafer reports that his store has a turnover rate of about 35 percent compared with the industry average of 80 percent. He also observes that the average tenure of employees is about one year and four months but it is about seven years for an employee with a disability. [43]

A *Canadian HR Reporter* survey revealed that about 50 percent of employers have a policy encouraging the hiring of people with disabilities and 70 percent have hired an individual who self-identified as having a disability. In terms of performance, 9 percent of respondents indicated that employees with disabilities performed better than other employees, almost 80 percent said there was no difference, and only 6 percent perceived that employees with disabilities performed worse than other workers. The three types of assistance that would be most beneficial include workplace support for employees with disabilities (such as a short-term job coach), disability awareness training for staff, and financial assistance with training and workplace modifications.[44]

Pardoned Convicts

The *Canadian Human Rights Act* prohibits discrimination against a convicted person if a pardon has been issued for the offence. Pardon may be granted by a parole board after five years following release, parole, or the completion of a sentence:

> A person convicted and paroled on a drug offence applied for a job with a government agency dealing with drug abuse. He was denied employment because of his conviction. Subsequently, the National Parole Board granted his request for a full pardon. The government agency maintained, however, that, pardoned or not, he remained a security risk and that being without a criminal record was a BFOR of a correctional service's staff. He appealed to the Canadian Human Rights Commission, and after the Commission's investigation, the government agency decided that a criminal record would not, in fact, inhibit the applicant's ability to meet the requirements of the job, and, satisfied that he was suitable, offered him the position. [45]

The CHRC has also been approached by persons who claim to have been refused employment on the basis of their arrest record, even when the arrest did not lead to a conviction. These persons are without legal protection, because the *Canadian Human Rights Act* does not address this type of discrimination. For the human resource manager, this does not mean that all applicants can be asked for their arrest record. It must still be shown that it is relevant to the job. For this reason, the Commission has advised employers under federal jurisdiction that applicants should not be asked, "Have you ever been convicted of an offence?" It is recommended—if such information is legitimately needed for employment purposes—that the question be phrased: "Have you ever been convicted of an offence for which you have not received a pardon?"

LO3 HRC 1, 4 & 5

Harassment

The *Canadian Human Rights Act* contains the following prohibition against harassment:

> It is a discriminatory practice,
>
> a) in the provision of goods, services, facilities or accommodation customarily available to the general public,
>
> b) in the provision of commercial premises or residential accommodation, or
>
> c) in matters related to employment,
>
> to harass an individual on a prohibited ground of discrimination.

Such behaviour may be verbal, physical, deliberate, unsolicited, or unwelcome; it may be one incident or a series of incidents. Protection against harassment extends to incidents occurring at or away from the workplace, during or outside normal working hours, provided such incidents are employment-related. [46] Consider a recent class action against the RCMP:

> A former member of the RCMP <http://www.rcmp-grc.gc.ca> initiated a class action lawsuit against the RCMP with the goal of purging the toxic attitude against women. Janet Merlo, who spent 19 years in the RCMP, alleges that she was subject to ongoing sexist comments, sexual pranks, derogatory remarks, and double standards. According to Merlo's lawyer David Klein, "Part of the problem is that the complaints women made were not taken seriously by the force. They need a new structure and it's something that has to come from the top down." [47]

As of the fall of 2014, approximately 335 women have joined the lawsuit. [48]

Although somewhat controversial, a website in the United States, eBossWatch <www.ebosswatch.com>, allows employees to provide anonymous ratings of their supervisors. While the founder of the website argues that this information will allow people to evaluate potential bosses, managerial candidates, and employers, there is the risk of false allegations or defamation complaints.[49]

What is harassment? **Harassment** may include

---

harassment

Occurs when a member of an organization treats an employee in a disparate manner because of that person's sex, race, religion, age, or other protective classification.

- verbal abuse or threats;
- unwelcome remarks, jokes, innuendo, or taunting about a person's body, attire, age, marital status, ethnic or national origin, religion, and so on;
- displaying of pornographic, racist, or other offensive or derogatory pictures;
- practical jokes that cause awkwardness or embarrassment;
- unwelcome invitations or requests, whether indirect or explicit, or intimidation;
- leering or other gestures;
- condescension or paternalism that undermines self-respect;
- unnecessary physical contact such as touching, patting, pinching, or punching; and
- physical assault.

It will be assumed that harassing behaviour has taken place if a "reasonable person ought to have known that such behaviour was unwelcome."[50]

A City of Woodstock parks department employee with 20 years of service and no previous disciplinary problems was demoted for sexually harassing a female employee and her co-workers during their summer employment. In addition to sexually inappropriate comments, the employee asked two female summer students (and one of the complainant's 16-year-old sister) to come to his hot tub, sent texts asking if all girls liked to be choked, and stated that he would like to marry the complainant. The employee's work computer also revealed he had pictures of the complainant taken away from the worksite and inappropriate pictures of her at work. The city decided to dismiss the employee who, through his union, grieved the dismissal (arguing that he was unaware that his behaviour was unwanted and that there was no policy prohibiting fraternization between supervisors with other workers). The arbitrator noted that the grievor had no previous disciplinary offences on his record and the harassment did not go beyond verbal and texted comments. As a result, the arbitrator gave the grievor a two-month suspension and an indefinite demotion to a non-supervisory position.[51]

Although most organizations have strong policies on harassment, an issue that is frequently overlooked is workplace ostracism. Ostracism is a form of bullying and can be overt or subtle but it is often omitted from harassment policies. It is important to make managers aware of the problem, provide training to employees, and emphasize that ostracism will not be tolerated.[52]

There is also growing concern about cyberbullying. An AVG Technologies study of employees in 10 countries revealed that about one-quarter of companies do not have a cyberbullying policy and only 37 percent of employees are aware of a comprehensive policy. Almost 10 percent of employees have had a manager use information against them that was obtained from a social media site, 53 percent believe that workplace privacy has been eroded due to social media, and 11 percent have had embarrassing photos or videos taken at a work event and then uploaded onto social media. Common forms of cyberbullying include sending unpleasant or defamatory remarks to or about a colleague and posting negative comments on a social media site about a colleague's appearance.[53]

From a policy perspective aimed at addressing cyberbullying, employers need to: (1) revise harassment and bullying policies to include cyberbullying, (2) create a procedure for investigating and reporting cyberbullying, (3) provide training on cyberbullying, (4) provide EAP support to employees who are victims of bullying, (5) have a zero tolerance policy, (5) respond to allegations in a timely manner, (6) raise awareness of cyberbullying, (7) make sure that you have a respectful workplace policy, (8) regularly monitor emails, social media, and text messages for incidents of cyberbullying, and (9) require employees to sign an antibullying agreement.[54]

Sexual harassment has become an important topic in human resource management, evidenced by the increased number of complaints lodged. A Canadian Human Rights Tribunal identified three characteristics of sexual harassment:

---

sexual harassment

Unsolicited or unwelcome sex- or gender-based conduct that has adverse employment consequences for the complainant.

---

1. the encounters must be unsolicited by the complainant, unwelcome to the complainant, and expressly or implicitly known by the respondent to be unwelcome;

2. the conduct must either continue despite the complainant's protests or, if the conduct stops, the complainant's protests must have led to negative employment consequences; and

3. the complainant's co-operation must be due to employment-related threats or promises.

How common is sexual harassment? An Angus Reid poll revealed that 28 percent of Canadians experienced unwelcome sexual advances, requests for sexual favours, or sexually-charged talk, with 43 percent of women and 12 percent of men reporting that they had been sexually harassed. One-quarter of participants who reported harassment indicated that management was unresponsive and dismissive, and three-quarters of the victims were harassed more than once. Also, 12 percent of women and 9 percent of men indicated that the harassment included unwanted sexual contact. Just under 80 percent of people experiencing sexual harassment did not report it to the employer.[55]

A landmark case involving sexual harassment was *Robichaud v. Department of National Defence (DND)*, which made its way up to the Supreme Court. The court ruled that the employer shared the responsibility for the actions of one of its supervisors who had sexually harassed Ms. Robichaud. It added that "only an employer can remedy undesirable effects [of discrimination]; only an employer can provide the most important remedy—a healthy work environment." The DND was ordered to pay Ms. Robichaud $5,000 for pain and suffering, to issue a written apology, and to post the written apology in all DND facilities.

Women are not the only employees who may be subjected to sexual harassment. Evidence from the United States Equal Employment Opportunity Commission <http://www.eeoc.gov> indicates that about 16 percent of all sexual harassment claims are by men and the percentage has doubled over the past 20 years. Most of the charges of sexual harassment filed by men involve men harassing other men:

R.R., a deckhand on a tugboat owned by Sea-West Holdings Ltd., was sexually harassed by the tug's skipper. He complained to the owner of Sea-West, but nothing was done. He was eventually fired. A tribunal held that the sexual harassment had created a poisoned work situation in which the individual is given a work environment which is intimidating, hostile, and offensive. The tribunal also felt that there is a duty upon the owner so informed (of harassment) to put an immediate stop to such practices. R.R. was awarded $2,000 for hurt feelings and $1,760 for lost wages.

The Jian Ghomeshi case has underscored the importance of having a clear policy on sexual harassment and conducting a proper investigation. According to lawyer Doug MacLeod, "if the employee believed that their complaint has been taken seriously and fairly investigated, then they're much less likely to go to the human rights tribunal."[56]

Employer Retaliation

It is a criminal act to retaliate in any way against those who exercise their rights according to the *Canadian Human Rights Act*. Those who file charges, testify, or otherwise participate in any human rights action are protected by law. If a supervisor tries to get even with an employee who filed charges, he or she violates the Act.

Enforcement

The responsibility for the administration of the *Canadian Human Rights Act* lies in the hands of the Canadian Human Rights Commission (CHRC). The Commission consists of up to eight members including the Chief Commissioner, who is a full-time member appointed for a term of not more than seven years. Other full-time members are also appointed for a term not to exceed seven years and part-time members are appointed for a term of not more than three years.

The role of the CHRC is to investigate and try to resolve allegations of discrimination in employment and the provision of services within the federal jurisdiction. The CHRC also administers the *Employment Equity Act*. The Commission is also mandated to develop and conduct information and prevention programs, to conduct and sponsor research, and to report annually to Parliament. The Commission is not a tribunal and does not rule on cases. If a complaint cannot be resolved, the Commission may recommend mediation or ultimately ask the Canadian Human Rights Tribunal to hear the case. Figure 4-3 describes some of the remedies available to the tribunal in settling a complaint. Should the tribunal find that the discriminatory practice was maintained purposely or recklessly, or that the victim's feelings or self-respect have suffered as a result of the practice, it may order the person or organization responsible to compensate the victim appropriately.

A person who obstructs an investigation or a tribunal, or fails to comply with the terms of a settlement, or reduces wages in order to eliminate a discriminatory practice, can be found guilty of an offence punishable by a fine or jail sentence or both. On summary conviction, such a person can be liable to a fine not exceeding $50,000.[57]

Spotlight *on* HRM

When a Manager Is Accused of Sexual Harassment

How you first respond to a complaint of sexual harassment filed against you is extremely critical. Knowing what to do and what not to do can have a big impact on the results of the investigation that follows.

Employers have an obligation to conduct an inquiry into the allegations when a complaint of sexual harassment has been lodged.

Although every case is different and the nature and extent of the investigation will depend on the circumstances, here are a few suggestions on how you should react if a complaint is filed against you:

(Continued)

Avoid any emotional reaction when first confronted with the complaint. It is not unusual for an accused person to become defensive, angry, threatening, or incoherent after being advised of a complaint. Restrain yourself from any overt behaviour that can later be categorized one way or the other. Try to keep the first meeting brief so you can leave to collect your thoughts and seek appropriate advice.

Never provide any response when first advised of the complaint. It will be hard to stay rational when you are first told about the complaint. You are at a disadvantage at this point; therefore, avoid any knee-jerk response that you may regret later.

It is important to understand the nature of the complaint. As an accused, you are entitled to know every allegation that has been made by both the complainant and any witnesses. Ask to be provided with a copy of the written complaint and any statement by witnesses.

If the complaint has not been recorded in writing, ask that the employer go back to the complainant and obtain a signed copy. This also applies to witnesses. The reason is that you want to confine the complaint and avoid any subsequent changes. And ask what the complainant is seeking by filing it.

Does the employer have a sexual or workplace harassment policy? Whether the conduct that you are accused of will be characterized as sexual harassment may depend on the definition in the company policy. It should outline how the investigation will be conducted and what types of corrective action could be taken by the employer if you are found guilty.

Retain an employment lawyer who has experience in sexual harassment cases. You are entitled to retain a lawyer, usually at your cost. An experienced counsel will provide you with a clear understanding of the law of sexual harassment and will assist you throughout the investigation. Your lawyer may not be permitted to accompany you during your interview with investigators. Still, you should press your employer for the right to have counsel present.

You have a right to respond to all allegations made against you. This will normally occur during your interview with investigators and it is usually done orally. However, circumstances may require that you provide a written response along with your oral interview. Be prepared to explain the context in which any behaviour occurred and to provide the names of any witnesses that you want the investigators to talk to.

You should avoid being uncooperative or engaging in any retaliatory behaviour. There could be serious consequences for you if you engage in this type of conduct. Cooperation does not mean waiving any of your rights, but you should always be respectful of the process and be honest in your approach.

Avoid any conduct that could be characterized as interfering with the investigation. This usually means trying to contact the complainant or any of the witnesses. Do not engage in any kind of retaliation against either of these parties. For example, changing the terms of employment or threatening to discipline or terminate the complainant or any witnesses could qualify as retaliation. Threatening to sue the complainant for defamation during the course of the investigation may also be considered a form of retaliation. Such conduct will usually be treated as a violation of company policy.

Avoid making denials where the truth is required. You may be surprised to know that just because you deny something occurred and there are no witnesses does not mean you can't be found guilty of sexual harassment. In many cases there are no witnesses and investigators must make a decision on the basis of conflicting evidence and credibility.

If there is no reasonable explanation for your conduct, be honest in your response and acknowledge any shortcomings in your behaviour. Misleading or lying to investigators can only make things worse for you. When a complaint of sexual harassment is filed against you, it is a very serious matter. It could result in discipline or even termination and, in most cases, would undermine your relationship with your co-workers and your reputation. The manner in which you respond may well determine your fate.

SOURCE: Courtesy of Malcolm MacKillop. Used with permission.

As mentioned previously, provinces have their own rules regarding human rights violations. Some employer lawyers are expressing concerns about the increasing awards associated with human rights cases. There appears to be a trend toward greater damages for injury to dignity and punitive damages.[58]

FIGURE 4-3

Remedies for Violations

> The Canadian Human Rights Tribunal has several remedies at its disposal. For example, it can order a violator to:
>
> - Stop the discriminatory practice.
>
> - Restore the rights, opportunities, and privileges denied the victim.
>
> - Compensate the victim for wages lost and any expenses incurred as a result of the discriminatory practice.
>
> - Compensate the victim for pain and suffering.
>
> - Develop and implement employment equity programs to equalize opportunity for certain groups that have suffered from discriminatory practices in the past.

HRC 5

Provincial Human Rights Laws and Human Rights Commissions

Most provinces and two territories (Northwest Territories and Yukon) have their own human rights laws and commissions with similar discrimination criteria, regulations, and procedures. British Columbia abolished its commission in 2003, but retained its Human Rights Tribunal. Nunavut has a human rights act and a tribunal and Ontario has both a commission and tribunal.

If a person feels discriminated against, he or she will contact a provincial human rights officer, who will investigate the complaint and attempt to reach a settlement that will satisfy all parties. Experience has shown that the majority of cases are settled at this stage. Should there be no agreement, the case will be presented to the provincial human rights commission. The members of that commission study the evidence and then submit a report to the minister in charge of administration of the relevant human rights legislation. Depending on the jurisdiction, a case may be sent to the relevant human rights tribunal or board of inquiry (which has powers similar to those of a tribunal). Noncompliance with the course of action prescribed by the board/tribunal may result in prosecution in a provincial court of law. Depending on the jurisdiction, individuals can be fined between $500 and $25,000. If an issue at hand has nationwide implications, a decision may ultimately be appealed to the Supreme Court of Canada.

There has been a trend recently to try and improve the dispute resolution programs administered by human rights commissions. For example, beginning in 2012, the Nova Scotia Human Rights Commission began using a "resolution conference" in an effort to deal with complaints better, faster, and in a manner helping to restore or repair relationships. The objective is to have the parties create their own solution to the complaint. If a resolution conference fails to resolve a complaint, information from it will be used to make a recommendation to commissioners who can dismiss the complaint or send it to a board of inquiry.[59]

Some jurisdictions, such as Ontario, have set up a human rights tribunal to deal with claims of discrimination. How do HR professionals view the tribunal's effectiveness? A survey of 235 HR professionals revealed that 76 percent perceive a bias against employers, 73 percent believe there are frivolous or nuisance claims, and 53 percent indicate that the process is too lengthy. According to one respondent, "the tribunal serves an important purpose but the reputation is it has a red carpet for complainants and a built-in bias for the employer."[60]

LO4 HRC 1 & 5

Employment Equity

The Abella Commission on Equality in Employment (chaired by Judge Rosalie Abella) was appointed in 1983 to inquire into the most effective, efficient, and equitable methods of promoting employment opportunities for four designated groups: women, persons with a disability, Aboriginal people, and members of a visible minority. The Commission recommended that all organizations set mandatory equality programs and urged the provincial and federal governments to pass equity legislation—a recommendation that has since been implemented by the federal and all provincial governments. The Commission also recommended to use the term *employment equity* in Canada to distinguish it from the U.S. term, *affirmative action*, because, in the opinion of the Commission, the latter carried too many negative associations.*

As a result of the Abella Commission's report, the federal government proclaimed the ***Employment Equity Act*** in August 1987. Its intent is to remove employment barriers and promote equality of the four designated group members. The Act requires employers with 100 and more employees under federal jurisdiction to develop annual plans setting out goals and timetables and to maintain these plans for three years. The Act requires further that each employer submit annual reports describing the progress in attaining the goals set out in the abovementioned plans. The Canada Employment and Immigration Commission forwards employer reports to the Human Rights Commission. Employers who do not comply may be investigated by the Human Rights Commission and, if necessary, prosecuted under the *Canadian Human Rights Act*.

Employment Equity Act
Federal law to remove employment barriers and to promote equality.

The *Employment Equity Act* was amended in 1996. It now contains two specific provisions regarding "reasonable accommodation." Section 5 provides that:

> "Every employer shall implement employment equity" by, among other measures, "making such reasonable accommodations as will ensure that persons in a designated group" achieve a degree of representation commensurate with their representation in the Canadian workforce and their availability to meet reasonable occupational requirements.

As noted above, the four designated groups are women, Aboriginal people, persons with a disability, and members of a visible minority. (This is in contrast to human rights legislation, which requires equal treatment of *all* groups.)

Section 10 of the Act specifies that an employer shall prepare an "employment equity plan" that provides for "reasonable accommodation ... to correct ... under-representation." Some examples of reasonable accommodation are

- providing a sign-language interpreter for a job interview with a deaf applicant;
- providing telephone or computer equipment to accommodate persons who are hard of hearing or blind;

---

*The major difference between Canadian employment equity and U.S. affirmative action programs is that the former are based on the principle of equitable access in all employment systems, while the latter are based on the principle of righting past wrongs.

- constructing a barrier-free worksite for wheelchair-bound employees;
- allowing religious minorities to alter their work schedules to accommodate religious obligations; and
- altering dress or grooming codes to allow Aboriginal people to wear braids.

The amended Act also established the CHRC as the monitoring agency that would carry out compliance audits for federally regulated public- and private-sector employers.

HRC 1, 2, 4, 5, 6 & 7

Functional Impact

Virtually every human resource function is affected by employment equity plans:

- *Human resource plans* must reflect the organization's employment equity goals.
- *Job descriptions* must not contain unneeded requirements that exclude members of protected classes.
- *Recruiting* must ensure that all types of applicants are sought without discriminating.
- *Selection* of applicants must use screening devices that are job-relevant and nondiscriminatory.
- *Training and developmental* opportunities must be made available for all workers, without discrimination.
- *Performance appraisal* must be free of biases that discriminate.
- *Compensation programs* must be based on skills, performance, and/or seniority and cannot discriminate against jobholders in other respects.

Even when human resource specialists know that their intent is not to discriminate, they must carefully review the results of these human resource functions to ensure that the results are not discriminatory. Otherwise, lawsuits may arise and the current employment equity plan may need to be revised or scrapped.

HRC 1 & 5

Employment Equity Programs

The *Employment Equity Act* gives the CHRC great latitude in pursuing the enforcement of the Act. One way for the Commission to comply with the intent of the Act to improve equal employment opportunities for special groups is for it to encourage **employment equity programs**.

employment equity programs

Developed by employers to undo past employment discrimination or to ensure equal employment opportunity in the future. Called affirmative action programs in the United States.

Section 16(1) of the *Canadian Human Rights Act* specifies special programs as a legitimate mechanism for improving the opportunities of a group through the elimination, reduction, or prevention of discrimination:

It is not a discriminatory practice for a person to adopt or carry out a special program, plan, or arrangement designed to prevent disadvantages that are likely to be suffered by, or to eliminate or reduce disadvantages that are suffered by, any group of individuals when those disadvantages would be based on or related to the prohibited grounds of discrimination, by improving opportunities respecting goods, services, facilities, accommodation, or employment in relation to that group.

Such programs are developed by employers to remedy past discrimination or to prevent discrimination in the future. For the organization, such a program usually involves a self-evaluation of its hiring, promotion, and compensation policies. If discrepancies are found, it would be good human resource practice to check the criteria used for different decisions, adjust them if necessary, and make sure that they are consistently applied.

Employment equity programs exist for several reasons. From a practical standpoint, employers seldom benefit by excluding people who belong to a particular group. To exclude an entire class of workers, such as women or visible minorities, limits the labour pool available to the human resource department. Open discrimination can also lead to negative public relations, boycotts by consumers, and government intervention. To ensure that such discrimination does not occur, employers often develop equity programs voluntarily.

It should be noted that mandated equity programs take place mainly at the federal level—that is, in organizations and industries under federal jurisdiction. At the provincial level, such programs are implemented almost exclusively on a voluntary basis, when organizations recognize an advantage in it. For example, at Saint Mary's University in Halifax, an employee equity program, approved by the Nova Scotia Human Rights Commission, was implemented to balance a perceived employment inequity between male and female faculty.

Regardless of the reasons or goals of such programs, human resource departments should adhere to the guidelines discussed below and summarized in Figure 4-4.

FIGURE 4-4

Major Steps in Employment Equity Programs

1. Exhibit strong employer commitment.
2. Appoint a high-ranking director.
3. Publicize commitment internally and externally.
4. Survey the workforce for underutilization and concentration.
5. Develop goals and timetables.
6. Design remedial, active, and preventive programs.
7. Establish control systems and reporting procedures.

- **Exhibit commitment.** No matter how favourably the human resource department is viewed by others in the organization, the CEO/president of the company should support the program in writing. Anything less than total support from top officials raises questions about the sincerity of the organization's commitment in the eyes of government agencies, courts, and employees. To exhibit this commitment forcefully, company officials may make raises, bonuses, and promotions dependent upon each manager's compliance.

- **Appoint a director.** Some member of the organization should be responsible for equity issues. Commonly, the vice-president of human resources is appointed director, although day-to-day implementation may be delegated to a compliance specialist in the human resource department.

- **Publicize commitment.** An employment equity program is ineffective unless publicized externally and internally. Outside the company, sources of potential recruits must be made aware of the new policy. School guidance counsellors, employment agencies, and officers of Canada

Employment Centres are likely candidates for notification. Organizations should include the phrase "An equal opportunity employer" on company stationery and in employment ads to further publicize its policy. Internally, the practice should be conveyed, in strong enough terms, to everyone involved in the hiring process. Otherwise, top management may pursue one policy and lower levels another.

- **Survey the workforce.** The human resource department needs to know how the composition of the employer's workforce compares with the composition of the workforce in the labour market. For example, if the employer's mix of male and female employees differs significantly from the labour market from which the employer attracts workers, it is possible that discrimination has occurred. When a survey of the employer's workforce indicates such differences, the employer may find examples of underutilization or concentration. **Underutilization** exists when a company or department has a smaller proportion of protected class members than is found in the labour market. For example, when a company has no female managers even though the labour market is 37 percent female, underutilization exists. **Concentration** is just the opposite, occurring when protected class members are concentrated in a few departments, out of proportion with their presence in the labour market.

---

underutilization

A condition that exists when a department or employer has a lesser proportion of members of a protected class than are found in the employer's labour market.

---

concentration

A condition that exists when a department or employer has a greater proportion of members of a protected class than are found in the employer's labour market.

- **Develop goals and timetables.** When, through surveys, underutilization and concentration are found (possibly as consequences of past discrimination), human resource specialists should set up goals and timetables to eliminate them.

- **Design specific programs.** To reach goals, human resource specialists must design remedial, active, and preventive programs. *Remedial programs* correct problems that already exist. *Active programs* imply that management goes beyond instructing supervisors about new hiring policies and waiting for things to happen. It means going to high schools in areas dominated by minorities, approaching community leaders in such areas for assistance, inviting residents to attend information sessions, and advertising in newspapers or other media outlets accessible to minorities and special target groups:

> The Law School at Dalhousie University in Halifax developed an Indigenous Black and Mi'kmaq Program to train more black and Mi'kmaq lawyers. It appointed a director and began a publication campaign aimed at these groups by advertising in local newspapers and association publications. The program director visits high schools and universities and holds information sessions at reserves and community centres. An advisory board made up of law school representatives, community leaders, and the two student groups assists in identifying ways to reach the target groups. [61]

Preventive programs are more proactive. They involve an assessment of human resource management policies and practices. Policies that discriminate (such as height rules) or practices that continue past discrimination (such as hiring exclusively from employee referrals) must be eliminated.

- **Establish controls.** An employment equity program is likely to fail unless controls are established. Human resource specialists and line managers must perceive their rewards as depending upon the success of the program. To evaluate that success, monthly, quarterly, and yearly benchmarks should be reported directly to the director of the program and to the CEO/president or another senior official.

HRC 1

Contract Compliance Policy

In addition to companies or agencies under federal jurisdiction, the federal government requires compliance with the *Employment Equity Act* from any company doing business with the federal government. Companies with 100 or more employees bidding on contracts for goods and services of $1,000,000 or more are subject to the employment equity criteria listed in the Act. Under this policy, companies are required to certify in writing at the tendering stage of a contract their commitment to implement employment equity. Employers will be subject to random reviews to ensure their compliance with the Act.

HRC 5 & 6

Pay Equity

Women aged 25–54 earn about 85 percent as much per hour compared to male employees. The gap is less for unionized workers (94 percent) and more for nonunion employees (79 percent).[62] There are many reasons for this pay gap, including differences in work experience, education, major field of study, occupation and industry of employment, as well as reasons that are still not understood. Pay equity legislation attempts to remedy these inequities. At the federal level, the *Canadian Human Rights Act* prohibits discrimination based on sex; it is therefore illegal to pay women less than men if their jobs are of equal value, a principle known as "equal pay for work of equal value," which is discussed in more detail in Chapter 9. Pay equity policy frameworks exist in British Columbia and Saskatchewan, and pay equity negotiations with public sector unions in Newfoundland. Legislation in Nova Scotia, Manitoba, New Brunswick, and PEI applies to public service employees but only Quebec and Ontario have laws covering the public and private sector. At the federal level, there is concern that the *Public Sector Equitable Compensation Act* represents a negative development for pay equity.[63]

That the "equal pay for work of equal value" concept can be very costly was shown in the case of 390 federal library science employees—mostly women—who earned less than historical researchers—mostly men—though the library science work was claimed to be of equal value. The settlement, requiring individual salary increases of up to $2,500 a year, cost the federal government $2.4 million.

On October 19, 1999, the longest and largest pay equity case was resolved when Mr. Justice John Evans upheld a Human Rights Tribunal's ruling that the federal government owed about 230,000 (mostly female) workers 13 years of back pay. The final settlement cost the Treasury Board over $3.5 billion. The federal government decided not to appeal this decision.

In November 2011, the Supreme Court of Canada decided in favour of female Canada Post workers in a pay equity case that was brought 28 years ago. Originally, about 2,300 employees worked in the affected classification (office workers) but about 6,000 employees (including some men) have been in the classification at some point in time. It is estimated that workers employed in the classification between 1983 and 2002 will share about $250 million. The main issue was whether it was appropriate for the Human Rights Commission to compare the office group with a male-dominated group that had some female members.[64]

The implication for human resource people is that they must make very sure the wage and salary system does not subtly discriminate on the basis of sex.

HRC 1, 2 & 5

Reverse Discrimination

The use of employment equity programs can lead to charges of reverse discrimination against employers. The charges usually arise when an employer seeks to hire or promote a member of a protected group over an equally (or better) qualified candidate who is not a member of a protected group. For example, if an employer has an employment equity program that gives preference to women over men when promotions occur, a qualified male may sue the employer and claim that he was discriminated against because of his sex.

Charges of reverse discrimination may put human resource departments in a difficult position. On the one hand, the human resource manager is responsible for eliminating concentration and underutilization. On the other hand, to give preference to members of a protected class (such as women) raises questions about whether the human resource department is being fair:

> In a landmark decision in 1984, the CHRC imposed a mandatory employment equity program on CN <http://www.cn.ca>. The company was ordered to hire women for one in four nontraditional or blue-collar jobs in its St. Lawrence region until women held 13 percent of such jobs. CN appealed the decision to the Supreme Court of Canada, which let stand the order for quotas. This ruling is important, as it allows employment equity programs as acceptable measures, even if they result in potential reverse discrimination.

Although preferential treatment will always raise questions of fairness, the *Canadian Human Rights Act* declares employment equity programs nondiscriminatory if they fulfill the spirit of the law.

HRC 5

The Principle of Natural Justice

Many people in an organization have the power of making decisions that can greatly affect the life or career of organization members. To ensure that a decision-making process is fair, the principle of **natural justice** has been accepted internationally—for example, as nonlegal guidelines for arbitrators or mediators, but also by courts in their legal judgment process. The rules of natural justice are minimum standards of fairness and are implied obligations for decision makers. Some of the rules are as follows:

---

natural justice

Minimum standards of fair decision making imposed on persons or bodies acting in a judicial capacity.

- the right to a fair hearing;
- the right to a bias-free proceeding (e.g., a person adjudicating a dispute should have no personal interest in the outcome of the proceedings);
- the right to present the opposing argument;

- the right of legal representation;
- the right of timely notice of a hearing; and
- the right to a timely process (according to the principle, "Justice delayed is justice denied").

Court decisions have decreed that natural justice rules supersede organizational policies and regulations. This means that human resource managers have to make sure that organizational procedures follow the above rules.

HRC 1, 4, 5, 6 & 8

Other Legal Challenges

This chapter has dealt mainly with legal discrimination and harassment issues. Of course, there are many other potential legal challenges, not all of which can be detailed here. The following are some of these relevant issues, most of which will be discussed in later chapters:

- **The *Canada Labour Code*.** The *Industrial Disputes Investigation Act* of 1907 was modified and re-enacted in 1971 as the *Canada Labour Code*. It regulates union certification, the right to organize, union prosecution, and mediation and arbitration procedures, all of which are discussed in more detail in Chapter 13. Provincial equivalents to the code are the *Employment* (or *Labour*) *Standards Acts*.

- **Dismissal.** According to common law, every employee has a contract with his or her employer, even if there is nothing in writing. An employee or employer can terminate an employment relationship by giving reasonable notice. An immediate dismissal is possible if an employee is compensated through appropriate severance pay (see Chapter 11).

- **Hours of work and overtime regulations.** The *Canada Labour Code* sets the standard workday at eight hours and the standard workweek at 40 hours, and overtime pay at one-and-a-half times the regular pay.

- **Minimum wages.** These are set by provincial and federal boards and discussed in Chapter 9.

- **Occupational health and safety.** The *Canada Labour Code* also regulates occupational health and safety issues, discussed in Chapter 12.

- **Weekly rest day.** The *Canada Labour Code* specifies that employees must be given at least one full day of rest during the week, preferably on Sunday.

- **Workplace Hazardous Material Information System (WHMIS).** WHMIS regulates the handling of dangerous material, discussed in Chapter 12.

These are some of the federal laws that have an impact on human resource managers. Most of them have their provincial equivalent. It is ultimately the human resource manager who is responsible for knowing and enforcing the law.

LO5   HRC 1

Strategic Implications of Legal Challenges

If there is one basic rule in human resource management, it is "Obey the law." The human resource manager must make sure all policies and rules take legal aspects into account (e.g., hiring and termination procedures, pay equity regulations, health and safety rules, and the handling of dangerous products). Given the current priority accorded employment equity, human resource managers also have to ensure that all long-range strategic plans that have an impact on staff and staffing follow employment equity requirements. Not doing so can be costly, as some of the examples given in this chapter have shown.

It is also desirable for a corporation to be perceived by the public as being a "good corporate citizen." One of the objectives of an organization is to project equity, which determines its attractiveness as perceived by job applicants (discussed in Chapters 5, 6, and 9).

Following legal requirements also has implications for training:

> A Sears employee in Winnipeg asked a customer to have his children get off of the lawn tractors on display. The employee also said "let me guess, you just came off the boat?" The two parties got into an argument and a part of the incident was captured on video. The employee was ultimately fired. The incident shows how quickly an issue can become viral and also points to the need for detailed customer service training. Sears has a code of conduct, a code of ethics, and a respect-in-the-workplace policy and every employee has to complete online training with exams every year. However, as business coach Janice Martin put it, "when you are faced with a ticked-off customer, you are not thinking of the role-playing you did months ago in training."[65]

Managers and supervisors have to be familiar with the laws as they apply to human resource management. Sexual harassment is an issue that has cost business and government organizations large amounts of money in fines, court costs, and compensation to the victims. Unjust dismissal is another prominent issue. More and more employees dismissed for unsatisfactory performance or other reasons have challenged their dismissal, and management has had to prove that the decision was valid.

LO6 HRC 1, 2, 4 & 5

Diversity Management

A combination of factors including governmental policies, demographic and labour force changes, increasing global operations, technological revolution, and radical changes in social values have fundamentally changed the way Canadian organizations work and whom they employ. The traditional "one size fits all" managerial policies of the past will no longer suffice.[66]

A diverse workforce requires managers with new leadership styles who understand their varying needs and creatively respond by offering flexible management policies and practices. Consider some of these statistics indicating major changes in the way we live and work:

- According to the 2011 census, Canada has a total of 64,475 same-sex common-law couples representing 0.8 percent of all couples in the country.[67] The number of same-sex couples increased by 42.6 percent between 2006 and 2011.

- With the legalization of same-sex marriage in July 2005, Canada became the third country in the world to legalize same-sex marriage after the Netherlands (2000) and Belgium (2003).

- 20.6 percent of Canadians were born outside the country and this is expected to increase to more than 25 percent by 2031.

- Nearly 6.3 million Canadians, or 19.1 percent of the total population (based on 2011 data), were visible minorities. About 70 percent of visible minorities live in Toronto, Montreal, or Vancouver.

- About 3.8 million Canadians (13.7 percent) reported having a disability in 2012. Women (14.9 percent) were more likely to report a disability than men (12.5 percent). [68]

Many women are hindered by lack of access to the **old boys' network**, the set of informal relationships that develop among male managers and executives.[69] This results in exclusive fraternizing of men with men that reinforces a "culture" of men without women's perspective and condones behaviour that devalues women. The friendships and contacts built through the network become the basis for assignments and promotions and the network becomes the informal communication link that provides vital information about business from which women are excluded. This means that many women never reach positions of power.

---

old boys' network

Set of informal relationships among male managers providing increased career advancement opportunities for men and reinforcing a male culture.

Even in judicial settings, women find themselves subject to harassment:

> Errol Massiah, an Oshawa Justice of the Peace, was found guilty of judicial misconduct for sexually harassing female court staff. Six complainants stated that Massiah made comments about their physical attributes during the period 2008 to 2010. A review by a panel of the Justices of the Peace Review Council considered Massiah's efforts to address his misconduct including writing letters of apology to the six complainants and attending sensitivity and remedial human rights training. However, Massiah was not terminated, but rather given a ten day suspension without pay but with benefits.[70]

According to the Conference Board of Canada, women made up about 48 percent of the Canadian workforce, but only 26,000 of 8 million working women (0.32 percent) had senior management positions. About 64 percent of men held management positions and since 1987, men have consistently been twice to three times as likely to occupy such positions. In terms of middle management, about 10 percent of men were at that level compared to 7 percent of women. According to Anne Golden, President and CEO of the Conference Board of Canada, "Between 1987 and 2009, the proportion of women in middle management rose by about 4 percent. At that rate, it will take approximately 151 years before the proportion of men and women at the management level is equal."[71]

A global study by Oliver Wyman revealed that 23 percent of executives at financial services firms in Canada are female, placing Canada third in the world behind Norway (35 percent) and Sweden (29 percent). Japan ranked last of 19 countries, with no women holding executive roles at major financial institutions. The Back to Bay Street program, which assists women returning to the financial sector after taking time off to have children, was cited as part of a web of support.[72]

The Canadian Board Diversity Council's Fifth Annual Report Card (2014) revealed that women held about 17 percent of board seats in FP500 companies (up from 13.7 percent in 2009). Women were more likely to be on the board of firms in the utilities (27.1 percent) and finance and insurance sectors (24.0 percent). However, only 14.0 percent of board seats in manufacturing and 9.7 percent in mining, oil, and gas were held by women. About 63 percent of respondents were in favour of an Ontario Securities Commission proposal to require companies to disclose their approach to increasing the number of women on their board.[73]

The federal government has established a goal of 30 percent female representation on boards within the next five years. Note that about 40 percent of public company boards have no female representation. In 2001, female representation on boards was about 11 percent, 13 percent by 2007, and 15 percent in 2011. At the current rate of change, it would take until the year 2097 to have gender parity in representation.[74] Although it is projected that visible minorities will make up about one-third of the country's population in 15 years, representation on the boards of public institutions and agencies tends to not be reflective of the community. An initiative called DiverseCity onBoard is aimed at addressing the issue by developing networks and providing boards with real-life candidates in front of them.[75]

The existing values, norms, and patterns of interactions among managers may also act as a **glass ceiling** that stunts the career growth of women and minority persons beyond a certain level. Promotional opportunities are visible, but invisible obstructions seem to block the way. The perception of the existence of a glass ceiling results in frustration, reduced job and career satisfaction, alienation from the workplace, and ultimately higher employee turnover. However, some organizations are making major strides in advancing promotional opportunities for female and visible minority employees.

glass ceiling

Invisible, but real obstructions to career advancement of women and people of visible minorities, resulting in frustration, career dissatisfaction, and increased turnover.

In 2011, Catalyst Canada recognized Michael Bach, Director of Diversity, Equity, and Inclusion at KPMG, for his activities in supporting the advancement of women in Canadian business. In 2007, KPMG examined the data concerning the advancement of women into its equity partnership. According to Bach, "they were at a glacier pace. The numbers had moved about 3 percent over the past ten years and were only at about 10 percent to begin with." The firm began to set targets for women becoming partners and now about 18 percent of partners are female and the proportion of women and visible minorities in new partner classes is at about 51 percent.[76]

Despite the transformation of Canadian cities and towns into multicultural mosaics, prejudices against visible minorities continue to exist in the workplace. In addition, the stereotypes faced by women belonging to specific religious groups prevent them from gaining even lower-level jobs:

Discriminatory hiring practices and workplace racism toward Muslim women are common in Toronto, according to a study by Women Working with Immigrant Women, a nonprofit organization that works with immigrants. Of the 32 Muslim women surveyed, 29 said that employers had commented on their hijab and 13 women reported an employer told them they would have to take the hijab off if they wanted a job. The study also included a field experiment where three teams of applicants—matched in every way except that one wore the hijab and one didn't—visited 16 job sites to apply for a job. At more than half of the sites, the applicant without the hijab was asked to fill out an application or leave a résumé while the applicant with a hijab was not. At two job sites, the woman without the hijab was told there was a job available while the woman with the hijab was told there weren't any jobs.[77]

Every year employers are honoured for their contribution to diversity. A list of organizations selected as one of Canada's Best Diversity Employers is available at <http://www.canadastop100.com/diversity>. Some of the 2015 winners include BC Hydro <https://www.bchydro.com>, City of Edmonton <http://www.edmonton.ca>, Mount Sinai Hospital <http://www.mountsinai.on.ca>, Loblaw Companies <http://www.loblaw.ca>, Xerox Canada, and YMCA of Greater Toronto. For each of the winners, one can read about the diversity initiatives in place at the organization as well as statistical data such as percentage of employees who are women, percentage of employees who are visible minorities, and average age.

HRC 1 & 5

Meaning of Diversity Management

Given the myriad differences among humans, it is very difficult to arrive at a broad and universally acceptable definition of diversity that is inclusive yet does not overwhelm us in the process. Broadly, **workplace diversity** may be defined to include important human characteristics that influence an employee's values, perceptions of self and others, behaviours, and interpretation of events around him or her. Diversity, at a minimum, includes age, ethnicity and culture, sex/gender, race, religion, sexual orientation, and mental and physical capabilities (see Figure 4-5). Several writers consider the above seven areas to be the **core dimensions of diversity** since they exert considerable impact on our early socialization and a powerful, sustained impact throughout our lives.

FIGURE 4-5

Core and Secondary Dimensions of Diversity

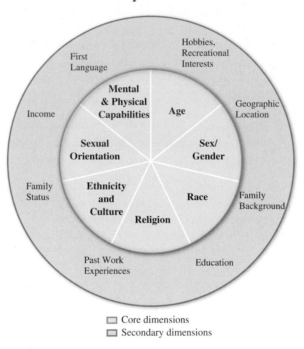

☐ Core dimensions
☐ Secondary dimensions

workplace diversity

Includes important human characteristics that influence employee values, their perceptions of self and others, behaviours, and interpretations of events.

core dimensions of diversity

Age, ethnicity and culture, sex/gender, race, religion, sexual orientation, and capabilities.

For example, regardless of whether a particular employee is currently 20, 40, or 60 years old, his or her age has a bearing on how that person is perceived by others as well as the individual's ability to learn, perform (several tasks), and relate to the environment. Age, thus, is a core dimension that affects an individual's workplace perceptions and behaviours.

Several other **secondary dimensions of diversity** such as education, family status, language, and even income levels play important roles in shaping our values, expectations, behaviours, and experiences. Hence, their impact on employee behaviours at the workplace should not be underestimated. They are, however, less visible, more mutable, and more variable in their impact on individual behaviours.

secondary dimensions of diversity
Education, status, language, and income levels.

According to Nancy Steele, Director of Technologies at American Express Canada <https://www.americanexpress.com/canada>, the company has had a diverse workforce for many years, but increased growth projections required the organization to do more to attract, retain, and develop skilled immigrants. Among the programs in place are mass recruitment days where 200 immigrants go through the recruitment process with 10 managers, language training for immigrants who want to improve their language skills, and cross-cultural training for managers.[78]

Canada's cultural mosaic raises several challenges for the manager who must successfully manage a diverse workforce. What advantages and disadvantages would a team made up of members from different cultures have?

Darryl Estrine/Getty Images RF.

Managing diversity recognizes that an organization is a mosaic where employees with varying beliefs, cultures, values, and behaviour patterns come together to create a whole organization and where these differences are acknowledged and accepted. Managing diversity has three major dimensions.[79] First, it assumes that effective management of diversity and differences among employees can add value to an organization; second, diversity includes all types of differences and not simply obvious ones such as sex/gender, race, and so on; and third, organization culture and working environments are key items to focus on in managing diversity.

managing diversity
Ability to manage individual employees with different cultural values and lead teams made up of diverse employees.

Managing diversity requires an organization to treat its employees as individuals rather than as numbers or categories. Most of us tend to group people using dimensions such as race, sex/gender, and age. However, it is important to recognize that the same person may belong to multiple categorical groups:

Thus, the same individual's identity can be composed of various facets: One can be an African-Canadian (race) woman (sex) who is older (age), married (marital status), and from a low-income family (income status).

This raises the important question: on which one or more of these identities should a human resource manager focus? Grouping people often results in **stereotyping**; yet, a grouping that gives added insights into the person's unique background, capabilities, and individuality is likely to generate better workplace outcomes. Further, the differences between groups need not be intrinsic or innate; they can be differences attributed to history or prevailing culture and subject to change.

stereotyping

The process of using a few observable characteristics to assign someone to a preconceived social category.

Organizations that carefully examine workplace practices may recognize the need to be more inclusive. For instance, some employers have moved away from having an annual Christmas party in favour of a "holiday party." As observed by Georgina Costa, Director of Human Resources at Sigma Systems <http://www.sigma-systems.com>, "We've become more neutral rather than focusing on Christianity. We wanted to just be more aware of the other cultures and beliefs that we have within our team. The holiday party does not focus on faith but is more of a celebration of the company's accomplishments throughout the year and a thank-you to employees for their hard work." A recent survey indicated that 64 percent of respondents believed that the holiday celebrations at their workplace should be more inclusive of all cultures and faiths. [80]

Such attributed differences play a key role in human interaction. Cultural conventions and values set "rules" when interacting with others and reduce uncertainty for individuals in a society. These largely unwritten rules themselves have been changing. For some people, many of these "rule changes" are welcome since they reduce inequity and injustice. For others, the pattern and pace of change heightens anxiety and discomfort because longstanding ideals are being eroded. How can we create workplace rules that enhance productivity, growth, and commitment and at the same time minimize anxiety and uncertainty? Herein lies the challenge of managing diversity.

HRC 1, 2, 4 & 5

Strategic Importance of Diversity Management

Several factors make diversity management strategically important.

Changing Workforce

As detailed in Chapters 1 and 3, the Canadian labour market is undergoing rapid and continuous transformation. The average member of the workforce of the past was male, white, approximately 30 years old, and usually held a high school diploma or lower. These men also worked within the region of their birth, were married, and had children. Typically, their wives stayed home to take care of their family. Today's workforce, in contrast, includes women, people of ethnic minorities, native Canadians, people with physical disabilities, and people with alternative lifestyles (for example, people with same-sex partners). If one includes other forms of heterogeneity (such as age and language differences), the workforce diversity is even more striking. Given this state of affairs, diversity management is not merely desirable, but mandatory if an organization is to effectively attract, utilize, and develop human resources.

The Edmonton-based PTI Group <http://www.ptigroup.com> has a strategic imperative to develop good relationships with Aboriginal communities. In 2010, the company hired almost 200 Aboriginal peoples and Sandy Sanderson, former Director of Aboriginal Relations, reported that the firm has retained almost 95 percent of those hires, which is a better retention rate than any other demographic within the organization. Sanderson found that while many Aboriginal peoples had the necessary qualifications for employment, a major barrier was obtaining transportation to PTI worksites. To overcome this obstacle, PTI worked with First Nations communities to establish a community-based transportation firm to drive workers between the reserves and the work locations. [81]

Importance of Human Capital

Changes in production technology have dramatically increased the importance of human capital. In today's world of "intellectual capitalism" and knowledge-intensive firms, it is not clear who owns the company, its tools, and its products. Often, today's organization may not even have a factory (and may be getting products manufactured by a subcontractor in Taiwan or Mexico). The only tools seen may be computers, smart phones, and fax machines. The knowledge worker may be the key to the success or failure of the firm. Often the departure of even a few key workers can spell disaster for the firm. The most valuable parts of the firm's operation may be reflected in human tasks of sensing, judging, and making decisions. In today's information age, no one can afford to use human capital inefficiently.

> The vast majority of employers believe that they have programs aimed at the successful integration of foreign-trained employees into their workplaces. However, a study of 560 professionals who earned their degrees outside of Canada, but have been in the country for between 6 and 15 years, found that only 49 percent of participants felt that the places they worked had policies to integrate non-Canadian employees. There was a perception that employer orientation programs should include more information on the culture at Canadian workplaces. Less than half of employers reported having a way to assess whether foreign credentials are adequate. [82]

Diversity as a Competitive Advantage

Proactive organizations recognize that competitive strength often lies in focusing on their employees and their clients. Globalization and changing domestic markets (because of demographic changes, immigration, etc.) mean that a firm's customers are no longer a homogeneous group of persons. For Canada, this is particularly important since our biggest trading partner, the United States, itself is undergoing rapid transformation in its population, resulting in greater workforce diversity.

Further, many of the growing export markets for Canadian firms are located in Asia, Latin America, and Africa. It is imperative that we understand the needs of a diverse population and respond effectively and in a timely fashion to maintain our competitive advantage.

Although the great majority of organizations report that diversity, inclusion, human rights and equity are strategic initiatives at their workplaces, a study by the Canadian Institute of Diversity and Inclusion revealed that only about 19 percent of employers are measuring the impact, efficiency, or return on investment (ROI) of their diversity initiatives. In addition, very few employers measure the diversity impact over an employee's life cycle. [83]

Increasing Role of Work Teams

Teams play a dominant role in modern organizations. Work teams are charged with task accomplishment to enable firms to distance themselves from the competitors and ensure survival. [84] While teams always reflected some degree of diversity, today the differences among members are even greater. Race, sex/gender, ethnicity, age, education levels, sexual orientation, and so on are among key factors that separate team members. The differences must be considered as "value added" rather than as "problematic" and the team leader today must have the skills to facilitate and inspire (rather than coach and control as in the past). Valuing differences can result in improved creativity and innovative problem solving.

> Does diversity matter? Based on a review of research on workplace diversity and firm performance published in nine leading journals from 2000–2009, McMahon found that the relationship was curvilinear, the effects

are stronger in more stable environments, and more dramatic in service industries compared to manufacturing. Diversity alone cannot explain firm performance—resources, capabilities, and core competencies are stronger predictors of performance. However, diversity that enhances these variables is associated with better performance.[85] Similarly, Herring, using data from a sample of for-profit firms in the United States, found that racial diversity was related to greater sales revenue and market share, higher relative profits, and more customers. In addition, gender diversity was associated with all of the above outcomes except for greater market share.[86]

Organizations that genuinely practise diversity recognize that diversity is more than a human resource management issue and affects all strategies and processes of the organization. Diversity management is tied to the strategic plan, and every employee from senior executives to the lowest-level employee contributes to fostering a diverse workforce.

LO7 HRC 4

Steps in Diversity Management

Jazz Aviation and National Bank are examples of organizations that took the notion of diversity management seriously:

> Each year, Mediacorp Canada <http://www.mediacorp.ca> recognizes 65 employers on its Canada's Best Diversity Employers list. Jazz Aviation <http://www.flyjazz.ca>, which made the most recent list, has introduced several diversity initiatives. For example, "heritage maps of the world" are hung at all locations and show the birthplace of employees and their ancestors. National Bank <http://www.nbc.ca>, which also made the most recent list, requires every senior manager to complete an action plan to address specific groups who are underrepresented in their business line (for instance, visible minorities or people with disabilities) and carry out strategies designed to achieve the targets.[87]

HRC 4

Transforming an organization's culture is a time-consuming process. Effective, systemwide changes require both attitudinal and behavioural changes. To generate a work climate that respects and builds on human differences may, at times, take several years of commitment. In almost all instances, diversity management efforts require four key steps (see Figure 4-6). These are discussed below.

FIGURE 4-6

Steps in Managing Diversity

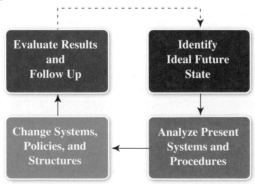

SOURCE: Adapted from Hari Das, *Strategic Organizational Design: For Canadian Firms in a Global Economy*, Scarborough, ON: Prentice Hall, 1998, p. 340. Reprinted with permission of Pearson Education Canada Inc.

Identify Ideal Future State

Implementing a diversity management program begins with an accurate portrayal of an organization's current workforce composition and a forecast of its future workforce.[88] Organizational members have to be identified accurately using demographic categories such as age, sex/gender, ethnicity, education, and disability. Some organizations also expand this to identify the number of employees belonging to other distinct groups on the basis of their language, race, sexual orientation, income level, social class, parental status, and marital status. Practical considerations that vary among firms determine which aspects of diversity can be accommodated. Once the firm has an accurate picture of its workforce composition (and likely future needs), it is critical to assess the values and needs of the workforce.

Analyze Present Systems and Procedures

The next step is to examine how the present systems are operating. Current policies, systems, practices, rules, and procedures have to be examined for their appropriateness for a diverse workforce. Included here are work assignments, recruitment and hiring, orientation, training, compensation, employee communication, human resource development, and performance appraisal. The validity and fairness of the various systems and rules for different cultures and their compatibility with different **cultural norms** are assessed at this stage:

cultural norms

Values and norms that determine behaviours of individuals and groups in different cultures.

Some organizations have developed programs aimed at retaining skilled immigrant employees. For example, Pythian <http://www.pythian.com>, a consulting services firm, pairs a newly hired employee who is trained internationally with a current employee with a similar background. The program, which helped Pythian win a 2012 Employer Excellence Award from Hire Immigrants Ottawa, helps new hires get answers to all kinds of questions that emerge when a person moves to a new country. Pythian's goal is to hire top talent around the world and having work experience in a specific country is not critical to success within the organization.[89]

Change Systems, Procedures, and Practices

All existing systems and practices have to be reviewed for their continued relevance to the organizational mission, strategy, and environmental demands. Those that are found lacking should be modified or even discontinued. Five factors are particularly critical in this context: senior management commitment, establishment of a diversity committee, education and retraining, wide communication of changes, and evaluation of results and follow-up.

Part of RBC's strategy of diversity is asking employees to examine their blind spots and banish their mind bugs. RBC's unconscious bias campaign is part of the company's commitment to progress in all areas of diversity including women, visible minorities, people with disabilities, LGBT, and Aboriginal communities. According to Senior-VP Rod Bolger, diversity has evolved from an initiative seen as "the right thing to do" to a business strategy conferring competitive advantage to today's drive for inclusiveness.[90]

Senior Management Commitment

Senior management commitment to diversity is one of the most important elements of ensuring the success of diversity efforts; so is whole-hearted support from the unions. Diversity efforts will fail unless all managers and employees see them as an integral part of the firm's business philosophy. This means that particular attention should be paid to communication, hiring, and reward structures to promote diversity. A number of managers do not know what their specific role is when it comes to managing diversity. According to Siu, "A lot of managers are saying 'I know how great diversity is but exactly what can I accomplish to prove that and align what I am doing with the senior management agenda?'"[91]

In the past, several organizations have confused diversity with hiring women, members of visible minorities, and people with disabilities. However, simply hiring more women or other minorities in the absence of a genuine commitment to diversity is not sufficient. Indeed, some recent research studies indicate that women often leave organizations and start their own companies to avoid "glass ceilings" at work.

Today's workforce includes more women participating in careers that were typically exclusive to men. Still, the glass ceiling remains. How can it be cracked?

Brand X/Fotosearch.

Sometimes, changes in the way an organization operates can result in simultaneous achievement of organizational goals and diversity targets. Consider the efforts of Vancity:

Vancity pays special attention to recruiting employees from lesbian, gay, bisexual, and transgendered/transsexual (LGBT) persons. It is also a lead sponsor of Vancouver's annual Pride Parade and a sponsor of the Queer Film Festival. A few years ago, it also introduced openly gay images in its advertising. It uses targeted recruitment ads in ethnic community newspapers and has working relationships with a number of community advocacy groups. Today, nearly two-thirds of its management employees are women, including the board chair, Virginia Weiler, and CEO Tamara Vrooman.[92]

At times, human resource practices represent major impediments to diversity and may discourage people for applying for a job. Consider the experience of applicants for firefighting jobs in Halifax:

A total of 94 applicants for firefighting jobs in Halifax were told that they would be removed from the primary eligibility list at the end of the current year because there were not enough minority applicants. All of the applicants were white males except for two women and two black men. There has been an employment equity program since 1999 and the recruiting service used outreach programs to try and increase the number of minority applicants. New applicants to the fire service may end up paying close to $1,000 for such things as an application fee, an aptitude test, an integrity interview, a physical agility test, and a polygraph test. The various tests had fees ranging from $50 to $350. In addition to the costs of the application, there was considerable criticism of the polygraph test, which asked candidates such questions as whether they had ever thought about committing suicide or had sex with animals.[93]

Figure 4-7 shows the areas where a firm must make changes if diversity initiatives are to succeed. Mere verbal support of system and policy changes is unlikely to produce tangible results. Linking diversity initiatives to business goals and incorporating diversity goals into performance criteria (reflected in salaries) ensures the accountability of managers for diversity.

FIGURE 4-7

Systems and Practices Requiring Modification during a Diversity Effort

- Recruitment and selection processes and criteria
- Orientation
- Work assignments
- Performance management
- Reward systems
- Employee communication systems
- Training
- Career and management development policies and programs
- Employee counselling practices
- Benefits policy
- Group and team practices
- Leadership skills and practices
- Job descriptions and specifications

Establishment of a Diversity Committee

One approach to increase employee involvement is through the establishment of a **diversity committee**. This committee will oversee diversity efforts, implement portions of the process, and serve as a communication link among employees, managers, and union officials. The number of members in the committee shows variation across organizations. Thus, small organizations may have only two or three members, while larger organizations typically employ six to eight members. What is perhaps even more important than size of the committee is its composition and power. Committee members should not be limited to the traditional "disadvantaged" groups (e.g., women, members of visible minorities), but should represent all employee groups broadly (e.g., occupational groups, geographic location, age groups). The committee should have power not only to identify budgets necessary for diversity efforts but also to hire outside experts, where necessary, to further diversify initiatives and oversee internal communication and education strategies.

diversity committee

A committee entrusted to oversee diversity efforts, implement processes, and serve as a communication link.

Education and Retraining

Training in the importance of diversity must be provided to all employees, from the CEO to the lowest-level employee. Different types of training and training methodologies are used to meet the unique needs of different work group segments. For example, a training approach to familiarize work supervisors with new appraisal procedures may employ role-plays and case studies. To train the same firm's assembly workers in communication with members of other cultures, these methods are likely to be less successful.

A diverse workforce, while adding to the strategic advantage of the firm, also provides a major managerial challenge. Many Canadians in the workforce today may have origins in cultures or ethnic groups that have vastly different assumptions about work, relationships, and group norms. Thus, a large number of Asians, Africans, Middle Easterners, Latin Americans, and Canadian Aboriginal persons who originate in rural-based societies have traditional ways of organizing reality and dealing with problems and events.[94] Similar value and behaviour differences can be seen between mainstream employees and other workforce segments as well (e.g., persons of different sexual orientation; persons who belong to different religious groups).

To sensitize workers to the cultural values and norms held by other groups, a variety of training and employee development techniques may have to be employed. Transference of learning to the workplace must be given particular importance when evaluating the effectiveness of alternate delivery mechanisms. Giving managers and employees new tools and information without permitting them to put them to use only creates frustration. Hence it is critical that key issues learned during training are incorporated into day-to-day work.

A survey revealed that only about 12 percent of organizations have a clearly defined policy aimed at integrating Internationally Educated Professionals (IEPs). About 46 percent of participants reported that the number of IEPs being hired has increased over the past 10 years. The major barriers to integrating IEPs include language (93 percent), recognition of foreign credentials (84 percent), cultural barriers (78 percent), and lack of Canadian work experience (61 percent).[95]

Wide Communication of Changes

Changes in internal systems and procedures must be communicated to all members. Information should be provided on what changes will occur, what the likely results will be, how important these changes are for the success of the organization, accomplishments until this point, and responses to questions related to diversity initiatives. More on employee communication strategies is discussed in Chapter 11.

> For a long time, Canada Post had a very stable and homogenous workforce. Over time, the organization attempted to enhance its diversity by recruiting more women, Aboriginal persons, and African-Canadians into its workforce. Today, women account for more than 50 percent of its employees, and 27.7 percent of senior managerial positions are held by women. Targeted initiatives such as the Progressive Aboriginal Relations Program helped the organization to attract more Aboriginal persons into its workforce. Members of visible minorities and persons with disabilities account for more than 15 percent of its workforce. To widely communicate its commitment to diversity, Canada Post runs special events such as celebrations around Aboriginal Day or Black History month.[96]

Evaluation of Results and Follow-up

Unless the firm monitors the progress of the diversity effort on a systematic basis, corrective actions may not follow. Monitoring will also ensure that quantitative and qualitative indices of change are available to the management, the union, and the workforce. These results should be widely communicated and the gaps between targets and accomplishments publicized along with the proposed corrective actions. Indices such as number of hires, promotions, absenteeism, turnover, salary levels, grievances, harassment complaints, and so on are useful for gauging progress, but should not be used exclusively since qualitative responses from employees may convey other dimensions of work climate and the intensity of employee feelings. More progressive organizations employ **diversity audits** on a regular basis to uncover the underlying dimensions, causes, and progress to date on diversity management matters. Prompt follow-up actions to accelerate accomplishments are necessary and should be planned in consultation with the senior managers and the unions to ensure success.

diversity audits
Audits to uncover underlying dimensions, causes, interdependencies, and progress-to-date on diversity management matters.

Current Industry Practices

About two-thirds of Canadian employers surveyed by Catalyst <http://www.catalyst.org>, a New York–based research and advisory organization that promotes women in business, indicated a stated commitment to diversity in their mission or vision statements; however, fewer than half of them had any policies or practices that in fact supported such a vision.[97] Many visible minority managers and professionals report lower satisfaction and more barriers to career advancement than their Caucasian counterparts. However, more progressive employers have adopted a variety of policies and practices to create an inclusive culture that welcomes everyone irrespective of their sex/gender, colour, and religious or other beliefs. As will be seen, the approaches are as varied as organizations. The choice of specific mechanisms should be made after a careful consideration of the unique challenges and constraints facing an organization.

Diversity Training Programs

Managers and lower-level supervisors need to learn new skills that will enable them to manage and motivate a diverse workforce. Often, outside experts are invited to mount **diversity training programs** in organizations. Indeed, in many firms this is one of the first actions taken to implement diversity management. Such training programs help to create awareness of the bottom-line impact of diversity management and the role of managers, supervisors, and co-workers in creating a work climate that is found comfortable by all employees, irrespective of their sex/gender, age, sexual orientation, racial or ethnic identity, and physical or mental capabilities.

diversity training programs

Training programs aimed at importing new skills to motivate and manage a diverse workforce.

Experts suggest two types of training: awareness training and skill-building training. **Awareness training** focuses on creating an understanding of the need for managing and valuing diversity. It is also meant to increase participants' self-awareness of diversity-related issues such as stereotyping and cross-cultural insensitivity.

awareness training

Training employees to develop their understanding of the need to manage and value diversity.

Once individuals develop an awareness, they can then monitor their feelings, reactions, etc. and make conscious decisions about their behaviour, often resulting in improved interpersonal communication. **Skill-building training** educates employees on specific cultural differences and how to respond to differences in the workplace. Often awareness and skill-building training are combined.

skill-building training

Training employees in interpersonal skills to correctly respond to cultural differences at the workplace.

Another issue to be resolved by a trainer in managing diversity is content versus process training. *Content training* relates to the question: "Should a training program focus solely on the knowledge and skills related to a single culture?" This would be appropriate for a manager working with a workforce consisting mainly of members of one culture. However, as mentioned before, statistics show that the Canadian workforce is becoming more culturally diverse; therefore, it will become more likely that managers will need to deal effectively with employees from several different cultures in a single organization.

In the long run, it is therefore more practical, although more difficult, to focus on *process training*; that is, supervisors and employees have to learn about diversity. Participants in a process-oriented diversity training program develop an understanding of how management style, the interpersonal communication process, teamwork, and other managerial issues are affected by diversity. After such a training program, participants may not have all the answers, but they will have plenty of questions.

Ideally the trainers themselves will reflect diversity. A team of male and female, white and black (or Asian) trainers could work together to cover different topics in a diversity training program. It probably would make participants from different minorities and racial and cultural backgrounds feel more comfortable.

Mentoring Programs

Some firms encourage **mentoring programs** where women or members of visible minorities and other disadvantaged groups are encouraged to work with a senior manager who acts like a friend, philosopher, and guide in achieving career success within the firm.

mentoring programs

Programs encouraging members of disadvantaged groups (e.g., women) to work with a senior manager who acts like a friend and guide in achieving career success.

Mentors may be identified formally or informally. Organizations can bring greater predictability into diversity outcomes by establishing formal mentoring systems since they result in greater tangible results and accountability on the part of both mentors and protegés.

One large Canadian bank lists all relevant details of its senior managers on its website. All new hires are encouraged to select someone from the list and contact him or her on a regular basis for receiving helpful hints for day-to-day performance and long-term career advice. Both the mentor and the protegé are encouraged to submit reports of their deliberations to the bank.

Alternate Work Arrangements

Often, removal of negative factors can enhance employee performance and career growth. This is especially so in the case of women who have multiple and conflicting role demands from work and family, or older workers who find the traditional work arrangements difficult. Several **alternate work arrangements** such as flexible work hours, telecommuting, extended leave, job sharing, etc. have been used in the past to accommodate the unique needs of employee groups. These arrangements were discussed in more detail in Chapter 3.

alternate work arrangements

Nontraditional work arrangements (e.g., flextime, telecommuting) that provide more flexibility to employees while meeting organizational goals.

Apprenticeships

Apprenticeships are similar to mentoring except that they relate to junior-level or technical jobs and often involve working with prospective employees before they formally join the organization. Such programs are particularly useful to attract members of visible minorities, women, people with disabilities, and other disadvantaged group members to nontraditional jobs within the firm:

> Temisan Boyo, a native of Nigeria with an interest in law, was pretty sure she would not want to work for a major corporate law firm like Blake, Cassels and Graydon. Boyo stated that she thought it would be "very white, very male, very formal, and very unaccepting of things that were not part of the status quo." However, Boyo became the recipient of an Equity & Diversity Pre-Law Internship at Blakes and she found out that the firm was very flexible and more diverse than she expected. Blakes is involved in several other initiatives such as their Indigenous Summer School program and supports a number of affinity groups including Women@Blakes, Pride@Blakes, and the Diversity and Inclusion Network.[98]

apprenticeships

A form of on-the-job training in which junior employees learn a trade from an experienced person.

Support Groups

Employees belonging to racial or other groups that are underrepresented in the organization may often feel lonely and uncomfortable at the workplace. Sometimes, this might be simply a feeling of loneliness and distance from mainstream workers. In other instances, the new employee may even face hostility from other members of the work group, especially when others perceive that the employee's minority status resulted in preferential treatment during hiring. Co-worker hostility is more likely to happen when a visible minority employee (or woman) is hired for a job that is nontraditional for that group. Often the result is employee alienation, which in turn results in high turnover.

To overcome this problem, one organization formed **support groups** that are designed to provide a nurturing climate for employees who may otherwise feel unwanted or shut out. Socialization in such groups enabled the newcomer not only to share concerns and problems but also to assimilate the organization's culture faster.

support groups

Groups of employees who provide emotional support to a new employee who shares a common attribute with the group (e.g., racial or ethnic membership).

Some employers use innovative approaches to make the new minority employee welcome.

ATI was a Toronto-based global manufacturer of graphics technology with 3,600 employees worldwide that attempted to create a culture that embraced immigrants. For example, when a woman was hired from Romania, the management sent an email to the employees. The Romanian community within ATI sent her emails welcoming her to the company. The result? The new employee felt welcome and at home even before actually arriving at the workplace.[99]

Communication Standards

Several organizations have established **communication standards**—formal protocols for internal messages and communication to avoid offending members of different sex/gender, racial, ethnic, age, or other groups.

communication standards

Formal protocols for internal communications within an organization to eliminate sex/gender, racial, age, or other biases in communications.

The use of "he" when referring to managers in policy manuals has the result of perpetuating the "male" image of a manager. There is no reason why a "chairman" of a meeting is a man; the more progressive organizations recognize this and use the term "chairperson." Similarly, there is no reason why automobiles, yachts, or some other equipment should be referred to as "she" rather than "it."

As the preceding discussion shows, at the present time, there is considerable interest in and focus on diversity management in Canadian industry. However, few organizations are prepared for the resistance that invariably follows the introduction of this concept at the workplace. Resistance to diversity management may emerge from employee groups, unions, work supervisors, and managers. Employee groups and unions fear the emergence of new systems that may bring in hiring quotas, employment and promotion criteria that result in reverse discrimination policies, and lowering of power, status, and rewards. Managers and supervisors share several of the same concerns and may also fear that the new procedures will alter internal systems and performance standards and reduce autonomy. In some instances, the resistance may originate from misperceptions, lack of understanding of the need for change, prevailing stereotypes, and even rumours about negative outcomes associated with diversity implementation elsewhere.

SUMMARY

Government is a significant variable that strongly shapes the role of human resource management. It influences human resources through laws governing the employment relationship. The application of the Charter of Rights and Freedoms was awaited with high expectations from both labour and management. However, its impact on the human resource management field has been mixed.

The two sources of equal employment laws are the federal and provincial human rights statutes. The *Canadian Human Rights Act* applies to federal government departments and agencies, Crown corporations, and businesses and industries under federal jurisdiction, such as banks, airlines, and railway companies. Areas not under federal jurisdiction are protected by provincial human rights laws. Each of Canada's provinces and territories has its own antidiscrimination laws that are broadly similar to the federal law.

To eliminate past discrimination and ensure future compliance, many organizations have developed employment equity programs. The programs identify areas of past and present discrimination, develop affirmative goals, and design remedial, active, and preventive programs.

To actively promote the employment of women, Aboriginal people, persons with a disability, members of a visible minority, the federal government introduced the *Employment Equity Act*, which requires employers with 100 or more employees under federal jurisdiction to develop plans and timetables for the employment of these groups. It also requires annual reports that have to be submitted to the Canadian Employment and Immigration Commission.

Managing a culturally diverse workforce is a major challenge facing Canadian employers. Workplace diversity includes important human characteristics that influence an employee's values, perceptions of self and others, behaviours, and interpretation of events around him or her. Diversity, at a minimum, includes age, ethnicity and culture, sex/gender, race, religion, sexual orientation, and mental and physical capabilities. Several writers consider the above seven areas to be the core dimensions of diversity since they exert considerable impact on our early socialization and a powerful, sustained impact throughout our lives.

To implement effective diversity management an organization has to go through four steps: identifying the ideal future state; analyzing present systems and procedures; changing systems, policies, and structures where necessary; and evaluating results and follow-up. Implementing a diversity management program begins with an accurate portrayal of its current workforce composition and a forecast of its future workforce. Organizational members have to be identified accurately using demographic categories such as age, sex/gender, ethnicity, education, and disability. Some organizations also expand this to identify the number of employees belonging to other distinct groups on the basis of their language, race, sexual orientation, income level, social class, parental status, and marital status. Current policies, systems, practices, rules, and procedures have to be examined (and perhaps modified or eliminated) in terms of their appropriateness for a diverse workforce. After this is done, all existing systems and practices have to be reviewed for their continued relevance to the organizational mission, strategy, and environmental demands, the progress of the diversity effort has to be monitored on a systematic basis, and corrective actions taken.

TERMS FOR REVIEW

alternate work arrangements
apprenticeships
awareness training
bona fide occupational requirement (BFOR)
Canadian Charter of Rights and Freedoms
Canadian Human Rights Act
Canadian Human Rights Commission (CHRC)
communication standards
concentration
core dimensions of diversity
cultural norms
diversity audits
diversity committee
diversity training programs
duty to accommodate
Employment Equity Act
employment equity programs
glass ceiling
harassment
managing diversity
mentoring programs
natural justice
old boys' network
provincial human rights laws
reasonable accommodation
regulations
secondary dimensions of diversity
sexual harassment
skill-building training
stereotyping
support groups
systemic discrimination
underutilization
workplace diversity

SELF-ASSESSMENT EXERCISE

How Knowledgeable Are You about Human Resource Legal Issues and Diversity Management?

1. Men are prohibited from filing sexual harassment complaints.   T   (F)

2. The Bank of Nova Scotia falls under the jurisdiction of the federal *Canadian Human Rights Act*.   (T)   F

(Continued)

3. Minimum height requirements are considered systemic discrimination.	T	F
4. The "duty to accommodate" means that an employer has to accommodate employees even if it involves "undue hardship."	T	F
5. Mandatory retirement is permitted in most provinces.	T	F
6. It is illegal to ask a candidate whether he or she has been convicted of a crime, unless it is job-related.	T	F
7. Drug dependency can be interpreted as a disability	T	F
8. If a supervisor harasses an employee, the employer can be held liable.	T	F
9. The term "old boys' network" has now been changed to "diversity network" to include women.	T	F
10. The percentage of minorities in Canadian companies is now typically similar to their percentage in the population.	T	F

SCORING

If you answered statements 1, 4, 5, 9, 10 as False you get one point each. All other statements are True, resulting again in one point each.

Scores of 8–10: Very good! Congratulations on a job well done.

Scores 5–7: You made it, but barely. It would be advisable for you to go over the chapter text again.

Scores of less than 5: Are you sure you read the chapter?

REVIEW AND DISCUSSION QUESTIONS

1. Suppose that during your first job interview after graduation you are asked, "Why should a company have an employment equity program?" How would you respond?

2. List the major prohibitions of the *Canadian Human Rights Act*.

3. Since a human resource department is not a legal department, what role does it play in the area of equal employment law?

4. Suppose that you are told that your first duty as a human resource specialist is to construct an employment equity program. What would you do? What types of information would you seek?

5. What conditions would have to be met before you could bring suit against an employer who discriminated against you because of your sex?

6. A job candidate answers "yes" to the question of whether she is a smoker. She is well qualified, but you decide not to hire her. Does she have legal recourse?

7. Why is management of diversity important for an organization today?

8. What are the steps in implementing a diversity management program?

CRITICAL THINKING QUESTIONS

1. If you are a supervisor in a bank and an employee demands to be allowed to miss work on Fridays for religious reasons, what would you do? Under what circumstances would you have to let the employee have time off? Under what circumstances could you prohibit it?

2. You have a job opening for a warehouse helper, a position that sometimes requires heavy lifting, up to 50 kilograms. A woman applies for the job and claims that she is able to do the work. She looks rather petite, and you are afraid that she may hurt herself. When you deny her the job, she threatens to complain to the Human Rights Commission. What do you do?

3. Choose an organization that you are familiar with. Are any of its rules, practices, or policies likely to be found undesirable by its female, minority, or older employees? Why?

4. If 40 percent of your employees are women, but if women account for only 2 percent of the executive group and 4 percent of the managerial group, what steps will you take to improve the status of women in your organization?

ETHICS QUESTION

Reverse discrimination has, so far, not been a salient issue in Canada, especially since human rights legislation allows employers to use employment equity programs "to correct past wrongs"—that is, hire more protected groups, such as women, members of a visible minority, and Aboriginal people, ideally to more accurately reflect the distribution of protected groups in the community in the makeup of the organization's staff. Despite the legality of employment equity programs, the question has been raised as to whether it is ethical to choose a less qualified candidate over a better qualified one. Shouldn't the "best" candidate get the job? Please comment.

WEB RESEARCH EXERCISE

1. Canadian Human Rights Commission

www.chrc-ccdp.ca

(a) Find and summarize three cases decided last year in favour of employers and three cases decided in favour of employees.

(b) What are the implications of the latest case decisions on gay rights for human resource managers?

2. Canadian Public Health Association

www.cpha.ca

(a) Go to the HIV/AIDS Information Centre and give a summary of the resources available to organizations to inform about AIDS.

3. Pay Equity Commission of Ontario

www.payequity.gov.on.ca

(a) How is progress in the pay equity process monitored?

4. Select any two industries and calculate the percentage of women and members of visible minorities and other disadvantaged groups who are employed in these sectors. What are the implications for diversity management practices in organizations in these sectors? (Hint: You may begin your research with the websites of Statistics Canada, Employment and Social Development Canada, and Industry Canada.)

INCIDENT 4-1

Metropolitan Hospital's Employment Equity Needs

A large metropolitan hospital in Ontario recently developed an employment equity program. Under the program, the hospital agreed to promote two women into supervisory ranks for each man promoted. This practice was to continue until 40 to 45 percent of all supervisory jobs in the hospital were held by women.

The need for the first supervisory promotion occurred in the medical records department. The manager of medical records was one of the few female managers in the hospital. Nevertheless, she argued that Roy Biggs should become a medical records supervisor, as he was best qualified. Roy had two years of medical school and was a graduate of a medical records program at the local community college. The assistant director of hospital operations agreed that Roy should get the promotion. The equal employment compliance specialist in the human resource department argued that Kate VanDam should get the promotion, because of the employment equity program and because she had more seniority and experience in the department than Roy. The records manager, the assistant administrator, and the compliance specialist decided that the human resource manager should make the final decision.

1. What weight would you give to (a) Kate's seniority and experience, (b) Roy's superior training, (c) the recommendation of the records manager, and (d) the new Employment Equity Program?

2. What are the implications for the equity program if Roy gets the job? What are the implications for the employees presently taking job-related courses if Kate gets the promotion?

3. What decision would you make if you were the human resource manager?

EXERCISE 4-1

Carver Jewellery Company

Carver Jewellery Company Ltd. has the following workforce composition:

Job Classes	Male	Female	White	Black	Asian	Native Peoples
Executive	9	1	10	0	0	0
Management	71	9	79	0	1	0
Salaried/commission	43	31	74	0	0	0
Hourly paid	24	164	168	10	8	2

An analysis of the local labour force from which Carver draws its employees is as follows:

Male	Female	White	Black	Asian	Native Peoples
53 percent	47 percent	84 percent	8 percent	3 percent	5 percent

On the basis of this information:

1. Identify which job classes at Carver exhibit underutilization.
2. Identify which job classes at Carver exhibit concentration.

CASE STUDY

Maple Leaf Shoes Ltd.

Legal Challenges

Maple Leaf Shoes Ltd. is a medium-sized manufacturer of leather and vinyl shoes located in Wilmington, Ontario. It was started in 1969 and currently employs about 400 persons in its Wilmington plant and some 380 more in offices and warehouses throughout Canada and internationally. More information on the firm and its operations is provided at the end of Chapter 1.

Eva White was the operator of a leather-cutting machine. When Eva heard the bell ring, indicating the end of the workday, she shut down her cutting machine and headed toward the women's locker room. It had been a long day and standing for eight hours on the machine didn't do her back any good. When she approached her locker, she saw that Rosetta Maurizio, who used the locker next to hers, was already there, changing into her street clothing. Eva and Rosetta had been hired together 10 months earlier. They had not known each other before, and, although they worked in different parts of the building, they kept each other company in the cafeteria during their lunch breaks. As her name indicated, Rosetta was of Italian descent. She had immigrated to Canada from Italy with her parents several years before, but her Italian accent was still quite noticeable.

Eva made some remarks about the hot day, when she noticed that Rosetta had red eyes, as if she had been crying. She asked Rosetta whether she had problems and whether she could be of any help. Rosetta seemed to be reluctant to talk, but when she finally responded she sounded quite agitated. The following dialogue developed:

Rosetta: As you know, I am one of the two women in the finishing section working with about 20 guys. They seem to enjoy making fun of me. It starts in the morning when I arrive. They call me risotto, which means "rice with gravy" in Italian, and give me some mock Italian greetings. They sometimes ask me whether I had a good time with my Italian boyfriend the night before and what we had done together. They also tell each other their own experiences with their girlfriends, each one bragging more than the other, but always so that I can hear it. I think they do it intentionally to embarrass me. I tend to blush and that seems to amuse them. When they tell a dirty joke, they ask me whether I understood it or whether I could tell one myself. Some of them have centrefolds pinned to the wall behind their machines. Today, one guy asked me whether I prefer Italian men over Canadian men; when I told him to let me alone and to mind his own business, he said that Italians are just braggarts, only good with their mouths. I was so angry that I had to go to the washroom to hide my tears. I am thinking of quitting this job; it is just getting too much.

Eva: Have you talked to Al, the supervisor, about that?

Rosetta: I don't want to talk to him about this. He's very friendly with the guys, and when they tell jokes when he's around, he laughs with them, which seems to encourage them. But they never tell him the types of jokes they tell me. I mentioned to him that I would like to find another job in the company. When he asked why, I told him that I had trouble breathing the vapour of the polish in the air. He said that he would find out whether there were other jobs open, but that was over a month ago. I do not dare to bring it up again.

Eva: You have to talk to him. Don't let it go on, otherwise you will suffer too much.

Rosetta: But when I complain to him and he talks to the guys, they will probably make it worse for me. No, I'd rather not.

Eva: Should I talk to him?

Rosetta: No, no, please don't. I will think about it.

Next morning, when they met in the changeroom again, Eva encouraged Rosetta once more to talk to her supervisor. She even offered to come with her if she wanted some support. Rosetta promised to do something, but declined Eva's offer.

In the evening, Eva noticed that Rosetta's locker was empty. The next day she asked the personnel department about what had happened to Rosetta and was told that Rosetta had quit, citing family reasons.

Eva was upset. She felt that Rosetta had been treated unfairly and that she should not be forced to quit her job because some co-workers had made her life miserable.

She decided to do something. She asked her own supervisor for a break and went over to the finishing workroom to talk to Al.

Al was sitting in his office when Eva walked in. He looked surprised when he saw her. He knew that she worked in the company, but had never talked to her. He offered her a seat and asked what he could do for her, and added quickly that if she was looking for a job in his division he had one opening, due to a recent vacancy.

Eva: That's not the reason I want to talk to you, although it is related to that vacant job. What happened to Rosetta?

He seemed to be taken aback by her aggressive tone, but kept his cool and answered: "Rosetta quit. She didn't like the job anymore."

Eva: Was that all she said?

Al: Well, she said that she didn't like to work in a place that made her feel uncomfortable. She mentioned that the guys in the finishing room were telling dirty jokes she didn't like and that they made fun of her. Well, I told her that I have been supervisor for 10 years in this division, and that I never heard an outright dirty joke, just some good old-fashioned fun jokes, nothing to be shocked by. I think she was just too sensitive. The guys just want to have a good time. The job is boring and they need something to distract them. They are not mean guys.

Eva: But there was more to this than just telling jokes. Rosetta told me that the guys also made fun of her Italian background.

Al: I think it's ridiculous to make that an issue. We have Ukrainians, Germans, British, Chinese, Indians, and some others. There has never been a problem. And as far as making fun of her, we all make fun of each other, but that's good-natured. I think she takes herself too seriously. My philosophy is that we have to be able to laugh at ourselves now and then. Life is tough enough.

Eva: But she did feel uncomfortable. She even cried because of what she went through. Don't you think that you have to accept some responsibility for that? I think that she has been treated unfairly and that you should have made an attempt to help her.

Al: I resent being called unfair. I think that I'm a very fair supervisor. We have the lowest number of grievances in our division, so I think that such a complaint is totally unjustified. She left of her own will, and I will not run after her.

Eva, angrily: Well, I don't think that you have heard the last of that.

Eva left, determined to take some action on behalf of Rosetta and her other female co-workers.

DISCUSSION QUESTIONS

1. Is there a case of sexual harassment in this situation or is it only fun?

2. If you were Eva, what would—and could—you do? What are the options? What is the probability of success of each option?

3. What are Al's responsibilities in this instance? Did he carry them out well? Why or why not?

CASE STUDY

Canadian Pacific and International Bank

Planning for Diversity at HBI*

Rhonda Dickoff looked at the memo in front of her one more time. As the manager of human resources at HBI, she knew it was her responsibility to ensure that the organization followed the general guidelines set forth by the parent company, Canadian Pacific and International Bank. Further, as a medium-sized financial institution, HBI was also required to submit a report on its efforts to diversify its workforce. Since its acquisition of HBI, the top management of CPIB had made it clear that HBI had to increase the number of protected groups (women, members of visible minorities, Aboriginal persons, and persons with a disability), and Mary Keddy (vice-president, human resources, with CPIB), had asked for a report on HBI's plans to diversify its workforce. The memo from Ms. Keddy indicated that this would be a topic of discussion at her next meeting (two weeks from now) with Rhonda Dickoff.

WORKFORCE DIVERSITY AT HBI

HBI is organized functionally into three major divisions: Operations, Marketing, and Administration. Of the 155 top and senior middle-level managers in the firm, five were women. Ms. Dickoff was the highest-ranking female manager at HBI. The other four were Patricia Kimble (senior portfolio analyst), Sheila Allen (senior accountant), Wendy Goodwin (advertising manager), and Theresa Reitman (manager, customer relations—consumer accounts). Both Sheila Allen and Wendy Goodwin had been with HBI for approximately five years while the other two were more recent entrants.

Dickoff knew that the overall picture at HBI (in terms of workforce diversity) was not very positive. While 90 percent of the nonmanagement employees were women, only 35 percent of junior managers and 21 percent of senior-middle-level managers were female. Dickoff was aware that while some of the male managers were open to increasing the diversity in the management cadres of HBI, most were skeptical of such initiatives. One of the senior male managers had told her recently: "We should desist from having token women and minority managers. I don't think we are doing them or ourselves a favour by promoting them before they are good and ready. ..." Another had mentioned that women cannot expect to reach top levels without having the necessary experience. Ms. Dickoff knew that these opinions were shared by others in the organization. So she had prepared a table of the proportion of women and men at each level at HBI and some other relevant information about the workforce. These are provided in Table 1. She had also gathered information on the leadership ratings of the senior-middle-level women managers (Table 2), but, given the short notice, had been unable to do so for the other female managers. However, she knew that the picture was similar at all levels of management.

HBI had been attempting to improve its workforce diversity for the past six years. In fact, it had started focusing on increasing the number of women and other protected group members being hired at management trainee level six years ago. At the management trainee level, nearly 20 percent of the hires in the past five years had been female and over 80 percent had remained with the firm.

This was slightly higher than the proportion for male management trainees. While some of these women had made it into junior and middle management, most of the women at these levels had over 15 years' experience. It had also begun recruiting males at entry level (nonmanagement cadre) before any other major financial institution. Several of these men had made it into supervisory and even junior management in the past few years.

Dickoff knew that she had to look into the numbers of other protected group members at HBI. HBI had hired some members of the other protected groups in the past six years, but only one—a visible minority person—had stayed with the firm. Mr. Johnson, in Marketing, had been with HBI for over five years and had a BA in Psychology. There were no other protected group members at HBI.

Dickoff looked at the memo again. "Two weeks ... that's not a long time. I have to get cracking ..." she said to herself.

DISCUSSION QUESTIONS

1. From the data provided, what conclusions can you form about the status of male and female employees (managerial and other) at HBI?

2. What suggestions do you have for Dickoff to diversify the workforce (managerial and other) at HBI?

*Case written by Professor Mallika Das of Mount Saint Vincent University, Halifax, as a basis for class discussion. All rights reserved by the author. Mallika Das © 2000.

TABLE 1

Workforce Composition at HBI

Level	Percent Female	Percent with University Education		Percent with 5+ Years' Experience		Age	
		F	M	F	M	F	M
Nonmanagement	90	25	25	42	20	39	30
Supervisory	70	43	36	54	33	38	35
Junior	35	87	85	63	58	40	39
Senior middle	21	100	75	40	40	45	43
Top management*	0	—	67	—	67	—	57

*Excluding Mr. John Hopkins.

TABLE 2

Profile of Senior-Middle-Level Managers at HBI

Division	Experience (months)		Leadership Rating		Percent with Univ. Education	
	Male	Female	Male	Female	Male	Female
Administration	46.0	60.5	7.0	8.5	60	100
Marketing	43.7	44.5	7.7	8.0	50	100
Operations	45.5	11.0	7.2	9.0	92	100

Recruitment

In this ever-changing, global, technologically demanding business environment, sourcing and retaining talent becomes the competitive battleground. Just as sports teams recruit aggressively for best athletes, business organizations in the future will compete aggressively for the best talent … Successful firms will be those most adept at attracting, developing and retaining individuals with the skills, perspective and experience sufficient to drive a global business.

DAVE ULRICH[1]

LEARNING OBJECTIVES

After studying this chapter, you should be able to:

LO1 Explain the strategic importance of the recruitment function.

LO2 Discuss the constraints facing a typical recruiter.

LO3 Identify the appropriate recruiting methods for different types of jobs.

LO4 Explain how to generate effective recruitment advertisements.

LO5 List key measures for evaluating the effectiveness of the recruitment function.

Finding new employees for the organization is a continuing challenge for most human resource departments. Sometimes the need for new workers is known well in advance because of detailed human resource plans. At other times, the human resource department is faced with urgent requests for replacements that must be filled as quickly as possible. In either case, finding qualified applicants is a key activity, as seen in the following example:

Consulting giant Accenture Inc. <http://www.accenture.com> is a leading employer in Canada with about 3,800 employees. Globally, Accenture hired approximately 70,000 employees in 2011 including about 1,000 new workers in Canada. With this fast-paced growth, Accenture faces one of the biggest human resource challenges: "attracting and retaining the best and brightest."[2]

Recruitment is the process of finding and attracting capable individuals to apply for employment and to accept a job offer if or when one is made to them. **Selection** involves the identification of candidates from this pool of applicants who best meet job requirements using tools such as application blanks, tests, and interviews. The recruitment process begins with generating a pool of applicants, continues during selection while decisions are made among applicants to choose the best one, and then extends after selection decisions have been made to convince candidates who have been made an offer to accept the job.[3]

---

recruitment

The process of finding and attracting capable applicants to apply for employment and accept job offers that are extended to them.

---

selection

The identification of candidates from a pool of recruits who best meet job requirements, using tools such as application blanks, tests, and interviews.

Recruitment includes all activities by an organization that affect an applicant's decision to apply for and to accept a position. These can be activities that the organization *purposefully* engages in to persuade applicants to want to work for them (such as recruitment websites), or *unintentional* things (like the length of time between when an applicant applies for the job and when they hear about an interview, or public relations fiascos such as the British Petroleum oil spill in the Gulf Coast in 2010[4]) that may affect applicant attraction to the organization.[5] Recruiting is a two-way street: it is a matching process between firms with jobs and individuals seeking jobs. The organization is trying to entice highly qualified people to consider working for their organization. Meanwhile, applicants are trying to learn learn about what it would be like to work for the organization. Work is a large part of most people's days, and can have a substantial impact on their well-being. How the organization treats them from the moment they first learn about it right through to a job offer being extended to them can impact whether or not they will choose to work there. Recruiting then segues into newcomer socialization.

Responsibility for recruitment usually belongs to the human resource department. This responsibility is important because the quality of an organization's human resources depends on the quality of its recruits. In organizations that recruit almost continuously, human resource departments will have dedicated recruitment specialists.

As Figure 5-1 illustrates, recruitment can be done only after the identification of job openings through human resource planning or requests by managers. As mentioned in Chapter 3, advanced knowledge of job openings allows the recruiter to be proactive.

After identifying openings, the recruiter learns what each job requires by reviewing job analysis information, particularly the job descriptions and specifications, and speaking with the requesting manager. This information tells the recruiter the characteristics of both the jobs and the future job incumbents. Knowing the job's requirements helps recruiters to choose methods of finding the right number and type of applicants.

Typically, most recruiters use more than one recruitment method to find suitable candidates for vacant job positions. Common recruitment methods include recruitment advertisements and postings on

FIGURE 5-1

An Overview of the Recruitment Process

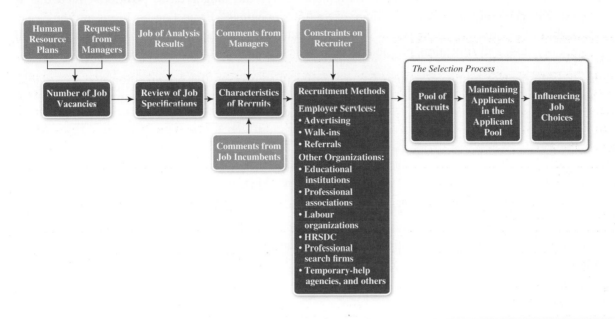

websites and job boards; school, college, and university campus visits; contacts with professional and labour associations; and use of government agencies such as Employment and Social Development Canada (ESDC). Sometimes, to attract high-quality applicants a recruiter may have to use unconventional procedures, as the following example shows:

> Inspector Kevin McQuiggin from the Vancouver Police Department <http://vancouver.ca/police> recognized that it was getting harder and harder to recruit IT talent to the force. In the past, the VPD averaged about a thousand applications a year from traditional recruitment sources like job fairs, putting ads in the newspaper, and word of mouth. In this new era, attracting tech-savvy applicants who will need to complete the two–three years of training to get up to speed, and then stick around for the long haul, is a rising challenge for police forces around the world. To alleviate the hiring crunch and attract a technologically adept crowd, McQuiggin held a recruiting seminar in Second Life <http://www.youtube.com/watch?v=HkJChEdCFDk>, a three-dimensional virtual world with millions of people around the globe participating through their avatars. The first VPD recruitment session was hosted by VPD avatars made in the images of the VPD real-life recruiters. It was attended by 30 avatars and produced four applications.[6]

Recruitment involves far more than just getting people to apply for jobs, and success in recruitment is not simply measured by the number of applications received. The right type of applicants is far more important than the number of applicants. The following section discusses the strategic importance of the recruitment function.

LO1   HRC 1 & 4

Strategic Importance of the Recruitment Function

In the recent past, recruitment has gained considerable attention among practitioners as well as in the media. Recruiting can be challenging because of a variety of factors including an aging population, which results in a large number of retirements; stiff competition for talent; growth in the Canadian economy; and rising compensation and aspiration levels of new entrants. Over the 2008–2017 period growth in Canada's economy is anticipated to create about 1.5 million new non-student jobs and a further 4 million positions to fill due to retirements. Over the longer term, positions freed due to retirement will generate an even higher share of total job openings.[7] Front-line positions are the easiest to fill, while executives, skilled trades, and high-tech jobs are the toughest for recruiters to fill. Managers in health and education, physicians, and nurses have the strongest shortage pressures.

Today, recruitment of human resources has a significant impact on the organization and its strategic success. The more important HR and organizational activities affected by recruitment are examined below.

HRC **1**

Gaining Competitive Advantage from Human Resources

Successful firms recognize that today, more than ever before, human resources spell the difference between success and failure. Despite the existence of state-of-the-art human resource systems and procedures, poorly qualified and motivated recruits often prove extremely costly to firms. In contrast, in today's global knowledge economy, the presence of highly skilled and motivated workers can be a real **competitive advantage**.

competitive advantage

A competitive advantage exists when the firm is able to deliver the same value and benefits as competitors but at a lower cost (cost advantage), or deliver more benefits or unique value that exceed those of competing products (differentiation advantage).

Experience working in a foreign country is considered a major asset by many employers. As one executive recruiter noted, "an international assignment on your CV gives you an edge over competitors because it shows breadth of experience and adaptability."[8] In one survey of 6,000 employees, 75 percent of the respondents considered foreign work credentials "essential" or "extremely useful."[9] However, managers with foreign country experience are also hard to come by. Only about 37 percent of 2,700 executives surveyed stated that they would consider taking an overseas assignment. This makes people with foreign work experience extremely valuable, which in turn makes recruiting them difficult.

Further, if applicants lack the necessary skills or aptitudes or both, considerable additional resources may have to be invested into selection, training and development, employee communication systems, and employee relations practices. A small pool of recruits also poses a major challenge to the selection procedure (which will be discussed in the next chapter).

HRC **1 & 4**

Reaping the Benefits of Diversity Management

Many Canadian firms recognize the vitality and competitive advantage that often accompanies a diverse workforce. Further, as discussed in Chapter 4, if the firm's workforce does not reflect the larger labour market composition, the firm may be asked to pursue an employment equity program to correct imbalances. Progressive employers monitor their environments continuously and adjust their recruitment strategies to deal with the emerging trends in a proactive manner. Faced with acute competition for valuable human resources, some employers are forming partnerships with social agencies and community associations to help them with their recruiting:

As a group, people with disabilities make up some 14.3 percent of the working age population and offer a major source for highly qualified employees for a variety of jobs. In a study involving 75 employers, a significant percentage of respondents were eager to hire qualified job seekers from this group, but were facing challenges in moving forward on this front. Many did not know how to communicate their hiring needs to people with disabilities. However, in Nova Scotia, Alberta, and British Columbia, employers have formed partnerships with a small number of organizations to convey their messages on a timely basis. For example, the Solutions Learning Centre <http://sollc.ca/category/home> in Nova Scotia and EmployAbilities <http://employabilities.ab.ca> in Edmonton have been successful in placing people with disabilities in a number of organizations. Employers also benefit because such targeted efforts result in speedier recruiting.[10]

Hiring from a larger, diverse pool of candidates offers a greater choice of job applicants to the firm. A diverse workforce also offers greater flexibility and additional capabilities in some instances. It reflects an organization's commitment to broader social goals and projects a better image of the firm to clients and other constituents.

HRC 4 & 7

Focusing on Employee Development

When recruiting (especially for middle- and upper-level jobs), a firm has a choice: it can either develop and promote internal candidates or hire from outside. The strategic choice of internal versus external recruitment has profound implications for an organization.

Figure 5-2 lists some of the advantages and weaknesses of each strategy. Needless to say, the specific strategy chosen by the firm has major implications for recruitment and salary costs, employee morale, and organizational innovation and change. One additional consideration is that, typically, promoting an employee will generate a job opening somewhere else in the organization. The internal promotion of a supervisor to a manager position results in a supervisor opening, which may in turn be filled by the internal promotion of a front-line worker. The front-line worker position may need to be filled by recruiting externally.

NCR Corporation <http://www.ncr.com>, a global Fortune 500 company, produces point-of-sale terminals, automated teller machines, cheque-processing systems, and barcode scanners, and is one of the largest providers of IT maintenance support services. It maintains its competitive edge by hiring employees at the entry level, retaining them, and promoting from within. Its Graduate Gateway program provides recent graduates with experience working in four key business areas during a two-year professional rotation program. Graduates gain experience in technical acumen, project management, business strategy, and leadership to prepare them for a successful career at NCR. The company actively seeks a competitive advantage through its employees by hiring top people and creating a work climate where they are highly productive.[12]

HRC 1 & 4

Investing Resources into Recruitment

The decision about the total recruitment budget affects the quality of recruits and the overall effectiveness of recruitment activity. It is important to note that the costs of recruitment are not simply the hiring costs (such as the costs of advertisement, recruiter's travel, and so on). Often the costs of a bad hire may not be translatable into monetary terms as there is no accurate way of measuring the number of lost customers or resources due to delays and inefficient handling of a situation.[11] Furthermore, inappropriate recruits often leave the organization, causing significant additional costs to hire and train replacements. Often such costs are not apparent. However, some organizations, such as NCR Corporation, have recognized the importance of the recruitment function and have found innovative ways to recruit qualified persons and reduce recruitment costs.

FIGURE 5-2

Internal versus External Recruiting

Internal Recruiting
Advantages
• Employee is familiar with the organization and its culture.
• Employee is "known" to the firm; the fit of this individual to the organization will be known as well.
• Improves workforce morale and motivation.
• Information about employee performance is known in addition to scores on selection tests; this improves the organization's ability to predict the person's success in the new job.
Weaknesses
• Internal rivalry and competition for higher positions; can reduce interpersonal and interdepartmental co-operation.
• No "new blood" is brought into the system, which can prevent creative solutions from emerging.
• Poor morale (leading to possible turnover) of employees who were not promoted.
• May be expensive to offer counselling, training, and development to employees who vied for, but did not get, the promotion.
• Performance evaluation records are only relevant to the extent that the promotion job is similar to the employee's current job.
External Recruiting
Advantages
• Organization is able to acquire skills or knowledge that may not be currently available within.
• Newer ideas and novel ways of solving problems may emerge.
Weaknesses
• Newcomers may not fit in with the organization and into its present culture.
• Newcomers take a longer time to learn about the organization's culture, policies, and practices.
• Usually, hiring from the outside is more expensive.
• Lowered morale and motivation levels of current employees who don't see any career growth possibilities within the firm.

Sources: M. Krakel, and A. Schottner, "Internal labor markets and worker rents," *Journal of Economic Behavior & Organization*, Vol. 84, 2012, pp. 491–509; C. R. McConnell, "Management recruiting: Inside versus outside," *Health Care Manager*, Vol. 29, Jan –March, 2010, pp. 1 -3.

Other investments into the recruiting process include selecting and training recruiters. When selecting recruiters, friendliness or personableness, knowledge of the job, organization, career-related issues, and enthusiasm are important characteristics.[13] Choices must also be made about whether recruiters should be HR professionals, line managers, or co-workers. HR professionals may be knowledgeable about career paths and the organization, but lack understanding of specific job details. Line managers, on the other hand, may know details of the job and company, but not necessarily career development opportunities. And co-workers may understand the job very well, but not necessarily the organization or career paths to the same extent as HR professionals. Depending on the areas of expertise of the recruiters, training may be needed for interviewing and interpersonal skills, job analysis, laws and regulations, and marketing and sales for creating advertisements and being persuasive to candidates.[14]

Key issues in the context of evaluating the effectiveness of the recruitment function and its contribution to organizational success will be discussed in a later section in this chapter. But first, it is important to recognize the several constraints a recruiter faces.

LO2 HRC 4

Constraints on Recruitment

A successful recruiter must be sensitive to the constraints on the recruitment process. These limits arise from the organization, the recruiter, and the external environment. Although the emphasis may vary from situation to situation, the next section describes the most common constraints, summarized in Figure 5-3:

FIGURE 5-3

Constraints on Recruiting

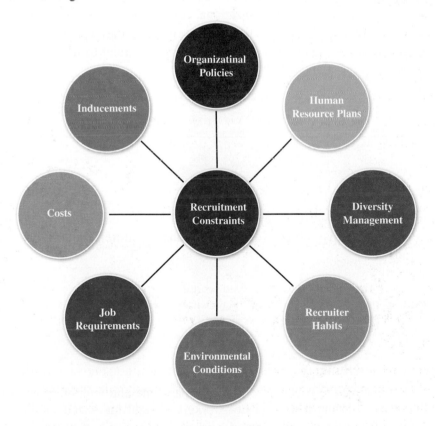

Organizational Policies

Organizational policies can constrain the recruiter. Policies seek to achieve uniformity, economies, public relations benefits, and other objectives unrelated to recruiting. Four policies that have implications for recruitment are highlighted below.

organizational policies

Internal policies that affect recruitment, such as "promote-from-within" policies.

1. Promote-from-within Policies

As already pointed out, promote-from-within policies are formulated to give present employees the first opportunity for job openings and facilitate their career growth. These policies are widespread. Searching for candidates internally versus external searching significantly impacts how recruiting is conducted. For instance, will recruitment ads be placed in the newspaper or posted in the lunchroom? Moreover, the content of the job postings will be different: substantially less information will be needed about the organization for internal as opposed to external candidates, and internal candidates may have a better sense of what a job entails than an external applicant.

Bypassing current employees to hire from outside can lead to employee dissatisfaction and turnover. On the other hand, promoting a positive organizational culture encourages people to join and stay with a firm.[15] Employees are likely to be loyal to their employer only if they believe the organization values them. Nevertheless, there may be generational differences in the extent to which workers plan to spend their careers with their current organizations:

> In a Conference Board of Canada report, 80 percent of Boomers reported planning to stay with their organization, whereas only 37 percent of Gen Xers and 24 percent of Gen Ys plan to stay.[16]

2. Compensation Policies

A common constraint faced by recruiters is pay policies. Organizations with human resource departments usually establish pay ranges for different jobs. Recruiters seldom have the authority to exceed stated pay ranges:

> If Charles Shaw at Ontario Electronics decides to recruit externally, the pay range will influence the job seeker's desire to become a serious applicant. For example, when the market rate for junior engineers is $3,500 to $3,800 per month, satisfactory applicants will be few if Charles can offer only $3,000 to $3,200 per month.

3. Employment Status Policies

Some companies have policies restricting the hiring of part-time and temporary employees. Although there is growing interest in hiring these types of workers, several unionized settings have limitations against hiring part-time, temporary, and contract workers, which can cause recruiters to reject all but those seeking full-time work. Likewise, policies against hiring employees who "moonlight" by having second jobs also inhibit recruiters. Prohibitions against holding extra jobs are intended to ensure a rested workforce.

4. International Hiring Policies

Policies in some countries, including Canada, may also require foreign job openings to be staffed with local citizens. The use of foreign nationals, however, does reduce relocation expenses, lessen the likelihood of nationalization, and if top jobs are held by local citizens, minimize charges of economic exploitation. Moreover, unlike relocated employees, foreign nationals are more apt to be involved in the local community and understand local customs and business practices.

Human Resource Plans

The **human resource plan** is another factor recruiters consider. Through skills inventories and promotion ladders, the plan outlines which jobs should be filled by recruiting and which ones should be filled internally. The plan helps recruiters because it summarizes future recruiting needs. This foresight can lead to economies in recruiting:

human resource plan

A firm's overall plan to fill existing and future vacancies, including decisions on whether to fill internally or to recruit from outside.

At Ontario Electronics, Charles Shaw checked the human resource plan before recruiting junior mechanical engineers. The plan indicated a projected need for three junior electrical engineers and a mechanical engineer during the next four months. Two internal candidates were hired for two of the junior positions. Charles decided to recruit mechanical engineering candidates at the same time when he was looking for the remaining junior electrical engineer. If advertisements were to be placed in the university newspaper, there would be no additional cost for seeking both types of engineers. Travel costs, advertising costs, and the time devoted to a second recruiting trip would be saved.

Diversity Management Programs

Where **diversity management** and employment equity programs exist, recruitment must also take these programs into account. As we saw in Chapter 4, employers cannot discriminate against people with physical disabilities unless the disability would prevent the person from doing the job after reasonable accommodation by the employer. Proactive employers such as the Vancouver International Airport use innovative recruitment programs to tap the skills of a diverse workforce:

diversity management

Recognizing differences among employees belonging to heterogeneous groups and creating a work environment in which members of diverse groups feel comfortable.

Results of a Statistics Canada survey show that compared to non-disabled co-workers, 90 percent of people with disabilities did as well or better at their jobs, 86 percent rated average or better in attendance, and retention rates are 72 percent higher. Furthermore, most require no workplace accommodations (or if required they were generally inexpensive and tax-deductible) [17] There are about 300,000 workers in British Columbia with disabilities, of whom 34,000 have college diplomas, 30,000 have trade certificates, and 28,000 have university degrees, yet people with disabilities are three times more likely to be unemployed than those without disabilities. Recognizing these facts and wanting to reflect the communities it serves, the Vancouver International Airport <http://www.yvr.ca> began actively recruiting people with disabilities to their "barrier-free" workplace. Now an entrenched hiring practice, YVR considers disability issues when designing and planning for new facilities and renovations, and staff understanding of disabilities creates a better travel experience for customers as well.[18]

Recruiter Habits

A recruiter's past success can lead to habits. While **recruiter habits** can eliminate time-consuming deliberations that reach the same answers, they may also perpetuate past mistakes or obscure more effective alternatives. So although recruiters need positive and negative feedback, they must guard against self-imposed constraints.

recruiter habits

The propensity of a recruiter to rely on methods, systems, or behaviours that led to past recruitment success.

Consider again the recruitment of the junior engineer at Ontario Electronics. Suppose that the engineering department expresses satisfaction with recruits from the nearby university. Such positive feedback encourages recruiters to make a habit of using this source for beginning engineers. Since all these engineers have a similar curriculum, they may also share strengths and weaknesses. As a result, the engineering department may suffer because of the educational uniformity of new recruits.

Environmental Conditions

External conditions strongly influence recruitment. Changes in the labour market and the challenges mentioned in Chapter 1 affect recruiting. The unemployment rate, the pace of the economy, spot shortages in specific skills, the size of the labour force, labour laws, and the recruiting activities of other employers—all of these factors affect the recruiter's efforts.

Faced with a labour market that had a severe shortage of experienced drivers, Coastal Pacific Xpress Inc. <http://www.cpx.ca>, a Surrey, British Columbia–based long-haul trucking firm, increased the pay of its owner-operators by 45 percent in four months to attract more recruits.[19]

Although these factors are considered in human resource planning, the economic environment can change quickly after the plan is finalized. To be sure that the plan's economic assumptions remain valid, recruiters can check three fast-changing measures.

1. Leading Economic Indicators

Statistics Canada routinely publishes the direction of the leading indicators. The economic indices suggest the future course of the national economy. If these indices signal a sudden downturn in the economy, recruiting plans may have to be modified. Other agencies such as ESDC, Industry Canada <http://www.ic.gc.ca/eic/site/icgc.nsf/eng/home>, the World Bank <http://www.worldbank.org>, and the International Monetary Fund <http://www.imf.org/external/index.htm> also publish information that is of great interest to national and international organizations.

2. Predicted versus Actual Sales

Since human resource plans are partially based upon the firm's predicted sales, variations between actual and predicted sales may indicate that these plans also are inaccurate. Thus, recruiting efforts may need to be changed accordingly.

3. Employment Statistics

Statistics Canada routinely reports various employment statistics. Periodically, it produces reports on the state of employment in different industry sectors.

Employers can also monitor competition for specific job groups by looking at the ads in major newspapers. For clerical and production workers, who are usually recruited on a local basis, the human resource department may want to create its own ads index to monitor local changes in ads.

Organizations worldwide are likely to face a spiraling employee attrition rate over the next decade or so.

> A survey of more than one million workers in 50 countries indicated that one-third of the global workforce will change employers in two years. Sixty-four percent of employees who reported being uncertain or not committed to staying with their employer actually left the company within five years.[20]

Tighter competition for applicants may require more vigorous recruiting. When business conditions decline, an opposite approach is called for, as the following example illustrates:

> After a decade of "explosive growth" in the construction sector, BuildForce <http://www.buildforce.ca/en> revised its 2014 projection from 22 percent growth in jobs over the following 10 years, to a 2015 projection of three years of job losses following the plunge in oil prices. Projections now call for steep job losses until late 2017 when economic recovery is forecast to begin.[21] Although human resource plans in this sector may have called for recruitment efforts, these are now being revised to include layoffs or more modest recruitment plans.

HRC 4

Job Requirements

Of course, the requirements of each job are a constraint. Highly specialized workers, for example, are more difficult to find than unskilled ones. Recruiters learn of a job's demands from the requesting manager's comments and job analysis information. Job analysis information is especially useful because it reveals the important characteristics of the job and of applicants. Knowledge of a job's requirements allows the recruiter to choose the best way to find recruits, given the constraints under which the recruiter must operate.

"Find the best and most experienced applicant you can" is often a constraint that is imposed on recruiters as though it were a job requirement. At first, this demand seems reasonable: all managers want to have the best and most experienced people working for them. But several potential problems exist with this innocent-sounding request. One problem in seeking out the "best and most experienced" applicant is cost. People with greater experience usually command higher salaries than less experienced people. If a high level of experience is not truly necessary, the recruit may become bored soon after being hired. Moreover, if the human resource department cannot show that a high degree of experience is needed, then experience may be an artificial requirement that discriminates against some applicants.

Another point about experience is worth remembering: for some people in some jobs, 10 years of experience is another way of saying 1 year of experience repeated 10 times. Someone with 10 years of experience may not be any better qualified than an applicant with only 1 year.

Costs

Like all other members of an organization, recruiters must also operate within budgets. The **costs** of identifying and attracting recruits are an ever-present limitation:

costs

Expenses related to attracting recruits.

Manitoba Engineering Company Ltd. found that the average cost of recruiting engineers in the company was more than $3,300 per hire. To hire senior engineers and managers, the cost was even higher. To fill a $70,000 per year position, the company often had to pay $5,000 to $6,000 to search firms. To monitor and control costs, the human resource manager of the company was asked to assess the effectiveness of the company's recruitment programs and costs of recruitment under alternative recruitment methods.

Careful human resource planning and forethought by recruiters can minimize these expenses. For example, recruiting for several job openings simultaneously may reduce the cost per recruit. Of course, a better solution would be to take action to reduce employee turnover, thus minimizing the need for recruiting. Proactive human resource management actions go far in achieving this objective.

Inducements

The recruiter is very much like a marketer—he or she is selling the company as a potential place of work to all eligible recruits. As with any marketing effort, **inducements** may be necessary to stimulate a potential recruit's interest. The growing global marketplace means that workers are also mobile, and attracting them may require unconventional incentives:

inducements

Monetary, nonmonetary, or even intangible incentives used by a firm to attract recruits.

Nurses at Health Canada <http://www.hc-sc.gc.ca> are offered up to a $4,500 inducement for working in remote and isolated First Nations communities.[22] KFC <http://www.kfc.com> in Japan developed a unique strategy for attracting qualified employees by offering them a trip to Hawaii. This enabled the company to meet local competition as well as competition from other international organizations, and look for Japanese workers effectively.[23]

Not all inducements are monetary or even tangible:

RBC Financial Group finds that its focus on workplace diversity has paid rich dividends when recruiting employees. It found that when job candidates come in for interviews at RBC, they often ask about the bank's diversity initiatives and whether resource groups exist. The fact that the bank has four resource groups is a big drawing factor when recruiting. The bank's Reach focuses on people with disabilities; Royal Eagles focuses on the needs of the Aboriginal people; Pride is for lesbian, gay, bisexual, and transgendered people; and Mosaic helps members of visible minorities and new Canadians to integrate into the workforce and the larger community.[24]

Flextime, high quality of life, and other initiatives can be potential selling points for a firm; in some instances, certain items (such as flextime) can also be a constraint if all major employers are using them. In such an instance, a firm needs to meet the prevailing standards. Inducements may be a response to overcoming other limitations faced by the recruiter:

> The fast-food industry, which employs a large percentage of young workers, typically experiences high employee turnover. To reduce turnover and thereby its recruiting costs, McDonald's introduced an educational assistance program. Employees can be reimbursed up to $5,250 per year in eligible expenses for grades 'C' and above.[25]

More recently, several employers have been using nontraditional benefits to attract and retain their employees:

> Some of the benefits offered today include fitness centre memberships, reimbursement of professional membership fees and course fees, on-site vaccination programs and daycare centres, employee mental health insurance, retiree health care benefits, financial planning assistance, and on-site parking.[26] Companies like Google <https://www.google.ca/intl/en/about/> provide free legal advice, dog-walking, free cafeterias, and extra time off when you have a baby.[27]

The key in all cases is to understand the needs and motivations of the target recruits and offer a set of inducements that appeal to them.

HRC 1 & 4

Applying for a Job

Traditionally, job seekers formally apply for a job through either submitting their résumé or completing a job application. The **résumé** (or curriculum vitae or CV) is a brief summary of the applicant's background. It typically includes a one- to two-page summary of the applicant's education, work experience, personal contact information, work goals, and related skills.

résumé

A brief voluntary listing of an applicant's work experience, education, personal data, and other information relevant to the job.

In the case of unsolicited applications, the résumé is the first piece of information about an applicant that a recruiter will see, and it will be used to determine whether the applicant is worthy of further consideration. This makes the résumé a vital part of a job search for any person. To help them sift through a large pile of résumés, many recruiters such as Home Depot and TD Canada Trust will scan paper résumés into an **applicant tracking system** or accept résumés electronically. They will then use résumé screening software to filter through and score the résumés according to key education and job requirements:

> Organizations such as MCI Telecommunications <http://www.mci.com> and Disneyland Resorts <http://disneyland.disney.go.com> use computer scanning to take advantage of the large number of résumés they receive. When résumés arrive at either MCI or Disneyland Resorts, clerks scan the résumés into a computer database. Later, recruiters can search the database for candidates with specific qualifications. Thus, job requirements such as "needs significant selling experience" and "should know French" can immediately be matched with applicant characteristics. The computer displays the number of résumés that meet the required criteria. If the number is too large or too small, the recruiter can change the required qualifications (e.g., if a search for candidates who have had 10 years of work experience yields only five résumés, the recruiter can change the search criterion to seven years of experience). Once the program finds a manageable

number of applicants, the recruiter can view the résumés or résumé summaries online and eliminate any that are not appropriate.

---

applicant tracking systems (ATS)

Databases of potential candidates that enable a good match between job requirements and applicant characteristics and also enlarge the recruitment pool.

The second way of formally applying for a job is by completing a **job application form**. Many people think that completing a job application form after submitting a résumé is redundant. Not so! The job application form collects information about recruits in a uniform manner, and hence is an important part of all recruitment efforts. Even when recruits volunteer detailed information about themselves on a résumé, job applications are often required so that the information gathered is comparable across candidates. Furthermore, job application forms designate the information the recruiters would like to have for each applicant, and may make indicators such as education credentials and gaps in employment history more readily apparent.

---

job application form

A company's form completed by a job applicant indicating their contact information, education, prior employment, references, special skills and other questions pertaining to the position.

Each human resource department generally designs its own form. Nevertheless, certain common features exist. Figure 5-4 provides a typical example of an application form and its major divisions.

Name and Address

Most application forms begin with a request for personal data. Name, address, and telephone number are nearly universal. But requests for some personal data, such as place of birth, marital status, number of dependants, sex, race, religion, or national origin, may lead to charges of discrimination. Since it is illegal to discriminate against applicants, an unsuccessful applicant may conclude that rejection was motivated by discrimination when discriminatory questions are asked. The human resource department must be able to show that these questions are job-related if it asks them.

When applications solicit information about health, height, weight, disabilities that relate to the job, major illnesses, and claims for injuries, potential legal problems exist. Discriminating against people with disabilities is prohibited under the *Canadian Human Rights Act*. The burden of proof that such questions are job-related falls on the employer.

Employment Status

Some questions on the application form concern the applicant's employment objective and availability. Included here are questions about the position sought, willingness to accept other positions, date available for work, salary or wages desired, and acceptability of part-time and full-time work schedules. This information helps a recruiter match the applicant's objective and the organization's needs. It may also cue the recruiter to be sensitive about an applicant's current employment status. Often applicants who are currently employed will not have their current place of employment contacted for a reference until they are close to receiving a job offer so that if they are not successful in obtaining the new job, their current employer does not know they were looking for an alternative.

FIGURE 5-4

A Typical Application Form

Kanata Electronics, Inc.

"An Equal-Opportunity Employer"
Application for Employment

Personal Data

1. Name _____

2. Address _____ 3. Phone number _____

Employment Status

4. Type of employment sought _____ Full-time _____ Part-time

   _____ Permanent _____ Temporary

5. Job or position sought _____

6. Date of availability, if hired _____

7. Are you willing to accept other employment if the position you seek is unavailable?

   _____ Yes _____ No

8. Approximate wages/salary desired $ _____ per month

Education and Skills

9. Circle the highest grade or years completed.

   9 10 11 12 13   1 2 3 4   1 2 3 4
   High School   University   Graduate School

10. Please provide the following information about your education.

    (Include only vocational schools and colleges.)

    a. School name _____ Degree(s) or diploma _____

       School address _____

       Date of admission _____ Date of completion _____

    b. School name _____ Degree(s) or diploma _____

       School address _____

       Date of admission _____ Date of completion _____

11. Please describe your work skills. (Include machines, tools, equipment, and other abilities you possess.)

Work History

Beginning with your most recent or current employer, please provide the following information about each employer. (If additional space is needed, please use an additional sheet.)

12. a. Employer _____ Dates of employment _____

       Employer's address _____

       Job title _____ Supervisor's name _____

       Job duties _____

       Starting pay _____ Ending pay _____

(Continued)

b. Employer _____   Dates of employment _____

Employer's address _____

Job title _____   Supervisor's name _____

Job duties _____

Starting pay _____   Ending pay _____

References

In the space provided, list three references who are not members of your family.

13. a. Name _____   Contact Information _____

Name _____   Contact Information _____

Name _____   Contact Information _____

14. Please feel free to add any other information you think should be considered in evaluating your application.

By my signature on this application, I:

a. Authorize the verification of the above information and any other necessary inquiries that may be needed to determine my suitability for employment.

b. Affirm that the above information is true to the best of my knowledge.

Applicant's Signature _____   Date _____

Education and Skills

The education and skills section of the application form is designed to uncover the job seeker's abilities. Traditionally, education has been a major criterion in evaluating job seekers. Educational attainment does imply certain abilities and is therefore a common request on virtually all applications. Questions about specific skills are also used to judge prospective employees. More than any other part of the application form, the skills section reveals the suitability of a candidate for a particular job.

Work History

Job seekers must frequently list their past jobs. From this information, a recruiter can tell whether the applicant is one who hops from job to job or is likely to be a long-service employee. A quick review of the stated job title, duties, responsibilities, and ending pay also shows whether the candidate is a potentially capable applicant. If this information does not coincide with what an experienced recruiter expects to see, the candidate may have exaggerated job titles, duties, responsibilities, or pay.

References

Besides the traditional references from friends or previous employers, applications may ask for other "reference-like" information. Questions may explore the job seeker's criminal record, credit history, friends and relatives who work for the employer, or previous employment with the organization. Information about criminal record, credit history, and whether the applicant has friends or relatives who work for the company may be important considerations if the job involves sensitive information, cash, or other valuables. Job-relatedness must be substantiated if these criteria disproportionately discriminate against some protected group. Previous employment with the organization means there are records of the applicant's performance.

Signature Line

Candidates are usually required to sign and date their applications. Adjacent to the signature line, a blanket authorization commonly appears. This authorization allows the employer to check references, verify medical, criminal, or financial records, and undertake any other necessary investigations. Another common provision of the signature line is a statement that the applicant affirms the information in the application to be true and accurate as far as is known. Although many people give this clause little thought, falsification of an application form or on a résumé is grounds for discharge (or worse) in most organizations:

> John Davy (a resident of British Columbia) was handed a jail term in New Zealand for lying on résumé. Davy fabricated a degree in business management and accounting from a non-existent U.S. university and lied about working for the B.C. Securities Commission.[28]

LO3

Recruitment Methods

To let job seekers know about job opportunities at the company, there are many options for recruiters. In most instances, recruiters will tend to use several methods at the same time in their search for applicants.

Walk-ins and Write-ins

Walk-ins are job seekers who arrive at the human resource department seeking to drop off their résumé or to complete a job application form. **Write-ins** are those who send a written inquiry by either mailing in their résumé or completing a job application online. Indeed, today, a significant percentage of human resource managers prefer to receive résumés and job applications electronically because of the ease of storage and retrieval.[29] Suitable résumés and applications are typically kept in an active file until an appropriate opening occurs or until the application is too old to be considered valid—usually six months. Larger firms relate information collected like this into their overall human resource information systems.

---

walk-ins/write-ins

Job seekers who arrive at or write to the human resource department in search of a job without prior referrals and not in response to a specific ad.

Employee Referrals

Present employees may refer job seekers to the human resource department. **Employee referrals** have several unique advantages. First, employees with hard-to-find job skills may know others who do the same work.

---

employee referrals

Recommendations by present employees to the recruiter about possible job applicants for a position.

The Canadian Forces have organized recruitment campaigns designed to attract more women to military careers. Should there be limitations as to choice—for example, wanting to be a submariner?

CP/Andrew Vaughan.

> RBC and KPMG <http://www.kpmg.com/ca> were chosen as two of Canada's Top Employers for 2012 (and again each year since), in part, because of their employee referral programs. RBC offers referral bonuses of up to $1,500 for some positions, with KPMG's referral bonuses reaching up to $5,000.[30]

Second, new recruits already know something about the organization from those employees who referred them. Thus, referred applicants may be more strongly attracted to the organization than are walk-ins. Third, employees tend to refer friends whom they identified through personal networking. These persons are likely to have similar work habits and work attitudes. Even if work values are different, these candidates may have a strong desire to work hard so that they do not let down the person who recommended them.

Employee referrals are an excellent and legal recruitment technique. However, recruiters must be careful that this method does not intentionally or unintentionally discriminate. The major problem with this recruiting method is that it tends to maintain the racial, religious, sex, and other features of the employer's workforce. Such results can be viewed as discriminatory.

LO4

Advertising

Advertising is an extremely common, effective method of seeking recruits. Since it can reach a wider audience than employee referrals or unsolicited walk-ins, many recruiters use it as a key part of their efforts.

Ads describe the job and the benefits, identify the employer, and tell those who are interested how to apply. They are the most familiar form of employment advertising. For highly specialized recruits, ads may be placed in professional journals or out-of-town newspapers located in areas with high concentrations of people with the desired skills.

---

ads

Advertisements in a newspaper, magazine, and so on that solicit job applicants for a position.

For example, recruiters in finance often advertise in Vancouver, Toronto, Montreal, and Halifax newspapers because these cities are major banking centres.

Ads have some significant drawbacks. They may lead to thousands of job seekers for one popular job opening, many of whom may not be qualified for the position.[31] Often the ideal recruits are already employed and not reading job ads. Finally, secretly advertising for a recruit to replace a current employee cannot easily be done with traditional ads.

These problems are avoided with **blind ads**. A blind ad does not identify the employer. Interested applicants are told to send their résumé to a post office box or to a non-corporate email account.

---

blind ads

Job ads that do not identify the employer.

The cost of most advertising is determined by the size of the advertisement (in general, larger ads cost more), and the size of the distribution of the advertisement (ads that are circulated to more people generally cost more than ads reaching fewer people). They may also be produced using various media. Radio and small print ads are typically the least expensive, followed by recruitment brochures and billboards, with television advertising as the most expensive form of recruiting. Typically, television advertising is only used for large hiring campaigns with a national focus. For instance, the Canadian Forces ran a TV ad campaign when they were looking to hire 30,000 recruits during one summer.

Because most readers will be travelling in a vehicle, the amount of information that can be conveyed on a billboard is limited. Another limitation of this approach is that it generally requires considerable lead time to prepare a sign. In deciding whether to use a billboard, the recruiter should consider the type of job to be advertised. If it is a job for which the firm is continuously recruiting, it may be worthwhile to have a billboard in visible locations.[32]

Transit advertising involves placing posters in buses, commuter trains, and subway stations. By and large these are only used by employers who have difficulty filling positions using traditional methods. Transit job advertising is relatively inexpensive. If it is placed in a specific geographic location (such as a particular bus stop), it allows an organization to target its advertising to a specific demographic or even ethnic group. If placed in a bus or train, a job advertisement can be seen by thousands of persons each week (or even day). In order to make it easy to respond, the organization should attach QR codes or physical coupons that can be torn off with information on how to apply.

Regardless of the advertising media, applicants prefer to learn basics about the job including hours of work, location, wages, and benefits right on the advertisement.[33] Job ads must contain not only information about the job but also information presented in a way that effectively portrays a message about the job, the work environment, management style, organizational climate, and future growth potential. This cannot be done if the ad contains information that explains only what responsibilities the job includes, who can be qualified, where it is located, and how and when to apply. Recruiters must also determine whether to portray the job only in an attractive manner so that applicants are enticed to apply for and accept the job, or whether to also include potential negative aspects of the job. Realistic recruitment messages portray the job and organization as it really is by including both positive and negative aspects. This "tell it like it is" philosophy may lead some applicants to decide not to apply, but applicants who choose to apply and eventually accept job offers may be more committed to the organization, and leave less frequently; they may be better able to cope with job demands; and they may avoid the disappointment of finding out negative aspects after they've accepted the job.[34]

The choice of whether to use an attractive or a realistic message may depend on the labour market and particular requirements of the job:

> If applicants are hard to find, then enticing prospects with an attractive message is likely best. And if there are lots of potential applicants, then having some applicants self-select out of the applicant pool by using a realistic message will leave recruiters with fewer applicants to sort through.

Traditional recruitment advertisements may be insufficient, particularly when recruiting people with hard-to-find skills or when labour markets are tight. Figure 5-5 lists some of the information contained in good job ads along with other desirable attributes.

As one can see, there are many decisions to be made about recruitment advertising. Regardless of the media and the message, the layout, design, and copy of an advertisement should reflect the image and character of the company and departments that are being represented.[35] This includes dimensions such as the size of the organization, the degree of decentralization seen in the firm, the degree of dynamism and progressive policies typical of the unit, and so on. This in turn means that an ad should emphasize the nature of the organization and the benefits of the package that it offers to attract the applications of qualified people, but at the same time be specific enough to screen out the wrong persons.

Internet Recruiting

The Internet is increasingly becoming one of the most important tools to match jobs with candidates—whether one is a recruiting firm or a job applicant. There are three major reasons for this. First, the Internet offers a cost-effective distribution of information to over 100 countries and millions of users and its information is accessible day and night. Second, by specifying the exact qualifications and job skills needed, the time needed to weed out unsuitable job candidates is minimized. Indeed, the applicants themselves may, on the basis of information supplied, decide not to apply for unsuitable positions. This also adds to the recruiting process the important attribute of timeliness. Third, it is relatively inexpensive. Compared to the commissions to be paid to an executive search firm or the travel expenses of a campus recruiter, the cost of putting an ad on the Internet is minimal, making it an attractive alternative for many organizations.

Internet recruiting has taken off in a number of areas. There are job board sites where job seekers can post their résumés and recruiters can post their job opportunities. Further, most organizations now have a Careers section on their corporate website that can be accessed in two clicks or less from their home pages.[36] Careers pages often contain detailed information about job opportunities, wages and benefits, the organization, and increasingly, employee testimonials about what it is like to work at the company.

To attract members of Generation Y to their careers, Safeway Canada <http://www.safeway.ca> worked with an HR and marketing consulting firm to create the Safeway Jobpod website <http://www.jobpod.ca>. The Jobpod site allows prospective applicants to visit links that appear like buttons on an iPhone. The site includes Generation Y video hosts and information on topics including student programs and educational reimbursement, different types of career opportunities at Safeway, what to expect on the first day, a calculator to help prospective applicants figure out how long it will take them to earn various amounts of money, and of course, a button to apply for jobs.

FIGURE 5-5

Attributes of Good Job Ads

Good job ads, in general, seem to have several common characteristics, such as the following:

1. They attract attention!

2. They address the audience and use a language that the applicant finds comfortable.

3. They use short sentences and familiar words that are action-oriented.

4. They contain all relevant information about the job and the firm. Some major items here are:
   - job title
   - working conditions
   - a clear description of the job
   - training offered
   - organizational and work culture
   - major skills, competencies, and educational requirements
   - career and personal development possibilities
   - location of the job
   - salary, benefits, and other incentives
   - travel and other requirements
   - company selling points

5. They sequence the content logically and in an engaging manner.

6. They respect provisions of human rights and other laws and the dignity of the readers.

7. They do not use sexist, racist, or otherwise unacceptable language. Even the use of adjectives that are normally associated with males or whites may be unacceptable to other groups (e.g., use of adjectives such as "assertive," "dominant," "aggressive," etc., usually connote male sex roles; while terms such as "compassionate," "gentle," and "sympathetic" signify female sex roles).[37]

8. They stand out from other advertisements with good copy layout, visual balance, visual tension, and colour contrast.

9. Their size and presentation should be cost-effective compared with other recruitment methods and considering size and location of target audience.

10. They should make a favourable projection of corporate image and activities without boasting or making unsupported claims.

The Internet has had such a significant impact on recruitment that over 50 percent of all résumés today are submitted electronically.[38]

To improve upon how résumés are searched on its job board site, Monster <http://www.monster.ca> has launched Power Résumé. Employers can use this product to search out job seekers with particular qualifications; the software then rates job seekers out of 10 and distills their résumés down to a short summary with education, skills, and years of experience that can be stacked side-by-side for easy comparison. Workopolis <http://www.workopolis.com>, an online career resource with job postings from across Canada, distributes its job postings automatically on Twitter.[39] With over 30,000 new résumés posted each month, Workopolis is now offering employers a creative new way to sell themselves to potential recruits—namely Workopolis TV, featuring career advice and employers talking about what makes their companies great places to work as they highlight available positions.[40]

Spotlight *on* ETHICS

Facing Recruitment Dilemmas

Like many other HR activities, recruitment often raises ethical dilemmas and questions. Consider the following situations. Do you believe that there are ethical issues here? Rate each item on a five-point scale with these anchors:

1. Very unethical

2. Somewhat unethical

3. Can't decide

4. Somewhat ethical

5. Very ethical

What values, beliefs, or other arguments justify your conclusion?

1. Because of a sudden spurt in demand for your products caused by the temporary closure of a competing plant, you need an additional manager. Your plant is located in a somewhat remote place devoid of many urban conveniences. You know that this is only a temporary position, but if you publicize it as such, you are unlikely to attract any competent candidates. In your advertisements and during the job interviews, you decide not to make any statements about the short-term nature of the position. You will not make any false statements, but also will not divulge that the position is going to be available for only about six months.

2. Of late, your firm, a designer clothing firm, has not been very successful in coming out with many innovative designs. If you do not make a breakthrough in the immediate future, the possibility exists that your firm may go under. You meet the chief designer of your competitor and offer an $8,000 raise to him in an effort to attract him to your firm and turn around your fortunes.

3. Your firm has been attempting to introduce diversity at your workplace. You have had a fair degree of success until now, except with members of one ethnic community who your HR department finds to be "troublemakers." Employees who belong to this community are found to be emotionally upset even over minor matters and are very vocal in their complaints. You find that a lot of productive time is wasted in managing conflicts and settling disputes. During a recent conversation with a professional colleague in another firm, you mentioned this matter. He confirmed similar experiences in his organization. He also told you that whenever he gets applications from members of this community (who can be identified from their names), he tends to pass them into the inactive file without serious consideration. He suggested that you follow the same practice until the situation improves.

(Continued)

4. Your firm, a successful software programmer with a 25 percent market share of a specific product, badly needs to know more about a competitor's patented program. While you do not intend to infringe their patents, a good knowledge of the intricacies of their program and future product plans can help you get a head start in the next phase of development and capture some of their market share. You offer a very attractive salary and a share of profits emerging from the new product to the star programmer with your competitor. You are hopeful that when she joins your firm, she will be able to tell you secrets of your competitor's success and future plans.

For some suggestions on how to recruit on the Internet, see the "Spotlight on HRM" below.

One caution with recruiting on the Internet is that a large portion of Canadians, especially those who are less educated or do not have broadband service access, cannot take full advantage of the Internet.[41] Further, since the Internet opens up recruiting to a global audience, great care has to be taken when designing ads and choosing hiring procedures.

Although many countries use English as their major language for business, there are vast differences in English usage across countries. For example, several words and expressions used in North America are alien to people in Hong Kong, Australia, or India, although many applicants in those countries are fluent in English. Many symbols and graphics also have vastly different meanings in different countries. For example, a thumbs-up gesture meant to signal a positive thought would be obscene in Sicily.[42] Job applicants in Holland and France expect that employers will ask them about personal details such as gender, age, and marital status, although such questions are illegal in Canada.

Spotlight *on* HRM

Recruiting on the Web

Effective recruiting online is dependent on the care and planning behind the strategy. This means that the message and tone conveyed can affect not only recruitment effectiveness but also the general public image of the company. Some of the suggestions for improving a firm's recruitment success recruiting online are as follows:

1. Make your postings attractive: In the past, print media costs and space constraints have forced recruiters to use brief job descriptions. Online job postings can be longer and more informative, visually more exciting, and interactive. Because the website has to compete for attention from surfers, it is important that the website be attention-grabbing, be easy to navigate, and have self-contained information. Researchers are now experimenting with how to tailor web-based recruitment based on individual applicant preferences.[43]

2. Using eye-tracking software, surveys, and having participants explain their thoughts while viewing websites, a recent study found that applicants pay more attention to information presented as hyperlinks on text than when it is presented as part of graphics or navigation tools. Content, site design, and communication features including social interaction with the website were all important. Information about the job opening, the organization, and geographic location should be obvious and easily accessible. Content found in text and hyperlinked information may be more important than providing lots on information on pretty graphics.[44]

3. Researchers recently found that presenting information about the organization's community involvement (including philanthropic efforts and supporting employees' volunteerism efforts) and to a lesser extent pro-environmentalism (policies and procedures toward eco-friendliness and sustainability) produced higher anticipated pride in working for a company and fit between the company's values and their own.[45] Highlight your organization's corporate social performance on web recruitment materials. Diversity information on web materials has also been found to increase viewing time and more attraction to the organization by minority applicants.[46]

(Continued)

4.   Publish your Web address on everything: Make sure that your URL is included in your traditional ads in the newspapers, marketing information, public relations notices, with published material for college, university, or trade school markets, on social media, and all other corporate communication devices. Continue to look for unconventional recruitment outlets: even when you announce job openings in less conventional locations (e.g., a minority language newspaper), include your URL in your message.[47]

5.   Use specialized recruitment websites: Today, a plethora of recruitment sites specialize in different kinds of personnel. By advertising on specialized websites, you are likely to target specific markets. Examples include the following:

   For teachers: <www.recruitingteachers.org>

   For fire and police personnel: <www.ifpra.com>

   For engineers: <www.engineeringjobs.org>

   For information technology personnel: <www.jobserve.com>

   Careers in oil and gas industry: <www.careersinoilandgas.com>

   For working from home: <www.hea-employment.com>

   For hospitality careers: <www.hcareers.ca>

6.   Target the websites in the province or territory where the job is: ESDC can give you a breakdown of applicants in each province for a specific job. There are also specialized websites for each province (e.g., for Government of Alberta recruitment:<www.jobs.alberta.ca>).

7.   When national recruitment efforts fail, consider attracting foreign nationals: Once again, there are many choices in terms of recruitment websites, including the following:

   For Australia: <http://www.seek.com.au>

   For the U.K.: <www.topjobs.co.uk>

   For the Philippines: <http://pni-recruitment.com>

8.   Post the recruitment ad in online newsgroups: They are free (at least most of them are). Because the newsgroups continuously update materials, you will need to periodically reinsert your ad. This also gives you an opportunity to revise your ad. One popular newsgroup is "can.jobs." Some of the other interesting websites (some originating in the United States) are:[48]

   CareerBuilder.com: <www.careerbuilder.com>

   Career Magazine: <www.careermag.com>

   MonsterTrak: <www.jobtrak.com>

   Irrespective of where the ad is listed, it should contain all key words likely to be used by a firm's recruits.[49]

9.   Take advantage of special online advertisement offers: Advertise your openings with popular online newspapers and magazines as their websites receive high traffic.

10.   List your ad with all major web-based job banks (including ESDC's): Use the various career sites to send applicants to you.[50] Included here are the following:

   <www.workopolis.com>

   <www.monster.ca>

   <www.recruitersonline.com>

11.   Remove the ad as soon as the position is filled: If the recruitment is for a one-time position, the advertisement should be removed as soon as the position is no longer available. The site should also indicate the period of time during which applications are kept active.

12.   Choose software carefully: Software that scans the résumés should be keyed for pertinent, job relevant words. A periodic review of the "screened out" applications indicates whether the software is deleting applications from protected employment groups systematically.

Social Media

To leverage technology, recruiting has also expanded to mobile devices. iPhone, BlackBerry, and Android have applications that allow job seekers to search and apply for jobs through their smartphones. Many organizations are also on Facebook <https://www.facebook.com>, where the average user is age 32, and LinkedIn <http://ca.linkedin.com>, where the average user is 37 years old.[51]

Social media can be used by recruiters in two primary ways. First, recruiters can post their opportunities and seek applicants using tools such as LinkedIn and Google+. While LinkedIn may have a greater number of users, it has limitations in terms of the conversations that can take place, and few comments are made despite many postings by 'thought leaders'. Google+, on the other hand, may allow for greater engagement, targeted audience networking, creation of a brand page, and help to direct traffic to the business from search engines, but there are currently fewer users. Some social media experts advocate that recruiters should leverage both of these tools and keep abreast of emerging tools; others recommend that recruiters need to know what tools their prospective recruits in their industry are using and focus their recruiting efforts on them.[52]

Second, recruiters may seek information about candidates and prospective candidates through social networking sites like Facebook, Twitter, Foursquare, blogs, wikis, online discussion boards, Google Groups, Tumblr, and video- and photo-sharing sites such as YouTube and Flickr. While recruiters may be able to learn more about applicants from these sites, much of what they learn may be unrelated to the job. For instance, information on these sites may relate to protected status such as age, gender, religion, race, political affiliation, national origin, disabilities, or sexual orientation. Furthermore, the information on these sites is not verified and the profile accessed may not even be for the correct person.[53]

The Society for Human Resource Management (SHRM) <http://www.shrm.org>, which has 275,000 HR professionals from around the world as members, revealed research showing that 57 percent of companies surveyed in 2013 did not have a policy about screening potential employees using social networking sites. Of those with a policy, there was an even split where 21 percent allow use and 21 percent prohibit use of the sites for screening candidates. SHRM research from 2011 revealed that 66 percent of HR professionals do not go to candidates' social media sites because they are afraid that they will discover information that they are not supposed to know. Compared to 54 percent of HR professionals reporting concern about the legality of screening candidates based on social networking sites in 2008, 74 percent expressed concern over screening based on social networking sites in 2013.[54]

Recall that recruiting includes all activities that may intentionally or unintentionally affect candidates' likelihood of applying for and accepting a job offer at a firm. The use of social media by employees of the firm may impact how candidates view an organization. Many organizations today are grappling with whether social media should be restricted to only those organizational functions that may need to use it (such as marketing, media relations, and HR), or promote its use by all employees. Regardless, HR may be involved with other functions (e.g., legal, marketing) in creating a social media use policy. An example of the social media guidelines by one progressive firm is reproduced in Figure 5-6.

Employment and Social Development Canada

Employment and Social Development Canada (ESDC) is the department of the Government of Canada responsible for developing, managing, and delivering social programs and services. The Skills and Employment branch provides programs and initiatives that:

- promote skills development, labour market participation and inclusiveness, and labour market efficiency

- address the employment and skills needs of those facing employment barriers, and contribute to lifelong learning and building a skilled inclusive labour force.

- support an efficient labour market including the labour market integration of recent immigrants, the entry of temporary foreign workers, the mobility of workers across Canada, and the dissemination of labour market information.

Further information about this fourth-largest department of the Canadian government is available on the ESDC website <http://www.esdc.gc.ca>.

Employment and Social Development Canada (ESDC)
Federal department that provides programs and services for employers and present and potential employees.

FIGURE 5-6

The Current and Official "IBM Social Computing Guidelines"

Introduction

Responsible engagement in innovation and dialogue

Whether or not an IBMer chooses to create or participate in a blog, wiki, online social network or any other form of online publishing or discussion is his or her own decision. However, emerging online collaboration platforms are fundamentally changing the way IBMers work and engage with each other, clients and partners.

IBM is increasingly exploring how online discourse through social computing can empower IBMers as global professionals, innovators and citizens. These individual interactions represent a new model: not mass communications, but masses of communicators.

Therefore, it is very much in IBM's interest—and, we believe, in each IBMer's own—to be aware of and participate in this sphere of information, interaction and idea exchange:

To learn: As an innovation-based company, we believe in the importance of open exchange and learning—between IBM and its clients, and among the many constituents of our emerging business and societal ecosystem. The rapidly growing phenomenon of user-generated web content—blogging, social web-applications and networking—are emerging important arenas for that kind of engagement and learning.

To contribute: IBM—as a business, as an innovator and as a corporate citizen—makes important contributions to the world, to the future of business and technology, and to public dialogue on a broad range of societal issues. As our business activities increasingly focus on the provision of transformational insight and high-value innovation—whether to business clients or those in the public, educational or health sectors—it becomes increasingly important for IBM and IBMers to share with the world the exciting things we're learning and doing, and to learn from others.

In 1997, IBM recommended that its employees get out onto the Internet—at a time when many companies were seeking to restrict their employees' Internet access. In 2005, the company made a strategic decision to embrace the blogosphere and to encourage IBMers to participate. We continue to advocate IBMers' responsible involvement today in this rapidly growing space of relationship, learning and collaboration.

IBM Social Computing Guidelines: Executive Summary

1. Know and follow IBM's Business Conduct Guidelines.

2. IBMers are personally responsible for the content they publish on blogs, wikis or any other form of user-generated media. Be mindful that what you publish will be public for a long time—protect your privacy.

3. Identify yourself—name and, when relevant, role at IBM—when you discuss IBM or IBM-related matters. And write in the first person. You must make it clear that you are speaking for yourself and not on behalf of IBM.

4. If you publish content to any website outside of IBM and it has something to do with work you do or subjects associated with IBM, use a disclaimer such as this: "The postings on this site are my own and don't necessarily represent IBM's positions, strategies or opinions."

5. Respect copyright, fair use and financial disclosure laws.

6. Don't provide IBM's or another's confidential or other proprietary information. Ask permission to publish or report on conversations that are meant to be private or internal to IBM.

(Continued)

7. Don't cite or reference clients, partners or suppliers without their approval. When you do make a reference, where possible link back to the source.

8. Respect your audience. Don't use ethnic slurs, personal insults, obscenity, or engage in any conduct that would not be acceptable in IBM's workplace. You should also show proper consideration for others' privacy and for topics that may be considered objectionable or inflammatory—such as politics and religion.

9. Find out who else is blogging or publishing on the topic, and cite them.

10. Be aware of your association with IBM in online social networks. If you identify yourself as an IBMer, ensure your profile and related content is consistent with how you wish to present yourself with colleagues and clients.

11. Don't pick fights, be the first to correct your own mistakes, and don't alter previous posts without indicating that you have done so.

12. Try to add value. Provide worthwhile information and perspective. IBM's brand is best represented by its people and what you publish may reflect on IBM's brand.

Reprint Courtesy of International Business Machines Corporation, © International Business Machines Corporation.

ESDC's mission is to build a stronger and more competitive Canada, to support Canadians in making choices that help them live productive and rewarding lives, and to improve Canadians' quality of life. Service Canada was created in 2005 to improve the delivery of government programs and services to Canadians, by making access to them faster, easier, and more convenient. Service Canada offers single-window access to a wide range of Government of Canada programs and services for citizens (including several of those from ESDC) through more than 600 points of service located across the country, call centres, and the Internet. ESDC offers specific programs and activities including the Jobs and the Workplace webpages and the Job Bank.[55]

Jobs and the Workplace

The Jobs and the Workplace pages <www.esdc.gc.ca/en/jobs/index.page> are designed to help Canadians find work, explore skills and training possibilities, make career decisions, plan for retirement, and apply for temporary financial assistance. On them, job seekers can explore job descriptions, examine wage rates and skills requirements, and find training and job opportunities. The information can be sorted by occupation and also within specific geographical regions. The site was designed to help Canadians choose career paths, explore educational options, and prepare for job searches and interviews. For employers, the site offers information on hiring and retaining workers, labour market information, advice on human resource management tools, and government program and regulatory information.

The Job Bank

The Job Bank provides a comprehensive database of thousands of jobs and work opportunities available across Canada. When an employer has a job opening, the human resource department voluntarily notifies ESDC of the job and its requirements, which are then posted at the website. Here, prospective employees can scan the job openings and discuss any vacancy with one of the counsellors available. When an applicant expresses interest in some particular job, counsellors interview that person. Over 40,000 employers use the services to advertise full-time, part-time, and summer job opportunities.[56]

Private Employment Agencies

Private employment agencies, which now exist in every major metropolitan area, arose to help employers find capable applicants. Placement firms take an employer's request for recruits and then solicit job seekers, usually through advertising or from walk-ins. Candidates are matched with employer requests and then told to report to the employer's human resource department. The matching process conducted by private agencies varies widely. Some placement services carefully screen applicants for their client. Others simply provide a stream of applicants and let the client's human resource department do most of the screening. Some of the private employment firms match their strategies to the emerging environmental trends, as the following illustration shows:

> A metropolitan placement agency marketed its services on the basis of skill, dedication, and ready availability of its temporary workers. When faced with a shortage of school students who worked part-time, the agency began looking at other population segments. One group met all the three requirements of the agency—recently retired and about-to-retire persons were skilled, dedicated, and prepared to accept temporary assignments. In a short while, the firm began to rely solely on this group for all its temporary staff needs.

Use of a private employment agency may be necessary when the employer needs only a few persons and on a temporary or irregular basis. Also, when the employer has a critical need to fill a position quickly this method can be very useful. In times of tight labour markets, it may be necessary to attract individuals who are already employed on a part-time basis. Private employment agencies can achieve this more cost-effectively, especially if the employer has limited experience in the local labour market.

In many provinces, it is either illegal for private employment agencies to charge applicants a fee for placement, or the fees charged are regulated. Most fees are paid by the agencies' clients—that is, the prospective employers. The fees commonly equal either 10 percent of the first year's salary or one month's wages, but the amount may vary with the volume of business provided by the client and the type of employee sought.

Professional Search Firms

Professional search firms are much more specialized than placement agencies. Search firms usually recruit only specific types of human resources for a fee paid by the employer. For example, some search firms specialize in executive talent, while others use their expertise to find technical and scientific personnel. Perhaps the most significant difference between search firms and placement agencies is their approach. Placement agencies hope to attract applicants through advertising, but search firms actively seek out recruits from among the employees of other companies. Although they may advertise, the direct contact is their primary tool for locating and attracting prospective recruits:

---

professional search firms

Agencies that, for a fee, recruit specialized personnel for a company.

> The Interlake-Eastern Regional Health Authority has hired a professional search firm to help fill physician vacancies in Eastern Manitoba. The region has relied on international medical grads to fill its openings, but most leave following two- or four-year commitments and successfully passing examinations to allow them to practice anywhere in Canada. The focus of the professional search firm is to recruit physicians who will want to remain in the communities.[57]

There are a couple of advantages to using professional search firms. First, search firms have in-depth experience that most human resource departments lack. Second, search firms are often willing to undertake actions that an employer would not, such as calling a competitor. Some human resource professionals consider the practice by search firms of "stealing" or "raiding" candidates from among their clients' competitors to be unethical, and refer to them as "headhunters."[58]

In the past few years, the number of executive recruiting firms in Canada has grown rapidly. Although most of them are located in large metropolitan cities such as Toronto, Montreal, or Vancouver, an increasing number of these firms are making an appearance in smaller cities and towns.

What is the reason for the growing popularity of executive search firms? Professional search firms may have greater understanding of niche requirements in particular industries, cost less per recruit, have access to candidates integrated into specific industries as well as passive job seekers, and result in an overall higher success rate in recruiting the right quality personnel.[59]

In one survey of 107 Canadian organizations, over 75 percent of the responding human resource departments indicated that executive search firms could reach applicants who were unreachable through other means. However, the same survey found that a majority of respondents felt search firms were more appropriate for larger firms. Over 60 percent also indicated that their own recruiters and departments had a better understanding of the firm's employment needs than search firms.[60]

When choosing a search firm, care must be taken to test the "fit" between the firm and the client organization. Some of the search firms, especially the smaller ones, are often highly specialized and may not be able to meet the general needs of a client. Checking the recruiting record of the firm and its reputation is, consequently, very important. The larger firms can be quite expensive, often charging 30 percent of the candidate's gross starting salary as fees (not inclusive of other expenses).[61] Some of the factors that should be considered in evaluating a recruiting firm include the size of the firm, staff qualifications, ability to meet time requirements, financial soundness of the firm, proven validity of the testing/selection instruments and practices, and provision of measurable results from previous contracts (track record and acceptable references).

Educational Institutions

For entry-level openings, **educational institutions** and **alumni associations** are another common source of recruits. Counsellors and teachers often provide recruiters with leads to desirable candidates in high schools. Many universities, community colleges, and technical schools offer their current students and alumni placement assistance. This assistance helps employers and graduates to meet and discuss employment opportunities and the applicant's interest.

---

educational institutions

High schools, technical schools, community colleges, and universities where applicants for job positions are sought.

---

alumni associations

Associations of alumni of schools, colleges, or other training facilities.

Campus recruitment is a very competitive activity. This is especially so for employers in the mining sector because so few students are graduating from mining engineering programs in Canada. A typical chemical engineering class will have several hundred students, but the mining engineering program at Dalhousie University <http://www.dal.ca> in Halifax had just 10 and the program at Queen's University <http://www.queensu.ca> in Kingston had only 30 in 2008. Graduates in mining engineering consequently have been able to pick and choose employers. The average job-offer acceptance rate across all industries was 82 percent, but it was just 59 percent for job offers in the mining industry.[62]

Past research studies indicate that students desire campus recruiters to be well informed, honest, and skilled. The title and age of the recruiter, and even whether the recruiter is an alumnus of the same institution, may also be important factors in creating a favourable impression on recruits.[63] Some other characteristics of successful campus recruiters are shown in Figure 5-7. However, not many recruiters are successful in getting the best talent during their campus visits. The recruitment cycle is getting shorter each year with top candidates often snapped up the September before they graduate. The National Association of Colleges and Employers (NACE) <http://www.naceweb.org> offers a number of suggestions on best practices for campus recruitment programs.[64]

Increasingly, organizations find that summer internships and co-operative education programs where students alternate between study and work terms significantly facilitate college and university recruitment efforts.

Summer internships are particularly popular in large companies such as Procter & Gamble <http://www.pg.com>, Aetna Life Insurance <http://www.aetna.com>, and Manitoba Liquor and Lotteries Corporation <http://www.mbll.ca>; however, even smaller organizations find that hiring students to complete summer projects helps them to identify qualified, motivated, and informed recruits for permanent placement.

FIGURE 5-7

A Profile of an Ideal Recruiter

- Hires for specific positions rather than looking for future recruits without any clear idea about job vacancies.
- Possesses considerable knowledge about the firm and the job position.
- Discusses strengths and limitations of the firm knowledgeably.
- Never exaggerates or oversells the employer.
- Studies the student's résumé carefully before the interview and asks specific questions.
- Validly assesses the student's awareness of and interest in the job and the company.
- Asks thought-provoking questions to measure the student's knowledge on relevant job matters.
- Expresses interest in the student as an individual.
- Is upbeat about the company and his or her own role in the firm.
- Displays good interpersonal skills and appears polite and sincere.
- Follows up promptly with feedback and evaluation.
- Is professional and ethical in demeanour.

SOURCE: Based partially on and expanded from John E. Steele, "A Profile of the Ideal Recruit," *Personnel Journal*, February 1997, pp. 58–59.

During their work terms, students are exposed to the organization and gain a clear idea of what to expect from the firm should they later join as full-time employees. Such "informed" recruits are less likely to leave the firm soon after they are hired. Employers can also assess the students' ability, attitudes, and performance without incurring any significant costs.[65]

Universities that provide business administration programs aimed at senior- and middle-level managers (such as executive MBA programs) are also a valuable source for recruiting managers. Keeping tapped into the alumni associations of schools, colleges, and even of prior employees can also be an excellent source for hiring experienced technical and managerial staff.[66]

Employers are required to reasonably accommodate people with physical disabilities. What if the accommodation requires the installation of an elevator for $100,000 in a branch of a national bank?

Pixtal/AGE Fotostock.

Professional Associations and Labour Organizations

Recruiters find that professional associations also can be a source of job seekers. Many associations conduct placement activities to help new and experienced professionals get jobs; some have publications that accept classified advertisements. Professionals who belong to the appropriate associations are considered more likely to remain informed of the latest developments in their field, and so this channel of recruitment may lead to higher-quality applicants. Another advantage of this source of applicants is that it helps recruiters zero in on specific specialties, particularly in hard-to-fill technical areas.

When recruiters want people with trade skills, local labour organizations have rosters of those people who are looking for employment. The local union of plumbers, for example, keeps a list of plumbers who are seeking jobs. In the construction industry, many contractors often hire on a per-project basis. A union hiring hall is a convenient channel for attracting large numbers of pre-trained recruits for new projects.

Canadian Forces

The Canadian Forces <http://www.forces.ca> trains personnel in almost every profession imaginable from trades to medical professionals to culinary arts. A veteran who joined the forces at 18 may be eligible for a full CF pension at 43 and some may seek to transition into a civilian career. Some veterans, such as those who have been trained as mechanics, welders, or pilots, have hard-to-find skills. Human resource departments that need skills similar to those found in the military often find nearby military installations a valuable source of recruits.

Military jets have the highest performing engines on the planet and disc-braking systems were developed for military aircraft. Audi's veteran hiring program recognizes the transferability of the skills gained working with adjusting and replacing disc brakes during military service to their high-performance car engines.[67]

Temporary-Help Agencies

Most large cities have **temporary-help agencies** that can respond quickly to an employer's need for help. These agencies do not provide recruits. Instead, they are a source of supplemental workers. The temporary help actually work for the agency and are "on loan" to the requesting employer. For temporary jobs—during vacations, peak seasons, illnesses, and so on—these agencies can be a better alternative than recruiting new workers for short periods of employment. Besides handling the recruiting and bookkeeping tasks caused by new employees, these agencies can often provide clerical and secretarial talent on short notice, sometimes within less than a day. And when the temporary shortage is over, there is no need to lay off surplus workers, because "temporaries" work for the agency, not the company.[68] Occasionally, temporary help are recruited to become permanent employees.

temporary-help agencies

Agencies that provide supplemental workers for temporary vacancies caused by employee leave, sickness, etc.

With over 50 branches in Canada, Adecco <http://www.adecco.ca> employs several thousand temporary Associates each day.[69] Adecco provides a pool of workers employed by the agency who can be loaned to local organizations for particular lengths of time. For instance, Adecco may lend one of its Associates to be the Senior Accountant at an Edmonton firm for a 10 month contract while its regular employee is on maternity leave, and may lend an Associate to a Net Developer for a 3–6 month contract in Kitchener/Waterloo. When their contracts are over, the Associates return to Adecco awaiting the next firms needing contract employment in their fields.

Departing Employees

An often overlooked source of recruits is among departing employees. These workers might gladly stay if they could rearrange their schedules or change the number of hours worked. Family responsibilities, health conditions, or other circumstances may lead a worker to quit when a transfer to a part-time job could retain valuable skills and training. Even if part-time work is not a solution, a temporary leave of absence may satisfy the employee and some future recruiting need of the employer.

An employee who leaves a company to pursue another job or venture and is later rehired is known as a "boomerang employee." As competition for top talent has intensified, the number of boomerang employees has grown vastly. A company such as Ernst & Young LLP <http://www.ey.com/CA>, a Toronto-based accounting firm, actively cultivates a continuing connection with its past employees. Former employees have access to webcasts sponsored by E&Y that discuss developments in the accounting field. A newsletter is sent a couple of times a year and several social events are held for former staff. When people leave the firm, they are even given a password to access the website, which includes a directory of current and former employees, details of what former employees are doing, and a place to post résumés. Encouraging former employees to reconsider E&Y is definitely one of the objectives of such efforts, according to a director of E&Y.[70]

A **buy-back** occurs when an employee resigns to take another job and the original employer outbids the new job offer, or renegotiates the terms of the employee's job contract. The following dialogue provides an example:

buy-back

A method of convincing an employee who is about to resign to stay in the employ of the organization, typically by offering an increased wage or salary.

Employee: I quit. I got a new job as a system analyst at International Plastics.

Manager: You're too valuable for us just to let you walk out the door. How much is International offering?

Employee: They're offering me $10,000 a year more!

Manager: Stay and I'll recommend a $6,000 raise.

Employee: No. I'm going.

Manager: How about $7,500 and an extra week of vacation?

Employee: Well, okay.

Even when the authority to enter into a bidding war exists, the manager may discover that other workers expect similar raises. Many HR practitioners are averse to this approach because of its ethical implications. Employees may also reject a buy-back attempt because of the ethical issue raised by not reporting to a job that has already been accepted.

Job Fairs

Attending **job fairs** can pay rich dividends to recruiters who are looking for specialized talents or a number of personnel. Over the years, budgetary constraints and the emergence of Internet recruitment have resulted in a decline in the popularity of job fairs. However, even today, there are examples of striking successes:

The job fair organized by the University of Waterloo <http://uwaterloo.ca>, Wilfrid Laurier University <http://www.wlu.ca>, Conestoga College <http://www.conestogac.on.ca>, and University of Guelph <http://www.uoguelph.ca> has tripled in size of attendees since it was first organized in 1994. The 2015 event is expected to attract 183 companies and 2,500 to 3,000 students, making it the largest job fair in Canada.[71]

Some job fairs are scheduled one year in advance; hence, employers should plan well ahead. More recently, it has also become popular to give out "swag," such as pens, notepads, USB sticks, and water bottles to visitors to promote the organization.[72]

job fairs
Trade show style fairs with many employers showcasing their companies and jobs to potential recruits.

Contract Workers

As discussed in Chapter 3, a very large segment of our labour market is composed of contract workers. Contract workers are useful when the work is of limited duration, so the firm can avoid fixed salary commitments; the employer pays a flat fee for the employees (and is not responsible for benefits). Contract workers, often, are compensated on the basis of task completion and hence need less supervision. Often, they also require lower training costs, making this an attractive proposition.

More organizations employ contract workers now than ever before. In many organizations, the proportion of the staff who were on contract is 7 to 10 percent, and two-thirds of HR professionals in Canada in a recent survey had seen an increase in the number of contract workers in the past five years. Reasons for the increase may include ability to better balance work–life needs, not being tied to a single employer, and the increasingly project-based nature of work.[73]

It should be noted that contract workers may not always be committed to the goals and philosophy of the organization. Because the workers are not part of an organization's regular workforce, they do not benefit from the statutory protections offered by various provincial employment laws. The contracting firm is also not responsible for remitting Canada Pension Plan premiums or withholding income tax. However, determining whether an individual is an independent contractor or an employee is not as easy as it appears. Courts and arbitrators have been increasingly monitoring contractual agreements to ensure that the employer is not using the independent contractor relationship to avoid its statutory and common law obligations.[74] Accordingly, it is important for the contracting parties to understand their rights and obligations.

Recruitment Abroad

With the growing labour shortages in Canada, many employers are looking abroad to secure skilled, hard-to-find employees.

Many high-tech and software companies today look at India as a major source of highly skilled programmers. Some of the software manufacturers have gone as far as locating their operations in Indian cities such as Bangalore and Hyderabad, while others have formed partnerships with Indian firms that periodically send their own staff to North America on a contract basis.

Many Canadian high-tech companies are taking advantage of India's low labour costs and highly skilled programmers, thus displacing local workers. What proportion of jobs should Canada export?

© FINDLAY KEMBER/AFP/Getty Images.

Recently, Canada has been recruiting a large number of skilled workers from other countries. Figure 5-8 shows the origins of 148,181 economic immigrants who entered the country in 2013. With an aging domestic workforce and a predicted shortage of technical and highly skilled employees, foreign nationals may become an important source of our workforce.

Foreign workers, especially those from developing countries, may be less expensive (at least initially). Relocation expenses may have to be paid in some instances, which can significantly add to the total cost. Firms hiring from abroad will need to train new recruits to adapt to local and organizational culture. The process of getting employment visas may also be time-consuming.

FIGURE 5-8

Origins of Canada's Skilled Immigrants, 2013

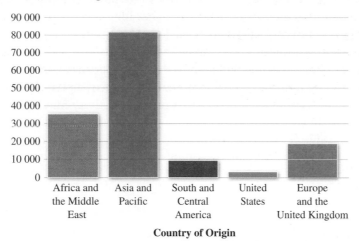

SOURCE: Chart prepared by the authors based on the data reported in Citizenship and Immigration Canada, "Immigration Overview: Permanent residents by category and source area," 2013, <http://www.cic.gc.ca/english/resources/statistics/facts2013/permanent/08.asp>, downloaded February 20, 2015.

Choosing Recruitment Sources

With all of the options available for sourcing potential applicants, how does a recruiter choose which method(s) to use? The choice of recruiting method may be assisted by answering the following six questions:[75]

1. How many recruits are needed? Some sources, such as advertising, will produce larger numbers of applicants whereas others are used when small numbers of recruits are needed (e.g., employment agencies).

2. What is the skill level required? If there is a high level of skill or experience required for the job, niche recruiting might be needed, for instance by approaching a professional association or using a professional search firm.

3. What sources are available in that industry and geographic region? Not all sources are available in all areas (e.g., a rural area might not have a temporary-help agency).

4. What has worked in the past? Tracking over time how well certain sources have worked may guide future recruitment efforts. For example, if advertising on an Internet job board has produced more applicants who have turned out to be good performers in the past than a community newspaper, the recruiter may choose to advertise new postings on the same job board.

5. How much is the budget? The budget will determine the methods the recruiter can afford to use. For instance, transit advertising may be too expensive to use for filling a single position.

6. Are there labour agreements in place that specify recruitment options? Collective agreements in place at the organization may obligate the recruiter to rely on internal versus external recruiting, and to use specific recruitment sources.

In competitive recruitment environments, recruiters will often employ multiple methods and then track each method to see the number of applicants, the quality of applicants, the number who eventually accept and perform the job well, and even retention rates. Producing a good system for tracking recruitment success saves time and effort down the road and can have a substantial impact on the organization's bottom line.

LO5 HRC 1 & 4 & 7

Evaluating the Recruitment Function

Like most other important functions, the recruiting activity in an organization should also be subjected to periodic evaluation. Typically, the recruitment process is expensive. Unless efforts are made to identify and control these costs, the potential benefits from the activity may end up being lower than the costs. Like all other corporate HR functions, recruiters will not be able to justify their own efforts unless these contribute to bottom-line financial performance. Recruitment also reflects a firm's overall human resource strategy. The more popular indices for evaluating the effectiveness of a firm's recruiting strategies are discussed below.

Cost per Hire

The dollar cost per person recruited is one possible measure of the effectiveness of the recruiting function. The costs should include not only the direct costs (e.g., recruiters' salaries, costs of advertisement, consultants' fees, and so on), but also apportioned costs and overheads (e.g., time of operating personnel, stationery, rent). However, often cost data are either not collected at all or are not interpreted so as to facilitate the evaluation of recruiting. Cost data collected from previous recruiting activities could serve as useful benchmarks for comparison.

Quality of Hires and Cost

A major criticism of using a simple dollar cost per hire as a measure of effectiveness is that it ignores the quality of the people hired. The performance, absenteeism, and motivation levels of employees recruited from one source (or using one media) may differ from those of other sources.

> Recruits selected through advertisements in professional journals and professional conventions may have qualitatively superior performance compared to those who were selected through campus recruitment efforts.

The number and quality of résumés and job applications received gives an indication of the overall effectiveness of a recruitment method or source.

Offers–Applicants Ratio

A somewhat better index is the ratio between the number of job offers extended and the total number of applicants calculated for each recruitment method or media. Even if a recruiting source brings in better-quality résumés, this may not be translated finally to job offers; an offers–applicants ratio gives a better picture of the overall quality of the applicant pool. The ratio of number of offers accepted to total number of job offers extended to applicants gives an indication of the overall effectiveness of the recruiting. However, caution is in order. The acceptance of a job offer is dependent on a number of extraneous variables, including the labour market situation, the compensation package offered by the organization and its competitors, and the firm's location. However, when used judiciously, this measure can point out weaknesses such as lack of professionalism and long delays in the recruiting process that could encourage a prospective employee to go elsewhere. This is particularly true for good candidates, who may receive multiple job offers from employers.

Time Lapsed per Hire

The number of days, weeks, or months taken to fill a position provides yet another measure of the effectiveness of the recruitment system. Clearly, a firm that takes a week to fill a position when the industry average is 10 days or two weeks is, in comparison, more efficient. Once again, several external and uncontrollable factors (including the nature of the job, labour market conditions, and location) affect the time for recruiting; consequently, this index should be used in conjunction with other information.

Figure 5-9 shows some of the more popular measures used to evaluate the recruiting function. Naturally, many of these measures are influenced by a firm's selection, training, and compensation systems. Indeed, an evaluation system that explicitly considers various factors related to the selection process and that contains job performance information (including tenure and value of job to the organization) may be very useful in several organizational settings. The next chapter will look at the various steps involved in the selection of personnel from the pool of applicants identified during recruiting.

FIGURE 5-9

Popular Measures Used for Evaluating Effectiveness of Recruitment Function

1. Total number of applications received
2. Time required to get applications
3. Time elapsed before filling positions
4. Costs per hire
5. Ratio of offers extended to number of applicants
6. Ratio of offers accepted to number of offers extended
7. Ratio of number of qualified applicants to total number of applicants
8. Performance rating of hires
9. Turnover of hires

SUMMARY

Recruitment is the process of finding and attracting capable applicants for employment, and then once the top candidates have been selected, recruiters seek to convince applicants to say "yes" to the job. Before recruiters can solicit applicants, they should be aware of organizational policies, human resource plans, employment equity plans, recruiter habits, environmental conditions, and the requirements of the job.

At the recruiter's disposal are a variety of methods to find and attract job seekers. Employer sources include walk-ins, write-ins, employee referrals, the Internet, and direct solicitations through ads and other forms of advertisement. Applicants can be found through referrals from Employment and Social Development Canada offices, private placement agencies, or search firms. Of course, recruits can be found through a variety of institutions, such as educational, professional, and labour organizations; the military; and government training programs. Some firms have reported success in converting temporary employees into permanent ones, on a full- or part-time basis, and in inducing departing employees to remain. Job fairs may inform prospective applicants about multiple companies and available positions and prompt them to submit applications.

The choice of sources used will depend on the quality and quantity of recruits needed, available sources, past successes with the source, the recruiting budget, and labour agreements. Over time, recruiters can track the success of each of their recruitment sources to guide them in future recruitment processes.

Applicants formally apply to organizations by submitting completed application forms or résumés. Application forms seek a variety of answers from recruits, including personal, employment, educational, and work history information. Questions may be asked about memberships, awards, and personal interests. References are usually solicited on the application form as well.

Like all other human resource functions, the recruitment activity also needs to be evaluated for its degree of effectiveness and efficiency. This is to ensure that the recruitment function achieves both organizational and individual objectives. A number of indices for evaluating the recruitment activity were suggested in this chapter. Bear in mind that all of these indices are affected by a firm's selection, training, compensation, and general human resource–related policies. With a pool of recruits and the information contained in completed application forms, the human resource department is now ready to assist line managers in the process of selecting new employees.

TERMS FOR REVIEW

ads
alumni associations
applicant tracking systems (ATS)
blind ads
buy-back
competitive advantage
costs
diversity management
educational institutions
employee referrals
Employment and Social Development Canada (ESDC)
human resource plan
inducements
job application form
job fairs
organizational policies
professional search firms
recruiter habits
recruitment
résumé
selection
temporary-help agencies
walk-ins/write-ins

SELF-ASSESSMENT EXERCISE

How Do You Recruit Employers?

Just as organizations have to recruit potential employees, most individuals also need to scan their environments for potential employers. Take this simple self-test to see how you go about collecting information about your future employers. Answer all questions on a five-point scale of strongly agree (SA), agree (A), undecided (U), disagree (D) and strongly disagree (SD).

Statement	Strongly Agree	Agree	Undecided	Disagree	Strongly Disagree
1. I have a clear idea of the type of job I want and the general competencies it requires.					
2. Looking at online job ads is a waste of time; most jobs are filled even before they are advertised anyway.					
3. I frequently look at job ads in newspapers circulating in the region I am interested in.					
4. I rarely (if ever) look at the annual reports of the firms where I would like to work in the future.					
5. I use social media to tell all my friends and acquaintances who work in the industry or profession that I am looking for a job in that field.					
6. I do not have a clear idea of the region or the industry where I want to work.					
7. I regularly look online to find out more about possible job openings in the industry or occupation I am interested in.					
8. I don't watch TV news or read newspapers.					

(Continued)

9. I keep in touch with my school and college friends, and network with them at social or professional events.					
10. In general, I never talk to others about their experiences in job hunting.					

SCORING

For the odd-numbered statements, give yourself a score of 5, 4, 3, 2, and 1 for SA, A, U, D, and SD, respectively. For the even-numbered statements, give a score of 1, 2, 3, 4, and 5 for SA, A, U, D, and SD, respectively. Add up all scores.

Your total score can lie anywhere from 10 to 50 in this exercise. If your score is 40 or above, you are doing a good job of keeping yourself abreast of the events in the job market. If you got a lower score, you may want to do some of the things indicated above. Getting the right job takes a lot of effort and time, and you have to begin efforts in that direction today!

REVIEW AND DISCUSSION QUESTIONS

1. What background information should a recruiter have before beginning to recruit job seekers?

2. Give three examples of how organizational policies affect the recruitment process. Explain how these influence a recruiter's actions.

3. Under what circumstances would a blind ad be a useful recruiting technique?

4. "If a job application form omits important questions, needed information about recruits will not be available. But if a needless question is asked, the information can be ignored by the recruiter without any other complications." Do you agree or disagree with this statement? Why?

5. Suppose your employer asks you, the human resource manager, to justify the relatively large recruiting budget that you have been historically assigned. What arguments would you provide? What indices or measures will you provide to show that your recruitment is cost effective?

CRITICAL THINKING QUESTIONS

1. After months of insufficient recognition (and two years without a raise), you accept an offer from another firm that involves a $2,000-a-year raise. When you tell your boss that you are resigning, you are told how crucial you are to the business and are offered a raise of $2,500 per year. What do you do? Why? What problems might exist if you accept the buy-back?

2. Suppose you are a manager who has just accepted the resignation of a crucial employee. After you send your request for a replacement to the human resource department, how could you help the recruiter do a more effective job?

3. If at your company the regular university recruiter became ill and you were assigned to recruit at six universities in two weeks, what information would you need before leaving on the trip?

4. In small businesses, managers usually handle their own recruiting. What methods would you use in the following situations? Why?

   (a) The regular janitor is going on vacation for three weeks.

   (b) Your office assistant who manages all appointments and handles all filing in your office has the flu and won't be in the office for two days.

   (c) Two more salespeople are needed: one for local customers and one to open a sales office in Victoria, British Columbia.

   (d) Your only chemist is retiring and must be replaced with a highly skilled person.

   (e) Your only computer programmer/analyst plans to go on a three-week leave to India to visit his sick mother next week. If his mother's health turns for the worse, he may be delayed by another week or two.

5. You are the human resource manager in a large auto-assembly unit employing 2,000 semiskilled and skilled employees. Each year, you recruit dozens of full-time and part-time workers. Recently, the vice-president (Finance) pointed out that recruitment costs in your firm are increasing steadily. She has proposed a freeze in the recruitment budget. What kind of information will you provide in an effort to change her mind on the matter?

ETHICS QUESTION

Darrow Thomas worked as a professional placement specialist for L.A. and D. Inc., an executive search firm. For the last three months, Darrow had not been very successful in finding high-level executives to fill the openings of L.A. and D.'s clients. Not only did his poor record affect his commissions, but the office manager at L.A. and D. was not very pleased with Darrow's performance. Since Darrow desperately needed to make a placement, he resolved that he would do everything he could to fill the new opening he had received that morning.

The opening was for a director of research and development at a major food processor. Darrow began by unsuccessfully reviewing the in-house directories of most of the large companies in this industry. Finally, he stumbled across the directory of a small food processor in the west. In the directory he found a listing for Suzanne Derby, assistant director of product development. He called her, and the following conversation took place:

Suzanne: Hello. P.D. Department, Suzanne Derby speaking.

Darrow: Hello. My name is Darrow Thomas, and I am with L.A. and D. One of my clients has an opening for a director of research and development at a well-known food processor. In discussions with people in the industry, your name was recommended as a likely candidate. I was…

Suzanne: Who recommended that you call me?

Darrow: I'm awfully sorry, but we treat references and candidates with the utmost confidentiality. I cannot reveal that name. But rest assured, he thought you were ready for a more challenging job.

Suzanne: What company is it? What does the job involve?

Darrow: Again, confidentiality requires that the company name go unmentioned for now. Before we go any further, would you mind answering a few questions? Once I feel confident you are the right candidate, I can reveal my client.

Suzanne: Well, okay.

Darrow: Good. How many people do you supervise?

Suzanne: Three professionals, seven technicians, and two clerks.

Darrow: Approximately how large a budget are you responsible for?

Suzanne: Oh, it's about two million dollars a year.

Darrow: What degree do you hold, and how many years have you been assistant director?

Suzanne: My undergraduate degree and Master's are in nutrition science. After I graduated in 2007, I came to work here as an applications researcher. In 2010, I was promoted to chief applications researcher. In 2013, I was appointed assistant director of product development.

Darrow: Good career progress, two degrees, and managerial experience. Your background sounds great! This is a little personal, but would you tell me your salary?

Suzanne: I make $79,500 a year.

Darrow: Oh, that is disappointing. The opening I have to fill is for $96,000. That would be such a substantial jump that my client would probably assume your past experience and responsibility are too limited to be considered.

Suzanne: What do you mean?

Darrow: Well, the ideal candidate would be making about $90,000 a year. That figure would indicate a higher level of responsibility than your lower salary. We could get around that problem.

Suzanne: How?

Darrow: On the data sheet I have filled out I could put down that you are making, oh, say $88,000. That sure would increase my client's interest. Besides, then they would know a salary of $96,000 was needed to attract you.

Suzanne: Wow! But when they checked on my salary history, they'd know that $88,000 was an inflated figure.

Darrow: No, they wouldn't. They wouldn't check. And even if they did, companies never reveal the salary information of past employees. Besides, my client is anxious to fill the job. I'll tell you what, let me send them the data sheet; I'm sure they'll be interested. Then we can talk about more of this. Okay?

Suzanne: Well, if you think it would mean a raise to $96,000, and they really need someone with my background, I guess I'd be interested.

1. Although "headhunters" do not necessarily engage in the practice of "inflating" an applicant's wage, it does happen occasionally. What would you do in Suzanne's place? Would you allow your name to be used?

2. Since most "headhunters" receive a commission that is a percentage of the successful applicant's starting salary, what safeguards would you suggest to prevent "headhunters" from inflating salaries?

3. If Suzanne goes along with Darrow's inflated salary figure and she is hired, what problems may she face?

WEB RESEARCH EXERCISE

Choose any two Internet recruiting sites. Select advertisements for two different job positions in each site (i.e., four in all). Compare their features and strengths. Do you expect different types of recruits to respond to these advertisements and sites? Why? Which of the four advertisements that you chose is the best? Which is the worst? Why? What suggestions do you have to enhance the effectiveness of poor ads? Report your findings to the class.

INCIDENT 5-1

Ontario Electronics Expansion

Ontario Electronics developed a revolutionary method of storing data electronically. The head of research and development, Guy Swensen, estimated that Ontario Electronics could become a supplier to every computer manufacturer in the world. The future success of the company seemed to hang on securing the broadest possible patents to cover the still-secret process.

The human resource director, Carol Kane, recommended that Swensen become a project leader in charge of developing and filing the necessary patent information. Swensen and Kane developed a list of specialists who would be needed to rush the patent applications through the final stages of development and the patent application process. Most of the needed skills were found among Ontario Electronics' present employees. However, after a preliminary review of skills inventories and staffing levels, a list of priority recruits was developed. It required the following:

- An experienced patent lawyer with a strong background in electronics technology.
- A patent lawyer who was familiar with the ins and outs of the patent process and the patent office in Hull, Quebec.
- Twelve engineers. Three had to be senior engineers with experience in the latest computer technology and design. Four had to be senior engineers with experience in photographic etching reduction. Five junior engineers were also requested in the belief that they could handle the routine computations for the senior engineers.
- An office manager, ten keyboard operators, and four secretaries to transcribe the engineering notebooks and prepare the patent applications.

Swensen wanted these 29 people recruited as promptly as possible.

DISCUSSION QUESTIONS

1. Assuming you are given the responsibility of recruiting these needed employees, what channels would you use to find and attract each type of recruit sought?

2. What other actions should the human resource department take now that there is the possibility of very rapid expansion?

CASE STUDY

Maple Leaf Shoes Ltd.

*A Case Study in Recruitment**

Robert Clark was a worried man.

He looked at the letter from Sam Polanyi, president of the Leather Workers' Union's local unit in Maple Leaf Shoes again. Polanyi had warned him of "dire consequences" if the firm did not proceed slowly on automation in its local plant. The union had urged its members to adopt a "work slow" tactic beginning next month. Worried by the decline and demise of giant organizations such as General Motors, Chrysler, and Nortel, Maple Leaf's workforce was strongly against any impending automation that could further reduce the workforce number at a time when the unemployment rates in various parts of Canada were at historical highs. In three months' time, the contract negotiations with the same union had to be concluded. Automation and the newly proposed workweek would surely be important bargaining items.

But what option did the firm have now? The competition from China, Korea, Indonesia, and Malaysia was devastating. Just in the last six months, the firm had lost two major retail suppliers in the United States, which had pointed out that Maple Leaf's shoes were too high-priced for its customers. Meanwhile, there were industry rumours that a major Indian footwear firm is planning to enter the North American market. When that materializes, Maple Leaf Shoes will likely face even greater competition at home. India has had a long history of producing quality footwear and can also take advantage of its cheap labour and emerging high-tech industries in producing high fashion, cheap dress shoes, and high-endurance "cross-trainer" footwear.

The recent warning from the local Human Rights Commission (HRC) did not help matters either. Apparently two female employees, who were denied promotion in the past, had complained to the Commission. They had argued that the promotion criteria employed by the firm for supervisory positions worked against women. When the HRC looked at the complaint, it did not consider their cases to be strong enough to proceed further. However, it had warned the company about the concentration of women in low-paid jobs and lack of clear job specifications for supervisory positions. The Commission had urged immediate remedial actions, including an in-depth look at supervisory competencies and job specifications. The firm was expected to come out with a remedial plan in the next 12 months.

To top it all, neither Pat Lim nor Jane Reynolds was there in Wilmington to help him. John McAllister, the firm's previous human resource manager, had resigned to take up a similar position in Western Canada. Maple Leaf Shoes had not hired a new manager in his place. Until now, Pat Lim, General Manager (Marketing) was overall in charge of the human resource function, although most of the routine decisions were made by Jane Reynolds, who in the past had served as special assistant to John McAllister. But recently Reynolds had been admitted to a local hospital for a surgical procedure. Clark has now been informed that Reynolds will not be returning for some time.

Given all the pressures, Clark decided to immediately fill the human resource manager's position. Clark retrieved the job ad the company had used when hiring John McAllister. He made some minor changes to it and decided to place it in local newspapers as soon as possible. A copy of the final advertisement that Clark prepared is shown in Exhibit 1.

It was after making arrangements for the newspaper ad that Clark remembered his childhood friend, Joy Flemming, who ran a temporary-help agency in Toronto. Clark and Flemming were schoolmates and had kept in touch with each other over the years. Flemming had built up a successful agency that supplied clerical and office staff on a temporary basis. While Clark knew that Flemming's agency primarily supplied clerical workers (and some technical/supervisory personnel), he was convinced that Flemming's years of experience in the local industry would have exposed her to successful human resource professionals elsewhere. He decided to hire Joy to also conduct a search.

Joy was certain to ask him what kind of a person he was looking for. In Clark's mind, he needed a tough individual—someone like John McAllister who could stand up to the unions and take charge. Clark personally disliked handling employee-related matters; he would like to hire someone who would consult him on major issues but who was capable of making decisions on his or her own. There was no formal job description for the HR manager's position in Maple Leaf Shoes, although a consultant was currently working on writing a detailed job description. However, Clark did not value such a document. He was a great believer that these documents meant little except adding to the paperwork. A good person was what he needed now—a well-rounded, tough, experienced person like John who would run a tight ship.

Oh, how much he missed John, Clark reflected sadly.

EXHIBIT 1

Maple Leaf Shoes Limited
REQUIRES
A HUMAN RESOURCE MANAGER

Maple Leaf Shoes Limited, the maker of Fluffy Puppy, Cariboo, Madonna, and other brands of high-quality footwear, which currently employs over 650 persons, requires a Human Resource Manager for its head office in Wilmington, Ontario. We are a fast-growing company with plans to expand operations to several provinces and countries in the near future. Currently, we export to the United States and a number of European countries.

As the Human Resource Manager, you will be responsible for overseeing all human resource functions for this large, expanding organization. You will be directly reporting to the President and be part of the top management team.

We are looking for an aggressive, results-oriented individual who can meet the organization's challenges and facilitate our growth plans in the 21st century. This is a senior position and the typical recruit for this position will have at least 15 years' experience in a senior management capacity. The salary and benefits will be commensurate with qualifications and experience.

We are an Equal Employment Opportunity Employer and welcome applications from qualified women and minority candidates.

Apply in confidence to:

Office of the President

Maple Leaf Shoes Limited

(Continued)

1, Crown Royal Lane, Maple Leaf Town

Wilmington, Ontario.

We help you put your best foot forward!

DISCUSSION QUESTIONS

1. What is your evaluation of the recruitment strategy used by Maple Leaf Shoes?
2. Evaluate the recruitment advertisement.
3. Design a new recruitment advertisement for the position of the human resource manager.
4. Design an application form to be used for hiring a human resource manager in the firm.

CASE STUDY

Canadian Pacific and International Bank

Evaluating Recruitment Function*

Canadian Pacific and International Bank (CPIB) had achieved significant expansion in its operations in the recent past and is currently a major global financial institution (see end of Chapter 1 for more details on the bank). One key component of its growth strategy was the acquisition of other financial institutions. While in most instances CPIB has been able to achieve a seamless merger of operations, there were times when the systems and culture of the newly acquired organization were at variance with CPIB's. This had necessitated routine internal audits of all major systems in newly acquired institutions.

Mary Keddy, vice-president of human resources, is currently looking through the results of an audit of the recruitment function in Ontario Financial Planners (OFP), an investment firm CPIB had acquired in the past. Table 1 shows a summary of relevant data for the last two years for two major groups of employees: investment managers and analysts, and sales staff. The other categories of staff (such as administrative and clerical) remained more or less stable across time. Several other activities in the firm were also contracted out to agencies or carried out by part-time employees. Other details of the workforce are given below.

OFP, which was begun by two brothers as a family business unit, had over time grown rapidly because of its professional approach to conducting business and friendly client relations. To ensure maximum predictability in employee behaviours, historically the firm had focused on employing family members, friends, and others referred by them. Over a period, however, this practice was replaced by several other recruiting methods. The firm also attempted to have representation from minority groups and women in all its job categories, although this has not always been successful. The financial planning industry has, by and large, always been a white-male-dominated profession— over 75 percent of the investment and financial planners in the industry were white males. The senior and middle-level managers were also mostly white males, Asian Canadians being one of the more

*Case prepared by Professor Hari Das of Saint Mary's University, Halifax. All rights retained by the author. Das © 2003. Revised 2009.

successful minorities to reach the position of portfolio or fund managers. The only exception to this general trend was commission-based sales jobs where women were making fast inroads, often reaching nearly one-half of total workforce in that category.

Getting well-qualified and competent financial planners was a challenging task since demand for proven analysts and managers was great until the stock market crash of 2008. During the global financial crash, banks were particularly affected. While CPIB had relatively minor investments in the risky portfolios that fatally affected several American and European banks, even CPIB's mutual funds division faced a significant and adverse decline in demand, necessitating reconfiguration of its workforce. This meant that the attrition of qualified persons was high, often reaching upwards of 20 percent for many firms. Hiring qualified analysts and investment managers was also fraught with considerable difficulties since the wrong hire could cause considerable damage to the company's reputation and customers' trust at a time when investment confidence was already at a low.

The average age of investment analysts and managers in OFP was in the low- to mid-forties. Hardly anyone had retired in that job category in the past year. In the sales category, the average age was slightly higher. One person had retired in the last year.

The figures in Table 1 reflect historical costs. The following recruitment methods are found to be more expensive currently, requiring upward adjustment.

Campus recruiting: increase by 15%

Advertisements: increase by 10%

Internet recruiting: increase by 5%

While common selection criteria were employed in hiring employees irrespective of the recruitment methods they came through, OFP's experience was that recruits from different sources required different levels of on-the-job training before they could be placed into job positions. The average cost of a day's training was approximately $700, which accounted for all costs including time lost. The firm's records show the following training statistics for various recruits:

Unsolicited applicants: 3 days

Recruits from ESDC, Internet, advertisements: 2 days

Campus recruits, applicants referred by current employees: 1 day

DISCUSSION QUESTIONS

1. Make your recommendation on the best recruitment method(s) for each type of workforce.

2. What other conclusions can you arrive at when looking at the figures provided in the case?

TABLE 1

Recruiting Method Used during the Past Year

	Investment Managers and Analyst	Sales Staff
Gender:		
Males	85%	60%
Females	15%	40%
Age:		
Less than 30 years	60%	30%
30–45 years	20%	45%
46–65 years	20%	25%
Education:		
High school or less	10%	60%
University degree or higher	90%	40%

Recruiting Method Used during the Past Two Years

	Unsolicited Applications	ESDC	Campus Recruitment	Advertisements	Internet Recruitment	Referrals from Employees
Total Number of Applications						
Investment managers	50	70	60	200	250	30
Sales staff	40	60	40	300	100	10
Number of Candidates Who Were Offered Jobs						
Investment managers	1	7	9	12	13	9
Sales staff	2	3	2	30	10	2
Number of Candidates Who Accepted Job Offers						
Investment managers	1	3	6	6	10	6
Sales staff	1	2	2	21	4	1

(Continued)

Cost per Recruit in Dollars (includes all overheads)						
Investment managers	45	36	66	60	16	26
Sales staff	42	30	63	48	17	23
Number of New Hires Who Left the Firm Within Two Years						
Investment managers	0	1	1	3	6	1
Sales staff	1	1	0	2	1	1

CHAPTER 6

Selection

The notion of trying to find "good employees" is not very helpful—organizations need to be as specific as possible about the precise attributes they are seeking ... the skills and abilities hired need to be carefully considered and consistent with particular job requirements and the organization's approach to its market. Simply hiring the "best and the brightest" may not make sense in all circumstances.

JEFFREY PFEFFER[1]

LEARNING OBJECTIVES

After studying this chapter, you should be able to:

LO1 Explain the strategic significance of the selection function.

LO2 Describe the various steps in the selection process.

LO3 Discuss the types and usefulness of applicant screening tools in selecting employees.

LO4 Explain the role of employment tests in the selection process.

LO5 Discuss the major approaches to test validation.

LO6 Outline the various steps in conducting an employment interview.

Once a pool of suitable applicants is created through recruiting, the process of selecting applicants begins. Consider the hiring process at Merrill Lynch:

Reliability
validity

Merrill Lynch <http://www.ml.com>, a global investment company owned by Bank of America with over 59 million customers in over 150 countries, pays considerable attention to the selection function. Applicants for the position of financial consultant in the past had to complete an application, take a written test, and go through an interview. In addition to this, the firm's financial consultant simulation exercise tested how applicants perform under stressful conditions similar to those that a real stockbroker faces. The test begins by giving each applicant a client book describing the accounts of a series of fictitious clients. In addition, the applicants are given a variety of unanswered emails and phone messages that they must sort through and decide how to treat. In the background, recorded sounds of a brokerage office are played to add an air of confusing noises, shouts, telephone rings, and other unexpected distractions. During the three hours, fictitious clients call and other messages and reports are dropped on the applicant's "desk."[2]

The simulation exercise is only one part of Merrill Lynch's selection process. Other steps precede and follow it. In the past, all aspiring recruits were encouraged to take a self-test available at the Merrill Lynch website. Only those who could truthfully answer "yes" to at least 15 of the 17 questions in the quiz were considered to "have what it takes to become a Merrill Lynch Financial Consultant" and encouraged to proceed. On its website, Merrill Lynch also provides very specific job information to different categories of applicants— undergraduate and graduate students, full-time positions, and summer internship assignees.[3]

Although many employers do not use such elaborate screening devices, all but the smallest employers put applicants through a variety of steps called the **selection process**. The selection process is a series of specific steps used to decide which recruits should be hired. The process begins when recruits apply for employment and ends with the hiring decision. And recall from Chapter 5 that the recruitment process continues during the selection process as recruiters try to maintain applicant interest in the organization while selection is occurring, and then convince chosen applicants to accept a job offer if one is presented to them. The steps in between match the employment needs of the applicant and the organization.

---

selection process

A series of specific steps used by an employer to decide which recruits should be hired.

LO1

Strategic Significance of the Selection Function

In many human resource departments, recruiting and selection are combined and called the *employment function*, or simply *recruiting*. In very small firms, the owner-manager typically does the hiring.[4] In larger departments, human resource managers or employment managers handle these duties. Whatever the title, in most firms, employment is associated closely with the human resource department.

A proper selection process is integral to the strategic success of firms. Below, we discuss the more critical dimensions of an organization's strategy that are affected by this function.

Successful Execution of an Organization's Strategy Depends on the Calibre of Its Employees

An organization's overall effectiveness and success depends on the quality and calibre of the employees it hires. Poor selection practices also result in the HR department not meeting the objectives specified in Chapter 1. In turn, an organization's mission and overall strategy affect the selection process and place major constraints on the human resource manager when selecting employees. This is because the skills and qualifications of the new hires need to closely match the organization's culture and strategic requirements, as the following example illustrates:

> A study of 243 small businesses found that firms have 7.5 percent higher revenue growth, 6.1 percent higher profit growth, and 17.1 percent lower turnover when they focus on attracting, finding, and selecting employees who fit the culture and values of the organization. When person–organization fit is integrated with a self-management strategy—as opposed to a controlling management strategy—within a family-like work atmosphere, retail firms had 74.7 percent lower turnover, low-skilled services had 57.9 percent lower turnover, and manufacturing firms watched 19.4 percent fewer employees walk out the door.[5]

An Organization's Selection Decisions Must Reflect Job Requirements

As we saw in Chapter 2, the results of job analysis help an organization to identify job duties, specifications, and performance standards. A mismatch between these and the selection criteria will not only result in poor hires but will also expose the organization to possible lawsuits from job applicants who believe that they have been discriminated against.

> Gian Singha, an immigrant from India who was fluent in four languages including English, held postgraduate degrees including a Ph.D. from Germany in environmental science, and was a co-author of two books and numerous research papers, applied for a mid-level position as a regulatory officer with the Land and Water Boards of the Mackenzie Valley <http://mvlwb.com>. He scored among the highest of the 12 applicants the Board chose to interview. Yet, to his shock a few days later, he was told that his application had been rejected because he was overqualified. The Board felt that he would become bored with the job's routine nature and quit prematurely. Mr. Singha complained to the Canadian Human Rights Tribunal, and in a groundbreaking decision, the Tribunal ruled that the Board's action discriminated against Mr. Singha and visible minority immigrants in general. Mr. Singha was awarded damages and, more significantly, it ordered the Board to cease using any hiring policies that would automatically disqualify visible minority immigrants on the grounds that they are overqualified.[6]

Today, the employer is required to show that the tools used for selecting employees are reliable and valid. "Feelings" or myths as in the above case where the Board members used unsupported assumptions to reject a qualified applicant are not valid arguments. This means that performance-based job descriptions[7] and valid selection tools are necessary in the context of selection. Figure 6-1 lists some of the popular myths in the context of hiring.

Selection Strategy Must Be Well Integrated with Organizational Priorities

As seen in Chapter 1, organizations differ in their strategic posture. Organizational characteristics—including such factors as product lines, market share, and culture—vary widely and are dynamic in nature. As a firm grows, different priorities start to emerge:

> A startup business typically has a few product lines and places heavy emphasis on entrepreneurship. In contrast, a multinational organization with operations in several different countries and cultures worries about achieving control over operations while providing adequate autonomy to local operations. An aging or declining organization needs to emphasize renewal if it is to survive. The type of employees sought are also somewhat different in each instance. An infant organization may attempt to hire entrepreneurial managers, while a mature organization needs managers who can continually search for economies of scale and implement efficient systems. In contrast, a declining organization may seek managers who can cut costs, generate revenues, rebuild the organization, and turn it around.

The specific needs of an organization are determined by a variety of factors (and not merely by its stage in the life cycle); however, an organization's stage in the life cycle provides a starting point in linking an organization's overall needs and its selection strategy.

FIGURE 6-1

Sample Myths in the Context of Hiring

Myth	Reality Emerging from Research Findings
Conscientiousness is a better predictor of employee performance than intelligence.	Several research studies indicate that intelligence, or general mental ability, is as or more important than conscientiousness.
Integrity tests don't work.	Although it is true that many people attempt to make themselves appear more ethical than they really are, a well-developed and validated integrity test can be a good predictor of a person's likely future job performance and counterproductive work behaviours such as absenteeism and lateness.
Integrity tests have adverse effects on racial minorities.	Racial and ethnic differences on integrity test scores are, typically, non significant. Well-developed and scientifically administered tests normally do not result in discrimination against specific racial groups.

SOURCE: Abridged, adapted and summarized from Sara L. Rynes, Kenneth G. Brown, and Amy E. Colbert, "Seven Common Misconceptions about Human Resource Practices: Research Findings versus Practitioner Beliefs," *Academy of Management Executive*, Vol. 16, No. 3, 2002.

Selection Strategy Must Recognize Organizational Constraints

All organizations have finite resources. This means that the systems employed for the selection of human resources should be cost-effective. The selection process is not an end; it is a means through which the organization achieves its objectives. Most organizations impose some limits, such as budgets and policies, which may hinder the selection process. Without budget limitations, selection procedures could be refined. But without limits, employment expenses could be so high that organizational effectiveness would suffer.

The firm's policies may expand existing challenges or simply add more constraints. Policies against discrimination reinforce external prohibitions, for example. Internal decrees may exceed legal demands from outside. For example, policies to hire ex-convicts further societal objectives (discussed in Chapter 1), but are not legally required. Such internal policies add still another challenge for employment specialists.

Selection Strategy Must Adapt to Labour Market Realities

It is important to have a large, qualified pool of recruits from which to select applicants. But some jobs are so hard to fill that there are few applicants per opening.

For example, notwithstanding current low oil prices, Fort McMurray in Alberta has experienced shortages in many jobs related to the oil and gas sector including drilling coordinators/production managers, land agents/purchasing agents, geologists and geophysicists, mining engineers, industrial electricians, and heavy-duty equipment mechanics. Thus, companies looking for these types of workers will face an unfavourable selection ratio. Shortages in one area of the country impact other areas in Canada as well, as favourable incentives may prompt workers from other areas to move for employment.[8]

A **selection ratio** is the relationship between the number of applicants hired and the total number of applicants available. A selection ratio such as 1:25 (compared to a selection ratio of 1:2) means there is a large number of applicants from which to select. In many instances a selection ratio such as 1:3 or 1:5 also means a low quality of recruits. The ratio is computed as follows:

$$\frac{\text{Number of applicants hired}}{\text{Total number of applicants}} = \text{Selection ratio}$$

selection ratio

The ratio of the number of applicants hired to the total number of applicants

Wes Klugh, an employment manager for a chain of motels, faced an adverse selection ratio for the third-shift desk clerk's job. Although it paid two dollars an hour more than the day or evening clerk jobs, few people applied for it. Wes decided to redesign the job by enriching it. The job was expanded to include responsibility for completing the daily financial report and other bookkeeping tasks. The additional duties justified the substantial raise and new title—night auditor. The result was more applicants.

The number of applicants for a position is also partially dependent on a firm's salary and benefit package compared to others in the industry. Industry information can be secured from Statistics Canada, Employment and Social Development Canada, or other associations.

Spotlight *on* ETHICS

Selection Practices Must Be Ethical

An organization's selection strategy should be ethical. Because employment specialists strongly influence the hiring decision, those decisions are shaped by their ethics. Consider the following situations and rate them as ethical or unethical. If unethical, what actions will you take to achieve the goals while at the same time maintaining high ethical standards?

Compare your answers with those of your friends. Do you see any differences? What accounts for the differences?

You are the human resource manager in a medium-sized firm and report to the director of human resources. Your boss gives you a lot of discretion in decision making and, in general, you are very happy with your job. However, more recently, the following three events have caused you some concern:

1. You are told to find "some positions" in the company for some of the executives' children for the coming summer months. You feel that disobeying the order may affect your career. However, you wonder whether hiring some of them would be an admission that you selected people on criteria other than merit.

2. An executive search firm, which your firm had hired in the past year to do a routine job search, has given you an expensive watch as a Christmas gift. Even a casual glance shows you that the watch was worth over $750. You wonder whether accepting it puts you under a moral obligation to the firm and taints your future decisions when hiring search firms. While you had no problems with the service provided by the firm, the firm by no means is the best service provider in the industry or region, nor the cheapest.

3. John McIntosh, your neighbour for 20 years now, indicated to you that his niece has applied for a position in your firm and it will be nice if "you can look into it." John has been a very kind neighbour

(Continued)

and has been of immense help to your family, which had to stay back in Canada while you were away on an international assignment last year. You looked at his niece's background. While she meets the minimum requirements, there are a number of candidates who are far better than her. Furthermore, some of the other candidates are known to a number of employees who will wonder why they were not hired.

Figure 6-2 summarizes the key factors that influence and are affected by a firm's selection strategy. As can be seen, selection affects virtually all major human resource functions within the organization. It should be noted that an organization's policies on other matters (e.g., compensation levels, training) have an impact on selection strategy at least in the long term. This fact is indicated by the dotted arrow in Figure 6-2.

FIGURE 6-2

Relationship between Selection Strategy and Other Organizational Variables

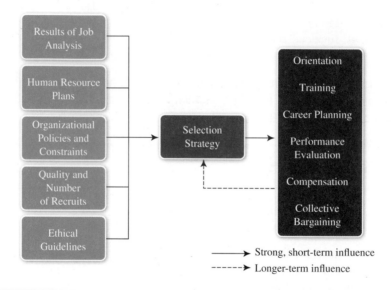

This chapter introduces various tools at the disposal of human resource managers in formulating an effective selection strategy. The next section begins the discussion by outlining major steps in the selection of human resources.

LO2 HRC 4

Steps in the Selection of Human Resources

The selection process is a series of steps through which applicants pass. Sometimes the process can be made simple and effective; however, simplicity should not be achieved at the cost of lower effectiveness. Consider this:

At a large bank, the selection process was simplified and automated in order to match present employees with internal openings. The specific tasks required of various jobs were computer-matched against the specific abilities of employees. Whenever job openings emerged, employees with the highest match for a given opening were then considered for the job.

A major shortcoming of a computerized matching process is the potential for other factors such as attitudes, personality, and the like to be ignored. To ensure that both task and nontask factors are considered, human resource departments commonly use a more involved sequence of steps, as shown in Figure 6-3. Note that these steps reflect considerable variation from one organization to the next. For example, in small organizations the hiring decision is based on a single interview by the owner or manager concerned. Further, depending on the unique constraints facing an organization, some of the stages may be combined or their sequence altered. For internal applicants, there is seldom a need to verify references from outsiders, or do a medical evaluation. As another example, some employers find it useful to introduce a realistic job preview at an earlier stage to save the time and expense of administering tests and interviews for applicants who are unlikely to fit the position. In most organizations, a medical evaluation, if done at all, is carried out only after a hiring decision is made. In such cases, the job offer is conditional on the applicant satisfactorily completing the medical evaluation. Note that an applicant may also be rejected at any step in the process.

FIGURE 6-3

Steps in the Selection Process

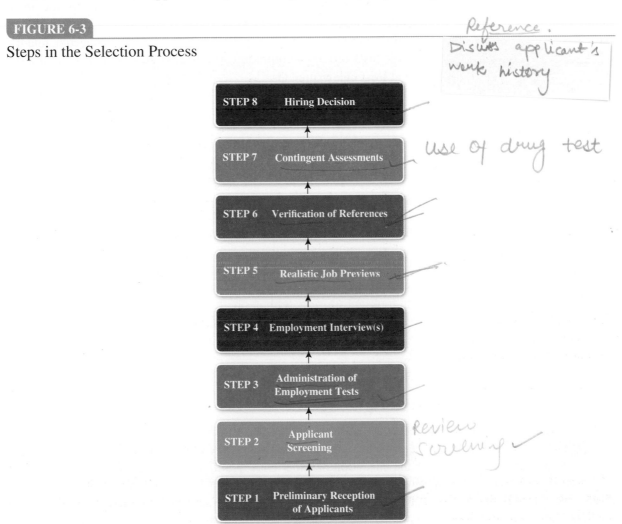

NOTE: The above sequence is likely to show some variation across organizations. Not all firms go through all the above steps or in the above sequence. In general, an applicant who disqualifies on a step does not advance to the next step.

The type of selection procedure used by an organization depends on a variety of factors including the size of the organization, the stage of its growth (e.g., new versus established for some time), and the jobs involved. There are also variations across industries. For example, use of honesty tests and checks for bondability are seen in the Canadian retail industry, but not in the education sector.

It is estimated that employee thefts are responsible for about a third of the $4 billion that Canadian firms lose annually to shrinkage. One study found that over a quarter of Canadian small- and mid-sized firms were victims of at least one instance of workplace fraud the previous year.[9] To overcome the problem, Canadian businesses have been doing more personal reference checks, honesty tests, credit and bondability assessments, and multiple interviews to screen out undesirable employees.

Using data from the Canadian Workplace and Employee Survey (with a sample of 23,639 employees from 1999 to 2005), one study reports that 79 percent of employees were given an interview, 10 percent were given a test of job-related knowledge, and 9 percent were given a personality test.[10] Other past surveys of employers indicate that letters of reference and weighted application blanks are most popular for the selection of white-collar professional workers while biographical information blanks are more frequently used for white-collar nonprofessional jobs. Personality tests are popular for selecting middle-management employees, and aptitude tests are most common for white-collar nonprofessional jobs. Nearly 50 percent of employers use at least one written test.[11]

Step 1: Preliminary Reception of Applicants

Job applicants may make initial contact either in person or in writing. When applicants "walk in," a preliminary interview–typically with a representative of the human resource department or the store manager in the case of a very small firm—is often granted as a courtesy. This "courtesy interview," as it is sometimes called, is unlikely to be as rigorous as otherwise, but it does attempt to screen out obvious "misfits" (e.g., someone who is not willing to travel but is interested in a salesperson's job with the firm requiring considerable travel). Such courtesy interviews are also an important part of good employer branding by the firm, as information conveyed during these meetings and the professionalism displayed by the HR manager during this early encounter may have lasting implications for its future recruitment and marketing success.[12] Candidates applying in writing are often sent a polite letter of acknowledgement. If the applicant looks promising (either on the basis of the initial letter or the courtesy interview), he or she is typically asked to complete a formal application form.

LO3

Step 2: Applicant Screening

At the applicant screening stage, the organization will have received a number of résumés or completed job application forms. The purpose of the screening stage is to remove from further consideration those applicants who do not meet either the education or experience qualifications required for the job. More fine-grained assessments of applicant qualities and their match to job specifications will be made during the later testing stages of the selection process; the goal of screening is merely to whittle the applicant pool down to only those applicants who meet minimum qualifications.

Résumés and job application forms, which were introduced in Chapter 5, can both be useful tools to screen out applicants who do not meet minimum specifications for a job. As discussed in Chapter 5, an application form may have additional utility over résumés when care is taken crafting the form.

One might suspect that some aspects of a person's background (e.g., years of education, previous experience in similar positions) would have a greater relationship to job success than some other factors (e.g., number of part-time jobs held while in school). A **weighted application blank (WAB)** technique provides a means of identifying which of these aspects reliably distinguish groups of satisfactory and unsatisfactory job incumbents.[13] Weights are assigned in accordance with the predictive power of each item so that a total "success score" can be calculated for each job applicant.

---

weighted application blank (WAB)

A job application form in which various items are given differential weights to reflect their relationship to criterion measures.

An office equipment firm in Toronto was seeking to lower its turnover rate. Over time, they observed that salespeople in their firm with university degrees were less likely to turn over than sales staff with post-secondary diplomas, or no post-secondary education. Furthermore, as number of years of sales experience went up, turnover rates decreased. The firm implemented a weighting scale to score the education and experience sections of their job applications. Using a scoring system on the education portion of 4 points for university degrees, 2 points for post-secondary diplomas, and 1 point for high school diplomas, and scores of 8 points for 4 or more years of sales experience, 5 points for 2 or 3 years of sales experience, and 2 points for 1 year or less of sales experience, the firm calculated a total score for each application. The firm identified a success score of 5 for applicants to continue in the selection process.

WABs have been found to be useful to predict a number of different indicators (including job performance, turnover, absenteeism, and accident rates). They are cost-effective, and may be particularly valuable for job positions where a large number of applicants apply for a few positions; however, they do not provide any insight into why relationships exist (for instance, why might higher education be associated with greater absenteeism?).[14]

Spotlight *on* ETHICS

A new policy by the Ontario Human Rights Commission in July 2013 states that requiring a job applicant to have "Canadian experience" is a form of discrimination. Ratna Omidvar, the President of Maytree Foundation <http://maytree.com>, a non-profit, Toronto-based organization aimed toward reducing poverty in Canada and enhancing diversity and leadership development, is encouraging Canadian organizations to consider anonymous job applications as an avenue toward bias-free hiring. By minimizing subjective reactions elicited from sex, name, and immigrant status, anonymous applications may produce a more diverse set of applicants for employment testing. Germany has piloted anonymous applications at freight company DHL <http://international.dhl.ca>, cosmetics company L'Oreal <http://www.lorealparis.ca>, and consumer goods giant Proctor & Gamble Co. Ecommerce retailer mydays <http://www.mydays.com> has continued with anonymous job applications following the pilot. What are the pros and cons of anonymous job applications in Canada?

SOURCE: Based on: Catherine Skrzypinski, "Will anonymous job applications end hiring discrimination in Canada?" Society for Human Resource Management, 2013, www.shrm.org/hrdisciplines/global/articles/pages/anonymous-job-applications-canada.aspx downloaded March 10, 2015.

Another applicant screening tool that is increasingly being used are **biographical information blanks (BIBs)**, also referred to as "biodata." The BIB is a questionnaire that applicants complete relating to their personal history and life experiences, such as their hobbies, family relations, accomplishments, values, reactions to stressful and disappointing experiences, and leisure-time pursuits. The items may range from early childhood to educational experiences to work experiences or current hobbies and relationships. Although primary emphasis is on past behaviours as a predictor of future behaviour, BIBs frequently also look at present behaviours and attitudes. Some sample questions from a BIB are presented in Figure 6-4.

FIGURE 6-4

Sample Biographical Information Blank Items

1. What is the level of supervision that you prefer?
   a. None
   b. Minimal
   c. Moderate
   d. Fairly close
   e. Very close

2. How many of your family members have been/are currently members of law enforcement?
   a. none
   b. one
   c. two
   d. three
   e. four or more

3. How many hours each week do you spend doing each of the following:
   a. _____ Music
   b. _____ Reading books and magazines
   c. _____ Socializing with friends
   d. _____ Watching TV
   e. _____ Home improvement projects
   f. _____ Outdoor activities

4. How many friends did you have in high school compared to other people?
   a. _____ Fewer
   b. _____ More
   c. _____ About the same

5. When faced with disappointment in your life, what is your typical reaction?
   a. Quietly reflect on the situation
   b. Talk to a friend or spouse
   c. Exercise or take a walk
   d. Try to forget about it
   e. Release your anger on something

6. In the last four years, how many employers have you had?
   a. more than 5
   b. 3 to 5
   c. 2
   d. 1
   e. 0

biographical information blank (BIB)

A type of application blank that uses a multiple-choice format to measure a job candidate's education, experiences, opinions, attitudes, and interests.

The items on the BIB are differentially weighted according to how well they separate high from low-performers. For instance, a company might identify that the leaders in their organization were all leaders in various roles in their communities (as sport team captains, or through Girl Guides or Scouts). They might also find that their employees who prefer to spend time with other people are more successful on the job than employees who prefer watching TV or reading books. More points would be granted on the BIB for candidates who have been in leadership positions in their communities and prefer spending time with other people as opposed to independent activities. Cut-off scores are then developed, with only the applications reaching the minimum score proceeding to the next stages of the selection process.

There are several considerations when determining whether or not to use a BIB. First, the items must not adversely affect any protected groups of Canadians (for instance, an item asking about whether someone has been a sport team captain may unintentionally discriminate against people with physical disabilities), and the items must be job-related. Second, BIB questions may be viewed by applicants as invasive and may have the unintended effect of turning off well-qualified applicants. Third, responses to BIB questions are not easily verifiable and thus, they can be faked by applicants. And fourth, typically BIBs will have to be developed for each organization; rarely do commercially available BIBs exist that will suit organizations' specific needs.[15]

Properly developed WABs and BIBs have been found to be useful in several occupations, including life insurance agents, sales clerks, engineers, research scientists, and architects. Reviews of studies that used biographical information as predictors of job success showed that over various occupations, the average validity was about .35.[16] Given this, carefully designed application blanks (especially in WAB and BIB format) seem to hold considerable potential as a selection tool.

Biographical information blanks often contain questions relating to a candidate's early life experiences, e.g., hobbies and interests. How would you feel if asked these types of questions when applying for a job?

John Fedele/Getty Images

Whatever the type of application form used, information given in an application form or résumé may contain elements of embellishment and even outright fabrication. Indeed, in recent years, *résumé fraud* (as it is called) has become a major concern of recruiters.

A newly hired Chief Administrative Officer of the City of Waterloo was fired because he had not disclosed critical information about his problems on the previous job. In a survey of 300 executive recruiters, it was found that "reasons for leaving prior jobs" was the item which was fabricated most, closely followed by "results and accomplishments on past jobs." Past salary, job responsibilities, education, dates of employment, and job titles were other major items where the candidates provided false information.[17]

This means that application forms and résumés have to be carefully analyzed for inconsistencies and checked against information coming from other sources such as references or background checks. In the case of several jobs, key KSAs (knowledge, skills, and abilities) are also assessed through standardized and validated tests. The following section discusses the use of employment tests to assess the key competencies required for a job.

LO4

Step 3: Administration of Employment Tests

Employment tests are useful for obtaining relatively objective information, which can be compared with that pertaining to other applicants and present jobholders. **Employment tests** are devices that assess the match between applicants and job requirements. Some are written tests; others are exercises that simulate work conditions. A math test for a bookkeeper is an example of a written test, and a manual-dexterity test for an assembly worker is an example of a simulation exercise.

employment tests

Devices that assess the probable match between applicants and job requirements.

Ultimately, through selection testing we are trying to identify people who are likely to perform well on the job. There are many options available including purchasing an already established test or making a new test specific for the organization. With all of the options available, how do we choose which test(s) to use? The use of tests should be guided by their reliability and validity. These are discussed in some detail below.

Reliability and Validity of Selection Tests

Testing became popular on a large scale during the First World War, when intelligence tests were given to army recruits. During the following 60 years, tests were developed for a wide range of employment uses, but many of these tests were assumed to be valid without sufficient proof. (For a discussion on testing and assessment, visit the American Psychological Association <http://www.apa.org/science/programs/testing/index.aspx>.)

For a test to be useful, it must meet the twin criteria of reliability and validity.

Reliability

Reliability means that the test yields consistent results.

reliability

A selection device's ability to yield consistent results over repeated measures. Also, internal consistency of a device or measure.

For example, a test of manual dexterity for assembly workers should give a similar score each time the same person takes the test. If the results vary widely with each retest because good scores depend on luck, the test is not reliable.

Reliability of a test may become low for a variety of reasons, including the following:

- The test questions may be hard to understand or ambiguous, thus resulting in different test takers reading different meanings into the same question or sentence. It is also possible that the same person may interpret a question differently on different occasions because of poor test construction.
- The test questions may be so hard or boring that the examinee loses all interest and begins to respond almost randomly or erratically.
- External factors (e.g., noise, smell), events (e.g., war), or personal characteristics (e.g., being ill at the time of test taking) may result in random errors.

Being aware of the above factors help the test maker to avoid them and improve reliability. However, high reliability alone does not ensure that a test is in fact valid or useful.

> If a clock gains exactly 5 minutes each day, the time is predictable; it will be 5 minutes late after the first day, 10 minutes late after the second day, and so on. However, the clock is still not an accurate device. Without knowing the number of days the clock ran uncorrected, we will not be able to predict the correct time.

Validity

Validity asks the question: "Is the test accurately measuring what it is purported to measure?"

---

validity

A key attribute of a selection device that indicates its accuracy and relationship to job-relevant criteria.

In the context of selection tests, validity requires that the test scores significantly relate to job performance or some other relevant criterion. The stronger the relationship between test results and performance, the more effective the test is as a selection tool. When scores and performance are unrelated, the test is invalid and should not be used for selection:

> An Ontario trucking company once gave all its applicants an extensive reading test. However, because the drivers received their instructions orally and were shown on a map where to go, the reading test had no relationship to job performance; it did not distinguish good drivers from bad ones. It only distinguished between those who could read English well and those who could not.

When tests are not reliable, they are also not valid, since they are not measuring the trait or competency with any degree of consistency. But the mere fact that the test is reliable does not ensure validity:

> As in our earlier clock example, the clock is reliable (it gains five minutes each day) but not valid (it does not tell the correct time).

To ensure that its tests are valid, human resource departments should conduct *validation studies*. These studies compare test results with performance of traits needed to perform the job. Figure 6-5 summarizes the most common approaches to validation.

LO5

FIGURE 6-5

An Explanation of Common Approaches to Test Validation

Empirical Approaches

Empirical approaches to test validation attempt to relate test scores with a job-related criterion, usually performance. If the test actually measures a job-related criterion, the test and the criterion exhibit a positive correlation between 0 and 1.0. The higher the correlation, the better the match.

* *Predictive validity* is determined by giving a test to a group of applicants. After these applicants have been hired and have mastered the job reasonably well, their performance is measured. This measurement and the test score are then correlated.

* *Concurrent validity* allows the human resource department to test present employees and correlate these scores with measures of their performance. This approach does not require the delay between hiring and mastery of the job.

Rational Approaches

When the number of subjects is too low to have a reasonable sample of people to test, rational approaches are used. These approaches are considered inferior to empirical techniques, but are acceptable validation strategies when empirical approaches are not feasible.

* *Content validity* is assumed to exist when the test contains an adequate and representative sample of items from the domain of the construct that it is attempting to measure. For example, a vocabulary test should contain a representative sample of words contained in an unabridged dictionary. If all the words in a test contain only words beginning with M or Q, or if they are all four-letter words containing the letter "e," the test is not content-valid.

* *Construct validity* is established by showing that the test measures the construct and only the construct under consideration. For example, an intelligence test should measure intelligence, not simply a person's reading ability or memory. Establishing construct validity is the hardest, since it can be done only over time by comparing the outcomes of the test with the outcomes of other tests and measures. For instance, the construct validity of a test on job stress may be established by comparing the scores on the test with other measures of stress or predicted outcomes of stress. Needless to say, such a relationship is established over time and by using theoretical arguments.

To ensure that selection tests are valid and reliable, over time organizations seek to accumulate evidence from both the empirical and rational approaches. Is it a lot of work to accumulate validity and reliability evidence? Yes! However, when an invalid test rejects people of a particular race, sex, religion, or national origin, it violates the *Canadian Human Rights Act* or related provincial legislation.[18] Evidence is necessary to know the test is not producing **differential validity**. When differential validity exists, a test may be valid for a large group (for instance, white male applicants), but not for subgroups of minorities or women. To know whether a test is generating differential validity, testing experts advise separate validation studies for different subgroups, such as women and minorities. The test should predict job performance (or absenteeism or counterproductive work behaviours) equally as well for multiple subgroups. Yet even when tests have been validated, the type of validation used is still important. Faulty procedures, no matter how well intentioned, cannot be relied on to prove a test's validity. An example of this point follows:

The Albemarle Corporation <http://www.albemarle.com>, a U.S. firm, gave several black applicants a battery of tests and then did not hire low scorers. The low scorers sued Albemarle, so the company then implemented a validation study. But the study had several weaknesses, and the court ruled the tests invalid and discriminatory.

The problems for Albemarle:

- It used the tests that had been validated for advanced jobs, not the entry-level positions to which tests were being applied. Such validation does not prove that tests are valid for entry-level jobs. Tests must be validated on those jobs to which tests are being applied.

- It validated the test on one group (white workers) and then applied the test to another group (black workers). Tests must be validated for all the groups to whom the test applies.[19]

---

differential validity

Test validation process aimed at discovering the validity of a test for various subgroups, e.g., females and members of visible minorities.

To assist in the collection of reliability and validity evidence, employment tests will have a test manual. The manual will contain information on the exact purpose of a test, its design, the directions for its administration, and its applications, and it should be reviewed before a test is used. The manual also reports the test's reliability and the results of validation efforts by the test designer. Today, many tests have been validated on large populations. Organizations may rely on—or generalize—the reliability and validity information contained within the manual to guide their selection test choices for their applicant pool and job.[20] This is called **validity generalization**—applying validity results amassed from many individual validity studies to guide test choices for a current organization and job. But human resource specialists should conduct their own studies (called "local validation studies") to make sure a particular test is valid for its planned use. The HR specialist should be also aware of the confounding effects of situational variables on a job applicant's performance in a specific test.

---

validity generalization

Using validity evidence accumulated for other jobs or applicant populations to guide employment test choices until local validation study results can be acquired.

Types of Tests

There is a wide variety of employment tests. Common categories of employment tests in Canada include: personality, ability, knowledge, performance, and integrity tests. Within each category, there are a number of tests and test publishers. Each type of test has a different purpose. Application forms, WABs, BIBs, and references discussed earlier may also be considered forms of employment tests most commonly used for broad screening of applicants (as opposed to making more fine-grained differentiations as with the tests described below). Figure 6-6 lists examples and a brief explanation of some of the employment-related tests by category along with the approximate frequency of use, cost, reliability, and validity of the testing category.

Personality Tests

Personality tests measure personality or temperament. Personalities are thought to be stable traits for individuals. That is, they do not change depending on the circumstances or context the person happens to be in at a particular moment, but rather they are constant over time. Early personality testing in an employment context used personality inventories that were developed to help diagnose psychological abnormalities. It is little wonder that an inventory such as the Minnesota Multiphasic Personality Inventory, which is designed to diagnose various psychoses (using items such as "I sometimes feel as though my limbs are falling off"), was not well-received in an employment context.

---

personality tests

Questionnaires designed to reveal aspects of an individual's character or temperament.

More recent personality tests have been designed with psychologically normal, working people in mind. Many of these inventories have centred on the "Big 5 Personality Factors," which include conscientiousness, agreeableness, neuroticism/emotional stability, openness to experience, and extraversion. A convenient acronym to help with remembering the Big 5 is CANOE.

> Of the Big 5 Personality Factors, conscientiousness (e.g., achievement-oriented, persistent, and organized) has the highest correlation to job performance ($r = .31$).[21] The personality factors have all been found to predict job performance in some occupations. For instance, extraversion (e.g., to seek and interact easily with others, likeable) predicts performance in occupations involving social interactions, such as sales,[22] and extraversion and openness to experience (e.g., imaginative, intellectually curious) predict training readiness and training success.[23] Although agreeableness (e.g., co-operative, eagerness to help) has shown some promise as a predictor of job performance, one can imagine that having an agreeable bill collector or police officer might not be the best choice! Additional research examining personality[24] as a predictor of job performance in additional occupations is needed, as well as an understanding of personality profiles (i.e., combinations of high and low scores on the personality factors).

Scores on personality tests have been linked to ratings of job performance, training performance, absenteeism, and counterproductive work behaviours. Although personality tests do not have the large differences between racial groups that are found with cognitive ability tests, one concern with personality testing is the potential for applicants to fake their responses. For instance, it is unlikely—even if the trait does not describe them—that candidates will respond with disagreement to the item "*I am a hard worker.*"[25]

Ability Tests

Ability tests aim to predict which job applicants have the skills, knowledge, and ability to do the job. Many different types of tests have been developed to measure specific human abilities and aptitudes, with some of the most common measuring cognitive ability (or intelligence) and specific physical abilities such as finger or manual dexterity and visual skills.

---

ability tests

Tests that assess an applicant's capacity or aptitude to function in a certain way.

FIGURE 6-6

Evaluation and Examples of Employment-Related Tests

Name	Application	Cost	Reliability	Validity
Personality Tests		Low	High	Moderate
NEO-PI-R	Measures the Big 5 Personality Factors in 12–99-year-olds			
HEXACO	Measures six factors of personality including honesty/humility			
16 PF	Measures personality and is used to provide vocational guidance, hiring, and promotion recommendations			
Hogan Personality Inventory	Measures normal personality and is used to predict job performance			
Ability Tests		Low	High	High
Wonderlic Contemporary Cognitive Ability Test	General mental ability; how easily individuals can be trained, how well they can adjust and solve problems on the job, and how well-satisfied they are likely to be with the demands of the job			
General Aptitude Test Battery	Measures nine distinct aptitudes including: general learning ability; verbal aptitude; numerical aptitude; spatial aptitude; form perception; clerical perception; motor coordination; finger dexterity; manual dexterity			
Minnesota Clerical Test	Clerical ability; perceptual speed and accuracy			
MacQuarrie Test for Mechanical Ability	Aptitude for acquiring manipulative skills including space relations, speed of decision and movement, hand–eye coordination, muscular control, and visual acuity			
Knowledge Tests		Moderate	High	High
How to Supervise?	Measures knowledge of supervisory practices			
Leadership Opinion Questionnaire	Measures knowledge of leadership consideration and structure practices			
Performance Tests		High	High	High
Stromberg Dexterity Test	Measures physical coordination			
Revised Minnesota Paper Form Board Test	Measures spatial visualization			
B-PAD	Situational judgment test assessing behavioural responses to video scenarios			
Job Simulation Tests, Assessment Centres	Measures a sample of "on the job" demands			
Integrity Tests		Low	High	Moderate
Stanton Survey	Measures honesty and integrity			
Reid Report	Measures attitudes and behaviours associated with high levels of integrity and responsible work habits			

Source: Created by the authors based on: H. Heneman III, T. Judge, V. Smith, and R. Summers, *Staffing Organizations*, 2nd Can. ed., 2010; J. W. Thacker and R. J. Cattaneo of the Faculty of Business Administration, University of Windsor, 1987; SHRM Research, 2005 Weekly Survey.

Cognitive ability tests were first adopted during World War I; the Army Alpha test was used to match recruits with various abilities to different military positions. For instance, high scorers on the Army Alpha test may have been made airplane pilots, and low scorers became infantry. More recently, paper-and-pencil or computerized versions of general cognitive ability tests are used to assess memory, reasoning, and verbal and mathematical abilities. Cognitive ability tests are one of the strongest predictors of job performance in many occupations (with an average predictive validity of $r = .50$),[26] in particular for highly complex jobs (such as managers and engineers). Below is an example of how a test of cognitive ability quickly and inexpensively helps to select applicants:

> The National Football League (NFL; <http://www.nfl.com>) has used the Wonderlic Contemporary Cognitive Ability Test to test its potential recruits since 1968. Along with tests of their football skill, the NFL administers the 12-minute Wonderlic test, at a cost of about $4 per test, to all prospects. Scores on the Wonderlic are out of 50 with an average score of 21 in the population. The NFL has average scores for each position ranging from 24 for quarterbacks and 26 for offensive tackles to 17 for wide receivers and fullbacks. Lower than average scores for a position may flag the applicant as potentially not able to meet the cognitive demands of the game.[27]

There is one serious potential issue with cognitive ability tests. There are racial differences in scores on cognitive ability tests disadvantaging blacks and Latinos compared to whites.[28] One strategy for selection specialists is to include measures without differential validity along with measures of cognitive ability to allow both good prediction of performance, but minimize racial biases.

Knowledge Tests

Knowledge tests measure a person's information or knowledge about job requirements.

---

knowledge tests

Tests that measure a person's information or knowledge.

> Arithmetic tests for an accountant, knowledge of tax laws for a tax specialist, and a weather test for a pilot are examples of knowledge tests.

Human resource specialists must be able to demonstrate that the knowledge is needed to perform the job. The Ontario trucking company example is a case wherein the tested knowledge (reading at an advanced level) was not needed.

Performance Tests

Performance tests (or work samples) measure the ability of applicants to do some parts of the work for which they are to be hired.

---

performance tests

Tests that measure the ability of job applicants to perform specific components of the job for which they are to be hired.

> A typing test for administrative assistants or a driving test for cab or truck drivers are obvious examples of performance tests.

Validity is often assumed when the test includes a representative sample of the work the applicant is to do when hired. The closer the demands of the test are to the demands of the job, the higher the fidelity of the test, and the better the test will be at predicting performance on the job.

One variation of performance tests is called a **situ** [...] ests, applicants are placed into hypothetical job scenari[...], and asked to select a behavioural response from a[...]. Their responses are then rated on their demonstration o[...] [situ]ational judgment tests have been found to predict job p[...] [the]y are relatively inexpensive compared to other perform[...] items is found in Figure 6-7.

situational judgment test

A test that places an applicant in hypothetical scena[...]d from a list of alternatives.

A second variation of performance tests for identifying managerial potential is an assessment centre (see Chapter 8). As one example, to assess the people skills of applicants to many police and fire departments in Canada and the U.S., many candidates take the Behavioral Personnel Assessment Device (B-PAD). B-PAD presents eight videos depicting scenarios that might be encountered on the job, and the candidate indicates how they would respond in each situation.[30]

Currently, assessment centres are used mostly at larger organizations such as Rio Tinto Alcan <http://www.riotintoalcan.com>, Manitoba Liquor and Lotteries Corporation, and Verizon <http://www.verizonwireless.com>, and are increasing in popularity in several municipal, provincial, and federal government units as well.

FIGURE 6-7

Sample Situational Judgment Test Items

1. You are currently working on several tasks, all of which are pressing. Your supervisor asks you to work on another assignment with an immediate deadline. She asks you to phone companies to obtain financial data. The list of companies is long and not yet complete. You would…

   a. Describe the pressing deadlines in which you are already involved and ask your supervisor to assign the new task to a less busy colleague.
   b. Complete those assignments on which you are already working, then concentrate on phoning the companies.
   c. Work on your other assignments and begin phoning companies only when you receive a complete list.
   d. Immediately phone the companies currently listed, then continue working on your other assignments; make the other phone calls as you are notified of company names.

2. You have just prepared a report that you have checked and rechecked for accuracy. Before you attend a meeting at which you will submit your report, you review the typed version and note many serious errors. You would…

   a. Show the original and the typed version to the person in charge of typing and demand that the errors be changed before the meeting.
   b. Present the report at the meeting, point out the errors and state they were due to the typist.
   c. Present the errors to the typist, ask him to make the corrections and explain to individuals at the meeting that your report is still being typed.
   d. Present your report at the meeting and make no mention of the errors but notify attendees of corrections after the meeting.

SOURCE: Adapted by the authors from Elaine D. Pulakos. "Selection Assessment Methods: A guide to implementing formal assessments to build a high quality workforce," Society for Human Resource Management (SHRM), 2005.

Assessment centres (ACs) use several methods of assessment, including written tests, job simulations, in-basket exercises, projective tests, interviews, personality inventories, and/or leaderless group discussions. Typically, the tests are used to measure intellectual ability, work orientation, and career orientation. Leaderless group discussions, role-playing, and in-basket exercises measure an applicant's administrative skill. However, ACs do more than simply test applicants. Through the use of multiple assessment techniques and multiple assessors (or panel judges), ACs are able to predict a candidate's future job behaviour, managerial potential, and training needs. In recent years, the AC technique has become increasingly popular for nonsupervisory and skilled labour as well.

> Candidates for managerial and executive jobs may participate in ACs lasting up to several days involving a combination of individual testing and evaluation and group-based exercises. The result is a profile of each applicant's strengths and weaknesses. For instance, the AC used by AT&T provides ratings on 25 separate dimensions of performance and effectiveness including job-related skills (e.g., planning, setting priorities), skills in dealing with others (e.g., oral communication, empathy), and information about candidate values and preferences. Organizations can then target training opportunities and job assignments toward developing areas noted as relative weaknesses at time of assessment.[31]

Research studies evaluating the validity of the assessment centre technique have reported positive conclusions, by and large, indicating a median .40 correlation coefficient between AC ratings and such criteria as career progress, salary advances, supervisor ratings, and evaluations of potential progress.[32]

Performance tests are increasingly being conducted using **computer-interactive performance tests**. During the tests, applicants' abilities, such as reaction time, ability to concentrate, ability to work under different time pressures, perceptual speed, spatial visualization, and so on, are measured. Candidates' reactions to the simulation, both mental (e.g., comprehension, coding, calculation) and motor (e.g., keying speed, accuracy) are assessed.[33] Research evidence seems to indicate high reliability for such interactive tests.[34] A computer-interactive test example is depicted in Figure 6-8.

---

computer-interactive performance tests

Performance tests using computer simulations that can measure skills, comprehension, spatial visualization, judgment, etc.

FIGURE 6-8

An Example of a Computer-Interactive Test

You are the human resource manager in our firm. At 8 a.m., when you walk into your office, you find the following email messages on your computer:

Sharon (your colleague): Can we start our meeting at 10? It should take two hours to get the Job Evaluation briefing sharpened up. As planned, we should be able to do the presentation in 90 minutes leaving 30 minutes for questions.

Chan (a manager): Can we meet for, say, one hour—no, make that one and a half hours—today? It is urgent. I am free any time between 9:30 and 12 and after 3 p.m.

Andre (your boss): Can you interview a job candidate this morning? She is in town only this morning; so you will have to meet her between 9 and 10:30 a.m. She looks really good for the position we advertised. So I would not want to miss this opportunity.

Jim (your secretary): Just to let you know that the Job Evaluation briefing to the staff is now moved up. It is going to be at 1 p.m. and not at 2 p.m. The message came in only as I was leaving the office at 6 p.m. Didn't want to call you at home and inform.

What is the earliest time you can meet with Chan?

a. 9:30   **b.** 3*   **c.** 4:30   **d.** 12:30   **e.** not possible today

*Correct answer. The computer will record the length of time between presentation of the question and the candidate's response.

Integrity Tests

Integrity tests, also called honesty tests, measure an applicant's honesty and trustworthiness. These tests are of great interest to employers for two reasons: first, if the candidate is not honest in filling out the job application form and in his or her answers during the job interview, much of the information collected to assess the applicant's suitability for the position is useless; second, all employers desire employees whom they can trust.

---

integrity tests

Employment tests that measure an applicant's honesty and trustworthiness.

The Retail Council of Canada <http://www.retailcouncil.org> found that theft and related costs/expenses cost retailers approximately $4 billion each year. In 2007, average retail shrink in Canada was 1.54 percent of net sales.[35] One U.S. study estimates that over 6 percent of job applicants may be involved in thefts in previous jobs.[36] Statistics such as these have prompted several employers to use tests and other devices to measure the integrity of job applicants.

Early integrity testing attempts used polygraphs, or lie detector tests. Use of lie detector tests for the purpose of employment is prohibited in some provinces (e.g., Ontario) under the *Employment Standards Act*.[37] Two types of written integrity tests are now typically used because of their ease of use and inexpensiveness (typically available at less than $20 per administration). With overt tests, applicants are asked direct questions about past thefts. With non-overt tests, applicants are asked to respond to questions about their risk-taking behaviours (such as driving cars over the speed limit and sky-diving), and their attitudes toward dishonest behaviours.

The Stanton Survey, an integrity survey administered by the Plotkin Group, was tested for its validity using 4,665 applicants. Fifty percent of the applicants were given the Stanton Survey, the other 50 percent were not. Of the applicants, 37 percent of those not tested were later dismissed for theft while only 22.6 percent of those tested with Stanton Survey were dismissed for the same reason. The number of policy violators in the untested group was 10.4 percent compared to 1.5 percent in the tested group. The average loss from the untested group was approximately $208 higher compared to the tested group.[38]

When confronted by direct questions, many individuals are not likely to openly admit theft. Are dishonest applicants likely to be honest about their dishonesty? In a recent meta-analysis of 104 studies, overt integrity tests have been found to predict job performance with a validity coefficient of .14, and to predict counterproductive behaviours (including theft, accidents, disciplinary problems, and absenteeism) with a validity of .38. Non-overt tests predict with an average validity coefficient of .18 for job performance, and .27 for counterproductive behaviours.[39] This indicates that integrity tests are better predictors of counterproductive behaviours than of job performance.

Integrity tests present human resource specialists with an inherent dilemma. On the one hand, these methods offer some additional screening tools to better ensure an optimal workforce. On the other hand, such tests are subject to errors: some honest applicants will be misclassified as having low integrity. Also, to many applicants and employees, these tests are an invasion of their privacy.

Besides specific cautions associated with individual tests, human resource specialists should realize that testing is not always feasible. Even when tests can be developed or bought, their cost may not be justified for jobs that have low selection ratios or that are seldom filled. Examples include technical, professional, and managerial jobs. Even when feasible, the use of tests must be flexible. They need not always be the first or last step in the selection process. Instead, human resource experts use tests during the selection process at the point they deem appropriate. Consider the comments of an experienced human resource manager of a large chain of grocery stores:

> Many human resource managers in other industries use testing only after other steps in the selection process. In the grocery business you must test first. Why waste time interviewing a grocery clerk who doesn't know that three for 88 cents is 30 cents apiece? Besides, when we take applications on Tuesdays, we may have 300 of them. Interviews would take 75 hours a week, and my staff consists of a clerk and myself. But through testing, we can test the entire group in an hour. Then we interview only those who score well.

Lastly, employment tests are only one of several techniques used in the selection process because they are limited to factors that can be tested and validated easily. Other items, not measurable through testing, may be equally important.

Step 4: Employment Interview(s)

The immediate supervisor is ultimately responsible for newly hired workers. Since that responsibility is ever-present, supervisors should have input into the final hiring decision. The supervisor is often better able to evaluate the applicant's technical abilities than is the human resource department. Likewise, the immediate supervisor can often answer the interviewee's specific job-related questions with greater precision.

When supervisors make the final decision, the role of the human resource department is to provide the supervisor with the best applicants available. From these two or three applicants, the supervisor decides whom to hire. Some organizations leave the final hiring decision to the human resource department, especially when applicants are hired into a training program instead of for a specific job.

In larger organizations, it is also common for the applicant to be interviewed by several persons (especially for supervisory and managerial positions) either consecutively or during a panel interview. The immediate work supervisor will still have considerable influence on the final decision; however, the "satisfactory" candidate also will have to satisfy larger organizational requirements and fit well with the culture of the organization.

Regardless of who has the final hiring authority, the personal commitment of supervisors is generally higher when they participate in the selection process. When the supervisor recommends hiring an individual, he or she has made a psychological commitment to assist the new employee. If the candidate turns out to be unsatisfactory, the supervisor is then more likely to accept some of the responsibility for failure.

Because interviewing is a critical step in the selection process, this will be discussed in some detail in a later section in this chapter.

Step 5: Realistic Job Previews

Often, the supervisory interview is supplemented with a realistic job preview. A **realistic job preview (RJP)** allows the potential employee to understand the job setting before the hiring decision is made—often by showing him or her the type of work, equipment, and working conditions involved.

---

realistic job preview (RJP)
Involves showing the candidate the type of work, equipment, and working conditions involved in the job before the hiring decision is final.

Unmet expectations about a job contribute to initial job dissatisfaction. The RJP attempts to prevent job dissatisfaction by giving the newcomer an insight into the job. RJPs indicate the positive or favourable aspects of the jobs along with negative and neutral aspects of the job. Recently hired employees who have had a RJP are less likely to be shocked by the job or the job setting on the first day they report to work. Two writers concluded the following:

> The RJP functions very much like a medical vaccination.... The typical medical vaccination injects one with a small, weakened dose of germs, so that one's body can develop a natural resistance to that disease. The RJP functions similarly by presenting job candidates with a small dose of "organizational reality." And, like the medical vaccination, the RJP is probably much less effective after a person has already entered a new organization.[40]

Previous research has found that RJPs help to lower turnover, improve performance, increase job satisfaction, and generate greater trust of the organization, which a recent study finds may be due to perceptions of organizational honesty.[41]

> Applicants to CIBC <https://www.cibc.com> can experience what it is like to work in the call centre during an online RJP. Within an hour, applicants can see what the job is like in terms of repetition, supervision, and potentially requiring them to deal with rude or unpleasant customers.[42] In New York, the Administration for Children's Services Department (ACS; <http://www.nyc.gov/html/acs/html/home/home.shtml>) implemented RJP ads in 500 subway cars. One of its sales pitches was "Wanted: Men and women willing to walk into strange buildings in dangerous neighbourhoods, be screamed at by unhinged individuals—perhaps in a language you do not understand—and, on occasion, forcibly remove a child from the custody of parents because the alternative could have tragic consequences." They also emphasized the importance of the position: "Our job is to keep children safe. You have to be able to walk into someone's home and get them to talk to you. You have to cope with unknown and troubling situations, and figure out the truth. It's all about how to protect a child. It's tough—but it's worth it." The first month after it began running the ads, inquiries were up about 200 percent.[43]

The adverse effect of RJPs may be more candidates declining job offers when the working conditions do not appear appealing. Many RJPs may also focus unduly on extrinsic and job-context factors rather than on job content (or intrinsic) factors. Also, RJPs are no substitute for continuous monitoring of working conditions and in-depth job analysis. Informing job applicants about unpleasant working conditions may increase the probability that they will remain on the job once hired; however, they are unlikely to be any more satisfied with the job than those who were not told and did not leave. This means that only a conscious and continuous effort at improving "irritants" at the workplace is a real, long-term solution.

Step 6: Verification of References

What type of person is the applicant? Is the applicant a good, reliable worker? To answer these questions, employment specialists use references. Many professionals have a very skeptical attitude toward references. *Personal references*—those that attest to the applicant's sound character—are usually provided by friends or family. Their objectivity and candour are certainly questionable. When a reference is in writing, the author usually emphasizes only positive points. Thus, personal references are not commonly used (see Figure 6-9).

FIGURE 6-9

Popularity of Reference Checks in Canadian Organizations

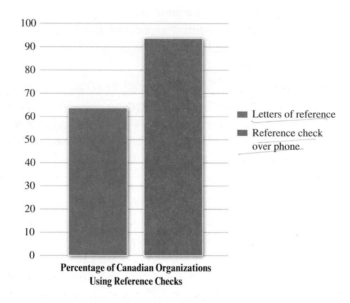

SOURCE: Chart prepared by the authors on the basis of a survey of 202 organizations reported by Sean Way and James Thacker in "Selection Practices: Where Are Canadian Organizations?" *HR Professional*, October/November, 1999, p. 35.

Employment references differ from personal references because they discuss the applicant's work history. Many human resource specialists doubt the usefulness of these references because former supervisors or teachers may not be completely candid, especially with negative information. Further, many managers do not seek the right information or ask the right questions while checking references.

---

employment references

Evaluations of an employee's past work performance and job-relevant behaviours provided by past employers.

One survey showed that 84 percent of companies have had to fire people for reasons that could have been discovered by proper reference checks. More than 93 percent of the respondents said they had found exaggerations on résumés and 86 percent had found outright misrepresentations.[44]

Often, many employment references are little more than confirmation of prior employment. Many employers are concerned about the risk of possible legal action by past employees who were not given positive references. In some cases, employers provide only basic information to protect themselves (e.g., simply stating that a person worked for them in the past in a certain capacity during specific dates). This lack of candour has caused some human resource specialists to omit this step entirely from the selection process. Other specialists have substituted phone inquiries for written references. Besides getting a faster response, often at lower cost, phone inquiries have the advantage of directness: voice inflections or hesitation over blunt questions may tip off the interviewer to underlying problems. In practice, however, only a small proportion of all reference checks seek negative information. Most reference checks are used to verify application information and gather additional data:

> John Adams impressed his interviewers a few minutes after the interview began. The position was that of a store manager in a large building supplies chain. His ready wit, ability to think on the spot, and keen mind appealed to the interviewers. Equally attractive was what his previous employers had to say about him. One of the references called him a "young dynamo" because of his drive and enthusiasm; another commented on John's ability to "come out with totally creative ideas" and his "methodical approach to problems." Adams, who was hired for the position by the firm, did perform true to these statements for the first three months. It was by sheer accident that one day a colleague noted a shortfall in the cash register. On investigation, it was found that Adams had been systematically stealing money from his employer. Even worse, he had a history of embezzling accounts with his three previous employers. One of the previous employers admitted being aware of a couple of incidents when Adams had received kickbacks from vendors. None of the references, however, made any mention of these facts in their letters.[45]

Lack of candour in **reference letters** may be due to a variety of reasons, including fear of legal reprisal, legal requirements (as in the United States) to show reference letters to an applicant, desire to get rid of an employee, and reluctance to pass judgment on a fellow human being. Given this state of affairs, an employer can get to the truth about a potential employee's character and work performance in a number of ways. Some of the possible strategies are shown in Figure 6-10.

---

reference letters

Written evaluations of a person's job-relevant skills, past experience, and work-relevant attitudes.

More recently, several firms have begun to include a background investigation as part of their selection process. Some applicants exaggerate their skills, education, and/or past work experience. While virtually every qualification listed in an application form or résumé can be verified, the cost of doing it may be prohibitive, especially for smaller employers. Some large organizations today use the services of specialized agencies to conduct background checks:

> In 2008 and 2009, BackCheck <http://www.backcheck.net>, one of Canada's leading pre-employment background check and employment verification organizations, screened over a half million Canadians, and placed "red flags" on between 25 and 50 percent of those screened.[47]

Another emerging trend is the use of social networking websites such as Facebook to learn more about the applicant's interests and behaviours. Although this practice has been outlawed in Germany[48] and caution has been warned in Alberta,[49] its use has not been tested legally yet in Canada:

> Several recruiters check applicants' backgrounds through search results on Google and other search engines. They can also access social networking sites such as Facebook or MySpace to learn more about an applicant's position on morality, drugs, sex, and various social phenomena as well as gather personal profiles that indicate age, sex, race, ethnicity, political affiliation, etc. Although it is illegal to use any of the latter in making a hiring decision, hiring decisions based on behaviours and self-stated opinions and other posted material may not be considered discriminatory.[50]

Whatever the approach, employers should be aware of their legal obligations when collecting and using employee information and abide by them. The federal *Personal Information Protection and Electronic*

Document Act (PIPEDA) applies to the collection, use, retention, and disclosure of "personal information" about employees in federally regulated organizations. In Alberta and British Columbia, there is a similar *Personal Information Protection Act* (PIPA). Broadly speaking, "personal information" has been interpreted to include all opinions, evaluations, comments, social status, and disciplinary actions. Only that part of personal information that is "reasonably required" in order to establish, manage, or terminate an employment relationship should be collected or disseminated to avoid possible legal challenges.[51]

FIGURE 6-10

How to Get the Truth Out of References

Use the phone: Most references are more likely to be honest over the phone or in person than in a formal letter or email.

Seek information on job-related behaviour: Ask for details on job behaviours, such as tardiness and absenteeism, rather than on personality traits, such as ambition and intelligence, which are hard to evaluate reliably.

Ask direct questions: Questions such as "Would you rehire this employee now?" or "How is this person's behaviour in a group setting?" and listen for how the referee responds including hesitations such as "ahh, umm."

Combine references with other predictors: Reference letters are no substitute for application blanks, tests, and interviews.

Use credible sources only: Former work supervisors are, typically, the most useful reference sources. Letters from acquaintances and friends are usually worthless for predicting future job success.

Note frequency of job changes: A person who has not stayed in any organization for more than a few months may be either an extremely successful employee or a problem employee. Persons who have been moving laterally across organizations without any apparent change in job challenge, rewards, or working conditions should be carefully watched.

Watch out for phrases with hidden meanings: Most references do not blatantly lie; they simply don't tell the whole truth. A person who is described as "deeply committed to family and friends" may be someone who will not work beyond five o'clock; an "individualist" may be a person who cannot work with others.

SOURCE: Adapted and summarized from Pamela Babcock, "It takes more than a reference check to weed out liars," Advice for Supervisors from the Society for Human Resource Management, 2004, SHRM; Hari Das and Mallika Das, "But He Had Excellent References: Refining the Reference Letter," *The Human Resource*, June/July 1988, pp. 15–16.

Step 7: Contingent Assessments

The selection process may include a contingent assessment. This occurs when a candidate has been selected and will receive a job offer provided they pass the contingent assessment. Although any type of selection method can be used contingently (for instance, a taxi company may verify a driving record before offering a driving position, and a security company may conduct a background check before offering a job to a new officer), drug testing and medical evaluations should be used exclusively as contingent methods for legal purposes.

Normally, a **medical evaluation** is a health checklist that asks the applicant to indicate health and accident information. The questionnaire is sometimes supplemented with a physical examination by a company nurse or physician. The medical evaluation may:

---

medical evaluation

Assessment of physical and/or mental health of an applicant through self-reports and/or medical examination by a preferred physician.

- entitle the employer to lower health or life insurance rates for company-paid insurance;
- be required by provincial or local health officials, particularly in food-handling operations where communicable diseases are a danger; and/or
- be useful to evaluate whether the applicant can handle the physical or mental stress of a job.

Employment references discuss the applicant's work history. Some employers refuse to answer questions relating to former employees on the phone. Are there ways to overcome this?

wavebreakmedia/Shutterstock

Many employers have done away with this step because of the costs involved. Also, if an applicant is rejected, charges of discrimination under the *Canadian Human Rights Act* or related provincial legislation may be brought. A congenital health condition may be considered a disability, and failure to hire may be seen as discrimination against the otherwise qualified applicant. If the employer wants a medical evaluation, it may be scheduled *after* the hiring decision. Medical examinations are usually conducted only if the job requires a clearly determined level of physical effort or other abilities (e.g., ability to climb poles). Even here, an applicant can be rejected only if reasonable accommodations cannot be made to allow the person to perform the job.

For example, imposing a height restriction for telephone installers on the grounds that short persons cannot get ladders from the truck would be deemed discriminatory. Provision of stools for workers to stand on while removing the ladders permit even short persons to perform the job.

The expertise with which the medical evidence was interpreted will also determine the strength of the employer's case in the event of a legal action by a rejected job applicant. Consider this example:

Tony Kearsley applied for a position as a firefighter with the city of St. Catharines. He was accepted, conditional upon passing a medical examination. During the medical examination, it was discovered that he had atrial fibrillation. The general medical practitioner refused to pass him, claiming that it increased the risk of a stroke by 1 to 5 percent a year. In addition, the medical examiner felt that Mr. Kearsley's condition might result in the heart not being able to pump sufficient blood to his organs during the extreme rigours of firefighting. Other experts whom the complainant consulted had advised him that it was a benign condition that would not impact on his ability to do the job. During the proceedings, the Ontario Human Rights Commission called in a medical expert in the area of atrial fibrillation, who testified that the increase in probability of a stroke for someone of Kearsley's age was inconsequential and possibly .2 percent per year. The expert also testified that there was no increased risk of heart failure in someone like Kearsley who was otherwise in good health. The Board asked the city to hire Kearsley within 75 days and pay him damages for the salary he lost until that date.[52]

In summary, to avoid possible allegations of discrimination, medical examinations should be conducted only when they are absolutely necessary. Guidelines for conducting medical examinations provided by Ontario Human Rights Commission include the following:[53]

- Where medical testing is appropriate, the employer should notify job applicants of this requirement at the time an offer of employment is made.

- There should be an objective, rational justification for the test. There should be an objective basis to believe that the degree, nature, scope, and probability of risk caused by the medical condition will adversely affect the safety of coworkers or the public.

- Medical testing should be conducted by qualified professionals and the results analyzed in a competent laboratory.

- Procedures should be instituted for the physician to review the test results with the employee concerned.

- All health assessment information should remain exclusively with the examining physician and separate from the employee's human resources file.

One noteworthy exception to the trend of fewer medical evaluations is **drug tests**. Increases in mortality rates, accidents, theft, and poor performance affect the employer's economic performance. Moreover, if the drug user's performance carries negative consequences for customers or fellow employees, lawsuits are likely. Through the analysis of urine, hair, or blood samples, laboratories are able to screen for the presence of drugs. Although professional and amateur intercollegiate athletes have been tested for many years to assure the absence of steroids and stimulants, their popularity in work organizations has been more recent.

---

drug tests

Tests that include whether a job applicant uses marijuana, cocaine, or other drugs.

In 2010, 76.5 percent of Canadians reported drinking, with 8.2 percent of males and 2.0 percent of females reporting frequent heavy drinking. Marijuana use was reported by 10.6 percent of Canadian adults in 2009 with heaviest usage on the east and west coasts, and 2 percent of Canadians reported using an illicit drug other than cannabis (e.g., heroin, cocaine, crystal meth).[54] Workplace substance abuse is estimated to cost Canadian employers $39.8 billion annually.[55] TD Canada Trust, Imperial Oil Limited <http://www.imperialoil.ca>, and Transport Canada <http://www.tc.gc.ca/eng/menu.htm> are among organizations that use drug testing in Canada.

Given these figures, it is not surprising that some companies are advocating the use of drug tests. Executives of TD Canada Trust argued that drug users are more likely to associate with criminal elements and are therefore more susceptible to criminal influence that might lead to blackmail and perhaps theft.

> TD's policies required all new and returning employees to undergo urinalysis within 48 hours of accepting an offer of employment. TD's aim was to address the potential impact of drugs on the health and work performance of the employees and preserve the safety of funds and employees. If habitual substance abusers refused to participate in rehabilitation services (funded by the bank or under government health plans) or those services were of no avail, the abuser faced dismissal. The same fate awaited casual users if they tested positive on three or more occasions and persisted in drug use. The bank paid full wages and benefits to employees in rehabilitation programs.[56]

In some jobs, even "one drink" may be too risky and lead to major workplace accidents. Should organizations abolish any alcohol usage during work hours?

S. Pearce/PhotoLink/Getty Images

The Canadian Civil Liberties Association called for an outright ban on employee drug tests, saying no person should "be required to share urine with a stranger" as a condition of employment.[57] It pointed out that there was no evidence to suggest that Canadian society has a serious drug problem or such a problem among those with full- or part-time employment. Nor "are drug tests totally reliable indicators of safe performance in the here-and-now—at best they show only that an employee may have used a particular drug at some point in the past, perhaps several weeks before."[58] The Association launched a complaint against the mandatory drug test imposed by TD Canada Trust but lost it.[59] However, the court did find the mandatory urinalysis intrusive. In 1998, the Federal Court of Appeal in a two-to-one decision found the bank's anti-drug program discriminatory. Justice F. Joseph Macdonald held that the bank's policy resulted in indirect discrimination against drug-dependent employees. While the bank's rule of three positive tests leading to dismissal applied to both new and returning employees, "the rule directly impacts more negatively on a protected class of individuals under the *Canadian Human Rights Act*—drug-dependent users."[60]

Drug-dependence is considered to be a disability, and no Canadian is to be discriminated against on the basis of a disability according to the *Canadian Charter of Human Rights and Freedoms*. This means that, today, an employer must delicately balance the individual rights of the employee against risk of liability and lack of safety at the workplace. Notably, the issue of whether casual or recreational users are protected under human rights legislation is still a matter of debate. However, several court cases have found that only dependent drug users have a disability and are accorded protection under human rights laws.[61] The Canadian Human Rights Commission has decreed that the following types of pre-employment testing are permissible:[62]

1. when an individual discloses an existing or recent history of drug or alcohol abuse;

2. where a pre-employment medical exam provides the physician with reasonable cause to believe that an individual may be abusing drugs or alcohol and therefore may become impaired on the job; and

3. drivers for commercial bus and truck operations.

However, employers cannot automatically withdraw offers of employment from candidates who fail alcohol or drug tests without offering accommodation. Canadian employers owe drug-dependent workers accommodation to the point that: (a) the accommodation would alter the nature of or viability of the enterprise, or (b) notwithstanding the accommodation efforts, there are serious health or safety risks to workers or members of the public. A relationship or rational connection between the drug or alcohol testing and job performance is an important component of any lawful drug or alcohol testing policy.

> In *Chiasson v. Kellogg Brown & Root (Canada) Co.*, a construction company terminated a new employee who failed a mandatory pre-employment drug test. The Alberta Court of Appeal upheld the employer's policy on the belief that such testing legitimately perceives that employees who are drug users are a safety risk in an already dangerous workplace. The court also pointed out that the effects of marijuana can linger for several days.[63]

Because most drug tests do not yield accurate data on current impairment or usage level and may be unreliable, even the pursuit of a productive, safe workplace may not justify universal, mandatory drug testing. If the testing policy is a bona fide occupational requirement of the job, particularly in a safety sensitive job position, an employer might have better luck defending it as policy.[64]

Step 8: Hiring Decision

Whether made by the supervisor or the human resource department, the final hiring decision marks the end of the selection process. When a single predictor such as a job interview is used, the decision is simple: whoever had the best interview performance is typically selected. However, when multiple predictors such as tests, interviews, and reference checks are used, the decision process becomes more complex. A brief discussion on the decision process is attempted in the following section.

Tradeoffs among Predictors

Alternate approaches to combine the scores on different predictors exist. Three popular approaches are the subjective approach, multiple cut-off approach, and compensatory approach.

Subjective Approach

In the **subjective approach**, also referred to as the clinical approach, the decision maker looks at the scores received by the various applicants on predictors, subjectively evaluates all of the information, and comes to an overall judgment.

---

subjective approach

An approach where the decision maker looks at the scores received by the various applicants on predictors, subjectively evaluates all of the information, and comes to an overall judgment.

Ontario Electronics had three finalists for a marketing position who received the following scores in a sales aptitude test and in the job interview, both scored out of a maximum of 100 points.

Candidate A: Sales Aptitude Test = 80, Interview = 50

Candidate B: Sales Aptitude Test = 40, Interview = 80

Candidate C: Sales Aptitude Test = 70, Interview = 70

The decision maker who looks at the above data may choose Candidate A if he believes that Sales Aptitude scores of the individual are the most critical in predicting future performance.[65]

It should be noted that another decision maker who looks at the same data may come to a different conclusion, especially if the person believes that interview performance is more important than aptitude. In that instance, Candidate B would be chosen. Similarly, a decision maker who believes that both are equally important and that a high score on one dimension does not compensate for a low score on another may come out with a totally different conclusion—namely, Candidate C. It is precisely the judgmental nature of the decision that causes confusion and potential problems. Decisions are based on gut feelings and may be hard to justify in the event of human rights complaints.

Multiple Cut-off Approach

In a **multiple cut-off approach**, cut-off scores are set for each predictor and each applicant evaluated on a pass–fail basis. Applicants are rejected if any one of their predictor scores fall below a set minimum score.

---

multiple cut-off approach

An approach where scores are set for each predictor and each applicant is evaluated on a pass–fail basis.

In the example of Ontario Electronics, if the employer has set a cut-off score of 60 for the test and 60 for interview scores, only Candidate C would qualify.

It is easy for managers to understand this approach, making the acceptance levels for this approach high. However, under this method, the deficiency in one predictor cannot be compensated by superior performance on another. The organization may reject a number of applicants who may be actually qualified to do the job. This can, in turn, result in poor public relations and possible legal challenges.

Compensatory Approach

In a **compensatory approach**, a higher score on a predictor may compensate for a low score on another. Predictors are assumed to be additive and to compensate for one another (in our above example, performing well on the test compensates for a relatively poorer performance on the interview). The applicant with the highest total score will be selected for the position.

compensatory approach

An approach where a higher score on a predictor may compensate a low score on another.

During selection, some organizations employ a sequential elimination process called the *multiple hurdles approach*, where an applicant has to pass a predictor satisfactorily before he or she can proceed to the next predictor.

> In the Ontario Electronics example, under the multiple hurdles approach, only those who achieve a satisfactory score in the sales aptitude test will be interviewed. Thus, if the organization has set up a minimum test score of 60 as satisfactory, then only Candidates A and C will be interviewed.

The multiple hurdles approach is particularly relevant to organizations when some of the predictors used are expensive (e.g., an expensive assessment centre evaluation, inviting job applicants from abroad). In such instances, by keeping these predictors in the latter half of the selection process, the firm is able to screen out candidates who are unlikely to meet organizational needs and thereby save considerable resources. However, the underlying assumption here (as in the case of the multiple cut-off model) is that a high score on one predictor does not compensate for a low score on another predictor. However, unlike in the case of other models, with multiple hurdles, as soon as an applicant receives a lower than desired score on a predictor, he or she shall be removed from further consideration and will not proceed to the next stage.

After Selection

Once the person is selected, the successful candidate has to be contacted immediately. Having a good employment contract is a must in most instances. When drawing up the employment contract, particular attention should be paid to the following areas:[66]

- **Specify probationary period if applicable.** A common misunderstanding is that all new employees are automatically subject to a probationary period, which is not the case.

- **Specify start date and terms of employment clearly.** In today's competitive labour market, employees move frequently from one job to another. If the employment contract does not specify the start date, under certain circumstances the employers may find themselves competing for the employee's service with a previous employer (especially if the required notice was not given by the employee).

- **Specify reasonable restrictive covenants.** Confidentiality of information and noncompete clauses should be specific, reasonable, and explicit.

- **Ensure that termination procedures are legally enforceable.** Ensure that termination procedures, if specified in the contract, meet the provincial minimum employment standards. (For information on employment law in Canada, visit: <www.employmentlawtoday.com>.)

Dispositioning of Applicants

Throughout the selection process, there will be applicants whom the organization no longer wishes to pursue. The organization's decision should be communicated to them at the earliest possible opportunity. From a public relations standpoint, unsuccessful applicants should be notified that they were not selected. However, the increased use of technology in the recruitment function has resulted in large volumes of job seekers applying for positions, making such a policy impractical. Several employers advise their applicants that only successful ones will be contacted. While this relieves the employer of the responsibility to contact all applicants it still may not be advisable from a public relations point of view. It is also important to pay careful attention to the wording of the rejection letter. The wording should be positive, and the reason offered for rejection should not be offensive or reduce the self-esteem of the applicant.

Employment specialists may also want to consider rejected applicants for other openings, since these applicants have already expressed an interest in the firm and may have gone through various stages of the selection process. Informing the applicants of such an action enhances public goodwill. Even if no openings are immediately available, applications of candidates with potential but who were not hired should be kept on file for future openings. Retaining these applications can also be useful if the employer is charged with employment discrimination.

The job applications of those hired should be carefully preserved as well. This not only enables the human resource department to update its HR information system (HRIS), but also helps to learn about the source of its applicants. Information on sex, race, and age of employees helps the human resource department assess the extent of underutilization and concentration (referred to in Chapter 4) and to take necessary corrective action proactively.

If some recruits prove unsatisfactory after they are hired, human resource specialists may be able to reconstruct the selection process beginning with the application. In their reconstruction, they may uncover invalid tests, improperly conducted interviews, or other flaws in the selection process.

The newly hired employee should be treated with respect and consideration. An employer does not get a second chance to make a good first impression with a new hire. The new hire's supervisor or co-worker should call the person a few days before the start date. Sending a welcome note to the entire family may be appropriate in some instances, especially if the employee's family is moving from another location. The time and place the new hire should report on arrival should be clearly communicated.[67] Some of the unwritten rules (such as dress code) should also be communicated so that the new hire does not arrive formally dressed on casual Friday, for example. A detailed orientation should follow on arrival. More on orientation and job placement will be discussed in the next chapter.

LO6 HRC 4

Employment Interview

The **employment interview** is a formal, in-depth conversation conducted to evaluate the applicant's acceptability. The interviewer seeks to answer two broad questions: Can the applicant do the job? How does the applicant compare with others who are applying for the job?

---

employment interview

A formal, in-depth, face-to-face, or more recently, a phone or video conference between an employer and a job applicant to assess the appropriateness of the applicant for the job under consideration.

Employment interviews are the most widely used selection technique. Their popularity stems from their flexibility. They can be adapted to unskilled, skilled managerial, and staff employees. They also allow a two-way exchange of information: interviewers learn about the applicant and the applicant learns about the employer.

Interviews do have shortcomings. The most noticeable flaw is their varying reliability and validity. Some early studies reported an average validity coefficient (i.e., the correlation between the interview assessment of candidates and their actual performance) of .10, or virtually nil.[68] More recently, validity coefficients of .37 are reported for unstructured interviews and as high as .59 when they are highly structured.[69] Reasons for the continued popularity of interviews include:

- An interview allows a personal impression. Besides assessing a candidate's ability to perform well on the job, an interviewer also wants to make sure that there is a match between the person's personality and the team with which he or she has to work. An interview provides an opportunity to do this.

- An interview offers the firm an opportunity to sell a job to a candidate. In high-demand areas such as engineering, electronics, and business administration, "selling" the company to top candidates assumes great importance. Typically, the employment policies, compensation, flexible work arrangements, career opportunities, and overall quality of work life are highlighted in an effort to convince top applicants to choose the firm.

- An interview offers the organization an opportunity to answer the candidate's questions regarding the job, career opportunities, and company policies.

High reliability means that the interpretation of the interview results should not vary from interviewer to interviewer. In reality, it is common for different interviewers to form different opinions. Reliability is improved when identical questions are asked, when interviewers are trained to record responses systematically, and when a scoring guide is provided to gauge the calibre of responses. Validity is questionable because few human resource departments conduct validation studies on their interview results. However, proactive human resource departments are beginning to realize this problem and are comparing interview results with actual performance or other criteria, such as stability of employment. More validation of interviews is needed because they may relate more to personal features of candidates than to the candidates' potential performance. Human rights tribunals also look for explicit links of job descriptions to interview questions,[70] and that there are no references to protected grounds (such as a note that a candidate was black and in her 50s)[71] when making decisions on discrimination cases.

Carefully structured interviews based on a thorough job analysis are more useful and valid than unstructured interviews that dwell on applicant opinions about topics not directly related to the job. Also, interviews that probe what the applicant has actually done in the past in situations similar to those described in the job analysis may be better predictors of future performance.

The following pages introduce you to types of interviews and the interview process. After this, the discussion turns to some of the common errors by interviewers and interviewees that you should recognize and avoid during interviews.

HRC **4**

Types of Interviews

Interviews are commonly conducted between the applicant and one or more interviewers on a one-to-one basis. Increasingly common are **panel interviews** wherein all interviewers meet with an applicant at the same time. This allows all interviewers to evaluate the individual(s) on the same questions and answers. Since the interviewers are more apt to reach the same conclusion, reliability is improved. A variation is a group interview where two or more applicants are interviewed together by one interviewer. This saves time, especially for busy executives. It also permits the answers of different applicants to be compared immediately.

panel interview

Interview using several interviewers with one applicant.

Whether a one-to-one, panel, or group interview, there are different interview formats that depend on the type of questions that are asked. Questions can be unstructured, or various types of structured questions including behavioural description and situational. Figure 6-11 compares these different formats. Most commonly, interviews will consist of a combination of question types. Figure 6-12 shows the relative popularity of different kinds of interviews in Canadian organizations.

FIGURE 6-11

Different Question Formats in Interviews

Interview Format	Types of Questions	Useful Applications
Unstructured	Few if any planned questions. Questions are made up during the interview.	Useful when trying to help interviewees solve personal problems or understand why they are not right for a job.
Structured	A predetermined checklist of questions, asked of all applicants.	Useful for valid results, especially when dealing with large numbers of applicants.
1. Behavioural Description	Questions are limited to actual behaviours. Evaluation is on the solution and the approach of the applicant	Useful to understand applicant's past work behaviour and abilities under specific work situations.
2. Situational	Questions focus on important situations likely to arise on the job and what the applicant would do in such situations.	Useful for understanding the applicant's behavioural propensities.
3. Stress-Producing	A series of harsh, rapid-fire questions intended to upset the applicant.	Useful for stressful jobs, such as handling complaints.

Unstructured Interviews

As the summary in Figure 6-11 indicates, **unstructured interviews** allow human resource specialists to develop questions as the interview proceeds. The interviewer goes into topic areas as they arise, and the end result is more like a friendly conversation. Unfortunately, this unstructured method lacks the reliability of a structured interview because each applicant is asked a different series of questions. Even worse, this approach may overlook key areas of the applicant's skills or background.

unstructured interviews

Interviews using few if any planned questions to enable the interviewer to pursue, in depth, the applicant's responses.

FIGURE 6-12

Popularity of Different Kinds of Interviews

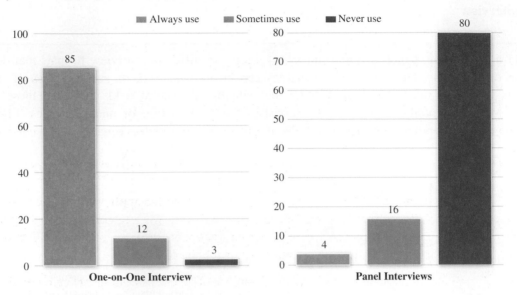

SOURCE: Chart prepared by the authors on the basis of data reported in Murray Axmith & Associates Ltd., *Survey 2000: Canadian Hiring, Retention and Dismissal Practices*, p. 13, Toronto/Courtesy of Right Axmith, a division of Right Management Consultants.

Structured Interviews

Structured interviews rely on a predetermined set of questions. The questions are developed before the interview begins and the same questions are asked of every applicant. Candidate responses are compared to a list of potential responses and scored according to a predetermined scoring guide. This approach improves the reliability of the interview process, but it does not allow the interviewer to follow up interesting or unusual responses. Here, the end result is an interview that seems quite mechanical to all concerned. The rigid format may even convey a lack of interest to applicants who are used to more flexible interviews. Situational and behavioural description interviews (discussed below) are two more useful forms of structured interviews.

structured interviews

Interviews wherein a predetermined checklist of questions usually asked of all applicants is used.

A survey of 300 human resource practitioners in Canada reveals that 78 percent prepare questions in advance, although 75.4 percent also add new questions during the interview. Only 12.6 percent of respondents use a rating scale. About 85.7 percent of respondents reported using behavioural questions most or all of the time, and 84.7 percent reported taking notes on candidate responses.[72]

Another survey of 592 interviewers from more than 500 Canadian and international organizations showed that trained interviewers are more standardized and formalized in their evaluation processes. They employ more sophisticated questioning strategies and are more consistent in their questioning practices. The study also identified four key factors to a structured interview: evaluation standardization, question consistency, question sophistication, and rapport building.[73]

Behavioural description interviews attempt to find out how job applicants responded to specific work situations in the past. Behavioural description interviews are based on the principle that the best predictor of people's future behaviour is their past behaviour in a similar circumstance. This is especially so if the behaviour being considered occurred most recently and, in addition, is of a long-enduring nature. The questions posed to the candidate could be along these lines:

To assess conflict resolution: "Tell me about the most serious disagreement that you have had with a co-worker in the past and how you dealt with it."

To assess motivation: "Tell me about a time in your last job (or in your present job) when you were asked to take on new duties and responsibilities even if they didn't appear in your job description and how you dealt with it."

To assess decision-making ability: "Tell me about the most unpopular decision you made on your last job."

behavioural description interviews

Interviews that attempt to find out how job applicants responded to specific work situations in the past.

The work situations chosen should be relevant to the job for which the applicant is under consideration. For instance, practically everyone who has worked in retail sales for any considerable length of time has had to deal with an angry customer. Everyone who has worked in an office would have faced a situation where they had to do something outside of their regular job duties.

Choosing *typical* situations such as the above is important when designing behavioural description questions. Figure 6-13 depicts a behavioural description interview question and a scoring key for the interviewer to use. Typically, the interviewer(s) would record the candidate's responses to each question, and then compare their response to the responses on the scoring guide. A numerical score is then given for each question, and the sum or scores for all questions produces a total interview score. The total interview score is then used to make comparisons across candidates.

FIGURE 6-13

Sample Behavioural Description Interview Question and Rating Criteria

Tell me about a time when you were able to establish rapport with someone when the situation made it difficult to do so. What were the circumstances? What did you do? What were the results?		
1 2	3	4 5
Low	**Moderate**	**High**
• Made minimal attempts to understand the person's perspective.	• Attempted to understand the other person's perspective.	• Effectively reached out to the person and actively sought to understand the person's perspective.
• Developed only a surface-level relationship in a simple situation.	• Developed a positive working relationship with the person in a moderately difficult situation.	• Developed an extremely positive relationship with the person in an extremely difficult or contentious situation.

SOURCE: Originally published as "Selection Assessment Methods: A guide to implementing formal assessments to build a high-quality workforce," by Elaine D. Pulakos, p.12. (c) 2005, Society for Human Resource Management, Alexandria, VA. Used with permission. All rights reserved.

Situational interviews attempt to assess a job applicant's likely future response to specific situations, which may or may not have been faced by the applicant in the past. In this type of interview, the interviewer describes situations that are likely to arise on the job and are important for effective job performance and then asks the job applicant what he or she would do in such situations. Here the "behavioural intentions" of the applicant are being assessed (unlike statements of actual behaviour in behavioural description interviews). For the purpose of interview questions, real events that describe either effective or ineffective work behaviour (called "critical incidents") are identified. These are situations faced or actions taken by actual workers on the job and may be gathered from past or present employees themselves, supervisors, clients, and others who come into contact with the persons doing the job. When it is not practical to collect such incidents, the interviewer may do a comparative analysis by considering the most effective and most ineffective employees in the same position. Whatever the approach, the focus is on getting information on relevant job behaviour during the employment interview:

situational interviews

Interviews that attempt to assess a job applicant's likely future response to specific situations, which may or may not have been faced by the applicant in the past.

For example, an organization that attempts to hire managers who must maintain tight cost controls may ask applicants to imagine themselves in a work situation where they faced escalating costs. The applicants' description of what they would do in that situation (e.g., co-operating with others to reduce costs, initiating own action plans to reduce costs, or seeking boss's advice on the matter) would be noted during the interview and evaluated against a pre-set scoring guide.

Behaviour description and situational interviews are claimed to be highly job-related because they reflect behavioural intentions of the job applicant and the critical behaviours needed for successful job performance. Research studies indicate improved reliability and validity for the situational and behavioural description interviews over traditional, unstructured interviews.[74] Whether one uses behavioural description or situational interviews, structured questions that are job relevant and assess a job applicant's future behavioural intentions are critical for gaining valid insights. Past studies recommend the following steps to improve the overall validity of an interview method:

1. Conduct a job analysis and develop critical incidents.

2. Select criteria for job success based on the results of the job analysis.

3. Select one or more incidents that indicate a specific performance criterion (for example, cost-consciousness in the previous illustration).

4. Turn each critical incident into a "What would you do when...?" question.

5. Develop a scoring guide to facilitate agreement among interviewers on what constitutes a good, acceptable, or unacceptable response to each question.

6. Evaluate the validity of the instrument and implement.

 HRC 4

The Interview Process

The five stages of a typical employment interview are listed in Figure 6-14. These **stages of an interview** are interviewer preparation, creation of rapport, information exchange, termination, and evaluation. Regardless of the type of interview used, each of these steps must occur for a successful interview to result. They are discussed briefly to illustrate how the actual interview process develops.

stages of an interview

Key phases in an employment interview: interview preparation, creation of rapport, information exchange, termination, and evaluation.

FIGURE 6-14

Stages in a Typical Employment Interview

Stage 1: Interviewer Preparation

Obviously, before the interview begins, the interviewer needs to prepare. This preparation requires that specific questions be developed. It is the answers to these questions that the interviewers will use in deciding the applicant's suitability. At the same time, the interviewers must consider what questions the applicant is likely to ask. Because the interview is used to persuade top applicants to accept subsequent job offers, the interviewer needs to be able to explain job duties, performance standards, pay, benefits, and other areas of interest.

A list of typical questions asked by recruiters and other interviewers appears in Figure 6-15. Note that several of these questions, while popular, are of questionable predictive power in assessing the future work performance of the applicant. Further, under the law, questions relating to sex, family status, race, etc., are prohibited. As can be seen from the list, these questions are intended to give the interviewer some insight into the applicant's interests, attitudes, and background. The same figure provides modified versions of the same questions that provide greater insights into an applicant's strengths and attitudes. Specific or technical questions are added to the list according to the type of job opening. These questions should be designed to assess specific tasks, duties, and competencies identified in the job analysis.

Spotlight *on* HRM

Technology-Mediated Interviews

Although interviews provide rich, face-to-face information, they are expensive to conduct—particularly if the interviewer(s) or applicant(s) have to travel to a single location. Apart from travel, subsistence, and lodging costs, there are additional soft or invisible costs such as lost time during travel.

To reduce time and monetary expenses, some employers are increasingly resorting to technology-mediated interviews. Options include sending a videotape of an interview and having the interviewer(s) watch the playback, and using teleconferencing, videoconferencing, Google Hangouts, or Skype for "real time" interviews. Some reasons for an increasing interest in technology-mediated interviewing include: expansion of national and international markets, satellite or virtual locations for many organizations, more employees teleworking, and greater competitiveness and lower recruiting budgets.

Although face-to-face interviews are still preferred by most employers, videoconferencing and Skype interviews are increasingly being used (e.g., when candidates would have to travel great distances for an interview). Employers using technology-mediated interviews believe they are able to gather relevant information on candidates and screen out those less qualified. There may even be a slight edge given to candidates who are interviewed using video technology. One study found that interviewers may attribute candidate pauses or lacklustre responses to the technology as opposed to the candidate.[75] Both employers and candidates indicate that using technology-mediated interviewing affords a wider pool of prospective employers and candidates in a smaller time commitment.

Although videoconference equipment rentals may cost $60 to $200 per hour, Skype and Google Hangouts are downloaded for free and simply require a computer with webcam and microphone—readily available hardware on most

(Continued)

personal computers. Sound and video quality may vary, however, depending on the bandwidth and number of simultaneous users.

Technology-mediated interviews are still quite new for most organizations and many managers may not be comfortable with the process and equipment. Thus, interviewer training on the technology is a must. The equipment should be tested before the interview starts to allow for a smooth interview process for both the candidate and interviewer(s). Notably, videoconferencing technology has advanced in sophistication. During panel interviews, the screen technology is sufficiently advanced such that eye contact can be made with each interviewer providing a higher fidelity experience than earlier videoconferencing technologies.

The future of technology-mediated interviews seems bright as technology continues to improve and candidates and interviewers become attuned to interviews being conducted without being in the same location. Growing demands on managerial time and competition for candidates may also heighten the demand for technology-mediated interviews. Additionally, in response to a White House call to develop practices aimed at recruiting and hiring the long-term unemployed, companies like Frontier Communications <https://frontier.com> successfully implemented video interviewing. Using video interviewing, they successfully hired more long-term unemployed people and found that these employees are promoted more quickly and have a lower turnover rate than other groups.

SOURCES: Robert Waghorn, "Internet puts new spin on traditional career fair," *Canadian HR Reporter*, November 2011, Vol. 24, p. 20; Roy Maurer, "Video Interviews help address long-term unemployment," SHRM, www.shrm.org/hrdisciplines/staffingmanagement/articles/pages/video-interviews-long-term-unemployment.aspx; downloaded March 15, 2015.

FIGURE 6-15

Popular Employment Interview Questions and Suggested Modifications

Popular Interview Questions	Suggested Modifications
1. Why do you want to work for our organization?	1. How do your skills and career goals match with our organizational activities?
2. What are your hobbies?	2. How do your hobbies/spare-time activities add to your value as an employee in this organization?
3. Describe your last job.	3. What were your duties in the last job? What measures of success or failure were employed? How did you fare on those criteria?
4. Tell me about a project you did recently.	4. Tell me about a project you were involved in the recent past. What was your role in the project? How might the skills and competencies you acquired on the project be used in the present position?
5. What was your favourite subject in school/college/university?	5. What was your favourite subject in school/college/university? Can you relate the subject matter to this job or other jobs that you might hold here?
6. Do you have any geographical preferences?	6. This job requires approximately two days of travel each month and periodic (typically, once in three years) relocations. Are there any factors that will prevent you from meeting this requirement?
7. What was your favourite sport at school/college/university?	7. Were you involved in any extracurricular activities at school/college/university? Do you think that the activity provided you with specific competencies that might be relevant for the present job?
8. Have you played any team sports?	8. Your ability to work in a team is critical for success in this position. Can you describe your work in a team that faced a conflict? How was the conflict resolved? What role did you play in the resolution of the conflict?

Before interviewing can begin, careful construction of interview questions designed to assess tasks, duties, and competencies identified in the job analysis is required along with an accompanying scoring guide for strong and weak responses to each question. Interview development may be done jointly between line management and HR specialists. Prior to the interview, interviewers should review scoring guide materials, the interview protocol (such as procedures for meeting the candidate, assigning interview questions to particular interviewers in the case of a panel interview, deciding who will answer candidate questions), and standard statements to tell the candidate such as interview length, next stages in the selection process, and timeline for communicating the hiring decision. Before the interview, interviewers should also review the application form and/or résumé before each candidate arrives.

With the average cost of hiring new employees often about 30 percent of the annual salary for managerial and professional employees,[76] the interviewers' preparation should be aimed at making the interview process efficient and comfortable for the applicant. Often the interviewer is one of the first representatives of the company with whom the applicant has an opportunity to talk. A strong and lasting impression of the company is likely to be formed at this stage. If the interviewer does not show courtesy to the applicant, that impression is certain to be negative. If the applicant is a promising candidate for the job, he or she likely has other job prospects.

Given the importance of interviewer preparation and skills in determining the overall effectiveness of the interview (as a selection tool), several organizations have begun to train their managers in interview techniques. Large companies often train their interviewers in matters such as human rights legislation and techniques to get more information from job candidates.[77] Interviewers should also be trained to link interview questions tightly to job analysis results, use a variety of questions, ask the same questions of each candidate, and anchor the rating scales for scoring answers with examples and illustrations.[78]

Stage 2: Creation of Rapport

Once the interview begins, the burden is on the interviewer to establish a relaxed rapport with the recruit. Without a relaxed rapport, the interviewer may not get a clear picture of the applicant's potential. Rapport is aided by beginning the interview on time and starting with nonthreatening questions such as, "Did you find parking all right?" At the same time, the interviewer may use body language to help relax the applicant. A smile, a handshake, relaxed posture, and moving paperwork aside all communicate without words; such nonverbal communications maintain rapport throughout the interview session. The interviewer has to act as the perfect host or hostess, greet the candidate with a warm smile showing him or her into the office, make small talk, and reduce the nervousness of the applicant by friendly conversation. Only in a relationship of mutual trust and comfort will a candidate talk freely. By projecting an image of confidence, competence, and concern, especially in the early stages of the interview, an interviewer can create trust.

Stage 3: Information Exchange

The heart of the interview process is the exchange of information. To help establish rapport, some interviewers may begin by asking the applicant if he or she has any questions. This establishes two-way communication and lets the interviewer begin to judge the recruit by the type of questions asked. Consider the following dialogue. Which response creates the most favourable impression?

Interviewer: Well, let's start with any questions you may have.

Applicant 1: I don't have any questions.

Applicant 2: I have several questions. How much does the job pay? Will I get two weeks' vacation at the end of the first year?

Applicant 3: What will the responsibilities be? I am hoping to find a job that offers me challenges now and career potential down the road.

Each response creates a different impression on the interviewer. But only Applicant 3 appears concerned about the job. The other two applicants appear to be either unconcerned or interested only in what benefits they will receive.

In general, an interviewer will ask questions worded to learn as much as possible. Questions that begin with how, what, why, compare, describe, expand, or "Could you tell me more about..." are likely to solicit an open response, while questions that can be answered with a simple "yes" or "no" do not give the interviewer much insight. Specific questions and areas of interest to an interviewer are suggested in Figure 6-15.

Both applicants and interviewers anticipate a selection interview. Would it seem unusual to you to get a job without having had an interview?

© Comstock Images/Getty Images

As already noted, asking specific behavioural description questions that assess an applicant's KSAs and other characteristics (such as work-shift availability, personality characteristics) significantly add to the validity of the information collected and define the essential job requirements as described in Chapter 2.

Stage 4: Termination of Interview

As the list of questions dwindles or available time ends, the interviewer must draw the session to a close. It is important to set candidate expectations at the start of the interview. For instance, state the number of questions, the total interview time, and when the candidate will be allowed to ask questions (first, throughout, or at the end of the interview). Nonverbal communication can also be useful. Sitting erect, turning toward the door, or glancing at a watch or clock all clue the applicant that the end is near. Some interviewers terminate the interview by asking, "Do you have any final questions?" At this point, the interviewer informs the applicant of the next step in the interview process, which may be to wait for a call or email.

Stage 5: Evaluation

Immediately after the interview ends, the interviewer should record the candidate's specific answers and general questions.

Interviewer Errors

Caution must be exercised to avoid some common **interviewer errors**, summarized in Figure 6-16, that decrease the effectiveness of the interview. When the applicant is judged based on interviewer errors or other personal biases, it reduces the validity and reliability of the interview and the results of the interview are misinterpreted. Applicants are accepted or rejected for reasons that may bear no relation to their potential performance. Biased interviews merely waste organizational resources and the applicant's time. Figure 6-17 summarizes some major dos and don'ts in the employment interview.

interviewer errors

Mistakes like biases and domination that reduce the validity and usefulness of the job interview.

FIGURE 6-16

Typical Interviewer Errors

Halo Effect
Interviewers who use limited information about an applicant to bias their evaluation of that person's other characteristics are subject to the halo effect. In other words, some information about the candidate plays a disproportionate part in the final evaluation of the candidate.

Examples:
- An applicant who has a pleasant smile and firm handshake is considered a leading candidate before the interview begins.
- An applicant who wears blue jeans to the interview is rejected mentally.

Leading Questions
Interviewers who "telegraph" the desired answer by the way they frame their questions are using leading questions

Examples:
- "Do you think you'll like this work?"
- "Do you agree that profits are necessary?"

Stereotypes
Interviewers who harbour prejudice against specific groups are exhibiting a personal bias based on stereotypical thinking.

Examples:
- "I prefer salespersons who are tall."
- "Accountants are not outgoing people."

Interviewer Domination
Interviewers who use the interview to oversell the applicant, brag about their successes, or carry on a social conversation instead of an interview are guilty of interviewer domination.

Examples:
- Spending the entire interview telling the applicant about the company plans or benefits.
- Using the interview to tell the applicant how important the interviewer's job is.

Contrast Errors
When interviewers compare candidates to those who came before instead of to an objective standard.

Examples:
- "This candidate did a better job responding to this question than that guy yesterday."

    "Of the three candidates we've seen, I like the second one best. I wonder how the next candidate will compare?

FIGURE 6-17

Some Do's and Don'ts of Conducting Employment Interviews

Do:

1. Collect only job-related information and not information on general personality traits.

2. Concentrate on securing information about the applicant's past job behaviour.

3. Use several interviewers (to interview each candidate) to increase the reliability of the interview process.

4. Treat all interviewees equally and impartially.

5. Have a checklist of questions to ask each job applicant.

6. Attempt to create a relaxed setting by asking easy, nonthreatening questions first and showing support to the applicant.

7. Provide job-related information to the candidate.

8. Compare your evaluation of each candidate with other interviewers and find out why discrepancies exist.

9. Compare the candidate's responses to objective standards (e.g., scoring guides).

Do Not:

1. Attempt to predict personality traits from a single interview.

2. Be guided by initial impressions (or nonverbal cues) and generalize them to all relevant work and nonwork behaviour of the applicant.

3. Allow your evaluation of the candidate's job performance to be influenced by a single characteristic (such as how well the applicant dresses).

4. Be tempted to make snap judgments of the candidate early in the interview, thus locking out further information.

5. Ask leading questions that communicate the correct or desired answer to the applicant (e.g., "Do you believe that women workers should be treated equally with males?").

6. Exhibit personal biases ("In my experience, good sales managers are all talkative").

7. Dominate the interview; rather, use the interview to collect relevant information about the candidate.

8. Compare the candidates to each other. Compare them to a standard instead.

Interviewee Errors

Interviewees make errors too. Some **interviewee errors** may be to cover job-related weaknesses. Others may emerge from simple nervousness. Although interviewers—especially those in the human resource department—may conduct hundreds of job interviews in a year, most applicants never experience that many in a lifetime. Common interview mistakes made by job candidates include: playing games, talking too much, boasting, not listening, and being unprepared.

interviewee errors

Interviewee mistakes such as boasting, not listening, or lack of preparation that reduce the validity and usefulness of an interview.

Playing games—for example, acting nonchalant—is often taken at face value: the candidate is not interested. The candidate may be excited or nervous and talk too much, especially about irrelevant topics such as sports or the weather. Instead, applicants should stick to the subject at hand.

Likewise, boasting also is a common mistake. Applicants need to "sell themselves," but credential distortion—even if just "embellishment"—about responsibilities and accomplishments or simply bragging too much can turn off the interviewer's interest. Failure to listen may result from anxiety about the interview. Unfortunately, it usually means missing the interviewer's questions and failing to maintain rapport. And, of course, being unprepared means asking poorly thought-out questions and even conveying a lack of interest, neither of which is likely to land the job being sought.

A recent survey of 400 hiring managers in Canada revealed that interviewers are prone to making snap judgments about applicants within the first 5 minutes (51 percent of interviewers) or 15 minutes (89 percent of interviewers). These quick decisions are often made on the basis of the applicant's body language, such as not making eye contact or not smiling, fidgeting or bad posture, playing with their hair or face, or a handshake that is too firm or too soft.[79]

Evaluating the Selection

How do you know whether the selection procedures in your organization are effective? How can you evaluate whether they achieved your organization's goals? Even if the procedures are effective (namely, they achieve the objective of hiring the right candidates), are they efficient and worth the costs and trouble?

In Chapter 1, it was pointed out that all human resource activities should be cost-effective. The department's contribution in various areas should also be at levels appropriate to an organization's needs. If the selection system is more or less sophisticated than the organization requires, then resources are wasted. This necessitates continuous monitoring of the effectiveness and efficiency of selection procedures.

The final outcome of the selection process is the people who are hired. As one writer pointed out, the goal of HR is "to get more productive workers who show up for work, who use better judgment, who don't harass anyone, who don't cost the company money, and who can inspire people."[80] If the pre-selection inputs are considered carefully and the major steps of the selection process have been followed correctly, then new employees are likely to be productive. And productive employees are the best evidence of an effective selection process. Some of the questions to ask in this context are as follows:

1. Are the superiors and peers of new hires indicating dissatisfaction with them?

2. Is the selection process too expensive?

3. Are the hiring criteria and practices showing too much variation across even similar jobs and regions?

4. Are the training costs of newer employees increasing?

5. Do managers spend too much time managing new hires?

6. Are the grievances, absenteeism, and turnover inordinately high?[81]

To evaluate both new employees and the selection process requires feedback. Feedback on successful employees is sometimes hard to find for employment managers, since supervisors often claim responsibility for their successes. Feedback on failures is ample. It can include displeased supervisors, growing employee turnover and absenteeism, poor performance, low employee satisfaction, union activity, and legal suits.

More constructive feedback is obtained through specific questions. How well does the new employee adapt to the organization? To the job? To the career of which the job is a part? And lastly, how well does the employee perform? Answers to each of these questions provide feedback about the employee and the selection process.

In the ultimate sense, the utility of a selection procedure is decided by looking at the quality and productivity of the workforce hired and the costs incurred in the process. An elaborate human resource audit is sometimes attempted.[82] The costs include not only the out-of-pocket costs (such as costs of testing, interviewing, postage, and stationery), but also the costs associated with errors in the decisions made. If the wrong candidate is hired or promoted, the costs are particularly high. However, an exhaustive look at all costs (actual and potential) associated with a selection system may be very difficult in real life. Appendix A to this chapter describes a procedure to assess the utility of the selection system.

SUMMARY

The selection process depends heavily upon inputs such as job analysis, human resource plans, and recruits. These inputs are used within the challenges of the external environment, ethics, and guidelines established by the organization.

The selection process then takes recruits and puts them through a series of steps to evaluate their potential. These steps vary from organization to organization and from one job opening to another. In general, the selection procedure relies on interviews for virtually every opening that is to be filled. References and application blanks are also other steps commonly found in the selection process of most employers. It was pointed out that weighted and biographical application blanks and situational interviews offer promise as reliable and valid instruments for screening applicants. The increasing popularity of drug tests in several organizations was also noted. However, the use of any tests that are not empirically justifiable by performance criteria is vulnerable to human rights violation charges.

The supervisor's role should include participation in the selection process, usually through provision of valid job-relevant information and an interview with job candidates. Through participation, the supervisor is more likely to be committed to the new worker's success.

Growing research evidence supports the use of a realistic job preview (RJP). After considerable expense and effort to recruit and select employees, the use of RJPs seems well advised as a means of reducing turnover among new employees.

Like all other human resource functions, the costs and benefits of the selection process also have to be compared periodically to evaluate the utility of various predictors. However, this is a very complex activity, often requiring fairly advanced mathematical skills. Notwithstanding, all human resource management systems have to implement evaluation studies to maintain their effectiveness and efficiency.

TERMS FOR REVIEW

ability tests
behavioural description interviews
biographical information blank (BIB)
compensatory approach
computer-interactive performance tests
differential validity
drug tests
employment interview
employment references
employment tests
integrity tests
interviewee errors
interviewer errors
knowledge tests
medical evaluation
multiple cut-off approach
panel interview
performance tests
personality tests
realistic job preview (RJP)
reference letters
reliability
selection process
selection ratio
situational interviews
situational judgment tests
stages of an interview
structured interviews
subjective approach
unstructured interviews
validity
validity generalization
weighted application blank (WAB)

SELF-ASSESSMENT EXERCISE

How Do You Fare As an Interviewee?

This short test helps you assess your behaviours as a job applicant in the context of job interviews. Indicate your behaviours on a scale of "Always," "Often," "Sometimes," and "Never." Do not omit any statements.

Statement	Always	Often	Sometimes	Never
1. Before attending an interview, I gather as much information about the employer as possible by consulting annual reports and newspapers, Internet searching, and/or talking to knowledgeable persons.				
2. During many interviews, I indicate how another employer has expressed interest in hiring me at this time.				
3. I carefully study the job responsibilities involved in the position and link my own competencies and training to each one of them before going for an interview.				
4. During the interview, I make sure that I talk a lot, even if that means I have to use "fillers" such as sports news or jokes.				
5. During the interview, I always maintain my composure and try to project a positive, can-do attitude.				
6. I often "sell" myself to the interviewer by mildly exaggerating my past accomplishments or work responsibilities.				
7. I utilize a part of the interview time to find out more about the job and focus on how I can contribute to its success.				
8. When the interviewer asks me, "Do you have any questions?" my typical response is, "Not really, thank you."				
9. I follow up the interview with a thank-you letter that also highlights my continuing interest in the position.				
10. At times during an interview, I flatter the interviewer and/or the employing organization. After all, is there a person out there who does not like flattery?				

SCORING

For the odd-numbered statements, give yourself a score of 4, 3, 2, and 1 for Always, Often, Sometimes, and Never, respectively. For the even-numbered statements, reverse the scoring. Now add up the scores for all 10 statements.

The total score may range anywhere from 10 to 40. If your score is 34 or above, you are currently doing well and have a general awareness of what is required for a successful interview. Scores below 20 require that you pay serious attention to developing interview skills.

REVIEW AND DISCUSSION QUESTIONS

1. What is the strategic importance of the selection function for an organization?

2. List and briefly discuss the various steps in the selection process.

3. What are the five stages of the employment interview? What specific actions should you, as an interviewer, take to conduct a proper interview?

4. What are the different types of validity? If you want to validate a new dexterity test (which measures physical coordination) for workers in an assembly plant, how will you go about it?

5. What attributes of behavioural description and situational interviews make them appear more promising than traditional interview formats?

6. What is a weighted application blank? How is it different from a traditional application form?

CRITICAL THINKING QUESTIONS

1. Suppose you are an employment specialist. Would you expect to have a large or small selection ratio for each of the following job openings?

    (a) Janitors

    (b) Nuclear engineers with five years' experience designing nuclear reactors

    (c) Pharmacists

    (d) Software programmers

    (e) Elementary-school teachers in the Yukon

    (f) Elementary-school teachers in Ontario

    What are the implications for human resource managers?

2. If a human resource manager asked you to streamline the firm's selection process for hourly paid workers, which steps described in this chapter would you eliminate? Why?

3. A Canadian university has been experiencing a high student dropout rate in recent years. One calculation showed that although the first-year enrollment in commerce courses increased from 650 to 980 students in the last four years, the dropout rate for first-year students has worsened from 9 percent to 15 percent. The university has been using uniform admission standards during the years and has not made any significant changes in the grading or instructional procedures. Based on what you've learned in this course until this point, what recommendations would you make to the university to improve its retention rates? Why?

4. If you are hired as a consultant to evaluate the selection process for salespersons in a large car dealership in the Toronto area, what kind of information will you collect?

5. Assume you are hired to improve the interview process employed by a large real estate organization when it hires sales and customer service representatives. When suggesting improvements, what factors will you focus on? What steps will you recommend to check whether your suggestions indeed result in better hires in the future?

6. Suppose you are approached by the human resource department in a large insurance firm that routinely hires dozens of clerical workers. Of the various types of tests discussed in the text,

which would you recommend? What are the steps you will suggest to validate the test(s) you recommended?

ETHICS QUESTION

You are the human resource manager in a large chain of grocery stores about to hire a new IT system programmer. Because of the downturn of the IT sector, you have received a large number of applications for the position. Mike, one of the applicants, is a nephew of your neighbour Mercy, a real estate agent. One day while you were working on your lawn, Mercy approached you and conveyed to you how "nice it would be to see Mike settled in a stable job like the one in your firm." Mercy knows that you are on the lookout for a new, larger house right now. During the conversation, she indicated that she will find one for you without charging you any commission. You looked at Mike's application and found him to have minimum qualifications necessary for the position. However, there are a large number of candidates who have better qualifications and experience. You know that your employer is making some major strategic changes now that will enhance the information needs of the firm significantly.

What considerations will you have in making the decision? What would you do right now?

WEB RESEARCH EXERCISE

Using the Employment and Social Development Canada website and others estimate the demand (and supply where available) of pharmacists, software programmers, accountants, salespersons, and financial analysts in Canada. What selection ratios do they indicate? What are the implications for human resource managers employed in the relevant sectors?

INCIDENT 6-1

A Selection Decision at Empire Inc.

At Empire Inc. the turnover rate is very high among assembly workers. Supervisors in the production department have told the human resource department that they do not have time to conduct a supervisory interview with the large number of applicants who are processed to fill assembly-line openings. As a result, the human resource department's employment specialists make the final hiring decisions. The profiles of three typical applicants are presented below.

The nature of the assembly jobs is rather simple. Training seldom takes more than an hour or two. Most people master the job and achieve an acceptable level of production during the second full day on the job. The tasks involve very little physical or mental effort. The employment test is valid, but has only a weak relationship between scores and actual performance.

1. What information would you consider irrelevant in the preceding selection profiles?

2. Are there any changes you would recommend in the selection process?

3. Which of the three candidates would you select, given the limited knowledge you possess? Why?

	Applicant A	Applicant B	Applicant C
Years of Experience	4	8	1
Education	1 year of university	Finished grade 8	High school diploma
Age	24	43	32
Test Score	77/100	74/100	82/100
Medical Evaluation	OK	OK	OK
Performance Evaluation	Very good	Excellent	Fair/good (last job)
Work History	Limited data	Stable	Stable
Ranking by:			
Interviewer 1	1	2	3
Interviewer 2	3	2	1
Apparent Eagerness	Moderate	Strong	Weak
Availability	4 weeks	2 weeks	Immediately

INCIDENT 6-2

National Food Brokers Selection Process

National Food Brokers buys carload orders of nonperishable food products for resale to food wholesalers. The sales staff take orders from major food wholesalers, write up the orders, and send them to the appropriate food producers. Nearly 90 of National's 130 employees work in the sales department. Since the job requires long hours on the phone to different accounts, the work is not very pleasant and turnover is high.

The manager of the sales department, Carol Decinni, made the following observations in the presence of the human resource manager, Craig Reems:

Most of the people who work in the department fall into two groups. There are those who have been here for two or more years. They seem reasonably content and are the top sellers we have. The other group consists of people who have been here for less than two years. Most of our turnover comes from this group. In fact, we lose one of every three new employees during the first two months. When I talk with the people who are quitting, most of them tell me that they had no idea how much time they had to spend on the phone. I am generally pleased with the quality of recruits the human resource department provides. But we cannot continue with this high turnover. My supervisors are spending most of their time training new workers. Is there anything the human resource department can do to hire more stable workers?

1. Suppose you are asked by the human resource manager to suggest some strategies for improving the selection process in order to hire more stable workers. What suggestions would you make?

2. What role should the supervisory interview play in the selection process? What information conveyed to the applicants can help reduce the future worker turnover rates?

EXERCISE 6-1

How Do You Select Your Friends?

Consider your closest friend. What are this person's attributes? (List as many items as you can think of including this person's education, age, race, family background, economic situation, interests, behaviours, attitudes, biases, and so on.)

Now consider another close friend you have. Do the same as above for this person.

Consider a person whom you like least at this point in time. Do the same as above in the case of this person.

Choose another person whom you dislike. What are this person's attributes?

Now compare the attributes of the persons whom you like and those you dislike. Are they different?

Now rate each attribute on a five-point scale (5 = extremely important from your point of view; 1 = least important).

Do the ratings give you an idea of your own values? Do you think your friends would value the same attributes?

CASE STUDY

Maple Leaf Shoes Ltd.

Selection of a Human Resource Manager[*]

Robert Clark, president and key shareholder of Maple Leaf Shoes, knew that he had a tough situation on his hands. In less than a month, Maple Leaf Shoes will have to negotiate a contract with a newly formed union in its plant, covering approximately 23 percent of the nonmanagerial workforce. A second and more militant union is due for contract negotiations a few months later. Recently, the firm's human resource manager, John McAllister, left the firm for a better position in Toronto. Despite its best recruitment efforts, Maple Leaf Shoes has not been able to fill the vacancy. The firm ran ads in *The Globe and Mail, National Post, Vancouver Sun*, and *Halifax Herald*. The ads yielded only 34 potential candidates, out of which a preliminary screening had reduced the number to nine (including a current employee of Maple Leaf Shoes). All nine were interviewed by Clark and five were eliminated from further consideration after this preliminary interview. The remaining four were interviewed a second time by Clark and three senior officers. Summaries of the résumés submitted by the four candidates are given in Exhibits 1 through 4.

Based on their résumés and on his impressions of the interviews with the four candidates, Robert Clark made the following mental evaluations of the applicants: Michael Anderson, Arthur Dougherty, Jane Reynolds, and Steven Robinson. Clark felt that each applicant had several strong points, but also possessed weaknesses.

---

[*] Case prepared by Professor Hari Das of Department of Management, Saint Mary's University, Halifax. All rights reserved by the author © 2003.

Michael Anderson: Anderson was the oldest of the lot (observed Clark). A widower with two grown-up children, he had the most diverse background. Anderson impressed Clark as a very interesting, if somewhat reserved, person. He had seven years' experience in the Canadian Armed Forces (with an outstanding record there) and knew several trades ("Jack of all trades"?). During the interview, Anderson came across as a results-oriented individual. As a previous employer noted, Corner Brook Arts and Crafts, where Anderson worked in the past, was about to be declared bankrupt when Anderson entered the company ("for peanuts money") and turned it around to become a successful firm by refining its planning and control systems. In Clark's mind, Anderson was someone who could take charge, but one of the references had warned about Anderson's "need for autonomy in his workplace." Clark felt that personally he would get along better with someone else (for example, Dougherty) than with Anderson. But then, his personal feelings shouldn't play that important a role in the hiring decision. Or should they?

Arthur Dougherty: Dougherty impressed Clark as the most gregarious of the four he interviewed. He was totally at ease with the interviewers and displayed the best interpersonal skills among the four. Not only was he comfortable in the presence of others, but he seemed to have the knack of making others feel comfortable as well. It was true that Dougherty's past experience was mostly in sales—he had moved to human resources after more than 15 years of a sales career ("I wanted bigger and more challenging things to do. You can only do so much selling shoes and steel"). He also had a good knowledge of the shoe industry. His references described Dougherty as "a very pleasant person to work with" and "always offering help to anyone who needs him." But Clark wondered whether Dougherty would be able to play the leader and catalyst role in HR at Maple Leaf. In favour of Dougherty was another fact: his children had all grown up, so he should be able to devote extra time to the new position. This job, with all these union contract negotiations ahead, was going to require a lot of 18-hour workdays!

EXHIBIT 1

Michael Anderson

Personal:	Age 53 years; widower, two children, Jason (25 years) and Jennifer (23 years)
Education:	Grade 12, Belvedere High School, Vancouver
	Two years in B.Com., University of B.C.
	Over 10 Extension courses in Human Resource Management in B.C. and Ontario. Subjects include Negotiation Skills, Human Resource Information Systems, Safety and Health, Employee Involvement, and Organizational Change
Experience:	7 years in Canadian Armed Forces; honorary discharge; outstanding record
	4 years, Production Scheduler, Corner Brook Arts & Crafts Ltd., Newfoundland
	6 years, Production Supervisor, Hamilton Steel Limited, Ontario
	12 years, Administrative Manager, De-Brook Safety Glasses Ltd., Mississauga, Ontario
	5 years, Assistant Human Resource Manager, U-Save Groceries Limited, Ontario
Other Activities:	Member, Council for Free Trade, Corner Brook (3 years)

(Continued)

	Initiated Young Entrepreneurs Program in association with a local bank, Mississauga
	Coach for the town soccer team (during the three years he coached, the team won all local games)

EXHIBIT 2

Arthur Dougherty

Personal:	Age 48 years; married for the last 23 years, three children, Jack (22), Liam (20), and Ava (17)
Education:	Grade 12 from St. John's High School, Mississauga, Ontario
	2 years in Bachelor of Arts Program, University of Toronto
	Dale Carnegie course
	Public Speaking workshop
	4 Human Resource Management courses (non-credit) at McMaster University, Hamilton, Ontario. Topics include Employee Relations, Diversity Management, Safety and Information systems
Experience:	2 years, Clerical (accounting), Great West Insurance Company, Toronto
	4 years, Sales Assistant, Classic Leather Shoes Ltd., Vancouver
	6 years, Sales Supervisor, Metro Auto Lines, Vancouver
	6 years, Senior Sales Supervisor, Fashion Foot Wear Ltd., Ontario
	4 years, Human Resource Supervisor, Ontario EngineeringWorks, Hamilton, Ontario
	4 years, Assistant Human Resource Manager, Madman McIsaac's Carpets and Home Furnishings Ltd., Hamilton, Ontario
Other Activities:	Member, Parish Council Executive (5 years)
	Member, Executive Committee for Trade, Vancouver Chamber of Commerce (3 years)
	Founding member of local animal shelter, Wanderbury, Ontario

EXHIBIT 3

Jane Reynolds

Personal:	Age 36 years; single, one child, Chase (8 years)
Education:	B.A. Sociology, University of New Brunswick (Dean's Honour List)
	6 credit courses in Human Resource Management, Saint Mary's University, Halifax, Nova Scotia. The courses were Human Resource Management, Industrial Relations, Wage and Salary Administration, Staffing and Training, Interpersonal Communication, and Organizational Theory and Design

(Continued)

	3 courses (Stress Management, Negotiation Skills and Interpersonal Communication) offered by Ontario Human Resources Association
Experience:	1 year, Employment Recruiter, Atlantic Fishery Products, Saint John
	2 years, Recruiter, Nova Brewery, Halifax
	1 year, Human Resource Assistant, Nova Scotia Power Corporation, Halifax
	3 years, Senior Human Resource Assistant, Ontario Steel Limited, Hamilton
	4 years, Human Resource Supervisor, Maple Leaf Shoes Ltd., Leaf Town
Other Activities:	Volunteer, United Way, Saint John (2 years)
	Leader, Girl Guides, Halifax (4 years)
	Member, Lions Club, Hamilton (3 years) and Leaf Town (2 years)

EXHIBIT 4

Steven Robinson

Personal:	Age 35 years; divorced, one child under Robinson's custody, Isabella (7 years)
Education:	B.A. (Honours) (Political Science), University of Alberta
	Certified Human Resources Professional, Alberta
	Two extension courses on Human Resources Information Systems and the Internet
Experience:	2 years, Correspondent for The Bugle, Calgary
	2 Years, Human Resources Assistant, The Bugle, Calgary
	4 years, Assistant Human Resource Manager, St. Xavier High School, Calgary
	4 years, Assistant Human Resource Manager, Bedford Town, Nova Scotia
Other Activities:	Member, Basketball Team, University of Alberta
	Organized literacy program for African-Canadians in Edmonton (2 years)
	Founding member and treasurer, African-Canadian Association, Calgary
	Member, Organizational Transitions Committee, Human Resources Association, Nova Scotia

Jane Reynolds: The fact that struck Clark about Reynolds every time he saw her was the way she dressed. She was so meticulously dressed and had impeccable manners (she reminded him of his German aunt who was very formal and methodical). Reynolds was popular among her colleagues, except for the finance manager, Tim McDonald, who didn't like her at all ("I can't stand that female! She is always asking me to do new things and she wants it yesterday!"). Considered a real "mover," Reynolds had been active at Maple Leaf Shoes, always working on some project or other. John McAllister, the previous human resource manager and Reynolds' boss, had, however, mixed evaluations of Reynolds' job performance ("She is very competent, I will say that; but her management style can alienate at least some folks here"). Reynolds was also probably quite junior for the position—after all, she had not held any senior administrative positions until this point. Will she be able to meet the challenges posed by Maple Leaf's growth and change? Clark did not know. Clark also had doubts about the wisdom of hiring a woman for the position. Can Reynolds really face up to Steven Mathews, the new leader of the Leather Workers' Association, who was known for his aggressive bargaining? Mathews had the reputation of being a tough, militant leader who was out to get results for his union. And while Clark didn't consider himself prudish, he still found it hard to accept having a child out of wedlock. Do other managers hold any prejudices against her? Will she fit into the team? The references from Reynolds' previous employers had given her consistently very high to outstanding ratings. There is a rumour that Reynolds has been offered a better position in another local firm and may move out soon. Reynolds impressed Clark as very career-minded.

Steven Robinson: The first thing that struck Clark about Robinson was what hiring him would do to the public's and employees' image of the company. Hiring an African-Canadian is just the thing to do right now—no one could criticize you any more about being insensitive to the multicultural mosaic of Canada. Just by hiring Robinson, he could create the impression of being a "progressive employer." Maple Leaf Shoes Limited has been facing a barrage of criticisms about human rights law violations; now, just by a single act of hiring Robinson, the firm could eliminate all those negative impressions. During the interview, Clark had received good "vibes" from Robinson. Robinson, who is divorced, has a small child. Robinson's mother lives with him to take care of the child. Robinson's referees gave him satisfactory recommendations, although not outstanding. Robinson was the youngest of all the four applicants and seemed full of energy and enthusiasm. Robinson was also the only one with a CHRP certification and extension courses in new information technology and the Internet. If the firm is to embrace new technology soon, Robinson will be the person to hire, Clark concluded.

Clark knew that he had a difficult decision to make. To complicate matters, there was not much agreement among the three managers who interviewed the four job applicants. The rankings given by the finance, marketing, and production managers to the four candidates are shown below (1 = first, 4 = last).

Interviewer	Applicant			
	Anderson	Dougherty	Reynolds	Robinson
Finance manager	2	1	4	3
Marketing manager	3	4	1	2
Production manager	1	3	2	4

Clark realized that he didn't approve of any one of the four applicants completely. Each also had specific strengths that others did not have. He also knew that he urgently needed an energetic, results-oriented person. The person selected should be able to deal with unions, redesign jobs to cut down costs, handle the growing number of employee complaints, and manage the challenges posed by the firm's growth. In the next three years, the firm was planning to expand its operations to other

Canadian provinces and two other countries. The firm's management cadre was expected to grow by roughly 3 percent each year for the next four to five years, and the need for management training existed now more than ever. This meant that the new person should be a mover and shaker, but at the same time be able to work with people without offending them.

"A tough problem to resolve," murmured Clark to himself as he sipped the seventh cup of coffee of the day. His doctor had warned him against having too much caffeine in his system due to his heart condition, but this was going to be one of those long, dreary days. In less than an hour, Clark had a meeting with Sam Polanyi, shop steward of the Vinyl and Leather Workers' Union, who wanted to talk about a "serious problem that exists in Plant 1." How much he wished he had a manager who could do all these thankless jobs!

DISCUSSION QUESTIONS

1. Based on the information given in the case, what education, experience, job skills, and other competencies would seem to be required for the future human resource manager of Maple Leaf Shoes?

2. How do the various candidates rate on these factors you identified?

3. What is your evaluation of the selection process employed by the firm (especially Robert Clark) in this instance? If you were in charge, would you have done anything differently? How?

4. Among the candidates, who (if any) would seem to be suitable for the position? What are the issues you should consider and tradeoffs you should make when selecting one of these candidates for the position?

CASE STUDY

CPIB

Canadian Pacific and International Bank

Evaluating a New Selection Test*

CPIB's rapid expansion into foreign markets had necessitated changes in its selection practices. Some of the factors considered by the bank when hiring employees (e.g., behaviour description interviews, assessment centre reports, reference checks over phone, and so on) were either not possible in some of the foreign countries (because of technical and infrastructural difficulties) or not valid due to cultural differences. In one Asian region, this challenge was particularly felt. In this region, in the past only 50 percent of the new hires were considered "satisfactory" by their supervisors. Although the bank expanded its orientation and initial job training program (which now costs the organization approximately $300 per employee), this still has not improved the success rate.

Recently, R. Dennison, CPIB's regional human resource director, attended a HR conference where she came across a selection test that appeared to have considerable promise. The Financial Services Aptitude Test, designed by a large international consulting firm, had a good validation record for job positions similar to those found in the bank. Initial concurrent validation studies at CPIB using two groups of employees also indicated the test's potential usefulness to the organization. The cost of the test per applicant was $30, which included all costs associated with the administration, scoring, and interpretation of test results.

CPIB added the test as an additional predictor in its selection kit. Table 1 shows the scores received by 100 applicants on the test, with a breakdown of number of applicants who were deemed "successful" on the job by their supervisors. The firm will continue to use its orientation and training program for all its selected employees.

TABLE 1

Financial Services Aptitude Test: Scores of "Successful" and "Unsuccessful" Candidates (n = 100)

Score	Number of Persons Who Received This Test Score	Number of Persons Deemed "Successful"	Number of Persons Deemed "Unsuccessful"
10	4	—	4
20	5	—	5
30	9	—	9
40	12	2	10
50	14	5	9
60	13	6	7
70	15	9	6
80	13	13	—
90	8	8	—
100	7	7	—
Total	100	50	50

Assume that the distribution of the test scores and "success rates" for the next 100 applicants will follow similar patterns as indicated in Table 1. At present, the firm wants to use these test results to fill 40 existing vacancies in the region.

DISCUSSION QUESTIONS

1. Calculate the cut-off test score that will minimize the overall cost of testing plus training.

2. To get 40 "successful" employees, how many persons will have to be hired who have:

   (a) a score of 70 or higher on the test?

   (b) a score of 60 or higher on the test?

3. What suggestions will you make to the bank in validating and using the above test?

PART-ENDING VIDEOS

Workwell Training: Harassment

SOURCE: © Workwell Training.

Manager's Hot Seat: "Beck 'N Call"

SOURCE: © MHHE Management Library.

"Scarf Eve"

SOURCE: The *National*, February 9, 2004, running time 9:11.

Go to Connect to access the videos.

ROLE-PLAY 3: IMPORTANCE OF HR MANAGEMENT ACTIVITIES

Time required: 40–50 minutes

OBJECTIVES OF THE ROLE-PLAY

1. To help the students understand the steps in conducting a behavioural interview.
2. To enhance their skills as interviewers.
3. To help them prepare for their role as interviewees.

PRIOR PREPARATION

1. Study Chapter 6 of the text.
2. Read descriptions of Maple Leaf Shoes Ltd. at the ends of Chapters 1, 2, and 6.

GUIDELINES FOR CONDUCTING THE ROLE-PLAY

In this role-play, Robert Clark is interviewing Jane Reynolds for the position of Human Resource Manager in the firm.

1. Two students, one for the role of Jane Reynolds and the other for Robert Clark, should be identified.
2. Students should read their own descriptions below along with the company details given at the ends of Chapters 1 and 2.
3. The instructor should signal the beginning and the end of the meeting. The interview will last about 25 minutes.
4. The remainder of the class time is used for discussion of the behaviours during the role-play and outcomes.

5. Observers should be asked to make notes against the questions listed below and discuss their findings at the end of the role-play.

6. Instructor should sum up by highlighting the importance of behaviourally based interviews to improve their reliability.

INSTRUCTIONS FOR OBSERVERS

As you observe the meeting between Jane Reynolds and Robert Clark, make notes against each of the questions below. Pay particular attention to the behaviours and verbal and nonverbal expressions of each person.

1. Were the two of them well prepared for the interview? Why?

2. How did Robert Clark begin the meeting?

3. Was there open communication between the two? Who spoke more? About what?

4. Was the sequence of his questions appropriate? Were the questions behavioural in nature? What could have been done better?

5. Did Jane present herself well during the interview? How? What would you do differently if you were Jane?

6. What is your assessment of the nonverbal behaviours of the interviewer and the interviewee? What changes would you recommend to each?

7. What other improvements to the interview would you recommend?

APPENDIX A

Utility Analysis

The utility of a selection procedure should be assessed only after considering a number of factors. The more important ones among these are (1) the validity of the predictor; (2) the variability in job performance; (3) the selection ratio; (4) the base rate of job success; and (5) selection costs.

1. VALIDITY OF THE PREDICTOR

Different predictors have differing validity coefficients. One study by Hunter and Hunter[83] showed that predictors such as tests and assessment centres had average validities in the range of .43 to .54, while others such as reference checks (.26) and interviews (.14) were much lower. Of course, when choosing between predictors with equal validity, the cost of the predictor becomes an important consideration; however, as one writer noted, the trade-off between the cost of a predictor and its validity should almost always be resolved in favour of validity.[84] This is because the potential cost of an error in the course of the test is extremely high.

2. VARIABILITY IN JOB PERFORMANCE

A useful measure of a job's value to the organization is the variability of job performance for a job expressed in dollar terms. For some jobs, the differences in performance ranges (example: "outstanding" to "totally incompetent") have relatively little effect in terms of dollar value to the organization. For example, the variability of performance of a receptionist or window cleaner is relatively less significant to the organization than that of a production planner or marketing manager.

Thus, a "good" receptionist may contribute, say, $6,000 over his or her salary and benefits to the organization, while a "poor" one may cost the firm, say, $2,000 in terms of lost sales because of disgruntled customers who have had bad experiences when paying visits to the organization. In the case of a marketing manager, the effects of outcomes may be far more serious. A good marketing manager may contribute $500,000 above his or her salary and benefits, while a poor one may cost the firm $200,000 in lost sales or decreased market share. The variability in performance in dollar terms for the receptionist is about $8,000; for the marketing manager's position, the corresponding figure may be $700,000. The statistical index used for computing this type of variability is the standard deviation of performance. Hunter and Schmidt's[85] research led them to conclude that a "40 percent rule" prevails for most common job positions—namely, the variability in job performance is typically 40 percent of the average annual salary of a position. Clearly, in the above example, an organization is more likely to spend $5,000 on improving the selection procedures for its marketing manager than for the receptionist.

3. SELECTION RATIO

As already mentioned in this chapter, a large selection ratio (such as 1:25) means that the firm can afford to be choosy, while a small ratio of 1:2 does not give much freedom to the organization to make selection decisions. On the one hand, a ratio such as 1:25 means that a large number of applicants must be tested and screened (thus adding to the selection costs). On the other hand, it also means that only the "cream" of the applicant group will be selected, thus implying that even a predictor with relatively low validity can be employed.

4. BASE RATE OF JOB SUCCESS

The base rate denotes the relative incidence of any given attribute or behaviour in the total population.[86] If 70 percent of the people between 22 and 40 years old are married, then the base rate for marriage for that segment of the society is 70. A low base rate of job success in an organization indicates that few employees reach an acceptable level of job performance. Typically, base rates of success tend to be high for easy and simple jobs. For complex jobs requiring many skills and years of training, the base rates tend to be lower. Generally, the usefulness of a selection procedure increases when it is able to increase the base rate of success for a job. If the base rate is already high at 80 or 90, it is very difficult to find a predictor that will improve on it as the typical validity coefficients for various predictors currently in use range from .15 to .60.

5. SELECTION COSTS

Selection costs may be actual or potential. Actual costs include costs of administering standardized tests, collecting and processing biographical blanks, conducting employment interviews, and offering money and other benefits to job candidates who are selected. The potential costs include cost of selection errors, as when the wrong person is hired for a job. The benefits of a selection process should also be defined broadly to include not only current benefits but also likely future events (e.g., potential of an employee to hold additional responsibility).

Clearly, a thorough evaluation of all the above variables is a very complex and difficult task. In the past, several writers have offered somewhat different algorithms and formulas to assess the usefulness of the selection procedure.[87] One formula suggested to calculate the utility of the selection procedure is:[88]

$P = (N) \times (T) \times (C) \times (S) \times (Z)$ where

P = increase in productivity in dollars

N = number of persons hired

T = average job tenure in years of those hired

C = the correlation between a selection predictor and job performance (or validity coefficient)

S = variability in job performance (measured by standard deviation of job performance in dollars, roughly 40 percent of annual wage)[89]

Z = the average predictor score of those selected (in standard score form)

As an illustration, consider the job position of marketing manager in a consumer goods organization.

Let us assume that the organization used an assessment centre technique (which had an estimated validity of .6) to hire 10 managers who are paid a salary of $80,000 each year. Further, let us assume that each manager will stay with the organization for five years. Assuming an average predictor score (standardized) of 1.4, it can be shown that the assessment centre procedure would increase productivity by $1.344 million over five years or an average of $268,800 each year of their tenure.

Utility analysis such as the above has been successfully used in a number of organizations and different work settings.[90] It should be noted that utility analysis does not require reducing all selection-decision outcomes to a dollar figure; indeed, what is more important may be identifying all possible outcomes of a decision and weighing their relative importance systematically.[91] The factors identified earlier in this section (namely, selection ratio, base rate of success, and so on) interact; hence they must be considered together. For example, typically the utility is higher with a low base rate of job success or when the variability in job performance is high. However, given identical base rates of job success, different selection ratios can make a major difference in the context of selection. For example, it can be mathematically shown that with a base rate of 50 percent and a validity coefficient of .40, a selection ratio of 70 percent will yield 58 percent successful employees. Keeping the other things the same, if the selection ratio is changed to 40 percent, the proportion of successful employees climbs to 66 percent, while for a 10 percent selection ratio the corresponding figure is a whopping 78 percent.[92] Such interdependence among the relevant selection variables makes utility analysis a very complex procedure indeed. Yet its contribution to an effective human resource management system should not be underestimated.

Placing, Developing, and Evaluating Human Resources

New employees need to know what is expected of them and what their responsibilities are, and they have to be trained properly to carry out these responsibilities effectively. A savvy employer will provide a career path for each employee and will provide opportunities to develop employees to their fullest potential. Also, employees need feedback on their performance to experience job satisfaction or to find out where they can improve. The next two chapters are about employee development and evaluation. As a student, you need to understand the human resource department's role in these activities. They affect you, whether you work in a human resource department or elsewhere in the organization. Understanding these activities will assist you to be a better employee or manager.

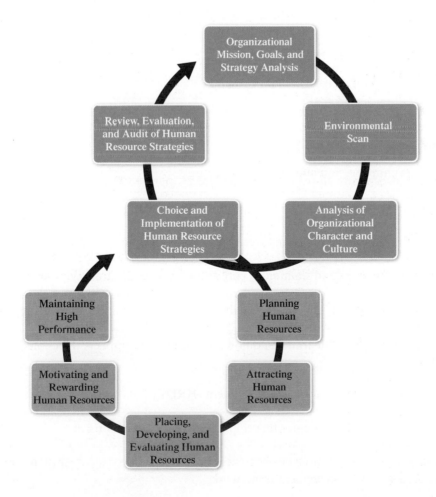

CHAPTER 7

Orientation, Training and Development, and Career Planning

Research and conventional wisdom both suggest that employees get about 90 days to prove themselves in a new job. The faster new hires feel welcome and prepared for their jobs, the faster they will be able to successfully contribute to the firm's mission.

TALYA BAUER[1]

In today's marketplace, a well-trained workforce is no longer a competitive advantage, it's a competitive necessity.

JOHN THOMAS HOWE[2]

LEARNING OBJECTIVES

After studying this chapter, you should be able to:

LO1 Explain the process of onboarding and why it is important.

LO2 List the key components of an employee orientation program.

LO3 Describe the importance of training as part of the long-range strategy of an organization.

LO4 Explain different approaches to needs analysis in designing training and development programs.

LO5 Explain the principles of learning and how this knowledge impacts the choice of training programs.

LO6 Define strategic human resource development (HRD).

LO7 List the developmental strategies that impact employee development.

LO8 Describe how human resource departments encourage and assist career planning as well as support the learning management framework.

Given the significant time spent on recruiting and selecting the best possible candidate, the next step in the process is to ensure that the organization uses its talent resources effectively. That means extending a warm welcome to the new hire, helping the employee to understand the organizational mission, vision, values, and how to do their job effectively, and communicating ways for the new hire to make continued contributions. Once on the job, the gap between employee performance and the job's characteristics and demands may require training. Furthermore, employees may need development to meet the firm's future strategic objectives.

The orientation, training, and development functions seek to match what the employee can do with job demands and tap employee potential for future job roles, while meeting the employee's career objectives. Although these efforts are time consuming and expensive, they reduce employee turnover, help new employees to be productive sooner, and contribute to overall employee satisfaction. The first part of this chapter discusses the concept of onboarding and the key steps involved in the orientation process. The next part discusses the training and development function and explains how human resource departments support the learning management framework. Finally, the chapter will address how the organization is able to assist employees to develop a progressive career plan.

LO1

Onboarding

Almost a quarter of employees experience some type of career transition each year and 50 percent of new hires leave an organization within the first four months.[3] To mitigate feelings of disappointment with their new job and organization, it is important for HR professionals to engage and onboard new employees.[4]

The term **onboarding** is used to describe the strategically aligned process of helping new hires adjust quickly and smoothly to the performance aspects of their new jobs and social aspects of the organization. It includes orientation, socialization, and training and development activities. It begins with the employment offer and lasts throughout the employee's first year.[5] The purpose of these programs is to help employees feel welcome, build relationships with peers and experienced workers, understand the organization's culture, and to leverage the skills and talent that a new hire brings.

---

onboarding

The process of integrating and acculturating new employees into the organization and providing them with the tools, resources, and knowledge to become successful and productive.[6]

For the new hire, the onboarding process builds knowledge of the organization at the individual, department, and job level. It is a commitment on the part of an organization to fully integrate employees into an organization. At the root of onboarding is the belief that human capital is one of the most important assets an organization possesses and that these individuals possess critical knowledge that an organization must leverage if it is to be successful.

Figure 7-1 provides a comprehensive onboarding model that illustrates the strategic focus of onboarding. It takes into account all the aspects of integrating and acculturating the employee from the initial interaction to the end of the first year.

FIGURE 7-1

Onboarding Model

Principles	**Align** to the mission and vision	**Connect** to culture, strategic goals, and priorities	**Integrate** across process owners	**Apply** to all employees

Roles		Process Owners	Process Champions	Employees

Process Phases & Key Activities

Prior to 1st Day	1st Day Orientation	1st Week	1st 90 Days	1st Year
• Extend personal welcome to employee • Communicate first day logistics to employee • Send paperwork in advance and/or online portal access • Prepare for employee	• Focus on sharing the mission and values • Incorporate senior leadership • Orient employee to organization and office norms • Introduce employee sponsor • Meet immediate requirements for employment	• Ensure direct managerial involvement • Set performance expectations and job scope • Assign meaningful work • Communicate resources or network required for work	• Provide essential training • Monitor performance and provide feedback • Obtain feedback through new hire survey and other means	• Recognize positive employee contributions • Provide formal and informal feedback on performance • Create employee development plan

Outcomes	High employee **job satisfaction** level	**Retention** of high-performing employees	Continued **employee engagement** and commitment	Faster time to **productivity**

SOURCE: Booz Allen Hamilton Inc. & The Partnership for Public Service.

If done properly, onboarding can serve several purposes:

Reduce Employee Turnover

When employees decide to join a firm they have expectations: if they contribute in a certain way they will receive certain rewards as a result. If these expectations are not managed properly there is a likelihood of employees feeling dissatisfied and wanting to leave the organization. As a general rule, turnover costs for non-exempt employees are between .25 and .5 times annual salaries plus benefits, for exempt employees between 1 and 1.5 times, and for executives between 3 and 5 times plus benefits. For a large firm, a few thousand dollars may seem inconsequential; but if thousands of employees leave every year, the costs can quickly escalate into millions, as shown in the following example:

> At the Royal Bank of Canada, the annual turnover averages 5 percent of its workforce. Compared to the national turnover rate of 10 to 16 percent across all industries[7], this may look quite reasonable. However, the size of the bank's workforce warrants action to reduce it. With a workforce of about 78,000, this means that approximately 4,000 employees leave the bank annually.[8]

When experienced, long-service employees quit, the loss may be incalculable because of the training, knowledge, and skills these workers take with them. Effective onboarding involves managing and meeting employee expectations. When this happens, both the employee and the organization will benefit:

> Research at Corning Incorporated <http://www.corning.com> revealed that new employees who had gone through a structured onboarding program were 69 percent more likely to be with the company three years later than those who had not.[9]

Reduce Errors and Save Time

Typically, new employees are less efficient than experienced employees.[10] This factor, combined with other additional costs involved in getting a new employee started (e.g., supervisor's time and attention), makes the **startup costs** of new employees very significant.[11] Well-onboarded employees know exactly what is expected of them and are less likely to make mistakes.

---

startup costs

The additional costs associated with a new employee because the new employee is typically less efficient than an experienced worker; the new worker also requires additional supervisory time.

Develop Clear Job and Organizational Expectations

For some jobs, the duties and job expectations are clear. However, for a majority of other jobs, this is simply not the case. There are no clear-cut lists of "desirable" behaviours, outcomes, and attitudes. Most new employees would like to know what it takes to survive and get ahead in an organization. In the absence of clear guidelines from their employer, they may have to find answers to their questions informally through the grapevine and by chatting with others. Unfortunately, in the latter instance, there is no guarantee that they will find the right answers. Effective onboarding is necessary to properly inform employees what the organization expects of them and what they can expect in return.[12]

Attain Acceptable Job Performance Levels Faster

Spelling out expected job performance standards at the beginning eliminates uncertainty about what is expected on the job, as shown in the following example:

> At Texas Instruments <http://www.ti.com>, employees who were carefully oriented to the organization and the job reached full productivity two months sooner than those who were not.[13]

Reduce Employee Anxiety and Increase Organizational Stability

New employees will experience less stress if an organization communicates with new employees openly, clarifies their roles, and familiarizes them with organizational objectives. Communicating policies and regulations to new employees early on clearly reduces undesirable behaviour and friction points.

Reduce Instances of Corrective Discipline Measures and Grievances

Onboarding activities clarify the rights and duties of employees, outline disciplinary regulations, and spell out the consequences of deviating from the prescribed path. Grievances often result from ambiguous job expectations and unclear responsibilities. Successful onboarding specifies both, leading to fewer corrective discipline measures and grievances.

Two activities common to effective onboarding include orientation and socialization. Both are described in more detail next.

Orientation

Orienting an employee into an organization is an important onboarding activity. It involves those activities that introduce the employee to the organization. Formal **orientation programs** familiarize new employees with their roles, with the organization, and with other employees.

---

orientation programs

Programs that familiarize new employees with their roles, the organization, its policies, and other employees.

LO2 HRC 4

There are various approaches to orienting new employees. Some organizations conduct orientation on an individual basis, although group orientation programs are used in larger organizations and firms where several employees are hired at the same time. Some organizations assign new hires a *buddy* or *sponsor* who is available to answer any questions they may have, and to direct the employee to the appropriate resources.

The delivery of these programs is varied. Some are delivered through the company intranet and others through a combination of online and face-to-face delivery. The length of time devoted to orientation also varies considerably depending on the size of the organization. Consider EllisDon's orientation program:

> EllisDon <http://www.ellisdon.com>, a large Canadian construction and project management firm, launched an online orientation program. A thousand employees across Canada can now access the system anytime, anywhere, and proceed through the program at their own pace. The orientation system starts with an automatic welcome message that is sent to the employee's email. Then the employee is told how to access the system and review the various modules at different stages within the first year. For example, week two's module for managers is designed to help with information specific to assist them in managing their team.[14]

For employers that hire workers only occasionally and in small numbers, there may be no formal orientation program. Instead, the new hire may be introduced to a senior worker who shows the new person around.

Formal programs explain orientation topics systematically. These programs are also more likely to create a favourable impression on new employees, which may explain why in a U.S. survey 72 percent of firms had formal programs.[15] A Canadian study showed that roughly 10 percent of orientations lasted one hour, but 51 percent took a day or longer. The same study reported that more than two-thirds of the firms conducted the orientation immediately after the employee reported to work.[16] There is ample research showing that formal orientation programs provide a myriad of favourable outcomes.[17]

A typical orientation program focuses on three main areas: organizational aspects, HR related policies and practices, and role expectations and performance. See Figure 7-2 for an overview of the content covered in each of these areas.

FIGURE 7-2

Topics Often Covered in Employee Orientation Programs

Organizational Issues	
History of employer	Product line or services provided
Organizational structure	Customers and competitors
Names and titles of key executives	Overview of production process
Employee's title and department	Company policies and rules
Layout of physical facilities	Disciplinary regulations
Probationary period	Safety procedures and enforcement
Tour of the locations	Code of conduct

HR Related Topics	
Pay scales and paydays	Employee benefits
Vacations and holidays	Insurance, retirement, employer-provided services
Training and education benefits	EAP services & counselling

(Continued)

Role Expectations & Performance	
Job location	Overview of job
Job tasks	Job objectives & accountabilities
Job safety requirements	Relationship to other jobs
	Internal and external customers

Of course, the experiences of employees during orientation can differ greatly. Here is an example of how an orientation can affect new employees:

Caroline Mathau: I reported to the human resource department 10 minutes early. I was told to have a seat and that someone would "show me around." An hour later I was led to an interview room. After a few minutes, the interviewer realized that I was not an applicant, but a new employee. After apologies, I was taken to meet my supervisor. The supervisor screamed for a claims processor to show me around. While I was being introduced to other people, the claims processor, Irv Porter, complained about what a grouch the supervisor was all the time. At lunch, I asked if I could get a transfer to another claims department. They told me that transfers were not permitted until after the three-month probation period. I am thinking about finding another job.

Harvey Jackson: My orientation was really super! When I arrived, I was shown to the auditorium. After coffee and a muffin, we were given an employee handbook that explained most of the company's benefits and policies. We also received some forms to complete and a brief lecture about company policies. The lecture was followed by a really interesting film that explained the company's history, facilities, and how different jobs related to one another. The following hour was spent on questions and answers. We had a tour of the plant and then we were treated to lunch by the company. At lunch, our supervisors joined us to answer questions and tell us about their departments. Afterward, the supervisors introduced us to the people in our departments and training began.

If Caroline's experience is a typical one in her company, employees probably begin work with low motivation, poor morale, and a lot of anxiety. The company is "saving" the cost of orientation, but it is paying a high price in employee attitudes and performance. Harvey's experience was significantly more favourable.

Socialization

An important aspect of ensuring effective integration into the workplace is to help employees understand "what it is really like to work around here"—the values and norms of the organization. This is an important part of introducing the employee to the organization culture.

Socialization is the continuing process by which an employee begins to understand and accept the values, norms, and beliefs held by others in the organization. New employees need to know, accept, and demonstrate behaviours that the organization views as desirable.

socialization

The process by which people adapt to an organization through learning and accepting the values, norms, and beliefs held by others in the organization.

During socialization, new hires are expected to build new relationships with their co-workers, get to know and understand the style and personality of their boss and co-workers, and understand the values espoused by the organization. What the employee learns is dependent on the new hires' social skills and efforts and the willingness of others to form a relationship with the newcomer.[18]

Socialization involves turning outsiders into insiders and helping the newcomer learn how to effectively fit into the organization. There are formal and informal ways in which employees learn about these norms and values. For example, in some organizations executives meet new hires and discuss the values that are important to the organization and the type of behaviour expected. Some organizations have recognition systems in place, which reinforce and reward employees for demonstrating valued organizational norms. Other socialization techniques are much less formal.

Consider the example of an employee being told that the hours of work are 9 a.m. to 5 p.m., but noticing after the first few weeks that no one in the department ever leaves before 6:30 p.m. Although a policy is developed, the actions may be more representative of the culture than the words. During socialization, observing the language, behaviours, dress, and other artifacts at the workplace will provide new hires with many clues on the expected behaviours and norms.

To ensure they are effective, the HR department may seek to gather reactions to orientation and socialization activities and to assess the new hires' attitudes (e.g., overall satisfaction with the organization and the job, work motivation, and so on) and behaviours (e.g., labour turnover, ability to carry out roles effectively, spontaneity visible in job performance, and so on). Tracking the extent to which onboarding materials are accessed as well as cost–benefit studies on orientation and socialization activities should be carried out continually.

In summary, the onboarding process, with related orientation and socialization activities, helps new hires to understand the social, technical, and cultural aspects of the workplace. As new employees are accepted they become part of the social fabric of the organization. Orientation and socialization programs help speed up the onboarding process and benefit both the employee and the organization.

LO3   HRC 1 & 7

Training and Development

As discussed in Chapter 1, organizations are under significant pressure to compete in regional, national, and international marketplaces. To be successful, they must boost workforce productivity and provide quality services and products. A firm's human resources bring a myriad of skills and competencies to the organization and it is critical for organizations to find a way to leverage these skills and competencies toward meaningful long-term contributions.

Many organizations now focus on becoming **learning organizations**.[19] Learning organizations are successful at managing the knowledge resident within their workforces and have advanced capacity to learn, adapt, and change in response to their environment. **Knowledge management** can be defined as the ability to use people's knowledge—the information stored in employees' heads.[20] Managing this knowledge denotes a significant commitment to learning and highlights the importance of HR's role in facilitating knowledge acquisition, knowledge sharing between employees, and knowledge retention. A true learning organization is one that is "skilled at creating, acquiring, interpreting, transferring, and retaining knowledge, one that adapts to change successfully by leveraging its knowledge base."[21]

learning organization

An organization that has an enhanced capacity to learn, adapt, and change.

knowledge management

The ability to use people's knowledge, that is, information stored in employees' heads.

HRC 7

A sustainable organization understands how to successfully tap its knowledge base and optimize its resources accordingly. It understands the increasingly more important role of HR to create processes that support the development of individuals and establish programs to optimize the meaningful contributions of employees.

Recognition of the value that employees bring to an organization has received considerable attention from executives and decision makers and has propelled the **human resource development (HRD)** function, also referred to as the *organizational development* or *employee development* function, into the limelight. The goal of HRD is to establish learning interventions that will enable individuals within organizations to optimally perform current and future jobs. Investments into human capital yield returns by improving employee skills and contributing to productivity improvements. HRD is an integral part of an organization's strategic plan to hone its competitive edge.[22]

human resource development (HRD)

A function of human resource management that integrates the use of training and employee and career development efforts to improve individual, group, and organizational effectiveness.

Especially for quality-oriented, high-performing companies, training and development are critical parts of a firm's overall long-range strategy. An example is EllisDon, one of the winners of Canada's Top 100 Employers to work for:

> EllisDon received an A+ in the training and development category in 2012. The company believes that knowledge is a vital resource and must be captured. At the same time, it recognizes that its employees have a thirst for knowledge. EllisDon has bridged these two needs by developing the EllisDon University (EDU). EDU is an in-house training program offering a variety of courses and programs for all employees, ranging from financial management to conflict resolution to Leadership in Environmental and Energy Design (LEED) certification. At EllisDon, employees receive tuition subsidies for courses related to their position and subsidies for professional accreditations. Also available are in-house training programs, online training programs, online employee skills inventories, formal mentoring programs, and career planning services.[23]

In 2013, the average amount of money spent on training per employee across industries and organizational size was $1208,[24] or 1.8 percent of payroll in Canada.[25] Small organizations with less than 500 people tend to spend more on training per employee than medium and large employers. However, large employers may be able to offer more training hours for the same cost due to economies of scale.[26] Sectors such as health/pharmaceuticals and technology spend more on average on training and development than sectors such as manufacturing. Training and development dollars are highly correlated with the economy with greater spending when the economy is strong and sharp cuts to training and development budgets at the first signs of economic slowdowns.[27]

Relationship between Training and Development

The terms training and development are often used interchangeably; however, there are several important differences. **Training** prepares people to do their *present* job. It is oriented for the short term to focus on the skills required to perform the immediate job or to improve or enhance performance of a current job or task. Because of its focus on improving current job performance, training efforts may be prioritized for employees who are not currently performing well.[28] Little benefit may come from providing training to employees who are performing well in their current roles.

training

Planned activities aimed to provide employees with enhanced skills to perform their current jobs.

Development prepares employees for future jobs. Development efforts may focus on building specific skills, but also competencies for future job roles. It is more about expanding an employee's potential through various learning processes so that that individual can, at some point, assume a future role. Development may be ongoing and occur through many learning experiences. While some organizations may seek to develop all employees, others will focus development efforts toward those employees determined to have the greatest potential.[29] Figure 7-3 highlights the differences between training and development.

development

Planned activities aimed to provide employees with enhanced skills and competencies for the future.

FIGURE 7-3

Differentiating Training & Development

	Training	Development
Time frame	Short term—immediate	Mid- to long term
Focus of activity	Current job/Skill development	Future roles and responsibilities/Competencies development, multiple learning experiences
Range	Individual	Group/organization
Goal	Enhance skills in current job	Optimize potential—future developmental/growth opportunities
Examples of methods used	Programmed instruction, role plays, job shadowing, simulation, self-study	Coaching, counselling, mentoring, conferences, case study, simulations, job rotations

This distinction between training and development is primarily one of intent, with training focusing on the present job and development focusing on the future contributions that an employee will make. It can be concluded that the *benefits of training* extend throughout a person's entire career and help develop that person for future responsibilities.

Training

As discussed, training is an investment in human capital. Canadian companies have to compete in a global economy and in a fast-changing business environment. This requires a workforce with the capability to respond quickly and reliably to new challenges. In turn, this makes training an important part of an organization's long-range strategy. Examples of the new requirements for survival include the following:

- Competing globally against companies from countries with low wage levels has forced many Canadian companies to flatten their organizational structure and to reduce the number of employees. A flatter organization—with fewer managers and supervisors—requires employees who are able to schedule their work, manage their team, and do their own quality control. Greater flexibility requires multiskilled (or cross-trained) employees who perform diverse tasks.

- Multiskilled employees prefer to be paid according to their competencies, not jobs performed. This requires a match to the company's compensation and performance appraisal systems. Multiskilled employees have to keep up-to-date on their skills and continue a lifelong learning process. The organizational environment must foster and support this new concept.

- Many immigrants come to Canada annually, mostly from Asian countries. This makes it essential that organizations understand the specific training needs of these new arrivals, and that Canadian managers learn to work with colleagues who hold different cultural values. Diversity training helps to alert supervisors and employees to the use of stereotypes and prejudices.

- Changing information technology and mobile technology applications, innovative multimedia training methods, the use of the Internet and intranets, and high-tech video- and web-conferencing technology require fresh skills, necessitating novel training programs and strategies.

HRC 7

The Training System

An effective training program benefits employees and the organization. Some of the benefits for the employees are skill improvement, self-development and stronger self-confidence, more effective handling of stress and conflicts, and a sense of growth. For the organization, the benefits may include improved profitability through higher productivity, improved morale, better corporate image, lower costs, stronger identification with corporate goals, and lower demands for managing poor performers including involuntary turnover.

To develop an effective training program, human resource specialists and managers must assess the needs, objectives, content, and learning principles associated with training. Figure 7-4 shows a training systems approach that describes the sequence of events to be followed before training begins.

FIGURE 7-4

A Training Systems Approach: Preliminary Steps in Preparing a Training Program

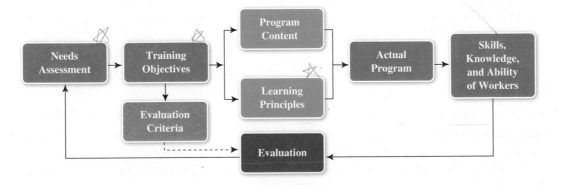

LO4 HRC 7

Needs Assessment

It is estimated that the cost of industrial training in Canada is around $4 billion annually, while federal and provincial governments spend over $40 billion on training and education.[30] To get maximum benefit from this staggering expenditure, HRD must concentrate on people and situations that can benefit most. **Needs assessment** diagnoses present problems and environmental challenges that can be met through training, or the future challenges to be met through long-term development. For example, changes in the external environment may present an organization with new challenges. The comments of one training director illustrate the impact of the external environment:

> Because of human rights legislation, we have to train every interviewer in the human resource department. This training is needed to ensure that our interviewers are not asking questions that might violate federal or provincial laws. When managers in other departments heard of the training, they, too, wanted to sign up. What was to be a one-time seminar became a monthly session for nearly three years. We evaluated the requests of these other managers and decided that they interviewed recruits and that they should be trained also.

---

needs assessment

 A diagnosis that presents problems and future challenges that can be met through training or development.

Sometimes a change in the organization's strategy can create a need for training. For example, new products or services usually require employees to learn new procedures. Sales personnel, programmers, and production workers have to be trained to produce, sell, and service a new product line. Training can also be used when high accident rates, low morale and motivation, or other problems are diagnosed.

Regardless of these challenges, needs assessment must consider each person. Needs may be determined by the HRD function, supervisors, or self-nomination. HRD specialists may find weaknesses among those who are hired or promoted. Supervisors are another source of recommendations for training. However, supervisors may suggest training to banish troublemakers, "hide" surplus employees who are temporarily expendable, or reward good workers. Because these are not valid reasons for training, the HRD specialists often review supervisory recommendations. Likewise, HR may also review self-nominations to determine whether training is actually needed.

Trainers are alert to other sources of information that may indicate a need for training. Production records, quality control reports, grievances, safety reports, absenteeism and turnover statistics, and exit interviews may indicate problems that should be addressed through training and development efforts. Training needs may also become apparent from career planning and development discussions or performance appraisal reviews, which will be discussed in Chapter 8. Regardless of how needs assessment takes place, it is important because the success of the remaining steps in Figure 7-4 depends on an accurate assessment. If the trainer's assessment of needs is not correct, training objectives and program content will not match.

Training Objectives

An evaluation of training needs results in training objectives. These statements serve as the standard against which individual performance and the program can be measured. These objectives should state the:

- Desired behaviour;
- Conditions under which training is to occur; and
- Acceptable performance criteria.

For example, the training objectives for an airline reservation agent might be stated as follows:

1. Provide flight information to call-in customers within 30 seconds.
2. Complete a one-city, round-trip reservation in 120 seconds after all information is obtained from the customer.

Objectives such as these give the trainer and the trainee specific goals that can be used by both to evaluate their success. If these objectives are not met, failure gives the human resource department feedback on the program and the participants.

Soldiers in the armed forces go through intensive and vigorous training exercises with clear training objectives. Should the training and acceptable performance criteria be the same for men and women?

CORBIS

Program Content

The program's content is shaped by the needs assessment and the learning objectives. This content may seek to teach specific skills, provide needed knowledge, or try to influence attitudes. Whatever the content, the program must meet the needs of the organization and the participants. If company goals are not furthered, resources are wasted. Similarly, participants must view the content as relevant to their needs, or their motivation to learn may be low.

LO5 HRC 7

Learning Principles

Perhaps the best way to understand learning is through the use of a **learning curve**, pictured in Figure 7-5. As the curve illustrates, learning takes place in bursts (from points A to B) and in plateaus (from points B to C). Trainers have two goals related to the shape of each employee's curve. First, they want it to reach a satisfactory level of performance, shown as a dashed line in the figure. Second, they want the curve to get to that level as quickly as possible.

learning curve

A visual representation of the rate at which one learns given material.

FIGURE 7-5

A Typical Learning Curve

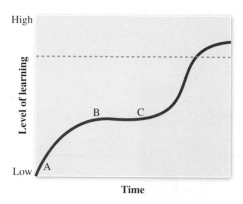

Although the rate at which an individual learns depends upon the person, the use of various learning principles helps speed up the learning process. **Learning principles** are guidelines to the ways in which people learn most effectively. The more they are included in training, the more effective training is likely to be. The principles are participation, repetition, relevance, transference, and feedback.

---

learning principles

Guidelines to the ways people learn most effectively.

- *Participation*. Learning is usually quicker and more long-lasting when the learner can participate actively. As a result of participation, we learn more quickly and retain that learning longer. For example, once they have learned, most people never forget how to ride a bicycle or drive a car.

- *Repetition*. Although it is seldom fun, repetition apparently etches a pattern into our memory. Studying for an examination, for example, involves memorization of key ideas to be recalled during the test. Likewise, most people learned the alphabet and the multiplication tables by repetition.

- *Relevance*. Learning is helped when the material to be learned is meaningful. For example, trainers usually explain the overall purpose of a job to trainees before explaining specific tasks. This explanation allows the worker to see the relevance of each task and the importance of following the given procedures.

- *Transference*. **Transference** is the application of training to actual job situations. The closer the demands of the training program match the demands of the job, the faster a person learns to master the job. For example, pilots are usually trained in flight simulators, because the simulators very closely resemble the actual cockpit and flight characteristics of the plane. The close match between the simulator and the plane allows the trainee to quickly transfer the learning in the simulator to actual flight conditions.

transference

Applicability of training to job situations; evaluated by how readily the trainee can transfer the learning to his or her job.

- *Feedback.* Feedback gives learners information on their progress. With feedback, motivated learners can adjust their behaviour to achieve the quickest possible learning curve. Without feedback, learners cannot gauge their progress and may become discouraged. Test grades are feedback on the study habits of test takers, for example.

HRC 7

Training Techniques

Before we review the various training techniques, it is important to remember that any method may be applied to both training and development. For example, a class on management techniques may be attended by supervisors and workers who are likely to be promoted to those positions. For supervisors, the class covers how to do their present job better. In the case of workers who have no management responsibilities, the classes are intended to develop them into supervisors. The classroom instruction would be identical for both groups, but it has two different purposes: training for supervisors and development for workers.

In selecting a particular training technique, there are several trade-offs. That is, no one technique is always best; the choice of method depends upon the following:

[handwritten: Types of Training evaluation criteria]

1. Cost-effectiveness;
2. Desired program content;
3. Appropriateness of the facilities;
4. Trainee preferences and capabilities;
5. Trainer preferences and capabilities; and
6. Learning principles.

[handwritten: ① Reaction ② Knowledge ③ Behaviour ④ Organisational results.]

The importance of these six trade-offs depends upon the situation. For example, cost-effectiveness may be a minor factor when training an airline pilot in emergency manoeuvres. Trainee preferences may be very important to certain employee demographics. For example, the Millennial generation may be more savvy with social networking than members of other generations. New mobile learning technologies may be better suited for this demographic than broader demographics.[31]

Equally as important as the type of technique is the delivery of that technique. Today many organizations are using sophisticated computer programs, applications, and learning management systems to deliver the content online in various types of formats. These formats can be a combination with some face-to-face training and some online training; they can be delivered solely online, all online, or hybrid (partially online and partially in class), which may be most effective.[32] They can be suited for mobile technology (e.g., smartphones or tablets) or even created in a virtual reality format.

On-the-Job Training

On-the-job training (OJT) is received directly on the job and is used primarily to teach workers how to do their present job. A trainer, supervisor, or co-worker serves as the instructor. This method includes each of the five learning principles (participation, repetition, relevance, transference, and feedback) in a series of carefully planned steps.

First, the participant receives an overview of the job, its purpose, and the desired outcomes, which emphasizes the relevance of the training. Then the trainer demonstrates the job to provide the employee with a model to copy. Since the employee is being shown the actions the job actually requires, the training is transferable. Next, the employee is allowed to mimic the trainer's example. Demonstrations by the trainer and practice by the trainee are repeated until the job is mastered by the trainee. Repeated demonstrations and practice provide the advantage of repetition and feedback. This training can be delivered online where appropriate. A common online method is an instructional video or an interactive simulation. Finally, the employee performs the job without supervision, although the trainer may visit the employee periodically to see if there are any lingering questions.

Job Rotation

As discussed in Chapter 2, to cross-train employees in a variety of jobs some trainers will move the trainee from job to job. Besides giving workers variety in their jobs, **cross-training** helps the organization when vacations, absences, and resignations occur. Learner participation and high job transferability are the learning advantages to job rotation.

---

cross-training

Training employees to perform operations in areas other than their assigned jobs.

Apprenticeships and Coaching

Apprenticeships, discussed in Chapter 4, involve learning from a more experienced employee or employees. Most tradespeople, such as plumbers, carpenters, and chefs, are trained through formal apprenticeship programs. Assistantships and internships are similar to apprenticeships. These approaches use high levels of participation by the trainee and have high transferability to the job.

Coaching is similar to apprenticeship in that the coach attempts to provide a model for the trainee to copy. Most companies use some coaching, especially for leadership development. It tends to be less formal than an apprenticeship program, because there are few formal classroom sessions, and the coaching is provided when needed rather than being part of a carefully planned program. Coaching is almost always handled by the supervisor or manager and not the human resource department. Participation, feedback, and job transference are likely to be high in this form of learning.

Off-the-Job Training

Lectures and Video Presentations

Lectures and other off-the-job techniques tend to rely more heavily on communications rather than modelling, which is used in on-the-job programs. These approaches are applied in both training and development. Presenting a lecture is a popular approach, because it offers relative economy and a meaningful organization of materials. However, participation, feedback, transference, and repetition are often low. Feedback and participation can be improved when discussion is permitted after the lecture. The lecture can be delivered with computer-mediation or face-to-face.

Job Labs and Simulations

So that training does not disrupt normal operations, some organizations use job lab training or simulations. Separate areas or vestibules are set up with the same kind of equipment that will be used on the job. This arrangement allows transference, repetition, and participation. The meaningful organization of materials and feedback are also possible:

> At the corporate training facilities of Best Western <http://www.bestwestern.com> motels and hotels, the job lab duplicates a typical motel room, a typical front desk, and a typical restaurant kitchen. This allows trainees to practise housekeeping, front-desk service, and kitchen skills without disrupting the operations of any one property.

Simulation exercises involve a mechanical simulator that replicates the major features of the work situation. Driving simulators used in driver's education programs are an example. This training method is similar to job lab training, except that the simulator more often provides instantaneous feedback on performance.

Role-Playing

Role-playing is a method that forces trainees to assume different identities. For example, a male worker and a female supervisor may trade roles. The result? Usually participants exaggerate each other's behaviour. Ideally, they both get to see themselves as others see them. The experience may create greater empathy and tolerance of individual differences. This technique seeks to change attitudes of trainees (such as racial understanding) and develop interpersonal skills. Although participation and feedback are present, the inclusion of other learning principles depends on the situation.

---

role-playing

A training technique that requires trainees to assume different identities in order to learn how others feel under different circumstances.

> The RCMP in British Columbia used role-playing exercises to reduce tensions between members of the force who are of Caucasian and Indian (mainly Sikh) origin. Friction between members of the different cultures on the force caused breakdowns in communications. The role-playing exercises required a small number of members of the two groups to assume the role of the other race. The role-playing leader gave each group an assignment and then directed them to carry it out as they thought members of the other race would do it. Through these exercises and the subsequent discussions, members of the different cultural groups were able to learn how their behaviour and attitudes affected each other. These role-playing exercises were an important step in reducing racial tensions.

Case Study

By studying a case, trainees learn about real or hypothetical circumstances and the actions others took under those circumstances. Besides learning from the content of the case, trainees can develop decision-making skills. When cases are meaningful and similar to work-related situations, there is some transference. There also is the advantage of participation through discussion of the case. Feedback and repetition are usually lacking. This technique is most effective for developing problem-solving skills.

Self-Study and Programmed Learning

Carefully planned instructional materials can be used to train and develop employees. These are particularly useful when employees are dispersed geographically or when learning requires little interaction. Self-study techniques range from manuals to prerecorded CDs, DVDs, or webcasts. The learning in this case is more knowledge-based and the employees learn at their own pace.

Programmed learning materials are another form of self-study. Commonly, these are printed booklets or online systems like the Connect and LearnSmart technology that accompanies this textbook. These materials contain a series of questions and answers. After a question is read, the answer can be uncovered immediately. If the reader was correct, he or she proceeds. If incorrect, the reader is directed to review accompanying materials. Programmed materials provide learning participation, repetition, relevance, and feedback. The major advantage appears to be the savings in training time.[33]

Web-based Learning/ELearning

Most of the above techniques can be delivered on the web. *Computer-based training (CBT)*, also known as *computer-assisted learning*, has gained significant prominence over the past several years. The terms *Internet training, Web-based training, virtual education*, and *elearning* all refer to the same concept: training or education delivered via the Internet or intranet. An intranet is a private and internal business network that enables employees to share information, collaborate, and improve their communications within an organization. The intranet is capable of delivering CBT, is flexible, allows for self-pacing, allows materials to be updated centrally, and ensures the content is more secure.

> Singapore's United Overseas Bank has over 500 offices in 19 countries. The bank has initiated a knowledge-based program called "i-learn." It is a virtual campus that has internally developed best practices. It also interfaces with external specialists and a suite of elearning modules created around key workplace skills.[34]

In a recent survey, 73 percent of chief learning officers said they plan on delivering more online learning and 52 percent plan on reducing in-class learning.[35] CBT offers the student control over the pace of learning and even other training contents in modular-type training programs. It offers the benefits of interactive learning, participation, and positive reinforcement during training.

There are many different ways to provide CBT delivery:

Web/computer training—The program is loaded on a hard drive and the user interacts with only one specific program.

Web/electronic performance support—Through an Internet connection, workers have access to various databases, online tools, and discussion forums that help them find solutions to work-related issues.

Web/virtual synchronous—Employees and trainers meet at a predetermined time. Demonstrations are displayed to the class with real-time access.

Web/virtual asynchronous—This is a classroom on the Internet. Here both employees and trainers can interact using email and discussion forums. Class materials are posted on a bulletin board or by uploading lecture notes. It is accessible anytime. Applications such as Illuminate allow students to interact with the teacher in real time and discussions to be recorded in an audio file so that the student can replay the content at another time. About 10–30 percent of training is offered in this way.[36]

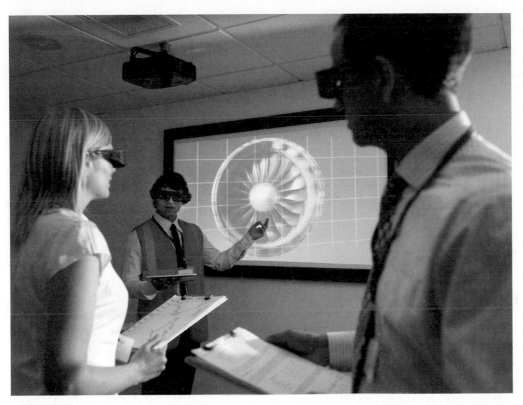

Trainees using virtual reality equipment train in a three-dimensional environment. What types of jobs may virtual reality technology be useful for?

© Monty Rakusen/cultura/Corbis.

Virtual reality also has application to training. It uses very realistic three-dimensional visual impressions of an actual work environment. It allows trainees to respond to job requirements as if they worked on the job, in a simulation. It allows companies to prepare trainees for job experiences that normally would involve high costs (e.g., flying an airplane); have the risk of costly damage to equipment (e.g., landing a plane on an aircraft carrier); or have the potential for injuries to the trainee (e.g., training in a race car).[37]

---

virtual reality

Use of modern computer technology to create a 3D environment.

Simulation provides real-time interactions and a trainee can simulate using many different modes: sensory, tactile, audio, and so on. However, while simulation deals with certain aspects of the job, virtual reality can combine all aspects of the job. It is taking something real and combining it with something artificial. The trainee works in a three-dimensional space and is able to interact with and manipulate objects in real time.

Popular Web-based Tools

The term "new media" has been described as interactive forms of communication available online that make it possible for anyone to create, modify, and share content with others using simple tools. There are several simple yet powerful tools that have been developed to facilitate the acquisition of learning. Some of these tools merely assist learning, others encourage collaboration and enable the learner to contribute to an existing knowledge base. Some of these are:

Blogs. Created by an individual or an organization, training **blogs** may contain comments, graphics, and videos, and are often interactive, allowing trainees to post comments on the material displayed. Some companies use blogs to enhance communication and its corporate culture, others for training and development purposes. The advantage of a blog is that trainees can choose the material they want to study.

> Sun Microsystems' CEO wrote blog entries from home. The blogs were translated into 10 languages and could reach 50,000 employees.[38]

---

blog

A web log—an online journal, diary, or serial published by a person or group of people.

RSS (Rich Site Summary). RSS is a format for delivering regularly changing Web content. Many news-related sites, blogs, and other online publishers syndicate their content as an RSS feed to whoever subscribes to it. It saves time by allowing users to retrieve the latest information from several sites without having to visit individual sites or rely on a newsletter.

Webcasts. Trainers can use this form of multimedia publishing to include audio or video clips that are automatically delivered to organization members or subscribers. Subscribers can then hand-pick the material they want to observe and have future episodes appear on their computer or MP3 player without taking any further action. Webcasting is becoming increasingly popular in education. It enables students and instructors to share information with anyone at any time. An absent student can download the webcast of the missed lesson. It can be a tool for instructors or administrators to communicate curriculum, assignments, and other information. Instructors can record team discussions and interviews and use it even with embedded slides.

> Computer storage leader EMC <http://canada.emc.com> produces 5–10 webcasts in a week for its employees. Using an RSS feed, employees subscribe to their favourite casts and can listen to them on their personal digital assistant while driving to client meetings.[39]

Wikis. A collaboration tool. Hawaiian for "quick," a **wiki** is a webpage with information available to everyone that also allows the reader to contribute to or change the information content. The collaborative encyclopedia Wikipedia is one of the best-known wikis. Wikis are used in business to create intranets and knowledge management systems.

---

wiki

A type of server program that allows multiple users to contribute to a website.

Social Networking Websites. Organizations are using social networks for information exchange, training and development, enhancing corporate culture, and motivating employees. Consider the following examples to illustrate how companies are using CBT to develop their employees and deliver training online.

> The Canadian Imperial Bank of Commerce abolished its $30 million training and development department and delegated the acquisition of relevant professional knowledge to its employees. It uses a competency model as a guide that describes approximately 50 skills that employees need to "provide value to customers."

Employees have access to books and software in training rooms, learn from co-workers via social networking sites, and can take courses as needed. They even track their own progress.[40]

Global Knowledge <http://www.globalknowledge.ca>, a leader in business and IT training, in conjunction with Deloitte <http://www.deloitte.ca>, a leading professional services firm, was awarded gold honours by the Canadian Society for Training and Development (CSTD) for their Managers 1 and 2 programs. These programs are designed to prepare the new managers to increase their confidence and capability. The program offered originality, instructional design, virtual class elearning, self-paced elearning, live labs, and a knowledge centre that included webinars, blogs, mobile apps, and special reports. The programs focused on the day-to-day realities that new managers face and provided them with the tools to manage these situations using technology.[41]

Spotlight *on* HRM

Using MOOCs in Corporate Training

Given the popularity of using massive open online courses (MOOCs) in higher education, it is no wonder that training executives and chief learning officers are excited about their potential in corporate settings. Although a 2013 study of a million MOOC students found low course engagement and high drop-out rates, with only 4 percent completing courses, corporate training experts believe business MOOCs may be valuable and cost-effective future training platforms.

MOOCs at AT&T

In 2013 AT&T partnered with MOOC-provider Udacity Inc. and Georgia Tech University to create one of the first accredited degree programs using the MOOC teaching model. With significantly lower tuition costs than an on-campus master's degree and tuition covered by the company, more than 200 AT&T employees have registered in the MOOC format Master's in Computer Science program.

The company needs more skilled software and network engineers to meet its evolving business in wireless, cloud-based products and services, and MOOCs can deliver leading-edge knowledge in those areas. AT&T senior vice president of human resources, Scott Smith, said "The MOOCs are a complement to the training we deliver internally, and they enable employees to access content 24/7 in ways that fit their work schedules and lifestyles. The format gives us a way to provide additional learning that in some cases may be too expensive to do internally, or when we may not have the instructors or content that a Georgia Tech or Udacity can offer."

Corporate MOOC Design

The key to MOOC success in the corporate domain may rest with motivated learners and MOOC design. Corporate learners may not seek to complete full courses, but rather seek information to address a specific issue or problem they are facing at work. So the drop-out rates that plague higher education MOOCs may not be of concern; learners will engage in the MOOC for only the portions providing the knowledge they seek. In organizations where MOOC completion is desired, some companies may provide "badges" for corporate profiles (e.g., AT&T) or certificates (Yahoo).

The promise of business MOOCs led CorpU to host a summit at the 2013 World Economic Forum. From the summit, a "college–employer collaborative" emerged with representation from 50 large companies and funding from the Bill & Melinda Gates Foundation for the purpose of creating new MOOC models for business. The focus is on bringing the best instruction from academia in leadership development and STEM skills—science, technology, engineering, and math—to the workplace. One of the collaborative's goals is to close the gap between critical STEM skills needed by their workforces and the skills new college graduates have. To improve learning outcomes, the collaborative is seeking to create MOOCs built on the EPIC acronym: Expert-led, Problem-based, Integrated with real work using a connected learning model, or Collaborative social learning.

Open University in the United Kingdom is pioneering a structure with promise for corporate settings as well. Through their design, it is possible to have trainees attend a MOOC with 10,000 people, but engage the dialogue and peer collaboration behind a company's firewall with only the people from that company participating. The assessment and collaboration are done inside the company's walls with the course instructions shared across many companies.

(Continued)

Business MOOCs will continue to evolve as corporate trainers take the best aspects of MOOCs from the post-secondary setting and innovate for corporate training effectiveness.

SOURCE: Adapted with permission from: Dave Zielinski, "Massive Open Online Courses at Work," April 7, 2014, http://www.shrm.org/hrdisciplines/orgempdev/articles/pages/massive-open-online-courses-at-work.aspx.

Benefits and Challenges of Online Learning

Organizations seek to match technology and training delivery and also try to take into consideration the individual nature of IT-supported training applications. There has been a fundamental shift in elearning from a one-size-fits-all approach toward a more individual, learner-centred approach, where the learning materials can be adjusted to the learner's needs and preferences (and even the learner's location by providing mobile access to the learning resources).[42] But is a learner-centred approach a benefit or a challenge?

Developing online training programs can be time consuming, but the costs are usually recovered quickly through savings in instructor time, travel, less or no time off the job, better retention, and higher general effectiveness.[43] The ability to provide "just-in-time" training or information allows the learner to learn when it is convenient; target the instruction to what the learner needs to know, when they need to know it. Online training can offer the learner significant flexibility in terms of pace of content and various media rich options.

However, when deciding whether to offer an online program, the principles of learning, trainee preferences, and type of content are important to consider. For example, if one has to learn a complex IT program, is it preferable to use an online teaching tool or a combination of in-class as well as online teaching methods? Is it preferable to have the content delivered over a series of weeks or one-week blocks? If the content is primarily fact based and can be learned sequentially, is it more effective to ask questions to a subject matter expert or follow the steps at one's own pace?

HRC 7

Employee Development — for future job / career development

To be successful, employees must acquire technical, human, and conceptual skills. Employee development is the process of providing employees with opportunities to grow within an organization. It helps to prepare the employee to assume greater responsibilities, power, and authority. Its focus is on developing competencies and skills that will enable the employee to be successful in a future role in the organization. Employee development does not always entail learning something new; the focus can also be on taking what the employee has already learned and applying it in innovative ways or to new levels of mastery.[44]

Many development programs focus on developing competencies, defined in Chapter 2. A competency approach allows management and employees to pinpoint unique personal and organizational characteristics that make the company successful in achieving a competitive advantage. For example, key competencies for a manager would be demonstrating a "results oriented" approach and development of coaching skills, and key competencies for HR professionals would be demonstrating that they are a "trusted adviser" and exhibit "strategic orientation." An advantage of using the competency framework is the opportunity for employees to understand what competencies are needed to get to the next level or to perform in a way that adds value to the business.

Reduces hoarding

The Conference Board of Canada developed an "Employability Skills Profile," listing critical skills required for success in current and future jobs in three different areas: fundamental skills, personal management skills, and teamwork skills (see Figure 7-6). This document identifies for students and educators what skills and competencies are critical for employers today. It signals to educators to build awareness, practice, and evaluation of these skills into their programs so the students are ready for the workforce. It is interesting to note that the board document puts much emphasis on interpersonal skills, such as communication and working with others, but also on the ability to think and learn, two crucial requirements for the future of more complex jobs.

FIGURE 7-6

Employability Skills Profile: The Critical Skills Required of the Canadian Workforce

Employability Skills 2000+

The skills you need to enter, stay in, and progress in the world of work—whether you work on your own or as a part of a team.

These skills can also be applied and used beyond the workplace in a range of daily activities.

Fundamental Skills	Personal Management Skills	Teamwork Skills
The skills needed as a base for further development	The personal skills, attitudes, and behaviours that drive one's potential for growth	The skills and attributes needed to contribute productively
You will be better prepared to progress in the world of work when you can:	*You will be able to offer yourself greater possibilities for achievement when you can:*	*You will be better prepared to add value to the outcomes of a task, project, or team when you can:*
Communicate <ul><li>read and understand information presented in a variety of forms (e.g., words, graphs, charts, diagrams)</li><li>write and speak so others pay attention and understand</li><li>listen and ask questions to understand and appreciate the points of view of others</li><li>share information using a range of information and communications technologies (e.g., voice, e-mail, computers)</li><li>use relevant scientific, technological, and mathematical knowledge and skills to explain or clarify ideas</li></ul> **Manage Information** <ul><li>locate, gather, and organize information using appropriate technology and information systems</li><li>access, analyze, and apply knowledge and skills from various disciplines (e.g., the arts, languages, science, technology,</li></ul>	**Demonstrate Positive Attitudes & Behaviours** <ul><li>feel good about yourself and be confident</li><li>deal with people, problems, and situations with honesty, integrity, and personal ethics</li><li>recognize your own and other people's good efforts</li><li>take care of your personal health</li><li>show interest, initiative, and effort</li></ul> **Be Responsible** <ul><li>set goals and priorities balancing work and personal life</li><li>plan and manage time, money, and other resources to achieve goals</li><li>assess, weigh, and manage risk</li><li>be accountable for your actions and the actions of your group</li><li>be socially responsible and contribute to your community</li></ul>	**Work with Others** <ul><li>understand and work within the dynamics of a group</li><li>ensure that a team's purpose and objectives are clear</li><li>be flexible: respect, be open to, and supportive of the thoughts, opinions, and contributions of others in a group</li><li>recognize and respect people's diversity, individual differences, and perspectives</li><li>accept and provide feedback in a constructive and considerate manner</li><li>contribute to a team by sharing information and expertise</li><li>lead or support when appropriate, motivating a group for high performance</li><li>understand the role of conflict in a group to reach solutions</li><li>manage and resolve conflict when appropriate</li></ul>

(Continued)

mathematics, social sciences, and the humanities)

Use Numbers
- decide what needs to be measured or calculated
- observe and record data using appropriate methods, tools, and technology
- make estimates and verify calculations

Think & Solve Problems
- assess situations and identify problems
- seek different points of view and evaluate them based on facts
- recognize the human, interpersonal, technical, scientific, and mathematical dimensions of a problem
- identify the root cause of a problem
- be creative and innovative in exploring possible solutions
- readily use science, technology, and mathematics as ways to think, gain, and share knowledge, solve problems, and make decisions
- evaluate solutions to make recommendations or decisions
- implement solutions
- check to see if a solution works, and act on opportunities for improvement

Be Adaptable
- work independently or as a part of a team
- carry out multiple tasks or projects
- be innovative and resourceful: identify and suggest alternative ways to achieve goals and get the job done
- be open and respond constructively to change
- learn from your mistakes and accept feedback
- cope with uncertainty

Learn Continuously
- be willing to continuously learn and grow
- assess personal strengths and areas for development
- set your own learning goals
- identify and access learning sources and opportunities
- plan for and achieve your learning goals

Work Safely
- be aware of personal and group health and safety practices and procedures, and act in accordance with these

Participate in Projects & Tasks
- plan, design, or carry out a project or task from start to finish with well-defined objectives and outcomes
- develop a plan, seek feedback, test, revise and implement
- work to agreed quality standards and specifications
- select and use appropriate tools and technology for a task or project
- adapt to changing requirements and information
- continuously monitor the success of a project or task and identify ways to improve

The Conference Board of Canada
255 Smyth Road, Ottawa
ON K1H 8M7 Canada
Tel: (613) 526-3280
Fac: (613) 526-4857
Internet:
www.conferenceboard.ca/education

SOURCE: *Employability Skills 2000+*, Brochure 2000 E/F (Ottawa: The Conference Board of Canada, 2000). Available at <http://www.conferenceboard.ca/Libraries/educ_public/esp2000.sflb>.

LO6 HRC 1 & 7

Strategic Human Resource Development—Linking Employee Development to Business Strategy

Strategic human resource development is the identification of essential job skills and the management of employees' learning for the long-range future in relation to explicit corporate and business strategies. The last part is the most critical in this sentence—namely the linkage between development needs and activities to the organization's mission and strategy.

strategic human resource development

The identification of needed skills and active management of employees' learning in relation to corporate strategies.

To prepare a pool of developed employees ready to meet future organizational challenges and opportunities, many organizations will focus a segment of their HR department on talent development, or establish a specific talent management group tasked with this responsibility. There may be specific policies and practices developed to manage employees with high and/or critical levels of talent (e.g., knowledge, skills, and abilities) that add value to the organization.[45] Managing development of future talent requires senior leaders to commit financial resources to talent development, even if there is no short-term payoff. Talent development makes good business sense, as these activities contribute to the creation of a robust and diverse talent pool from which the organization can draw when resources are needed. Research has indicated that organizations that invest in their employees have a higher retention rate, employees themselves experience greater job satisfaction and commitment to the organization, and turnover rates are significantly reduced.[46] A recent study found that 63 percent of Canadian executives agree that having talent management processes closely linked to business strategy is critical to help an organization achieve its goals.[47]

One of the key development decisions is whom to develop. Some organizations have focused on developing employees deemed to have high future potential from primarily within the management ranks or in key positions. For instance, the focus is on developing the top 10 percent of employees deemed to have the highest potential.[48] Other organizations have spread development efforts more broadly. There are advantages and disadvantages to both approaches. Those receiving development may anticipate compensation benefits to accompany their expanding breadth of skills and expect future promotions. With fewer positions available at higher ranks, more people developed may mean more disappointed employees when compensation and promotion expectations are not met. On the other hand, some employees may emerge as having high future potential only following development efforts. Talent managers must balance these considerations when determining with top management whom to develop.[49]

A recent survey found that 67 percent of the respondents noted senior leadership as a key talent segment. The respondents identified other talent segments as follows: 61 percent indicated mid-level potential leaders, 59 percent indicated high performers, 55 percent indicated key contributors/technical experts, 48 percent identified those in roles critical to delivering the business strategy, and 36 percent indicated employees whose skills are in short supply and high demand.[50] Talent shortages, retention of high performers, and ensuring that an organization optimizes its knowledge base are all critical factors to consider when determining who should be developed to maintain organizational sustainability.

Steps to Create Employee Development Plans (EDP)

There are several steps to consider when developing an employee development plan, as outlined below:

1. **Assess employees' needs.** The first step toward creating a plan is to understand the employee's interests and the type of work they are most interested in doing. To obtain information about employees' needs, HR managers have access to several sources. An employee's performance

appraisal is one, using an assessment centre that would provide interest and ability testing another. A third is engaging the employee in a career planning discussion.

2. **Link competencies and skills to business goals.** Organizations seek to develop employees in accord with their business goals. In other words, the organization should benefit from the development. For example, if the organization seeks to implement a new system, and an employee has good project management skills and wants to develop them in a larger scope, then the organization will be interested in helping to develop such skills. Typically, an objective is written and measurable terms specified. For example, "Julie needs to learn to manage projects greater than $1 million in revenue by the first quarter of next year."

3. **Identify learning and development activities.** This relates to what activities and learning methods the organization chooses to offer. To choose applicable methods, the HR or talent manager must consider the type of development that would be appropriate.

4. **Determine resources.** This step focuses on who will be involved, costs, time, and what support is needed to ensure success.

5. **Identify barriers.** As with any plan there may be obstacles. Consideration must be given to any hurdles that the employee may face and how best to manage them.[51]

LO7 HRC 7

Developmental Strategies—Identifying Learning and Development Activities

The types of development activities to offer will depend on whether the areas to develop are cognitive, behavioural, or environmental in nature.[52] Figure 7-7 describes examples of instruments and programs that are used in each developmental strategy.

FIGURE 7-7

Training and Development Strategies

Strategies	Definition	Instruments/Programs
Cognitive	Being concerned with altering thoughts and ideas (knowledge, new processes).	Articles, lectures, videos, university courses, management seminars _least effective ; most passive method_
Behavioural	Attempts to change behaviour (e.g., management/interpersonal style).	Role-playing, behaviour modelling, Leadership Grid, sensitivity training, outdoor adventures, team building, mentoring, coaching
Environmental	Strategies to change attitudes and values.	Job rotation, organizational development, the learning organization concept, temporary assignments, employee exchange programs, matrix management, project team, internal consulting, cross-cultural management training

most promising, hard to implement (because involves changing environment))

The *cognitive strategy* is part of the ongoing information-sharing process necessary in an "organic" organization, the adaptable skills needed in a fast-changing business environment. Cognitive development implies constant learning and upgrading, principles strongly advocated in the learning organization concept discussed in this chapter.

The cognitive strategy is probably the least effective in employee development. The methods used are relatively passive: lectures, seminars, and academic education. While this approach tends to increase the knowledge and expertise of individuals, it does little to change a person's behaviour, attitudes, and values—important elements of an employee's development. This approach fulfills at least part of the definition of employee development: it adds to the value of the person. However, increased knowledge and expertise are necessary, but not sufficient, attributes of an effective employee. Unfortunately, this seems to be the dominant strategy in employee development.

The ideal organizational setting continuously reinforces desirable behaviour, the second of the development strategies. Desirable behaviour includes the appropriate management style (modelled after top management and being part of the corporate culture), proper leadership style (strongly influenced by the CEO), type of communication, conflict resolution, and interaction with customers.

Behavioural strategies aim at making individuals more competent in interacting with their environment, for example, with colleagues, subordinates, or customers. Some common instruments or programs used in this strategy are outlined below:

- *Behaviour modelling* teaches a desired behaviour effectively by providing the trainee with a vivid and detailed display of desirable behaviour by a manager (the model), often with strong social reinforcement.[53]

Many companies are sending their employees on outdoor exercises to build teamwork and trust. How can white-water rafting or rock-climbing increase trust in a team?

© Stephanie Godin/Workbook Stock/Getty Images.

- *The Leadership Grid* (formerly known as the Managerial Grid) approach is an example of attempting to change the dominant management style in an organization—for example, to make managers more person- or task-oriented to increase their effectiveness.[54]

- *Sensitivity training* is considered a very effective method for making managers more aware of the impact of their own behaviour on others or to prepare them for more effective interactions with staff in foreign subsidiaries or joint ventures.[55]

- *Team building* helps team members to diagnose group processes and to devise solutions to problems.[56] There are many different types of team-building exercises. Using team-related activities that take place outdoors or in the wilderness are popular (e.g., mountain climbing, white-water rafting, even surviving in a jungle). The objective is to develop a strong team spirit and to help people learn how to maximize their strengths and stretch their potential.[57]

- *Mentoring* involves establishing a close relationship with a boss or someone more experienced who takes a personal interest in the employee's career and who guides and sponsors it.[58] The person being mentored is less experienced that the mentee, but not necessarily younger. There are formal and informal relationships that can exist. Formal mentorships are established by the organization. Typically, HR creates a mentorship program and there is a formal process as to who is assigned to a mentor. Informal mentor arrangements are spontaneous and arise due to the common interests of both parties.

The behavioural strategy undoubtedly has a greater impact on the development of employees than the cognitive approach. The *environmental approach* is concerned with providing the organizational setting in which employees can thrive and develop. Here is an example of how effective it can be:

The Great Little Box Company (GLBC; <http://www.greatlittlebox.com>) began in 1982 as a small enterprise with seven employees in Vancouver, British Columbia, but by 2005 it had grown into the largest independent corrugated-sheet plant in western Canada with over 200 employees and offices in Vancouver, Victoria, Kelowna, British Columbia and in Everett, Washington. What made the company so successful? Robert Meggy, the owner, says, "Everything we do has to be by people who are well motivated. I see it in the bottom line for us. Turnover is very low. If you've got people who enjoy working together, they don't leave."

Robert's "people first" approach included improving teamwork and boosting morale by applying the principles of open-book management. It is designed to get employees involved in running the company. At monthly meetings, management shares all corporate and financial information. In the beginning, Robert had to explain what a balance sheet was and the implications of a high or low income-to-debt ratio. He wants every employee to know how the company is doing and why. "Everyone works together to reach the same target," says Maintenance Manager Philip Lim, who has been with the Great Little Box Company for 14 years. "The company cares about the employees and, in turn, the employees care about the company."[59] It will come as no surprise that GLBC was chosen again in 2015 to be among Canada's 100 Top Employers.

The environmental approach seems to be the most promising developmental strategy. It involves a variety of methods, such as the following:

- *Job rotation* is extremely useful in developing managers with a systems concept in their decision-making style (e.g., the Japanese system of rotating management trainees for two years through all departments of an organization).[60]

- *Organizational development* is a system-wide effort applying behavioural science knowledge to the planned creation and reinforcement of organizational strategies, structures, and processes for improving an organization's effectiveness.[61]

- *The learning organization* creates a knowledge network where employees can share ideas and learn more about content that is important to their development.

- *Temporary assignments* allow management trainees to gain valuable special experiences they could not have had in one job (e.g., a salesperson assigned for a period of time to the engineering department to assist in the development of a saleable product).

- *Employee exchange programs* have been implemented by companies such as Bell Canada, IBM, and Xerox, and the federal government of Canada. Usually, a manager takes a one-year leave (either paid or unpaid, depending on the arrangement with the host organization, with the stipulation that the exchange manager does not lose money) and joins another organization. The manager, the host, and the parent organization all tend to gain from this experience.

- *Matrix management* combines the use of different specialists while maintaining functional units. This approach is best suited for project management with fluctuating workloads. For example, a company might work on several projects. A project manager will "borrow" staff necessary to complete the project from different functional units. These specialists will report for the duration of the project to the project manager, but will maintain their affiliation to their respective functional departments.[62]

- *Project teams* differ from matrix management in that the functional manager has no involvement with the team for the duration of the project. For example, when IBM developed the personal computer, it put together a project team whose members were independent from their functional units. This strategy allows for a highly concentrated effort.[63]

- *Internal consulting (or troubleshooting assignments)* allows organizational needs and individual development needs to be combined simultaneously. For example, an expert in management information systems may assist the human resource department in developing a human resource information system, not only enhancing the effectiveness of the department but also gaining valuable personal experience.

- *Lateral transfer* is the movement of an employee from one position to another in the same class, but under another supervisor or in another department; or the movement of an employee to a position in a different class that has substantially the same level of duties, responsibility, and salary.

- *Job redefinition/reclassification* allows management—with the consent of the job incumbent—to change an employee's job responsibilities, often to avoid a layoff.

- *Cross-cultural management training* prepares employees to work in a different cultural environment (detailed discussion in Chapter 4).

- *Diversity training* deals specifically with preparing supervisors to manage employees from different cultures. It also sensitizes managers and employees in gender-dominated industries to work with colleagues from the opposite sex, for example in engineering or nursing (diversity management is discussed in Chapter 4).

Spotlight *on* HRM

Trojan Technologies Tackles Training to Build Loyalty and Leaders

Companies are often wary of investing too much time and money in training employees because of concerns these well-trained workers will walk out the door as soon as they get a better job offer elsewhere. But a company's commitment to employee development often trumps salary incentives come decision-making time.

Trojan Technologies <http://www.trojantechnologies.com> in London, Ontario, specializes in the design, manufacture, and sale of ultraviolet disinfection systems for wastewater, drinking water, and environmental contaminant treatment. It needs to attract and retain employees with specialized skills who are willing to grow with an ever-expanding enterprise.

(Continued)

What does this mean? First, Trojan has to find people who thrive in an environment that's constantly changing. Second, Trojan has to provide ongoing opportunities to learn. These include structured programs at colleges and universities and on-the-job training in industry-specific technical skills.

Every engineering employee at Trojan has a development plan and meets with a career leader once a month. Last year, more than 95 percent of the 20 associates in Gary Dénomme's career group were engaged in some kind of training. "Our people want assignments that are challenging and different. We have automated the repetitive work as much as possible to free up employees to do assignments that are more interesting to them," says Dénomme, product engineering manager and mechanical engineering career leader at Trojan.

Training Helps Workers Move into New Roles

At Trojan Technologies, an in-house leadership development program was created for all leaders and potential leaders. In July 2007, 52 leaders successfully graduated from phase one of the program. The program continued in 2008 with phase two.

Leaders also work with associates in developing a plan that identifies the elements for success, such as projects they should take on, study required, and the behaviours necessary to move into a leadership role. Many technical professionals have developed their leadership skills to take on a management position.

In addition, several employees are making lateral moves across the organization. This includes a manager who, with the support of the company, expanded his knowledge through higher business education and moved from engineering to business development.

Trojan feels succession planning is crucial in building the organization's future leaders. Dénomme is building his team to develop them as future successors for his role and others. His role is continually changing and he now spends much of his time working with associates in international offices in Europe, China, and India. The bottom line is "people feel more secure and satisfied about their jobs when they're developing in their career," he says.

All employees, even younger ones, want job security. In a recent survey of more than 27,000 university students (from Learning to Work, 2008), 51 percent identified security and stability as key factors in deciding where to work. And when questioned about whom they would like to work for, the top five companies were the Government of Canada, Health Canada, Google, provincial governments, and Apple.

"These organizations are seen as companies that have a commitment to keeping and growing their talent... This was identified as the number one influencer for making an employment decision by 56 per cent of the students surveyed," says Eric Meerkamper of DECODE, the Toronto research firm that conducted the study.

If an organization is looking for loyal employees, it needs to give them what they want. Right now, that means professional development. Employees view learning and growth as the pathway to a successful and secure future.

SOURCE: Excerpts from: © Lynn Johnston, "Employees put high price on learning, development," *Canadian HR Reporter,* Vol. 21, No. 19, 2008, p. 29. Retrieved from http://search.proquest.com/docview/220810293? accountid=14569 by permission of Carswell, Toronto, Ontario, 1-800-387-5164, <www.hrreporter.com>.

HRC 7

Evaluation of Training and Development—Did Learning Actually Take Place?

Training and development serve as transformational processes. Untrained employees are transformed into capable workers, and present workers may be trained to assume new responsibilities. To verify the program's success, human resource managers increasingly demand that training activities be evaluated systematically.

A lack of evaluation may be the most serious flaw in most training efforts. Simply stated, human resource professionals too seldom ask, "Did the program achieve the objectives established for it?"

They often assume it had value because the content seemed important. Or trainers may rely on the evaluation of trainees who comment on how enjoyable the experience was for them, but who cannot yet determine how valuable it is.

To determine whether the training was successful there are four types of evaluation criteria that can be used to assess training outcomes:[64]

1. **Reaction.** Also known as the happiness or smile sheet, participant reactions are the most widely used criteria in training evaluation. The usual question asked is, "How satisfied are you with the program?" or "Would you recommend it to a colleague?" This measure evaluates the setup of the program, but not its effectiveness. However, it can provide valuable information for the organizers of programs as to the proper training environment, seating arrangement, satisfaction with training facilities, food, and accommodation.

2. **Knowledge/Skill.** Consider the learning aspect—what skills and knowledge were acquired? Very popular in learning institutions (exams), evaluating on the basis of knowledge is legitimate if an increase in knowledge is the intended objective of a training program (e.g., improved product knowledge). However, it can be reliably assessed only if before and after tests are used. Otherwise, it is uncertain whether a high score means the program was effective or whether the students knew the material beforehand.

3. **Behaviour.** Here we look at the "actions" of an employee to assess behavioural change. For example, if the employee is expected to learn to be more collaborative, do the individuals who interact with this employee observe this change? For the measurement of behaviour change, self-reports and observations by others are used (e.g., neutral observers, superiors, peers, subordinates, or customers). Supervisor observation of behaviour change is more effective, but this approach has an inherent weakness. It is usually the supervisor who sent the employee to the training program and, because of this, is less likely to admit that he or she made an error in judgment.

4. **Organizational Results.** Organizational results would be ideal measurements were it not for the difficulty in determining the cause–effect relationship between training programs and organizational results. The time difference between a training program and the availability of reports on organizational results can be many months. Who is then to say whether it was the training program or some other event that caused the results?

Evaluation Methodology

To evaluate whether training was effective, a popular method is to give participants a test at the end of a training program. There are inherent problems with this method. We do not know whether a high score was because the training was effective, or whether perhaps the participants were already experienced and did not need the training in the first place.

A more effective approach is the pre-test/post-test design, in which the instructor applies tests at the beginning and at the end of the training program to measure first the precondition (baseline characteristic) of the participants and then the outcome:

$$O \qquad\qquad T \qquad\qquad O$$
(observation/test)   (training)   (repeat observation/test)

Spotlight *on* ETHICS

Was It Really That Good?

A training specialist is asked by his human resource manager to give her an assessment of the effectiveness of the company's training programs for a report to the president, who wants to know "how much bang we get for our training buck." The HR manager was a benefits officer prior to her promotion and knows little about training techniques and evaluation; the president has a sales background. The programs are usually offered in a nearby resort hotel very much liked by the trainees.

So far, the training specialist has assessed training outcomes through reaction measurements, because they were cheap and easy to do, and, more importantly, they tended to be very positive. He suspects that the positive results were largely based on the relaxing hotel environment, but he is sure that the HR manager and the president would be quite happy with this kind of feedback.

Please comment.

This allows a more realistic assessment of the outcomes of a training program. Examples of the two approaches are given below:

> One of the authors recently conducted a human resource management seminar in Slovakia. At the end of the 10-day seminar, the organizers used a reaction sheet to assess the outcome of the program. Although it was obvious that participants enjoyed it very much, nobody could say how effective the program really was or whether it had achieved its objectives.

> A similar seminar was offered the following year. This time the author suggested to the organizers that a pre-test/post-test method be used. At the beginning, a knowledge test and an application test (case) were given to the participants, and equivalent tests were given at the end of the program. The average score at the beginning was 23 out of 100 points; the average score at the end was 66, an almost 300 percent improvement. It was concluded that the training had been effective.

A pre- and post-test design will produce a more valid assessment of training effectiveness.

Cost–Benefit Analysis

A training investment should be treated like any other investment decision and be subject to a **cost–benefit analysis**. Such an analysis assesses the cost-effectiveness of a project or program. It also assists a trainer or talent manager in demonstrating the contribution the training or department makes to the organization's profit.

---

cost–benefit analysis

Analysis undertaken to assess the cost-effectiveness of a project or program.

Contributions to profit can be made through increasing revenues or by decreasing expenditures according to the formula:

$$\text{Revenue} - \text{Costs} = \text{Profit}$$

Training and development can contribute to increased revenue by improving the performance of revenue-producing employees, by increasing output or by reducing production costs, or by both. If training is used to increase productivity, training costs have to be included in the pricing of the product. Figure 7-8 presents factors associated with different training activities. It should be mentioned that companies, depending on industry, spend between 1.7 to 6 percent of their payroll expenditures on training.[65]

Training Costs and Benefits

Activities	Costs
Needs analysis	Labour: consultant, clerical staff
Program development	Labour: consultant, clerical staff Material; office material; video films Equipment rental Other potential costs: travel; accommodation; per diem expenses
Course delivery	Equipment Room rental Food Trainers' salaries Trainees' salaries Lost production
Program evaluation	Evaluator's fee Travel and accommodation (assuming external evaluator) Overhead costs: staff and clerical support, office

Examples of Financial Benefits Derived after Training
Increased productivity (widgets/hr or $/hr)
Reduced labour costs ($/hr or per year)
Reduced error rate ($/hr or per year)
Higher sales ($/year)
Reduced accident rate (days lost, reduced absenteeism in $)

HRC 4 & 7

Career Planning and Development

Inseparably linked with employee development is career planning and career management. To be ready for career opportunities, successful people develop career plans and then take action to achieve their plans. A global study found that if organizations are going to attract and retain talent, they must help employees with their career planning and offer employees opportunity for development. The study found that one of the five top attractions across all generations was career advancement. In terms of retention, one of the top five motivators globally was employees who felt engaged and very clearly understood the many potential career tracts available.[66]

As shown in the following example, meeting employees' career development objectives can alleviate other organizational concerns such as retention:

IBM was losing employees due to the perception that there were not enough career advancement opportunities. Management devised a plan to create a more formal and consistent way of providing people with new skills and connecting them to business opportunities within IBM through a job bank, called "Blue

Opportunities." The program was designed to electronically connect employees through a system with direct employee and manager feedback. Employees were able to learn about opportunities by shadowing other employees as they performed their jobs anywhere in the world and speaking with them virtually about their work or with the manager of a department. [67]

Career Planning and Development Overview

The term **career planning** refers to the process through which individuals become more aware of their interests, needs, and motivations in terms of their job life. **Career management** is a series of formal and less formal activities designed and managed by the organization to influence the career development of one or more employees.[68] Well-planned and managed careers tend to result in greater job satisfaction and career commitment. **Career development** is a lifelong series of activities undertaken by individuals in their pursuit of a career. A well-designed career development system effectively taps a firm's resources and is effective in matching an individual's skills with organizational needs. This matching is an important concept from an employee commitment and engagement perspective as is shown in the relational diagram in Figure 7-9.[69] When employers encourage career planning, employees are more likely to set goals. In turn, these goals may motivate employees to pursue further education, training, or other career development activities. These activities then improve the value of employees to the organization and give the human resource department a larger pool of qualified applicants from which to fill internal job openings.

career planning

The process through which someone becomes more aware of their interests and needs, motivations, etc. in terms of their career.

career management

A series of formal and less formal activities designed and managed by the organization to influence the career development of one or more employees.

career development

A lifelong series of activities undertaken by individuals in their pursuit of a career.

HRC 1, 3, 4, & 7

FIGURE 7-9

A Model of Career Development

HRC 7

Individual Career Development

In decades gone by, employees expected that if they were loyal and hard-working, their employer would "take care of them." The current psychological contract suggests that the employer and employee meet each other's needs for the moment, but neither one is making any long-term commitments. Employers now focus on employability and recognize that employees are focused on and committed to their personal growth. The trend is geared toward having employees create a career portfolio—one that illustrates not just promotions, but includes horizontal or lateral movement, and the ability to enhance one's skills and competencies through job rotations, projects, volunteering and other activities.[70]

The starting point for career development is the individual employee, who is responsible for transforming his or her career path by playing an active role in managing a career. Once a personal commitment has been made, there are several actions that employees typically take to direct their personal development:

- **Demonstrate Exceptional Job Performance.** The most effective action an employee can undertake is good job performance. When performance is substandard, even modest career goals are usually unattainable, because low performers are quickly excluded from promotion considerations.

- **Increase Visibility and Exposure within the Organization.** Being known—and held in high regard—by those who decide on promotion and other career opportunities make an employee more likely to be considered for an advancement.[71] It used to be considered that putting in "face time" (or hours in the workplace visible to others) was required to obtain exposure. Indeed, Yahoo decided in 2013 to drop its work from home policy in favour of more time at the office.[72] However, several reports suggest that visibility and exposure may best be attained through strong performance results shared with colleagues and bosses rather than merely face time at the workplace.[73]

- **Leave the Organization to Seek a Better Job.** Some employees— perhaps young professionals in particular—change employers as part of a conscious career strategy. Also called "job hopping," changing employers every few years often comes with a promotion, a pay increase, and a new experience; however, it may also indicate low commitment and be a warning sign to future employers. While astute managers and professionals formerly used this technique sparingly to avoid a "job hopper" stigma, a recent survey by Accountemps suggests that especially younger Canadian workers believe the benefits of changing jobs every few years may outweigh the potential bad reputation.[74]

- **Demonstrate Organizational Commitment.** Low levels of organizational loyalty are common among recent university graduates (whose high expectations often lead to disappointment with their first employer) and professionals (whose first loyalty is often to their profession).[75] Career-long dedication to the same organization complements the HR department's objective of reducing employee turnover.

- **Seek Mentors, Sponsors, and Coaches.** A **mentor** is someone who offers informal career advice. If the mentor can nominate the employee for career development activities, such as training programs, transfers, or promotion, the mentor becomes a **sponsor**, someone in the organization who can create career development opportunities for others. *Coaching* was discussed earlier in this chapter in connection with apprenticeship training, and is common with corporate executives. However, as *The Globe and Mail* observed, "All kinds of people, from entrepreneurs to new hires to the recently retired, use coaches to move into second careers, to prepare for promotion, to refocus, or to refine communication skills."[76]

---

mentor

Someone who offers informed career guidance and support on a regular basis.

---

sponsor

A person in an organization who can create career development opportunities for others.

- **Seek Growth Opportunities.** By working on a project, volunteering to run a United Way campaign, sitting on a board of directors for an agency, or entering into a management development program, individuals may advance their career.

To assist in their career development, employees expect organizations to provide the following:

1. **Career Equity.** Employees want to perceive equity in the organization's performance/promotion system with respect to career advancement opportunities.

2. **Supervisory Concern.** Employees want their supervisors to play an active role in career development and provide timely performance feedback.

3. **Awareness of Opportunities.** Employees want knowledge of the career advancement opportunities that exist in their organization.

How Do Employees Measure Career Success?

Being satisfied with one's career encompasses both objective and subjective criteria, such as promotions, status, salary, the development of new skills, work–life balance, challenge, and purpose.[77] Researchers have determined that there are four general outcome measures that employees use to evaluate success: advancement, learning, employability, and the evidence of positive psychological factors.[78]

- *Advancement* refers to the ability to gain a sense of power or status, the ability to develop a positive reputation, achieve a sense of autonomy and entrepreneurship.

- *Learning* refers to the acquisition of new skills and competencies that individual's value and see as important in their development.

- *Employability* relates to being able to make money to survive and have the applicable experiences so that obtaining meaningful work will be possible.

- *Psychological factors* include focusing on internal motivational drivers such as recognition, self-esteem, engagement, satisfaction, and self-actualization.

Consider how this Proctor and Gamble employee defines career success after attending a course from the company's business school in Massimiliano, Italy:

"When I was selected for the EFS (European Financial Seminar), I took for granted that I would have had fun, met a group of outstanding international students, and had the opportunity to take a close peek at the work of P&G employees. Well, all this happened. That definitely makes the EFS one of the most valuable experiences I have had so far in my whole life. From the number of resources and amount of time the company spent for the organization of the event, I could see how P&G values talent and looks after its reputation as an employer—we could closely feel the firm's commitment to making us live an unforgettable experience. To conclude, I would suggest even to the most skeptical student to apply for the EFS 2010—the risk–reward profile is nothing, but attractive!"[79]

It is important to note that these outcomes are not necessarily important to everyone in equal measure, nor do all employees possess the same expectations regarding what organizations offer in terms of career planning programs. Employees value these programs in varying degrees, based on their contextual and interpersonal characteristics. The next section will address some of these factors affecting career choice.

Factors Affecting Individual Career Choices

When determining career aspirations and direction, individual values, attitudes and abilities may vary along eight anchors: technical competence; managerial competence; security and stability; entrepreneurship and creativity; autonomy and independence; dedication to a cause; pure challenge; and lifestyle.[80] Researchers have found that everyone has a propensity toward one or more of these elements. When considering what type of developmental opportunities to offer to an employee, it is important for HR to recognize and pay attention to individual differences in anchors and personality types, and to offer employee development opportunities that match. Below are three examples of individual differences and examples of how HR professionals can offer career experiences to match:

Social or Environmental Concern

Some individuals especially value social or environmental concerns (i.e., the dedication to a cause anchor). For instance, a recent study indicated that 61 percent of Millennials (born 1978 to 1995) see themselves as accountable for making a difference in the world, and 78 percent feel that their employer should join them.[81] Companies may meet their employees' career objectives through echoing their social or environmental concerns, as shown in the following example:

Patagonia <http://www.patagonia.com> recognizes how important ecological and environmental concerns are to some workers. In 1993, the company established an employee internship program. Through the program, employees can leave their jobs for up to one month to work for the environmental group of their choice. This program will pay employees' salaries and benefits while they're gone, and environmental groups worldwide get them for free. To date, more than 850 employees have taken part in the program.[82]

Work–Life Balance

While some employees are happy to put in long hours at the workplace, more and more workers are seeking a balance between their home and work lives; their anchor is lifestyle. Offering development opportunities that maintain work–life balance will be important when choosing development activities for lifestyle-focused employees. Read what Randolph Williams, Process Engineer at Genesis Systems Group, has to say about his company's understanding of work–life balance:

"There are several reasons why I like working for Genesis Systems Group <http://www.genesis-systems.com>, some of which include the investment the organization makes in its employees, the balance between work and home life, and the "team" culture in the organization. Genesis invests in its employees and supports training activities of all types that will improve our ability to contribute to the organization. Genesis also provides an excellent work/life balance. The organization recognizes the hard work and dedication its employees give to our customers and for that they understand when we have to balance our home life with work. There is also a "team" culture in the organization. No employee is ever alone to resolve an issue or to work through a tough assignment. There is always a co-worker or two, who are willing to offer assistance."[83]

Personality—Job Fit

One career development model developed back in the 1960s and still relevant today identified individual occupational preferences based on personality types. The model suggests that certain personality types may be well-suited for particular occupations. For example, if someone was outgoing, extroverted, co-operative, and liked people then occupations such as teacher, social worker, clergy, or sales representative might fit. If a personality was more analytical, reflective, curious, and precise, a more applicable occupation might be an investigator, dentist, or systems analyst. In addition to understanding their anchors, career counsellors use this theory to augment their discussions with their clients to help individuals think through what type of work would be the best fit with their personalities. The theory is called the RIASEC model (as is shown in Figure 7-10) and the types are: Realistic, Investigative, Artistic, Social, Enterprising, and Conventional.[84]

FIGURE 7-10

The RIASEC Model

John Holland's Occupational Type	Personality Type— Characteristics	Sample Occupations
Realistic	Practical, stable	Firefighter, farmer, mechanic, dentist
Investigative	Analytical, precise, curious	Systems analyst, CSI investigator, economist
Artistic	Creative, innovative	Advertising, marketing, artist, graphic designer
Social	Co-operative, outgoing, extravert	Clergy, teacher, social worker
Enterprising	Ambitious, seeks out novel experiences	Small business owner, entrepreneur, franchisers
Conventional	Practical	Banker, accountant

Savvy HR professionals will seek to match employee personality with the personality characteristics of the occupation or specific career paths.

LO8   HRC 7

Human Resource Departments and Career Management

As mentioned earlier, career management refers to the programs, processes, and assistance provided by the organization to optimize employees' opportunity for success in their careers.[85] It is the HR department's role to ensure that the applicable processes and practices are developed.

HR managers encourage career development in a number of ways: they encourage management support; they devise communication plans that incorporate HR tools to raise awareness of career options, provide education to employees about career opportunities, and offer career counselling services; they establish and maintain HR related processes that align with career planning efforts; and they utilize technology effectively to facilitate employees' developmental processes.

Encourage Management Commitment and Support

If a manager does not value development, then employees will receive little reinforcement for their efforts. In addition, efforts by the human resource department to encourage career development have little impact unless supported by managers. Ideally, this effort is advanced by the practice of evaluating managers on their ability to develop their subordinates:

> The Ford Motor Company has made it part of its performance appraisal for managers that they are assessed on how well they succeeded in developing a successor for themselves. The company is aware of the danger that if the "successors" have to wait too long for a promotion, they will look for opportunities elsewhere. However, the company has the experience that many of those who move return later with significantly more knowledge.[86]

Devise Communication Plans through HR Tools to Raise Awareness of Career Options

Workshops/Seminars

Conducting workshops and seminars on career planning increases employee interest by pointing out the key concepts associated with career planning. Workshops help the employee set career goals, identify career paths, and uncover specific career development activities. These educational activities may be supplemented by information on career planning and establishing a career planning record (see Figure 7-11) for employees to review and discuss with their managers and mentors. This record can be reviewed once a year, facilitating a career planning discussions.

FIGURE 7-11

Career Planning Record

Employee's Name: Date Record Initiated:

Job Title:

Personal Development Assessment

List at least two major strengths:

List the two most important skills that require additional development in order to contribute effectively in the desired job or to attain future career goals:

Career Planning Goals

A. No Career Development Activity Required: no change; focus on existing level of job requirements.

B. Job Enrichment: current position, more variety through assignments, joining task forces, etc.

C. Job Enlargement: current position, more accountability, complexity.

D. Secondment: temporary move to another position.

E. Lateral Transfer: permanent move to another position at the existing band and level of accountability.

F. Promotion: increased level of accountability and authority to next higher band.

Goals: Now–12 months	(indicate A–F)
13–24 months	(indicate A–F)
Over 24 months	(indicate A–F)

Development Plan
(Indicate the specific development plans or career moves required within the next two years.)
Specific plans / career actions:

Timing:

Further Comment:
(List anything about your qualifications, aspirations, needs that you would like to add to this Career Planning Record.)

Job Posting

Offering an internal job posting process and ensuring that job descriptions and specifications are accurately documented and are easily accessible can be helpful to employees who are thinking about their next move.

Career Paths

HR professionals create career paths and link these paths to the type of training required to move to the next step. They ensure that these paths are available for employees to view and encourage discussion with employees about applicable paths to follow. Career paths are a valuable information source to help employees understand "what their next step" might be in their area of interest.

> For example, consider the possible career paths faced by Leslie Stevens, who works at a newspaper. In this type of work, the jobs of advertising assistant, assistant account representative, and account manager call for similar characteristics. But Leslie, an advertising assistant, may not realize that her skills could be applied to a position that may earn her twice as much. Understanding what type of additional training is needed and which skills and competencies are required to move along to the next level, are important considerations.

Career Counselling

Offering career counselling to employees is another way that HR helps to raise awareness of options. Some organizations have onsite counsellors, whereas other organizations outsource this function. Counsellors will help employees establish career goals and find appropriate career paths. They will inform employees of changes that may affect their career choices and help them explore the various opportunities that exist. The counsellor may simply be someone who has the employee's interests in mind and provides the specific job-related information, or she may be more active in terms of helping an employee by offering options such as seeking training for new skills, accepting special assignments, job rotation, lateral moves, sabbaticals, or even a career change.

In addition, the counsellor may help employees discover their interests by administering and interpreting aptitude and skill tests. Two tests in particular, the *Kuder Preference Record* and the *Strong Interest Inventory*, are useful for guiding people into occupations likely to be of interest. Other tests are also available to measure individual abilities and interests in specific types of work. But to be truly successful, career counsellors must get employees to assess themselves and their environment. See Figure 7-12 to view a self-interest inventory. In addition they may create a career development record to help employees track and document their career planning efforts (as is seen in Figure 7-11).

FIGURE 7-12

A Self-Inventory for Career Planning

	Low				High
Work Interests and Aptitudes	1	2	3	4	5
Physical work (fixing, building, using hands)	1	2	3	4	5
Written work (writing, reading, using words)	1	2	3	4	5
Oral work (talking, giving speeches, using words)	1	2	3	4	5
Quantitative work (calculating, doing accounting, using numbers)	1	2	3	4	5
Visual work (watching, inspecting, using eyes)	1	2	3	4	5
Interpersonal work (counselling, interviewing)	1	2	3	4	5

(Continued)

Creative work (inventing, designing, ideas)	1	2	3	4	5
Analytical work (doing research, solving problems)	1	2	3	4	5
Managerial work (initiating, directing, coordinating)	1	2	3	4	5
Clerical (keeping records)	1	2	3	4	5
Outdoor work (farming, travelling, doing athletics)	1	2	3	4	5
Mechanical (repairing, fixing, tinkering)	1	2	3	4	5

Work Skills and Abilities List below specialized skills, unique personal assets, enjoyable experiences, and major accomplishments. Then check the skills and abilities required.	Physical	Written	Oral	Quantitative	Visual	Interpersonal	Creative	Analytical	Managerial	Clerical	Outdoor	Mechanical
1.												
2.												
3.												
4.												
5.												

Align HR Processes to Facilitate Career Planning

There are several HR related processes that contribute to employee development. Some of the processes are: succession planning, human resource planning, training and development, and performance management.

Succession Planning

It is the responsibility of the human resource department to engage in **succession planning**—that is, to ensure that there are a sufficient number of candidates for key positions ready to take over if an unexpected vacancy occurs, be it because of someone leaving the company, sickness, or death.

---

succession planning

The process of making long-range management development plans to fill human resource needs.

A number of years ago, a small plane with seven executives of a Calgary-based oil company on a flight to New York crashed, killing all seven and the crew. It was a catastrophic event for the company, but the company survived because it had a sufficient number of trained managers ready. This event is oft-cited in numerous industries when engaging in succession planning efforts—and in designing corporate travel policies.

As the example shows, having well-developed employees ready to take on critical responsibilities in case of an emergency can be crucial for the survival of a company.

Human Resource Planning

Designing a robust planning process that considers a number of different programs to balance demand and supply is important for helping individuals plan their careers. Organizations who plan effectively will greatly contribute to the career planning efforts of its employees as the opportunities to move into different roles will be transparent and communicated in a timely fashion. See Figure 7-11 for an example of a career planning record to see how one company connects its career discussions to its planning efforts.

Training & Development Function

As discussed throughout this chapter the relationship between training and development is highly interdependent. Aligning the needs of the employee with the organizational needs and managing the talent within an organization is critical for sustainability.

Performance Management

A well-run performance management program is critical to ensuring that employees receive effective feedback with respect to their performance. An integral component of these programs is to ensure a tight link between performance feedback, employee development, and career planning efforts. This information is invaluable in terms of helping the employees understand their strengths and areas of development and what the employee must do to enhance their value to the organization. Chapter 8 discusses the performance management process in greater detail.

HRC 2

4 ### Use Technology to Support Career Planning Efforts

[handwritten: Intranet / application from robust enterprise / webcasts]

Technology now plays a significant role in career planning and career development. Robust enterprisewide applications have Career Planning Modules where organizations are able to place their career paths online through a secure portal. They can create default career paths and design individual plans for employees. Employees can see what type of training would be required to move up to the next level and what development activities are required and a suggested time it would take to build these skills.

Many organizations now use an intranet for career counselling purposes. The Bank of Montreal's virtual Career Possibilities Centre is a good example of this approach of shifting from employee direct counselling to letting them handle their own career management by providing the necessary tools on the intranet, such as self-testing and workshops on organizational change and how to cope with it. Professional career consultants are still available if employees need special advice.[87]

Many organizations are using various forms of technology to engage employees in career planning. Consider how Deloitte is using technology to help its employees and potential new hires think about "a career." They have several webcasts of existing employees who "tell their story about what they do" and they ask the viewer to "consider where they might fit."

As a result of HR's active involvement in career planning, the contribution that HR makes toward employee engagement and satisfaction and to overall talent management can be evidenced in several ways. Active career planning:

- **Develops Promotable Employees.** Career planning helps to develop internal supplies of promotable talent.
- **Lowers Turnover.** The increased attention to and concern for individual careers generates more organizational loyalty and therefore lower employee turnover.
- **Furthers Employee Growth.** Career plans and goals motivate employees to grow and develop.
- **Reduces Hoarding.** Without career planning, it is easier for managers to hoard key subordinates. Career planning causes employees, managers, and the human resource department to become aware of employee qualifications.

- **Satisfies Employee Needs.** With less hoarding and improved growth opportunities for employees, individual needs for recognition and accomplishment are more readily satisfied, and self-esteem is boosted.

- **Assists Organizations Meet Legal Requirements such as Employment Equity Plans.** Career planning can help members of protected employee groups prepare for more important jobs.

- **Taps Employee Potential.** Career planning encourages employees to tap more of their potential abilities, because they have specific career goals.

- **Optimizes Organizational Potential**. This helps create a talent pipeline, a pool of talent that ensures that organizations have the needed skills when and where they need their respective human resources.

SUMMARY

After workers are selected, they are seldom ready to perform successfully. They must be integrated into the social and work environment of the organization. Orientation programs help a worker begin this socialization process. The organization benefits because training time and costs are lowered, employee satisfaction is higher, and initial turnover is lower.

Training is an essential part of an organization's long-range strategy. If a company wants to survive in a competitive global environment, it requires an efficient and flexible workforce that is adaptable to fast-changing technologies and new approaches to doing business. Canadian managers also have to learn to manage a diverse workforce, made up of new immigrants from very different cultures. Flatter organizations necessitate new skills for employees, who have to shoulder more responsibilities. This, in turn, leads to greater emphasis on employees' competencies, resulting in the need for lifelong learning.

Training begins with an assessment of training needs. Specific training objectives can then be set. These objectives give direction to the training program and serve to evaluate the training program at its completion. The content of the program depends upon the training objectives. The design of the training should consider such learning principles as participation, repetition, relevance, transference, and feedback.

External and internal pressures have changed the skill and attitude requirements for managers. Top management is expected to work with leaner organizations, requiring sharing of power and delegation of authority. This in turn necessitates that lower-level managers must assume greater responsibilities, for which they have to be prepared. It is essential that top management make strategic human resource development a key component in its long-range strategic business plan.

Similarly, if management wants to meet the global challenge and keep the organization competitive, if it wants its managers to be prepared for constant change, new skill requirements, and higher willingness to accept risks, it has to make employee development plans a part of its overall strategic business plan.

Different development strategies may be employed, at the cognitive, behavioural, and environmental levels, with the cognitive method being the least promising and the environmental method the most promising approach.

Once training and development programs are completed, it is essential that they be evaluated. Without evaluation, a company does not know what it gets in return for its training and development investment.

Career planning and development are relatively new concepts to human resource specialists. In recent years, human resource departments have begun to recognize the need for more proactive efforts in this area. As a result, some (mostly large) departments provide career education, information, and counselling. But the primary responsibility for career planning and development rests with the individual employee. The planning process enables employees to identify career goals and the paths to those goals. Then, through developmental activities, the workers seek ways to improve themselves and further their career goals.

Career planning does not guarantee success. But without it, employees are seldom ready for career opportunities that arise. Because of this, their career progress may be slowed and the human resource department may be unable to fill openings internally.

TERMS FOR REVIEW

blog
career development
career management
career planning
cost–benefit analysis
cross-training
development
human resource development (HRD)
knowledge management
learning curve
learning organization
learning principles
mentor
needs assessment
onboarding
orientation programs
role-playing
sponsor
startup costs
strategic human resource development
succession planning
training
transference
virtual reality
wiki

SELF-ASSESSMENT EXERCISE

Test Your Knowledge of Orientation, Training and Development, and Career Planning

1. Because of the importance of managing a diverse workforce, most Canadian managers have been trained in this type of management.   T   F

2. Training programs focus on skill developments.   T   F

3. A training needs assessment includes learning principles.   T   F

4. Training focuses on management skills; development focuses on interpersonal skills.   T   F

5. Strategic human resource development focuses on training future executives.   T   F

6. Coaching is mainly used in team building.   T   F

7. Virtual reality training uses a real-time approach.   T   F

8. A *knowledge worker* is defined as an employee who has scored at least 60 percent on a knowledge test.   T   F

9. The fourth level of training evaluation is called "Training & Development Audit."   T   F
   → org results.

10. A person's career plan requires an environmental assessment.   T   F

SCORING

If you marked statements 2, 3, 7, and 10 as *True*, give yourself one point for each. If you marked statements 1, 4, 5, 6, 8, and 9 as *False*, give yourself one point for each.

Scores of 8–10: Very good! You seem to have a good understanding of the concepts. Congratulations.

Scores of 5–7: Okay, that keeps you in the running, but you may want to reread the chapter to improve your score.

Scores of less than 5: It may be advisable for you to spend more time studying the concepts and their application.

REVIEW AND DISCUSSION QUESTIONS

1. "If employees are properly selected, there should be no need for an orientation program or training." Do you agree or disagree? Why?

2. What are the organizational and employee benefits that result from a comprehensive onboarding process?

3. For each of the following occupations, which training techniques do you recommend? Why?

   (a) a cashier in a grocery store

   (b) a welder

   (c) an assembly-line worker

   (d) an inexperienced supervisor

4. Assume you were hired to manage a research department. After a few weeks, you noticed that some researchers were more effective than others, and that the less effective ones received little recognition from their more productive counterparts. What forms of training would you consider for both groups?

5. What is the purpose of a cost–benefit analysis?

6. Discuss why a linkage between an organization's human resource development needs and its mission and strategy is so important.

7. Explain the differences between the cognitive, behavioural, and environmental approaches to strategic employee development.

8. In what way does a "learning" organization differ from a "traditional" organization?

9. Why should a human resource department be concerned about career planning, especially when employee plans may conflict with the organization's objectives? What advantages does a human resource department expect to receive from assisting career planning?

10. Suppose you are in a management training position after completing university. Your career goal is not very clear, but you would like to become a top manager in your firm. What type of information would you seek from the human resource department to help you develop your career plan?

11. Why is employee feedback an important element of any organization's attempt to encourage career development?

12. Suppose a hard-working and loyal employee is passed over for promotion. What would you tell this person?

CRITICAL THINKING QUESTIONS

1. Before you entered your college or university, you had certain ideas about what your values and expectations would be as a student. How did the institution's socialization process change those values and expectations?

2. Your company is desperately looking for a systems analyst. You know that your competitor invested heavily in training and has a highly competent systems analyst, who indicated to you privately that she would switch if you paid her $10,000 more. Your boss thinks that this is a bargain and tells you, "Get her!" It surely would hurt the competitor. What issues does this raise?

3. You are the training and development manager. Your president calls you in and tells you that the employee development budget has to be cut because of the company's financial situation. What arguments can you use to persuade your boss that development money is well spent?

ETHICS QUESTION

1. **Orientation:** You are about to give an orientation session to new employees and you plan to stress ethical behaviour as outlined in a company brochure. You know that company executives have recently been convicted in a foreign country of bribing government officials. Will you mention this?

2. **Training**: During a training program, which requires taking tests to measure progress, you notice that one of the participants, who struggled in some early tests, suddenly submits tests without mistakes. She is a probationary employee. You notice too that she is dating a staff member in your department, who has access to the test solutions. What do you plan to do?

3. **Development:** Should employees who are to retire soon have access to development programs, if they so desire? Please comment.

4. **Career planning:** You are the HR manager and one of your staff members asks you for career advice on this company. She wants to get ahead and is willing to take courses fitting your company's special needs. You have strongly encouraged such moves in the past. You know that the company is doing badly in its market and has probably less than a year to survive. How will you advise her?

WEB RESEARCH EXERCISE

ONBOARDING

1. **University of Minnesota**

   http://www1.umn.edu/ohr/training/index.html

   (a) Under the training and development tab, take a look at the University's onboarding process. Do you think it is comprehensive?

   (b) What are some of the major components covered?

EMPLOYEE ORIENTATION

1. **Robert Bacal of Bacal & Associates**

   http://work911.com/articles/orient.htm

   (a) In this quick guide to employee orientation, what does Bacal have to say about the outcomes of an effective orientation program?

   (b) What different types of orientation programs does he describe? How do they differ?

TRAINING AND DEVELOPMENT

1. **Canadian Society for Training and Development**

   www.cstd.ca

   (a) Give a summary of training publications and resources available from the CSTD. What type of assistance do they offer to trainers? What are they good for?

(b) Discuss the advantages and disadvantages of the designation Certified Training & Development Professional (CTDP) offered by the CSTD. Should all trainers be certified?

2. **Employment and Social Development Canada (ESDC)**

http://www.esdc.gc.ca/en/jobs/index.page

Explore the "Career choices" and "Training" links. Give an overview of what types of career and training resources are available from the Government of Canada. Which ones would be relevant for you? Why?

3. **Service Canada**

www.jobsetc.ca

Go to "Training/Learning," then to "Training and Careers Features," then to "How Do I Learn Best?" take the quizzes and checklists there to assess your unique learning style.

CAREER

1. **Career Planning**

http://careerplanning.about.com/od/selfassessment/Self_Assessment.htm

Explore the self-assessments there including the financial literacy test and personality type test.

(a) Do you agree with the results/recommendations?

(b) Assume that you want to pursue a career in accounting. What steps will you follow?

2. **Another Career Self-Assessment Instrument**

www.keirsey.com/sorter/register.aspx

Do the self-assessment. Do you agree with the results?

CASE STUDY

Maple Leaf Shoes Ltd.

Developing a Training Program

Maple Leaf Shoes Ltd. is a medium-sized manufacturer of leather and vinyl shoes located in Wilmington, Ontario. It was started in 1973 and currently employs about 500 persons in its Ontario plant and some 200 more in offices and warehouses throughout Canada.

"How can we develop a training program that will have a significant impact on our manufacturing staff?"

Jane Reynolds, special assistant in the personnel department, faced that challenge from a vice president of the largest division of Maple Leaf Shoes, manufacturing. Training had never been a high priority at Maple Leaf Shoes, having always been viewed as an expense item, not an investment. If skilled workers were needed, Maple Leaf Shoes preferred to raid other companies to save training costs. If raiding was not successful, a quick on-the-job training was provided by more experienced employees—limited to essential skills, since there was little incentive for the employees to be more involved.

However, when the vice president attended a convention of shoe manufacturers, he was surprised to learn how cost-efficient some other shoe producers were, especially in Italy and France. Although wages there were similar to the wages paid in Canada, the productivity of the Italian and French workers was significantly higher. The VP found that the Italian and French companies invested heavily in training, allowing them to use cross-trained, flexible staff.

The VP asked Reynolds to develop a training plan, suitable to improve the overall skill level of Maple Leaf Shoes' employees. Reynolds vaguely remembered something about training from her few courses in human resource management quite some time ago, but she felt that it was not sufficient to develop a training program on her own. Besides, she knew nothing about the skill requirements in the manufacturing division.

She decided to ask Russ Summers, manager of the cutting operation, to chair a committee of first-line supervisors to assist her in the program development.

DISCUSSION QUESTIONS

1. You are Russ. Describe the steps you would recommend that Reynolds go through before actually designing the content of the training.

2. What training methods would you suggest be used to train production workers? (First you might ask: What determines the methods?)

3. How would you evaluate the training program to determine how effective it was? (What criteria would you use?)

4. Do you think the first-line supervisors are the appropriate people to design the training program? Whom else would you add, if anyone, to this group?

CASE STUDY

Canadian Pacific and International Bank

Mary Keddy, senior vice president of human resources, felt somewhat embarrassed. She had just received a call from Michael Bennett, the CEO of the bank. He had asked a blunt question: "Mary, how is our return on investment in training?" At first she had not understood what he meant, but he explained that the board of directors had discussed her proposal to increase the training budget to 4 percent of payroll, and that one board member had asked whether the bank really knew how effective its training programs were and whether the money was well spent. She had to admit that she did not know. Bennett then had asked her to come up with an answer in time for the board meeting next month.

Mary had expected this question to arise sooner or later, but had hoped it would not happen so soon. She had been occupied with breaking the glass ceiling in the bank hierarchy and had been quite successful with it—so much so that even the Canadian Human Rights Commission had praised the bank for its employment equity program, which targeted women and minorities. Training had a high priority in the bank's strategy, as evidenced by its training budget, which exceeded 3 percent of payroll, much more than the average Canadian company and even its bank competitors spent.

The evaluation of its training programs had not been a high priority. So far, training sessions had been assessed mainly by using reaction measurements and the occasional feedback requested from supervisors sometime after sessions. Mary remembered from her HR courses that in order to assess the effectiveness of training programs, somewhat more sophisticated instruments and methods had to be used. Now she had to come up with some good ideas.

DISCUSSION QUESTIONS

1. You are Mary Keddy. Develop a proposal that Michael Bennett could present to the board. Consider also the practicality of the plan.

2. As a general rule, 5 to 10 percent of the cost of a training program should be used for the evaluation part of a program, depending on the complexity of the assessment. (The cost is an experience-based figure. The first author of this book worked for five years as the training director for a German company with 2,000 employees, and for 25 years as an instructor, trainer, and consultant for Canadian government and private company programs.) Please develop a "cheap" and an "expensive" proposal. A brief description of your approach and reasons will suffice (e.g., why would one method be cheaper or more expensive than the other?).

ADVANCED QUESTION, REQUIRING EXTRA READINGS

3. If you wanted to recommend a "foolproof" evaluation—that is, rule out other causes of success than the training program itself—what approach would you suggest?

CHAPTER 8

Performance Management

Performance management helps an organization define and achieve long-term and short-term goals vital to its success.

HARI DAS[1]

LEARNING OBJECTIVES

After studying this chapter, you should be able to:

LO1 Explain the purpose of performance management.

LO2 Identify the issues that influence the selection of a performance management process.

LO3 Describe the characteristics of effective performance measurement.

LO4 Describe commonly used appraisal methods.

LO5 Discuss rater biases in performance appraisals.

LO6 Describe the guidelines for effective performance evaluation interviews.

LO7 Explain how the results of performance appraisal affect human resource management.

LO1 `HRC 1`

Performance Management

A comprehensive **performance management** system involves much more than just **performance appraisal**. To achieve the organization's strategic objectives, individual employees need to meet their individual performance goals. Employees meeting their individual goals together all contribute to an organization achieving its objectives. When any employee does not play their role, the organization will not perform at its best. Performance management involves using performance data to mutually inform corporate culture, organizational benchmarks, human capital potential, systems and processes, resources, current policies, and program directions. It also involves sharing the results with all stakeholders and asking for stakeholders' input.

---

performance management

The use of performance data to effect organizational culture, systems, and processes, set goals, allocate resources, affect policies and programs, and share results.

---

performance appraisal

The process by which organizations evaluate employee job performance.

Here the human resource function has the potential of creating an enormous influence through development and maintenance of a sound performance management program. It requires that human resource professionals run performance management strategically—to align each employee's performance management plan with the strategy for the organization—whether the strategic focus of the organization is safe working, competitive pricing, high quality, or exemplary customer service.

The ideal performance management system provides incentives for employees to concentrate on improving things that contribute most to value creation, ranging from hiring the right people to producing high-quality goods or services to using the most effective training and development programs. The two examples below illustrate the importance of having a performance management system that aligns with a good business strategy:

> The first author of this book remembers his first visit as an engineering student to the famous Hannover Machine Tool Exhibition. There he saw a Russian lathe that was the heaviest in its category, more than double the weight of competing lathes. A discussion with the Russian exhibitors revealed that the manufacturing managers were rewarded by the Russian government for tonnage of production. No wonder that managers concentrated their effort on producing machines as heavy as possible.

This measurement was simple, but hardly appropriate. No doubt a measurement of the quality of the lathes produced rather than their weight would have been more effective. At Microsoft, a companywide integrated approach links rewards to performance based on corporate strategy:

> At Microsoft, three inputs determine a single performance rating for each employee: (a) what employees did during the year versus their commitments and goals as compared to the achievements of their peers, (b) the behaviour used to achieve their results as provided in feedback from peers and managers, and (c) employees' proven capabilities based on their work inputs plus their long-term performance record. The single rating triggers increases in merit pay, bonus, and restricted stock units, with the size linked to job family and discipline. The company can target its compensation investment to critical positions and disciplines, such as engineering research and development, which are most significant in the company's success. Employees are able to see how their compensation would shift based on different performance ratings through the interactive intranet portal. With the clear line of sight between performance and pay, the quality of conversations about performance expectations went up, as did pay satisfaction.[2]

This example shows how incentives can be used to reinforce performance that matches desired business strategy. Business strategy, performance management, and compensation systems should be carefully linked.

HRC **1**

Performance Management System Goals

Organizations concerned with running an efficient and effective performance management system will try to achieve the following objectives:

- Transform organizational objectives into clearly understood, measurable outcomes that define success and are shared with stakeholders in and outside the organization.
- Provide instruments for measuring, managing, and improving the overall health and success of the organization.
- Include measures of quality, cost, speed, customer service, and employee satisfaction, motivation, and skills to provide an in-depth, predictive performance management system.
- Shift from prescriptive, audit- and compliance-based management to an ongoing, forward-looking strategic partnership between top and middle management and employees.

Sound performance management programs make clear the connection between company goals and employee objectives and work plans, as well as criteria for success.[3] One approach is to have organizational goals cascade into refined goals and expectations at the unit, team, and individual levels. With this approach, high-level executives will develop goals for their division that align with the organizational goals. Then, mid-level managers will develop unit goals to meet the division goals, followed by managers developing team goals to meet the unit goals, and so on until the goals are cascaded down to individuals.[4] The left side of Figure 8-1 shows the cascade approach to setting performance goals.

FIGURE 8-1

Cascading versus Linking Up Approaches to Aligning Organizational and Individual Performance Goals

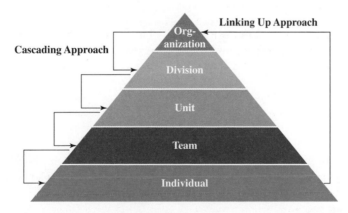

Although cascading goals are used to ensure line of sight between organizational objectives and individual work, they can be time-consuming to set up (each level is dependent on the level above to complete their goals in a timely manner) and they risk being distorted down the chain until the individual goal no longer contributes to the organizational goal. In the "linking up" approach, each unit and employee clearly links their goals to the organization's objectives (see the right side of Figure 8-1).

The linking up approach may be faster than the cascading approach, and it allows for a more direct line of sight between the individual's goals and the organization's objectives, which may produce more meaningful and clearer goals.[5] In either approach, the goal is for performance management plans to provide clarity for what is expected of the employee and how the work of the employee contributes to the overall functioning of the organization.

To assess the performance of the overall organization, one popular system—the **balanced scorecard**—integrates financial measures with other key performance indicators around customer satisfaction, internal organizational processes, and organizational growth, learning, and innovation.[6] The performance measures, targets, and initiatives for each of these areas all align with the organization's vision and mission to ensure that all aspects of the organization are moving forward together. Figure 8-2 provides an example of a balanced scorecard.

balanced scorecard

An integrated organizational performance measuring approach that looks at organizational learning and innovation, financial management, internal operations, and customer management.

FIGURE 8-2

A Balanced Scorecard Example

Mission: Dedication to the highest quality of Customer Service delivered with a sense of warmth, friendliness, individual pride, and company spirit.

Vision: Continue building on our unique position–the *only* short haul, low-fare, high-frequency, point-to-point carrier in America.

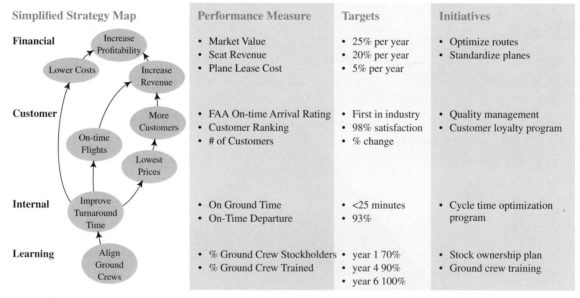

Courtesy of Balanced Scorecard Institute.

Reprinted with permission from Balanced Scorecard Institute, a Strategy Management Group Company. Copyright 2008.

Human resources play a critical part in an organization's performance, of course. HR has direct links to innovation and learning, but it also influences customer satisfaction, quality improvement programs, and other internal processes. One survey found that "people management" made by far the greatest contribution to profitability and productivity compared with "other critical success factors." Factors highly associated with success were employee skills and job design, which promoted autonomy, flexibility, and problem solving.[7]

LO2 HRC 1

Variations of the balanced scorecard have been developed to focus on particular HR functions including the HR scorecard and the leadership scorecard. Designed to align HR's twin imperatives of cost control and value creation, the HR scorecard aims to identify HR deliverables, align HR systems through the use of high-performance work systems, align the HR system with the organizational strategy, and identify HR efficiency measures.[8] In short, the HR scorecard tracks how well the HR function as a whole is meeting the organization's objectives.

Performance Appraisals as Part of Managerial Strategy

Within a performance management system, it is critical to assess whether the employee is meeting their individual performance goals (as they fit within the goals of the team, unit, division, and organization as a whole). Assessing the strengths and weaknesses of the human resources in the organization is part of the performance management process. Thorough performance analyses offer management the necessary data to assess the current skill, experience, and performance level of every employee, as well as performance standards critical for future requirements. Such data may have a significant impact on human resource planning, training and development programs, career development, and compensation expense forecasts.

Just as the engineering department is concerned with designing equipment, the maintenance department is concerned with running equipment, and manufacturing is concerned with turning out a quality product at minimal cost, the human resource department should be concerned with identifying what the people in engineering, maintenance, and manufacturing must do (*behaviour*) to be proficient in their respective functions. Similarly, they should determine what top management must do to implement the strategic plan once it has been formulated.

> Whereas some people may groan during performance appraisal season, it may be surprising that a recent Ceridian Canada survey reports that 71 percent of the 800 respondents said that their review made them feel valued, and 91 percent felt that their performance appraisal process met or exceeded their expectations. However, only 51 percent reported the performance reviews provided a clear path for the future.[9]

The uses of performance appraisals are outlined in Figure 8-3. Accurate performance evaluations show employees where they are deficient. For the HR department, appraisals make compensation, placement, training, development, and career guidance decisions more effective. At the same time, the department obtains feedback on its development activities, which can be used to set training objectives and to assess the staffing process and job designs. In short, performance appraisals serve as a quality control check on employee and human resource department performance.

Without an effective appraisal system, promotions, transfers, terminations, and other employee-related decisions become subject to trial and error. Career planning and human resource development suffer because there is no systematic performance feedback. Moreover, the human resource department lacks adequate information to evaluate its performance objectively. This lack of feedback can cause the human resource department to miss its objectives. Sometimes, the consequences of this failure are severe:

A large agricultural co-operative association in the western provinces rated employees twice a year. But employees were evaluated on personality characteristics, such as attitude, co-operation, and other factors that were only indirectly related to actual performance. Employees who were well liked by their managers received higher ratings. As a result, promotions, pay raises, and other employee-related decisions were biased by personalities. Eventually, several employees filed charges against the co-operative, alleging racial and sexual discrimination. When company lawyers defended past decisions as unbiased, they lost the case, because they could not show how the ratings related to job performance.

FIGURE 8-3

Uses of Performance Appraisals

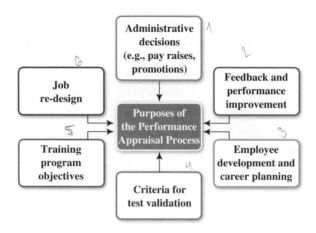

As this example emphasizes, an organization cannot have just any appraisal system. It must be effective, accepted by employees and management, and consistent with employment standards. If effective and accepted, it can identify developmental and career planning needs (see Chapter 7). It also can help with replacement summaries (discussed in Chapter 3), along with the other uses illustrated in Figure 8-3.

Elements of the Performance Appraisal System

Figure 8-4 shows the elements of an acceptable appraisal system. The approach must identify performance-related criteria, measure those criteria, and then give feedback to employees and the human resource department. If performance measures are not job-related, the evaluation can lead to inaccurate or biased results. Not only is performance feedback distorted, but errors in employee records can lead to incorrect human resource decisions, as happened in the above example of the agricultural co-operative.

HRC 1

Key Elements of Performance Appraisal Systems

The human resource department usually develops performance appraisals for employees in all departments. This centralization is meant to ensure uniformity. With uniformity in design and implementation, results are more likely to be comparable among similar groups of employees.

Although the human resource department may develop different approaches for managers and workers, uniformity within each group is needed to ensure useful results.

FIGURE 8-4

Key Elements of Performance Appraisal Systems

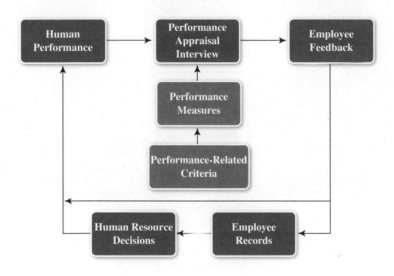

So important is the evaluation of performance that 85 percent of all companies surveyed in one Canadian study used appraisals for their clerical, professional, supervisory, and management employees.[10] To explain the importance of this widely used tool of human resource management, the remainder of this chapter examines the preparation, methods, and implications of performance appraisals.

The appraisal should create an accurate picture of an individual's job performance. To achieve this goal, appraisal systems should be job-related, be practical, have standards, and use dependable measures. *Job-related* means that the system evaluates critical behaviours that constitute job success. If the evaluation is not job-related, it is invalid and probably unreliable. Without validity and reliability, the system may discriminate in violation of antidiscrimination laws. Even when discrimination does not occur, appraisals are inaccurate and useless if they are not job-related, such as if an assessment of a manager's performance is based on whether the manager has a college degree.

In addition, a job-related approach also must be *practical*. A practical system is one that, first of all, is understood by evaluators and employees; a complicated, impractical approach may cause resentment and non-use. The confusion can lead to inaccuracies that reduce the effectiveness of the appraisal. An example of a simple and practical approach would be to judge an employee's performance on production—for example, number of widgets.

Performance evaluation requires **performance standards**—benchmarks against which performance is measured. To be effective, they should relate to the desired results of each job; they cannot be set arbitrarily. Knowledge of these standards is collected through job analysis. As discussed in Chapter 2, job analysis uncovers specific performance criteria by analyzing the performance of existing employees.

performance standards
The benchmarks against which performance is measured.

Performance feedback is crucial for the motivation of employees. Ongoing feedback is also ideal for another motivational tool. Which one? (*Hint:* Setting …)

© Rob Daly/OJO Images/Getty Images.

From the duties and standards listed in the job description, the analyst can decide which behaviours are critical and should be evaluated. If this information is lacking or unclear, standards may be developed from observation of the job or discussion with the immediate supervisor.

Performance evaluation also requires dependable **performance measures**, the ratings used to evaluate performance. To be useful, they must be *easy to use, be reliable*, and *report on the critical behaviours* that determine performance. For example, a call centre supervisor must observe the following in each representative:

- use of company procedures—following the appropriate script, verifying customer identity, and following company rules and regulations
- phone manners—speaking clearly and courteously, staying calm
- accuracy—providing accurate answers to customer questions and offering complementary service options to meet customer needs

performance measures
The ratings used to evaluate employee performance.

Such observations can be made either directly or indirectly. *Direct observation* occurs when the rater actually sees the performance. *Indirect observation* occurs when the rater can evaluate only substitutes for actual performance. For example, a supervisor's monitoring of a representative's calls is direct observation; a written test on company procedures for handling calls from difficult customers is indirect observation. Likewise, hearing a report about performance from a second-hand source is another form of indirect observation.[11] Indirect observations are usually less accurate, because they evaluate substitutes for actual performance:

> To test how well operators might respond to calls from difficult customers, a call centre developed a test. The test was intended to determine if each representative knew exactly how to proceed when calls were received from angry or belligerent customers. After several hundred representatives were tested, it was noticed that fast readers scored better. The human resource department decided to scrap the test and use false difficult calls to evaluate the representatives.

Another dimension of performance measures is whether they are objective or subjective. *Objective* performance measures are those indications of job performance that are verifiable by others. For example, the average length of calls to solve customers' problems. The results are objective and verifiable. Usually, objective measures are quantitative. They typically include items such as gross units produced, net units approved by quality control, scrap rates, number of computational errors, number of customer complaints, or some other mathematically precise measure of performance. Objective measures are not available in all jobs, however. For instance, how would you objectively measure the performance of many white-collar jobs? A measure of minutes sitting at a computer or number of keystrokes would not give a very good indication of performance!

Subjective performance measures are those ratings that are based on opinion or perception. Usually, such measures are the rater's personal opinions. Subjective measures are low in accuracy. When subjective measures are also indirect, accuracy becomes even lower. For example, measurement of a representative's phone manner is done subjectively, since supervisors must use their personal opinions of good or bad manners. Because the evaluation is subjective, accuracy is usually low even if the supervisor directly observes the representative. Accuracy is likely to be even lower when the rater uses an indirect measure, such as an electronic test of phone manners. Whenever possible, human resource specialists prefer objective and direct measures of performance.

LO3 HRC **1**

Considerations for Designing an Effective Performance Management Process

There are many considerations for the HR department when designing the performance management process. These range from determining the types of decisions that the appraisals are intended to inform (e.g., terminations, promotions, compensation), deciding whom to have involved in the process, and ensuring that the targets set are acceptable and achievable. Further discussion of 12 of these considerations is presented next:

1. **Validity.** Validity (relevance) is of utmost importance. Invalid (job-irrelevant) criteria lead to biased assessments. Results are the most valid criteria as they tend to be objective. It would be difficult, for example, to question the relevance of a 10 percent increase in profits for a performance assessment of a manager in charge of a department. Job-related behaviours are also relevant. However, some still widely used personality traits, such as leadership or intelligence, are of questionable value for performance assessment. They are characteristics the employee brings to the job, not a job outcome. Even though traits may relate to performance—a more intelligent employee will probably do better than a less intelligent one—this does not justify their use as performance measures any more than the use of intelligence scores as substitutes for school grades. [12]

Valid, or job-related, performance criteria must be based on a thorough job analysis (discussed in Chapter 2) and documented in the job description for each position. Validity is also crucial for the validation of any selection test (discussed in Chapter 6). And finally, validity is essential for any court challenge of performance criteria—for example, in case of a wrongful dismissal suit in which an employee's performance is an issue.

2. **Reliability.** Reliability (consistency), although highly desirable, is difficult to achieve in an organizational setting because of different raters, different instruments, and changing work environments. As a consequence, reliability can be looked at only as a distant aim.[13] However, it is important to know that *valid criteria tend to be reliable, but reliable criteria are not necessarily valid.*

> Early craniologists believed that the circumference of the human skull was a measure of intelligence (which is without foundation). It is an example of an absolutely reliable measure (every time one measures the circumference, one gets the same result), but without any validity.

3. **Input into System Development.** Employee participation in the development of performance criteria, appraisal instruments, and the system that manages them significantly increases the probability of acceptance of the system by both supervisors and employees. It gives employees a feeling of ownership. It is true that employees hired after a system has been installed will not have had input into it, but the knowledge that it was developed with the input of those who are rated by it will make it more acceptable.[14]

4. **Acceptable Performance Standards.** How often do supervisors make the mistake of using their own performance standards to assess an employee's performance? The temptation is high, but this approach mostly backfires. Performance standards are derived from a job analysis (discussed in Chapter 2). If standards are set unilaterally by management, they become "management's standards" and get little or no commitment from the employees. This does not mean that employees should set their own performance standards, but rather that the standards should be set with the employees to gain their commitment. It may be necessary for a manager to start out with a lower standard for a new employee until he or she has developed some experience and more self-confidence. Here, the manager's coaching skills become crucial, as do open communication, trust, and support by colleagues.[15]

5. **Acceptable Goals.** Similarly to performance standards, performance goals are often set unilaterally by managers, sometimes too high for an employee. Goals derive from the strategic business plans of the organization, operationalized at the department level by the manager. It is the responsibility of the manager, as coach and counsellor, to set goals seen by the employee as achievable; otherwise, the employee will be discouraged, often resulting in a self-fulfilling prophecy: "That's too high for me, I can't do it." Studies have consistently found that when supervisors set specific goals, performance improves twice as much as when they set general goals.[16] Increasingly, supervisors and employees set goals together at the beginning of the appraisal period and establish a *performance management plan*, also known as a PMP. Then, after the review period (and hopefully ongoing feedback and dialogue between the supervisor and employee), they meet again to review the employee's progress against the goals set forth in the PMP.

6. **Control of Standards.** Current performance standards used in appraisals often seem to be based on the assumption that the job in question is independent of other jobs. However, several studies have shown that most jobs are highly interdependent, which means that job incumbents have to rely on the contributions or co-operation of their colleagues. A standard of performance that is not fully under the control of the employee is not valid.[17] When performance standards across jobs are intertwined, employees may engage collaboratively to meet joint goals thereby enhancing team or unit performance.

7. **Frequency of Feedback.** Most appraisals take place once a year. Ideally, performance feedback would be given by the supervisor immediately after effective or ineffective job behaviour was observed. However, this is challenging in many organizational settings where both employee and supervisor are busy completing their job tasks, and may not be nearby when performance events occur. A compromise may be feedback sessions on a monthly, quarterly, or at least twice-yearly basis. It is important to note, however, that the most effective performance management sees feedback as an ongoing activity to ensure that expectations are communicated on a regular basis, feedback is provided in real time as it occurs, and to help employees develop and realize their full potential.[18]

8. **Rater Training.** Raters need to be trained in observation techniques and categorization skills (e.g., the use of diaries or critical incidents and how to group job behaviours or apply organizational performance standards). Frame-of-reference (FOR) training aims at improving these skills.[19] Raters also have to be familiar with the many potential rating errors (e.g., the halo effect, leniency) and the ways to minimize them. Research has shown that rater training reduces such errors.[20]

A maître d', a server, and a wine steward all do restaurant-related work, but each of their performance evaluations uses different criteria. Do you recognize some criteria that they may have in common?

Steve Debenport/Getty Images RF.

9. **Ratee Training.** If management wants to ensure that the performance management process is well understood and accepted by employees, it should consider training the ratees in addition to the raters. The ratee training might be part of the process of developing the system, thereby serving two purposes.

10. **Input into Interview Process.** Allowing employees to have a high level of participation in the appraisal interview increases employee satisfaction and morale.[21]

11. **Appraisal Consequences.** Appraisals without consequences lose their effectiveness very quickly. Employees as well as supervisors have to see that appraisal results are taken seriously by management and are followed up on. All too often, evaluation results end up in the employee's HR file unread, leading to cynical employees and frustrated supervisors.[22] Of course, there is a crucial link to a merit pay system. Especially high-performing employees expect to be rewarded for their effort.[23]

12. **Different Sources (Raters).** Relying on the judgment of one person increases the risk of biases (rating errors). Using different sources either confirms an assessment if all or a majority point in the same direction, or it raises a caution flag if assessments are at variance. Appraisal information can be gathered from the direct supervisor, secondary supervisors, self, peers, subordinates, and clients or customers. Raters from different levels of the organization will have different but valid views of a job and the performance of the incumbent.[24]

Performance appraisal systems can use different types of appraisal techniques. For ease of discussion, we have grouped these techniques into those that focus on comparisons between employees and noncomparative appraisals.

LO4 HRC 1

Comparative Evaluation Methods

Comparative evaluation methods are a collection of different methods that compare one person's performance with that of co-workers. Usually, comparative evaluations are conducted by the supervisor. They are useful for deciding merit pay increases, promotions, and organizational rewards because they can result in a ranking of employees from best to worst. The most common forms of comparative evaluations are the ranking method and forced distributions. Although these methods are practical and easily standardized, they too are subject to bias and offer little job-related feedback.

---

comparative evaluation methods

A collection of different methods that compare one person's performance with that of co-workers.

Many large companies use an elaborate group evaluation method. This method reduces biases because multiple raters are used, and some feedback results when managers and professionals learn how they compared with others on each critical factor. However, these comparative results are often not shared with the employee, because the supervisor and the HR department want to create an atmosphere of co-operation among employees, and to share comparative rankings might lead to internal competition instead of co-operation. Nevertheless, two arguments in favour of comparative approaches merit mention before discussing specific methods:

Arguments for a comparative approach are simple and powerful. The simple part of it is that organizations do it anyway, all the time. Whenever human resource decisions are made, the performance of the individuals being considered is ranked and compared. People are not promoted because they achieve their objectives, but rather because they achieve their objectives better than others.

The second reason (the powerful one) for using comparative as opposed to noncomparative methods is that they are far more reliable. This is because reliability is controlled by the rating process itself, not by rules, policies, and other external constraints.[25]

Ranking Method

The **ranking method** has the rater place each employee in order from best to worst. All the HR department knows is that certain employees are better than others. It does not know by how much. The employee ranked second may be almost as good as the one who was first or considerably worse. This method is subject to the halo and recency effects (discussed later in this chapter) although rankings by two or more raters can be averaged to help reduce biases. Its advantages include ease of administration and explanation.

---

ranking method

A method of evaluating employees that ranks them from best to worst on some trait.

Forced Distributions

Forced distributions require raters to sort employees into different classifications. Usually a certain proportion must be put in each category. Figure 8-5 shows how a rater may classify 10 subordinates, and Figure 8-6 shows these ratings plotted in a typical bell curve. As with the ranking method, relative differences among employees are unknown, but this method does overcome the biases of central tendency, leniency, and strictness. Some workers and supervisors strongly dislike this method because employees are often rated lower than they or their supervisor/rater think to be correct because the HR department's forced distribution requires some employees to be rated low.

---

forced distributions

A method of evaluating employees that requires raters to categorize employees.

FIGURE 8-5

The Forced Distribution Method of Appraisal of 10 Subordinates

Captone Fisheries Ltd. Forced Distribution Rating				
Classification: Overall Performance				
Lowest 10% of Subordinates	Next 20% of Subordinates	Middle 40% of Subordinates	Next 20% of Subordinates	Best 10% of Subordinates
A. Wilson	G. Carrs	B. Johnson	K. McDougal	W. Smythe
	M. Lopez	E. Wilson	L. Ray	
		C. Grant		
		T. Valley		

FIGURE 8-6

Plotting Performance onto the Bell Curve

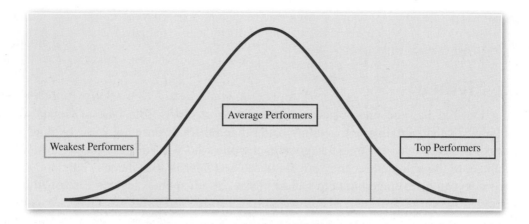

A famous example of a forced distribution is the "Vitality Curve" used by GE under its legendary CEO Jack ("Neutron Bomb") Welch:

> Jack Welch insisted that all managers categorize their employees into categories of "Top 20," "The Vital 70," and "Bottom 10" and that the latter be fired every year, regardless of actual performance. It is understandable that many managers strongly resisted this demand, but they had no choice. It should be noted that under Jack Welch's reign, GE <http://www.ge.com> had over 400,000 employees.[26]

HR departments may use comparative methods, like forced distributions along a bell curve, to inform compensation decisions, wherein the top performers are granted bonuses or higher raises than average performers. Top performers may be offered development opportunities, recognition, or promotions. The weakest performers may be targeted for dismissal, remedial training, or performance improvement plans.[27]

Noncomparative Evaluation Methods

Noncomparative evaluation methods, as the name implies, do not compare one employee against another, but use scales or reports with performance criteria developed by supervisors or a committee. Such methods include the following:

- the rating scale
- behaviourally anchored rating scales BARS
- performance tests and observations
- management by objectives
- assessment centres

noncomparative evaluation methods

Appraisal methods that evaluate an employee's performance according to preset data, and not by comparing one person's performance with that of co-workers.

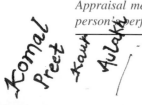

When evaluating an employee's past performance, significant consideration is also given to who should be conducting the evaluation: should ratings be made by the employee's supervisor or other potential raters as well? This section also includes a discussion on 360-degree performance appraisals.

Rating Scale

Perhaps the oldest and most widely used form of performance appraisal is the **rating scale**, which requires the rater to provide a subjective evaluation of an individual's performance along a scale from low to high. An example appears in Figure 8-7. As the figure indicates, the evaluation is subjective in nature. Although subordinates or peers may use it, the immediate supervisor usually completes the form.

rating scale
A scale that requires the rater to provide a subjective evaluation of an individual's performance.

The form is completed by checking the most appropriate response for each performance factor. Responses may be given numerical values to enable an average score to be computed and compared for each employee. The advantages of this method are that it is inexpensive to develop and administer, raters need little training or time to complete the form, and it can be applied to a large number of employees.

FIGURE 8-7

A Sample of a Rating Scale for Performance Evaluation

NutriGrow Organic Foods		
Instructions: For the following performance factors, please indicate your rating and the basis for your evaluation.		
Employee's Name _____ Department _____		
Rater's Name _____ Date _____		
Rating Definitions and Score Points		
5 Outstanding (clearly superior performance)		
4 Very good (exceeds expectations)		
3 Good (meets expectations)		
2 Marginal (needs improvement)		
1 Poor (unsatisfactory)		
Factors	**Score**	**Comments**
1. Dependability (reliability of employee)	_____	
2. Initiative (willingness to take action)	_____	
3. Overall output (productivity of employee)	_____	
4. Attendance (overall attendance, punctuality)	_____	
. . . . .		
. . . . .		
. . . . .		
20. Quality of work (accuracy, thoroughness, etc.)	_____	
Total	_____	

The disadvantages, however, are numerous. A rater's biases are likely to be reflected in a subjective instrument of this type. Specific performance criteria might be omitted to make the form applicable to a variety of jobs. For example, "maintenance of equipment" might be left off because it applies to only a few workers. But for some employees, that item may be the most important part of the job. These omissions tend to limit specific feedback. Also, descriptive evaluations are subject to individual interpretations that vary widely. And when specific performance criteria are hard to identify, the form may rely on irrelevant personality variables that dilute the meaning of the evaluation. The result is a standardized form and procedure that is not always job-related.

To ameliorate some of the criticisms that have been levied against rating scales, some proponents now advocate for streamlined rating scales. Specifically, limiting the number of performance ratings to only those that are critical to job performance and using a simplified rating scale[28] such as the one presented in Figure 8-8.

FIGURE 8-8

A Simplified Rating Scale Example

Unacceptable	Failed to meet technical quality standards; work was incomplete, poorly conceived, error ridden or not well targeted; work performed unsatisfactorily or in an unresponsive manner.
Successful	Products and services met expectations, were complete, well targeted and understandable; work performed was responsive and competent.
Outstanding	Surpassed quality standards and expectations; products were thorough, error-free, ideally targeted and maximally responsive to needs.

SOURCE: Elaine Pulakos, Rose Mueller-Hanson, Ryan O'Leary, and Michael Meyrowitz, "Building a high-performance culture: A fresh look at performance management," SHRM Foundation's Effective Practice Guidelines Series, 2012, http://www.shrm.org/about/foundation/products/documents/perf%20mgmt%20epg-final%20for%20web.pdf, downloaded March 26, 2015.

Behaviourally Anchored Rating Scales

Behaviourally anchored rating scales (BARS) attempt to reduce the subjectivity and biases of subjective performance measures. From descriptions of effective and ineffective performance provided by incumbents, peers, and supervisors, job analysts or knowledgeable employees group these examples into performance-related categories such as employee knowledge, customer relations, and the like. Then specific examples of these behaviours are placed along a scale (usually from 1 to 7).

behaviourally anchored rating scales (BARS)

Evaluation tools that rate employees along a rating scale by means of specific behaviour examples on the scale.

Actual behaviours for a bank branch manager are illustrated on the rating scale shown in Figure 8-9. Since the positions on the scale are described in terms of job-related behaviour, an objective evaluation along the scale is more likely. The form also cites specific behaviours that can be used to provide performance feedback to employees. The BARS are job-related, practical, and standardized for similar jobs. But the rater's personal biases may still cause ratings to be high or low, although the specific behaviours that "anchor" the scale provide some criteria to guide the sincere rater.[29] If the rater collects specific incidents during the rating period, the evaluation is apt to be more accurate and more legally defensible, besides being a more effective counselling tool. One serious limitation of BARS is that they only look at a limited number of performance categories, such as customer relations or human resource management. Also, each of these categories has only a limited number of specific behaviours. To improve the effectiveness of this approach when it comes time to counsel the employee, it is important that supervisors maintain records of performance events that occurred throughout the rating period.

FIGURE 8-9

Behaviourally Anchored Rating Scale for Bank Branch Manager

Human Resource Management		Bank of Ontario
Outstanding Performance	—7—	Can be expected to praise publicly for tasks completed well, and constructively criticizes in private those individuals who have produced less than adequate results.
Good Performance	—6—	Can be expected to show great confidence in subordinates, and openly displays this with the result that they develop to meet expectations.
Fairly Good Performance	—5—	Can be expected to ensure that human resource management records are kept right up to date, that reports are written on time, and that salary reviews are not overlooked.
Acceptable Performance	—4—	Can be expected to admit a personal mistake, thus showing that he or she is human too.
Fairly Poor Performance	—3—	Can be expected to make "surprise" performance appraisals of subordinates.
Poor Performance	—2—	Can be expected not to support decisions made by a subordinate (makes exceptions to rules).
Extremely Poor Performance	—1—	Can be expected not to accept responsibility for errors and to pass blame to subordinates.

A slightly different, and less common, method is the *Behaviour Observation Scale (BOS)*. Like BARS, BOS uses critical incidents. Instead of making a judgment about whether a specific job behaviour is expected to occur, however, it measures the frequency of the observed behaviours with scales ranging from high to low.

Performance Tests and Observations

With a limited number of jobs, performance appraisal may be based upon a test of knowledge or skills. The test may be of the paper-and-pencil variety or an actual demonstration of skills. The test must be reliable and valid to be useful. For the method to be job-related, observations should be made under circumstances likely to be encountered. Practicality may suffer when the cost of test development is high:

Pilots of all major airlines are subject to evaluation by airline raters and Transport Canada. Evaluations of flying ability are usually made both in a flight simulator and while being observed during an actual flight. The evaluation is based on how well the pilot follows prescribed flight procedures and safety rules. Although this approach is expensive, public safety makes it practical, as well as job-related and standardized.

360-Degree Performance Appraisals

Even though the human resource department usually designs the appraisal system, it seldom does the actual evaluation of performance. Instead, research shows that the employee's immediate supervisor participates in the evaluation 95 percent of the time.[30] More recently, recognizing that managers are not the only source of information about employee performance, human resource professionals have begun implementing 360-degree performance appraisals. Pictured in Figure 8-10, the **360-degree performance appraisal**, or "multi-source feedback," is a popular method of assessment. There can be little doubt that the combination of self, peer, supervisor, and subordinate evaluation will provide feedback on different aspects of the job, since every contributor probably has a different focus.[31] The trend toward 360-degree appraisals is also in line with the trend toward a flatter organization, which tends to result in a wider span of control. With fewer managers having to supervise more employees, it becomes more difficult to assess everybody's performance accurately. And there is the trend of today's managers toward teamwork and participative management, which makes the historic approach of one supervisor providing performance feedback look obsolete.[32]

FIGURE 8-10

360-Degree Performance Appraisals

360-degree performance appraisal

Combination of self, peer, supervisor, and subordinate performance evaluation.

The Greater Toronto Airports Authority (GTAA; <http://www.torontopearson.com>), which operates Canada's busiest airport (Pearson handled about 38.5 million passengers in 2014), needed to align its human resources with its customer-centric strategy. Over a two-year period, HR completed 360-degree feedback sessions with all 1,200 employees. They were able to address the identified shortcomings in how staff related to its customers through their core competency training. The result was more consistent and effective leadership at the GTAA.[33]

Not everybody shares the enthusiasm about the 360-degree approach. It requires a suitable corporate culture,[34] and is better suited for performance appraisal systems that are developmental (i.e., to improve performance) as opposed to administrative (e.g., to determine pay raises and promotions) in focus. Each of the rating sources may offer a different perspective on the employee's performance, and there are many considerations around integrating ratings by different sources such as how to preserve anonymity yet provide specific feedback.

Self-Appraisals

Getting employees to conduct a self-appraisal can be a useful evaluation technique if the goal of evaluation is to further self-development. When employees evaluate themselves, defensive behaviour is less likely to occur. Thus, self-improvement is more likely. When self-appraisals are used to determine areas of needed improvement, they can help users set personal goals for future development.

Not only does it get the employee involved in forming a self-appraisal of improvement areas, but the completed sheet indicates to the supervisor what he or she needs to do to "eliminate roadblocks to meeting or exceeding job standards."[35]

Peer Appraisals

Employees' peers may have more opportunities to observe their performance, and to observe their typical performance such as when they are not on their "best behaviour" because their boss is present. There is a high correlation between ratings made by peers and ratings made by supervisors.[36] Peer ratings may also positively impact open communication, motivation, group cohesion, and employee satisfaction, even if the feedback provided is negative.[37]

Direct Report Appraisals

Many employees are in a good position to evaluate the performance of their supervisors. No one is in a better position to assess how a supervisor provides praise or feedback, autonomy and guidance to an employee than the employee him- or herself.[38] More and more organizations are including direct report appraisals, or upward feedback, in their performance appraisal systems. Direct report appraisals may help to identify potential leadership or management issues, and are valuable for developmental (more than administrative) purposes. Many direct reports may be concerned about providing feedback and ratings to their supervisors for fear of potential retribution if their responses are identified. However, direct report and peer ratings of supervisors are typically comparable, and thus, there may not be significant rating inflation despite these concerns.

The above approaches evaluate past performance; they examine what the employee's behaviours have been over the previous performance appraisal period. The next two approaches evaluate employee potential for future performance and focus on setting future performance goals. They are the management-by-objectives approach and the assessment centre technique.

Management-by-Objectives Approach

The heart of the **management-by-objectives (MBO) approach** is that each employee and superior jointly establish performance goals for the future.[39] Ideally, these goals are mutually agreed upon and objectively measurable. If both conditions are met, employees are apt to be more motivated to achieve the goal, since they have participated in setting it. Moreover, they can periodically adjust their behaviour to ensure attainment of an objective if they can measure their progress toward the objective. But to adjust their efforts, performance feedback must be available on a regular basis.

---

management-by-objectives (MBO) approach

Requires an employee and superior to jointly establish performance goals for the future. Employees are subsequently evaluated on how well they have obtained these objectives.

When future objectives are set, employees gain the motivational benefit of a specific target to organize and direct their efforts. Objectives also help the employee and supervisor discuss specific developmental needs of the employee. When done correctly, performance discussions focus on the job's objectives and not personality variables. Biases are reduced to the extent that goal attainment can be measured objectively.

In practice, some challenges with MBO programs include objectives that are too ambitious or too narrow. The result is frustrated employees or overlooked areas of performance. For example, employees may set objectives that are measured by quantity rather than quality, because quality, while it may be equally important, is often more difficult to measure. When employees and managers do focus on subjectively measured objectives, special care is needed to ensure that biases do not distort the manager's evaluation. Figure 8-11 shows the annual assessment of the performance of a salesperson, using an MBO approach. The Spotlight on HRM provides an example of the successful implementation of a MBO process at Agilent Technologies.

FIGURE 8-11

MBO Evaluation Report for a Salesperson

Objectives Set	Period Objective	Accomplishments	Variance
1. Number of sales calls	85	98	+15%
2. Number of new customers	10	8	–20%
3. Sales of product xx	2,500	3,100	+24%
4. Sales of product yy	1,500	1,350	–10%
5. Customer complaints	10	22	+120%
6. Number of training courses taken	5	3	–40%
7. Number of monthly reports on time	12	11	–8%

Spotlight *on* HRM

Management by Objectives at Agilent Technologies

With 18,500 employees in 110 countries, test and measurement giant Agilent Technologies <http://www.agilent.ca> (the now wholly independent former test and measurement division of Hewlett Packard) has values including dedication to innovation; trust, respect, and teamwork; uncompromising integrity; speed, focus, and accountability to meet customer needs; and a culture of performance drawing on the full range of its employees' skills and aspirations. However, its pay practices and training tools were not having the desired impact. Facing high attrition, the need to increase employee engagement and plan for employee development, and most importantly, to make HR a strategic decision-making partner, Agilent developed a Management by Objectives performance management system. Its purpose is to give employees freedom to do their work in the manner that suits them, make them responsible and accountable for their objectives and results, and create visibility for how their individual work contributes to the objectives of the organization.

The MBO process at Agilent involves four steps:

Step 1: Define the Measures of Success
The broad measures of success at Agilent lay in four quadrants: Customer Satisfaction (create loyal customers); Employees, Leadership and Culture (speed to opportunity); Financial (leverage the operating model); and Markets (accelerate profitable growth). These four quadrants are further subdivided to set priorities for each Group, Business Unit, and Department within a performance plan defining individual priority objectives and development. Following this step, employee deliverables are clear, as is their link to achieving organizational objectives.

(Continued)

Step 2: Quarterly MAPS Process

The objective of MAPS (short for My Accountability and Performance Standards) is to ensure that employees are crystal clear about what is expected of them, where they stand, and what their manager is doing to support their development. The focus is on open dialogue on areas where employees are performing well and where they need to improve. During the strategic MAPS conversations, the idea is to not only make employees understand where they stand, but also chart a development plan for improvement based on feedback. The conversations are documented and uploaded onto the MAPS website for future reference. Function-wide reports are also published to share and increase accountability. The entire process is transparent, providing clarity and ownership of the objectives.

Step 3: HR Analytics

Quarterly meetings are held between HR and the function leads to discuss the function's HR data. Data points discussed include: rank and level attrition data, a compensation ratio (calculated as the average of the employee's actual pay divided by the pay range mid-point of the job grade), percentage of employees below the minimum compensation ratio, comparison of attrition/pay between new, existing, and exited employees, and employees on a corrective action plan. These meetings help function leads understand and own the HR data in their departments. HR's role is then to help them with tools, consultation, and brainstorming, and to partner with them on creating and executing programs. This process helps the function leads to make prudent HR decisions such as distribution of wages, and provides information to HR that can be used to improve business processes or inform policy changes.

Step 4: Leadership Audit Survey

The purpose of the Leadership Audit Survey is to provide feedback from employees to each manager through a twice-annual survey of all Agilent employees. It provides each manager with accountability based on their rating by their employees. The survey measures four aspects of employee engagement: Customer Orientation (to surpass customer expectations), Speed and Decisiveness (for addressing conflicts and making decisions), Risk Taking (to allow employees freedom to take informed risks), and Engagement (through feedback and clear links between their performance and the performance of Agilent as a whole). The survey provides leaders with feedback and allows managers with perfect scores to share their stories with managers who are not doing as well to help them learn and improve performance. Development support is provided to managers requiring improvement.

Agilent has recognized the importance of paying employees well to keep them engaged, happy, and motivated. It also provides intangible motivators like work/life flexibility where employees are able to work from home once a week. The company's philosophy is to manage by objectives and not by the number of hours in the office. It also believes in differentiation with feedback and letting employees know where they stand with respect to their performance.

Since adopting MBO, attrition has dropped significantly below market, they have best-in-class engagement scores, industry recognition through awards such as a top 10 Great Place to Work (in 2011), and a successful culture of differentiation within the company.

SOURCE: Excerpts taken and adapted from: SHRM India Case Study, "Agilent Technologies – Measures for Excellence," November 29, 2011, http://www.shrm.org/india/hr-topics-and-strategy/performance-management/performance-planning/pages/agilent%20technologies%20-%20measures%20for%20excellence.aspx, downloaded March 27, 2015.

Assessment Centre Technique

Assessment centres are a method of evaluating employee potential. Assessment centres (ACs) are a standardized form of employee appraisal that relies on multiple types of evaluation and multiple assessors. Also discussed in Chapter 6 on selection, ACs in the performance appraisal context are usually applied to groups of middle-level managers who appear to have potential to perform at more responsible levels in the organization. During a brief stay at the assessment centre facility, candidate potential is individually evaluated through in-depth interviews, personal background histories, peer ratings by other attendees, leaderless group discussions, ratings by psychologists and managers, and simulated work exercises. The simulated work experiences usually include in-basket exercises, decision-making exercises, computer-based business games, and other job-like opportunities that test the employee in realistic ways.

---

assessment centres

A standardized form of employee appraisal that relies on several types of evaluation and multiple assessors.

These activities are usually conducted for a few days at a location physically removed from the job site. During this time, the psychologists and managers who do the rating attempt to estimate the strengths, weaknesses, and potential of each attendee.[40] They then pool their estimates to arrive at some conclusion about each member of the group being assessed.

Some critics question whether the procedures used are objective and job-related, especially as rater biases are possible in forming the subjective opinions of attendees.[41] Nevertheless, ACs have gained widespread use, and human resource researchers are finding ways to validate the process. Interestingly, research indicates that the results of ACs are a good prediction of actual on-the-job performance in 75 percent of all cases.[42] Unfortunately, this accurate method is expensive, since it usually requires a separate facility and the time of multiple raters.

Other Developments

Web-based performance appraisal has moved from being a leading edge tool used by large organizations to a mainstream industry standard for all sizes of firms. These systems are developed by experts, adaptable to an organization's needs, easy to use, and result in data that are easily analyzed, stored, and retrieved.[43] Ideally, such a program would be part of an enterprise-wide software system, and even that is already available.[44] It means that all human resource aspects, such as application data, interview guides for selection decisions, computer-based training, performance appraisal, payroll, job evaluation, as well as other organizational functions such as finance, purchasing, distribution, manufacturing, and more, are part of one software package. The development and application of such an integrated software system is often the result of "business process reengineering," a radical rethinking of organizational functions to achieve higher efficiency, quality improvement, and better service.[45]

The advantage of such an integrated system is that everyone in the organization receives the same information:

> The concept of entering data once, at source, saves time (there is no or very little duplication of data entry) and ensures that data can be treated as a corporate resource, used by any and all who have a need (and have authorized access). Through this horizontal integration of information, issues about whose/which data is correct are avoided, time is saved, and the organization as a whole wins.[46]

The disadvantages are that the implementation of such a system is time-consuming, complex, and costly. However, it appears that the savings and higher efficiency make it worthwhile.[47]

Another development is the difficulties associated with the change to paying employees for their *competencies* instead of their job performance (and assessing them on that basis). Historically, it has been the performance standards set in job descriptions that have guided supervisors in their assessment. Now the tendency is to focus more on skill levels than job performance (see discussion on compensation in Chapter 9). As a consequence, employee assessment tends to involve tests rather than supervisor evaluations.

One problem that still has to be addressed is assessing the performance of contingency employees (for a more detailed discussion on the use of contingency workers, see Chapter 3). Since such employees are hired only for the duration of a project, it makes little sense to sit down with them to develop long-range performance objectives. They also tend to have, by definition, little knowledge of the work culture of the organization, the supervisor's expectations, and their specific job responsibilities and performance standards. It is perhaps easiest to limit their performance assessment to very specific tasks, which have been communicated to them, and to tie rewards to the satisfactory completion of these tasks.

Within the human resource management field, one recent development is a focus on talent management. As discussed in Chapter 7, talent management involves identifying and developing specific individuals within the organization who are seen as having high potential. The concept comes from recognizing that employees who are top performers are not necessarily the people with the highest potential for working in key organizational positions or areas, or for moving up in the organization.

One tool for conversing about the development opportunities that could be provided to employees who might have high potential within an organization is the 9-box grid.[48] Figure 8-12 shows an example of a 9-box grid. Employees categorized into the "future star," "consistent star," and "current star" boxes may be targeted for specific developmental opportunities. Opportunities granted may include: (a) specific work assignments designed to give them the opportunity to grow their skills in a particular area such as a key business unit or overseas assignment (often referred to as "stretch assignments"), (b) educational opportunities such as advanced degree or certificate programs, or organization-specific leadership or other training opportunities, and/or (c) inclusion in events or mentor activities that will give the employee visibility and access to senior employees of the organization.[49]

FIGURE 8-12

A 9-Box Grid Depicting Performance by Potential

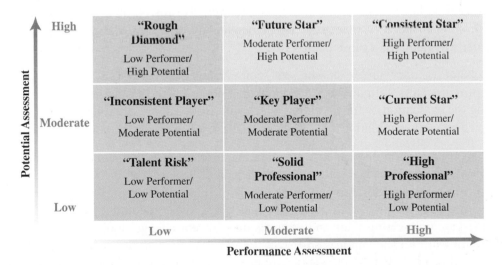

Many global organizations, such as Pepsi Co. <http://www.pepsico.ca>, CitiBank <https://online.citibank.com>, and S. C. Johnson <http://www.scjohnson.ca>, and Canadian organizations[50] including National Bank in Montreal, Xerox Canada, and TD Bank Group, now have a talent management department or talent management group within their HR department.[51] Many times, employees will receive evaluations of potential along with ratings of performance. Both cues can be used by the HR department to inform their decisions such as development and compensation.

HRC **1 & 2**

Implications of the Appraisal Process

The appraisal system design and its procedures are usually handled by the human resource department. The specific approach is influenced by previous procedures and the purpose of the new appraisal. If the goal is to evaluate past performance to allocate rewards, comparative approaches may be preferred. Similarly, other methods of evaluating past performance may be best if the appraisal system exists primarily to give employees counselling about their behaviour. Methods aimed at targeting future performance may focus on specific goals, as is the case with MBO techniques. Assessment centres may seek to uncover a specific weakness or help with internal placement. Regardless of the technique selected by the department, however, the approach must be converted into an ongoing practice among the line managers. Raters are often unfamiliar with the procedures or the forms and have to be taught how to use them properly.

Evaluation systems that involve employees in their design may gain greater acceptance. Human rights legislation supports having employees involved in the design of the appraisal system. Involvement may increase interest and understanding of whatever performance appraisal system the human resource department eventually administers. However, to operate the performance appraisal system may require training for those who serve as raters.

Training Raters and Employees

Whether a simple comparative method or a sophisticated assessment centre is used, raters and employees alike need knowledge of the system and its purpose. Just knowing whether the appraisal is to be used for compensation or placement recommendations versus for developmental purposes may change the rater's evaluation of those being rated.

A major problem is rater understanding and consistency of evaluations. Some human resource departments provide raters with a rater's handbook that describes the employer's approach. Guidelines for conducting the evaluation or for providing ratees with feedback are often included in the handbook. Key terms, such as "shows initiative" or "provides leadership," may also be defined in the handbook.

Although in the past rater training has focused on rating errors such as the halo effect, leniency bias, and central tendency, the emphasis has shifted now to the cognitive aspect of the rating process, that is, the ability of raters to make valid judgments on the basis of relatively complex information.[52] Likewise, the focus is now on training both managers and employees, including a deeper focus on the knowing/doing gap, uncovering fears and attitudes that prevent change, tools to facilitate change, and accountability for learning and application.[53]

LO5

Rater Biases

The problem with subjective measures is the opportunity for bias. Bias is the distortion of a measurement. Despite the best of intentions, common rater biases include the following:

- the halo effect
- the error of central tendency
- the leniency and strictness biases
- personal prejudice
- the recency effect
- contrast errors

The Halo Effect

The **halo effect** (discussed in Chapter 6) occurs when the rater's personal opinion of the employee sways the rater's measurement of performance. For example, if a supervisor likes an employee, that opinion may distort the supervisor's estimate of the employee's performance. The problem is most severe when raters must evaluate their friends:

> Sam was Jim's supervisor. They had been friends in school and had played together in a minor league baseball team for years. Jim was a happy-go-lucky guy and his job performance was so-so, but he was very good with people. When Sam had to write a performance evaluation, he praised Jim for his "excellent social" and "superior communication" skills, but overlooked his shortcomings in productivity aspects. Sam felt that he "could not let down" his friend.

halo effect

A bias that occurs when an evaluation allows some information to disproportionately affect the final evaluation.

The Error of Central Tendency

Some raters do not like to judge employees as "effective" or "ineffective," so they avoid checking extremes—very poor or excellent—and instead place their marks near the centre of the rating sheet so that employees appear to be "average." Thus, the term **error of central tendency** has been applied to this bias. Human resource departments sometimes unintentionally encourage this behaviour by requiring raters to justify extremely high or low ratings.

error of central tendency

An error in rating employees that consists of evaluating employees as neither good nor poor performers even when some employees perform exceptionally well or poorly.

> The first author of this book did his Ph.D. dissertation on performance appraisals in Canadian banks. When he surveyed over 2,000 appraisals, all of which used 7-point scales, he did not find a single evaluation that used the 1 or 7 anchors.[54]

Leniency and Strictness Biases

The **leniency bias** occurs when raters are too easy in evaluating employee performance. The **strictness bias** is just the opposite; it results from raters being too harsh in their evaluation of performance. Both errors more commonly occur when performance standards are vague. The leniency bias is much more common.

leniency bias

A tendency to rate employees higher than their performance justifies.

strictness bias

A tendency to rate employees lower than their performance justifies.

The "average" performance assessment of officers in the Canadian Armed Forces is about 80 percent.[55]

Personal Prejudice

A rater's dislike for a person or group may distort the ratings. One study found that women line workers received lower performance ratings than women in staff jobs or than men in either line or staff jobs. Promoted women received higher performance ratings than promoted men, suggesting that women are held to higher standards in promotion.[56] Sometimes raters are unaware of their prejudice, which makes such biases even more difficult to overcome. Nevertheless, human resource specialists should pay close attention to prejudice in appraisals, since it prevents effective evaluations and violates antidiscrimination laws.

Ann was the only female welder in a maintenance team, and she was good. She had passed her welder's certification with flying colours and was chosen over a number of male applicants. Tom, the team's foreman, had opposed her hiring, saying that women would not fit into the team, but the HR manager insisted on "hiring the best person." Ann noticed that Tom scrutinized her work much more closely than that of other team members and publicly complained about even her minor mistakes. In her first annual performance assessment she was judged "average, with potential for improvement."

The Recency Effect

When using subjective performance measures, ratings are affected strongly by the employee's most recent actions. Recent actions—good or bad—are more likely to be remembered by the rater. This is known as the **recency effect**.

recency effect

A rater bias that occurs when the rater allows recent employee performance to sway the overall evaluation of the employee's performance unduly.

John had been an average nurse, paying more attention to his female colleagues than his patients. However, a few weeks ago, by sheer coincidence, he had saved a patient's life. During the recent performance appraisal, Jennifer, the head nurse, concentrated on this one-time event and lavishly praised John's overall job performance.

Contrast Errors

When raters compare employees to each other rather than to a performance standard, they are committing **contrast errors**.

contrast error

A rater bias occurring when a rater compares employees to each other rather than to a performance standard.

When subjective measures must be used, human resource specialists can reduce the distortion from biases through training, feedback, and the proper selection of performance appraisal techniques. Training for raters should involve three steps. First, biases and their causes should be discussed. Second, the role of performance appraisals in employee decisions should be explained to stress the need for impartiality and objectivity. Third, raters should be allowed to apply subjective performance measures as part of their training. For example, classroom exercises may require evaluation of the trainer or videos of various workers. Mistakes uncovered during simulated evaluations then can be corrected through additional training or counselling.

Once raters are trained, the appraisal process can begin. But the results of the appraisal process do little to improve employee performance unless employees receive feedback on their appraisals. This feedback process is called the *evaluation interview*.

LO6

Evaluation Interviews

Evaluation interviews are performance management sessions that give employees feedback about their past performance or future potential. The evaluator may provide this feedback through several approaches: tell and sell, tell and listen, and problem solving. The *tell-and-sell approach* reviews the employee's performance and tries to convince the employee to perform better. It is best used on new employees. The *tell-and-listen* approach allows the employee to explain reasons, excuses, and defensive feelings about performance. It attempts to overcome these reactions by counselling the employee on how to perform better. The *problem-solving approach* identifies problems that are interfering with employee performance. Then through training, coaching, or counselling, efforts are made to remove these deficiencies, often by setting goals for future performance.

evaluation interviews

Performance review sessions that give employees feedback about their past performance or future potential.

Regardless of which approach is used to give employees feedback, the guidelines listed in Figure 8-13 can help make the performance review session more effective.[57] The intent of these suggestions is to make the interview a positive, performance-improving dialogue. By stressing desirable aspects of employee performance, the evaluator can give the employee renewed confidence in his or her ability to perform satisfactorily. This positive approach also enables the employee to keep desirable and undesirable performance in perspective, because it prevents the individual from feeling that performance review sessions are entirely negative. When negative comments are made, they focus on work performance and not the individual's personality. Specific, rather than vague generalities, examples of the employee's shortcomings are used, so that the individual knows exactly what behaviours need to be changed. The review session concludes by focusing on actions that the employee can take to improve areas of poor performance. In that concluding discussion, the evaluator usually offers to provide whatever assistance the employee needs to overcome the deficiencies discussed.

Spotlight *on* ETHICS

On Probation

You have recently been hired as a supervisor and accepted a six-month probationary period. You have earned a Certificate in Human Resource Management from a well-known university. Your arrival coincides with performance appraisal time in the company. You quickly realize that the currently used appraisal instrument is of little value, because it consists mainly of subjective measures. The appraisal instrument is the brainchild of the CEO, who is very proud of "his baby," as he explained when he hired you. One of the tasks given to you is the training of supervisors in assessing performance. You know that any training with this instrument is a waste of time, but if you criticize it, there is a danger that you will not survive the probationary period. What will you do?

FIGURE 8-13

Guidelines for Effective Performance Evaluation Interviews

1. *Emphasize* positive aspects of employee performance.
2. *Tell* each employee that the evaluation session is to improve performance, not to discipline.
3. *Provide* immediate positive and developmental feedback in a private location, and explicitly state that you are providing the employee with performance feedback.
4. *Review* performance formally at least annually and more frequently for new employees or those who are performing poorly. Ongoing and regular feedback is optimal.
5. *Make* criticisms specific, not general and vague.
6. *Focus* criticisms on performance, not on personality characteristics.
7. *Stay* calm and do not argue with the person being evaluated.
8. *Identify* specific actions the employee can take to improve performance, and discuss the manager's role in supporting future development and career planning.
9. *Emphasize* the evaluator's willingness to assist the employee's efforts and to improve performance.
10. *End* the evaluation session by stressing the positive aspects of the employee's performance and reviewing plans to improve performance.

Having managers provide guidance and feedback is not only linked to employee performance, but also has a significant impact on employee engagement.[58]

Establishing a Performance Improvement Plan

Notwithstanding strong training, development, and feedback efforts, there are often employees who are not meeting acceptable performance standards. There are multiple reasons for poor performance such as insufficient or inadequate training, unclear job expectations, or roadblocks preventing effective performance. A *Performance Improvement Plan* (PIP) is an effective way of giving an employee struggling to meet performance standards the opportunity to succeed, while still holding them accountable for past performance.

Below are six steps for creating a PIP adapted from the How To Guides offered by the Society for Human Resource Management:[59]

1. **Getting Started**. The first step for establishing a PIP is to document the employee's current performance and the areas that require improvement. This documentation should include the main performance issues expressed specifically and objectively using facts, examples, and patterns of performance concerns.

   Important questions for the supervisor to address in advance include: ensuring that the performance expectations set were clear, ensuring that the employee has the tools, resources, and skills necessary to be successful, ensuring the background information needed to document the performance deficit is gathered, that the employee has been provided with feedback and that it is non-personal in nature, and that the employee has had the opportunity to respond.[60]

2. **Develop an Action Plan**. The manager should next develop an action plan for improvement. The action plan should contain specific goals. For instance, "the employee should not be late for work once during this 90-day performance improvement cycle." For each goal, the manager should contemplate whether additional resources, time, training, or coaching is necessary to meet the

objectives. This action plan should help set performance expectations, and include the consequences for not meeting the objectives. Action plans are typically 60 or 90 days in duration.[61]

3. **Review the Performance Improvement Plan**. Before meeting with the employee, the manager should seek assistance from the HR department or other knowledgeable professional. The HR department should ensure that the plan is clear, specific, unemotional, and attainable within the set timeframe. This is an important step in the event that the employee does not meet the performance improvement objectives and may proceed toward termination.

4. **Meet with the Employee**. When meeting with the employee, the manager should clearly lay out the areas for improvement and the action plan. Following the employee's feedback and input, the action plan may need some modification. After the changes are implemented, both the manager and employee should sign the PIP.

5. **Follow Up**. Regular follow up meetings on a weekly or bi-weekly basis should be set for the manager and employee. These meetings should discuss any potential roadblocks encountered, required tools or training, and provide the opportunity for the employee to ask questions or to seek guidance or clarification.

6. **PIP Conclusion**. Following the PIP period, if the employee was able to meet the objectives, then the PIP is closed and the employee continues employment. If the employee was unable to improve and meet the objectives in the plan, then the employer should close the PIP and terminate employment. When the employee does improve some but perhaps did not quite meet performance expectations set out in the PIP, there are several options. First, the employer may agree to extend the PIP for another few weeks or months. Second, the employer may seek to revise the objectives believing in retrospect that the objectives were too challenging or not within the employee's control. In this case, the employer may end the PIP or extend the PIP period. Third, the employer may terminate employment because the standards simply were not met.

When terminating an employee for not meeting performance expectations, documentation is pivotally important. Engaging the HR department to ensure proper processes are followed is key.

LO7 HRC 1 & 2 & 4

Human Resource Management Feedback

The performance appraisal process also provides insight into the effectiveness of the human resource management function. If the appraisal process indicates that poor performance is widespread, many employees are excluded from internal placement decisions. They will not be promoted or transferred. In fact, they may be excluded from the organization through termination.

Unacceptably high numbers of poor performers may indicate errors elsewhere in the human resource management function. For example, human resource development may be failing to fulfill career plans because the people who are hired during the selection process are screened poorly. Or the human resource plan may be in error because the job analysis information is wrong or the employment equity plan seeks the wrong objectives. Likewise, the human resource department may be failing to respond to the challenges of the external environment or effective job design. Sometimes, the human resource function is pursuing the wrong objectives. Or the appraisal system itself may be faulty because of management resistance, incorrect performance standards or measures, or a lack of constructive feedback.

Finally, focusing on future performance targets allows the human resource department to provide feedback to employees as to the status of their career progression. If an employee's performance is inadequate, the cause has to be investigated. If it is a lack of skill or experience, the necessary improvements have to be made part of the goals discussed with the employee. Ideally, a step-by-step plan will be the outcome of the interview process.

Legal Aspects of Performance Appraisal

A performance appraisal form is a legal document. The implication is that raters have to be careful to use only performance criteria that are relevant to the job. In a court challenge, for example, where an employee loses a job as a result of inadequate job performance, the human resource manager has to prove that the performance criteria used were *valid* and were used *consistently*. Nonrelevant criteria can be avoided if performance standards are established through a thorough job analysis and recorded in a job description.[62]

It is also a legal requirement that a reasonable time frame be set for performance improvement.[63] The length of time would depend on the job. While it may be reasonable to expect an office clerk to improve his or her performance within a few weeks or months, it might take a manager a year or more to show improvement.

Well-documented performance shortcomings can avoid serious embarrassments, and feedback interviews have been viewed favourably in court or with arbitrators.

SUMMARY

Performance management is an ongoing process, which integrates an organization's vision with performance objectives and performance measurements. It requires a well-developed communication system that provides feedback to managers and employees, a training program that corrects deficiencies, and appropriate rewards for motivation purposes (discussed in the following chapter).

Performance appraisal is a critical part of a performance management system. Its goal is to provide an accurate picture of past, future, or both past and future employee performance. To do this, performance standards are established. Standards are based on job-related criteria that best determine successful job performance. Where possible, actual performance is then measured directly and objectively. From a wide variety of appraisal techniques, human resource specialists select those methods that most effectively measure employee performance against the previously set standards. Techniques can be selected both to review past performance and to anticipate performance in the future.

The appraisal process is usually designed by the human resource department, often with little consultation from other parts of the organization. When it is time to implement a new appraisal approach, those who do the rating usually have little idea about the appraisal process or its objectives. To overcome this shortcoming, the department may design and deliver appraisal workshops to train managers.

A necessary requirement of the appraisal process is employee feedback through an evaluation interview. The interviewer tries to balance positive areas of performance and those areas where performance is deficient, so that the employee receives a realistic view of performance. Perhaps the most significant challenge raised by performance appraisals is the feedback they provide about human resource department performance. Human resource specialists need to be keenly aware that poor performance, especially when it is widespread, may reflect problems with previous human resource management activities that are malfunctioning.

TERMS FOR REVIEW

360-degree performance appraisal
assessment centres
balanced scorecard
behaviourally anchored rating scales (BARS)
comparative evaluation methods
contrast error
error of central tendency
evaluation interviews
forced distributions
halo effect
leniency bias
management-by-objectives (MBO) approach
noncomparative evaluation methods
performance appraisal
performance management
performance measures
performance standards
ranking method
rating scale
recency effect
strictness bias

SELF-ASSESSMENT EXERCISE

Performance Appraisal as a Crucial Management Skill

		T	F
1. Performance appraisal includes assessing managerial attitudes.		T	F
2. One application of performance appraisals is to discipline employees		T	F
3. One of the key elements of a performance appraisal system is a training needs analysis.		T	F
4. Effective performance standards are determined through a survey in ensure employee input.		T	F

(Continued)

5. The halo effect occurs when raters are too easy on employees in evaluating their performance. → leniency. F	T	(F)
6. The reliability of a performance appraisal instrument is the most crucial characteristic. validity F	T	F
7. Because of potential personal biases, performance appraisal results cannot be used in courts. F	T	F
8. A weighted checklist weighs the performance evaluation made by a department head higher than that of a direct supervisor. F	T	F
9. The critical incident method uses employee self-reports of critical events they experience on the job. F	T	(F)
10. Self-appraisal is the preferred performance appraisal method for executives. F	T	F

SCORING

Of course, you realized that all of the above statements are false. If not, it is advisable to reread the sections where the mistake originated.

REVIEW AND DISCUSSION QUESTIONS

1. Discuss the differences between performance management and performance appraisal.

2. Explain why Agilent is a good example of effective performance management. What did management do to make it one of the great employers?

3. What are the uses of performance appraisals?

4. Suppose that a company for which you work uses a rating scale. The items on the scale are generally personality characteristics. What criticisms would you have of this method?

5. If you were asked to recommend a replacement for the rating scale, what actions would you take before selecting another appraisal technique?

6. Why are direct and objective measures of performance usually considered superior to indirect and subjective measures?

7. If your organization were to use subjective measures to evaluate employee performance, what instructions would you give evaluators about the biases they may encounter?

8. Describe how you would conduct a typical performance evaluation interview.

9. How do the results of performance appraisals affect other human resource management activities?

10. Describe the characteristics of a 360-degree performance appraisal.

11. In what ways is the linking up approach a useful performance management process?

12. What is the relationship between a performance appraisal system and a selection system?

13. Explain how you would go about establishing a performance improvement plan?

14. Explain the legal aspect of a performance appraisal system. Under what circumstances could it become a crucial document?

CRITICAL THINKING QUESTIONS

1. If the dean of your faculty asked you to serve on a committee to develop a performance appraisal system for evaluating the faculty, what performance criteria would you identify? Of these criteria, which ones do you think are most likely to determine the faculty members' success at your school? What standards would you recommend to the dean, regardless of the specific evaluation instrument selected?

2. Your organization has dismissed an employee for not performing up to par. She sues the company for unjust dismissal, claiming that the company's performance appraisal instrument is not a valid assessment tool, since no woman had served on the committee responsible for developing it. Are you able to persuade a judge that, despite the fact that no woman served on the committee, your appraisal instrument is a valid one?

3. Can one performance appraisal instrument be used for all levels in an organization—that is, executives, middle managers, and employees? Why or why not?

ETHICS QUESTION

You are a branch manager, and one of your supervisors is a good friend of yours, the friendship going back to your high school years. His normally average performance has been deteriorating over the last two years, mainly because of his sick wife, a situation that causes him to miss many working days. He also has five children. You know that money is a big issue for him, and if you give him above-average performance ratings he would receive significant bonuses.

Discuss the ethical issues involved.

WEB RESEARCH EXERCISE

1. Helpful Tips for Performance Appraisal

   http://www.flowhelp.com/pa/performance_appraisal.html

   Dexter Hansen describes how traditional performance appraisals can hurt quality and teamwork. What suggestions do you have to avoid this outcome?

2. 360-Degree Performance Appraisal

   http://performance-appraisals.org/faq/index360.htm

   What are the strengths and weaknesses of a 360-degree performance appraisal? Would you be comfortable using it if you were a manager? Why or why not?

3. Matthew Effect

   www.performance-appraisal.com/bias.htm

   What is the Matthew Effect in performance appraisals? Where does the name come from? Can it be avoided? How?

4. "Ten Stupid Things Managers Do to Screw Up Performance Appraisals"

http://performance-appraisals.org/Bacalsappraisalarticles/articles/stupman.htm

Are the 10 "stupid" things some managers do based on research, or do they represent the personal opinion of the author? How valid are they? If they are valid, are there remedies?

5. "Seven Stupid Things Human Resource Departments Do to Screw Up Performance Appraisals"

http://performance-appraisals.org/Bacalsappraisalarticles/articles/stupemp.htm

In what way are these seven "stupid" things different from the 10 "stupid" things managers do (see above)? Who would initiate remedies?

6. About.com

http://humanresources.about.com/od/performancemanagement

Tips about many topics, one of which is on performance management.

INCIDENT 8-1

The Malfunctioning Regional Human Resource Department

For one month, the corporate human resource department of Universal Insurance Ltd. had two specialists review the operations of their regional human resource department in Vancouver. The review of the regional office centred on the department's human resource information base. A brief summary of their findings listed the following observations:

- Each employee's performance appraisal showed little change from the previous year. Poor performers rated poor year in and year out.

- Nearly 70 percent of the appraisals were not initialled by the employee even though company policy required employees to do so after they had discussed their review with the rater.

- Of those employees who initialled the evaluations, several commented that the work standards were irrelevant and unfair.

- A survey of past employees conducted by corporate office specialists revealed that 35 percent of them believed performance feedback was too infrequent.

- Another 30 percent complained about the lack of advancement opportunities because most openings were filled from outside, and no one ever told these workers they were unpromotable.

The corporate and regional human resource directors were dismayed by the findings. Each thought the problems facing the regional office were different.

1. What do you think is the major problem with the performance appraisal process in the regional office?

2. What problems do you think exist with the regional office's (a) job analysis information, (b) human resource planning, (c) training and development, and (d) career planning?

EXERCISE 8-1

Developing a Performance Appraisal System

Time: 1 hour. Form groups of five to six. Assume that your group is the Faculty Evaluation Committee assigned the task to assess the performance of the course instructor.

1. Define at least three performance criteria for the instructor.

2. How would you measure them so that the results would be useful for a tenure and promotion decision?

3. Which type of instrument or method do you suggest? Why?

4. Who should be the appraisers?

5. Time permitting, compare the results in your group with those of another group.

CASE STUDY

Maple Leaf Shoes Ltd.

Performance Appraisal Issues

Maple Leaf Shoes Ltd. is a medium-sized manufacturer of leather and vinyl shoes located in Wilmington, Ontario. It was started in 1973, and currently employs about 500 persons in its Wilmington plant and some 200 more in offices and warehouses throughout Ontario.

It is time for the annual performance appraisal, the "ritual" as some managers call it. They have received the appraisal forms sent by the personnel department one week prior to the deadline. The current system was developed by John McAllister, the previous personnel manager, who recently left the company for a similar job in Toronto. McAllister believes that performance appraisal forms should be simple to understand and easy to complete, so he made one up himself (see Table 1).

Supervisors have to assess each employee by August 31. The assessment is supposed to be discussed with the employee and then returned to the personnel department for filing in the employee's personnel records. If promotions come up, the cumulative ratings are to be considered at that time. The ratings are also supposed to be used as a check when raises are given.

Jane Reynolds, special assistant in the personnel department at Maple Leaf Shoes, looks at the pile of completed rating forms in front of her and shakes her head. She dislikes the way performance evaluation in this company is conducted, and would have preferred to come up with a new approach. However, Robert Clark, the company president, has so far resisted any change and she feels hesitant to tell him what she thinks of it.

A month ago, Reynolds conducted an informal survey to find out how managers and employees felt about the current system. The results confirmed her hunch. Over 60 percent of the managers and more than 75 percent of the employees felt either indifferent or negative about the assessment system. Close to 50 percent of the supervisors filled out the forms in three minutes or less and returned the form to personnel without discussing the results with their staff. Another 40 percent spent sometime with the employees for feedback, but without much discussion. Only 10 percent tried to do an effective performance feedback job by giving each employee detailed feedback and setting new objectives.

TABLE 1

Performance Evaluation Form of Maple Leaf Shoes Ltd.

Performance Evaluation

Supervisors: Please complete this form for each of your employees. Evaluate each performance aspect separately. Return this form by September 1.

	5	4	3	2	1	Score
Quantity of work	Excellent	Good	Average	Fair	Poor	
Quality of work	Excellent	Good	Average	Fair	Poor	
Dependability at work	Excellent	Good	Average	Fair	Poor	
Initiative at work	Excellent	Good	Average	Fair	Poor	
Co-operativeness	Excellent	Good	Average	Fair	Poor	
Communication	Excellent	Good	Average	Fair	Poor	
Energy and enthusiasm	Excellent	Good	Average	Fair	Poor	
Getting along with co-workers	Excellent	Good	Average	Fair	Poor	
					Total	_____
Supervisor's signature						
Employee's name						
Employee number _____						

Reynolds knows from her experience at the company that the forms were rarely retrieved for promotion or pay-raise analyses by her previous boss, McAllister. Because of this, most supervisors may feel the evaluation program is a useless ritual.

The company has never offered any training for its supervisors on how to conduct performance reviews.

Then she thinks of Tim Lance, the consultant. Once, Clark had hired Lance to "look into the present and future role of Maple Leaf Shoes personnel department and suggest appropriate action plans to improve its contribution to the organization and help the company meet its future challenges." In his final report, Lance had made a number of recommendations, but Clark had put off any change until a new personnel manager was hired.

Reynolds remembers that, among other items, the consultant recommended a new approach to appraising employee performance. She feels that this gives her a good reason to push for a revision of the current system. Time is a big issue. She has to prepare for contract negotiations with two separate unions next month. Two more are coming up a month later. She is confident that Clark will accept her recommendation to hire Lance again to come up with a new performance appraisal system.

DISCUSSION QUESTIONS

1. You are Tim Lance. Write an assessment of Maple Leaf Shoes' performance evaluation system.

2. What changes would you recommend to the company? Why?

CASE STUDY

Canadian Pacific and International Bank

Part I

The results were in and Mary Keddy, senior vice-president of human resources, was quite pleased. She was looking at the latest employee attitude survey. The vast majority of the bank's employees felt that the CPIB was a good place to work (which, of course, was borne out by a very low turnover rate, 2 percent lower than that of other banks). Satisfaction with supervision, as measured by the JDI,* was also high, a score of 46 out of 54. The last survey two years ago had a score of 38, so this was a significant improvement. She was also intrigued by the results of the measurement on the quality of communication between supervisors and employees, which was seen as close to excellent, 4.6 on a 5-point scale. That was really good news. Perhaps it was time to think of implementing a pet idea of hers: a 360-degree performance appraisal system. She had toyed with it for several years, but she had felt that the time was not right. But the current survey results were very encouraging. She knew that it was a somewhat daring undertaking, given the high risk of failure, but on the other hand, if it worked the positive outcomes would be significant.

She remembered the attempt to introduce an "all round" feedback system by her previous employer, a large steel company in Ontario, an attempt that had failed miserably. It had been the idea of a quite progressive CEO, but only a handful of middle managers had supported the idea, while a majority of the managers feared that the approach would lead to backstabbing and would be seen by many employees as an opportunity to "get back" at their supervisors.

Given that experience, she wanted to make sure her own attempt at the bank would succeed, since she knew a failure would hurt her career. She felt confident that she had the full support of the CEO and her VP colleagues. She was less confident about the willingness of the bank's middle managers to embrace such a new approach. Being evaluated by subordinates, colleagues, and customers—in addition to the direct supervisor, of course—required a strong degree of self-confidence and significant trust in colleagues and subordinates. The result of the employee survey seemed to

---

*The Job Descriptive Index (JDI) is undoubtedly the best-validated measure of job satisfaction. It includes five measures of satisfaction with nature of work, supervision, peers, advancement opportunities, and pay. It is copyrighted by, and available from, the Psychology Department of Bowling Green University, Bowling Green, OH.

indicate that the trust was there. How about self-confidence? She was not so sure about that part. She certainly had to take this into account in her plan.

She thought it was interesting that she had greater confidence in the employees' acceptance of the new approach. When she had taken her plan for greater diversity to the employees three years ago, she had been pleasantly surprised about the positive reception the plan had received. Of course, she had carefully planned the introduction through staff meetings and training sessions. She had to come up with something similar now.

DISCUSSION QUESTIONS

If you were in Mary Keddy's position, what would you do? Outline a step-by-step plan for the introduction and implementation of a 360-degree performance evaluation system. Include in your plan measures to overcome the anticipated resistance by middle managers.

Part II

There was another issue relating to performance appraisal Mary Keddy had to deal with. In a recent decision, an arbitrator had ruled to reinstate an employee who had been dismissed for inadequate performance. His ruling was somewhat of an embarrassment for the bank, because the arbitrator had argued that the two performance evaluations given the employee over the two years of her employment had rated her performance as below standard, but promising. There was nothing in the written assessment that indicated serious shortcomings. The supervisor had argued she had given the employee several verbal warnings after repeated mistakes, but had not recorded it because she had not wanted to put a blemish on the employee's personnel record. However, after another, more serious mistake, she had decided enough was enough and let the employee go. The union grieved on behalf of the employee, and the case went to arbitration with the above result. Michael Bennett, the CEO, had asked Mary to make sure that such a case did not happen again.

DISCUSSION QUESTION

How can the bank develop a system that will be legally foolproof?

PART-ENDING VIDEOS

"HotJobs.com"

SOURCE: © MHHE Management Library.

Go to Connect to access the video.

ROLE-PLAY 4: PROVIDING PERFORMANCE FEEDBACK

Time required: 30–40 minutes

OBJECTIVES OF THE ROLE-PLAY

1. To give students some experience in providing feedback, which for many supervisors is an unpleasant task, although it can be an effective motivating tool if done properly.

2. To provide an opportunity to improve oral communication skills, since peers and the instructor will give feedback.

PRIOR PREPARATION

1. Study Chapter 8.

2. Read role-play instructions.

GUIDELINES FOR CONDUCTING THE ROLE-PLAY

The performance feedback meeting involves Carl Monahan, Production Manager at Maple Leaf Shoes, and Al Sweeny, Supervisor of the Finishing Operation.

1. Two students play the roles of Carl Monahan and Al Sweeny.

2. Each student reads his or her role description.

3. The instructor signals the beginning and end of the meeting. The meeting should last about 30 minutes. It may end earlier.

4. The remainder of the class time is used for discussion of the behaviours during the role-play and outcomes.

5. Observers are asked to make notes against the questions listed below and discuss their findings at the end of the role-play.

6. The instructor discusses the strong and weak points during the interview.

INSTRUCTIONS FOR OBSERVERS

Please read the questions below and write down your observations. Pay particular attention to the verbal and nonverbal communication between Carl and Al.

Observe the manner in which Carl begins the interview.

1. What, if anything, does Carl do to create a cordial atmosphere?

2. Does Carl state the purpose of the interview early in the session?

3. Is the purpose of the interview stated clearly and concisely?

Observe how the interview is conducted.

1. To what extent does Carl learn how Al feels about his job in general?

2. Does Carl use broad, general questions at the outset?

3. Does Carl criticize Al?

4. Does Carl praise Al?

5. Does Carl accept Al's feelings and ideas?

6. Who talked most?

Observe and evaluate the outcome of the interview.

1. To what extent did Carl arrive at a fairer and more accurate evaluation of Al as a result of the interview?

2. What things did Carl do, if any, to motivate Al to improve?

3. Were relations better or worse after the interview? If worse, why?

4. How might Carl have done a better job?

Canada Labour Code.
i) Industrial Relations
ii) Occupational Safety & Health regulations
iii) Deals with standard

More 90% business covered by → Federal

Objectives of compensation

Effective compensation
- Control cost
- Reward behaviour
- Ensure Equity
- Retain employees
- Acquire personnel
- Legal compliance
- Administrative efficiency.

Challenges affecting of compensation
- Union power - Huge influence.
- Productivity
- Wage & salary policies
- Prevailing wage rate
- Govt. constraints - Minimum pay.

Motivating and Rewarding Human Resources

Employees have to be compensated for their performance fairly and equitably. The human resource department assists managers in assessing the value of a job and determining an appropriate salary, and it will administer the proper benefits. It is also one of the responsibilities of a human resource manager to create a motivating job environment.

Each of these topics is discussed in Part 5. They are important management tools for human resource specialists and managers alike. Regardless of your job, you will find that these tools are helpful ways to ensure effective performance.

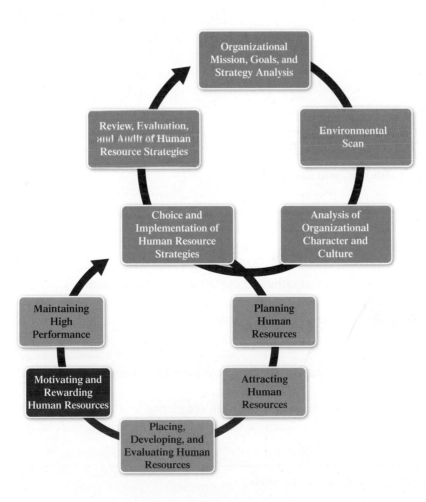

CHAPTER 9

Compensation Management

Management's challenge is to create an environment which stimulates people in their jobs and fosters company growth, and a key aspect of the environment is compensation.

LANCE A. BERGER AND DOROTHY R. BERGER[1]

Genuine and lasting employee motivation is not something management does, but rather a process that management fosters and allows to happen.

MICHAEL KAVANAGH[2]

LEARNING OBJECTIVES

After studying this chapter, you should be able to:

LO1 Explain the objectives of effective compensation management.

LO2 Describe how wages and salaries are determined.

LO3 Identify the major issues that influence compensation management.

LO4 Explain the differences between "equal pay for equal work" and "equal pay for work of equal value."

LO5 Evaluate the advantages and disadvantages of incentive systems.

LO6 Explain the major approaches to group incentive plans.

LO7 Define total compensation.

LO8 Describe pay and organizational strategy.

One way the human resource department improves employee performance, motivation, and satisfaction is through the development, implementation, and administration of compensation systems, which tie rewards to the achievement of company objectives. Compensation is the cash and noncash rewards employees receive in exchange for their work. When the system is properly administered, employees are more likely to be satisfied and motivated to contribute to the achievement of organizational objectives. But when employees perceive their compensation to be inappropriate, performance, motivation, and satisfaction may decline dramatically. The following dialogue is an example of how not to administer pay policy:

> Joan Swensen walked into Al Jorgeson's office, slammed down her clipboard, and said, "I quit!"
>
> "What's the matter, Joan?" Al questioned. "You've been here two years, and I've never seen you so mad."
>
> "That's just the problem. I've been here two years, and this morning I found out that the new man you hired last week, Kurt, is making the same pay that I am," Joan said.
>
> "Well, he does the same work, he works the same hours, and he has the same responsibilities. Would it be fair to pay him less?" Al asked.
>
> "Doesn't experience count for anything around here? When you brought him into the shop, you told me to show him the ropes. So not only did I have more experience, but I am also responsible for training him," Joan responded.
>
> "Okay, okay, I'll talk with Human Resources this afternoon and see if I can get you a raise," Al conceded.
>
> "Don't bother. I'm quitting," Joan asserted, still fuming. "If this company doesn't want to do what is right voluntarily, I'd rather work someplace else."

Compensation programs help to maintain an organization's human resources. When wages and salaries are not administered properly, the firm may lose employees and the money spent to recruit, select, train, and develop them. Even if workers do not quit, as Joan did, they may become dissatisfied with the company.

Dissatisfaction arises because employee needs are affected by *absolute* and *relative* levels of pay. When the total, or absolute, amount of pay is too low, employees cannot meet their physiological or security needs. In industrial societies, the absolute level of pay usually is high enough to meet these basic needs, at least minimally. A more common source of dissatisfaction centres on relative pay, which is an employee's pay compared with that of other workers. For example, Joan's concern was over the relative amount of her salary in comparison with the new, less experienced employee, Kurt. Her additional experience and training responsibilities were not reflected in her pay as compared with Kurt's pay. She felt that her esteem needs were affected, because she did not get the recognition she thought she deserved.

Because compensation affects the organization and its employees, this chapter examines the requirements for an effective compensation system. The chapter also discusses the objectives and procedures used to administer compensation. It concludes with a review of financial incentives.

LO1 HRC 1 & 6

Objectives of Compensation Management

The management of compensation must meet numerous objectives. Sometimes, the ones listed in Figure 9-1 conflict with each other and trade-offs must be made. For example, to retain employees and ensure equity, wage and salary analysts pay similar amounts for jobs of similar value. But a recruiter may want to offer an unusually high salary to attract a qualified recruit. At this point, the hiring manager (the manager of the line department) must make a trade-off between the recruiting objectives and the internal equity objectives, with the guidance of the human resource department.

FIGURE 9-1

Objectives Sought through Effective Compensation Management

- *Acquire qualified personnel.* Compensation needs to be high enough to attract applicants. Since companies compete in the labour market, pay levels must respond to the supply and demand of workers. But sometimes a premium wage rate is needed to attract applicants who are already employed in other firms.   PIRACY

- *Retain present employees.* When compensation levels are not competitive, some employees quit. To prevent employee turnover, pay must be kept competitive with that of other employers.

- *Ensure equity.* The management of wages and salaries strives for internal and external equity. Internal equity requires that pay be related to the relative worth of jobs. That is, jobs of similar value get similar pay. External equity involves paying workers at a rate perceived to be fair compared to what the market pays. Internal equity, also called internal consistency, refers to comparisons among jobs or skills levels inside a single organization. The focus is on comparing jobs and skills in terms of their relative contributions to the organization's objectives.

- *Reward desired behaviour.* Pay should reinforce desired behaviours. Good performance, experience, loyalty, new responsibilities, and other behaviours can be rewarded through an effective compensation plan.

- *Control costs.* A rational compensation program helps an organization to obtain and retain its workforce at a reasonable cost. Without a systematic wage and salary structure, the organization might overpay or underpay its employees.

- *Comply with legal regulations.* As with other aspects of human resource management, wage and salary management faces legal constraints. A sound pay program considers these constraints and ensures compliance with all government regulations that affect employee compensation.

- *Further administrative efficiency.* In pursuing the other objectives of effective compensation management, wage and salary specialists try to design the program so that it can be efficiently administered. Administrative efficiency, however, should be a secondary consideration compared with other objectives.

Other objectives of compensation are to reward desired behaviour and to control costs. These objectives can conflict, too. For example, a department manager might want to reward outstanding performance with a raise, but every raise adds to costs. Here again, the human resource manager must decide between two conflicting goals.

Regardless of the trade-offs, an overriding objective is to maintain legal compliance. For example, the *Canada Labour Code* requires employers to pay minimum wages and time-and-a-half for overtime. Periodically, federal and provincial governments raise minimum wages, and employers must comply regardless of other objectives being sought.

Compensation objectives are not rules, they are guidelines. But the less these guidelines are violated, the more effective wage and salary management can be. To meet these objectives, compensation specialists evaluate every job, conduct wage and salary surveys, and price each job. Through these steps, the appropriate pay level for each job is determined. Figure 9-2 depicts the three major phases of compensation management that take place after the initial job analysis phase. Each phase is discussed in the following sections. Finally, the compensation system has to be part of the overall organizational strategy. The implications are discussed later in this chapter.

FIGURE 9-2

Major Phases of Compensation Management

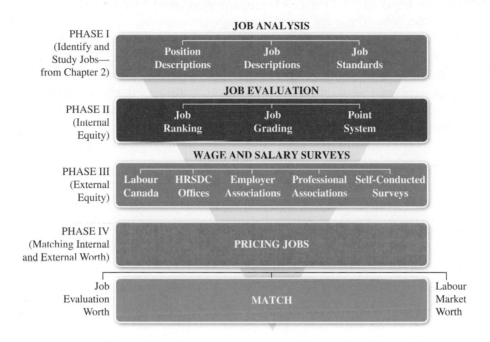

Job Evaluation

Job evaluations are systematic procedures to determine the relative worth or value of jobs. Although evaluations take several different approaches, each one considers the duties, responsibilities, and working conditions of the job. The purpose of job evaluation is to identify which jobs should be paid more than others. Because the process of evaluation is subjective, it is conducted by a group of subject-matter experts. This job evaluation committee is usually made up of compensation specialists and representatives of line management responsible for the job(s) being evaluated.[3] They begin with a review of job analysis information to learn about the duties, responsibilities, and working conditions that shape their evaluation. With this knowledge, the relative worth of jobs is determined by selecting a job evaluation method. Before the enactment of pay equity legislation, there were a number of job evaluation methods, such as job ranking, job grading, and the point system. Now the point system is, by far, the most commonly used evaluation method as it provides, relatively, the best information regarding job values.[4] (See <www.hr-guide.com/jobevaluation.htm> for examples of job evaluation forms.) For comparison purposes, we provide brief descriptions of some of the other evaluation methods, but we focus on the point system.

---

job evaluations

Systematic process of assessing job content and ranking jobs according to a consistent set of job characteristics and worker traits.

Job Ranking

The simplest and least precise method of job evaluation is **job ranking**. Specialists review the job analysis information for each job. Then each job is ranked subjectively according to its importance in comparison with other jobs. These are overall rankings, although raters may consider the responsibility, skill, effort, and working conditions of each job. It is quite possible that important elements of some jobs may be overlooked while unimportant items are weighted too heavily. What is even more damaging, these rankings do not differentiate the relative importance of jobs. For example, the job of janitor might be ranked as 1, the secretary's job might get a 2, and the office manager might rank as a 3. But the secretarial position might be three times as important as the janitorial job and half as important as the job of office manager. The job ranking approach does not allow for these relative differences between jobs. Pay scales based on these broad rankings ensure that more important jobs are paid more. But since the rankings lack precision, the resulting pay levels may be inaccurate.

job ranking

A form of job evaluation in which jobs are ranked subjectively according to their overall worth to the organization.

Job Grading

Job grading, or job classification, is a slightly more sophisticated method than job ranking, but it, too, is not very precise. It works by assigning each job a grade, as explained in Figure 9-3. The standard description in the figure that most nearly matches the job description determines the grade of the job. Once again, more important jobs are paid more. But the lack of precision can lead to inaccurate pay levels. The largest user of this approach has been the Public Service Commission of Canada <http://www.psc-cfp.gc.ca/index-eng.htm>, which is gradually replacing this approach with more sophisticated methods.

job grading

A form of job evaluation that assigns jobs to predetermined job classifications according to their relative worth to the organization.

 HRC 6

Point System

As mentioned before, research shows that the **point system** is used more than any other evaluation method. It evaluates the critical—also called compensable—factors of each job, determines different levels or degrees for each factor, and allocates points to each level. Although it is more difficult to develop initially, it is more precise than other methods because it can handle critical factors in more detail. It is usually done by a job evaluation committee or an individual analyst. In most cases, organizations use a system that has predetermined job factors and assigned points to each factor. This system requires six steps to implement. It is very rare that a company develops a system from scratch.

point system

A form of job evaluation that assesses the relative importance of the job's key factors in order to arrive at the relative worth of jobs.

FIGURE 9-3

A Job Classification Schedule for Use with the Job Grading Method

Empire Machine Shop	
Job Classification Schedule	
Directions: To determine appropriate job grade, match standard description with job description.	
Job Grade	**Standard Description**
I	Work is simple and highly repetitive, done under close supervision, requiring minimal training and little responsibility or initiative. *Examples:* Janitor, file clerk
II	Work is simple and repetitive, done under close supervision, requiring some training or skill. Employee is expected to assume responsibility or exhibit initiative only rarely. *Examples:* Administrative assistant I, machine cleaner
III	Work is simple, with little variation, done under general supervision. Training or skill required. Employee has minimum responsibilities and must take some initiative to perform satisfactorily. *Examples:* Parts expediter, machine oiler, administrative assistant II
IV	Work is moderately complex, with some variation, done under general supervision. High level of skill required. Employee is responsible for equipment or safety; regularly exhibits initiative. *Examples:* Machine operator I, tool-and-die apprentice
V	Work is complex, varied, done under general supervision. Advanced skill level required. Employee is responsible for equipment and safety; shows high degree of initiative. *Examples:* Machine operator II, tool-and-die specialist

Step 1: Determine Compensable Factors

Figure 9-4 shows how the factor of responsibility can be broken down into the following components:

- safety of others
- equipment and materials
- assisting trainees
- product/service quality

Step 2: Determine Levels (or Degrees) of Factors

Because the extent of responsibility or other factors may vary from job to job, the point system creates several levels (or degrees) associated with each factor. Figure 9-4 shows four levels, although more or fewer may be used. These levels help analysts to reward different degrees of responsibility, skills, and other critical factors.

Step 3: Allocate Points to Subfactors

With the factors listed down one side and the levels placed across the top as in Figure 9-4, the result is a point system matrix. Points are then assigned to each subfactor to reflect the relative importance of different subfactors. Analysts start with Level IV and weight each subfactor with the number of points they think it deserves. This allocation allows them to give very precise weights to each element of the job. For example, if assisting trainees is twice as important as product/service quality, it is assigned twice as many points, 80 versus 40.

FIGURE 9-4

Point System Matrix

Critical Factors	Levels or Degrees				Factor Points
	I	II	III	IV	
1. Responsibility (weight 40%)					**400**
Subfactors:					
a. Safety of others	20	80	140	200	
b. Equipment and materials	8	24	56	80	
c. Assisting trainees	8	24	56	80	
d. Product/service quality	4	16	28	40	
2. Skill (weight 30%)					**300**
Subfactors:					
a. Experience	18	72	126	180	
b. Education/training	12	48	84	120	
3. Effort (weight 20%)					**200**
Subfactors:					
a. Physical	8	32	56	80	
b. Mental	12	48	84	120	
4. Working conditions (weight 10%)					**100**
Subfactors:					
a. Unpleasant conditions	3	12	21	30	
b. Hazards	7	28	49	70	
				Total points	**1,000**

A detailed calculation of the data in Figure 9-4 is provided in Appendix A at the end of this chapter.

Spotlight *on* HRM

Profit-Sharing Plans Help Keep Great Workers

By Larry Ginsberg

Successful entrepreneurs understand that their prosperity depends upon hiring and retaining great employees. One of the key concerns for workers is their compensation package. Compensation will usually include a base salary, commissions (if the position is related to sales or marketing), benefits, employee profit-sharing plans, and, if appropriate, stock option plans. To build and keep a winning team, you must determine an appropriate compensation package. Here's what to consider:

(Continued)

Base Salary and Benefits

Your industry association will have information regarding the common base salary and benefits for your business. Confirm this information by talking to your peers. Another significant source is executive search consultants that specialize in your industry. The main advantages of using these consultants from time to time are that they are professionally obliged to not steal your employees to fill other positions and they have a great deal of information about your industry.

As a general rule, you should pay somewhere in the third quartile (about 75 percent) of the range for a particular position. For example, if the range is $28,000 to $40,000, your starting salary should be about $37,000. If you pay in the low part of the range, it is easy for new employees to move on to a competitor for much more money—after you have invested the time and effort to train them. Similarly, your benefits package should be at least comparable to the norm for the industry.

If a commission is paid to an employee, as opposed to salary, the employee may be able to claim certain tax-deductible expenses that are allowed as an employee.

Employee Profit-Sharing Plans

There are basically two types of employee profit-sharing plans. The first is an annual bonus that is generally based upon overall company profit and/or tied to specific items, such as sales, that an employee can influence. A bonus can be set up as a liability in your company books at your fiscal year-end. For the bonus to be tax-deductible to the firm in the fiscal year, Canada Customs and Revenue Agency requires you to pay it within 180 days of your year-end.

The second type of plan is a trust that is set up to allow an employer to share profit from the business with some or all employees. This trust is called an Employees' Profit Sharing Plan, or EPSP. An EPSP allows an employer to deduct in the current fiscal year all monies paid to the trust within 120 days of the fiscal year-end. Employer contributions are determined using a formula that is tied to the company's profit.

Funds contributed are allocated among employees who are members of the plan. In addition, money earned by the trust and any capital gains or losses of the trust are allocated to the employees, who are taxed on these amounts.

The plan can be established to vest the benefits over time. This helps guarantee employee loyalty, as the funds are not available until they have been vested by the terms of the plan. For example, if the current-year profit allocation is set up to vest 50 percent in the second year and 50 percent in the third year from the date of the contribution, employees who choose to leave after one year receive no money. They only get a credit on their personal tax return for the tax paid on amounts not received. This plan is ideal to help knowledge-based companies retain their vital assets: employees.

The major advantages of an EPSP are that a company receives a current-year deduction but only needs to make the payment within 120 days of the fiscal year-end, that employees who leave voluntarily lose the opportunity to participate in the plan, that funds in the plan are invested by the trustees and earn interest, and that this plan does not affect any other employee compensation or retirement arrangement. But any company should consult with an accountant before setting up a plan.

Smart entrepreneurs are careful to structure their employee compensation packages to ensure they maintain the benefit from the training and experience they give their employees. Hiring a new employee is expensive and the related training is time-consuming; protecting this investment is critical to the long-term success of any venture.

SOURCE: Larry Ginsberg is co-author of *Small Business, Big Money*. He can be reached at ginsberg@ginsorg.com.

Step 4: Allocate Points to Levels (Degrees)

Once the points for each job element are satisfactory under column IV, analysts allocate points across each row to reflect the importance of the different levels. Usually equal point differences are used, but analysts or job evaluation committees may decide to use variable differences. See Appendix A at the end of this chapter for a calculation of equal differences.

Step 5: Develop the Point Manual

The point manual contains a written explanation of each job element, as shown in Figure 9-5 for responsibility of equipment and materials. It also defines what is expected for the four levels (degrees) of each subfactor. This information is needed to assign jobs to their appropriate level.

Step 6: Apply the Point System

When the point matrix and manual are ready, the relative value of each job can be determined. This process is subjective. It requires specialists to compare job descriptions with the point manual for each subfactor. The match between the job description and the point manual statement reveals the level and points for each subfactor of every job. Once completed, the points for each subfactor are added to find the total number of points for the job. An example of this matching process for Machine Operator I appears below:

The job description of Machine Operator I states: "[O]perator is responsible for performing preventive maintenance (such as cleaning, oiling, and adjusting belts) and repairs." The sample point manual excerpt in Figure 9-5 states: "Level III: … performs preventive maintenance and repairs. …" Since the job description and the point manual match at Level III, the points for the equipment subfactor are 55. Repeating this matching process for each subfactor yields the total points for the job of Machine Operator I.

FIGURE 9-5

Point Manual Description of "Responsibility: Equipment and Materials"

1. Responsibility …

b. *Equipment and Materials.* Each employee is responsible for conserving the company's equipment and materials. This includes reporting malfunctioning equipment or defective materials, keeping equipment and materials cleaned or in proper order, and maintaining, repairing, or modifying equipment and materials according to individual job duties. The company recognizes that the degree of responsibility for equipment and materials varies widely throughout the organization.

Level I.   Employee reports malfunctioning equipment or defective materials to immediate superior.

Level II.   Employee maintains the appearance of equipment or order of materials and has responsibility for the security of such equipment or materials.

Level III. Employee performs preventive maintenance and repairs on equipment or corrects defects in materials.

Level IV. Employee makes replacement and purchasing decisions and is in control of the "equipment and materials" factor.

After the total points for each job are known, the jobs are ranked. As with the job ranking and job grading systems, this relative ranking should be reviewed by department managers to ensure that it is appropriate.

Beyond the three job evaluation methods discussed in this section, many other variations exist. Large organizations often modify standard approaches to create unique in-house variations. The "Hay Plan," <http://en.wikipedia.org/wiki/Hay_Guide_Chart> for example, is one variation widely used by Canadian and U.S. firms. This proprietary method, marketed by the large consulting firm Hay and Associates, relies on a committee evaluation of critical job factors to determine each job's relative worth. Although other job evaluation approaches exist, all effective job evaluation schemes attempt to determine a job's relative worth to ensure internal equity.

Spotlight *on* ETHICS

Job Evaluation

You are the human resource director of a large grocery chain. As part of a restructuring of its compensation system, and to comply with pay equity legislation, the company has recently switched from the job ranking

(Continued)

system to the point system. You are chairing the Job Evaluation Committee, which is ready to allocate points to the cashier job category, the largest category in the company. The discussion so far has focused on how many points to allocate to the responsibility factor, and the committee is essentially split 50–50 on the numbers. As it so happened, there are three women and three men on the committee. The women argue that cashiers have the same responsibility as the accounting clerks, who are all male, in the office. The male members of the committee, on the other hand, disagreed, suggesting that a cashier's responsibility is to balance the cash register, not accounts, a more difficult task. You seem to have the deciding vote. The dilemma from your point of view is that all the cashiers are women while the three accounting clerks are all male. In your assessment you agree that the accounting clerks carry a higher responsibility and deserve more points. If you support the male members of the committee you are pretty sure that the cashiers will launch a pay equity grievance, usually a costly and time-consuming affair. If you agree with the female members it means cashiers will fall into a higher pay category, increasing payroll expenses significantly. You know very well that the competition in the food market is fierce, with low profit margins (2 to 3 percent). A pay increase would have a direct impact on the bottom line. What do you do?

LO2

Wage and Salary Surveys

All job evaluation techniques result in a ranking of jobs based upon their perceived relative worth. This assures **internal equity**; that is, jobs that are worth more will be paid more. But how much should be paid? What constitutes **external equity**?

internal equity   *equity within org.*
Perceived equity of a pay system in an organization.

external equity
Perceived fairness in pay relative to what other employers are paying for the same type of work.

To determine a fair rate of compensation, most firms rely on **wage and salary surveys**, which discover what other employers in the same labour market are paying for specific key jobs. The *labour market*—the area from which the employer recruits—is generally the local community; however, firms may have to compete for some workers in a wider market. Consider how the president of one large university viewed the market:

> Our labour market depends on the type of position we are trying to fill. For the hourly paid jobs such as janitor, data entry clerk, and secretary, the labour market is the surrounding metropolitan community. When we hire professors, our labour market is Canada. We have to compete with universities in other provinces to get the type of faculty member we seek. When we have the funds to hire a distinguished professor, our labour market is the whole world.

wage and salary surveys
Studies made of wages and salaries paid by other organizations within the employer's labour market.

Sources of Compensation Data

Wage and salary data are benchmarks against which analysts compare compensation levels. Sources for this information include the following:

- Employment and Social Development Canada
- Canadian Human Resource Centres

- Employee associations
- Professional associations
- Private consultants

The major problem with all these published surveys is their varying comparability. Analysts cannot always be sure that their jobs match those reported in the survey. Just matching job titles may be misleading; federal, provincial, and association job descriptions using the same title may be considerably different. Since most government-published surveys rely on the National Occupational Classification (NOC), any job description should be compared with descriptions in the NOC.

At this point, all jobs are ranked according to their relative worth, as a result of the job evaluation process. Through wage and salary surveys, the rate for key jobs in the labour market is also known. This leaves the last phase of wage and salary management, pricing the jobs.

<hr />

 6

Pricing Jobs

Pricing jobs includes two activities: establishing the appropriate pay level for each job and grouping the different pay levels into a structure that can be managed effectively.

Brian Gable/The Globe and Mail. Reprinted with permission from The Globe and Mail/CP Images

Pay Levels

The appropriate pay level for any job reflects its relative and absolute worth. A job's relative worth is determined by its ranking through the job evaluation process. The absolute worth of a job is influenced by what the labour market pays similar jobs. To set the right pay level means combining the job evaluation rankings and the survey wage rates. Of course, many other considerations will determine the final pay level, for example, the organization's pay policy.

This information is combined through the use of a graph called a *scattergram*. As Figure 9-6 illustrates, its vertical axis shows the pay rates. If the point system is used to determine the ranking of jobs, the horizontal axis is in points. The scattergram is created by plotting the total points and wage level for each **key job**. Thus, each dot represents the intersection of the point value and the wage rate for a particular key job. For example, key Job A in Figure 9-6 is worth 500 points and is paid $22 an hour.

key job

A job that is similar and common in the organization and its labour market—for example, accountant, tool-and-die maker.

FIGURE 9-6

The Development of a Wage-Trend Line

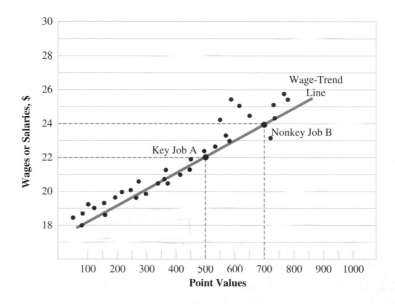

Through the dots that represent key jobs, a *wage-trend line* is drawn as close to as many points as possible. (This line can be done freehand or, more accurately, by a statistical technique called the *least squares method*.[5]) The wage-trend line uses two steps to help determine the wage rates for nonkey jobs. First, the point value for the nonkey job is located on the horizontal axis. Second, a line is traced vertically to the wage-trend line, then horizontally to the dollar scale. The amount on the vertical scale is the appropriate wage rate for the nonkey job. For example, nonkey Job B is worth 700 points. By tracing a vertical line up to the wage-trend line and then horizontally to the vertical (dollar) scale, it can be seen in Figure 9-6 that the appropriate wage rate for Job B is $24 per hour.

The Compensation Structure

A medium-sized organization with 2,000 workers and 325 separately identifiable jobs would present the wage and salary analyst with complex problems. The existence of 325 separate wage rates would be meaningless, because the differences in wages between each job might be no more than a few cents.

Compensation analysts find it more convenient to lump jobs together into job classes. In the job grade approach, jobs are already grouped into predetermined categories. With other methods, the grouping is done by creating job grades based on the previous ranking, pay, or points. In the point system, for example, classifications are based on point ranges: 0 to 100, 101 to 150, 151 to 200, and so forth. This grouping causes the wage-trend line to be replaced with a series of ascending dashes, as shown in Figure 9-7. Thus, all jobs in the same class receive the same wage rate. A job valued at 105 points, for example, is paid the same as a job with 145 points. Having too many grades defeats the purpose of grouping; having too few groupings results in workers with jobs of widely varying importance receiving the same pay.

FIGURE 9-7

The Impact of Job Classes on the Wage-Trend Line

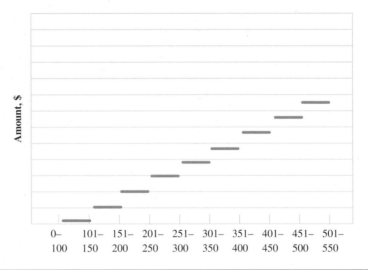

The problem with flat rates for each job class is that exceptional performance cannot be rewarded. To give a worker a merit increase requires moving the employee into a higher job class. This upsets the entire balance of internal equity developed through job evaluations. To solve these problems, most firms use rate ranges for each class. A **rate range** is simply a pay range for each job class.

rate range

A pay range for each job class.

For example, suppose that the wage-trend line indicates $24 is the average hourly rate for a particular job class. Every employee in that class gets $24, if a flat rate is paid. With a rate range of $3 for each class, a marginal performer can be paid $21 at the bottom of the range, as indicated in Figure 9-8. Then an average performer is placed at midpoint in the rate range, or $24. When performance appraisals indicate above-average performance, the employee may be given a **merit raise** of, say, $1.00 per hour for the exceptional performance. If this performance continues, another merit raise of $1.00 can be granted. Once the employee reaches the top of the rate range, no more wage increases will be forthcoming. Either a promotion or a general across-the-board pay raise needs to occur for this worker's wage to exceed $27. An across-the-board increase moves the entire wage-trend line upward.

merit raise

A pay increase given to individual workers according to an evaluation of their performance.

FIGURE 9-8

Varying Wage Ranges for Job

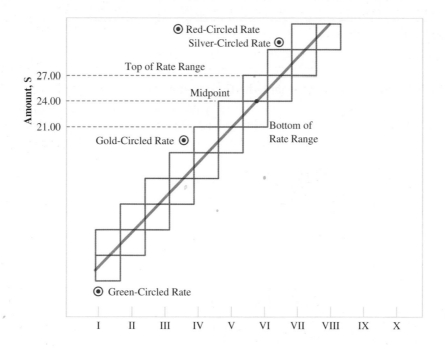

As new jobs are created, the wage and salary section performs a job evaluation. From this evaluation, the new job is assigned to an appropriate job class. If the rate ranges are used, the new employee will start at the bottom of the range and receive raises, where appropriate, to the top of the rate range.

LO3 HRC 1 & 3 & 6

Challenges Affecting Compensation

Even the most rational methods of determining pay must be tempered by several challenges. The implications of these contingencies may cause wage and salary analysts to make further adjustments to employee compensation.

Prevailing Wage Rates

Some jobs must be paid more than is indicated by their relative worth because of market forces. In the 1990s, there was a scarcity of software specialists. Fitting these jobs onto a wage-trend line often resulted in a wage rate below their prevailing wage rate. Because demand outstripped supply, market forces caused wage rates for these specialists to rise above their relative worth when compared with other jobs. Firms that needed these talents were forced to pay a premium. Diagrammatically, these rates appear on a wage chart as a **red-circled rate**, as seen in Figure 9-8. The term arises from the practice of marking out-of-line rates with a red circle on the chart. In the early 2000s, the shortage of information technology professionals was so serious that firms first offered huge hiring bonuses, but were then eventually forced to raise salaries for these jobs, even at the entry level.[6] Some companies pay more than the maximum salary level to employees with long job tenure. This salary level appears then as *silver-circled*. *Gold-circled* salaries indicate payments beyond the maximum level if an employee receives a special merit pay that does not fit into the established range.

---

red-circled rate

A rate of pay higher than the contractual, or formerly established, rate for the job.

Some jobs may be paid less than the established minimum. This happens when an organization uses salary caps (limits). For example, a company may pay newly hired employees with no experience rates 10 to 20 percent below the pay minimum until they have "learned the ropes." This level is *green-circled*.

Electricians belong to a dominant union, which is why their wage rates are so high. Is it justified to pay an electrician double—or close to double—what a carpenter makes?

Ryan McVay/Getty Images.

Union Power

When unions represent a portion of the workforce, they may be able to use their power to obtain wage rates out of proportion to their relative worth. For example, wage and salary studies may determine that

$20 an hour is appropriate for a truck driver. But if the union insists on $22, the human resource department may believe paying the higher rate is less expensive than a strike. Sometimes the union controls most or all of a particular skill, such as carpentry or plumbing. This enables the union actually to raise the prevailing rate for those jobs.

Productivity

Companies must make a profit to survive. Without profits, the company cannot attract the investors necessary to remain competitive. Therefore, a company cannot pay workers more than they contribute back to the firm through their productivity. When this happens (because of scarcity or union power), companies usually redesign those jobs, train new workers to increase their supply, or automate.

Wage and Salary Policies

Most organizations have policies that cause wages and salaries to be adjusted. One common policy is to give nonunion workers the same raise as that received by unionized workers. Some companies have a policy of paying a premium above the prevailing wages to minimize turnover or to recruit the best workers. Also, some companies have automatic cost-of-living clauses that give employees automatic raises when the Statistics Canada cost-of-living index increases. Raises or policies that increase employee compensation move the wage-trend line upward.

A useful index for salary administrators is the **compa-ratio**, an indicator of how the salary of an employee relates to the midpoint of the relevant pay grade. A compa-ratio of above or below 1 shows that the individual's salary is above or below the midpoint of the pay grade. The pay-grade midpoint can be viewed as a benchmark for salary decision criteria such as performance, tenure, and experience. The formula for the individual compa-ratio is:

$$\text{Compa-ratio} = \frac{\text{Salary of the employee}}{\text{Midpoint of the pay grade}}$$

compa-ratio

An index that indicates how an individual's or a group's salary relates to the midpoint of their relevant pay grades.

Also of interest to salary administrators is the compa-ratio for groups. A ratio above 1 indicates that a large number of employees are bunched at the top of the pay grade (top-heavy). A ratio below 1 may be caused by many new employees or may be an indication of high turnover. The formula for the group compa-ratio is:

$$\text{Compa-ratio} = \frac{\text{Average of salaries paid}}{\text{Midpoint of the pay grade}}$$

Government Constraints

Canada is a nation of wage-earners. What people earn bears a direct relationship to the economy and general welfare of the population. Since the 1930s, the federal government has regulated some aspects of compensation.

The *Canada Labour Code* in its revised version of 1971 is the most comprehensive law affecting compensation rights for organizations under federal jurisdiction. It sets requirements for minimum wage, overtime pay, equal pay, child labour, and record keeping. The minimum wage (see below) and overtime provisions require employers to pay at least a minimum hourly rate of pay regardless of the worth of the job. (When the minimum is increased by law, it may mean adjusting upward the wages of those who already earn above the minimum. If those just above minimum wage do not also get raises, wage differentials will be squeezed together. This is called *wage compression*.) For every covered job, the organization must pay one-and-a-half times the employee's regular pay rate for all hours over 40 per week. Executive, administrative, professional, and other employees are exempt from the overtime provisions. Laws involving similar regulations have been enacted by each province for organizations under their jurisdiction.

Canada Labour Code
Federal law regulating labour relations under federal jurisdiction.

Minimum Wages

All the provinces have minimum-wage legislation that applies to most classes of workers, other than farm labourers and domestic servants. The legislation provides for a board to set minimum-wage rates, and these rates are imposed by means of minimum-wage orders that are periodically issued.[7] Wide discretion is given to all provincial boards for determination of the classes of employees for which minimum wages are to be established. The current minimum-wage rates at the provincial and federal levels can be found at <http://srv116.services.gc.ca/dimt-wid/sm-mw/rpt1.aspx?lang=eng>. The rates shown are typical for persons 18 years of age and over. For employees under 18, the rates are somewhat lower.

The federal government passed the *Minimum Wages Act* in 1935, in compliance with one of the three conventions adopted by the International Labour Organization. However, under the *Constitution Act, 1867* (formerly the *British North America Act*), minimum-wage legislation comes under provincial jurisdiction. The federal *Minimum Wages Act* currently applies to all government agencies, Crown corporations, and some selected industries as mentioned in Chapter 4.

Contracts with the Government

The *Fair Wages and Hours of Labour Act* applies to contracts made with the Government of Canada for all types of work. It is mandatory on the part of contractors dealing with the Government of Canada to pay fair wages and establish an eight-hour workday during all such work.[8]

Staff Records

The Canada Labour Code requires every employer in those industries falling under federal jurisdiction to furnish information relating to wages of employees, their hours of work, general holidays, annual vacation, and conditions of employment whenever the Ministry of Labour demands it. Similar provisions exist in the provincial legislation. Accurate records are also to be kept, for example, on maternity leave and severance pay relating to all affected employees. This is to ensure that all provisions of the legislation relating to such things as minimum wages, maximum weekly hours, and overtime payments are strictly adhered to by each employer.

Criticisms of Minimum-Wage Regulations

It has been pointed out by some that minimum-wage regulations increase the cost of production in Canada. This may eventually work against the workers rather than for them, as Marc Law argues:

> In recent years, minimum wages across Canada have risen more than the average increase in manufacturing wages. And some economists are suggesting … [that] it could lead to an intolerable increase [in unemployment] and cause the major burdens to fall precisely on the workers it was designed to help.[9]

Increases in minimum wages are usually accompanied by increases in unemployment figures of low-skilled and young persons in the workforce. It is also pointed out by some that continual increases in minimum-wage rates may actually contribute to the inflationary trends in the economy.[10] There is, however, no conclusive evidence on the matter one way or the other at this time.

LO4 HRC 1 & 2 & 3 & 6

Pay Equity

In 1977, the *Canada Labour Code*, Part I, was repealed and replaced by the *Canadian Human Rights Act*. Since this act prohibits, among other things, discrimination because of sex, it is illegal for companies to pay women less than men if their jobs involve equal skills, effort, responsibilities, and conditions. The government enforces these provisions by requiring wrongdoers to equalize pay and make up past discrepancies.

As first mentioned in Chapter 4, an important issue in compensation management and equal opportunity is **equal pay for work of equal value,** the concept that jobs of comparable worth to the organization should be equally paid (referred to as **pay equity**). The idea goes beyond **equal pay for equal work** (referred to as *equal pay*), part of the *Canada Labour Code* since 1971, which requires an employer to pay men and women the same wage or salary when they do the same work. Exceptions to equal pay of both types are allowed when a valid seniority or merit system exists. Employers can pay more for seniority or to workers who perform better and merit higher pay. Exceptions are also allowed when pay is determined by the employee's production, such as sales commissions.

equal pay for work of equal value *(pay equity)*

The principle of equal pay for men and women in jobs with comparable content; based on criteria of skill, effort, responsibility, and working conditions; part of the Canadian Human Rights Act.

pay equity

A policy to eliminate the gap between income of men and women, ensuring that salary ranges correspond to value of work performed.

equal pay for equal work *(equal pay)*

The principle or policy of equal rates of pay for all employees in an establishment performing the same kind and amount of work, regardless of sex, race, or other characteristics of individual workers not related to ability or performance.

The pay equity concept, however, takes a different perspective. It became law in an amendment to the *Canadian Human Rights Act* in 1978. It makes it illegal to discriminate on the basis of job value (or content). For example, if a nurse and an electrician both received approximately the same number of job evaluation points under the point system, they would have to be paid the same wage or salary, regardless of market conditions. This approach to compensation is sought by governments as a means of eliminating the historical gap between the income of men and women, which results in women in Canada earning about 74 percent as much as men.[11] This gap exists in part because women have traditionally found work in lower-paying occupations, such as teaching, retailing, nursing, and secretarial work, and in such positions as receptionist and telephone operator.

It should be emphasized, however, that the above-mentioned figure of 74 percent as the earning gap between men and women is misleading, although it is widely used by proponents of equal pay to point to the "discrimination" in pay against women. This figure emerges if one compares all men and women wage-earners regardless of job tenure and skill level. But this is not an appropriate comparison. If a woman chooses to leave the labour force to have children and to bring them up and then returns to continue her career, she will have missed many training and advancement opportunities in her organization as compared to her male colleague who presumably continued to grow and advance in his career.

By using comparable groups, the pay gap decreases to between 5 to 10 percent, depending on the group studied.[12] For example, the income of single women aged 35 to 44 was 94.5 percent of that earned by men of the same age. (If one looks only at the most educated members of that age group–single females with a university degree–women actually made 6 percent more than their male counterparts.) Taking all of the above factors into account, it still leaves a gap of between 5 and 10 percent that cannot be explained. There is no evidence, however, that there is a conspiracy among entrepreneurs and managers to keep the wages of female-dominated jobs down. (*Note:* A job is gender-dominated if, depending on jurisdiction, 60 to 70 percent of the job occupants are from one sex.)

Pay equity ensures equal pay for work of equal value. Why is it then that women workers in Canada make only 74 cents compared to the $1 men make?

Jupiterimages/Stockbyte/Thinkstock

Then what keeps women's wages below comparable men's wages? Society's expectations about the role of women in our culture have determined, to a large degree, women's job choices. Traditionally, it was the son who, after high school, would go on to study for a profession and pursue a career, while the daughter had to be content to learn household skills, such as cooking and sewing, or, at the most, secretarial skills, such as typing and shorthand. This attitude has changed, as enrollments in our business, engineering, law, and medical schools demonstrate. But even today, a woman's job choice is often influenced by her role as a homemaker and mother, as evidenced in the following study:

Two researchers were asked to examine a manufacturing company whose management wanted to find out why in some jobs there were so few women despite the company's sincere employment equity program. They found that some of the higher-paying jobs were not attractive to women because of overtime requirements, shift work, and heavy lifting. Women felt that they had a stronger responsibility toward the family and could not afford to work overtime or do shift work. This study—and other studies—shows that some contextual factors such as family considerations, which do not enter the job evaluation process, have a strong impact on job choices.[13]

What makes the issue of equal pay for work of equal value very tricky is the lack of any generally acceptable definition of "equal value" and how it can be measured. The definition offered in the guidelines issued by the Canadian Human Rights Commission is not of much help:

Value of work is the value which the work performed by an employee in a given establishment represents in relation to the value of work of another employee, or group of employees, the value being determined on the basis of approved criteria, without the wage market or negotiated wage rates being taken into account.[14]

The approved criteria referred to above are skill, effort, responsibility, and working conditions. These criteria will be considered together; that is, they will form a composite measure. This does not mean that employees must be paid the same salary, even if their jobs are considered equal. The equal wage guidelines define seven "reasonable factors" that can justify differences in wages:

1. different performance ratings (ratings must be based on a formal appraisal system and be brought to the attention of each employee);

2. seniority (based on length of service);

3. red-circling (because of job re-evaluation);

4. rehabilitation assignment (e.g., after lengthy absence because of sickness);

5. demotion pay procedures (because of unsatisfactory work performance, or reassignment because of labour force surplus);

6. procedure of phased-in wage reductions; and

7. temporary training positions.[15]

These factors justify a difference in wages only if they are applied consistently and equitably. It must be clearly demonstrable that existing wage differences are not based on sex.

Where does this leave the human resource manager? The *Canadian Human Rights Act* applies only to organizations under federal jurisdiction, such as federal government departments and Crown agencies, the RCMP, the Canadian Armed Forces, banks, airlines, most railway companies, and communication firms. In addition, most provinces have enacted pay equity legislation (Newfoundland and Saskatchewan are exceptions), which means organizations under their jurisdiction have to comply with these laws (in Ontario and Quebec the laws also apply to the private sector). Fortunately, these laws are modelled on the federal one, and use similar criteria.

A human resource manager has to make sure that the company's pay system is in line with the province's or the federal government's legislation. The following measures are suggested:

• Review the organization's human resource policies, procedures, and practices with the objective of determining relevance and consistency of application.

- Review recruiting and promotional decisions and track career trends, particularly with respect to compensation levels; examine how the organization has treated employees in the past.

- Review human resource planning techniques and procedures to determine consistency of application throughout the organization.

- Review the underlying philosophy and rationale of the job evaluation plan(s) currently used (e.g., are they appropriate for the organization today; has the evaluation process been as objective as possible; what "groups" fall under which plan, and is this appropriate?).

- By specific position, examine the differential between earnings of men and women in the organization.

- By salary grade, examine the differential between earnings of men and women.

- For groups of positions performing work of "relative importance," examine the differential between earnings of men and women.

- Examine all employee benefits practices across the organization, including those in place for plant and hourly rated employees, to determine if inequalities exist (e.g., to determine if overtime, vacation, and other benefit levels are consistently applied).

Should inequalities be found, it would be advisable to eliminate them; or if the organization is large, it may be useful to implement an employment equity program. Initiation of such a program would not imply any past wrongdoing on the part of the organization, but it is encouraged by federal and provincial human rights commissions. For an overview of pay equity in various Canadian jurisdictions, see <http://www.payequity.gov.on.ca>.

Provincial Legislation

As mentioned, most provinces have enacted pay equity legislation. Manitoba, Nova Scotia, and Ontario legislators took a new approach to pay equity legislation by creating a Pay Equity Bureau, or, in Ontario's and Nova Scotia's case, Pay Equity Commissions, that are responsible for the administration and implementation of the laws. All three also take a proactive approach by requiring employers to evaluate all jobs in an organization under a single, gender-neutral job evaluation scheme, and to apply the scheme to classes of work where one sex predominates. In contrast, the laws of the remaining provinces are reactive, since they deal with inequities only if the latter are brought to the attention of the appropriate human rights commissions. For a discussion of provincial pay equity legislation, see <http://www.canadianlabour.ca/news-room/publications/quick-education-pay-equity-womens-economic-equality> or <http://en.wikipedia.org/wiki/Equal_pay_for_women>.

HRC 6

The Pay-for-Performance Model

Incentive systems provide the clearest link between pay and performance or productivity (*performance* is the accomplishment of assigned tasks; *productivity* is the measure of output). **Incentive pay** is directly linked to an employee's performance or productivity. Employees who work under a financial incentive system find that their performance (productivity) determines, in whole or part, their income. A typical example of an incentive pay is a salesperson's commission. The more the salesperson sells, the more he or she earns.

pay to encourage desirable behaviors.

incentive pay

Compensation that is directly tied to an employee's performance, productivity, or both.

One of the most significant benefits of financial incentives is that better performance is reinforced on a regular basis. Unlike raises and promotions, the reinforcement is generally quick and frequent—usually with each paycheque. Since the worker sees the results of the desired behaviour quickly, that behaviour is more likely to continue. The employer benefits, because wages are given in proportion to performance, not for the indirect measure of time worked. And if employees are motivated by the system to expand their output, recruiting expenses for additional employees and capital outlays for new workstations are minimized. A switch from hourly to direct incentive pay can be quite dramatic as one study shows:

> Professor Lazear, Stanford University <http://www.stanford.edu>, followed the changeover from an hourly pay system to piece rate at Safelite Glass Corporation in 1995 and found that productivity increased by 44 percent per worker. He could break down the increase into three components: (1) higher output per worker; (2) lower quitting rates among the highest output workers; and (3) the company's ability to hire more productive workers.[16]

Offsetting these advantages are significant problems. The administration of an incentive system can be complex. As with any control system, standards have to be established and results measured. For many jobs, the standards and measures are too imprecise or too costly to develop. This means that the incentive system may result in inequities. Some incentive systems require less effort than other systems that pay the same. Sometimes, workers make more than their supervisors, who are on salary. Another problem is that the employee may not achieve the standard because of uncontrollable forces, such as work delays or machine breakdowns.

Unions often resist incentive systems, because they fear management will change the standard(s) for the incentive system, and workers will have to work harder for the same pay. This fear of a speedup often leads to peer pressure against anyone who exceeds the group's output norms. The advantages of the incentive system are essentially lost when group pressures restrict output. And incentives tend to focus efforts on only one aspect (output, sales, or stock prices), sometimes to the exclusion of other dimensions (quality, service, and long-term objectives). Some of the more common incentive systems are outlined below.

LO5 HRC 6

Individual Incentive Plans

Piecework

Piecework is an incentive system that compensates the worker for each unit of output. Daily or weekly pay is determined by multiplying the output in units times the piece rate per unit. For example, in agricultural labour, workers are often paid a specific amount per bushel of produce picked. Piecework does not always mean higher productivity, however. Group norms may have a more significant impact if peer pressure works against higher productivity. And in many jobs, it may be difficult to measure the person's productive contribution (e.g., receptionist), or the employee may not be able to control the rate of output (e.g., an assembly-line worker).

piecework

A type of incentive system that compensates workers for each unit of output.

Production Bonuses

Production bonuses are incentives paid to workers for exceeding a specified level of output. They are used in conjunction with a base wage rate or salary. Under one approach, the employee receives a predetermined salary or wage. Through extra effort that results in output above the standard, the base compensation is supplemented by a bonus, usually figured at a given rate for each unit of production over the standard. A variation rewards the employee for saving time. For example, if the standard time for replacing an automobile transmission is four hours and the mechanic does it in three, the mechanic may be paid for four hours.

---

production bonuses

A type of incentive system that provides employees with additional compensation when they surpass stated production goals.

A third method combines production bonuses with piecework by compensating workers on an hourly basis, plus an incentive payment for each unit produced. In some cases, the employee may get a higher piece rate once a minimum number of units are produced. For example, the employee may be paid $15 an hour plus $0.30 per unit for the first 30 units each day. Beginning with the 31st unit, the bonus may become $0.40.

Commissions

In sales jobs, the salesperson may be paid a percentage of the selling price or a flat amount for each unit sold. When no base compensation is paid, the salesperson's total earnings come from commissions. Real estate agents and car salespeople are often paid this form of straight commission. Figure 9-9 shows examples of different types of sales commission and bonus plans.

FIGURE 9-9

Examples of Sales Commission and Bonus Plans

Sales Plan Type	Content
Base salary only	No other compensation is offered.
Commission only	Total compensation is based on established commission schedule.
Base salary plus commission	The commission is over and above the guaranteed base salary. The salary commission mix varies with the type of product, territory, and sales support.
Base salary plus bonus	The bonus is over and above the guaranteed base salary. The bonus is usually based on task achievement; it is earned only when the established sales quota is met.

SOURCE: J. A. Colleti and D. Cichelly, "Increasing Sales-Force Effectiveness Through the Compensation Plan," in Milton L. Rock and Lance A. Berger, eds., *The Compensation Handbook*, New York, NY: McGraw-Hill, 1991, pp. 290–303. Used with permission.

Executive Incentives

Executive incentives vary widely <http://payroll.naukrihub.com/compensation/incentive-management/executive-incentive/>. Young and middle-aged executives are likely to want cash bonuses to meet the needs of a growing or maturing family. As they get older, the need for present income is offset by retirement considerations. Here, bonuses may be deferred until the executive reaches the lower tax rates of retirement.

Executives are sometimes granted *stock options,* that is, the right to purchase the company's stock at a predetermined price. This price may be set at, below, or above the market value of the stock. Thus, the executive has an incentive to improve the company's performance in order to enhance the value of the stock options. Generally, it is considered appropriate to give stock options only to those executives who can have a significant effect on company profits.

Other forms of executive incentives exist, including incentive systems that allow executives to design their own compensation package. The common element in most executive incentive plans, however, is their relation to the performance of the organization. When these systems do not relate the incentive to performance, they are not incentive plans, no matter what they are called. Increasingly, executive incentives are being geared to promote long-term performance.[17]

Team- (or Group-) Based Pay

When students graduate and join an organization, there is a high probability that they will work as part of a team rather than working alone; their performance will then be measured by how much they contribute to the team results. According to one study, 87 percent of the Fortune 1000 companies have created project teams, and 47 percent have permanent teams.[18] The team concept seems to work best in high-tech companies, where groups of engineers collaborate on solving problems or designing software. A former director of human relations for Coopers & Lybrand (now PricewaterhouseCoopers), has an interesting view: "When I try to build a team environment, I say: individuals win trophies, teams win championships."[19] Figure 9-10 compares characteristics of team-based merit pay and individual merit pay.

FIGURE 9-10

Contrasting Approaches to Merit Pay

Team-Based Merit Pay	Individual Merit Pay
Rewards teamwork and co-operation	Creates internal competition
Encourages group to improve work systems	Individuals try to improve system—results in failure
Increases flexibility and ability to respond to changing needs	Decreases flexibility
Not incorporated in base pay	Incorporated into base pay
Encourages information sharing and communication	Encourages withholding of information
Focus on wider organization	No focus on wider organization

SOURCE: Reproduced with permission: Institute for Employment Studies. "Team Working and Pay," Thompson, M. IES Report 281, 1995.

There can be a number of advantages in a team-based pay system. For example, in project teams, many jobs are interrelated; that is, they depend on each other for making progress. A team approach tends to foster group cohesion and organizational commitment. Communication in cohesive teams tends to be more open, and decision making can be more effective if a consensus approach is in the team's interest. Team-based pay often includes rewards for developing better interpersonal skills to improve co-operation and incentives for cross-training.

There can be disadvantages to team-based pay systems. If team cohesiveness is not strong, a "freeloader effect" may take place. As in any group, individual contributions to team goals vary. Some put in more effort, others less. If these differences are significant and the high performers do not receive satisfaction for their input, they may cut back their contributions. Usually, however, high-input members get their satisfaction from being recognized as team leaders or higher-status members, for example as experts or specialists. Another potential drawback is social pressure on high performers to lower their input to avoid drawing management's attention to the low performers. This issue will most likely occur in a hostile management–union environment. It is also possible that the team approach may be too effective, resulting in competition between teams and undesirable consequences, such as hoarding of resources or withholding of important information.

LO6

Team- (or Group-) Based Incentive Plans

Several plans have been developed to provide incentives for teamwork. Most fall into one of the following categories: team results, production incentives, profit sharing, stock ownership, or cost-reduction plans.

Team Results

Under team-based pay plans, employee bonuses and salary increases are based on a team's overall results and are often shared equally. However, a team can also vote shares of a bonus pool to its various members, much like a Stanley Cup or Grey Cup winner votes its members full or partial shares of its championship reward, depending on individual contributions.

Production Incentive Plans

These plans allow groups of workers to receive bonuses for exceeding predetermined levels of output. They tend to be short-range and related to very specific production goals. A work team may be offered a bonus for exceeding predetermined production levels, or may receive a per-unit incentive that results in a group piece rate.

Profit-Sharing Plans

A **profit-sharing plan** shares company profits with the workers. The effectiveness of these plans may suffer, because profitability is not always related to employee performance; a recession or new competitors may have a more significant impact. Even when outside sources do not seriously affect results, it is often difficult for employees to perceive their efforts as making much difference. Some companies further reduce the effectiveness of the incentive by diverting the employees' share of profits into retirement plans. Thus, the immediate reinforcement value of the incentive is reduced, because the incentive is delayed. However, when these plans work well they can have a dramatic impact on the organization, because profit-sharing plans can create a sense of trust and a feeling of common fate among workers and management.

profit-sharing plan
A system whereby an employer pays compensation or benefits to employees, usually on an annual basis, in addition to their regular wage, on the basis of the profits of the company.

In Canada, the number of profit-sharing plans increased from approximately 2,000 registered plans in the mid-1950s to more than 60,000 by 2000. Since a recent study found that more than 50 percent of all profit-sharing plans are cash plans that do not require registration, the number of profit-sharing plans in Canada is probably well beyond 60,000.

How effective are profit-sharing plans in motivating employees? The evidence is not that clear-cut. Although companies with profit-sharing plans tend to be more profitable, it is by no means certain that the plan is the cause of increased profitability.[20] As usual, many factors play a role.

Studies show that the profitable companies with profit-sharing plans also tend to have open and two-way communication between management and employees. In addition, in these companies, management tends to practise a participative management style, resulting in a supportive and satisfying work environment.[21] In summary, it can be said that profit sharing tends to contribute to higher motivation and productivity, but it does so in conjunction with other factors.[22] For a more complete discussion about the effectiveness of profit-sharing plans, see <http://www.sozofirm.com/reward-your-hard-working-employees-with-a-profit-sharing-plan/>.

Employee Stock Ownership Plans (ESOPs)

Employee stock ownership plans (ESOPs) have become very popular in North America. One study indicates that over 11,000 of such plans cover almost 9 million employees, who own more than US$200 billion in assets.[23] Because of a lack of tax incentives, only 25 percent of Canadian companies offer an ESOP.[24] Unlike the more traditional profit-sharing plans, ESOPs give employees genuine ownership and voting power when it comes to major decisions relating to the company's future.

> Ten years ago, General Printers <http://www.generalprinters.ca> was an operation chronically in the red, with absentee owners, employees who didn't care about their work, and the need for round-the-clock supervision.
>
> Today, the value of the Oshawa, Ontario, company has grown by 80 percent, and employees do a first-rate job with no managers on-site for two-thirds of the 24-hour workday. The icing on the cake was being named 1997 Business of the Year by the local chamber of commerce. The latest recognition was the Award of Excellence, earned at the 2005 Ontario Printing and Imaging Competition.
>
> The dramatic turnaround can be traced to one key change: the workers became co-owners of the commercial print shop. An ESOP was established that made them not just workers earning a wage, but investors in the firm with a stake in its success.[25]

ESOPs can be modelled to fit the special needs of a company. This may include the need to do the following:

- attract and retain employees, especially in high-tech, knowledge-based industries;
- motivate employees and improve their productivity;
- rescue a failing firm;
- provide a source of additional financing; or
- create something for firms to offer in lieu of wage and salary increases.

Some recent studies show some very positive results regarding the impact of ESOPs on employee motivation, productivity, and turnover, among other items, and their impact on companies' overall sales, sales per employee, and long-term growth. In fact, about 40 percent of Canada's fastest growing companies offer some type of employee ownership plan.[26] For an overview, see <http://esopcanada.com>.

As might be expected, events involving companies such as Enron and Lehman Brothers, in which executives received huge stock options that they sold before their companies folded, have had serious repercussions. A number of Canadian companies have given up on the idea of using stock options as an incentive. Among them are Sobeys <http://www.sobeys.com> and its parent company Empire Co. <http://www.empireco.ca>, Winpak <http://www.winpak.com>, St. Lawrence Cement (now Holcim

Inc., <http://www.holcim.ca>), Calian Technology Ltd. <http://www.calian.com>, and Leon's Furniture <http://www.leons.ca>. Instead of ESOPs, these companies rely on cash bonuses or share purchase plans to reward their executives, doing away with any incentive to manipulate the price of their options.[27]

Cost-Reduction Plans

Some critics of group incentive plans argue that profit-sharing schemes do not always reward the employees' efforts if profits fall for reasons beyond the employees' control. For example, the average bonus received by workers at Lincoln Electric <http://www.lincolnelectric.com/enus/Pages/default.aspx>, a company with a cost-reduction plan, fell from $22,690 one year to $15,460 the next because of a slowdown in the economy. Although $15,460 is a considerable bonus, the bonus is influenced by forces outside the employees' control.

Another approach is to reward employees for something they can control: labour costs. Most cost-reduction plans seek to tap employee effort and ideas for ways to reduce costs. Often a committee of employees is formed to open new lines of communication that allow employee ideas to be heard, while the plan allows greater psychological and financial participation in the firm's day-to-day operations. Perhaps the best-known of these approaches is the **Scanlon Plan** <http://www.scanlon.org/>, which bases bonuses on improvements in labour costs, as compared with historical norms.[28] Under a Scanlon Plan group incentive, employees aim to reduce costs, and then they share in those savings. If, for example, employee productivity increases at the Canadian Valve and Hydrant Manufacturing Company, the ratio of payroll costs to net sales revenue improves. These savings are then shared with employees in the form of a bonus. *Rucker* and *Improshare* plans are similar, but they differ in how bonuses are calculated and in other administrative matters. All three approaches differ from profit sharing in that they focus on something the employee can influence (costs), and not on something that employees may control only indirectly (profitability).

Scanlon Plan

An incentive plan developed by Joseph Scanlon that has as its general objective the reduction of labour costs through increased efficiency and the sharing of resultant savings among workers.

Nonmonetary Rewards

How important is money compared to nonmonetary rewards? A number of studies seem to indicate that money is not as important as, say, a challenging job. One should be cautious about such results, because the answer often depends on how the question is phrased. For example, "high" pay is rated lower than "fair" pay. Of importance is also whether the reward is public—that is, known. Such rewards have much higher status than secret ones. In addition, some people are reluctant to admit that pay is important to them. It seems obvious also that during a recession, job security becomes more important than cash bonuses. It is fair to say that "good old-fashioned cash" is still one of the best incentives.[29]

While monetary rewards are obviously important, research indicates that nonmonetary rewards can be highly motivational, for example praise and recognition. See more on this topic in the section "Tailor-Made Perks" later in this chapter.

Pay Secrecy

Pay secrecy is a touchy topic. Many employers prefer not to publish salary levels to avoid having to defend their pay decisions. If a pay policy is indefensible, disclosure may cause significant dissatisfaction among employees. Research has shown that employees generally prefer secrecy about individual salaries, but favour disclosure of pay ranges and pay policies.[30] Figure 9-11 shows the advantages and disadvantages of insisting on secrecy.

pay secrecy

A management policy not to discuss or publish individual salaries.

FIGURE 9-11

Advantages and Disadvantages of Pay Secrecy

Advantages	Disadvantages
Most employees prefer to have their pay kept secret	May generate distrust in the pay system
Gives managers greater freedom	Employees may perceive that there is no relationship between pay and performance
Covers up inequities in the internal pay structure	

According to Edward Lawler, founder and director of the Center for Effective Organizations <http://ceo.usc.edu>, pay secrecy has two major effects: (1) it lowers the pay satisfaction of employees and (2) it reduces the employees' motivation to perform.[31] It is practically unavoidable that employees will talk about and compare salaries. On the basis of rumours and speculations, employees tend to overestimate the salaries of their colleagues, causing feelings of unfairness, inequity, and resentment. Pay secrecy also prevents employees from perceiving the connection between their performance and their pay.

HRC 1 & 6

New Approaches to Pay

So far, this chapter has dealt with the traditional approach to compensation: paying for the job done. It means that once employees are hired, they are paid for doing what their job descriptions list as job responsibilities or tasks. The amount paid is determined through the process of job evaluation.

A new way of thinking about paying employees is based on the skills or knowledge they have. **Skill- or knowledge-based pay** requires, first, the identification of the tasks that have to be performed in the organization. Second, the skills required to complete the tasks have to be identified. Third, skills have to be priced so that pay rates can be determined. Typically, employees are paid only for those skills they are able to perform, but there is always an incentive to broaden one's skill level:

skill- or knowledge-based pay

A pay system based on the skills or knowledge that an employee has (in contrast to the more common job-based pay).

NCR Canada's Engineering and Manufacturing Facility in Waterloo, Ontario, employs a staff of over 30,000 to develop and manufacture products and systems for the document processing market. In 1988, management introduced the concept of work teams. Every employee learns all the seven basic functions in the production process. They rotate across the functions every six weeks to first learn and later hone other skills. Wages are based on learning and performing all of the functions in a cell on a regular rotational basis. Individual and team performance is measured and rewarded.[32]

Many companies, especially in the manufacturing industry, provide incentives for the horizontal learning of skills, similar to the job enlargement principle. Workers learn a greater variety of skills so that they are able to perform different jobs. Volvo in Sweden has taken another approach. There, workers are encouraged to learn vertical skills. Volvo gives every member of a work group an increase if the group is able to function without a supervisor, a powerful motivation for the development of **autonomous work groups** (also known as *leaderless work groups*). A similar approach has been taken by Shell Canada <http://www.shell.ca> in its Brockville, Ontario, plant as described below:

> Fewer than 100 people are employed in this ultramodern plant, which produces lubricants. Information technology is the key for the design of this plant, putting a computer at the fingertips of every worker. This has drastically changed the working relationships in this plant. Missing are the traditional foremen and supervisors who tell people what to do and how to do it. Every worker, or team operator, is a supervisor of sorts. Operators must master all the jobs within his or her team, plus at least one skill in two other groups. Pay is based on a number of defined skills. The impact on pay was significant. The average salary increased by 22 percent, and some employees almost doubled their income.[33]

---

autonomous work groups

Any of a variety of arrangements that allow employees to decide democratically how they will meet their group's work objectives.

The greatest advantage of skill-based pay is the flexibility of the workforce. This includes filling in after turnovers and covering for absenteeism, for employees who are being trained, and for those who are in meetings. Also, if a company's production or service process is changing frequently, it is very desirable to have a highly trained workforce that can adapt smoothly to changes. This advantage is likely to become increasingly important in the future because of the shorter life cycles of products, the increasing demand for product customization, and the need to respond quickly to market changes.[34] Lawler cites an example in which a highly skilled workforce made a major difference:

> As part of some work I did with Johnson & Johnson <http://www.jnjcanada.com>, I designed a skill-based pay system for a plant that makes Tylenol. As a result of the Tylenol poisoning tragedy, J&J decided to completely redo its packaging of Tylenol to add greater safety. The skill-based plant quickly installed the new technology needed and got back into production. Not so with its sister plant, which was a traditional, job-based seniority-driven plant. Seniority rights and traditional pay grades got in the way of people's flexibility in adapting to the new technology.[35]

Other advantages come from the fact that skill-based pay may lead to leaner organizations. If multiskilled employees are able to fill in, the organization does not need to have as many extra employees to cover for absenteeism.

Disadvantages lie in the higher pay rates skill-based pay systems tend to generate. This does not mean total wage costs have to be higher; if the organization can make better use of its people, total costs can be significantly lower.[36]

Variable Pay

There is strong evidence that Canadian companies are shifting toward a more performance-linked compensation approach. A survey by Hewitt Associates, a human resource consulting firm, found that of 420 large Canadian companies surveyed in 2008, 86 percent use variable pay as part of their compensation system.[37] Figure 9-12 shows what type of variable pay programs are used by these companies.

FIGURE 9-12

Types of Variable Pay Plans Used by Canadian Companies

Plan Type	2002	2005
Business incentive	69%	64%
Special recognition	42%	55%
Individual performance	27%	45%
Cash profit sharing	38%	42%
Stock options	37%	28%
Team/group	12%	15%
Gainsharing	15%	13%

The objectives of variable pay are (1) to improve business performance through changed employee behaviour, (2) to keep compensation competitive, and (3) to control labour costs. The advantage of the variable compensation approach is that it is performance linked. Unlike merit pay, it is able to incorporate the performance of individuals, groups, business units, and corporate financial and stock price performances. The great advantage of a variable pay plan is that the award must be re-earned every year and does not permanently increase base salary.

LO7   HRC 1 & 6

Total Reward Model

In the past few years we have seen the increased popularity of a **total reward model** in the compensation field. It is defined as the use as rewards of everything an employee values in an employment relationship. Figure 9-13 lists 13 components of such a system.

total reward model

Inclusion of everything employees value in an employment relationship.

The total reward approach requires a reward system tailor-made for the organization, a major undertaking and a reason few organizations have implemented it, although those who did found it to be to their great advantage. Studies have shown that such companies enjoy easier recruitment of high-quality staff, reduced costs because of lower turnover, higher employee performance, and an enhanced reputation as an employer of choice.[38]

HRC 6

Broadbanding

Traditionally, salaries were grouped into a large number of pay grades. It was a system well suited for narrow and specialized jobs. In some organizations, the grade number has become a status symbol. Any additional responsibility usually resulted in a new job evaluation and a move up in the pay grades. With the increased focus on knowledge workers and skill-based pay, **broadbanding** has become a popular alternative. It is defined as a strategy for salary structures that consolidate a large number of pay grades into a few "broad bands." The advantages are several. Broadbanding does the following:

- Assists in flattening large, hierarchical organizations.
- Encourages employees to broaden their skills and abilities.
- Allows for a more flexible workforce and organization.
- De-emphasizes promotion.
- Eases internal transfers.
- Supports a new organizational climate.
- Simplifies paperwork.

broadbanding

Consolidation of a large number of pay grades into a few "broad bands."

FIGURE 9-13

Components of a Total Reward System

1. Compensation	Wages, commissions, and bonuses
2. Benefits	Vacations, health insurance
3. Social interaction	Friendly workplace
4. Security	Stable, consistent position and rewards
5. Status/recognition	Respect, prominence
6. Work variety	Opportunity to experience different things
7. Workload	Right amount of work (not too much, not too little)
8. Work importance	Is work valued by society?
9. Authority/control/autonomy	Ability to influence others; control own destiny
10. Advancement	Chance to get ahead
11. Feedback	Receive information helping to improve performance
12. Work conditions	Hazard free
13. Development opportunity	Formal and informal training to learn new knowledge/skills/abilities

SOURCE: George T. Milkovich, Jerry M. Newman, Nina Cole, and Margaret Yap, *Compensation*, Fourth Canadian ed., Toronto: McGraw-Hill Ryerson, 2013, p. 224. Used with permission.

Broadbanding is not a cure-all. With its high salary-range maximums, it does not have the salary control features of the traditional salary structure. Maintaining pay equity might also be more difficult. If two employees are in the same broad salary band doing similar work, and one is paid near the bottom of the range (because of lack of broader skills) and the other is paid near the top, how does one justify the salary differential to the employees?[39] For a broader discussion of the pros and cons of broadbanding, see <http://www.auxillium.com/broadbn2.shtml>.

Tailor-Made Perks

The latest trend in reward plans is to allow employees to choose their rewards. Before it was dissolved, Nortel Networks came up with the idea to thank employees by allowing supervisors and peers to recommend employees for special points that can be converted into money. The recommendations had to be approved by two managers to avoid "back-scratching" between friends. For example, 5,000 points would be a modest thank-you, worth about $100. Points can be cashed in or exchanged for merchandise or saved for higher-value prizes, such as a trip to the National Basketball Association all-star game, valued at 160,000 points. While the plan was innovative, it did not prevent the company's demise.[40]

HRC 6

International Pay

"Think globally, act locally!" has become a popular part of business strategies of international companies. For HR managers, this policy has become quite a challenge. Traditionally, when companies went international, they imposed the "home-country system" on their overseas operations. It often led to quite serious discrepancies in HR policies. For example, it was possible that a Canadian middle manager in a Canadian subsidiary in Japan could be earning $150,000 (with generous "overseas benefits") while the Japanese counterpart, having the same job title and responsibilities, may be paid a quarter of the expatriate's salary—surely a cause for frictions.

HRC 6

The next generation of international enterprises were the multinational corporations (MNCs). For most of these, the strategy was to have each country's operation choose HR policies based on local customs and values. However, this approach made it impossible to integrate transnational organizational objectives. An integrated "global" strategy requires a common framework, but not a one-size-fits-all solution, which is quite a challenge when it comes to pay.

A good example is the differences in pay policies in the United States and Japan. U.S. base pay levels and merit increases are highly individualized and based on performance. Contrast this to Japan, where salary differences among those in the same job or level are more reflective of family size (number of dependents), age, and experience (job tenure) than performance differences. Also, in the United States, individual contributions (e.g., as indicated by performance appraisal ratings) tend to play a significant role in an employee's remuneration. In contrast, Japan's semi-annual bonuses, measured in months of salary, tend to be far less affected by individual differences.[41]

The third generation of international companies, the truly global enterprises, will preserve national cultural differences while maintaining organizational values that allow the application of a global strategy. For example, these companies hire employees on the basis of their expertise, not nationality. A Japanese employee may work for a Canadian company in Germany. The Japanese employee would be expected to adapt to the German culture, while maintaining his Japanese values. The company, in turn, would have developed a corporate culture, policies, and strategies that would allow it to do business in any country of the world.[42] Pay policies will play a crucial role in the effectiveness of the organization.

The challenge for global HR managers is clear: develop HR policies that take into account global needs, national cultures, and individual differences—a difficult task. There is more discussion on these issues in Chapter 14, Global Human Resource Management.

LO8 HRC 1 & 3 & 6

Pay and Organizational Strategy

In the past, internal equity has been the major concern of organizations. Because of increased competitiveness, nationally and internationally, the focus is shifting now to maintaining a competitive advantage. The prerequisite for developing a strategic pay plan is a clear corporate strategic agenda.[43] Only then is it possible to identify the behaviours and skills needed for the organization to be successful.

Lawler suggests a concentration on seven areas that affect pay systems:

1. **Motivating Performance.** Money is still a strong motivator. Studies show that effective incentive systems can improve the motivation of individuals to perform by as much as 40 percent.[44] A key determinant of the effectiveness of a pay system is the way performance is measured. Top management has to be able to define the organizational behaviour it wants in accordance with its strategic plan.

2. **Identifying Valued Rewards.** As mentioned, pay is an important motivator, partially because it leads to other rewards, such as status and prestige. Because pay means different things to different people, management has to understand how and why it is important to individuals. Only then is it possible to develop an effective reward system for all employees in the organization.

3. **Relating Rewards to Performance.** It is essential for employees to perceive a connection between their pay and their performance.[45] This relationship is the more effective the closer the tie is between the reward and the performance. The common year-end bonus does little to make individuals aware of any performance–reward connection.

4. **Setting Performance Goals.** Reward systems often fail because the goals are simply set too high. Effective goals have to be acceptable and attainable. Employee participation in setting goals tends to increase goal acceptance and in many cases leads to increased productivity.[46]

5. **Motivation and Punishment.** An individual's motivation to perform is strongly influenced by the consequences of missing set objectives. If the consequences are particularly negative, an individual may not even attempt to succeed. This point is especially relevant in organizations that encourage risk taking in managerial decision making.[47] Organizations have to make sure that their reward system allows for occasional failures. A good example is the 3M Company, which has a reward system that encourages its managers to take risks. They are rewarded on the basis of their long-term track record rather than the immediate success or failure of a venture.

6. **Motivating Skill and Knowledge Development.** A crucial issue for an organization is to develop the right mix of skills for its business objectives. A company in a knowledge work field needs different skills than a company in a service business. The pay system chosen has to reinforce the development of the skills needed, and it has to work for all levels of the organization. The appropriate kinds of skills are determined to a large degree by the management style used in the organization as well as the type of business it is in. An organization managed in a participative way needs very different skills than one managed in a top-down, autocratic way.

7. **Fostering Attraction and Retention.** The pay and reward system of an organization has a major impact on the attraction of individuals to work for it and on the retention of those individuals.

Simply stated, companies that offer the most valued rewards tend to have the best attraction and retention rates.[48]

How these broad compensation strategies translate into more specific pay objectives is shown in Figure 9-14. It illustrates a pay philosophy that consists of four basic pay objectives and four basic pay principles.

FIGURE 9-14

Sample Pay Philosophy

Pay Objectives

- To attract the best person available for each job.
- To encourage growth both on an individual basis and as a participant on a work team.
- To recognize the importance of high-quality work performance and to reward it accordingly.
- To encourage a career-long commitment to the company.

Pay Principles

- Pay must be fully competitive in the market, as defined by each business.
- Each individual's pay must be fair in relationship to the pay other employees receive within the same business unit.
- Pay must be communicated. That communication must explain general pay principles, the specific pay system applicable, and the process used to determine individual levels under that system.

The compensation principles originate from two sources: the overall strategy of the organization and its corporate values. If a company has as part of its strategy a strong emphasis on quality of customer service, the core principles have to focus on rewards that reinforce such behaviour. If, on the other hand, top management wants its managers to behave like entrepreneurs, the reward system has to promote risk-taking behaviour, without punishment for failure.

SUMMARY

Employee compensation, if properly administered, can be an effective tool to improve employee performance, motivation, and satisfaction. Mismanaged pay programs can lead to high turnover and absenteeism, more grievances, poor performance, and job dissatisfaction.

For compensation to be appropriate, it must be internally and externally equitable. Through job evaluation techniques, the relative worth of jobs is determined. This assures internal equity. Wage and salary surveys are used to determine external equity. With knowledge of the relative worth of jobs and external pay levels, each job can be properly priced.

The process of wage and salary administration is affected by several challenges, including union power, the productivity of workers, the company's compensation policies, and government constraints on pay. The *Canada Labour Code* is the major federal law affecting compensation management, regulating minimum wages, overtime, and child labour. The *Canadian Human Rights Act* seeks to eliminate sex-based pay differentials. All provinces have similar laws—labour codes and human rights legislation—for their jurisdictions. (A good example of government constraints on pay is wage and price controls. In 1975, the federal government introduced such a program to fight inflation. Pay and price increases were limited to a certain percentage and were controlled by an anti-inflation board. The program was abolished in 1978.)[49] Pay equity has become a major issue in the past few years. When the *Canadian Human Rights Act* was passed in 1977, it introduced the new concept of "equal pay for work of equal value," which requires employers to compare the content of jobs when determining pay scales and to pay equal wages for jobs of comparable value. The Canadian Human Rights Commission specifies four criteria by which jobs can be evaluated: skill, effort, responsibility, and working conditions. Provincial equal pay legislation is usually modelled after the federal law.

Financial incentives are another dimension of compensation management. Individual incentives attempt to relate pay to productivity. Group plans have the same objectives, but the relationship is often not as direct or obvious to workers. Some approaches pay a bonus for reaching a production target, others share the company's profits with workers, and still others share savings in labour costs.

The human resource function is directly and indirectly involved with employee motivation and job satisfaction. Human resource policies and programs have a major effect on organizational motivation.

Compensation consists of more than wages, salaries, and bonuses. Remuneration includes an ever-growing list of fringe benefits and services. Although these benefits are referred to as "noncash compensation," they are a significant part of the total labour cost of most employers. The next chapter describes the range of benefits and services offered by employers.

TERMS FOR REVIEW

autonomous work groups
broadbanding
Canada Labour Code
compa-ratio
equal pay for equal work
equal pay for work of equal value
external equity
incentive pay
internal equity
job evaluations
job grading
job ranking
key jobs
merit raise
pay equity
pay secrecy
piecework
point system
production bonuses
profit-sharing plan

rate range
red-circled rate
Scanlon Plan
skill- or knowledge-based pay
total reward model
wage and salary surveys

SELF-ASSESSMENT EXERCISE

Examining Compensation Issues

1. One objective of compensation administration is to ensure administrative efficiency.	**(T)**	**F**
2. Job evaluation committees set wage and salary policies.	**T**	**(F)**
3. Job ranking is a superior evaluation method because it compares jobs directly.	**T**	**(F)**
4. The labour market for salary surveys is generally considered to be the local community.	**(T)**	**F**
5. Unions insist that nonunionized employees do not receive the same increases as union members.	**T**	**(F)**
6. Under no circumstances can an employee legally be paid less than minimum wage.	**(T)**	**F**
7. The pay equity concept specifies that women are paid the same as men for the same work. *equal work*	**T**	**(F)**
8. The wage gap between males and females is between 5 and 10 percent for comparable groups.	**(T)**	**F**
9. Profit-sharing plans are ideal instruments for motivating employees. *merit pay / incentive pay.*	**T**	**(F)**
10. The variable pay concept emphasizes a linkage between pay and performance.	**(T)**	**F**

SCORING

If you answered statements 2, 3, 5, 7, and 9 as false, you get one point each. All other statements are true, resulting again in one point each.

Scores of 8–10: Very good! Congratulations.

Scores 5–7: You made it, but barely. It is advisable that you go over the chapter text again.

REVIEW AND DISCUSSION QUESTIONS

1. What is the difference between absolute and relative pay?

2. Why is job analysis information, discussed in Chapter 2, necessary before job evaluations can be performed?

3. Suppose that when you interview new employees, you ask them what they think is a fair wage or salary. If you hire them, you pay them that amount as long as it is reasonable and not below minimum-wage laws. What problems might you expect?

4. Assume that your company has a properly conducted compensation program. If a group of employees asks you why they receive different hourly pay rates even though they perform the same job, how would you respond?

5. Why is the point system superior to all other systems? Discuss the advantages and disadvantages of the system.

6. If you are told to find out what competitors in your area are paying their employees, how would you get this information without conducting a wage and salary survey?

7. Even after jobs are first priced using a wage-trend line, what other challenges may cause you to adjust some rates upward?

8. Since financial incentives give employees feedback for good performance and they relate pay to performance, why do most companies pay wages and salaries rather than financial incentives?

9. Explain the difference between "equal pay for equal work" and "equal pay for work of equal value," and the implications of the difference for a human resource manager.

10. Under what circumstances are pay differentials justified?

11. Why is it so important to explain to employees the performance–reward relationship?

12. In what ways does the total reward model differ from the regular compensation approach?

CRITICAL THINKING QUESTIONS

1. Suppose that you manage a small business with 30 employees. You discover that some people are much more motivated by money and others are more motivated by security. Is it possible to satisfy the needs of both groups? What difficulties may arise?

2. "Money is a strong motivator" and "In surveys on what employees want from their job, money ranks low." How can you reconcile these two statements?

3. Obviously, profit-sharing plans are not an option as an incentive plan in nonprofit and government organizations. Can you think of incentive plans that will fulfill a similar function?

4. "Minimum wages increase unemployment." Please comment on this statement often made by many economists. Do you agree?

5. How should an HR manager find out what employees value as rewards? Is it acceptable to ask employees directly? Discuss. Are other methods preferable? Which? Why?

ETHICS QUESTION

The issue of the wage gap between the sexes has been discussed for decades, and pay equity legislation is supposed to take care of it. However, Statistics Canada reports that there is still a gap of about 20 percent in average salaries across jobs and provinces. It has been argued that women will never achieve pay equity, because their role in society often requires them to interrupt a career, have children, and stay home to bring them up. How ethical is it to expect women to make this sacrifice and then pay for it in terms of lower average compensation?

WEB RESEARCH EXERCISE

1. The National Center for Employee Ownership (U.S.)

   www.nceo.org

   (a) What are the characteristics of an effective employee ownership plan? What steps should be followed in its development?

   (b) Research seems to indicate that employee ownership plans have a different effectiveness depending on the size of the company. Try to determine what the relationship of the effect is to size and why there may be a difference in effectiveness.

2. An interactive program on employee ownership

   www.nceo.org/pages/interactive.cgi?nextpage=1

   Take the demonstration training program.

3. The Conference Board of Canada

   www.conferenceboard.ca

   What different types of information are available to Canadian managers regarding incentive plans?

4. Gainsharing: Different types of plans

   www.hr-guide.com/data/G443.htm

   www.qualitydigest.com/jul/gainshre.html

   Summarize the research studies on the effectiveness of gainsharing programs.

5. Chartered Institute of Personnel and Development

   www.cipd.co.uk/subjects/pay/general/totrewd.htm

   How many other total reward models can you identify? How do they differ?

INCIDENT 9-1

Compensation Administration at Reynolds Plastic Products

The family-owned Reynolds Plastic Products Co. in London, Ontario, was recently purchased by a much larger company, International Plastics Ltd. When the human resource director of International Plastics, Hans Himmelman, looked at Reynolds Plastic compensation policies, he became concerned that some of them were questionable and in some cases actually seemed to violate the law. When he asked the plant manager, an engineer, who also acted as an HR manager, how he determined pay rates, the manager explained that he would ask applicants what they earned in their previous job and just add 25 or 50 cents to this amount, depending on job experiences they had. To make matters worse, two recently hired female machinists complained that they were paid less for the same work than their male colleagues. The machine shop supervisor disputed their claim, asserting that the male employees had more work experience and deserved higher pay. Himmelman also discovered that productivity in the subsidiary was lower than in other plants of International Plastics.

An HR consultant was hired to assess the compensation system of the Reynolds Plastic subsidiary. The key points of her report are summarized below:

- Executives in the past have received an annual bonus determined by the owner at his discretion.

- Wages for hourly employees ranged from $16.00 for employees during their probationary period to $28.00 per hour for the more skilled or experienced ones.

- The amount of overtime paid by Reynolds was very modest; overtime was paid for all hours over 180 per month.

- The wage rates for different workers varied widely even on the same job; those employees who were heads of households received approximately 18 percent more than those workers who were not. Most heads of households were men.

- Female employees were paid 10 to 20 percent less in all job categories.

- On highly technical jobs, the firm paid a rate of 20 percent above the prevailing wage rate for these jobs. All other jobs were paid an average of 15 percent below the prevailing rate.

- Production workers were eligible for a $200 draw each month if there were no accidents during the month.

- Sales personnel were paid a commission and received a $200 bonus for every new customer.

- Whenever sales went up 10 percent, all the hourly employees got a day off with pay or could work one day at the double-time rate.

- Turnover averaged a modest 12 percent. However, in technical jobs turnover was less than 2 percent; in nontechnical jobs turnover was nearly 20 percent.

- Absenteeism followed the same pattern.

DISCUSSION QUESTIONS

1. What laws were probably being violated?

2. What problems do you see with the incentives for (a) executives? (b) production workers? (c) salespeople? (d) hourly employees?

3. Himmelman read about new approaches to pay policies like broadbanding, variable pay, and profit sharing, and wondered whether either one would be a suitable solution for the subsidiary, especially profit sharing to increase low productivity. How would you advise him?

4. Develop a step-by-step plan of actions you would take and the order in which you would undertake them if you were made human resource director of the Reynolds subsidiary.

EXERCISE 9-1

A Realistic Job Evaluation Simulation

Form groups of three to five. (Three students may need approximately 20 minutes, five students about 45 minutes for the exercise.)

Use the following rules:

1. Have each student choose a job he or she is familiar with (ideally, a job description would be available, but is not essential). The jobs should be different, but from a single organization (e.g., hospital, school, manufacturing plant).

2. Use the table below to record numbers.

Critical Factors	Job 1	Job 2	Job 3	Job 4	Job 5
1. Responsibility					
a. Safety of others					
b. Equipment and materials					
c. Assisting trainees					
d. Product/service quality					
2. Skill					
a. Experience					
b. Education/training					
3. Effort					
a. Physical					
b. Mental					
4. Working conditions					
a. Unpleasant conditions					
b. Hazards					

3. Using Figure 9-4, find consensus in your group in choosing the most appropriate point level for each job.

   Example: For the job of a janitor, what level of responsibility for the safety of others (critical factor) is appropriate? Probably not a high one, so a good choice might be Level I, 25 points. For a bus driver or an emergency room nurse, the appropriate choice might be Level IV, or 100 points.

4. Choose one of the above jobs, called a "key job"—a well-known job, ideally common in many organizations (e.g., secretary, accountant, tool-and-die maker in the manufacturing industry, and so on). Conduct a simulated wage survey. In this exercise it is sufficient to take an educated guess on what the key job is paid in the job market.

   It does not matter whether you choose an hourly wage or a monthly or annual salary, but it must be the same for each job.

5. Calculate the pay coefficient by dividing the estimated wage by the point total of the key job, according to the formula:

$$\text{Pay coefficient (pc)} = \frac{\text{Wage of Key jobs}}{\text{Point total for key jobs}} = \frac{\$}{\text{Point}}$$

6. Multiply all job point totals by the pay coefficient. The results are the wages/salaries for all the above jobs. (In reality, this procedure would have to be done by the job evaluation committee for all jobs in the organization, often in the hundreds.)

COMMENT

This exercise is a fairly realistic simulation of what is going on in a job evaluation committee. In all probability, the opinions in your group were very diverse when it came to determining the level for each job. The results, of course, are not realistic, since the point table has been created artificially and not by a job evaluation committee and the pay level of the key job has been estimated by you. Nevertheless, this exercise should give you a good feel for the job evaluation process, using the point method. It also demonstrates the need to choose members of the committee who are knowledgeable about the jobs in the organization and are trained in the application of the point method. One more point: up to the wage survey, money was not part of the discussion, only points.

CASE STUDY

Maple Leaf Shoes Ltd.

Compensation Policy

Maple Leaf Shoes Ltd. is a medium-sized manufacturer of leather and vinyl shoes located in Wilmington, Ontario. It was started in 1973 and currently employs about 500 persons in its Ontario plant and some 200 more in offices and warehouses throughout Canada.

Recently, the company has been facing a number of issues and challenges that require immediate attention by its management. First, the cost of production at Maple Leaf Shoes has been rising slowly but steadily. Labour costs currently account for over 53 percent of manufacturing costs and have been increasing rapidly. The productivity levels of workers have not shown any increase in the past three years. If the present trend continues, the firm is likely to lose its price advantage over its competitors. Already, in two out of six popular brands sold by Maple Leaf Shoes, the prices for the firm's products are equal to or higher than those of its competition.

Second, over 70 percent of the company's staff are unionized. There are indications that remaining nonmanagerial staff are also about to be unionized. Management believes that this will reduce the already limited autonomy it possesses in hiring, terminating, and managing employees.

Robert Clark, president and majority shareholder of Maple Leaf Shoes, has recently begun reading about profit-sharing (PS) plans. Some time ago, in an airport VIP lounge, he met a CEO of a company that had a PS plan. The CEO marvelled at the productivity of his employees, their commitment, quality-consciousness, concern for customers, low absenteeism, and low turnover. That really got Clark's attention. The more he learned about this incentive system, the more he liked it, and the more he had talked to his managers about it. Since the idea came from him, they tend to support it and even show some enthusiasm. Among themselves, however, most are only lukewarm to the idea of letting workers have part of the company's profits. Managers, yes—they make the company profitable—but blue-collar workers?

So far, Maple Leaf Shoes' workers are paid the straight union wages negotiated two years ago, when the old contract expired. At that time, management tried to introduce a piece-rate incentive system, but no agreement could be reached on how the base rate would be set, something industrial engineers had to do. The unions did not trust Maple Leaf Shoes' engineers, whom they thought to be on management's side.

Recently, Clark asked Jane Reynolds, his special assistant in the Personnel Department, whether she knew much about PS plans. She had taken some human resource management courses and remembered that PS plans had been discussed, but she could not remember whether PS plans were more effective than other incentive plans. Clark then decided to call Tim Lance, the HR consultant, to look into the pros and cons of having a PS plan at Maple Leaf Shoes. He wanted to have the plan ready as soon as possible, since two unions were about to start contract negotiations and he thought it would be a good bargaining tool. He hoped that union representatives would embrace the idea of sharing profit and perhaps moderate their wage demands.

However, he was in for a rude awakening. He once mentioned casually the concept of profit sharing to one of the union presidents, without revealing his ideas of introducing such a plan at Maple Leaf Shoes. He received the following response: "Profit sharing? Forget it. That is a management gimmick. Its only purpose is to make workers work harder and make the company more profitable. And the risk is too great that there are no or low profits. What do we have then? Nothing. We want our negotiated wages and nothing more."

Clark wonders whether it would still be possible to introduce a PS plan. The other CEO has mentioned that his union is a strong supporter of the plan. How can he sell his unions on this concept? Would Tim Lance know a solution?

DISCUSSION QUESTIONS

1. You are the consultant. Clark has asked you to submit a proposal for a PS plan for Maple Leaf Shoes. You wonder about the appropriateness of such an incentive system for Maple Leaf Shoes, but you promised to look into it. What will you tell Robert Clark?

2. Do you see a possibility of convincing Maple Leaf Shoes' unions to buy in on a PS plan?

3. What other incentive plans are suitable for Maple Leaf Shoes?

CASE STUDY

Canadian Pacific and International Bank

Ernie Kemball, an instructor in CPIB's training and development division, specialized in training managers and supervisors in developing human resource skills. One of his favourite topics was "How to motivate employees," an interesting but, as he well knew, difficult topic to teach, because everyone is motivated by different needs.

To get managers involved immediately and to arouse their interest Ernie preferred to use the case-study approach. His opening remark to every motivation seminar was to quote Professor Kavanagh: "Genuine and lasting employee motivation is not something management does, but rather a process that management fosters and allows to happen." He would then proceed to introduce the first case:

"Let's begin by looking at what not to do in terms of creating a motivating work environment. Here is an excellent case and, let me add, a real one. It was written by Dr. Craig Pinder, a professor at the Faculty of Business Administration, University of Victoria.* It is based on an interview with 'Pamela Jones,' a bank employee in Vancouver. Use the expectancy model and answer the following questions:

- Did management make the "right" hiring decision?
- How did management fare with respect to providing a motivating work environment?
- To what degree did management fulfill the expectations of Pamela?
- Was the performance–reward connection clear to her?
- What should management have done to create a truly motivating work environment?"

PAMELA JONES

Pamela Jones enjoyed banking. She had taken a battery of personal aptitude and interest tests that suggested she might like and do well in either banking or librarianship. She applied for employment with a large chartered bank, the Bank of Winnipeg, and was quickly accepted.

Her early experiences in banking were almost always challenging and rewarding. She was enrolled in the bank's management development program because of her education (a B.A. in languages and some postgraduate training in business administration), her previous job experience, and her obvious intelligence and drive.

During her first year in the training program, Pamela attended classes on banking procedures and policies and worked her way through a series of low-level positions in her branch. She was repeatedly told by her manager that her work was above average. Similarly, the training officer who worked out of the main office and coordinated the development of junior officers in the program frequently told Pamela that she was "among the best three" of her cohort of 20 trainees. She was proud to be a banker and proud to be a member of the Bank of Winnipeg.

After one year in the management development program, however, Pamela found she was not learning anything new about banking or the bank itself. She was shuffled from one job to another at her own branch, cycling back over many positions several times to help meet temporary problems caused by absences, overloads, and turnover. Turnover—a rampant problem in banking—amazed Pamela. She could not understand for many months why so many people started careers "in the service" of banking, only to leave after one or two years.

After her first year, the repeated promises of moving her into her own position at another branch started to ring hollow. The training officer claimed that there were no openings at other branches suitable for her. On two occasions when openings did occur, the manager of each of the branches in question rejected Pamela, sight unseen, presumably because she had not been in banking long enough.

---

* This case was reproduced, with permission, from C.C. Pinder, *Work Motivation*, Glenview, IL: Scott, Foresman, 1984. All rights reserved by the author.

Pamela was not the only unhappy person at her branch. Her immediate supervisor, George Burns, complained that because of the bank's economy drive, vacated customer service positions were left unfilled. As branch accountant, Burns was responsible for day-to-day customer service. Eventually, George Burns left the bank to work for a trust company, earning $200 a month more for work similar to that he had been performing at the Bank of Winnipeg. This left Pamela in the position of having to supervise the same tellers who had trained her only a few months earlier. Pamela was amazed at all the mistakes the tellers made, but found it difficult to do much to correct their poor work habits. All disciplinary procedures had to be administered with the approval of head office.

After several calls to her training officer, Pamela was finally transferred to her first "real" position in her own branch. Still keen and dedicated, Pamela was soon to lose her enthusiasm.

At her new branch, Pamela was made assistant accountant. Her duties included the supervision of the seven tellers, some customer service, and a great deal of paperwork. The same economy drive that she had witnessed at her training branch resulted in the failure to replace customer service personnel. Pamela was expected to "pick up the slack" at the front desk, neglecting her own work. Her tellers seldom balanced their own cash, so Pamela stayed late almost every night to find their errors. To save on overtime, the manager sent the tellers home while Pamela stayed late, first to correct the tellers' imbalances, and then to finish her own paperwork. He told Pamela that as an officer of the bank, she was expected to stay until the work of her subordinates, and her own work, was satisfactorily completed. Pamela realized that most of her counterparts in other branches were willing to give this sort of dedication; therefore, so should she. This situation lasted six months, with little sign of change in sight.

One day, Pamela learned from a phone conversation with a friend at another branch that she would be transferred to Hope, British Columbia, to fill an opening that had arisen. Pamela's husband was a professional, employed by a large corporation headquartered in Vancouver. His company did not have an office in Hope; moreover, his training was very specialized so that he could probably find employment only in large cities anyway.

Accepting transfers was expected of junior officers who wanted to get ahead in the bank. Pamela inquired at head office and learned that the rumour was true. Her training officer told her, however, that she could decline the transfer if she wished, but he could not say how soon her next promotion opportunity would come about.

Depressed, annoyed, disappointed, and frustrated, Pamela quit the bank.

APPENDIX A

Calculation of Data in Point System Matrix (Replication of Figure 9-4)

Critical Factors	Levels or Degrees				Factor Points
	I	II	III	IV	
1. Responsibility (weight 40%)					**400**
Subfactors:					
a. Safety of others	20	80	140	200	
b. Equipment and materials	8	32	56	80	
c. Assisting trainees	8	32	56	80	
d. Product/service quality	4	16	28	40	
2. Skill (weight 30%)					**300**
Subfactors:					
a. Experience	18	72	126	180	
b. Education/training	12	48	84	120	
3. Effort (weight 20%)					**200**
Subfactors:					
a. Physical	8	32	56	80	
b. Mental	12	48	94	120	
4. Working conditions (weight 10%)					**100**
Subfactors:					
a. Unpleasant conditions	3	12	21	30	
b. Hazards	7	28	49	70	
			Total points		**1,000**

STEP 1. DETERMINE TOTAL POINT MATRIX NUMBER

How many points to be used for allocation purposes is a personal choice. A rule of thumb is the number of compensable factors times 250. Another formula takes the highest-paid job and divides its wage rate by the wage rate of the lowest-paid job times 100. For example, if the president is paid $200,000 and the lowest job $20,000, the result is 10 ($200,000 : $20,000). Multiplying by 100 results in a total of 1,000 points for the point system. (For convenience, numbers are rounded.)

STEP 2. DETERMINE INDIVIDUAL FACTOR WEIGHTS

This decision is made by the Job Evaluation Committee. In this example the committee decided on the following weight distribution:

Responsibility	40%
Skill	30%
Effort	20%
Working conditions	10%
	100%

Multiplying 1,000 points by the weights results in:

Responsibility	400 points
Skill	300
Effort	200
Working conditions	100

STEP 3. DETERMINE SUBFACTOR WEIGHTS AND ALLOCATION OF SUBFACTOR POINTS

Again, the job evaluation committee has to decide the weight of each subfactor.

Responsibility

Safety of others	50%
Equipment and materials	20%
Assisting trainees	20%
Product/service quality	10%

Skill

Experience	60%
Education/training	40%

Effort

Physical	40%
Mental	60%

Working conditions

Unpleasant conditions	30%
Hazards	70%

Now the factor points are multiplied by the subfactor weights. We will use only the first factor, responsibility, for this example.

Safety of others: 400 points × 50% = 200 points

Equipment and materials: 400 points × 20% = 80 points

Assisting trainees: 400 points × 20% = 80 points

Product/service quality: 400 points × 10% = 40 points

The highest subfactor points are always given to the highest level, in this case IV.

The lowest-level point value is calculated by the formula: Subfactor weight × Factor weight.

Safety of others: 50% × 40% = 20 points

Equipment and materials: 20% × 40% = 8 points

Assisting trainees: 20% × 40% = 8 points

Product/service quality: 10% × 40% = 4 points

STEP 4. DETERMINE INCREMENTS BETWEEN LEVELS

This is calculated by the formula:
(Highest-level points – Lowest-level points)/(Number of levels –1).
For subfactor "Safety of others," this means:

$$\frac{200 - 20}{4 - 1} = \frac{180}{3} = 60 \text{ points}$$

The steps are: 20, 80, 140, 200 (see table at beginning of this Appendix). This assumes equal distance between levels. However, if the job evaluation committee feels that this does not reflect reality, it is free to determine the point differences between levels. *What is important is that employees perceive this judgment to be fair.*

CHAPTER 10

Employee Benefits and Services

In many respects Canada's position in the area of fringe benefits is unique, striking a balance between the situation prevailing in the U.S. and that in Europe.

BILL MEGALLI[1]

LEARNING OBJECTIVES

After studying this chapter, you should be able to:

LO1 Describe the objectives of indirect compensation.

LO2 Explain how government furthers employee security and which major Canadian laws relate to it.

LO3 Discuss the key issues in designing pension plans.

LO4 Explain the differences between legal and voluntary benefits.

LO5 Discuss the benefits and services that are likely to become more common in the future.

LO6 Describe the cost of employee benefits and ways to control them.

LO7 Describe the advantages and disadvantages of flexible benefit plans.

LO8 Identify the administrative problems of employee benefits and services and suggest improvements.

Employee Benefits

To many people, compensation means pay. Anything else an employer might provide is often considered so minor that it is called a "fringe benefit." The reality is, however, that most employers now make benefits an important part of the total compensation package and increasingly use it as a tool to attract, motivate, and keep key personnel. Some employers even go so far as to tailor-make benefit packages for individual employees to satisfy their special needs.

"Did you receive another job offer?" Carla asked her brother.

"Yes. I received a letter yesterday from a bank in Vancouver. That's my problem; I don't know which to accept," Ed responded. "The pay, working conditions, and job duties are almost identical. The people I met at both banks seem equally pleasant."

"What about fringe benefits?" Carla asked.

"What about them? They're only the extras. They don't make much difference," Ed answered.

"They don't make much difference? Are you kidding?" Carla questioned. "Some companies spend half as much on benefits as they do on wages."

"Now who's kidding? They're just fringes," Ed asserted.

"I'm not kidding. Let me give you an example. Suppose one bank pays all your supplementary health and life insurance and the other pays half. At a cost of $2,000 a year, you would be $1,200 better off with the bank that pays all of your benefits," Carla said confidently.

Ed interrupted, "You mean $1,000."

"Don't forget taxes," Carla added. "To pay your half of the $2,000 you would have to come up with $1,000, true. But to have $1,000, you would probably have to earn $1,200 before taxes. And that is $100 a month."

"Maybe I should find out more about their benefits before I decide," Ed pondered.

When employees like Ed ignore benefits and services, they exclude from consideration all other forms of compensation except pay. Admittedly, pay is a major concern to employees. But since the typical organization spends a considerable share of its labour costs on benefits and services, ignorance like Ed's raises questions about the role of pay and benefits. Simply put, what is the difference between pay and benefits?

Pay is called *direct compensation* because it is based on critical job factors or performance.

Benefits and services are *indirect compensation*, because they are usually extended as a condition of employment and are not directly related to performance. They include insurance, income security, time off, and scheduling benefits, in addition to educational, financial, and social services.

To explain the broad scope of benefits and services, this chapter discusses the objectives of indirect compensation. We follow this with an examination of legally required benefits. The chapter concludes with a description of voluntary benefit programs.

Benefits and Corporate Strategy

Benefit programs have become a very significant part of a company's compensation system, slowly approaching the 50 percent mark of annual payroll expenses, as compared to about 15 percent in the early 1950s. This means that when we talk about an employee's annual salary of $50,000 we are really talking about $75,000 in actual payroll expenses for the company. What once were called "fringe benefits" are not "fringe" anymore.

Benefit policies can have a significant impact on the issue of attracting and retaining key and high-performing employees. Benefits will not replace performance incentives as motivators, but—especially for older employees—health and pension benefits can make a great difference in corporate loyalty.

> To make benefits an important part of the company's compensation strategy has paid off tremendously for Husky Injection Molding Systems Ltd. <http://www.husky.ca> in Bolton, Ontario. The firm spends more than $4 million a year on its 2,800 employees at a time when most companies are considering cutting back. However, Husky managers say that the program more than pays for itself in higher productivity and, ultimately, in lower costs.
>
> Husky's voluntary turnover rate is about 15 percent, or 5 percent below the industry average. Absenteeism averages 4 days a year in contrast with an industry average of 7.3 days. And injury claims are 1.2 for every 200,000 hours worked, as against an industry average of 5.8, according to Dirk Schlimm, Husky's Vice-President of Corporate Affairs.

It is obvious from this example that benefits can play a critical part of a company's staffing strategy.

LO1 HRC 1 & 6

The Role of Indirect Compensation

Employee benefits and services seek to satisfy several objectives. These include societal, organizational, and employee objectives.

Societal Objectives

Industrial societies have changed from rural nations of independent farmers and small businesses to urban nations of interdependent wage earners. This interdependence was illustrated forcefully by the mass unemployment of the Great Depression of the 1930s. Since that time, industrial societies have sought group solutions to societal problems.

To solve social problems and provide security for interdependent wage earners, governments rely on the support of employers. Through favourable tax treatment, employees can receive most benefits tax-free, while employers can deduct the cost of benefits as a regular business expense. The result has been a rapid growth in indirect compensation since the Second World War.

Today, benefits and services give many employees financial security against illness, disability, and retirement. In fact, the growth of benefits since the Second World War means that the average employer spends more than one-third of its payroll costs on benefits and services. No longer are benefits those "little extras" or "fringes." These outlays are a major and growing cost of doing business. If this trend continues, benefits and services could amount to over one-half of most firms' payroll costs in the near future.

HRC 1 & 6

Organizational Objectives

What do employers gain for these large outlays for benefits? Companies must offer some benefits if they are to be able to recruit successfully in the labour market. If a company did not offer retirement plans and paid vacations, recruits and present employees would work for competitors who did offer these "fringes." Similarly, many employees will stay with a company because they do not want to give up benefits, so employee turnover is lowered. For example, employees may stay to save pension credits or their rights to the extended vacations that typically come with greater seniority.

Vacations, along with holidays and rest breaks, help employees reduce fatigue and may enhance productivity during the hours the employees do work. Similarly, retirement, health care, and disability benefits may allow workers to be more productive by freeing them from concern about medical and retirement costs. Likewise, if these benefits were not available to employees, they might elect to form a union and collectively bargain with the employer. (Although collective action is legal, many nonunion employers prefer to remain nonunion.) Therefore, it is accurate to state that indirect compensation may do the following:

- reduce fatigue
- discourage labour unrest
- satisfy employee objectives
- aid recruitment
- reduce turnover
- minimize overtime costs

 HRC 6

Employee Objectives

Employees usually seek employer-provided benefits and services because of lower costs and availability. For example, company insurance benefits are usually less expensive because the employer may pay some or all of the costs. Even when the workers must pay the entire premium, rates are often lower because group plans save the insurer the administrative and selling costs of many individual policies. With group plans, the insurer also can reduce the adverse selection of insuring just those who need the insurance. Actuaries—the specialists who compute insurance rates—can factor these savings into lower premiums for policyholders.

For some employees, the primary objective may be to obtain benefits and services—especially supplementary health and life insurance. Without employer-provided insurance, these policies may not be obtainable if the employee has a pre-existing medical condition.

The objectives of society, organizations, and employees have encouraged rapid growth of benefits and services. This growth has affected all areas of benefits and services, including insurance, income security, and time-off benefits. There are two types of benefits and services: those that are legally required and those that an employer voluntarily gives. This chapter will focus first on the required type.

HRC 1 & 6

Legally Required Benefits

Financial security
Health Insurance
Holidays & vacations

Legally required benefits and services are imposed upon organizations by the government; employers must comply with the law and its procedures. Most of these benefits and services are designed to help employees. In general, government seeks to ensure minimum levels of financial security for the nation's workforce. Figure 10-1 shows that the objective of providing financial security is to ease the monetary burdens of retirement, death, long-term disability, and unemployment. The loss of income from these causes is cushioned by the security provisions. The financial problems of *involuntary unemployment* are lessened by unemployment compensation. And job-related injuries and death are compensated under workers' compensation laws. None of these programs fully reimburses the affected workers; nevertheless, each worker does get a financial base to which additional protection can be added.

FIGURE 10-1

Sources of Financial Protection for Workers

Protection for Workers	Sources of Protection	Legislating Government
Fair remuneration	Minimum-wage acts	Federal and provincial
Retirement	Canada Pension Plan	Federal (except in Quebec)
Involuntary unemployment	Employment Insurance	Federal
Industrial accidents	Workers' compensation acts	Federal and provincial
Medical care	Health insurance plans	Provincial
Child sustenance	Family allowances	Federal

Legally required benefits and services are important to the human resource department for two reasons. First, top management holds the human resource department responsible for meeting these legal obligations. If the department is to meet this responsibility, it must ensure that the firm is in compliance with the law. Second, if the obligations are improperly handled, the result can be severe fines and more taxes. None of these outcomes contributes to the organization's objectives.

LO2 HRC 6

Financial Security

A large majority of Canadians are financially dependent on their monthly paycheques. Only a small percentage of the population is self-employed; most others work for another person or organization. To protect the well-being of society, governmental regulations on retirement plans, employment insurance, disability compensation, and health care are imperative. The major legal provisions concerning the above matters will be discussed below. It should be emphasized that in Canada (unlike in the United States or in some other Western countries), many of these regulations are provincially administered. To suit the specific work environments, many of these statutes and provisions vary from province to province.

The Canada Pension Plan (CPP) and the Quebec Pension Plan (QPP)

The **Canada Pension Plan (CPP)** (Quebec Pension Plan in the province of Quebec), which came into effect on January 1, 1966, is a mandatory plan for all self-employed persons and employees in Canada. Both CPP and QPP are **contributory plans**—that is, both the employer and the employee pay part of the costs. **Portability clauses** are applicable to the plans in Canada, meaning that pension rights are not affected by changes of job or residence. The plans are also tied to cost-of-living changes.

Canada Pension Plan (CPP)

A mandatory, contributory, and portable pension plan applicable to all employees and self-employed persons in Canada, except those working for the federal government.

---

contributory plans

Benefits that require the employer to contribute to the cost of the benefit.

portability clauses

Allow accumulated pension rights to be transferred to another employer when an employee changes employers.

In May 1999, the Supreme Court of Canada ruled that governments cannot limit benefits by discriminating against same-sex common-law relationships, since it would be contrary to the principles enshrined in the Canadian Charter of Rights and Freedoms as well as the *Canadian Human Rights Act.* Following this ruling the federal government enacted in June 2000 the *Modernization of Benefits and Obligations Act* to ensure that common-law relationships (both opposite- and same-sex) are treated equally under federal law. All provinces and territories have issued similar laws.

The latest information about amendments to the CPP can be found at <http://www.esdc.gc.ca/en/reports /pension/cpp_amendments.page>.

 HRC 6

Employment Insurance (EI)

In 1940, Canada started a program called Unemployment Insurance (UI), renamed **Employment Insurance (EI)** in 1995, to help alleviate people's financial problems during the transition from one job to another. The *Unemployment Insurance Act* of 1971 significantly changed and added to the program. Since 1971, there have been several modifications to eligibility criteria and payment schedules. Currently, approximately 11 million Canadians are covered by the scheme. Most salaried and hourly workers who are employed for a minimum number of hours, depending on regional unemployment rates, are covered by EI. The self-employed have not been eligible for benefits in the past, but in 2009 the *Fairness for the Self-Employed Act* made them eligible for maternity, parental, adoption, medical, and compassionate-care benefits.

Employment Insurance (EI)

A program to help alleviate the financial problems of workers in Canada during the transition from one job to another.

The *Employment Act* became fully implemented in 2001–2002. It has been fundamentally restructured. Key features include the following:

- benefits based on hours rather than on weeks worked;
- collection of premiums based on first dollar earned;
- reduction in the maximum benefit entitlement period;
- increased eligibility requirements for people entering the labour market;
- reduction in benefit rate based on an individual's claim history;
- a family income supplement top-up for claimants in low-income families; and
- a lower income threshold for the clawback of benefits.

For more in-depth information on EI, visit <http://www.servicecanada.gc.ca/eng/sc/ei/index.shtml>.

Workers' Compensation Acts

All provinces and the territories have some act or other (usually called *Workers' Compensation Act* or *Ordinance*) that entitles workers to **workers' compensation** in the event of personal injury by accident during their regular work. The administration is done provincially, and all the provincial acts are of the "collective liability" type: that is, compensation is payable by employers collectively. The industries covered by the act are classified into groups according to their special hazards, and all employers in each group are collectively liable for payment of compensation to all workers employed in that group. The annual contribution rate (a percentage of payroll) is determined on the basis of an employer's total annual payroll figures. However, an employer can also be charged a higher rate of contribution if there are many workers' compensation claims.

workers' compensation

Compensation payable by employers collectively for injuries sustained by workers in the course of their employment.

Spotlight *on* HRM

Trust Betrayed

You are the HR manager of a medium-sized, family-owned company. You discovered that a long-time, trusted employee, a purchasing officer, had been embezzling company funds for several years to the tune of close to $20,000. It was found out only because she went on vacation and a replacement had taken over her job for that time. She was known to be hard-working, and it had been the first vacation she had taken in many years. You and all the staff had always admired her dedication and commitment to the company. The company owner did not want to press charges, because of her length of service and because, in his opinion, the loss was not that significant. He also blamed himself for not installing more effective controls. The purchase officer's excuse was that she had had a bad divorce and that her husband did not provide sufficient support for herself and her children to continue their lifestyle.

When you wanted to dismiss her for cause, she cried and asked you to consider her situation and think of her children. She asked whether you could give as the official reason for her leaving the company a company reorganization and elimination of her job, so that she would be able to draw unemployment benefits and have a better chance to find another job. There has been a precedent for this, when the owner did not press charges against an employee who had stolen company property and who had been officially "laid off for lack of work" and had been receiving unemployment benefits. You feel sorry for her that she has ruined her life and career and you think of her children. What are you going to do?

Health Insurance Plans

Canada's health and medical insurance, also referred to as simply **health insurance**, is provided by provincial governments with assistance from the federal government. In April 1972, the scope of the *Medical Care Act* of 1966 was widened to include all of Canada. Since then, a major part of the cost of medical care has been paid for by taxes collected at the federal level. Detailed explanations of health insurance plans in all provinces can be found at <http://www.cic.gc.ca/english/newcomers/after-health.asp>. Supplementary health plans are discussed below under "Voluntary Benefits."

health insurance

Health and medical insurance provided by provincial governments with assistance from the federal government.

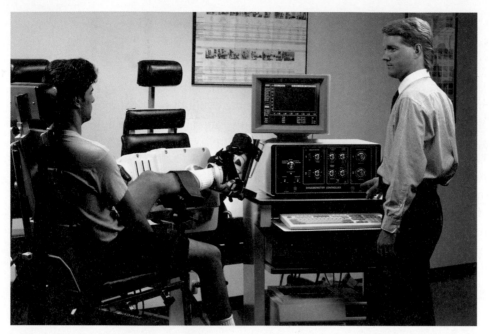

Workers' compensation covers a wide variety of benefits, but the law stipulates that workers cannot sue their employers in case of injury. Is this just?

CORBIS.

 HRC 6

Holidays and Vacations

Vacations are usually based on the employee's length of service, but federal and provincial laws specify a two-week (in Saskatchewan, three-week) minimum vacation entitlement. In some regions, this increases to three weeks (in Saskatchewan, four) after five, six, or ten years of service. Holidays are also federally and provincially regulated. For a listing of federal and provincial holidays, see <http://en.wikipedia.org/wiki/Holidays_in_Canada>.

 HRC 6

Voluntary Benefits   = inducement to work, not mandatory.

Insurance Benefits

Insurance benefits spread the financial risks encountered by employees and their families. These risks are shared by pooling funds in the form of insurance premiums. Then, when an insured risk occurs, the covered employees or their families are compensated.

Life Insurance

Life insurance was the first form of insurance offered to workers by employers. As a result, group life insurance has become a practically universal element in corporate employee benefit programs. Several surveys show that 99 percent of Canadian companies provide a group life insurance program for all of their employees.[2] There are two types of plans. Under the first, the deceased's family receives a lump sum payment. Under the second, the family receives a generally lower lump sum than in the first case, plus a survivor's pension payable to the deceased's spouse for life. This amount is supplemented by family allowance benefits, CPP benefits, workers' compensation if the death is caused by a work-related accident or illness, and, in certain provinces, automobile insurance act benefits if death is the result of a traffic accident.

Employers generally pay the cost of these life insurance plans. Coverage is commonly based on the employee's pay, often 100 or 200 percent of annual pay. Optional expanded coverage is usually available.

Health-Related Insurance

All Canadian citizens—and landed immigrants—are covered by provincial health care programs. For this reason, employers in Canada offer only supplementary health insurance plans. This is in contrast to the United States, where health insurance is the most common form of coverage.[3]

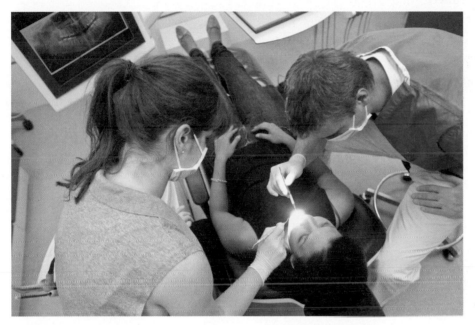

Dental insurance is a common benefit offered by many companies to their employees, but it is a voluntary one. Should it be mandatory?

© Anderson Ross/Getty Images.

In addition to the provincial health insurance, group life and disability insurance is widely provided as an employee benefit. Some firms still offer major medical insurance for their employees whenever they travel outside the province or country. Increasingly, many organizations have also been providing dental insurance to their employees. In many cases, the cost of health and dental premiums is shared between the employer and the employee.

Salary Continuation Plans

If an employee misses a few days because of illness, it is usually not crucial from a financial point of view, since most employers grant paid sick leave for a limited time. It becomes more of a problem when an employee becomes disabled for a longer period of time or even permanently. Canadian companies offer short-term and long-term disability plans.

A **short-term disability plan** typically involves crediting or allocating a certain number of days to an employee, to be used as sick leave for nonoccupational accidents or illnesses. Sick leave credits may be cumulative or noncumulative. A plan is cumulative if insured credits earned during one year may be transferred to the following year; it is noncumulative when the employee's entitlement is reviewed on a yearly basis or after each illness.

---

short-term disability plan

A benefit plan crediting a number of days to be used as sick leave.

For workers who are disabled for a prolonged time, employers offer some form of **long-term disability insurance**. Such plans generally have a long waiting period (six months is very common), and they pay the employee a smaller amount (usually 50 or 60 percent) of the employee's working income. Under most plans, these payments, if necessary, are made until the normal retirement age is reached.

---

long-term disability insurance

A benefit plan providing the employee with an income in the case of long-term illness or injury.

Employee Security Benefits

In addition to insurance, there are noninsurance benefits that enhance employee security. These benefits seek to ensure an income before and after retirement.

Employment Income Security

Discharges or layoffs may entail severe economic consequences for an employee; the impact, however, can be cushioned by employer-provided benefits. If employees have not been given at least two weeks' notice, and if the dismissal was not for just cause, according to the *Canada Labour Code* they are entitled to severance pay equal to two weeks' regular wages. For executives, who usually work on a contract basis, **severance pay** can reach six months' or a year's compensation.

---

severance pay

Payment to a worker upon permanent separation from a company.

Layoffs may be eased by accrued vacation pay. A few companies go so far as to provide a **guaranteed annual wage (GAW)**. These plans assure the worker of receiving some minimum amount of work or pay. For example, employees may be promised a minimum of 1,500 hours of work or pay a year (compare this with the "normal" 52 forty-hour weeks for a total of 2,080 hours). Some employers guarantee 30 hours per week. Even on layoff, the employees draw some income.

---

guaranteed annual wage (GAW)

A benefits plan by which an employer assures employees that they will receive a minimum annual income regardless of layoffs or a lack of work.

The auto industry is a leader in another method, **supplemental unemployment benefits (SUB)**. When employees are out of work, employment insurance benefits are supplemented by the employer from monies previously paid to the SUB fund. This assures covered employees an income almost equal to their previous earnings for as long as the SUB fund remains solvent.

supplemental unemployment benefits (SUB)
Private plans providing compensation for wage loss to laid-off workers.

LO3

Retirement Security

Retirement plans were originally designed to reward long-service employees. Through employer generosity and union pressure, retirement plans have grown in scope and coverage, so that in Canada the average firm spends 6.3 percent of its total payroll costs on government and private pension plans alone.[4]

Registered Pension Plans (RPP)

As of April 2011, 32 percent of all Canadian employees are covered by RPP, so called because they have to be registered with Revenue Canada for preferential tax considerations.[5] Most employers contribute to such plans. Integrated RPP—which make up approximately two-thirds of all RPP—take into account benefits received from the CPP.[6] (See the discussion in the latter part of this chapter.)

DEFINED BENEFITS (DB) PLANS With a **defined benefits (DB) plan**, the employee receives a fixed dollar amount as a pension, depending on age and length of service. Many employees and unions prefer DB plans because of their predictable outcomes. These type of plans are also strictly regulated by the *Employee Retirement Income Security Act*. The advantage for employees is that they know in advance what their retirement benefits will be. For the employer the advantage is that by providing a predictable, guaranteed benefit at retirement that is valued by workers, such a plan can promote worker loyalty and help retain valuable workers.

defined benefits (DB) plan
A benefits plan whose benefits are defined by a formula based on age and length of service, with the employer assuming responsibility for funding.

DEFINED CONTRIBUTION (DC) PLANS When employer and employee contribute to a pension plan, it is called a **defined contribution (DC) plan**; if only the employer makes the contributions, it is called a *noncontributory plan*. In a *contributory plan*, the employee makes a commitment to make regular payments, which are matched by the employer. A typical arrangement would be that the employee allows monthly or weekly deductions from his or her salary, say 5 percent, and the employer either matches this or makes a higher contribution, up to a specific level. These amounts are usually invested in secure funds. After the employee's retirement the money is used to purchase an annuity or may be invested in other approved financial arrangements that pay a regular income to the retiree.

defined contribution (DC) plan
A benefits plan based on amounts contributed by the employer and the employee, the final pension depending on amounts contributed, investment income, and economic conditions at retirement.

For employees, a DC plan may mean greater benefits, especially if it is started at a younger age (longer investment horizon). This is true even if employees leave the organization, since accumulations continue to participate in the accounts' investment. (In a DB plan, accrued benefits are frozen when the employee leaves. With inflation, benefits can lose much of their value by the time the employee retires.) With a DC plan employees also have more control over their investment, because they own their retirement account individually, and it is portable—that is, the investment can be moved to another organization.

Two significant problems have developed in the administration of pension plans. *First*, some employers go out of business, leaving the pension plan unfunded or only partially funded. *Second*, some companies minimize their pension costs by having very long vesting periods. **Vesting** gives the workers the right to pension benefits even if they leave the company. Thus, an employee who quits or is fired before the vesting period has passed often has no pension rights. Since both of these problems may impose hardships on employees and on the nation's welfare programs, Parliament has passed the *Pension Benefits Standards Act*.

---

vesting

A provision in employer-provided retirement plans that gives workers the right to a pension after a specified number of years of service.

For answers to frequently asked question about RPPs, see <http://www.cra-arc.gc.ca/tx/rgstrd/rpp-rpa/menu-eng.html>.

Pension Benefits Standards Act

The ***Pension Benefits Standards Act*** regulates pension plans in industries under the jurisdiction of the Government of Canada, such as banks, railways, shipping companies, and radio and other communications companies. In addition, eight provinces (Alberta, Saskatchewan, Manitoba, New Brunswick, Ontario, Quebec, Nova Scotia, and Newfoundland and Labrador) have enacted their own pension benefits acts that in content are similar to the federal act. Pension plans in the remaining provinces, to qualify for tax deductions, must conform to certain standards set forth in the federal legislation. The *Pension Benefits Standards Act* requires that pension funds be held in trust for members, and that the funds not be held under the complete custody and control of either the employer or the employees. To accomplish this, the funding of a private pension plan must be carried out by one or more of the following means:

- an insurance contract with a company authorized to conduct a life insurance business in Canada;

- a trust in Canada whose trustees are either a trust company or a group of individuals, at least three of whom live in Canada and one of whom must be independent of the employer and employees;

- a corporate pension society; and

- an arrangement administered by the Government of Canada or a provincial government.

Pension Benefits Standards Act

A federal act regulating pension plans in industries under the jurisdiction of the Government of Canada.

LO4   HRC 6

Paid Time-Off Benefits

Time periods during which the employee is not working, but is getting paid, are the result of time-off benefits. Time-off benefits include legal (such as statutory holidays and vacation) and voluntary benefits (such as wash-up time). Although these benefits may seem minor, according to one survey they were the costliest major category, making up 15 percent of gross annual payroll.[7]

On-the-Job Breaks

Some of the most common forms of time-off benefits are those found on the job. Examples include rest breaks, meal breaks, and wash-up time. Through a break in the physical and mental effort of a job, productivity may be increased. The major problem for human resource and line managers is the tendency of employees to stretch these time-off periods:

> When one human resource manager was confronted by a supervisor with the problem of stretched breaks, she suggested a simple solution. Each employee was assigned a specific break time—from 9:15 to 9:30 a.m., or 9:30 to 9:45 a.m., for example—but could not leave for break until the preceding employee returned. Since each clerk was anxious to go on break, the peer group policed the length of breaks and the stretched breaks ended.

Paid Sick Leave

Absences from work are unavoidable. Today, most companies pay workers when they are absent for medical reasons by granting a limited number of days of sick leave per year. Unfortunately, this is one of the most abused benefits; many workers take the attitude that these are simply extra days off. If the human resource policies prohibit employees from crediting unused sick leave to next year's account, absences increase near the end of the year. To minimize abuses, some companies require medical verifications of illness or pay employees for unused sick leave.

A few firms avoid the abuse question by granting "personal leave days." This approach allows an employee to skip work for any reason and get paid, up to a specified number of days per year. Sick leave banks allow employees to "borrow" extra days above the specified number when they use up their individual allocation. Then when they earn additional days, the days are repaid to the sick leave bank.

©David Anderson

Holidays and Vacations

As mentioned under federally and provincially regulated holidays and vacation days, most employers grant vacation days beyond the minimum required number, depending on tenure.[8] Like sick leave, however, this benefit is subject to abuse. Employees sometimes try to stretch the holiday by missing the workday before or after the holiday. Policies that require attendance the day before and after a holiday as a condition of holiday pay lessen this problem.

Policies for vacations vary widely. Some companies allow employees to use vacation days a few at a time. Other companies insist that the worker take the vacation all at once. A few employers actually close down during designated periods and require vacations to be taken during this period. Still other companies negate the reason for vacations completely by allowing employees to work and then receive vacation pay as a bonus.

Employee Services

Some companies go beyond pay and traditional benefits. They also provide educational, financial, and social services for their employees.

Educational Assistance

Tuition refund programs are among the more common employer services. These programs partially or completely reimburse employees for furthering their education. They may be limited only to courses that are related to the employee's job, or the employer may reimburse workers for any educational expenditure. In the future, more companies may follow the lead of Kimberly-Clark Corporation in the United States:

> Kimberly-Clark <http://www.kimberly-clark.com> created an educational savings account for employees and their dependants. The company gives employees credits for each year of service. Then when an employee or dependant wants to go to college, he or she can be reimbursed partially from the educational savings account established by the company.

Financial Services

Probably the oldest service is employee discount plans. These programs, common among retail stores and consumer goods manufacturers, allow workers to buy products from the company at a discount.

Credit unions are another well-established employee service. The interest collected by the credit union on loans and investments is distributed to members in the form of dividends. The dividends (interest payments) are allocated in proportion to the amount employees have in their share (savings) account. The lower interest rate on loans, the higher interest on deposits, and payroll deductions for savings or loan repayments are the major employee advantages.

Stock purchase programs are another financial service. These plans enable employees to buy company stock, usually through payroll deductions. In some stock purchase programs, employee outlays may be matched by company contributions.

Social Services

Employers provide a wide range of social services. At one extreme are simple interest groups such as bowling leagues and softball teams; at the other are comprehensive **employee assistance programs (EAP)** designed to assist employees with personal problems, for example child care, transportation assistance, individual and group counselling, employee quarrels, family disputes, or even assisting managers in dealing with employee complaints.

employee assistance programs (EAP)

Comprehensive company program that seeks to help employees and their family members overcome personal and work-related problems.

Employee assistance programs are becoming more common. Human resource managers realize that employee problems affect company performance.[9] Employer services that can lessen these problems offer potential dividends in employee performance, loyalty, and reduced turnover.

One employer service with a growing record of success is alcohol and drug rehabilitation. For example, human resource experts formerly recommended the discharge of alcoholic workers. Over the past 10 years, however, an increasing number of human resource departments have implemented alcohol and drug rehabilitation programs. This service has saved many otherwise good employees in companies such as Canadian National Railway (CN, <https://www.cn.ca>). CN spends over $1 million annually on EAPs, which include alcohol and drug rehabilitation programs.[10] When rehabilitation has been effective the company usually gains a hard-working, loyal employee.

Spotlight *on* HRM

Women's Work

By Kathryn Dorrell

Juggling the roles of mom, daughter, wife and employee is taking its toll as women's absenteeism outpaces men's. Plan sponsors can implement strategies that acknowledge this reality.

A recent profile of Barbara Stymiest, president and chief executive officer of the Toronto Stock Exchange, in a prominent business magazine discussed the executive's demanding hours in the context of the fact that she has a young daughter. As the mom of an 18-month-old, I was interested in how Stymiest juggled a career and family. But at the same time, I couldn't help bristle at the realization that discussions of businessmen who also happen to be dads seldom delve into this territory.

Balancing work and family life isn't the juggling act for most working men that it is for women. This seemingly sexist statement is a reality in many organizations, and it's backed up by a new Statistics Canada report, *Women in Canada 2000*.

In 1999, three times as many working women took time off to deal with personal and family issues than men. Female workers missed an average of seven days because of such commitments—up from two days in the mid-'70s—whereas working men missed one day, about the same as two decades ago. Meanwhile, 28 percent of women worked fewer than 30 hours a week compared to 10 percent of men, and 20 percent of these women say they did so because of personal and family responsibilities.

Putting some hard numbers behind the old adage that a woman's work is never done isn't about male bashing or even trying to change what are obviously still ingrained societal trends. (No, I'm not about to suggest that plan sponsors offer

(Continued)

lunch-and-learn sessions teaching dads how to take their sick babies to the doctor.) With a growing number of women dominating the workforce—46 percent in 1999, up from 37 percent in 1976—and in increasingly senior positions, it simply makes good business sense for plan sponsors to acknowledge and confront this issue.

The Royal Bank has done just that. Three-quarters of its employees are women and it has implemented the kind of progressive benefits strategies that not only keep talented female employees in the working world but help them climb the proverbial ladder, even if it's with a baby or two and an aging parent in tow.

The bank offers leaves, that have ranged from one day to a year and are sometimes paid, for employees to deal with family matters. In addition, 30 percent of all employees are currently enjoying some sort of flexible working arrangement—be it flex hours or job sharing. And if a supervisor doesn't appear to be supportive of these initiatives, workers can take up the issue using an employee ombudsman phone service.

Norma Tombari, manager of workforce solutions at the Royal Bank, believes that if the company didn't offer these programs it would lose many of its best workers to the competition. "I would love to see more men using these options," she adds. "But right now it's mostly women."

Another beacon of progress is the arrival of Catalyst on the Canadian consulting scene. The New York–based firm, which opened a Toronto office recently and has worked with Bell Canada, specializes in identifying barriers and opportunities for women in the workplace.

However, the best benefit for working women may actually be as simple as creating a work environment and communications strategy that conveys the message that organizations recognize men have personal and family commitments too.

"There is still such a stigma around men taking time off for family matters. It's a huge cultural shift that men are trying to fight. They don't want to say they can't stay for the 5 p.m. meeting because they have to pick up the kids for fear of how they will be viewed," says Judy Hauserman, senior vice-president at Aon Consulting. "If we approach this issue from only a gender perspective, we miss the point."

SOURCE: © 2000 Rogers Media. This article first appeared in the November 2000 edition of *Benefits Canada* magazine. Kathryn Dorrell is associate editor of *Benefits Canada*. She can be reached at kdorrell@rmpublishing.com.

Relocation programs are the support in dollars or services a company provides to its transferred or new employees. At minimum, this benefit includes payment for moving expenses. Some employees receive fully paid house-hunting trips with their spouse to the new location before the move, subsidized home mortgages, placement assistance for working spouses, and even family counselling to reduce the stress of the move. A transferred employee also may be able to sell his or her home to the employer for the appraised value to avoid having to sell it on the market.[11]

relocation programs

A company-sponsored benefit that assists employees who must move in connection with their job.

Employee assistance programs have traditionally involved personal interaction; especially if they were concerned with counselling services, face-to-face communication was important. However, with the advancement of technology, especially the Internet, employers can respond to their employees' needs not only faster, but also more effectively and efficiently. The most prominent of the recent developments in this field is **online service delivery**. The scope of possibilities is vast: opportunities for live chat rooms, one-on-one video counselling, group-help bulletin boards, and online self-help applications are only the tip of the technological iceberg. The goal of online assistance programs is not to replace counselling, but mostly to provide an enhancement to services already offered.[12]

online service delivery

EAP services available to employees through the Internet and by intranet.

Additional assistance activities are discussed in Chapter 11 in connection with counselling.

LO5 HRC 1 & 6

Emerging Services and Trends

Several studies have attempted to predict the types of benefits that will be in demand over the next 10 years.[13] The more popular options for employees seem to be the following:

- above all, increased medical coverage, dental plans, and optometrist services;
- greater assumption of costs of medical coverage by employers;
- more and longer vacations, coupled with reduced length of service requirements;
- more holidays;
- increased pension coverage, with greater contributions by employers;
- cost-of-living adjustments of pension plans;
- improved portability of pension rights and earlier vesting;
- sabbatical leaves for managers, and paid educational leave for rank-and-file employees;
- child care, with the employer providing either fully or partially subsidized care facilities and staff;
- elder care, offering employees time off to take care of aging and dependent relatives, often coupled with counselling and special assistance;
- all benefits to same-sex couples, in accordance with federal and provincial legislation;
- benefits to part-time employees as well as to retirees; and
- prepaid legal advice.

Some companies will go to extremes when it comes to retaining key employees, offering such nontraditional benefits as free laundry, backup child care, or dog walking services.[14]

KPMG's 26,000 employees in its 125 U.S. offices were recently given convenience services through LesConcierges <http://www.lesconcierges.com>. One call to an 800 number and employees may ask for "anything that's legal, ethical, and doesn't harm anyone else," says Kathie Linge, work/life director for KPMG. She used the service to find an electrician on the day after Thanksgiving and to hire an excavator to align the front of her house. She says that studies show that employees who use this program are more productive, more loyal, and more likely to recommend the company to other job applicants.[15]

The recent recessionary economy does not hold promise that these popular wants will in fact be offered. However, current trends indicate that indirect compensation will form a greater proportion of total compensation offered. Perhaps the employer share of contributions to the various current benefit plans will rise without any new types of benefits being added. Employees may also be able to make choices among benefits, and it may well become easier for employees to enroll in benefit plans through liberalized eligibility requirements.

Given the trends outlined above, it will be critical for top management in general and the human resource manager in particular to adopt a total compensation approach when decisions have to be made relating to pay. Organizations cannot afford to treat employee benefits and services independent of direct compensation, especially since they are growing at twice the pace of wages and salaries.

A number of companies have already taken steps to extend benefits to part-time workers. A survey done by Hewitt Associates found that only 9 percent of companies responding did not offer any benefits to part-timers. Two-thirds provide the same health coverage as to full-time employees.[16] It is interesting to note that some respondents are considering or are already offering flexible benefits to their part-time employees. One of those companies is Shell Canada, whose benefits propelled it into the Canada's Top 100 Employers listing. To see a compilation of these benefits visit <http://www.eluta.ca/top-employer-shell-canada>.

Child care, with the employer providing either full or partially subsidized care facilities and staff, is emerging as an extended benefit for employees. What advantages does this benefit offer to workers?

© IT Stock Free.

Part-time work is also possible with job sharing (discussed in Chapter 3), where the duties of a job are shared by two or more employees. It is an increasingly popular arrangement for employers, who want to reduce employment, and for employees, who prefer to work fewer hours.[17]

Finally, management has to take into account the changes in the labour force that will take place over the next 10 to 20 years. The average age of the labour force will increase, which will result in greater emphasis on pensions as part of the benefit package. More women will be working, and more will do so longer, making their job a career. What impact will this have on benefits and services (paid maternity leave, day care centres, nurseries, etc.)? Part-time work also will become more common, with still unforeseeable consequences, since traditionally part-timers received few or no benefits. There can be little doubt that the issue of employee benefits and services will require more attention and occupy more of management's time than ever before.

LO6   HRC 1 & 6

Management of Voluntary Benefit and Service Programs

A serious shortcoming of human resource management has been poor management of indirect compensation. Even in otherwise well-managed human resource departments, benefits and services have grown in a haphazard manner. Those costly supplements were introduced in response to social trends, union demands, employee pressures, and management wishes, and so human resource departments seldom established objectives, systematic plans, and standards to determine the appropriateness of benefits and services. This patchwork of benefits and services has caused several problems.

Problems in Administration

The central problem in supplementary compensation is a lack of employee involvement. Once a benefit program is designed by the human resource department and the labour union (if there is one), employees have little discretion. For example, pension and maternity benefits usually are granted to all workers equally. Younger employees see pensions as distant and largely irrelevant; older workers find maternity benefits are not needed. This uniformity fails to recognize individual differences and wishes. Admittedly, uniformity leads to administrative and actuarial economies; but when employees receive benefits they neither want nor need, these economies are questionable.

Because employees have little choice in their individual benefit package, most workers are unaware of all the benefits to which they are entitled:

> Two researchers designed a study to learn how knowledgeable selected workers were about their benefits. In two different plants—one with a union and one without—they asked employees to list all the benefits that they could recall. The average worker could not recall 15 percent of the employer-provided benefits.[18]

Ignorance and the inability to influence the mix of benefits often lead to pressure from employees for more benefits to meet their needs. For example, older workers may request improved retirement plans, while younger workers seek improved insurance coverage of dependants. Often the result is a proliferation of benefits and increased employer costs. These costs, which represented 15.1 percent of an employer's gross annual payroll in 1953, escalated to about 40 percent in 2010.[19] Still, employee ignorance and confusion can lead to complaints and dissatisfaction about their benefit package.

Traditional Remedies

The traditional remedy to benefit problems has been to increase employee awareness, usually through publicizing employee benefits. This publicity starts with orientation sessions that explain the benefit programs and provide employee handbooks. Company newspapers, special mailings, employee meetings, bulletin-board announcements, and responses to employee questions are also used to further publicize the organization's benefit package.

LO7 HRC 6

A Proactive Solution: Flexible Benefits = cafeteria benefit programs

Flexible benefit programs, also known as *cafeteria benefit programs*, allow employees to select benefits and services that match their individual needs. Workers are provided a benefit and services account with a specified number of dollars in the account. Through deductions from this account, employees shop for specific benefits from among those offered by the employer. The types and prices of benefits are provided to each employee in the form of a cost sheet that describes each benefit. Then, as illustrated in Figure 10-2, employees select their package of benefits and services for the coming year.

---

flexible benefit programs

Programs that allow employees to select the mix of benefits and services that will answer their individual needs. Also known as cafeteria benefit programs.

Figure 10-2 indicates how two different workers might spend the $5,845 the company grants each worker. Workers A and B select two different sets of benefits because their personal situations differ dramatically. Worker A is a young parent who is supporting a family and her husband. A dental plan will assist in defraying the high expenses for dental work, especially if they plan to have another child. Worker B allocated fewer dollars for weekly income benefits. Instead, he put a large portion of his benefit monies into the company pension plan. Although this approach creates additional administrative costs and an obligation for the human resource department to advise employees, there are several advantages. The main advantage is employee participation. Through participation, employees come to understand exactly what benefits the employer is offering, and employees can better match their benefits with their needs. [20]

Flexible benefits, until recently, have offered the usual choices of better long-term disability insurance, dental or vision care, prescription drug coverage, life insurance, group legal services, etc., but it has become now more common that employers offer the opportunity to "purchase" more vacation. Not only this, but it is even possible to sell vacation time. [21] In the past, cafeteria plans often had different choices for single and married employees. The trend now is to offer the choices independent of marital status.

Technology is changing the way companies handle flexible benefits enrollment and communication. In the early days, paper enrollment forms and written communication pieces were the norm. While paper still plays a role in the process in many companies, *interactive voice response systems (IVRs)* and Web-based technologies are becoming the norm for the administration of flexible benefit plans, making the communication process more effective. [22]

FIGURE 10-2

Hypothetical Benefit Selection of Two Different Workers

	Worker A	Worker B
	Age 27, female, married with one child. Husband in graduate school.	Age 56, male, married with two grown and married children. Wife does not work outside the home.
Supplemental health insurance:		
Supplemental dental insurance	$ 545	$ 0
Maternity	345	0
$100 deductible	1,035	0
Prescription drug coverage	0	1,025
Life insurance:		
$100,000 for worker	300	300
$50,000 for spouse	250	0
Vacations	900	1,800
Holidays	500	500
Pension plan	400	1,615
Jury duty pay	0	0
Disability insurance	300	300
Weekly income benefit	1,270	305
Total	$5,845	$5,845

Blue Cross Canada <http://www.bluecross.ca> now offers Health Spending Account administration services for companies with flexible benefit plans. It saves these companies the headaches of administering the plans and claims to be cheaper than if the company managed the plan on its own.[23]

LO8 HRC 1 & 2 & 6

Implications for Human Resource Management

Change in the field of employee benefits has been dramatic over the last decade. Retirement plans have been and are under constant legal review, tax reforms have added complexity, health care policies have changed and their expenses gone up, all adding to the responsibilities of the human resource professional. Advances in computer hardware technology and the tremendous growth in the range of "friendly" software have resulted in human resource practitioners being able to develop their own applications.

To find the right approach for the administration of benefit plans, a needs analysis is an essential first step. The analysis should deal with five basic questions:

1. What tasks need to be performed, how often, and how quickly?

2. Who currently performs these tasks, and what does it cost now to perform them (including internal as well as external costs)?

3. What alternative ways of performing these tasks are possible and practical?

4. What will each alternative cost, both to install and to maintain?

5. How long will it take to implement each option, and can the implementation ever be truly completed?

The objective of the needs analysis is to identify the best administrative methodology to meet both the short-term and long-term needs of the employer. The result of the analysis should be a report that can be used by decision makers as a reference document against which a detailed implementation process can be tested.

The implications of financial security plans for human resource departments are several. First, human resource managers should make sure that the firm adheres to all provisions relating to minimum wages and pension deductions. For example, the *Canada Labour Code* requires every employer to furnish, from time to time, information relating to employee wages, hours of work, general holidays, annual vacations, and conditions of employment. As well, the Canada Labour Standards Regulations require that each employee's social insurance number, sex, and occupational classification be recorded and kept ready for inspection. Accurate records of maternity leave, overtime, and termination should also be maintained.

Second, to avoid duplication, human resource managers need to consider CPP and other benefits available to employees when designing their firm's own benefit and service plans. In many provinces, some of the items included in private group insurance plans are already covered under the workers' compensation and health insurance plans.

Third, human resource specialists also need to be concerned about reducing accidents in order to lower the cost of workers' compensation. These costs are directly related to the claims made against the company by employees. The more that must be paid to these employees, the greater the cost. Yet even aside from cost considerations, many managers feel a moral obligation to provide a safe working environment.

A fourth approach is to challenge all unjustified claims for employment compensation made against employers. Those claims that are successfully challenged may reduce costs in the future:

> Kevin Hirtsman was fired for stealing from the company, since the employee manual stated that stealing was grounds for immediate dismissal. When his claim for employment insurance was sent to the company for its comments, the human resource manager wrote back that Kevin was terminated for cause. Kevin's claim for employment compensation was denied.

To keep ballooning health costs under control, William M. Mercer, a benefit consulting company, recommends that employers take the following measures:

- Instead of having a set employee-paid deductible, ask staff to pay 20 percent of any treatment.

- Stop out-of-country medical coverage for personal travel, or set a 30-day limit or a dollar maximum.

- Remember that many dental plans were designed in pre-fluoride days. Six-month checkups may not be necessary anymore.

- Where they are available, pay only for generic drugs, saving an average of 6 percent on drug plans.

- With "maintenance drugs," such as birth control pills, ask employees to get larger amounts to save on dispensing fees.

- An employer who builds a series of these alternatives into its benefit plans could probably save 15 percent of costs.[24]

 **HRC 3 & 6**

Retention

The question has been raised earlier what role benefits play in retaining employees. **Retention** of key employees has become a major issue, especially in high-tech companies.[25] Several studies have shown that innovative and flexible benefit plans are very effective tools in attracting and retaining highly skilled staff.[26] "My sense is that benefits become increasingly important as a competitive advantage if you can't negotiate around the total compensation package," said Ann O'Neill, director of the Certified Employee Benefits Specialist program at Dalhousie University in Halifax.[27] This view is confirmed by a recent Canadian survey of over 1,800 employees.[28]

---

retention

A company's ability to keep employees.

Benefit Audit

Often, the administration of benefit plans still leaves room for improvement. One approach that readily identifies inefficiencies is a **benefit audit**. It usually consists of two components: a claims audit, which examines claims and claim trends, and an organization audit, which examines the efficiency and effectiveness of handling employee benefits within the employer organization, including dealings with an insurer or third-party administrator.

benefit audit
A system to control the efficiency of a benefit program.

A benefit audit enables employers to do the following:

- identify opportunities for financial and human resource savings;
- ensure that insurers or third-party administrators are doing a good job;
- exert effective control over their benefits area;
- identify who is in control of the benefits budget; and
- check how their employee claiming habits compare against other Canadian employers.

Goods and Services Tax Application to Benefits

Since 1991, the GST applies to some benefits, but not to others. Generally, GST has to be paid on the following benefits:

- company cars (if also used for private purposes)
- car operating costs
- tax return preparation
- short-term residential accommodation
- holiday trips within continental North America
- frequent flyer points
- financial counselling
- parking

Not affected are awards, health benefits, stock options, low-interest or no-interest loans, tuition fees, child care, a Christmas turkey, and gifts under $100.

HRC 3 & 6

Benefits and Strategy Implications

As is outlined in Chapter 1, management has to look at the long-term objectives of the organization and match these with organizational conditions to create the necessary environment for reaching the objectives. Specifically, the following steps have to be taken:

- Define the objectives of the organization.
- Link objectives of the human resource department with the objectives of the organization.
- Assess the needs of the employees.
- Assess the legal requirements to ensure that laws are followed.
- Compare the company's benefits with those of the competition.
- Make sure the benefits are valued by the employees.
- Conduct an annual benefit audit.

It is important for human resource managers to integrate benefits into the wage and salary package. This compensation package has to fulfill both short-term and long-term goals. The short-term goals, for example, high motivation and productivity, are usually satisfied with merit pay and incentive systems that reward high performers. A common long-term goal is to retain good employees, an objective that can be achieved by a valued pension or a profit-sharing plan. Another strategy may address the need for downsizing by using an appropriate severance package. These are just a few items of a comprehensive pay strategy.[29]

SUMMARY

Employee benefits and services are the fastest-growing component of compensation. The Canadian government has instituted compulsory programs that provide citizens with certain benefits and services. Financial security is achieved partially through such benefits as the Canada Pension Plan, employment insurance, and workers' compensation. The CPP provides income at retirement or upon disability. It also provides the family members of a deceased worker with a death benefit and a survivor's annuity, under certain conditions.

Employment insurance pays the worker a modest income to reduce the hardships of losing a job. These payments go to employees who are involuntarily separated from their jobs. Payments last until the worker finds suitable employment or until the worker receives the maximum number of payments permitted by the government.

Workers' compensation pays employees who are injured in the course of their employment. The payments are made to prevent the employee from having to sue to be compensated for injuries. If an employee dies, benefits are paid to the employee's survivors.

Health and medical insurance is provided by provincial governments with assistance from the federal government. In addition to the provincial health insurance, group life and disability insurance is widely provided as an employee benefit. More and more companies are also providing dental insurance for their employees.

Voluntary benefits include insurance, security, and time-off benefits. Employee services encompass educational, financial, and social programs. This diversity contributes to several serious administrative problems. The most significant problem is the orientation of managers and human resource specialists toward cost savings. In pursuit of administrative and actuarial economies, most companies and unions do not allow individualized benefit packages in indirect compensation programs.

A major issue is ballooning health care costs. Management has to pay more attention to the efficient administration of such plans and to the control of their costs. Some studies have shown that savings of up to 15 percent can be achieved if management pays attention to health benefit costs.

A significant development in the field of benefit administration is the benefit audit, consisting of a claims and an organization audit. The audit examines the efficiency and effectiveness of handling employee benefits, including insurers and third-party administrators.

If management wants to be up-to-date in benefits, it has to be aware of the trends in the field. Changing demographics make changing demands on benefit systems: extra medical coverage, company pension plans with better portability and earlier vesting, child care, and elder care are some of the new developments in this field. In all probability, increased part-time work will necessitate offering benefits even to these employees. These developments will make it necessary for top management to adopt a total compensation package as part of a pay strategy.

TERMS FOR REVIEW

benefit audit
Canada Pension Plan (CPP)
contributory plans
defined benefits (DB) plan
defined contribution (DC) plan
employee assistance programs (EAP)
Employment Insurance (EI)
flexible benefit programs
guaranteed annual wage (GAW)
health insurance
long-term disability insurance
online service delivery
Pension Benefits Standards Act
portability clauses
relocation programs
retention
severance pay
short-term disability plan
supplemental unemployment benefits (SUB)
vesting
workers' compensation

SELF-ASSESSMENT EXERCISE

Understanding Benefits

Benefits tend to be neglected when it comes to considerations of labour costs, but with the average benefit package in Canada now being close to 35 percent of payroll, HR managers are well advised to pay special attention to the management of benefits. Test yourself on your expertise.

1. If the current trend continues, soon benefits will make up over one-half of most firms' payroll.	**T**	**F**
2. Vacations, along with holidays and rest breaks to reduce fatigue and enhance productivity, are part of employees' objectives.	**T**	**F**
3. Salaried, hourly paid, and self-employed persons are eligible for unemployment benefits.	**T**	**F**
4. In Canada, like in the U.S., health insurance is the most common form of insurance coverage.	**T**	**F**

(Continued)

5. Vesting gives workers the right to pension benefits even if they leave the company.	(T)	F
6. Meal breaks, rest breaks, wash-up time, sick leave, holidays, and vacations make up the costliest major category of benefits.	(T)	F
7. Cafeteria benefits allow employees free meals.	T	(F)
8. Benefits play a major role in retaining employees.	(T)	F
9. Benefits cannot be taxed.	T	(F)
10. Benefits and services are the fastest-growing component of compensation.	(T)	F

SCORING

If you marked statements 1, 5, 6, 8, and 10 as true, give yourself one point each. The remaining statements are false.

Scores of 8–10: Very good! Congratulations for your thorough understanding of the content in this chapter.

Scores of 5–7: Well … it's okay, but rereading this chapter could help you do better.

Scores of less than 5: Oops … add this chapter to your reading list again.

REVIEW AND DISCUSSION QUESTIONS

1. Why has government been interested in providing financial security to workers through laws? What areas do you think are likely to receive government attention in the future to ensure employee financial security?

2. Some people believe that employment insurance has over a period of time worked against workers rather than for them. What is your opinion of employment insurance? Why?

3. Suppose a friend of yours contracted lead poisoning on the job. What sources of income could this person rely on while recovering during the next two months? What if it took two years for your friend to recover? Are other sources of income available?

4. Besides retirement income, what other benefits are provided through the Canada Pension Plan?

5. What changes should be made to the employment insurance system to eliminate its present weaknesses?

6. What factors have contributed to the rapid growth of benefits since the Second World War?

7. Briefly describe the benefits that an organization might give employees to provide them with greater financial security.

8. Why was the *Pension Benefits Standards Act* needed? What are its major provisions?

9. What are the common problems you would expect to find with the benefits and services program of a large company?

10. If you were asked to increase employee awareness of benefits, what actions would you take without changing the way the company provides benefits? If you could change the entire benefit program, what other methods would you use to increase employee awareness?

CRITICAL THINKING QUESTIONS

1. Suppose you are asked to explain why employees are better off receiving pay and benefits rather than just getting larger paycheques that include the monetary value of benefits. What arguments will you use?

2. For each of the following groups of employees, what types of problems are likely to occur if a company goes from a five-day, 40-hour week to a four-day, 40-hour week: (a) working mothers, (b) labourers, (c) assembly-line workers?

3. Should companies pay educational assistance? Assume that it was for a degree in information technology. What if a competitor offers a higher salary to the successful graduate? How could you make sure the company's investment remains in the organization?

ETHICS QUESTION

It is quite common for fish-processing companies in the Atlantic Provinces to allow employees to work the number of weeks required to qualify for Employment Insurance (EI), then lay them off and hire other family members to let them qualify for EI. Discuss the ethical issues involved.

WEB RESEARCH EXERCISE

1. What are the characteristics of an effective Retirement Savings Program? Look at the following website:

   www.benefits.org/interface/benefit/retire.htm

2. What are the advantages of a flexible benefit plan? Have a look at:

   www.benefits.org/interface/benefit/flex.htm

3. Employee Assistance Programs have become very popular with small and large companies. Give some good reasons for the introduction of an EAP. See (search for "eap"):

   http://www.benefits.org/coverage/health-care/employee-assistance

4. What are the eligibility criteria for the new Employment Insurance program? Give details.

   http://www.servicecanada.gc.ca/eng/sc/ei/benefits/regular.shtml

INCIDENT 10-1

Soap Producers and Distributors Ltd.

Soap Producers and Distributors Ltd. faced an employee turnover problem. The company's annual turnover rate was nearly 20 percent among technical and white-collar workers. Among hourly paid employees, the rate was nearly 30 percent.

Wage and salary surveys repeatedly showed that the company's pay levels were 10 to 11 percent above those of comparable jobs in the labour market. The benefit program was not as impressive, but management thought it was competitive. Employees received supplementary health and life insurance, paid vacations and holidays, and a Christmas bonus of $1,000.

Although some employees complained about the company's benefits, complaints varied widely and no one benefit or lack of benefit seemed to be the key issue.

To make Soap Producers and Distributors' problems worse, they operated in a tight labour market, which meant jobs sometimes took weeks to fill. To hire specialized workers almost always meant recruiting them from other cities and paying their moving expenses.

DISCUSSION QUESTIONS

1. What additions do you think should be made to the company's benefit program? (Hint: what is missing?)

2. What problems in the incident might be solved by a cafeteria approach? Think of specific interest groups.

3. To overcome the company's recruitment problems, what other changes do you suggest? What are the trends in benefit programs?

CASE STUDY

Maple Leaf Shoes Ltd.

Flexible Benefit Program

Maple Leaf Shoes Ltd. is a medium-sized manufacturer of leather and vinyl shoes located in Wilmington, Ontario. It was started in 1973 and currently employs about 500 persons in its Ontario plant and some 200 more in offices and warehouses throughout Canada.

Sam Polanyi, President of Maple Leaf Shoes' Leather Workers Union, was working on a draft of his plan for the upcoming negotiations with management. He knew that he had to be prepared for some tough bargaining; Robert Clark, the company's president and chief negotiator, was no pushover. Almost all negotiations in the past had gone to the wire, sometimes just hours away from a strike, but so far there had always been a last-minute settlement.

Some of Sam's members had approached him to discuss the advantages of a flexible benefit plan. Apparently, some of the workers' spouses worked in companies that had such a plan, and the workers seemed to like it. It meant they could choose the kind of benefits most useful to them, which was not possible under the rigid "one size fits all" system the company was using now. Could he convince Bob Clark that it would be to the company's advantage? A flexible—or cafeteria—plan would certainly be more expensive, and that was the rub. Sam was willing to compromise on other issues to get the plan, but how could he sell Clark on it?

(Continued)

DISCUSSION QUESTIONS

Can you assist Sam Polanyi in his attempt to sell Robert Clark on a flexible benefit plan? What are the advantages and disadvantages of such plans?

CASE STUDY

CPIB

Canadian Pacific and International Bank

Mary Keddy, Senior Vice-President HR, was facing Michael Bennett, the bank's CEO, in his office. He had called her to an urgent meeting regarding the bank's benefit expenses. He showed her some figures he had received from the Internal Auditor. The data indicated that the bank's benefit expenses had reached almost 40 percent of the bank's payroll. He also produced benchmark data from a survey, which showed that the industry average was close to 30 percent. "Why is it our benefit expenses are so much higher than those of our competitors?" he asked.

Mary pointed out that the data had assessed the financial services industry, not just banks, and that the industry included some trust companies with much lower benefit levels than banks—which, by and large, had benefit expenses similar to those of the CPIB—although the CPIB certainly occupied the high end of the scale.

Mr. Bennett wondered whether these expenses were really justified. "Where is the payoff?" he asked. Mary had no problems defending the bank's benefit outlays. She pointed out that the CPIB had the lowest turnover rate among banks, 2 percent lower than any other, and that every employee attitude survey showed that the CPIB staff felt the bank to be a very good place to work and that job satisfaction was high. She also mentioned that the bank had no difficulties attracting top-flight applicants. She was convinced that the bank's generous benefit package contributed significantly to this level of satisfaction. She concluded her explanation by saying: "Mike, look at the level of customer satisfaction. We beat out every other bank on this measure. I am sure the reason is that happy employees mean happy customers. And there is the main payoff."

Bennett appreciated Mary's explanation. He always had been proud when he saw the results of internal surveys. There was no doubt that people liked to work for the CPIB. "Still," he wondered, "are there ways to cut the expenses without doing too much damage to employee satisfaction?" Mary agreed to look into that matter and to make suggestions regarding more efficient methods of delivering benefit services. She had heard and read about the use of the intranet and the Internet as more effective ways to administer benefit plans, but felt that she did not know enough about it to come up with convincing recommendations. It was obvious that she needed some expert advice.

ADDITIONAL INFORMATION

The last time a benefit audit had been done was seven years ago—a year before Mary joined the bank. Ever since her arrival, Mary had been too busy introducing strategic changes in areas such as selection, diversity management, and training. In the past five years, the bank had also acquired several other financial institutions and expanded into other countries. But the need for a benefit audit had been on her mind for some time.

The bank's flexible benefit package included, besides the usual supplementary health and life insurances, child care, elder care, a drug payment plan, wellness programs (the bank had its own exercise centre), personal counselling service (drugs, alcohol, smoking cessation), educational support, and financial advising. It was also possible to purchase more vacation time. There were three full-time employees responsible for administering the flexible benefit package. The administration expenses, including communication, were close to $300,000 annually. The bank used a quite-effective intranet mainly for training and public announcements.

DISCUSSION QUESTIONS

1. Use Web research to find arguments for and against using the Internet and the bank's intranet for the administration and delivery of its benefit services.

2. Is outsourcing benefit administration advisable? Why? What criteria should be used in making the decision?

3. If Mary asks for a benefit audit, what would the auditor look at?

PART-ENDING VIDEOS

"21st Century Ventures: Corporate Drumming Up Business"

SOURCE: *Venture*, show number 914, February 15, 2004, running time 3:10.

"Finding and Keeping the Best Employees"

SOURCE: © MHHE Management Library.

Go to Connect to access the videos.

ROLE-PLAY 5: FLEXIBLE BENEFITS

Time required: 40–50 minutes

OBJECTIVES OF THE ROLE-PLAY

1. To help the students understand the pros and cons of flexible benefits.

2. To enhance their skills to listen and respond to employee concerns.

3. To help them prepare for their role as human resource managers.

PRIOR PREPARATION

1. Study Chapter 10 of the text.

2. Read descriptions of Maple Leaf Shoes Ltd. at the end of Chapters 1 and 2.

GUIDELINES FOR CONDUCTING THE ROLE-PLAY

In this role-play, an employee, Megan Litkoff, is meeting with Jane Reynolds to inquire into the possibility of a flexible work hours and benefit plan.

1. Two students, one for the role of Jane Reynolds and the other for Megan Litkoff, should be identified.

2. Students should read their respective descriptions (see the Instructor Resource Manual), along with the company details given at the end of Chapters 1 and 2.

3. The instructor should signal the beginning and end of the meeting. The interview will last about 25 to 30 minutes.

4. The remainder of the class time is used for discussion of the behaviours during the role-play and outcomes.

5. Observers should be asked to make notes against the questions listed below and discuss their findings at the end of the role-play.

6. Instructor should sum up by highlighting the advantages and disadvantages of flexible benefit plans.

INSTRUCTIONS FOR OBSERVERS

As you observe the meeting between Jane Reynolds and Megan Litkoff, make notes regarding each of the questions below. Pay particular attention to the behaviours (both verbal and nonverbal) of each person.

1. How did Jane begin the meeting?

2. Was there open communication between the two? Who spoke more? About what?

3. Was each party listening to the other? Were their concerns realistic? What could have been done better?

4. What is your assessment of the nonverbal expressions of each? What changes would you recommend to each?

5. What other improvements would you recommend?

Maintaining High Performance

An organization's culture and working environment has an effect on the motivation and job satisfaction of its employees. To maintain good relationships, an effective communication process is essential. Good interpersonal relations also require appropriate and fair discipline procedures. Workplace safety is also very important. Managing in a union environment requires familiarity with the legal requirements in dealing with unions, the collective bargaining process, and administration of the collective agreement.

The three chapters in Part 6 discuss ways to create a positive work environment, maintain proper discipline, ensure a safe workforce, and deal with union management issues.

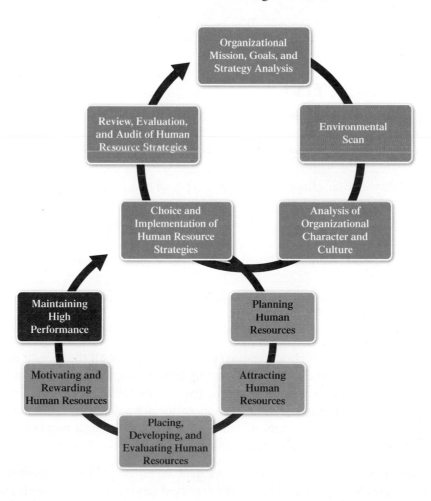

CHAPTER 11

Managing Employee Relations

Although the concept and measurement of high-performance organizations are relatively new to management theory, they have roots that extend at least back to the beginning of the Industrial Revolution.

AMERICAN MANAGEMENT ASSOCIATION[1]

LEARNING OBJECTIVES

After studying this chapter, you should be able to:

LO1 Discuss the importance of downward and upward communication in organizational settings.

LO2 Define employee counselling and the major types of counselling.

LO3 Describe how progressive discipline and wrongful dismissal work.

LO4 Explain the different techniques available to improve quality of work life.

LO5 Outline the major issues relating to downsizing the workforce and their implications for strategic human resource management.

In many ways, this entire book is about employee relations. How well the human resource department handles human resource planning, placement, training and development, evaluation, and compensation largely determines the state of employee relations. Even when these activities are performed properly, solid employee relations demand careful attention to organizational communication, employee counselling, discipline, and management of work groups. In addition, a number of organizations are becoming high-involvement workplaces that emphasize human resource management.

A number of employees express frustration with their employer and their manager/supervisor. In a study of Canadian employees, only 15 percent reported having jobs with both clear feedback and a significant impact (that is, the work is important). Almost 25 percent of employees indicated that their job had both little recognition and low satisfaction. According to study author Paul Fairlie, "Engagement, commitment, and performance are important, but these are outputs. They don't happen unless employees view their work as meaningful."[2]

A *Canadian HR Reporter* survey on problem managers revealed that 46 percent of respondents viewed problem managers as a big problem and 27 percent reported that they are a huge problem. More than half of the respondents said that one in 10 managers is a problem manager. The survey identified what types of behaviours create the most problems: inappropriate comments (74 percent), showing favouritism (70 percent), failing to follow due process (63 percent), treating employees in a disrespectful manner (62 percent), and bullying or intimidation (57 percent). About 35 percent of participants indicated that their organization tolerates just about anything if the manager delivers results, while about 14 percent reported little tolerance for managerial misbehaviour. Only about 17 percent of respondents stated that they were able to get problem managers to change their behaviour most of the time.[3]

A study by Watson Wyatt Worldwide (now Towers Watson; <http://www.towerswatson.com>) identified the following seven factors as important in building employee commitment: trust in senior leadership, a chance to use skills on the job, job security, competitiveness of rewards, the quality of the organization's products/services, the absence of work related stress, and the honesty and integrity of the employer's business conduct.[4]

Although the focus of this chapter is on employee relations, an effective organization also pays considerable attention to relationships among workers. Several human resource initiatives, such as policies on workplace and sexual harassment, conflict resolution procedures, and employee involvement programs, play an important role in enhancing human relations.

HRC 1, 2, 5 & 8

Strategic Importance of Employee Relations Practices

"Employee relations" is a complex blend of organizational culture, human resource practices, and individual perceptions. Virtually everything the human resource department does affects employee relations, directly or indirectly. But many human resource activities (such as recruitment, selection, and benefits administration) go largely unnoticed by employees. Other important human resource functions affect employees only periodically, as in the case of performance appraisal and salary review sessions. This necessitates ongoing activities to foster good employer–employee relations.

Why are employee relations practices important? At least four major reasons can be offered:

1. *Good employee relations practices improve productivity.* Employee productivity is significantly affected by two factors: ability and attitude. Ability is simply whether the employee is able to perform the job. Ability is influenced by such things as training, education, innate aptitude, tools, and work environments. Attitude, on the other hand, refers to an individual's willingness to perform the job. Attitude is affected by a myriad of factors, such as level of motivation, job satisfaction, and commitment to work. Good employee relations practices help improve both the ability and attitude of the employee. The result is an improvement in employee productivity:

   A University of Melbourne (Australia; <http://www.unimelb.edu.au>) study suggests twittering or using Facebook during office hours may actually increase employee productivity. The study indicates that employees who use the Internet for personal reasons while working are about 9 percent more productive than those who do not. According to the study author, Brent Coker, "people need to zone out a bit to get their concentration back. Short and unobtrusive breaks, such as a quick surf of the Internet, enables the mind to rest itself."[5]

2. *Good employee relations ensure implementation of organizational strategies.* In Chapter 1, the importance of the role that human resource activities play in achieving organizational goals was discussed. Good employee relations practices ensure that organizational goals and strategies are properly communicated to the employees and receive their commitment.

3. *Good employee relations practices reduce employment costs.* When concern for and interest in employees becomes part of the overall organizational culture, significant cost savings in terms of reduced absenteeism and turnover can emerge. Good employee relations practices also give employers a recruiting advantage as most job applicants prefer to work for an organization that treats them fairly and offers them a challenging job with potential for career growth.

4. *Good employee relations help employees grow and develop.* As discussed in Chapter 1, an important goal of human resource departments today is to help employees achieve their personal goals. A keen interest in the employee's work-related and career goals not only brings benefits to the organization (in terms of improved employee morale, loyalty, improved productivity, ready availability of skilled personnel within), but also helps it meet its social objectives.

A recent study by CareerBuilder <http://www.careerbuilder.ca> indicated that just under 60 percent of employees are satisfied at work but about 20 percent plan to change jobs by next year. Individuals planning to stay reported that it was because they like the people they work with (54 percent), and they are satisfied with their benefits (49 percent) and salary (43 percent). Among workers who were very dissatisfied, almost 60 percent indicated a desire to change jobs. The sources of dissatisfaction included concerns over salary (66 percent), a feeling of not being valued (65 percent), limited advancement opportunities (45 percent), a lack of work–life balance (39 percent), and a poor opinion of their supervisor or manager's performance (37 percent).[6]

As Figure 11-1 shows, there are five major components of effective employee relations: communication, counselling, discipline, rights, and involvement. Each of these will be discussed in some detail below. In addition, a section of the chapter will address the issues of employee retention, job security, and organizational downsizing.

FIGURE 11-1

Five Key Dimensions of Employee Relations

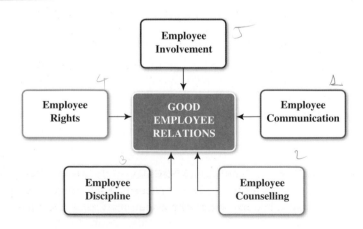

LO1   HRC 2, 3, 5 & 9

Effective Employee Communication

Information about the organization, its environment, its products and services, and its people is essential to management and employees. Without information, managers cannot make effective decisions about markets or resources, particularly human resources. Likewise, insufficient information may cause stress and dissatisfaction among employees. Moreover, effective communication is an essential component of learning organizations.

The need for information is met through an organization's communication system. In small or less-sophisticated firms, communication may be informal, but in large multibillion-dollar enterprises, specialists may serve as employee communications directors or as chief information officers.

Most organizations use a blend of formal, systematically designed communication efforts and informal ad hoc arrangements. For convenience, most of these approaches can be divided into *downward communication systems*, which exist to get information to employees, and *upward communication systems*, which exist to obtain information from employees.

Downward Communication Systems

Human resource professionals try to facilitate an open, two-way flow of information, although often messages are of the top-down variety. **Downward communication** is information that begins at some point in the organization and proceeds down the organizational hierarchy to inform or influence others. Top-down methods are necessary for decision makers to have their decisions carried out. These communications also help give employees knowledge about the organization and feedback on how their efforts are perceived.

---

downward communication

Information that begins at some point in the organization and feeds down the organization hierarchy to inform or influence others.

Organizations use a variety of downward communication methods because multiple channels are more likely to overcome barriers and reach the intended receivers. For example, limiting messages to email or text messaging may exclude large numbers of employees. Some common examples of downward communication approaches include in-house publications, information booklets, employee bulletins, prerecorded messages, email, and jobholder reports and meetings. Failing to communicate effectively can be very costly:

> According to James Hoggan, a Vancouver public relations expert, "the right communication strategy can help organizations maintain or rebuild corporate credibility that has been hit hard in recent months. Multimillionaire Wall Street CEOs, whose out-of-control mortgage businesses have undermined markets and economies around the world, insisted their companies were healthy only days before their collapse. Whether they were incompetent or dishonest, their actions have shattered public trust in private institutions."[7]

In-House Publications and Prerecorded Messages

Many organizations publish internal magazines, newspapers, or information booklets for employees (in hard copy or electronic formats or both). Their purpose is to inform employees about current developments and to foster a long-term understanding about objectives and mission:

At Air Canada <http://www.aircanada.com>, keeping employees in the loop is critical. In addition to a daily newsletter of current information and a weekly newsletter from the chief operating officer, the organization also has a monthly magazine, *Horizons*, to keep the almost 27,000 employees worldwide in touch. Employees can also check out a Yammer social networking site that addresses such topics as flight issues and offers ideas to the company on a page titled "Creative Juices."[8]

Human resource departments often distribute information on various subjects to employees. For instance, an employee handbook is often given to new employees to inform them about regulations and benefits. It is important that the information in employee handbooks be updated regularly and carefully reviewed—in some instances, information contained in employee handbooks has been used by former employees in litigation against the organization.

Information on specialized subjects relating to human resource activities, such as suggestion programs, employee assistance programs, occupational health and safety, wage incentives, retirement, and fringe benefits is also frequently provided, often as online publications. Also, a number of organizations develop internal video programs for employees to access.

Electronic Communication

Using email as a means of communicating with employees is taken for granted in many organizations. However, it is important to realize that email may not be appropriate for all types of communication:

Esthetician Crystal Bell of Kelowna, British Columbia, checked her Facebook account one morning as she was getting ready for work and discovered that she had been terminated (cybersacked). Bell, who had only been employed for two weeks, showed up for work because she thought her employer was kidding. According to Bell, "it is not the human way to go. I think that using any kind of texting or emailing to let people go is a coward's way out." Ruth Haag, author of *Hiring and Firing*, states that "doing an email is quickest and easiest but people forget that it is the most public way to communicate because it can be around the world in minutes and you're looking like a jerk for firing someone that way."[9]

In addition, more and more employers are using intranets (internal communications systems that function like a smaller version of the World Wide Web). Denis Zenkin, an E2.0 expert, calls intranets and HR a "perfect match":

Zenkin identifies several uses of an intranet by HR specialists including information dissemination of HR documents and collection of employee information, HR transactions (use of eforms), training (such as a slideshow, video, or text embedded in a wiki), collecting feedback information (such as surveys and blog posts), community building (for example, tracking birthdays and organizing special events), performance management, and recruitment.[10]

Firms use intranets for a variety of purposes ranging from tracking benefit enrollments to providing copies of employee handbooks, policy manuals, and company newsletters.[11] Human resource departments have found intranet communication to be particularly effective as a means of updating handbooks and manuals and in eliminating some of the administrative burden associated with forms management. Examples of human resource departments using intranets include creating an electronic employee directory, setting up training registration information, using electronic pay stubs, updating of employee accounts, mapping performance achievements, managing succession planning, and creating discussion groups:[12]

How can HR be made greener? According to Environment Canada, paper still accounts for about one-third of all waste. There are several options available to HR to reduce the use of paper, including online statement delivery (such as payroll information), self-service technology, and electronic solutions (to track HR information such as payroll, time, attendance, and performance management data). These are a few examples of the Green HRM approach.[13]

With intranet communication, the traditional top-down communication system is altered, with communication opportunities extended to a much larger group of employees. However, the use of technology needs to be carefully managed. One study found that HR technology (including employee self-service) reduced transaction costs for employers by 43 percent. But employee portals regularly fail to meet the goals companies hoped for: almost all employers participating in one study anticipated productivity improvements, but only 54 percent reported some productivity gains and 31 percent of human resource executives indicated that getting employees to use self-service was their most pressing technology-related issue.[14] Still, technology can be a very valuable tool:

> Some organizations are increasing their use of "assistive technology" (software and/or hardware) to help both individuals with disabilities and nondisabled employees. Examples of assistive technology include electronic pointing devices, closed-caption television broadcasting, speech and/or voice recognition software, and text-to-speech or speech synthesizers that allow blind or low-vision employees to hear their email and read web pages.[15]

Many employers have developed policies on Internet usage. Among the issues to consider are the restriction of the Internet to business purposes, the right of employers to monitor employee usage of the Internet, and specific prohibitions (relating to such concerns as copyright, distribution of viruses, or the posting or downloading of material that is threatening, abusive, defamatory, or obscene). In addition, firms must be concerned about hackers obtaining confidential company and employee data.

A seven-step plan to protect the organization from the misuse of electronic communications includes (1) developing and implementing a policy addressing electronic communications; (2) being aware of legal issues and limitations associated with monitoring electronic communications; (3) training employees and managers concerning the policy; (4) encouraging prompt reporting of policy violations and immediately addressing all complaints; (5) understanding your system; (6) examining the available tools for controlling Internet access; and (7) developing a policy for telecommuting.[16]

A survey of more than 10,000 employees indicated that 70 percent found instant messaging distracting and 10 percent had never heard of it. Sixty percent reported that texting was distracting and 16 percent had never sent a text message, and 90 percent found social networking sites a nuisance. It appears that employees are concerned about their jobs and don't want to do anything to jeopardize them.[17] However, some employers are encouraging the use of electronic communication:

> Shannon Boudjema, a business manager for marketing communications firm Bond Brand Loyalty <https://bondbrandloyalty.com>, posted a message on Twitter asking for help in finding research on young consumers. On returning to work the next day, she had dozens of tweets. Bond Brand Loyalty is encouraging employees to find ways to use social networking to help the company. While several Canadian companies block access to IM and social networking sites, other employers believe that using such sites can increase productivity and employee value.[18]

How often do Canadians use the web? A new study by comScore Inc. <http://www.comscore.com> shows that Canadians spend more time online than individuals in any other country (an average of 36.3 hours a month—the United States was second at 35.2 hours per month). About 49 percent of the time online is now spent on mobile devices. There are about 24 million mobile subscribers and around 80 percent have a smartphone. The most common uses of smartphones were instant messaging, games, and social media (such as Twitter and Snapchat), while the top uses of tablets were taking and managing photos, using social media, and listening to Internet radio.[19]

An issue that has caused some concern for employers revolves around employee blogs (web logs). From an organizational perspective, employers are worried about employees leaking confidential information about the company (intentionally or unintentionally), hurting the organization's reputation, describing the business in a negative way, or exposing the employer to potential liability. Rather than simply trying to ban employees from blogging, some organizations are developing a blogging policy; typical guidelines include writing in the first person (using I) to make it clear that the views are not those of the company, being aware of the responsibilities with respect to corporate information, and adhering to professional standards.[20] Fredrik Racka outlines four rules for employees: understand that you're personally responsible, abide by existing rules, keep secrets, and use common sense.[21] However, these rules are not always followed.

Workplace social media policies are gaining more and more attention as employers become growingly concerned about employee abuse of social media at work to the detriment of the brand and image of the organization. A recent study on professionalism in the workplace indicated that about half of HR professionals believed that IT abuses had increased over the past five years, with about two-thirds indicating problems with excess tweeting and Facebook use.[22]

Social Media and the Use of Mobile Devices

An issue for human resource professionals is the growing use of social media by employees. According to the Society for Human Resource Management, slightly more than two-thirds of employers have employees who use social media to communicate with groups such as customers and prospective employees. However, just under 75 percent of such employers do not provide training to such employees, and few HR professionals view social media as being very effective for meeting such goals as sharing information or improving traffic to the employer's website.[23]

A major concern with the increased use of mobile devices, such as laptops and tablets, is the security of networks and data. Experts are calling for good mobility management as part of an enterprise security management system. Concerns include protecting precious data from attacks and human error and meeting ongoing changes to privacy laws. From an HR perspective, it is critical that employees are aware of policies addressing the use of mobile devices; while about 95 percent of large organizations report having a policy on usage, only about 30 percent of employees are very aware of such policies.[24]

A *Canadian HR Reporter* survey of more than 775 HR professionals addressed several issues related to social media. Almost two-thirds of participants reported that employee use of social media has garnered a fair bit of attention within organizations, and about 60 percent agreed that the time employees spend on social media sites is of some or a big concern. About 60 percent of respondents indicate that their organization has a policy on social media use, and a similar percentage has made moves to block access to some websites. In addition, about 56 percent of employers monitor employee web usage during work hours.[25] However, not everyone wants to be connected:

> An OfficeTeam <http://www.roberthalf.ca/en/officeteam> study of executives revealed that 71 percent of participants were uncomfortable being "friended" by their boss on Facebook, 66 percent do not want to be Facebook friends with people they manage, and 63 percent do not want to connect on Facebook with their clients.[26]

A BMO survey of small businesses revealed that close to 60 percent use social media, with 46 percent using it to promote their firm's brand and 38 percent using it to sell products and services. In addition, 38 percent use it to crowd source suggestions and ideas, 35 percent track what is being reported about their business, and one in four track sentiment about competitors. LinkedIn and Facebook are used by 28 percent and 43 percent of small firms respectively.[27]

With the growth in the use of social media comes a dramatic increase in social media hacking. According to Mark Nunnikhoven, VP of cloud and emerging technologies at Trend Micro in Ottawa <http://www.trendmicro.ca>, social media hacking "usually comes down to financial gain. Over the last two or three years, cybercrime has shifted to be a big business, so this is organized criminals who are in it for profit." Being hacked has several consequences for organizations including damage to a brand's reputation, declining employee engagement, and a loss of trust by customers.[28]

A study of executives revealed that 33 percent of respondents reported having a social media policy, 40 percent were considering developing a policy or had other related policies, and 27 percent had no policy or plans to develop one. While 71 percent of participants indicated that their company was concerned about risks associated with social media, only 36 percent provided any type of social media training. The four biggest concerns were damage to the employer brand, disclosure of confidential or proprietary information, corporate identity theft, and legal/regulatory and compliance violations. Almost 60 percent of organizations did not have a social media risk assessment plan in place.[29]

With increased reliance on social media and the concern by organizations about their reputation, more and more employers are hiring a chief reputation officer. Most employers do not have anyone directly responsible for reputation management with the expertise to address issues related to the reputation of the business.[30] Having individuals or departments address reputation issues on an ad hoc basis may result in inconsistent application of policies by employees who may not have proper training in reputation management.

The growth in cloud-based tools provides new challenges for organizations with particular impacts on sharing of information, conducting meetings, and communication throughout the organization. Among the issues for human resource professionals are social communication (such as integrating social networking capabilities, blogs, wikis and activity feeds), unified communication (for instance, instant messaging, conferencing enterprise voice capabilities using PC, browser, and mobile devices), rich communication services (such as audio/video calling and rich online meetings), and accessible software (for instance, being able to access PowerPoint or Excel from a mobile device or browser).[31]

Some employers are using social media in creative and innovative ways to communicate with employees:

> ICBC <http://www.icbc.com>, an auto-insurance Crown corporation with 5,400 employees, has been using social media in a fairly intensive way over the past few years. According to Len Posniak, VP of Human Resources, "Every morning we are using Twitter to promote any positions that we are having difficulty filling. And it's very inexpensive to use so it's a good way of getting our message out there. We want people to be able to speak across the company and through levels of the management structure."[32]

However, employers must also be aware that social media must be used responsibly. There is an increasing trend among employers meeting a new job candidate or client to Google the person or check the individual out on Facebook, Twitter, or other social networking sites. There are risks to using social media to check an individual's background. The information may not be accurate or up-to-date or one might be obtaining information about the wrong person. Employers need consent to collect certain information under privacy laws, and collecting information pertaining to an individual's background (age, sex, race, etc.) may make the organization susceptible to a claim of discrimination by the individual. Under the privacy guidelines, simply viewing the information is considered collection.[33]

Information Sharing and Open-Book Management

Some employers provide reports to employees about the organization's economic performance. The reasoning is that economic information is as important to employees as it is to shareholders. The report is presented in the same style as the annual report, except that it shows how the annual economic results affect workers. The release of the report may be followed by meetings that are organized and conducted in the same way as shareholder meetings. Top management attends the meetings, and all employees are invited. Management formally presents the report, and employees are invited to question management and make proposals in the same way that owners do in stockholder meetings. These meetings improve communication and give jobholders a stronger feeling of belonging.

While many companies believe that the financial performance and budget goals of the firm are not the business of employees, some firms have adopted an approach of sharing such information with employees (for example, a Statistics Canada study indicates that about 36 percent of employers follow a practice of sharing information with workers).[34] Using *open-book management*, some firms are making employees assume more responsibility for the success of the firm. The basic concepts involve educating employees about how the firm earns profits, giving workers a stake in the performance of the business, and providing feedback on how the company is doing.

> Xilinx <http://www.xilinx.com> has a people-centric culture that starts with the CEO, who spends up to 20 percent of his time communicating with employees. He moves offices on a regular basis in order to get to know employees better, has monthly meetings with workers, has a Q&A feature on the company's website, and encourages storytelling where employees get together and relate stories showing how the company's values affect decision making.[35]

Some actions by organizations to improve communications internally and to enhance the link between employees and the organization (and its customers or clients) include the following:

- conduct more research/employee surveys to understand employee attitudes toward communication and what is working (and not working)

- issue "total rewards" communication that addresses the numerous benefits of working for the employer

- provide performance-oriented communication that outlines performance standards for employees and the effect of employee performance on the organization and its customers

- offer communications training for managers and employees

- regularly review or audit the communication system[36]

Should employees be required to respond to email around the clock? A recent collective agreement in France contained a provision that addressed the issue, limiting employee obligations to respond to emails sent after 6 p.m. Among the concerns associated with after-hours emails are demands by employees for overtime pay, allegations of harassment, higher error-rates if people are tired, and increased employee stress and burnout. In response to such concerns, Edelman Canada's Toronto office established a "7 to 7 rule" prohibiting emails outside of the hours of 7 a.m. to 7 p.m.[37]

HRC 3 & 5

Upward Communication Systems

Perhaps no area of communication is more in need of improvement in most organizations than upward communication. **Upward communication** consists of information initiated by people who seek to inform or influence those higher up in the organization's hierarchy. The cornerstone of all such messages is the employee and the supervisor. When a free flow of information travels between an employee and the supervisor, informal day-to-day communication is often sufficient for most situations. If open communication does not exist, or exists only for a limited range of issues, other approaches are needed.

---

upward communication

Communication that begins in the organization and proceeds up the hierarchy to inform or influence others.

How do organizations create open, upward communication? No universal formula exists—the type of approach used may vary depending on the situation. However, one common element in many organizations is a genuine concern for employee well-being combined with meaningful opportunities for ideas to flow up the organization's hierarchy. Some of the more common upward communication channels include the grapevine, in-house complaint procedures, manager–employee meetings, suggestion systems, and attitude survey feedback.

Grapevine

Grapevine communication is an informal system that arises spontaneously from the social interaction of people in the organization. It is the people-to-people system that arises naturally from human desires to make friends and share ideas. For instance, two employees chatting at the water cooler about their problems with a supervisor is a grapevine communication.

---

grapevine communication

Informal communication within an organization that arises from normal social interaction.

The grapevine provides a large amount of useful off-the-record feedback from employees. There are many opportunities for feedback because human resource specialists are in regular contact with employees as they discuss benefits, counsel employees, and perform other functions. Employees feel somewhat free to talk with human resource specialists since the occupation of human resource management is oriented toward helping people and human resource specialists do not directly supervise employees in other departments. Some of the types of grapevine feedback that come to the human resource department include information about employee problems, the quality of labour–management relations, important grievance issues, areas of job dissatisfaction, difficulties with supervisors, and acceptance by employees of changes within the organization. However, the Internet and the use of social media are changing how employees communicate:

An informal gathering around the water cooler or coffee station is one method by which employees exchange information, but also gossip and rumours. What can management do to keep rumours down?

© Leon/Getty Images.

Social networking used to involve gossip around the water cooler or lunchroom chats. However, sites like Facebook, YouTube, and Twitter have changed the rules. HR professionals need to be aware of the new social media and the rights of both employers and employees relating to the use of electronic social networking. What an employee posts online could constitute discrimination, bullying, or harassment. In addition, an employee could intentionally or inadvertently divulge private company information. What about employees posting information outside of regular work hours? If the employer can show that its legitimate business interests are affected by the material posted by the employee, the employee may be liable and subject to discipline.[38]

Human Resource Management and Technology

Although the issue of electronic communication has been discussed in detail earlier in the chapter, it is important to recognize that email, intranets, social media, and discussion groups are also very useful in facilitating upward communication. Again, the importance of issues such as security of use, monitoring of employee messages, rules of conduct, and the need for a policy on email and Internet usage needs to be emphasized.[39]

> At a lab outside New York, a group of mathematicians spy on IBM's workforce. They are the subject of a book by Stephen Baker called *The Numerati*. Monitoring company email servers allows employers to determine who is networking with whom, who might be meeting with a competitor, and who is checking sports scores or chatting with friends online. Supermarkets are also using data to track customer preferences.[40]

Having a record of email communications may be helpful to a party involved in litigation—in the case described below, an examination of email messages may be more helpful to the dismissed employee:

> During a wrongful dismissal trial in which a CIBC portfolio manager was terminated after a margin-related glitch cost his clients $35 million, a judge ordered that the approximately 3,500 emails in the employee's account should be made available by CIBC to his lawyers. The judge stated that the emails could aid the court in determining whether trades made by the employee were properly authorized by CIBC.[41]

More and more organizations are implementing human resource management systems (HRMS). This is not surprising considering that mastering HR technology has recently been identified as one of the five competency domains for human resource management (along with business knowledge, HR delivery, strategic contribution, and personal credibility).[42] Still, many HRMS are being used for maintaining employee records rather than for strategic human resource issues and communication purposes.[43]

HR departments and professionals are using cloud computing for a wide range of tasks and activities including payroll administration, employee communication and self-service applications, and employee file and records management. For example, Toronto marketing firm Ariad's <http://ariad.ca> movement to the cloud resulted in cost savings and efficiencies, streamlined HR activities, and provided ready access to management and employees of HR information and employment data.[44]

While a lot of focus on the use of social media has been on the concern of abuse, social media may prove to be a valuable tool for HR professionals. Some of the benefits cited include mentoring (such as one-to-many using blogs or many-to-many with forums), performance management (and the provision of timely feedback), leadership (transparency and visibility), e-recruiting (trying to attract both the active and passive candidates), and communications (timely messages, information, and feedback to employees and customers).[45]

An issue that is beginning to impact employers is the growing use of "wearables" at the workplace. Wearables include activity monitors (which can track an individual's body behaviour), head-mounted displays (such as Google Glass and GoPro), and smart watches. Associated with such devices are key questions relating to privacy. For example, while a device that monitors employee health conditions may allow an employer to improve productivity, reduce injuries, and enhance employee wellness, there are major issues relating to employee privacy and concerns over hacking and data theft, who can access the data, and the use of the information against a current or prospective employee.[46]

In-House Complaint Procedures

How does an employee solve a problem if the supervisor is not willing to discuss it? In some organizations, the employee has no other option except to talk with the supervisor's superior. Although that may seem reasonable, most people in organizations are very reluctant to do that because they do not want to create negative feelings between themselves and their supervisor. To lessen the burden of "going over the supervisor's head," some organizations have installed **in-house complaint procedures**.

---

in-house complaint procedures

Formal methods through which an employee can register a complaint.

In-house complaint procedures are formal methods through which an employee can register a complaint. Normally these procedures are operated by the human resource department and require the employee to submit the complaint in writing. Then, an employee relations specialist investigates the complaint and advises the employee of the results. In some companies, the employee's name is known only by the employee relations investigator. However, if a supervisor is questioned about the issue, it may be obvious who filed the complaint.

In recent years, there has been growing interest in *alternative dispute resolution* (ADR) programs. The goal of ADR is to resolve disputes in a timely, cost-effective manner. Some types of ADR programs include the following:

1. An **open-door policy** in which an employee is encouraged to meet with his or her supervisor or another member of management to resolve workplace conflict.

---

open-door policy

A company policy that encourages employees to address their problems to higher levels of management.

---

2. A *peer review panel* or ombudsperson who hears an employee's presentation of the problem and makes recommendations. While the composition of the peer review panel may vary, a typical structure involves two individuals from a similar job classification as the employee and one management representative. It is estimated that about 90 percent of disputes getting to peer review are settled at this level.

3. *Mediation* in which a neutral third party meets with the parties and tries to resolve the issue. Although the mediator cannot impose a settlement, his or her involvement is often instrumental in resolving the conflict.

4. *Arbitration* in which a neutral third party hears both parties' views of the case and makes a binding decision. While arbitration is common in unionized environments, it is also becoming more popular as a means of resolving disputes in nonunion settings.[47]

The previous two decades have seen considerable growth in the presence of a grievance system for nonunion employees. A nonunion grievance procedure can be defined as one that is in writing, guarantees employees the right to present complaints to management, and is communicated to employees.[48] For

Farcus

by David Waisglass
Gordon Coulthart

© 1992 Farcus Cartoons   WAISGLASS/COULTHART   www.farcus.com

**"... and now I'd like to discuss new ways
to fight our absenteeism problem."**

Farcus®, printed with permission of Universal Uclick.

example, a study of Canadian firms revealed that about 31 percent had a grievance procedure for nonunion employees, with the typical procedure consisting of a three- or four-step process.[49] In setting up a nonunion grievance procedure, several issues exist. Some questions to consider:

- What subjects may be grieved? For example, can disciplinary actions be grieved?

- Are all nonunion employees eligible to participate in the procedure?

- Are employees protected from retaliation if they use the procedure?

- Must the grievance be filed in writing? Are there time limits for employee filing and management response?

- How many steps will the grievance procedure contain? Can an employee bypass his or her supervisor? What are the specific steps in the procedure?

- Does the employee have the right to be present throughout the procedure? Can the employee have someone else (such as another employee, human resource staff member, lawyer) present the case? Can the employee call witnesses?

- What is the final step in the procedure? For instance, who ultimately resolves the issue? Some options include a senior line manager, HR professional, a panel (which can be comprised of just managers, managers and employees, or just employees), or outside arbitration.[50]

Manager–Employee Meetings

Closely related to in-house complaint procedures are meetings between managers and groups of employees to discuss complaints, suggestions, opinions, or questions. These meetings may begin with some information sharing by management to inform the group about developments in the company. However, the primary purpose of these meetings is to encourage upward communication, often with several levels of employees and lower-level management in attendance at the same time. Attendance at such meetings varies according to how the meetings are planned. In small facilities, it may be possible to get all the employees together annually or semi-annually; however, this does not reduce the need to keep in touch with employees on a regular basis. In some organizations, there is a growing focus on virtual meetings. Depending on the employer structure, different meeting formats may be needed:

> One major bank's Open Meeting Program arranges meetings of about a dozen employees at a time. Meetings are held with different groups until at least one in five employees from each department attends. Employees are selected randomly and may decline to participate if they wish. A human resource specialist coordinates each meeting and develops the group report on a newsprint sheet in open discussions with the group. No employee names are used on the report, which becomes the basis of action plans with management. The program is repeated annually, and it has significantly improved upward communication.

Does an employer have the right to record performance review or disciplinary meetings? Invariably, there is the need to balance employer rights to operate with employee rights to privacy. Calgary lawyer Tim Mitchell notes that in a number of recent cases, employers engaging in non-consensual recording of employee meetings have been prevented from using the evidence or ordered to refrain from continuing the practice.[51]

Suggestion Systems

Suggestion systems are a formal method for generating, evaluating, and implementing employee ideas. All three of these elements are crucial to a successful suggestion system.

---

suggestion systems

A formal method of generating, evaluating, and implementing employee ideas.

A successful suggestion system begins with the employee's idea and a discussion with the supervisor. Once the suggestion form is completed, the supervisor reviews and signs the form, indicating awareness of the suggestion, but not necessarily approval. The suggestion system office or committee receives the idea and informs the employee that it has received the suggestion. The idea is then evaluated, and the decision is communicated to the employee. If it is considered a good idea, implementation follows, with the employee receiving recognition and usually some award (often awards are equal to about 10 percent of the first year's savings from the suggestion).

Although most suggestion systems pay employees a percentage of the first-year savings, some companies pay a flat dollar amount in order to minimize the need for precision in evaluating the suggestion's exact dollar savings. This approach means that employees receive feedback about their suggestions much faster. In addition, organizations that place a higher focus on teamwork may need to revamp their suggestion system program to reflect a group contribution.

For suggestion systems to work, management must provide prompt and fair assessment of the ideas, supervisors must be trained to encourage employee suggestions, and top management must actively support the program. Unfortunately, this source of upward communication is ineffective in many companies because evaluations often take months or supervisors see suggestions as more work for them with few personal benefits.

While suggestion systems can work in government, there is some evidence that they are harder to implement because management changes when a new administration takes over. This results in variations in the types of suggestions that are made. For example, in the case of Toyota, the focus is on organization-centred factors to encourage employee participation in solving job-related problems.

However, suggestion systems in government are more likely to emphasize employee factors that make the conditions appropriate for employees to make larger improvements in their jobs.[52]

Employee Attitude/Opinion Surveys

What do employees think about the organization? Do they have problems or concerns? How engaged are the employees? Do they understand the human resource department's benefit plan? Compensation program? Career planning efforts? Answers to these and many other questions can make a useful addition to the human resource department's information system.

An **employee attitude/opinion survey** is a systematic method of determining what employees think about their organization. While surveys may be conducted through face-to-face interviews, they are usually done through questionnaires that employees complete anonymously. Many organizations are now using web technology to conduct employee surveys.

---

employee attitude/opinion survey

A systematic method of determining what employees think of their organization.   ⟶ web tech

---

An employee survey typically seeks to learn what employees think about working conditions, supervision, human resource policies, and other organizational issues. New programs or special concerns to management also may be a source of questions. The resulting information can be used to evaluate specific concerns, such as how individual managers are perceived by their employees.

Attitude/opinion surveys can be a frustrating experience for employees if they do not receive any information on the survey results. Without feedback, the survey has little meaning to workers and they may be reluctant to participate in a follow-up survey. Therefore, a summary of the survey results should be provided to employees for their reaction. However, feedback is not enough. Employees need to see that the survey findings result in problems being solved. Feedback of the results and action on the problem areas make survey feedback a powerful communication tool:

> FedEx Canada, along with other FedEx businesses in 210 countries, participates in a global employee satisfaction survey that allows them to see how they compare to sister companies. Response rates to the survey are around 98 percent and the survey results are linked to managers' performance appraisals and, in turn, to their base and variable pay. Managers whose scores are low have to submit action plans that are signed off on by their manager, their reports, and an employee relations representative. This is all part of FedEx's People First philosophy. According to the Managing Director of Human Resources, "an engaged employee is an employee who is satisfied, who is committed, and who gives that above-and-beyond discretionary effort."[53]

LO2 `HRC 2 & 3`

Employee Counselling

Counselling is the discussion of a problem with an employee, with the general objective of helping the worker resolve the issue or cope with the situation so that the person can become more effective both at work and away from the workplace:

---

counselling

The discussion of a problem with an employee, with the general objective of helping the worker resolve the issue or cope with the situation so that he or she can become more effective.

One company has a program available to employees and their families that covers both personal and work-related problems. The company maintains a 24-hour hotline and uses both company counsellors and community agencies. The service is strictly confidential. An average of 750 employees use the service each month. Many successes have been reported, although the program is unable to solve every employee problem. A study of alcoholic employees reported a remarkable 85 percent reduction in lost work hours, a 47 percent reduction in sick leave, and a 72 percent reduction in sickness and accident benefit payments. In a survey, 93 percent of the employees reported that they believe that counselling is a worthwhile service.

Some firms advise managers to avoid giving personal advice to employees that is not related to the job because the managers are not professionally qualified to do so. There is a chance that they will give inappropriate or wrong advice that aggravates an employee's problem. A growing number of organizations have formal arrangements with outside professional counselling agencies to help their employees.

HRC 2 & 8

Employee Assistance Programs (EAP)

Organizations may establish an employee assistance program (EAP) to assist employees with personal problems (such as family or marital difficulties, substance abuse, or stress) that may be affecting their performance at work.

While a number of employees may prefer a face-to-face meeting with an EAP counsellor, there is a substantial growth in digital EAPs (such as chat messaging, ecounselling, video counselling, and mobile apps). Privacy, security, and quality issues are obviously important, but digital EAPs allow workers to get assistance around the clock from local and remote locations.[54] However, it should be recognized that online services are not appropriate for every case; rather, they represent one of a number of alternative approaches to providing EAP services.

LO3   HRC 2 & 5

Employee Discipline

Even after counselling, there are instances where an employee's behaviour remains inappropriately disruptive or performance is unacceptable. Under these circumstances, discipline is needed. **Discipline** is management action to encourage compliance with organization standards. It is a type of action that seeks to inform employees about organizational expectations and change worker attitudes and behaviour.

---

discipline

Management action to encourage compliance with organization standards.

About 90 percent of the 500 largest employers in the United States have a policy prohibiting employees from downloading child pornography on company computers, and one study indicated that 50 percent of the companies applied the policy after finding inappropriate images on at least one of their computers. Of the firms making formal investigations, 44 percent of the employers terminated employees who violated the policy.[55] It should also be noted that a number of Canadian jurisdictions are placing an obligation on employers to report the presence of child pornography on their computer systems.[56]

There are two types of discipline: preventive and corrective.

HRC 2 & 5

Preventive Discipline

Preventive discipline is action prior to an infraction taken to encourage employees to follow standards and rules. The basic objective is to encourage self-discipline among employees. In this way, employees maintain their own discipline, rather than having management impose it.

---

preventive discipline

Action taken prior to an infraction to encourage employees to follow standards and rules.

Management has the responsibility for building a climate of preventive discipline. If employees do not know what standards are expected, their conduct is likely to be erratic or misdirected. Employees will better support standards that they have helped to create. They will also give more support to standards stated positively instead of negatively, such as "Safety first!" rather than "Don't be careless!"

The human resource department has a major responsibility for preventive discipline. For example, it develops programs to manage absenteeism and employee grievances. It communicates standards to employees and encourages employees to follow them. It also provides training programs to explain the reasons behind standards and to build a positive spirit of self-discipline.

HRC 2 & 5

Corrective Discipline

Corrective discipline is an action that follows a rule infraction. It seeks to discourage further infractions so that future acts are in compliance with standards. Typically the corrective action is a penalty of some type and is called a *disciplinary action*. Examples are a warning or suspension without pay. The objectives of disciplinary action are:

- to reform the offender;
- to deter others from similar actions; and
- to maintain consistent, effective group standards.

---

corrective discipline

Discipline that follows a rule infraction.

The objectives of disciplinary action are positive, educational, and corrective. The goal is to improve the future rather than punish past acts. The corrective disciplinary interview often follows a "sandwich model," which means that a corrective comment is sandwiched between two positive comments in order to make the corrective comment more acceptable. An example: "Your attendance is excellent, Jason (a positive comment), but your late return from coffee breaks disrupts our repair operations (negative). Otherwise, your work is among the best in our department (positive)." The supervisor then focuses on ways in which the two of them can work together to correct the problem. However, corrective discipline is frequently not used or not used properly. Many managers receive little or no training addressing employee discipline and the consequences if the disciplinary process is not managed effectively.

HRC 2 & 5

Restrictions on Discipline

The ability to discipline may be restricted by union contracts and government legislation. Corrective discipline is an especially sensitive subject with unions who may see it as an area where employees need protection from unreasonable management authority. In addition, the union wants to show employees that the union leadership cares for their interests.

Government legislation makes it illegal for an employer to discipline a worker who is asserting rights protected by law. For example, an employee cannot be disciplined or dismissed for union activities (the right to participate in union activities is protected under labour relations statutes) or for refusing to perform work that is hazardous, unsafe, or unlawful. Other employment restrictions may also apply, depending on the circumstances and the laws of the provinces concerned.

Due process for discipline may be required of the employer by courts of law, arbitrators, and labour unions. **Due process** means that established rules and procedures for disciplinary action need to be followed and that employees are provided an opportunity to respond to allegations or complaints made against them.[57] It is the human resource department's responsibility to ensure that all parties in a disciplinary action follow the proper rules and procedures so that due process will be used.

---

due process

In a disciplinary situation, the following of proper, established rules and procedures, and giving employees the opportunity to respond to allegations.

If a disciplinary action is challenged, the human resource department must have sufficient documentation to support the action; therefore, human resource policy should require proper documentation for all employer disciplinary actions.

Proper documentation should be specific, beginning with the date, time, and location of an incident. It should also describe the nature of the undesirable performance or behaviour and how it relates to job and organizational performance. Specific rules and regulations that relate to the incident must be identified. Documentation should include what the manager said to the employee and how the employee responded, including specific words and actions. If there were witnesses, they should be identified. All documentation must be recorded promptly, when the incident is still fresh in the memories of the parties. The evidence recorded should be objective, based on observations and not impressions.

A useful guide for corrective discipline is the **hot-stove rule**. The hot-stove rule states that disciplinary action should have the same characteristics as the penalty a person receives from touching a hot stove. These characteristics are that discipline should be with warning, immediate, consistent, and impersonal.

---

hot-stove rule

The principle that disciplinary action should be like what happens when you touch a hot stove: it is with warning, immediate, consistent, and impersonal.

HRC 2 & 5

Progressive Discipline

Most employers apply a policy of **progressive discipline**, which means that there are stronger penalties for repeated offences. The purpose of this is to give an employee an opportunity to take corrective action before more serious penalties are applied. Progressive discipline also gives management time to work with an employee to help correct infractions:

> When Margaret Stoner had two unauthorized absences, the human resource department provided counselling. It also arranged for her to join a ride pool that allowed her to leave home 30 minutes later than with public transportation. Eventually her unauthorized absences stopped.

progressive discipline

The use of stronger and stronger penalties for repeated offences.

A typical progressive discipline system is shown in Figure 11-2. The first infraction leads to a verbal reprimand by the supervisor. The next infraction leads to a written reprimand, with a record placed in the file. Further infractions result in stronger discipline, leading finally to discharge. Usually the human resource department becomes involved at the third step or earlier to ensure that company policy is applied consistently in all departments.

FIGURE 11-2

A Progressive Discipline System

1. Verbal reprimand by supervisor
2. Written reprimand, with a record in file
3. One- to three-day suspension from work
4. Suspension for one week or longer
5. Discharge for cause

It is essential that employers document efforts made to help employees. One possible program involves four steps:

1. Clearly indicate in writing the nature of the problem and the impact of the employee's performance or conduct on the organization.

2. Provide the employee with a clear and unequivocal warning that failure to improve behaviour will result in discipline (up to and including termination).

3. Establish through progressive discipline that the employee's performance was still unacceptable despite repeated warnings.

4. Demonstrate that discipline was applied in a fair and consistent manner.[58]

Some progressive systems allow minor offences to be removed from the employee's record after a period of time (typically between one and five years). However, serious offences, such as fighting or theft, are usually not dealt with by means of progressive discipline. An employee who commits these offences may be discharged on the first offence.

In some organizations, lawyers play an important role in the disciplinary process while in others they are consulted after a problem arises. More than one-quarter of HR professionals view their lawyer or legal team as a strategic partner while 46 percent only use lawyers for transactional assistance. A

Canadian HR Reporter survey indicated that lawyers are most likely to be consulted for certain issues such as terminations (87 percent), wrongful dismissal lawsuits (40 percent), employment contracts and hiring (37 percent), accommodation and return to work (32 percent), and harassment claims (31 percent).[59]

HRC 2 & 5

Positive Discipline

Instead of using punishment to discipline employees, some organizations employ an approach called *positive discipline*, which involves an acceptance on the part of the employee that a problem exists, an acknowledgement by the employee that he or she must assume responsibility for the behaviour, and the use of a problem-solving approach to resolve the problem. The key steps in using positive discipline are as follows:

1. Focus on the specific problem rather than the employee's attitude or personality.

2. Gain agreement with the employee that a performance problem exists and that the employee is responsible for changing his or her behaviour.

3. Approach discipline as a problem-solving process.

4. Document suggested changes or commitments by the employee.

5. Follow up to ensure that the employee is living up to his or her commitments and to reduce the likelihood of having to take more severe action.[60]

HRC 2 & 5

Dismissal

The ultimate disciplinary action is dismissal, which is separation from the employer. Michael Wilson, former CEO of Agrium Inc. notes:

> Building a new culture also means you get rid of people who aren't prepared to accept best practices and move toward that. You cannot afford to have a naysayer on the team. If someone's not in support, you have to take them out of the company.[61]

A nonunion employer who does not have just cause for dismissing an employee may be sued for **wrongful dismissal**. Consider the experience of one small business:

> The owner of a small business with 18 employees terminated a manager who had been with the firm for 22 years. Although there was no documented evidence to support his claim, the owner said that the manager's performance had been slipping over the past few years. Shortly after being released, the employee contacted an employment lawyer and the parties settled out of court for in excess of $100,000. The business owner had never heard of the law of wrongful dismissal and the settlement put the business in jeopardy.

---

wrongful dismissal

Terminating an employee without just cause or without giving the employee reasonable notice or compensation in lieu of notice.

The law of wrongful dismissal is very complicated and human resource professionals without considerable expertise in this area are advised to seek prudent legal advice. Note that the dismissal of unionized employees (slightly less than 30 percent of the non-agricultural workforce) is governed by the provisions of the collective agreement and the remedy exists with the grievance arbitration process (see Chapter 13). Save for a few exceptions, an employer can terminate a nonunion employee at any time if just cause exists; however, in the absence of just cause, the employer is usually obligated to give the former employee "reasonable notice" or compensation in lieu of notice.

All provinces and the federal jurisdiction have employment standards legislation providing minimum periods of notice for employees terminated without cause. The amount of advance notice an employer is required to give an individual is dependent on the employee's length of service with the employer, and some jurisdictions have specific notice periods that apply if the employer engages in a mass layoff or termination. However, it should be noted that the provisions under employment standards legislation are statutory *minimums* and the amount of reasonable notice awarded by the courts frequently exceeds such provisions.

> One human resource management manager indicated that the company's practice was to provide the minimum notice provisions under employment standards legislation if terminating an employee. The reason for this approach was simply that the manager was uninformed about the law of wrongful dismissal.

Three jurisdictions (federal, Quebec, and Nova Scotia) provide an alternative forum for some wrongfully dismissed employees meeting specified period of service requirements (10 years in Nova Scotia, 5 years in Quebec, and 1 year for the federal jurisdiction). While the provisions of the statutes vary, the thrust of the legislation is to permit employees to bring their cases to an adjudication process in which the adjudicator may order reinstatement and damages if sufficient cause for dismissal does not exist. The specifics of the legislation are quite detailed and legal assistance is advised.

HRC **2 & 5**

Determining Just Cause

Cause for dismissal under common law includes any act by the employee that could have serious negative effects on the operation or reputation of the organization. This typically includes incompetence and employee misconduct (such as fraud, drunkenness, dishonesty, insubordination, or refusal to obey reasonable orders). The onus for proving the existence of **just cause** is on the employer.[62] Ideally, there is a carefully planned termination interview to ensure that the separation is as positive and constructive as possible—the Supreme Court of Canada has ruled that an employer must act in a way that demonstrates good faith and fair dealing in the dismissal of employees.[63]

---

just cause

Legal grounds for termination such as employee misconduct or incompetence.

While an employer may terminate an employee at any time if just cause exists, the courts' interpretation of what constitutes just cause for dismissal is often much different from managers' perceptions of cause. Although employers argued just cause for dismissal in 44 percent of wrongful dismissal cases over a 15-year period, the court found that just cause existed in only 37 percent of the decisions—in other words, while employers often believe just cause was present, this belief is frequently not supported by the courts.[64] However, some recent decisions suggest that the pendulum has swung back toward the employer side.[65] Note that in many instances, cases are settled out of court:

An executive of the Nova Scotia Liquor Corporation <http://www.mynslc.com> was terminated after eight months of service. The employer asserted that the individual did not fit in and failed to get along with other executives. The former employee was given a severance package that included six months' pay and a bonus (for a total compensation package of $62,000).[66]

When considering federally-regulated employees, the recent decision of the Federal Court of Appeal in *Wilson v. Atomic Energy of Canada* held that such federally-regulated employees may be dismissed without cause. Previously, it was generally accepted that employees covered by the *Canada Labour Code* could only be dismissed for cause. However, there is the possibility that the *Wilson* decision could be appealed to the Supreme Court of Canada.[67]

Incompetent Work Performance

When considering dismissal on the basis of incompetence, the employment contract contains an implied warranty that the employee is "reasonably competent" and able to perform the work for which the person was hired. If the employee proves to be incompetent, the employer may dismiss the employee on the basis of just cause.

However, employers and the courts often differ in their assessment with respect to cause involving dismissal for incompetence. Employers were able to establish employee incompetence in less than 25 percent of the cases in which they argued just cause for termination on the basis of incompetence—establishing cause on the grounds of incompetence is not easy (see Figure 11-3).

FIGURE 11-3

Requirements in Dismissing an Incompetent Employee

1. The employer must provide reasonable, objective standards of performance in a clear and understandable manner.

2. The employee must fail to meet those standards.

3. The employer must have given the employee a clear and unequivocal warning that she or he has failed to meet the standards, including particulars to the specific deficiency.

4. The warning must clearly indicate the employee will be dismissed if she or he fails to meet the requisite standards.

SOURCE: Andrew Treash, "Terminating Underperforming Employees A Delicate Act," *Canadian HR Reporter*, September 26, 2011, p. 26 Reprinted by permission of Canadian HR Reporter. © Copyright Thomson Reuters Canada Ltd., (2015), Toronto, Ontario, 1-800-387-5164. Web: http://www.hrreporter.com

---

Kathleen Fisher, who had worked at Lakeland Mills Ltd. <http://www.lakelandmills.ca> for 18 years, informed company president Keith Anderson of her intention to stay with the company upon turning 65 years of age. Anderson responded "you can stay with our company for as long as you wish." A year later, the office manager wanted to replace Fisher with someone who was more versatile. In addition to her accounting position, Fisher was asked to back up the shipping clerk—the job required certain computer skills which Fisher did not have, but she expressed a desire to acquire the necessary skills. The company then argued that her performance was not up to standards and that it was going to hire someone to take over part of her accounting work unless she retired. Fisher resigned and sued for constructive dismissal. The BC Court agreed that Fisher was wrongfully dismissed and awarded her 10 months' severance with bonus and benefits.[68]

The employer must establish *real* incompetence, an inability to carry out job duties, or substandard work performance that fails to improve even after the employee has been put on notice that his or her performance is not adequate. Performance standards must be nondiscriminatory, reasonable, and applied fairly, while warnings must clearly describe what constitutes acceptable performance and what specific actions the employee should take to improve performance. Merely giving an employee average or substandard ratings is not enough. Also, the employer should make it clear to the employee that his or her job is at risk if performance does not improve. A single incident of incompetence will rarely justify dismissal, especially if the incident is a single blemish on an otherwise clean work record.

Employee Misconduct

The courts have repeatedly found that an allegation of employee misconduct must be decided with reference to the unique factors of each case. Four classes of misconduct identified in the case law include (1) unfaithful service to the employer; (2) misconduct of a general nature; (3) theft, fraud, or dishonesty; and (4) willful disobedience of a reasonable and lawful order.

Acts of unfaithful service, such as conspiracy and competition against the employer or serious conflict of interest, are generally regarded as being in that class of misconduct justifying immediate dismissal. The employer's case is relatively straightforward when there is an intent on the part of the employee to commit an act of unfaithful service and the threat of loss to the employer is real.

What about cases involving drug or alcohol abuse; abuse of co-workers, clients, or customers; or improper activity outside the workplace? In determining whether the misconduct is sufficient to justify dismissal, the courts consider both the nature of the misconduct and the employee's position within the organization. A serious act of misconduct may justify immediate discharge. In addition, employees in senior management or in positions of trust (such as a teacher) may be held to higher standards of conduct regarding misconduct both at and away from the workplace.

> Consider the following case and decide if there is cause for dismissal. The case involved two Research in Motion (now BlackBerry; <http://ca.blackberry.com>) vice-presidents who became drunk and disorderly on an Air Canada flight from Beijing to Toronto. Their behaviour became so bad that flight attendants and passengers had to subdue the two men, one of whom even chewed through his plastic handcuffs. The men received suspended sentences, one year probation and a requirement that each pay about $35,000 to Air Canada. In this case, RIM fired the two executives.[69]

Theft, fraud, and dishonesty are among the most serious grounds for dismissal because they call into question the honesty and integrity of the employee. Depending on the circumstances, a single isolated act of theft, dishonesty, or fraud may justify dismissal, but the court carefully reviews any explanation for the employee's behaviour. Employers may be justified in worrying about employee theft and fraud:

> A survey of almost 3,500 employees in the United States, United Kingdom, and Australia revealed that 22 percent of American, 29 percent of Australian, and 48 percent of British workers with access to employer or client confidential data would feel comfortable doing something (intentionally or accidentally) with that data, and 10 percent of American, 12 percent of Australian, and 27 percent of British workers reported that they would be willing to forward the data to a non-employee.[70]

Willful disobedience (which may include absenteeism, tardiness, or a breach of rules or policy) is considered to constitute a repudiation of the employment contract. An employee who refuses to obey the lawful and reasonable order of the employer is in breach of the employment contract. However, disobedience must be seen to be willful or deliberate; petty disagreements and personality conflicts usually do not amount to cause. Furthermore, a reasonable excuse for disobedience will negate the intent required for cause.[71]

A survey on employee misconduct by ClearView revealed that 42 percent of Canadian workers have witnessed incidents of misconduct. Among the violations were misuse of company property (28 percent), harm to other employees (25 percent), privacy violations (17 percent), fraud (17 percent), conflict of interest (13 percent), environmental violations (12 percent) and bribery, corruption, or both (9 percent). However, 48 percent of employees witnessing misconduct did not report it due to such reasons as a lack of faith that an investigation would be conducted properly (69 percent), a perception that disciplinary measures would not be consistently applied (66 percent), or a fear of retaliation or negative consequences (23 percent).[72]

Business or Economic Reasons

Contrary to the impressions of many managers, courts have consistently held that terminating an employee because of business or economic factors is not just cause for dismissal because such factors are not related to the employee's behaviour. It is critical that employers seeking to dismiss employees due to declining demand or as a result of an organizational downsizing ensure that terminated employees are provided with reasonable notice or appropriate compensation. It is advisable to seek legal assistance to review the process and compensation or severance package offered to terminated employees.

 HRC **2 & 5**

Constructive Dismissal

Rather than terminate an employee, an employer may decide to change the individual's job in such a way that the employee decides to quit. A major change in the employment terms that results in an employee resigning may be considered as **constructive dismissal**. Some examples of constructive dismissal include a significant change in job function, a demotion, a demand for an employee's resignation, or a forced transfer.[73] The law relating to constructive dismissal is technical in nature and human resource professionals are advised to seek legal advice prior to changing a major term of an employment contract. Consider the case of a manager at Sobeys:

> Debbie Gillis, a 47-year-old food experience manager, started with the company as a teenage cashier and worked her way up to a management position at head office. As part of a restructuring, her position was eliminated, but the company made it clear that it wanted to retain her as an employee and presented her with two job alternatives—an assistant store manager position or a demo-coordinator. Both positions paid less money than her original job, but the company agreed, for the first year, to pay a lump sum equal to the salary differential and maintain her current vacation and benefits. Gillis believed that both positions represented a demotion and, after coming to work for part of a day, went home and did not return. She sued for constructive dismissal. The court held that while the demo-coordinator position represented a demotion, the assistant store manager job did not as it involved working with more employees, more responsibilities, and a competitive, but lower salary. Even though the salary was lower, the opportunities for further advancement were strong and the court held that Gillis had not been constructively dismissed.[74]

constructive dismissal

A major change in the terms of the employment contract that results in an employee resigning.

In its 2015 decision in *Potter v. New Brunswick Legal Aid Services Commission*, the Supreme Court of Canada identified two branches of constructive dismissal (a single act by the employer that breaches an essential term of the contract or a series of acts that, in combination, show that the employer no longer wants to be bound by the employment contract). The court made it clear that an administrative suspension cannot be justified if there is no basic communication with the employee or no reason for suspension is given. The court also underscored the importance of an employer acting in good faith in dealing with an employee and that this requires being honest, forthright, candid, and reasonable.[75]

HRC **2 & 5**

Reasonable Notice

severance pay

An employer that does not have just cause for dismissal must provide a dismissed employee with "reasonable notice" or compensation (typically salary, benefits, and reasonable job search expenses) in lieu of notice. While several managers believe that the organization need only provide the minimum notice period outlined under employment standards legislation, it should be emphasized that these provisions are only minimums and courts may (and frequently do) award much greater notice periods. Further, establishing just cause at common law does not mean that an employer will also always have sufficient cause under provincial labour or employment standards legislation to avoid providing minimum statutory severance.[76]

The major factors used to predict notice include the following:

- *The former employee's age, length of service, salary, and occupational status*: on average, older employees, long-service employees, more highly paid employees, and employees occupying more senior positions in the organization tend to receive higher periods of notice. However, the character of employment variable (an employee's position and responsibilities) has come under criticism in recent case law.

- *An attempt to mitigate losses*: employees who are terminated must make reasonable efforts to find similar alternative employment.

- *A less favourable labour market*: when alternative employment opportunities are limited, courts tend to award greater notice periods.

While each case is settled based on its own particular facts, some guidelines relating to wrongful dismissal have been developed. However, it should be underscored that these are only guidelines to provide some guidance to students relating to wrongful dismissal awards. Based on the guidelines, an employee in a clerical/blue-collar position will receive about two weeks' notice (or compensation in lieu of notice) for each year of service, an employee in a supervisory or lower-level management position will receive three weeks' notice (or compensation) for each year of service, and senior management and professional employees will receive one month's notice (or compensation) for each year of service. In the past, it has been rare (but not unheard of) for notice periods to exceed 24 months.[77]

The law firm of Samfiru Tumarkin has developed an app (<www.severancepaycalculator.com>) to calculate severance pay. The app looks at factors such as an employee's union status, age, salary, length of service and type of job to give an estimate of severance.

Do employees have to give notice? Depending on the jurisdiction, the labour or employment standards code may specify a minimum notice period (usually a week or two depending on length of service). However, the Ontario Court of Appeal upheld a decision awarding damages of almost $20 million against four key employees who resigned from GasTOPS <http://www.gastops.com>, an Ottawa company involved in supplying control and condition assessment systems for industrial machinery. After resigning, the employees set up a competing business and hired away 12 employees originally with the company. The Ontario Superior Court of Justice noted that the employees had breached their fiduciary duty of good faith by misappropriating confidential company information and corporate opportunities, ruled that 10 months would have constituted reasonable notice, and awarded over $19.5 million in damages. The case sends a message to employees that a few weeks' notice may not be appropriate, particularly if the employer may have difficulty finding a reasonable replacement.[78] Consider the following case:

> Sebastien Marineau-Mes, an executive with BlackBerry, signed a contract with the company. Among the terms of the agreement was a provision providing for the right to resign at any time upon providing six months' prior written notice and the obligation to provide active service during the notice period. Marineau-Mes wasn't happy at BlackBerry and decided to join Apple without giving the six month notice. An Ontario court held that the notice period was reasonable and the contract was binding, thus requiring Marineau-Mes to satisfy the terms of the agreement.[79]

An employer has the right to provide "working notice" and have employees continue working during the notice period. The Target withdrawal from Canada included a minimum of 16 weeks compensation to employees. However, the company had employees continue working for at least some of the notice period and then receive payment from a $70 million trust fund as a top-up or pay in lieu of notice. An employee refusing to work would have been viewed as having resigned and would not have been entitled to additional compensation. Having employees work during the notice period may be cost effective but often results in lower morale, reduced productivity, and sometimes even sabotage.[80]

HRC 2 & 5

The "Wallace Effect"

The 1997 decision of the Supreme Court of Canada in *Wallace v. United Grain Growers* has led to the awarding of extended periods of notice in a number of wrongful dismissal cases in which the employer was found to have terminated an employee in bad faith. In the *Wallace* case, the court ruled that the employer had dismissed Wallace in "bad faith" and thus added an additional 9 months onto a reasonable notice award of 15 months. However, as MacKillop, Nieuland, and Ferris-Miles observe, the trend in recent decisions has been to close the floodgates relating to punitive damage claims.[81]

In the *Honda Canada v. Keays* case, the Supreme Court of Canada addressed the issue of *Wallace* damages. As noted by employment lawyer Stuart Rudner:

> The Supreme Court of Canada completely revamped the manner in which bad-faith damages are calculated. The court replaced the notice extension with a compensatory approach that appears to require the employee to prove not only that the employer acted in bad faith but that the employee actually suffered damages as a result. The court also determined that punitive damages are restricted to advertent wrongful acts that are so malicious and outrageous that they are deserving of punishment on their own.[82]

HRC 2 & 5

Managing the Dismissal

There are several guidelines to follow in dismissing an employee:

- Prepare for the interview and conduct a rehearsal.
- Conduct the interview in private.
- Consider the dismissal process from the employee's perspective and ask, "How would I like to be treated in such a situation?"
- Get to the point. Some experts suggest that you convey the message of termination within the first few sentences.

- Select the time and place. Experts often suggest a meeting in the morning and during the middle of the week.

- Have any necessary information ready (such as a severance package and outplacement counselling assistance).

- Notify others in the organization and ensure that the individual's duties are covered.

- In some instances, special security arrangements may be necessary.

- Discuss the process with other colleagues who have had to terminate employees.[83]

Should employers specify a notice period in employment contracts? As lawyer Tim Mitchell points out, this practice is not without its dangers and any attempt to limit the notice period to statutory minimum periods outlined in employment or labour standards legislation must be based on clear and unambiguous language. According to Mitchell, it is essential to recognize "the importance of careful drafting in an employment contract and the importance of reviewing the contract periodically, particularly where some change has occurred. The providing of a specific notice entitlement is a dangerous practice based on the jurisprudence."[84]

What should an employer do when terminating an employee who may be potentially violent? Among the suggestions are trying to identify the high-risk worker (What are the common characteristics of such individuals? Are there warning signs?), protecting the organization and employees during and after the termination, protecting the intellectual property of the employer, and tracking or monitoring the social media and communication activities of the former employee immediately after the dismissal.[85]

What if an employee reveals terms of a confidential settlement? In a recent decision, the Ontario Divisional Court upheld a decision of an arbitrator who had ordered Jan Wong, a former reporter with *The Globe and Mail*, to pay back a settlement of $209,912 to the paper after she disclosed some of the confidential terms of the settlement in a book. Ms. Wong wrote about her experiences in her 2012 memoir but the court did not support her argument that it was acceptable to discuss the settlement as long as she did not reveal that actual settlement amount.[86]

Employee Rights

Employee rights refer to those rights desired by employees relating to working conditions and job security. Some of these rights are protected under law, others under the collective agreement with the union (if one exists), and yet others may be listed in the letter of appointment given to the employee at the time of hiring. Regardless of whether these rights are recorded in writing or currently protected by law and agreements, they have a significant impact on the human resource management activities of an organization. Progressive human resource managers recognize this and strive to provide fair and equitable working conditions that help the employee to maintain dignity on the job. Would you be willing to have a computer chip implanted into your body? Consider the following:

> The CEO and two other employees of a surveillance company in Cincinnati, Ohio, had computer chips implanted in their upper arms as a security measure to limit access to a room holding confidential police and government documents. The implanted chip is slightly longer than a grain of rice. Privacy experts in the United States are concerned that if acceptance of the technology grows, there will be pressure on employees to have to accept the chips.[87]

Are employees becoming more litigious? What are the implications for human resource professionals? A *Canadian HR Reporter* survey revealed that 84 percent of 533 participants believe that competence in dealing with litigation has become somewhat or much more important for HR professionals in the past five years. About 70 percent of respondents perceived that employees are becoming somewhat or much more litigious compared to five years ago and almost 69 percent believe that when in court, the playing field is slanted in favour of the employee. The issues that are most problematic include wrongful dismissal (68 percent), termination and severance pay (58 percent), human rights issues (54 percent), and reasonable accommodation (31 percent). As Robert Smith, managing partner of Injury Management Solutions, observes, once a legal action has started, it is imperative that HR gather witness statements and all of the appropriate documentation as soon as possible—the longer the delay, the less likely HR will get the true story.[88]

Spotlight *on* HRM

Great Television Doesn't Translate into Great Policy

By Natalie C. MacDonald

"You're fired." Real estate tycoon Donald Trump's catch phrase has captured the attention of the world. Millions of viewers tuned in every week to watch *The Apprentice*, a hit reality show where individuals competed for the ultimate prize of being Trump's apprentice.

Contestants were put into teams. Winners received a prize, the losers earned a trip to the boardroom to explain why they lost. Every week, at least one person was "fired."

In Trump's termination process, he and two of his advisors confronted the contestants, pummelling each of them with questions about their performance. He sent the contestants out while he deliberated about who would be terminated. The contestants returned to the boardroom where he handed down his decision, listing all of the reasons why he was about to terminate one of them. The drama and the tension built until he made his final choice.

While this makes for great television, it is not, nor should it inspire, a great way to terminate someone's employment. If employers in Canada were to adopt Trump's method, they would undoubtedly be on the hook for significant damages. Trump's television terminations were insensitive and callous, making the employee's firing much more difficult than it needs to be.

Trump's 10 Biggest Termination Mistakes

In the course of his terminations, Trump committed a number of serious mistakes. Here's a look at 10 of the most serious errors Trump made that should never be emulated in a Canadian workplace:

- The person being terminated is brought into a boardroom where she is with her peers and is being terminated in front of her peers, not in private just with Trump.
- She is being terminated not only in front of her peers, but also with two of Trump's advisors watching, thereby creating a firing-squad like atmosphere, rather than simply being in front of one advisor and Trump.
- Prior to the termination, all of the team members know that one of the select group being pulled into the boardroom will be terminated, instead of the termination being kept secret among only senior management.
- The person being terminated is advised of all the things she did wrong, but is never given a warning and the chance to correct the behaviour before being fired.
- She is terminated for cause where there is likely no legal cause for her termination.
- She is terminated without being provided what she is entitled to under applicable employment standards legislation.

(Continued)

- She is terminated without reasonable notice of the termination or compensation in lieu of notice pursuant to the employer's obligation under the common law.

- She is not provided with a letter of reference, outplacement counselling, or anything which will assist her in the transition to new employment.

- She may have been enticed to leave secure employment to be "employed" with Trump, which would increase Trump's liability when firing her.

- An employee terminated in this manner would likely be entitled to significant Wallace damages. That's because she was ostracized in front of her peers and Trump's advisors, terminated with cause when there was no cause and made to feel worthless. This is exactly what the Supreme Court of Canada warned against in its decision in *Wallace v. United Grain Growers Ltd.* ...

If any of the contestants on *The Apprentice* had been real employees and had sued for wrongful dismissal it is likely that each would be successful in a claim for *Wallace* damages. A court would likely not hesitate in lengthening the notice period because of Trump's actions. In fact, a firing handled like Trump's television ones may even result in a successful claim for mental distress damages.

Steps Employers Should Take

To avoid creating a scenario like Trump's boardroom, it is recommended employers:

- Keep the termination a secret: Ensure the termination is only known to those terminating the employee or those involved in the decision.

- Keep the termination small: Bring the person being terminated into a room without anyone else except another senior manager as a witness. Never terminate someone in front of her colleagues.

- Do not allege cause: If an employer does not have cause, it should not allege it.

- Do not list: Don't get into a long list of what the employee has already done wrong.

- Have a severance package ready: Have a package ready for the employee, including provision of entitlements pursuant to employment standards legislation and under the common law.

- Provide transitional assistance: If the employee is not terminated for cause, consider providing transitional assistance to find another job, including a letter of reference and outplacement counselling.

- Know the person's employment history: The employer should have accounted for this person's particular circumstances, especially what happened before she was hired. If the employee was lured away from secure employment, take that into account.

- Be sensitive: Being fired is one of the most difficult things for an individual to hear and it is usually a major blow to self-esteem. Those doing the firing should remember the golden rule and treat the worker as they would want to be treated in a similar circumstance.

The Apprentice is only a television show, but if Trump's methods become a reality for employers, it will cause them significant grief. When terminating someone's employment, all the employer has to do is act in good faith and not make the termination more difficult than need be.

Natalie MacDonald is an associate with Grosman, Grosman & Gale <http://www.grosman.com>, a Toronto-based law firm specializing in employment law. She can be reached at 416-364-9599 or nmacdonald@grosman.com.

HRC **2 & 5**

Right to Privacy

Employer concerns about employee privacy rights mean that many employers are careful to collect only job-related information at the point of hiring. There is an increasing realization among employers that collecting nonwork information is an unnecessary intrusion into the private lives of job applicants.

Even when such additional information is not considered illegal, many employers feel that such an action constitutes a moral violation of workers' rights.

> In Saanich, British Columbia, the privacy commissioner, Elizabeth Denman, ruled that employees' privacy rights were violated when the organization installed employee monitoring software. Mayor of Saanich, Richard Atwell, initiated the complaint and refused to use his work computer until the software was removed. According to Denman, "the district can only collect personal information that is directly related to and necessary for the protection of the IT systems. An employee's every stroke and email, or screen captures of computing activities at 30-second intervals clearly exceeds that purpose and is not authorized by privacy law."[89]

A number of recent high-profile cases have demonstrated that the lines between workplace and private rights are blurring and conduct away from the workplace may lead to discipline or dismissal. The Supreme Court of Canada, in *Bhasin v. Hrynew*, imposed an obligation on both employers and employees to deal with each other honestly and in good faith. As lawyer David Whitten notes, "Employees should always be mindful that comments and postings on the Internet are permanent and publicly accessible. Therefore, they really need to consider whether the content they post is appropriate by asking "would an employer care?"[90]

The *Personal Information Protection and Electronic Documents Act* (PIPEDA) came into force in January 2004 in every province without its own privacy legislation. The aims of the legislation include requiring organizations to hold personal information about individuals in a responsible manner, permitting individuals to access and correct personal information, and allowing individuals control over the handling of information about them (see Figure 11-4).

FIGURE 11-4

The 10 Principles of the *Personal Information Protection and Electronic Documents Act*

Principle 1: Accountability
An organization is responsible for personal information under its control and shall designate an individual or individuals who are accountable for the organization's compliance with the following principles.

Principle 2: Identifying Purposes
The purposes for which personal information is collected shall be identified by the organization at or before the time the information is collected.

Principle 3: Consent
The knowledge and consent of the individual are required for the collection, use, or disclosure of personal information, except where inappropriate.

Principle 4: Limiting Collection
The collection of personal information shall be limited to that which is necessary for the purposes identified by the organization. Information shall be collected by fair and lawful means.

Principle 5: Limiting Use, Disclosure, and Retention
Personal information shall not be used or disclosed for purposes other than those for which it was collected, except with the consent of the individual or as required by law. Personal information shall be retained only as long as necessary for the fulfillment of those purposes.

Principle 6: Accuracy
Personal information shall be as accurate, complete, and up-to-date as is necessary for the purposes for which it is to be used.

Principle 7: Safeguards
Personal information shall be protected by security safeguards appropriate to the sensitivity of the information.

(Continued)

Principle 8: Openness
An organization shall make readily available to individuals specific information about its policies and practices relating to the management of personal information.

Principle 9: Individual Access
Upon request, an individual shall be informed of the existence, use, and disclosure of his or her personal information and shall be given access to that information. An individual shall be able to challenge the accuracy and completeness of the information and have it amended as appropriate.

Principle 10: Challenging Compliance
An individual shall be able to address a challenge concerning compliance with the above principles to the designated individual or individuals accountable for the organization's compliance.

SOURCE: Adapted from Office of the Privacy Commissioner of Canada, Privacy Principles, www.priv.gc.ca, downloaded March 31, 2015.

What is personal information? As defined in PIPEDA, personal information is "factual information, recorded or not, about an individual." Under PIPEDA and provincial privacy legislation, information should only be kept as long as required for the purpose for which it was intended. The main problems with information security often revolve around security expertise and responsibility for security, poor enforcement of policies and procedures, outdated security software, and poor hiring (about 70 percent of identity theft occurs at the workplace).

> The privacy commissioner held that Health Canada violated privacy laws by disclosing personal health information of more than 40,000 Canadians. In November of 2013, Health Canada sent notices in oversized envelopes to individuals outlining changes to the Marijuana Medical Access Plan (MMAP). The return address included the words "Health Canada - Marijuana Medical Access Plan". More than 300 individuals complained to the privacy commissioner who concluded that Health Canada had mishandled patients' personal information.[91]

> An employee of the Bank of Montreal won a lawsuit permitting her to sue for damages on the basis of invasion of privacy. A co-worker, who was involved in a relationship with the employee's ex-husband, looked at the employee's bank records at least 174 times over a four year period. While the co-worker was suspended without pay for a week and denied a bonus, such a decision does not address the rights of the employee. Although the bank is under PIPEDA, the act does not apply to privacy rights between two individuals. The case stresses the importance of having a privacy policy and enforcing it on a consistent basis.[92]

In an article to celebrate Data Privacy Day (January 28), Federal privacy commissioner Daniel Therrien stated that about one-third of the PIPEDA complaints to his office involve small businesses with fewer than 100 employees. In a recent poll, more than 50 percent of participants indicated they would do business with an organization specifically because it does not collect personal data but only 16 percent perceive that employers take their obligation to protect personal information very seriously. According to Therrien, firms should limit the information they collect to what is necessary for delivering the product or service, and should make it clear why such information is needed (through a privacy policy). The most common complaints involve the use and disclosure of personal information for purposes other than specified or when an employee has accessed a person's file without authorization. A survey by Therrien's office revealed that 55 percent of companies do not have a privacy policy and 67 percent did not have policies or procedures designed to assess the privacy implications of new products, services, and technologies.[93]

While a survey of Canadian employees revealed that 33 percent of men and 25 percent of women felt that it was acceptable for employers to look at their social media activity,[94] not everyone believes that an employer has the right to an individual's social media communications:

> The Maryland Department of Public Safety and Correctional Services recently asked a corrections officer returning to work, after being on a leave of absence due to the death of his mother, to turn over his Facebook

username and password as a condition of being reinstated to his job. The department subsequently decided to suspend the practice for 45 days as it looked into the implications of its actions. Similarly, Justin Bassett, during the course of an employment interview, was asked for his Facebook login information when the interviewer couldn't see his private profile when she went to his Facebook page. Bassett refused and decided to withdraw from the job search because he didn't want to work for a company that would track personal employee information. Jurisdictions in the United States and Canada have made it illegal or are considering making it illegal to ask for private employee passwords. [95]

Privacy in the workplace is becoming an extremely sensitive issue and HR professionals must be aware of the legal and ethical challenges surrounding it. A 2007 survey by the American Management Association revealed that 24 percent of employers had employee email and instant messages (IM) subpoenaed in the course of a lawsuit or regulatory investigation and 15 percent had a lawsuit (for instance, on the basis of sexual harassment or a hostile work environment allegation) as a result of employee email.[96]

The Supreme Court of Canada is immersed in the privacy debate. The case of *R. v Cole* involved a charge of possession of child pornography when a computer technician performing maintenance on a teacher's computer found a hidden folder containing nude pictures of an underage female student. The court held that employees may have a reasonable, but limited, expectation of privacy in their work computer, but the court did not specifically address employer monitoring of employee computers. In *R. v. Telus Communications*, the court found that text messages are considered private communications, and in *R. v. Vu*, the court ruled that police must have specific authorization in a search warrant to search data in a computer. These cases are quite complex and HR professionals are advised to seek legal advice in developing and administering privacy policies at work.[97]

Employers need to balance employee privacy rights with operational requirements. Advice to employers includes: (1) communicating to employees what personal information will be collected, used and disclosed, and for what purposes; (2) disclosing to employees the use of any recording or surveillance, and that the information can be used for specific purposes such as safety or discipline; (3) developing a clear written policy and communicating it to employees if the employer is going to monitor employees. The policy, which should be signed by employees, needs to explain that employees should not have any expectation of privacy and the use of the information by the employer may be used for performance, conduct, and workplace security monitoring.[98]

A 2007 AMA survey on electronic monitoring and surveillance showed that employers are particularly concerned about inappropriate web surfing, with 66 percent monitoring employee website connections. Just under two-thirds of employers have software to block connections to inappropriate websites (a 27 percent increase from 2001). Employers blocking web access are most concerned about employees visiting adult sites with sexual or pornographic content (96 percent), game sites (61 percent), and social networking sites (50 percent). Computer monitoring includes tracking content, key strokes, and time spent at the keyboard (used by 45 percent of employers); storing and reviewing computer files (43 percent); and monitoring the blogosphere (12 percent) to see what is being written about the organization. Most employers (more than 83 percent) inform employees that their activities are being monitored. Approximately 30 percent of the organizations report terminating employees for misuse of the Internet, 28 percent fired employees for email abuse, and 6 percent have dismissed employees for improper use of the telephone. About 48 percent of the companies participating in the AMA study use video monitoring to reduce or eliminate theft, violence, or sabotage (up from 33 percent in 2001), slightly more than 8 percent use global satellite positioning technology to track employee productivity and movement, and 52 percent use smart card technology to control access to buildings.[99]

Colleen Colwell, a commercial manager with Cornerstone Properties, had been employed with the company for more than seven years when she discovered that a hidden camera had been installed in the ceiling of her office a year earlier. Her boss, VP of Finance Trent Krauel, asserted that the camera was used to detect theft by maintenance staff. Colwell sought medical attention because she felt emotionally violated and psychologically distraught. Krauel insisted he had a legal right to install the camera and did not owe Colwell an apology. Ultimately, Colwell resigned and sued for wrongful dismissal. The court concluded that the secret installation of the camera, Krauel's unwillingness to apologize, his assertion of a right to install the camera without advising Colwell, and his preposterous explanation of the reason for installing the camera made it impossible for Colwell to stay in her job. While employers may have the right to install cameras in the workplace, the right is limited by the need to exercise it in good faith and fair dealing.[100]

Canada introduced new anti-spam legislation which came into effect on July 1, 2014, and on January 1, 2015, new rules came into effect that make it illegal to install programs, such as malware, on someone's computer without consent. The definition of spam is "any electronic commercial message sent without the express or implied consent of the recipient." The legislation has major implications for businesses that now need to obtain consent from members of the public before sending a message. There is concern that the legislation is particularly problematic for small businesses who may be unaware of the legislation and lack the expertise or resources to comply with the law. From an HR perspective, it may be necessary to develop a policy to address the legislation or amend an existing social media policy as well as provide training for employees to make sure that they understand their rights and responsibilities.[101]

Using GPS tracking and surveillance, the City of Hamilton discovered that a group of city workers were visiting coffee shops, having downtime at home, and running personal errands on company time. As a result, 29 employees were dismissed and two were suspended for 30 days. According to lawyer Daniel Michaluk, when it comes to GPS devices, employers have prevailed for the most part. On the other hand, video-surveillance can collect more sensitive information and one-half of the arbitrators in Ontario will ask employers to justify its use. For major investigations, HR rarely handles the issue itself.[102]

The need for training on privacy is critical. The Office of the Privacy Commissioner of Canada, which oversees PIPEDA, asserts that organizations should provide training for both management and front-line workers. Although training should vary depending on the organization, Rick Shields, an Ottawa-based privacy lawyer, suggests that the training should include some background information on privacy, the meaning of key terms and key privacy concepts, the organization's activities with regard to privacy, a review of policies and procedures, introduction to the employer's privacy officer or team, and highlighting each person's role and responsibilities relating to privacy.[103]

HRC **5**

Right to Fair Treatment

Earlier in this book we saw that an individual's age, race, sex/gender, religion, physical disability, and so on, should not be considered when hiring unless it is a *bona fide job requirement*. As previously noted, an employer has an obligation to make reasonable accommodation to meet employee needs. The right of employees to fair treatment requires that these principles govern the actual work once the applicants are hired. Thus, employees have the right not to be discriminated against in all employment decisions (such as compensation, training, and promotion issues) as well as the right to work in a safe and harassment-free environment. In a split decision, the Supreme Court of Canada held that an Irving Oil policy providing for random alcohol testing of unionized employees in "safety-sensitive positions" is not justified in the absence of evidence that there was a problem with alcohol use at work. The court concluded that Irving was only able to cite eight alcohol-related incidents over a decade and a half, thus there was insufficient evidence of a serious enough problem to warrant an invasion of union workers' privacy in the absence of consent by the union.[104] Proactive employers continuously monitor working conditions through employee surveys, open-door policies, and the presence of grievance committees. They also initiate new programs and policies to meet the changing needs of the workforce:

> Today, many organizations emphasize a pollution-free work environment. Employers have banned smoking in any part of the workplace; others have rules governing the use of air sprays and perfumes. Several organizations respect the employees' right to be environmentally conscious by providing recycling bins and helping cut down waste. Other organizations have focused on reducing the noise level at the workplace.

LO4 HRC 2 & 5

Employee Involvement

To increase employee productivity and satisfaction, human resource departments often attempt to improve the satisfaction of employees at the workplace. Most of the approaches to employee involvement focus on the increased participation of workers. The quality of an employee's life while at work is affected by many factors including the quality of supervision, working conditions, pay and benefits, and an interesting and rewarding job:

> A survey conducted during the global financial crisis indicated that 89 percent of employers introduced strategies to try to improve employee morale. What were companies doing? About 49 percent reported increasing the frequency and quality of communication, 28 percent provided additional professional development opportunities, 25 percent gave additional financial rewards, 20 percent enhanced employee recognition programs, and 20 percent conducted additional team building activities.[105]

Does morale really matter? A Sirota study found that companies with high morale (75th percentile or higher) outperformed their competitors by 368 percent with regard to year-over-year stock returns (15.1 percent improvement in stock price for high-morale companies versus 4.1 percent for competitors). Not surprisingly, companies with low morale (below the 25th percentile) were about 166 percent below their industry counterparts.[106]

A popular method used to improve the quality of work life is employee involvement. *Employee involvement* (EI) consists of a variety of systematic methods that empower employees to participate in the decisions that affect them and their relationship with the organization. Through EI, employees feel a sense of responsibility or even "ownership" of decisions in which they participate. To be successful, however, EI must be more than just a systematic approach; it must become part of the organization's culture and management philosophy.[107] Today, some North American organizations provide employees with considerable involvement in the decision-making process:

> EllisDon appears regularly on the Best Employers in Canada list. According to consultant Ted Emond, "A company like EllisDon has so instilled into the DNA of the organization what it is that engages employees. We believe it's going to help them manage the sacrifices and challenges that will be asked of employees on the downsize." At EllisDon, a construction firm with 1,400 employees, workers are given access to financial information and the business plan, and have the opportunity to ask questions. Feedback from employees has led to changes in the performance management system.[108]

EI is based on two important principles. First, individuals tend to support systems or decisions that they helped to make. For example, if an employee was actively involved in developing a new credit collection procedure, then this individual is more likely to ensure that the new procedure is carried out correctly. Second, employees who actually perform a task know more about it than anyone else, including their supervisor. Asking for information from employees who actually perform the job can provide insights not available from their supervisors or outside experts. Some firms are strong believers in employee involvement:

> High Liner Foods <http://www.highlinerfoods.com>, a Nova Scotia Top Employers 2015 winner, is committed to its employees. According to VP of Human Resources Joanne Brown, "we are an employer that provides opportunities for our employees to grow." A recent initiative, the Seafood Savvy Program, is a two and a-half day program that provides employees with an insight into all aspects of High Liner's operations, from when a fish is bought until it ends up on the shelf of the supermarket.[109]

While it has been argued that employee loyalty is an outdated concept (and a recent study by Bain and Company <http://www.bain.com> revealed that less than half of employees believe that their organization deserves their loyalty), there is evidence that employee loyalty does matter. According to Fred Reichheld, author of *Loyalty Rules*:

> For the average company, loyalty is dying. Of course, this means that the average company is dying. Employees spend half their waking hours working at a company that they don't really believe in. The key to success is building mutually beneficial relationships, a give and take in which employees are offered opportunities to grow, learn, and make money—but only if they contribute to custom value creation and the bottom line.[110]

Employee Involvement Interventions

A number of different interventions have been used to increase employee involvement and improve overall employee satisfaction at work.

Self-Directed Work Teams or Groups

A common approach to EI is **self-directed work teams or groups**. Self-directed work teams are teams of workers without a formal, company-appointed supervisor who decide among themselves most matters traditionally handled by a supervisor. These groups of workers typically decide daily work assignments, the use of job rotation, orientation for new employees, training, and production schedules. Some groups even handle recruitment, selection, and discipline.

---

self-directed work teams (groups)

Teams of workers without a formal, employer-appointed supervisor who decide among themselves most matters traditionally handled by a supervisor.

Some observers are critical of the increased focus on innovation and workplace teams. In a number of organizations, managers "stress the system" by speeding up the line, cutting the number of employees or machines, or having workers take on more tasks (at times through "multiskilling"). Under such systems, workers may be required to act like machines. While management by stress may help in raising productivity (at least over the short-term), workers often experience considerable personal stress and a sense of being "dehumanized."[111]

How is technology shaping how teams operate? A study of U.S. and Canadian employers revealed that about 23 percent use virtual teams and 57 percent are planning on using more virtual teams (defined as "employees from different functions of an organization distributed across disparate locations and between companies"). About 72 percent of respondents cite cost savings as a major reason for the use of virtual teams. Concerning HR's role, major issues include the need for more training relating to virtual teams, the requirement of additional communication (particularly cross-cultural), and time zone and distance concerns.[112]

HRC 2 & 5

High-Involvement Work Practices

There is growing evidence that human resource management practices do matter and are related to organizational performance. In one study, **high-involvement work practices** were related to lower turnover, higher productivity, and improved financial performance. In another study, "low road" practices (such as use of short-term contracts, low levels of training, little commitment to job security, and low levels of HR sophistication) were negatively associated with corporate performance while "high road" practices (characterized by high-commitment human resource management) were strongly related to a high level of organizational performance. The thrust of the work in this area has been away from focusing on any single human resource practice in favour of studying systems or bundles of practices and the strategic impact of human resource management on organizational performance. In addition, a growing number of researchers are examining employee perceptions of high-involvement work systems and the roles that workers play in both low and high-involvement workplaces.[113]

high-involvement work practices

A set of human resource practices aimed at increasing employee performance.

AON's <http://www.aon.com> *Trends in Global Engagement* 2014 study from 6,000 employers in 155 countries revealed that 61 percent of employees were engaged. The three key drivers (in order) were career opportunities, managing performance, and organization reputation. Baby boomers were the most engaged (66 percent), followed by Generation X (60 percent) and Millennials (56 percent). While engagement is important, high-performing employers also had strong leadership, a performance orientation, and a positive reputation.[114]

Quality circles involve a small group of employee volunteers with a common leader who meet regularly to identify and solve work-related problems. Why the emphasis on volunteers?

© Stuart O'Sullivan/Getty Images.

What does this mean for human resource management? The human resource function must focus on business-level outcomes and problems, become a strategic core competency with the ability to understand the human capital dimension of the organization's major business priorities, and develop a systems perspective of human resource management.[115] Seven practices of successful organizations are (1) a focus on employment security, (2) selective hiring, (3) self-managed teams and decentralization of accountability and responsibility as basic elements of organizational design, (4) comparatively high compensation contingent on organizational performance, (5) extensive training, (6) the reduction of status differentials, and (7) the sharing of information with employees.[116]

To what extent are Canadian organizations pursuing high-involvement workplace strategies? The results of one study are presented in Figure 11-5. A survey of more than 600 Canadian workplaces found that 50 percent had problem-solving groups, just over one-quarter had a total quality management (or similar) program, and just under 40 percent had training in EI. About 70 percent reported having project teams.

FIGURE 11-5

Employee Involvement Programs in Canadian Organizations

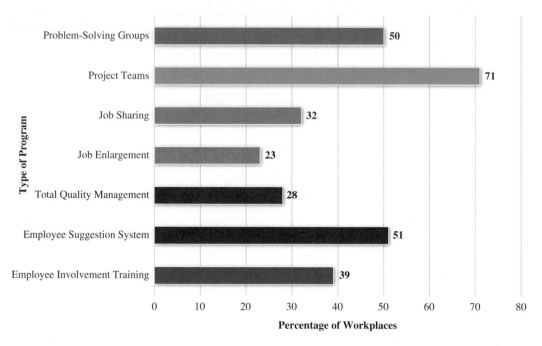

SOURCE: Terry H. Wagar, *Human Resource Management and Workplace Change*, Saint Mary's University, 2009.

HRC 2 & 6 & 8

Employee Self-Service

Although employee self-service was a fairly new concept a decade ago, a growing number of organizations are introducing self-service as a means of reducing the amount of administrative work performed by human resource professionals.

Currently, human resource activities that can be addressed by employee self-service have been divided into two groups:[117]

- **Productivity Applications.** This includes *management of personal data, retirement plans*, and *health and benefits management*. In addition, productivity applications for managers may include the use of management reports and approval applications. For example, an employee seeking an approval to participate in a training program could request such an approval electronically and the process could be set up to route the request by email to the appropriate manager.

Spotlight *on* ETHICS

The High-Involvement Workplace Dilemma

Consider the following situation and make a note of your answer on a separate sheet of paper.

You are a human resource management associate at a manufacturing company with just under 800 employees. You report to the human resource manager who, in turn, reports to the vice-president of human resource management. Neither you nor the manager is part of the senior executive team. Your most recent project involves an assessment of whether your organization should incorporate a high-involvement workplace strategy.

A few days ago, the following memo appeared (by mistake) in your email inbox:

All members of the senior executive team:

As you are aware, we are carefully considering the implementation of a high-involvement workplace system. The key to making this project succeed is to get employee buy-in. I have had chats with some other friends in our industry, and the gist of what they are saying is that if we sell this right, we can really save ourselves on labour costs. One company set up workplace teams and rewarded employees for coming up with labour-saving ideas—nine months later, the firm was able to cut almost 20 percent of the workforce. I figure we can follow a similar approach and will be able to get rid of between 125 and 150 jobs. Of course, we can't let the employees find out about this.

Maggie Pool (Vice-President of Human Resources)

You are unsure what you should do in this situation. On one hand, it is not illegal for a company to reduce the size of its workforce. On the other hand, both you and the human resource manager believe that the organization is interested in considering a high-involvement strategy as a way of increasing employer performance and employee satisfaction (not as a tool for reducing labour costs and cutting jobs).

- **Strategic Applications.** This includes *online recruitment and skills management applications*. By way of example, there are a growing number of programs designed to increase management productivity and free up time for more strategic initiatives.

While employee self-service applications are becoming more common in larger companies, it is expected that their use will increase noticeably in the next five years.

LO5   HRC 1 & 5

Job Security, Downsizing, and Employee Retention

No-Layoff Policies

In the past, loyal, hardworking employees could expect a secure job in return for dedicated work for the organization. However, this is no longer the case and the traditional psychological contract (the unwritten commitments between employers and employees) has been radically rewritten.[118] This new employment relationship has been described as follows:

> You're expendable. We don't want to fire you, but we will if we have to. Competition is brutal, so we must redesign the way we work to do more with less. Sorry, that's just the way it is. And one more thing—you're invaluable … We're depending on you to be innovative, risk-taking, and committed to our goals.[119]

Contrary to the downsizing trend of the 1990s, some organizations are developing no-layoff policies. These firms are using such policies as part of an integrated system of progressive HR practices—the idea is that employees who have job security are more receptive to change, more likely to be innovative and suggest changes that will improve the organization, and are more willing to "go the extra mile."

HRC 1 & 5

Organizational Downsizing

In many organizations, lifetime employment has been replaced by job insecurity. For example, in early 2015, Tim Horton's cut 350 office staff following their merger with Burger King, Target pulled out of Canada leaving 17,000 without jobs, and Sony <http://www.sony.com> announced the closure of all 14 of its retail stores. The declining price of oil also led to major restructuring and layoffs in the oil and gas industry with Suncor <http://www.suncor.com> cutting its 2015 budget by $1 billion and slashing about 1,000 jobs.[120]

Downsizing may be defined as "a deliberate organizational decision to reduce the workforce that is intended to improve organizational performance."[121] It has also been described as a set of activities undertaken on the part of management and designed to improve organizational efficiency, productivity, and/or competitiveness."[122] It is possible to identify three types of downsizing strategies:

1. **Workforce Reduction.** This is a short-term strategy focused on cutting the number of employees through programs such as attrition, early retirement or voluntary severance incentive packages, or layoffs.

2. **Work Redesign.** This strategy takes somewhat longer to implement and requires that organizations critically examine the work processes and evaluate whether specific functions, products, or services should be changed or eliminated.

3. **Systematic Change.** This is a long-term strategy requiring a change in the culture and attitudes and values of employees with the ongoing goal of reducing costs and improving quality. This strategy takes a long time to implement and thus the benefits only accrue over time.[123]

---

downsizing

Reducing employment to improve efficiency, productivity, and competitiveness.

While firms frequently believe that downsizing will enhance organizational performance, study after study shows that "following a downsizing, surviving employees become narrow-minded, self-absorbed, and risk averse. Morale sinks, productivity drops, and survivors distrust management."[124] Employee responses can be severe:

> At HMV, an employee hijacked the firm's Twitter account and gave live updates about the termination including "There are over 60 of us being fired at once! Mass execution, of loyal employees who love the brand."[125]

Downsizing and layoffs often cause a drop in employee morale and lower productivity. What are the ways to avoid these consequences, or at least to reduce the negative impact?

© Ariel Skelley/Getty Images.

In addition, there is growing evidence that firms engaging in downsizing do not perform better financially—the bulk of the research indicates that the stock price of downsized firms often declines after a layoff announcement is made.[126]

Downsizing efforts often fail to meet organizational objectives. This is not surprising, considering that many workforce reductions are carried out with little strategic planning or consideration of the costs to the individuals and employer. Frequently, cutting jobs is a short-term response to a much more serious problem. In several instances, little attention is given to carefully examining and resolving critical human resource issues.

> In April of 2014, Liat Honey, a married mother of two children, showed up at the Cobequid Children's Centre where she had worked for two years to find that the doors were locked and she was out of work. In addition to the need to fight for wages and vacation pay she was due, Liat was devastated by the loss of her job. In her words: "I was very, very angry, and I was very depressed. I was crying for literally two months. Now I am doing a lot better, but I was very angry that they didn't let us know. I understand businesses go down, but why wouldn't they tell us before, to give us time to plan?"[127]

While downsizing may be an appropriate strategic response for some organizations, it is not a "quick fix" remedy. Before implementing such a program, it is critical to carefully consider the decision, plan the process, and assess the consequences from the perspectives of the organization, the customer, the "survivors" (those employees that remain), and the victims (those that lose their jobs).

> Don Walker has more than 33 years in the forest industry. However, in the summer of 2008, he lost his job as a hydraulic log loader when his employer closed down. Walker says he has taken all he can and no longer has the will to pull himself back up after losing his job. He is running out of money and suffering from depression. "I've been beaten down my whole life and pulled myself back up off the ground so many times, but I just don't give a damn anymore. There are zero prospects—I've applied everywhere."[128]

Of those organizations who engage in the workforce-reduction stage of downsizing, many ignore the critical elements of redesigning the organization and implementing cultural change.[129] One organization had planned to contract out the maintenance of vehicles to local garages. While huge savings were projected, several of the local garages did not have repair bays big enough to accommodate the vehicles and the hoists were not strong enough to support the trucks. From a best practices perspective, six key principles deserve attention:

1. Change should be initiated from the top but requires hands-on involvement from all employees.

2. Workforce reduction must be selective in application and long term in emphasis.

3. There is a need to pay special attention both to those who lose their jobs and to the survivors who remain with the organization.

4. It is critical that decision makers identify precisely where redundancies, excess costs, and inefficiencies exist and attack those specific areas.

5. Downsizing should result in the formation of small semiautonomous organizations within the broader organization.

6. Downsizing must be a proactive strategy focused on increasing performance.[130]

Human resource professionals have an important role to play in downsizing efforts and should be involved in the strategic process. HR people are often in a good position to advise on the impact of restructuring an organization (from a variety of perspectives including work groups, teams, departments, and individuals) to maximize productivity and retain quality performers. Similarly, HR can develop skill inventories and planning charts to evaluate the effects on human resource needs and projected capabilities.

> At the JDS Uniphase <http://www.jdsu.com> plant in Victoria, British Columbia, the firm developed a 112-page directory with biographical sketches of the 180 or more employees who were the victims of a downsizing. The directory was sent to more than 400 employers in Western Canada. According to HR Director Arlene Keis, "The company is determined to treat employees well during good times and bad times." Other assistance to former employees included career transition help, courses for upgrading skills, and a job bulletin board.[131]

Moreover, in light of the compelling evidence that most downsizings have dramatically negative impacts on those who survive, human resource experts can assist in coordinating and communicating the downsizing decision. There is growing evidence that effective communication can reduce some of the negative consequences associated with downsizing:[132]

A number of employers are developing social media policies and limiting who can speak to the media but experts agree it is not possible to prevent all employees and former workers from accessing social media. However, Professor Aneil Mishra provides an excellent example of effectively handing a downsizing—when etailer Zappos had to lay off about 8 percent of its staff, its CEO sent an email to employees explaining why layoffs were necessary and the severance packages available to workers and began blogging and tweeting about the challenges and difficulty he had to endure as a result of the layoffs.[133]

More and more, former employees who have been downsized or terminated air their views on social media. According to Stacy Parker, Managing Director of the Blu Ivy Group <http://bluivygroup.com>, "The reality is that most people will use social media, particularly when they are not so happy with the way things have taken place. Especially during a downsizing, it is a very challenging time for the entire employment culture."[134]

Finally, HR can assist in evaluating the downsizing program. Issues include monitoring who left the organization and who remains, job design and redesign, worker adjustment to change, the need for employee counselling, organizational communication, and a comprehensive review of the appropriateness of existing HRM policies and programs (such as training, compensation and benefits, and orientation of employees into the "new" organization).[135] However, research has shown that downsizing employees is professionally demanding and the "downsizers" may experience social and organizational isolation, a decrease in personal well-being, and poorer family functioning.[136]

HRC 1 & 6

Retaining Top Performers

Keeping high-performing employees is often a challenge for both growing and downsized organizations. A study by Right Management <http://www.right.com> indicated that a shortage of talent was the top HR challenge (identified by 34 percent of Canadian executives), followed by low engagement/productivity (24 percent of respondents).[137] Many companies lose half of their employees in three to four years and half their customers in five years —keeping employees is as critical as retaining customers because without loyal employees, you won't have loyal customers.[138] A survey of about 4,000 Canadian workers found that about 50 percent of people expect to change careers in the next five years. The primary reasons for changing include changing personal interests, a desire for improved work–life balance, and the need for higher income.[139]

Of course, some organizations may adopt a strategy in which people are not important and are easily replaceable and thus they may be willing to accept high levels of employee turnover. One study suggests that the number one reason employees leave their jobs is "shock"—some precipitating event (such as a heated argument with the boss, uncertainty over a corporate merger, or an unexpected and unsolicited job offer) is more likely than job dissatisfaction to cause an employee to leave his or her current job.[140]

BMO's 2014 Labour Day survey looked to the strategies being used by Canadian organizations to retain talented employees. The most common practices included flexible work hours (76 percent), education, training, and development (66 percent), increased health and dental benefits (36 percent), increased paid vacation (29 percent), tuition assistance (27 percent), and telecommuting (25 percent). There were noticeable differences based on firm size; large businesses were clearly more likely to offer telecommuting (50 percent as compared to 24 percent for small firms) and tuition assistance (49 percent versus 26 percent respectively).[141]

A study by Professor Tim Gardner indicates that employees who are thinking of quitting often give off behavioural cues and start disengaging at the workplace. The 10 characteristics identified in the research included:

1. Offering fewer constructive contributions in meetings.

2. Being reluctant to commit to long-term projects.

3. Acting more reserved and quiet.

4. Being less interested in advancing in the organization.

5. Showing less interest in pleasing the boss than before.

6. Avoiding social interactions with the boss and other members of management.

7. Suggesting fewer new ideas or innovative approaches.

8. Doing the minimum amount of work needed and no longer going beyond the call of duty.

9. Participating less in training and development programs.

10. Demonstrating a drop in work productivity.

Gardner found if an employee exhibited at least six of these behaviours, his model could predict with 80 percent accuracy that the employee was going to quit.[142]

A Canadian study examining high potential ("HIPO") employee programs revealed that only 10 percent of more than 200 participants believed that senior managers are "highly effective" at spotting talent. About 85 percent of participants indicated that their organization had some type of HIPO program; most of the programs involved identifying high performers (say the top 10 percent) and providing such individuals with leadership development opportunities. More than 80 percent of organizations have not formally evaluated the accuracy of the method used to identify high potential employees. The most common methods used to identify high performers were current job performance (88 percent), supervisor recommendation (70 percent), and upper-level management recommendation (68 percent).[143]

What do employees want in a job? Based on research conducted by the Canadian Policy Research Networks and EKOS Research Associates <http://www.ekos.com>, the top five factors in terms of importance were: being treated with respect, having interesting work, having work that results in a feeling of accomplishment, having good communications among co-workers, and having a balance between work and family issues. Having a job that pays well was rated ninth out of fifteen factors. While the values of younger and older workers did not vary much, women placed more attention on workplace issues such as communication, co-worker relations, and work–family balance relative to their male counterparts. In short, female employees were especially concerned about a supportive work climate.

Among the factors in retaining key employees are the following:

• Developing a planned approach to employee retention (which examines the usual company benefits, addresses individual needs, focuses on the long term, is part of the vision of the organization, and is based on investment in employees).

- Becoming an employer of choice with a goal of retaining employees from the day they join the organization.

- Communicating the organizational vision and values frequently and in a clear and consistent manner.

- Rewarding supervisors and managers for keeping good people.

- Using exit interviews to obtain information as to why people are leaving the organization.[144]

A number of recent studies have examined whether there is a relationship between the human resource management practices of an organization and employee retention. The findings suggest that employers with high-involvement human resource systems tend to have lower employee turnover.[145]

SUMMARY

The human resource department's role in organizational communication is to create an open two-way flow of information. Part of the foundation of any organizational communication effort is the view held by management of employees. If that view is one that sincerely strives to provide an effective downward and upward flow of information, then the human resource department can help develop and maintain appropriate communication systems.

Downward communication approaches include in-house publications, information booklets, employee bulletins, prerecorded messages, email, jobholder reports, and open-book management. Multiple channels are used to help ensure that each message reaches the intended receivers. Perhaps the greatest difficulty in organizational communication is to provide an effective upward flow of information. In-house complaint procedures, manager–employee meetings, suggestion systems, and attitude survey feedback are commonly used tools.

Counselling is the discussion of a problem with an employee to help the worker cope with the situation. It is performed by human resource department professionals as well as supervisors. Counselling programs provide a support service for both job and personal problems, and there is extensive co-operation with community counselling agencies.

Discipline is management action to enforce organizational standards, and it is both preventive and corrective. The hot-stove rule is a useful general guide for corrective discipline. Most disciplinary action is progressive, with stronger penalties for repeated offences. Some disciplinary programs primarily emphasize a counselling approach.

Employee involvement efforts are systematic attempts by organizations to give workers a greater opportunity to take part in decisions that affect the way they do their job and the contribution they make to their organization's overall effectiveness. They are not a substitute for good, sound human resource practices and policies. However, effective EI efforts can supplement other human resource actions and lead to improved employee motivation, satisfaction, and productivity. Whether that involvement is in solving workplace problems or participating in the design of jobs, employees want to know that their contribution makes a difference.

In this era of downsizing and restructuring, it is important to understand the basic principles relating to wrongful dismissal law. Also, there is evidence that many downsizing efforts fail to meet organizational objectives. Human resource professionals have an important role to play in both growing and downsized workplaces.

TERMS FOR REVIEW

constructive dismissal
corrective discipline
counselling
discipline
downsizing
downward communication
due process
employee attitude/opinion survey
grapevine communication
high-involvement work practices
hot-stove rule
in-house complaint procedures
just cause
open-door policy
preventive discipline
progressive discipline
self-directed work teams (groups)
suggestion systems
upward communication
wrongful dismissal

SELF-ASSESSMENT EXERCISE

Procedural and Distributive Justice in the Classroom

Consider a grade you obtained in a course. Research suggests that individuals are concerned with not only the outcome—that is, the grade ("distributive justice")—but also the procedures leading to the decision ("procedural justice"). The following self-test gives you a quick assessment of both procedural and distributive justice. Read each statement and give it a score from 1 to 5 (1 indicating that you strongly disagree with the statement and 5 indicating that you strongly agree with the statement).

1. The grading procedures used to arrive at my grade were applied consistently. _____

2. The grading procedures used to arrive at my grade were free of bias. _____

3. The grading procedures used to arrive at my grade were based on accurate information. _____

4. I was able to express my views and feelings during the grading process. _____

5. The grade I obtained reflected the amount of effort I put into my work. _____

6. The grade I obtained reflected my contribution in the course. _____

7. The grade I obtained is appropriate when I consider the amount of work I did in the course. _____

8. The grade I obtained is fair, given my performance in the course. _____

SCORING

First add up your scores for statements 1 through 4. These statements address the issue of "procedural justice." A higher score is associated with a stronger perception that the procedures used in grading your work were fair. Then add up your scores for statements 5 through 8. These statements measure "distributive justice." A higher score is associated with a belief that the grade you obtained was appropriate, given your contribution.

Note: This survey is adapted from Jason Colquitt, "On the Dimensionality of Organizational Justice: A Construct Validation of a Measure," *Journal of Applied Psychology*, Vol. 86, 2001, pp. 386–400.

REVIEW AND DISCUSSION QUESTIONS

1. Think of a situation in which you learned some new information from the grapevine and took action on the basis of that information. Discuss.

2. List and describe the different types of programs that can be used by the human resource department to improve communication.

3. Discuss differences between preventive and corrective discipline. What examples of either one were applied to you on the last job you had?

4. What is progressive discipline? How does it work? Is its basic approach realistic in work situations? Explain your answer.

CRITICAL THINKING QUESTIONS

1. Employee involvement has become a popular concept. As a manager, what steps would you take to increase EI in your organization?

2. Suppose you are a plant or division manager and you want to improve the quality of work life in your division. What steps would you take?

3. Think of an organization that you have worked in. What high-involvement work practices could be implemented to improve performance?

4. Assume you have been asked to terminate an employee. How would you conduct the termination interview?

ETHICS QUESTION

You are the human resource manager, and the CEO has just told you that the company is in a financial crisis and has to downsize staff by 500 employees (out of 2,000) to survive. You are asked to prepare for the dismissal and your suggestions as to who should be chosen. It is a family-owned, nonunion firm. There is a precedent: a few years ago, 50 employees had to be let go, and the main criterion was low performance. It seems to be obvious that this time the performance criterion will not be sufficient. Many of the employees have 20 to 30 years of tenure; some have large families, with at least five children; there are single mothers; and a few have sick spouses or parents to take care of. When you ask some of the supervisors, you are told that they prefer to keep the younger employees who seem to be more productive (and are less expensive to employ). Develop a plan to save the company. What ethical issues are involved?

WEB RESEARCH EXERCISE

1. Visit the websites of three employee assistance program (EAP) providers. Compare the programs and approaches of the three providers. What similarities and differences do you observe?

2. Laws relating to dismissal vary among countries. Using the Internet, examine dismissal law websites in Canada, the United States, and one other country. Compare the laws regarding dismissal among the three countries.

INCIDENT 11-1

The Machinist's Abusive Comments to the Supervisor

William Lee, a machine operator, worked as a machinist for Horace Gray, a supervisor. Horace told William to pick up some garbage that had fallen from William's work area, and William replied, "I won't do the janitor's work." Horace replied: "When you drop it, you pick it up." William became angry and abusive, calling Horace a number of uncomplimentary names in a loud voice and refusing to pick up the garbage. All employees in the department heard William's comments.

The situation was as follows: Horace had been trying for two weeks to get his employees to pick up garbage in order to have a cleaner workplace and prevent accidents. He talked with all employees in a weekly department meeting and to each employee individually at least once. He stated that he was following the instructions of the superintendent. Only William objected with the comment, "I'm not here to do the janitor's work. I'm a machinist."

William had been in the department for six months and with the company for three years. Horace had spoken to him twice about excessive horseplay, but otherwise his record was good. He was known to have a quick temper.

After William finished his abusive outburst, Horace told him to come to the office and suspended him for one day for insubordination and abusive language to a supervisor. The discipline was within company policy, and similar acts had been disciplined in other departments.

When William walked out of Horace's office, Horace called the human resource director, reported what he had done, and said that he was sending a copy of his action for William's file.

1. As human resource director, what comments would you make?

2. What follow-up actions should the human resource director take or recommend that Horace take? For example, do you recommend counselling for William? Would you reconsider disciplinary procedures and policies?

CASE STUDY

Maple Leaf Shoes Ltd.

Addressing Employee Relations

As she sat in her office in Winnipeg, Britney MacPherson thumbed through a textbook on human resource management. As manager of the Winnipeg location of Maple Leaf Shoes, she was responsible for the day-to-day operations of the facility. However, Britney was finding her job particularly challenging—although she had a B.Com., which she received in 1994 from a well-known Ontario university, her training had been focused on accounting and finance and she had had only one course in human resource management. Things were unravelling in Winnipeg, and Britney knew that she needed help. Unfortunately, her phone calls and emails to head office in Wilmington, Ontario, brought little assistance.

The company policy regarding employee communications was quite simple: "What goes on at the company stays at the company." This policy was communicated regularly to all employees. However, Joan Jorgenson, a clerk in the office, had violated this policy. A couple of weeks ago, Joan had struck up a conversation with a co-worker, Natalie King. During their talk, Natalie had mentioned that she had recently moved from Wilmington to Winnipeg, because, according to Natalie, a senior member of management in the Wilmington office had become enraged when Natalie refused his sexual advances. He had threatened Natalie with dismissal, but after a short discussion an agreement was reached that Natalie would move to the Winnipeg location. Joan became enraged when she heard Natalie's story, and immediately notified not only employees of the human rights commission in Ontario but also the media in both Winnipeg and Wilmington. Britney is now trying to decide how she should handle the situation.

Max MacSweeney is a 31-year-old accountant who has been employed by Maple Leaf Shoes for seven years (three years in Wilmington and the last four years in Winnipeg). Although Max is based in Winnipeg, he travels throughout western Canada as part of his job. Max is considered a very good employee. He is well known in the business community, is very involved in the local association of management accountants, and is a highly visible member of a number of charitable organizations in the Winnipeg area. Max is married and has two children.

About three weeks ago, head office started monitoring the Internet usage of employees. Much to their surprise, they found that Max had visited several pornographic web sites on four different evenings (while on business at the Wilmington office). The records revealed that he had spent an average of about three hours on each of the four evenings visiting such sites. While Max used company property (the computer he accessed the sites from was in an office assigned to him while in Wilmington) when visiting the "undesirable" sites, such visits were made outside of regular working hours. While the company has been providing Internet access to employees for a number of years, it had not developed a policy on Internet usage. Head office personnel in Wilmington have asked Britney to deal with the issue.

As they say, "Problems come in threes." Britney's head was aching as the phone rang. On the line was Rob McEwen from head office in Wilmington. He wanted to find out what Britney was going to do about Paul Bertuzzi. Paul is a 44-year-old warehouse supervisor at the Winnipeg facility. He supervises eight employees, has been with Maple Leaf Shoes for just over 11 years, and earns $49,600 a year. Paul's performance evaluations are among the highest at the Winnipeg office, he attends night school and is two credits away from his B.A., and he is well liked by his co-workers.

One month ago, Paul went to Toronto to attend a two-day training program for warehouse supervisors. After the first day of sessions, Paul and two other warehouse supervisors (from the Montreal and Toronto facilities) went out for dinner. During the meal, the other two supervisors revealed to Paul that they had developed a scheme in which they wrote off a small portion of the shoe inventory as wastage but actually kept the shoes and sold them to a friend at a discount. As one of the individuals said: "We're not talking about big money, Paul. However, I'm sure you could use an extra $125 to $175 a week. After all, we're all underpaid and our salaries are not keeping pace with inflation." In addition, they told Paul of a new moneymaking scheme and asked if he was interested in joining their "team." It appears that a shoe manufacturer overseas was interested in mass-producing Maple Leaf Shoes products—however, the new company needed more information on the latest shoe designs and production techniques. Under the scheme, the warehouse supervisors were going to get information for the overseas company in return for part-ownership in the business.

One week ago, an auditor uncovered the scheme. The two warehouse supervisors from Montreal and Toronto were fired. While the audit confirmed that no other Maple Leaf Shoes employees were involved in the scheme, Paul (and one other Maple Leaf Shoes employee) admitted knowing about the fraud. In discussions with top management, the point was raised of whether Paul had a duty to report the fraud. Again, Britney has been asked to deal with the matter.

DISCUSSION QUESTIONS

1. Consider the three issues Britney needs to address. Which one should be addressed first? Last? Explain your reasoning.

2. How should Britney deal with the Joan Jorgenson incident? What suggestions would you make to improve the policy on employee communications?

3. What disciplinary action (if any) would you recommend that Britney take with respect to the case involving Max MacSweeney?

4. Develop a company policy on Internet usage.

5. Do you recommend that Paul Bertuzzi be dismissed? Is there just cause for dismissal?

6. What would be "reasonable notice" in the event that a court ruled that your organization did not have just cause to terminate Paul? Explain your answer.

7. If you were in Paul Bertuzzi's position, would you have reported the scheme to senior management?

CASE STUDY

A Matter of Security at Canadian Pacific and International Bank

Brenda Reid joined Canadian Pacific and International Bank (CPIB) in 2002 and has been employed with CPIB since that time. Brenda, who is 38 years old, is a single mom with two young children (Norris, age seven, and Morris, age five). Brenda graduated from Mount Allison University in 1995 with a B.Com., worked almost five years with another bank (from 1995 to 2000), and returned to school in 2000. She earned a Master of Business Administration from University of Saskatoon in 2002, specializing in finance and information systems. Upon graduation, she joined CPIB as an assistant manager and is now the manager of the main branch in Halifax (a position she assumed three years ago).

Brenda is considered a very strong performer, and senior bank officials believe that she has senior upper-management potential. Brenda has participated in several management training programs and within the next year the bank had planned to send her to the Advanced Management Seminar provided by the London University Business School. The Advanced Management Seminar is a prestigious program for international bankers with at least 10 years' experience.

Brenda earns just over $110,000 a year, and her performance is very solid (she has consistently ranked within the top 20 percent of bank managers). The only disciplinary incident in her file involved a written warning two years ago for misplacing her security pass card to the main Halifax branch. The card was ultimately found in a CPIB policy and procedures manual that she had borrowed.

On a Friday afternoon three weeks ago, Brenda decided to take home two files, each of which contained detailed financial and corporate information on a major CPIB corporate client in the Atlantic region. Brenda was scheduled to meet with representatives from each of the two companies the following Monday, and removed the files from the bank in order to review them over the weekend. According to Brenda, taking files home to review was not unusual—several managers did it regularly.

After leaving work on the Friday afternoon, Brenda met a few friends and went out for dinner in downtown Halifax. Later, the group attended a play at Neptune Theatre. When the play was over, Brenda returned to her minivan to find that her briefcase containing the two files had been stolen from the van (which she had locked). Brenda had put the briefcase under the front seat of the van. While Brenda's empty briefcase was found in the parking garage, its contents have not been recovered.

Although CPIB does not have a detailed policy relating to the removal of property from the bank offices, the CPIB handbook contains a provision informing all personnel to exercise extreme caution and care when removing CPIB property from the office. Interviews with loans officers and managers indicate that the typical procedure is to either keep the property on their person or secure the property in the trunk of a vehicle.

Brenda was devastated by the theft and reported it immediately to her supervisor. She broke into tears when discussing the incident with CPIB management, apologized profusely for her mistake, and promised that it would never happen again.

DISCUSSION QUESTIONS

1. Would you recommend disciplinary action in this case? Why or why not?

2. Are there long-term implications for the human resource function as a result of this incident?

3. Assume that head office has demanded a new policy addressing the security of bank property. Discuss the merits and drawbacks of having such a policy.

4. Develop a policy for CPIB.

CHAPTER 12

Ensuring Health and Safety at the Workplace

Those who suffer (from work-related injuries) include not only the injured worker but his or her family and friends as well. Also, the impact of work injuries on human productivity reaches well beyond the workplace and includes a worker's ability to contribute to family and community.

JULIAN BARLING AND MICHAEL FRONE[1]

LEARNING OBJECTIVES

After studying this chapter, you should be able to:

LO1 Describe the major Canadian laws relating to occupational health and safety.

LO2 Assess the traditional thinking with respect to occupational health and safety issues.

LO3 Explain the new thinking with respect to employee rights relating to occupational health and safety issues.

LO4 Outline the safety and health responsibilities of employers and employees.

LO5 Discuss the impact of stress on employees and the workplace.

LO6 Summarize the relationship between health and safety issues and human resource management.

HRC 8

Even today, too many employees are injured at the workplace. Employers, supervisors, and employees must work together to reduce on-the-job injuries and illness:

Vernon Theriault was a miner at the Westray coal mine. On May 9, 1992, he was getting ready to go to work and begin his shift when an explosion at the mine led to the death of 26 miners. As he reflects on what happened at Westray, he believes that politicians have not done enough to make workplaces safer. As Theriault notes, "The bottom line is, the reason I went there is they said it was going to be 20, 25 years of work and you could work all the overtime you want and (make) $60,000 to $80,000 a year. I was looking after my family and that was No. 1 for me."[2]

At the turn of the twentieth century, the thinking and attitudes of employers and employees toward accident prevention were quite different from today. Comments made during this period by employers illustrate this:

- "I don't have money for frills like safety."

- "Some people are just accident prone, and no matter what you do they'll hurt themselves some way."

- "Ninety percent of all accidents are caused by just plain carelessness."

- "We are not in business for safety."[3]

During this period, the courts used a legal expression, **assumption of risk**, meaning that the worker accepted all the customary risks associated with the occupation he or she worked in. Workers were instructed to protect themselves from special hazards such as extreme heat or molten and sharp metal. Furthermore, the attitudes of employees paralleled those of the employers. Scars and stumps on fingers and hands were often proudly referred to as badges of honour. The thought that safety was a matter of "luck" was frequently reflected in such statements as "I never thought he'd get it; he was always one of the lucky ones," or "When your number's up, there's not much you can do."

---

assumption of risk

The worker accepts all the customary risks associated with his or her occupation.

Over a four-year period in the early 1900s, records of one steel company show that 1,600 of its 2,200 employees lost time from work because of injury. In other words, 75 percent of this plant's entire workforce lost time from work because of accidents on the job.[4]

The early approach to safety at work used the **careless worker model**. It assumed that most accidents were due to workers' failure to be careful or to protect themselves. Even if training was provided to make workers more aware of the dangers in the workplace, this approach still assumed that it was mainly the worker's fault if an accident happened. A new approach, the **shared responsibility model**, assumes that the best method to reduce accident rates relies on the co-operation of the two main partners: the employer and the employees (who may be represented by a union).[5] Accident rates are reduced when the following occurs:

- management is committed to safety in the workplace;

- employees are informed about accident prevention;

- consultation between the employer and employees takes place on a regular basis (for example, the creation of a health and safety committee);

- there is a trusting relationship between the employer and staff; and

---

careless worker model

The early approach to safety in the workplace, which assumed that most accidents were due to workers' failure to be careful or to protect themselves.

---

shared responsibility model

A newer approach to safety in the workplace that assumes the best method to reduce accident rates relies on the co-operation of the employer and the employees (who may be represented by a union).

- employees have actual input into the decision-making process.

In Chapter 10, one of the topics was workers' compensation, which has as its aim the compensation of an employee for injuries suffered on the job. These programs have a serious defect: they are after-the-fact efforts. They attempt to compensate employees for accidents and illnesses that have already occurred. Many early supporters of these laws had hoped that costs would force employees to become more safety-conscious. Yet even with greater efforts by employers, accident rates continue to remain high. In addition, toxins and unhealthy work environments continue to create new health hazards.

A home building company and contractor were charged in Alberta after a workplace accident left a father of two paralyzed from the waist down. The employee severed his spinal cord after falling 6 metres through an open stairwell at a construction site. According to a spokesperson for Occupational Health (Alberta), "The prime employer is always on the hook. If there's another company directing work, they can also be accountable." The contractor who hired the employee (a personal friend for several years) said that the charges were an insult. "It was a tragic accident. If it could have been avoided, it would have been. That is why they're called accidents."[6]

A 19-year-old Ontario man who was distributing pay slips died at a Kanata construction site when he was crushed between a backhoe and a large excavator. The employee was new on the job, but had worked for the employer the previous summer. The company president stated that they had been in business for 36 years and "this is the first time anything like this has happened. We've got a great safety record and we train our employees well. This is a family company. We really care for our employees."[7]

 HRC 8

Workplace Injuries and Health Hazards

It is estimated that about three Canadian workers die every working day from an occupational injury or disease. However, the number of work-related injuries has dropped dramatically since the 1980s with the number of work-related injuries dropping from about 50 per 1,000 employed workers in 1986 to about 15 per 1,000 workers today. Every minute worked costs the Canadian economy more than $60,000 in compensation payments to injured workers. Workplace accidents and occupation-related illnesses cost more than $8 billion annually in compensation payments alone. The total cost is more than $19 billion a year when indirect expenses are taken into account, and this does not include the incalculable social toll associated with workplace-related accidents.[8] Employers interested in calculating the direct and indirect costs of workplace accidents and injuries can use an injury cost calculator available from different provincial websites (see, for instance, <http://www.work.alberta.ca>).

Accidents at work are caused by a complex combination of unsafe employee behaviour and unsafe working conditions. Several factors contribute to the complexity of managing safety in the workplace: the effects of some industrial diseases do not show up for years; employers may "clean up" a health or safety problem before an inspector arrives; companies may fail to monitor or disclose health risks; or employees may fail to follow safe practices at the workplace or engage in dangerous behaviour (such as drinking alcohol or taking drugs while on the job).

It is also critical that organizations consider the safety of members of the public who enter onto company property.

In November 2000, two 14-year-old children were killed during the Take Our Kids to Work Day at the John Deere <http://www.deere.com> plant in Welland, Ontario. The fatal accident occurred when they crashed the small vehicle they were driving. An inquest into the accident resulted in several recommendations including the use of an informed consent form containing health and safety messages and requiring the signature of both the student and a parent or guardian, a requirement that children are under adult supervision at all times, refusing to allow a student to operate a motorized vehicle, and a mandatory orientation program for student participants which addresses health and safety issues.[9]

Workplace Injuries

Data from the Association of Workers' Compensation Boards of Canada provide some perspective on the extent of workplace injury and illness in Canada. While the number of workplace injuries has declined and then levelled off in recent years, the direct cost of injuries (such as lost wages, first aid and medical treatment, rehabilitation, and disability compensation) has not. Moreover, workplace injuries result in several indirect costs (including lost production, recruiting, selecting, and training of new employees, and damage to facilities and equipment) that are incurred by the employer.

FIGURE 12-1

Number of Accepted Time-Loss Injuries (1994–2013)

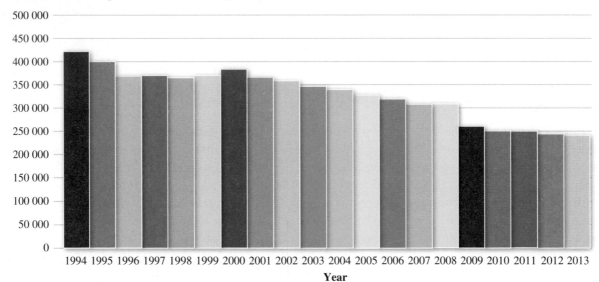

Source: Number of Accepted Time-Loss Injuries: Association of Workers' Compensation Boards of Canada, "National Work Injuries Statistics Program," Association of Workers' Compensation Boards of Canada (AWCBC), National Work Injury/Disease Statistics Program (NWISP)

Research on the number of time-loss injuries is provided in Figure 12-1 and information on the number of workplace fatalities is contained in Figure 12-2. There are approximately 775,000 occupational injury claims each year and more than one-third of these claims are accepted time-loss injuries warranting compensation. In 2013, 902 workers died as a result of a workplace injury (an average of about three workers each day of the year). April 28 is the National Day of Mourning to commemorate employees killed or injured on the job.

Exposure to asbestos is responsible for about one in three workplace deaths each year since 1996. The 368 deaths for 2013 represent more fatalities than from highway accidents, fires, and chemical exposures combined. Health professionals believe that the long latency period associated with asbestos (often from

20 to 40 years) will lead to higher death rates. According to Health Canada, "asbestos poses potential health risks only when fibres are present in the air people breathe. The problem is there's no way of ensuring that all products are always bound or enclosed. Brake pads wear down, renos stir up dust, while pipes and tiles get sawed."[10]

When considering injury incidence for 2013, there was an injury for about every 68 workers. Men were more likely than women to have a time-loss injury; when measured per 1,000 workers, 18.8 cases involved men and 11.2 cases involved women.[11]

Fishing, construction, manufacturing, and transportation are among the most dangerous industries when considering time-loss injury rates. The most common type of injury involves strains and sprains, followed by cuts, contusions, crushing, or bruises. Evidence from British Columbia reveals that the most common body part involving time lost cases was the back (24 percent of cases). Other common injuries included fingers (11 percent), legs (9 percent), shoulders (8 percent), and ankles (5 percent).[12]

> Reynold Hert, now CEO of the BC Forest Safety Council <http://www.bcforestsafe.org>, remembers being a sawmill manager about two decades ago and watching an operator of a lumber-trimming machine stick his hands into the equipment to straighten out a board. Fortunately, the man was not injured but could easily have lost fingers, a hand, or an arm. The man said that taking risks was necessary to avoid costly work disruptions. Hert told him to follow safety procedures and the man had to shut down his machine 90 times during his next shift to straighten out boards, reducing his productivity by about 33 percent. When Hert asked an engineer and maintenance employee to examine the issue, they found that the machine had a timing flaw, and were able to fix the problem. The previous year, there were 21 fatalities and approximately 7,000 injuries in the BC forest industry. Hert recognizes that some of the 4,000 employers in the industry may cut corners in order to keep bids as low as possible. According to Hert, investing in safety training may increase short-term costs but the contractors that don't pay attention to safety will find it hard to get work. "When you are staring at the spot where a person died, you realize it is preventable."[13]

FIGURE 12-2

Number of Fatalities (1994–2013)

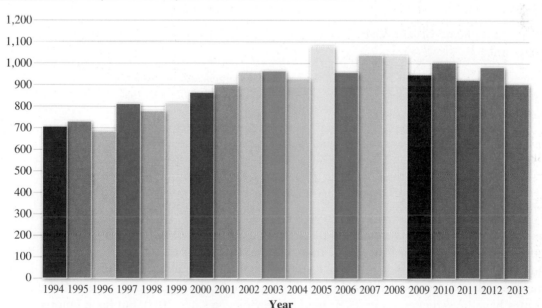

Source: Number of Fatalities: Association of Workers' Compensation Boards of Canada, "National Work Injuries Statistics Program," Association of Workers' Compensation Boards of Canada (AWCBC), National Work Injury/Disease Statistics Program (NWISP)

Health Hazards

It is possible to combine the various health hazards into three categories:[14]

1. **Physical Agents.** Exposure to physical elements such as noise, temperature, lighting, vibrations, and radiation.

2. **Biological Agents/Biohazards and Chemicals.** Exposure to such natural organisms as parasites, bacteria, insects, viruses, and so on; exposure to chemical compounds or other harmful toxic substances:

   > Health and safety charges were brought against the owners and operators of a British Columbia mushroom farm after three workers died. The workers allegedly died due to the presence of toxic gases while they were working in a confined space.[15]

3. **Ergonomically Related Injuries.** Caused by the work environment and including repetitive strain, stress, over exertion/fatigue, and back injuries. In simple terms, *ergonomics* involves the "study of the relationship between people and their jobs." More specifically, ergonomics uses scientific principles to examine the nature of the task that the employee is doing, the equipment or machinery needed to carry out the task, and the environment in which the task is carried out. Some ways in which ergonomics has been applied include preventing back injuries, developing proper work positions, organizing the work space, and managing the light at work.[16]

Awareness of health hazards is very important. Consider the example involving letter carriers:

> Residents of a Montreal suburb were asked by Canada Post to remove the Christmas garlands from the hand-rails on their front steps. While some residents complained, Canada Post noted that a letter carrier nearly lost a finger when she slipped and caught her hand on a garland wire. In Quebec, letter carriers had almost 600 work accidents during the year, with 80 percent resulting from slips and falls on private property.[17]

Moreover, a number of employers have given little (if any) thought to preparing for emerging health hazards:

> Although Ebola and measles have been in the news, many organizations do not have a pandemic plan in place and policies relating to sick leave and time off. Health Canada estimates that a major influenza pandemic would result in up to 35 percent of the workforce being unable to work at least half a day and absenteeism rates of up to 60 percent for a period of up to four weeks with people too sick to work or staying at home to care for family members. Many small and medium-sized firms have not considered the implications of a pandemic and their obligations to take reasonable steps to protect employees. Even some large companies are unprepared for emergencies—a 2008 survey revealed that half of Canadian companies with 500 or more employees do not have a pandemic plan and among those with a plan, only 1 percent have the 15 key components identified by experts.[18]

In addition, some rather dangerous workplaces may not be subject to the same scrutiny as others. For example, one observer argues that NHL rinks are unsafe workplaces. He asks, "when will authorities responsible for occupational health and safety turn their attention to the professional hockey rink which, after all, is a workplace and subject to regulation?" He argues that British Columbia's health authorities have investigated 43 cases of workplace violence since 2010, but have ignored professional sport. He asserts that while hockey involves some inherent risks, injury resulting from fighting, illegal use of the stick, and head shots render the hockey rink an unsafe workplace.[19]

HRC 8

Younger Workers and Workplace Safety

There is growing emphasis on the health and safety of young workers. About one in seven young workers is injured on the job and approximately one-fourth of all workplace injuries involve employees in the 15 to 29 age group. Among injured workers who are under 25 years of age, more than 50 percent were injured during the first six months of employment and nearly 20 percent of the injuries and fatalities occur during the first month on the job. The most common injuries affecting young workers include electrocution and machine injuries. According to the Canadian Centre for Occupational Health and Safety (CCOHS) <http://www.ccohs.ca>, a number of younger workers are not aware of their health and safety rights and responsibilities at the workplace.

> Across the country, governments are trying to make young workers aware of workplace safety. For instance, Alberta has followed the lead of other provinces and introduced the Work Safe Alberta Video Contest in which high school students submit videos addressing issues relating to safe work. The first place prize is $2,000, with $1,500 for second and $1,000 for third place. The winning videos are available on the Work Safe Alberta webpage (see <http://work.alberta.ca/occupational-health-safety/3608.html>).

Many employees fail to appreciate the wide range of health and safety hazards while performing a job. Consider, for example, a student working part-time as a cook at a small restaurant or fast-food outlet. Potential hazards include exposure to biological and chemical elements, ergonomic issues, and a wide variety of safety risks including electrical shock, cuts, burns, collisions with co-workers, getting a limb or hair caught in a piece of equipment, and so on. For example, a Tim Horton's employee was injured when a car passing through the drive-thru lane hit the worker who was leaning out the window.[20] The CCOHS documents the risks associated with several jobs often performed by younger workers.

> A 16-year-old Grade 10 student got his first summer job at RONA <http://www.rona.ca/en>. On his second shift as a foot soldier in the lumberyard, he hopped on a forklift driven by a friend and co-worker. The 2,300 kilogram forklift was not meant to carry passengers and consequently tipped over and crushed him. He died before paramedics could help him. An online safety campaign <http://work.alberta.ca/occupational-health-safety/bloodylucky.html> focuses on young workers and the importance of safety at work.[21]

LO1 HRC 8

Federal and Provincial Safety Regulations

Each province as well as the federal jurisdiction has detailed legislation addressing health and safety, and most employers and employees are governed by provincial legislation. Although this chapter examines safety legislation at the federal level, students interested in learning about the specific legislation in their province can obtain such information by contacting the relevant provincial government department. Provincial government websites typically contain both the legislative provisions and detailed guides to understanding health and safety law.

At the federal level, the *Canada Labour Code* (Part II) details the elements of an industrial safety program and provides for regulations to deal with various types of occupational safety problems. All provinces and the territories have similar legislation. Part II of the *Code* establishes three fundamental employee rights:

1. The right to know about hazards in the workplace.

2.   The right to participate in correcting those hazards.

3.   The right to refuse dangerous work.

A key element of health and safety laws is the **workplace health and safety committee**, which is usually required in every workplace with 20 or more employees. These committees have a broad range of responsibilities. Some of the major powers and duties of committees under federal jurisdiction include:

- Meeting at least nine times a year, at regular intervals and during regular working hours.

- Considering and expeditiously disposing of health and safety complaints.

- Participating in all of the inquiries, investigations, studies, and inspections pertaining to employee health and safety.

- Ensuring that adequate records are kept on workplace accidents, injuries, and health hazards.

- Participating in the implementation of changes that might affect occupational health and safety.

- Inspecting, each month, all or part of the workplace, so that every part of the workplace is inspected at least once a year.[22]

---

workplace health and safety committee

A group consisting of representatives of the employer and employees that meets regularly in order to reduce accident rates.

Some other relevant federal laws are the *Hazardous Products Act*, the *Transportation of Dangerous Goods Act*, and the *Canadian Centre for Occupational Health and Safety Act*.

Part of the *Hazardous Products Act* and associated regulations concerns hazard classification and communication. The primary objectives of Canada's national hazard communication standard, the **Workplace Hazardous Material Information System (WHMIS)**, include hazard classification, cautionary labelling of containers, the provision of (material) safety data sheets or (M)SDSs, and worker education and training.[23]

Workplace Hazardous Materials Information System (WHMIS)

Legislation that requires suppliers to label all hazardous products and provide a (material) safety data sheet on each.

Although WHMIS provides information on the use of hazardous materials, other countries have different requirements and this is problematic with global trade. In an effort to standardize hazardous materials requirement and communications around the globe, the Globally Harmonized System of Classification and Labelling of Chemicals (GHS) was introduced. Consequently, in February 2015, the Hazardous Products Regulations were amended to incorporate the GHS for workplace chemicals (known as WHMIS 2015, see Figure 12-3). This has resulted in new harmonized criteria for hazard classification and safety data sheets. However, there is a transition period to allow employers and workers to adjust to WHMIS 2015.[24]

The *Transportation of Dangerous Goods Act* makes Transport Canada, a federal government agency, responsible for handling and transporting dangerous materials by federally regulated shipping and transportation companies. It requires that such goods be identified, that a carrier be informed of them, and that they be classified according to a coding system.

FIGURE 12-3

WHMIS Class and Division Hazard Symbols

	Exploding bomb (for explosion or reactivity hazards)		**Flame** (for fire hazards)		**Flame over circle** (for oxidizing hazards)
	Gas cylinder (for gases under pressure)		**Corrosion** (for corrosive damage to metals, as well as skin, eyes)		**Skull and Crossbones** (can cause death or toxicity with short exposure to small amounts)
	Health hazard (may cause or suspected of causing serious health effects)		**Exclamation mark** (may cause less serious health effects of damage the ozone layer*)		**Environment*** (may cause damage to the aquatic anvironment)
	Biohazardous Infectious Materials (for organisms or toxins that can cause diseases in people or animals)				

*The GHS system also defines an Environmental hazards group. This group (and its classes) was not adopted in WHMIS 2015. However, you may see the environmental classes listed on labels and Safety Data Sheets (SDSs). Including information about environmental hazards is allowed by WHIMS 2015.

The *Canadian Centre for Occupational Health and Safety Act* established a public corporation with the following objectives:

(a) to promote health and safety in the workplace in Canada and the physical and mental health of working people in Canada;

(b) to facilitate

   (i) consultation and co-operation among federal, provincial, and territorial jurisdictions, and

   (ii) participation by labour and management in the establishment and maintenance of high standards of occupational health and safety appropriate to the Canadian situation;

(c) to assist in the development and maintenance of policies and programs aimed at the reduction or elimination of occupational hazards; and

(d) to serve as a national centre for statistics and other information relating to occupational health and safety.[25]

The CCOHS is supervised by a board of governors made up of representatives of the federal government, labour, and employers. Several hundred organizations are now connected electronically with the centre and have access to information relating to health and safety generally and to hazardous materials specifically.

The administration of safety programs comes mainly under provincial jurisdiction. Each province has legislated specific programs for the various industries and occupations within it. Across the country, provinces are following a trend of consolidating health and safety legislation and streamlining the enforcement of the relevant statutes by combining different agencies into one body.[26]

Safety Enforcement

In the federal jurisdiction, there have been some significant changes to the *Canada Labour Code* as it relates to health and safety. Among the changes is the removal of references to "health and safety officers," replaced by "the Minister." This change would make the Minister responsible for exercising the duties historically performed by health and safety inspectors or delegating the duties to another party. Section 141 of the *Canada Labour Code* (Part II) details these powers:

1. The Minister may, in carrying out the Minister's duties and at any reasonable time, enter any work place controlled by an employer and, in respect of any work place, may:

   (a) conduct examinations, tests, inquiries, investigations and inspections or direct the employer to conduct them;

   (b) take or remove for analysis, samples of any material or substance or any biological, chemical or physical agent;

   (c) be accompanied or assisted by any person and bring any equipment that the officer deems necessary to carry out the Minister's duties;

   (d) take or remove, for testing, material or equipment if there is no reasonable alternative to doing so;

   (e) take photographs and make sketches;

   (f) direct the employer to ensure that any place or thing specified by the Minister not be disturbed for a reasonable period of time pending an examination, test, inquiry, investigation or inspection in relation to the place or thing;

   (g) direct any person not to disturb any place or thing specified by the Minister for a reasonable period pending an examination, test, inquiry, investigation, or inspection in relation to the place or thing;

   (h) direct the employer to produce documents and information relating to the health and safety of the employer's employees or the safety of the workplace and to permit the Minister to examine and make copies or take extracts from those documents and that information;

   (i) direct the employer or an employee to make or provide statements, in the form and manner that the Minister may specify, respecting working conditions and material and equipment that affect the health or safety of employees;

   (j) direct the employer or an employee or a person designated by either of them to accompany the Minister while the Minister is in the workplace; and

   (k) meet with any person in private or, at the request of the person, in the presence of the person's legal counsel or union representative.[27]

Provincial laws provide similar powers to safety officers under their jurisdiction.

Syncrude Canada <http://www.syncrude.ca> was fined $365,000 when a worker in Alberta died. The employee, who was using steam to clear ice on pipes, was struck by a large slab of ice, weighing several hundred kilograms, and was crushed against the metal railings. Most of the money was targeted toward developing a new course at Keyano College in Fort McMurray and $100,000 was set aside to be used for scholarships in the deceased worker's name.[28]

In Alberta, the introduction of administrative penalties and tickets is leading to the levying of fines to employers and employees. Penalties can include a fine of up to $10,000 a day for each safety violation. On-the-spot tickets to employers, contractors, employees, and suppliers can range from $100 to $500. Mark Hill of the Yukon Workers Compensation Health and Safety Board <https://wcb.yk.ca> reports that in the Yukon, "fines have had a dramatic effect on workplace behaviour, with the vast majority of workplaces now ensuring appropriate personal protective equipment is worn (not long ago, this was the exception rather than the rule)." However, safety consultant Alan Quilley disagrees when he asserts that "from my perspective, there is nothing in human history that says we can fine ourselves into excellence."[29]

A Nova Scotia employee fell to his death from the sixth floor of an apartment building under construction in the fall of 2013. The Nova Scotia Occupational Health and Safety division has laid charges against the employer, Parkland Construction, with failing to provide adequate fall protection, fall protection training, and a safe work plan. A company supervisor has also been charged with failing to provide fall protection and failing to take every precaution to protect an employee's health. The company could be fined up to $500,000 and the supervisor could receive a jail term of up to two years.[30]

As a general principle, an occupational health and safety inspector may enter a business to carry out his or her duties without notice or a warrant. When an OHS (Occupational Health and Safety) inspector arrives at the workplace the employer should do the following:

1. Be diligent—take notes on everything the inspector says and answer questions directly without a lot of narrative.

2. Be prepared—have the documentation for due diligence in order and follow your safety procedures to the letter (as the inspector may be testing the employer to see if the rules are actually followed).

3. Stay covered—post the safety policy inside the front door and easily visible to the safety inspector and choose an employee who will be designated to deal with the inspector.[31]

On the other hand, there are examples where safety standards may not be rigorously enforced:

Two explosions at British Columbia sawmills a few months apart resulted in four deaths and 40 other workers being badly injured. However, in both cases, the Criminal Justice Branch has been unable to bring charges because WorkSafeBC did not warn the sawmills about the hazards associated with high levels of combustible sawdust and then failed to investigate the incidents properly.[32] In a 2012–2013 review of the health and safety division, Nova Scotia auditor general Jacques Lapointe found that, over a one year period, more than 1,225 orders (about 32 percent of the total) were not complied with and just 27 of the 100 workplaces with the highest safety risk rating were inspected. According to Lapointe, "you have only a limited number of inspectors with a lot of work to do…part of it involves focusing a little better on inspecting targeted workplaces. And make sure inspectors do follow up."[33]

LO2 HRC 8

Responsibility for Health and Safety

So far the focus in this chapter has been on the legal requirements for maintaining a safe and healthy work environment. It should be emphasized, however, that these must be seen as the minimum requirements for employers. A major purpose of occupational health and safety laws is to prevent injuries from happening.

> An electrician working on a switchboard in a sewage treatment facility in Dartmouth, Nova Scotia, was badly burned due to electrical arcing resulting from the build-up of silver fines. The electrician successfully sued the Halifax Regional Municipality <http://www.region.halifax.ns.ca> and was awarded a settlement of $90,000 for extreme pain and loss of his profession, $68,119 for lost income, and $1,713 in special damages. In finding the City liable, Nova Scotia Supreme Court Justice Gerald Moir stated that "the content of the duty of care to the employee included reasonably regular inspection and cleaning of the motor control centres. The failure to inspect or clean for years, if not decades, caused the silver fines to go undetected."[34]

> The list of 2015 *Canada's Top 100 Employers* revealed that leading organizations place considerable attention on safety. At steelmaker ArcelorMittal <http://corporate.arcelormittal.com>, safety is a key component of the healthy workplace strategy. According to millwright Giovanni Cisternino, "There is an open door policy. Zero accidents is one of our big goals. If there's an accident at a brother or sister plant across the globe, we'll discuss how to prevent that type of accident." Enerflex <http://www.enerflex.com>, which supplies products and services to the oil and gas industry, is also highly committed to safety. In the words of engineering manager Ryan Hesketh, "Another company principle is 'Everyone Home. Every Night.' This focuses on safety, not hours of work. No matter where home is that night, we want our people to get there safely, for themselves and their families."[35]

Historically, it was believed that the responsibility for health and safety rested primarily with the employer. However, this view is changing. A number of jurisdictions have legislation requiring the establishment of joint health and safety committees or health and safety representatives as mentioned above. The requirement of establishing a joint committee varies among the provinces; for example, a committee may be required if a workplace has a minimum number of employees (typically 10 or 20 workers). The relevant legislation will outline the duties of the committee (such as maintaining records, conducting meetings, inspecting the workplace, and so on) and the makeup of the committee (number of members, employee representation on the committee, and so on).

As pointed out above, there is also a focus on educating young employees about workplace safety. Several programs exist to make young workers aware of safety issues, to educate them about safety, and to provide information on rights and obligations under safety legislation.[36]

No law, by itself, can make a workplace safe. It is far more effective—and less costly in the long run—if the responsibility for safety becomes a concern for everyone: top management, supervisors, and employees.

> A bus driver was attacked from behind and punched in the face and shoulder by an intoxicated female passenger while driving down a Winnipeg street. The union representing transit drivers has argued for the provision of face shields to drivers and training in self-defence. Winnipeg Transit <http://winnipegtransit.com/en>has installed on-bus video-and audio-recording devices and is revising employee training to include basic self-defence skills. While the use of face shields is being studied, there are concerns that they may impact on the ability of the drivers to operate buses and provide quality customer service.[37]

Many organizations neglect safety issues when designing orientation programs. A comprehensive safety orientation program will address several issues such as fire safety, smoking at the workplace, accident procedures, personal clothing, protective equipment, material and chemical hazards, waste disposal, safety representatives and the safety committee, occupational health, and the safety policy or policies in existence. It is important that employees understand the various issues and know how to respond in a crisis situation.[38]

Similarly, employers often fail to consider the safety issues related with shift work. According to the Institute for Work and Health <http://www.iwh.on.ca>, about 30 percent of Canadians work shift work or are on call. Shift workers may experience higher stress and may be prone to an increase in accidents and mistakes due to such factors as sleepiness and fatigue. One study indicated that individuals working outside of regular daytime hours are 1.5 times more likely to be injured at work and this rate rises around 2.5 times if a person alternates working between day and night shifts. In addition, shiftworkers may not eat properly and those on longer shifts may be at a greater risk resulting from exposure to health hazards. Of particular note is that shift workers are most at risk when they are driving home from work.[39]

Research from the University of Pennsylvania study revealed that chronic disruptions in a person's sleep cycle, which is often experienced by shift workers, could lead to damaged neurons in the brain and permanent brain damage. There is also evidence that shift workers are more likely to have a higher risk of injury at work and preliminary studies suggest a link with heart disease, mental health issues, and certain types of cancers.[40] A Global Corporate Challenge Insights study reported that about one in five employees is sleep deprived. Also, 93 percent of poor sleepers were more likely to show signs of workplace fatigue which is a common symptom of "excessive daytime sleepiness" (EDS). EDS, in turn, is associated with higher rates of absenteeism and greater accident and injury rates at work.[41]

LO3

Top Management

Top management must set policies and make concern for health and safety part of the organization's culture and strategy. This ensures that health and safety aspects will be considered whenever business decisions are made and training programs developed. A failure on the part of managers to pay attention to health and safety issues is being considered seriously by the courts in Canada. Consider the following cases:

> Petro-Canada <http://www.petro-canada.ca> was fined $150,000 after a worker at a refinery was severely burned when steam and scalding water poured out of a tank. Shaw Cable Systems <http://www.shaw.ca> was fined $75,000 when an employee was severely burned after making contact with an unguarded and uninsulated power line. The company failed to appoint a safety watcher and failed to provide safety equipment where there was a high-voltage hazard. TDL Spring and Suspension Specialists was fined $120,000 for violating safety regulations after an employee died when a sidebin on a recycling truck he was working on fell and crushed the worker. The sidebin had blocking pins to prevent the bin from falling, but they were not used and the employer failed to provide proper tools to prevent the bin from falling.[42]

Some organizations, recognizing that they lack the internal expertise to address safety issues, are now outsourcing some health and safety needs. Options for such firms include hiring a health and safety expert on a part-time or contract basis or seeking the assistance of a firm that specializes in health and safety. While the cost of a health and safety consultant generally ranges from about $50 to $150 or more per hour, companies often save three to five times the cost of the consulting bill by reducing the number of safety incidents at the workplace. According to one safety consultant:

Safety gear, such as that worn by construction workers, is essential to reducing work injuries. Should penalties be imposed for not wearing it?

> We get invited to a workplace that has just bought all new work stations and ergonomic chairs. And they would have ended up saving all that money, and prevented musculoskeletal injuries, if they had just asked for advice beforehand. The earlier an ergonomist is brought in, the cheaper it is. For every dollar you spend at the design stage, it will cost you a hundred times more to fix it at the implementation stage.[43]

The Bill C-45 amendments to the *Criminal Code* imposed a new duty on individuals and organizations. Section 217.1 of the *Criminal Code* states:

> Everyone who undertakes, or has the authority, to direct how another person does or performs work or performs a task is under a legal duty to take reasonable steps to prevent bodily harm to that person, or any other person, arising from that work or task.

The first Bill C-45 conviction involved the death of an employee in Quebec:

> Transpavé <http://www.transpave.com>, a stone-paving manufacturer, was fined $110,000 for criminal negligence causing death after a 23-year-old employee was crushed by a machine being used with an unplugged safety device. The employee's mother was disappointed with the amount of the fine, saying that she expected a fine to be millions of dollars.[44]

There has been a lot of criticism about Bill C-45, which celebrated its 10th anniversary in 2014, and relatively few cases have resulted from the legislation. In the *R. v Metron Construction* case, six employees got on a swing stage to go down 14 stories. The swing, which had only two lifelines, collapsed and four of the workers died in the fall. Subsequent investigation revealed that the swing stage was defective and failed to meet Ontario safety standards. In addition, three employees, including the site supervisor, had marijuana in their system. Metron pleaded guilty to criminal negligence charges and the judge imposed a $200,000 fine. However, the Court of Appeal felt that the fine did not reflect the moral blameworthiness and gravity of Metron's conduct and substituted a fine of $750,000. [45]

Other countries are also developing legislation making safety violations a criminal offence:

> A British firm was the first company to be charged with corporate manslaughter under the United Kingdom's 2007 *Corporate Manslaughter Act*. A 27-year-old geologist was killed when the pit he was working near collapsed. Cotswold Geotechnical Holdings director Peter Eaton was charged and convicted of gross negligence manslaughter and fined £385,000. An organization is guilty of corporate manslaughter if "the way senior management organizes or manages the business activities causes a person's death and amounts to a gross breach of the firm's duty of care owed to the person who died."

Since the legislation was passed, there have only been four convictions. However, there is a proposal to introduce tougher sentencing guidelines and a maximum fine of up to £20 million. [46]

One CEO, Robert Watson of SaskPower <http://www.saskpower.com>, tendered his resignation after a report indicated that workplace safety was not enough of a priority. SaskPower was ordered to remove more than 100,000 smart meters that had been installed in homes after it was found that at least eight of the meters caught fire. The province's Economy Minister stated that "Watson took responsibility for the problems experienced with this project. He felt it was time that there was new leadership." A review revealed that the meter project was rushed, no one was responsible for the overall program, and there was insufficient attention to customer safety. [47]

Supervisors

As part of their management training, supervisors must become proficient in managing safety, which means knowing about health and safety laws, safety regulations, training in observing safety violations, and learning communication skills to convey the necessary information to their employees.

> A roofing company in Dartmouth, Nova Scotia, was fined $25,000 and a victim surcharge of $3,750 and a supervisor was fined $8,000 and a surcharge of $1,200 after they pleaded guilty to failing to reasonably ensure the health and safety of an employee who died after falling through a hole in the roof of a school. Plywood originally covering a skylight opening had been taken away and the employee fell through the foam insulation covering the hole. The company admitted that the accident could possibly have been avoided if more stringent safety procedures were in place. The accident was particularly hard on the employee's supervisor, who was a friend of the employee and got him employment with the company while they were working at the school. [48]

The ingredients of an effective safety training program include the following:

- accident investigation and analysis;
- communication skills and report writing;
- overview of legislative requirements;
- meeting with management and objective setting;
- organization and responsibility of joint health and safety committee;
- team problem-solving/problem-solving techniques;
- audits and inspections;

- principles of occupational health and safety; and

- ergonomics.

An issue that supervisors may have to deal with, but feel uncomfortable about, involves an employee's right to refuse unsafe work. It is important that the supervisor know the provincial legislation relating to work refusals and recognize the importance of taking every work refusal seriously (even if the supervisor believes that the work is safe).

> David Law, a lawyer specializing in health and safety, believes that "whenever employees feel so concerned about their health risks that they would resort to such a drastic measure as refusing to work, the first thing you do is shut up and listen. To dismiss out of hand would be disrespectful about an issue that, in the employee's perception, could have serious, harmful consequences. People are often very poor judges of risk, but if we don't listen to them, what can they conclude except that we don't care?"[49]

Almost 90 percent of safety professionals report seeing workers not wearing personal protective equipment (PPE) when they should have, with 29 percent reporting that this has happened on numerous occasions. The most common compliance challenges involving PPE relate to eye protection, hearing guards, and respiratory protection or masks. The two most pressing workplace issues relating to safety involve worker compliance and managing safety with fewer workers.[50]

There are also examples where supervisors do not assume proper responsibility for safety. A British Columbia mine run by Imperial Metals Corp. <http://www.imperialmetals.com> spilled millions of cubic metres of waste into nearby waterways. According to a local United Steelworkers executive, workers had warned company officials of safety issues months before the spill. In his words, "not everybody's saying it, but you get guys coming in who are saying that it's looking dangerous." It was not known whether the warnings stayed with supervisors or went higher up the organization.[51]

Employees

While employers are responsible for providing a safe work environment, and supervisors are responsible for the safety of their people in the workplace, employees are responsible for working safely. Employees must be trained to understand safety rules and how to operate equipment safely.

> Teenager Sarah Wheelan began working part-time at a deli counter of a supermarket. Standard practice was to clean the machines between each use. Rather than taking the machine apart and washing the blade, the practice was to hold one's hand to a spinning blade and clean the blade. While Wheelan did not lose any fingers or suffer any injuries, it took her about two months to get up the courage to confront her supervisor, concerned that she would look stupid or unable to handle the pressure and responsibility of the job. Her supervisor, a butcher, told her that new butchers would frequently nick themselves or lose a finger—that was just the nature of the job. One week later, Wheelan quit.[52]

It is also important that a system of enforcement is in place, understood, and followed. If necessary, progressive discipline has to be applied for violation of safety rules in the same way as for other rule violations.

There is a growing, but fairly recent, recognition that employers need to consider the needs of female employees when it comes to health and safety. For example, safety protection gear and equipment such as tools and harnesses may not be suitable for female employees. In addition, training programs need to be examined—how to carry equipment, for instance, may differ depending on a person's height, weight, and strength.[53]

Good safety performance should be recognized and rewarded by managers. On the other side, unsatisfactory practices should be documented and corrected. Rewarding good performance is preferable. The objective of safety incentives should be to promote safety awareness and should therefore benefit as many workers as possible. Group awards may help to reinforce safety-consciousness through peer pressure. In addition, the importance of safety training cannot be overemphasized:

> Thirty-two miners in Esterhazy, Saskatchewan, were trapped one kilometre below ground while a fire burned at the Mosaic <http://www.mosaicco.com> potash mine. The miners stayed in "refuge stations" (chambers that can be sealed off and are equipped with food, water, and beds) and waited to be rescued. The situation ended with the rescue of the miners, and it was acknowledged that their safety training was invaluable. As one miner said, "Follow every rule you were taught, even if they don't make sense, and it all works out in the end."[54]

A typical OHS training session may involve a day or more of in-class training and more than 500 slides that are communicated to the participants. Recognizing that traditional programs were not meeting their objectives in terms of keeping employees safe at work, the Canadian Manufacturers and Exporters <http://www.cme-mec.ca> set up a two-year project to examine OHS training. The result was a new training program offered both face-to-face and over the Internet with homework assignments completed at the workplace. Among the features of the training were videos showing employees how to conduct a task-and-hazard analysis, role play simulations, and training set up for workers with low levels of literacy or understanding of English.[55]

The failure to train can have serious consequences:

> A 17 year-old boy suffered an asthmatic attack at a Tim Horton's in London, Ontario. The teenager was able to say "help" and "phone" but the staff told him that the phone was not for public use and directed him to a pay phone across the street. A customer witnessing the incident called 911 and stayed with the boy until medical help arrived. Norm Keith, a Toronto lawyer, noted that "employers have a general duty to ensure that everyone, not just workers, are safe in the workplace. Assuming the worst—a pandemic, health concerns, someone fainting at work because of a health incident—you have to have a plan that deals with that." As a result of the incident, Tim Horton's employees will be given a refresher course and training on what to do in an emergency situation.[56]

Organizations operating in foreign countries may need to provide specialized training to workers going to such locations. To meet this requirement, progressive employers are recognizing the importance of employee training in global hotspots (areas of political, social, or civil unrest that are potentially dangerous).[57]

LO4 HRC 8

Implications for Human Resource Management

Human resource professionals should ensure consistent enforcement of all safety and health rules. If one worker is allowed to violate safety rules, other workers may follow—and if an accident results, the employer may be subject to penalties.

> In the United States, Walmart was fined $2 million after a temporary maintenance employee was trampled to death by bargain-hungry shoppers. Although the company was not charged criminally, it implemented a new crowd-management plan.[58]

> Transocean Ltd. <http://www.deepwater.com> rewarded top executives with bonuses for achieving "the best year in safety performance in our company's history." Most senior managers received two-thirds of their maximum safety bonus despite the fact that an explosion of a company oil rig killed 11 people and spilled

more than 750 million litres of oil into the Gulf of Mexico. The company said that it still had an exemplary safety record, because it met or exceeded a number of internal safety targets.[59]

Health and safety law permits an employee to refuse to work when working conditions are perceived to be unsafe. In such instances, the employee should report the circumstances of the matter to his or her supervisor or to the supervisor's manager and to the safety committee in the firm. In most jurisdictions, an employee with reasonable cause to believe that the work is unsafe will not receive any loss in pay for refusing to work.

Recent changes in Ontario law now make safety training mandatory. All supervisors and employees covered by the OHSA are required to complete a one-hour training program which is designed to inform the parties of their rights and responsibilities in creating a culture of safety. As noted by Rob Ellis of MySafeWork <http://www.mysafework.com>, "most Canadians still don't understand that they have the right to say no to unsafe work, and I find it shocking that most Canadians still fear putting up their hand and reporting unsafe work."[60]

When charged with a health and safety offence, a company's best defence is "due diligence," which means that the company took all reasonable steps to avoid the particular event. In examining the organization's behaviour, the court considers several factors including the magnitude of the risks involved and the nature of the potential harm, with a focus on the part of the safety program designed to prevent the accident in question. An effective safety program only helps establish due diligence—preparing a defence based on due diligence begins well before an accident ever happens.[61]

Health and Safety Audit

With increased attention on health and safety, more and more organizations are having a health and safety audit conducted. Some of these audits are voluntary and others are as a result of being targeted by government health and safety officials. While health and safety audits vary, they may include a review of the employer's occupational health and safety documentation (such as training records, manuals, etc.), a tour of the workplace, and interviews (and/or surveys) of front-line employees, supervisors, and senior management.

Of course, some employers may decide to take the risk and not comply with health and safety standards. As one lawyer stated:

> I think that there has always been a lack of enforcement and that has been well known and for many employers that is all they need to know. No matter how good the laws are, they know that they will not be enforced.[62]

However, failing to comply may be a risky proposition:

> The Transportation Safety Board of Canada (TSB) <http://www.bst-tsb.gc.ca/eng> found that 254 incidents involving Canadian National, Canadian Pacific <http://www.cpr.ca/en>, and Montreal, Maine and Atlantic (the railway involved in the Lac-Megantic Quebec derailment that killed 47 people) were not reported over a seven-year period. The TSB has made it clear that the railroads are expected to comply with the regulations and a spokesperson for Canadian National stated that "CN will continue to focus on every safety incident as a leading indicator of potentially more serious accidents."[63]

Consequently, a growing number of employers are being more proactive and rather than waiting for a provincial audit, they are either conducting internal audits or hiring consultants to assess the health and safety system. A number of provinces, such as Nova Scotia, provide detailed information on how to establish and evaluate a health and safety system.[64]

HRC 8

Safety Climate

According to an HR manager for a Calgary road-building company, "Safety is all about the way you run your business. Wherever you see poor safety there is always a poor-run company. The unfortunate aspect is that the ownership isn't even aware that it is poorly run. If a company has a poor attitude toward safety, it makes us wonder if that attitude is indicative of other aspects of their business."[65]

Why should employers and human resource professionals be concerned with safety climate? There is growing evidence that safety climate is an important factor affecting safety knowledge and motivation. Neal and Griffin, two leading scholars specializing in workplace safety, have developed a framework for conceptualizing safety climate (perceptions about the value of safety in an organization) and safety behaviour.[66] They assert that safety climate is an important factor affecting safety knowledge and motivation, which in turn impacts on safety behaviour (see Figure 12-4).

About seven years ago, and faced with one of the worst injury rates in the country, Saskatchewan introduced a new educational campaign called "Mission Zero" in an effort to reduce workplace deaths and injuries. The chair of the Saskatchewan Workers Compensation Board (WCB) <http://www.wcbsask.com>, noted that safety requires that employers and employees work together with the same goal of a safe work environment and asserted that safety is "an attitude thing" with a culture where safety is out front. The program is still going strong—according to Donna Kane, VP of HR and Communications at WCB, "we believe every injury is preventable and that's why Mission Zero is core to everything we do."[67]

FIGURE 12-4

A Framework for Conceptualizing Safety Climate and Safety Behaviour

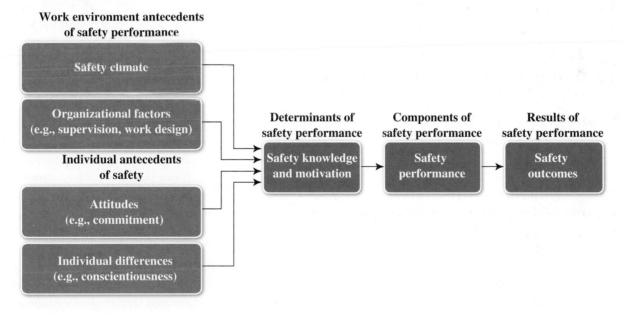

SOURCE: Andrew Neal and Mark Griffin, "Safety Climate and Safety at Work," in Julian Barling and Michael Frone (Eds.), *The Psychology of Workplace Safety*, Washington, DC: American Psychological Association, 2004, p. 17.

Neal and Griffin outline eight dimensions of safety climate. Organizational level dimensions include the following:

- management commitment to safety (does management place a high priority on safety and communicate and act on safety issues effectively?)

- human resource management practices (to what extent are the HRM practices of the organization perceived to enhance safety?)

- safety systems (to what extent are hazard management systems, incident investigation, and safety policies and procedures perceived to be effective and of high quality?)

Local work group dimensions include the following:

- supervisor support for safety (including placing a high priority on safety and responding to safety issues)

- internal group processes (communication and support for safety issues within the group)

- boundary management (quality of communication between the group and other stakeholders)

- risk (are the work tasks perceived to be hazardous, dangerous, or unsafe?)

- work pressure (is workload perceived to exceed the employee's capacity to perform the work safely?)

The importance of top management commitment is critical:

> A report to the House of Commons described the "culture of fear" at Canadian National Railways. CN received a score of 1 out of 5 when evaluated on its efforts to implementing the safety management standards introduced as an update to the *Railway Safety Act*. Railway workers described how difficult it was to develop a safety culture when they were working in a culture of fear in which they feared reprisals and disciplinary action if they voiced concerns relating to safety. There was evidence that safety management systems were getting little more than lip service, thus increasing the risk of train derailments and other accidents. According to one former employee, "we had it drummed into our heads if trains aren't running on time, somebody would want to know why and it could mean our jobs."[68]

HRC 1 & 2 & 4 & 8

Downsizing and Safety

Another issue that is beginning to attract attention is the relationship between downsizing and employee safety. This is particularly relevant in light of the number of downsizings announced in recent years. The research evidence suggests that downsizing creates job insecurity, which is strongly associated with low levels of job satisfaction. Low job satisfaction, in turn, is related to *safety motivation* (the motivation to perform a job in a safe manner) and *safety knowledge* (an understanding of safe operating procedures). When safety motivation is low, employees are less likely to comply with safety procedures and carry out their work in a safe manner (what is known as *safety compliance*). Finally, lower levels of safety compliance are associated with more workplace accidents. It is suggested that during a downsizing, employees concerned with keeping their jobs view productivity as more important than safety. However, in downsizings in which employees perceived that the safety climate was positive and the organization viewed safety as very important, the negative outcomes associated with job insecurity were not seen.[69]

Spotlight *on* ETHICS

A Question of Safety

Consider the following situation and make a note of your answer on a separate sheet of paper.

You are a supervisor at a local dairy. Your job involves supervising employees who work in the dairy while another individual is responsible for supervising the employees who deliver milk to various stores. In the past six months, the labour market has been fairly tight and your company has been having problems attracting and retaining good delivery people.

Two weeks ago, the human resource management department hired a new milk delivery employee named Lucy Lynn. Lucy's job involves driving a milk van and making deliveries to grocery stores. By all accounts, Lucy is a very competent and reliable employee, and the human resource professional who hired her did so without any hesitation. Lucy is also the mother of one of your best friends. Lucy, who is 54 years of age, was recently downsized from her job as a delivery person at a large courier company.

Two days ago, you were invited to dinner at Lucy's house. Lucy commented on how much she was enjoying her new job and how grateful she was to obtain employment so quickly. Lucy had recently gone through a messy divorce, and you were aware that she was having some financial problems.

Just after dinner, you went out to the kitchen and found Lucy sitting on a chair with her head resting on the kitchen table. When you asked whether she was okay, she replied that "Everything is fine. It's just that over the last few months, I have been getting really bad headaches and have had three or four dizzy spells. When my head starts whirling, I just need to sit down and put my head between my knees. it's no big deal—the dizziness passes in a few minutes. I'm telling you this in confidence. Please don't tell anyone at work. I can't afford to lose my job."

What are you going to do? Complicating the decision is that you know the company asks individuals who will be driving company vehicles to provide a detailed medical history. The questions include whether the individual has experienced dizzy spells and severe headaches. After completing the form, individuals are required to sign that they have answered the questions honestly and to the best of their ability.

LO5 HRC 8

Workplace Stress

The term *stress management* is now part of the regular vocabulary of managers and employees, but what is "workplace stress"? *Workplace stress* is "the harmful physical and emotional responses that can happen when there is a conflict between job demands of the employee and the amount of control the employee has over meeting those demands."[70] Although high levels of stress are usually associated with poorer job performance, it should be emphasized that not all stress is harmful. Moderate levels of stress may actually increase workplace performance.

A ComPsych survey indicated that 64 percent of employees have high levels of stress, with extreme fatigue / feeling out of control, 31 percent report having constant but manageable stress, and 5 percent indicate having low stress levels. In terms of the impact of stress, 35 percent of employees report losing 1 hour or more a day in productivity due to stress, 55 percent miss 1 to 2 days due to stress, 29 percent miss 3 to 6 days, and 16 percent more than 6 days a year.[71]

Similarly, a study of more than 7,300 employees by Globe Careers / Howatt HR Consulting revealed that about 6 out of 10 people felt stressed and on edge. Respondents were placed in one of five categories (Calm to Losing It) based on their scores on a Quality of Life scale. In the Calm group, 26 percent were senior managers or executives, 96 percent said they put 80 percent or more effort into their job each day, 2 percent indicated suffering from a mental health issue and 16 percent reported calling in sick more than four days a year. For the Losing It group, only 9 percent were senior managers or executives, 52 percent said they put 80 percent or more effort into their job every day, 4 percent responded that they suffered from a mental health issue, and 48 percent stated that they called in sick more than four days a year. The Losing It group were more likely to report not being a good fit for their job, that the work culture was not positive, that they had trouble sleeping, suffered from headaches, did not receive adequate performance feedback, and would leave the organization if they could. [72]

It is estimated that stress-related absences cost the Canadian economy more than $4.5 billion a year, have increased more than threefold since 1995, and average about 20 days in length. Health Canada suggests that each dollar invested in the prevention of stress is worth about $3.40 in future savings.[73]

The actual experience or the perceived threat of a corporate takeover, merger, downsizing, or plant closing, all of which could put large numbers of employees out of jobs, can lead to a variety of symptoms of stress that can harm employees' job performance. These symptoms involve both mental health and physical health. Persons who are stressed may become nervous, easily provoked to anger, and chronically worried about things.

Too much stress on the job can lead to employee burnout. What measures can an employer take to reduce stress? Can stress be avoided?

Tom Grill/Getty Images.

There is a growing body of research indicating that stress may be associated with cardiovascular disease (in particular, among employees in psychologically demanding jobs that allow workers little control over the work process), musculoskeletal disorders (such as back injuries), psychological disorders (for example, depression and burnout), workplace injuries, suicide, cancer, ulcers, and impaired immune functions.[74] In addition, employer immunity from lawsuits as a result of contributing to the workers' compensation system is being eroded as more courts allow employees to sue their employers for stress resulting from a poisoned work environment.

Although there has been a lot of effort aimed at protecting employees from physical harm at work, experts are now calling for greater attention to psychological safety at work. According to Lorne Zon, former CEO of the Canadian Mental Health Association <https://www.cmha.ca> (Ontario Division), "we expect psychological safety in our schools and communities, and we should be able to count on it in the workplace. If employees don't feel safe speaking to their managers or co-workers, because they are afraid of recrimination, the workplace is not psychologically safe and productivity will be affected."[75]

In early 2013, the National Standard on Psychological Health and Safety in the Workplace was published. The purposes of the National Standard are to identify and eliminate hazards in the workplace that pose a risk of psychological harm to a worker and assess and control the risks associated with hazards that cannot be eliminated, implement structures and practices that support and promote psychological health and safety in the workplace, and foster a culture that promotes psychological health and safety in the workplace.[76]

Causes of Stress at Work

A model of job stress has been developed by the National Institute for Occupational Safety and Health <http://www.cdc.gov/niosh> in the United States.[77] According to the model, exposure to stressful working conditions (called "job stressors") can directly influence the health and safety of employees. However, the model also recognizes that individual and situational factors can intervene to strengthen or weaken the relationship between stressful job conditions and the risk of injury or illness. Examples of individual and situational factors include one's outlook or attitude, the presence of a support network of co-workers or friends, and the balance between work and family life. Although major distress can occur from only one stressor, usually **stressors** combine to affect an employee in a variety of ways until distress develops.

stressors

Stressful working conditions that can directly influence the health and safety of employees.

While almost any job condition may cause stress (depending upon an employee's reaction to it), there are, however, a number of job conditions that frequently cause stress for employees. Some of the major causes of workplace stress are outlined in Figure 12-5.

It is also possible to distinguish between *acute stressors*, which occur infrequently but are extremely stressful events (such as a major organizational change), and *chronic stressors*, which are the ongoing, daily problems and hassles that occur at work. While many wellness programs are aimed at chronic stress, organizations regularly ignore the impacts on employees associated with major organizational changes.

FIGURE 12-5

Causes of Workplace Stress

Factors Unique to the Job	**Relationships at Work**
• Workload	• Supervisors/co-workers/subordinates
• Work pace/variety/meaningfulness of work	• Threat of violence, harassment, and so on
• Autonomy	**Organizational Climate**
• Hours of work/shift work	• Participation (or nonparticipation) in decision making
• Physical environment (noise, air quality, etc.)	• Management style
• Isolation (physical or emotional)	• Communication patterns
Role in the Organization	**Career Development**
• Role conflict/role ambiguity	• Under- or overpromotion
• Level of responsibility	• Job security
	• Career-development opportunities
	• Overall job satisfaction

SOURCE: Based on "Major Causes of Workplace Stress." Adapted from L.R. Murphy, "Occupational Stress Management: Current Status and Future Direction," *Trends in Organizational Behavior*, 1995, pp. 1–14.

With many employers cutting back on staff, employees are being told to work smarter, but there is evidence that many are not able to face the added pressure. One study found that as people work longer hours, their risk of injury and illness goes up. This includes workplace accidents, depression, hypertension, stress, cardiovascular disease, and chronic infections.[78]

Recent evidence from Statistics Canada revealed that more than one in four workers (about 3.7 million working adults) reported life as being "highly stressed." For highly stressed individuals, the main source of stress was, in fact, work (63 percent), followed by finances (12 percent), time (12 percent), and family issues (8 percent). Respondents with poorer physical and mental health were more likely to be highly stressed. Workers who were mainly stressed about work tended to be well-educated and have white-collar jobs, workers anxious about finances had lower incomes and less skilled jobs, and women were more likely to be stressed about family matters.[79]

What are the most stressful jobs? A 2015 CareerCast study revealed that the most stressful jobs are fire fighter, enlisted military personnel, military general, airline pilot, and police officer. The least stressful jobs included hair stylist, audiologist, university professor, medical records technician, and jeweller.[80]

Poor supervision can cause stress. For example, the following stressful conditions are mostly created by poor supervision: an insecure workplace climate, lack of performance feedback, and inadequate authority to match one's responsibilities. Workers frequently complain in private about "bad bosses."

A study of workers in Finland revealed that a bad boss may be hazardous to employee health. Employees who perceived that they were being treated fairly at work by their supervisors had a 30 percent lower risk of coronary heart disease compared with co-workers who did not believe that their supervisors treated them fairly.[81]

A general and widely recognized cause of stress is *change of any type*, because it requires adaptation by employees. Change tends to be especially stressful when it is major, unusual, or frequent. One particular type of change that dominated the 1990s and is becoming more common since the global financial crisis is *organizational* downsizing. In many organizations, the "survivors" of workplace change are being asked to work longer hours and do more with limited resources. Working in such an environment may increase both employee stress and the probability of having an accident. As well, downsizing may have an impact on an employee's family. Research suggests that the job loss of a parent affects their children. Perceptions of the job insecurity of a parent were associated with negative attitudes toward work and lower grades on exams.[82]

Evidence from the Global Business and Economic Roundtable on Addiction and Mental Health indicates that about 18 to 25 percent of American and Canadian workers suffer from depression, and employers are losing billions of dollars due to lost productivity and a lower capacity to compete. In order to build a healthy workplace, CEOs must value a psychologically healthy and safe workplace and be willing to walk the talk.[83] Consider the impact of stress on Canadian call centre workers:

> A study of call centre employees revealed that employees in the industry suffer higher rates of stress and emotional difficulty than workers in other industries. The call centre industry currently employs about half a million Canadians. It is estimated that among 100 recent hires at a call centre, 14 percent may experience high levels of stress and 10 percent may experience high levels of depression. Each day about 10 percent of employees call in sick, turnover may run as high as 50 percent or more a year, and the cost of training a replacement employee is more than $6,000. As observed by Karen Seward, senior vice-president at Shepell-fgi <http://www.shepellfgi.com>, "It doesn't take long to do the math to figure out the impact of this on a company's profits."[84]

Burnout

Burnout is a condition of mental, emotional, and sometimes physical exhaustion that results from substantial and prolonged stress. It can occur for any type of employee, whether one is a professional employee, secretary, or labourer. There is growing concern over what has become known as *presenteeism*, which describes an employee who is able to come to work but is inhibited from achieving optimal levels of productivity due to ongoing health issues.[85] One employee described a burned-out associate in the following way: "His body is here today, but his mind stayed home." Employers cannot merely ignore requests by an employee for help:

> Suzanne Zorn-Smith, a 21-year employee of a Canadian bank, suffered from burnout due to the heavy workload placed on her. She sought EAP counselling and then applied for short-term disability, citing exhaustion, inability to focus, and feeling overwhelmed. The bank took the position that the injury was not totally disabling and demanded that she return to work on a specified date or they would assume that the employment relationship was over. Zorn-Smith did not return to work by the specified date and sued the bank for wrongful dismissal. The court found that she was entitled to a 16-month notice period (or compensation in lieu of notice) and also awarded $15,000 for intentional infliction of mental suffering. The court noted that the bank was aware of the staffing shortage, knew about Zorn-Smith's burnout and requests for relief, and chose to do nothing about the situation.[86]

burnout

A condition of mental, emotional, and sometimes physical exhaustion that results from substantial and prolonged stress.

With respect to burnout, the human resource department's role is a proactive one to help employees prevent burnout before it occurs. For example, the human resource department can train supervisors to recognize stress and rearrange work assignments to reduce it. Jobs may be redesigned, staff conflicts resolved, counselling provided, and temporary leaves arranged. Weeks or months of rest, reassignment, or treatment may be required before recovery occurs. Some emotional or health damage can be permanent. Preventive strategies can be very important:

> Civilian employees of the Department of National Defence who are responsible for monitoring billions of dollars of military equipment projects are facing burnout and low morale. Compounding the problem is that about 18 percent of the civilian workforce is eligible to retire within the coming year. The problems identified in the department's HR plan include heavy workloads, long-term high levels of stress, and declining morale, leading to increased sick leave, higher error rates due to burnout, and poorer labour relations. The plan to address the problem includes improved training and professional development and better succession planning.[87]

Stress and Job Performance

Stress can be either helpful or harmful to job performance. When there is no stress, job challenges are absent and performance tends to be low. As stress increases, performance tends to increase, because stress helps a person call up resources to meet job requirements. It is a healthy stimulus to encourage employees to respond to challenges. Eventually it reaches a plateau that represents approximately a person's top day-to-day performance capability. At this point, additional stress tends to produce no more improvement. Finally, if stress becomes too great, performance begins to decline, because stress interferes with it. An employee loses the ability to cope, becomes unable to make decisions, and is erratic in behaviour.

There are several solutions to the problem of workplace stress. Curative solutions try to correct the outcome of stress, while preventive solutions attempt to change the cause of stress. In terms of *curative measures*, some employers give employees the opportunity to relax through such activities as aerobic exercises, yoga, and meditation. Some companies have counselling professionals on staff, employ an external consulting service that provides assistance in diagnosing the causes of stress and developing ways to cope with it, and are looking at or using video counselling as a means of helping employees. While video counselling is at times the only option for employees in remote locations, it also gives employees more flexibility in scheduling counselling sessions. However, it is important that the counselling platform meets privacy requirements (such as PIPEDA), has appropriate technology support, and allows for multiple participants.[88]

With regard to *preventive measures*, there are different approaches to dealing with stress at the workplace. First, organizations can establish stress management training sessions and EAP assistance to help workers deal with stress. Second, some organizations are looking at improving working conditions in order to reduce stress at work—the employer needs to identify stressful situations and design strategies to reduce or eliminate the stressors. In managing stress, it may be necessary to bring in outside experts.[89]

Management should look at the structure of the organization and the design of jobs. Several Canadian organizations have developed programs that provide workers with more diversified tasks, greater control over decisions that affect their work, and a chance for wider participation in the overall production process. Figure 12-6 shows some of the specific actions that the human resource department should take to reduce employee stress and burnout.

FIGURE 12-6

Actions to Reduce Stress

- Ensure that an employee's workload is compatible with the individual's capabilities and resources.

- Design jobs to provide meaningful opportunities for employees to use their skills.

- Clearly define employee roles and responsibilities.

- Provide workers with the opportunity to participate in decision making.

- Improve the communications process.

- Increase opportunities for social interaction among employees.

- Develop appropriate work schedules.

- Train managers and employees to be sensitive to the symptoms of stress.

- Establish a stress management policy.

SOURCE: National Institute for Occupational Health and Safety, *Stress at Work.*

Spotlight *on* HRM

Parents' Job Anxiety Wreaks Havoc on Children

A Queen's University researcher has documented a relationship that HR specialists have long recognized—children absorb the job anxieties of their parents. Business professor Dr. Julian Barling surveyed 154 commerce undergraduates and their parents and found that children's perceptions of their parents' job insecurities affect their attitudes about work and jobs and, indirectly, their grades.

Barling, an expert in work and family relationships at the Kingston, Ontario, university, said that he undertook the study because "we need to be aware of how the next generation is being affected by current insecurity in the workplace." In his study, he found a close correlation between students' perceptions and their midterm grades. Barling considers school performance to be a matter of great concern because "how children perform at school affects their self-esteem and how they are perceived by peers, teachers, and families. And, in the long term, grades obtained will influence the educational and occupational opportunities open to them."

In a companion study …in the *Journal of Applied Psychology,* Barling writes that children's perceptions of their parents' job insecurity also affect their beliefs and attitudes toward work. He notes that the waves of layoffs in both the public and private sectors in the last decade may produce "a generation of young people with pre-existing negative work beliefs and attitudes which may not be amenable to change."

Parents Anxious Over More Than Security

Barling is not alone in his observations. "Professor Barling has quantified something I have been observing for well over a decade—children are sponges and readily absorb their parents' anxiety and ambivalence about work," said Barbara Moses, president of BBM Human Resource Consultants, Inc., and author of *Career Intelligence.* She added that parental anxieties extend beyond job insecurity to include dissatisfaction with promotions, wages, workload, and perquisites.

"Is it any wonder that children are ambivalent? They see their parents tired and complaining, or more likely, they rarely see their parents. They grow to feel their parents are abused by work, and work denies them access to their parents. They see their parents as victims of their jobs and careers. And, despite these sacrifices, their employers treat them badly and let them go."

(Continued)

HR's Role Goes beyond EAPs

Moses said HR professionals have a role to play in reducing employee anxiety and the communication of this anxiety to sons and daughters. "At a minimum, HR should ensure that corporate communications do not unnecessarily incite job anxiety among employees," she said. "In addition, HR can promote career management among employees. Career support services reassure employees that they will be okay even if they lose their jobs. Encourage them to talk the language of employability rather than job security."

The assistance can be provided through support groups and Employee Assistance Programs, although Moses and others say EAPs are insufficient because they are reactive rather than proactive, and fail to address the needs of employees who do not identify themselves as anxious.

Sam Klarreich, president of the Berkeley Centre for Wellness, described the success of a support group he was involved with a few years ago at Imperial Oil. "We set up a group to help employees deal with on-the-job stress. We brought guest speakers, reprinted and shared articles on stress, held group discussions, published a newsletter. By working together the group members learned better ways to cope with stress. The program was such a success the group grew from an initial membership of 20 to over 200."

SOURCE: © Canadian HR Reporter, December 29, 1997, pp. 16, 20. Reprinted by permission of Canadian HR Reporter. © Copyright Thomson Reuters Canada Ltd., (2015), Toronto, Ontario, 1-800-387-5164. Web: www.hrreporter.com

The Stress Audit

Human resource managers must be sensitive to the many possible sources and causes of stress at the workplace. It is possible to evaluate the extent of dysfunctional stress by performing a stress audit, which assists in identifying the causes of stress.[90] The stress audit asks the following questions:

- Do any individuals demonstrate physiological symptoms?
- Is job satisfaction low, or are job tension, turnover, absenteeism, strikes, or accident proneness high?
- Does the organization's design contribute to the symptoms described?
- Do interpersonal relations contribute to the symptoms described?
- Do career-development variables contribute to the symptoms described?
- What effects do personality, socio-cultural influences, and the nonwork environment have on the relationship between the stressors—individual careers, interpersonal relations, and organizational design—and stress?

Mental Health

It is estimated that mental health problems and illnesses cost the Canadian economy about $50 billion a year directly and $6 billion annually for lost productivity resulting from related absenteeism. Approximately 6.7 million Canadians have a mental health problem or illness, about half a million Canadians are absent in any given week as a result of mental health issues, and around 30 percent of disability claims and 70 percent of disability costs are attributable to mental illness.[91] A Conference Board of Canada report indicated that about 44 percent of Canadians experienced a mental health issue and only 26 percent perceived that their supervisor "effectively managed mental health issues." The report also revealed that employees on disability leave for more than 12 weeks have about a 1 in 2 chance of returning to work.[92] However, some employers are making major strides in helping employees:

Willow Bean Café in Vancouver has six employees, all of whom are also clients of the Canadian Mental Health Association. According to Elisha Brodeur, employment support coordinator for the café, the program "trains clients of CMHA in an actual café setting. They're people who have maybe faced more barriers to finding employment due to mental health problems or struggles with mental illness."[93]

A 2014 Sun Life Health Index report indicated that about 23 percent of Canadians were impacted by a mental health issue and 66 percent indicate that deteriorating health is a top concern as people age. More than three-quarters of participants indicated that they are stressed out with the most important factors being personal or household finances (41 percent), trying to maintain a budget (31 percent), unexpected expenses (30 percent), personal relationships (29 percent), and work life (25 percent). About 29 percent of respondents reported never or rarely participating in at least 30 minutes of physical activity a day.[94]

In order to get a more complete picture of mental health in the workplace, it is important to also consider the influence of life at home. A recent study of almost 2,000 employees from 63 organizations reveals that mental health in an organization does not exist in a vacuum. Fewer mental health problems were associated with living with a partner, in households with young children, with higher household incomes, fewer work–family conflicts, and greater access to social network support away from work. In addition, work-related factors (including support for employees, higher use of skills, job security, and meeting expectations of job recognition) were also related with fewer mental health issues.[95]

HR professionals may need to develop a greater understanding of mental illness issues and diagnoses. The Diagnostic and Statistical Manual of Mental Disorders (DSM), which is considered to be the authoritative source for the diagnosis of mental illness, had its first major revision in nearly 20 years. Major changes include new diagnostic criteria, greater attention to culture and gender, and a developmental focus. The DSM is used by several parties including arbitrators, employers and HR professionals, workers compensation decision-makers, and mental health professionals.[96] Consider the following arbitration case:

> A 38-year-old labourer at a Toronto dairy manufacturing plant was diagnosed with severe mental health conditions. The employee's behaviour became quite erratic and the employer ultimately terminated the worker because of the safety risk. An arbitrator ruled that the employer had examined accommodation to the point of undue hardship and concluded that the employee should not be reinstated to active duty. However, the company was ordered to reinstate the employee for three months without compensation solely for the purpose of allowing the employee to apply for long-term disability benefits.[97]

Fitness and Employee Wellness Programs

Fitness, wellness, and lifestyle programs have become quite popular in organizations and have been shown to have a positive impact on reducing stress and absenteeism and increasing productivity. A recent UK study of more than 1,000 employees revealed that 39 percent of employees reported that losing weight was their top health issue, followed by managing stress (26 percent) and getting more exercise (17 percent).[98]

Many employees want access to health promotion programs in the workplace and the National Wellness Survey Report for 2013 indicates that more than 90 percent of Canadian organizations with 50 or more employees and almost 60 percent of smaller employers offer at least one type of wellness initiative. The most common wellness initiatives were flexible work programs (49 percent), first aid/CPR courses (36 percent), staff appreciation events (28 percent), time off in lieu of overtime (27 percent), involvement of employees in work scheduling (27 percent), and flu shot programs (24 percent). However, 87 percent of employers do not measure the health status of employees and 75 percent are not confident that they have the knowledge or support to effectively address employee mental health needs. About 47 percent of employers are using incentive programs to encourage participation in wellness initiatives. The biggest barriers to adopting wellness initiatives were lack of budget (28 percent), lack of staffing (21 percent), lack of ability to quantify benefits (19 percent), little knowledge of wellness (19 percent), and lack of conviction of cost savings (18 percent). [99]

Starting in 2011, the safest employers in Canada have been recognized at the Canada's Safest Employer Awards ceremony, In addition to awards in 10 industries, there is also a wellness and psychological safety award and, beginning in 2015, a young worker safety and best health and safety culture award. For example, Powerstream <http://www.powerstream.ca>, an energy company in Vaughn, Ontario, was the 2014 Wellness award winner. In developing an annual wellness plan, Powerstream uses survey data and statistics from the benefits plan (including usage of medications and accessing of the family and employee assistance plan). According to organizational improvement coordinator Daniella Cogliano, wellness is "in our DNA."[100]

A recent Aon Hewitt survey of Canadian employers indicated that about 92 percent of employers believe that an integrated approach to managing health is essential but only 20 percent see their programs as in the top ranges of integration. Among the most common wellness initiatives were: employee assistance program (93 percent), lunch and learns (59 percent), health spending account (55 percent), newsletters (45 percent), and fitness memberships (42 percent). About 39 percent had online fitness classes and 23 percent had a smoking cessation program. [101]

Is an employer allowed to restrict job applicants to non-smokers? According to Krista McMullin of Smoke-Free Nova Scotia, "having smokers can mean more lost time, indirect health care costs, longer breaks, and less productivity." However, providing support for smokers indicates that an employer cares about its employees. While the law is currently unsettled, it can be argued that an addiction to smoking is a disability, thus raising the possibility of a human rights complaint.[102]

The average annual cost to an employer for each smoker is estimated by the Conference Board of Canada to be $4,256. Part of the cost is related to absenteeism with smokers, on average, taking more than two extra sick days a year than non-smokers. In addition, unsanctioned smoke breaks result in a loss of $3,842 per employee. Further, smokers and those who recently quit smoking are 2.3 times more likely to be off work for three months or more a year due to chronic health issues.[103]

How effective are wellness programs? While most evaluations have come from large American corporations with comprehensive programs, the evidence indicates that such programs:

- improve employee health
- decrease health care costs
- improve employee satisfaction
- decrease absenteeism and turnover
- improve corporate image
- reduce disability claims

A review of 73 published studies revealed an average savings-to-cost ratio of $3.50 to $1.00 due to reduced absenteeism and health care costs. A meta-analysis of 43 studies indicated an average reduction of 28 percent in sick leave absenteeism and a 30 percent reduction in workers'compensation and

More and more companies are promoting health by providing health programs. Would the money be better spent by paying bonuses that serve to motivate employees?

Lifesize/Getty Images.

disability management claims associated with health promotion.[104] Specific programs also show significant benefits:

> In an effort to enhance its wellness efforts and combat growing obesity, Standard Life <http://www.standardlife.ca/en> wanted a program that everyone could participate in, regardless of the employee's current level of fitness. The company opted to join the Global Corporate Challenge, which challenges employees to take 10,000 steps a day. The program goes for 16 weeks beginning each May, participants are grouped in teams of seven, everyone is given a pedometer to measure their performance, and as employees enter the number of steps online, their team is taken on a virtual walking journey around the world. At Standard Life, 95 percent of employees indicated that their health had improved, 80 percent reported more energy, 82 percent indicated that morale had increased, and 52 percent reported higher productivity. Just under half of the participants lost weight, with an average loss of eight pounds.[105]

In evaluating the success of wellness programs, employers are focusing on positive feedback from participants, good participation, improved employee morale, and reduced absenteeism. Only 19 percent of organizations were using a positive return on investment as a measure of success. When asked to identify health risk concerns, the three biggest issues included poor stress management skills, lack of exercise by employees, and an inability to balance work and family issues.[106] Some employers are being creative in trying to help workers get healthier:

> One approach involves imitating digital games and having employees track health performance online. In many instances, employees form teams and monitor their results. There is some concern that employees may feel manipulated or pressured by co-workers to help the team win. In one organization, employees posted messages criticizing co-workers who were dragging the team down.[107]

Although labour unions have been strong supporters of health and safety initiatives, organized labour has not always been an advocate of wellness programs: unions are often skeptical about employer motivations behind wellness programs and there is a concern that employee information may be collected and tracked to be used in attendance management. However, the number of wellness and healthy workplace initiatives was noticeably higher when the labour–management relationship was better.[108]

Other Contemporary Safety Issues

Workplace Security

The events of September 11, 2001, have increased employer and employee awareness of workplace security issues. This has led to a reassessment of security policies used to make workplaces safe. In addition to terror concerns, other issues include preparations for a disaster (such as an earthquake or flood) and access to workplace property by an intruder:

> While schools are generally well prepared for a lockdown, many employers are not. However, the attack at the National War Memorial and subsequent firing of shots on Parliament Hill in October 2014 have made employers more aware of the importance of having a lockdown procedure. According to Ann Wyganowski, Director of the Toronto Disaster Recovery Information Exchange, "employers should conduct a proper internal and external assessment ahead of time. Training is also important. You need to do the drills."[109]

A number of organizations have developed emergency plans (such as evacuation of buildings), implemented training programs associated with security issues, assessed the work site for hazards and security shortcomings, and established safety competencies for managers and supervisors.[110] However, not all employees feel secure at work:

> Letter carriers in Montreal have been subject to at least 12 attacks by assailants seeking keys to mailboxes to steal credit cards, passports, and other documents. The keys provide access to grey boxes, community mail boxes, and apartments. There is concern that the movement to community boxes will lead to increased thefts and CUPW local president Alain Duguay stated that there had been more than 4,800 thefts at community boxes in British Columbia in recent years.[111]

Some firms have taken proactive measures to increase security for employees:

> During the global financial crisis, TD Bank became concerned about robberies. Consequently, it trained 33,000 employees in robbery prevention. A training needs assessment was completed and the company also partnered with the RCMP and an armed robbery prevention association with the goal of making the training as realistic as possible. The training included elearning, instructor-led discussions, role-plays, informal discussions, and ongoing coaching. The bank has seen several benefits from the training including a reduction in robberies, increased safety to employees and customers, and a positive return on investment.[112]

Sick Building Syndrome (SBS)

Sick building syndrome is used to describe situations in which employees experience acute health and comfort effects that appear to be linked to the length of time spent in a building but no specific illness or cause can be identified. However, the term *building-related illness* is used when symptoms of diagnosable illness are identified and are attributable directly to airborne contaminants in a building.[113]

People spend up to 90 percent of their lives indoors and a growing number report becoming sick while working in a particular building. Symptoms range from headaches to dizziness to nausea to eye, ear, or throat irritation, to allergic reactions. Sick building syndrome may be caused by major combustion pollutants (caused, for instance, by malfunctioning heating systems), biological air pollutants (such as mites, mould, and dander), volatile organic compounds (including pesticides, solvents, and cleaners), and heavy metals (such as lead). Human resource professionals should take proactive steps to prevent sick building syndrome.[114] However, sick building syndrome is not always easy to detect:

> The Alberta Court of Appeal building has been abandoned since 2001. Following renovations to the building, there were numerous complaints from lawyers, judges and other workers of watery eyes, fatigue, and irritated lungs. It took a considerable time to figure out the problem but eventually it was determined that air quality was the problem—the new, airtight building trapped moisture inside the walls, leading to the growth of toxic mould. It is estimated that about 4 percent of the population react to mould spores and that between 30 to 50 percent of new or refurbished buildings cause sick building syndrome.[115]

HRC 8

Workplace Violence

One area of safety management that has been neglected to some extent concerns workplace violence. However, a scan of newspapers and television reports indicates that workplace violence is not a rare event. In this era of restructuring and productivity improvement, there have been a number of accounts of terminated employees returning to the workplace and injuring or killing other employees. For example, Chuang "Ray" Li, a computer programmer at Ceridian Canada <http://www.ceridian.ca> in Toronto, allegedly stabbed four of his former co-workers after being fired from employment and is facing several charges including attempted murder. As a result, jurisdictions across the country have developed legislation to address the issue.[116] Consider the experiences of health care workers:

> A study of on-the-job abuse by patients revealed that 46 percent of male nurses and 33 percent of female nurses reported being physically assaulted by a patient in the previous year. In addition, 55 percent of male nurses and 46 percent of female nurses had been emotionally abused.[117]

> At the Toronto East General Hospital <http://www.tegh.on.ca>, there are about two "code whites" a week, indicating a violent situation within the hospital. Six months ago, the hospital introduced a zero-tolerance approach to workplace violence and has reduced the average security response time from 2.5 minutes to 59 seconds. What is making the difference is a small wireless device that can be clipped on a shirt or worn on a lanyard. A double-click of the device opens up a two-way communication between the employee and every security officer in the building. It saves the employee from having to find a phone, make a call, and explain what is happening and where the incident is occurring.[118]

Evidence from the United States indicates that about 9 percent of workplace deaths were homicides, with four-fifths of the deaths resulting from gunshots. Workplace violence is the second-highest cause of workplace death for women (behind traffic accidents), with 22 percent of the fatal workplace injuries to women resulting from homicide. In terms of deaths per 100,000 workers, U.S. evidence indicates that the highest-risk jobs (in order of risk of death) include taxi drivers, law enforcement officers, hotel clerks, gas station attendants and security guards, liquor store workers, detective or protective service workers, and jewellery store workers. The jobs with the greatest risk of workplace violence are police officers, security guards, taxi drivers, prison guards, bartenders, mental health professionals, gas station attendants, and convenience or liquor store clerks.[119] Measures aimed at preventing or reducing the incidence of workplace violence include an anti-violence/zero-tolerance policy, self-defence training, and safety and security measures.

A 2012 study from the United States indicates that 36 percent of organizations had at least one incident of workplace violence during the past five years. In the event of a threat of violence from an employee, the HR department (90 percent) and management staff (45 percent) were most commonly identified as being responsible to handle the issue. Verbal threats are most common, followed by pushing or shoving, robbery, fist-fighting, and stalking.[120]

Additional U.S. research on workplace violence revealed that about 52 percent of employees had witnessed, experienced, or heard about an incident of workplace violence. Approximately 28 percent had personally experienced a violent event while working (such as hostility, threats, or abusive language) but about 29 percent failed to report the incident. Just under 95 percent of employers take some action upon a complaint of workplace violence with the most common actions being holding an employee meeting, meeting with the employee who was the victim, taking some disciplinary action, and providing employee and supervisor training. The most common action taken by employees was to report the incident to their supervisor or human resources.[121]

A study entitled *Violence and Aggression in the Workplace* involved a survey of Canadian CEOs. The results indicated that the three most common incidents of workplace violence were loud screaming or yelling, destruction of employer property during a fit of anger, and throwing a telephone, pen, or some other office object in anger. Based on CEO perceptions, the top three contributors to workplace violence were consumption of drugs and alcohol, lack of management authority, and poor morale.[122]

With the growth of the Internet and social media, one of the most recent threats at the workplace involves "cyberstalking," which is the use of electronic communications to harass or threaten another individual. Based on 2013 data, the most common ways in which cyberstalking escalated included Facebook (29 percent), phone (25 percent), text messaging (24 percent), and Twitter (17 percent).[123] Although one might expect that careful selection of new hires may be an important step in reducing workplace violence, a recent study places more attention on situational factors and poor management:

> According to Julian Barling, co-author of a recent study entitled *Supervisor-Targeted Aggression*, "in trying to understand why people behave aggressively in the workplace, we should give primary responsibility to situational rather than personal considerations." Barling believes that in creating a healthy work environment where workers are treated fairly, quality supervision is important to reducing workplace violence. Moreover, when an act of workplace violence does occur, he suggests looking inside the workplace for a potential cause rather than assuming that the worker has a psychological problem.[124]

In workplace violence lawsuits, courts in the United States are placing a much heavier onus on employers to take reasonable care in making sure that the workplace is safe. Factors considered by the courts include the crime rate in the neighbourhood, the security measures in place at the business, the lighting of the buildings and grounds, the architectural design of the buildings, and recommendations from security consultants:

> A store manager at a shopping centre in the United States was robbed, beaten, and suffered permanent brain damage. In a lawsuit by the victim's family against the shopping centre, it was shown that a security consultant recommended a 24-hour foot patrol of the property because of the difficulty in controlling access to the various stores. The shopping centre owner decided to have a guard patrol the mall on a part-time basis using an automobile. The lawsuit was settled out of court for $9.25 million.[125]

It is estimated that workplace violence costs well over $8 billion a year, with costs including medical care, disability and worker's compensation, higher insurance rates, negative public relations and company image, consulting fees, greater security measures, and lower morale and productivity. Experts point out that under Bill C-45, employers and executives may be criminally liable for failing to take reasonable steps to prevent workplace violence and accidents. Proactive suggestions include careful employee selection, development of a comprehensive policy on workplace violence, employee training, assessment of the likelihood of workplace violence, and rigorous security standards.[126]

> Jamie Pasieka, who worked at a Loblaw warehouse in Edmonton, stopped at a military surplus store on his way to work, purchased two large knives, and allegedly attacked several co-workers, leaving two dead and four injured. According to Glenn French of the Canadian Initiative on Workplace Violence, an incident of workplace violence is very complex because "there is an environmental impact, there's witness and bystander impact, and, of course, there's the impact on the individual (victim) and the individual's family."[127]
>
> In September 2005, an Ottawa teenager was killed shortly after midnight while walking home after her shift had ended at a Wendy's <http://www.wendys.ca> restaurant. Emile Therien, President of the Canada Safety Council <http://canadasafetycouncil.org> at the time, stated that getting workers home safely should be an employer responsibility. "You are asking very young kids—most of them under 19—to leave these places at very late hours when there's no public transportation. There's no assurance that they'll get home safely." While some organizations are reviewing their policies, McDonald's already has a program to ensure that an employee has a pre-arranged ride home or door-to-door transportation with a manager, co-worker, or parent. If this is not possible, transportation by taxi will be arranged and paid for by McDonald's.[128]

Workplace bullying can cause mental health problems yet many employers are not aware of national standards aimed at protecting the psychological health of employees. Consultant Valerie Cade notes that there is no well-established definition of bullying, but her definition is: "workplace bullying is deliberate, disrespectful, and repeated behaviour toward someone or many people, for the bully's gain." According to Cade, envy is at the root of all bullying and nice, effective people are frequently targeted. The bully's goal is to take something away from the victim (such as praise from somebody or relationships at work).[129]

Another issue that is gaining more attention is the link between domestic violence and other facets of an employee's life, including their life at work. A study by Western University and the Canadian Labour Congress <http://canadianlabour.ca> revealed that about one in three respondents said that they had experienced a domestic violence incident during their lives (17 percent of men, 38 percent of women, and 65 percent of participants in the transgender/other category). Prevalence of domestic violence was particularly high for respondents with disabilities, Aboriginal respondents, and individuals indicating that their sexual orientation was not heterosexual. Almost 54 percent of participants who reported experiencing domestic violence said that at least one abusive act occurred at or close to their workplace, 38 percent reported that domestic violence affected their ability to get to work, and just under 9 percent reported losing a job because of domestic violence. The most common abuse acts at or near the workplace included abusive phone calls or text messages (41 percent), stalking or harassment near the workplace (21 percent), and the abuser coming to the workplace (18 percent).[130]

HRC 8

Ergonomics

An area of health and safety that is attracting more attention is ergonomics (also known as *human factors engineering*). As discussed in Chapter 2, ergonomics focuses on the interaction between employees and their total working environment.[131] An ergonomics program seeks to ensure that the physical and behavioural characteristics of the employee are compatible with the work system (including methods of work, machines and equipment, the work environment, and the workplace or work station layout).[132]

While a number of organizations wait until employees complain about the work system or sustain an injury, proactive employers aim to ensure that the work system is compatible with employees; recent research indicates that it is important to incorporate wellness initiatives into ergonomic and safety programs.[133] Consultants specializing in ergonomics can assist organizations in the design and implementation of the work system.

> Software called ErgoWATch evaluates the risk of repetitive-stress injuries in workers' hands and arms. The software can evaluate the load or impact of a task and estimate the potential physical demands as well as the risk of injury. In addition, the software examines risk factors over the whole day because the probability of injury is also related to fatigue. Four different measurement tools estimate and interpret the physical loading associated with different jobs.[134]

Two common types of injuries that may be reduced by the application of ergonomic principles are (1) overexertion and lower back injury and (2) repetitive-strain injuries (RSI), which may include cumulative trauma disorder (CTD), overuse syndrome (OS), and musculoskeletal injury (MSI). Repetitive-strain injuries are caused by repeated actions resulting in muscle or skeletal strain.

Research suggests that the most rapidly growing category of workplace illnesses involves ergonomic disorders. In 1981, when the IBM PC was introduced, 18 percent of all illnesses reported to the Occupational Health and Safety Administration in the United States involved repetitive-strain injuries. Three years later, that figure had grown to 28 percent, and to 52 percent by 1992. Now it is estimated that about 70 percent of all occupational illnesses will be repetitive-strain injuries and $1 of every $3 spent on compensation costs is associated with improper ergonomics.[135]

The treatment of repetitive-strain injuries is complex and varied. Some of the approaches used include physical treatments (such as physiotherapy or chiropractic treatments), postural treatments (often aimed at correcting bad habits relating to posture), relaxation (such as meditation), exercise and stretching, acupuncture, and cognitive behavioural therapy (with a focus on coping with pain).[136] A properly designed work station can play a major role in reducing workplace injuries. The key factors in designing an ergonomically sound work station relate to the layout of the work station, the characteristics of control and display panels, seating arrangements at the work station, and lighting quality and quantity.[137] While a number of organizations have moved to an open-office concept, workers complain about such things as reduced privacy and noise spillover:

> One woman at a public relations firm could not concentrate while a co-worker in an adjoining cubicle completed the ritual of clipping his nails. Another employee complained about the lack of privacy when she spoke on the phone to a former boyfriend, while a different employee lamented hearing a co-worker blurt out a crude phrase to tell a client he had to use the washroom.[138]

One group of employees often overlooked in terms of ergonomics is teleworkers. It is estimated that almost 1.5 million Canadians are involved in telework, but many employers do not have policies, procedures, and training for employees working from their homes. As a consequence, teleworkers may suffer from repetitive stress, eye strain, and back injuries. Employers should be aware of their obligation to provide a safe work environment and balance the requirement of due diligence with employee privacy concerns.[139]

AIDS

A chapter on occupational health and safety would be incomplete if no reference was made to the acquired immune deficiency syndrome (AIDS) or the human immunodeficiency virus (HIV) that causes AIDS. There are an estimated 70,000 individuals in Canada living with AIDS.[140] Both HIV and AIDS have a potentially immense impact on the human resource function.[141]

AIDS and Human Resource Management

Consider the following case that occurred more than 25 years ago:

> Ron Lentz was hired January 4, 1988, by the Toronto Western Hospital as a nurse and fired on January 23. He complained to the Ontario Human Rights Commission that he was discriminated against because he was HIV-positive. The commission agreed and negotiated with the hospital a settlement that included reinstatement, about $14,000 in back pay, $1,400 in benefits, $5,000 in legal fees, restoration of seniority, and a clean employment record.[142]

This case points to challenges that human resource managers have to face if one of their employees is HIV-positive, develops AIDS, or if a job applicant happens to mention that he or she has an HIV-related infection. It is a breach of human rights laws to discriminate against that person. But what if colleagues refuse to work with that person? What if a supervisor expressed concern about the employee's contact with customers? To be prepared for such questions, each employer should establish a policy and have an action plan in place before a case arises among employees or their dependants. Some recommendations on how to set up a successful AIDS program are outlined below.

1. A *policy* regarding HIV-infected employees should
   - protect an employee's right to privacy;
   - guarantee the employee will not be isolated from other workers; and
   - keep those diagnosed with AIDS productive as long as they are able.

2. *Mandatory training* for managers, supervisors, and union leaders should
   - present facts on HIV;
   - address personal concerns about AIDS in the workplace;
   - reiterate the company's policy;
   - help with job restructuring; and
   - discuss how to manage co-worker concerns.

3. *Education programs* for all employees should
   - explain policy;
   - present facts on transmission and prevention;
   - encourage empathy for those with AIDS; and
   - provide workshops or forums for frank, open discussion.

4. *Counselling and support* should be provided to
   - help employees with AIDS cope with their disease;
   - assist others in coming to terms with an HIV-infected co-worker; and

- explore with supervisors the issues involved in managing AIDS.[143]

Despite the considerable amount of information on HIV and AIDS, many individuals are still not well informed about the disease. One of the problems human resource managers must deal with is the lack of knowledge on the part of employees. There are still questions asked such as "Can I get AIDS from germs in the air? From touching an infected worker? From a toilet seat? From infected water in a swimming pool? From insect bites?" It has been found that a comprehensive education program for co-workers can halt the hysteria that often results when a colleague is diagnosed with HIV or AIDS.[144]

LO6   HRC 1 & 2 & 8

Occupational Health and Safety Strategy

It must be continually stressed that top management's involvement in setting health and safety policies is essential. If it does not assume a leadership role, it sets an example by its inaction, and middle managers, first-line supervisors, and employees will behave accordingly. Part of an effective occupational health and safety strategy is to clearly assign responsibilities for plant safety and health programs to ensure that the company's policies are carried out. An occupational health and safety committee with enforcement authority is a very helpful tool to implement health and safety policies. Such a committee should be made up of representatives of management and employees, ideally with balanced representation. This increases the probability that the committee's decisions are accepted as fair by the employees.

It is important to have a control process in place. Causes of accidents should be identified and either eliminated or controlled to prevent recurrence. The human resource department should use its information system to monitor for patterns of accidents or health problems that may be otherwise overlooked. An effective training program is another critical part of a good occupational health and safety program. Moreover, a number of organizations are hiring occupational health and safety specialists to design and administer comprehensive workplace health and safety programs. Finally, management should continually encourage safety awareness on the part of supervisors and employees.

SUMMARY

Occupational health and safety has become an important aspect of organizations and will have an even higher priority for human resource managers in the future. The federal and provincial governments have created a variety of laws that require the attention of human resource professionals. Most occupational health and safety acts now require the establishment of safety committees in companies with 20 or more employees.

The Workplace Hazardous Materials Information System (WHMIS) is a comprehensive plan that requires suppliers to provide detailed information about any danger their material may pose, but it also asks the user to make sure that the information is available and that employees are trained to understand it.

Accident prevention is a major concern, but human resource managers should not forget to look at the psychological aspect of the work environment. Stress-related losses—absenteeism, turnover, low productivity, accidents, and so on—cost Canada billions of dollars each year. Preventive programs such as employee assistance programs, professional counselling, time management, and fitness programs can go a long way to reduce stress-related costs.

(Continued)

AIDS and the workplace is an important issue facing human resource managers. Some organizations will experience individual cases of AIDS or HIV that, given present experiences, can lead to severe friction among work groups and irrational actions from some frightened employees. Human resource managers should be prepared for this by appropriate training and communication programs.

TERMS FOR REVIEW

assumption of risk
burnout
careless worker model
shared responsibility model
stressors
Workplace Hazardous Materials Information System (WHMIS)
workplace health and safety committee

SELF-ASSESSMENT EXERCISE

Work–Life Balance Quiz

Do you find it difficult to balance the different roles in your life? If so, you're not alone—58 percent of Canadians report "overload" as a result of the pressures associated with work, home and family, friends, physical health, and volunteer and community service.

Take this quiz to see if you're in balance.

ARE YOU IN BALANCE?

More than ever before, Canadians play many different roles in their lives. They are workers, parents, spouses, friends, caregivers of elderly relatives, and volunteers in their communities. They must also make room in their lives for taking care of their own physical and mental well-being. Not surprisingly, achieving balance among all these competing priorities can be difficult. This overload can be heightened by new technologies that were actually intended to make our work lives easier—through email, cell phones, and other electronic devices, many workers are expected to be available 24/7, making the achievement of a balance between work and the rest of our lives even more difficult.

Achieving work–life balance means having equilibrium among all the priorities in your life—this state of balance is different for every person. But, as difficult as work–life balance is to define, most of us know when we're out of balance. To find out more about your own personal balance:

TAKE THE WORK–LIFE BALANCE QUIZ

Disclaimer
This is not a scientific test. Information provided is not a substitute for professional advice. If you feel that you may need advice, please consult a qualified health care professional.

WORK/LIFE BALANCE QUIZ

	Agree	Disagree
1. I feel like I have little or no control over my work life.	○	⊗
2. I regularly enjoy hobbies or interests outside of work.	⊗	○
3. I often feel guilty because I can't make time for everything I want to.	○	⊗
4. I frequently feel anxious or upset because of what is happening at work.	○	⊗
5. I usually have enough time to spend with my loved ones.	⊗	○
6. When I'm at home, I feel relaxed and comfortable.	⊗	○
7. I have time to do something just for me every week.	⊗	○
8. On most days, I feel over-whelmed and overcommitted.	○	⊗
9. I rarely lose my temper at work.	○	⊗
10. I never use all my allotted vacation days.	○	⊗
11. I often feel exhausted – even early in the week.	○	⊗
12. Usually, I work through my lunch break.	○	⊗
13. I rarely miss out on important family events because of work.	○	⊗
14. I frequently think about work when I'm not working.	○	⊗
15. My family is frequently upset with me about how much time I spend working.	○	⊗

WHAT YOUR SCORE MEANS

Give yourself one point for agreeing with statements 2, 5, 6, 7, 9, and 13. Give yourself one point for disagreeing with statements 1, 3, 4, 8, 10, 11, 12, 14, and 15.

0 – 5: Your life is out of balance—you need to make significant changes to find your equilibrium. But you can take control!

6 – 10: You're keeping things under control—but only barely. Now is the time to take action before you're knocked off balance.

11 – 15: You're on the right track! You've been able to achieve work–life balance—now, make sure you protect it.

Source: Canadian Mental Health Association: http://www.cmha.ca/

REVIEW AND DISCUSSION QUESTIONS

1. Explain the legal term *assumption of risk*.

2. What factors affect occupational accidents?

3. What responsibilities do joint occupational health and safety committees have?

4. Explain the requirements of the Workplace Hazardous Materials Information System (WHMIS).

CRITICAL THINKING QUESTIONS

1. Develop a strategy and identify the implementation steps you would follow to lower the incidence of workplace accidents in your organization.

2. Think about a time when you felt under considerable stress. What were the causes of that stress? What efforts (by you and/or others) were or could have been taken to reduce the stress?

3. What can be done to prepare an organization for an AIDS case?

4. Consider an organization that you have worked in. Critically review its safety procedures and training. Evaluate the organization in terms of the presence of physical, biological, and chemical hazards. Also be sure to address issues relating to ergonomics.

ETHICS QUESTION

You are a maintenance worker in a refinery where smoking is strictly prohibited and any violation is punished by immediate dismissal. The refinery has had several accidents based on secret—and careless— smoking, resulting in injury and even death. Just now, when you go to a machine room to do some repairs, you surprise two of your colleagues who are smoking. Both are long-time employees, and you have known them well for many years. You even belong to the same bowling club, and your family socializes with theirs. When you challenge them, they respond, "Don't worry. This is a safe room, nothing flammable is stored here. You won't report us, will you?" If you report them, they will be dismissed. Both have families with children. If you do not report them, you are sure that they will continue to violate the no-smoking policy and thus endanger the lives of others. What do you do?

WEB RESEARCH EXERCISE

1. Visit the Justice Laws Website <http://www.laws-lois.justice.gc.ca> and examine the relevant sections of the *Canada Labour Code* that deal with occupational health and safety. Also, explore other websites that address health and safety law within your province.

2. Go to the website of the American Institute of Stress <http://www.stress.org>. Check out three other websites that also have information on workplace stress. Compare the information from the various sites.

INCIDENT 12-1

Safety at Canada Chemicals Ltd.

Canada Chemicals Ltd. is a large wholesaler of industrial chemicals in Ontario. It handles swimming pool supplies, industrial solvents, fertilizers, and special lubricants. The sales and clerical operations caused few safety worries, but the warehouse facilities caused Sam Peterson sleepless nights. Sam's title was manager of safety and security. He had worked in the human resource department since his job was created in 1992.

His biggest problem was the warehouse manager, Garfield McKenney. Gar simply did not appreciate safety. Nearly every action Sam took to improve safety resulted in objections from Gar, especially if it meant warehouse workers were to be slowed or delayed in their jobs. Most of the workers liked Sam, but they paid more attention to Gar. The only time employees wore their safety goggles, shoes, and acid-resistant gloves was when Sam was around. They knew Gar did not care and would not discipline good workers for safety violations unless company property was damaged.

One day a case of sulphuric acid was dropped, badly burning a new employee. The employee recovered after four weeks and two plastic surgery operations. Immediately after the accident, Sam requested a meeting with Gar, the human resource manager, and the general manager.

1. If you were the general manager, what would you do to gain greater co-operation on safety from (a) Gar and (b) the workers under him?

2. Should Sam be given authority to discipline those who violate safety rules?

CASE STUDY

Maple Leaf Shoes Ltd.

Safety at the Workplace

As he sat in his cubicle (what some would call an office) sipping what remained of a cold cup of coffee, Jon Atherton thought about his family back home in Vancouver. He missed his wife and two young daughters, and at times, he longed for his old job and his life back in British Columbia. On the other hand, his family would be joining him in Wilmington in a couple of months, and the job that he had left six weeks ago in Vancouver had ceased to provide much challenge. Although his job as a supervisor on the shop floor of a small manufacturing firm gave him some experience in the area of health and safety, his new position in Wilmington was that of safety coordinator. Deep down, he knew that he loved the work—it was just that upon his arrival in Wilmington, everything seemed to be in turmoil. As soon as he solved one problem, another one would pop up.

THE FIRST ISSUE

A week ago, Jon met with Sam Johnson, a 42-year-old man who has been with Maple Leaf Shoes for eight years. Sam is one of two nonunion employees working at the snack bar—his job requires that he serve customers and prepare "snack" foods (such as toast, muffins, and cold sandwiches) for employees. The snack bar is located in the employee lounge, a common hangout for employees on break or having lunch. Fellow employees get along well with Sam—he is always cheerful and his laugh can be heard throughout the lounge on a regular basis. As well, Sam's supervisor says that Sam is a solid performer. Jon also recalled that Sam is taking computer courses on a part-time basis at a nearby community college.

Jon thought back to his talk with Sam a week ago. Sam appeared to be uneasy and reserved when he entered Jon's office and told Jon he had something very important to tell him. Jon recalled how they struggled to get through the conversation—ultimately, Sam revealed to Jon that he had become infected with the AIDS virus and asked Jon for advice. Jon and Sam had arranged to meet in a week's time.

Catherine Reading, who is 56 years of age and has been with Maple Leaf Shoes for 12 years, is the other employee who works with Sam at the snack bar. Catherine is a dependable worker, and while she and Sam are not close friends, they get along well at work. Aside from getting a warning for being 14 minutes late a few years ago, Catherine has a clean work record. Shortly after meeting with Jon, Sam told Catherine that he had been infected with the AIDS virus (saying "Since you work with me, I felt I had to tell you"). Catherine was very troubled by this information. The next day, she reported for work but refused to work with Sam. Her supervisor asked Catherine if she was refusing to obey his orders. Catherine replied "Yes, I am. I am scared, and I'll never work with someone who has AIDS." The supervisor told Catherine that refusing to carry out his request amounted to insubordination. He sent Catherine home and went to see Jon for advice.

DISCUSSION QUESTIONS

1. Does Maple Leaf Shoes have just cause to dismiss Sam? Catherine?

2. What should Jon do in this case?

3. Develop a policy on AIDS and describe how you would administer this new policy.

THE SECOND ISSUE

Alexandra (Alex) Dixon, a 26-year-old employee at Maple Leaf Shoes, has been employed in her current secretarial position for almost two years. Prior to receiving the promotion to this position, Alex worked with Maple Leaf for six years as an office assistant. She is a single mother with a five-year-old daughter. Note that the secretarial staff is unionized.

Alex's performance evaluations have been slightly above average. However, her personnel file indicates that 18 months ago she received a three-day suspension because she and another employee were caught drinking on the job during regular working hours ("just a couple of drinks on a boring Friday afternoon," according to Alex).

Over the past few years, Maple Leaf Shoes has had some problems with substance abuse at work (although the problems have been confined almost entirely to employees in the production and warehouse facilities). In one case, a forklift operator under the influence of cocaine dropped a wooden pallet loaded with shoes from about 15 feet in the air—luckily, no one was seriously hurt. Six months ago, Alex's supervisor called in all of her staff to let them know that the company was concerned about safety and would not tolerate the use of drugs at work. There had not been problems of drug use among the office staff, and the topic of drug use was not mentioned again.

Two weeks ago, Alex's supervisor thought that she saw Alex take a puff on a marijuana cigarette on company property (actually on the far side of the company parking lot) at the end of the day. The next day, the supervisor confronted Alex at her workstation and accused her of taking drugs while at work. This meeting was witnessed by six other office employees. Alex admitted smoking the cigarette (saying that she only had about three puffs while on company property), made it clear that she was on her own time ("It was well past quitting time"), said that she was very sorry, and promised never to do it again. However, the supervisor told Alex that the company was clamping down on drug use and terminated her.

The union is filing a grievance about Alex's discharge. The collective agreement gives Maple Leaf Shoes the right to discipline or discharge an employee for "just cause."

DISCUSSION QUESTIONS

1. Does Maple Leaf Shoes have just cause to terminate Alex?

2. In discharge cases, the grievance procedure at Maple Leaf Shoes goes directly to the third step, a meeting between senior union and management representatives. The management side is looking to Jon for advice on how to proceed. Help Jon formulate an appropriate strategy.

CASE STUDY

Canadian Pacific and International Bank

Stressful Times at a CPIB Branch

The downtown branch of the Canadian Pacific and International Bank in Brandon, Manitoba, is known for its friendly service and high levels of employee morale. Although the branch gets very busy at times, the employees regard it as a good place to work. There is a spirit of co-operation among the employees, and the bank manager, Marsha Cobourg, is well liked by the staff.

Roselynn Barkhouse, a 26-year-old customer service representative, has been employed at the Brandon branch for just over nine months. In general, co-workers describe Roselynn as a good, solid worker, but most also agree that she is somewhat shy.

Three weeks ago, Roselynn was working at the counter when Roy Romanowski came in to deposit money into his business account. Roy has operated his small convenience store, which is located about three blocks from the bank, for 31 years. He is a loyal CPIB client and visits the bank at least once a day. Everyone in the area knows Roy—while he is a very hard worker, he is also an impatient man and not overly friendly. Some area residents refuse to buy anything from Roy's store because, in the words of one woman who lives near the store, "He is just so unfriendly, cold, and abrupt, I will never support his store." However, Roy's wife and children, who also work in the family store, are well liked in the community.

Roy approached Roselynn's counter and gave her his deposit bag. A careful count of the money revealed that Roy had $2,314 to deposit. Roselynn filled out the deposit slip for Roy, had him initial it, and went to the computer to enter the transaction. However, Roselynn mistakenly pressed the withdrawal button (instead of the deposit button), so when Roy looked at his passbook, it showed a withdrawal from his account of $2,314. He noticed the error immediately because he always keeps a close eye on his account.

Upon seeing the error, Roy started to scream at Roselynn. The following conversation ensued:

Roy: "What are you doing? Are you stupid or something? You trying to steal my money? I work real hard for my money."

Roselynn: "I am very sorry, Mr. Romanowski. I will fix up the mistake right away."

Roy: "How can I trust you? I have always gone to this bank, and they always treated me right. Now, this happens. How many mistakes have you made before? I want to see the manager. I want to get you fired. There is no room in the bank for stupid people."

At this point, two other employees and the manager, Marsha Cobourg, arrived at Roselynn's counter. Roselynn was in tears, and once again apologized to Roy. Within seconds, the error was corrected, and Cobourg also offered her apologies to Roy and walked him to the door.

Since the incident, however, Roy has continued to come into the bank at least daily (and more often when his store is busier). Whenever he enters the store, he makes a rude comment to Roselynn if she is working. Often, his comments are overheard by other customers. At times, he also tells other people to avoid going to Roselynn's counter. Both Marsha Cobourg and Roselynn's co-workers have reassured her that her work is fine and have advised her just to ignore Roy.

Two days ago, Roy entered the bank and, as luck would have it, Roselynn was the next available representative. Roy, however, refused to go to her workstation and made this known to all the customers around him. The bank was very busy at the time, and Roselynn burst into tears, left her counter, and went home. The next day, she called Cobourg and told Marsha: "I am totally stressed out and just can't take it anymore. I'm quitting and am going to look for work somewhere else. The job is just not worth it." Marsha tried to comfort Roselynn and after much discussion, was able to get Roselynn to come in for a meeting the next day.

DISCUSSION QUESTIONS

1. The day of the meeting between Roselynn and Marsha has arrived. Was arranging such a meeting a good idea?

2. What should Marsha try and achieve during the meeting? Were there any steps that could have been taken to prevent this incident from occurring?

The meeting with Roselynn ended at 11 a.m., and Marsha Cobourg went back to her office. Forty minutes later, as she glanced out her office door, she saw a man wearing dark glasses and a baseball hat burst into the bank. At the time, there were six bank employees and seven customers in the bank.

The man was waving a shotgun and yelling, "Everyone on the floor. Don't look up and don't try and stop me. No one will get hurt." He swore several times and ran to the cash station. "Open the drawer and give me the money." The bank representative at the cash station complied with his request, and in a matter of seconds the bank robber had run out the door.

Within a few minutes, the police arrived, as Marsha had pressed the silent alarm in her office. Everyone was told to remain calm, and the bank doors were locked. No new customers were allowed into the bank, and everyone present when the robbery occurred had to remain inside. Each customer was interviewed by the police. Marsha also asked each customer how they were. Three of the customers were very upset—one woman who was in the bank with her one-year-old son was particularly distraught.

A number of the bank employees were also visibly upset. Others seemed to take a deep breath and appeared ready to deal with the business at hand.

One customer commented on how the atmosphere in the branch had changed so rapidly. Prior to the robbery, everyone was relaxed and people were chatting.

During the robbery, there was extreme tension. Then, the aftermath of the robbery was very different—some people were in shock, some seemed emotionally drained, and others were trying to think through what had occurred. The customer also noted that while a number of the bank employees were terribly upset, they seemed in total control during the robbery: "It was like they knew what to do. I only caught a glimpse of what happened but there was no show of fear or panic on the employees' faces. It was almost like they were doing a drill, but in real life."

After about 45 minutes, the customers were permitted to leave the bank. As Marsha returned to her office, she received a phone call from the police notifying her that they had just arrested a suspect as he was preparing to rob another bank.

DISCUSSION QUESTIONS

1. Develop a safety training program for bank employees. What are the basic components of the program? What requirements would you build into such a program?

2. As a result of the robbery, a number of employees and customers may feel traumatized. What should the bank do in such a situation? Be sure to consider both short- and long-term suggestions.

CHAPTER 13

The Union–Management Framework

HRM focuses on the shared interests of workers and managers in the success of their enterprise. Conflict is de-emphasized in favour of "win–win" scenarios where problems are solved or put aside to fulfill organizational objectives. By contrast, industrial relations assumes conflict is inherent in the employment relationship.

DAPHNE GOTTLIEB TARAS, ALLEN PONAK, AND MORLEY GUNDERSON[1]

LEARNING OBJECTIVES

After studying this chapter, you should be able to:

LO1 Discuss the major reasons why workers join unions.

LO2 Describe the structure of Canadian unions.

LO3 Summarize the core legal principles relating to collective bargaining.

LO4 Explain how a union organizing campaign is carried out.

LO5 Outline the key steps in negotiating a union contract.

LO6 List common techniques to resolve disputes.

LO7 Describe how unions affect the human resource management environment.

LO8 Suggest ways to build union–management co-operation.

Workers may join together and form a union. A **union** is an organization with the legal authority to represent workers, negotiate the terms and conditions of employment with the employer, and administer the collective agreement.

union

An organization with the legal authority to represent workers, negotiate the terms and conditions of employment with the employer, and administer the collective agreement.

Many successful companies have one or more unions among their employees. While unionized organizations are often lumped together, there is growing evidence that the quality of the relationship between an employer and union is a major factor in predicting firm performance. Still, the presence of a union places limits on the role of human resource management and many managers find these new limitations hard to accept:

> CUPE Local 118 in Saint John, New Brunswick, had a clause in its contract with the city that guaranteed a minimum of 293 full-time outside employees. The clause, which was introduced in the early 1980s, has been renewed several times to avoid damaging union–management relations and labour unrest. Terry Totten, former City Manager for more than 15 years, believed that the clause was fundamentally wrong and impaired the ability of the city to save money by contracting out services. Totten asserted that the clause will only be removed when the economic climate is right and council have the political will to remove the clause. Union officials report that the clause was introduced to stop corruption, poor quality work, and kickback schemes with outside contractors, and believe that the clause has benefited both employees and taxpayers. [2]

As shown in Figure 13-1, the industrial relations and human resource perspectives on workplace conflict are somewhat different.

FIGURE 13-1

Industrial Relations and Human Resource Perspectives on Workplace Conflict

Industrial Relations Perspective

1. Conflict stems from an employer–employee power imbalance.

2. Conflict between labour and management is enduring.

3. Correcting the power imbalance between labour and management often requires institutional intervention in the forms of union representation and legislation.

4. Conflict can be constructive even when the conflict is addressed in an adversarial, non-problem-solving fashion.

Human Resource Perspective

1. Conflict stems from poor management.

2. Conflict can be partially reduced by organizational and workplace innovations that build an employer–employee unity of interests.

3. Conflict can further be reduced by co-operative, mutual gains-oriented problem-solving techniques.

4. As a result of improved management, conflict will fade from the employment relationship.

SOURCE: Adapted from D. Lewin, "IR and HR Perspectives on Workplace Conflict: What Can Each Learn from the Other?" *Human Resource Management Review*, Vol. 11, 2001, pp. 453–85.

LO1 HRC 5

Why Employees Seek Union Representation

Unions do not just happen. They are frequently caused by some management action or inaction that workers perceive as unfair. For example, in a 6:1 decision, the Supreme Court of Canada recently found that the RCMP's internal system for negotiating workplace issues is grossly unfair and gave Mounties the right to join a union.[3] Once a union is organized, it becomes the employees' bargaining agent and the employer is legally obligated to meet with the union and bargain a labour contract called a **collective agreement**. The collective agreement, which is known as the "rule book" by some managers and union officials, addresses a variety of issues such as wages and benefits, hours of work, working conditions, and related issues such as grievance procedures, safety standards, probationary periods, and work assignments. The collective agreement is usually negotiated between the local union's bargaining committee and the human resource or industrial relations department.

collective agreement

A labour contract that addresses a variety of issues such as wages and benefits, hours of work, working conditions, grievance procedures, safety standards, probationary periods, and work assignments. Usually negotiated between the local union's bargaining committee and the human resource or industrial relations department.

The collective agreement places restrictions on management's rights in managing the workplace. When a new collective agreement is negotiated, it is important that supervisors and managers dealing with unionized employees are made aware of the terms of the agreement and provided with training regarding the interpretation and application of the new agreement. All too often, a union grievance arises because the supervisor did not understand the terms of the collective agreement.

HRC 5

Causes of Unionization

Why do employees join unions? The reasons for joining a union vary from person to person and there is no single force that motivates people to join unions. Instead, perceptions are shaped by a variety of reasons. The *union push explanation* asserts that some employees are pushed or forced into joining a union because of employer treatment of the workforce, peer pressure by co-workers to join a union, or collective agreement provisions requiring an employee to join if he or she wants the job in question. The *union pull explanation* states that employees are pulled into the union because of the benefits of union representation (such as higher wages, greater benefits, job security, and grievance representation).

Consider the following organizing drive at a Halifax coffee shop.

In April 2013, Just Us! Coffee Roasters Co-op was presented with unfair labour practice charges relating to the dismissal of two employees who were alleging that they were terminated for trying to start a union. Just Us! was started by two social workers and sold itself as a fair-trade workers' co-op. While there was a health care plan, an employee had to work 30 hours a week to meet the full-time requirement. In addition, the store manager was responsible for scheduling, and employees who weren't close to the manager got fewer shifts, more night or weekend shifts, and "clopens" or split shifts requiring employees to open and close the store.

The Service Employees International Union commenced an organizing drive at Just Us! and 90 percent of the employees voted for the union. The parties got down to serious but "amicable" bargaining and struck a three-year deal that addressed such issues as work scheduling, wages, worker control of tips, and an improved grievance procedure. One employee stated: "unionizing was a transformative process. We realized we don't have to sit back and take whatever management gives us." Debra Moore, one of the company's founders, noted that "with the union things are so much clearer and better. We can go to the union if we are not happy. The down side is that we can't be flexible. We have to stick to the contract." [4]

When considering union joining, it is important to distinguish between the desire for union representation and the opportunity to do so.[5] Three factors—job dissatisfaction, individual attitudes toward unions in general, and perceived union instrumentality (beliefs about what unions can do for an employee)—appear to be most important in the decision of an individual to join a union.[6]

Reasons for not joining a union are equally diverse. Workers who want to become managers may believe union membership damages their chances for promotion. Other employees view unions as "just another boss" that leads to extra costs, such as union dues or lost wages from strikes. Likewise, past experiences or isolated stories of union wrongdoing may cause some people to form a negative opinion of collective action. Also, employer policies and supervisory treatment may be fair and consequently, employees are not motivated to join a union.

As the following example shows, people within a community may have vastly differing views concerning unionization:

In the small town of Brooks, Alberta, a strike shut down the Lakeside Packers slaughterhouse. Management was determined to open the plant (which employed about one-quarter of the town's population) during the dispute, which divided the town. While some citizens strongly supported the employees and their union, others were concerned that the strike would hurt other businesses in the community and leave lasting divisions among the town's residents. Striking workers were very upset—despite an Alberta Labour Relations Board order that banned strikers from doing more than delaying vehicles seeking to enter the plant, workers were committed to restricting access to the facility. As one worker stated, "If they kill us, they can go in. This is modern slavery for me." [7]

Having a union means strikes and walkouts. Are unions necessary in today's organizational environment, with labour and pay equity laws safeguarding workers?

CP/Fred Lunn.

Canadians' Views toward Unions

A recent (2013) survey by Leger polled 1,400 Canadian adults concerning their attitudes toward unions. While the survey provides important information, it should be emphasized that the results are aggregated and important differences may exist among workers based on demographic characteristics. For a few of the questions, responses from a 2008 Nanos survey are presented. Some of the major findings with regard to attitudes toward work and employers are reported below:

- Among Canadians who are not unionized, 19 percent reported that they were very or somewhat interested in being unionized, 2 percent don't know or refused to respond, and 79 percent do not want to be unionized.

- Among current union members, 71 percent would prefer to be unionized. Among formerly unionized workers 46 percent would prefer to be unionized.

- Among respondents, 71 percent of current union members believed that unions are as relevant today as they have ever been. Support for this statement dropped to 46 percent for former union members and 42 percent for respondents who had never been in a union.

- When forming or removing a union from the workplace, 86 percent of current union employees and 83 percent of nonunion employees believe that a secret ballot vote should be required.[8]

Incidents reported in the media may impact on the views of individuals. Consider, for instance, the decision by Caterpillar to shut down an Ontario plant:

In February of 2012, Caterpillar <http://www.cat.com> announced that it would close its Electro-Motive plant in London, Ontario. The announcement came about a month after the company had locked out 450 workers when they refused a 50 percent pay cut. Caterpillar argued that the closure was necessary because the plant was unsustainable. Shortly before the closure, Caterpillar announced that its quarterly earnings were up 58 percent and it had a record profit of almost $5 billion. According to Ken Lewenz, president of the Canadian Auto Workers (CAW) at the time, "The closure was a callous move. From Day 1, we believed that Caterpillar was trying to provoke a crisis by forcing deep cuts that were not possible." Ontario Federation of Labour <http://ofl.ca> president Sid Ryan observed that "job loss like this is going to decimate towns across the country."[9]

Employer Views toward Unions

A *Canadian HR Reporter* survey of human resource professionals examined their views toward unions. The study revealed several important trends:

- 27 percent of participants think the union has the upper hand in bargaining, while 52 percent do not.

- 52 percent believe that economic conditions have pitted unionized workers against management.

- 42 percent report that the number of grievances has increased over the past three years, 44 percent indicate no change, and 13 percent believe there has been a decrease.

- 62 percent perceive that there is a growing trend for employers and unions to work together to find solutions to problems.

- 19 percent of respondents believe that unions have had a large financial impact on the employer, while 57 percent indicated that the financial impact of unions was small.

- 36 percent of participants think that the employer's relationship with the union will get worse over the next five years, 39 percent believe that it will stay about the same, and 24 percent think it will improve.[10]

The bitter labour disputes of the past few years have attracted considerable media and public attention. Some commentators argue that unions are fighting to survive. Ken Georgetti, former president of the Canadian Labour Congress, stated "There used to be a time when we had great respect from the public. But we've lost that. There's this notion that unions are just out for themselves and not for society. You get that label hung on you, and you have to work to get rid of it."[11] It is argued that unions must engage the new workforce if they are to survive. While strikes and threats of strikes have been common in the past, Jim Stanford, an economist with Unifor <http://www.unifor.org>, observes that "the confrontations are overwhelmingly driven by the employers' side. Almost all of the strikes and conflicts have been defensive from the perspective of the union. They're trying to hang on to what they have."[12]

LO2 HRC 5

Labour Unions: Goals and Structure

Labour unions alter the work environment. Their presence changes the relationship between employees and the organization, and the human resource department's involvement in union-related issues is not always well received by lower levels of management who believe that their ability to make workplace decisions has been eroded.

Unions have a major effect on the work environment, but in many other ways the environment remains unchanged. Supervisors and managers retain their primary responsibility for employee performance. Profit objectives and budgetary goals are often not shared with the union (although this is changing in some organizations). Nor do unions reduce the need for effective human resource policies and procedures. In short, management must still manage, and the union does not assume the responsibilities of the human resource department. To understand how and why unions influence human resource management, it is necessary to examine their goals and structure.

Union Goals and Philosophy

A union's objectives are influenced internally by the wishes of their members, the aspirations of their leaders, and the financial and membership strength of the union. Like other organizations, unions are open social systems that are affected by their external environment: the financial condition of the employer, the gains of other unions, the inflation and unemployment rates, and government policies all influence the union's objectives.

Yet among all these internal and external considerations, there exists a common core of widely agreed-upon objectives. Writing almost 100 years ago, one prominent labour leader stated that the mission for the labour movement was to protect workers, increase their pay, improve their working conditions, and help workers in general.[13] This approach has become known as **business unionism**, primarily because it recognizes that a union can survive only if it delivers a needed service to its members in a businesslike manner. But some unions have chosen to address broader social issues of politics and economics when such concerns are in the best interest of their members. This second kind of union, engaged in what is called **social (or reform) unionism**, tries to influence the economic and social policies of government at all levels—municipal, provincial, and federal.[14] In practice, union leaders pursue the objectives of social unionism by speaking out for or against government programs. For example, many union leaders oppose substantial government intervention into collective bargaining because it takes away or limits the right of the union to engage in free collective bargaining with management.

---

business unionism

A type of unionism whose mission is to protect workers, increase their pay, improve their working conditions, and help workers in general. Recognizes that a union can survive only if it delivers a needed service to its members in a businesslike manner.

---

social (reform) unionism

A type of unionism that tries to influence the economic and social policies of government at all levels. In practice, union leaders pursue such objectives by speaking out for or against government programs.

A number of unions have developed programs to help members deal with issues at the workplace. Consider, for example, the Women's Advocate program:

> The program, which was developed by the Canadian Auto Workers (now part of Unifor), is aimed at providing trained workplace advocates / representatives to help women (and men) deal with such issues as partner abuse and workplace harassment by making workers aware of community resources and workplace supports. The importance of employer support is noted. According to Julie White, the union's women's director: "It's really important we have that management support person to go through because, ultimately, if a woman needs time off work, it's not the union that can authorize that, it's the management support system."[15]

Human resource management is influenced by both business and social unionism goals. The growth of benefits discussed in Chapter 10 has resulted partly from union pressure. Even nonunionized employers have added many benefits in order to remain competitive in the labour market or to forestall unionization among their employees.

Union Structure and Functions

It has been argued that employees lost direct contact with business owners as organizations grew larger, so unions emerged to help workers influence workplace decisions.[16] Through unions, workers were able to exert control over their jobs and their work environment.[17] Then, when attempts were made by employers to cut wages or employment, the employees relied on unions to resist these actions.[18] The most important levels of union structure are local unions, national and international unions, and labour congresses.

Local Unions

For most union members and industrial relations practitioners, the **local unions**, or locals, are the most important part of the union structure. They provide the members, the revenue, and the power of the entire union movement. Historically, the two major types of unions were craft and industrial unions. **Craft unions** are composed of workers who possess the same skills or trades; these include, for example, all the carpenters who work in the same geographical area. **Industrial unions** include the unskilled and semiskilled workers at a particular location. When an employer has several locations that are unionized, employees at each location are usually represented by a different local union. An example would be the United Food and Commercial Workers.

local union

A branch of a union that is locally based and forms part of a larger (often national or international) union.

craft union

A type of union composed of workers who possess the same skills or trades.

industrial union

A type of union that includes the unskilled and semiskilled workers at a particular location.

Figure 13-2 shows the structure of a typical local. The union steward is usually elected by the workers and helps them present their problems to management. If the steward of an industrial union cannot help the employee, the problem is given to the grievance committee, which takes the issue to higher levels of management or to the human resource department. In craft unions, the steward, who is also called the representative, usually takes the issue directly to the business agent, who is often a full-time employee of the union.

FIGURE 13-2

Structure of a Typical Local Union

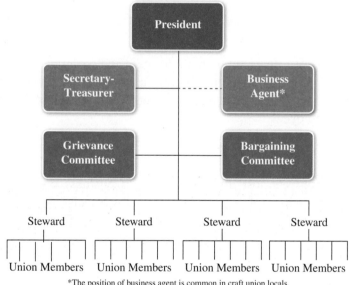

*The position of business agent is common in craft union locals.

Based on Human Resources and Social Development Canada, "Structure of a Typical Union", Public Works and Government Services Canada, 2003.

National and International Unions

Many local unions are part of a larger union, which may be a *national union*, such as Unifor or the Canadian Union of Public Employees <http://cupe.ca/>, or an *international union*, such as the United Steelworkers <http://www.usw.ca> or the International Brotherhood of Teamsters <http://www.teamster.org>. National unions are based in Canada, while international unions have their headquarters outside of the country (typically in the United States).

National and international unions exist to organize and help local unions. They also pursue social objectives of interest to their members and frequently maintain a staff that assists the local unions with negotiations, grievance handling, and expert advice. Some national and international unions leave many key decisions (including bargaining a collective agreement) with their local unions. In other relationships, the national or international union plays a very active role in local union affairs. Figure 13-3 shows the membership of the largest unions in Canada. Note that the two largest unions represent public sector employees.

FIGURE 13-3

Membership in Canada's Largest Unions (2013)

Union	Membership (000s)
Canadian Union of Public Employees	630
National Union of Public and General Employees	340
Unifor	308
United Food and Commercial Workers Canada	245
United Steelworkers of America	231
Public Service Alliance of Canada	188
Social Affairs Federation	129
Service Employees International Union	119
Teamsters Canada	93
Alberta Union of Provincial Employees	80

Based on Workplace Information and Research Division, Strategic Policy, Analysis, and Workplace Information Directorate, Labour Program, Employment and Social Development Canada.

Canadian Labour Congress

The **Canadian Labour Congress (CLC)** represents many unions in Canada, and has about 3.3 million members. The president, Hassan Yussuff, was elected in 2014. The CLC has five main functions: (1) representing Canada at the International Labour Organization, (2) influencing public policy at the federal level, (3) enforcing the code of ethics set out in its constitution, (4) providing services (such as research and education) for its member unions, and (5) resolving jurisdictional disputes among its member unions.

Canadian Labour Congress (CLC)

An organization, with a membership of about 3.3 million, that represents many unions in Canada.

While the Canadian Labour Congress is the largest labour federation, it is not the only one. In addition to other federations at the national level, there are also federations operating at the provincial and municipal or regional level (for instance, the Quebec Federation of Labour <http://ftq.qc.ca> and the Ottawa and District Labour Council <http://www.ottawalabour.org>).

Secession

In 1960, about two-thirds of union members belonged to an international union. Over the past half-century, that percentage has declined noticeably so that now only about 25 percent of union members belong to international unions.[19] This trend, referred to as *secession*, has been motivated, in part, by a desire for more autonomy on the part of Canadian locals and the development of policies aimed at specifically addressing the needs of Canadian workers. The most dramatic breakaway occurred in 1985 when the Canadian Auto Workers union (now part of Unifor), led by former president Bob White, severed ties with the United Auto Workers and held its founding convention in Toronto. Canadian members of international unions have often complained that they receive a disproportionately small share of union benefits.

Trends in Union Membership

Union Growth and Decline

In 2012, about 4.7 million workers were covered by collective agreements (union coverage rate of 30 percent). In terms of industry sector, education was the most highly unionized at 68 percent, followed closely by public administration (67 percent), utilities (63 percent), and health care and social assistance (54 percent). The lowest rates of unionization were in the agricultural (3.6 percent), scientific and technical services (4.4 percent), and accommodation / food services sectors (6.7 percent). [20]

A number of employers in small business and the service sector (such as retail) have been determined to remain union free:

> Almost 10 years ago, the United Food and Commercial Workers (UFCW) <http://www.ufcw.ca> began an organizing drive at Walmart in Weyburn, Saskatchewan. The union and employer were unable to reach an agreement during bargaining and a decertification vote was commenced. The UFCW objected to the vote but the Supreme Court of Canada refused to hear the case, and by a vote of 51 to 5, the union was decertified. According to local union president Norm Neault, "the process has been really, totally frustrating. Nine years battling this out in the courts, that's not very consistent of how you would see labour relations go between a union and an employer." [21]

However, unions are placing greater emphasis on organizing service employers:

> The United Food and Commercial Workers union, which represents most of the employees at Loblaws (Canada's largest food retailer), turned its efforts to organizing the second-largest food retailer (Sobeys). Sobeys sent a letter to employees indicating that the union merely wants their dues money and emphasized the good and open relationship the company has with employees. Loblaws executives indicated that they would welcome the move to remove the competitive disadvantage of paying 35 percent higher wage payments to employees. By 2014, the UFCW represented employees at more than 350 Sobeys, Safeway, IGA, and Freshco stores and at a number of distribution warehouses across Canada. [22]

In recent years, the number of women members in Canadian unions has been increasing rapidly. In 1967, women made up only 20 percent of total union membership; now, more than 50 percent of union members are female—the unionization rate for women surpassed that for men for the first time in 2004. While about one in six female employees belonged to a union in 1967, that ratio has doubled over 35 years and now about 1 in 3 women are union members. Thirty years ago, 4 out of 10 male employees were union members; today that proportion has fallen to under 3 in 10. In terms of age, the density rate is 15 percent for workers from 17 to 24, 28 percent for those between 25 and 34, 31 percent for workers from 35 to 44, 36 percent for workers from 45 to 54, and 36 percent for those between 55 and 64 years of age.

Unions today are acknowledging that traditional approaches to organizing and collective bargaining are becoming less relevant today. Many Canadians view union workers as being in a blue-collar or government occupation so there is a growing recognition of the need to appeal to other employees. For example, Unifor has decided to try and attract young workers to the union movement. According to

Anna Goldfinch of the Canadian Federation of Students <http://cfs-fcee.ca>, "there is more and more underemployment, precarious employment for youth. Unions need to start communicating that they're applicable in any workforce—and that unions will reflect young people more and more as young people start to participate in them."[23]

There are some structural changes happening within organized labour as some unions explore consolidating with other unions:

> Two major unions, the Canadian Auto Workers and the Communications, Energy and Paperworkers Union, merged in 2013 to form a new union called Unifor. Unifor represents more than 300,000 employees and is looking to grow. In discussing the merger, Dave Coles, National President of CEP at the time of the merger, said that "the new union is modern, forward-looking, and open to everyone."[24] There is also a trend within some unions of creating "super locals." For example, two UFCW locals combined to create a new local of approximately 60,000 members, many of whom work in the grocery sector. As noted by UFCW Canada Director Wayne Hanley, "if we pool our resources, we can give better service."[25]

In comparing unionization across provinces, Newfoundland had the highest rate (38 percent), followed closely by Quebec (37 percent), while the lowest union density was in Alberta (22 percent). Also of note is the lower probability that a part-time worker will be unionized (the union density rate for full-time workers is 31 percent compared with 23 percent for their part-time counterparts). In addition, larger workplaces are more likely to be unionized—about 13 percent of employees in firms with less than 20 employees were unionized, 30 percent in firms with 20 to 99 employees, 41 percent in firms with 100 to 500 employees, and 54 percent in firms with more than 500 employees.[26]

On the global scene, a number of countries have experienced a decline in union density (that is, union members as a percentage of the paid non-agricultural workforce). Explanations for the decline in union representation include (1) the decline in the manufacturing sector, (2) the constraints that globalization of financial markets have put on macroeconomic policies, and (3) competition from developing countries with low labour costs, resulting in the loss of low-skilled, labour-intensive jobs in high-wage countries.[27]

The Impact of Union Representation

Strikes

Members of the public frequently associate unions with strikes. However, the reality is that most collective agreements are settled without the union resorting to strike action or the employer locking out the workers. Still, there are exceptions:

> In 2009, approximately 1,800 City of Windsor (Ontario) inside and outside workers went on strike. By the six-week mark of the strike, frustration was setting in. A bar owner reported that her employees were harassed by city workers for removing the bar's garbage during the strike and a newspaper columnist said his car was vandalized after he wrote an article about taking garbage to a private firm. There were allegations of individuals putting clothes hangers in tall grass to prevent it from being mowed and spreading nails on the road leading to a private waste disposal site. The local CUPE president insisted that there are no reports of union picketers doing anything. Rather, one CUPE member stated that he suffered a broken ankle and cuts to his face after a confrontation with a private contractor cutting grass and other picketers revealed that they had been nudged by people seeking to drive past the picket line. One picketer was the victim of a hit-and-run and another was put in a headlock by an irate driver.[28]

In studying why strikes occur, it is possible to classify strikes into one of two categories:

1. **Strikes as Mistakes/Misjudgment.** At least some strikes occur because the parties have uncertain and imperfect information when trying to negotiate an agreement or because one or both negotiation teams are inexperienced negotiators. For example, some negotiators become frustrated easily when bargaining and make their "final offer" too early or without carefully considering the implications of shutting down bargaining.

2. **Strikes as Collective Voice.** In a number of instances, the decision to go out on strike is not because of a mistake or misjudgment but because of a perception on the part of workers that they are not being treated fairly. A strike is considered a mechanism by which to voice discontent to management:[29]

A prolonged strike between the City of Ottawa and OC Transpo <http://www.octranspo1.com> showed how adversarial a dispute can become and its impact on labour–management relations. The city wanted more control over route assignments and scheduling in an effort to improve the quality of the transit service, but the union was strongly opposed. As one union member stated, "This offer is going to destroy my family life. I won't be home for my family." The scheduling issue had the most impact on drivers with more seniority, and some of the other employees were anxious to return to work. According to one attendant, "In this economy, I don't think anybody wants to be out of work for a long period of time."[30]

In a strike environment, there are several issues to consider. An extended strike puts considerable financial pressure on employees. As well, the family is at risk for more than just financial reasons; normal family patterns and routines are seriously disrupted. Physical and emotional harm may also be an issue. Once the dispute is settled, employees have to return to a workplace and work teams that just a few days before were divided by a fundamental conflict. While companies need to get on with business, the human issues do not go away by themselves. It can take four to six weeks to return to normal working conditions, and some workplaces are never really the same:[31]

A series of wildcat strikes in the Quebec construction industry hit more than 100 work sites. At one Montreal site, workers knocked down a chain-link gate and chased away non-striking employees. A strike at Fortress Paper <http://www.fortresspaper.com> was estimated to cost the business between $500,000 and $600,000 in foregone profits.[32]

What factors distinguish firms with lower strike activity? Strikes were less common in smaller firms and in organizations where

- workers had more autonomy in the workplace;
- the employer introduced progressive human resource management practices;
- the union was in a strategically weak position; and
- employers have a large share of the market.[33]

How common are strikes and lockouts? Data on the number of strikes and lockouts, the number of workers involved, and the person-days not worked are provided in Figure 13-4. Over the 2009–2013 period, the greatest number of strikes and lockouts was in 2012, but 2009 had the largest number of person-days not worked. Obviously, a small number of large strikes in a given year can markedly affect these results. In addition, the cost of a strike can be substantial:

A bitter three-week strike between the *Toronto Star* <http://www.thestar.com> and its 2,000 newspaper carriers was estimated to cost the newspaper more than $30 million. The company was able to proceed with the outsourcing of home-delivery service after agreeing to guarantee jobs to carriers with the distributors for six months at their current wage rate. Union leader John Deverell estimated the costs to the paper to include about $19 million for buyouts, $3 million for strike replacement workers, $6 million for advertising discounts, and $3 million for half-price subscriptions to home-delivery subscribers. Outsourcing newspaper delivery was estimated to save the *Toronto Star* $6 million annually. [34]

FIGURE 13-4

Strikes and Lockouts in Canada

Year	Number of Strikes and Lockouts	Workers Involved (000)	Person-Days Not Worked (000)
1995	328	149	1,583
1996	330	276	3,269
1997	284	258	3,607
1998	381	244	2,440
1999	413	160	2,441
2000	378	143	1,644
2001	381	221	2,203
2002	294	166	2,986
2003	266	79	1,730
2004	297	259	3,185
2005	260	199	4,148
2006	151	42	793
2007	206	66	1,771
2008	188	41	875
2009	157	67	2,162
2010	174	58	1,202
2011	149	91	1,351
2012	281	137	904
2013	165	205	1,491

Based on Strategic Policy, Analysis, and Workplace Information Directorate, Labour Program, ESDC.

Quebec and British Columbia prohibit the use of replacement workers if there is a strike or lockout. However, some employer groups are arguing that the ban on replacement workers does not reduce the number of strikes or lockouts or days lost due to work stoppages. In addition, employers argue that the legislation discourages investment by employers in Quebec. [35]

Some strikes can take well over a year to resolve. Employees at the Voisey's Bay (Newfoundland) nickel mine finally settled with Brazilian mining firm Vale <http://www.vale.com>, ending a very bitter 18-month strike. According to United Steelworkers spokesperson Boyd Bussey, the use of replacement workers by Vale made the dispute particularly nasty. In Bussey's words, "It's been a cold couple of years on the picket line. At the end of the day, these workers resolved to take on the company and they came through with flying colours."[36]

Sometimes workers do not go out on strike, but come up with other approaches to put pressure on an employer. Air Canada was forced to cancel a number of flights a few years ago when several pilots "booked-off" by calling in sick. The airline said it supports the right of pilots to call in sick if they are not well or unable to work, but cannot permit such actions as part of industrial action.[37]

Two recent Supreme Court of Canada decisions address important issues relating to strikes. First, the court struck down Saskatchewan legislation that prevented public sector workers from going on strike. According to Lori Johb of the Saskatchewan Federation of Labour <http://www.sfl.sk.ca>, "workers aren't generally keen to strike. Without that right, we really had no power, we had no ability to achieve fair, collective bargaining for all the members."[38] The court also ruled that a part of Alberta's privacy legislation violated the right of a union to free speech by prohibiting the union from videotaping employees crossing a picket line. The court recognized the importance of freedom of expression in labour disputes with picketing representing a particularly critical form of expression.[39]

One issue that frequently comes up after a strike is settled concerns rebuilding the labour–management relationship. A strike changes the relationship, often leads to workplace conflict, and typically destroys the trust between the parties:

When a seven-week strike at CBC ended, management announced plans to hire consultants to "reintegrate" the workers with their managers. The reaction from most employees was "they've got to be [expletive] kidding." According to one consultant, "there is always a dramatic erosion in trust of management after a strike, which creates lingering resentment, and lack of productivity unless it is addressed properly." While each strike is different, some companies have outside consultants with expertise in psychology and social work conduct confidential debriefing sessions for employees. As well, some organizations have "return to work" training programs (again run by consultants) for managers; the programs focus on role plays, dealing with employees, and getting the team back and running. In addition, employees should be made aware of the EAP program and other assistance available to them.[40]

Wages and Benefits

What are the effects of unions on wages and benefits? The average hourly wage for full-time unionized employees at the end of 2014 was $28.33 an hour (compared with $23.47 for nonunion workers). This difference was more dramatic when comparing part-time workers: $22.09 for unionized employees and $14.02 for nonunion workers.[41] Moreover, as indicated in Figure 13-5, unionized employees tend to have more comprehensive benefit plan coverage.

FIGURE 13-5

Union Status and Work Conditions

Work Condition	Union Employees	Nonunion Employees
% of employees with pension coverage	82.8	32.9
% of employees with supplemental health plan coverage	83.7	44.4
% of employees with dental plan coverage	77.0	41.9
% of employees with paid sick leave	77.2	44.7
% of employees with paid vacation leave	84.1	65.3

(Continued)

% of employees with flextime option	16.7	27.1
% of employees in job sharing arrangement	12.1	6.8
Average annual paid vacation leave (days)	20.9	15.1

SOURCE: "Strikes and Lockouts in Canada" adapted from the Statistics Canada publication "Perspectives on Labour and Income," Catalogue No. 75-001, Autumn, 2000.

Spotlight *on* HRM

Making Peace at Work

Communication is vital to rebuilding a workplace after a labour dispute, the experts say. Here are tips from Steve Kennedy, Ottawa-based mental-health practitioner for employee assistance provider FGIworld:

- Before employees return, managers should discuss how the new agreement changes the workplace and how they will welcome back the staff.

- Employees and managers may need counselling to help them recover if they experienced conflicts at the picket line. "It's important from the get-go to acknowledge that both sides have a legal right to do what they did," Mr. Kennedy says.

- As soon as possible after employees return, managers should acknowledge that the strike caused stresses and that efforts will be made to relieve them. A full-scale staff meeting is best.

- Attendance at the meeting should be mandatory. "The message is not 'Come if you want to,'" Mr. Kennedy says. Employees usually are anxious to participate.

- To help employees refocus, managers should state goals clearly and express optimism. They should also commit to supporting employees and trying to better resolve issues in the future.

- Allow ample time for employee questions and discussions.

- Managers should set up processes to discuss and resolve any outstanding issues among teams or individuals.

- Employees should be encouraged to take stock of their role and consider what they can do to create a better work environment. They should also remember that managers are human, too.

Based on Wallace Immen, "How to Heal a Bruised Workplace," *The Globe and Mail*, October 5, 2005, pp. C1, C2.

 HRC 5

Unions and Productivity

One major issue of interest for human resource management and industrial relations practitioners is the relationship between unionization and productivity. On one hand, it can be argued that unions have a "monopoly" face that creates economic inefficiency by introducing restrictive and inflexible work rules, withdrawing labour in the form of a strike if an employer fails to meet union demands, and increasing compensation costs. On the other hand, it can also be asserted that unions have a "voice" face that increases productivity by reducing turnover, enhancing employee morale, improving communications with workers, and "shocking" management into employing more efficient workplace practices.[42] Studies have shown that unions:

- reduce employee turnover (fewer quits);
- increase tenure with the firm; and

- raise productivity or output per worker.[43]

However, the relationship between unionization and productivity is open to considerable debate and has not been universally agreed upon. In fact, management perceptions are opposite to some of the empirical work: while managers from both the union and nonunion sectors tend to believe that unions lower productivity, some studies indicate that in a number of industries, productivity is actually higher in unionized firms. There is also evidence that unions recognize the importance of increasing productivity:

> The International Boilermakers Union <http://boilermakers.ca> believed that union members who were shutting down work sites illegally, sleeping on the job, and being disrespectful were giving the union a bad name. As a result, the union got tough and decided to adopt a zero-tolerance policy for poor worker behaviour. As one senior union official stated, "a majority of our members are honest, hard-working, skilled tradespeople. Unfortunately, a small group are destroying other members' careers with their personal agenda of bad attitudes, late starts, early quits, poor productivity, absenteeism, and job disruptions." The union implemented a new policy with strict guidelines addressing union member behaviour.[44]

One issue that comes up during a strike is whether the employer should use replacement workers:

> The PotashCorp <http://www.potashcorp.com> Allan mine chose to operate using nonunion labour during a strike. The company's Director of Communications indicated that while management is running the mine, there were some jobs (such as operating machinery at the hoist and steam plant) that management is not trained to do. A representative from the United Steel Workers union expressed concerns about the safety of the managers working, noting that people have been injured when managers have been operating equipment during other labour disputes.[45]

In most jurisdictions, employers have the right to operate during a strike but some choose not to:

> According to one labour relations expert: "The employer has to calculate very carefully if bringing in replacement workers is going to exacerbate the bitterness of the dispute. After a strike it takes a while to put the relationship back together. There's a lot of bitterness left over. The employer takes some chance of exacerbating that when they bring in replacement workers—at a substantial cost to the labour–management relationship over the long term."[46]

LO3 HRC 5

The Legal Environment

Government shapes the union management framework through both the enactment of laws and in their role as employer. Unlike the United States, where employers and unions across the country are regulated by the *National Labour Relations Act*, in Canada the federal government and each province has its own labour legislation. This division of responsibilities for trade union law is a result of the *British North America Act* (now the *Constitution Act, 1867*), which specifies the powers of the federal government and the provinces.

The issue of jurisdiction over labour relations is significant for human resource practitioners. The Canadian Parliament is restricted in its jurisdiction over labour relations matters to organizations involved in interprovincial trade and commerce (e.g., banks, airlines, railways, and federal government agencies). All other organizations fall under the jurisdiction of the provinces. It has been estimated that less than 10 percent of the Canadian labour force comes under federal jurisdiction. Consequently, it is important that human resource practitioners are aware of the appropriate legislation.

Although the traditional view is that the employer and union should be free to sit down and negotiate a collective agreement, we are seeing increasing government intervention in the bargaining process at both the provincial and national level. For instance, Alberta's Bill 46 gives the province the right to bypass arbitration and impose a collective agreement if it is unable to reach a deal with the Alberta Union of Provincial Employees (AUPE) <http://www.aupe.org>. According to Guy Smith, president of AUPE, "this is a government that is being extremely heavy-handed and dictatorial."[47] Buzz Hargrove, former president of the Canadian Autoworkers Union, stated: "there's no respect left for the collective bargaining process. It's about government coming in on behalf of employers and defending employers, almost guaranteeing they're going to win the dispute…it's so anti-democratic, it's so un-Canadian."[48]

The Common Core of Canadian Labour Legislation

The fact that each province and the federal jurisdiction all have their own labour relations statutes makes dealing with unions somewhat more difficult, particularly for employers operating in more than one province. Some of the key aspects of Canadian labour law (which will be discussed in more detail later) include the following:

- **Right to Join a Union.** Employees have the right to join a trade union of their choice and participate in the union's activities.

- **Good Faith Bargaining.** In attempting to negotiate a collective agreement, both labour and management have a duty to "bargain in good faith."

- **No Strikes or Lockouts during the Life of the Collective Agreement.** It is illegal for a union to strike or an employer to lock out employees during the life of the contract.

- **Prohibition on Unfair Labour Practices.** All jurisdictions have legislation prohibiting unfair labour practices by employers and unions.

- **Conciliation.** The right of a union to strike or an employer to lock out employees is (in most provinces) delayed until the conciliation process has been exhausted.

While each province and the federal jurisdiction have some unique features in their labour law, there is a "common core" of provisions contained in the various labour relations acts (refer to Figure 13-6).[49]

FIGURE 13-6

Common Characteristics of Federal and Provincial Labour Legislation

1. All jurisdictions create labour relations boards to decide who has the right to participate in collective bargaining and what bargaining unit should be permitted to represent those who are organized.

2. Most jurisdictions prohibit strikes during the life of an agreement.

3. Most jurisdictions contain regulations that delay strike action until a conciliation effort has been made and has failed.

4. All jurisdictions require that a collective agreement be in force for at least one year.

5. All jurisdictions specify and prohibit certain "unfair labour practices" by management and unions.

Labour Relations Boards

To enforce labour legislation, the federal and all provincial governments have created **labour relations boards (LRBs)**. These agencies investigate violations of the law and have the power to determine: (1) whether a person is an employee for the purposes of the law; (2) whether an employee is a member of a trade union; (3) whether an organization is an appropriate bargaining agent for bargaining purposes; (4) whether a collective agreement is in force; and (5) whether any given party is bound by it. The enforcement procedures of an LRB relating to unfair labour practice allegations are summarized in Figure 13-7.

labour relations boards (LRBs)

Boards set up in the federal and provincial jurisdictions to administer labour relations legislation.

FIGURE 13-7

LRB Procedures for Redressing Unfair Labour Practices

1. The aggrieved individual or organization contacts the appropriate LRB office (federal or provincial) and explains the alleged violation.

2. If the case appears to have merit, the LRB informs the other party of the complaint and asks for a response.

3. The LRB gives the parties involved the opportunity to present evidence and to make representations. If the complaint cannot be solved informally, the LRB conducts an official hearing with the interested parties present and usually represented by legal counsel.

4. On the basis of the evidence, the board will either dismiss the case or, if one party is found guilty of a violation, issue a cease-and-desist order. In the event of noncompliance, this order is enforceable in a court of law.

5. It is up to the courts to decide whether a verdict can be appealed or not. In any case, an appeal can be made in matters of jurisdiction, failure to pursue legitimate complaints, and procedural irregularities.

In comparison to traditional courts of law, LRBs are more flexible in their procedures for resolving a conflict. They may rely on expert evidence instead of adhering to precedents, suggest a compromise, or even impose a solution upon the parties. In all jurisdictions, the boards' decisions are final and binding and cannot be appealed except on procedural matters.

When charges have been filed against an employer, the human resource department usually assists the organization's lawyer in preparing the case. For example, the HR department may be involved in compiling job descriptions, performance appraisals, attendance records, and other documents that help the company prove its case. Consider the following:

Patrick Veinot was an employee of Vale Canada, a nickel mining and metals company, and vice-president of his local union. During a long and bitter strike, Veinot was charged with criminal harassment after an employee, who crossed the picket line, was assaulted. Vale investigated the incident, concluded that Veinot had verbally harassed the employee and encouraged another striking worker to assault the employee, and terminated Veinot's employment (but Veinot was subsequently acquitted of the charges). Veinot was also prohibited from going onto the employer's property. After the strike ended, Veinot was appointed a vice-president of the local union—the company would contact him by phone to discuss grievances but refused to let Veinot on the company property. The union grieved the employer's action and the labour board held that banning Veinot from company property was interference with union activities. The company was ordered to stop such interference and allow Veinot on the property for the purpose of union meetings.[50]

LO4 HRC 5

The Collective Bargaining Process

Union Organizing

It is worth remembering that a union exists only when workers create it. While unions may use professional organizers, the outcome of the organizing drive depends primarily upon the employees. As George Meany, the first president of the AFL-CIO in the United States, once commented:

> Despite the well-worn trade union phrase, an organizer does not organize a plant. Now, as in the beginning, the workers must organize themselves. The organizer can serve only as an educator; what he or she organizes is the thinking of the workers.[51]

In addition to professional organizers, employees interested in unionization often play an important role in convincing co-workers to join the union. During regular working hours, employees are not allowed to discuss unionization with co-workers. However, several other techniques are used to encourage workers to sign **authorization cards**, including handbills, speeches, conversations, and even home visits. Depending on the jurisdiction, a union is typically certified either on the basis of card signatures or as a result of an election. Some unions are particularly creative in the organizing process:

> The United Food and Commercial Workers (UFCW) have developed a Youth Internship Program which involves youth activists who are given the opportunity to work with union representatives to learn negotiating skills and experience hands-on union organizing campaigns. Travel and accommodation expenses as well as lost wages are covered by the union. The UFCW also have a program—Talking Union—where union representatives and members visit high schools, colleges, and universities and provide students who are new to the workforce with information on labour history and workplace rights.[52]

authorization cards

Cards signed by workers to join a union. Depending on the jurisdiction, a union may be certified either on the basis of card signatures or as a result of an election.

Union organizers educate the workers by explaining how the union can help employees and reduce mistreatment of workers. However, professionals only assist workers; they do not cause workers to join a union. Even experienced organizers find it difficult to organize a well-managed and growing company with proactive human resource practices.[53] Still, some unions are using new technology to help organize workers:

> Some union activists are advocating using the Internet to build support through virtual organizing and virtual picketing. Derek Blackadder, a CUPE organizer, tried to organize a group of workers using Facebook but was banned from the network for having too many friends. However, an email campaign by a colleague was used to have Facebook administrators restore his privileges. Some experts believe social networks are particularly appropriate for union organizing as unions are very committed to increasing membership of young people (who are primary users of social networks).[54]

Prior to many union organizing campaigns, there are signs of employee interest in union representation. Of particular importance is the work environment. For example, are the turnover and absenteeism rates higher than the norms for the industry and community? Is morale poor? Are pay and benefits below average for the industry? Does the employer have a procedure for resolving employee complaints or issues and if so, is the process used by workers? Changes in employee behaviour may also suggest that a union drive is under way (see Figure 13-8). It is important to remember that these are only indications of a *possible* union drive.

FIGURE 13-8

Employee Behaviour That Suggests Union Activity

- Groups of employees in huddled conversations that end when a manager walks by

- More time in washrooms (where union cards are frequently signed)

- Problems being created or magnified by a few workers

- More militant employee behaviour

- An increase in questions about company policies and benefits

- Sudden disappearance of sources of gossip and information

Based on Howard Levitt, "Keep in Touch If You Want to Keep the Union at Bay," *Financial Post*, September 13, 1999, p. C11.

An organizing drive at a Denny's <http://www.dennys.ca> restaurant signalled the use of class-action litigation as a new organizing strategy for unions. The Denny's case involved the charging of agency fees by companies recruiting temporary foreign workers for the restaurant. The BC Supreme Court supported the filing of a class-action lawsuit, a strategy that has been used in the United States with difficult-to-organize and exploited workers who may be unable or unwilling to bring a case on their own against their employer.[55]

Spotlight *on* ETHICS

Hiring a Union Supporter

Consider the following situation and make a note of your answer on a separate sheet of paper.

You are a recent university graduate and three months ago started working for a small manufacturing firm. The company currently has 17 employees, including 10 labourers who are responsible for product assembly. Although wage levels in the firm are slightly above average when compared to the competition in the immediate area, the business owner is known as a tough manager who isn't exactly a "people person."

While your official title is assistant manager of operations, your job involves some aspects of production as well as marketing. Although the hours are long, you have found the job to be quite rewarding and have enjoyed the exposure to the "real world of business." Four days ago, the owner of the business came to you and asked you to also assume responsibility for human resources, saying, "I'm not into all that people management stuff but we are expanding and I know we've got to have somebody do it. You can pretty much do what you want when it comes to hiring—the only thing that's important to me is that we don't ever get a union around here."

(Continued)

Yesterday, the owner dropped by your office to tell you that the company was going to need to hire two labourers. He said, "Here's a chance for you to use some of that stuff you learned in university. I've been doing most of the hiring around here but I'm just getting too busy. As I mentioned the other day, the only thing I want is to be sure that we don't get a union around here. Oh, also, the people you hire better be good! I'll let you in on a little secret—when you bring someone in for an interview, ask them the usual stuff about qualifications and so on. Then, carefully bring the conversation around to unions. But you've got to be careful—I don't want the labour board down here bothering us. I usually bring up some labour dispute—the NHL collective bargaining situation, a strike by the post office or nurses, or some other union issue. If you are careful, you can find out what the person really thinks about unions. And, obviously, if you think that they are sympathetic to unions, don't hire them. It's worked for me for more than 25 years. Whatever you do, don't mess this up!"

On one hand, you know the views of the business owner concerning unions. On the other hand, you are fully aware that under Canadian labour law, employees have the right to join a union and participate in its activities and that it is illegal to discriminate against an employee or job candidate because they are interested in union representation. What are you going to do in this situation?

Once a union drive begins, management's choice of responses becomes limited in several important ways. A labour relations board (LRB) will protect workers from management reprisals. For example, the discipline of union supporters is illegal, unless the employer can prove the basis for punishment was not involvement in a union but improper behaviour.

Employer lawyer Jamie Knight identified three stages to an employer's defence in the event that an employer is committed to remaining union free. Stage 1 involves removing the incentive to unionize through effective human resource management (such as competitive wages and benefits, fair and reasonable policies, excellent communication with employees, and a complaint and suggestion system that allows employees to voice their concerns without the threat of reprisal). Stage 2, which occurs when card signing begins, involves discussing the impacts of unionization (such as the union becoming the exclusive bargaining agent, the requirement for employees to pay dues, and the need to carefully assess union promises) and the need to avoid unfair labour practice charges. In Stage 3, when an election is about to be held, the employer is advised to encourage employees to get out and vote because the chance of a union victory may decline as voter turnout increases.[56]

When unions are organizing, labour relations boards pay particularly close attention to the actions of employers. Unlike the United States, Canadian labour law provides employers with relatively little freedom to counter a union organizing drive.[57] Both the context and content of statements about unionization are carefully examined by LRBs. Consequently, employers are well advised to obtain prudent legal advice in the wake of a union organizing campaign.

Canadian LRBs are quite vigilant in enforcing unfair labour relations practices. Human resource administrators should stress to every member of management, from supervisor to chief executive officer, the following two cautions:

1. Can management actions be judged as unfair labour practices by the LRB?

2. Will management actions provide fuel for the organizing drive?

HRC 5

In Prince Edward Island, two fish processing plants were closed down upon the arrival of union organizers. The P.E.I. Labour Relations Board ordered the employer, Polar Foods <http://www.polarfoods.com>, to compensate 150 workers for lost wages (a total settlement of almost $500,000) following evidence at an unfair labour practices hearing that Polar Foods closed the plants to avoid unionization.[58]

When an unfair labour practice is committed by any member of management, it can lead to expensive, time-consuming lawsuits and (in some instances) automatic certification of the union. Moreover, union supporters can point to management violations as further justification for a union.

Unfair Labour Practices

To prevent employers from interfering with employee rights, the law prohibits specific **unfair labour practices** by management. These legal prohibitions are summarized in Figure 13-9. They require that management neither interfere with nor discriminate against employees who undertake collective action.

unfair labour practices

Practices by management such as interfering with or discriminating against employees who undertake collective action. Unions may also commit unfair labour practices.

FIGURE 13-9

Unfair Labour Practices by Management

Every jurisdiction in Canada has specific provisions dealing with unfair labour practices by management. Some of the most common provisions addressing unfair labour practices are provided below. Activities that management may not engage in include:

1. Interfering in the formation of a union or contributing to it financially (although there have been allowances for the providing of an office for the union to conduct business and for paid leave for union officials conducting union business)
2. Discriminating against an employee because the individual is or is not a member of a trade union
3. Discriminating against an employee because that individual chooses to exercise rights granted by labour relations statutes
4. Intimidating or coercing an employee to become or not become a member of a union

Labour legislation also makes company-dominated unions illegal. In the past, some employers believed that if they could not prevent their employees from organizing, the next best thing would be to encourage a union they could dominate. Through threats, bribes, or infiltration, some companies tried to control union activities.

Unfair labour practices by unions are also prohibited. A summary of such practices is provided in Figure 13-10.

FIGURE 13-10

Unfair Labour Practices by Unions

While every jurisdiction has laws regulating trade union conduct, some of the most important unfair labour practice provisions are presented below. Activities that a union is not permitted to engage in include:

1. Seeking to compel an employer to bargain collectively with the union if the union is not the certified bargaining agent
2. Attempting, at the workplace and during working hours, to persuade an employee to become or not become a union member
3. Intimidating, coercing, or penalizing an individual because he or she has filed a complaint or testified in any proceedings pursuant to the relevant labour relations statute
4. Engaging in, encouraging, or threatening illegal strikes
5. Failing to represent employees fairly

HRC 5

Obtaining Bargaining Rights

Legal recognition or bargaining rights may be obtained in three ways: (1) voluntary recognition, (2) through certification by a labour relations board, and (3) a prehearing vote or automatic certification resulting from unfair labour practice.

1. **Voluntary recognition** occurs if a union has organized a majority of employees and the employer is satisfied that the union did not apply undue pressure in the organization process. The employer then accepts the union as the legal bargaining agent without any involvement of a third party.

2. **Regular certification** may take different forms (depending on the jurisdiction):

   - In some provinces, if a substantial number of employees (usually between 50 and 65 percent, depending on jurisdiction) sign union cards, the labour relations board may certify the unit without an election. If the union is unable to get enough employees to sign cards to qualify for automatic certification but still gets a significant number of card signatures (typically between 35 and 45 percent of bargaining-unit members, again depending on the jurisdiction), an election is mandatory. A secret ballot is taken under the supervision of the labour relations board at the employer's place of business. If the union loses, another election among the same employees cannot be held for one year. If the union wins (that is, the majority of eligible employees who vote cast ballots in favour of the union), then the employer must prepare to negotiate with the union and attempt to reach a collective agreement.

   - Five provinces (Alberta, British Columbia, Nova Scotia, Ontario, and Saskatchewan) do not automatically certify unions based on card signatures. Rather, an election is held if there is sufficient support for the union in the form of signed cards. Again, the union is certified if the majority of the ballots cast are in favour of the union. Similarly, recent changes to the *Canada Labour Code* (what has been referred to as the *Employees' Voting Rights Act*), result in a similar procedure for a union attempting to organize federally regulated employers. While employers generally favour a mandatory secret ballot vote for certification, the legislative change away from certification on the basis of card signatures was strongly opposed by unions.

3. **Prehearing votes** are taken in cases when there are significant indications that an employer has committed unfair labour practices to prevent unionization. In such a case a union can ask an LRB to conduct a prehearing vote. In addition, most jurisdictions provide for automatic certification if employer actions (in the form of unfair labour practices) are such that the true wishes of employees may not be known.[59]

In Jonquiere, Quebec, a Walmart suddenly closed down a few months after the employees became the first Walmart store to unionize in 2004. The closure was on the day an arbitrator was selected to resolve the dispute. A legal battle that took about a decade was ultimately decided when the Supreme Court of Canada ruled that the employees were entitled to compensation.[60]

LO5 HRC 5

Negotiating a Collective Agreement

Once a union is certified, the various labour relations statutes require both the union and management to bargain in good faith. This means that both sides are required to make a reasonable effort to negotiate a collective agreement. The failure of either party to do so can lead to unfair labour practice charges.

The collective bargaining process has three overlapping phases. Preparation for negotiations is the first and often the most critical stage. The success of the second stage, face-to-face negotiations, largely depends on how well each side has prepared, the skill of the management and union negotiators, and the bargaining power of each side. The third phase involves the follow-up activities of contract administration. An organization may establish an industrial relations department or create a labour relations specialist position within the human resources department to administer the collective agreement and coordinate contract negotiations. On occasion, some organizations choose to use outside negotiators:

> Moving away from traditional practice, the City of Halifax decided to hire an outside lawyer to negotiate with its firefighting and police unions. According to the city, they required some expertise in labour relations and any expenditure for the lawyers' fees would be part of the typical operating budget. The Halifax Regional Police Association was opposed to the appointment, indicating that it was unaware of issues with the city's internal legal department and expressed concern over the costs to taxpayers of bringing in an outside lawyer.[61]

Postal strikes tend to have a serious impact on customers, especially small businesses. Should postal strikes be prohibited? Could such prohibitions be done legally?

CP/Sean Kilpatrick.

Preparing for Negotiations

The purpose of negotiations is to achieve a *collective agreement*. The agreement specifies the rights and responsibilities of management and the union. Detailed preparations are required if each party is to achieve its objectives.[62]

Labour relations specialists need to monitor the environment to obtain information about likely union demands. A number of strategies can be employed. The labour relations department must be sensitive to the rate of inflation and the settlements made by other unions.

One set of bargaining issues revolves around **management rights**. These rights provide management with the freedom to operate the business subject to any terms in the collective agreement.[63] They often include the right to reassign employees to different jobs, to make hiring decisions, and to decide other matters important to management.

---

management rights

Rights that provide management with the freedom to operate the business subject to any terms in the collective agreement.

Under what is known as the *residual rights theory* of management, employers argue that they have the authority over all issues not contained in the collective agreement. On the other hand, union leaders assert that residual rights do not exist and that they are free to bargain over any issue affecting workers. Most collective agreements have a *management rights clause*. A typical clause might be:

> Nothing in this agreement shall be deemed to restrict management in any way in the performance of all functions of management except those specifically abridged or modified by this agreement.[64]

In negotiating a collective agreement, management may want to include contract language that increases their flexibility at the workplace. For example, supervisors may want all job descriptions to include the phrase "and other duties assigned by management." This clause prevents workers from refusing work because it is not in their job description. The clause also gives supervisors greater freedom in assigning employees. Labour relations specialists in the human resource department may use a variety of sources (such as surveys, discussions, focus groups, provisions in other collective agreements, and information from grievance claims) to discover which rights are important.

Negotiating with the Union

After preparing for bargaining, the second phase of negotiations is face-to-face bargaining with the union. Discussions often start as much as 60 to 90 days before the end of the present contract. If the negotiations are for a first contract, they begin after the union is recognized by the employer or wins a certification election.

Negotiations cover a variety of issues relating to terms and conditions of employment including wages, hours of work, and working conditions. These areas are interpreted broadly. *Wages* means all forms of compensation such as pay, insurance plans, retirement programs, and other benefits and services. *Hours of work* include the length of the workday, breaks, holidays, vacations, and any other component of the work schedule. *Working conditions* involve such issues as safety, supervisory treatment, and other elements of the work environment. The contents of a collective agreement are only limited by the ingenuity of the parties. For instance:

Canadian Blood Services <https://www.blood.ca> (Edmonton) permits employees to take up to three days off to attend their wedding. In PEI, the Labourers International Union <http://www.liuna.ca> negotiated a clause that prohibits the use of cellphones and smart phones during work hours and in Quebec, CBC and Groupe TVA <http://groupetva.ca> agreed to a clause guaranteeing an employee salary and benefits if the individual is incarcerated for refusing to divulge a confidential source.[65]

Union leaders, like politicians, are elected. Are there other similarities?

THE CANADIAN PRESS/Frank Gunn.

Successful bargaining usually begins with easy issues in order to build a pattern of give-and-take. Negotiations almost always take place in private, permitting more open discussion of the issues. When deadlocks occur, several tactics can keep negotiations moving toward a peaceful settlement. By settling easy issues first, bargainers often point to this progress and say, "We've come too far to give up on this impasse. Surely, we can find a solution." This sense of past progress may increase the resolve of both sides to find a compromise.

Richard Dixon, vice-president and human resources officer at NAV-Canada <http://www.navcanada.ca>, stated: "In any unionized environment, if you're sitting at the collective bargaining table, you're sitting across from individuals who know the business very well. When trying to introduce a new business process or negotiate a more streamlined way of doing things, the HR professionals who don't know the business as well as the people on the other side of the table could have their pockets picked."[66]

Compromises may be achieved by offering counterproposals that take into account the needs of the other party. For example, Air Canada and its pilots reached an agreement without resorting to strike action or arbitration for the first time since 1996. In addition to reopener clauses, the contract also provides for profit sharing for union members using a formula similar to that applied for executive bonuses.[67]

Sometimes progress is made by simply dropping the issue temporarily and moving on to other items. Further progress on other issues may lead to compromises regarding earlier impasses. If no progress results, bargainers may request the assistance of federal or provincial mediators or conciliators.

Many management teams will exclude top executives. They are kept out of negotiations because top managers are often not experienced in collective bargaining. Also, their exclusion gives management bargainers a reason to ask for a temporary adjournment when the union introduces demands that require a careful review. Rather than refusing the union's suggestion, management bargainers may ask for a recess to confer with top management (using the old adage "my hands are tied").

Experienced bargainers realize that the other side must achieve some of its objectives. If the employer is powerful enough to force an unacceptable contract on the union negotiating team, the union membership may refuse to ratify the contract, or union officials and members may refuse to co-operate with management once the collective agreement goes into effect. In addition, if management does not bargain in good faith, the union may file unfair labour practice charges.

Mutual Gains Bargaining

Rather than use the traditional adversarial approach to negotiating a collective agreement, some unions and employers are employing *mutual gains bargaining*. This approach moves away from the us-versus-them or win–lose attitude in favour of a win–win approach in which both parties work together to solve common problems. However, labour unions are often skeptical about win–win bargaining. According to one senior union official:

> It has been our experience that most employers only become "less adversarial" and talk about co-operation when they want something that will benefit them. Many employers have approached unions wanting to extract concessions, normally accompanied by promises of future employer co-operation. It is also usually followed by an acute case of amnesia on the part of the company. Any level of co-operation between the union and company must be accompanied by a commitment that front-line supervisors are prepared to treat our members with dignity and respect on the shop floor. Without that commitment, co-operation between the union and company is meaningless. [68]

Note that mutual gains bargaining does not mean "soft" bargaining or one side giving in. Rather, both parties sit down at the bargaining table as equals and engage in joint problem-solving activities. The process is usually preceded by training in conflict resolution for both employer and union representatives. In addition, mutual gains bargaining requires substantial commitment, trust, and respect, and a long-term focus on the part of both labour and management.

What does a mutual gains enterprise need to succeed? At the workplace level, it is important to have high standards of employee selection, broad design of tasks and a focus on teamwork, employee involvement in problem solving, and a climate based on co-operation and trust. At the human resource policy level, key elements include a commitment to employment stabilization, investment in training and development, and a contingent compensation strategy that emphasizes participation, co-operation, and contribution. Finally, at the strategic level, there must be a strong commitment from top management to the mutual gains concept, business strategies that support and are aligned with the mutual gains model, and an effective voice for human resource management in strategy making. [69]

Research by the Conference Board of Canada revealed that 36 percent of employers and 42 percent of unions have attempted interest-based or mutual gains bargaining techniques.[70]

Still, many labour relations experts are somewhat skeptical about interest-based bargaining. According to one labour lawyer:

> If you ask seasoned negotiators (about interest-based bargaining), they'll give you the look of death and say, "Are you crazy?" Mutual gains bargaining requires both sides to invest so much time and energy in being trained in things like "What do you need?" "What are our needs?" "How do we negotiate in a collaborative fashion?" But to go from traditional bargaining into mutual interest takes a diametric mind-shift. You need to invest the resources and the relationship has to be mature enough.[71]

Approving the Proposed Agreement

The bargaining stage of negotiations is completed when the agreement has been approved. Often final approval for the employer rests with top management. Negotiations are not complete until the union also approves the proposed agreement. Typically, the union bargaining team submits the proposal to the membership for ratification. If a majority of the members vote for the proposal, it replaces the previous collective agreement. If members reject it, union and management bargainers reopen negotiations. Administration of the collective agreement begins when both sides sign it.

LO6 HRC 5

Conciliation and Mediation

What happens in the event that negotiations between labour and management break down? In their legislation, all jurisdictions provide for **conciliation** and mediation services. Actually, in most provinces, no strike action is permitted before a conciliation effort has been made and has failed.[72] A 10-year review of conciliation cases in Nova Scotia revealed that conciliation officers settled more than 90 percent of the cases.[73] However, the results vary among provinces and some jurisdictions have not come close to matching the 90 percent figure.

conciliation
Use of a government-appointed third party to explore solutions to a labour–management dispute.

Conciliators are appointed by the federal or provincial minister of labour, at the request of either one or both of the parties involved or at the discretion of the ministers. A conciliator is requested to submit a report to the minister within a specified time period. If conciliation fails, strikes or lockouts can legally commence, usually two weeks after the submission of the conciliator's report. Although labour relations legislation may include an option to have a conciliation board meet with the parties, this is used infrequently.

With reference to **mediation**, often a mediator will meet separately with each bargaining team, especially when the negotiations take place in a hostile atmosphere. Effective mediation requires a high degree of sensitivity, patience, and expertise in the psychology of negotiation.

mediation
Use of a neutral third party to help settle a labour–management dispute.

Administering the Collective Agreement

Upon ratification by union members and approval by management, the parties begin living with the collective agreement. What happens if the parties have a disagreement regarding the interpretation of a term of the agreement? As discussed below, alleged violations of the agreement typically go through the **grievance procedure**. A *grievance* is defined as a complaint by an employee or employer that alleges that some aspect of a collective agreement has been violated. Almost every collective agreement in Canada contains some type of formalized procedure for resolving disputes. Furthermore, labour legislation typically requires that a grievance that cannot be resolved between the parties be submitted to an arbitrator or arbitration board whose decision is final and binding. To give an example, consider the following case:

> A 46-year-old Ottawa city worker was found to have altered the water meter at both his current and former residence. The employer met with the worker who admitted to tampering with the meter and agreed to reimbursing the city for almost $7,000 to cover unrecorded water usage. The employee admitted turning off the meter on several occasions (such as on heavy laundry days or when filling his pool). Although the employee had 23 years of service without performance or disciplinary issues and the misconduct was off-duty and not directly related to his employment, an arbitrator upheld the termination of the employee.[74]

grievance procedure

A formalized procedure for resolving disputes if the parties have a disagreement regarding the interpretation of a term of the collective agreement.

Grievance Procedures

While either management or the union may file a grievance when the collective agreement is violated, most workplace decisions are made by management. Consequently, most grievances are filed by the union. The grievance procedure consists of an ordered series of steps. Figure 13-11 describes the steps through which an employee's grievance typically passes. An example further demonstrates how a grievance may proceed:

> One winter day, a bus driver for the Hamilton Street Railway Company was following another bus closely as they were to begin their routes. The road conditions were poor and when the bus in front stopped, the bus driver slid her bus into it. Both drivers were injured and both buses were damaged. The collective agreement listed several infractions that would "conclusively be deemed to be sufficient cause for dismissal." One such infraction was for accidents due to "carelessness, negligence, or disregard to normal safety precautions." The driver had been involved in two other accidents over the past four months, so the company decided to terminate her. The union grieved the dismissal and an arbitrator overturned the termination. The company appealed the decision and the Ontario Superior Court of Justice held that termination was appropriate, because the collective agreement clearly spelled out dismissal as the specific penalty for carelessness or negligence. Consequently, the arbitrator lacked jurisdiction to substitute a lesser penalty.[75]

The number of steps in the grievance procedure and the staff involved at each step will vary from organization to organization, but most grievance procedures have between three and five steps. The purpose of a multistep grievance procedure is to allow higher-level managers and union representatives to look at the issue from different perspectives and to assess the consequences of pursing the matter further. This approach increases the chance that the dispute gets resolved without going to arbitration.

FIGURE 13-11

Typical Steps in a Union–Management Grievance Procedure

- *Preliminary discussion*. The aggrieved employee discusses the complaint with the immediate supervisor with or without a union representative. At this stage, or at any other step in the process, management may resolve the grievance to the satisfaction of the union or the union may decide to drop the grievance. Otherwise, the grievance proceeds to the next step in the process.

- *Step 1*. The complaint is put in writing and formally presented by the shop steward to the first-level supervisor. Normally, the supervisor must respond in writing within a contractually specified time period, usually two to five days.

- *Step 2*. The chief steward takes the complaint to the department superintendent. A written response is required, usually within a week.

- *Step 3*. The complaint is submitted to the plant manager/chief administrative officer by the union plant or grievance committee. Again, a written response is typically required.

- *Step 4*. If Step 3 does not solve the dispute, arrangements are made for an arbitrator or an arbitration board to settle the matter.

HRC 5

Handling Grievances

Once a grievance has been filed, management should seek to resolve it fairly and quickly. Failure to do so can be seen as a disregard for employee needs and is not conducive to building and maintaining effective labour relations. However, in resolving grievances, management should consider several issues. Most important, grievances should be settled on their merits. Complaints need to be carefully investigated and decided on the facts. Second, the cause of each grievance should be recorded. A large number of grievances coming from one or two departments may indicate poor supervision or a lack of understanding of the contract. Third, the final solution to the grievance needs to be explained to those affected:

> Shahab Makholi, an immigrant from Iran, was hired as a welder by a Mississauga company that manufactures fire doors. Makholi injured his hand at work and had to have a splint put on it. He continued working and was ultimately assigned alternate duties. Eventually, his lead hand assigned Makholi to do work that he couldn't perform and he went to the production manager's office to complain. After some discussion, the employer concluded that Makholi wanted to be laid off and documentation was prepared. Makholi was dismissed and ultimately grieved. The arbitrator, in reinstating Makholi, noted that Makholi could not read or write English, the company did not make a substantial effort to explain the importance of the dismissal documentation, no union representative was present at the termination meeting although the agreement required that the union be notified of any layoffs, and Makholi was instructed not to tell the union what had happened.[76]

In late October of 2014, CBC ended its relationship with radio host Jian Ghomeshi. One issue that has drawn the attention of human resource and legal experts revolves around the right of Ghomeshi and his union to grieve his dismissal. The collective agreement gives CBC the right to terminate for just and sufficient cause. According to lawyer Ron Minken, "cause termination essentially is when a worker does something outrageous and one would have to consider the conduct and whether the termination for cause is proportional to it."[77]

Arbitration

All jurisdictions require that collective agreements include a provision for final settlement by **arbitration**, without stoppage of work, of all differences concerning the interpretation or administration of a contract. This means that as long as a collective agreement is in force, any strike or lockout is illegal. An arbitrator may be selected from a list provided by the appropriate ministry of labour, or the parties may agree to the selection of an arbitrator. The arbitrator's decision is final and cannot be changed or revised, except in rare instances (such as corruption, fraud, or a breach of natural justice).[78] There is growing concern that the arbitration process is becoming too costly, too slow (some cases take two years or more to be resolved), and too legalistic.[79]

---

arbitration

The settling of a dispute between labour and management by a third party.

Arbitration holds two potential problems for labour relations practitioners: costs and unacceptable solutions. An arbitration case can cost both the union and employer several thousand dollars. There are also time commitment costs in terms of preparing for arbitration, attending the actual hearings, and case follow-up. From the perspective of management, a potential problem occurs when an arbitrator renders a decision that is against management's best interest. Since the ruling is binding, it may alter drastically management's rights and set a precedent for future cases. For example, if an arbitrator accepts the union's argument of extenuating circumstances in a disciplinary case, those extenuating circumstances may be cited in future cases. Consider the following case and decide if the employee should be terminated:

> An Ontario pilot worked for Wasaya Airlines, which was owned and operated by First Nations persons. After making negative comments about First Nations people on his Facebook page, the pilot was terminated. The pilot had made the comments while off-duty, the comments were limited to a single posting, and the pilot was remorseful. The airline felt dismissal was appropriate and it was aware of situations in the past where First Nations people refused to deal with people who had been disrespectful of their culture. An arbitrator ruled that the pilot's conduct was clearly inappropriate, but opted to replace the dismissal with a lengthy suspension.[80]

This decision shows that once an employer goes to arbitration, the decision is turned over to a third party. In dismissal cases, the union will typically argue that discharge is an inappropriate penalty and there exists the possibility that an arbitrator may agree with the union position. Consequently, it is important that an employee grievance is treated seriously by management representatives and that the organization attempts to resolve grievances with the union in a fair and timely matter. However, there may be some instances where arbitration is unavoidable.

Contract Provisions

Every collective agreement contains specific terms and provisions. A number of the most common ones are listed in Figure 13-12. These clauses are important because they define the rights and obligations of the employer and the union. For instance, union security is a very important issue from the union's perspective. In addition, some of the most frequent disputes concern seniority and discipline.

Common Provisions in Union–Management Agreements

- *Union recognition.* Normally near the beginning of a contract, this clause states management's acceptance of the union as the sole representative of designated employees.

- *Union security.* To ensure that the union maintains members as new employees are hired and present employees quit, a union security clause is commonly demanded by the union. Union security provisions are discussed later in the chapter.

- *Wage rates.* The amount of wages to be paid to workers (or classes of workers) is specified in the wage clause.

- *Cost of living.* Unions may negotiate automatic wage increases for workers when price levels go up. For example, one approach is for wages to go up in response to an increase in the consumer price index above some specified amount.

- *Insurance benefits.* This section specifies which insurance benefits the employer provides and how much the employer contributes toward these benefits. Frequently included benefits are life and supplemental hospitalization insurance and dental plans.

- *Pension benefits.* The amount of retirement income, years of service required, penalties for early retirement, employer and employee contributions, and vesting provisions are described in this section if a pension plan exists.

- *Income maintenance.* To provide workers with economic security, some contracts give guarantees of minimum income or minimum work. Other income maintenance provisions include severance pay and supplements to employment insurance.

- *Time-off benefits.* Vacations, holidays, rest breaks, washup periods, and leave-of-absence provisions typically are specified in this clause.

- *Seniority clause.* Unions seek contract terms that require human resource decisions to be made on the basis of seniority. Often, senior workers are given preferential treatment in job assignments, promotions, layoffs, vacation scheduling, overtime, and shift preferences.

- *Management rights.* Management must retain certain rights to do an effective job. These may include the ability to require overtime work, decide on promotions, design jobs, and select employees. This clause reserves to management the right to make decisions that management thinks are necessary for the organization's success.

- *Discipline.* Prohibited employee actions, penalties, and disciplinary procedures are either stated in the contract or included in the agreement by reference to those documents that contain the information.

- *Dispute resolution.* Disagreements between the union and management are resolved through procedures specified in the contract.

- *Duration of agreement.* Union and management agree on a time period during which the collective agreement is in force.

HRC 5

Union Security

Can an employee be required to join a union as a condition of employment? An employer and union can negotiate clauses dealing with union security and, in some jurisdictions, compulsory dues checkoff is required.

The highest form of union security is the *closed shop* (found in about 8 percent of agreements), which requires an employee to be a union member prior to obtaining employment and to pay dues to the union. The closed shop, which is frequently operated through a hiring hall, is common in construction and longshore industries.

Under a **union shop** security arrangement, the employer is free to hire an individual but as a condition of employment the new hire must join the union within a specified period of time after being hired and pay union dues. If the individual refuses to join the union, the employer is required to terminate the worker's employment. About 40 percent of agreements have a union shop provision.[81]

union shop

A union security provision in which employers may hire anyone they want, but all new employees must join the union within a specified period and pay dues.

The *Rand Formula* requires an employer to deduct union dues at source from the wages of an employee and remit the funds to the union. However, the employee is not required to join the union. In some jurisdictions, dues checkoff clauses must be negotiated; in other jurisdictions, compulsory dues checkoff is enshrined in law.

While the amount of dues varies, it is typically in the range of about 1 to 1.5 percent of an employee's earnings. Most workers covered by a collective agreement are subject to a dues checkoff requirement.[82] Some jurisdictions allow workers who object to joining a union on the basis of religious grounds to pay the equivalent amount to a registered charity.

In an *open shop*, an individual does not have to join the union and is not required to pay dues.

Seniority

Unions typically prefer to have employee-related decisions determined by the length of the worker's employment, called **seniority**. Seniority assures that promotions, overtime, layoffs, and other employee concerns are handled without favouritism. As well, the influence of seniority is not restricted to the union environment; several nonunion organizations also place considerable weight on seniority in making human resource decisions.

seniority

Length of the worker's employment, which may be used for determining order of promotion, layoffs, vacation, etc.

Seniority is often very important in deciding layoff rights. For example, when a company plans a layoff, the most recently hired workers are typically the first to go. The remaining employees probably receive higher wages if there is a premium for service with the organization. Thus, the higher-paid employees are retained, even though the layoff may have been implemented as a cost-reduction measure. Moreover, layoffs may undermine a company's employment equity plan, since employees hired through the employment equity program may have low seniority.

Discipline

Unions often challenge the discipline of a union member. Due to the difficulty of trying to list employee behaviours that may warrant discipline, many collective agreements provide the employer with the right to discipline or discharge if "just cause" exists. In any disciplinary action, management must abide by the terms of the collective agreement. Arbitration cases are frequently lost because management failed to establish grounds for disciplinary action, neglected to document past disciplinary procedures, and failed to adhere to the provisions of the collective agreement.

In deciding discipline and discharge cases, the starting point is the collective agreement. However, many collective agreements have a provision indicating that the employer must have "just cause" to discipline or discharge an employee. In determining just cause, a number of factors may be important:

- nature and seriousness of the offence
- due process and procedure
- past record of the grievor
- seniority and age of the grievor
- knowledge of rules
- previous warnings from management
- lax enforcement/condonation by management in the past
- unequal treatment of employees
- provocation by management
- isolated incident
- sincere apology/remorse on the part of the grievor[83]

Although an employer may believe that clear grounds for discipline or dismissal exist, arbitrators consider a number of issues in making their decisions:

> A Brewers Retail <http://www.thebeerstore.ca> employee in Ontario took a Toronto Maple Leafs shirt from a case of beer being returned by a customer. Cases of beer containing Maple Leaf shirts were part of a special promotion and the employee's daughter was a big Leafs fan. The employee put the shirt in his coat pocket (with part of it hanging out) and went to serve a customer. The employer terminated the employee as part of its zero-tolerance theft policy while the employee argued that he had intended to ask his supervisor whether he could keep the shirt. An arbitrator ruled that the employee, who had 23 years of service with the employer, had not intended to steal the shirt and replaced the termination with a three-day suspension.[84]

 HRC 5

Past Practice

The actions of managers and union officials sometimes change the meaning of the agreement. A **precedent** is a new standard that arises from the past practices of either party. Once a precedent results from unequal enforcement of disciplinary rules, the new standard may affect similar cases in the future.

precedent

A new standard that arises from the past practices of either the company or the union.

The fear of past practices usually causes two changes in human resource policies and procedures. First, employee-related decisions are often centralized in the human resource department. Supervisors are stripped of their authority to make decisions on layoffs, discipline, and other employee matters. Instead, supervisors are required to make recommendations to the human resource department to ensure uniformity and consistency of application and to prevent precedents.

The second change is to increase the training of supervisors in the administration of the contract. Training is needed to ensure that supervisors administer the collective agreement in a consistent manner. For example, if each supervisor applies a different standard to tardiness, some employees may be disciplined while others with more lenient supervisors may not receive any penalty. In time, the union might argue that unequal treatment makes it unfair to discipline those who are late. Through centralization and training, human resource departments create a more uniform enforcement of the contract.

Public Sector Bargaining

When Parliament passed the ***Public Service Staff Relations Act*** **(PSSRA)** in 1967, it essentially gave federal civil servants bargaining rights similar to those granted workers in the private sector—usually the right to bargain for wages, hours, and certain working conditions. More important, it also gave them the right to strike. This is in contrast to civil servants in the United States, who since 1962 have had the right to bargain collectively, but not to withhold their services. Under the PSSRA, the methods of conflict resolution are different from those in the private sector. Before a bargaining agent can give notice that it wishes to bargain, a decision must be made as to whether a conciliation-strike procedure or a binding-arbitration procedure will be used should a deadlock occur. The union has the right to choose different procedures for each subsequent collective agreement. If the strike route has been chosen, conciliation procedures must be followed before a strike can begin.

Public Service Staff Relations Act **(PSSRA)**
Provides federal public servants with the right to unionize and either opt for compulsory arbitration or strike if a deadlock in bargaining occurs.

Another difference from the private sector is that the law allows the employer to designate certain employees as performing essential services, thus divesting them of the right to strike. The union, however, may challenge the list of "designated employees," in which case the Public Service Staff Relations Board makes the final decision.

A comparison of the federal and provincial legislation for government employees reveals little uniformity across Canada. While municipal government employees generally fall under the same legislation as private sector workers, the legislation applicable to provincial civil servants varies markedly. For instance, Saskatchewan government employees come under the same legislation as private sector employees, in some provinces there is specific legislation applicable only to provincial government employees, and in other jurisdictions, there may be two or more statutes applicable to government employees. In addition, some provinces markedly restrict or prohibit strikes by public sector workers.[85]

Over the last couple of years, a number of provinces have introduced legislation which is being challenged or vehemently opposed by unions. For example, Alberta's Bill 45 provides for a fine of up to $1 million a day if a union engages in a wildcat strike and then-Premier Jim Prentice announced that he wanted to overhaul the collective bargaining approach for public sector unions and institute a more consistent and centralized approach. He stated that the high wages paid to government workers were a problem and due, at least in part, to a lack of coordination among government negotiators.[86]

In Nova Scotia, the Liberal government's *Health Authorities Act* was introduced in September 2014 to reduce the number of health care bargaining units from 50 to 4. The expectation was that each of the four existing unions would be assigned to one of the units. The parties were, not surprisingly, unable to reach agreement, so well-known arbitrator James Dorsey was hired to settle the dispute using mediation–arbitration. After mediation failed, Dorsey arbitrated the dispute. In his report, Dorsey delayed deciding which union would represent nursing and support bargaining units, so he was fired by the province.

After threatening to legislate an outcome, the province finally reached a deal with the four unions that will allow each union to retain its members and bargain as councils.[87]

LO7 HRC 5

Human Resource Practices in the Union Environment

A study by the Industrial Relations Centre at Queen's University provides insights on the labour relations profession in Canada. Among the major findings are the following:

- the four activities labour relations professionals are most involved in are conflict resolution management, coaching with regard to labour relations best practices, administration of the collective agreement, and grievance settlement.

- from a knowledge perspective, the most important areas are understanding the union–management perspective, conflict resolution, labour statutes, and negotiation.

- in terms of skills required to perform day-to-day work, the top four skills included communication, active listening, relationship building, and collective agreement interpretation.

- when considering the labour relations profession, 59 percent are optimistic about the future of the profession, 15 percent are pessimistic, and 26 percent are unsure.

- the top three perceived opportunities for the profession are talent management, union–management collaboration and partnership, and strategic labour relations.[88]

While there is a significant and growing body of information about human resource management from the perspective of the employer, less attention has been paid to examining what human resource management practices are found within unionized workgroups.

A key issue for human resource management practitioners involves obtaining union involvement in managing change. Bob White, former president of the Canadian Labour Congress, had this to say about unions and change:

> For workers, change will be judged to be positive if higher productivity is shared in the form of better wages and benefits; if change results in more rather than less security of employment; if change gives workers access to new skills and opportunities; and if change improves the overall quality of working life in terms of the ability of workers to make a productive contribution.[89]

A survey of Canadian union officials examined a number of human resource issues in the unionized environment. Concerning human resource management policies, union officials were asked to indicate whether a number of specific HRM programs or practices applied to bargaining-unit employees. As revealed in Figure 13-13, more than 95 percent of units had a policy addressing sexual harassment, 86 percent had an orientation program for new hires, 86 percent had an employee assistance plan (EAP), and 66 percent had some type of formal performance appraisal system. About 51 percent of respondents reported that the employer shared business information with union members.

Union officials were also asked to indicate whether bargaining-unit employees were involved in a number of specific team-based and incentive programs (Figure 13-13). As the figure reveals, 28 percent of the union locals reported having work teams, 22 percent had quality circles and 40 percent had problem-solving groups. Unions have generally stayed away from contingency compensation plans such as profit sharing, productivity sharing, and employee stock ownership plans; overall, less than 20 percent of respondents reported having such plans.

FIGURE 13-13

HRM Practices/Programs among Canadian Unions

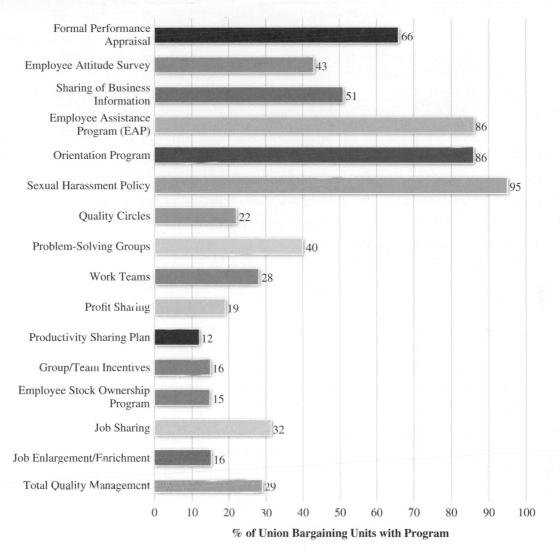

SOURCE: Terry H. Wagar, *Human Resource Management and Workplace Safety: A Study of Canadian Union Officials*, unpublished report, Saint Mary's University, 2009.

Implications of Union Avoidance Approaches

In nonunion facilities, an implicit objective of many employers is to remain nonunion. Employers frequently adopt either a *union suppression* or a *union substitution* approach in order to avoid unionization. The union suppression approach involves fighting union representation. An employer may try to intimidate workers, threaten closing or moving the plant or facility, or discriminate against union supporters.

An employer in the food services industry heard that four of the workers were discussing unionization as a means of improving wages and working conditions. Senior management learned about the issue and decided to terminate six employees—the four union activists and two other employees who were considered poor performers. The termination notices were issued under the guise of incompetent work performance.

The union substitution approach examines what unions bring to the employment relationship and then tries to introduce such features into the nonunion workplace. This approach requires that human resource specialists do the following:

- Design jobs that are personally satisfying to workers.

- Develop plans that maximize individual opportunities while minimizing the possibility of layoffs.

- Select workers who are well qualified.

- Establish fair, meaningful, and objective standards of individual performance.

- Train workers and managers to enable them to achieve expected levels of performance.

- Evaluate and reward behaviour on the basis of actual performance.

- Provide employees with a "voice" in the workplace.

- Implement a compensation plan in which wages/salary and benefits parallel those available in the union sector.

The union substitution approach is advocated by many HR practitioners, consultants, and labour lawyers. According to employer lawyer Jamie Knight:

Nonunion companies that want to remain nonunion should steal some of their best features from their competitors' collective agreements. Often a collective agreement will contain provisions that do not contradict an efficient and effective operation. Employers should have a nonunion dispute resolution process. Dealing with complaints is the biggest challenge in a nonunion workplace.[90]

On the other hand, Canadian labour relations legislation requires that workers need to take the initiative in establishing collective bargaining relationships knowing that many employers are opposed to unions. Consequently, the beginning of the new union–management relationship is already characterized by conflict and adversarialism.[91] Roy Adams, Professor Emeritus of Industrial Relations at McMaster University, argues that the practice of union avoidance sabotages the right to bargain collectively and contravenes the International Labour Organization's Declaration of Fundamental Principles and Rights at Work which includes the effective recognition of the right to bargain collectively. In North America, this right is generally not available until workers go through an arduous certification procedure which results in an adversarial relationship.[92]

LO8 HRC 5

Managing in a Union Environment

When unions are present, the human resource function is changed. In many organizations, the human resource department is expanded by the addition of specialists in labour relations who deal with such critical areas as negotiations and contract administration, while human resource professionals attend to their more traditional roles. Although some organizations establish separate industrial relations departments to deal with labour relations issues, industrial relations is often considered a subset of human resource management.

Unionization may be associated with greater centralization of employee record-keeping and discipline to ensure uniformity of application. This change can mean that line managers lose some of their authority to the human resource department. They may also find their jobs more difficult because of the new rules imposed by the contract—while management has the right to act, the union may have the right, under the contract, to react to management's actions.

Line managers may become dissatisfied because their authority diminishes while their responsibility increases. These added responsibilities are likely to result from requests of human resource professionals, who may need to monitor the work environment more closely and need more information from the line managers. For example, the line manager may have to compile new reports on such issues as absenteeism, lateness, productivity, and employee grievances (a growing number of organizations are using computer technology to collect such information). Such demands on supervisors may create friction between line managers and human resource staff members.

The presence of a union means that management has less freedom to make unilateral changes. No longer can an employer simply decide what changes to implement. Instead, collective agreement provisions and labour laws must also be considered.

Labour–Management Co-operation

Some unions and employers are moving toward greater co-operation and there is increasing acceptance that labour and management must work together if they are to survive and prosper in the highly competitive global economy.[93]

> As noted by the Conference Board of Canada, "There is a high degree of maturity within Canadian labour relations; both parties now openly acknowledge that their individual interests are inextricably linked. Management is making more of an effort to provide unions with high-level information and generally making more of an effort to involve the unions with the business. Similarly, unions have a better sense of business realities and no longer make the 'knee-jerk' reactions they once did."[94]

There is growing evidence that organizational performance is enhanced when labour and management co-operate. For example, research using data from both employers and unions indicated that a more positive labour climate was associated with perceptions of higher productivity, enhanced product or service quality, and greater customer or client satisfaction.[95] However, co-operation is a very challenging process:

> A recent survey of Vancouver's 10,000 municipal employees indicated low levels of morale despite efforts to change the employment culture. A Hay Group study revealed problems relating to workload and stress, with particular concerns about city leadership and a lack of strategic direction. Moreover, only 6 percent of respondents from the Vancouver Fire Department reported having confidence in the fire chief and his managers.[96]

Obstacles to Co-operation

Industrial relations specialists often seek union co-operation to improve the organization's effectiveness. However, co-operation may not be politically attractive to union leaders who see little gain in co-operating with management. In fact, if leaders do co-operate, they may be accused by workers of forgetting the union's interests. These accusations can mean defeat by political opponents within the union. Thus, co-operation may not be in the union leader's best interest.

In addition to political obstacles, union leaders may mistrust management. For example, bitter remarks during an organizing drive or arbitration case may convince union officials that human resource specialists are anti-union. Within this climate, co-operative gestures are often seen as tricks or gimmicks aimed at hurting the union. If co-operative proposals threaten the members or leaders, mistrust increases and co-operation usually fails.

While employers often have good reasons for seeking more co-operation with their unionized workforce, a number of co-operative programs have the underlying goal of increasing managerial domination in the workplace. As well, some employers use co-operation to "stress the system" by reducing employees or resources, giving workers more tasks, or speeding up the assembly line; such practices may dramatically increase the stress level of workers and dehumanize the workplace.[97]

HRC 5

Support for Co-operative Programs

In one study, employer and union participants were asked to indicate their perceptions of the degree of support for co-operative programs (using a six-point scale where 1 = no support and 6 = strong support for co-operative programs) for the five groups referred to in Figure 13-14. Although there was modest support for co-operative programs, one interesting finding was that employers perceived that the greatest opposition to co-operative programs came from national and international union leaders while union officials reported that management (supervisors and upper management) were most opposed to co-operative efforts.

FIGURE 13-14

Support for Co-operative Programs

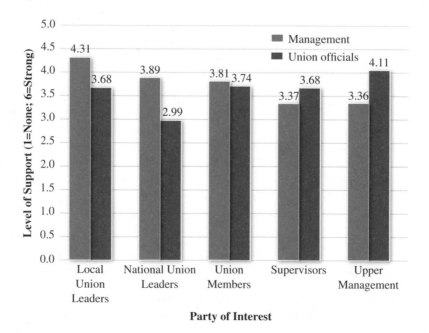

SOURCES: Terry H. Wagar, *Human Resource Management, Strategy and Organization Change: Evidence from Canadian Employers*, unpublished report, Saint Mary's University, 2003; Terry H. Wagar, *Examining Labour Relations in Canada: Evidence from Union Officials*, unpublished report, Saint Mary's University, 2003.

An employer and union interested in greater labour–management co-operation have several options to consider. Some of the most common co-operative efforts are summarized in Figure 13-15. One of the most basic actions is prior consultation with the union. While not every management decision must be approved by the union, actions that affect unionized employees may result in grievance filing unless explained in advance to the union.

A growing number of unionized organizations are among the Best Workplaces in Canada winners. Some observers believe that co-operation between unions and employers is key as the parties move away from the "us-versus-them" mentality. For example, at Toronto East General Hospital, employees and union stewards are involved in all joint committees with managers, including the staff satisfaction committee. General Mills <http://www.generalmills.ca> believes that all employees need to have a sense of ownership of the company's success. The company shares minutes from weekly executive team meetings with all employees and encourages employee input into decisions.[98]

FIGURE 13-15

Methods of Building Labour–Management Co-operation

Managers and human resource specialists can build co-operation between the employer and the union through:

- *Prior consultation* with union leaders to defuse problems before they become formal grievances

- *Sincere concern* for employee problems and welfare even when management is not obligated to do so by the collective agreement

- *Training programs* that objectively communicate the intent of union and management bargainers and reduce biases and misunderstandings

- *Joint study committees* that allow management and union officials to find solutions to common problems

- *Third parties* who can provide guidance and programs that bring union leaders and managers closer together to pursue common objectives

Human resource specialists can also build co-operation through a sincere concern for employees. This concern may be shown through the prompt settlement of grievances. As well, employers can establish programs (such as employee assistance programs and job counselling) that assist employees who are experiencing personal difficulties.

Training programs are another way to build co-operation. After a new contract is signed, the human resource department often trains just managers. The union does the same for its leaders. The result is that both sides continue their biases and misunderstandings. If human resource management sponsors training for both the union and management, a common understanding of the contract is more likely to be brought about. The training can be as simple as taking turns paraphrasing the contract or outside neutrals can be hired to do the training. Either way, supervisors and union officials end the training with a common understanding of the contract and a new basis for co-operation.

When a complex problem confronts the union and employer, *joint study committees* are sometimes formed. For example, one organization recently set up a joint committee with its union to establish a policy on sexual harassment. Other employers use joint study committees to address such issues as workplace rules, quality of work life, technological change, budget reduction strategies, and safety. However, union participation and support is absolutely essential:

At Toronto Hydro <http://www.torontohydro.com>, the company implemented a recognition program in which employees who demonstrated certain behaviours that reduced costs, improved productivity, or surpassed performance standards would receive a nonmonetary reward of up to $300. The union strongly opposed the program on the grounds that it pitted workers against each other and violated the union's right to be the exclusive bargaining agent for the employees, refused management's offer to develop the program, and filed a grievance. The arbitrator found in favour of the union. HR Consultant Eric Cousineau commented, "What Toronto Hydro should have done right from the start is to do it with the union, not to the union."[99]

A final method of building co-operation is through the use of third parties, such as consultants or government agencies, who may act as change agents or catalysts to co-operation. For example, in Nova Scotia, the provincial government has established and delivers a variety of joint union–management programs (including grievance mediation, joint supervisor–steward training, and labour–management committees) with the goal of increasing co-operation in the workplace.

There is no single best approach to building co-operation. Since each relationship is unique, the methods used will depend upon the situation. Improving union management relations is an important function that can be addressed by human resource professionals in unionized organizations.

SUMMARY

The labour–management framework consists of unions, government, and management. Although each union is unique, unions share the common objectives of protecting and improving their members' wages, hours, and working conditions. To further these objectives, the union movement has created local, national, and international structures, plus federations at the provincial and federal levels.

In Canada, the federal government has jurisdiction in labour relations matters over Crown corporations, airlines, most railways, communication companies, and federal government agencies—or approximately 10 percent of the labour force. All other organizations fall under the jurisdiction of the provinces, which have enacted separate but similar legislation.

Unionization often occurs when workers perceive the need for a union as a response to unsatisfactory treatment by management. During the organizing process, management's response is limited by laws and employee reactions. The employer's primary defence is sound policies implemented by competent supervisors before unionization begins.

If workers form a union, federal or provincial law requires management and the union to bargain in good faith. The success of the employer at the bargaining table is affected by its actions before negotiations begin. Negotiations with the union usually result in a "collective agreement" that must be approved by union members and top management. Once negotiated, the collective agreement is administered by the union and management.

In administering the agreement, human resource specialists face several challenges. For example, contract clauses place limits on management, day-to-day administration of the contract can lead to precedents, and limitations often result from the resolution of disputes through the grievance procedure or arbitration.

Although unions may represent the employees, management remains ultimately responsible for organizational performance and effectively utilizing the human resources. Through prior consultation, sincere concern for employees, training programs, joint study committees, or third parties, human resource specialists can lay the foundations of a co-operative union–management relationship.

TERMS FOR REVIEW

arbitration
authorization cards
business unionism
Canadian Labour Congress (CLC)
collective agreement
conciliation
craft union
grievance procedure
industrial union
labour relations boards (LRBs)
local union
management rights
mediation
precedent
Public Service Staff Relations Act (PSSRA)
seniority
social (reform) unionism
unfair labour practices
union
union shop

SELF-ASSESSMENT EXERCISE

What Are Your Views toward Unions?

The following self-test gives you a quick assessment of your attitudes toward unions. Read each statement and give it a score from 1 to 5 (with 1 indicating that you strongly disagree with the statement and 5 indicating that you strongly agree with the statement).

1. Unions give members their money's worth.	_____
2. Unions improve job security for their members.	_____
3. Unions protect workers against unfair actions by the employer.	_____
4. Unions represent the wishes of their members.	_____
5. Unions are a positive force in our society.	_____
6. Unions are still needed today.	_____
7. Unions need more power.	_____
8. Laws should be changed to make it easier to get a union at the workplace	_____
9. I would prefer to work in a unionized job.	_____
10. If a union was organizing my workplace, I would vote for the union.	_____

SCORE

Add up your score for each of the statements. A higher score is associated with a more positive view of unions.

REVIEW AND DISCUSSION QUESTIONS

1. In your own words, summarize the primary objectives of unions.

2. What distinguishes craft and industrial unions from each other?

3. What roles do Labour Relations Boards serve in labour–management relations?

4. In preparing to negotiate an agreement with a union, what types of information would you gather before arriving at the bargaining table?

5. If you were asked to explain why various types of people are on the employer's bargaining team, what reasons would you give for (a) the company lawyer, (b) the director of industrial relations, (c) a wage and salary specialist, (d) a benefit specialist, and (e) the assistant plant manager?

6. Since grievance procedures are found in most contracts, both managers and unions must want them. Explain why both managers and unions want grievance procedures.

CRITICAL THINKING QUESTIONS

1. "Unions do not happen, they are caused by management." Do you agree or disagree with this statement? Why?

2. If you had to advise the manager of a small chain of bakeries how to prepare for a possible strike, what would you suggest?

3. Suppose an employee in your department is an active member of the union, but is performing improperly. After several sessions with the employee, performance is still unacceptable. What type of support would you want to gather before you terminated that employee? What legal complications might result from your action?

4. If you worked in the human resource department of a small company that is suddenly unionized, what changes would you expect to occur in the human resource department?

5. What role do you think federal and provincial governments will play in future labour–management relations? What actions can unions and management take to reduce the probability of future government involvement?

6. Obtain a copy of two different collective agreements. Compare and contrast the contract items and the grievance procedure.

ETHICS QUESTION

You are the HR manager in a small, private specialty-steel mill that is nonunionized. Over the years, the company has been quite profitable and has shared profits with its employees through a profit sharing plan. Last year, however, due to global economic conditions, the company incurred its first loss in a decade, so there were no profits to share. The United Steelworkers Union (USU), a union with a reputation for militancy, saw this as a great opportunity to try to organize your company again—its fifth attempt. In the past, their attempts have been abysmal failures, but they keep trying. This time, however, because of the discontent of the employees about the missing bonus, you perceive that the union might have a real chance to win enough votes for certification. You know who the union activist is: a loudmouthed individual who has been disciplined several times for abusive behaviour and foul language directed at supervisors. You know too that it would be easy to provoke him to be abusive again, giving you an excuse for his dismissal; the last time he had had an encounter with his supervisor, he had been warned in writing that one more provocation would result in dismissal. The supervisor even volunteers to find an excuse for an encounter. If the union lost its internal organizer, there is a very good chance that the certification drive would fail again. Temptation is great. What do you do?

WEB RESEARCH EXERCISE

1. Visit the website of the International Labour Organization <http://www.ilo.org>. What are the major objectives of the ILO? What are some of the major issues affecting workers around the world?

2. Go to the website for the Canadian Labour Congress. Also visit the website for a provincial federation of labour (for instance, the Nova Scotia Federation of Labour <http://nslabour.ca>). Compare and contrast the functions of the two federations. What similarities and differences exist? What assistance do the federations provide to organized labour?

INCIDENT 13-1

A Routine Discharge at ITC

Four months ago, Pete Ross was discharged from ITC. The supervisor requested that the human resource department discharge Pete because he was caught drinking alcohol in the employee locker room. Drinking on company property was prohibited, as it had been since publication of the ITC Employees' Handbook in 1990.

All employees of ITC were given a copy, and whenever new employees joined, as had Pete in 1999, they too were given one as part of the orientation program. The handbook stated in part: "The consumption of alcoholic beverages on company premises is grounds for immediate termination."

The discharge appeared rather routine to the human resource manager and to the plant manager. Although drinking violations were uncommon, the plant manager believed clear-cut violations of company policy should be punished. Besides, he was frequently heard to say, "We must support our first-line managers."

Pete's fellow machinists did not see it as a "routine discharge." John Briggs, a fellow machinist, summed up the group's feelings: "Pete was a darn good machinist. He was seldom tardy, never absent, and always did a first-class job. If Pete did it, it was done right! That bugged George [the supervisor] because George would pressure Pete to get out the work and say, 'Don't worry about the quality; they only measure quantity.' But Pete wasn't slow. He'd turn out a quality product as fast as some people turned out junk. I don't think George liked Pete. I don't know if Pete took a drink before leaving the plant Wednesday evening, but I think George just wanted to can Pete."

The following Monday, John Briggs spent his rest breaks and lunch hour talking with the other machinists, telling them that "If we don't want to end up like Pete, we'd better get a union." He even had authorization cards from the International Association of Machinists Union. By Monday evening, Briggs had 32 signed cards. There were 39 machinists in the shop.

On Tuesday morning, John Briggs was called into the supervisor's office. The plant manager and the supervisor grilled him. They asked him if he had been distributing authorization cards, who had signed them, and how many he had obtained. Briggs simply replied by saying, "That is none of your business." The plant manager adjourned the meeting without saying a word.

On Thursday (payday at ITC), Briggs received a termination notice with his paycheque. The notice was effective immediately. The notice said termination was for low productivity and excessive absences during the previous 12 months.

1. What unfair labour practices may have occurred?

2. Should management offer reinstatement to Pete Ross or John Briggs?

3. Was Briggs correct when he answered, "That is none of your business," to the questions about the authorization cards?

CASE STUDY

Maple Leaf Shoes Ltd.

Absenteeism at Maple Leaf Shoes

Another busy day for Jane Reynolds, special assistant to the human resource manager. Pat Lim, the general manager of marketing (who has also assumed responsibility for the human resource function), had sent yet another memo to Jane (see below).

Memorandum Maple Leaf Shoes

To: Jane Reynolds

From: Pat Lim

Re: Absenteeism Case/Absenteeism Policy

Dear Jane:

As you are aware, we're having trouble with absenteeism at the plant. Could you look into the following grievance involving Glenda Feltham, discuss it with the union, and see if we can resolve it?

Also, the problem is much deeper than simply a single grievance. Please review the relevant part of the collective agreement and the absenteeism policy that we developed some years ago with the union. Meet with the union and see if we can put together a more proactive policy.

Don't hesitate to contact me if you need my assistance.

Regards,

Pat

First things first. Jane decided that resolving the Feltham grievance was her first priority. While she recognized the importance of developing a good attendance policy, that would take some time. At 11 a.m., Jane met with the employee, Glenda Feltham, and her union steward, Shaun Robberman. The facts of the Feltham grievance are reported below.

THE FELTHAM GRIEVANCE

Ms. Glenda Feltham, 32 years of age, has worked at Maple Leaf Shoes for six years. During the past year, as a result of family and health problems, she was absent or late on a number of occasions. The collective agreement between Maple Leaf Shoes and the union does not specifically address the issue of absence from work; it merely states that "no employee may be given a written reprimand or written warning, or be suspended, demoted, or dismissed unless the employer has just cause."

The absenteeism policy at Maple Leaf Shoes, which was developed several years ago as a joint effort between union and management, requires the application of progressive discipline for offences involving tardiness or absenteeism. The policy also provides for "wiping the slate clean" if an employee's attendance is satisfactory for a one-year period. Both union and management acknowledge that, at times over the years, the policy has not been strictly enforced. However, four months ago, Maple Leaf management notified the union that it would strictly enforce the policy.

A review of Glenda Feltham's file showed that she has received the following disciplinary penalties:

- Fourteen months ago—oral warning for being 22 minutes late.

- Nine months ago—written warning for being absent for two days. Glenda failed to call in sick or provide any explanation for her absence upon returning to work.

- Seven months ago—one-day suspension for being 1 hour and 14 minutes late.

- Six months ago—five-day suspension for being absent for one day. Again, Glenda failed to call in sick or explain the reason for her absence.

It appeared that the five-day suspension had alerted Glenda to the fact that unexplained absenteeism and lateness are not acceptable behaviours at Maple Leaf Shoes. After this suspension, Glenda was not late or absent for almost six months. However, one week ago, Glenda failed to show up at work or call in sick. When her supervisor called Glenda's home, no one answered. The next day, Glenda called in sick, but was reportedly seen that afternoon entering a local fitness club. The following day, Glenda showed up for work, met with her supervisor, and explained that her absence was due to the fact that her boyfriend of six years had told her he was moving out of their apartment and ending their relationship. She said that she was so upset she couldn't face coming to work or trying to explain her absence over the telephone.

INSTRUCTIONS

Assume the role of management representatives (Jane Reynolds' perspective) or union representatives (Shaun Robberman's perspective). The first objective of this case is to ask the parties to meet and try to negotiate a resolution to the Glenda Feltham grievance.

THE POLICY ON ABSENTEEISM

Prior to meeting with the union to address the development of a new policy on absenteeism, Jane reviewed the absence records for the plant. She found that, on average, employees missed about 7.9

days a year. A recent consulting report for the industry indicated that the absence rate for the industry as a whole was 6.7 days a year. Jane realized that the number of absences varied among individuals, but still she was troubled by the high absenteeism rate at the Maple Leaf plant. A review of the absenteeism policy indicated that the policy was very short and had not been updated in several years. The policy read as follows:

1. The need for managing absenteeism is recognized by both the employer and union. While some absence from work is unavoidable, management is concerned that an employee absence creates more work for other employees. Management also believes that it is important to acknowledge both healthy and sick employees.

2. In instances of absenteeism or lateness, the employer will apply principles of progressive discipline. If an employee is able to maintain a satisfactory attendance record for one year, all previous disciplinary infractions relating to attendance issues will be removed from the employee's file.

3. Management has the right to discipline employees for "excessive absenteeism." In the event that an employee will be late for work or absent from work, the employee is required to make a reasonable effort to contact the employer and indicate that he or she will be late or not present at work. Upon returning to work, the employee is required to provide an explanation for his or her lateness or absence. Depending on the circumstances, the employee may be asked to provide a doctor's note in support of the explanation.

INSTRUCTIONS

The second objective of the case involves the joint meeting of union and management representatives in order to develop a new policy on absenteeism. Work in two groups—management and union—and develop a new policy on absenteeism. Several sources on the Internet are extremely helpful in developing an absenteeism policy.

CASE STUDY

Canadian Pacific and International Bank

Labour–Management Relations: CPIB and the Maple Leaf Trust Acquisition

The acquisition of Maple Leaf Trust has given Mary Keddy, Senior Vice-President of Human Resources, some cause for concern. She has assigned two senior human resource management employees to review labour relations at Maple Leaf, with a particular focus on the Credit Card Centre, located in Mississauga, Ontario. The Credit Card Centre, which has been unionized for about four years, has had some labour turmoil since the certification of the Canadian Union of Bank Employees (CUBE). Negotiations for a first contract were very difficult, but Maple Leaf Trust and CUBE were able to reach a two-year agreement without resorting to strike action. About 18 months ago, the parties negotiated a second contract (also two years in duration) that was settled after a short (two-day) strike. Approximately 285 unionized workers are employed at the Credit Card Centre, performing a variety of clerical and administrative tasks. Keddy believes that successful integration of the Credit Card Centre employees is very important, but that it represents a major challenge to the human resources department.

A few weeks ago, Keddy met with Pat Jameson, the human resource manager responsible for labour relations issues at the Credit Card Centre. In addition to discussing the adversarial relationship between labour and management, Keddy was able to obtain some data addressing labour relations issues at the Credit Card Centre. This information is summarized below.

Over the four years that the Credit Card Centre has been unionized, employee grievances have increased by about 12 percent a year. Jameson echoed the concern of the company with respect to the amount of time being spent by company officials, union representatives, and employees in contract negotiations and administering the collective agreement. According to Jameson, "During contract negotiations, we met with the union bargaining team on a weekly basis. Each meeting was a good six or seven hours, and it took us almost four months to ultimately hammer out a contract. Things were further complicated by the strike, and we also spent three days in conciliation. Furthermore, we seem to be spending way too much time dealing with grievances. While our wages are competitive, the morale at the Credit Card Centre is low and turnover is clearly a problem."

A review of company records revealed the following grievance pattern:

Total grievances filed	398
Number settled at:	
Step 1—First-level supervisor stage	55
Step 2—Second-level supervisor stage	232
Step 3—Senior HR manager stage	104
Arbitration	7

While some of the grievances involved more than one issue, most of them were single issue matters. The breakdown of grievances based on the type of issue was also available:

Grievance Issues	
Lateness or absenteeism	154
Overtime allocation	88
Other discipline or discharge	34
Job scheduling	67
Job posting	22
Multiple-issue disputes	33

Jameson also provided Keddy with the results of a recent survey of managers and employees at the Credit Card Centre. All of the managers and 266 of the 285 unionized employees completed the survey. The survey was conducted by a Toronto consultant and was supported by both the company and union (with the understanding that the completed survey forms would go directly to the consultant and the survey results would be provided in summary form to both the company and union). As Jameson noted, "We didn't think the union would co-operate, and we needed them on board in order to survey the unionized workers. I'm getting a sense that both management and the union are getting concerned about the impact of the negative labour relations climate on our ability to compete. And this is even more of an issue since we are now a part of CPIB." Some of the initial findings from the survey are provided below.

1. Assume that you are one of the two senior HRM employees assigned to examining labour relations at the Credit Card Centre. Review the material for Mary Keddy and briefly summarize your major findings.

2. What specific recommendations would you give Mary? Are there any programs or initiatives that you would suggest?

Initial Results from the Labour–Management Survey

Part A:

Workplace Performance Measures	Average Management Response	Average Union Response
Workplace productivity	3.66	3.54
Service quality	3.78	3.45
Union member morale	3.64	2.43
Union member job satisfaction	3.75	2.38
Quality of union member/supervisor relations	3.98	2.93

Note: Each of these questions uses a 5-point scale (1 = Very low; 5 = Very high).

Part B:

Labour Climate Measures	Average Management Response	Average Union Response
Grievances are settled promptly	4.01	2.87
The working conditions are fair	4.22	3.21
The parties co-operate to solve problems	3.88	2.63
The parties share information	3.66	2.44
The relationship is adversarial	2.94	4.09

Note: Each of these questions uses a 5-point scale (1 = Strongly disagree; 5 = Strongly agree).

PART-ENDING VIDEOS

Workwell Training: Conflict Communication Skills

SOURCE: © Workwell Training

Workwell Training: Violence: Keeping It Out of the Workplace

SOURCE: © Workwell Training

The Power of Positive Discipline

SOURCE: © 2012. Produced by Kantola Productions. Copyright protected by Kantola Productions and cannot be duplicated, transmitted, or placed on a network without prior written permission.

Go to Connect to access the videos.

ROLE-PLAY 6: EMPLOYEE DISMISSAL INTERVIEW

Time required: 30–45 minutes

OBJECTIVES OF THE ROLE-PLAY

1. To help the students understand the steps in conducting a dismissal interview.

2. To enhance their skills as interviewers.

3. To help them understand the challenges involved in dismissing an employee.

PRIOR PREPARATION

1. Study Chapter 11 of the text.

2. Read descriptions of Maple Leaf Shoes Ltd. at the ends of Chapters 1, 2, and 6.

GUIDELINES FOR CONDUCTING THE ROLE-PLAY

In this role-play, a sales manager (Matt Duritzski) is being terminated from his employment at Maple Leaf Shoes. Note that Matt Duritzski is a nonunion employee. Jane Reynolds will be responsible for conducting the dismissal interview.

1. Two students, one for the role of Jane Reynolds and the other for Matt Duritzski, should be identified.

2. Students should read their own role description in the Instructor Resource Manual along with the company details given at the end of Chapters 1 and 2.

3. The instructor should signal the beginning and the end of the meeting. The length of the interview will vary depending on the approaches taken by Jane Reynolds and Matt Duritzski.

4. The remainder of the class time is used for discussion of what happened during the interview and for reviewing the proper procedure for conducting a dismissal interview.

5. Observers should be asked to make notes against the questions listed below and discuss their findings at the end of the role-play.

6. The instructor should sum up by highlighting the important issues relating to employee dismissal. In addition to reviewing how to conduct a dismissal interview, the instructor should also discuss the concepts of "just cause" and "reasonable notice."

INSTRUCTIONS FOR OBSERVERS

As you observe the meeting between Jane Reynolds and Matt Duritzski, make notes against each of the questions below. Pay particular attention to the behaviours (verbal and nonverbal) of each person.

1. Were the two participants well prepared for the interview? Why?

2. How did Jane Reynolds begin the meeting?

3. Was there open communication between Reynolds and Duritzski? Who spoke more? About what? Did one party control the interview?

4. Was the sequence of his questions appropriate? Was the interview too short or too long? Did Reynolds give Duritzski the opportunity to argue that he should not have been terminated? What could have been done better?

5. Did Jane Reynolds present herself well during the interview? How? What would you do differently if you were Jane? What would you do differently if you were Matt Duritzski?

6. What other improvements to the interview would you recommend?

Human Resource Management in a Global Context

PART

7

Our world has become smaller. Trade is not just across borders, but intercontinental. A small company operating in Ontario, with a subsidiary in Michigan, can justifiably call itself an international enterprise, but more and more companies have subsidiaries in many countries and continents and are truly global in their business dealings. Human resource managers have to adjust to new demands in terms of expertise and become knowledgeable about HR practices on an international level. Do we send locals to other countries or do we hire foreign nationals to do our business there? How do we select employees to be sent abroad? How do we adjust our compensation system to international requirements? These, and many more questions regarding international and global business, will be discussed in this final chapter.

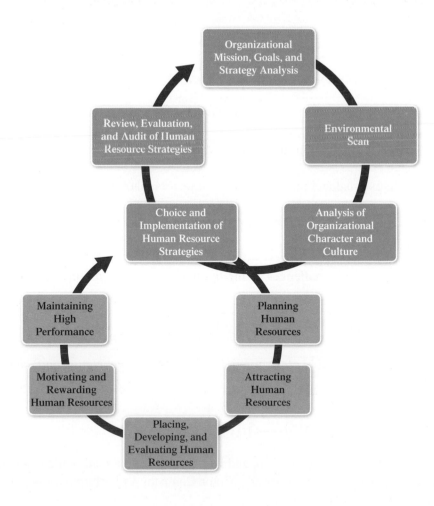

CHAPTER 14

Global Human Resource Management

> The ability to diagnose the beneficial attributes of a culture, and then use them to motivate strategically important behavior, is one of the key factors that differentiate peak-performing organizations from the also-rans in their field.
>
> JON KATZENBACH AND ASHLEY HARSHAK
> PARTNERS WITH BOOZ & COMPANY, NEW YORK AND LONDON[1]

LEARNING OBJECTIVES

After studying this chapter, you should be able to:

LO1 Differentiate between the terms *International HRM* and *Global HRM*.

LO2 Describe the evolution of a firm's operations and the impact on HRM.

LO3 Identify the external and internal contextual factors that influence global HRM.

LO4 Explain the differences between a firm's domestic HRM policies and practices and the policies and practices of a global firm.

LO5 Describe the staffing challenges facing multinational organizations and the staffing options available.

LO6 List what constitutes a successful expatriate experience.

LO7 Discuss the changing role of corporate HR in a global organization and emerging HR competencies.

A Global Company—Honda

The Civic, Accord, Odyssey, Shadow 750, and Honda Goldwing are all models of cars and motorcycles, and all are highly profitable lines for Honda Motor Company Ltd. <http://www.honda.ca>. Founded in

1948, Honda has grown to be one of the world's leading manufacturers of automobiles and motorcycles, and is the third-largest car manufacturer in Japan after Toyota and Nissan <http://www.nissan.ca>. Honda is a truly global company, with a network of 454 subsidiaries and affiliates, 145,000 employees, and operations in Japan, South America, Asia, North and Central America, Europe, Middle East, Africa, and China.[2]

Honda management operates under the principle of respect for the individual and believes that everyone who comes into contact with Honda, whether it be selling or buying, should share a sense of joy through that experience.[3] It is a company that provides high-quality products at reasonable prices for worldwide customers. In addition, management takes its commitment to corporate social responsibility very seriously. A key phrase, "Together for Tomorrow," illustrates Honda's concern for, and commitment to, the communities in which it operates, to create a safe and healthy environment.[4]

Honda anticipates increased demand for its products and is expanding its facilities. This growth is evidenced by the number of plants it recently opened, or are slated to open, around the globe. It just dedicated a new automobile transmission plant in Hamamatsu, Japan.[5] To fulfill the growing demand in the motorcycle market in Malaysia, Honda entered into a joint venture with Oriental Holdings Berhad and built a new plant in 2013 with an annual production capacity of 350,000 units.[6] Honda continues the expansion of its manufacturing operations with plans for a new plant in 2015 in Mexico for the production of fuel efficient subcompact cars, employing approximately 3,200 workers, and a new automobile production plant in the city of Itirapina in the state of San Paolo, Brazil.[7] It is clear that Honda's global presence is rapidly expanding.

A company like Honda faces a number of challenges if it wants to operate globally. International HR managers have to understand local cultures and follow host-country labour legislation and trade regulations. They have to decide whether to hire locally or transfer current employees, what compensation to pay, how to integrate employees from headquarters into the local society, and how to manage performance from afar. International HR management (IHRM) is about HR managers' understanding of economic and legal characteristics of each county, and the cultural and ethical issues that arise as firms participate and plan in a global economy.

LO1
Human Resources in a Multinational Enterprise

The globalization of business has increased significantly over the past decade. National borders are no longer barriers to trade, and more and more organizations are exploring ways to enhance their markets, manage cost, and control efficiencies around the globe. For 2025, McKinsey has projected that one-half of the billion-dollar-plus companies worldwide will originate from the emerging markets and will contribute significantly to the global gross national product.[8]

New buzzwords about strategic planning have emerged. Terms such as "co-evolution," "business ecosystem," and "white space" are being used to describe how global firms capitalize on these opportunities. A **business ecosystem** is a series of tightly knit intercompany relationships that allow the business to attain a competitive advantage. These terms describe organizations as a system—one that interacts with many stakeholders, such as customers, suppliers, and even competitors. Successful companies will be those that get others in their network to buy into their vision, find opportunities that will be of mutual benefit, and create a win–win scenario for all. Leading organizations do this by pursuing mergers and acquisitions, joint ventures, and strategic alliances. These opportunities can be anywhere, anytime, with anyone, and require organizations to be very flexible, adaptable, and ready to seize the chance.[9]

business ecosystem

A series of tightly knit intercompany relationships, allowing a business to attain a competitive advantage.

For example, the Bank of Montreal expanded further into wealth management in China. It recently purchased a minority stake in Cofco Trust Company <http://www.cofco.com/en/about/21888.html>, a state-owned Beijing-based investment firm, establishing a strategic alliance benefiting both parties and expanding its wealth management capability in China.[10] To seize these opportunities, managers must clearly understand the human management challenges and the impact operating globally has on HRM practices and policies.

International human resource management (IHRM) is about the worldwide management of talent from a staffing perspective. It provides HR support for different nationals and across different countries.[11] Traditionally, IHRM's focus has been on staffing across borders. It addressed the needs of people working abroad (expatriates), frequent commuters, cross-cultural team members, and expatriates. Its activities were primarily focused on the recruitment and selection processes. However, with increasing globalization and demands on HRM to deliver more strategic, value-added programs and services, IHRM has adopted a far more comprehensive and macro approach.

international human resource management (IHRM)

The worldwide management of talent from a staffing perspective, including HR support across many countries and the employment of different nationals.

The term **global human resource management (GHRM)** has been used to describe a broader IHRM process. It views HRM in a global context and less traditional sense, as one that focuses on organizational capabilities. GHRM is not only concerned with staffing, but also with organizational efficiency, information exchange, and knowledge transfer.

global human resource management (GHRM)

An IHRM process that views HRM in a global context as one that contributes to organizational capabilities.

GHRM is a broad concept. It takes into account distinct local and national characteristics and is sensitive to the balance between global integration and local management. GHRM recognizes that HR practices must adjust accordingly.

Firms differ in the way they participate in global competition. The degree of internationalization of an organization can be defined by the number of countries in which it operates. As organizations grow, HR must grow, offering more value-added services and resources across a wide range of geographic locations.[12]

LO2 HRC 1

Four Stages of Corporate Evolution

There are four stages of corporate evolution: domestic, international, multinational, and global/transnational. Each stage brings with it increasingly different and more complex HR-related practices and challenges, affecting resource planning in different ways.[13] Figure 14-1 provides an overview of the four stages, their characteristics, and HRM implications.[14]

FIGURE 14-1

The Four Stages of Corporate Evolution and the HR Implications

Stage of Growth	Characteristics	HRM Implications
Domestic Firms	• Focus on domestic market • Operates locally • Importance of international business is minimal	• Staffing is primarily local/regional • HR policies relate to the local country in which the firm operates • Range of HR activities are limited • HR administers HR programs belonging to a single nationality
International Firms	• Firms choose to operate internationally when foreign sales reach 10–20 percent of total revenue • Firms often form divisions which are responsible for all international operations	• Resources planning becomes more complex as the firms' available pool of talent expands • Some employees begin to be sent on short-term assignments abroad • Some relocation from home country • Emergence of national staffing categories—PCN/HCN/TCN (see below for definition) • HRM has to deal with more external factors, e.g., different country government regulations • Compensation differences between countries are explored
Multinational Firms	• Branches and subsidiaries in many countries • Each subsidiary operates independently • Focus on economies of scale	• Global HRP begins • Employees sent with increasing frequency on international assignments • HR provides relocation services and deals with international compensation and benefit issues • Worldwide policies are developed and formalized • Performance management programs are focused on identifying the value of international experiences, and key international competencies
Global/Transnational Firms	• No borders • Headquarters can be anywhere • Firms are comprised of employees from many different cultures • Focus on economies of scale • Emphasis on flexibility and mass customization of products to meet the needs of particular clients	• Maximum leverage of talent pool • Worldwide HR policies formalized and communicated • Employees are hired anywhere in the world, wherever the skills and competencies are • Management promotions require managers to have international experience • HR becomes sophisticated in terms of its global knowledge in all HR functions and service delivery coordination • Corporate headquarters develops programs, using country managers, while maintaining a focus on local importance

Domestic Firms

This firm focuses on domestic markets. It operates locally, but some larger domestic firms may export their products or services as they expand. The importance of international business is minimal.

Resource planning is local. The firm's practices are dictated by local legislation and the focus is typically on meeting legislative requirements, such as employment equity. Cross-cultural issues are negligible. Staffing is primarily local/regional, depending on the firm's demand/supply requirements. As firms grow, they may need to fill some key positions nationally. Staffing involves mainly employees within a national boundary.[15]

International Firms

In this stage, exports become part of organizational plans. A firm may choose to form international divisions when its foreign sales reach 10–20 percent of total revenues.[16] Initially, the choice will involve only exporting to foreign customers in one country or importing one or few products. The international activity has little impact on business as foreign operations are viewed as sites that copy procedures and policies from home. These firms typically expand to the nearest border and their focus becomes marketing. As the firm expands beyond national boundaries, the focus is on two national categories: the home country, referring to where the firm is headquartered, and the host country, referring to subsidiaries in another country.[17]

Resource planning becomes more sophisticated as the firm's available pool of talent expands significantly. Employees are sent abroad on short-term assignments and some individuals will be temporarily relocated from their home country. The firm typically relies on a few key managers and technical experts to deal with overseas linkages and transfer technology. Cultural sensitivity becomes more important and managers require some training in understanding cultural differences. Human resources practices are dictated from home office and divisions abroad tend to align with parent company practices. A major HRM challenge is ensuring that those internal management resources are *ready* to go abroad when needed, that they receive cultural sensitivity training, and that the distractive elements are taken care of, for example work permits. The managers sent on these assignments are not necessarily senior personnel. They are chosen to help manage and maintain a secure link between the home office and the division or for their technical expertise. To ensure a smooth transition and equitable treatment, HR-related policies addressing travel and expenses are formalized and communicated.

In this stage, various national staffing categories emerge and three distinct types of employees become available to IHRM professionals.[18] These categories are **parent country nationals (PCNs)**, **host country nationals (HCNs)**, and **third country nationals (TCNs)**. PCNs are citizens of the country where the headquarters is located, HCNs are citizens of a county of a foreign subsidiary, hired to work at a subsidiary located in their home country, and TCNs are citizens of a country other than the parent country or the host country.[19]

---

parent country national (PCN)

Citizen of the country where the headquarters is located.

---

host country national (HCN)

Citizen of a county of a foreign subsidiary, hired to work at a subsidiary located in their home country.

---

third country national (TCN)

Citizen of a country other than the parent country or the host country.

Multinational Firms

Multinational enterprises (MNEs) are those organizations that have operations and subsidiaries around the globe. Each subsidiary typically operates independently of its parent company and operations in other countries. MNEs tend to focus on economies of scale, building facilities in different countries with an attempt to take advantage of lower production and distribution costs.[20] Staff working together from different parts of the organization and across boundaries require the development of cross-cultural skills. The cultures in these types of organizations are less unified and less dominated by a single national culture. These firms develop strategic capabilities that allow them to be very sensitive and responsive to differences in national environments.[21]

---

multinational enterprise (MNE)

An organization that has operations and subsidiaries around the globe.

It is at this point that firms begin to engage in *global HR planning*. As they increase their global presence, organizations send employees on international assignments with increased frequency. These are viewed as significant developmental opportunities for high-potential employees. Managers who are sent to these subsidiaries are typically senior and hold high positions in the organization and are seen as an important link to headquarters.

The HR role at this stage becomes more involved, providing services such as relocation, and dealing with international compensation and benefits issues for individuals who have been assigned to foreign locations. HR may coordinate activities and practices of many subsidiaries. At this point in their evolution, companies typically conform to local HR practices, which are largely decentralized. Corporate HR tries to find consistency with culture and policies of the parent company. Firms establish a global set of rules and processes to coordinate their efforts to establish recruitment processes and develop selection criteria for candidates. HR planning tends to focus on greater integration of key personnel into the local culture, choosing from a variety of staffing options, weighing costs and benefits, and ensuring that candidates are ready when the need arises.

Global and Transnational Firms

Global firms do not have any borders. They operate on the assumption that products or services can be created anywhere, and the world is seen as one big market to be tapped for resources. They manage subsidiaries in many countries, seek economies of scale, and spread development costs over a large area. The emphasis is on flexibility and mass customization of products to meet the needs of specific clients. Headquarters can be located in any country and people working in subsidiaries can be from anywhere. These firms are comprised of employees used to working in the international arena. Managers are sent abroad to ensure a common strategy. They are chosen from a high talent pool and are ready for the next step in their careers.[22]

Transnational firms are similar to global firms, but are more complex. Like global companies, they tend to have central headquarters, but they delegate decision-making power, research and development, and marketing to individual foreign markets. It can be said that they create synergies through cultural differences.[23]

Brazil's Embraer <http://www.embraer.com>, which builds aircraft, is an example of a truly global aerospace company. Although its headquarters is located in Sao Paulo, 93 percent of its profits originate from outside Brazil.

Techtronic Industries <http://www.ttigroup.com> of Hong Kong is another such firm. Using manufacturing and engineering expertise in many countries, this firm is cost efficient and on the cutting edge of innovation. It manufactures cordless power tools and distributes them around the globe.[24]

Walmart Stores Inc. is an example of a transnational company. It has branches all over the world and has established alliances with local companies on every continent, using national talents and resources to run its business.[25]

For a global firm, the most significant HR planning challenge is helping the global organization optimize its human resource capability, using whatever resource options makes the best sense from a cost/benefit perspective. There is a significant emphasis on valuing cross-cultural diversity and developing training programs to foster knowledge of cultural differences. Global HR planning is "managing the balance between overall coordinated systems and sensitivity to local needs."[26]

Spotlight *on* HRM

HR in the News: Can Women In the Workplace Save Japan?[27]

There is a major concern in Japan about the availability of labour and the aging population. The size of the working group ages 15–64 has been projected to fall from its peak of 87 million in 1995 to 55 million in 2050. Contributing to this shortage is the fact that women are underemployed at managerial levels. It has been reported that the number of female managers is strikingly low—only 9 percent compared to 43 percent in the United States.

It is increasingly difficult for women in Japan to balance working and raising a family. The HR policies are inflexible, with many companies not allowing shorter working hours, and if they do there is a general reluctance to work part-time hours due to the atmosphere at work. The general view of taking time off to deal with childcare responsibilities is not highly supported in Japan and there is limited availability of domestic help. Government policies are restrictive and the culture is not highly supportive of women in career stream roles with only 6 percent of career track employees being female.

Surprisingly, the labour rate at the start of a women's career is as high as comparable countries, but sharply drops off within the child-rearing years. The female participation rate is 24 percent lower than that of males, which is typical for other Asian countries as well. For example, in Korea the female participation rate is 22 percent.

Government policies do make a major difference. In Sweden, for example, there are several supportive policies in place and a greater focus on money being allocated to childcare programs. Sweden has a comprehensive parental leave policy, a highly subsidized childcare system, and a strict policy for shorter working hours for women.

There has been progress in Japan. In 2010 the Bank of Japan <https://www.boj.or.jp/en> hired its first female branch manager, Daiwa Securities <http://www.daiwa-grp.jp/english> placed four women on their board, and Shiseido <http://www.shiseido.com> created diversity and inclusion policies and established supportive measures for women's activities to help them with their careers. In 2013, Shiseido set a goal to increase the number of female managers by 30 percent and as at April 2014 they are at 26.4 percent of their target.[28]

Raising female participation rates by focusing on diversity and inclusion and providing supportive policies will provide Japan with valued resources to support its growth. As an IHR professional it is important to understand the labour market and government support systems and to bring best practices from the host country to ensure a balanced diverse workforce.

LO3 HRC 1

Contextual Factors

The challenges of an MNE are great as it grows through the establishment of subsidiaries and divisions in other countries. The impact of firms extending their global reach has a significant impact on HRM policies and practices.

To fully comprehend the implications to HRM one has to consider external and internal context factors. External factors are culture, labour economy, labour legislation, and immigration policies. Internal factors refer to a firm's preferences to local responsiveness versus global integration, managerial staffing decisions, and its commitment to global corporate social responsibility (CSR),[29] as is shown in Figure 14-2. Consider how Indian business context has affected IHRM policies and practices:

> Over the last decade, India has emerged as a major country in the economic global arena. If foreign investors operating in India are going to be successful, they must understand the Indian business context and develop applicable human resource systems. For example, over half the population is under the age of 25 and one-third is under the age of 15, making it one of the largest working populations in the world. The median age is currently 24.8, compared to 30 in China, 38 in Europe, and 41 in Japan. With labour costs lower than China, Brazil, and Thailand, India is an attractive location for businesses. From an HR perspective, it means designing attraction and retention mechanisms that appeal to this demographic makeup. Typically in India, selection, promotion, and transfer decisions are based on ascribed status and on social and political connections as opposed to merit. In addition, the society is highly collective, resulting in family and group taking precedence over work outcomes. These cultural differences contrast starkly to typical North American ways.[30]

FIGURE 14-2

External and Internal Contextual Factors

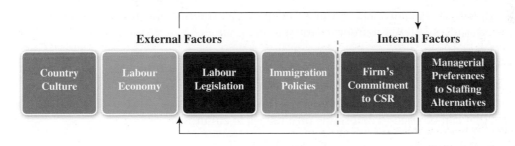

External Contextual Factors

The four external contextual factors are country culture, labour economy, labour legislation, and immigration policies.

Country Culture

Arguably the most significant cross-cultural research to date focuses on country culture and the importance of HRM developing a greater understanding of a culturally diverse work environment with its varying degrees of work ethics, norms, values, and business protocols.[31] The diversity of a global talent pool necessitates that HR educate its mobile workforce on cultural diversity. It must train and develop its employees to be sensitive to differing cultures and to develop tools and processes to ensure the workforce is ready to work with others from diverse backgrounds and to appreciate and value local differences. The development of these cross-cultural competencies is imperative as organizations expand their global reach and engage a mobile workforce.

Employing managers from different countries means that organizations have the potential to draw on a wealth of knowledge about customs and country requirements. It also increases the diversity of viewpoints in terms of defining problems and can increase decision quality. However, when people lack intercultural skills, miscommunications can occur, leading to poor business relationships and ultimately to diminished productivity.

Countries across the globe are very different in terms of their history, beliefs, laws, and behaviour patterns. Understanding these values is important so that conflicts can be avoided. Culture is one of the most important factors affecting the success of MNEs.[32]

> For example, in France it is very common for work to stop for a few hours during the lunch break. In Canada, on the other hand, it is quite common to have short lunch breaks and to rush to get back to work. Adapting to a different culture can be a challenge for employees who are sent abroad.
>
> A particularly surprising example is about an employee who worked for an MNE. He was caught stealing and was fired by the manager. Company policy dictated notifying local authorities. To the manager's horrific surprise, this employee was then subsequently executed.[33]

Managing successfully with an increasingly diverse workforce can be a major challenge for HR and executives of MNEs and is a key priority today.[34] In a recent study conducted by Korn Ferry <http://www.kornferry.com>, China was one of the easiest countries to attract executives to, but one of the most difficult to succeed in. The most common reason was lack of cultural fit. Some countries are easier to adapt to than others. Western Europe, North America, and South East Asia were locations where executives were more successful in adapting to cultural differences, whereas in North Asia, Japan, and South Korea it was harder for them to integrate.[35]

Cultural Dimensions

The Global Leadership and Organizational Behaviour Effectiveness study (GLOBE), an ongoing research project into leadership and culture from 825 organizations in 62 countries, identified nine key dimensions that can be used to determine differences in cultures.

1. Assertiveness

2. Gender differentiation

3. Uncertainty avoidance

4. Power distance

5. In-group collectivism

6. Performance orientation

7. Humane orientation

8. Institutional collectivism

9. Future orientation[36]

Assertiveness focuses on how assertive people are in society and the degree to which they are confrontational. **Gender differentiation** focuses on how society views differences in gender roles and affords higher status to certain roles. **Uncertainty avoidance** refers to the degree to which people are consistent and seek structure in their lives. **Power distance** focuses on the degree to which people are separated by power and authority. **In-group collectivism** focuses on the degree to which a society feels loyal either toward their family or other collective groups. **Performance orientation** focuses on the extent to which society recognizes and rewards performance. **Humane orientation** focuses on the degree to which societies focus on altruistic behaviour and generosity. **Institutional collectivism** refers to the degree to which institutions want individuals to integrate into the larger structure, even if this is at the cost of individual freedom. **Future orientation** refers to the degree to which people are willing to delay rewards.[37]

---

assertiveness

Focuses on how assertive people are in society and the degree to which they are confrontational.

---

gender differentiation

How society views differences in gender roles and affords higher status to certain roles.

---

uncertainty avoidance

Degree to which people are consistent and seek structure in their lives.

---

power distance

Degree to which people are separated by power and authority.

---

in-group collectivism

Degree to which a society feels loyal toward their family or other collective groups.

---

performance orientation

Extent to which society recognizes and rewards performance.

---

humane orientation

Degree to which societies focus on altruistic behaviour and generosity.

---

institutional collectivism

Degree to which institutions want individuals to integrate into the larger structure, even at the cost of individual freedom.

---

future orientation

The degree to which people are willing to delay rewards.

It is important to understand these dimensions, because they can have a significant effect on a firm's action in a specific country, e.g., the decisions whether to staff locally or with employees from other countries. Understanding a country's values assists HR in designing the most appropriate programs.

Communication and Language

It is important to understand the various cultural communication styles: direct–indirect, high–low context, nonverbal, avoiding conflict, and saving face. Direct communication prefers clear, succinct messages that are to the point. Australia is an example of a direct culture. France, on the other hand, prefers indirect communication. It is typical to have many speeches and much discussion before focusing on the outcome.[38]

Body language can be a cause of miscommunication. Greeks and Indians, when shaking their head, mean something positive, while Canadians will interpret it to mean no.[39] In the Middle East, raising one's eyebrows with the head tilted back and clicking the tongue to make a "tsk" sound, is a negative response.[40] North Americans would probably not know how to interpret such a gesture.

Even using the same language can result in miscommunication. In the United Kingdom, to "table" a topic at a meeting means to discuss it now, but in Canada it means to postpone it.

 HRC 5 & 9

Labour Economy

For MNEs, the complexity of operating in countries with a different labour economy is an added challenge.

The points below illustrate some examples of how global labour information can potentially add very valuable input into a firm's global human resource planning and help to balance its demand and supply across its subsidiaries.

- Skill Shortages in India's Call Centre Industry—According to Gartner Consulting <http://www.gartner.com>, there is a skill shortage in the call centre industry in India. This shortage is going to get worse and the Indian government has determined that there is a need for one million trained and qualified employees in call centres. This shortage can potentially impact MNEs who are located in India anticipating a stream of workers.[41]

- Software and IT Services Industry Growth in China—The Chinese IT and telecom markets are growing exponentially. Research conducted by the China Electronic and Information Development Academy predicts continued growth for the combined industries in the range of 16 percent over the next five years. Is now the right time to expand into the Chinese IT market?[42]

- Labour Costs in Emerging Economies—Labour demand is strong and rising in Asia and Central and Southern Europe, and labour costs have been reported as 20 to 80 percent below U.S. labour costs. Firms that are focused on cost control might consider these regions to expand their operations, and HR professionals should proactively explore the labour situations within these emerging countries.[43]

- Labour Force Participation—China has the highest labour force participation rates for both men and women. Brazil and India's rates for women are below 50 percent. Mexico and Korea had the lowest rates of unemployment.[44] Developing countries are experiencing a significant increase in the working age population and there are a significant number of young people entering the workforce. The reverse is true in developed countries where economists have reported slowing rates of population growth. This fact, combined with increased health in midlife, has increased the working age population toward mature groups.[45] Labour force participation rates are useful indicators of labour supply.

Labour Legislation

Another factor affecting global HRM is labour legislation as it differs around the globe. Each country has its own rules regarding employment standards such as hours of work, rest periods, overtime, termination provisions, and vacation. When planning to expand into a country, or perhaps planning to reduce the number of employees within a particular country, HR planners must be cognizant of these laws and how they affect their global resource plan. In addition, knowledge of legislation has an impact on employee relations as the organization must decide whether it is ethically comfortable with employment practices in the host country and the balance between headquarters' policies and local policies. The following examples illustrate some of these differences and the resource and labour cost implications.

In Ontario, Canadian employees receive two weeks' vacation after one year of service and eight statutory holidays. In France, employees receive 25 days leave and 11 public holidays, the Netherlands have 31.5 days of leave and 8 public holidays, and Ireland gets 20 days with 9 public holidays. The issues involved for the resource planner are the costs associated with increased vacation, coverage when employees are not working, and lost productivity.[46]

What if labour laws are so onerous as to impede a company's sustainability? Lee Cooper <https://www.leecooper.com>, a British jeans manufacturer, experienced exactly that in Indonesia. After several years of poor revenues, management decided to lay off some of its workers. However, due to Indonesia's inflexible labour laws, it found that this was difficult as the legislation required that dismissed workers receive up to several years in severance pay. Even employees who quit were entitled to payouts. Because these costs were deemed excessive, Lee Cooper decided to close the plant.[47] Severance provisions in each country differ. Finland requires one to three months of notice and a minimum of one-month salary for lower level employees and up to ten months of salary for senior. In France, an inspector must approve all terminations, and payment to seniors can exceed three months' salary.[48]

Human rights legislation differs in each country. In Canada, the United States, and the United Kingdom, these laws are highly developed. Most countries ban discrimination based on gender, ethnic orientation, and race, but in matters of sexual orientation, age, social class, and disability laws vary considerably. For example, a common form of gender discrimination is sexual harassment. In South Korea and Hong Kong it is considered a criminal offence, whereas in Sri Lanka it is not.[49] In China, women are protected from harassment, but employers still can ask the sex, age, and marital status of an applicant.[50]

Immigration Policies

Countries tend to control immigration tightly since it has a direct impact on their labour market. HR planners must be aware of countries' immigration policies when planning for resources as it affects a firm's recruitment and staffing policies. HR staff also has to understand the various types of visas required, procedures that must be followed, details to be obtained from the applicant, length of time that it takes to seek approval, renewal requirements, and potential road-blocks that may impede this process.

Internal Contextual Factors

The two internal factors that can influence HRM decisions are a firm's commitment to CSR and management's preference regarding staffing. The latter issue relates to the HR policy on how much control top management wants to maintain over its subsidiaries in foreign countries.

Commitment to Corporate Social Responsibility

Corporate social responsibility (CSR) is a way to demonstrate, through proactive programs, a company's commitment to economic, social, and environmental issues which influence its operations and ethical approach to labour.

---

corporate social responsibility (CSR)

A company's sense of responsibility toward the community and environment in which it operates.

How a firm demonstrates its commitment is an important factor influencing a firm's resource plan. It is not uncommon for the parent firm (headquarters) of a large MNE to set the overarching CSR principles. However, it is often the responsibility of subsidiaries to align its programs accordingly. CSR can have a wide range of meanings and the tools, which are employed to enhance a firm's performance in this regard, vary considerably.[51]

It is no surprise that countries across the globe can have very different views about the importance of being socially responsible. Global firms make decisions with respect to what country they will operate in and how they will conduct themselves with respect to employment practices. Choices are made regarding where work will be done and who will carry out the work. In addition, a firm may decide to outsource the work to another company in another country and must decide its level of comfort with the firm that it outsources to. Some global firms establish "hyper norms," broad-based universal principles, and are very demanding regarding conformity. Ernst and Young, a professional services accounting firm, has a global code of conduct that it requires all of its subsidiaries to adhere to. Honda adheres to global standards with respect to safety and environmental issues.

Spotlight *on* ETHICS

The Hidden Cost of Fast Fashion within the Garment Industry[52]

The development of the garment industry in Indonesia and Cambodia has given rise to a number of issues regarding social responsibility practices and ethical considerations. Many questions have been raised about factory conditions and unsafe employment conditions.

Labour shortages, poverty, significant product demand, lack of a universal birth registration system, and the requirements of producing "fast fashion" (chains introducing style changes every two weeks) have created a labour environment that is rife with problems.[53] A recent report from the UN Refugee Agency on human rights practices in Cambodia indicated that the government was not effective in enforcing standards on overtime and hours worked. Work-related injuries are very common.[54]

As a result we see the rise of a new role called "Compliance Officer." This individual works in partnership with human resource officers employed by companies and with third party auditors and staff recruited from major brands to monitor compliance with rules established by governments and other national and international organizations.. A key requirement of these officers is that they must be familiar with HR practices and labour laws and that their actions support safe conditions by encouraging dialogue between managers and workers.[55]

The *Wall Street Journal* reports that underage labour is a major issue in the garment industry, especially involving teenaged workers who are able to pass themselves off as 18 or older. The law prohibits children under 18 from working with harmful chemical agents, but does not specify the types of chemicals. It also prohibits workers under 18 from working overtime or night shifts or doing hazardous work that compromises their health. These underage workers cannot sign employment contracts without their guardian's consent. However, it is reported that many teens are lying about their birth dates to get jobs and that parents and companies look the other way.[56]

Many people believe it is acceptable to lie to get a job. Having secured employment keeps young people from entering the sex trade and it enables them to help their families. Proponents of "fast fashion" recognize the dark side of doing business, but many turn a blind eye to the consequences. Due to the constant demand for product changes every two weeks, factories are forced to focus on production schedules as opposed to workers' rights. To meet these goals requires factories to engage in excessive overtime, additional shifts, and inadequate monitoring of human resource legislation, knowing full well that some of the workers are underage. It has been reported that the government of Cambodia enforces standards selectively.[57]

The ethical issue here is: Is having a job more important than work safety? What if life is endangered?

Staffing Preferences

Staffing preferences relates to the degree of control an organization feels it should have over its subsidiary. Executives are always concerned about how to optimally balance and coordinate a firm's global standards, set by the parent company, with local practices.[58] Staffing preferences bring to light the issue of how much local presence is important; researchers have debated for quite some time the degree to which headquarter policies and manpower should be present in a local market. These preferences are referred to as ethnocentrism, polycentrism, geocentrism, and regiocentrism.[59] See Figure 14-3 for a breakdown of which staffing alternatives are most commonly used in each preference.

FIGURE 14-3

Managerial Preferences in Staffing Alternatives

Staffing Preference	Standard Followed	Host-Country Positions Filled By:
Ethnocentrism	Home-country standards	PCN (Parent Country National)
Polycentrism	Home-country standards	HCN (Host Country National)
Geocentrism	Global strategy to fit standards across countries	Combination of PCN, HCN, and TCNs (Third Country National)
Regiocentrism	Host-country standards	HCN (Host Country National)

Ethnocentrism refers to the view in which managers use a home-country standard as reference for managing activities. Individuals from headquarters fill key positions in subsidiaries. Decision making is centralized and is driven from the home country where control over operations is exercised. Subsidiaries are controlled by the PCN and there are very few opportunities for HCNs to hold key positions or be promoted outside their operation.[60] This strategy is based on transferring and adapting the parent company's knowledge and expertise to foreign markets while maintaining considerable influence.[61]

ethnocentrism

A view in which managers use a home-country standard as reference for managing activities.

Polycentrism describes policies under which subsidiaries are staffed by host-country managers and are characterized by decentralized and autonomous operations. Subsidiaries are managed via tight financial and operational controls from headquarters. The opportunity for promotion within subsidiaries is available, but limited externally.

polycentrism

Characterized by firms that are staffed by host-country managers and are typically decentralized and autonomous operations.

Geocentrism focuses on creating a global network, following a strategy that integrates and is dependent on the global firm's strengths. It is of the view that the best person for the job can be found anywhere.[62]

geocentrism

A managerial outlook that focuses on creating a global network and follows a strategy that integrates and is dependent on the global firm's strengths.

Regiocentrism focuses on organizations in terms of the regions they operate in, choosing the best manager in the region. Transfers within the region are common.

regiocentrism

A focus on the regions in which organizations operate.

LO4

Human Resource Planning & Staffing in a Global Context

There are commonalities between domestic and IHRM practices. However, the main distinction lies in the fact that domestic HRM is involved with employees within one national boundary, while IHRM manages employees from many different countries and cultures. Its scope is much broader, its programs are significantly enhanced to address cultural differences, the human resource problems are far more complex, and the decisions as to how to effectively balance corporate head office and local customs is an important consideration. Figure 14-4 provides an overview of some of the important considerations in global staffing.

FIGURE 14-4

Global Staffing Considerations

Staffing
- Consider the advantages and disadvantages of staffing alternatives: HCN, TCN, PCN
- Establish an inventory of core competencies expected of an international candidate and assess candidates accordingly
- Become knowledgeable of country specific visa requirements and turnaround times
- Create a well-structured repatriation program

Chapter 3 discussed how human resource planning is about ensuring that organizations have the right skills at the right time in the right place. For global firms the goal of human resource planning does not change. What is different is the size of its talent pool, the geographic reach, the economic and legal differences of each country, and the major cultural and ethical issues that arise as firms participate and plan in a global economy. **Global HR planning** estimates employment needs and develops plans for meeting those needs from the available global labour force and the viability of MNEs in their ability to align their workforce forecasts with the supply for global talent.[63]

global HR planning

Estimates employment needs and develops plans for meeting those needs from the available global labour force and the viability of MNEs in their ability to align their workforce forecasts with the supply for global talent.

From a resource planning perspective, global HR planning is about leveraging a firm's talent pools, creating career development and succession programs, and optimizing a firm's resource supply while balancing the need to attract local talent to meet demand.[64] A major advantage for these global firms is that they potentially have a significant supply of talent across the globe to choose from. However, the challenge is how to transfer and exchange knowledge so that learning is deployed across its global units and how to effectively utilize these skills on a real-time basis.[65]

Successful staffing on a global level requires HR programs that promote cross-cultural competencies. In what ways would hiring for international positions differ from hiring for local jobs?

iStockphoto/ThinkStock.

Effective global HR planning means that HR planners must understand the human resource capabilities resident within their global enterprise. They must leverage their talent pool across many geographic boundaries and develop a talent pipeline of available skills and competencies so that the organization will have the optimum resources to meet its strategic goals. They must be aware of any legislative changes within the countries where they conduct business and the challenges they face regarding employment rules. Currently one top-of-mind challenge facing organizations is the hiring of temporary foreign workers (TFW). For example, consider the reforms announced by the Minister of Employment and Social Development: as of June 2014 there are significant changes to the TFWP programs in Canada. Some of the major changes involve a cap on low-wage TFW, using wage levels instead of National Occupational Classification (NOC) as a core criterion for administering the TFWP, and revising the test that allows employers to bring workers into Canada (moving from a labour market option to an assessment protocol that is rigorous and through).[66]

LO5 HRC 4

The Staffing Mix

It has often been said that high-performing organizations "think globally, but act locally." There are a number of staffing options that reflect that advice, each with advantages and disadvantages. Figure 14-5 provides an overview of these staffing choices.

Advantages and Disadvantages of Staffing Choices

Staffing Choice / Nationality	Advantages	Disadvantages
Host Country National—HCN		
• Employees of the MNE who are citizens of the host country	• Knows local culture and politics and economic situation • Shares common language and can communicate effectively • Less expensive than bringing an employee from the home country	• Lacks familiarity with parent country's culture
Parent Country National—PCN		
• Employees of the MNE who are citizens of the country where the MNE corporate headquarters resides	• Familiar with MNE corporate culture • Can communicate well with headquarters • Ensures that the MNE strategic objectives are understood and complied with	• Can be expensive to send • Resentment due to possible inequities regarding reward/compensation packages between PCN and HCN • Limited awareness of local culture • Work permit issues
Third Country National—TCN		
• Neither citizens of home or host country	• Identifies with the global firm • Mobile • Culturally sensitive • Highly developed language and cultural skills	• May not be perceived as legitimate representatives of headquarters • May be culturally biased if TCN is from a country with a history of conflict

Host Country National—Local Presence

Using host country nationals (HCNs) has many advantages. These employees know the culture, local politics, and economic conditions. They share a common language and can communicate effectively. They are also less expensive than bringing someone over from the home country. On the other hand, they may lack familiarity with the parent country's culture. In this way HCNs can help PCNs better understand the local environment and how best to integrate corporate practices. Managing without an expatriate also means less coordination between headquarters and the subsidiary. Ideally, organizations hire locals together with transfers from the parent country.[67] In this way the PCNs help support the new HCNs.

Parent Country Nationals—Integrating Global Standards.

Parent country nationals (PCNs) are employees of the MNE who are citizens of the country where the MNE has its corporate headquarters. Utilizing PCNs can be beneficial as they are familiar with the MNE's corporate culture, can communicate effectively with headquarters, are able to exert control over the subsidiary's operations, and will ensure that the MNE's strategic objectives, policies, and goals will be understood and complied with.[68] MNEs continue to send PCNs as technical troubleshooters, structure reproducers, and general management operatives. Other important reasons PCNs are used are:

- To fill positions when HCNs are not available;

- To develop and mentor others;

- To support organizational development and change efforts; and

- To provide lead-time for HCNs to reach acceptable performance standards.

Some possible disadvantages to using PCNs is that they can be expensive and there may be perceived reward inequities between how the HCNs and the PCNs are compensated. In addition, PCNs may have limited awareness of local culture.[69]

Third Country Nationals

Third country nationals (TCNs) are not citizens of the country in which the MNE is headquartered, nor citizens of the country where the foreign subsidiary is located. TCNs identify with a global firm and do not overly identify with either the parent or the host country. They may not be as expensive as a PCN and they tend to be mobile and culturally sensitive. They typically have better language and cross-cultural skills than headquarter expatriates and can make an important contribution in the cultural socialization of management. They may be chosen for their language ability rather than for their managerial or technical abilities. While TCNs may have greater linguistic and cross-cultural skills, TCNs may not be perceived as legitimate representatives of their headquarters and there may be cultural biases if the TCN comes from a country where there is a history of conflict. Another possible disadvantage to using this group relates to the fact that it may experience work permit obstacles.[70]

Recently, a fourth pool of expatriate candidates has been identified, referred to as TCK–*third culture kids*. **Third culture kids (TCK)** are the children of parents who have been sent on global work assignments and have become comfortable with many different cultures. Having spent their formative adolescent years in several different cultures living abroad, these individuals do not subscribe to any particular culture fully.[71]

---

third culture kids (TCK)

Children who accompany their parents on global work assignments and become familiar with more than one culture.

No matter which staffing option organizations decide to choose, the ultimate goal is to *optimize their talent pool* and do so in the most *cost-efficient and effective manner*.

 HRC 4

Current Trends in Staffing Global Organizations—"The Assignment"

Assignments have become a popular staffing option as technology enables communication across wide boundaries. There are many different types of assignments that organizations may consider, depending on business needs, for example, short or long-term or frequent or infrequent. There are many different variables that determine the type of assignment. Researchers have categorized assignments in four ways: short-term, international commuter, frequent flyer, and expatriate.

The term **international commuter** refers to employees who frequently commute from their home country to a place of work in another country, typically on a weekly or biweekly basis. A **frequent flyer** travels often on international business trips to accomplish a specific task. The term **flexpatriate** describes a person on a short-term assignment who engages in frequent travel without relocation. Typically, short-term assignments are for less than one year, which is also true for the international commuter and frequent flyer.

---

international commuter

An employee who frequently commutes from a home country to a place of work in another country, typically on a weekly or biweekly basis.

---

frequent flyer

An employee who travels often on international business trips to accomplish a specific task.

---

flexpatriate

A person who is on a short-term assignment and engages in frequent travel without relocation.

Expatriates are individuals who are sent on an assignment outside of their home country for a period of time, usually for more than one year. Expatriates are of special concern for organizations because of questions regarding whether they have to relocate, can travel back home or bring their family, or the length of their assignment.[72] **Inpatriates** are TCN or HCN employees who relocate from a foreign subsidiary or joint venture to the parent company.[73]

---

expatriate

An individual who is sent on an assignment outside the home country for a period of time.

---

inpatriate

Third country national (TCN) or host country national (HCN) employee who relocates from a foreign subsidiary or joint venture to the parent company.

LO6

Key Elements of a Successful Expatriate Experience

There are several considerations that must be taken into account when IHR managers face global staffing challenges. Of critical importance are clearly defined hiring criteria and the development of a well–thought-out plan for the return of an expatriate to the parent company. Equally important is the development of formalized IHRM policies such as travel, relocation policies, compensation, performance management, and training and development policies, supported by a well-structured and consistent administrative process. Figure 14-6 depicts the key elements of a successful expatriate experience.

A recent survey conducted by PwC indicated that less than 50 percent of companies surveyed had formalized policies in place regarding tax, social security, and visa requirements. Of those who did respond, 50 percent indicated that they followed one policy and did not differentiate between the different types of assignments. Over 80 percent of those surveyed felt changes to their existing policies needed to be made.[74]

FIGURE 14-6

Key Elements of a Successful Expatriate Experience

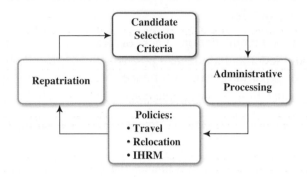

Travel and Relocation

IHRM Policies

Some of the HR policies that are relevant to the expatriate are training and development, compensation, and performance management. In terms of training and development policies, firms must consider the types of cultural and language training and cultural sensitivity experiences needed to sensitize the individual to cultural differences, and whether there are any special country conditions that must be understood (e.g., a country where there may be safety and security issues). The degree and level of training will differ, based on the type of assignment. Performance management is another area of consideration. Objectives and standards have to be set and developed. Supervisors have to be educated on the special skill requirements for expatriate candidates. Pay policies must be developed to ensure that they are locally relevant and globally equitable. Compensation for a short-term assignment will be easier to determine than one where an individual is going to relocate to a particular country on a long-term assignment, since factors such as cost of living need to be taken into account in the latter case.[75]

Travel

Issues have to be dealt with about the number of trips expatriates can take back to their home country and at what cost per trip. Will the company allow individuals to fly first class or economy? If employees are on a short-term assignment, consideration must be given to their daily allowance for meals, entertainment, etc., whether this allowance will fluctuate based on the country, and if the allowance will be unlimited or have a cap set.

Relocation Policies

Relocation has been cited as one of the most stressful situations an employee can encounter. The focus of a formal relocation policy is to transport an employee, the family, and the household goods to the new site with minimal disruption. The policy typically includes housing, cost-of-living adjustments, temporary living expenses, spousal assistance, cross-cultural training, and set-up services.[76] Relocation can be very costly. According to a recent study by Atlas Van Lines <http://www.atlasvanlines.ca>, the average cost of relocation is about \$45,000 for a domestic move and twice that for an international move.[77] Firms such as Runzheimer International <https://www.runzheimer.com> and Brookfield Global Relocation Services <http://www.brookfieldgrs.com> are specialists in helping employees relocate.

Administrative Processing

Another important element is administration. Lack of attention to detail and potential errors in administrative processes can hinder an individual's positive experience and has been cited as one of the most frustrating issues that expatriates can experience. Managing the basics is an expectation of everyone working for an organization. Some simple considerations include ensuring that:

- The assignment terms and conditions are documented and that the individual agrees to these new terms and conditions;

- Payroll processing and tax administration is managed according to the new agreement;

- The organization offers assistance with the visa application to ensure that the documentation compiled is complete according to the immigration regulations; and

- Any spouse and or dependent issues and concerns have been looked after.

In addition, providing administrative support with respect to relocation is very important. Considerations have to be given to such items as engaging a relocation firm to help the assignee find suitable accommodation, managing the vendors who will be providing services to the assignee, and building in supports to help with family concerns such as schools to attend or community groups to join.[78]

Candidate Selection Criteria

Arguably, one of the most critical considerations is whether the individual chosen is the best fit for the assignment. Large multinational firms that do this well have established specific criteria for candidate selection, giving thought to the importance of nationality and whether sending a HCN, a PCN, or a TCN will enhance the fit for the position and the achievement of the firm's objectives.[79] These firms document and communicate the criteria to potential candidates. One of the most important criterion to consider is the degree to which an individual possesses cultural intelligence (CQ). Cultural intelligence refers to an individual's ability to successfully adapt to new and unfamiliar cultural settings and to function effectively in situations characterized by cultural diversity.[80] It applies across all cultures and has been defined with both process components, such as skills, and content components, such as knowledge and mindfulness.[81]

A recent study conducted on expatriates in Malaysia found that expatriates performed more effectively in their jobs if they had a greater awareness and understanding of their own thought processes, used higher order thinking such as analytical skills, and adapted their verbal and nonverbal behaviours appropriately so that they could fit within the diverse culture.[82] Other factors to consider when choosing a suitable candidate are gender, previous work experience, and level of interest and competencies such as adaptability, flexibility, and personality characteristics.

The skills and competencies that a successful expatriate candidate should possess are listed in Figure 14-7.

FIGURE 14-7

Core Competencies of an Expatriate Manager

Past writings indicate that successful expatriate managers possess several core competencies. Here are the key ones:

Multidimensional Perspective

Ability to consider multiple dimensions of a problem and their interrelationships and ability to integrate them. Ability to conceptualize and resolve a problem at multifunctional, multiproduct, multi-industry, and multicountry levels.

Cultural Adaptability

Ability to understand and adapt to local cultural norms and practices without losing track of one's objectives.

Decision-Making Ability

Strategic-thinking ability, ability to process information and identify creative alternatives to problems, evaluate and test alternatives for their feasibility, and ability to modify own decision process to suit the needs of the situation.

Team-Building and Leadership Ability

Ability to understand the motivations of a culturally diverse workforce, bring them together as a high-performing team to accomplish organizational objectives.

Resourcefulness

Ability to adapt own actions and practices to the needs of the situation. Ability to accurately gauge the various political, cultural, technological, and other constraints surrounding own firm and find creative solutions to meet them.

Negotiation Skills

Ability to conduct successful strategic business negotiations in a multicultural and political environment. An understanding of the motivations of the "other side" at the bargaining table and ability to identify solutions that result in win–win solutions.

Change-Agent Skills

Ability to bring about changes in a foreign setting and influence others into newer ways of thinking and acting. Ability to understand the cultural parameters surrounding oneself and adapt one's change strategy to meet these cultural requirements.

SOURCES: *HR Magazine* published by the Society for Human Resource Management, Alexandria, VA. © January 1990, Vol. 44, No. 1; Training and Development, American Society of Training & Development; Allan Bird and Roger Dunbar, "Getting the Job Done over There: Improving Expatriate Productivity," *National Productivity Review,* Vol. 10, No. 2, Spring, 1991, pp. 145–56 © 1991; reprinted from Rosalie Tung, "Selection and Training of Personnel for Overseas Assignments," *Columbia Journal of World Business,* Vol. 16, No. 1, Spring, 1981, pp. 68–78.

Repatriation

The final consideration is how effective an organization is at reintegrating an expatriate into the home-country firm. These individuals can be a major resource within a company as they have significant expertise that they have built up over time. If their knowledge is fully employed, these individuals can play a significant role in helping firms sustain their competitive advantage. However, there is ample evidence to suggest that when expatriates return from an extended assignment, it is often difficult for them to adjust back to the parent company and home country. This phenomenon has been referred to as **reverse culture shock**. This experience refers to how individuals adjust to their home culture and environment upon return, after growing accustomed to the host's culture. They may miss the special benefits they received while working abroad. For example, in some countries having a chauffeur is common and even necessary if there are safety issues. Another common problem is that the individual often expects a promotion upon return and this may not happen in a timely fashion. In addition, the returning individual may feel disconnected and on the periphery, as the company may have hired new personnel who have become an integral part of the team, but the returning individual does not know them or understand their role.[83] All of this may contribute to an individual's decision to leave the organization.[84] One survey suggested that as many as 25 percent of expatriates leave their companies within two years of returning home.[85]

---

reverse culture shock

Returning home after having been accustomed to another culture. Also called re-entry shock.

The repercussions from an organization not addressing these issues can significantly affect the individual's experience on an assignment. Poorly managed policies and practices can have a profound effect on an individual's perception as to just how effective an organization is when dealing with its employees abroad. Individuals may choose to pass on assignments and the word *assignment* can take on a negative tone. If employees do not value a job experience abroad, the organization will have difficulties finding candidates for such positions. Individuals who are already on an assignment may feel frustrated and decide to quit. Such loss of personnel will ultimately hurt a firm, as valuable knowledge "walks out the door." In addition, labour costs may rise due to turnover, as it is likely that the firm will have to hire new employees.[86]

Orientation, Training, and Development

A significant activity of effective talent management is the development of proper training programs. Some specific concerns relate to what type of training would be most effective and whether to export training programs from headquarters or develop them locally. A recent survey by Worldwide ERC <http://www.worldwideerc.org>, the association for workforce mobility and the Hong Kong Institute of HRM <http://www.hkihrm.org> examined the major challenges facing expats moving to China for a long-term assignment and the necessity for specific types of training. They found that helping to build language capability, aiding the expat to find comparable medical services to their home country, and providing enhanced cross-cultural training helps to mitigate culture shock, enabling the expat to perform more effectively.[87] Figure 14-8 provides an overview of some of the major considerations.

FIGURE 14-8

Orientation, Training, and Development in a Global Context

| Orientation, Training, & Development | • Consider the length and complexity of expatriate assignment and the type of training, language, and sensitivity programs that are applicable
• Develop global leadership and multicultural team building skills
• Create an onboarding progam with specific consideration as to the length of assignment
• Develop awareness of country specific cultural dimensions |

Orientation: The Importance of Predeparture Training

Unlike new employee orientations in a domestic firm, international orientations may begin weeks or even months before and last several weeks after an assignment starts. This is called *predeparture training*. The focus is on developing cultural awareness. These programs help to develop an appreciation of a foreign culture and help the expat develop coping mechanisms. The components vary from country to country, but common elements include details of the culture, language, local customs, attitudes toward time and punctuality, power, teamwork, use of titles, social taboos, and degree of formality in interaction with the local population.

Depending on the length of the assignment, training on each of these elements will be greater in depth and this "acculturation" will continue once the employee is at the assignment. The orientation provides information on the policies, place, procedures, and people that the new job incumbent will encounter in the near future.

Copyright Grantland Enterprises; www.grantland.nct.

One large firm with global operations invites the spouse of the employee to be sent abroad to all orientation events. An integral part of the orientation in this firm is a two-week language and culture orientation course for both. It often includes a briefing from an expatriate employee or spouse. Apart from the personal touch, repatriated families are likely to have keen insights about a particular culture.[88]

Cross-Cultural Training Methods

A number of training methods aimed at preparing employees for a foreign work environment have been tried. Some of the more promising approaches are described below.

Sensitivity Training

This has been successfully used by several organizations to prepare managers for overseas assignments. The objective of sensitivity training is to increase self-awareness and the ability to assess the impact of one's own behaviour on others. (This method was discussed in Chapter 7.)

Culture Assimilators

These consist of a series of episodes dealing with interpersonal issues in a cross-cultural situation. By responding to individual episodes and referring to explanations describing why their responses were appropriate or not, trainees have an opportunity to test their cross-cultural effectiveness and to learn about the appropriate responses in a specific culture. Studies have shown that assimilator-trained employees performed better in another culture than employees who did not receive such training. The following is an example of a culture assimilator episode:

You offer a Japanese manager a generous gift if he would be helpful in getting your sales bid accepted by his boss. He reacts by sucking air through his teeth. Do you assume that:

a)   He is pleasantly surprised;

b)   He is deeply embarrassed;

c)   He is unsure how to respond and would prefer more information and clarification; or

d)   It is a sign that the value of the proposed gift is insufficient to obtain his support.

The correct answer is (b). Japanese respond to embarrassing situations by sucking air through their clenched teeth. This reaction is often accompanied by the comment: "That will be difficult," which to the Japan expert means, "No, don't bother."

Critical Incidents

These are brief descriptions of effective or ineffective behaviours that illustrate problems an expatriate employee may encounter in an organization abroad. Below are examples of an effective and an ineffective behaviour:

When a newly appointed Canadian manager began his job in Mexico, he was complimented by his employees for his mastery of the Spanish language. He explained that he had studied the language for six months intensively before coming to Mexico.

The Japanese employees of an international company suggested to the foreign CEO that a new company building should be dedicated on *taian*, a day of good luck. The CEO rejected the idea because it would have meant waiting another three weeks.

The Japanese often use a decision-making process known as *ringisei*, which is decision making by consensus, but it usually takes longer to reach it. Is that positive or negative for the decision-making process?

© Hans Neleman/Getty Images.

Cases

Cases are more detailed and complex than critical incidents. They illustrate a variety of cross-cultural problems in management within a single setting. The Maple Leaf Shoes Ltd. case at the end of this chapter provides a good example of the challenges of working in a multinational, multiracial team.

Role-Play

Role-play is a semi-structured activity. Participants are given a description of a situation with specific role instructions, but no script, forcing the participants to improvise their reactions to the setting. The results usually reveal personal values and biases that can be analyzed and discussed. A significant learning experience can be achieved if participants are asked to advocate a position that is contrary to their own beliefs. Studies indicate that this method is relatively effective in changing a person's attitudes.[89]

Simulation

Simulation is a common cross-cultural training method.

> A popular simulation game is *Ba Fa' Ba Fa'*.[90] Participants are divided into two cultures: Alpha and Beta. After learning the "rules" of their own culture, participants have to interact with members of the other culture. Since the interaction rules for each culture are different, confusion and frustration, even hostility, result. These experiences are then discussed at a debriefing session.

It is unlikely that any single method will be sufficient to prepare an employee for the complex experiences that lie ahead when going abroad.[91] More likely, a combination of the methods described will be most effective, as people react differently to different methods. Whatever the method(s) chosen, effective cross-cultural training aims to develop a **global mindset** for managers. Mindsets can be defined as the different ways the subject at hand is perceived, understood, reasoned about, and acted upon by individuals. Persons with a global mindset are able to do the following:

- Look at events in the context of the bigger, broader picture;
- Recognize the diversity and inherent contradictory forces that exist in any situation;
- Appreciate and even welcome ambiguity and surprises; and
- Understand the need for change and establish processes that facilitate change.

---

global mindset
Capacity to scan the world with a broad view, to value diversity, and to appreciate change.

A global mindset thus indicates the capacity to scan the world with a broad view—always looking for unexpected trends and opportunities to achieve the firm's and the individual manager's objectives.[92] In today's global marketplace, this is perhaps what distinguishes a leading enterprise from other organizations.

 HRC 2 & 7

Performance Appraisal

Employees in international operations need to be evaluated and, just like any other employee, require assistance in career planning. Performance appraisal is particularly difficult in **home-country evaluations** because the evaluator in the home country may be thousands of kilometres away and may not fully understand the challenges faced by the person being evaluated.[93] Geographical and cultural distance pose severe communication problems for expatriates and home-country managers. While improvements in information technology have significantly reduced the distance and time barriers, this has not always made communication easier between an individual and the superior at the home office.

A conscious effort to overcome this communication problem is often required as in the case of the Dow Chemical Company <http://www.dow.com>:

> At Dow Chemical, a senior manager in the same function is assigned to the role of godfather to an employee. The employee and his mentor (or "godfather") are expected to keep each other informed about performance and other matters that affect the person's career. The godfather then becomes involved with pay raises and locating a job in the home country when the employee is repatriated.[94]

home-country evaluations

Performance appraisals carried out by an expatriate's home office.

When **host-country evaluations** take place, the evaluator has a better awareness of the constraints under which an expatriate works. However, even here problems exist. Local cultural values may bias one's perception of the manager's effectiveness.

host-country evaluations

Performance appraisals carried out by an expatriate's local (or host) office.

> For example, a manager who uses a participative or consultative style of leadership may be considered as "weak" or ineffective by members of a culture that in the past have been under autocratic leaders and expect their leader to make all important decisions.

Further, local evaluators may not possess adequate information about the larger organizational priorities. Even actions that are not suitable from the point of view of local operations may be desirable for the long-term growth and success of the parent organization in the region.

Given this, the appraisals should attempt to balance the two sources of appraisal information.[95] While the host-country managers are in a good position to observe day-to-day behaviours of the employee concerned, the individual is likely still formally tied to the parent organization for pay, career development, and other decisions. This factor should be kept in mind when designing an appraisal system. Figure 14-9 lists four steps in developing a global performance management system.

FIGURE 14-9

Steps in Global Performance Management

Performance Management	• Establish a management performance process using multiple performance criteria • Develop a professional profile clearly identifying expatriates' productivity standards • Develop applicable tools and assign the raters taking into consideration local and corporate expectations • Ensure raters are trained and understand the impact of local challenges on expatriate performance

HRC 6

Global Compensation

International compensation goes well beyond pay and benefits. Pay is expanded to compensate for additional taxes, living expenses, and personal costs. Incentives may be added, especially for assignments to less desirable locations. Supplements may be given to cover extra costs of educating children in private schools that follow the curriculum of the home country, making return trips to the home country, and special medical services. Benefits may include a company car, a driver, club memberships, housing, and other "perks" normally reserved for top management. Several firms also offer *relocation assistance*, which can range from buying the employee's home at market value to shipping household goods, cars, and other possessions abroad.

A few of the human resource department's concerns at a large international firm in the area of compensation management include:

- Developing an overseas compensation and benefits plan;
- Taking into account cost-of-living differences;
- Considering any special needs;
- Giving tax advice and financial counselling; and
- Supervising the sometimes extensive paperwork involved.

When designing international compensation systems, HR professionals have to consider the value different cultures place on rewards, monetary or otherwise. While nonfinancial incentives such as independence and prestige are powerful motivators, money may be a key driving force for others. In some cultures, however, security, family, respect, and social recognition may be more valued. A recent survey conducted by Mercer <http://www.mercer.ca> described the various mindsets of different country cultures:

> In Australia, 84 percent of workers indicated the importance of benefits and that the type of benefits influenced whether they would join a company. In France, employees indicated the importance of base pay as highly valued, but ranked incentives much lower. Due to increasing turnover of key talent, in China career development opportunities are highly valued.[96]

Companies are reconsidering their global compensation strategies, shifting to more centralized compensation and benefit structures. This is to help ensure that executives and employees worldwide are treated equitably.[97] The packages for expatriate compensation can be complex. One approach is to compensate expatriates so that their spending power is maintained as if they were in their home country. This is called the *balance sheet approach*. This method typically includes a benefit package that would be the same as if the person were at home.

Another approach is to focus on local compensation. With this approach employers give the expatriate the same compensation as the local talent equivalent would receive. A concern with this approach is that local policies are difficult to implement and 72 percent of companies who have these policies do not strictly follow them. According to a recent survey, localization is arguably most important in such countries as Malaysia and Hong Kong, where the retention rate for employees after two years on a localized package is over 80 percent.[98]

An emerging approach to compensation is to design a system using the concept of *local plus*. It offers a competitive local salary package with extras that are not provided to locals. It is proving to be an effective attraction method to secure nonlocal talent and to localize long-term expatriates. This approach can be attractive to younger employees in large business centres such as Hong Kong, Beijing, and Shanghai.[99] Consider how Tetra Pak Corporation has chosen to compensate its globally mobile employees:

> Tetra Pak <http://www.tetrapak.com> has established a global employment company called "Tetra Pak Global Resources." Every employee who goes out on an assignment has a contract with this company. This arrangement establishes a common basis for expatriates, in which, no matter where they are in the world, they receive a base salary that is a combination of the company's top seven markets. The structure of the base

salary and the incentive is the same for everyone, but the incentive does vary depending on location. Employees also receive an offshore pension, location allowance, and cost-of-living adjustments.[100]

The field of international compensation is a specialty discipline. Figure 14-10 provides an overview of important considerations for IHR managers in global compensation.

FIGURE 14-10

Global Compensation Considerations

Compensation	• Communicate compensation philosophy • Balance local and global compensation considerations • Consider country-specific cost of living, tax, and social security systems • Take into account country specific challenges (e.g., security and safety issues) • Consider additional supplements (e.g., housing, education)

LO7 HRC 1

The Changing Role of HR in Global Organizations

This chapter has highlighted the challenges facing IHRM in a global environment. In contrast to HR managers responsible for domestic staff, managers supervising employees abroad have to have a broader perspective, because international HR issues are more complex. They are managing the problems of many different nationalities and are more involved in the personal lives of their employees. However, it is important to note that the importance of developing a global mindset is no longer defined only as being able to operate outside the country. Given our diverse populations within Canada, HR professionals and managers often have to address a significant number of issues dealing with differing value systems and attitudes. Growing international diversity is the first step in developing key competencies and skills for managing within a global context.[101]

In arranging international assignments they must deal with family issues, health care, relocation challenges, and different national staffing categories of employees. There exists an increased risk of failure from both the human and financial perspective and requires IHR managers to become highly knowledgeable about potential problems.[102]

IHR managers also have to adjust domestic HR practices, processes, and systems to international requirements. Developing internal coordination and control mechanisms and being able to replicate these across a firm's foreign subsidiaries provides firms with a significant competitive advantage. Consider how Intel Corp. has attempted to integrate its global workforce with its corporate culture:

> Intel has established a corporate value system shared by its employees worldwide. Everyone understands the definition of work, commitment, and corporate values in the same way. From the moment employees join Intel they are instilled with Intel's values, operating philosophy, and standards of behaviour. To support this common view even the facilities across the world look the same.[103] This strong culture is reinforced by consistent HR policies and processes that enable managers to have a corporate framework as they address specific cultural differences within their countries.[104]

The three key responsibilities of the IHR manager, and the emerging competencies that set them apart from their domestic counterparts, are shown in Figure 14-11.

FIGURE 14-11

The Changing Role of HR in Global Organizations

HRC 1

Foster a Global Mindset

Fostering a global mindset means developing *global wisdom and collaboration* into the fabric of the workforce.[105]

Across the enterprise, IHR managers must work to help the organization view others' perspectives; recognizing that the same reality may be perceived very differently by other cultures. It is imperative that IHR build training programs that will enhance the ability of its global employees to manage intercultural communication, to recognize how cultural dimensions influence interactions with people from other cultures, and to inculcate the view that one's perceptions can be limiting. This requires IHR managers to possess exceptional communication skills and preferably be multilingual. Being knowledgeable about global training methods and learning styles of various cultures would be an important asset.

HRC 4

Managing the Talent Pipeline

Staffing a global organization with competent leaders is a major challenge. Ensuring that the organization has a pool of talent with unique skills and competencies and that these resources are available across the organization is a major responsibility of the IHR manager. **Global talent management** is defined as the strategic integration of resourcing and development at the international level, which involves the proactive identification and development and strategic deployment of high-performing and high-potential employees on a global scale.[106]

global talent management

Strategic integration of resourcing and development at the international level, which involves the proactive identification, development, and strategic deployment of high-performing and high-potential employees on a global scale.

Global talent management means that IHR managers must increase the quantity and quality of linkages and improve communication across all stakeholders. They are expected to build the applicable mechanisms to not only identify critical skills needed, but also to develop high-potential employees so the firm can be ready to meet any business challenge with the appropriate resources. Creating a learning culture and building systems and programs to share knowledge across the organization are critical activities that IHRM is accountable for as organizations extend their global reach.

Whether firms are operating domestically, internationally, or on a global basis, HR must demonstrate that IHRM programs have an impact on the bottom line. Figure 14-12 outlines some of the critical emerging competencies that IHR managers must possess.

FIGURE 14-12

Emerging Competencies for IHR Managers Supporting Global Operations

- Cultural literacy; understands how to work with people from diverse cultures
- High degree of flexibility; deals with multiple perspectives and demonstrates ability to adjust to local and geographic differences
- Strong persuasion skills
- Multilingual
- Strategic thinker; expertise in alignment with HR policies, practices, and systems across geographic regions
- Knowledge of internal and external contextual factors that affect global operations
- Politically and culturally astute; understands emerging market demographics
- Experience in delivering global HR programs
- Expertise in developing communication plans and supporting social and learning networks across many geographic regions
- Knowledge of global training principles, learning styles, and practices
- Knowledge of local compensation differences and social security systems
- Knowledge of enterprisewide HR applications and demonstrated ability to utilize IT resources to support management decision making, learning, and development
- Expertise in designing talent management programs to leverage a firm's resources across its global enterprise

HRC 2 & 7

Think Globally, Act Locally

Globalization requires IHR to develop effective coordination and control mechanisms. To maintain control from headquarters, IHR managers have to:

- Develop and implement formal systems to improve worldwide communication;
- Implement and effectively utilize an enterprisewide HRIS;
- Implement recruitment and staffing strategies to attract the best talent worldwide; and
- Develop policies that effectively balance equity across the global enterprise.

Flexibility of IHR practices refers to the extent to which a firm's domestic policies and practices can be adapted across many nations and the speed of adaption and application.[107] Consider the example below of how Scotiabank is aligning its policies and practices with its organizational values:

> Scotiabank's "Advancement of Women's Initiative" (AoW) is one example of how a multinational corporation has worked to align its practices with organizational outcomes. Scotiabank has a long history of supporting diversity in the workplace. Part of its overall commitment to being a global employer of choice is to further the advancement of women and to make strides in the representation of women at all levels within the bank. In 2003, Scotiabank launched its "Advancement of Women Initiative" to address the barriers to advancement that women face worldwide. At that time, the data indicated that only 18.9 percent of women held senior management positions. By 2007, the company had made significant progress, raising the number to 31.5 percent. It has extended this initiative around the world by establishing local AoW committees and organizing networks, and mentor and career advancement programs at many of its worldwide locations.[108]

SUMMARY

Corporations have become increasingly more complex with respect to the markets they serve and the human resource planning challenges they face. As firms grow, they move through four stages: domestic, international, multinational, and global. As organizations expand their global reach, their available pool of talent expands, and the complexities with respect to managing employees with diverse cultures and in different countries increases exponentially.

HRM has responded to these challenges and, as a discipline, has evolved from providing solely domestic support to providing services on a global basis. International human resource management (IHRM) is about the worldwide management of talent. It is about providing HR support across many different countries and the employment of many different national categories of employees. Primarily, the focus for IHRM has been on staffing across borders.

Recently, the term global human resource management (GHRM) has been used to describe a broader IHRM process. It views IIRM in a global context and in a less traditional sense, as one that contributes and delivers on organizational capabilities. GHRM focuses not just on staffing, but on those activities that contribute to organizational efficiency, information exchange, knowledge transfer, and to the convergence of core business processes. Global HR planning determines employment needs and develops plans for meeting these needs from the available global labour force.

Managers have several options when deciding how to staff a multinational enterprise (MNE): use host country nationals (HCNs), parent country nationals (PCNs), or third country nationals (TCNs). Deciding which category is most appropriate will depend on managerial preference and staffing needs. There are various types of global staffing assignments which managers of MNEs consider. These include short-term, international commuter, frequent flyer, and expatriate.

To ensure a successful expatriate experience, there are several policies that need to be well documented and consistently applied to each employee involved in the assignment. Expatriates must be given cultural sensitivity and language training and be compensated accordingly. The firm's travel and relocation policies must be clear. In addition, companies need to manage the basics such as documenting the arrangement and helping expatriates and their families find appropriate accommodation, fulfill visa requirements, and cover moving costs to ensure a smooth transition.

IHRM has developed specific competencies and skills to manage in a global environment. It must foster a global mindset, think globally, act locally, develop and align HR policies and practices with organizational outcomes, and manage the talent pipeline globally to contribute to organizational sustainability.

TERMS FOR REVIEW

assertiveness
business ecosystem
corporate social responsibility (CSR)
ethnocentrism
expatriate
flexpatriate
frequent flyer
future orientation
gender differentiation
geocentrism
global HR planning
global human resource management (GHRM)
global mindset
global talent management
home-country evaluations
host country national (HCN)
host-country evaluations
humane orientation
in-group collectivism
inpatriate
institutional collectivism
international commuter
international human resource management (IHRM)
multinational enterprise (MNE)
parent country national (PCN)
performance orientation
polycentrism
power distance
regiocentrism
reverse culture shock
third country national (TCN)
third culture kids (TCK)
uncertainty avoidance

SELF-ASSESSMENT EXERCISE

Thinking Locally, Acting Globally

1. A company, operating in Windsor, Ontario, and having a sales office in Detroit, U.S.A., can be called an international company.	T	F
2. A company, operating in Vancouver and having subsidiaries in Seattle, U.S.A., and Mexico City, Mexico, is an example of a global enterprise.	T	F
3. Uncertainty avoidance refers to the degree to which people are consistent and seek structure in their lives.	T	F
4. The terms international and global human resource management are interchangeable.	T	F
5. Third country nationals are neither citizens of the country in which the MNE is headquartered, nor citizens of the country where the foreign subsidiary is located.	T	F
6. In IHRM, a *frequent flyer* refers to an employee commuting to work by plane.	T	F
7. A Japanese sucking air through his teeth expresses embarrassment.	T	F
8. Critical incidents refers to examples of effective or ineffective work behaviour.	T	F
9. Home-country evaluation means that product prices are set by the parent company.	T	F
10. Think locally, act globally is the ideal characteristic of a global HR manager.	T	F

If you circled 1, 3, 5, 7, 8 as true, and 2, 4, 6, 9, and 10 as false, you are correct.

REVIEW AND DISCUSSION QUESTIONS

1. What are the four categories used to describe the evolution of an MNE firm?

2. What are the four external contextual factors that influence IHRM practices?

3. What are the two internal contextual factors that HR professionals must consider?

4. Managers have a specific orientation with respect to staffing its subsidiaries. What are the preferences?

5. There are advantages and disadvantages to consider when employing a PCN, a TCN, or an HCN. What are the reasons why a manager would choose one option versus another?

6. A successful expatriate experience requires that the organization considers several elements. What are these elements?

7. International compensations can be complex. What are the various mechanisms used to compensate expatriates?

8. What are the key elements to be considered when designing a global performance appraisal system?

CRITICAL THINKING QUESTIONS

1. Why would you hire a third culture kid (TCK)?

2. How useful are expatriates in transferring knowledge and skills to their home countries?

3. What are some the ethical issues that would arise when working in a country like China?

4. What are the competencies of an international manager?

5. Why is predeparture training so crucial?

6. What does "Think globally, act locally" mean?

ETHICS QUESTION

You are the project manager of a multidisciplinary team of software developers. You have been called by one of your customers to work on a software problem that must be resolved within 48 hours. You review the competencies of your available developers and choose to assemble a team of your most competent developers from Italy, England, and the United States. You send each of these individuals an email telling them about the project that they are assigned to.

Just as you are about to leave for the airport you get a call from the U.S. developer, Rick. Rick says that he cannot commit to working with "this team" and in particular "his Italian counterpart," Roberto. He tells you that he has heard from others that this individual is emotionally unstable and that he is overly "expressive" with his views, especially when working under time constraints. Rick tells you that, although he appreciates different working styles, trying to get the job done within 48 hours working with someone "like this" just won't work and that he won't be part of the team.

You feel that it is improper to allow one employee to taint the reputation of another employee based on gossip and you need the expertise of both Rick and Roberto to solve the customer's problem. What do you do?

WEB RESEARCH EXERCISE

Many global companies are developing programs to help expatriates prepare for the experience of working abroad and to help them become adjusted once in a new country. For example, KPMG International has invested in a "buddy system" to help expatriates manage the stress of moving to a foreign country.[109]

1. Find three articles that describe what some global companies are doing to help make this a positive experience. Consider the types of programs these companies offer and the type of training/support they provide to their expatriates. Some companies to consider are: DuPont Chemical, KPMG, and General Electric (GE).

RESOURCES:

http://royaldutchshellplc.com/2014/01/17/when-expats-return-home-whats-next/

http://www2.dupont.com/corporate/en-us/careers/career-paths/human-resources.html

http://www.expat.or.id/info/mythsofexpatlife.html

2. Go to <http://www.youtube.com> and view a podcast called "Mobility Matters at Ernst and Young." Discuss the impact that the international assignment had on the employee. What benefits do you think the employee received from the assignment? What did the employee learn from this assignment?

INCIDENT 14-1

Is Importing Workers from China the Answer to Mining's Labour Shortage?

Canadian Dehau International Mines Group Inc. <http://www.dehua.ca> is embarking on a coal-mining project in northern British Columbia. They plan to have a mine up and running by 2015 and they have proposed to bring in 400 workers from China to staff the mine.

It is no surprise that the mining industry has faced a severe labour shortage and has had to find creative ways to staff its facilities. However, the idea of bringing workers from China with specific skills in underground mining has been challenged as perhaps not an optimum way to manage this shortage.

Concerns have been raised from labour groups and the Mining Association of British Columbia <http://www.mining.bc.ca> about bringing in foreign workers into northern British Columbia towns, and what a significant influx of Chinese people would have on the cultural and social ramifications of a small community. The projected site is northwest of Chetwynd, which has a population of 2,500, and there are native reserves nearby that have significant traditional ties to the areas. Concerns have also been raised about the decision to bring in workers from foreign countries versus developing local talent. Currently, Aboriginals are underrepresented in mining and could be a source for the labour pool. Wages are also an issue in terms of whether the workers would accept less than the going rate of $20.00 to $30.00 an hour and the impacts this would have on the industry.[110]

1. Discuss the cultural impacts on the northern communities if 400 workers were hired.

2. Discuss the ethical and corporate social responsibility issues that the company is facing. Discuss the health and safety concerns as well.

3. Is this the answer to Dehau's labour problems? What other staffing options might Dehau consider? Where would they find suitable labour?

CASE STUDY

Maple Leaf Shoes Ltd.

International Expansion

Maple Leaf Shoes Ltd. is a medium-sized manufacturer of shoes located in Wilmington, Ontario. It was started in 1969 and currently employs about 400 persons in its Wilmington plant and some 380 more in offices and warehouses throughout Canada. A conglomerate bought the firm from its founder in 1985. Eventually, control of the company passed to Robert Clark. Clark is both the CEO of the company and its key shareholder.

Maple Leaf is in a difficult market situation. Most shoes sold in Canada are now manufactured abroad to take advantage of lower labour rates offshore. Maple Leaf has tried various strategies to compete against foreign products. The company has tried to make its manufacturing more efficient by upgrading its technology. It has shifted some of its labour from full-time unionized employees to part-time contract employees. It has formalized its systems to make them more cost-effective. It has even moved to computer-aided techniques to reduce the number of employees needed in the manufacturing process.

About 70 percent of the non-management employees in the firm are unionized. Jane Reynolds, the company's HR manager, has worked for Maple Leaf Shoes for several years. Jane is aware that Maple Leaf faces ever-increasing foreign competition. The company's profit margins and market share have declined for the last five years. Jane has worked closely with Bob Smith, the Operations Manager, to find ways to increase productivity of the labour force. They have had some success with their programs but, nonetheless, the competitive position of the company has continued to erode.

Robert Clark has been considering what kinds of strategies the company can pursue to deal with its competitive situation. A month ago, he received a report from a consulting firm that analyzed various alternatives including opening a plant in Southeast Asia or Mexico. Clark has had several meetings with Bob Smith and Tim McDonald, the CFO, to consider the findings in the report. Although the consultant's work was supposed to be performed on a confidential basis, rumours of the report have spread through the company. As a result, employees have expressed considerable anxiety. Today, Jane has been asked to join Clark, Smith, and McDonald to discuss the future of the business. Jane has reasonably good relationships with Clark and Smith, but over the years, she has had some difficulties with McDonald. She knows McDonald tends to see her as not always being strategic and focusing on the bottom line. Below is the dialogue that transpired at this meeting:

Robert Clark: "Jane, you know we have been considering opening a plant outside of Canada for economic reasons. First of all, our labour costs are high. If we can't significantly reduce our labour costs, there is a good chance the company won't survive. Second, our market in Canada is not growing very fast. If we can open a plant in a market with stronger population growth, we may be able to benefit."

Jane: "I understand that. Most of our competition no longer makes shoes in Canada."

Bob Smith: "That's correct. And it's a real pity. This company was built to provide a good product to Canadians, made by Canadians. My concern is how we're going to exercise quality control if we're operating a plant 4,000 kilometres from here."

Tim McDonald: "It's going to be difficult, Bob. No doubt about it, but we really don't have a choice. This company has been dancing around the labour issue for more than a decade. We can't solve it the way it's been going. You and Jane have tried everything possible to make our current mode of operations work. That's why Maple Leaf, almost alone in the industry, still manufactures solely in Canada. But it's a fight that can't be won. Everything we do to keep jobs in Canada simply makes the unions more difficult to deal with. This isn't a question of what we want to do. It's a question of what we have to do."

Robert: "That brings us back to you, Jane. It's a labour cost issue that has brought us to this point and making the shift is going to have some major human resource implications. We need your help in our planning. We think our best bet will be to expand into Mexico, in a suburb of Mexico City. That's the conclusion that our consultant has come up with and we agree. The consultant wrote the report from the perspective of our financial concerns. That was the mandate that Tim and I gave them. From the financial side, some form of international expansion makes a lot of sense. In fact, it more than makes sense. We're going to have to do it if this company is going to remain a manufacturer. Tim is absolutely right about that. But we haven't really turned our minds to the human resources side of the ledger. We need to understand how to make this work from the people perspective. We need your expertise in that area.

"The question is, where do we go from here? What are our next steps? The obvious things are that we should look for a plant to buy or land to build one on. And after that we need to obtain the machinery. Tim and Bob have assured me we can manage this. What we don't understand well are the human resource challenges we will face in Mexico. Bob and I are thinking we will need to send at least one senior manager from head office and one senior human resource staff to help manage operations. We are thinking that maybe we should hire some local staff to help us more fully understand the culture. Of course, there is the issue of cost. If we can do this with less personnel that would be wonderful. But we don't want to damage the expansion by not spending the money we need to up front."

Tim McDonald: "We don't want to overspend, either, Jane. We need to do this as economically as possible."

Robert Clark: "That's right, Tim. So Jane, we need your help. How do we deal with the human resource issues?"

Jane: "This is a lot to take in all at once. I'll have to do some research and get back to you all. There are cultural and legal aspects to the expansion that must be dealt with. Can I provide you with my initial report in say, two weeks?"

Robert Clark: "That's exactly the timeframe we were thinking of. It goes without saying that this should be your main priority for the next little while. And one more thing. Keep your work absolutely confidential. We don't want word of this project leaking out prematurely. It's going to be a difficult sell when we come to discuss it with the employees. I don't want to lose control of the timing. And I don't want to have to explain our thinking before we're certain what our final decision will be."

Jane: "Understood, of course."

Jane was upset when she left the meeting and it took her some time to gather her thoughts. Although she had expected to hear that the consultant had recommended some kind of foreign expansion, she hadn't expected the senior team's thinking to be so far advanced—and without her involvement. She had worked hard to provide analytical tools to help operations in Canada, but she had never dealt with working in a non-Canadian environment. That would be a challenge for her, but one which she welcomed. It was time for her to expand her knowledge and this would be a good opportunity to do so.

The difficulties would not just be about dealing with Mexican issues. Once the employees understood what management was considering, there would be a backlash. At least Robert and Bob understood that. On the other hand, Tim didn't seem to worry much about that aspect of the situation.

Jane had worked hard to develop a trusting relationship with the employees and she felt the production efficiency of the company depended on that. She understood that the unions would oppose the move, no matter what she said, and she wondered how the unions in Mexico would respond. Like Bob, she cared about the manufacturing tradition of the company and its history of providing local jobs. She didn't want the Mexican expansion to increase the vulnerability of Canadian operations.

She also understood that those considerations would have to wait. Now she had an assignment to deal with. She picked up her pad and began to jot down ideas.

DISCUSSION QUESTIONS

1. Identify some of the challenges Maple Leaf will face if it were to open a plant in Mexico. What specific issues should Jane discuss in her report?

2. Robert Clark and Bob Smith are considering whom to send on an expatriate assignment from headquarters to Mexico. They have identified two possible openings at this point: one position is for a manager and one position is for an HR specialist. They have asked Jane to make some recommendations. What should the selection criteria be? What specific competencies should be considered?

3. Jane Reynolds will need to set up a performance appraisal program. She has asked you to summarize what she needs to do to ensure that the EPA (expat performance appraisal) experience is positive.

4. What actions can Jane take to demonstrate to Tim McDonald that she is a strategic thinker and understands the bottom line repercussions?

EXTENSION QUESTION:

1. Discuss the labour relation issues Maple Leaf will face in Canada.

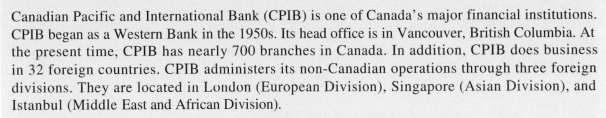

CASE STUDY

Canadian Pacific and International Bank

International Expansion

Canadian Pacific and International Bank (CPIB) is one of Canada's major financial institutions. CPIB began as a Western Bank in the 1950s. Its head office is in Vancouver, British Columbia. At the present time, CPIB has nearly 700 branches in Canada. In addition, CPIB does business in 32 foreign countries. CPIB administers its non-Canadian operations through three foreign divisions. They are located in London (European Division), Singapore (Asian Division), and Istanbul (Middle East and African Division).

The senior team of the bank has been spending much of its time reflecting on the impact of non-Canadian business to CPIB. In the late 1990s a foreign debt crisis hit Asia and many Asian currencies were devalued. As a result, Asian debt and Asian businesses declined in value. In 2008, the United States went through a financial crisis that led to bailouts of the automobile industry and financial services. Many individuals were forced into personal bankruptcy and lost their homes. Soon after that, similar problems engulfed many of the European economies—leading to a debt crisis in Europe that may take a decade or more to resolve. In 2011, social unrest in the Middle East resulted in the change of several countries' governments. The results of the Arab Spring are not yet known, but there is a risk of increased instability in the Middle East.

Despite those problems, the bank's foreign operations have continued to expand. Projections state that much of the bank's future growth will occur outside of Canada. It is acknowledged that as foreign business becomes a larger factor in the bank's performance, more management attention will have to be spent on the bank's non-Canadian operations.

The bank's strategic plan calls for a greater emphasis on foreign growth. It also discusses the possibility of outsourcing some functions to offshore locations. It has been suggested that call centres and data input could be more efficiently and more cheaply provided from locations offshore.

The bank's CEO recently had a meeting with Mary Keddy, Senior VP for Human Resources. At that time, the CEO advised Keddy that she felt it was time for the bank's head office to become more involved in human resource issues in foreign jurisdictions. The CEO is well aware that doing business in non-Canadian locations exposes the bank staff to different cultural norms. Many jurisdictions have a different approach to labour law and human rights legislation than Canada does. At the end of the meeting, the CEO asked Mary to provide her with a plan to create an International HR Management group within her staff.

DISCUSSION QUESTIONS:

1. What are the various staffing categories that Mary Keddy should consider?

2. What are the internal and external factors that will influence how the company will proceed?

3. What are the implications for the IHR function as CPIB expands?

4. Mary Keddy plans to offer one of her staff a promotion to lead the IHR group. She has asked you to prepare an internal job posting and to discuss the details with her prior to release. Discuss the roles and competencies expected of this position and prepare a job posting.

PART-ENDING VIDEOS

Cirque du Soleil

SOURCE: © MHHE Management Library

Go to Connect to access the videos.

References

CHAPTER 1

1. Leif Edvinsson, http://hrfirst.co.in; downloaded February 3, 2012.
2. How stuff works, http://www.howstuffworks.com/innovation/inventions/top-5-nasa-inventions.htm#page=1; downloaded March 12, 2015.
3. National Aeronautical and Space Administration, http://mars.jpl.nasa.gov/mars2020/; downloaded March 12, 2015
4. James Harder, "Engage your long-time employees to improve performance," *Harvard Business Review,* downloaded March 23, 2015, from: https://hbr.org/2015/03/engage-your-long-time-employees-to-improve-performance.
5. Dave Ulrich and Wayne Brockbank, *The HR Value Proposition.* Harvard Business Press: Boston, MA, 2005.
6. C. Brewster, G. Wood, M. Brookes, and J. Van Ommeren, J., "What determines the size of the HR function? A cross-national analysis," *Human Resource Management,* Vol. 45, No. 1, 2006, p. 3–21.
7. B. E. Becker and M. A. Ulrich, *The HR scorecard: Linking people, strategy, and performance,* Boston, MA: Harvard Business School Press, 2001.
8. R. S. Kaplan and D. P. Norton, *Strategy maps: Converting intangible assets into tangible results,* Boston, MA.: Harvard Business School Publishing Corporation, 2004.
9. Charles W. L. Hill and Gareth R. Jones. *Strategic Management Theory,* 8th ed., Boston, MA: Houghton Mifflin Company, 2008.
10. Walmart, http://cdn.corporate.walmart.com/66/e5/9ff9a87445949173fde56316ac5f/2014-annual-report.pdf; downloaded March 24, 2015.
11. Target, https://corporate.target.com/about/mission-values; downloaded March 24, 2015.
12. SHRM, "Salaries as a percentage of operating expenses," 2008, http://www.shrm.org/research/articles/articles/pages/metricofthemonthsalariesaspercentageofoperatingexpense.aspx; downloaded March 24, 2015.
13. David Brown, "HR Issues Top of Mind for Execs Worldwide: Study," *Canadian HR Reporter,* May 5, 2003, p. 1.
14. H. Das, *Strategic Organization Design,* Scarborough ON: Prentice Hall, 1998.
15. Canada's 50 Best, https://www.canadas50best.com/en/Pages/Home.aspx; downloaded February 12, 2012.
16. Department of Finance, http://www.fin.gc.ca/efp-pef/2011/efp-pef-01-eng.asp; downloaded February 8, 2012.
17. Department of Finance, http://www.budget.gc.ca/2014/docs/jobs-emplois/jobs-emplois-eng.html#_Toc379482620; downloaded March 27, 2014.

18. Ibid.
19. Ibid.
20. World Economic Forum, *The Global Competitiveness Report 2014–2015,* http://www.weforum.org/reports/global-competitiveness-report-2014-2015; downloaded March 27, 2015.
21. Bruce Little, "We're Less Dependent but More Entangled," *The Globe and Mail,* May 15, 2000, p. A2.
22. Saba Colakoglu, Dave P. Lepak, and Ying Hong, "Measuring HRM Effectiveness: Considering a global context," *Human Resource Management Review,* Vol. 17, 2006, pp. 77–92.
23. World Economic Forum, *The Global Competitiveness Report 2014–2015,* http://www.weforum.org/reports/global-competitiveness-report-2014-2015; downloaded March 27, 2015.
24. Conference Board of Canada, "Innovation Overview," February 2010, http://sso.conferenceboard.ca/HCP/overview/Innovation-overview.aspx; downloaded February 18, 2012.
25. Conference Board of Canada, http://www.conferenceboard.ca/Libraries/NETWORK_PUBLIC/CIC_brochure.sflb; downloaded March 27, 2015.
26. Elizabeth Church, "Canada's Progress in Science, Innovation Mediocre, Study Finds," *The Globe and Mail,* May 6, 2009, p. A6.
27. Conference Board of Canada, "Innovation: Share of World Patents," October 2008, www.conferenceboard.ca/hcp/details/innovation/share-of-world-patents.aspx; downloaded October 1, 2009.
28. Conference Board of Canada, "Innovation Overview," February 2010, http://sso.conferenceboard.ca/HCP/overview/Innovation-overview.aspx; downloaded February 18, 2012.
29. Bloomberg.com, http://www.bloomberg.com/news/print/2012-01-19/kodak-photography-pioneer-files-for-bankruptcy-protection-1-.html; downloaded March 15, 2012.
30. Internet World Stats, "Canada Internet Usage, Broadband and Telecommunication Reports," www.internetworldstats.com/am/ca.htm; downloaded April 15, 2009. See also: Simon Tuck, "Internet Milestone Set as 50% Connected in Canada," *The Globe and Mail,* May 1, 1999, p. B1.
31. Internet World Stats, "North America Telecoms and Telecommunications Market," http://www.internetworldstats.com/america2.htm; downloaded February 18, 2012.
32. "Working from Home Cuts Employee Stress, Study Finds," *The Globe and Mail,* November 16, 1994, p. B19.
33. Statistics Canada, http://www12.statcan.gc.ca/nhs-enm/2011/dp-pd/dt-td/Rp-eng.cfm?LANG=E&APATH=3&DETAIL=0&DIM=0&FL=A&FREE=0&GC=0&

GID=0&GK=0&GRP=1&PID=105617&PRID=0&PTYPE=105277&S=0&SHOWALL=0&SUB=0&Temporal=2013&THEME=96&VID=0&VNAMEE=&VNAMEF=; downloaded March 27, 2015.
34. Working.com, http://www.working.com/story_print.html?id=bc7b53a1-4cf4-4624-9c23-b28c6ee8e559&sponsor; downloaded March 30, 2012.
35. "5 Telework Pitfalls to Avoid," *Canadian HR Reporter,* October 20, 2008, p. 2.
36. D. Mota, "Keeping data safe takes several solutions," 2015, http://insurancenewsnet.com/oarticle/2015/03/02/keeping-data-safe-takes-several-solutions-a-602265.html#.VRX1bPnF-OM; downloaded March 27, 2015.
37. "McCarthy's Reinvents the Practice," *The Globe and Mail,* December 6, 1999, p. M1.
38. R. Dobbs, S. Ramaswamy, e. Stephenson, F., and S. P. Viguerie, "Management institution for the next 50 years," *McKinsey Quarterly.* 2014, http://www.mckinsey.com/insights/strategy/management_intuition_for_the_next_50_years?cid=other-eml-ttn-mip-mck-oth-1410; downloaded March 27, 2015.
39. J. Bersin, "Big data in human resources: A world of haves and have-nots," 2013, http://www.forbes.com/sites/joshbersin/2013/10/07/big-data-in-human-resources-a-world-of-haves-and-have-nots/; downloaded March 27, 2015.
40. Sandra Mingail, "Technology No Longer the Driver," *Canadian HR Reporter,* April 11, 2005, p. 11.
41. CBC Television, Venture, undated.
42. Adapted from Statistics Canada, "Labour Force Survey Estimates by sex and detailed age group," CANSIM, table 282-0008. http://www5.statcan.gc.ca/cansim/a47; downloaded March 27, 2015.
43. Ibid.
44. Ross Laver, "Kids, Bosses and Work," *Maclean's,* February 24, 1997, p. 38.
45. Human Resources Development Canada (Applied Research), *Quarterly Labour Market and Income Review,* Vol. 3, No.1, Summer 2002, pp. 14–15.
46. Statistics Canada, "Labour force survey estimates by sex and detailed age group," CANSIM, table 282-0002. http://www5.statcan.gc.ca/cansim/a47; downloaded March 27, 2015
47. "Employment Trends in the Information Economy," *Applied Research Bulletin,* Vol. 3, No. 2, 1997; HRDC site, www.hrdc-drhc.gc.ca.
48. Alberta Government, http://employment.alberta.ca/documents/occupational-demand-and-supply-outlook.pdf; downloaded February 22, 2012.
49. C. J. Dahlman, and J. E. Aubert, *China and the knowledge economy: Seizing the 21st century.* The World Bank, 2001.

References

50. Catherine Connelly, David Zweig, Jane Webster, and John P. Trougakos, "Knowledge hiding in organizations," *Journal of Organizational Behavior,* Vol. 33, No. 1, January 2012, pp. 64–88.

51. Human Resources and Skills Development Canada. "Indicators of well-being in Canada, Learning-Educational Attainment," http://www4.hrsdc.gc.ca/.3ndic.1t.4r@-eng.jsp?iid=29; downloaded February 18, 2012.

52. Human Resources Development Canada, *Quarterly Labour Market and Income Review,* Vol. 3, No. 1, Summer 2002, p. 13.

53. Canadian School Boards Association, "Pisa Results: Canadian students score high in performance, Canadian education system scores high in equity," http://cdnsba.org/all/education-in-canada/pisa-results-canadian-students-score-high-in-performance-canadian-education-system-scores-high-in-equity; downloaded February 18, 2012.

54. Statistics Canada, "Adult literacy and life skills survey," *The Daily,* 2005, http://www.statcan.gc.ca/daily-quotidien/050511/dq050511b-eng.htm; downloaded March 27, 2015.

55. Human Resources Development Canada, *Quarterly Labour Market and Income Review,* Vol. 3, No. 1, Summer 2002, p. 18.

56. Adapted from Statistics Canada, "Labour Force Survey Estimates by sex and detailed age group," CANSIM, table 282-0004. http://www5.statcan.gc.ca/cansim/a26; downloaded March 27, 2015.

57. Workplace Education–PEI, "Creating Partnerships with Business and Industry," Charlottetown: April 2000.

58. Corporate Council on Education, "Employability Skills Profile," a program of the National Business and Education Centre, Ottawa: The Conference Board of Canada, undated.

59. "Our Coming Old Age Crisis," *Maclean's,* January 17, 1983, p. 24.

60. Adapted from Statistics Canada, "Projected population, by projection scenario, age and sex, as of July 1, Canada, provinces and territories," CANSIM, 52-0005 http://www5.statcan.gc.ca/cansim/pick-choisir.

61. Adapted from Statistics Canada, "Projected population, by projection scenario, age and sex, as of July 1, Canada, provinces and territories," CANSIM, 52-0005 http://www5.statcan.gc.ca/cansim/pick-choisir.

62. Statistics Canada, "Labour Force Survey Estimates retirement age by class of worker and sex," CANSIM, table 282-0051 http://www5.statcan.gc.ca/cansim/pick-choisir.

63. Susan Singh, "Globalization Puts Focus on HR," *Canadian HR Reporter,* June 6, 2005, pp. 1, 15.

64. Paul Nyhof, "Managing Generation X: The Millennial Challenge," *Canadian HR Reporter* Vol. 13, No. 10, May 22, 2000, pp. 7–8.

65. For a good exposition of the difference between two age groups, see Claire Raine and Jim Hunt, *The X-ers and the Boomers,* Berkely, CA: Crisp Publications, 2000, pp. 32–39; J. A. Cordeniz, "Recruitment, retention, and management of generation X:

A focus on nursing professionals," *Journal of Healthcare Management/American College of Healthcare Executives,* 2002, Vol. 47, No. 4, pp. 237–49.

66. Barbara Kofman and Kaitlin Eckler, "They Are Your Future: Attracting and Retaining Generation Y," *Canadian HR Reporter,* April 25, 2005, pp. 7, 10.

67. CBC, True Canadians: Multiculturalism in Canada debated, http://www.cbc.ca/archives/categories/politics/language-culture/making-the-mosaic-multiculturalism-in-canada/true-canadians.html; downloaded March 28, 2015.

68. Statistics Canada, Canada's Ethnocultural Mosaic, 2006 Census.

69. John Porter, *The Vertical Mosaic: An Analysis of Social Class and Power in Canada,* Toronto: University of Toronto Press, 1965; see also V. V. Murray, "Canadian Cultural Values and Personnel Administration," in Harish Jain, ed., *Contemporary Issues in Canadian Personnel Administration,* Scarborough, ON: Prentice-Hall, 1974; B. Kalman, *Canada: The Culture,* Crabtree Publications, 2010.

70. Statistics Canada, 2011 Census.

71. KPMG's Ethics Survey 2000, Managing for Ethical Practice, cited in Leslie Young, "Companies Not Doing Right by Their Ethics Codes," *Canadian HR Reporter,* Vol. 13, No 7, April 10, 2000, p. 17.

72. Ibid.

73. L. Kohlberg, "Moral Stages and Moralization: The Cognitive-Development Approach." In T. Lickona, ed., *Moral Developmental and Behavior: Theory, Research, and Social Issues.* New York: Holt, Rinehart and Winston, 1976, pp. 31–35.

74. 2003 Business Ethics Survey conducted by the Society for Human Resource Management, reported in *Canadian HR Reporter,* May 19, 2003, p. 1.

75. Hari Das, *Strategic Organizational Design,* Scarborough, ON: Prentice-Hall, 1998, pp. 324–329; J. P. Birnholtz, M. D. Cohen, and S. V. Hoch, "Organizational character: on the regeneration of Camp Poplar Grove," *Organizational Science,* Vol. 18, 2007, pp. 315–332.

76. Uyen Vu, "'Strategic' Overused in HR," *Canadian HR Reporter,* July 14, 2008, p. 8.

77. D.P. Lepak and S.A. Snell, "The Strategic Management of Human Capital: Determinants and Implications of Different Relationships," *Academy of Management Review,* Vol. 24, No. 1,1999, pp. 1–18.

78. Peter Bamberger and Ilan Meshoulam, *Human Resource Strategy,* Thousand Oaks, CA: Sage Publications, 2000, p. 57.

79. Uyen Vu, "Standing up to the Bad Boss," *Canadian HR Reporter,* February 13, 2006, p. 5.

80. Gordon Sova, "What Do the Stats Tell Us?" *Canadian HR Reporter,* February 27, 2006, p. 9.

81. Managing Tomorrow's People: The Future of Work in 2020, report by PricewaterhouseCoopers, UK, cited by Shannon Klie, "What Will Working World Look Like in 2020?" *Canadian HR Reporter,* September 22, 2008, pp. 1, 8.

82. David Brown, "Innovative HR Ineffective in Manufacturing Firms," *Canadian HR Reporter,* April 7, 2003, p. 1.

83. John Gibbons and Christopher Woock, "Evidence-Based HR in Action," *Canadian HR Reporter,* March 23, 2009, pp. 16, 20.

84. Christopher Bartlett, "Companies Must Gear Up for a Management Revolution," *The Globe and Mail,* January 16, 1998, p. B23.

85. James W. Thacker and R. Julian Cattaneo, *Survey of Personnel Practices in Canadian Organizations,* unpublished manuscript, University of Windsor, Faculty of Business Administration, March 1993.

86. Terry Wagar, *Human Resource Management and Labour Relations: A Study of Canadian Organizations,* Halifax: Department of Management, Saint Mary's University, October 1993, pp. 11–13.

87. BC Human Resource Management Association, http://www.hrmetricsservice.org/; downloaded March 3, 2012.

88. Deloitte & Touche Human Resource Consulting Services, *The State of the Human Resources Management Function in Canada,* 1994, p. ii.

89. Arthur Young, Wayne Brockbank, and Dave Ulrich, "Lower Cost, Higher Value: Human Resource Function in Transformation," *Human Resource Planning,* Vol. 17, No. 3, 1994, pp. 10–12.

90. Arthur Young, Wayne Brockbank, and Dave Ulrich, "Lower Cost, Higher Value: Human Resource Function in Transformation," *Human Resource Planning,* Vol. 17, No. 3, 1994, pp. 10–12.

91. Shannon Klie, "Do You Have What It Takes?" *Canadian HR Reporter,* November 17, 2008, p. 17.

92. Ibid.

93. Human Resource Professional Association, http://www.hrpa.ca/Documents/HRPA_KB_CEO_Perspective_Research_Highlight.pdf; downloaded March 17, 2012.

94. Peoplefluent (2014). *The evolving role of HR.* White paper.

95. For a good discussion on HR's emerging role, see Seyed-Mahmoud Aghazadeh, "Human Resource Management: Issues and Challenges in the New Millennium," *Management Research News,* Vol. 22, No. 12, 1999, pp. 19–32.

96. Peter Drucker, "The End of Money?" *The Globe and Mail,* May 13, 2000, p. A16.

97. "'Love Bug' Hits World's E-mail," *The Globe and Mail,* May 5, 2000, p. A1.

98. Richard Blackwell, "Banks Give Shareholders a Voice," *The Globe and Mail,* March 3, 2000, p. B10.

99. "Finance Minister to Have Wide Bank Powers," *The Globe and Mail,* June 1, 2000, p. B1.

100. Mary Janigan, "Feud without End," *Maclean's,* April 24, 2000, p. 60.

101. "Scotiabank Warns of 'Intrusive' Consumer Regulation," *The Globe and Mail,* March 1, 2000, p. B3.

102. Keith McArthur and Dawn Walton, "Protecting What Is Right," *The Globe and Mail,* February 15, 2000, p. B16.

CHAPTER 2

1. Philip C. Grant, "What Use Is a Job Description?" *Personnel Journal*, Vol. 67, No. 2, February 1988, p. 50.
2. Uyen Vu, "How Purolator dealt with skyrocketing costs," *Canadian Human Rights Reporter*, Vol. 19, March 2006, pp. 9–10.
3. SHRM, Survey Findings: Job Analysis Activities, December 11, 2014, http://www.shrm.org/research/surveyfindings/articles/pages/2014-Job-Analysis-Activities.aspx.
4. Economic Research Institute, "Conducting Job Analysis," 2012, http://www.erieri.com/pdf/conductingjobanalysis.pdf, downloaded February 2, 2015.
5. William Wooten, "Using Knowledge, Skill and Ability (KSA) Data to Identify Career Planning Opportunities: An Application of Job Analysis to Internal Manpower Planning," *Public Personnel Administrator*, Vol. 22, No. 4, 1993, pp. 551–63.
6. *Canadian Human Rights Reporter*, Vol. 6, 1985, p. 6.
7. IC&RC, "IC&RC Announces Updated Alcohol and Drug Counselor (ADC) Job Analysis," http://internationalcredentialing.org/Resources/Documents/ADC_JA_Finished_Announcement.pdf; downloaded March 11, 2015.
8. Michael T. Brannick and Edward L. Levine, *Job Analysis: Methods, Research, and Applications for Human Resource Management in the New Millennium*, London, UK: Sage Publications, Inc., 2002.
9. Purdue Research Foundation, *Position Analysis Questionnaire*, West Lafayette, IN: 1989; see also: Position Analysis Questionnaire, http://www.paq.com/?FuseAction=bulletins.job-analysis-questionnaire; downloaded January 30, 2015.
10. E. C. Dierdorff and M. A. Wilson, "A meta analysis of job analysis reliability," *Journal of Applied Psychology*, Vol. 88, 2003, pp. 635–646.
11. CBC News story, "CP freight train derails near Golden, B.C.," http://www.cbc.ca/news/canada/british-columbia/story/2011/12/27/bc-cp-train-derailment.html; downloaded January 30, 2015.
12. O*Net OnLine, "Summary Report for Locomotive Engineers," http://www.onetonline.org/link/summary/53-4011.00; downloaded February 3, 2015.
13. E. L. Levine, R. A. Ash, and N. Bennett, "Explorative Comparative Study of Four Job Analysis Methods," *Journal of Applied Psychology*, Vol. 65, 1980, pp. 524–35; and J. Sanchez and E. L. Levine, "The Analysis of Work in the 20th and 21st Centuries" in N. Anderson, D. Ones, H.K. Sinangil, and C. Viswesvaran (Eds), *Handbook of Industrial, Work and Organizational Psychology*, Vol. 1, London, UK: Sage Publications, Inc., 2002, pp. 71–89.
14. SHRM Survey Findings: Job Analysis Activities. December 11, 2014. http://www.shrm.org/research/surveyfindings/articles/pages/2014-Job-Analysis-Activities.aspx
15. Human Resources and Skills Development Canada, National Occupational Classification, 2011, www5.hrsdc.gc.ca/NOC/; downloaded February 3, 2015.
16. Entrepreneur Media, "How to Write a Job Analysis and Description," *Start Your Own Business: The Only Start-Up Book You'll Ever Need*, 5th ed., October 2010, http://www.entrepreneur.com/article/56490; downloaded February 3, 2015.
17. Filip Gilbert and Gary Gerstner, "Chapter 7: Benchmarking," in Jason Geller and Arthur H. Mazur (Eds.), *Global Business Driven HR Transformation: The Journey Continues*, Deloitte Development LLC, 2011.
18. Kenneth Carlton Cooper, *Effective Competency Modeling & Reporting*, New York: AMACOM, AMA Publications, 2000; Joan Hill, "Competency model helps HR build value," *Canadian Human Rights Reporter*, Vol. 25, No. 2, January, 2012, pp. 20–21.
19. G. P. Hollenbeck, M. W. McCall, and R. F. Silzer, "Leadership competency models," *The Leadership Quarterly*, Vol. 17, No. 4, 2006, pp. 398–413.
20. Joan Hill, "Competency model helps HR build value," *Canadian Human Rights Reporter*, Vol. 25 No. 2, January, 2012, pp. 20–21.
21. F. P. Morgeson and S. E. Humphrey, "The Work Design Questionnaire (WDQ): developing and validating a comprehensive measure for assessing job design and the nature of work," *Journal of Applied Psychology*, Vol. 91, 2006, p. 1321; A. M. Grant, "Relational job design and the motivation to make a prosocial difference," *Academy of Management Review*, Vol. 32, No. 2, 2007, pp. 393–417.
22. C. Passariello, "Louis Vuitton tries modern methods on factory line," *The Wall Street Journal*, October 9, 2006, pp. A1, A15.
23. Michael Losey, "HR Comes of Age," *HR Magazine*, 50th Anniversary Issue, 1998, pp. 40–53.
24. Robert Inman, "Workflow," *Transactions*, Vol. 28, No. 7, July 1996, pp. 555–56.
25. G. Salvendy, *Handbook of Human Factors and Ergonomics*, John Wiley & Sons, 2012.
26. S. Chahardoli, M. Motamedzade, Y. Hamidi, R. Golmohammadi, and A. R. Soltanian, "Relationship between job design, performance and job satisfaction among Bank employees," *Journal of Health and Safety at Work*, Vol. 4, No. 3, 2014, pp. 75–84.
27. Glenn Harrington, "Ergonomics Preaches Prevention as Alternative to High Cost Injuries," *Canadian HR Reporter*, September 9, 1996, p. 22.
28. AWCBC Online Community—Annual KSM Standard Report 2013. Retrieved from: https://aoc.awcbc.org/KsmReporting/KsmSubmissionReport/2; downloaded February 3, 2015.
29. Glenn Harrington, "Older Workers Need Ergonomic Aid," *Canadian HR Reporter*, November 17, 1997, p. 20.
30. Statistics Canada, "Canada's population estimates: Age and sex, 2014," *The Daily*, September 26, 2014, http://www.statcan.gc.ca/daily-quotidien/140926/dq140926b-eng.htm; downloaded February 4, 2015.
31. G. Salvendy, *Handbook of Human Factors and Ergonomics*, John Wiley & Sons, 2012.
32. Patricia Chisholm, "Redesigning Work," *Maclean's*, March 5, 2001, p. 36.
33. J. R. Hackman and G. Oldham, *Work Redesign*, Reading, MA: Addison-Wesley, 1980; Paul Sparrow, "New Employee Behaviours, Work Designs and Forms of Work Organization: What Is in Store for Future of Work?" *Journal of Managerial Psychology*, Vol. 15, No. 3, 2000, pp. 202–218.
34. Richard W. Woodward and John J. Sherwood, "A Comprehensive Look at Job Design," *Personnel Journal*, August 1977, p. 386.
35. Robert D. Mohr and Cindy Zoghi, "Is Job Enrichment Really Enriching?" working paper, University of Chicago, January 2006, http://www.bls.gov/ore/pdf/ec060010.pdf.
36. P. Booth, *Challenge and Change: Embracing the Team Concept*, Ottawa: Conference Board of Canada, 1994; Abraham Sagie and Zeynep Aycan, "A cross-cultural analysis of participative decision-making in organizations," *Human Relations*, April 2003, pp. 453–473.
37. P. Engardio, "Managing a global workforce," *Business Week*, August 20, 2007, pp. 48–51; J. Marquez, "Connecting a virtual workforce," *Workforce Management*, September 22, 2008, pp. 18–28.
38. Ageeth Balkema and Eric Molleman, "Barriers to the Development of Self-Organizing Teams," *Journal of Managerial Psychology*, Vol. 14, No. 2, 1999, pp. 134–50.
39. For instance, see Paul Sparrow, "New Employee Behaviours, Work Designs and Forms of Work Organization: What Is in Store for Future of Work?" *Journal of Managerial Psychology*, Vol. 15, No. 3, 2000, pp. 202–218.
40. William Bridges, "The End of the Job," *Fortune*, September 19, 1994, p. 64.
41. Peter Coy, "The 21st Century Organization," *Business Week*, August 28, 2000
42. Karen May, "Work in the 21st Century: Implications for Job Analysis," *The Industrial-Organizational Psychologist*, The Society for Industrial and Organizational Psychology, December 18, 2000, www.siop.org.

CHAPTER 3

1. A. Rahman bin Idris and D. Eldridge, "Reconceptualising Human Resource Planning in Response to Institutional Change," *International Journal of Manpower*, Vol. 19, No. 5, 1998, p. 346.
2. IBM Corporate website, http://www.ibm.com/annualreport/2013/strategy.html; downloaded March 30, 2015.
3. W.J. Rothwell, *Effective Succession Planning*, 3rd ed., New York: Amacom, 2005.
4. Ibid.; J. W. Boroski, "Putting it together: HR planning in '3D' at Eastman Kodak," [Electronic version], *Human Resource Planning*, Vol. 13, No. 1, 1990, pp. 45–56; J. W. Walker, *Human Resource Strategy*, The United States: McGraw-Hill, Inc., 1992.

References

5. B. J. Smith, J. W. Boroski, and G. E. Davis, "Human resource planning," [Electronic version], *Human Resource Management,* Vol. 31, No. 1/2, 1992, pp. 81–93.

6. C. Edwards, "Inside Intel," *BusinessWeek,* January 9, 2006, p. 46.

7. T. Krisher, "Ford reports worst loss in auto maker's history," *Toronto Star,* January 26, 2007, p. F3.

8. T. Van Alphen, "800 New Toyota Jobs for Ontario: A second shift at assembly operations in Woodstock will start producing RAV4 sport utility vehicle in March." *Toronto Star,* December 11, 2009, p. B1.

9. Marina Stauss, "Nordstrom to plant Canadian flagship in Toronto," *The Globe and Mail,* January 15, 2014.

10. Market Wired. http://www.marketwired.com /press-release/laura-hamill-phd-appointed -chief-people-officer-at-limeade-2003269.htm; downloaded March 30, 2015.

11. D. Q. Mills, "Planning with people in mind," *Harvard Business Review,* 2001, pp. 97–105.

12. D. Hoeffler, How to predict employee turnover using SAP InfiniteInsight, 2015, http://scn.sap.com/community/predictive -analysis/blog/2014/12/01/how-to-predict -employee-turnover-using-sap-infiniteinsight; downloaded March 30, 2015.

13. J. Boudreau, "Predict what employees will do without freaking them out," *Harvard Business Review,* September 5, 2014.

14. M. Effron, R. Gandossy, and M. Goldsmith (Eds.), *Human Resources in the 21st Century,* Hoboeken, NJ: John Wiley and Sons, 2003.

15. Judith Cooksey, "Workforce Challenges for Dentists and Pharmacists," Fall 1999, www.hrsa.dhhs.gov/newsroom/features /workforcechallenges.htm, downloaded May 8, 2012; E. Brynjolfsson, and A. McAfee, *Race against the machine: How the digital revolution is accelerating innovation, driving productivity, and irreversibly transforming employment and the economy,* Digital Frontier Press, October 17, 2011.

16. "Good Jobs, No Jobs," *The Globe and Mail,* January 15, 1997, p. B3.

17. News from Canada Newswire quoted by www.globeinvestor.com, June 29, 2000.

18. A. L. Delbecq, A. H. Van de Ven, and D. H. Gustafson. *Group Techniques for Progress Planning: A Guide to Nominal and Delphi Process,* Glenview, IL: Scott, Foresman, 1975; J. M. Bartwrek and J. K. Muringhan, "The Nominal Group Technique: Expanding the Basic Procedure and Underlying Assumptions," *Group and Organizational Studies,* Vol. 9, 1984, pp. 417–432.

19. Cognology, www.cognology.com.au; downloaded March 31, 2015.

20. B. Z. Posner and J. M. Kouzes, Leadership Practices Inventory (LPI): A self-assessment and analysis, 1987, https://www.lpionline. com/lpi_individual.html.

21. J. Walker, "Human Resource Planning: Managerial Concerns and Practices," *Business Horizons,* June, 1976, pp. 56–57; See also G. Odiorne, "The Crystal Ball of HR Strategy," *Personnel Administrator,* December 1986, pp. 103–106; J. Byrne and A. Cowan, "Should Companies Groom New Leaders or Buy Them?" *BusinessWeek,* September 1986, pp. 94–96.

22. J. Hooper and R. F. Catalanello, "Markov Analysis Applied to Forecasting Technical Personnel," *Human Resource Planning,* Vol. 4, 1981, pp. 41–47.

23. R. Niehaus, "Human Resource Planning Flow Models," *Human Resource Planning,* Vol. 3, 1980, pp. 177–187.

24. Government of Alberta, "Alberta's short-term employment forecast 2014–2016," http:// work.alberta.ca/documents/short-term -employment-forecast.pdf; downloaded March 31, 2015.

25. Government of Alberta, "Alberta's occupational demand and supply outlook 2013–2023," http://work.alberta.ca /documents/occupational-demand-and-supply -outlook-2013-2023.pdf; downloaded March 31, 2015.

26. Government of Alberta, "2012 Alberta labour mobility survey report," http://work.alberta .ca/documents/2012-alberta-labour-mobility -survey-report.pdf; downloaded March 31, 2015.

27. Statistics Canada, "The migration of infrastructure tradespersons," http://www .statcan.gc.ca/pub/75-006-x/2014001 /article/14011-eng.htm; downloaded March 31, 2015.

28. H. Yen and H. Dreier, "Rural population shrinking for the first time in U.S. History, Census finds," *Huffington Post,* 2013, http:// www.huffingtonpost.com/2013/06/13/rural -us-population-goes-down_n_3433855.html; downloaded March 31, 2015.

29. W. Roth, "COPS: A Presentation of Results Using a Revised Framework," Research Paper Series T-95-3, HRDC, August 2009, www .hrdc-drhc.gc.ca; downloaded August 2009.

30. Human Resources and Skills Development Canada, "New COPS Occupational Projection Methodology," September 8, 2006, http://www.hrsdc.gc.ca/eng/employment /ei/reports/eimar_2011/chapter4_1.shtml; downloaded May 8, 2012.

31. Employment and Social Development Canada, Temporary Foreign Worker Program, http://www.esdc.gc.ca/eng/jobs/foreign _workers/index.shtml; downloaded March 31, 2015.

32. Employment and Social Development Canada, Reform Report for Temporary Foreign Worker Program, http://www.esdc .gc.ca/eng/jobs/foreign_workers/reform /overhauling_TFW.pdf; downloaded March 31, 2015.

33. P. Koven, "Agrium Inc. targeted by another activist investor," *Financial Post,* 2014, http:// business.financialpost.com/news/mining /agrium-inc-in-crosshairs-of-another-activist -investor/; downloaded March 31, 2015.

34. L. Berkow, "Tech labour crunch looming in Canada," *Financial Post,* March 29, 2011, http://business.financialpost.com/2011/03/29 /tech-labour-crunch-looming-in-canada/.

35. "Shipping Industry faces severe labour shortage over next decade," *Daily Commercial News and Construction Record,* January 8, 2008, http://www.dailycommercialnews.ca/%20 article/id25940.

36. HRSDC, http://www23.hrsdc.gc.ca /w.2lc.4m.2@-eng.jsp; downloaded March 31, 2015.

37. Ontario Ministry of Labour, http://www .labour.gov.on.ca/english/es/; downloaded May 8, 2012.

38. D. Howell, "Heavy oil industry needs 'lifestyle change,' conference told," *Edmonton Journal,* 2015, http://www. edmontonjournal.com /Heavy+industry+needs+lifestyle +change+conference+told/10916187/story .html; downloaded March 31, 2015.

39. Investopedia, http://www.investopedia.com /terms/p/phased-retirement.asp#axzz1uJouTga0; downloaded May 8, 2012.

40. McGill University Pension Plan, http://www .mcgill.ca/pensions/; downloaded May 8, 2012.

41. Norma Tombari, "The Bottom–Line for Work/Life Leadership: Linking Diversity and Organizational Culture," *Ivey Business Journal,* http://wwwold.iveybusinessjournal .com/about_us/our_writers/author .asp?intAuthor_ID=751; downloaded May 8, 2012.

42. ESDC, http://www.esdc.gc.ca/eng/jobs /ei/reports/mar2012/chapter2_5.shtml; downloaded May 8, 2012.

43. P. Booth, "Contingent Work: Trends, Issues and Challenges for Employers," The Conference Board of Canada, 1997.

44. B. Lankard Brown, "Part-Time Work and Other Flexible Options," ERIC Digest #192, 1998, http://www.eric.ed.gov /ERICWebPortal/search/detailmini .jsp?_nfpb=true&_&ERICExtSearch _SearchValue_0= ED418247&ERICExtSearch _SearchType_ 0=no&accno=ED418247; downloaded May 8, 2012.

45. G. Schellenberg, "The Changing Nature of Part-Time Work," The Canadian Council on Social Development, November 17, 1997, http://www.ccsd.ca/pubs/archive/ptw /xs_pt.htm; downloaded May 8, 2012.

46. CBC News, April 2, 2012, http://www.cbc.ca /news/canada/windsor/story/ 2012/04/02/wdr -service-industry-windsor.html; downloaded May 8, 2012.

47. S. Klie, "Part-Timers Could Go Full Time at Grocery Giant," *Canadian HR Reporter,* March 23, 2009, p. 1.

48. J. Fantini and L. de Piante, "Temporary Lay-offs Risk Dismissal Claims," *Canadian HR Reporter,* March 23, 2009, p. 5, https://library.villanova.edu/Find /Summon/Record?id=FETCH-proquest _dll_16807468411; downloaded May 8, 2012.

49. P. A. S. Milley, "Well, what did you expect? Setting expectations for probationary employees," 2015, http://www.smss .com/abcnewsletter/AEC/2015_Spring /A2. html?utm_source=Mondaq&utm _medium=syndication&utm_campaign=View -Original; downloaded March 31, 2015.

50. Government of Saskatchewan, "Benefits for Part-Time Employees," Rights & Responsibilities Guide,

Saskatchewan Labour site, http://www
.lrws.gov.sk.ca/search?c=all&q=part
-time+benefits&x=16&y=5; downloaded
May 8, 2012.

51. Neil Sutton, "BMO hands over HR in
$750 million outsourcing deal,"
Computing Canada, Vol. 29 No. 9,
May 9, 2003, http://www.itbusiness
.ca/it/client/en/Home/News
.asp?id=5164; downloaded May 8, 2012.

52. Armina Ligaya, "Canadian interactive
studio to produce Marvel's e-magazine for
blockbuster movies," *Financial Post*, 2014,
http://business.financialpost.com
/entrepreneur/canadian-interactive-studio-to
-produce-marvels-e-magazine-for-blockbuster
-movies/; downloaded March 31, 2015.

53. People for a Shorter Workweek and
Sustainable Life, January 30, 2006, http://
shorterworkweek.blogspot.ca/2006/01
/indiana-company-has-3040-plan-for.html;
downloaded May 8, 2012.

54. Ken Dychtwald, Tamara J. Erickson,
Robert Morison, *Workforce Crisis: How
to Beat the Coming Shortage of Skills and
Talent*, Harvard Business Press/Google
eBook, 2006, http://books.google.ca
/books?id=YOiqKakrS2oC&dq=
william+mercer+study+flexible
+retirement& source=gbs_navlinks_s;
downloaded May 9, 2012.

55. Donald C. Dowling, Jr., Global HR Hot
Topic: Solutions to "Floating" Employees
Issues "Floating" Employees Working in
Overseas "Permanent Establishments"
(Part 3), November 2008, http://www
.whitecase.com/hrhottopic_1108/;
downloaded May 9, 2012.

56. William Schieman, "Measuring and
Managing Your People Equity," *Human
Resources*, 2009, http://www
.humanresourceiq.com/metrics/articles
/measuring-and-managing-your-people
-equity/; downloaded May 9, 2012.

57. T. H. Davenport, *Process Innovation*.
Boston, MA: Harvard Business School Press,
1993.

58. Srinivas R. Kandula, *Human Resource
Management in Practice: With 300 Models,
Techniques and Tools*, PHI Learning Pvt.,
2004, http://books.google.ca
/books?id=dcsLkvhujLoC&printsec=
frontcover#v=onepage&q&f=false;
downloaded May 9, 2012.

59. S. F. Gale, "Special report: HRMS vendors
say, 'Hey, you, get onto my cloud.',"
Workforce, 2014, http://www.workforce.com
/articles/20692-special-report-hrms-vendors
-say-hey-you-get-onto-my-cloud;
downloaded March 31, 2015.

60. Sage Software Systems, http://www
.sagehrms.com/; downloaded May 9, 2012.

61. University of Manitoba, What VIP Means—
Human Resources Information System, (n.d.),
http://umanitoba.ca/computing/ist/internal
/admin_sys/appsupport/banner/HRIS_VIP.
html; downloaded May 9, 2012.

62. Predictive Analysis World, Predictive
Analysis Guide, http://www.predictive
analyticsworld.com/predictive_analytics.php;
downloaded May 9, 2012.

63. J. W. Boudreau and P. M. Ramstead,
"Talentship and the new paradigm for human
resource management: From professional
practices to strategic talent decision science,"
[Electronic version], *HR. Human Resource
Planning*, Vol. 28, No. 2, 2005, pp. 17–26.

64. N. Chaudhry and M. Roomi, "Accounting
for the development of human capital in
manufacturing organizations: A study of the
Pakistani textile sector," *Journal of HRCA:
Human Resource Costing & Accounting*,
Vol. 14, No. 3, 2010, pp. 178–195. Retrieved
from ProQuest.

65. H. Das and M. Das, "One More Time:
How Do We Place a Value Tag on Our
Employees? Some Issues in Human Resource
Accounting," *Human Resource Planning*,
Vol. 2, No. 2, 1979, pp. 91–101.

66. See ibid. for a discussion of the various
models.

67. D. Zabarenko, "Arctic thawing faster than
forecast," *Toronto Star*, May 2, 2007, p. A3;
M. Mittelstaedt, "The fallout of global
warming: 1000 years," *The Globe and Mail*,
January 31, 2007, p. A1.

CHAPTER 4

1. Canadian Charter of Rights and Freedoms, as
part of the *Constitution Act* of 1982.

2. Ibid.

3. Sarah Dobson, "24-hour Shift for Medical
Residents Quashed," *Canadian HR Reporter*,
September 26, 2011, pp. 1, 11.

4. "A Guide to the Human Rights Act,"
Canadian Human Rights Commission, www
.chrc-ccdp.gc.ca/pdf/chraaguiode.pdf; see
also: Canadian Human Rights Commission,
Annual Report 2010, www.chrc-ccdp.ca/pdf
/ar_2010_ra_eng.pdf.

5. Steve Lambert, "Waitress Fired for Shaving
Head," *Chronicle Herald*, January 28, 2011,
p. A10.

6. *Canadian Human Rights Act*, Paragraph 2,
Subsection (a).

7. See Canadian Human Rights Commission,
2013 Annual Report to Parliament, www
.chrc-ccdp.gc.ca; New Brunswick Human
Rights Commission, *Annual Report 2013*-14,
www.gnb.ca.

8. Liz Bernier, "No Easy Answer for Competing
Rights Cases," *Canadian HR Reporter*,
February 10, 2014, pp. 1, 8.

9. Doreen Pitkeathly, "Phoenix Rising," *Human
Resource Professional*, February 1990,
pp. 16–18.

10. Canadian Human Rights Commission,
Annual Report 1991, p. 59, www.chrc-ccdp
.ca/publications/2001_ar/default-en.asp;
downloaded September 5, 2006; see also:
"A Place for All: A Guide to Creating an
Inclusive Workplace," Catalogue No. HR21-
55/2001, Ottawa: Minister of Public Works
and Government Services, 2001, www
.chrc-ccdp.ca/pdf/chrc_place_for_all.pdf;
downloaded September 5, 2006.

11. This case and the following cases have
been taken from either Canadian Human
Rights Commission, *Legal Reports*, Ottawa:
Government of Canada, 1979 to present, or
the annual reports of the Canadian Human

Rights Commission, Ottawa: Government
of Canada, 1980 to 2012. As of May 15,
2012, many of these reports are available at
http://www.chrc-ccdp.ca/publications
/anti_discrimination_case-eng.aspx.

12. Pulse Survey, *Canadian HR Reporter*,
October 24, 2011, p. 14.

13. Canadian Press, "Tribunal Orders Penalty
Against Firm That Said It Only Hired White
Men," *Chronicle Herald*, September 9, 2014,
p. A13.

14. Amanda Silliker, "Matthew, You're Hired.
Good Luck Next Time, Samir," *Canadian
HR Reporter*, November 21, 2012, pp. 1.
20. A report of the full study *Why Do Some
Employers Prefer to Interview Matthew
but Not Samir?* is available at http://mbc.me
tropolis.net/assets/uploads/files/wp/2011
/WP11-13.pdf.

15. "Accommodating Employees' Religious
Beliefs," *The Worklife Report*, Vol. 7, No. 5,
p. 8, Kingston, ON: IR Research Services,
1990. For more examples, see annual report
of the Canadian Human Rights Commission,
2004, www.chrc-ccdp.ca/publications/reports
_ archive_rapports-en.asp, downloaded
September 5, 2006. Also see, Robert Hatfield,
"Duty to Accommodate," *Just Labour*, Vol. 5,
2005, pp. 23–33.

16. Amanda Silliker, "7 in 10 Firms Not Hiring
Older Workers," *Canadian HR Reporter*,
January 14, 2013, pp. 1, 10.

17. Kathryn Blaze Carlson, "Tories End Forced
Retirement, Decades of Age Discrimination,"
National Post, December 18, 2011.

18. Janice Rubin, "Ageism Not Easy to
Circumnavigate," *Canadian HR Reporter*,
June 2, 2014, p. 12; Sun Life Canada,
2015 Canadian Unretirement Index Report,
www.cdn.sunlife.com; downloaded 2015.

19. "The Aging Workforce," *Canadian HR
Reporter*, November 18, 2013, p. 11.

20. Liz Bernier, "Retirement Incentives: Proceed
with Caution," *Canadian HR Reporter*,
December 16, 2013, pp. 3, 8.

21. "Fired Pregnant Woman to get $15,000,"
Chronicle Herald, February 8, 2012, p. B2.

22. Jeffrey Smith, "Pregnant Server Not On Tap
for Bar Owner," *Canadian HR Reporter*,
November 3, 2014, p. 5.

23. Liz Bernier, "Discrimination Alive and
Well Around Pregnancy, Breastfeeding,"
Canadian HR Reporter, December 1, 2014,
pp. 3, 6.

24. Liz Bernier, "Pregnant Workers More
Vulnerable to Health Risks," *Canadian HR
Reporter*, June 16, 2014, p. 3.

25. Sarah Dobson, "Male-wanted Job Ads,"
Canadian HR Reporter, May 5, 2014,
pp. 1, 10.

26. Catalyst, "Women Offered Fewer Career-
Advancing 'Hot Jobs' New Catalyst Report
Finds," www.catalyst.org, 2012.

27. CHRC, *Annual Report 1999*, pp. 6–7, www
.chrc-ccdp.ca/publications/reports_archive
_rapports-en.asp, downloaded September 5,
2006. Also see Canadian Heritage, "Sexual
Orientation and Human Rights," www.pch
.gc.ca.

28. Gwen Brodsky, Shelagh Day and Yvonne
Peters, *Accommodation in the 21st Century*,

References

(March 2012), Online: Canadian Human Rights Commission http://chrc-ccdp.gc.ca /proactive_initiatives/default=eng.aspx, p. 42.

29. Sarah Dobson, "Employer on the Hook for Lost Wages, Damages in Vile Case," *Canadian HR Reporter*, September 9, 2013, pp. 1, 2.

30. Kevin Bourassa and Joe Varnell, "It's a Quiet Thing: Equal Marriage Is Law," Equal Marriage for Same-Sex Couples site, July 21, 2005, www.samesexmarriage.ca/legal /qui210705.htm; downloaded September 5, 2006.

31. See Amanda Silliker, "LGBT Staff Still Face Bias," *Canadian HR Reporter*, December 19, 2011, pp. 1, 9. For more information about the Canadian Gay and Lesbian Chamber of Commerce, see www.cglcc.ca.

32. Trans Equality Society of Alberta, "Human Rights Across Canada," www.tesaonline .org; see also: Josh Wingrove, "Transgender Bill Languishes in Senate," *The Globe and Mail*, November 29, 2014, p. A7.

33. Brian Kreissl, "Coping with Gender Reassignment Surgery," *Canadian HR Reporter*, February 25, 2013, p. 27.

34. Melissa Beaumont, "When Childcare Interferes with Work: When Is an Employer's Duty to Accommodate Triggered?" Thompson, Doreman, and Sweatman, www .tdslaw,com; downloaded August 26, 2014.

35. "Starbucks Settles with Dwarf Fired from Barista Job," *Reuters*, August 18, 2011.

36. Tavia Grant, "The (Dis)Ability Edge," *The Globe and Mail*, February 28, 2014, pp. B6, B7.

37. Ibid.

38. Kathryn Filsinger, *Employment Law for Business and Human Resources Professionals*, 2nd ed., Toronto: Emond Montgomery, 2010, pp. 128–130.

39. CHRC, *Annual Report 2001*, p. 12, available at: www.chrc-ccdp.ca/ publications/reports_archive_rapports-en. asp, downloaded September 5, 2006. See also: "Submission of the Ontario Human Rights Commission Concerning Barrier-Free Access Requirements in the Ontario Building Code: March 1, 2002," 2002, Ontario Human Rights Commission site, www.ohrc.on.ca/english/publications /building-code-submission.shtml, downloaded September 5, 2006.

40. Francis Jewett and Nicole Cormier, "AODA Compliance: The Next Phase," *Canadian HR Reporter*, January 16, 2012, p. 12. For more details, see: www.mcss.gov .on.ca/en/mcss/programs/accessibility /customerService/.

41. Laurie Monsebraaten, "Ontario to Reduce Enforcement of Accessibility Law," *Toronto Star*, www.thestar.com, downloaded February 24, 2015,

42. Amanda Silliker, "People with Episodic Disabilities Valuable Talent," *Canadian HR Reporter*, February 13, 2012, pp. 1, 19.

43. "Workers with Disabilities," *Canadian HR Reporter*, June 6, 2011, p. 10.

44. Amanda Silliker, "70 Percent of Employers Hire Workers with Disabilities," *Canadian HR Reporter*, May 6, 2013, pp. 1, 9.

45. "Correctional Service Agrees to Hire Ex-convict," news release, a publication of the Canadian Human Rights Commission, Ottawa: Government of Canada, undated.

46. For a nice summary of the historic Janzen and Govereau sexual harassment case see Stephen Hammond, "The Historic Fight Against Sexual Harassment," *Canadian HR Reporter*, August 15, 2011, p. 31.

47. Terri Theodore, "RCMP Faces Suit by Female Officers," *Chronicle Herald*, March 28, 2012: B1, B3.

48. Lori Culbert, "More Than 330 RCMP Women Allege On-the-Job Harassment," *Vancouver Sun*, www.vancouversun.com; downloaded September 20, 2014.

49. Sarah Dobson, "Bad Bosses Targeted on Web Site," *Canadian HR Reporter*, September 6, 2010, pp. 3, 10, available at: www .ebosswatch.com.

50. CHRC, "Harassment and the *Canadian Human Rights Act*," 2005, Canadian Human Rights Commission site, www.chrc-ccdp.ca /pdf/publications/har-chra.pdf, downloaded September 5, 2006.

51. Jeffrey Smith, "When Banter Crosses the Harassment Line," *Canadian HR Reporter*, November 29, 2010, pp. 5, 27.

52. Liz Bernier, "Ostracism an Often-Overlooked Form of Workplace Bullying, Finds Study," *Canadian HR Reporter*, July 14, 2014, p. 3.

53. AVG Technologies, "Social Media Stokes Workplace Privacy Fears," www.now.avg .com; downloaded January 31, 2013.

54. Lisa Barrow, "Unmasking the Face of Workplace Cyber-bullying," *Canadian HR Reporter*, March 10, 2014, p. 10.

55. CBC, "Sexual Misconduct Complaints Mostly Ignored by Employers, Survey Suggest," www .cbc.ca; downloaded December 5, 2014.

56. Sarah Dobson, "Sexual Harassment Investigations No Easy Task," *Canadian HR Reporter*, January 26, 2015, pp. 1, 2.

57. *Canadian Human Rights Act*, Paragraph 60, Section 2.

58. Sarah Dobson, "Human Rights Costs Growing Concern," *Canadian HR Reporter*, July 12, 2010, pp. 1, 16.

59. See Nova Scotia Human Rights Commission, "Changes to the Dispute Resolution Program," www.humanrights.gov.ns.ca.

60. Sarah Dobson, "Bias Problematic at Human Rights Tribunal: Survey," *Canadian HR Reporter*, August 15, 2011, pp. 1, 18.

61. See law.dal.ca/Prospective_Students /Indigenous Blacks & Mi'kmaq Initiative.

62. Julie Cook, "Wage Gap Between Men and Women," Social Affairs Division, Publication Number 2010-30E, July 29, 2010; see also Rene Morissette, Garnett Picot, and Yuqian Lu, "The Evolution of Canadian Wages Over the Last Three Decades," Social Analysis Division, Catalogue no. 11F0019M.

63. See Women's Legal Education and Action Fund, "Pay Equity," http://leaf.ca /wordpress/wp-content/uploads/2011/01/ PayEquityFactSheet.pdf; see also Pay Equity Commission (Ontario), "An Overview of Pay Equity in Various Jurisdictions–October

2011," www.payequity.gov.on.ca/en/about /pubs/genderwage/pe_survey.php.

64. CBC News, "Postal Workers Win 28-Year Pay Equity Fight," November 17, 2011.

65. Sarah Dobson, "Ugly, Racist Altercation Caught on Video at Sears," *Canadian HR Reporter*, March 24, 2014, pp. 1, 12.

66. Mallika Das, "Workforce 2000: Diversity in the Workplace," in *Managing Diversity: Gender and Other Issues*, 3rd. ed., Halifax: Mount Saint Vincent University, 1997, p. 4.

67. Statistics Canada, Same-sex Couples and Sexual Orientation…by the Numbers, June 20, 2014.

68. Statistics Canada, *Projections of the Diversity of the Canadian Population: 2006–2031*, Catalogue No. 91-551-x; see also Statistics Canada, *Immigration and Ethnocultural Diversity in Canada*, Catalogue No. 99-010-X2011001; and Employment and Social Development Canada, *Canadians in Context – People with Disabilities*, www4.rhdcc .gc.ca, 2015.

69. A. DePalma, "Women Can Be Hindered by Lack of 'Boys' Network." *Boulder Daily Camera*, November 12, 1991, p. B9.

70. Anita Li, "Justice of the Peace Suspended for Sexually Harassing Female Court Staff," *Toronto Star*, April 12, 2012.

71. Conference Board of Canada, "Women Still Missing in Action from Senior Management Positions in Canadian Organizations," News Release 12–29, August 31, 2011.

72. Janet McFarland, "Canada's Bank Sector Lauded for Gender Diversity in World Ranking," *The Globe and Mail*, December 5, 2014, p. B4.

73. Canadian Board Diversity Council, "2014 Annual Report Card," www.boarddiversity.ca.

74. Liz Bernier, "Federal Government Gets on Board with Female Leaders," *Canadian HR Reporter*, October 6, 2014, p. 3; see also Sarah Dobson, "Is Board Gender Parity a Pipe Dream?" *Canadian HR Reporter*, January 13, 2014, pp. 1, 2.

75. Joe Friesen, "Program Aims for Diversity on Boards," *The Globe and Mail*. February 26, 2015, p. A4.

76. Sarah Dobson, "Catalyst Honours Champions of Women in Business," *Canadian HR Reporter*, November 7, 2011, pp. 1, 17.

77. Shannon Klie, "Muslims Face Discrimination in Workplace," *Canadian HR Reporter*, February 27, 2006, pp. 1, 16.

78. Amanda Silliker, "Firms Honoured for Work with Skilled Immigrants," *Canadian HR Reporter*, March 28, 2011, pp. 1, 20.

79. R. Kandola, "Managing Diversity: New Broom or Old Hat?" *International Review of Industrial and Organizational Psychology*, Vol. 10, 1995, pp. 131–167.

80. Amanda Silliker, "Holiday Parties Should be More Inclusive: Survey," *Canadian HR Reporter*, November 7, 2011, pp. 1, 32.

81. Shannon Klie, "Aboriginals a Strategic Imperative," *Canadian HR Reporter*, April 25, 2011, pp. 1, 8.

82. Wallace Immen, "Immigrants Looking for a Better Welcome in Canadian

Workplaces," *The Globe and Mail*, February 11, 2012, p. B17.

83. Canadian Institute of Diversity and Inclusion, "What Gets Measured Gets Done: Measuring the Return on Investment of Diversity and Inclusion," www.cidi-icdi.ca; downloaded 2013.

84. Lee Gardenswartz and Anita Rowe, *Diverse Teams at Work*, Chicago, IL: Irwin, 1994, p. 17.

85. Ann McMahon, "Does Workplace Diversity Matter? A Survey of Empirical Studies on Diversity and Firm Performance, 2000–09," *Journal of Diversity Management*, 2010, Vol. 5, No. 3, pp. 37–48.

86. Cedric Herring, "Does Diversity Pay?: Race, Gender and the Business Case for Diversity," *American Sociological Review*, 2009, Vol. 74, No. 2, pp. 208–224.

87. Amanda Silliker, "Employers Recognized for Diversity," *Canadian HR Reporter*, March 26, 2012, pp. 3, 5.

88. Hari Das, *Strategic Organization Design: For Canadian Firms in a Global Economy*, Scarborough, Ontario: Prentice-Hall, 1998, p. 340.

89. Amanda Silliker, "Pythian, Algonquin Recognized for Skilled Immigrant Retention Practices," *Canadian HR Reporter*, April 9, 2012, p. 10.

90. "RBC Addressing Unconscious Bias to Root Out Blind Spots," *The Globe and Mail*, March 31, 2015; and Mediacorp, *2015 Canada's Best Diversity Employers*, 2015, p. 18.

91. Bobby Siu, *HR Manager's Guide to Managing Diversity and Employment Equity*, Carswell, 2011; see also Amanda Silliker, "Making Managers Accountable for Diversity," *Canadian HR Reporter*, August 15, 2011, pp. 12, 14.

92. Sarah Dobson, "Employers Rewarded for Diversity," *Canadian HR Reporter*, March 9, 2009, p. 6.

93. Dan Arsenault, "Firefighting Hiring Plan Under Fire," *The Chronicle Herald*, February 1, 2011, pp. A1, A2; see also Michael Lightstone, "HRM to Change Fire Service Recruiting Process," *The Chronicle Herald*, March 9, 2011: A6.

94. "Managing Diversity: A Guide to Effective Staff Management," *The McDonald Series*, Winnipeg: Cross Cultural Communications International Inc., undated, p. 24.

95. Amanda Silliker, "Majority of Employers Lack IEP Integration Policies," *Canadian HR Reporter*, January 28, 2013, pp. 1, 10.

96. Sarah Dobson, "Employers Rewarded for Diversity," *Canadian HR Reporter*, March 9, 2009, p. 3; see also Canada Post, *2013 Social Responsibility Report*, https://www.canadapost.ca/cpo/mc/assets/pdf/aboutus/csr/2013_csrreport_en.pdf.

97. Catalyst study quoted by Shannon Klie, "Firms Short on Diversity Practices: Report," *Canadian HR Reporter*, March 23, 2009; see also *Career Advancements in Corporate Canada: A Focus on Visible Minorities*, a report from Catalyst, New York, 2008.

98. "Blakes Builds a Diverse Pipeline to Corporate Law," *The Globe and Mail*, March 31, 2015; Mediacorp, *2015 Canada's Best Diversity Employers*, 2015, p11.

99. Todd Humber, "Making Immigrants Feel at Home," in Report on Recruitment and Staffing, *Canadian HR Reporter*, December 5, 2005, p. R3.

CHAPTER 5

1. Dave Ulrich, *Human Resource Champions*, Boston, MA: Harvard Business School Press, 1997, p. 13.

2. Marjo Johne, "The hunt for talent at an emerging giant," *The Globe and Mail*, October 7, 2011.

3. Krista L. Uggerslev, Neil E. Fassina, and David Kraichy, *2012* "Recruiting through the stages: A meta-analytic test of predictors of applicant attraction at different stages of the recruiting process," *Personnel Psychology*, Vol. 65, pp. 597–660; Alan Saks, and Krista Uggerslev, "Sequential and combined effects of recruitment information on applicant attraction," *Journal of Business and Psychology*, Vol. 25, 2010, pp. 351–365.

4. Michael Liedtke, "5 PR Nightmares That Were Handled Better than the BP Oil Spill," *The Huffington Post*, June 14, 2010, http://www.huffingtonpost.com/2010/06/14/5-pr-disasters-handled-be_n_611010.html#s99783&title=Exxon_Valdez_Spill, downloaded February 6, 2015.

5. Derek Chapman, Krista Uggerslev, Sarah Carroll, Kelly Piasentin, and David Jones, "Applicant attraction to organizations and job choice: A meta-analytic review of the correlates of recruiting outcomes," *Journal of Applied Psychology*, Vol. 90, 2005, pp. 928–944.

6. David Carey, "Using the virtual world of Second Life to snag young IT talent," Itbusiness.ca, http://www.itbusiness.ca/it/client/en/home/News.asp?id=49854, downloaded February 6, 2015.

7. Employment and Social Development Canada, Publications Centre "Looking-Ahead: A 10-Year Outlook for the Canadian Labour Market (2008–2017)," November 2008, http://www.hrsdc.gc.ca/en/publications_resources/research/index.shtml; downloaded February 6, 2015.

8. Tom Long, Toronto-based partner of executive recruiter Egon Zehnder International Inc. quoted by Wallace Immen, "Going Abroad to Get Ahead," *The Globe and Mail*, February 22, 2006, p. C1.

9. Results of surveys by Global Recruitment Consultancy Robert Walters, Korn/Ferry International, 2005 Survey of Executives Worldwide reported in Wallace Immen, "Going Abroad to Get Ahead," *The Globe and Mail*, February 22, 2006, p. C1.

10. Alar Prost, "Successful Recruiting from an Untapped Resource," *Canadian HR Reporter*, January 16, 2006, p. 11.

11. For example, see J. A. Bellizzi and R. W. Hasty, "The Effects of Hiring Decisions on the Level of Discipline Used in Response to Poor Performance," *Management Decision*, Vol. 38, No. 3, 2000, pp. 154–159.

12. NCR Graduate Gateway, http://www.ncr.com/careers/job-types/graduate/graduate-gateway; downloaded February 6, 2015.

13. Todd Humber, "Recruitment Isn't Getting Any Easier: Report on Recruitment and Staffing," Special supplement to *Canadian HR Reporter*, May 23, 2005, p. R2; Krista L. Uggerslev, Neil E. Fassina, and David Kraichy, "Recruiting through the stages: A meta-analytic test of predictors of applicant attraction at different stages of the recruiting process," *Personnel Psychology*, Vol. 65, 2012, pp. 597–660.

14. Herbert Heneman, Timothy Judge, Vicky Smith, and Russel Summers, *Staffing Organizations*, 2nd ed., Canada: McGraw-Hill Ryerson, 2010.

15. Lisa Butler, "Corporate Culture Can Be Your Key to Success on the Hiring Front," *Canadian HR Reporter*, May 3, 1999, p. 22.

16. The Conference Board of Canada, "Winning the "Generation Wars: Making the Most of Generational Differences and Similarities in the Workplace," November, 2009.

17. Canadian Labour Congress, December, 2008, "Toward Inclusion of People with Disabilities in the Workplace," http://www.canadianlabour.ca/sites/default/files/pdfs/Toward-Inclusion-of-People-with-Disabilities-EN.pdf; downloaded February 6, 2015.

18. "Vancouver International Airport: Recruiting People with Disabilities," go2hr, https://www.go2hr.ca/articles/vancouver-international-airport-recruiting-people-disabilities; downloaded February 6, 2015.

19. Virginia Galt, "Better Shifts, Better Training, Better Pay," *The Globe and Mail*, February 24, 2006, p. C1.

20. Rod Nutt, "There's a War on for Talent Out There," *The Globe and Mail*, May 12, 2001, p. D3.

21. Tamsin McMahon, "Alberta's construction industry facing three years of job losses," *The Globe and Mail*, March 16, 2015.

22. Nursing Profiles, http://www.hc-sc.gc.ca/fniah-spnia/services/nurs-infirm/empl/profil-eng.php; downloaded February 13, 2015.

23. C. S. Manegold, Bill Powell, and Yuriko Hoshiai, "Hanging the Help-Wanted Sign," *Newsweek*, July 16, 1990, p. 39.

24. Shannon Klie, "Diversity Makes Employers More Attractive to Candidates," *Canadian HR Reporter*, April 20, 2009, p. 20.

25. "McDonald's FAQs," www.aboutmcdonalds.com/mcd/corporate_careers/benefits/highlights_of_what_we_offer/balance_work_and_life.html; downloaded March 17, 2015.

26. "What Benefits Are Companies Offering Now?" *HR Focus*, Vol. 77, No. 6, June 2000, p. 5.

27. Google Career Benefits, https://www.google.ca/about/careers/lifeatgoogle/benefits, downloaded February 6, 2015.

28. P. Luke, "Lying your way into a job is entering a minefield," *The Province*, June 23, 2002, http://search.proquest.com.proxy.lib

References

.sfu.ca/docview/269329772?accountid=13800; downloaded March 17, 2015.

29. "E-mail Is Now the Preferred Way to Receive Resumes," *HR Focus,* Vol. 77, Issue 7, July 2000, p. 8.

30. "Top employers–the list: Canada's top 100 employers for 2012," *The Globe and Mail,* http://www.canadastop100.com/; downloaded February 13, 2015.

31. Brian Dineen, Juan Ling, Steven Ash, and Devon DelVecchio, "Aesthetic properties and message customization: Navigating the dark side of web recruitment," *Journal of Applied Psychology, Vol. 92, No.* 2, 2007, pp. 356–372.

32. James Breaugh, 2012, "Recruiting and attracting talent: A guide to understanding and managing the recruitment process." SHRM Foundation's Effective Practice Guidelines Series, pp. 1–43.

33. Alan M. Saks, and Krista L. Uggerslev, "Sequential and combined effects of recruitment information on applicant attraction," *Journal of Business and Psychology,* Vol. 25, 2010, pp. 351–365.

34. James Breaugh, "Employee recruitment: Current knowledge and important areas for future research," *Human Resource Management Review,* Vol. 18, 2008, pp. 103–118; Alan M. Saks, "The impracticality of recruitment research," In A. Evers, O. Smit-Voskuyl, and N. Anderson (Eds.), *Handbook of Personnel Selection,* Oxford, UK: Basil Blackwell, 2005, pp. 47–72.

35. James Breaugh, "Recruiting and attracting talent: A guide to understanding and managing the recruitment process." SHRM Foundation's Effective Practice Guidelines Series, 2012, pp. 1-43.

36. Alice Snell, "Best practices for Web site recruiting," *Canadian HR Reporter,* February 26, 2001, p. G7.

37. S. L. Bem, *Bem Sex Role Inventory: Professional Manual,* Palo Alto, CA: Consulting Psychologists Press, 1981.

38. "Half of Resumes coming by Email," *Canadian HR Reporter,* February 23, 2004, p. 2.

39. Sarah Dobson, "Recruitment technology evolving," *Canadian HR Reporter,* April 5, 2010, p. 14.

40. Shannon Klie, "Lights, Camera and Recruitment," *Canadian HR Reporter,* December 19, 2005, p. 1.

41. Mark Swartz, "Jobs Are Online: What About Job Seekers?" *Canadian HR Reporter,* June 2, 1997, p. 21.

42. Anne Freedman, "The Web Worldwide," *Human Resource Executive,* March 6, 2002, pp. 44–48.

43. David Kraichy and Derek Chapman, "Tailoring web-based recruiting messages: Individual differences in the persuasiveness of affective and cognitive messages," *Journal of Business and Psychology,* Vol. 29, 2014, pp. 253–268.

44. D. G. Allen, J. E. Biggane, R. Otondo, and J. Van Scotter, "Reactions to recruitment web sites: Visual and verbal attention, attraction, and intentions to pursue employment,"

Journal of Business and Psychology, Vol. 28, No. 3, 2013, pp. 263–285.

45. David Jones, Chelsea Willness and S. Madey, "Why are job seekers attracted by corporate social performance? Experimental and field tests of three signal-based mechanisms," *Academy of Management Journal,* Vol. 57, 2014, pp. 383-404.

46. H. J. Walker, H. S. Feild, J. B. Bernerth, and J. B. Becton, "Diversity cues on recruitment websites: Investigating the effects on job seekers' information processing," *Journal of Applied Psychology,* Vol. 97, No. 1, 2012, pp. 214–224, http://dx.doi.org/10.1037/a0025847

47. Al Doran, "The Site Is Up: Now How Do You Attract Job Seekers?" *Canadian HR Reporter,* September 8, 1997, p. 9.

48. Richard Nelson Bolles, *Job-Hunting on the Internet,* Berkeley, CA: Ten Speed Press, 1997.

49. Gabriel Bouchard, "A Panoply of Web Recruiting Ideas," *Canadian HR Reporter,* January 12, 1998, p. 4.

50. Debbie McGrath, "Is Your Internet Recruiting Strategy Sending Qualified Candidates to Your Competitors?" *Canadian HR Reporter,* Guide to HR Technology, October 6, 1997, pp. G22–G23.

51. Dave Crisp, "Highlights from the HRPS global conference," *Canadian HR Reporter,* July 14, 2008, p. 11.

52. Lin Grensing-Pophal. "Which Is Best For HR Consultants—LinkedIn or Google+?" September 9, 2013, http://www.shrm.org /india/hr-topics-and-strategy/hr-and-social -media/social-media-and-networking/pages /which%20is%20best%20for%20hr%20 consultants%E2%80%94linkedin%20or%20 google+_.aspx; downloaded February 13, 2015.

53. Aliah D. Wright. "Time to Revamp Your Social Media Policy," August 19, 2013, http:// www.shrm.org/india/hr-topics-and-strategy /hr-and-social-media/social-media-and -networking/pages/time%20to%20 revamp%20your%20social%20media%20 policy.aspx; downloaded February 13, 2015.

54. Aliah D. Wright. "Time to Revamp Your Social Media Policy," August 19, 2013, http://www .shrm.org/india/hr-topics-and-strategy/hr-and -social-media/social-media-and-networking /pages/time%20to%20revamp%20your%20 social%20media%20policy.aspx; downloaded February 13, 2015.

55. Employment and Social Development Canada website, http://www.esdc.gc.ca/eng/about /index.shtml; downloaded February 20, 2015.

56. "Government of Canada Services for You," Catalogue No. PF4-2/2000, Minister of Public Works and Government Services, 2000.

57. Larry Kusch, "Headhunter hired to fill physician vacancies. Eastern health authority counting on results," *Winnipeg Free Press,* August 22, 2014, http://www .winnipegfreepress.com/local/headhunter -hired-to-fill-physician-vacancies-272262331 .html; downloaded March 17, 2015.

58. Brian Kreissl, "Problems with employee referrals," *Canadian HR Reporter,* October 4, 2010, p. 34.

59. Amanda Curtis, "Filling those niche roles," *Canadian HR Reporter,* May 23, 2011, p. 17; "Benefits to using specialty recruitment firms," *Canadian HR Reporter,* May 23, 2011, p. 17.

60. Pamela d'Eon Scott and Hari Das, "Searching for a Search Firm," *Journal of Academy of Business Administration,* July 2000, pp. 25–31.

61. V. Catano, S. Cronshaw, W. Wiesner, R. Hackett, and L. Methot, *Recruitment and Selection in Canada,* 3rd edition. Toronto: ITP Nelson, 2005, p. 256.

62. Shannon Klie, "Mining for New Graduate Hires," *Canadian HR Reporter,* November 17, 2008, p. 1.

63. Daniel Turban, "Organizational attractiveness as an employer on college campuses: An examination of the applicant population," *Journal of Vocational Behavior,* Vol. 58, 2001, pp. 293–312; Daniel Cable and Trevor Yu (Eds.), *The Oxford Handbook of Recruitment* (in press); "Top 5 Best Practices for Information Sessions," http:// haskaynecareerconnections.wordpress.com /category/campus-recruitment-best-practices/; downloaded March 12, 2012.

64. Stephen Jackson, "Performance Based Selection Nets Top Performers," *Canadian HR Reporter,* January 25, 1999, p. 6; "Best Practices for Campus Recruitment Centres," NACE, http:// www.naceweb.org/KnowledgeCenter .aspx?fid=786&menuID=88&ispub =False&nodetype=3&navurl=; downloaded March 12, 2012.

65. Nathan Laurie and Mark Laurie, "No Holds Barred in Fight for Students to Fill Internship Programs," *Canadian HR Reporter,* January 17, 2000, p. 15.

66. Sarah Dobson, "Staying in touch with alumni networks," *Canadian HR Reporter,* September 20, 2010, pp. 19–22.

67. Bill Leonard, "Hiring vets the right way," SHRM Articles, December 20, 2013, www .shrm.org/hrdisciplines/staffingmanagement /articles/pages/hiring-vets-the-right-way.aspx; downloaded March 8, 2015.

68. Murad Hemmadi, "The freelance economy prompts the rise of a new kind of temp agency," *Canadian Business,* Vol. 88, pp.14–16, http://www.canadianbusiness .com/innovation/the-new-temp-agency/; downloaded March 17, 2015.

69. Retrieved from www.adecco.ca, March 22, 2012.

70. Ann Kerr, "Accounting Firm Makes Sure to Stay in Touch with Past Staff," *The Globe and Mail,* June 30, 2004, p. C1.

71. P4E Career Fair 2015, https://www .partners4employment.ca/home.htm; downloaded March 17, 2015.

72. "Giving Job Fairs a Fair Shot," *Canadian HR Reporter,* November 17, 2008, p. 21.

73. Amanda Silliker, "More firms hiring contract workers," *Canadian HR Reporter,* May 7, 2012, http://www.hrreporter.com /articleview/13016-more-firms-hiring -contract-workers; downloaded March 17, 2015.

74. Anthony Moffat, "The line between employees and temps," *Canadian HR Reporter,* May 4, 2009, pp. 18–19.

75. Herbert Heneman, Timothy Judge, Vicky Smith, and Russel Summers, *Staffing Organizations,* 2nd edition, 2010, Canada: McGraw-Hill Ryerson.

CHAPTER 6

1. Jeffrey Pfeffer, *Human Equation,* Boston: Harvard Business School Press, 1998, pp. 70–71.

2. The "'Extra Things' Merill Wants," June 2005, Retrieved from Bloomberg Business Week, http://www.businessweek.com/bschools /mbapremium/Jun2005/bs20050621_6285 _bs053.htm; downloaded March 23, 2012.

3. Merrill Lynch website, March 23, 2012, www.ml.com.

4. Ben Lupton, "Pouring the Coffee at Interviews?" *Personnel Review,* Vol. 29, No.1, 2000, pp. 48–68.

5. Christopher Collins, *Research report on phase 5 of Cornell University/Gevity Institute Study: Human resource management practices and firm performance in small businesses: A look at differences across industries* (CAHRS Working Paper #07-10), March, 2007. Ithaca, NY: Cornell University, School of Industrial and Labor Relations, Center for Advanced Human Resource Studies, http:// digitalcommons.ilr.cornell.edu/cahrswp/465.

6. Michael Valpy, "Human-Rights Victory Brings Little Relief," *The Globe and Mail,* February 27, 2006, p. A6.

7. Canadian Human Rights Commission. March, 2007. A Guide to Screening and Selection in Employment, http://www.chrc-ccdp.ca/pdf /screen.pdf; downloaded March 23, 2012.

8. Petroleum Human Resources Council of Canada, Alberta, 2011, http://www .petrohrsc.ca/council-projects/project-list /labour-market-information/provincial -analysis/alberta.aspx; March 8, 2012.

9. Sharon Lebrun, "Retailers Lose $3 Million a Day to Employees," *Canadian HR Reporter,* May 5, 1997, pp. 1–2.

10. Sara L. Mann, and James Chowhan, "Selection Practices in Canadian Firms: An Empirical Investigation," *International Journal of Selection and Assessment,* December 2011, 19, pp. 435–437.

11. Society for Human Resource Management Research, SHRM Weekly Online Survey, March 15, 2005, www.shrm .org/research/surveyfindings/documents /which_20methods_20does_20your _20organizations_20use, downloaded March 8, 2015; J. W. Thacker and R. J. Cattaneo, "Survey of Personnel Practices in Canadian Organizations," Working Paper No. W-87-03, University of Windsor, Faculty of Business Administration, April 1987.

12. Amy Gulati, "The hidden benefits of employer branding," *SHRM Articles.* February 26, 2015, http://www.shrm.org /hrdisciplines/staffingmanagement/articles /pages/benefits-employer-branding.aspx; downloaded March 8, 2015.

13. David G. Allen, "Retaining talent: A guide to analyzing and managing employee turnover," SHRM Foundation's Effective Practice Guidelines Series, 2008; P. W. Hom and R. W. Griffeth, *Employee Turnover,* Cincinnati, OH: South-Western College Publishing, 1995.

14. David G. Allen, "Retaining talent: A guide to analyzing and managing employee turnover," SHRM Foundation's Effective Practice Guidelines Series, 2008.

15. Victor M. Catano, Willi H Wieser, Rick D. Hackett, and Laura L. Methot, *Recruitment and Selection in Canada, 4th ed.,* Canada: Nelson Education Ltd, 2010; H. Heneman III, T. Judge, V. Smith, and R. Summers, *Staffing Organizations,* 2nd Can. ed., McGraw Hill Ryerson, 2010.

16. J. E. Hunter and R. F. Hunter, "Validity and Utility of Alternative Predictors of Job Performance," *Psychological Bulletin,* Vol. 96, 1984, pp. 72–98. David G. Allen, "Retaining talent: A guide to analyzing and managing employee turnover," SHRM Foundation's Effective Practice Guidelines Series, 2008.

17. David Brown, "Waterloo Forced to Fire Top Bureaucrat Weeks After Hiring," *Canadian HR Reporter,* October 11, 2004, p. 3.

18. Canadian Human Rights Commission, A Guide to Screening and Selection in Employment, March 2007, http://www.chrc -ccdp.ca/eng/content/guide-screening-and -selection-employment; downloaded March 10, 2015.

19. James Leduinka and Lyle F. Schoenfeldt, "Legal Development in Employment Testing: Albermarle and Beyond," *Personnel Psychology,* Spring 1978, pp. 1–13.

20. Henryk Krajewski, and Richard Goffin, "Choosing the right personality test for the job," *Canadian HR Reporter,* August 2009, 22, p. 14.

21. Robert R. McCrae, Paul T. Costa, Jr., and Thomas A. Martin, "The NEO–PI–3: A More Readable Revised NEO Personality Inventory," *Journal of Personality Assessment,* Vol. 84, No. 3, 2005, pp 261–270; Robert R. McCrae and Paul T. Costa, Jr., *NEO Inventories for the NEO Personality Inventory-3, NEO Five-Factor Model 3, and NEO Personality Inventory-Revised,* Psychological Assessment Resources Inc, Florida, USA, 2010.

22. Murray R. Barrick, G. L. Stewart, and M. Piotrowski, "Personality and job performance: Test of the mediating effects of motivation among sales representatives," *Journal of Applied Psychology,* Vol. 87, 2002, 432002.51; G. Blickle, S. Wendel, and G. R. Ferris, "Political skill as moderator of personality–Job performance relationships in socioanalytic theory: Test of the getting ahead motive in automobile sales," *Journal of Vocational Behavior,* Vol. 76, 2010, pp. 326–335.

23. B. Griffin and B. Hesketh, "Why openness to experience is not a good predictor of job performance," *International Journal of Selection and Assessment,* Vol. 12, 2004, pp.

243–251; T. A. Timmerman, "Relationships between NEO-PI-R personality measures and job performance ratings of inbound call center employees," *Applied Human Resource Management Research,* Vol. 9, 2004, pp. 35–38.

24. Kibeom Lee and Michael C. Ashton, "The HEXACO Personality Inventory: A new measure of the major dimensions of personality," *Multivariate Behavioral Research,* Vol. 39, 2004, pp. 329–358; Michael C. Ashton and Kibeom Lee, "The HEXACO-60: A short measure of the major dimensions of personality," *Journal of Personality Assessment,* Vol. 91, 2009, pp. 340–345.

25. Steven J. Rogelberg. "Personality Assessment," *Encyclopedia of Industrial and Organizational Psychology,* Thousand Oaks, CA: Sage Publications, 2007, pp. 612–615.

26. J. F. Salgado, N. Anderson, S. Moscoso, C. Bertua, F. de Fruyt, and J. P. Rolland, "A meta-analytic study of general mental ability validity for different occupations in the European community," *Journal of Applied Psychology,* Vol. 88, 2003, pp. 1068–1081.

27. "NFL Combine 2012. 10 of the Most Pathetic Wonderlic Scores Ever," February 14, 2012, http://bleacherreport.com/articles/1065284 -nfl-combine-2012-10-most-pathetic- wonderlic-scores-ever; downloaded March 30, 2012.

28. Kevin R. Murphy, B. E. Cronin, and A. P. Tam, "Controversy and consensus regarding the use of cognitive ability testing in organizations," *Journal of Applied Psychology,* Vol. 88, 2003, pp. 660–671.

29. M. A. McDaniel, F. P. Morgeson, E. B. Finnegan, M. A. Campion, and E. P. Braverman, "Use of situational judgment tests to predict job performance: A clarification of the literature," *Journal of Applied Psychology,* Vol. 86, 2003, pp. 730–740; M. A. McDaniel, and N. T. Nguyen, "Situational judgment tests: A review of practice and constructs assessed," *International Journal of Selection and Assessment,* Vol. 9, 2001, pp. 103–113.

30. William G. Doerner and Terry Nowell, "The Reliability of the Behavioural-Personnel Assessment Device (B-PAD) in Selecting Police Recruits," *Policing: An International Journal of Police Strategies and Management,* Vol. 22, No. 3, 1999, pp. 343–52.

31. American Psychological Association, "Assessment Centers Help Companies Identify Future Managers," May 2004, http:// www.apa.org/research/action/managers.aspx; downloaded March 11, 2015.

32. W. Arthur, E. A. Day, T. L. McNelly, and P. S. Edens, "A meta-analysis of the criterion-related validity of assessment center dimensions," *Personnel Psychology,* Vol. 56, 2003, pp. 125–154; J. M. Collins, F. L. Schmidt, K. M. Sanchez, M. A. McDaniel, and H. Le, "Can basic individual differences shed light on the construct meaning of assessment center evaluations?" *International Journal of Selection and Assessment,* Vol. 11, 2003, pp. 17–29.

33. I. Cook, "The gamification of human resources," *Canadian HR Reporter*, Vol. 25, No. 2, 2012, pp. 31–32; S. Jackson, "Hire top performing managers with performance-based micro assessments," *Canadian HR Reporter*, Vol. 13, No. 7, 2000, pp. 11–12; S. Sillup, "Applicant Screening Cuts Turnover Costs," *Personnel Journal*, 1992, pp. 115–116.

34. For example, see, R. C. Overton, H. J. Harms, L. R. Taylor, and M. J. Zickar, "Adapting to Adaptive Testing," *Personnel Psychology*, Vol. 50, 1997, pp. 171–185.

35. Advocacy & Policy: Nova Scotia: Submissions, May 4th, 2009. Retrieved from: http://www.retailcouncil.org /advocacy/ns/issues/submissions/submission _nssecurityservices_lpinretail.asp; downloaded March 30, 2012.

36. "Should You Tell All?" *Parade Magazine*, May 27, 1990, p. 5.

37. *Ontario Employment Standards Act*, 2000, http://www.e-laws.gov.on.ca/html/statutes /english/elaws_statutes_00e41_e.htm; downloaded March 10, 2015.

38. Bison Security Group website, www.bsgcorp .com/journal/journal.html; downloaded December 25, 2000. More information about the Stanton Survey can be found at http:// www.plotkingroup.com/Employment_ Prescreening/Stanton_Survey.php.

39. Chad Van Iddekinge, Philip Roth, Patrick Raymark, and Heather Odle-Dusseau, "The Criterion-related validity of integrity tests: An Updated Meta-analysis," *Journal of Applied Psychology*, Vol. 97, No. 3, May 2012, pp. 499–530.

40. Paula Popovich and John P. Wanous, "The Realistic Job Preview as a Persuasive Communication," *Academy of Management Review*, October 1982, p. 571.

41. James A. Breaugh, "Recruiting and Attracting Talent: A guide to understanding and managing the recruitment process," *SHRM Foundation's Effective Practice Guidelines Series*, 2009; D. R. Earnest, D. G. Allen, and R. S. Landis, "Mechanism linking realistic job previews with turnover: A meta-analytic path analysis," *Personnel Psychology*, Vol. 64, 2011, pp. 865–897.

42. Igor Kotlyar and Ravit Abelman, "Simulation turns recruitment into a two-way street: Applicants can get a better sense of the job while the company gets a sampling of how the candidate will perform," *Canadian HR Reporter*, Vol. 16, No. 21, December 2003, p. G6.

43. M. Santora, "To recruit caseworkers, a dose of reality," *New York Times*, March 3, 2008, B3; J. Mooney, "The faces of those who knock on difficult doors," *New York Times*, April 20, 2008, B1.

44. Lesley Young, "Reference Checking Skills Sorely Lacking," *Canadian HR Reporter*, January 25, 1999, p. 1.

45. Hari Das and Mallika Das, "But He Had Excellent References: Refining the Reference Letter," *The Human Resource*, June–July 1988, pp. 15–16.

46. Stephen Jackson, "Objective Descriptions– Not Opinions–Should Be Aim of Reference Checks," *Canadian HR Reporter*, April 21, 1997, p. 10.

47. "Notable Trends from BackCheck," March 17, 2010, http://www.backcheck.net/notable -trends-from-backcheck.htm; downloaded April 1, 2012.

48. Helen Leggatt, "Germany bans Facebook as employee screening tool," *BizReport*, September, 2010.

49. Amanda Silliker, "Tread Carefully with Social Media Checks," Human Resources Institute of Alberta, www.hria.ca/news-resources/e -source-article-3-march-2012; downloaded March 31, 2012.

50. L. Shiffman, "Employers Use Facebook Information When Hiring," *North by Northwestern*, November 12, 2007, http:// www.northbynorthwestern.com/story /employers-use-facebook-information-when -hiring/; downloaded March 10, 2015.

51. Anthony Moffatt, "The Danger of Digging Too Deep," *Canadian HR Reporter*, August 11, 2008, p. 5.

52. Kearsley v. City of St. Catharines, Board of Inquiry decision on April 2, 2002, Ontario Human Rights Commission, www .ohrc.on.ca/English/cases/summary-2002 .shtml;downloaded September 5, 2006.

53. Ontario Human Rights Commission, "Human Rights at Work," approved by Commission on September 22, 1999, pp. 58–60. See also www.obrc.on.ca.

54. Barbara Butler & Associates Inc., Canadian Alcohol and Drug Use Monitoring Survey, as reported in, "Brief Analysis of Current Workplace Alcohol and Drug Issues and Activities in Canada," March 2011, http://www.ccsa.ca/2004%20CCSA%20 Documents/extl-011055-2004.pdf; downloaded April 2, 2012.

55. Canadian Centre for Occupational Health and Safety, http://www.ccohs.ca/oshanswers /psychosocial/substance.html; downloaded March 9, 2015.

56. Jeffrey Miller, "Drug Testing Dealt a Blow by Federal Court," *Canadian HR Reporter*, September 21, 1998, p. 5.

57. Virginia Galt, "Total Ban Sought on Drug Testing by Employers," *The Globe and Mail*, February 22, 1992.

58. Canadian Human Rights Commission, *Annual Report 1993*, Ottawa: Minister of Supply and Services Canada, 1994, pp. 35–36.

59. "The Case Against Drug Testing," editorial, *The Globe and Mail*, August 19, 1994, p. A18.

60. Jeffrey Miller, "Drug Testing Dealt a Blow by Federal Court," *Canadian HR Reporter*, September 21, 1998, p. 5.

61. *Milazzo v Autocar Connaisseur* (2003) 47 C.H.R.R. D/468. More recently, the Tribunal followed this finding in *Dennis v Eskasoni Band Council* (September 2008); *Alberta (Human Rights and Citizenship Commission) v Kellogg Brown & Root* (2007) ABCA 426. Leave to appeal denied by SCC May 29, 2008.

62. "Canadian Human Rights Commission Policy on Alcohol and Drug Testing," October 2009,

http://www.chrc-ccdp.gc.ca/sites/default/files /padt_pdda_eng_2.pdf; downloaded March 10, 2015.

63. Jakki Warkentin, "Kellogg Brown & Root: Discrimination and pre-employment drug testing," April 17, 2008, The Court, Osgoode Hall Law School, York University, http:// www.thecourt.ca/2008/04/17/kellogg-brown -root-discrimination-and-pre-employment -drug-testing/; downloaded March 10, 2015.

64. Janice Rubin and Sharaf Sultan, "Drug and Alcohol Testing: Where Are We Now?" *Canadian HR Reporter*, March 9, 2009, p. 15.

65. Adapted from Hari Das, *Recruitment, Selection and Deployment*, Toronto: Pearson Education, 2006, p. 320.

66. David Whitten, "Steering Clear of Contract Landmines," *Canadian HR Reporter*, June 20, 2005, p. 5.

67. Marc Belaiche, "Put Your Company's Best Foot Forward with New Hires," *Canadian HR Reporter*, September 21, 1998, p. 66.

68. See Hermann F. Schwind, "How Well Do Interviews Predict Future Performance?" *The Human Resource*, June–July 1987, pp. 19–20; G. P. Latham, L. M. Saari, E. D. Pursell, and M. A. Champion, "The Situational Interview," *Journal of Applied Psychology*, Vol. 65, No. 4, 1989, pp. 422–27.

69. Timothy Judge, Chad Higgins, and Daniel Cable, "The employment interview: A review of recent research and recommendations for future research," *Human Resource Management Review*, Vol. 10, 2000, pp. 383–406; J. M. Conway, R. A. Jako, and D. F. Goodman, "A meta-analysis of interrater and internal consistency reliability of selection interviews," *Journal of Applied Psychology*, Vol. 80, 1995, pp. 565–579.

70. Helen Gardiner and Rick Hackett, "Employment Interviewing: A Review and Analysis of Canadian Human Rights Cases," Jacques Barrette, ed., *ASAC 1997 (Human Resource Division) Proceedings*, Vol. 18, No. 9, 1997, pp. 46–55.

71. Shannon Klie, "Biases creep into interviews," *Canadian HR Reporter*, April, 2008, p. 2.

72. Canadian Human Rights Commission, "A Guide to Screening and Selection in Employment," March 2007, http://www.chrc -ccdp.ca/pdf/screen.pdf; downloaded March 23, 2012.

73. Survey by Professors David Zweig and Derek Chapman quoted by Shannon Klie, "Armchair Psychology' Doesn't Make for Good Hiring Choices," *Canadian HR Reporter*, December 19, 2005, Page 3.

74. M. A. Campion, J. E. Campion, and J. P. Hudson, "Structured Interviewing: A Note on Incremental Validity and Alternative Question Types," *Journal of Applied Psychology*, Vol. 79, 1994, pp. 998–1002; E. D. Pulakos and N. Schmitt, "Experience and Situational Based Interview Questions: Studies of Validity," *Personnel Psychology*, Vol. 48, 1995, pp. 289–308; Elaine D. Pulakos, "Selection Assessment Methods: A guide to implementing formal assessments to build a high-quality workforce," 2005, Society for Human Resource Management (SHRM);

Timothy Judge, Chad Higgins, and Daniel Cable, "The employment interview: A review of recent research and recommendations for future research," *Human Resource Management Review,* Vol. 10, 2000, pp. 383–406.

75. Derek S. Chapman, Krista L. Uggerslev, and Jane Webster, "Applicant reactions to technology-mediated interviews: A field investigation," *Journal of Applied Psychology,* Vol. 88, December 2003, pp. 944–953.

76. Tammy Williams, "The true cost of hiring," *Canadian HR Reporter,* September 2002, Vol. 15, p. 16.

77. Shannon Klie, "Biases creep into interviews," *Canadian HR Reporter,* April, 2008, Vol. 21, p. 8.

78. Canadian Human Rights Commission, "A Guide to Screening and Selection in Employment," March 2007, http://www.chrc-ccdp.ca/pdf/screen.pdf; downloaded March 23, 2012.

79. "Employers know within 5 minutes if candidate good fit," *National Journal of Human Resource Management,* March 6, 2015, http://www.hrreporter.com/articleview/23713-employers-know-within-5-minutes-if-candidate-good-fit#sthash.SOgMlUrq.dpuf; downloaded March 11, 2015.

80. Anthropologist Jennifer James quoted by Bob Rosner, "Coming of Age in HR," *Workforce,* August 2000, p. 61.

81. Stephen Jackson, "If Low Performers Outnumber High Performers, It's Time to Review Your Selection Process," *Canadian HR Reporter,* March 8, 1999, p. 8.

82. Sharon Ifill and Neil Moreland, "Auditing Recruitment and Selection Using Generic Benchmarking: A Case Study," *The TQM Magazine,* Vol. 11, No. 5, 1999, pp. 333–340.

83. J. E. Hunter and R. F. Hunter, "Validity and Utility of Alternative Predictors of Job Performance," *Psychological Bulletin,* Vol. 96, 1984, pp. 72–98; see also Hermann F. Schwind, "How Well Do Interviews Predict Future Performance?" *The Human Resource,* June–July 1987, pp. 19–20.

84. Wayne Cascio, *Managing Human Resources,* 7th ed., New York: McGraw-Hill Irwin, 2006, p. 199.

85. J. E. Hunter and F. L. Schmidt, "Quantifying the Effects of Psychological Interventions on Employee Job Performance and Work Force Productivity," *American Psychologist,* Vol. 38, 1983, pp. 473–478; see also J. E. Hunter and F. L. Schmidt, "Fitting People to Jobs: The Impact of Personnel Selection on National Productivity," in Marvin D. Dunnette and E.A. Fleishman, eds., *Human Capability Assessment,* Hillsdale, NJ: Lawrence Erlbaum Associates, 1982.

86. Marvin D. Dunnette, "Personnel Selection and Placement," *Personnel Selection and Placement,* Belmont, CA: Wadsworth, 1966.

87. J. E. Hunter and F. L. Schmidt, "Fitting People to Jobs: The Impact of Personnel Selection on National Productivity," in Marvin D. Dunnette and E.A. Fleishman, eds., *Human Capability Assessment,*

Hillsdale, NJ: Lawrence Erlbaum Associates, 1982; F. L. Schmidt, J. E. Hunter, R. C. McKenzie, and T. W. Muldrow, "Impact of Valid Selection Procedures on Work Force Productivity," *Journal of Applied Psychology,* Vol. 64, 1979, pp. 609–626; Ralph B. Alexander and Murray R. Barrick, "Estimating the Standard Error of Projected Dollar Gains in Utility Analysis," *Journal of Applied Psychology,* Vol. 72, 1987, pp. 463–474; J. E. Hunter, *The Economic Benefits of Personnel Selection Using Ability Tests: A State of the Art Review Including a Detailed Analysis of the Dollar Benefit of U.S. Employment Service Placement and a Critique of the Low Cutoff Method of Test Use,* Washington, DC: U.S. Employment Service, U.S. Department of Labor, January 15, 1981; F. L. Schmidt, J. E. Hunter, and K. Pearlman, "Assessing the Economic Impact of Personnel Programs on Work Force Productivity," *Personnel Psychology,* Vol. 35, No. 3, 1982, pp. 333–343; Wayne F. Cascio, *Costing Human Resources: The Financial Impact of Behaviour in Organizations,* Boston, MA: Kent Publishing, 1982; W. F. Cascio and V. Silbey, "Utility of the Assessment Centre as a Selection Device," *Journal of Applied Psychology,* Vol. 64, pp. 107–118; W. F. Cascio and N. F. Philips, "Performance Testing: A Rose Among Thorns? *Personnel Psychology,* Vol. 32, pp. 751–766.

88. Adapted from Wayne Cascio, *Managing Human Resources,* 7th ed., New York: McGraw-Hill Irwin, 2006, p. 199.

89. J. E. Hunter and F. L. Schmidt, "Quantifying the Effects of Psychological Interventions on Employee Job Performance and Work Force Productivity," *American Psychologist,* Vol. 38, 1983, pp. 474–477.

90. See, for example, J. E. Hunter and F. L. Schmidt, "Fitting People to Jobs: The Impact of Personnel Selection on National Productivity," in Marvin D. Dunnette and E.A. Fleishman, eds., *Human Capability Assessment,* Hillsdale, NJ: Lawrence Erlbaum Associates, 1982; F. L. Schmidt, J. E. Hunter, R. C. McKenzie, and T. W. Muldrow, "Impact of Valid Selection Procedures on Work Force Productivity," *Journal of Applied Psychology,* Vol. 64, 1979, pp. 609–626; Wayne Cascio, *Managing Human Resources,* 7th ed., New York: McGraw-Hill Irwin, 2006; F. L. Schmidt, J. E. Hunter, and K. Pearlman, "Assessing the Economic Impact of Personnel Programs on Work Force Productivity," *Personnel Psychology,* Vol. 35, No. 3, 1982, pp. 333–343. See also Steven F. Cranshaw, "The Utility of Employment Testing for Clerical/Administrative Trades in the Canadian Military," *Canadian Journal of Administrative Sciences,* Vol. 3, No. 2, 1986, pp. 376–385; Steven F. Cranshaw, Ralph A. Alexander, Willi H. Weisner, and Murray R. Barrick, "Incorporating Risk into Selection Utility: Two Models of Sensitivity Analysis and Risk Simulation," *Organizational Behaviour and Decision Processes,* Vol. 40, 987, pp. 270–286.

91. Marvin D. Dunnette, "Personnel Selection and Placement," *Personnel Selection and Placement,* Belmont, CA: Wadsworth, 1966, p. 174.

92. H. C. Taylor and J. T. Russell, "The Relationship of Validity Coefficients to the Practical Effectiveness of Tests in Selection: Discussion and Tables," *Journal of Applied Psychology,* Vol. 23, 1939, pp. 565–578.

CHAPTER 7

1. Talya Bauer, "Onboarding new employees: Maximizing success," SHRM Foundation's Effective Practice Guidelines Series, 2010.

2. J. Howe, "What's Right for You?" *Canadian HR Reporter,* May 17, 1999, pp. G3, G6.

3. Talya Bauer, "Onboarding new employees: Maximizing success," SHRM Foundation's Effective Practice Guidelines Series, 2010; K. Rollag, S. Parise, and R. Cross, "Getting new hires up to speed quickly," *MIT Sloan Management Review,* Vol. 46, 2005, pp. 35–41.

4. S. Dunn and D. Jasinski, "The role of new hire orientation programs," *Journal of Employment Counseling,* Vol. 46, September 2009, pp. 115–127.

5. Conference Board of Canada, "Bringing New Hires Up to Speed: How Structured Onboarding Can Help," Briefing, August 2011.

6. Booz, Allen & Hamilton, *Getting On Board: A Model for Integrating and Engaging Employees,* May 2008, http://www.boozallen.com/media/file/Getting_On_Board.pdf.

7. "What costs over $250K/yr but is not on any budget?" *Ignite,* April 19, 2011, http://ignitetechnical.com/blog/what-costs-over-250kyr-but-is-not-on-any-budget; downloaded May 4, 2012.

8. Royal Bank of Canada, "RBC at a glance: Q1/2015," http://www.rbc.com/investorrelations/pdf/rbcglance15q1.pdf; downloaded March 19, 2015.

9. R. Ganzel, "Putting Out the Welcome Mat," *Training Magazine,* (citing research at Corning Glass Works [1981] and Texas Instruments [1981]), March 1998.

10. E. Lowe, "Understanding the Costs of Employee Turnover," Edward Lowe Foundation, http://edwardlowe.org/index.peer?page=main& storyid=0010; downloaded September 5, 2006.

11. J. Howe, "What's Right for You?" *Canadian HR Reporter,* May 17, 1999, pp. G3, G6.

12. H. Heneman III, T. Judge, V. Smith, and R. Summers, *Staffing Organizations,* 2nd Can. ed., Toronto: McGraw Hill Ryerson, 2010.

13. R. Ganzel, "Putting Out the Welcome Mat," *Training Magazine,* (citing research at Corning Glass Works [1981] and Texas Instruments [1981]), March 1998.

14. S. Dobson, "Mix of online, face-to-face programs ensure success in orientation," *Canadian HR Reporter, Vol. 24, No. 6,* March 28, 2011, pp. 13, 17.

15. "Industry Report," *Training,* Vol. 36, No. 11, October 1999, p. 58. For more recent survey results, see www.westwood-dynamics

References

.com/all_about_orientation/surveys_north _american.htm; downloaded September 5, 2006.

16. S. L. McShane and T. Baal, "Employee Socialization Practices on Canada's West Coast: A Management Report," *Faculty Research*, December 1984, Burnaby, BC: Faculty of Business Administration, Simon Fraser University.

17. T. N. Bauer, T. Bodner, B. Erdogan, D. M. Truxillo, and J. S. Tucker, "Newcomer adjustment during organizational socialization: A meta-analytic review of antecedents, outcomes and methods," *Journal of Applied Psychology*, Vol. 92, 2007, pp. 707–721; T. Kim, D. M. Cable, and S. Kim, "Socialization tactics, employee proactivity, and person-organization fit," *Journal of Applied Psychology*, Vol. 90, 2005, pp. 232—241; H. J. Klein and N. A. Weaver, "The Effectiveness of an Organizational-Level Orientation Training Program in the Socialization of New Hires," *Personnel Psychology*, Vol. 53, No. 1, 2000, pp. 44–62; A. M. Saks, K. L. Uggerslev, and N. E. Fassina, "Socialization tactics and newcomer adjustment: A meta-analytic review and test of a model," *Journal of Vocational Behavior*, Vol. 70, 2007, pp. 413–446.

18. R. Korte. "First, get to know them: a relational view of organizational socialization," *Human Resource Development International*, Vol. 13, No. 1, February 2010, pp. 27–43.

19. Peter Senge, *The Fifth Discipline: The Art and Practice of the Learning Organization*, Doubleday/Currency, 2006.

20. Knowledge Management Network, www .brint.com/km, downloaded September 5, 2006; See also "Managing Knowledge Workers: Brain Teasing," *The Economist*, October 13, 2005, www.economist .com/business/globalexecutive/reading /displayStory.cfm?story_id=5016986; downloaded September 5, 2006.

21. M. Grant and D. Hughes, "Learning and Development Outlook 2007: Are We Learning Enough?" *The Conference Board of Canada*, April 2007.

22. M. Grant and D. Hughes, "Learning and Development Outlook 2007: Are We Learning Enough?" *The Conference Board of Canada*, April 2007.

23. R. Yerema and K. Leung, *Employer Review: EllisDon Corporation*, October 6, 2011, http://www.eluta.ca /top-employer-ellisdon.

24. Association for Talent Development, "2014: State of the Industry," 2014, https://www.td.org/publications/research-Reports/2014/2014-State-of-the-Industry, downloaded March 19, 2015.

25. M. Grant and D. Hughes, "Learning and Development Outlook 2007: Are We Learning Enough?" *The Conference Board of Canada*, April 2007; see also A. Campbell and D. Hughes, "Learning and Development Outlook 2009: Learning in Tough Times," *The Conference Board of Canada*, August 2009.

26. Association for Talent Development, "2014: State of the Industry," 2014, https://www.td.org/publications/research -Reports/2014/2014-State-of-the-Industry; downloaded March 19, 2015

27. A. Campbell and D. Hughes, "Learning and Development Outlook 2009: Learning in Tough Times," *The Conference Board of Canada*, August 2009.

28. H. Aguinis, and K. Kraiger, "Benefits of training and development for individuals and teams, organizations, and society," *Annual Review of Psychology*, Vol. 60, 2009, pp. 451–474; H. Aguinis and E. O'Boyle, "Star Performers in Twenty-First Century Organizations," *Personnel Psychology*, Vol. 67, No. 2, 2014, pp. 313–350; W. Arthur Jr., W. Bennett Jr., P. S. Edens, and S. T. Bell, "Effectiveness of training in organizations: A meta-analysis of design and evaluation features," *Journal of Applied Psychology*, Vol. 88, 2003, pp. 234–245.

29. D. Vloeberghs, R. Pepermans, and K. Thielemans, "High-potential development policies: An empirical study among Belgian companies," *Journal of Management Development*, Vol. 24, 2005, pp. 546–558; T. J. Maurer, "Employee Learning and Development Orientation: Toward an Integrative Model of Involvement in Continuous Learning," *Human Resource Development Review*, Vol. 1, No. 1, March 2002, pp. 9–44.

30. O. Parker, "The Real Bottom Line on Training: It's How, Not How Much," Ottawa: The Conference Board of Canada, www .conferenceboard.ca/humanresource/training -inside.htm; downloaded September 5, 2006.

31. I. Goldstein and K. Ford, *Training in Organizations: Needs Assessment, Development, Evaluation*, 4th ed., Belmont, CA: Thomson-Wadsworth Publishing, 2002, p. 272.

32. Sarah Dobson, "Mix of online, face-to-face programs ensure success in orientation," *Canadian HR Reporter*, Vol. 24, No. 6, 2011, pp. 13–17, http://search.proquest.com /docview/861493598?accountid=14569

33. L. Rowan, "Change and Stasis in Learning Delivery," Chief Learning Office: Solutions for Enterprise Productivity, July 2005, http:// clomedia.com/articles/view /change_and_stasis_in_learning_delivery/1.

34. P. Harris, "Learning You Can Bank On," *T+D*, Vol. 65, No. 10, October 2011, pp. 40–42.

35. L. Rowan, *"Change and Stasis in Learning Delivery,"* Chief Learning Office: Solutions for Enterprise Productivity, July 2005 http://clomedia.com/articles/view /change_and_stasis_in_learning_delivery/1

36. L. Rowan, *"Change and Stasis in Learning Delivery,"* Chief Learning Office: Solutions for Enterprise Productivity, July 2005 http://clomedia.com/articles/view /change_and_stasis_in_learning_delivery/1

37. T. Middleton, "The Potential of Virtual Reality Technology for Training," *The Journal of Interactive Instructional Development*, Spring 1992, pp. 8–12; see also

Ken Mark, "Virtual Training–At Your Pace, in Your Space," *Human Resource Professional*, February/March 1998, pp. 15–17; Defence Research and Development Canada, "DRDC Develops Virtual Reality Simulator for Use in Helicopter Deck-Landing Training," July 2002, www.drdc-rddc.gc.ca/newsevents /newstand/release/020701farn_e.asp; downloaded September 5, 2006.

38. A. Gronstedt, "All Aboard! The Web 3D Train Is Leaving the Station," *T+D*, 2008, pp. 22–24.

39. A. Gronstedt, "All Aboard! The Web 3D Train Is Leaving the Station," *T+D*, 2008, pp. 22–24.

40. V. Allee, "Principles of Knowledge Management," American Society for Training and Development, www.providersedge. com/docs/km_articles/12_Principles_of _Knowledge_Management.pdf; downloaded September 5, 2006.

41. "Global Knowledge and Deloitte Win Gold for Training Excellence in Internal Learning," *Business Wire*, November 23, 2010.

42. B. Little, "Trends in learning content management," *Industrial and Commercial Training*, Vol. 4, No. 5, 2008, pp. 261–265.

43. J. Surveyer, "Net-Based Learning Goes Mainstream," *The Computer Paper*, Eastern ed., July 2000, p. 68; Eugene Sadler-Smith, Simon Down, and Jonathan Lean, "Modern Learning Methods: Rhetoric and Reality," *Personnel Review*, April 29, 2000, pp. 474– 490; "What Is Web-Based Training?" *Web-Based Training*, July 27, 2000, Web-Based Training Information Center site, www.wbtic.com/home.aspx.

44. W. Costen, M. Johanson, and D. Poisson, "The Development of Quality Managers in the Hospitality Industry: Do Employee Development Programs Make Cents?" *Journal of Human Resources in Hospitality & Tourism*, Vol. 9, 2010, pp. 131–141.

45. I. Tarique and R. S. Schuler, "Global talent management: Literature review, integrative framework, and suggestions for further research," *Journal of World Business*, Vol. 45, No. 2, 2010, pp. 122–133; V. Vaiman, H. Scullion, and D. Collings, "Talent management decision making," *Management Decision*, Vol. 50, 2012, pp. 925–941; R. Silzer, and A. Church, "Identifying and assessing high-potential talent: Current organizational practices," in R. Silzer and B. E. Dowell (Eds). *Strategy Driven Talent Management: A Leadership Imperative*, San Francisco, CA: Jossey-Bass, 2009, pp. 213–280.

46. Towers Watson, *"Canadian Companies Poorly Prepared to Manage Future Talent Needs, Says Towers Perrin Study,"* November 10, 2009, http://www .towersperrin.com/tp/showdctmdoc .jsp?url=Master_Brand_2/CANE/Press _Releases/20091110/2009_11_10.htm.

47. Ibraiz Tarique and Randall Schuler, "Global Talent Management Literature Review," SHRM Foundation, September 15, 2012.

48. H. Aguinis and E. O'Boyle, "Star Performers in Twenty-First Century Organizations,"

Personnel Psychology, Vol. 67, No. 2, 2014, pp. 313–350; B. E. Becker, M. A. Huselid, and R. W. Beatty, *The differentiated workforce: Transforming talent into strategic impact,* Harvard Business Press, 2009.

49. M. Thunnissen, P. Boselie, and B. Fruytier, "Talent management and the relevance of context: Towards a pluralistic approach," *Human Resource Management Review,* Vol. 23, No. 4, 2013, pp. 326–336; G. C. Thornton, III, G. P. Hollenbeck, and S. K. Johnson, "Selecting leaders: Executives and high potentials," in J. L. Farr and N. T. Tippins (Ed.). *Handbook of employee selection,* New York, NY: Routledge/Taylor & Francis Group, 2010, pp. 823–840; C. Tansley and S. Tietze, "Rites of passage through talent management progression stages: an identity work perspective," *The International Journal of Human Resource Management,* Vol. 24, 2013, pp. 1799–1815.

50. Towers Watson, "Canadian Companies Poorly Prepared to Manage Future Talent Needs, Says Towers Perrin Study," November 10, 2009, http://www.towersperrin.com/tp/showdctmdoc.jsp?url=Master_Brand 2/CANE/Press_Releases/20091110/2009_11_10.htm.

51. P. T. Brown, "Having Their Backs: Improving Managers' Skills in Developing Others," *T+D,* 2010, pp. 61–64.

52. K. N. Wexley and G. P. Latham, *Developing and Training Human Resources in Organizations,* 3rd ed., 2001. New York: Prentice Hall.

53. A. Pescuric and W.C. Byham, "The New Look of Behavior Modeling," *Training & Development,* July 1996, pp. 24–30; see also M. M. Najjar and J. W. Boudreau, "The Effect of Behavior Modelling Training," paper provided by Center for Advanced Human Resource Studies, Cornell University, 1996.

54. R. R. Blake and A. A. McCanse, *Leadership Dilemmas– Grid Solutions,* Houston: Gulf Publishing Co., 1994; Robert R. Blake and Rachel Kelly McKee, *Solution Selling: The Grid Science Approach,* Houston: Gulf Publishing Company.

55. K. B. Majumdar and L. A. Cuttress, "Cultural Sensitivity Training Among Foreign Medical Graduates," *Medical Education,* Vol. 33, No. 3, March 2009, p. 177.

56. D. Whitney, A. Trosten, J. Cherney, and R. Frey, *Appreciative Team Building: Positive Questions to Bring Out the Best of Your Team,* Lincoln, NB: Universe, Inc., 2004.

57. G. Kroehnert, *Games Trainers Play Outdoors,* McGraw-Hill Education, 2002.

58. S. Butyn. "Mentoring Your Way to Improved Retention," *Canadian HR Reporter,* January 27, 2003, pp. 13–15.

59. Search Top Employers, http://www.eluta.ca/top-employer-great-little-box-company, July 2012.

60. D. MacLeod and E. Kennedy, "Job Rotation System," Consulting report, 1993, Dan MacLeod's Ergo website, www.danmacleod.com/Articles/job%20rotation.htm; downloaded September 5, 2006. Md Lazim Mohd Zin, Faridahwati Mohd Shamsudin, and Chandrakantan Subramaniam, *International Journal of Business and Society,* Vol. 14, No. 1, 2013, pp. 135–148.

61. T. G. Cummings and C. G. Worley, *Organization Development and Change,* 8th ed. Mason, OH: South-Western, Thompson Publishing, 2005.

62. S. L. McShane, *Canadian Organizational Behaviour,* 5th ed., Toronto: McGraw-Hill Ryerson, 2004, pp. 439–441.

63. R. Finney, "Winning Project Teams," white paper, itmWEB, www.itmweb.com/essay003.htm, downloaded September 5, 2006.

64. D. L. Kirkpatrick, "Techniques for Evaluating Training Programs," *Journal of the American Society of Training Directors,* Vol. 13, 1959, pp. 3–9, 21–26; Vol. 14, 1960, pp. 13–18, 28–32.

65. S. Killian, "What Percentage of Salary Should Go to Training?" January 2, 2009, http://hrthought leaders.org/2009/01/02/what-percentage-of-salary-should-go-to-training/; downloaded October 1, 2009.

66. Towers Perrin, "*Closing the Engagement Gap: A Road Map for Driving Superior Business Performance,*" Towers Perrin Global Workforce Study 2007–2008, 2008, http://www.towersperrin.com/tp/getwebcachedoc?webc=HRS/USA/2008/200803/GWS_Global_Report20072008_31208.pdf.

67. J. Wiscombe, IBM Corp. 2010 WINNER: *Global Outlook,* Resource Library, December 1, 2010, http://findarticles.com/p/articles/mi_m0FXS/is_12_89/ai_n56452408/.

68. J. Chew and A. Girardi, "Is Career Management the Panacea to Retaining Vital Staff?" *International Journal of Management and Marketing Research,* Vol. 1, No. 1, 2008, pp. 83–98; S. Sullivan and Y. Baruch, "Advances in Career Theory and Research: A Critical Review and Agenda for Future Exploration," *Journal of Management,* Vol. 35, No. 6, 2009, pp. 1542–1571.

69. B. Adekola, "Career Planning and Career Management as Correlates for Career Development and Job Satisfaction—A Case Study of Nigerian Bank Employees," *Australian Journal of Business and Management Research,* Vol. 1, No. 2, May 2011, pp. 100–112.

70. J. Chew and A. Girardi, "Is Career Management the Panacea to Retaining Vital Staff?" *International Journal of Management and Marketing Research,* Vol. 1, No. 1, 2008, pp. 83–98.

71. J. Hunt and J.R. Weintraub, *The Coaching Manager: Developing Top Talent in Business,* Sage Publications Inc., 2002.

72. Kara Swisher, "'Physically Together': Here's the Internal Yahoo No-Work-From-Home Memo for Remote Workers and Maybe More," February 22, 2013, http://allthingsd.com/?p=297562&ak_action=printable; downloaded March 23, 2015.

73. Catherine Albison and Shelley Correll, "Benefit of office face time a myth," reported on CNN, March 13, 2013, http://www.cnn.com/2013/03/13/opinion/albison-correll-women-face-time/, downloaded March 23, 2015; Sara Sutton Fell, "How "Face Time" hurts productivity and why remote work can help," April 7, 2014, https://www.linkedin.com/pulse/20140407183936-60144-how-face-time-hurts-productivity-and-remote-work-helps; downloaded March 23, 2015.

74. "Is Job Hopping Losing Its Stigma?" Canada NewsWire [Ottawa]. December 18, 2014, http://search.proquest.com/docview/1637580188?accountid=14569; downloaded March 23, 2015.

75. C. Kanchier, "Loyal Workers Reward Companies," *National Post,* December 3, 2005.

76. C. Adams, "Coaches Offer More Than Game Plan," *The Globe and Mail,* July 8, 2002, p. 1.

77. B. Barnett and L. Bradley, "The impact of organizational support for career development on career satisfaction," *Career Development International,* Vol. 12, No. 7, 2007, pp. 617–636.

78. Y. Baruch, *Managing Careers–Theory and Practice,* Essex: Pearson Education Limited, 2004, p. 78.

79. Proctor & Gamble, P&G Business School, 2011, P&G Live Events–Testimonials, http://www.pgbusinessschool.com/testimonials.php?from=financial_seminar.

80. E. H. Schein and E Schein, *Career dynamics: Matching individual and organizational needs,* Vol. 24, Reading, MA: Addison-Wesley, 1978; E. H. Schein, "Career anchors revisited: Implications for career development in the 21st century," *The Academy of Management Executive,* Vol. 10, No. 4, pp. 80–88.

81. A. Glass, "Understanding generational differences for competitive success," *Industrial and Commercial Training,* Vol. 39, No. 2, 2007, pp. 98–103.

82. Patagonia, *Environmentalism: What We Do– Environmental Internships,* 2011, http://www.patagonia.com/us/patagonia.go?assetid=1963.

83. Genesis Systems Group, *Employee Testimonials,* 2011, http://www.genesis-systems.com/how-we-do-it/company-info/employee-testimonials.

84. Y. Baruch, *Managing Careers—Theory and Practice,* Essex: Pearson Education Limited, 2004.

85. J. Sampson, "Modern and Postmodern Career Theories: The Unnecessary Divorce," *The Career Development Quarterly,* Vol. 51, No. 1, 2009, pp. 91–96; Y. Baruch, *Managing Careers—Theory and Practice,* Essex: Pearson Education Limited, 2009; B. Barnett and L. Bradley, "The impact of organisational support for career development on career satisfaction," *Career Development International,* Vol. 12, No. 7, 2007, pp. 617–636.

86. Personal communication by the first author with a Ford HR executive at the Cologne plant in Germany.

87. Chartered Institute of Personnel and Development, Annual Survey Report 2005 on Training and Development. www.cipd.co.uk/NR/rdonlyres/271CD424-507C-4E4A-99B6-1FAD80573E4A/0/traindevtsurvrept05.pdf, downloaded October 1, 2009.

CHAPTER 8

1. Hari Das, *Performance Management,* Toronto: Prentice Hall, 2003.
2. Stephen Miller, "Integrating performance management and rewards at Microsoft," May 25, 2012, http://www.shrm.org /india/hr-topics-and-strategy/performance -management/performance-planning /pages/integrating%20performance%20 management%20and%20rewards%20at%20 microsoft.aspx; downloaded March 26, 2015.
3. Sandra Chiodo, "Objective performance development," *Canadian HR Reporter,* December 2010, pp. 28, 34.
4. Elaine D. Pulakos, Performance Management: A roadmap for developing, implementing and evaluating performance management systems, Alexandria, VA: SHRM Foundation, 2004.
5. Rose Mueller Hanson and Elaine Pulakos, "Putting the "Performance" back in performance management," SHRM-SIOP Science of HR White Paper Series, http://www. shrm.org/Research/Documents/SHRM -SIOP%20Performance%20Management.pdf; downloaded March 25, 2015.
6. Howard Rohm, "Using the Balanced Scorecard to Align Your Organization," Balanced Scorecard Institute, January 2008; Robert S. Kaplan and David P. Norton, *The Balanced Scorecard: Translating Strategy into Action,* Boston, MA: Harvard Business School Press, 1992; Robert S. Kaplan and David P. Norton, *The Strategy-Focused Organization: How Balanced Scorecard Companies Thrive in the New Business Environment,* Boston, MA: Harvard Business School Press, 2000.
7. Richard H. Hopf et al., "Guide to a Balanced Scorecard: Performance Management Methodology," U.S. Department of Commerce, 1999, Acquisition Community Connection site, https://acc.dau.mil/ GetAttachment .aspx?id=46158&pname=file&aid=13701, downloaded September 5, 2006.
8. SHRM Foundation, "Scorecard: What is a Balanced Scorecard?" May 25, 2012, http:// www.shrm.org/india/hr-topics-and-strategy /performance-management/business-strategy -deployment-including-balanced-score-card /pages/scorecard_%20what%20is%20a%20 balanced%20scorecard_.aspx; downloaded March 26, 2015.
9. Sarah Dobson, "Performance reviews valued by employees: Poll," *Canadian HR Reporter,* Vol. 24, December 2011, p. 22.
10. Terry H. Wagar, "Union Status, Organization Size and Progressive Decision-Making Ideology as Predictors of Human Resource Management Practices," *International Journal of Employment Studies,* April 1996, pp. 79–93.
11. Krista Uggerslev and Lorne Sulsky, "Presentation modality and indirect performance information: Effects on ratings, reactions, and memory," *Journal of Applied Psychology,* Vol. 87, 2002, pp. 940–950.
12. Theresa J. B. Kline and Lorne M. Sulsky, "Measurement and assessment issues in performance appraisal," *Canadian Psychology/Psychologie canadienne,* Vol. 50, No. 3, 2009, p. 161.
13. Theresa J. B. Kline, and Lorne M. Sulsky. "Measurement and assessment issues in performance appraisal," *Canadian Psychology/Psychologie canadienne,* Vol. 50, No. 3, 2009, p. 161.
14. H. A. Richardson and S. G. Taylor, "Understanding Input Events: A Model of Employees' Responses to Requests for Their Input," *Academy of Management Review,* Vol. 37, No. 3, 2012, pp. 471–491.
15. Hermann F. Schwind, "Performance Appraisal: The State of the Art," in S.L. Dolan and R.S. Schuler, eds., *Personnel and Human Resources Management in Canada,* Minneapolis/St. Paul: West Publishing, 1987, pp. 197–210.
16. Eran Vigoda-Gadot and Larisa Angert, "Goal Setting Theory, Job Feedback, and OCB: Lessons from a Longitudinal Study," *Basic and Applied Social Psychology,* Vol. 29, No. 2, 2007, pp. 119–128, DOI: 10.1080/01973530701331536.
17. Andrew E. Schwartz and Deborah Zemke, "Performance Management," Barron's Educations Series, October 1999; see also A. M. Mohrman, S. M. Resnick-West, and E. E. Lawler, *Designing Performance Appraisal Systems,* San Francisco, CA: Jossey-Bass, 1989.
18. Elaine Pulakos, Rose Mueller-Hanson, Ryan O'Leary, and Michael Meyrowitz, "Building a high-performance culture: A fresh look at performance management," SHRM Foundation's Effective Practice Guidelines Series, 2012, http://www.shrm.org/about/ foundation/products/documents/perf%20 mgmt%20epg-final%20for%20web.pdf; downloaded March 26, 2015.
19. Krista L. Uggerslev and Lorne M. Sulsky, "Using Frame-of-Reference training to understand the implications of rater idiosyncrasy for rating accuracy," *Journal of Applied Psychology,* Vol. 93, 2008, pp. 711–719; see also Sylvia G. Roch and Brian J. O'Sullivan, "Frame of Reference Rater Training Issues: Recall, Time and Behavior Observation Training," *International Journal of Training and Development,* Vol. 7, June 2003, pp. 93–1007.
20. Paul E. Levy and Jane R. Williams, "The social context of performance appraisal: A review and framework for the future," *Journal of Management,* Vol. 30, No. 6, 2004, pp. 881–905; Deidra J. Schleicher and David V. Day, "A Cognitive Evaluation of Frame-of-Reference Rater Training: Content and Process Issues," *Organizational Behavior and Human Decision Processes,* Vol. 73, No. 1, January 1998, pp. 76–101.
21. G. E. Roberts, "Employee performance appraisal system participation: A technique that works." *Public Personnel Management,* Vol. 32, No. 1, 2003, pp. 89–98; Taehee Kim and Marc Holzer, "Public Employees and Performance Appraisal A Study of Antecedents to Employees' Perception of the Process," *Review of Public Personnel Administration,* 2014, DOI: 0734371X14549673.
22. Gary P. Latham and Kenneth N. Wexley, *Increasing Productivity Through Performance Appraisal,* 2nd ed., Reading, MA: Addison-Wesley, 1994.
23. Kyungwon Kang, Shezeen Oah, and Alyce M. Dickinson, "The Relative Effects of Different Frequencies of Feedback on Work Performance," *Journal of Organizational Behavior Management,* Vol. 23, No. 4, 2005, pp. 21–53, DOI: 10.1300/J075v23n04_02.
24. J. W. Smither, M. London, and R. R. Reilly, "Does performance improve following multisource feedback? A theoretical model, meta-analysis, and review of empirical findings," *Personnel Psychology,* Vol. 58, No. 1, 2005, pp. 33–66.
25. J. Peter Graves, "Let's Put Appraisal Back in Performance Appraisal: II," *Personnel Journal,* December 1982, p. 918.
26. Jack Welch, *Straight from the Gut,* New York: Warner Business Books, 2001.
27. Abhinaya Chakkirala, "HR professionals' love-hate equation with the bell curve," January 22, 2013, http://www.shrm.org /india/hr-topics-and-strategy/performance -management/business-strategy-deployment -including-balanced-score-card/pages/hr%20 professional%e2%80%99s%20love-hate%20 equation%20with%20the%20bell%20curve .aspx; downloaded March 26, 2015.
28. Elaine Pulakos, Rose Mueller-Hanson, Ryan O'Leary, and Michael Meyrowitz, "Building a high-performance culture: A fresh look at performance management," SHRM Foundation's Effective Practice Guidelines Series, 2012, http://www.shrm.org/about /foundation/products/documents/perf%20 mgmt%20epg-final%20for%20web.pdf; downloaded March 26, 2015.
29. K. R. Murphy and J. I. Constans, "Behavioral Anchors as a Source of Bias in Rating," *Journal of Applied Psychology,* Vol. 72, November 1987, pp. 573–586.
30. Richard C. Grote, "Performance Appraisal Reappraised," *Harvard Business Review,* January 1, 2000.
31. Elaine D. Pulakos, Performance Management: A roadmap for developing, implementing and evaluating performance management systems, SHRM Foundation, Alexandria, VA, 2004.
32. Elaine D. Pulakos, Performance Management: A roadmap for developing, implementing and evaluating performance management systems, SHRM Foundation, Alexandria, VA, 2004.
33. Shannon Klie, "Shift in strategy requires new leadership skills," *Canadian HR Reporter,* January 2011, p. 14; Toronto Pearson Passenger Data, http://www.torontopearson .com/uploadedFiles/GTAA/Content/About _GTAA/Statistics/04-Apr15-passenger.pdf; downloaded 13 July 2015.
34. Mehrdad Derayeh and Stephane Brutus, "Learning from Others' 360-Degree Experiences," *Canadian HR Reporter,* February 10, 2003, pp. 18, 23.
35. Jeanne D. Makiney and Paul E. Levy, "The Influence of Self-Ratings Versus Peer Ratings on Supervisors' Performance Judgments," *Organizational Behavior and Human Decision Processes,* Vol. 74, No. 3, June 1998, pp. 212–28.

36. Michael M. Harris and John Schaubroeck, "A meta-analysis of self-supervisor, self-peer, and peer-supervisor ratings," *Personnel Psychology,* Vol. 41, 1988, pp. 43–62.

37. V. V. Druskat and S. B. Wolff, "Effect and timing of developmental peer appraisals in self-managing work groups," *Journal of Applied Psychology,* Vol. 84, 1999, pp. 58–74.

38. Amanda Silliker, "Management behaviours closely linked to engagement: Study," *Canadian HR Reporter,* Vol. 24, No. 8, 2011, pp. 3, 6.

39. R. Rodgers and J. E. Hunter, "Impact of Management by Objectives on Organizational Productivity," *Journal of Applied Psychology,* Vol. 77, No. 2, 1991, pp. 322–336.

40. W. Arthur, E. A. Day, T. L. McNelly, and P. S. Edens, "A meta-analysis of the criterion-related validity of assessment center dimensions," *Personnel Psychology,* Vol. 56, 2003, pp. 125–154; J. M. Collins, F. L. Schmidt, K. M. Sanchez, M. A. McDaniel, and H. Le, "Can basic individual differences shed light on the construct meaning of assessment center evaluations?" *International Journal of Selection and Assessment,* Vol. 11, 2003, pp. 17–29.

41. American Psychological Association, "Assessment Centers Help Companies Identify Future Managers," May 2004, http://www.apa.org/research/action/managers.aspx; downloaded March 11, 2015.

42. Gail J. Gunderson and Bill R. Haynes, "Assessment Technology: Its Use in Improving Leadership and Management Performance," *Journal of Extension,* Vol. 38, No. 6, December 2000.

43. Paul Loucks, "Plugging into performance management," *Canadian HR Reporter,* Vol. 20, February 2007, p. 4.

44. Ian Turnbull, "Enterprise-wide Software Gaining Popularity," *Canadian HR Reporter,* June 16, 1997, pp. 10–11; see also special supplement "Guide to HR Technology," *Canadian HR Reporter,* March 10, 2003.

45. Michael Hammer and James Champy, *Reengineering the Corporation: A Manifesto for Business Revolution,* New York: HarperCollins, 1993.

46. Ian Turnbull, "Enterprise-wide Software Gaining Popularity," *Canadian HR Reporter,* June 16, 1997, pp. 10–11.

47. Ian Turnbull, "Enterprise-wide Software Gaining Popularity," *Canadian HR Reporter,* June 16, 1997, pp. 10–11.

48. Rob Silzer and Ben E. Dowell, ed., *Strategy-Driven Talent Management: A Leadership Imperative,* San Francisco: Jossey-Bass, 2010.

49. Thomas Ruddy and Pooja Anand, "Managing Talent in Global Organizations," in Rob Silzer and Ben E. Dowell (Eds.), *Strategy-Driven Talent Management: A Leadership Imperative,* San Francisco: Jossey-Bass, 2010.

50. Karen Gorsline, "Talent management comes of age," *Canadian HR Reporter,* Vol. 23, No. 14, 2010, p. 9; Rob Silzer and Ben E. Dowell, ed., *Strategy-Driven Talent Management:*

A Leadership Imperative, San Francisco: Jossey-Bass, 2010.

51. Ian Hendry, "Hail talent management," *Canadian HR Reporter,* Vol. 24, No. 13, 2011, pp. 13–14.

52. "Managing Employee Performance," *Society for Human Resource Management,* February 2012, http://shrm.org/templatestools/toolkits/pages/managingemployeeperformance.aspx, downloaded May 3, 2012.

53. Elaine Pulakos, Rose Mueller-Hanson, Ryan O'Leary, and Michael Meyrowitz, "Building a high-performance culture: A fresh look at performance management," SHRM Foundation's Effective Practice Guidelines Series, 2012, http://www.shrm.org/about/foundation/products/documents/perf%20mgmt%20epg-final%20for%20web.pdf; downloaded March 26, 2015.

54. Hermann F. Schwind, "Developing and Evaluating a New Performance Appraisal and Training Evaluation Instrument: The Behaviour Description Index," unpublished Ph.D. dissertation, University of British Columbia, 1978.

55. Testimony from several members of the Canadian Armed Forces, all officers, in classes of the first author.

56. Karen S. Lyness and Madeline E. Heilman, "When fit is fundamental: performance evaluations and promotions of upper-level female and male managers," *Journal of Applied Psychology* Vol. 91, 2006, p. 777.

57. Jacques Gaumond, "5 tips to perfecting performance reviews," *Canadian HR Reporter,* Vol. 21, January 2008, p. 2; Sandra Chiodo, "Objective performance development," *Canadian HR Reporter,* Vol. 23, December 2010, p. 22.

58. Amanda Silliker, "Management behaviours closely linked to engagement: Study," *Canadian HR Reporter,* Vol. 24, p. 8.

59. "How To Guides: How to Establish a Performance Improvement Plan," Society for Human Resource Management How To Guides, June 7, 2010, http://www.shrm.org/india/hr-topics-and-strategy/performance-management/managing-poor-performance-including-exits/pages/how%20to%20guides_%20how%20to%20establish%20a%20performance%20improvement%20plan.aspx; downloaded March 27, 2015.

60. Lin Grensing-Pophal, "Functional feedback: Working with performance-challenged employees," May 17, 2011, http://www.shrm.org/india/hr-topics-and-strategy/performance-management/managing-poor-performance-including-exits/pages/functional%20feedback_%20working%20with%20performance-challenged%20employees.aspx; downloaded March 27, 2015.

61. Hugh Secord, "Performance Improvement Plan Guidelines," *Canadian Labour Relations and Employment Law Topics,* March 2008, http://www.cch.ca/newsletters/Business/March2008/Article2.htm; downloaded March 27, 2015.

62. James D. Grant and Terry H. Wagar, "Dismissal for Incompetence: An Analysis of the Factors Used by Canadian Courts in Determining Just Cause of Termination,"

in Natalie Lam, ed., *Proceedings of the Administrative Science Association of Canada, Personnel and Human Resource Division,* 1991, pp. 1–10.

63. Robert Olson, "Terminating a worker for poor performance," *Canadian HR Reporter,* Vol. 24, November, 2011, p. 19.

CHAPTER 9

1. Lance A. Berger and Dorothy R. Berger, eds., *Handbook of Wage and Salary Administration,* 4th ed., New York: McGraw-Hill, 2000, p. xiii.

2. Michael Kavanagh, "In Search of Motivation," in T. T. Herbert, *Organizational Behavior: Readings and Cases,* New York: Macmillan, 1976.

3. James F. Reda, *Compensation Committee Handbook,* Mississauga, ON: John Wiley and Sons Canada, Ltd., December 2001; see also Rabindra Kanungo and Manuel Mendonca, *Compensation–Effective Reward Management,* Mississauga, ON: John Wiley and Sons Canada, Ltd., 1997, pp. 264–265.

4. Rabindra Kanungo and Manuel Mendonca, *Compensation–Effective Reward Management,* Mississauga, ON: John Wiley and Sons Canada, Ltd., 1997, p. 257.

5. The least squares method is explained in any introductory statistics book.

6. See Gwyn Morgan, "Rising to the challenge of Canada's skills shortage," *The Globe and Mail,* April 6, 2014, for an overview of current skill shortages.

7. Employment and Social Development Canada, "Current and Forthcoming Minimum Hourly Wage Rates for Experienced Adult Workers in Canada," http://srv116.services.gc.ca/dimt-wid/sm-mw/rpt1.aspx?lang=eng; downloaded February 15, 2015.

8. Employment and Social Development Canada, "The Procurement Process," https://buyandsell.gc.ca/for-businesses/selling-to-the-government-of-canada/the-procurement-process; downloaded February 15, 2015.

9. Marc Law, "The Economics of Minimum Wage Laws," Vancouver: The Fraser Institute, February 9, 1999. As a counterpoint, see Morley Gunderson, "Minimum Wages: Issues And Options For Ontario," from http://www.fin.gov.on.ca/en/publications/2007/Gunderson/; downloaded February 15, 2015.

10. Arthur Macewan, "The Minimum Wage and Inflation," *Dollars and Sense,* July/August 2014, http://dollarsandsense.org/archives/2014/0714macewan.html; downloaded February 15, 2015.

11. Emanuela Heyninck, "Women's Day in Canada: Much to celebrate, much more work to do" *The Globe and Mail,* March 8, 2014.

12. "Equal Pay For Equal Work? A Look At The Wage Gap Between Men And Women In The U.S. And Canada," CBC, February 15, 2013, http://www.cbc.ca/strombo/news/equal-pay-for-equal-work-a-look-at-the-wage-gap-between-men-and-women-in-va; downloaded February 16, 2014; see also Marina Adshade, "Do women choose lower pay? (The gender wage gap explained)," *Canadian Business,* January 22, 2013,

http://www.canadianbusiness.com/blogs-and -comment/gender-wage-gap/; downloaded February 16, 2014.

13. C. C. Hoffmann and K. P. Hoffmann, "Does Comparable Worth Obscure the Real Issues?" *Personnel Journal*, Vol. 66, No. 1, January 1987, pp. 82–95.

14. "Equal Pay for Male and Female Employees Who Are Performing Work of Equal Value," interpretation guide for Section 11 of the *Canadian Human Rights Act*, Ottawa: Canadian Human Rights Commission, undated.

15. Ibid.

16. Edward Lazear, "Performance Pay and Productivity," *American Economic Review*, 2000, Vol. 90, No. 5, pp. 1346–1361.

17. David Brown, "Pay for Performance Better for Executives, Companies," *Canadian HR Reporter*, March 25, 2002; see also Ray Murrill, "Stock Options Still the Preferred Incentive," *Canadian HR Reporter*, June 21, 2005.

18. Edward E. Lawler, *Rewarding Excellence: Pay Strategies for the New Economy*, San Francisco: Jossey-Bass, February 2008.

19. Steve Ginsberg, "Team Pay Rewards the Players Behind the Superstars," *San Francisco Business Times*, August 15, 1997.

20. David E. Tyson, *Profit Sharing in Canada*, Toronto: John Wiley and Sons, 1996; see also John N. Reynolds, *Sharing Profits: The Ethics of Remuneration, Taxes and Shareholder Return*, New York: Palgrave Macmillan, 2014.

21. Brad Cherniak , "How to share profits with your staff without running into problems," *Financial Post*, October 15, 2013; see also Hermann F. Schwind, "Do Profit Sharing Plans Motivate Employees?" *Profit sharing in Canada*, Vol. 1, No. 1, Autumn 1996, pp. 6–7.

22. Hermann F. Schwind, "Do Profit Sharing Plans Motivate Employees?" *Profit sharing in Canada*, Vol. 1, No. 1, Autumn 1996, pp. 6–7; see also Michel Magnan and Sylvie St-Onge, "The Impact of Profit-Sharing on the Performance of Financial Services Firms," *Journal of Management Studies*, Vol. 42, No. 4, June 2005, pp. 761–791; Michel Magnan, Sylvie St-Onge, and Denis Cormier, "The Adoption and Success of Profit-Sharing Plans in Strategic Business Units: Opportunism or Contingency?" *International Journal of Productivity and Performance Management*, Vol. 54, No. 5/6, 2005, pp. 355–369.

23. Kate Robertson "Leave your company in good hands," *The Globe and Mail*, November 23, 2010.

24. Sharon Lebrun, "ESOP Saves the Day," *Canadian HR Reporter*, November 1997, pp. 1–2.

25. ESOP Builders Inc., "An Information Circular on a Workplace Option for the New Economy–Employee Share Ownership Plans," 2001, www.esopbuilders.com/media .html; downloaded February 13, 2015.

26. The National Center for Employee Ownership, "Employee Ownership and Corporate Performance," Research Report, April 2006, www.nceo.org/library/corpperf .html, downloaded September 5, 2006;

see also Sylvie St-Onge, Michel Magnan, Sophie Raymond, and Linda Thorne, "The Effectiveness of Stock Option Plans: A Field Investigation of Senior Executives," *Journal of Management Inquiry*, Vol. 10, No. 3, 2001, pp. 250–266; Stephane Renaud, Sylvie St-Onge, and Michel Magnan, "The Impact of Stock Purchase Plan Participation on Workers' Individual Cash Compensation," *Industrial Relations (Berkeley)*, Vol. 43, No. 1, 2004, pp. 120–147; see also: http://www. profitguide.com/manage-grow/human -resources/employee-ownership-smarter -ways-to-share-30176; downloaded February 19, 2015.

27. Janet McFarland, "How to Build a Better Option Plan," *The Globe and Mail*, November 20, 2002, p. B2. See also Gordon Pitts, "Calian Head Keen on Good Governance," *The Globe and Mail*, November 18, 2002, p. B3; Ray Murrill, "Stock Options Still the Preferred Incentive," *Canadian HR Reporter*, June 20, 2005, pp. 12–13; Marjo Johne, "When employees have skin in the game," *The Globe and Mail*, March 22, 2012, p. B16.

28. Carl F. Frost, John H. Wakeley, and Robert A. Ruh, *The Scanlon Plan for Organizational Development*, Ann Arbor, MI: University of Michigan Press, 2000. For more information about Scanlon plans, see www.scanlonleader .org.

29. Sherry Ryan, "Rewards and Recognition," Allison Rossett's home page, EdWeb, http:// edweb.sdsu.edu/people/ARossett /pie/Interventions/incentivesrewards_2.htm; downloaded February 19, 2014.

30. "Tossing the Coin—Pay Secrecy," ManageMentor website, www .themanagementor.com/enlightenmentorareas /hr/rr/tossingthecoin.htm; downloaded February 19, 2015.

31. Edward E. Lawler, *Rewarding Excellence: Pay Strategies for the New Economy*, San Francisco: Jossey-Bass, February 2008.

32. NCR home page, www.ncr.com; November 2002; see also "NCR Canada Recognized for Workplace Health," *The Mississauga News*, September 22, 2002.

33. Bruce Little, "How to Make a Small, Smart Factory," *The Globe and Mail*, February 2, 1993, p. B24; see also "Shell upgrades Brockville lubricants plant," http://www .trucknews.com/features/shell-upgrades -brockville-lubricants-plant/; downloaded February 19, 2015.

34. Edward E. Lawler, *Rewarding Excellence: Pay Strategies for the New Economy*, San Francisco: Jossey-Bass, February 2008.

35. Ibid.

36. Ibid.

37. Hewitt Associates, "Effective Compensation Programs Involve More than Base Salary, According to Hewitt Survey," September 24, 2008, Hewitt Associates, www .hewittassociates.com/Intl/NA/en-CA /AboutHewitt/Newsroom/PressReleaseDetail .aspx?cid=5606, downloaded October 1, 2009; see also Ken Abosch, Marilu Malague, "Getting it Right—Paying for Performance Through Variable Pay,"

www.aon.com/attachments/thought -leadership/GettingItRight.pdf, downloaded March 12, 2015; see also Stephen Miller, "Variable Pay Spending Spikes to Record High," SHRM, http://www.shrm.org /hrdisciplines/compensation/articles/pages /variable-pay-high.aspx#sthash.v4hVxvgr .dpuf; downloaded March 12, 2015.

38. "Managing Total Rewards Across the EMEA Region - Can One Size Fit All?" Towers Watson, November 2012, http://www .towerswatson.com/en-za/insights/ic-types /survey-research-results/2012/11/managing -total-rewards-across-the-emea-region-can -one-size-fit-all, downloaded February 21, 2015.

39. Edwin W. Arnold, Clyde J. Scott, "Does Broad Banding Improve Pay System Effectiveness?" *Southern Business Review*, Vol. 27, No. 2 , Spring 2002.

40. Elizabeth Church, "Nortel Workers Pick Tailor-Made Perks," *The Globe and Mail*, December 8, 2000, p. B11.

41. Hideo Inohara, *Human Resource Development in Japanese Companies*, 2nd ed., Tokyo: Asian Productivity Organization, 1998.

42. Nancy Adler, Allison Gundersen, *International Dimensions of Organizational Behavior*, Cengage Learning, June 29, 2007.

43. Richard Long, *Strategic Compensation in Canada*, 5th Edition, Nelson Publishing, Toronto, 2014.

44. Alan S. Binder, *Paying for Productivity: A Look at the Evidence*, Washington, DC: Brookings Institution, 1998.

45. David Hume, *Reward Management: Employee Performance, Motivation and Pay*, Oxford: Blackwell Publishers, November 1995.

46. Ibid.

47. Edward E. Lawler, *Rewarding Excellence: Pay Strategies for the New Economy*, San Francisco: Jossey-Bass, February 2008.

48. Ibid.

49. Allan M. Maslow and Gene Swimmer, *Wage Controls in Canada, 1975–78: A Study of Public Decision Making*, Toronto: Institute for Research on Public Policy, 1982.

CHAPTER 10

1. Bill Megalli, "The Fringe Benefit Debate," *The Labour Gazette*, July 1978, p. 313.

2. William M. Mercer, "2005/2006– Canada–Corporate Boards 2005/2006: Insights into Director Compensation," www.mercerhr.com/summary .jhtml?idContent=1210475&originUrl =/home.jhtml, downloaded April 2006.

3. Health Insurance Coverage in the U.S., Wikipedia, http://en.wikipedia.org/wiki /Health_insurance_in_the_United_States; downloaded February 24, 2015.

4. "36th Annual Canadian Salary Survey," Toronto: Watson Wyatt Consulting, 2005, www.watsonwyatt.com/canada-english /research/anss36/default.asp; downloaded September 5, 2006.

5. Office of the Superintendent of Financial Institutions, "Registered Pension Plan (RPP)

and Retirement Savings Coverage (Canada)," http://www.osfi-bsif.gc.ca/eng/oca-bac /fs-fr/pages/fs_rpp_2013.aspx; downloaded February 24, 2015.

6. William M. Mercer, "2005/2006–Canada–Corporate Boards 2005/2006: Insights into Director Compensation," www.mercerhr.com/summary .jhtml?idContent=1210475&originUrl =/home.jhtml, downloaded April 2006.

7. William M. Mercer, "Reducing Costs, Improving Productivity," www.mercerhr.com /summary.jhtml?idContent=1089885.

8. Human Resources and Social Development Canada, "Vacations and Statutory Holidays," April 2006, www.sdc.gc.ca/en/lp/spila/wlb /wfp/ 18Vacations_and_Statutory_Holidays .shtml, downloaded September 5, 2006; Canadian Heritage, "Public Holidays and Other Important Dates," www.pch.gc.ca/progs /cpsc-ccsp/jfa-ha/index_e.cfm; downloaded September 5, 2006.

9. Barb Jaworski, "Employee Assistance: I'll Have My People Call Your People," *Canadian HR Reporter,* March 27, 2006, p. 13; see also Susan Pinker, "SOS? Call your EAP," *The Globe and Mail,* December 11, 2002.

10. Personal communication with Sheila Hagen-Bloxham, Western Regional Coordinator of CN EAPs.

11. Runzheimer International, Family Assistance Programs for Transferees, "Runzheimer Reports on Relocation," Vol. 23, No. 1, June 2004, www.runzheimer.com/web /publications/RRR/ RRR-2004-06.pdf; downloaded September 6, 2006.

12. Scott Ion, "Are You Ready for Online EAP Services?" *Canadian HR Reporter,* May 3, 1999, pp. 17–19; see also Ceridian Corporation, "First-Ever Study Finds Employees Highly Motivated to Use Online EAP and Work Life Services," press release, March 7, 2002, www.ceridian.com/corp /printer/friendly/1,2878,10963-52769,00. html; downloaded September 6, 2006.

13. Jon J. Meyer, "The Future of Flexible Benefit Plans," *Employee Benefits Journal,* June 2000, pp. 3–7; see also Gaelyn Mitchell, "E-Benefits: Taking It Online," *Employee Benefits Journal,* June 2000, pp. 42–44; "What's in the Future for Employee Benefits?" *Workforce,* May 2000, www .findarticles.com/p/articles/mi_m0FXS /is_5_79/ai_62792459, downloaded September 6, 2006; Manulife of Canada, "Predicting the Future of Your Benefits Plan," http://groupbenefits.manulife.com/canada /GB_V2. nsf/LookupFiles /EBNQ106Predictingthefuture/$File/ predictingfuture_Q106.htm, downloaded April 2006; Barb Jaworski, "Employee Assistance: I'll Have My People Call Your People," *Canadian HR Reporter,* March 27, 2006, p. 13.

14. Jill Elswick, "Never Enough Fluff," *Employee Benefit News,* May 2000, www .benefitnews.com/subscriber/00_05/feature2 .html, downloaded September 6, 2006; see also Jill Elswick, "Green Without Envy," *Employee Benefit News,* June 15, 2002,

www.benefitnews.com/subscriber/Article .cfm?id=37880708, downloaded September 6, 2006.

15. Elswick, loc. cit.

16. "Royal Bank Gives Benefits to Part-Timers," *The Globe and Mail,* September 4, 1996.

17. Oliver Bertin, "Part-Time Work: Boon or Bust?" Workopolis.com, November 6, 2002, http://globeandmail.workopolis.com/servlet /Content/qprinter/20021106/CANJOBS, downloaded September 6, 2006.

18. William H. Holley, Jr. and Earl Ingram II, "Communicating Fringe Benefits," *Personnel Administrator,* March/April 1973, pp. 21–22; see also "3rd Annual Communications Awards," *Benefits Canada Magazine,* June 2000; Charles Benayon, "Lack of EAP Awareness–What's It Costing You?" *Canadian HR Reporter,* December 14, 1998, pp. 25–27; Jim Browning, "The EAP Conundrum: It Doesn't Pay to Cut Costs in Employee Communication," *Canadian HR Reporter,* May 3, 1999, pp. 18–19; Canada's DC Forum, "Employee Communication Linked to Financial Performance," *Benefits Canada,* March 2006, p. 5.

19. Watson Wyatt Consulting, 34th Annual Canadian Salary Survey.

20. "Flexible Benefit Plans Continue to Gain Momentum in Canada, Says Hewitt Associates," July 6, 2005, http://was4 .hewitt.com/hewitt/resource/newsroom /pressrel/2005/07-06-05eng.htm, downloaded April 2006.

21. Jon J. Meyer, "The Future of Flexible Benefit Plans," *Employee Benefits Journal,* June 2000, pp. 3–7.

22. Ibid.

23. Blue Cross Canada, www.bluecross.ca.

24. William M. Mercer, "2005/2006–Canada–Corporate Boards 2005/2006: Insights into Director Compensation," www.mercerhr .com/summary.jhtml?idContent=1210475& originUrl=/home.jhtml, downloaded April 2006.

25. Chrisy Wilson, "Benefits column: How to retain employees," *Benefits Canada,* September 26, 2014, http://www .benefitscanada.com/benefits/other/benefits -column-how-to-retain-employees-56197, downloaded March 1, 2015; see also Stephen Bruce, "Voluntary Benefits: Low Cost, High Reward!" *HR Daily Advisor,* http:// hrdailyadvisor.blr.com/2015/02/25/voluntary -benefits-low-cost-high-reward/#more-10002, downloaded February 25, 2015.

26. Craig Gunsauley, "Benefits Are Key to Successful Retention Strategies," *Employee Benefit News,* August 2000, www .benefitnews.com/subscriber/00_08/quality1. html, downloaded March 1, 2015.

27. Jody White, "Benefits 101," *Benefits Canada,* July 11, 2008, http://www .benefitscanada.com/news/benefits-101-2394, downloaded March 1, 2015.

28. Mark Swartz, "Why People Leave Their Jobs," Workforce Management, Monster, http://hiring.monster.ca/hr/hr-best-practices /workforce-management/employee-retention -strategies/why-people-leave-their-jobs-ca .aspx; downloaded March 1, 2015.

29. Deborah Cameron, "Design your benefits to drive behavior," *Benefits Canada,* http://www. benefitscanada.com/benefits/health -benefits/design-your-benefits-to-drive -behaviour-25492; downloaded March 1, 2015.

CHAPTER 11

1. American Management Association, "How to Build a High-Performance Organization," *AMA,* 1997, p. 1, www.amanet.org.

2. Paul Fairlie, "Five Must-Haves of Meaningful Work," *Canadian HR Reporter,* June 15, 2009.

3. Claude Balthazard, "Problem Managers: It Doesn't Take Many to Spoil the Bunch," *Canadian HR Professional,* January 17, 2011, p. 11.

4. What Drives Employee Commitment (and the Higher Productivity That Follows)," *HRFocus,* April 2000, p. 9.

5. Internet Use Boosts Productivity, Study Finds," *Times-Colonist* (Victoria), April 10, 2009, p. C12.

6. A Forbes, "Why Your Top Talent is Leaving in 2014, and What It'll Take to Retain Them," www.forbes.com, downloaded January 24, 2014.

7. "10 Tips for Communicating in Tough Times," *Canadian HR Reporter,* November 13, 2008.

8. "The High Flyers of Air Canada Impress the World," Canada's Top Employers 2015 Winners, *The Globe and Mail* and Mediacorp, 2014, p. 13.

9. Janice Tibbetts, "Fired on Facebook, Spa Worker Cries Foul as Controversy Rages," *Edmonton Journal,* January 5, 2009, p. A5.

10. "8 Uses of the Intranet for HR," Noodle: The Social Intranet, www.vialect.com, downloaded September 12, 2012.

11. Martha I. Finney, "Harness the Power Within," *IIR Magazine,* January 1997, pp. 66–74.

12. Samuel Greengard, "12 Ways to Use an Intranet," *Workforce,* March 1997, p. 94.

13. Janice MacLellan, "Electronic Solutions a Greener Option," *Canadian HR Reporter,* April 20, 2009.

14. Andrew McIlvaine, "Encouraging Repeat Self-Service Use," www.workindex.com; downloaded August 2004.

15. Frank Jossi, "High Tech Enables Employees," *HR Magazine,* Vol. 51, No. 2, February 1, 2006, www.dors.state.md.us/NR /rdonlyres/96523EAE-E2F6-466C-B938 -8DF2FE8400BA/0/HRM Magazine.pdf; see also "Types of Assistive Technology Products," www.microsoft.com.

16. "How to Protect Your Company from Misuse of Electronic Communications," *HRFocus,* April 2000, p.7.

17. "Fear of Losing Jobs Has Workers Avoiding Facebook, IM and Texting at Work," *National Post,* May 27, 2009, p. FP12; see also Laura McMullen, "8 Ways to Destroy Workplace Distractions," U.S. News, www.money.usnews.com, downloaded October 1, 2014.

18. Wallace Immen, "Tweet at Work, Your Boss May Thank You," *The Globe and Mail,* June 3, 2009, p. B14.

19. CBC News, "Internet Use by Canadians Highest in World, comScore Says," www.cbc.ca, downloaded March 27, 2015.

20. Annie Massey, "Blogging Phobia Hits Employers," *Canadian HR Reporter,* September 26, 2005, pp. 15, 17.

21. See www.corporateblogging.info.

22. Anthonia Akitunde, "Employees Gone Wild: 8 Reasons You Need a Social Media Policy Today," www.openforum.com, downloaded August 15, 2013.

23. "Social Media Training Needs Boost," *Canadian HR Reporter,* December 19, 2011, p. 4.

24. "Dangers Lurking in Mobile Devices," *Canadian HR Reporter,* November 7, 2011, pp. 19, 25.

25. Shannon Klie, "Employers Wary of Social Media," *Canadian HR Reporter,* July 12, 2010, pp. 14–15.

26. "Facebook for Pleasure, Not Business," *Canadian HR Reporter,* September 9, 2013, p. 2.

27. BMO, "Use of Social Media among Canada's Small Business Owners Up 42% from 2012," October 25, 2013, www.newsroom.bmo.com.

28. Liz Bernier, "Held Hostage," *Canadian HR Reporter,* December 15, 2014, pp. 1, 8.

29. Amy Gesenhues, "Survey: 71% of Companies Concerned Over Social Media Risks, But Only 36% Provide Employee Training," Marketing Land, www.marketingland.com, downloaded September 27, 2013.

30. Harvey Schachter, "Why You Need a Chief Reputation Officer," *The Globe and Mail,* January 5, 2015, p. B6.

31. Carolyn Buccongello, "Technology Presents Challenges, Opportunities," *Canadian HR Reporter,* September 23, 2013, pp. 14, 18.

32. "How is HR Using Social Media?" *Canadian HR Reporter,* November 21, 2011, p. 15.

33. Amanda Silliker, "Tread Carefully with Social Media Checks," *Canadian HR Reporter,* January 30, 2012, pp. 1, 11.

34. Statistics Canada, *Workplace and Employee Survey Compendium,* Ottawa: Statistics Canada, 2005.

35. Graham Lowe, "Want to Reach Staff? Tell Them a Story," *Canadian HR Reporter,* September 12, 2005, pp. 16, 20.

36. See Claudine Kapel and Maggie Thompson, "Effective Communications Link Employees to Business and Customers," *Canadian HR Reporter,* January 17, 2005, p. 12.

37. Liz Bernier, "Before You Hit Send," *Canadian HR Reporter,* June 2, 2014, pp. 1, 8.

38. Vita Lobo, "Dealing with the Social Media Monster," *Canadian HR Reporter,* June 6, 2009.

39. For more information on privacy issues see Thomas Keenan, *Technocreep,* Greystone, 2014.

40. Eddie Evans, "New Age Makes Serfs of Us All: Numerati Track Our Every Move," *Windsor Star,* September 15, 2008, p. B6.

41. Bruce Erskine, "CIBC Emails Will Be Used as Evidence at Trial," *Chronicle Herald,* February 7, 2012, p. C6.

42. Wayne Brookbank and David Ulrich, *Competencies for the New HR,* Ann Arbor,

MI: University of Michigan Business School, 2003.

43. A detailed examination of the use of HR technology is found in "Guide to HR Technology," supplement to *Canadian HR Reporter,* October 22, 2001.

44. David McIninch, "Managing HR in the Cloud," *Canadian HR Reporter,* September 9, 2013, pp. 21, 22.

45. Liz Bernier, "5 Areas Where Social Media Shines," *Canadian HR Reporter,* January 27, 2014, pp. 12, 14.

46. Jess Sloss, "New Tools, New Rules," *Canadian HR Reporter,* November 3, 2014, p. 15.

47. Shari Caudron, "Blow the Whistle on Employment Disputes," *Workforce,* May 1997, pp. 50–57; see also William Roche, Paul Teague, and Alexander Colvin, *The Oxford Handbook of Conflict Management in Organizations,* Oxford University Press, 2015.

48. See Peter Feuille and Denise R. Chachere, "Looking Fair or Being Fair: Remedial Voice Procedures in Nonunion Workplaces," *Journal of Management,* Vol. 21, 1995, pp. 27–42; and Alexander Colvin, "An Empirical Study of Employment Arbitration: Case Outcomes and Processes," *Journal of Legal Empirical Studies,* Vol. 8, 2011, pp. 1–23.

49. Terry H. Wagar, "Grievance Procedures in the Non-Union Environment," *Labour Arbitration Yearbook,* 2001, pp. 127–136; see also Alexander Colvin, "The Relationship Between Employee Involvement and Workplace Dispute Resolution," *Relations Industrielles,* Vol. 59, 2004, pp. 681–702.

50. These are just some of the issues discussed in Peter Feuille and Denise R. Chachere, "Looking Fair or Being Fair: Remedial Voice Procedures in Nonunion Workplaces," *Journal of Management,* Vol. 21, 1995, pp. 27–42.

51. Tim Mitchell, "Is This Thing On?" *Canadian HR Reporter,* September 8, 2014, p. 27.

52. Phillip Marksberry, Joshua Church, and Michael Schmidt, "The Employee Suggestion System: A New Approach Using Latent Semantic Analysis," *Human Factors and Ergonomics in Manufacturing and Service Industries,* Vol. 24, 2014, pp. 29–39.

53. See "Employee Engagement," *Canadian HR Reporter,* September 12, 2005, pp. 7–8. For further details, see www.fedex.com/ma/about/overview/philisophy.html. See also Jeff Cattel, "FedEx: A Pioneer in Developing, Measuring Employee Culture," Corporate Learning Network, www.corporatelearningnetwork.com, downloaded October 24, 2013.

54. Barb Veder, "If You Build It, They Will Come," *Canadian HR Reporter,* August 12, 2013, p. 16.

55. "Downloading of Child Porn Still a Workplace Problem," *The Globe and Mail,* July 22, 2005, p. C1.

56. Yosie Saint-Cyr, "Employers Obligated to Report Child Porn Found on Their Computer Systems," www.slaw.ca.

57. Howard A. Levitt, *The Law of Dismissal in Canada,* 3rd ed., Aurora, ON: Canada Law Book, 2009.

58. Paul Falcone, "The Fundamentals of Progressive Discipline," *HR Magazine,* February 1997, pp. 90–94.

59. Amanda Silliker, "HR, Lawyers Working Hand-in-Hand," *Canadian HR Reporter,* June 17, 2013, pp. 1, 8.

60. This material is based largely on the video *Discipline without Punishment (Revised),* which was released in 1996 by Owen Stewart Performance Resources. Also see Tom Watson, "Discipline Without Punishment: A Best Practices Approach to Disciplining Employees," www.watson-training.com, downloaded April 15, 2014.

61. "CEOs Talk," *Canadian HR Reporter,* December 6, 2004, p. 10.

62. Howard A. Levitt, *The Law of Dismissal in Canada,* 3rd ed., Aurora, ON: Canada Law Book, 2009.

63. *Wallace v. United Grain Growers Ltd.,* Supreme Court of Canada, October 30, 1997; see also Potter v. New Brunswick Legal Aid Services Commission, March 6, 2015.

64. Terry H. Wagar, "Wrongful Dismissal: Perception vs. Reality," *Human Resources Professional,* June 1996, pp. 8, 10.

65. See Stuart Rudner, "Just Cause—Back From the Dead," *Canadian HR Reporter,* September 22, 2008; Natalie MacDonald, "Progressing Toward Just Cause," *Canadian HR Reporter,* September 22, 2008; Kathryn Filsinger, *Employment Law for Business and Human Resources Professionals,* Toronto: Emond Montgomery, 2010.

66. David Jackson, "6 Months' Severance for 8 Months Work," *Chronicle Herald* (Halifax), March 15, 2006, pp. 1, 2.

67. Jennifer Brown, "Federally Regulated Employers Can Dismiss Without Cause: Court," *Canadian HR Reporter,* February 23, 2015, pp. 1, 6.

68. Howard Levitt, "Promise of Job for Life Proves Costly for Employer," *Times-Colonist* (Victoria), March 18, 2009, p. B7.

69. Sarah Dobson, "Employees Behaving Badly," *Canadian HR Reporter,* January 16, 2012, pp. 1, 8.

70. "Possibility of Internal Sabotage Alarming," *Canadian HR Reporter,* August 15, 2011, p. 4.

71. For more information on just cause see Randall Scott and Matthew L.O. Certosimo, *Just Cause: The Law of Summary Dismissal in Canada,* Aurora, ON: Canada Law Book, 2002; and Howard A. Levitt, *The Law of Dismissal in Canada,* 3rd ed., Aurora, ON: Canada Law Book, 2009.

72. ClearView Strategic Partners, "Theft, Abuse and Cooking the Books: 42% of Canadians Admit Witnessing Misconduct at Work," www.clearviewpartners.com., downloaded July 3, 2013.

73. Howard A. Levitt, *The Law of Dismissal in Canada,* 3rd ed., Aurora, ON: Canada Law Book, 2009.

74. Jeffrey Smith, "Opportunity Knocks but Employee Does Not Answer," *Canadian HR Reporter,* January 30, 2012, pp. 5, 8.

75. Sharah Sultan, "Keeping the Good Faith: The Supreme Court Clarifies Constructive Dismissal and Emphasizes Honesty, Candidness and Communication," Ontario Bar Association, www.oba.org, downloaded March 23, 2015.

76. Peter Straszynski, "Proving Just Cause Just Not Enough," *Canadian HR Reporter,* June 20, 2011, p. 10.

77. An excellent source of information on reasonable notice awards is John Sproat, *Wrongful Dismissal Handbook,* 6th ed., Toronto: Carswell, 2012; see also Howard Levitt, "Four Factors Drive Severance Packages," *Telegraph-Journal* (Saint John), March 7, 2009, p. E7; and MacLeod Law Firm, "Wrongful Dismissal Update: What is Reasonable Notice of Termination," www.macleodlaw.ca, downloaded January 8, 2013.

78. Malcolm MacKillop, Hendrik Nieuland, and Meighan Ferris-Miles, *Employment Law Solutions,* Markham, Ontario: LexisNexis, 2010.

79. Jeffrey Smith, "6-Month Notice of Resignation Upheld for BlackBerry Executive Keen to Join Apple," *Canadian HR Reporter,* May 19, 2014, p. 5.

80. Sarah Dobson, "Target Bows Out," *Canadian HR Reporter,* February 9, 2015, pp. 1, 2.

81. Ron Minken, "$20 Million Award Upheld by Appeal Court," *Canadian HR Reporter,* March 26, 2012, p. 5.

82. Stuart Rudner, "Just Cause—Back from the Dead," *Canadian HR Reporter,* September 22, 2008.

83. More detail on these points is provided in Jeffrey Connor, "Disarming Terminated Employees," *HR Magazine,* January 2000, pp. 113–116; see also David Bell, "No Easy Way to Say You're Fired," *Canadian HR Reporter,* June 15, 2009; Donna Nebenzahl, "Ethics of Dismissal: Boss Must Do It in Person and with Privacy," *The Province* (Vancouver), May 31, 2009, p. A39.

84. Tim Mitchell, "A Look at the Various Pitfalls of Specifying Notice Periods in Contract," *Canadian HR Reporter,* October 6, 2014, p. 15.

85. Martin Jaekel and Linda Bilotta, "Tempering High Risk Terminations," *Canadian HR Reporter,* February 24, 2014, pp. 17, 20.

86. Jeff Gray, "Court Sides with Globe in Dispute Over Settlement," *The Globe and Mail,* November 4, 2014, p. B2.

87. Estanislao Oziewicz, "Would Chip Implant Get Under Your Skin?" *The Globe and Mail,* February 14, 2006, p. A14.

88. Shannon Klie, "Employees More Litigious: Survey," *Canadian HR Reporter,* November 19, 2010, pp. 10–11.

89. Jen St. Denis, "Saanich Monitoring Software Was Violation of Employees' Privacy Rights: Privacy Watchdog," *Business Vancouver,* www.biv.com, downloaded March 30, 2015.

90. Leah Eichler, "What You Do After Hours Matters, Too," *The Globe and Mail,* November 1, 2014, p. B17.

91. "Privacy Commissioner: Health Canada Violated Privacy Laws by Disclosing Personal Health Information of Over 40,000 Canadians," Canadian Privacy Law Blog, www.blog.privacylawyer.ca, downloaded March 16, 2015.

92. Danielle Harder, "Court Ruling Opens Doors to Privacy Lawsuits," *Canadian HR Reporter, February 27, 2012, pp. 1–2.*

93. Daniel Therrien, "In Business, Privacy Is Money," *Chronicle Herald,* January 29, 2015, p. A11.

94. "Gender Differences in Social Media," *Canadian HR Reporter,* February 14, 2011, p. 4.

95. Todd Humber, "Here's the Memo on Facebook–Again," *Canadian HR Reporter,* March 14, 2011, p. 18; see also "Some US Employers Asking for Applicants' Facebook Login Info," *Chronicle Herald,* March 21, 2012, p. C6; David Doorey, "Ontario Human Rights Commission Issues Statement on Employer Requests for Facebook Passwords," The Law of Work, www.lawofwork.ca, downloaded March 16, 2015.

96. See American Management Association, "2007 Electronic Monitoring and Surveillance Survey," 2008, www.amanet.org.

97. *R. v. Cole,* Supreme Court of Canada, October 19, 2012; *R v. Telus Communications,* Supreme Court of Canada, March 27, 2013; *R v. Vu,* Supreme Court of Canada, November 7, 2013.

98. Stuart Rudner and Natalie MacDonald, "The Law, Surveillance and Employee Privacy," *The Globe and Mail,* Monday, June 9, 2014.

99. See American Management Association, "2007 Electronic Monitoring and Surveillance Survey," 2008, www.amanet.org.

100. Howard Levitt, "Spy without Cause–and Pay Price," *Vancouver Sun,* January 24, 2009, p. H5.

101. See www.fightspam.gc.ca for more information; see also Brenda Bouw, "New Anti-spam Law 'A Big Deal' for Small Business," *The Globe and Mail,* March 24, 2014.

102. Sarah Dobson, "Hamilton Workers Caught in the Act," *Canadian HR Reporter,* February 25, 2013, pp. 1, 12.

103. Rick Shields, "Training Around Privacy," *Canadian HR Reporter,* May 5, 2014, p. 12.

104. Jeff Gray, "Ruling Could Make Random Alcohol Testing Tougher," *The Globe and Mail,* June 14, 2013.

105. "Employers Boost Morale," *Canadian HR Reporter,* February 24, 2009.

106. Sirota, "Companies Profit by Giving Employees What They Want," www.sirota.com, downloaded October 9, 2013.

107. Brian E. Becker, Mark A. Huselid, Peter S. Pickus, and Michael F. Spratt, "HR as a Source of Shareholder Value: Research and Recommendations," *Human Resource Management,* Spring 1997, pp. 39–47.

108. Sarah Dobson, "Engagement Drives Top Employers," *Canadian HR Reporter,* January 26, 2009.

109. Carol Dobson, "High Liner Foods Takes the High Road with Employees," *Chronicle Herald–Nova Scotia's Top Employers 2012,* November 19, 2011, p. 8.

110. Asha Tomlinson, "Loyalty Isn't Dead But It Does Need Some Critical Care," *Canadian HR Reporter,* November 5, 2001, p. 3. or more information on Fred Reichheld's work on loyalty, see www.loyaltyeffect.com.

111. A good review of this perspective is presented in Mike Parker and Jane Slaughter, "Management by Stress," *Technology Review,* October 1988, pp. 37–44; see also D. Mehri, "The Darker Side of Lean: An Insider's Perspective on the Realities of the Toyota Production System," *Academy of Management Perspectives,* Vol. 20, 2006, pp. 21–42.

112. Sarah Dobson, "Virtual Teams Expected to Grow: Survey," *Canadian HR Reporter,* October 10, 2011, p. 3.

113. Mark Huselid, "The Impact of Human Resource Management Practices on Turnover, Productivity, and Corporate Financial Performance," *Academy of Management Journal,* June 1995, pp. 635–672; see also Jeffrey Pfeffer, "Producing Sustainable Competitive Advantage Through the Effective Management of People," *Academy of Management Executive,* Vol. 19, 2005, pp. 95–108; Jonathan Michie and Maura Sheehan-Quinn, "Labour Market Flexibility, Human Resource Management and Corporate Performance," *British Journal of Management,* Vol. 12, 2001, pp. 2187–2306; Brian Becker and Mark Huselid, "Strategic Human Resources Management: Where Do We Go From Here?" *Journal of Management,* Vol. 32, 2006, pp. 898–925; Jake Messersmith, Pankaj Patel, and David Lepak, "Unlocking the Black Box: Exploring the Link Between High-Performance Work Systems and Performance," *Journal of Applied Psychology,* 2011, Vol. 96, pp. 1105–1118; Duckjung Shin and Alison Konrad, "Causality Between High-Performance Work Systems and Organizational Performance," *Journal of Management,* forthcoming.

114. AON, "AON Hewitt Research Reveals Steady Progression in Global Employee Engagement Levels," April 30, 2014, aon.mediaroom.com.

115. Brian E. Becker, Mark A. Huselid, Peter S. Pickus, and Michael F. Spratt, "HR as a Source of Shareholder Value: Research and Recommendations," *Human Resource Management,* Spring 1997, pp. 39–47.

116. Jeffrey Pfeffer and John Veiga, "Putting People First for Organizational Success," *Academy of Management Executive,* May 1999, p. 43.

117. David Link, "HR Self Service Applications Grow in Number and Depth," *Canadian HR Reporter,* August 11, 2003, pp. 9, 11

118. Denise Rousseau, "Changing the Deal While Keeping the People," *Academy of Management Executive,* Vol. 10, 1996, pp. 50–59.

119. B. O'Reilly, "The New Deal: What Companies and Employees Owe One Another," *Fortune,* June 13, 1994, p. 44.

120. "Tim Horton's Cuts 350 Office Staff," *The Globe and Mail,* January 30, 2015, p. B3;

"Target's Canadian Retreat: A 20-Million-Square-Foot-Hole," *The Globe and Mail,* January 16, 2015, pp. B1, B7; "Sony Shutters Canadian Stores," *The Globe and Mail,* January 16, 2015, p. B4; "Suncor Cuts Deep as Oil Plunges," *The Globe and Mail,* January 14, 2015, pp. B1, B7.

121. Steve W.J. Kozlowski, Georgia T. Chao, Eleanor M. Smith, and Jennifer Hedlund, "Organizational Downsizing: Strategies, Interventions, and Research Implications," in C.L. Cooper and I.T. Robertson, eds., *International Review of Industrial and Organizational Psychology,* Vol. 8, 1993, pp. 263–332.

122. Kim Cameron, "Strategies for Successful Organizational Downsizing," *Human Resource Management,* Summer 1994, p. 192.

123. Ibid.

124. Wayne Cascio, *Responsible Restructuring: Creative and Responsible Alternatives to Layoffs,* San Francisco: Berrett-Koehler, 2002.

125. "X Factor Firing Goes Viral as Employee Hijacks Twitter Account," *National Post,* January 31, 2013, news.nationalpost.com.

126. See, for instance, Robert D. Nixon, Michael A. Hitt, Ho-Uk Lee, and Eui Jeong, "Market Reactions to Announcements of Corporate Downsizing Actions and Implementation Strategies," *Strategic Management Journal,* Vol. 25, 2004, pp. 1121–1129; E. Geoffrey Love and Nitin Nohria, "Reducing Slack: The Performance Consequences of Downsizing by Large Industrial Firms," *Strategic Management Journal,* Vol. 26, 2005, pp. 1087–1108. A very good review of the literature is in Deepak Datta, James Guthrie, Dynah Basuil, and Alankrita Pandey, "Causes and Effects of Employee Downsizing: A Review and Synthesis," *Journal of Management,* Vol. 36, 2010, pp. 281–348.

127. Patricia Brooks Arenburg, "Shock of a Sudden Job Loss," *Chronicle Herald,* January 13, 2015, pp. B1, B4.

128. Andrew Duffy, "Forest Workers Lose Hope as Downturn Deepens; Log Loader No Longer Gives a Damn," *Times-Colonist* (Victoria), March 14, 2009, p. B1.

129. Kim Cameron, "Strategies for Successful Organizational Downsizing," *Human Resource Management,* Summer 1994, p. 192.

130. Kim Cameron, Sarah Freeman, and Anil Mishra, "Best Practices in White Collar Downsizing: Managing Contradictions," *Academy of Management Executive,* Vol. 5, 1991, pp. 57–73.

131. David Brown, "Take My Workers—Please," *Canadian HR Reporter,* February 11, 2002, p. 3.

132. See, for instance, Terry H. Wagar, "What Do We Know about Downsizing?" *Benefits and Pensions Monitor,* June 1996, pp. 19–20, 69.

133. Aneil Mishra, "Zappos Uses Social Networks for Announcing Downsizing," www.trustiseverything.com, downloaded January 17, 2009.

134. Liz Bernier, "Your Employer Brand in 140 Characters," *Canadian HR Reporter,* September 8, 2014, p. 11.

135. These issues are discussed in more detail in Mark Mone, "Relationships between Self-Concepts, Aspirations, Emotional Responses, and Intent to Leave a Downsizing Organization," *Human Resource Management,* Summer 1994, pp. 281–298.

136. Barry Wright and Julian Barling, "The Executioners' Song: Listening to Downsizers Reflect on their Experiences," *Canadian Journal of Administrative Sciences,* December 1998, pp. 339–355; see also J. Clair and R. Dufresne, "Playing the Grim Reaper: How Employees Experience Carrying Out a Downsizing," *Human Relations,* Vol. 57, 2004, pp. 1597–1625.

137. "What's the Top HR Challenge?" *Canadian HR Reporter,* March 12, 2012, p. 4.

138. This is discussed in more detail in Frederick F. Reichheld, *The Loyalty Effect,* Boston: Harvard Business School Press, 1996.

139. "Many Workers Plan to Switch Careers in 5 Years," *Canadian HR Reporter,* September 12, 2011, p. 4.

140. Virginia Galt, "Shock: The Number 1 Reason People Leave Their Jobs," *The Globe and Mail,* September 10, 2005, p. B10.

141. Bank of Montreal, "Annual BMO Labour Day Survey: How Are Canadian Businesses Retaining Talented Employees?" www.newsroom.bmo.com, downloaded August 28, 2014.

142. Chad Brooks, "10 Signs Your Employee is Ready to Quit," *Business News Daily,* www.businessnewsdaily, downloaded February 21, 2014.

143. Len Karakowsky and Igor Kotlyar, "Think You Know Your High Performers?" *Canadian HR Reporter,* December 5, 2011, p. 23.

144. Charlene M. Solomon, "Keep Them! Don't Let Your Best People Get Away," *Workforce,* August 1997, pp. 46–51.

145. See, for example, Rosemary Batt, "Managing Customer Services: Human Resource Practices, Quit Rates, and Sales Growth," *Academy of Management Journal,* Vol. 45, 2002, pp. 587–597; Lisa Hughes, "The Effects of Human Resource Management and Union Member Status on Employees' Intentions to Quit," Queen's University Industrial Relations Centre Research Program, January 2006.

CHAPTER 12

1. Julian Barling and Michael Frone (Eds.), *The Psychology of Workplace Safety,* Washington: APA, 2004, p. 4.

2. Michael Gorman, "Westray Miner: Workplace Safety Still Lags," *Chronicle Herald,* May 9, 2011, p. A3; see also Michael Gorman, "Westray Legacy: Better Safety, In Theory," *Chronicle Herald,* May 9, 2012, p. A3.

3. F. E. Bird, Jr., *Management Guide to Loss Control,* Atlanta, GA: Institute Press, 1974.

4. Ibid.

5. E. Kevin Kelloway, Lori Francis, and James Montgomery, *Management of Occupational Health and Safety,* 3rd ed., Toronto: Nelson, 2006.

6. "Charges Laid in Workplace Accident," *Calgary Herald,* November 13, 2008, p. B5.

7. "Worker, 19, Dies in Accident at Kanata Construction Site," *Ottawa Citizen,* March 19, 2009, p. C2.

8. David Schwartz, "Workplace Safety by the Numbers," www.cbc.ca, April 28, 2014; see also Human Resources and Social Development Canada, Occupational Injuries and Diseases in Canada: 1996–2008, Ottawa, ON: Government of Canada, 2010.

9. Joyce Grant, "Inquest Reports on Kids At Work Tragedy," *Canadian HR Reporter,* June 18, 2001, p. 13.

10. Tavia Grant, "Asbestos Top Source of Workplace Deaths in Canada," *The Globe and Mail,* December 5, 2014, pp. A1, A6.

11. Human Resources and Development Canada, *Work Safely for a Healthy Future.*

12. See Association of Workers' Compensation Boards of Canada site, www.awcbc.org; "It Hurts Where?" *Canadian HR Reporter,* September 9, 2013, p. 4.

13. Paul Luke, "Safety Yields Bigger Returns," *The Province* (Vancouver), March 15, 2009, p. A28.

14. Kevin Kelloway and Lori Francis, *Management of Occupational Health and Safety,* 5th edition, Toronto: Nelson, 2010.

15. "Charges Filed in Farm Accident," *Canadian HR Reporter,* October 4, 2010, p. 3.

16. See also E. Kevin Kelloway, Lori Francis, and James Montgomery, *Management of Occupational Health and Safety,* 3rd ed., Toronto: Nelson, 2006.

17. Les Perreaux, "For Letter Carriers, 'Tis the Season to Be Cautious," *The Globe and Mail,* December 24, 2010, p. A7.

18. See Jim Middlemiss, "Don't Panic, Prepare; Employers Have Obligation to Protect Workers," *National Post,* May 19, 2009, p. FP7; Sarah Dobson, "Employers Prepare for Worst," *Canadian HR Reporter,* May 18, 2009.

19. Stephen Hume, "NHL Rinks Are an Unsafe Workplace," *Vancouver Sun,* April 5, 2012.

20. "Tim's Worker Hurt," *Chronicle Herald,* November 4, 2014, p. A7.

21. Jamie Hall, "Keeping Teenagers on the Job; Provincial Ad Campaign Emphasizes Workplace Safety," *Edmonton Journal,* November 1, 2008, p. A1.

22. For more information, see Justice Laws Website, "Canada Labour Code, Part II," www.laws-lois.justice.ca.

23. Health Canada, Workplace Hazardous Materials Information System, www.hc-sc.gc.ca.

24. Jessie Callaghan, "GHS Set to Replace WHMIS – Sort Of – In 2015," *Canadian HR Reporter,* October 21, 2013, p. 12.

25. More information on the Canadian Centre for Occupational Health and Safety is available from the Centre's website, www.ccohs.ca, and from their annual reports.

26. The websites for the various provincial governments are very informative.

27. For a full copy of the *Canada Labour Code*, see http://laws-lois.justice.gc.ca/eng /acts/L-2/.

28. "Syncrude Fined for Worker's Death," *Chronicle Herald*, February 22, 2011, p. E2.

29. "Some Canadian Facts on Workplace Safety," www.win.ualberta.ca; see also Sarah Dobson, "Alberta OHL Levying Cash Fines Against Employers, Workers," *Canadian HR Reporter*, October 21, 2013, p. 6.

30. Jennifer Henderson, "Parkland Construction Charged after Worker Alan Fraser's Death," www.cbc.ca, February 18, 2015.

31. Anna Aceto-Guerin, "What To Do When An OHS Inspector Shows Up," *Canadian HR Reporter*, March 11, 2013, p. 13.

32. Justine Hunter, "Safety Board Blamed for Lack of Prosecution in Deadly Blast," *The Globe and Mail*, April 15, 2014, pp. A1, A12.

33. David Jackson, "AG: Safety Process Lax," *Chronicle Herald*, November 21, 2013, pp. B1, B2.

34. Sherri Borden Colley, "HRM Must Pay Badly Burned Worker," *Chronicle Herald* (Halifax), June 21, 2005, p. B1.

35. Canada's Top 100 Employers 2015 Winners, *The Globe and Mail* and Mediacorp, 2014, pp. 14, 26.

36. See, for example, Ontario's Young Worker Awareness Program. More information about the program is available at www.yworker. com. In addition, the CANOSH website has links for all of the jurisdictions in Canada at www.canoshweb.org/en/young_workers.html.

37. Gabrielle Giroday, "Face Shields for Bus Drivers Sought," *Winnipeg Free Press*, May 6, 2009, p. B1.

38. Bill Pomfret, "Sound Employee Orientation Program Boosts Productivity and Safety," *Canadian HR Reporter*, January 25, 1999, pp. 17, 19.

39. See Institute for Work and Health site, www .iwh.on.ca; see also Patricia Brooks Arenburg, "Tough Haul of Shiftwork," *Chronicle Herald*, January 30, 2015, pp. B1, B2.

40. Liz Bernier, "Losing Sleep Over Losing Sleep," *Canadian HR Reporter*, April 21, 2014, pp. 1, 7.

41. Sandy Smith, "Stress, Fatigue and Reduced Productivity: The True Cost of Sleepless Workers," *EHS Today*, December 22, 2014, www.ehstoday.com.

42. See "Petro-Canada Fined After Worker Burned," *Times-Colonist* (Victoria), December 11, 2008, p. A7; Daryl Slade, "Shaw Fined $75K After Employee Burned," *Calgary Herald*, March 21, 2009, p. B2; "Truck Repair Firm Fined $120K After Worker Killed on Job," *Ottawa Citizen*, May 13, 2009, p. D4.

43. Lesley Young, "Are You Sure You've Got Health and Safety Covered?" *Canadian HR Reporter*, May 17, 1999, pp. 18–19.

44. "First Bill C-45 Conviction and Fine," *Daily Commercial News*, April 30, 2008.

45. Michelle McCann, "ONCA: $750,000 Fine Under Bill C-45," www.stewartmckelveyblogs. com, September 25, 2013.

46. "British Firm First to Be Charged with Corporate Manslaughter," *Canadian HR Reporter*, April 23, 2009; BBC News, 2011, http://www.bbc.co.uk/uk-england-gloucestershire-13367855, accessed August 10, 2012; see also, Owen Bowcott, "Corporate Manslaughter Fines Should Be Up To £20m, Says Sentencing Council," *The Guardian*, November 13, 2014.

47. Clare Grant, "SaskPower Head Quits After Study of Safety," *Chronicle Herald*, October 28, 2014, p. B6.

48. Ian Fairclough, "Firm Fined for Death," *Chronicle Herald* (Halifax), April 13, 2005, p. B5.

49. Uyen Vu, "Right to Refuse Dangerous Work Expands," *Canadian HR Reporter*, August 9, 2004, pp. 1, 2.

50. "High Rate of Non-compliance with Safety Protocols," *Canadian HR Reporter*, August 15, 2011, p. 4.

51. Sunny Dhillon, "Mine Workers Said To Have Reported Safety Worries In Months Before Spill," *The Globe and Mail*, August 9, 2014, p. A7.

52. Todd Humber, "Target: Zero Fatalities," *Canadian HR Reporter*, October 20, 2008.

53. Sarah Dobson, "Making Sure the Shoe—and Hard Hat—Fits," *Canadian HR Reporter*, October 10, 2011, pp. 20, 26.

54. Tim Cook, "Miners' Safety Training Paid Off," *Chronicle Herald* (Halifax), January 31, 2006, p. A3.

55. Johanna Faulk, "Conveying Safety Messages—In Any Language," *Canadian HR Reporter*, March 12, 2012, pp. 11, 18.

56. Amanda Silliker, "Will Your Staff Help if a Customer Falls Ill?" *Canadian HR Reporter*, April 8, 2013, pp. 1, 12.

57. Sarah Kenning, "Employee Safety in Global Hot Spots," *Canadian HR Reporter*, May 20, 2013, p. 16.

58. "Walmart to Pay $2 Million After Employee Trampled to Death," *Canadian HR Reporter*, May 14, 2009.

59. Jordan Robertson, "Firm Gives Kudos Despite Spill," *Chronicle Herald*, April 3, 2011, p. A8.

60. Liz Bernier, "Safety Training to be Mandatory in Ontario," *Canadian HR Reporter*, December 16, 2013, pp. 1, 6.

61. Daniel Black, "Due Diligence: Your Company's Best Defence Against an Occupational Health and Safety Offence," *Canadian HR Reporter*, May 31, 1999, pp. 17, 19.

62. Joyce Grant and David Brown, "The Inspector Cometh," *Canadian HR Reporter*, January 31, 2005, pp. 13, 17.

63. Andy Blatchford, "Safety Board Seeks Rail Accident Data," *Chronicle Herald*, October 28, 2014, p. B4.

64. "Occupational Health and Safety: Policy and Program Guide," Workers' Compensation Board of Nova Scotia, June 14, 2012, www .wcb.ns.ca//app/DocRepository/1/Prevention /Education/ohspolicy.pdf.

65. Rob Stewart, "The Challenge of Creating a Culture of Safety," *Canadian HR Reporter*, March 28, 2005, p. 11.

66. Andrew Neal and Mark Griffin, "Safety Climate and Safety at Work," in Julian Barling and Michael Frone (Eds.), *The Psychology of Workplace Safety*, Washington: APA, 2004, pp. 15–34.

67. Will Chabun, "Safety a State of Mind," *Leader Post* (Regina), May 11, 2009, p. D1. See also "Saskatchewan's Top Employers 2015," *Star Phoenix and Leader Post*, p. 11.

68. Scott Simpson, "Report Attacks CN's Approach to Safety," *Vancouver Sun*, May 31, 2008, p. A3; see also John Nicol and Dave Seglins, "CN Hiding Derailment, Falsifying Stats, Employees Allege," *CBC News*, October 24, 2013.

69. For an interesting review of the safety–job insecurity issue, see T. Probst, "Job Insecurity: Exploring a New Threat to Employee Safety," in Julian Barling and Michael Frone (Eds.), *The Psychology of Workplace Safety*, Washington: APA, 2004, pp. 63–80; see also Jennie McKelvey and Jim Colwick, "Leading Through Downsizing," *Occupational Health and Safety*, October 1, 2009, www.ohsonline.com.

70. Canadian Centre for Occupational Health and Safety, "Workplace Stress," April 28, 2000, www.ccohs.ca/oshanswers/psychosocial /stress.html.

71. ComPsych, 2014 StressPulse Survey, November 12, 2014, www.compsych.com.

72. Gillian Livingston, "Survey Says: We're Stressed and Can't Cope," *The Globe and Mail*, February 7, 2015, p. B17; see also www.tgam.ca/yourlifeatwork and Tavia Grant, "Working It Out," *The Globe and Mail*, February 2, 2015, p. L1, L6.

73. See "Managing Stress At Work: A How-to for Employers," Canadian Federation of Independent Business, www.cfib-fcei.ca.

74. International Labour Organization, *Encyclopaedia of Occupational Health and Safety*, 4th ed., Waldorf, MA: ILO. This volume can be accessed at www.ilo.org /encyclopaedia/.

75. "Mental Health Association Calling for Psychological Safety in Workplaces," *The Globe and Mail*, December 7, 2010, p. E7.

76. For more information and to download the National Standard see www .mentalhealthcommission.ca.

77. National Institute for Occupational Safety and Health, *Stress at Work*, Washington, DC: U.S. Department of Health and Human Services, 1999. This publication can be accessed at www .cdc.gov/niosh/stresswk.html.

78. Sarah Boesveld, "Exhaustion, Longer Hours, Heavier Workload, Greater Responsibility, Unbearable Stress Juggling," *The Globe and Mail*, March 2, 2009, p. L1.

79. Susan Crompton, "What's Stressing the Stressed? Main Sources of Stress Among Workers," *Canadian Social Trends*, Statistics Canada, www.statcan.gc.ca, October 13, 2011.

80. CareerCast, "The Most Stressful Jobs of 2015," www.careercast.com.

81. "Bad Bosses May Affect Health of Workers," *The Globe and Mail*, October 28, 2005, p. C2.

82. Doug Burn, "Parents' Job Anxiety Wreaks Havoc on Children," *Canadian HR Reporter*, December 29, 1997, pp. 16, 20.

References

83. Amanda Silliker, "Employers in Best Position to Fight Depression," *Canadian HR Reporter*, January 30, 2012, pp. 3, 8.

84. Helen Morris, "Study Finds High Levels of Stress at Call Centres," *Ottawa Citizen*, September 2, 2008, p. D8.

85. Employers Feeling the Pain of Poor Worker Health, But Concern Not Translating Into Action," news release, 2005 Watson Wyatt Staying@Work Survey, September 29, 2005, www.watsonwyatt.com/canada-english /news/press.asp?ID=15216.

86. Natalie C. MacDonald, "Paying for Pain," *Canadian HR Reporter*, April 19, 2004, pp. 17, 20.

87. David Pugliese, "Defence Procurement Staff Struggle with Burnout," *Ottawa Citizen*, November 23, 2014.

88. Barb Veder and Kelly Beaudoin, "Face-to-face – But Not in Person," *Canadian HR Reporter*, March 24, 2014, p. 20.

89. National Institute for Occupational Safety and Health, *Stress at Work*, Washington, DC: U.S. Department of Health and Human Services, 1999. This publication can be accessed at www.cdc.gov/niosh/stresswk.html.

90. Ibid.

91. Mental Health Commission of Canada, *Making the Case for Investing in Mental Health in Canada*, www .mentalhealthcommission.ca.

92. Charles Boyer and Louise Chenier, "Does Workplace Wellness Really Matter?" *Canadian HR Reporter*, November 17. 2014, p. 19.

93. Liz Bernier, "Breaking Down Barriers – 1 Cup at a Time," *Canadian HR Reporter*, November 4, 2013, pp. 18, 20.

94. Sun Life Health Index, 2014, cdn.sunlife .com.

95. Alain Marchand, Pierre Durand, Victor Haines, and Steve Harvey, "The Multilevel Determinants of Worker Mental Health: Results from the SALVEO Study," *Social Psychiatry and Psychiatric Epidemiology*, 2014.

96. Sarah Dobson, "Mental Health Bible Overhauled," *Canadian HR Reporter*, September 23, 2013, pp. 1, 11.

97. Jeffrey Smith, "Safety Trumps Accommodation for Worker with Mental Illness," *Canadian HR Reporter*, February 11, 2013, p. 5.

98. ComPsych, "ComPsych Tell It Now," www.compsych.com, January 14, 2013.

99. *Sun Life Buffet National Wellness Survey*, *2013*.

100. See Canada's Safest Employers, www. safestemployers.com.

101. AonHewitt, Rapid Response Survey on Wellness, www.aon.com, March 2013.

102. Sarah Dobson, "Smokers Need Not Apply," *Canadian HR Reporter*, May 6, 2013.

103. Jennifer Elia, "Butting Out for Good," *Canadian HR Reporter*, June 2, 2014, p. 9.

104. Creative Wellness Solutions, "Building the Business Case for Workplace Health" http://www.wellnesssolutions.ca/index. php?id=66&spage=234, downloaded October 1, 2009.

105. Amanda Silliker, "Global Corporate Challenge Combats Obesity," *Canadian HR Reporter*, December 19, 2011, pp. 6, 19; see also www.getheworldmoving.com.

106. See *Canadian HR Reporter*, April 11, 2005, p. 20. See also www.worksmartlivesmart.com.

107. Anna Wilde Mathews, "Ready, Set, Exercise...For a Day Off and Other Perks," *The Globe and Mail*, May 7, 2012, p. L6.

108. See Psychologically Healthy Workplace Collaborative site, www.phwc.ca.

109. Sarah Dobson, "Are You Prepared for a Lockdown?" *Canadian HR Reporter*, November 17, 2014, pp. 1, 8.

110. "Safety Strategies for a Post-Sept. 11 World," *HRFocus*, October 2002, pp. 3–5.

111. Peter Rakobowchuk, "Several Attacks Leave Letter Carriers Worried," *Chronicle Herald*, March 6, 2015, p. A12.

112. Sarah Dobson, "Learning to Avoid the Bad Guys," *Canadian HR Reporter*, November 29, 2010, pp. 24, 26.

113. This material is taken from the U.S. Environmental Protection Agency, see www.epa.gov/iaq/pubs/sbs.html.

114. This information is based on an article by Kat Morgan, "Sick Building Syndrome," *Human Resources Professional*, February– March 1998, pp. 39–40.

115. Ellie Zolfagharifard, "Are Energy Efficient Homes Making Us Ill?" *Daily Mail Online*, February 18, 2014, www.dailymail.co.uk.

116. See The Canadian Initiative on Workplace Violence, www.workplaceviolence.ca; see also Liz Bernier, "Termination Nightmare: Stabbing Rampage Raises Unsettling Questions," *Canadian HR Reporter*, May 5, 2014, pp. 1, 8.

117. Tiffany Crawford, "Male Nurses Take Brunt of Patient Abuse," *Calgary Herald*, April 16, 2009, p. A12.

118. Theresa Boyle, "Toronto East General Goes High-Tech to Fight Violence," *Toronto Star*, February 17, 2009, p. GT1.

119. www.vault.com and http://crimeprevention .rutgers.edu/crime/violence/workplace /riskyjobs.htm (this site has some excellent resource material pertaining to workplace violence); see also Greg Botelho, "Workplace Violence: Know the Numbers, Risk Factors and Possible Warning Signs," www.cnn.com, September 28, 2014.

120. See www.shrm.org; see also Society for Human Resource Management, *1999 Workplace Violence Survey*, Alexandria, VI: SHRM, 1999.

121. "Workplace Violence Common," *Canadian HR Reporter*, March 26, 2012, p. 4.

122. COMPAS, "Violence and Aggression in the Workplace," http://bdo.ca.

123. "Most Common Ways in Which Cyber Stalking Cases Escalated in 2013," www .statista.com.

124. Shannon Klie, "Screening New Hires Won't End Workplace Violence, Study Says," *Canadian HR Reporter*, November 21, 2005, pp. 1, 3.

125. Milo Geyelin, "Firms Often Blamed for Violence at Work," *The Globe and Mail*, March 18, 2002, p. C2.

126. Paul Viollis and Chris Mathers, "Companies Need to Re-engineer Their Cultural Thinking About Workplace Violence," *Canadian HR Reporter*, March 14, 2005, p. 19.

127. Liz Bernier, "Picking up the Pieces," *Canadian HR Reporter*, April 7, 2014, pp. 1, 8.

128. Uyen Vu, "Teen's Death Prompts Calls for Late-shift Policies," *Canadian HR Reporter*, October 10, 2005, pp. 1, 2.

129. Clare Mellor, "Battling Bullies," *Chronicle Herald*, May 31, 2014, pp. B1, B2.

130. Western University and Canadian Labour Congress, "Can Work Be Safe, When Home Isn't?" www.canadianlabour.ca, 2014.

131. Kevin Kelloway and Lori Francis, *Management of Occupational Health and Safety*, 5th ed., Toronto: Nelson, 2010.

132. Philip Hagan, John Montgomery, and James O'Reilly, *Accident Prevention Manual for Business and Industry*, 13th ed., Washington, DC: National Safety Council, 2009.

133. Don't Forget to Tie Workplace Wellness Programs into Ergonomics and Safety Programs, www.kelbyergodesign.com.

134. For more details on ErgoWATch, see www .ahs.uwaterloo.ca.

135. See "Repetitive Strain Injuries–The Hidden Cost of Computing," WebReference.com, October 1, 2009, www.webreference.com /rsi.html.

136. For further information, see http://www. tifaq.org/information/rsi.html.

137. Ergonomic issues are discussed in much more detail in E. Kevin Kelloway, Lori Francis, and James Montgomery, *Management of Occupational Health and Safety*, 3rd ed., Toronto: Nelson, 2006.

138. Nancy Stuart, "Open Offices Drive Workers up the Wall," *The Globe and Mail*, October 6, 2000, p. B11.

139. Bob Fortier, "Ergonomics for Teleworkers Often Overlooked," *Canadian HR Reporter*, June 6, 2005, pp. 18, 21.

140. See www.avert.org/canada-aids.htm.

141. Information on AIDS can be obtained from the Canadian AIDS Society's various publications available at www.cdnaids.ca; see also UNAIDS 2011 World Aids Day Report available from the www.unaids .org site.

142. J. J. Breckenridge, "Nurse with AIDS Gets Job Back, But Row Over Dismissal Goes On," *The Globe and Mail*, June 29, 1988, p. A10.

143. *Business Week*, February 1, 1993, p. 53; see also the "HIV/AIDS Toolkit" developed by the Society for Human Resource Management at www.worksupport.com /resources/printview.cfm/335, downloaded June 15, 2012.

144. The Canadian Human Rights Commission has considerable information about AIDS on its website, www.chrc-ccdp.ca. Similarly, information is readily available from provincial human rights commissions. For example, see the Ontario Human Rights Commission's "Policy on HIV/Aids-Related Discrimination" at www.ohrc.on.ca/en /policy-hivaids-related-discrimination.

CHAPTER 13

1. Morley Gunderson, Allen Ponak, and Daphne Gottlieb Taras, *Union–Management Relations in Canada,* 4th ed., Toronto: Pearson, 2005, p. 10.

2. John Chilibeck, "Clause That Clogs the Wheel," *Telegraph Journal,* December 23, 2008, p. C1.

3. Sean Fine, "Mounties Win the Right to Unionize," *The Globe and Mail,* January 17, 2015, p. A10.

4. Stephen Kimber, "Brewhaha," *Atlantic Business,* January–February 2015, pp. 26–34.

5. Gregor Murray, "Unions: Membership, Structure and Actions," in Morley Gunderson and Allen Ponak (Eds.), *Union–Management Relations in Canada,* 3rd ed., Don Mills, ON: Addison-Wesley, 1995.

6. Julian Barling, Clive Fullagar, and Kevin Kelloway, *The Union and Its Members: A Psychological Approach,* New York: Oxford University Press, 1992.

7. Patrick Brethour, "Bitter Strike Divides Alberta Town," *The Globe and Mail,* October 17, 2005, pp. 1, 7.

8. Leger, Labour Watch State of the Unions 2013, October 2013, www.labourwatch.com.

9. Keith Leslie, "Caterpillar Closes Plant after Lockout," *Chronicle Herald,* February 4, 2012, p. B2. For a review of the Caterpillar closure and its implications see Tavia Grant, "The Caterpillar Shutdown's Stark Warning for the Industrial Heartland," *The Globe and Mail,* February 22, 2012, pp. A8–A9.

10. Amanda Silliker, "Canada's Labour Relations at the Crossroads," *Canadian HR Reporter,* December 5, 2011, pp. 1, 9.

11. John Allemang, "Organized Labour is Fighting to Survive," *The Globe and Mail,* March 24, 2012.

12. Jane Taber, "Union Tensions on the Rise," *The Globe and Mail,* March 7, 2012, pp. A1, A4.

13. Samuel Gompers, *Labor and the Common Welfare,* Freeport, NY: Books for Libraries Press, 1919, p. 20.

14. An editorial in *Canadian Labour,* June 1968, p. 5.

15. Sarah Dobson, "CAW's Women's Advocate Program Presented at UN Session," *Canadian HR Reporter,* April 8, 2013, p. 3.

16. Frank Tannenbaum, *The Labour Movement, Its Conservative Functions and Consequences,* New York: Alfred A. Knopf, 1921.

17. Selig Perlman, *A Theory of the Labour Movement,* New York: Macmillan, 1928.

18. Charles Lipton, *The Trade Union Movement in Canada, 1827–1959,* Montreal, QC: Canadian Social Publications, 1967, p. 4.

19. "Union Coverage in Canada–2013," Workplace Information and Research Division, Labour Program, Employment and Social Development Canada, June 2014.

20. Dianne Galarneau and Thao Sohn, *Unionization 2012,* Statistics Canada, November 2013.

21. Sabrina Nanji, "Walmart Workers Reject Union," *Canadian HR Reporter,* September 9, 2013, pp. 1, 11.

22. Gordon Sova, "Union Targeting Second-Largest Food Retailer," *Canadian HR Reporter,* January 15, 2009; see also "Canada's Leading Union Committed to Representing Members Impacted by Sobeys Announcement," June 30, 2014, www.ufcw.ca.

23. Sabrina Nanji, "Labour Pains," *Canadian HR Reporter,* January 27, 2014, pp. 16–17.

24. "CAW, CEP Merge to Form Unifor," *Canadian HR Reporter,* June 17, 2013, p. 6.

25. Danielle Harder, "UFCW Creates Super Local of 60,000," *Canadian HR Reporter,* August 15, 2011, p. 8.

26. Sharanjit Uppal, *Unionization 2011,* October 2011, www.statcan.gc.ca.

27. More information on international union density trends is available in International Labour Organization, *World Labour Report: Industrial Relations, Democracy and Social Stability (1997–98),* Geneva: ILO, 1997; see also Peter Hall-Jones, "Unionism and Economic Performance," www.newunionism.net.

28. Trevor Wilhelm, "Tension Rising on the Line: City Strike Turns Ugly," *Windsor Star,* May 22, 2009, p. A1.

29. John Godard, "Strikes as Collective Voice: A Behavioral Analysis of Strike Activity," *Industrial and Labor Relations Review,* October 1992, pp. 161–175.

30. Mohammed Adam and Bruce Deachman, "Transit Workers Vow to Strike as Long as it Takes," *Ottawa Citizen,* January 6, 2009, p. A1.

31. Don Herald, "Back to Work Doesn't Mean Back to Normal," *Canadian HR Reporter,* September 9, 2002, pp. 8, 11.

32. Real Seguin and Bertrand Marotte, "Wildcat Construction Strikes Continue for Second Day," *The Globe and Mail,* October 26, 2011, p. A10.

33. John Godard, "Strikes as Collective Voice: A Behavioral Analysis of Strike Activity," *Industrial and Labor Relations Review,* October 1992, pp. 161–175.

34. Oliver Bertin, "Star Ends Bitter Three-week Carrier Strike," *The Globe and Mail,* April 16, 2001, p. B3.

35. Shannon Klie, "Labour Debate Rages in Quebec," *Canadian HR Reporter,* February 28, 2011, pp. 1, 2.

36. "Voisey's Bay Mine Strike Over," *Chronicle Herald,* February 1, 2011, p. C3.

37. See Brent Jang, "Air Canada Duels with Its Pilots," *The Globe and Mail,* March 19, 2012, pp. A1, A3; "Air Canada: Pilot 'Book-offs' Disruptive," *Chronicle Herald,* March 19, 2012, pp. B1, B7.

38. Mike Blanchfield, "Top Court OKs Right to Strike," *Chronicle Herald,* January 31, 2015, p. A5.

39. Jeff Gray and Jordan Fletcher, "Top Court's Ruling on Union Rights Hailed as Victory for Freedom of Expression," *The Globe and Mail,* November 16, 2013, p. A19.

40. Wallace Immen, "How to Heal a Bruised Workplace," *The Globe and Mail,* October 5, 2005, pp. C1, C2.

41. Statistics Canada, Average Hourly Wages of Employees by Selected Characteristics, February 2015; see also Sharanjit Uppal, *Unionization 2011,* October 2011, www.statcan.gc.ca.

42. Richard B. Freeman and James L. Medoff, *What Do Unions Do?* New York: Basic Books, 1984.

43. Morley Gunderson and Douglas Hyatt, "Union Impact on Compensation, Productivity, and Management of the Organization," in Morley Gunderson and Daphne Gottlieb Taras, (Eds.), *Canadian Labour and Employment Relations,* 6th ed., Toronto: Pearson, 2009.

44. Asha Tomlinson, "Union Cracks Down on Workers with Bad Habits," *Canadian HR Reporter,* August 12, 2002, pp. 1, 11.

45. Ashleigh Mattern, "Allan Mine Hires Non-Union Workers," *Leader Post,* August 28, 2008, p. D1.

46. Shannon Klie, "Replacement Workers Put Pressure on the Union But at What Cost?" *Canadian HR Professional,* October 24, 2005, pp. 11, 12.

47. Sabrina Nanji, "Alberta's Labour Laws Spawn Legal Challenge," *Canadian HR Reporter,* January 27, 2014, pp. 8, 14.

48. Sarah Dobson, "Collective Bargaining Under Fire: Hargrove," *Canadian HR Reporter,* November 7, 2011, pp. 3, 18.

49. George W. Adams, *Canadian Labour Law,* 2nd ed., Aurora, ON: Canada Law Book, 2012.

50. Jeffrey Smith, "Vale Must Open Its Gates to Fired Worker: Board," *Canadian HR Reporter,* February 13, 2012, pp. 5, 8.

51. George Meany, "Organizing a Continuing Effort," *The American Federationist,* July, 1976, p. 1.

52. See www.ufcw1000a.com for more information about these initiatives.

53. For an interesting view of union organizing in the United States, see William E. Fulmer, "Step by Step Through an Organizing Campaign," *Harvard Business Review,* 1991, Vol. 59, pp. 94–102.

54. Lorna Harris, "Technology Providing Organizing Options," *Canadian HR Reporter,* June 25, 2008.

55. Tom Roper, "Class-action Litigation—New Tool for Unions," *Canadian HR Reporter,* February 25, 2013, pp. 23, 24.

56. Jamie Knight, "What You Can Do If a Union Comes Knocking," *Canadian HR Reporter,* October 21, 2013, p. 5.

57. George W. Adams, *Canadian Labour Law,* 2nd ed., Aurora, ON: Canada Law Book, 2012.

58. "Fish Processor Pays for Union-Busting Closures," *Canadian HR Reporter,* December 5, 2005, p. 2.

59. George W. Adams, *Canadian Labour Law,* 2nd ed., Aurora, ON: Canada Law Book, 2012.

60. Stephanie Marin, "Wal-Mart Staff Win Case," *Chronicle Herald,* June 28, 2014, p. A14.

61. "Unions Question City's Strategy," *Chronicle Herald,* November 11, 2014, p. A4.

62. Richard E. Walton, Joel E. Cutcher-Gershenfeld, and Robert B. McKersie, *Strategic Negotiations: A Theory of Change in Labor–Management Relations,* Boston: Harvard Business School Press, 1994.

63. Fiona McQuarrie, *Industrial Relations in Canada*, 3rd ed., Mississauga: Wiley, 2011.

64. Jon Peirce, *Canadian Industrial Relations*, 2nd ed., Scarborough, Prentice Hall, 2003.

65. Sabrina Nanji and Liz Foster, "With This Contract, I Thee Wed," *Canadian HR Reporter*, February 24, 2014, p. 15.

66. "Developing HR's Business Skills," *Canadian HR Reporter*, September 13, 2004, p. 9.

67. Greg Keenan, "Air Canada, Pilots Reach Tentative 10-Year Agreement," *The Globe and Mail*, October 7, 2014, p. B4.

68. Michael J. Fraser, "Labour Skeptical About Win-Win," *Canadian HR Reporter*, September 10, 2001, pp. 11, 12.

69. Thomas A. Kochan and Paul Osterman, *The Mutual Gains Enterprise*, Boston, MA: Harvard Business School Press, 1994.

70. Judy Lendvay-Zwickl, *The Canadian Industrial Relations System: Current Challenges and Future Options*, Ottawa: Conference Board of Canada, 2005.

71. Uyen Vu, "Interest Wanes on Interest-Based?" *Canadian HR Reporter*, February 28, 2005, pp. 6, 9.

72. Each jurisdiction has defined procedures relating to conciliation and mediation. As well, the distinction between these terms has been blurred. Consequently, human resource professionals need to consult the relevant legislation for their jurisdiction.

73. See the Nova Scotia Department of Labour Annual Reports for the 1992 to 2001 period.

74. Jeffrey Smith, "City Worker's Water Use Doesn't Wash," *Canadian HR Reporter*, May 5, 2014, p. 5.

75. Jeffrey Smith, "Collective Agreement Gave Transit Company Discretion to Fire Driver After Accident," *Canadian HR Reporter*, December 16, 2008.

76. Jeffrey Smith, "Employee's Complaint Wasn't Layoff Request," *Canadian HR Reporter*, October 7, 2013, pp. 5, 6.

77. Sarah Dobson, "Ghomeshi's Legal HR Quadmire," *Canadian HR Reporter*, November 17, 2014, pp. 1, 12.

78. The judicial review of labour board and arbitration decisions is a very technical area of labour law. For an in-depth treatment, see Richard L. Charney and Thomas E.F. Brady, *Judicial Review in Labour Law*, Aurora, ON: Canada Law Book, 2008.

79. These issues are discussed in more detail in Terry H. Wagar, "The Arbitration Process: Employer and Union Views," in W. Kaplan, J. Sack, and M. Gunderson, (Eds.), *Labour Arbitration Yearbook 1996–1997*, Toronto: Lancaster House, pp. 3–11; see also Fiona McQuarrie, *Industrial Relations in Canada*, 3rd ed., Mississauga: Wiley, 2011.

80. Madeleine Loewenberg, "Balancing Risks, Benefits of Social Media," *Canadian HR Reporter*, January 31, 2011, pp. 29, 31.

81. Anthony Giles and Akivah Starkman, "The Collective Agreement," in Morley Gunderson, Allen Ponak, and Daphne Gottlieb Taras, *Union–Management Relations in Canada*, 5th ed., Toronto: Pearson Addison Wesley, 2005, p. 306.

82. Ibid.

83. For a comprehensive review of the arbitration process, see Donald J.M Brown and David M. Beatty, *Canadian Labour Arbitration*, 4th. ed., Aurora, ON: Canada Law Book, 2011.

84. Lorna Harris, "Promotional T-shirt Runs Afoul of Zero Tolerance," *Canadian HR Reporter*, November 8, 2004, p. 5.

85. An excellent summary of the legislative requirements applicable to public sector workers is found in George W. Adams, *Canadian Labour Law*, 2nd ed., Aurora, ON: Canada Law Book, 2012.

86. Justin Giovannetti, "Premier, Public Sector Unions at Odds," *The Globe and Mail*, March 3, 2015, p. A4.

87. See Michael Gorman, "Dorsey Rule on Union Despite Being Fired," *Chronicle Herald*, February 26, 2015, p. A3; see also Michael Gorman, "Province Strikes Deal with Health-Care Unions," *Chronicle Herald*, March 14, 2015, p. A3.

88. Paul Juniper, Alison Hill and Tahreem Raza, *An Inquiry into the State of Labour Relations in Canada*, Kingston, ON: Queen's University IRC, 2012.

89. This quote is taken from Human Resources Development Canada and the Organisation for Economic Co-operation and Development, *Changing Workplace Strategies: Achieving Better Outcomes for Enterprises, Workers and Society*, Hull: HRDC, 1997.

90. Virginia Galt, "Benefits Seen in Union-like Workplace," *The Globe and Mail*, February 18, 2002, p. C1.

91. Roy Adams, "Canadian Industrial Relations at the Dawn of the 21st Century—Prospects for Reform," *Workplace Gazette*, Vol. 3, 2000, pp. 109–115.

92. Roy Adams, *Labour Left Out: Canada's Failure to Protect and Promote Collective Bargaining as a Human Right*, Ottawa: Canadian Centre for Policy Alternatives, 2006.

93. See, for instance, William N. Cooke, *Labor–Management Cooperation*, Kalamazoo, MI: W.E. Upjohn Institute, 1990; Thomas A. Kochan and Paul Osterman, *The Mutual Gains Enterprise*, Boston, MA: Harvard Business School Press, 1994.

94. "Industrial Relations Outlook," Ottawa: Conference Board of Canada, 2002.

95. See, for instance, Terry H. Wagar, "Is Labor–Management Climate Important? Some Canadian Evidence," *Journal of Labor Research*, Winter 1997, pp. 101–112; and Ali Dastmalchian, "Industrial Relations Climate," in Paul Blyton, Nicolas Bacon, Jack Fiorito, and Edmund Heery (Eds.), *The Sage Handbook of Industrial Relations*, London, UK: Sage, 2008, pp. 548–568.

96. Steve Mertl, "Vancouver City Employees, Especially Firefighters, Suffer from Poor Morale," January 16, 2014, www.ca.news.yahoo.com.

97. Guillermo Grenier and Raymond Hogler, "Labor Law and Managerial Ideology: Employee Participation as a Social Control System," *Work and Occupations*, August 1991, pp. 313–333. For an excellent discussion of management by stress, see Mike Parker and Jane Slaughter, "Management by Stress," *Technology Review*, October 1988, pp. 37–44.

98. "Unionized Organizations Make Their Mark," *The Globe and Mail*, April 13, 2010, pp. GPTW1, GPTW9.

99. David Brown, "Union Says Recognition Divides Workers," *Canadian HR Reporter*, March 11, 2002, pp. 1, 13.

CHAPTER 14

1. Jon Katzenbach and Ashley Harshak, "Stop Blaming Your Culture," *strategy + business*, January 19, 2011, http://www.strategy-business.com/article/11108?gko=f4e8d.

2. "Honda Motor: 2007 company profile edition 1: SWOT analysis," *Just Auto*, 2007, www.just-auto.com, pp. 15–16.

3. Honda, "Company overview, Details of Honda's head office," http://world.honda.com/profile/overview, downloaded May 18, 2007.

4. Honda, "Community, The key phrase: Together for tomorrow," http://world.honda.com/community, downloaded May 18, 2007.

5. Honda, *Honda Marks Completion of New Transmission Plant at Hamamatsu Factory*," http://world.honda.com/news/2010/c100908New-Transmission-Plant-Hamamatsu-Factory/, September 8, 2010.

6. Honda, "Honda to Build New Motorcycle Production Plant in Malaysia–Renewing production capability with the transfer of existing production," http://world.honda.com/news/2011/c110922Motorcycle-Production-Plant-Malaysia/index.html, downloaded September 22, 2011.

7. Honda, "Honda Increases North American Manufacturing Footprint with Production Start of Fuel-Efficient, Subcompact Vehicles at New Auto Plant in Mexico," http://www.honda.com/newsandviews/article.aspx?id=7629-en, downloaded February 21, 2014.

8. R.L. Tung, "Distinguished Scholar Invited Essay Requisites to and Ways of Developing a Global Mindset: Implications for Research on Leadership and Organizations," *Journal of Leadership & Organizational Studies*, Vol. 21, No. 4, 2014, pp. 329–337.

9. J. Byrne, "Strategic planning," August 26, 1996, http://www.businessweek.com/1996/35/b34901.htm.

10. BMO Financial Group, "BMO Completes Strategic Investment in COFCO Trust Co.: Expands BMO's wealth management capability in China," news release, August 2, 2012, http://newsroom.bmo.com/press-releases/bmo-completes-strategic-investment-in-cofco-trust--tsx-bmo-201208020809398004.

11. D. G. Collings, H. Scullion, and M. J. Morley, "Changing patterns of global staffing in the multinational enterprise: Challenges to the conventional expatriate assignment and emerging alternatives," *Journal of World Business*, Vol. 42, 2007, pp. 198–213.

12. C. Brewster, P. Sparrow, and H. Harris, "Towards a new model of globalizing HRM,"

International Journal of Human Resource Management, Vol. 16, No. 6, June 2005, pp. 940–970.

13. N. J. Adler, "Globalization and human resource management: Strategic international human resource development," *Pacific Region Forum,* 1990; I. Tarique, R. Schuler, and Y. Gong, "A model of multinational enterprise subsidiary staffing composition," *International Journal of Human Resource Management,* Vol. 17, No. 2, 2006, pp. 207–224.

14. A. McWilliams, D. D. Fleet, and P. M. Wright, "Strategic Management of Human Resources for Global Competitive Advantage," *Journal of Business Strategies,* Vol. 18, No. 1, 2001.

15. N. J. Adler, "Globalization and human resource management: Strategic international human resource development," *Pacific Region Forum,* 1990; I. Tarique, R. Schuler, and Y. Gong, "A model of multinational enterprise subsidiary staffing composition," *International Journal of Human Resource Management,* Vol. 17, No. 2, 2006, pp. 207–224.

16. Ibid.

17. Ibid.

18. Ibid.

19. I. Tarique, R. Schuler, and Y. Gong, "A model of multinational enterprise subsidiary staffing composition," *International Journal of Human Resource Management,* Vol. 17, No. 2, 2006, pp. 207–224.

20. A. McWilliams, D. D. Fleet, and P. M. Wright, "Strategic Management of Human Resources for Global Competitive Advantage," *Journal of Business Strategies,* Vol. 18, No. 1, 2001.

21. M. E. Mor Borak, *Managing Diversity toward a Globally Inclusive Workplace,* Thousand Oaks, CA: Sage Publications Inc., 2005.

22. C. A. Bartlett and S. Ghoshal, "What is a global manager?" *Harvard Business Review,* Vol. 70, No. 5, 1992, pp. 124–132.

23. A. McWilliams, D. D. Fleet, and P. M. Wright, "Strategic Management of Human Resources for Global Competitive Advantage," *Journal of Business Strategies,* Vol. 18, No. 1, 2001.

24. P. Engardio, M. Arndt, and G. Smith, "Emerging giants," *Businessweek,* July 31, 2006, pp. 40–49.

25. R. Mahapatra, "Wal-Mart juggernaut gets set to roll into India," *Toronto Star,* November 28, 2006, p. D3.

26. C. Brewster, P. Sparrow and H. Harris, "Towards a new model of globalizing HRM" *International Journal of Human Resource Management,* Vol. 16, No. 6, 2005, pp. 949–970.

27. C. Steinberg, "Can Women Save Japan (and ASIA Too)?" *Finance & Development:* A quarterly magazine of the IMF, Vol. 49, No. 3, 2012.

28. Shiseido Group, *Diversity & Inclusion: Support Measures for Women's Activities,* http://www.shiseidogroup.com/csr/labor/diversity.html.

29. I. Tarique, R. Schuler, and Y. Gong, "A model of multinational enterprise subsidiary staffing composition" *International Journal of Human Resource Management,* Vol. 17,

No. 2, 2006, pp. 207–224; D. Wiechmann, A. Ryan, and M. Hemingway, "Designing and implementing global staffing systems: Part I–leaders in global staffing," *Human Resource Management,* Vol. 42, No. 1, 2003, p. 79; C. Brewster, P. Sparrow, and H. Harris, "Towards a new model of globalizing HRM," *International Journal of Human Resource Management,* Vol. 16, No. 6, 2005, pp. 949–970; D. R. Briscoe and R. S. Schuler, *International Human Resource Management,* 2nd ed., 2004. New York: Routledge.

30. P. S. Budhwar and A. Varma, "Emerging HR management trends in India and the way forward," *Organizational Dynamics,* Vol. 40, 2011, pp. 317–325.

31. "Selected cross-cultural factors in human resource management," Resource Library (findarticles.com), *HR Magazine,* September 2008, http://findarticles.com/ p/articles /mi_m3495/is_9_53/ai_n29460531/?tag= content;col1.

32. D. R. Briscoe and R. S. Schuler, *International Human Resource Management,* 2nd ed., 2004, New York: Routledge.

33. Ibid, p. 176

34. M. E. Mor Borak, *Managing Diversity toward a Globally Inclusive Workplace,* Thousand Oaks, CA: Sage Publications Inc., 2005.

35. J. Marshall and E. M. Heffes, "China: Recruiting easy, but success difficult" *Financial Executive,* Vol. 22, No. 10, 2006, p. 12.

36. M. Javidan and R. J. House, "Cultural acumen for the global manager: Lessons from Project GLOBE," *Organizational Dynamics,* Vol. 29, No. 4, 2001, p. 289.

37. M. Javidan, G. K. Stahl, F. Brodbeck, and C. P. M. Wilderom, "Cross-border transfer of knowledge: Cultural lessons from Project GLOBE," *Academy of Management Executive,* Vol. 19, No. 2, 2005, pp. 59–75.

38. C. Solomon and M. S. Schell, *Managing Across Cultures: The Seven Keys to Doing Business with a Global Mindset,* McGraw-Hill, 2009, pp. 144–150.

39. "Selected cross-cultural factors in human resource management," Resource Library (findarticles.com): *HR Magazine,* September 2008, http://findarticles.com/p/articles /mi_m3495/is_9_53/ai_n29460531 /? tag=content;col1.

40. C. Solomon and M. S. Schell, *Managing Across Cultures: The Seven Keys to Doing Business With a Global Mindset,* McGraw-Hill, 2009, p.150.

41. "Indian labour shortage may affect offshoring, says Gartner," *Out-Law News,* 2005, http://www.out-law.com/page-6116-theme=print, downloaded May 13, 2007.

42. "Employment trends and opportunities" *Going Global Career Guides,* 2006, pp. 18–33.

43. K. Hansen, "Balancing the global workforce," *Workforce Management,* Vol. 85, No. 23, 2006, p. 44.

44. M. Guillard, "A visual essay: International labor market comparisons," *Monthly Labor Review,* 2006, pp. 33–40.

45. M. E. Mor Borak, *Managing Diversity toward a Globally Inclusive Workplace,* Thousand Oaks, CA: Sage Publications Inc., 2005.

46. M. Carley, "Industrial relations in the EU, Japan and USA, 2001," *Eurofound, 2003,* http://www.eurofound.europa.eu/ eiro/2002/12/feature/tn0212101f.html, downloaded March 14, 2007.

47. T. Wright, "Indonesia Chained by Labour Law," *The Globe and Mail,* December 7, 2006, p. B19.

48. D. R. Briscoe and R. S. Schuler, *International Human Resource Management,* 2nd ed., 2004, New York: Routledge, p.151.

49. M. E. Mor Borak, *Managing Diversity toward a Globally Inclusive Workplace,* Thousand Oaks, CA: Sage Publications Inc., 2005.

50. C. Woodhams, B. Lupton, and H. Xian, "The persistence of gender discrimination in China – evidence from recruitment advertisements," *The International Journal of Human Resource Management,* Vol. 20, No. 10, October 2009, pp. 2084–2109.

51. *Industry Canada, Corporate social responsibility, 2005,* http://strategis.ic.gc.ca /epic/site/csr-rse.nsf/en/Home, downloaded June 8, 2007.

52. R. Dudley, A. Devnath, and M. Townsend, "The Hidden Cost of Fast Fashion: Worker Safety," Bloomberg Businessweek, February 7, 2013, http://www.bloomberg.com /bw/articles/2013-02-07/the-hidden-cost-of -fast-fashion-worker-safety.

53. Ibid.

54. United States Department of State, *2013 Country Reports on Human Rights Practices – Cambodia,* February 27, 2014, http://www. refworld.org/docid/53284b4c3.html.

55. International Labor Organization, "Better Work Indonesia: Improving capacity of HR and compliance practitioners in the Indonesian garment industry," November 14, 2012, http://www.ilo.org/jakarta/info /public/pr/WCMS_193188/lang--en/index .htm.

56. K. O'Keefe, "Cambodia Factories Grapple with Issue of Underage Workers," *The Wall Street Journal,* December 29, 2013, http:// www.wsj.com/articles/SB1000142405270230 3799404579287353595133592.

57. United States Department of State, *2013 Country Reports on Human Rights Practices – Cambodia,* February 27, 2014, http://www .refworld.org/docid/53284b4c3.html.

58. K. Kamouche, "The integration-differentiation puzzle: A resource-capability perspective in international human resource management," *The International Journal of Human Resource Management,* Vol. 7, No. 1, 1996, pp. 230–243.

59. D. G. Collings, H. Scullion and M. J. Morley, "Changing patterns of global staffing in the multinational enterprise: Challenges to the conventional expatriate assignment and emerging alternatives," *Journal of World Business,* Vol. 42, 2007, pp. 198–213.

60. Ibid.

61. M. E. Mor Borak, *Managing Diversity toward a Globally Inclusive Workplace,* Thousand Oaks, CA: Sage Publications Inc., 2005.

62. D. R. Briscoe and R. S. Schuler, *International Human Resource Management,* 2nd ed., 2004, New York: Routledge, p. 55.

63. Ibid, p. 202.

64. C. Brewster, P. Sparrow, and H. Harris, "Towards a new model of globalizing HRM," *International Journal of Human Resource Management,* Vol. 16, No. 6, 2005, pp. 949–970.

65. Ibid; Y. Ling and B. Jaw, "The influence of international human capital on global initiatives and financial performance," *International Journal of Human Resource Management,* Vol. 17, No. 3, 2006, pp. 379–398; R. S. Schuler, P. S. Budhwar, and G. W. Florkowski, "International human resource management: Review and critique," *International Journal of Management Reviews,* Vol. 4, No. 1, 2002, pp. 41–70.

66. Employment and Social Development Canada, "New Reforms for the Temporary Foreign Worker Program," December 31, 2014, http://www.esdc.gc.ca/eng/jobs /foreign_workers/reform/highlights.shtml.

67. I. Tarique, R. Schuler, and Y. Gong, "A model of multinational enterprise subsidiary staffing composition," *International Journal of Human Resource Management,* Vol. 17, No. 2, 2006, pp. 207–224; D. G. Collings, H. Scullion, and M. J. Morley, "Changing patterns of global staffing in the multinational enterprise: Challenges to the conventional expatriate assignment and emerging alternatives," *Journal of World Business,* 42, 2007, pp. 198–213.

68. D. R. Briscoe and R. S. Schuler, *International Human Resource Management,* 2nd ed., 2004, New York: Routledge, p. 55; I. Tarique, R. Schuler, and Y. Gong, "A model of multinational enterprise subsidiary staffing composition," *International Journal of Human Resource Management,* Vol. 17, No. 2, 2006, pp. 207–224.

69. H. Scullion and D. G. Collings, *Global Staffing.* New York: Routledge, 2006.

70. C. Reynolds, "Strategic employment of third country nationals," *HR. Human Resource Planning,* Vol. 20, No. 1, 1997, pp. 33–39; H. Scullion and D. G. Collings, *Global staffing.* New York: Routledge, 2006.

71. H. Scullion and D. G. Collings, *Global staffing.* New York: Routledge, 2006.

72. H. Mayerhofer, L. C. Hartmann, G. Michelitsch-Riedl, and I. Kollinger, "Flexpatriate assignments: A neglected issue in global staffing," *International Journal of Human Resource Management,* Vol. 15, No. 8, 2004, pp. 1371–1389.

73. D. R. Briscoe and R. S. Schuler, *International Human Resource Management,* 2nd ed., 2004, New York: Routledge, p. 252.

74. D. G. Collings, H. Scullion, and M. J. Morley, "Changing patterns of global staffing in the multinational enterprise: Challenges to the conventional expatriate assignment and emerging alternatives," *Journal of World Business,* Vol. 42, 2007, pp. 198–213.

75. Ibid.

76. C. Moakler and G. Reinhart, "Apply international lessons to domestic moves," *Canadian HR Reporter,* Vol. 16, No. 21, 2003, p. 21.

77. J. S. Mumma, "How to control relocation costs," *HR Magazine,* Vol. 38, No. 8, 1993, pp. 67–69.

78. R. S. Schuler, P. S. Budhwar, and G. W. Florkowski, "International human resource management: Review and critique," *International Journal of Management Reviews,* Vol. 4, No. 1, 2002, pp. 41–70.

79. Ibid; D. G. Collings, H. Scullion, and M. J. Morley, "Changing patterns of global staffing in the multinational enterprise: Challenges to the conventional expatriate assignment and emerging alternatives," *Journal of World Business,* 42, 2007, pp. 198–213.

80. R. C. Rose, S. S. Ramalu, J. Uli, and N. Kumar. "Doing Business in Global Arena: An Examination of the Relationship Between Cultural Intelligence and Cross-Cultural Adjustment," *Asian Academy of Management Journal,* Vol. 15, No. 1, 2010, pp. 79–97.

81. K. Crowne, "The relationships among social intelligence, emotional intelligence and cultural intelligence," *Organizational Management Journal,* Vol. 6, 2009, pp. 148–163.

82. R. C. Rose, S. S. Ramalu, J. Uli, and N. Kumar. "Expatriate Performance in International Assignments: The Role of Cultural Intelligence as Dynamic Intercultural Competency," *International Journal of Business and Management,* Vol. 5, No. 8, 2010, pp. 76–85.

83. C. D. Contreras and F. Bravo, "Should you accept an international assignment?" *Chemical Engineering Process,* Vol. 99, No. 8, 2003, p. 67.

84. G. Fink, S. Meierewert, and U. Rohr, "The use of repatriate knowledge in organizations," *HR. Human Resource Planning,* Vol. 28, No. 4, 2005, pp. 30–36.

85. C. D. Contreras and F. Bravo, "Should you accept an international assignment?" *Chemical Engineering Process,* Vol. 99, No. 8, 2003, p. 67.

86. D. G. Collings, H. Scullion, and M. J. Morley, "Changing patterns of global staffing in the multinational enterprise: Challenges to the conventional expatriate assignment and emerging alternatives," *Journal of World Business,* Vol. 42, 2007, pp. 198–213.

87. Worldwide ERC: The Workforce Mobility Association, *Attention to Family Issues Eases International Assignments to Mainland China: Worldwide ERC and HKIHRM Release Survey,* July 20, 2006, http://www .worldwideerc.org/Newsroom/pressreleases /Pages/07-20-06_china.aspx.

88. Nancy Napier and Richard Peterson, "Expatriate Re-entry: What do Repatriates Have to Say?" *Human Resource Planning,* March 1991, pp. 19–28.

89. B. T. King and I. L. Janis. "Comparison of the Effectiveness of Improvised versus Non-Improvised Role-Playing in Producing Opinion Change," *Human Relations,* May 1956, pp. 177–86; see also W. A. Scott,

"Attitude Change Through Reward of Verbal Behaviour," *Journal of Abnormal and Social Psychology,* Vol. 55, July 1957, pp. 72–75.

90. R. G. Shirts, *Ba Fa' Ba Fa', A Cross-Cultural Simulation,* Del Mar, CA: Sirrile, 1977.

91. H. F. Schwind, "The State of the Art in Cross-Cultural Management Training," in R. Doktor (Ed.), *International HRD Annual,* Vol. 1, Washington DC: American Society for Training and Development, 1985.

92. S. Rhinesmith, "Global Mindsets for Global Managers," *Training and Development,* October 1992, pp. 63–68.

93. R. S. Schuler, J. R. Fulkerson, and P. J. Bowling, "Strategic Performance Measurement and Management in Multinational Corporations," *Human Resource Management,* Vol. 30, No. 3, Fall 1991, pp. 365–392.

94. C. D. Contreras and F. Bravo, "Should you accept an international assignment?" *Chemical Engineering Process,* Vol. 99, No. 8, 2003, p. 67.

95. S. Black and H. Gregersen, "Serving Two Masters: Managing the Dual Allegiance of Expatriate Employees," *Sloan Management Review,* Vol. 33, No. 4, Summer 1992, pp. 61–71.

96. Mercer, *Compensation Planning 2012,* http:// www.imercer.com/uploads/Europe/pdfs /mercer_compplanning2012_pov.pdf, 2011.

97. "More Multinationals Embracing Centralized Compensation Structures," *Workspan,* November 2006, p. 10.

98. P. Stanley and T. Farmer, *Localization and Local Plus Packages: An Alternative Deal for Foreign Talent,* July 29, 2011, http://www .mercer.com/webcasts/1417565, 2012.

99. Ibid.

100. Mercer, *Expatriate Management Policy Trends,* http://www.imercer.com/content /august-2011-pov.aspx.

101. R. L. Tung, "Distinguished Scholar Invited Essay Requisites to and Ways of Developing a Global Mindset: Implications for Research on Leadership and Organizations," *Journal of Leadership & Organizational Studies,* Vol. 21, No. 4, 2014, pp. 329–337.

102. A. J. Plessis, "International Human Resource Management: An Overview of its Effect on Managers in Global Organisations," *Interdisciplinary Journal of Contemporary Research in Business,* Vol. 2, No. 4, 2010.

103. C. Solomon and M. S. Schell, *Managing Across Cultures: The Seven Keys to Doing Business With a Global Mindset,* McGraw-Hill, 2009, p. 275.

104. M. M. Novicevic and M. Harvey, "The changing role of the corporate HR function in global organizations of the twenty-first century," *The International Journal of Human Resource Management,* Vol. 12, No. 8, 2001, pp. 1251–1268.

105. C. Solomon and M. S. Schell, *Managing Across Cultures: The Seven Keys to Doing Business With a Global Mindset,* McGraw-Hill, 2009, p. 17.

106. E. Farndale, H. Scullion, and P. Sparrow, "The role of the corporate HR function in global talent management," *Journal of World Business*, Vol. 45, 2010, pp. 161–168.

107. H.-Y. Ngo and R. Loi, "Human resource flexibility, organizational culture and firm performance: an investigation of multinational firms in Hong Kong," *The International Journal of Human Resource Management*, Vol. 19, No. 9, September 2008, pp. 1654–1666.

108. Scotiabank Canada, *Advancement of Women, 2012*, http://www.scotiabank.com/ca/en/0,2727,00.html; see also *Scotiabank Antigua and Barbuda, Advancement of Women, 2012*, http://scotiabank.com/ag/cda/content/0,1679,CCDag_CID4805_LIDen_SID98_YID23,00.html.

109. E. Krell, "Budding Relationships: Formal Global Buddy Programs Can Help Ease the Transition for Expatriates and Improve Retention and Productivity," *HR Magazine*, 2005, downloaded November 2, 2007.

110. W. Stueck, "Coal Company Wants to Hire Chinese Workers for B.C. Mine," *The Globe and Mail*, May 28, 2007, p. B1.

Glossary

360-degree performance appraisal Combination of self, peer, supervisor, and subordinate performance evaluation.

ability tests Tests that assess an applicant's capacity or aptitude to function in a certain way.

ads Advertisements in a newspaper, magazine, and so on that solicit job applicants for a position.

alternate work arrangements Nontraditional work arrangements (e.g., flextime, telecommuting) that provide more flexibility to employees while meeting organizational goals.

alumni associations Associations of alumni of schools, colleges, or other training facilities.

applicant tracking systems (ATS) Databases of potential candidates that enable a good match between job requirements and applicant characteristics and also enlarge the recruitment pool.

apprenticeships A form of on-the-job training in which junior employees learn a trade from an experienced person.

arbitration The settling of a dispute between labour and management by a third party.

assertiveness Focuses on how assertive people are in society and the degree to which they are confrontational.

assessment centres A standardized form of employee appraisal that relies on several types of evaluation and multiple assessors.

assumption of risk The worker accepts all the customary risks associated with his or her occupation. For example, workers may be instructed to protect themselves from special hazards such as heat extremes or molten and sharp metal.

attrition Loss of employees due to their voluntary departures from the firm through resignation, retirement, or death.

authorization cards Cards signed by workers to join a union. Depending on the jurisdiction, a union may be certified either on the basis of card signatures or as a result of an election.

autonomous work groups Any of a variety of arrangements that allow employees to decide democratically how they will meet their group's work objectives.

autonomy In a job context, independence—having control over one's work and one's response to the work environment.

awareness training Training employees to develop their understanding of the need to manage and value diversity.

balanced scorecard An integrated organizational performance measuring approach, that looks at organizational learning and innovation, financial management, internal operations, and customer management.

behavioural description interviews Interviews that attempt to find out how job applicants responded to specific work situations in the past.

behaviourally anchored rating scales (BARS) Evaluation tools that rate employees along a rating scale by means of specific behaviour examples on the scale.

benefit audit A system to control the efficiency of a benefit program.

biographical information blank (BIB) A type of application blank that uses a multiple-choice format to measure a job candidate's education, experiences, opinions, attitudes, and interests.

blind ads Job ads that do not identify the employer.

blog A web log—an online journal, diary, or serial published by a person or group of people.

bona fide occupational requirement (BFOR) A justified business reason for discriminating against a member of a protected class. Also known as a bona fide occupational qualification (BFOQ).

broadbanding Consolidation of a large number of pay grades into a few "broad bands."

burnout A condition of mental, emotional, and sometimes physical exhaustion that results from substantial and prolonged stress.

business ecosystem A series of tightly knit intercompany relationships, allowing a business to attain a competitive advantage.

business unionism A type of unionism whose mission is to protect workers, increase their pay, improve their working conditions, and help workers in general. Recognizes that a union can survive only if it delivers a needed service to its members in a businesslike manner.

buy-back A method of convincing an employee who is about to resign to stay in the employ of the organization, typically by offering an increased wage or salary.

Canada Labour Code Federal law regulating labour relations under federal jurisdiction.

Canada Pension Plan (CPP) A mandatory, contributory, and portable pension plan applicable to all employees and self-employed persons in Canada, except those working for the federal government.

Canadian Charter of Rights and Freedoms Federal law enacted in 1982, guaranteeing individuals equal rights before the law.

Canadian Human Rights Act A federal law prohibiting discrimination.

Canadian Human Rights Commission (CHRC) Supervises the implementation and adjudication of the *Canadian Human Rights Act.*

Canadian Labour Congress (CLC) An organization, with a membership of about 3.3 million, that represents many unions in Canada.

Canadian Occupational Projection System (COPS) Provides up to 10-year projection of Canadian economy and human resource needs.

career development A lifelong series of activities undertaken by individuals in their pursuit of a career.

career management A series of formal and less formal activities designed and managed by the organization to influence the career development of one or more employees.

career planning The process through which someone becomes more aware of their interests and needs, motivations, etc. in terms of their career.

careless worker model The early approach to safety in the workplace, which assumed that most accidents were due to workers' failure to be careful or to protect themselves.

Certified Human Resources Professional (CHRP) Human resource practitioner, formally accredited to practice, who reflects a threshold professional level of practice.

collective agreement A labour contract that addresses a variety of issues such as wages and benefits, hours of work, working conditions, grievance procedures, safety standards, probationary periods, and work assignments. Usually negotiated between the local union's bargaining committee and the human resource or industrial relations department.

combination Concurrent use of two or more job analysis techniques (e.g., interviews and observation).

communication standards Formal protocols for internal communications within an organization to eliminate sex/gender, racial, age, or other biases in communications.

compa-ratio An index that indicates how an individual's or a group's salary relates to the midpoint of their relevant pay grades.

comparative evaluation methods A collection of different methods that compare one person's performance with that of co-workers.

compensatory approach An approach where a higher score on a predictor may compensate a low score on another.

competency A knowledge, skill, ability, or characteristic associated with successful job performance.

competency matrix A list of the level of each competency required for each of a number of jobs.

competency model (competency framework) A list of competencies required in a particular job.

competitive advantage A competitive advantage exists when the firm is able to deliver the same value and benefits as competitors but at a lower cost (cost advantage), or deliver more benefits or unique value that exceed those of competing products (differentiation advantage).

computer-interactive performance tests Performance tests using computer simulations that can measure skills, comprehension, spatial visualization, judgment, etc.

concentration A condition that exists when a department or employer has a greater proportion of members of a protected class than are found in the employer's labour market.

conciliation Use of a government-appointed third party to explore solutions to a labour–management dispute.

constructive dismissal A major change in the terms of the employment contract that results in an employee resigning.

consultants Professionals who provide expert advice and counsel in a particular area.

contract (or contingent) worker A freelancer (self-employed, temporary, or leased employee) who is not part of the regular workforce who provides goods or services to another entity under the terms of a specific contract.

contrast error A rater bias occurring when a rater compares employees to each other rather than to a performance standard.

contributory plans Benefits that require the employer to contribute to the cost of the benefit.

core dimensions of diversity Age, ethnicity and culture, sex/gender, race, religion, sexual orientation, and capabilities.

corporate social responsibility (CSR) A company's sense of responsibility toward the community and environment in which it operates.

corrective discipline Discipline that follows a rule infraction.

cost leadership strategy Strategy to gain competitive advantage through lower costs of operations and lower prices for products.

cost–benefit analysis Analysis undertaken to assess the cost-effectiveness of a project or program.

costs Expenses related to attracting recruits.

counselling The discussion of a problem with an employee, with the general objective of helping the worker resolve the issue or cope with the situation so that he or she can become more effective.

craft union A type of union composed of workers who possess the same skills or trades.

cross-training Training employees to perform operations in areas other than their assigned jobs.

crowdsourcing The act of a company or institution taking a function once performed by employees and outsourcing it to an undefined (and generally large) network of people in the form of an open call.

cultural forces Challenges facing a firm's decision makers because of cultural differences among employees or changes in core cultural or social values occurring at the larger societal level.

cultural mosaic Canadian ideal of encouraging each ethnic, racial, and social group to maintain its own cultural heritage, forming a national mosaic of different cultures.

cultural norms Values and norms that determine behaviours of individuals and groups in different cultures.

defined benefits (DB) plan A benefits plan whose benefits are defined by a formula based on age and length of service, with the employer assuming responsibility for funding.

defined contribution (DC) plan A benefits plan based on amounts contributed by the employer and the employee, the final pension depending on amounts contributed, investment income, and economic conditions at retirement.

Delphi technique The soliciting of predictions about specified future events from a panel of experts, using repeated surveys until convergence in opinions occurs.

demographic changes Changes in the demographics of the labour force (e.g., education levels, age levels, participation rates) that occur slowly and are usually known in advance.

development Planned activities aimed to provide employees with enhanced skills and competencies for the future.

differential validity Test validation process aimed at discovering the validity of a test for various subgroups, e.g., females and members of visible minorities.

differentiation strategy Strategy to gain competitive advantage by creating a distinct product or offering a unique service.

discipline Management action to encourage compliance with organization standards.

diversity audits Audits to uncover underlying dimensions, causes, interdependencies, and progress-to-date on diversity management matters.

diversity committee A committee entrusted to oversee diversity efforts, implement processes, and serve as a communication link.

diversity management Recognizing differences among employees belonging to heterogeneous groups and creating a work environment in which members of diverse groups feel comfortable.

diversity training programs Training programs aimed at importing new skills to motivate and manage a diverse workforce.

downsizing Reducing employment to improve efficiency, productivity, and competitiveness.

downward communication Information that begins at some point in the organization and feeds down the organization hierarchy to inform or influence others.

drug tests Tests that include whether a job applicant uses marijuana, cocaine, or other drugs.

due process In a disciplinary situation, the following of proper, established rules and procedures, and giving employees the opportunity to respond to allegations.

duty to accommodate Requirement that an employer must accommodate the employee to the point of "undue hardship."

economic forces Economic factors facing Canadian business today, including global trade forces and the force to increase one's own competitiveness and productivity levels.

educational attainment The highest educational level attained by an individual worker, employee group, or population.

educational institutions High schools, technical schools, community colleges, and universities where applicants for job positions are sought.

efficiency Achieving maximal output with minimal input.

employee assistance programs (EAP) Comprehensive company program that seeks to help employees and their family members overcome personal and work-related problems.

employee attitude/opinion survey A systematic method of determining what employees think of their organization.

employee log Approach to collecting job- and performance-related information by asking the jobholder to summarize tasks, activities, and challenges in a diary format.

employee referrals Recommendations by present employees to the recruiter about possible job applications for a position.

employee self-service (ESS) A feature of an HRIS that allows employees to access and view their own records and make changes where applicable.

Employment and Social Development Canada (ESDC) Federal department that provides programs and services for employers and present and potential employees.

Employment Equity Act Federal law to remove employment barriers and to promote equality.

employment equity programs Developed by employers to undo past employment discrimination or to ensure equal employment opportunity in the future. Called affirmative action programs in the United States.

Employment Insurance (EI) A program to help alleviate the financial problems of workers in Canada during the transition from one job to another.

...iew A formal, in-depth, ...more recently, a phone or ...nce between an employer and a ...ant to assess the appropriateness of the ...cant for the job under consideration.

employment references Evaluations of an employee's past work performance and job-relevant behaviours provided by past employers.

employment tests Devices that assess the probable match between applicants and job requirements.

enterprise-wide systems Link an organization's entire software application environment into a single enterprise solution.

environmental considerations The influence of the external environment on job design. Includes employee ability, availability, and social expectations.

equal pay for equal work The principle or policy of equal rates of pay for all employees in an establishment performing the same kind and amount of work, regardless of sex, race, or other characteristics of individual workers not related to ability or performance.

equal pay for work of equal value The principle of equal pay for men and women in jobs with comparable content; based on criteria of skill, effort, responsibility, and working conditions; part of the *Canadian Human Rights Act.*

ergonomics The study of relationships between physical attributes of workers and their work environment to reduce physical and mental strain and increase productivity and quality of work life.

error of central tendency An error in rating employees that consists of evaluating employees as neither good nor poor performers even when some employees perform exceptionally well or poorly.

ethnocentrism A view in which managers use a home-country standard as reference for managing activities.

evaluation interviews Performance review sessions that give employees feedback about their past performance or future potential.

expatriate An individual who is sent on an assignment outside the home country for a period of time.

external equity Perceived fairness in pay relative to what other employers are paying for the same type of work.

extrapolation Extending past rates of change into the future.

feedback Information that helps evaluate the success or failure of an action or system.

flexible benefit programs Programs that allow employees to select the mix of benefits and services that will answer their individual needs. Also known as *cafeteria benefit programs.*

flexible retirement Programs that provide retirees with the opportunity to work after they have retired and provide them with significant flexibility in terms of how they work, what they work on, when they work, and where.

flexpatriate A person who is on a short-term assignment and engages in frequent travel without relocation.

focus group A face-to-face meeting with five to seven knowledgeable experts on a job and a facilitator to collect job and performance-related information.

focus strategy Strategy to gain a competitive advantage by focusing on the needs of a specific segment of the total market.

forced distributions A method of evaluating employees that requires raters to categorize employees.

forecasts Estimates of future resource needs and changes.

frequent flyer An employee who travels often on international business trips to accomplish a specific task.

full-time employees Work 37.5 to 40 hours in a workweek.

functional authority Authority that allows staff experts to make decisions and take actions normally reserved for line managers.

future orientation The degree to which people are willing to delay rewards.

gender differentiation How society views differences in gender roles and affords higher status to certain roles.

geocentrism A managerial outlook that focuses on creating a global network and follows a strategy that integrates and is dependent on the global firm's strengths.

glass ceiling Invisible, but real obstructions to career advancement of women and people of visible minorities, resulting in frustration, career dissatisfaction, and increased turnover.

global HR planning Estimates employment needs and develops plans for meeting those needs from the available global labour force and the viability of MNEs in their ability to align their workforce forecasts with the supply for global talent.

global human resource management (GHRM) An IHRM process that views HRM in a global context as one that contributes to organizational capabilities.

global mindset The capacity to scan the world with a broad view, to value diversity, and to appreciate change.

global talent management Strategic integration of resourcing and development at the international level, which involves the proactive identification, development, and strategic deployment of high-performing and high-potential employees on a global scale.

grapevine communication Informal communication within an organization that arise from normal social interaction.

grievance procedure A formalized procedure for resolving disputes if the parties have a disagreement regarding the interpretation of a term of the collective agreement.

guaranteed annual wage (GAW) A benefits plan by which an employer assures employees that they will receive a minimum annual income regardless of layoffs or a lack of work.

halo effect A bias that occurs when an evaluation allows some information to disproportionately affect the final evaluation.

harassment Occurs when a member of an organization treats an employee in a disparate manner because of that person's sex, race, religion, age, or other protective classification.

health insurance Health and medical insurance provided by provincial governments with assistance from the federal government.

high-involvement work practices A set of human resource practices aimed at increasing employee performance.

home-country evaluations Performance appraisals carried out by an expatriate's home office.

host country national (HCN) Citizen of a county of a foreign subsidiary, hired to work at a subsidiary located in their home country.

host-country evaluations Performance appraisals carried out by an expatriate's local (or host) office.

hot-stove rule The principle that disciplinary action should be like what happens when you touch a hot stove: it is with warning, immediate, consistent, and impersonal.

human resource accounting (HRA) A process to measure the present cost and value of human resources as well as their future worth to the organization.

human resource audit An examination of the human resource policies, practices, and systems of a firm (or division) to eliminate deficiencies and improve ways to achieve goals.

human resource development (HRD) A function of human resource management that integrates the use of training and employee and career development efforts to improve individual, group, and organizational effectiveness.

human resource information system (HRIS) Gathers, analyzes, summarizes, and reports important data for formulating and implementing strategies by HR specialists and line managers.

human resource management The leadership and management of people within an organization using systems, methods, processes, and procedures that enable employees to optimize their performance and in turn their contribution to the organization and its goals.

human resource plan A firm's overall plan to fill existing and future vacancies, including decisions on whether to fill internally or by recruiting from outside.

human resource planning A process used to determine future human resource requirements by anticipating future business demands, analyzing the impacts of these demands on the organization, determining the current availability of human resources, and making decisions on how to effectively acquire and utilize firms' human resources.

humane orientation Degree to which societies focus on altruistic behaviour and generosity.

incentive pay Compensation that is directly tied to an employee's performance, productivity, or both.

indexation A method of estimating future employment needs by matching employment growth with a selected index, such as the ratio of production employees to sales.

inducements Monetary, nonmonetary, or even intangible incentives used by a firm to attract recruits.

industrial union A type of union that includes the unskilled and semiskilled workers at a particular location.

in-group collectivism Degree to which a society feels loyal toward their family or other collective groups.

In-house complaint procedures Formal methods through which an employee can register a complaint.

inpatriate Third country national (TCN) or host country national (HCN) employee who relocates from a foreign subsidiary or joint venture to the parent company.

institutional collectivism Degree to which institutions want individuals to integrate into the larger structure, even at the cost of individual freedom.

integrity tests Employment tests that measure an applicant's honesty and trustworthiness.

internal equity Perceived equity of a pay system in an organization.

international commuter An employee who frequently commutes from a home country to a place of work in another country, typically on a weekly or biweekly basis.

international human resource management (IHRM) The worldwide management of talent from a staffing perspective, including HR support across many countries and the employment of different nationals.

interview Approach to collecting job- and performance-related information by a face-to-face meeting with jobholder, typically using a standardized checklist of questions.

interviewee errors Interviewee mistakes such as boasting, not listening, or lack of preparation that reduce the validity and usefulness of an interview.

interviewer errors Mistakes like biases and domination that reduce the validity and usefulness of the job interview.

intranet An organization-specific internal computer network.

job Group of related activities and duties.

job analysis Systematic study of a job to discover its specifications, skill requirements, and so on, for wage-setting, recruitment, training, or job-design purposes.

job analysis questionnaires Checklists used to collect information about jobs in a uniform manner.

job application form A company's form completed by a job applicant indicating their contact information, education, prior employment, references, special skills and other questions pertaining to the position.

job code A code that uses numbers, letters, or both to provide a quick summary of the job and its content.

job description A recognized list of functions, tasks, accountabilities, working conditions, and competencies for a particular occupation or job.

job design Identification of job duties, characteristics, competencies, and sequences taking into consideration technology, workforce, organization character, and environment.

job enlargement Adding more tasks to a job to increase the job cycle and draw on a wider range of employee skills.

job enrichment Adding more responsibilities and autonomy to a job, giving the worker greater powers to plan, do, and evaluate job performance.

job evaluations Systematic process of assessing job content and ranking jobs according to a consistent set of job characteristics and worker traits.

job fairs Trade show style fairs with many employers showcasing their companies and jobs to potential recruits.

job families Groups of different jobs that are closely related by similar duties, responsibilities, skills, or job elements.

job grading A form of job evaluation that assigns jobs to predetermined job classifications according to their relative worth to the organization.

job identity Key part of a job description, including job title, location, and status.

job performance standards The work performance expected from an employee on a particular job.

job ranking A form of job evaluation in which jobs are ranked subjectively according to their overall worth to the organization.

job rotation Moving employees from one job to another to allow them more variety and to learn new skills.

job sharing A plan whereby available work is spread among all workers in a group to reduce the extent of layoffs when production requirements cause substantial decline in available work.

job specification A written statement that explains what a job demands of jobholders and the human skills and factors required.

just cause Legal grounds for termination such as employee misconduct or incompetence.

key job A job that is similar and common in the organization and its labour market—for example, accountant, tool-and-die maker.

knowledge management The ability to use people's knowledge, that is, information stored in employees' heads.

knowledge tests Tests that measure a person's information or knowledge.

knowledge workers Members of occupations generating, processing, analyzing, or synthesizing ideas and information (such as scientists and management consultants).

labour market analysis The study of a firm's labour market to evaluate the present or future availability of different types of workers.

labour relations boards (LRBs) Board set up in the federal and provincial jurisdictions to administer labour relations legislation.

labour shortage Insufficient supply of qualified talent to fill the demand for labour.

learning curve A visual representation of the rate at which one learns given material.

learning organization An organization that has an enhanced capacity to learn, adapt, and change.

learning principles Guidelines to the ways people learn most effectively.

leniency bias A tendency to rate employees higher than their performance justifies.

line authority Authority to make decisions about production, performance, and people.

local union A branch of a union that is locally based and forms part of a larger (often national or international) union.

long-term disability insurance A benefit plan providing the employee with an income in the case of long-term illness or injury.

management or leadership inventory Comprehensive reports of available management capabilities in the organization.

management rights Rights that provide management with the freedom to operate the business subject to any terms in the collective agreement.

management-by-objectives (MBO) approach Requires an employee and superior to jointly establish performance goals for the future. Employees are subsequently evaluated on how well they have obtained these objectives.

manager self-service (MSS) A feature of an HRIS that allows managers to view and access their employee's records and add relevant information.

managing diversity Ability to manage individual employees with different cultural values and lead teams made up of diverse employees.

Markov analysis Forecast of a firm's future human resource supplies, using transitional probability matrices reflecting historical or expected movements of employees across jobs.

mechanization The shift toward converting work that was traditionally done by hand to being completed by mechanical or electronic devices.

mediation Use of a neutral third party to help settle a labour–management dispute.

medical evaluation Assessment of physical and/or mental health of an applicant through self reports and/or medical examination by a preferred physician.

mentor Someone who offers informed career guidance and support on a regular basis.

mentoring programs Programs encouraging members of disadvantaged groups (e.g., women) to work with a senior manager who acts like a friend and guide in achieving career success.

merit raise A pay increase given to individual workers according to an evaluation of their performance.

mission statement Statement outlining the purpose, long-term objectives, and activities the organization will pursue and the course for the future.

multinational enterprise (MNE) An organization that has operations and subsidiaries around the globe.

multiple cut-off approach An approach where scores are set for each predictor and each applicant is evaluated on a pass–fail basis.

National Occupational Classification (NOC) An occupational classification created by federal government, using skill level and skill types of jobs.

natural justice Minimum standards of fair decision making imposed on persons or bodies acting in a judicial capacity.

needs assessment A diagnosis that presents problems and future challenges that can be met through training or development.

nominal group technique A focused group discussion where members meet face-to-face, write down their ideas, and share them. All new thoughts on a topic are recorded and ranked for importance.

noncomparative evaluation methods Appraisal methods that evaluate an employee's performance according to preset data, and not by comparing one person's performance with that of co-workers.

observation An approach to collecting job- and performance-related information by direct observation of jobholder by a specialist.

old boys' network Set of informal relationships among male managers providing increased career advancement opportunities for men and reinforcing a male culture.

onboarding The process of integrating and acculturating new employees into the organization and providing them with the tools, resources, and knowledge to become successful and productive.

online service delivery EAP services available to employees through the Internet and by intranet.

open-door policy A company policy that encourages employees to address their problems to higher levels of management.

organization character The product of all the organization's features—people, objectives, technology, size, age, unions, policies, successes, and failures.

organizational culture The core beliefs and assumptions that are widely shared by all organizational members.

organizational goals An organization's short- and long-term goals that human resource management aims to support and enable.

organizational policies Internal policies that affect recruitment, such as "promote-from-within" policies.

orientation programs Programs that familiarize new employees with their roles, the organization, its policies, and other employees.

outplacement Assisting employees to find jobs with other employers.

outsourcing Contracting tasks to outside agencies or persons.

panel interview Interview using several interviewers with one applicant.

parent country national (PCN) Citizen of the country where the headquarters is located.

part-time employees Persons working fewer than the required hours for categorization as full-time workers and who are ineligible for many supplementary benefits offered by employers.

pay equity A policy to eliminate the gap between income of men and women, ensuring salary ranges correspond to value of work performed.

pay secrecy A management policy not to discuss or publish individual salaries.

Pension Benefits Standards Act A federal act regulating pension plans in industries under the jurisdiction of the Government of Canada.

people equity How organizations measure and manage their human capital to maximize its value.

performance appraisal The process by which organizations evaluate employee job performance.

performance management The use of performance data to effect organizational culture, systems, and processes, set goals, allocate resources, affect policies and programs, and share results.

performance measures The ratings used to evaluate employee performance.

performance orientation Extent to which society recognizes and rewards performance.

performance standards The benchmarks against which performance is measured.

performance tests Tests that measure the ability of job applicants to perform the job for which they are to be hired.

personality tests Questionnaires designed to reveal aspects of an individual's character or temperament.

phased retirement Gradual phase into retirement with loss or reduction of pension benefits.

piecework A type of incentive system that compensates workers for each unit of output.

point system A form of job evaluation that assesses the relative importance of the job's key factors in order to arrive at the relative worth of jobs.

polycentrism Characterized by firms that are staffed by host country managers and are typically decentralized and autonomous operations.

portability clauses Allow accumulated pension rights to be transferred to another employer when an employee changes employers.

position Collection of tasks and responsibilities performed by an individual.

power distance Degree to which people are separated by power and authority.

precedent A new standard that arises from the past practices of either the company or the union.

predictive analysis The process of selecting, exploring, analyzing, and modelling data to create better business outcomes.

preventive discipline Action taken prior to an infraction to encourage employees to follow standards and rules.

proactive human resource management A human resources management approach wherein decision makers anticipate problems or challenges both inside and outside the organization and take action before they impact the organization.

production bonuses A type of incentive system that provides employees with additional compensation when they surpass stated production goals.

productivity The ratio of a firm's outputs (goods and services) divided by its inputs (people, capital, materials, energy).

professional search firms Agencies that, for a fee, recruit specialized personnel for a company.

profit-sharing plan A system whereby an employer pays compensation or benefits to employees, usually on an annual basis, in addition to their regular wage, on the basis of the profits of the company.

progressive discipline The use of stronger and stronger penalties for repeated offences.